Lecture Notes in Artificial Intelligence 13196

Subseries of Lecture Notes in Computer Science

More information about this subseries at https://link.springer.com/bookseries/1244

Stefania Bandini · Francesca Gasparini ·
Viviana Mascardi · Matteo Palmonari ·
Giuseppe Vizzari (Eds.)

AIxIA 2021 – Advances in Artificial Intelligence

20th International Conference
of the Italian Association for Artificial Intelligence
Virtual Event, December 1–3, 2021
Revised Selected Papers

Springer

Editors
Stefania Bandini
Department of Informatics, Systems
and Communication
University of Milano-Bicocca
Milan, Italy

Francesca Gasparini
Department of Informatics, Systems
and Communication
University of Milano-Bicocca
Milan, Italy

Viviana Mascardi
Department of Informatics, Bioengineering,
Robotics and Systems Engineering
University of Genoa
Genova, Italy

Matteo Palmonari
Department of Informatics, Systems
and Communication
University of Milano-Bicocca
Milan, Italy

Giuseppe Vizzari
Department of Informatics, Systems
and Communication
University of Milano-Bicocca
Milan, Italy

ISSN 0302-9743 ISSN 1611-3349 (electronic)
Lecture Notes in Artificial Intelligence
ISBN 978-3-031-08420-1 ISBN 978-3-031-08421-8 (eBook)
https://doi.org/10.1007/978-3-031-08421-8

LNCS Sublibrary: SL7 – Artificial Intelligence

This Springer imprint is published by the registered company Springer Nature Switzerland AG
The registered company address is: Gewerbestrasse 11, 6330 Cham, Switzerland

Preface

The 20th International Conference of the Italian Association for Artificial Intelligence (AIxIA 2021), held during November 29 – December 3, 2021, was organized by the Associazione Italiana per l'Intelligenza Artificiale (AIxIA), a non-profit scientific association founded in 1998 fostering artificial intelligence (AI) through academic, social, and production environments. The association aims at increasing the public awareness of AI, encouraging teaching, and promoting advanced research in the field.

AIxIA 2021 (https://aixia2021.disco.unimib.it/home-page) featured a main track and a set of 12 thematic workshops, grouping the communities working on various research areas of the field. Keynote speakers, award events, and open satellite events completed the conference. Two invited keynote speakers kindly gave their lectures at the conference: Evelina Fedorenko (Massachusetts Institute of Technology, USA) addressed "The language system in the human brain" and Pascal Hitzler (Kansas State University, USA) spoke about "Neuro-Symbolic Deep Deductive Reasoning".

The main track hosted a set of sessions focusing on planning and strategies; constraints and logic programming; knowledge representation, reasoning, and learning; natural language processing; AI for content and social media analysis; signal processing: images, videos, and speech; machine learning for argumentation, explanation, and exploration; machine learning and applications; and AI and applications.

The conference received 58 submissions, and each paper was reviewed by at least two Program Committee members in a single blind review process. In total, 47 papers were selected, of which 36 are included in this volume and 11 in a separate Discussion Papers publication.

AIxIA 2021 also covered many aspects of theoretical and applied AI through a series of workshops dedicated to specific topics and grouping the related AI communities:

- 5th Workshop on Advances in Argumentation in Artificial Intelligence (AI^3 2021)
- 10th Italian Workshop on Machine Learning and Data Mining (MLDM 2021)
- 5th Workshop on Natural Language for Artificial Intelligence (NL4AI 2021)
- Towards smarter health care: can Artificial Intelligence help? (SMARTERCARE 2021)
- 2nd Italian Workshop on Artificial Intelligence for an Ageing Society (AIxAS 2021)
- 28th RCRA International Workshop on Experimental Evaluation of Algorithms for Solving Problems with Combinatorial Explosion (RCRA 2021)
- 1st International Workshop on Causality (Causal-ITALY 2021)
- 2nd Italian Workshop on Explainable Artificial Intelligence (XAI.it 2021)
- 2nd Workshop on Evolutionary and Population-based Optimization (WEPO 2021)
- 9th Italian Workshop on Planning and Scheduling (IPS 2021)
- Italian Workshop on Artificial Intelligence and Applications for Business and Industry (AIABI 2021)
- 8th Italian Workshop on Artificial Intelligence and Robotics (AIRO 2021)

The workshop proceedings are published independently; however, 12 papers selected from the workshops are also included in this volume; following the original (single blind) reviewing and selection process adopted by the workshops, these papers have been further revised and extended. The additional papers have been included together with the papers from the main conference in the relevant sections.

To cater for the growing interest in AI and its applications, the conference hosted four open events for the general public (in Italian):

- Intelligenza Artificiale per lo Sviluppo Sostenibile (Chair: Piero Poccianti)
- Intelligenza Artificiale e impatti di genere: una questione urgente (Chair: Chiara Lupi)
- Il rilievo politico dell'Intelligenza Artificiale (Chair: Francesco Varanini)
- Intelligenza Artificiale: quali benefici per l'Area delle Risorse Umane? (Chair: ASSINTEL)

As is the tradition of AIxIA, the conference hosted the presentations of the winners of three awards, whose selection was coordinated by Stefania Costantini: Elena Bellodi and Riccardo Guidotti received the "Marco Somalvico" young researchers award; Alberto Maria Metelli received the "Marco Cadoli" PhD award; and Giorgio Franceschelli received the "Leonardo Lesmo" MS award.

We would like to thank all individuals, institutions, and sponsors that supported AIxIA 2021: the Artificial Intelligence Journal for the "Funding Opportunities for Promoting AI Research" program; the European Commission (DG CNECT - DG for Communications Networks, Content and Technology); the Department of Informatics, Systems and Communication (University of Milano-Bicocca) for the website hosting; and Angelo Ferrando (University of Genoa) for his collaboration and assistance with the website. We thank all the authors for submitting high-quality research papers and the reviewers for their contribution in the selection of the papers. We are also indebted to the workshop coordination chairs (Fabio Stella, Gabriella Cortellessa, and Silvia Rossi), the members of the workshop program committees, and the additional reviewers that spent their valuable time providing careful reviews and recommendations. A special acknowledgement goes to Daniela Briola, Stefano Ferilli, and Marta Giltri for their indispensable support to the organization of the whole event. Finally, a special thanks to Piero Poccianti, the President of the AIxIA, for his constant effort in supporting this event and the association activities.

April 2022

Stefania Bandini
Francesca Gasparini
Viviana Mascardi
Matteo Palmonari
Giuseppe Vizzari

Organization

General Chair

Stefania Bandini	University of Milano-Bicocca, Italy, and RCAST - The University of Tokyo, Japan

Program Committee Chairs

Viviana Mascardi	University of Genova, Italy
Matteo Palmonari	University of Milano-Bicocca, Italy
Giuseppe Vizzari	University of Milano-Bicocca, Italy

Organizing Committee

Francesca Gasparini	University of Milano-Bicocca, Italy
Stefano Ferilli	University of Bari, Italy
Marta Giltri	University of Milano-Bicocca, Italy
Daniela Briola	University of Insubria, Italy

Publicity and Communication Committee

Elisabetta Fersini	University of Milano-Bicocca, Italy
Angelo Ferrando	University of Genova, Italy
Francesca A. Lisi	University of Bari, Italy
Giovanni Stilo	University of L'Aquila, Italy
Marco Viviani	University of Milano-Bicocca, Italy

Workshop Chairs

Gabriella Cortellessa	ISTC-CNR, Italy
Silvia Rossi	University of Naples Federico II, Italy
Fabio Stella	University of Milano-Bicocca, Italy

Program Committee

Farshad Badie	Berlin School of Business and Innovation, Germany
Matteo Baldoni	University of Turin, Italy
Roberto Basili	University of Rome Tor Vergata, Italy

Ana L. C. Bazzan	Universidade Federal do Rio Grande do Sul, Brazil
Federico Bergenti	University of Parma, Italy
Stefano Bistarelli	University of Perugia, Italy
Rafael H. Bordini	Pontifícia Universidade Católica do Rio Grande do Sul, Brazil
Andrea Burattin	Technical University of Denmark, Denmark
Elena Cabrio	Université Côte d'Azur, France
Stefano Cagnoni	University of Parma, Italy
Diego Calvanese	Free University of Bozen-Bolzano, Italy
Luigia Carlucci Aiello	Sapienza University of Rome, Italy
Federico Chesani	University of Bologna, Italy
Flavio S. Correa Da Silva	University of São Paulo, Brazil
Stefania Costantini	University of L'Aquila, Italy
Claudio Di Ciccio	Sapienza University of Rome, Italy
Ivana Dusparic	Trinity College Dublin, Ireland
Johannes K. Fichte	TU Wien, Austria
Giancarlo Fortino	University of Calabria, Italy
Salvatore Gaglio	University of Palermo, Italy
Nicola Gatti	Politecnico di Milano, Italy
Marco Gavanelli	University of Ferrara, Italy
Chiara Ghidini	Fondazione Bruno Kessler, Italy
Laura Giordano	University of Piemonte Orientale, Italy
Gianluigi Greco	University of Calabria, Italy
Ernesto Jimenez-Ruiz	City, University of London, UK
Antonio Lieto	University of Turin, Italy
Francesca A. Lisi	University of Bari "Aldo Moro", Italy
Marin Lujak	University Rey Juan Carlos, Spain
Bernardo Magnini	Fondazione Bruno Kessler, Italy
Marco Maratea	University of Genova, Italy
Fulvio Mastrogiovanni	University of Genova, Italy
Alessio Micheli	University of Pisa, Italy
Angelo Oddi	ISTC-CNR, Italy
Viviana Patti	University of Turin, Italy
Piero Poccianti	Consorzio Operativo Gruppo MPS, Italy
Gian Luca Pozzato	University of Turin, Italy
Francesco Ricca	University of Calabria, Italy
Fabrizio Riguzzi	University of Ferrara, Italy
Andrea Roli	University of Bologna, Italy
Silvia Rossi	University of Naples Federico II, Italy
Paolo Rosso	Universitat Politècnica de València, Spain
Salvatore Ruggieri	University of Pisa, Italy

Emanuel Sallinger	TU Wien, Austria
Francesco Scarcello	University of Calabria, Italy
Giovanni Semeraro	University of Bari "Aldo Moro", Italy
Luciano Serafini	Fondazione Bruno Kessler, Italy
Mauro Vallati	University of Huddersfield, UK
Eloisa Vargiu	CETaqua, Spain
Serena Villata	CNRS, France
Antonius Weinzierl	TU Wien, Austria

Additional Reviewers

Gennaro Vessio	University of Bari "Aldo Moro", Italy
Daniele Peri	University of Palermo, Italy
Alessandra Rossi	University of Hertfordshire, UK
Marco Polignano	University of Bari "Aldo Moro", Italy
Chenxi Whitehouse	City, University of London, UK
Jose Alvarez	University of Pisa, Italy
Sultan Daud Khan	National University of Technology, Pakistan
Antonio Origlia	University of Naples Federico II, Italy
Carlo Taticchi	University of Perugia, Italy
Giovanni Ercolano	University of Naples Federico II, Italy
Paolo Didier Alfano	University of Genova, Italy
Salvatore Vitabile	University of Palermo, Italy
Francesco Faloci	University of Camerino, Italy

Contents

Planning and Strategies

Task Allocation for Multi-robot Task and Motion Planning: A Case for Object Picking in Cluttered Workspaces ... 3
Hossein Karami, Antony Thomas, and Fulvio Mastrogiovanni

A Sound (But Incomplete) Polynomial Translation from Discretised PDDL+ to Numeric Planning ... 18
Francesco Percassi, Enrico Scala, and Mauro Vallati

Enhancing Telepresence Robots with AI: Combining Services to Personalize and React ... 32
Riccardo De Benedictis, Gloria Beraldo, Rami Reddy Devaram, Amedeo Cesta, and Gabriella Cortellessa

Tafl-ES: Exploring Evolution Strategies for Asymmetrical Board Games ... 46
Roberto Gallotta and Roberto Capobianco

Constraints, Argumentation, and Logic Programming

Combining DCOP and MILP for Complex Local Optimization Problems ... 61
Fernanda N. T. Furukita, Fernando J. M. Marcellino, and Jaime Sichman

Automated Design of Elevator Systems: Experimenting with Constraint-Based Approaches ... 77
Stefano Demarchi, Marco Menapace, and Armando Tacchella

Modular Logic Argumentation in Arg-tuProlog ... 91
Roberta Calegari, Giuseppe Contissa, Giuseppe Pisano, Galileo Sartor, and Giovanni Sartor

Burden of Persuasion in Meta-argumentation ... 104
Giuseppe Pisano, Roberta Calegari, Andrea Omicini, and Giovanni Sartor

Knowledge Representation, Reasoning, and Learning

Reasoning About Smart Contracts Encoded in LTL ... 123
Valeria Fionda, Gianluigi Greco, and Marco Antonio Mastratisi

A Combinatorial Approach to Weighted Model Counting in the Two-Variable Fragment with Cardinality Constraints ... 137
Sagar Malhotra and Luciano Serafini

Option Discovery for Autonomous Generation of Symbolic Knowledge ... 153
Gabriele Sartor, Davide Zollo, Marta Cialdea Mayer, Angelo Oddi, Riccardo Rasconi, and Vieri Giuliano Santucci

Natural Language Processing

A Neural-Machine-Translation System Resilient to Out of Vocabulary Words for Translating Natural Language to SPARQL ... 171
Manuel Borroto, Francesco Ricca, and Bernardo Cuteri

Exploiting Textual Similarity Techniques in Harmonization of Laws ... 185
Emilio Sulis, Llio Bryn Humphreys, Davide Audrito, and Luigi Di Caro

Easy Semantification of Bioassays ... 198
Marco Anteghini, Jennifer D'Souza, Vitor A. P. Martins dos Santos, and Sören Auer

Pruned Graph Neural Network for Short Story Ordering ... 213
Melika Golestani, Zeinab Borhanifard, Farnaz Tahmasebian, and Heshaam Faili

Multi-task and Generative Adversarial Learning for Robust and Sustainable Text Classification ... 228
Claudia Breazzano, Danilo Croce, and Roberto Basili

Punctuation Restoration in Spoken Italian Transcripts with Transformers ... 245
Alessio Miaschi, Andrea Amelio Ravelli, and Felice Dell'Orletta

AI for Content and Social Media Analysis

On the Impact of Social Media Recommendations on Opinion Consensus ... 263
Vincenzo Auletta, Antonio Coppola, and Diodato Ferraioli

Misogynous MEME Recognition: A Preliminary Study ... 279
Elisabetta Fersini, Giulia Rizzi, Aurora Saibene, and Francesca Gasparini

Signal Processing: Images, Videos and Speech

A Relevance-Based CNN Trimming Method for Low-Resources Embedded Vision ... 297
Dalila Ressi, Mara Pistellato, Andrea Albarelli, and Filippo Bergamasco

Vision-Based Holistic Scene Understanding for Context-Aware Human-Robot Interaction 310
Giorgio De Magistris, Riccardo Caprari, Giulia Castro, Samuele Russo, Luca Iocchi, Daniele Nardi, and Christian Napoli

Human Detection in Drone Images Using YOLO for Search-and-Rescue Operations 326
Sergio Caputo, Giovanna Castellano, Francesco Greco, Corrado Mencar, Niccolò Petti, and Gennaro Vessio

ArabCeleb: Speaker Recognition in Arabic 338
Simone Bianco, Luigi Celona, Intissar Khalifa, Paolo Napoletano, Alexey Petrovsky, Flavio Piccoli, Raimondo Schettini, and Ivan Shanin

Static, Dynamic and Acceleration Features for CNN-Based Speech Emotion Recognition 348
Intissar Khalifa, Ridha Ejbali, Paolo Napoletano, Raimondo Schettini, and Mourad Zaied

EEG-Based BCIs for Elderly Rehabilitation Enhancement Exploiting Artificial Data 359
Aurora Saibene, Francesca Gasparini, and Jordi Solé-Casals

Machine Learning for Argumentation, Explanation, and Exploration

Supporting Trustworthy Artificial Intelligence via Bayesian Argumentation 377
Federico Cerutti

Logic Constraints to Feature Importance 389
Nicola Picchiotti and Marco Gori

Clustering-Based Interpretation of Deep ReLU Network 403
Nicola Picchiotti and Marco Gori

Exploration-Intensive Distractors: Two Environment Proposals and a Benchmarking 413
Jim Martin Catacora Ocana, Roberto Capobianco, and Daniele Nardi

Neural QBAFs: Explaining Neural Networks Under LRP-Based Argumentation Frameworks 429
Purin Sukpanichnant, Antonio Rago, Piyawat Lertvittayakumjorn, and Francesca Toni

Machine Learning and Applications

Domino Saliency Metrics: Improving Existing Channel Saliency Metrics with Structural Information 447
Kaveena Persand, Andrew Anderson, and David Gregg

Learned Sorted Table Search and Static Indexes in Small Model Space 462
Domenico Amato, Giosué Lo Bosco, and Raffaele Giancarlo

Siamese Networks with Transfer Learning for Change Detection in Sentinel-2 Images 478
Giuseppina Andresini, Annalisa Appice, Domenico Dell'Olio, and Donato Malerba

Adversarial Machine Learning in e-Health: Attacking a Smart Prescription System 490
Salvatore Gaglio, Andrea Giammanco, Giuseppe Lo Re, and Marco Morana

Deep Learning of Recurrence Texture in Physiological Signals 503
Tuan D. Pham

Highlighting the Importance of Reducing Research Bias and Carbon Emissions in CNNs 515
Ahmed Badar, Arnav Varma, Adrian Staniec, Mahmoud Gamal, Omar Magdy, Haris Iqbal, Elahe Arani, and Bahram Zonooz

Generating Local Textual Explanations for CNNs: A Semantic Approach Based on Knowledge Graphs 532
Vitor A. C. Horta and Alessandra Mileo

Detection Accuracy for Evaluating Compositional Explanations of Units 550
Sayo M. Makinwa, Biagio La Rosa, and Roberto Capobianco

Knowledge-Based Neural Pre-training for Intelligent Document Management 564
Daniele Margiotta, Danilo Croce, Marco Rotoloni, Barbara Cacciamani, and Roberto Basili

Improving Machine Translation of Arabic Dialects Through Multi-task Learning 580
Youness Moukafih, Nada Sbihi, Mounir Ghogho, and Kamel Smaili

Continuous Defect Prediction in CI/CD Pipelines: A Machine Learning-Based Framework 591
Lazzarinetti Giorgio, Massarenti Nicola, Sgrò Fabio, and Salafia Andrea

AI Applications

Robust Optimization Models For Local Flexibility Characterization of Virtual Power Plants 609
Allegra De Filippo, Michele Lombardi, and Michela Milano

Explainable Artificial Intelligence for Technology Policy Making Using Attribution Networks 624
Feras A. Batarseh, Dominick Perini, Qasim Wani, and Laura Freeman

A Comparative Study of AI Search Methods for Personalised Cancer Therapy Synthesis in COPASI 638
Marco Esposito and Leonardo Picchiami

Effective Analysis of Industry-Relevant Cyber-Physical Systems via Statistical Model Checking 655
Angela Pappagallo

An ASP-Based Approach to Scheduling Pre-operative Assessment Clinic 671
Simone Caruso, Giuseppe Galatà, Marco Maratea, Marco Mochi, and Ivan Porro

Solving the Dial-a-Ride Problem Using an Adapted Genetic Algorithm 689
Stjepan Zelić, Marko Đurasević, Domagoj Jakobović, and Lucija Planinić

Unstructured Data in Predictive Process Monitoring: Lexicographic and Semantic Mapping to ICD-9-CM Codes for the Home Hospitalization Service 700
Massimiliano Ronzani, Roger Ferrod, Chiara Di Francescomarino, Emilio Sulis, Roberto Aringhieri, Guido Boella, Enrico Brunetti, Luigi Di Caro, Mauro Dragoni, Chiara Ghidini, and Renata Marinello

Author Index 717

Planning and Strategies

Task Allocation for Multi-robot Task and Motion Planning: A Case for Object Picking in Cluttered Workspaces

Hossein Karami, Antony Thomas(✉), and Fulvio Mastrogiovanni

Department of Informatics, Bioengineering, Robotics, and Systems Engineering, University of Genoa, Via Opera Pia 13, 16145 Genoa, Italy
hossein.karami@edu.unige.it, antony.thomas@dibris.unige.it, fulvio.mastrogiovanni@unige.it

Abstract. We present an AND/OR graph-based, integrated multi-robot task and motion planning approach which (i) performs task allocation coordinating the activity of a given number of robots, and (ii) is capable of handling tasks which involve an *a priori* unknown number of object re-arrangements, such as those involved in retrieving objects from cluttered workspaces. Such situations may arise, for example, in search and rescue scenarios, while locating/picking a cluttered object of interest. The corresponding problem falls under the category of *planning in clutter*. One of the challenges while planning in clutter is that the number of object re-arrangements required to pick the target object is not known beforehand, in general. Moreover, such tasks can be decomposed in a variety of ways, since different cluttering object re-arrangements are possible to reach the target object. In our approach, task allocation and decomposition is achieved by maximizing a *combined* utility function. The allocated tasks are performed by an integrated task and motion planner, which is robust to the requirement of an unknown number of re-arrangement tasks. We demonstrate our results with experiments in simulation on two Franka Emika manipulators.

Keywords: Task and motion planning · Manipulation planning · Multi-robot system

1 Introduction

Humans trivially perform complex manipulation tasks, such as picking up a tool from a cluttered toolbox, or grabbing a book from a shelf by re-arranging occluding objects. For us, as humans, these tasks seem to be routine, and they do not require much thought. Yet, for robots, this is not the case. Such complex manipulation tasks require symbolic reasoning to decide which objects to re-arrange so as to reach a target object with motion planning to account for the geometric feasibility of the discrete actions. This interaction between symbolic reasoning and motion planning is the subject of integrated Task and Motion

S. Bandini et al. (Eds.): AIxIA 2021, LNAI 13196, pp. 3–17, 2022.
https://doi.org/10.1007/978-3-031-08421-8_1

Planning (TMP). Single-robot TMP has been an area of active research. Yet, current approaches do not naturally account for the capabilities afforded by the presence of multiple robots, such as tasks that can be decomposed in a variety of ways, task allocation involving many robots, or collision avoidance among robots and between each robot and the workspace. A naive extension of single-robot TMP approaches to the multi-robot case would have to treat the multi-robot system as a combined set of single-robot system, which becomes computationally intractable as the number of robots increases.

TMP finds applications in a variety of areas. In search and rescue, locating/picking an object of interest may require re-arranging cluttering objects in debris. This presents two main challenges: (i) the amount of debris to be re-arranged before being able to reach and pick the target object is unknown beforehand, (ii) the debris should be safely re-arranged so that it poses no further impediment to reaching the target. In this paper, we address the above two challenges from a multi-robot perspective, that is, how multiple robots can interact to achieve reaching a target object in clutter while (i) and (ii) hold. As for challenge (i), in scenarios such as search and rescue, one may not always be interested in finding optimal solutions. Therefore, currently we are not concerned with optimality in terms of the number of object re-arrangements or load-balancing among the involved robots. To tackle challenge (ii), in this work we assume the availability of a safe region where the objects to be re-arranged are placed so that they pose no further challenge to reach the target object.

We present an approach for multi-robot integrated task and motion planning which first allocates tasks to the available robots, and then plans via AND/OR graphs a sequence of actions for the multiply decomposable tasks that are optimal with respect to an available utility function for the multi-robot system. As a case in point, we focus on re-arranging clutter in manipulation tasks using multiple manipulators. Specifically, we consider a cluttered table-top where different target objects are to be picked by the robots by re-arranging occluding objects, as in Fig. 1. This requires task allocation among the available robots, followed by a TMP method to complete the allocated tasks. It is noteworthy that to achieve each task, that is, picking a target object, the number of cluttering object re-arrangements is not known beforehand. Though off-the-shelf Planning Domain Definition Language (PDDL) [23] based planners are available for task planning, one needs additional expertise to incorporate task-motion interaction that comply with the state-space search of the planner. Moreover, integrating multi-robot capabilities still remains a challenge. As it will be discussed in Sect. 3, we address these challenges by encoding the task-level abstractions efficiently and compactly within an AND/OR graph that grows iteratively to a tree.

2 Background

2.1 Related Work

Single-robot TMP is an area of research which has received considerable attention in the literature, and spanning two main areas—TMP for manipulation [4,8,

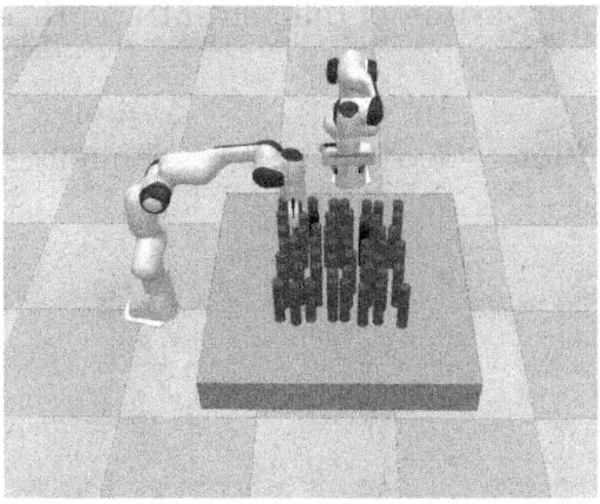

Fig. 1. Cluttered table-top with two target objects (in black) and other objects in red. The multi-robot system consists of two Franka Emika manipulators. The target objects are allocated to each robot or a single robot depending on the utility function. Each target object is then picked by re-arranging clutter via a TMP method. (Color figure online)

9,15,32,39] and TMP for navigation [14,22,27,33,37]. These approaches combine symbolic-level action selection of task planning with the continuous trajectory generation of motion planning [20]. Yet, such methods do not consider the implication of having multiple robots in task allocation and collision avoidance, and would have to treat the multi-robot system as a combined single-robot system, which becomes intractable as the number of robots increases.

Current TMP approaches for multi-arm robot systems focus on coordinated planning strategies, and consider simple pick-and-place or assembly tasks. As such, these methods do not scale to complex manipulation tasks [29,40]. TMP for multi-arm robot systems in the context of welding is considered in [1], whereas [40] discusses an approach for multi-arm TMP manipulation. However, the considered manipulation task is a simple pick-and-place operation involving bringing an object from an initial position to a goal position, where two tables and a cylindrical object form the obstacles. A centralized inverse kinematics solver is employed in [24]. Motion planning for a multi-arm surgical robot is presented in [28] using predefined motion primitives. Yet, a fine tuning of such primitives towards real experimental platforms remains a challenge.

TMP for multi-robot systems has not been addressed thoroughly, and therefore the literature is not sufficiently developed. Henkel *et al.* [13] consider multi-robot transportation problems using a Task Conflict-Based Search (TCBS) algorithm. Such an approach solves a combined task allocation and path planning problem, but assigns a single sub-task at a time and hence may not scale well to an increased number of robots. Interaction Templates (IT) for robot interactions during transportation tasks are presented in [25]. The interactions enable handing over payloads from one robot to another, but the method does not take into account the availability of robots and assumes that there is always a robot available for such an handover. Thus, while considering many tasks at a time this framework does not fare well since a robot may not be immediately available for an handover. A distributed multi-robot TMP method for mobile robot navigation is presented in [38]. However, they define task-level actions for a pair

Table 1. Comparison of different MR TMP methods.

Considered method	Task allocation	Task decomposition	Motion planning	Unknown number of sub-tasks
TCBS [13]	✓			
IT [25]	✓	✓		
[38]	✓		✓	
TMP-CBS [26]	✓	✓	✓	
Our	✓	✓	✓	✓

of robots and therefore optimal solutions are available for an even number of tasks, and only suboptimal solutions are returned for an odd number of tasks. Motes *et al.* [26] present TMP-CBS, a multi-robot TMP approach with sub-task dependencies. They employ a CBS method [31] in the context of transportation tasks. Constructing a conflict tree for CBS requires the knowledge of different constraints which depend on the sub-task conflicts, for example, two robots being present at a given location at the same time. However, in the table-top scenario considered in this paper, the number of sub-tasks is not known beforehand. The capabilities of the discussed methods are summarized in Table 1.

2.2 Task-Motion Planning and AND/OR Graphs

Task planning or classical planning is the process of finding a discrete sequence of actions from the current state to a desired goal state [12].

Definition 1. *A task domain Ω can be represented as a state transition system and is a tuple $\Omega = \langle S, A, \gamma, s_0, S_g \rangle$ where:*

- *S is a finite set of states;*
- *A is a finite set of actions;*
- *$\gamma : S \times A \rightarrow S$ such that $s' = \gamma(s, a)$;*
- *$s_0 \in S$ is the start state;*
- *$S_g \subseteq S$ is the set of goal states.*

Definition 2. *The task plan for a task domain Ω is the sequence of actions $a_0, \ldots, a_m$ such that $s_{i+1} = \gamma(s_i, a_i)$, for $i = 0, \ldots, m$ and s_{m+1} satisfies S_g.*

Motion planning finds a sequence of collision free configurations from a given start configuration to a desired goal [21].

Definition 3. *A motion planning domain is a tuple $M = \langle C, f, q_0, G \rangle$ where:*

- *C is the configuration space;*
- *$f = \{0, 1\}$, for collision $f = 0$, else $f = 1$;*
- *$q_0 \in C$ is the initial configuration;*
- *$G \in C$ is the set of goal configurations.*

Definition 4. *A motion plan for M finds a collision free trajectory in C from q_0 to $q_n \in G$ such that $f = 1$ for $q_0, ..., q_n$. Alternatively, a motion plan for M is a function of the form $\tau : [0, 1] \rightarrow C_{free}$ such that $\tau(0) = q_0$ and $\tau(1) \in G$, where $C_{free} \subset C$ is the configurations where the robot does not collide with other objects or itself.*

TMP combines discrete task planning and continuous motion planning to facilitate efficient interaction between the two domains. Below we define the TMP problem formally.

Definition 5. *A task-motion planning with task domain Ω and motion planning domain M is a tuple $\Psi = \langle C, \Omega, \phi, \xi, q_0 \rangle$ where:*

- *$\phi : S \rightarrow 2^C$, maps states to the configuration space;*
- *$\xi : A \rightarrow 2^C$, maps actions to motion plans.*

Definition 6. *The TMP problem for the TMP domain Ψ is to find a sequence of discrete actions $a_0, ..., a_n$ such that $s_{i+1} = \gamma(s_i, a_i)$, $s_{n+1} \in S_g$ and a corresponding sequence of motion plans $\tau_0, ..., \tau_n$ such that for $i = 0, ..., n$, it holds that (i) $\tau_i(0) \in \phi(s_i)$ and $\tau_i(1) \in \phi(s_{i+1})$, (ii) $\tau_{i+1}(0) = \tau_i(1)$, and (iii) $\tau_i \in \xi(a_i)$.*

We now provide a brief overview of AND/OR graphs [5,16]. An AND/OR graph is a graph which represents a problem-solving process [3].

Definition 7. *An AND/OR graph G is a directed graph represented by the tuple $G = \langle N, H \rangle$ where:*

- *N is a set of nodes;*
- *H is a set of hyper-arcs.*

For a given AND/OR graph G, we have that $H = \{h_1, \ldots, h_m\}$, where h_i is a many-to-one mapping from a set of child nodes to a parent node. In that sense, a hyper-arc induces a logical *and* relationship between the child nodes/states, that is, all the child states should be satisfied to achieve the parent state. Similarly, a single parent node can be the co-domain for different hyper-arcs h_i. These hyper-arcs are in logical *or* with the parent node. Nodes without any successors or children are called the *terminal* nodes. The terminal nodes are either a success node or a failure node. We now mathematically define an AND/OR graph network, a detailed treatment of which can be found in [17].

Definition 8. *For an AND/OR graph $G = \langle N, H \rangle$, an augmented AND/OR graph G^a is a directed graph represented by the tuple $G^a = \langle N^a, H^a \rangle$ where:*

- *$N^a = \{N, n^v\}$ with n_v being the virtual node;*
- *$H^a = \{H, H^v\}$ with $H^v = \{h_i^v\}_{1 \leq i \leq |H^v|}$.*

Definition 9. *An AND/OR graph network Γ is a directed graph $\Gamma = \langle \mathcal{G}, T \rangle$ where:*

- *$\mathcal{G} = \{G_1^a, \ldots, G_{n'}^a\}$ is a set of augmented AND/OR graphs G_i^a;*
- *$T = \{t_1, \ldots, t_{n'-1}\}$ is a set of transitions such that $G_{i+1}^a = t_i(G_i^a)$, $1 \leq i \leq n' - 1$;*

where n' is the total number of graphs in the network. Alternatively, n' is also the depth of the network.

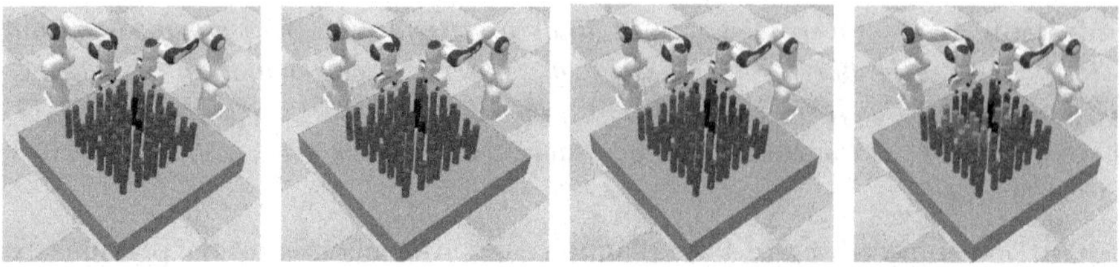

(a) (b) (c) (d)

Fig. 2. Illustration of the obstacle selection method: (a) a cluttered table-top scenario with two robots r1 (right), r2 (left) and the target objects in black; (b) a valid grasping angle range is computed by discretizing a fixed grasping angle range of $-\frac{\pi}{2}$ to $\frac{\pi}{2}$; the objects that fall within the grasping angle range of r1 (one target) are shown in blue; (c) blue objects within the grasping angle range of r1, considering both the targets; (d) Objects within the grasping range of both r1 (blue) and r2 (green), considering both the targets for each robot. (Color figure online)

2.3 Problem Definition

We present a framework which (i) allocates T manipulation tasks to a set of R robots, and (ii) plans for a sequence of motions-actions for each robot to achieve the respective tasks. To this end, we consider a multi-robot setting with a cluttered table-top wherein different target objects need to be picked by re-arranging the clutter. Thus, each manipulation task corresponds to picking up a target object.

In order to carry out each task, objects need to be re-arranged – depending on the clutter *degree* – and the number of objects to be re-arranged is not known beforehand. By representing the task-level abstractions within an AND/OR graph network (see Sect. 3), we can overcome this issue.

3 Multi-robot Task and Motion Planning

In this Section, we detail our multi-robot TMP method. We begin by describing a heuristic approach providing a rough estimate of the objects to be re-arranged to pick a target object. The approach allows us to define a combined utility function for the multi-robot system to perform task allocation. Allocated tasks are then carried out using a TMP method based on an AND/OR graph network and a sampling based motion planner.

3.1 Obstacles Selection

An overview of the method can be seen in Fig. 2. First, it finds different feasible plans to the target, each one corresponding to different grasping angles, by ignoring all the obstacles in the workspace. This is done by discretising the set of graspable angles, that is $\left[-\frac{\pi}{2}, \frac{\pi}{2}\right]$ (the axis is located at the center of the target). It is noteworthy that we consider only side grasps to make the scenario more challenging. Among the available plans, the maximum and minimum grasping angles, namely α and β, are then obtained. The method then constructs two lines starting at the center of the target object and towards the robot with the corresponding angles α and β. The lines are terminated when there are no more obstacles along their paths. The end-points are then joined to form a triangle. This triangle is then enlarged on all the three sides by the radius of the bounding volume sphere of the end-effector. The objects within the constructed triangle are the objects to be re-arranged to facilitate the target grasp.

We note that what we describe here is an approximate method to identify the objects to be re-arranged. The actual set of objects depend on other such factors as the degrees of freedom of the robot, the size of the links and the end-effector, or the *degree* of clutter. As it will be discussed later, for all practical purposes we are interested only in an approximate measure so as to perform multi-robot task allocation.

3.2 Task Allocation

Let R be the number of available robots, and T the number of tasks to be allocated, that is, we have T target objects to be picked, such that $T \geq R$. Task allocation is performed offline and we assume that each task, that is, picking up a target object from clutter, is performed by a single robot, and that each robot is able to execute only one task at a time. We also recall here our assumption from the Introduction that the objects to be re-arranged to reach and pick a target are placed in a *safe* region. Our task allocation strategy falls under the Single-Task, Single-Robot, Time-extended Assignment (ST-SR-TA) taxonomy of Gerkey and Matarić [11], since the multi-robot system contains more tasks than robots. In order to allocate tasks, we define $U_{r_i t_j}$ as the utility function for a robot $r_i \in R$ executing a task $t_j \in T$. In this work, utility is inversely proportional to the number of object re-arrangements required to grasp the target object. To determine such a measure, we first (randomly) select a target object t_1, and then for each robot r_i we run the obstacles selection algorithm described above. For each r_i, such a run returns the set of objects to be re-arranged to reach t_1. Let us denote this set by $O_{r_i t_1}$ (and by $O_{r_i t_j}$ for the jth task). The robot r_k whose set $O_{r_k t_1}$ is of minimum cardinality (i.e., maximum utility) is then allocated task t_1. For the next target t_2 this step is repeated. We note here that $O_{r_k t_2}$ is computed offline and returns the number of objects to be re-arranged by robot r_k to execute task t_2. However, it may be the case that some objects appear in both $O_{r_k t_1}$ and $O_{r_k t_2}$, that is, $O_{r_k t_1} \cap O_{r_k t_2} \neq \{\emptyset\}$. Since each robot executes one task at a time, r_k can execute t_2 only after having performed t_1. Thus, during the execution phase, r_k may have already removed the common objects while executing t_1, and therefore these objects may be ignored to avoid *intra-robot* double counting while computing the utility $U_{r_k t_2}$ offline.

Once each robot is allocated a task, the set of remaining tasks T' is completed only after the execution of the assigned tasks. For the remaining T' tasks, the *inter-robot* or robot-robot double counting must be considered. Reasoning in a similar manner for intra-robot double counting, the set $O_{r_i t_j}$ restricted to

$T \setminus T' < j \leq T$ for the remaining T' tasks may have common objects with respect to $O_{r_i t_j}$ restricted to $1 < j \leq T'$ of the assigned tasks. Thus, the total number of objects to be re-arranged for robot r_i to execute task t_j is

$$O^c_{r_i t_j} = |O_{r_i t_j}| - \sum_k |O_{r_i t_j t_k}| - \sum_k \sum_l |O_{r_i r_k t_j t_l}| \tag{1}$$

where $|\cdot|$ denotes the cardinality of a set,

$$O_{r_i t_j t_k} = \begin{cases} O_{r_i t_j} \cap O_{r_i t_k} & \text{if } r_i \text{ allotted } t_k \text{ previously,} \\ 0 & \text{otherwise.} \end{cases} \tag{2}$$

and

$$O_{r_i r_k t_j t_l} = \begin{cases} O_{r_i t_j} \cap O_{r_k t_l} & \text{if } r_k \text{ allotted } t_l \text{ previously,} \\ 0 & \text{otherwise,} \end{cases} \tag{3}$$

with the terms $|O_{r_i t_j t_k}|$ and $|O_{r_i r_k t_j t_l}|$ modeling the intra-robot and inter-robot double counting, respectively. We therefore have the following utility function

$$U_{r_i t_j} = \frac{1}{1 + O^c_{r_i t_j}}. \tag{4}$$

The maximum utility of $U_{r_i t_j} = 1$ is therefore achieved when no object re-arrangement is required to execute task t_j, that is, $O^c_{r_i t_j} = 0$. Using the taxonomy in [18], we thus have In-schedule Dependencies (ID) – the effective utility of an agent for a task depends on what other tasks that agent is performing as well as Cross-schedule Dependencies (XD) – the effective utility of an agent for a task depends not only on its own task but also on the tasks of other agents.

We now define the combined utility of the multi-robot system, which consists of maximising

$$\sum_{i \in R} \sum_{j \in T} U_{r_i t_j} x_{r_i t_j} \tag{5}$$

$$\begin{aligned} \text{such that} \sum_{i \in R} x_{r_i t_j} &= 1 \\ \text{where}\, x_{r_i t_j} &\in \{0, 1\}. \end{aligned} \tag{6}$$

From (4) and (5) we see that the robot with the minimum number of object re-arrangements for a given task is thus assigned the maximum utility. In case of a tie, we select the robot which has not been allocated any task. If all the robots with the same utility have been allocated tasks already, or if none has been allotted, then a robot is selected randomly.

3.3 Task Decomposition

Each manipulation task is decomposed into a set of sub-tasks which correspond to pick-and-place tasks, that is, re-arrangement of the objects that hinder the target grasp. As seen above, the number of sub-tasks for a given task are not known beforehand. Moreover, *multiple decomposability* [41] is possible since the clutter can be re-arranged in different ways. We seek a decomposition minimizing the number of sub-tasks for the multi-robot system. This can be achieved during task allocation since utility is computed based on the obstacles selection method. In this work, we consider *complex task decomposition* [41] – a multiply decomposable task for which there exists at least one decomposition that is a set of multi-robot allocatable sub-tasks. Though in this work we ignore the multi-robot allocatability property, this can be incorporated trivially. For example, let us consider the case where two robots have the same utility to perform a task t_j. In this case, the sub-tasks can be equally divided to achieve multi-robot allocatability or one robot may be selected randomly (or depending on previous allocation) to perform the entire task.

3.4 Task and Motion Planning

PDDL [23] is the *de facto* standard for task planning, and most TMP approaches resort to it. Integrated TMP requires a mapping between the task space and the motion space. Semantic attachments are used in [4,6,7,37] to associate algorithms to functions and predicate symbols via external procedures. However, it is assumed by these approaches that the workspace be known in advance. Moreover, they reduce motion space to a finite space since the robot configuration, the grasp poses, and other geometrical constraints need to be specified in advance. This issue is addressed in [10] using *streams*, which enable procedures within PDDL to sample values of continuous variables, therefore encoding an infinite set of actions. Though off-the-shelf PDDL planners are available, one needs additional expertise to incorporate semantic attachments or streams complying with the planner semantics. Furthermore, for the cluttered table-top scenario, the number of objects that need to be re-arranged is not known beforehand. As a result, one would need observation based re-planning within the PDDL framework, which require additional mapping between the PDDL action space and the observation space of the robot [2].

A cluttered table-top scenario in the context of single-robot TMP is considered in [17,36]. To address the above mentioned challenges associated with PDDL modeling, in [17] the task-level abstractions of the TMP problem is efficiently and compactly encoded within an augmented AND/OR graph (see Sect. 2) that grows iteratively until solutions are found, where each iteration is meant at managing a sub-task as defined above.

In general, AND/OR graphs are constructed offline. However, the number of objects to be re-arranged depends on the clutter degree and is not known beforehand. [17] introduces AND/OR graph networks, consisting of augmented AND/OR graphs which iteratively deepen at run-time till a solution to the modeled problem is found. The key idea is that the set of task-level abstractions, i.e., the states (nodes) and actions (hyper-arcs) of the AND/OR graph defined for the robot remain the same irrespective of the number of re-arrangements, i.e., sub-tasks. Therefore, one can define an initial AND/OR graph encoding task-level actions, which is augmented with the initial workspace configuration. The augmented graph is then iteratively expanded with the updated workspace configuration as long as sub-tasks are carried out resulting in a network of AND/OR graphs. In this work, we use this AND/OR graph network based task planner and customize it for multi-robot task planning. For motion planning, we simply use MoveIt [34], which supports RRT [19] from OMPL [35]. The motion planner is first employed to execute the obstacles selection algorithm. Once the tasks are allocated, the motion planner is called to (i) achieve the re-arrangement of each sub-task identified by the task planner (i.e., the AND/OR graph network) and (ii) to grasp the target object.

3.5 The Multi-robot Task-Motion Planning Loop

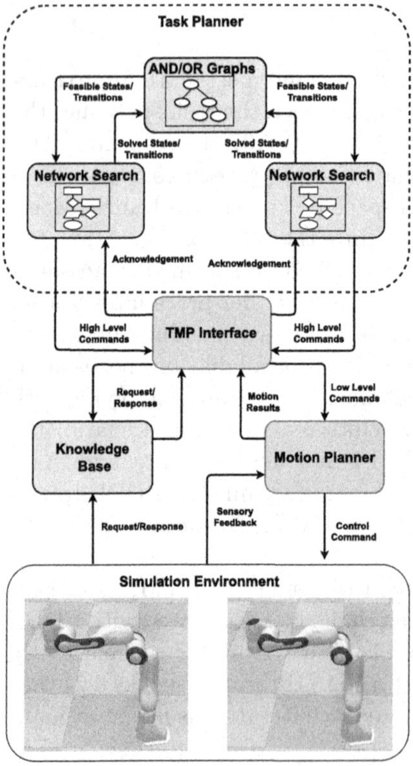

Fig. 3. System's architecture.

Figure 3 depicts the overall system's architecture of our multi-robot TMP method. Once the tasks have been allocated, *Task Planner* selects the abstract actions whose geometric execution feasibility is checked by *Motion Planner*. The *Task Planner* layer consists of the *AND/OR Graphs* module – the initial augmented AND/OR graphs for the robots, and the *Network Search* module – the search procedure iterating the initial augmented graphs. As discussed in Sect. 3.4, the initial augmented AND/OR graph consists of the task-level actions for each robot augmented with the current workspace configuration. *AND/OR Graphs* provides a set of achievable transitions between the states to *Network Search*, and receives the set of allowed states and transitions as the graph is expanded. *Task Planner* then associates each state or state transition with an ordered set of actions in accordance with the workspace and robot configurations. The *Knowledge Base* module stores the information regarding the current workspace configuration, that is, the objects and their locations in the workspace as well as the robot configuration. This module augments the graphs with the current workspace configuration to facilitate *Network Search*. Since we consider here two robots and their respective configurations need to be updated, we have two *Network Search* modules corresponding to each robot.

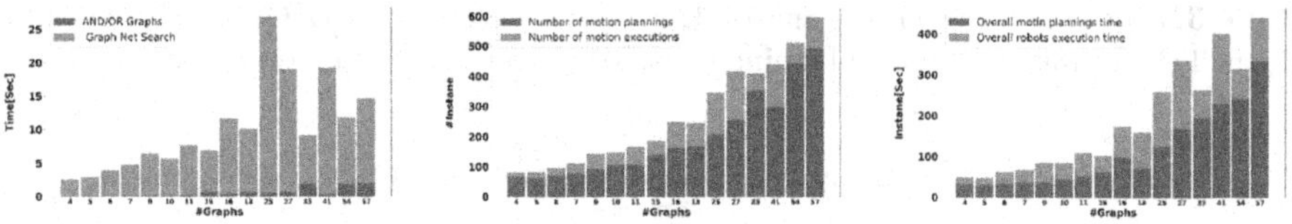

(a) (b) (c)

Fig. 4. Various histograms with and increasing AND/OR graph network depth.

TMP interface acts as a bridge between the task planning and the motion planning layers. It receives action commands from *Task Planner*, converts them to their geometric values (for example, a grasping command requires various geometric values such as the target pose or the robot base pose), and passes them on to *Motion Planner* to check motion feasibility. To this end, the module retrieves information regarding both the workspace and robots from *Knowledge Base*. If an action is found to be feasible, it is then sent for execution. Upon execution, *Task Planner* receives an acknowledgment regarding action completion and the *Knowledge Base* is updated accordingly.

4 Experimental Results

Table 2. Average computation times for different modules.

Activity	Average [s]	Std. dev. [s]
AND/OR graphs	0.03213	0.02174
Network search	0.8992	0.1862
Motion planner (attempts)	18.320	6.450
Motion execution (attempts)	6.3126	0.8176
Motion planner (time)	0.8010	0.2170
Motion execution (time)	4.7490	2.0240

We validate and demonstrate the performance of our multi-robot TMP approach by performing experiments in the state-of-the-art robotics simulator CoppeliaSim [30], employing two Franka Emika manipulators. As seen in Fig. 1, we consider a cluttered table-top scenario where manipulation tasks correspond to picking up different target objects. For each task, the sub-tasks consist of removing objects hindering each target grasp. In this work, such objects are picked and placed outside the working area, in a *safe* space. The number of objects to be removed is unknown (and therefore likewise the number of sub-tasks) at planning time. Experiments are conducted on a workstation equipped with an Intel(R) core i7-8700@3.2 GHz × 12 CPU's and 16 GB of RAM. The architecture is developed using C++ and Python under ROS Kinetic. A video demonstrating the results can be found at https://youtu.be/nkB_LHorg1g. We begin with 6 objects in the workspace with two of them being target objects. To test the scalability to an increasing number of objects, we perform experiments with up to 64 objects. For a given number of objects the experiment is conducted 3 times, and in each experiment the target objects are chosen randomly. Table 2 reports the average combined planning and execution times for robots r_1 and r_2, focusing on the architecture's modules. AND/OR graph and

Table 3. Statistics for robots r_1 and r_2. Legenda: d - average AND/OR graph network depth, TP - average total task planning time, MP - average total motion planning time.

Objects	d	r_1				r_2			
		TP [s]	MP [s]	MP attempts	Objects re-arranged	TP [s]	MP [s]	MP attempts	Objects re-arranged
6	2.33	1.5505	16.339	36.66	1.66	1.1201	13.207	31.33	1.0
8	2.66	1.422	13.721	32.66	1.66	1.1478	18.154	28.66	1.0
9	2.33	1.3532	16.909	30.66	1.0	2.415	18.520	40.0	2.33
12	4	2.4025	20.3363	42.66	2.66	2.0532	17.825	37.66	2.33
16	4.66	2.755	20.1718	47.66	3.33	2.6326	22.830	45.66	3.33
20	3.66	2.125	17.618	42.33	2.66	4.022	25.182	61.33	5.33
30	5.75	3.464	25.854	56.75	4.25	4.748	45.226	83.75	5.75
49	17	8.642	81.361	147.0	6.33	6.886	49.593	106.66	10.66
64	22.6	9.053	132.179	203.0	12.2	5.271	66.994	109.875	7.0

graph network search times are per number of grown graphs. It must be noted that motion planning failures due to actuation errors or grasping failures lead to re-plans, and therefore to a larger number of motion planning attempts.

Table 3 report the average network depth d, the average total task planning time, the average total motion planning time, the average number of motion planning attempts, and the average number of objects to be re-arranged for robots r_1 and r_2, respectively. As the AND/OR graph network depth d increases, task planning times are *almost* linear with respect to d. This is so because for an AND/OR graph network with each graph consisting of n nodes, the time complexity is only $O(nd)$ [17]. In contrast, PDDL-based planners are characterized by a search complexity of $O(n \log n)$, where $n \approx 2^{13}$ for the table-top scenario. Figure 4 shows different histograms for an increasing network depth d. In particular, Fig. 4(a) shows the total task planning time with d. One can readily observes that the linearity in planning time is not strictly followed. For example, the time for $d = 25$ is greater than the time for $d = 41$. In many cases, due to motion planning failures a new graph is expanded before reaching the terminal node, which implies that more nodes are traversed for $d = 25$ compared to $d = 41$, therefore explaining the variations. Figure 4(b) plots the number of motion planning attempts and the total executions with an increasing d. An increase in d in most cases correspond to a higher degree of clutter. Therefore, as depth d or the graphs increase the motion planning attempts increases as well. However, motion planning failures can also increase the depth d since a new graph need to be expanded. This explains the slight deviation in the trend. Figure 4(c) reports the total motion planning and execution times with an increasing d, and the plot readily follows from the discussions above.

5 Conclusion

We present a task allocation approach for integrated multi-robot task and motion planning capable of handling tasks with an unknown number of sub-tasks. Our obstacles selection strategy combined with the introduced utility function allocates task to the available robots. Allocated tasks are then achieved by our TMP method, which comprises an AND/OR graph network based task planner that is robust to the issue of an unknown number of sub-tasks. We show that our method is capable of handling varying degree of clutter, i.e., the number of objects in the workspace. Currently, the objects hindering each tasks are removed from the workspace. As a result, subsequent tasks need not consider theses objects while computing the utility. There may be situations in which removing objects from the workspace will not be possible, and the planner will have to select free space for object placement. Future work will seek to develop a non-myopic technique to predict possible future trajectories based on the previous ones and the current environment configuration so as to enable the selection of smart object placements.

References

1. Basile, F., Caccavale, F., Chiacchio, P., Coppola, J., Curatella, C.: Task-oriented motion planning for multi-arm robotic systems. Robot. Comput.-Integr. Manuf. **28**(5), 569–582 (2012)
2. Bertolucci, R., et al.: Manipulation of articulated objects using dual-arm robots via answer set programming. Theory Pract. Logic Program. **21**(3), 372–401 (2021)
3. Chang, C.L., Slagle, J.R.: An admissible and optimal algorithm for searching AND/OR graphs. Artif. Intell. **2**(2), 117–128 (1971)
4. Dantam, N.T., Kingston, Z.K., Chaudhuri, S., Kavraki, L.E.: Incremental task and motion planning: a constraint-based approach. In: Robotics: Science and Systems (2016)
5. Darvish, K., Simetti, E., Mastrogiovanni, F., Casalino, G.: A hierarchical architecture for human-robot cooperation processes. IEEE Trans. Robot. **37**, 567–586 (2020)
6. Dornhege, C., Eyerich, P., Keller, T., Trüg, S., Brenner, M., Nebel, B.: Semantic attachments for domain-independent planning systems. In: International Conference on Automated Planning and Scheduling (ICAPS), Thessaloniki, Greece, pp. 114–121, September 2009
7. Dornhege, C., Gissler, M., Teschner, M., Nebel, B.: Integrating symbolic and geometric planning for mobile manipulation. In: IEEE International Workshop on Safety, Security & Rescue Robotics (SSRR), pp. 1–6. IEEE (2009)
8. Erdem, E., Haspalamutgil, K., Palaz, C., Patoglu, V., Uras, T.: Combining high-level causal reasoning with low-level geometric reasoning and motion planning for robotic manipulation. In: 2011 IEEE International Conference on Robotics and Automation, pp. 4575–4581. IEEE (2011)
9. Garrett, C.R., Lozano-Perez, T., Kaelbling, L.P.: FFRob: leveraging symbolic planning for efficient task and motion planning. Int. J. Robot. Res. **37**(1), 104–136 (2018)
10. Garrett, C.R., Lozano-Pérez, T., Kaelbling, L.P.: PDDLStream: integrating symbolic planners and blackbox samplers via optimistic adaptive planning. In: Proceedings of the International Conference on Automated Planning and Scheduling, vol. 30, pp. 440–448 (2020)

11. Gerkey, B.P., Matarić, M.J.: A formal analysis and taxonomy of task allocation in multi-robot systems. Int. J. Robot. Res. **23**(9), 939–954 (2004)
12. Ghallab, M., Nau, D., Traverso, P.: Automated Planning and Acting. Cambridge University Press, Cambridge (2016)
13. Henkel, C., Abbenseth, J., Toussaintl, M.: An optimal algorithm to solve the combined task allocation and path finding problem. In: 2019 IEEE/RSJ International Conference on Intelligent Robots and Systems (IROS), pp. 4140–4146. IEEE (2019)
14. Jiang, Y., Yang, F., Zhang, S., Stone, P.: Task-motion planning with reinforcement learning for adaptable mobile service robots. In: IROS, pp. 7529–7534 (2019)
15. Kaelbling, L.P., Lozano-Pérez, T.: Integrated task and motion planning in belief space. Int. J. Robot. Res. **32**(9–10), 1194–1227 (2013)
16. Karami, H., Darvish, K., Mastrogiovanni, F.: A task allocation approach for human-robot collaboration in product defects inspection scenarios. In: 2020 29th IEEE International Conference on Robot and Human Interactive Communication (RO-MAN), pp. 1127–1134. IEEE (2020)
17. Karami, H., Thomas, A., Mastrogiovanni, F.: A task-motion planning framework using iteratively deepened AND/OR graph networks. arXiv preprint arXiv:2104.01549 (2021)
18. Korsah, G.A., Stentz, A., Dias, M.B.: A comprehensive taxonomy for multi-robot task allocation. Int. J. Robot. Res. **32**(12), 1495–1512 (2013)
19. Kuffner, J.J., LaValle, S.M.: RRT-connect: an efficient approach to single-query path planning. In: Proceedings of the ICRA 2000 IEEE International Conference on Robotics and Automation, vol. 2, pp. 995–1001. IEEE (2000)
20. Lagriffoul, F., Dantam, N.T., Garrett, C., Akbari, A., Srivastava, S., Kavraki, L.E.: Platform-independent benchmarks for task and motion planning. Robot. Autom. Lett. **3**, 3765–3772 (2018)
21. Latombe, J.C.: Robot Motion Planning. Kluwer Academic Publishers (1991)
22. Lo, S.Y., Zhang, S., Stone, P.: PETLON: planning efficiently for task-level-optimal navigation. In: Proceedings of the 17th International Conference on Autonomous Agents and MultiAgent Systems, pp. 220–228. International Foundation for Autonomous Agents and Multiagent Systems (2018)
23. McDermott, D., et al.: PDDL- the planning domain definition language. In: AIPS 1998 Planning Competition Committee (1998)
24. Mirrazavi Salehian, S.S., Figueroa, N., Billard, A.: A unified framework for coordinated multi-arm motion planning. Int. J. Robot. Res. **37**(10), 1205–1232 (2018)
25. Motes, J., Sandström, R., Adams, W., Ogunyale, T., Thomas, S., Amato, N.M.: Interaction templates for multi-robot systems. IEEE Robot. Autom. Lett. **4**(3), 2926–2933 (2019)
26. Motes, J., Sandström, R., Lee, H., Thomas, S., Amato, N.M.: Multi-robot task and motion planning with subtask dependencies. IEEE Robot. Autom. Lett. **5**(2), 3338–3345 (2020)
27. Muñoz, P., R-Moreno, M.D., Barrero, D.F.: Unified framework for path-planning and task-planning for autonomous robots. Robot. Autonom. Syst. **82**, 1–14 (2016)
28. Preda, N., Manurung, A., Lambercy, O., Gassert, R., Bonfè, M.: Motion planning for a multi-arm surgical robot using both sampling-based algorithms and motion primitives. In: 2015 IEEE/RSJ International Conference on Intelligent Robots and Systems (IROS), pp. 1422–1427. IEEE (2015)
29. Rodríguez, C., Suárez, R.: Combining motion planning and task assignment for a dual-arm system. In: 2016 IEEE/RSJ International Conference on Intelligent Robots and Systems (IROS), pp. 4238–4243. IEEE (2016)

30. Rohmer, E., Singh, S.P.N., Freese, M.: CoppeliaSim (formerly V-REP): a versatile and scalable robot simulation framework. In: Proceedings of the International Conference on Intelligent Robots and Systems (IROS) (2013). www.coppeliarobotics.com
31. Sharon, G., Stern, R., Felner, A., Sturtevant, N.R.: Conflict-based search for optimal multi-agent pathfinding. Artif. Intell. **219**, 40–66 (2015)
32. Srivastava, S., Fang, E., Riano, L., Chitnis, R., Russell, S., Abbeel, P.: Combined task and motion planning through an extensible planner-independent interface layer. In: IEEE International Conference on Robotics and Automation (ICRA), pp. 639–646. IEEE (2014)
33. Stilman, M., Kuffner, J.: Planning among movable obstacles with artificial constraints. Int. J. Robot. Res. **27**(11–12), 1295–1307 (2008)
34. Sucan, I.A., Chitta, S.: Moveit! (2013)
35. Şucan, I.A., Moll, M., Kavraki, L.E.: The open motion planning library. IEEE Robot. Autom. Mag. **19**(4), 72–82 (2012). https://doi.org/10.1109/MRA.2012.2205651. https://ompl.kavrakilab.org
36. Thomas, A., Karami, H., Mastrogiovanni, F.: Iterative AND/OR graphs for task-motion planning. In: Italian Conference on Robotics and Intelligent Machines (I-RIM) (2020)
37. Thomas, A., Mastrogiovanni, F., Baglietto, M.: Task-motion planning for navigation in belief space. In: Asfour, T., Yoshida, E., Park, J., Christensen, H., Khatib, O. (eds.) ISRR 2019. SPAR, vol. 20, pp. 542–558. Springer, Cham (2022). https://doi.org/10.1007/978-3-030-95459-8_33
38. Thomas, A., Mastrogiovanni, F., Baglietto, M.: Towards multi-robot task-motion planning for navigation in belief space. In: European Starting AI Researchers' Symposium. CEUR (2020)
39. Toussaint, M.: Logic-geometric programming: an optimization-based approach to combined task and motion planning. In: Twenty-Fourth International Joint Conference on Artificial Intelligence (2015)
40. Umay, I., Fidan, B., Melek, W.: An integrated task and motion planning technique for multi-robot-systems. In: 2019 IEEE International Symposium on Robotic and Sensors Environments (ROSE), pp. 1–7. IEEE (2019)
41. Zlot, R.: An auction-based approach to complex task allocation for multirobot teams. Ph.D. thesis. Robotics Institute, Carnegie Mellon University (2006)

A Sound (But Incomplete) Polynomial Translation from Discretised PDDL+ to Numeric Planning

Francesco Percassi[1](✉), Enrico Scala[2], and Mauro Vallati[1]

[1] University of Huddersfield, Huddersfield, UK
f.percassi@hud.ac.uk

[2] Università degli Studi di Brescia, Brescia, Italy

Abstract. PDDL+ is an expressive planning formalism that enables the modelling of domains having both discrete and continuous dynamics. Recently, two mappings for translating discretised PDDL+ problems into a numeric a-temporal task have been proposed. Such translations produce a task of exponential or polynomial size w.r.t. the size of the native task. In this work, starting from the above-mentioned polynomial translation, we introduce a sound but not generally complete variant that has the potential to improve the performance of numeric planning engines. We define the subclass of problems where the variant is safely applicable, and we assess the advantages of such a translation.

Keywords: Automated planning for hybrid systems · Planning via translation

1 Introduction

Automated planning is a solid branch of artificial intelligence that aims to design methodologies for synthesising a sequence of actions capable to transform a given state, i.e., the initial state, into the desired state, i.e., a goal state.

Many real-world systems are *hybrid* in nature, as they are characterised by the coexistence of a discrete and continuous dynamic.

In automated planning, hybrid systems can be represented and modelled using the PDDL+ formalism [5]. PDDL+ provides a representation that elegantly puts together an agent, via an action-oriented formalisation, with an explicit representation of the environment and its exogenous dynamics. However, PDDL+ planning problems are notoriously difficult to be solved, and there is a restricted set of planning engines that can natively support PDDL+.

Recently, to increase the pool of planning engines that can tackle PDDL+ planning problems, an exponential and a polynomial translation schemata have been proposed [11]. The aim of such translations is to transform a PDDL+ problem into a simpler problem, more precisely, a discrete a-temporal numeric planning problem represented using the PDDL2.1 formalism [4].

S. Bandini et al. (Eds.): AIxIA 2021, LNAI 13196, pp. 18–31, 2022.
https://doi.org/10.1007/978-3-031-08421-8_2

This approach is part of a broader family of approaches aimed at solving problems represented in highly-expressive languages by means of translation into some less expressive languages (see, e.g., [2,3,6,8–10,12,14]). This way, any solver that can tackle the simpler case can be used to solve the more expressive case as well.

In this work, we present a variant of the polynomial (POLY) scheme proposed in [11]. This variant starts from the observation that in many planning problems the continuous effects of PDDL+ processes can be decomposed to obtain translations that are lighter and more approachable by numeric, a-temporal planners. We study this variant, that we name POLY$^-$, both theoretically and practically. Our theoretical results indicate that POLY$^-$ is sound, but generally incomplete for a general discretised PDDL+ planning problem. After having formally presented the POLY$^-$ translation, we first identify which kinds of solution are excluded from the search space induced by the novel transformation, and second, we outline in which class of planning problems POLY$^-$ is complete, too. From a practical point of view, we study this translation against the original POLY. Our experimental analysis indicates that POLY$^-$ is competitive and well complements existing approaches to PDDL+. Further, even in cases when the variant does not guarantee the completeness, it can still speed up the planning process if used in a portfolio-based approach.

2 Background

In this section we report on the PDDL+ problem [5] interpreted over a discrete timeline [11], and the problem of numeric planning as the one that can be specified in PDDL2.1 (level 2) [4]. Then, we introduce the polynomial translation. We borrow notation and the semantics from [11], and focus here on the description of those aspects that are crucial to understand this work. We detail our problems using propositional formulas over comparisons and Boolean variables[1]. A comparison is $\xi \bowtie 0$ where ξ is a mathematical expression, and $\bowtie \in \{\leq, <, =, >, \geq\}$.

Definition 1. *A* PDDL+ problem Π *is a tuple* $\langle F, X, I, G, A, E, P \rangle$ *where:* F *and* X *are the sets of Boolean and numeric variables, respectively;* I *and* G *are the description of the initial state, expressed as a full assignment to all variables in* X *and* F*, and the description of the goal, expressed as a formula, respectively;* A *and* E *are the sets of actions and events, respectively. Actions and events are pairs* $\langle p, e \rangle$ *where* p *is a propositional formula and* e *is a set of conditional effects of the form* $c \triangleright e$ *where (i)* c *is a formula and (ii)* e *is a set of Boolean* ($f = \{\bot, \top\}$) *or numeric* ($\langle \{asgn, inc, dec\}, x, \xi \rangle$*, where* ξ *is an expression over* X) *assignments; Finally,* P *is a set of processes. A process is a pair* $\langle p, e' \rangle$ *where* p *is a formula and* e' *is a set of numeric continuous effects expressed as pairs* $\langle x, \xi \rangle$*, with the meaning that* ξ *represents the time-derivative of* x*, with* $x \in X$*.*

[1] We use positive and negative literals to short-cut the assignments $f = \top$ and $f = \bot$.

Let $a = \langle p, e \rangle$ be an action/event/process, *pre*(a) is the precondition p of a, and *eff*(a) the effect of a. In the following we will use a, ρ, and ε for denoting an action, process, and event, respectively.

A plan for a PDDL+ problem is an ordered set of timed actions plus a time envelope, organised formally as follows.

Definition 2. *A* PDDL+ plan π_t *is a pair* $\langle \pi, \langle t_s, t_e \rangle \rangle$ *where:* $\pi = \langle \langle a_0, t_0 \rangle, \langle a_1, t_1 \rangle, ..., \langle a_{n-1}, t_{n-1} \rangle \rangle$*, with* $t_i \in \mathbb{R}$*, is a sequence of time-stamped actions;* $\langle t_s, t_e \rangle$*, with* $t_s, t_e \in \mathbb{R}$*, is a real interval, called envelope, within which* π *is performed.*

PDDL2.1 is the subclass of PDDL+ where we only have actions and no explicit management of metric time.

Definition 3. *A* PDDL2.1 problem Π *is a tuple* $\langle F, X, I, G, A, c \rangle$ *where all elements are as for* PDDL+*, yet there are neither processes nor events and* c *associates to each action a rational cost.*

Definition 4. *A* PDDL2.1 plan *is a sequence of actions* $\langle a_0, ..., a_{n-1} \rangle$*. The cost of the plan* π *is the sum of all action costs in* π*,* $cost(\pi) = \sum_{a \, in \, \pi} c(a)$.

$\gamma(s, \cdot)$ denotes the state resulting by applying either an action/event ($\gamma(s, a)$) or a sequence of action/events ($\gamma(s, \langle a_0, \ldots, a_n \rangle)$) in state s. As for formal specification [4], an action is valid if no numeric variable appears as left hand side of the effect (lvalue) in more than one effect.

The semantics of a discretised PDDL+ is defined through the notion of a time point, histories and the induced discrete projection of a plan given a domain. A time point T is a pair $\langle t, n \rangle$ where $t \in \mathbb{R}$ and $n \in \mathbb{N}$. Time points over $\mathbb{R} \times \mathbb{N}$ are ordered lexicographically. A history $\mathcal{H}$ over $\mathcal{I} = [T_s, T_e]$ maps each time point in $\mathcal{I}$ into a situation. A "situation at time T" is the tuple $\mathcal{H}(T) = \langle \mathcal{H}_A(T), \mathcal{H}_s(T) \rangle$, where $\mathcal{H}_A(T)$ is the set of actions executed at time T and $\mathcal{H}_s(T)$ is a state, i.e., an assignment to all variables in X and F at time T. We denote by $\mathcal{H}_s(T)[v]$ and $\mathcal{H}_s(T)[\xi]$ the value assumed in the state at time T by $v \in F \cup X$ and by a numeric expression ξ, respectively. $E_{trigg}(T)$ indicates the set of active events in T. T is a significant time point (hereinafter STP) of $\mathcal{H}$ over $[T_s, T_e]$ iff, in such a time point, an action is applied, an event is triggered, a process has started or stopped or there has been a discrete change just before. A history $\mathcal{H}$ is monotonous over a real interval $\mathcal{I}_t$ if there are no significant time points in $\mathcal{I}_t$.

We use $\Delta(\xi, \delta)$ to denote the discretised expression of the derivative value ξ. For example, let $\dot{x} = 1.5 \cdot y$ and $\delta = 2$ be a continuous effect and a discretisation parameter. The discretised expression $\Delta(1.5 \cdot y, \delta) = 3 \cdot y$.

Definition 5 (Induced discrete projection). *Let* $\delta \in \mathbb{Q}$*, let* $\mathbb{H}^{\pi}$ *be a history, let* I *be an initial state and let* π_t *be a* PDDL+ *plan. We say that* $\mathbb{H}^{\pi}$ *is a* discrete projection of π_t which starts in I *iff* $\mathbb{H}^{\pi}$ *induces the significant time points*

$T_{\mathbb{H}} = \langle T_0 = \langle t_0, n_0 \rangle, \cdots, T_m = \langle t_m, n_m \rangle \rangle$ *where either* $t_{i+1} = t_i + \delta$ *or* $t_{i+1} = t_i$ *and, for all* $0 \leq i < m$, *the following rules hold:*

R1 $E_{trigg}(T_i) \neq \langle\rangle$ *iff* $\mathbb{H}^{\pi}_{s}(T_{i+1}) = \gamma(\mathbb{H}^{\pi}_{s}(T_i), E_{trigg}(T_i))$, $\mathbb{H}^{\pi}_{A}(T_i) = \langle\rangle$, $t_{i+1} = t_i$ *and* $n_{i+1} = n_i + 1$;
R2 $\mathbb{H}^{\pi}_{A}(T_i) \neq \langle\rangle$ *iff* $\mathbb{H}^{\pi}_{s}(T_{i+1}) = \gamma(\mathbb{H}^{\pi}_{s}(T_i), \mathbb{H}^{\pi}_{A}(T_i))$, $E_{trigg}(T_i) = \langle\rangle$, $t_{i+1} = t_i$ *and* $n_{i+1} = n_i + 1$;
R3 *for each* $\langle a_i, t_i \rangle, \langle a_j, t_j \rangle$ *in* π, *with* $i < j$ *and* $t_i = t_j$ *there exists* $T_k, T_z \in T_{\mathbb{H}}$ *such that* a_i *in* $\mathbb{H}^{\pi}_{A}(T_k)$ *and* a_j *in* $\mathbb{H}^{\pi}_{A}(T_z)$ *where* $t_k = t_z = t_i$ *and* $n_k < n_z$;
R4 *for each pair of contiguous significant time points* $T_i = \langle t_i, n_i \rangle$, $T_{i+1} = \langle t_{i+1}, 0 \rangle$ *such that* $t_{i+1} = t_i + \delta$, *the value of each numeric variable* $x \in X$ *is updated as:*

$$\mathbb{H}^{\pi}_{s}(T_{i+1})[x] = \mathbb{H}^{\pi}_{s}(T_i)[x] + \sum_{\substack{\langle x', \xi \rangle \in eff(\rho),\ x' = x \\ \rho \in \{\rho \in P,\ \mathbb{H}^{\pi}_{s}(T_i) \models pre(\rho)\}}} \mathbb{H}^{\pi}_{s}(T_i)[\Delta(\xi, \delta)]$$

and values of unaffected variables remain unchanged (frame-axiom).

Definition 6 (Valid PDDL+ plan under δ discretisation). *A* PDDL+ *plan* π_t *is a* valid plan for a PDDL+ problem Π under δ discretisation *iff* $\mathbb{H}^{\pi}_{s}(T_m) \models G$ *and, for each* $T \in \mathcal{I}$ *such that* $\mathbb{H}^{\pi}_{A}(T) \neq \langle\rangle$, *then* $\mathcal{H}^{\pi}_{s}(T) \models pre(a)$ *for each* a *in* $\mathbb{H}^{\pi}_{A}(T)$.

The validity of a plan for PDDL2.1 can be formalised in a much simpler way.

Definition 7 (Valid PDDL2.1 plan). *A* PDDL2.1 *plan* $\pi = \langle a_0, ..., a_{n-1} \rangle$ *is a* valid plan for a PDDL2.1 problem Π *if the trajectory of states* $\langle s_0 = I, s_1, \ldots, s_n \rangle$ *generated applying actions from* π *iteratively is such that each action* a_i *with* $0 < i \leq n$ *is executable in* s_{i-1} *and* $s_n \models G$.

2.1 Polynomial Translation

As shown in [11], it is possible to translate a discretised PDDL+ into a PDDL2.1 that is only polynomial w.r.t. the size of the PDDL+. The key idea in POLY consists in simulating the progress of a discrete amount of time $\delta \in \mathbb{Q}$ by means of a sequence of actions. In what follows, and without loss of generality, we focus on the first step of such a translation, which assumes that the PDDL+ problem has no event. Events can be captured by adding an extra-step of translation [11] that does not impact the variant proposed in this paper.

Let $\Pi = \langle F, X, I, G, A, \emptyset, P \rangle$ be an event-free PDDL+ problem, and a discretisation parameter $t = \delta$, POLY generates a new PDDL2.1 problem $\Pi_{\text{POLY}} = \langle F \cup D \cup \{pause\}, X \cup X^{cp}, I, G \wedge \neg pause, A_c \cup A_P \cup \{start, end\}, c \rangle$ such that:

$$X^{cp} = \{x^{copy} \mid x \in X\}$$
$$D = \bigcup_{\substack{ne \in \mathit{eff}(\rho) \\ \rho \in P}} \{done_{ne}\}$$
$$A_c = \{\langle pre(a) \wedge \neg pause, \mathit{eff}(a)\rangle \mid a \in A\}$$
$$start = \langle \neg pause, \{pause\} \cup \bigcup_{x \in X} \{\langle asgn, x^{copy}, x\rangle\}\rangle$$
$$end = \langle \bigwedge_{done \in D} done \wedge pause, \{\neg pause\} \cup \bigcup_{done \in D} \{\neg done\}\rangle$$
$$A_P = \bigcup_{\substack{ne:\langle x,\xi\rangle \in \mathit{eff}(\rho) \\ \rho \in P}} \{\langle pause \wedge \neg done_{ne}, \{\sigma(pre(\rho), X^{cp}) \triangleright$$
$$\{\langle inc, x, \Delta(\delta, \sigma(\xi, X^{cp}))\rangle\}\} \cup \{done_{ne}\}\rangle\}$$

Whenever the passage of a discrete amount of time δ has to be simulated within Π_{POLY}, the sequence of actions $wait = \langle start, seq(A_P), end\rangle$, where $seq(A_P)$ is any permutation of all A_P actions, has to be performed. Such simulation consists of the following steps: (i) *start*, this action enables the execution of all A_P actions and, at the same time, disables all those that do not belong to A_P through the use of the *pause* predicate; (ii) $seq(A_P)$, this sequence modifies the state of the world according to the dynamics of the active processes; to prevent the A_P actions from interfering with each other, the *start* action performs a copy of all the numeric variables X, assigning the current value to the corresponding X^{cp} variables; this allows to correctly modify the state of the world, regardless of the specific sorting chosen for $seq(A_P)$; (iii) *end*, this actions closes the simulation and can be executed, by using the *done* predicates, if all the A_P actions have been executed.

3 POLY$^-$: A Sound (but Incomplete) Translation

For an event-free PDDL+ problem Π, POLY$^-$ generates a PDDL2.1 problem $\Pi_{\text{POLY}^-} = \langle F, X, I, G, A \cup \{SIM\}, c\rangle$, discretised in $t = \delta$. Π_{POLY^-} is almost identical to Π but for the absence of processes and the presence of the special action *SIM* playing the role of the simulator, i.e., what changes when time goes forward (similarly to the *wait* sequence for POLY translation). *SIM* is defined as follows:

$$pre(SIM) = \top$$
$$\mathit{eff}(SIM) = \bigcup_{\rho \in P} \{pre(\rho) \triangleright \bigcup_{\langle x,\xi\rangle \in \mathit{eff}(\rho)} \{\langle inc, x, \Delta(\xi, \delta)\rangle\}\}$$

SIM action is always applicable and features a conditional effect for each process $\rho \in P$. Such conditional effect is triggered if the precondition of ρ holds when *SIM* is applied, modifying, for each $\langle x, \xi\rangle \in \mathit{eff}(\rho)$, the affected numeric variable x according to the discretised effect expression, i.e. $\Delta(\xi, \delta)$.

Hereinafter when we say "Π admits a valid solution" we imply "under discrete interpretation".

Proposition 1 (Soundness of POLY$^-$). *Let Π be a* PDDL+ *problem, and let Π_{POLY^-} be the* PDDL2.1 *problem obtained by using the* POLY$^-$ *translation discretised in $t = \delta$. If Π_{POLY^-} admits a solution then so does Π.*

Proof (Sketch). Note that every plan solving Π_{POLY^-} is structured alternating an agent's action and a sequence (possibly empty) of *SIM* actions. Let $\pi_{\text{POLY}^-} = \langle\langle SIM\rangle \times \frac{t_0}{\delta}, a'_0, \langle SIM\rangle \times \frac{t_1-t_0}{\delta}, ..., a'_{n-1}, \langle SIM\rangle \times \frac{t_e-t_{n-1}}{\delta}\rangle$ be such a plan. We can construct a valid PDDL+ plan $\pi_t = \langle \pi, \langle 0, t_e\rangle\rangle$ as follows: i) for each action a'_i *in* π_{POLY^-} such that $a'_i \neq SIM$ then $\langle a_i, t_i\rangle$ *in* π, where t_i is equal to δ multiplied for the occurrences of *SIM* in π_{POLY^-} before a'_i; ii) for each a'_i, a'_j such that $a'_i \prec a'_j$ in π_{POLY^-} then $\langle a_i, t_i\rangle \prec \langle a_j, t_j\rangle$ in π and iii) t_e is equal to δ multiplied by the number of *SIM* in π_{POLY^-}. The plan we get by using this construction is:

$$\pi_t = \langle\langle \pi = \langle a_0, t_0\rangle, \langle a_1, t_1\rangle, ..., \langle a_{n-1}, t_{n-1}\rangle\rangle, \langle 0, t_e\rangle\rangle$$

In order to show the validity of π_t, we reason on the discrete projection $\mathbb{H}^\pi$ of π_t which is built by using the rules provided in Definition 5. Once we have built $\mathbb{H}^\pi$ (see [11], Lemma 1, for further details) we can generate τ as the sequence of states associated to each STP of $\mathbb{H}^\pi$. Let $\tau' = \langle s_0, ..., s_{m-1}\rangle$ be the sequences of states executing π_{POLY^-}. Knowing that π_{POLY^-} is valid for Π_{POLY^-} we show that π_t is valid too by noticing that $\mathbb{H}^\pi_s(T_i)$ and s_i are equivalent for each $0 \leq i \leq m-1$, i.e. they agree over $F \cup X$. To do this we proceed by induction over τ and τ' in a similar way to what was done for Lemma 1 in [11]. The base case and the inductive for the *instantaneous transition* are inherited straightforwardly from the aforementioned proof, while the *temporal transition* remains to be demonstrated.

Temporal Transition. Let i be an index such that $T_i = \langle t_i, n_i\rangle$ and $T_{i+1} = \langle t_i + \delta, 0\rangle$ are two STPs of $\mathbb{H}^\pi$. We denote with SIM_i the application of *SIM* in the i-th state of τ'. State s_i induces the context $\mathcal{C}(s_i) = \{\rho \in P,\ s_i \models pre(\rho)\}$ and then $SIM_i = \langle \top, \bigcup_{\substack{\langle x,\xi\rangle \in eff(\rho) \\ \rho \in \mathcal{C}(s_i)}} \{\langle inc, x, \Delta(\xi, \delta)\rangle\}\rangle$, since the conditional effects that are not triggered in s_i have been removed. To show that the state produced by the application of SIM_i in s_i is equivalent to that produced according to the discrete PDDL+ semantic, when a quantum of δ time passes, it is sufficient to focus on a single variable $x \in X$, and then generalise to all the numeric ones. Propositional variables can be neglected as they are not affected by processes.

Since π_{POLY^-} is valid for Π_{POLY^-} then every occurrence of *SIM* in π_{POLY^-} is applicable. Therefore in s_i, for each $x \in X$, at most one conditional effect affecting x is triggered, i.e. $\langle inc, x, \Delta(\xi, \delta)\rangle \in eff(SIM_i)$, which corresponds to enforce the transition as the following:

$$s_{i+1}[x] = \gamma(s_i, SIM_i)[x] = s_i[x] + s_i[\Delta(\xi, \delta)] \tag{1}$$

According to Rule 4 of Definition 5, each numeric variable $x \in X$ changes over δ according to the active processes but, since $\mathbb{H}^\pi(T_i) \equiv s_i$, due to the inductive hypothesis, then there exists at most a single numeric continuous effects affecting x in s_i, i.e., $\langle x, \xi \rangle$, and then the update-rule for x can be simplified as follows:

$$\mathbb{H}^\pi_s(T_{i+1})[x] = \mathbb{H}^\pi_s(T_i)[x] + \mathbb{H}^\pi_s(T_i)[\Delta(\xi, \delta)]. \quad (2)$$

Since $s_i \equiv \mathbb{H}^\pi_s(T_i)$ by inductive hypothesis, the right-hand side expressions of Formulae 2–1 are the same. Thus s_{i+1} and $\mathbb{H}^\pi_s(T_{i+1})$ are equivalent. □

Proposition 2 (Incompleteness of POLY$^-$). *Let Π be a* PDDL+ *problem, and let Π_{POLY^-} be the* PDDL2.1 *problem obtained by using the* POLY$^-$ *translation discretised in $t = \delta$. If Π admits a solution then Π_{POLY^-} may not admit it.*

Proof (Sketch). To show the correctness of the proposition we build the simplest case in which a solution π_t for Π does not admit a corresponding solution π' for Π_{POLY^-}. Let $\pi_t = \langle \pi, (0, t_e) \rangle$ be a valid solution for Π (assume w.l.o.g. $t_s = 0$) under δ discretisation and assume that π_t induces, according to Definition 5, a discrete projection $\mathbb{H}^\pi$ in which the following conditions are satisfied:

- in the first STP of $\mathbb{H}^\pi$, i.e., $T_0 = \langle 0, 0 \rangle$, two numeric continuous effects affecting the same variable $x \in X$ are active, i.e., $\mathbb{H}^\pi_s(T_0) \models pre(\rho) \wedge pre(\rho')$ with $\rho, \rho' \in P$, $\langle x, \xi \rangle \in eff(\rho)$ and $\langle x, \xi' \rangle \in eff(\rho')$;
- $\mathbb{H}^\pi$ is monotonous over $(0, \delta)$.

Using the translation POLY$^-$, we get a PDDL2.1 planning problem Π_{POLY^-} where the action *SIM* has, w.r.t. ρ and ρ', the following conditional effects:

$$eff(SIM) = \{pre(\rho) \triangleright \{\langle op, x, \Delta(\xi, \delta) \rangle\}, pre(\rho') \triangleright \{\langle op', x, \Delta(\delta, \xi') \rangle\}, ...\}$$

Let π' be a PDDL2.1 plan constructed in such a way that: i) for each $\langle a, t \rangle$ *in* π then a' *in* π' (where a' is the compiled version of a); ii) for each $\langle a_i, t_i \rangle, \langle a_j, t_j \rangle$ with $a_i \prec a_j$ in π then $a'_i \prec a'_j$ in π' iii) a sequence, possibly empty, of *SIM* actions has to be placed before each action a'_i *in* π' and at the end of π' according to the following structure:

$$\pi' = \langle \langle SIM \rangle \times \frac{t_0}{\delta}, a'_0, \langle SIM \rangle \times \frac{t_1 - t_0}{\delta}, ..., a'_{n-1}, \langle SIM \rangle \times \frac{t_e - t_{n-1}}{\delta} \rangle$$

where $\langle SIM \rangle \times k$ indicates k repetitions of *SIM*.

By using this mapping from π_t to π', we get that the first action of π' is *SIM*, which is used to simulate the passage of time from 0 to δ. Π and Π_{POLY^-} have the same initial state and then *SIM* is applied in a state $I \models pre(\rho) \wedge pre(\rho')$, thus activating the aforementioned conditional effects which both affect x. The state thus generated has to be considered, according to the PDDL2.1 semantic, inconsistent and it has to be pruned from the search space induced by Π_{POLY^-}. It follows that the action *SIM* is not applicable in I within Π_{POLY^-}, and then π' is not a valid solution for Π_{POLY^-}. □

Above, we have shown an example where the translation scheme POLY$^-$ generates a numeric problem whose induced search space does not contain some of the states present and reachable in the original problem. The next definition formalises this aspect in general terms through the notion of forbidden states.

Definition 8. *Let Π and Π_{POLY^-} be a* PDDL+ *and a* PDDL2.1 *problem obtained by using the* POLY$^-$ *translation discretised in $t = \delta$. Let $FP(\Pi) = \{\langle \rho, \rho' \rangle \mid \langle x, \xi \rangle \in eff(\rho), \langle x', \xi' \rangle \in eff(\rho'), x = x',\ \rho \neq \rho'\}$ and $states(\Pi) = \{\bot, \top\}^{|F|} \times (\mathbb{R} \cup \{\bot\})^{|X|}$, we define the set of forbidden states for Π_{POLY^-} as follows:*

$$FS(\Pi_{\text{POLY}^-}) = \{s \mid s \in states(\Pi), s \models \bigvee_{\langle \rho, \rho' \rangle \in FP(\Pi)} pre(\rho) \wedge pre(\rho')\}$$

The set of forbidden states for Π_{POLY^-} is defined as the set of states over $X \cup V$ where there exists at least one pair of active forbidden processes. A pair of processes $\langle \rho, \rho' \rangle$ is said to be forbidden, i.e., $\langle \rho, \rho' \rangle \in FP(\Pi)$, iff ρ and ρ' have continuous numeric effects having the same variable as right-hand side value.

Note that these states are labeled as *forbidden* in the sense that, once reached, it is not possible to apply the *SIM* action as its execution would cause the generation of an undefined state. This means that a π' plan solving Π_{POLY^-} can induce a forbidden state as long as no *SIM* action is applied in it.

Also note that Definition 8 is independent of I, G or of the reachability of such states. Therefore we could have a Π problem such that $FS(\Pi_{\text{POLY}^-}) \neq \emptyset$ but in which such states are unreachable.

In the following we outline a syntactic property for a PDDL+ problem that, if satisfied, ensures that POLY$^-$ is complete other than sound.

Definition 9. *Let Π be a* PDDL+ *problem. We say that Π is* a mono left-hand PDDL+ side problem *(shortened in 1-lhs) if it does not have two processes having numeric continuous effects having as left-hand side value the same numeric variable.*

Proposition 3 (Completeness of POLY$^-$ over *1-lhs* problems). *Let Π be a 1-lhs* PDDL+ *problem, and let Π_{POLY^-} be the* PDDL2.1 *problem obtained by using the* POLY$^-$ *translation discretised in $t = \delta$. If Π admits a solution then also Π_{POLY^-} admits it.*

Proof (Sketch). Let $\pi_t = \langle \pi, \langle 0, t_e \rangle \rangle$ be a valid solution for Π (assume w.l.o.g. that $t_s = 0$). Let π_{POLY^-} be a PDDL2.1 plan constructed in such a way that: i) for each $\langle a, t \rangle$ *in* π then a' *in* π_{POLY^-} (where a' is the compiled version of a); ii) for each $\langle a_i, t_i \rangle, \langle a_j, t_j \rangle$ with $a_i \prec a_j$ in π then $a'_i \prec a'_j$ in π_{POLY^-} iii) a sequence, possibly empty, of *SIM* actions has to be placed before each action a'_i *in* π_{POLY^-} and at the end of π_{POLY^-} according to the following structure

$$\pi_{\text{POLY}^-} = \langle \langle SIM \rangle \times \frac{t_0}{\delta}, a'_0, \langle SIM \rangle \times \frac{t_1 - t_0}{\delta}, ..., a'_{n-1}, \langle SIM \rangle \times \frac{t_e - t_{n-1}}{\delta} \rangle$$

where $\langle SIM \rangle \times k$ indicates k repetitions of *SIM*.

In order to prove that π_{POLY^-} is a valid solution for Π_{POLY^-}, it suffices to show that the states belonging to τ and τ', and having the same position, are equivalent. This is proved by induction on τ' and τ' in a similar way to the opposite direction. The structure of the proof remains unchanged except for the discussion of *temporal transitions* exploiting the *1-lhs* property.

Temporal Transition Let i be an index such that $T_i = \langle t_i, n_i \rangle$ and $T_{i+1} = \langle t_i + \delta, 0 \rangle$ are two STPs of $\mathbb{H}^\pi$. Again, we focus the discussion on a single numeric variable $x \in X$. According to Rule 4 of Definition 5, each numeric variable $x \in X$ changes over δ according to the active processes in $\mathcal{C}(\mathbb{H}^\pi_s(T_i))$ but, since Π is by hypothesis a *1-lhs* task, then there exists at most a single numeric effects affecting x, i.e., $\langle x, \xi \rangle$, and the update-rule for x can be simplified as follows:

$$\mathbb{H}^\pi_s(T_{i+1})[x] = \mathbb{H}^\pi_s(T_i)[x] + \mathbb{H}^\pi_s(T_i)[\Delta(\xi, \delta)]. \tag{3}$$

Since $s_i \equiv \mathbb{H}^\pi_s(T_i)$ by inductive hypothesis, then each effect of SIM_i has to refer to one and only one variable. Therefore $\langle inc, x, \Delta(\xi, \delta) \rangle \in \mathit{eff}(SIM_i)$, which corresponds to enforce the transition as the following:

$$s_{i+1}[x] = \gamma(s_i, SIM_i)[x] = s_i[x] + s_i[\Delta(\xi, \delta)] \tag{4}$$

Since $s_i = \mathbb{H}^\pi_s(T_i)$ by inductive hypothesis, then the right-hand side expressions of Formulae 3–4 are the same. Thus s_{i+1} and $\mathbb{H}^\pi_s(T_{i+1})$ are equivalent. □

The property of completeness stated in Proposition 3 derives from the definition of *1-lhs* domain which implies that the set of forbidden states is necessarily empty as forbidden pair processes cannot exist. The syntactic property of being *1-lhs* is sufficient but not necessary (in the sense that there may be problems that are not *1-lhs* where POLY$^-$ is sound and complete).

In the following, we study in what relationship the solution space of Π and Π_{POLY^-} are in order to actually understand what we can expect if we use POLY$^-$. To do so, let us denote with $\pi_{\text{POLY}^-} = map^{-1}(\pi_t)$ the procedure used in Proposition 1 to generate a PDDL2.1 starting from a PDDL+ one.

Definition 10. *Let Π be a 1-lhs* PDDL+ *problem, and let Π_{POLY^-} be the* PDDL2.1 *problem obtained by using the* POLY$^-$ *translation discretised in* $t = \delta$. *We define* the solution space of Π and Π_{POLY^-} *as follows:*

$$SS(\Pi) = \{\pi_t \mid \pi_t \textit{ is a valid solution for } \Pi\},$$
$$SS(\Pi_{\text{POLY}^-}) = \{map^{-1}(\pi_{\text{POLY}^-}) \mid \pi_{\text{POLY}^-} \textit{ is a valid solution for } \Pi_{\text{POLY}^-}\}$$

Observation 1. *Let Π be a* PDDL+ *problem, and let Π_{POLY^-} be the* PDDL2.1 *problem obtained by using the* POLY$^-$ *translation discretised in* $t = \delta$, *then the following relationship hold:*

i. in the general case it holds that $SS(\Pi_{\text{POLY}^-}) \subseteq SS(\Pi)$;
ii. if Π is 1-lhs, then $SS(\Pi_{\text{POLY}^-}) = SS(\Pi)$;

iii. if Π is not 1-lhs and there exists a plan π for Π whose execution generates a $s \in FS(\Pi)$, in which time has to pass, then $\pi \notin SS(\Pi_{\text{POLY}^-})$ and thus $SS(\Pi_{\text{POLY}^-}) \subset SS(\Pi)$;

iv. if Π is not 1-lhs and each $\pi \in SS(\Pi)$ generates a state $s \in FS(\Pi)$, in which time has to pass, $SS(\Pi_{\text{POLY}^-}) = \emptyset$.

In the general case (i), without any assumption about the structure of Π, $SS(\Pi_{\text{POLY}^-})$ is always a subset of $SS(\Pi)$ and in some cases such sets could be equal. If Π is *1-lhs* (ii), then there is a one-to-one correspondence between the valid plans for Π and Π_{POLY^-}, respectively. If Π is not *1-lhs*, and there is a solution traversing a forbidden state (iii), then $SS(\Pi_{\text{POLY}^-})$ is a strict subset of $SS(\Pi)$ because all solutions of Π having this feature do not admit a valid equivalent for Π_{POLY^-}. Finally, if Π is not *1-lhs*, and each valid plan for Π traverses a forbidden state (iv), then Π_{POLY^-} becomes unsolvable since any solution for Π do not admit a valid equivalent for Π_{POLY^-}.

Example 1. *Let $\Pi = \langle F, X, I, G, A, \emptyset, P\rangle$ be a* PDDL+ *problem without events encompassing one Boolean variable, i.e., $F = \{f_1\}$, four numeric variables, i.e., $X = \{x_1, x_2, x_3, x_4\}$ and two processes $P = \{\rho_1, \rho_2\}$ such that:*

$$\rho_1 = \langle x_1 > 0, \{\langle x_2, x_3\rangle\}\rangle,\ \rho_2 = \langle f_1, \{\langle x_2, x_4\rangle\}\rangle$$

According to R4 of Definition 5, ρ_1 affects x_2 according to $\dot{x_2} = x_3$ when $x_1 > 0$ holds and, similarly, ρ_1 affects x_2 according to $\dot{x_2} = x_4$ when f_1 holds. Finally, if $x_1 > 0 \wedge f_1$, then $\dot{x_2} = x_3 + x_4$.

POLY *Let $ne_1 = \langle x_2, x_3\rangle$ and $ne_2 = \langle x_2, x_4\rangle$ be the numeric continuous effects of ρ_1 and ρ_2, respectively. The* PDDL2.1 *problem obtained using* POLY *discretised in $t = \delta$ is $\Pi_{\text{POLY}} = \langle F \cup \{done_{ne_1}, done_{ne_2}\} \cup \{pause\}, X \cup \{x_1^{copy}, x_2^{copy}, x_3^{copy}, x_4^{copy}\}, I, G \wedge \neg pause, A_c \cup \{SIM\text{-}ne_1, SIM\text{-}ne_2\} \cup \{start, end\}, c\rangle$ such that:*

$$\begin{aligned}
start =& \langle \neg pause, \{\langle ass, x_1^{copy}, x_1\rangle, \langle ass, x_2^{copy}, x_2\rangle,\\
& \langle ass, x_3^{copy}, x_3\rangle, \langle ass, x_4^{copy}, x_4\rangle, pause\}\rangle\\
SIM\text{-}ne_1 =& \langle pause \wedge \neg done_{ne_1}, \{(x_1^{copy} > 0) \triangleright \{\langle inc, x_2, x_3^{copy} \cdot \delta\rangle\}, done_{ne_1}\}\rangle\\
SIM\text{-}ne_2 =& \langle pause \wedge \neg done_{ne_2}, \{f_1 \triangleright \{\langle inc, x_2, x_4^{copy} \cdot \delta\rangle\}, done_{ne_2}\}\rangle\\
end =& \langle pause \wedge done_{ne_1} \wedge done_{ne_2}, \{\neg pause, \neg done_{ne_1}, \neg done_{ne_2}\}\rangle
\end{aligned}$$

POLY$^-$ *The* PDDL2.1 *problem obtained using* POLY$^-$ *discretised in $t = \delta$ is $\Pi_{\text{POLY}^-} = \langle F, X, I, G, A \cup \{SIM\}, c\rangle$ such that:*

$$SIM = \langle \top, x_1 > 0 \triangleright \{\langle inc, x_2, x_3 \cdot \delta\rangle\}, f_1 \triangleright \{\langle inc, x_2, x_4 \cdot \delta\rangle\}\rangle$$

Note that Π is not a 1-lhs because ne_1 and ne_2 affect the same variable, i.e., x_2, and so the transformation POLY$^-$ *could not preserve the solution space of Π. We can define the set of forbidden states for Π_{POLY^-} as follows:*

$$FS(\Pi_{\text{POLY}^-}) = \{s \in states(\Pi),\ s \models f_1 \wedge x_1 > 0\}$$

Table 1. Performance achieved by METRIC-FF when run on models generated using the POLY and POLY⁻ translations. Results are presented in terms of coverage (number of solved instances), average runtime, average makespan, and average number of nodes evaluated during the search process. Averages are calculated considering instances solved by all approaches. "—" indicates that no instances can be considered for the average calculation. ✗ is used to indicate domain models that do not satisfy the *1-lhs* property.

Domain	Coverage		Search time (seconds)		Makespan		Eval. nodes (×1000)	
	POLY	POLY⁻	POLY	POLY⁻	POLY	POLY⁻	POLY	POLY⁻
Rover (20)	19	**20**	61.4	**12.4**	**500.0**	**500.0**	14.0	**4.0**
Lin-Car (10)	**10**	**10**	7.0	**3.8**	16.1	**14.9**	2.6	**0.4**
Lin-Gen (10) ✗	**10**	—	—	—	—	—	—	—
UTC (10) ✗	**7**	—	—	—	—	—	—	—
Baxter (20) ✗	**19**	**19**	**12.2**	12.4	17.7	**14.6**	**27.1**	68.3
OT-Car (20)	18	**19**	14.1	**6.2**	43.1	**24.6**	106.3	**15.3**

4 Experimental Analysis

Our experimental analysis aims to evaluate the benefit that the proposed translation can provide to a numeric planning engine, with particular regards to the polynomial translation proposed in [11].

We consider the well-known numeric planning system METRIC-FF [7], and compare the performance of such a system with both the complete and the incomplete polynomial schemata followed by the (unchanged) translation that handles events. Our experiments were run on an Intel Xeon Gold 6140M CPUs with 2.30 GHz. For each instance, we set a cutoff time of 900 s, and RAM was limited to 8 GB. As benchmarks, we consider the same suite examined in [11] which includes the following domains: Solar-Rover (Rover), Linear-Car (Lin-Car), Linear-Generator (Lin-Gen), Urban-Traffic-Control (UTC) from [15], Baxter from [1] and Overtaking-Car (OT-Car). The benchmark suite is available at: https://bit.ly/30gMyNW. Out of the considered benchmark domains, 3 satisfy the *1-lhs* property: Solar-Rover, Linear-Car, and Overtaking-Car. The remaining domains, i.e. Linear-Generator, UTC, and Baxter, do not satisfy the mentioned property.

Table 1 shows how the POLY⁻ translation performs compared to the POLY translation. It is worth reminding that POLY⁻ is a translation that does not guarantee completeness, unless the *1-lhs* property is satisfied for the PDDL+ domain model. In UTC and Lin-Gen, METRIC-FF is not able to solve any instance when using the models generated using the POLY⁻ translation. However, in Baxter, POLY⁻ allows METRIC-FF to deliver good coverage and plan quality performance: this is due to the fact that Baxter instances can be solved in numerous different ways, and therefore the incompleteness is not removing all the paths

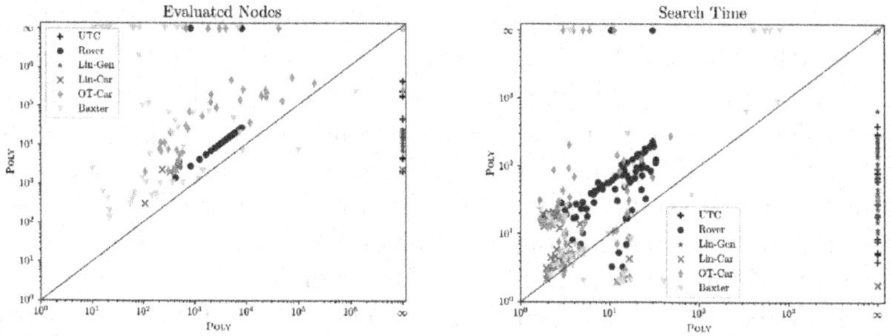

Fig. 1. Scatter plots comparing the number of nodes evaluated (left) and the search time (right) needed by METRIC-FF when run using models generated by the POLY translation (y-axis) or the POLY$^-$ translation (x-axis).

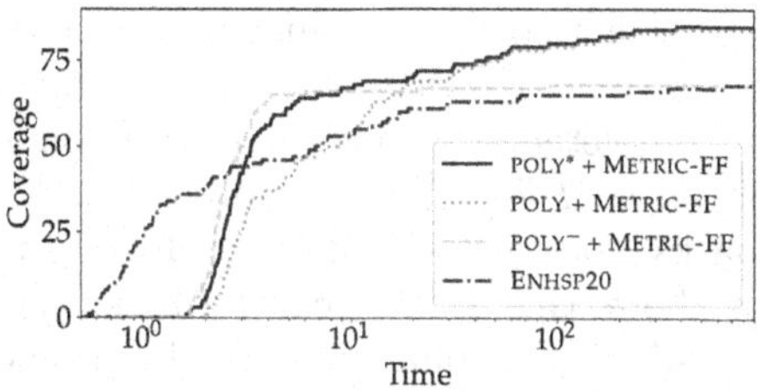

Fig. 2. Coverage over time of METRIC-FF when using POLY, POLY$^-$, or a portfolio approach combining them (POLY*).

to goal states. However, the use of POLY$^-$ in Baxter forces the planning engine to explore a larger chunk of the search space, resulting in a higher runtime. In the other domains, where the *1-lhs* property is satisfied, POLY$^-$ always allows METRIC-FF to deliver much better performance than POLY in terms of runtime.

Results presented in Table 1 suggest that there is a trade-off to consider when selecting between POLY and POLY$^-$. The former provides guarantees of completeness, but the latter can generate translations that are more amenable to be exploited by the selected PDDL2.1 planning engine. This trade-off is easily observed when the number of evaluated nodes is compared. Figure 1 compares the number of nodes evaluated and the search time of METRIC-FF when using POLY (y-axis) or POLY$^-$ (x-axis): besides the instances where the use of POLY$^-$ does not allow to generate a solution, in almost all cases it allows the planning engine to find a solution while expanding a significantly smaller number of nodes, and requiring less CPU-time.

Given the results presented in Table 1 and Fig. 1, a question naturally arises: is it possible to combine the strengths of POLY and POLY$^-$? Interestingly, the fact that a PDDL+ domain model satisfies the *1-lhs* property can be straightforwardly checked while parsing the model. This opens the way to the combination of the POLY and POLY$^-$ translations into a portfolio approach, where POLY$^-$ is used on a considered instance if the *1-lhs* property is satisfied, and POLY is exploited otherwise. Figure 2 shows the coverage over time of METRIC-FF when the above described portfolio (POLY*) is in use, compared to the performance achieved by using only POLY or POLY$^-$. For reference, we include also the performance achieved by ENHSP20 [13], a native PDDL+ state-of-the-art planning engine, when run on the original PDDL+ models. As expected, the combination of the translations allows to exploit the strengths of POLY$^-$, in terms of quickly solving a large number of instances, without the drawback of limited coverage due to the incompleteness of the translation. Even when a significant amount of CPU-time is made available to the planning engine, the combination of the translations can be beneficial in terms of overall coverage.

5 Conclusion

We introduced a sound but not complete translation from discretised PDDL+ to numeric planning. The introduced POLY$^-$ translation can generate more compact encodings, but its completeness is guaranteed only on a subclass of PDDL+ problems, that we defined as *1-lhs*. Our experimental analysis, run on a variety of PDDL+ benchmarks, confirms the benefits of using the proposed POLY$^-$ translation. Further, it shows that POLY$^-$ can be beneficial also in some cases where the model is not *1-lhs*, if the solution space of a problem admits solutions that do not require intermediate states in which two continuous numeric effects that affect the same variable are simultaneously active.

Future work will focus on optimising the considered polynomial translations, and in investigating advanced ways for selecting and combining different translations at runtime.

Acknowledgements. Francesco Percassi and Mauro Vallati were supported by a UKRI Future Leaders Fellowship [grant number MR/T041196/1].

References

1. Bertolucci, R., Capitanelli, A., Maratea, M., Mastrogiovanni, F., Vallati, M.: Automated planning encodings for the manipulation of articulated objects in 3D with gravity. In: Alviano, M., Greco, G., Scarcello, F. (eds.) AI*IA 2019. LNCS (LNAI), vol. 11946, pp. 135–150. Springer, Cham (2019). https://doi.org/10.1007/978-3-030-35166-3_10
2. Bonassi, L., Gerevini, A.E., Percassi, F., Scala, E.: On planning with qualitative state-trajectory constraints in PDDL3 by compiling them away. In: Proceedings of the Thirty-First International Conference on Automated Planning and Scheduling, ICAPS 2021, pp. 46–50 (2021)
3. Cooper, M.C., Maris, F., Régnier, P.: Compilation of a high-level temporal planning language into PDDL 2.1. In: Twenty-Second IEEE International Conference on Tools with Artificial Intelligence, ICTAI 2010, pp. 181–188 (2010)
4. Fox, M., Long, D.: PDDL2.1: an extension to PDDL for expressing temporal planning domains. J. Artif. Intell. Res. **20**, 61–124 (2003)

5. Fox, M., Long, D.: Modelling mixed discrete-continuous domains for planning. J. Artif. Intell. Res. **27**, 235–297 (2006)
6. Grastien, A., Scala, E.: Intelligent belief state sampling for conformant planning. In: Proceedings of the Twenty-Sixth International Joint Conference on Artificial Intelligence, IJCAI 2017, pp. 4317–4323 (2017)
7. Hoffmann, J.: The metric-FF planning system: translating "ignoring delete lists" to numeric state variables. J. Artif. Intell. Res. **20**, 291–341 (2003)
8. Keyder, E., Geffner, H.: Soft goals can be compiled away. J. Artif. Intell. Res. **36**, 547–556 (2009)
9. Palacios, H., Geffner, H.: Compiling uncertainty away in conformant planning problems with bounded width. J. Artif. Intell. Res. **35**, 623–675 (2009)
10. Percassi, F., Gerevini, A.E.: On compiling away PDDL3 soft trajectory constraints without using automata. In: Proceedings of the Twenty-Ninth International Conference on Automated Planning and Scheduling, ICAPS 2019, pp. 320–328 (2019)
11. Percassi, F., Scala, E., Vallati, M.: Translations from discretised PDDL+ to numeric planning. In: Proceedings of the Thirty-First International Conference on Automated Planning and Scheduling, ICAPS 2021, pp. 252–261 (2021)
12. Scala, E., Grastien, A.: Non-deterministic conformant planning using a counterexample-guided incremental compilation to classical planning. In: Proceedings of the Thirty-First International Conference on Automated Planning and Scheduling, ICAPS 2021, pp. 299–307 (2021)
13. Scala, E., Haslum, P., Thiébaux, S., Ramírez, M.: Interval-based relaxation for general numeric planning. In: Proceedings of the Twenty-Second European Conference on Artificial Intelligence, ECAI 2016, vol. 285, pp. 655–663 (2016)
14. Taig, R., Brafman, R.I.: Compiling conformant probabilistic planning problems into classical planning. In: Proceedings of the Twenty-Third International Conference on Automated Planning and Scheduling, ICAPS 2013, pp. 197–205 (2013)
15. Vallati, M., Magazzeni, D., Schutter, B.D., Chrpa, L., McCluskey, T.L.: Efficient macroscopic urban traffic models for reducing congestion: a PDDL+ planning approach. In: Proceedings of the Thirtieth AAAI Conference on Artificial Intelligence, AAAI 2016, pp. 3188–3194 (2016)

Enhancing Telepresence Robots with AI: Combining Services to Personalize and React

Riccardo De Benedictis(✉), Gloria Beraldo, Rami Reddy Devaram, Amedeo Cesta, and Gabriella Cortellessa

CNR-ISTC, National Research Council of Italy, Institute of Cognitive Sciences and Technologies, Via S. Martino della Battaglia 44, 00185 Rome, Italy
{riccardo.benedictis,gloria.beraldo,rami.devaram,amedeo.cesta, gabriella.cortellessa}@istc.cnr.it

Abstract. Mobile Telepresence Robots represent a class of robotic platforms, characterized by a video conferencing system mounted on a mobile robotic base, which allows a pilot user to move around in the robot's environment. These commercially available platforms are relatively cheap and straightforward, yet robust enough to operate continuously in a dynamic environment. Their simplicity and robustness make them particularly suitable for the application in an elderly care context. Although the technology used on these robotic platforms has evolved considerably in recent years, these tools are meant to have no or minimal autonomy and are, hence, mostly relegated to provide pure telepresence services for video calls between the older users and their carers.

This work aims to lay the foundations to increase the autonomy of mobile telepresence robots, both by supporting teleoperation through shared approaches and offering services to users in total autonomy. To this purpose, different artificial intelligence technologies such as Reasoning, Knowledge Representation, Automated Planning, Machine Learning, Natural Language Processing, Advanced Perception and Navigation must coexist on limited hardware. An architecture aiming to integrate these technologies is proposed together with backbone services that integrate classical and innovative AI with robotics. Additionally, the problems that arise from the integration of heterogeneous technologies such as plan adaptation needs, shared navigation challenges and the generation of data-driven models able to run on not-performant hardware, are presented along with possible solutions exemplified on the older users assistance domain.

Keywords: Enhanced telepresence · Robotics and perception · Planning and execution · Active ageing

1 Introduction

Mobile Telepresence Robots represent a class of multipurpose robots that, among other uses, enable mitigating the isolation of elderly people living alone [7,25].

Authors are supported by projects: SI-Robotics, Cleverness, FocAAL.

S. Bandini et al. (Eds.): AIxIA 2021, LNAI 13196, pp. 32–45, 2022.
https://doi.org/10.1007/978-3-031-08421-8_3

In order to become very user-effective, however, there is the need to integrate the robotic progress with additional technology to create an end-to-end system that can help live better. The technology used on these robotic platforms has evolved considerably in recent years [12], nevertheless, such tools are basically relegated to provide telepresence services on different mobile robotic platforms that can be controlled remotely [14,19,26], having, as an example, no or minimal autonomy [22]. Usability and acceptability of these platforms, indeed, require that they achieve a certain level of autonomy, supporting their teleoperation by people typically not very familiar with technology (e.g., including family members of the assisted persons, doctors and nurses), as well as endowing the robots with proactive services and capabilities, exploitable when they are not remotely teleoperated [12,16,23,27].

Suppose, for example, we want to use a telepresence robot to administer, autonomously, a cognitive rehabilitation therapy to a user. The task requires the ability for the robot to plan, based on the user's characteristics, a personalized therapy over time, the ability to navigate in a dynamic environment, the ability to recognize the user and to follow him/her in order to offer, day by day, the planned cognitive exercise. Furthermore, in natural language, the administration of the cognitive exercise should dynamically adapt to the responses proposed by the user and to his/her current emotional state. Finally, the administration of the planned exercise could "fail", as a consequence of the state of the environment (e.g., the user is not at home) or as a consequence of the interaction with the user (e.g., the user does not want to carry out the planned exercise), requiring a readjustment of the rehabilitation plan.

Various Artificial Intelligence technologies could augment the robot capability and deliver new services to the users. However, integrating these technologies with a telepresence platform poses several challenges that stress the expected behaviour of the existing solutions. For example, knowledge Representation and Reasoning and Automated Planning represent very expressive domain-independent tools and, as such, can be relatively slow in producing solutions to the problems posed to them. Moreover, once a solution has been generated, it should possibly adapt to the emerging and unpredicted evolution of the environment to avoid an expensive regeneration of new solutions from scratch. Furthermore, navigation skills must range from autonomous to shared, considering both the high-level plans generated by semantic and causal reasoning technologies and the changes that dynamically occur in the environment. Finally, machine learning technologies must cope with the limited computational resources offered by the hardware, that needs to be cheap to enable a widespread use.

We are currently facing these research topics inside the SI-ROBOTICS (SocIal ROBOTics for active and healthy ageing) project whose general goal is to design and develop customizable tools integrating robots, sensors and AI software. The goal of the project consists in creating a holistic system that includes multivariate services that range from monitoring the physiological measurements of *primary user* (i.e., the older adult at home) to performing cognitive and physical exercises through the robot, from telepresence services to advanced remote teleoperation to keep in contact with *secondary users* (e.g., doctors, medical staff, family, friends). We here specifically consider a commercial telepresence robot and work at enhancing it with a backbone of services that integrate classical and innovative AI with robotics. Additionally, the problems that arise from the integration of heterogeneous technologies, such as plan adaptation needs, shared navigation challenges and the generation of data-driven models able to run on not-performant hardware, are addressed along with possible solutions exemplified the SI-ROBOTICS scenario.

2 An Architecture to Enhance Robotic Telepresence

To better understand our architectural choices, we start with a sketchy idea of the comprehensive system (Fig. 1). A telepresence robot is assigned to each older adult who lives in the same environment. The telepresence robot can be teleoperated from outside. In addition to the robot, in the house there can be different *sensors*, both environmental (e.g., motion, pressure, contact and brightness) and physiological (e.g., blood pressure, weight, oximeter and thermometer), whose data are collected and processed by a local gateway (*fog*) which, besides, can also control some *actuators* inside the house (e.g., motorized shutters and smart lamps). Inside the houses, the robots, the environmental and physiological sensors, and actuators, constitute our *edge* infrastructure.

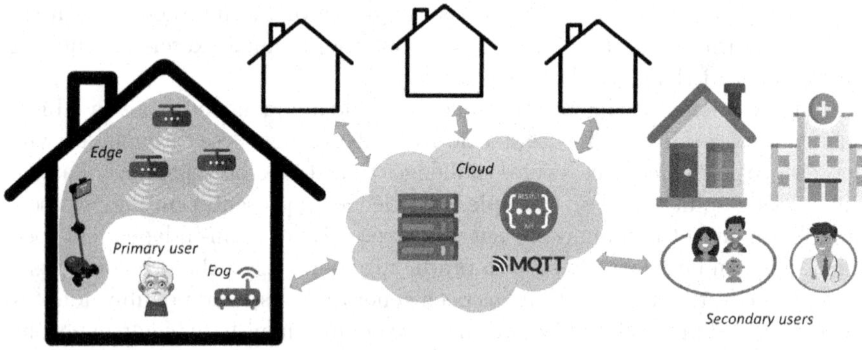

Fig. 1. A sketch of the SI-ROBOTICS ecology.

Outside the houses, a cloud infrastructure exposes some REST microservices for allowing the different component a read/write access to a shared database, responsible for keeping information regarding the different users, their roles and, for the assisted users, those characteristics which are relevant for the generation of personalized plans (e.g., any physical and/or cognitive problem). The database also contains information regarding the houses, the users who have access to the structure, the environmental and physiological sensors, and the available robotic platforms. Finally, the cloud infrastructure offers an MQTT-based messaging service that allows the exchange of messages among the different components of the system and a web user interface that allows secondary users an entry point to the system. It is worth noticing, in particular, that the presence of sensors and

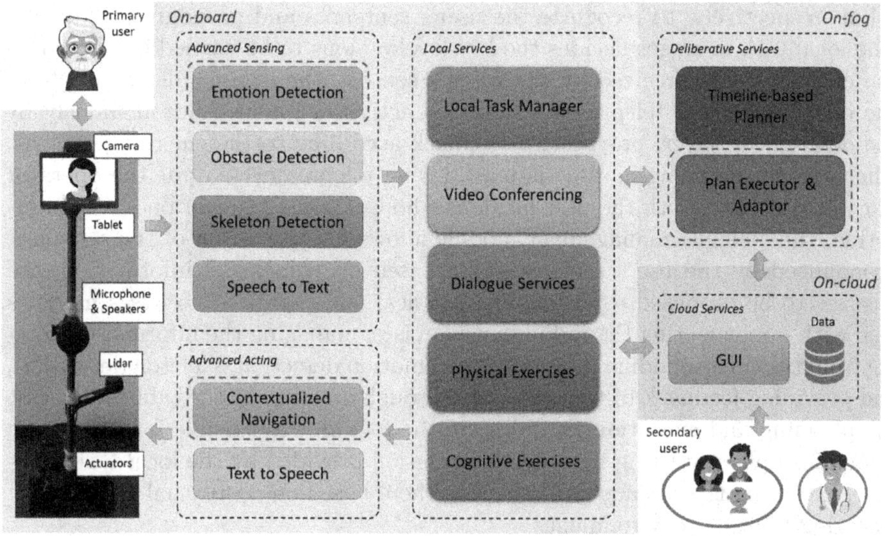

Fig. 2. The architecture proposing different intelligent components and services grouped according to functionalities.

actuators inside the house also requires joint coordination between the different intelligent components. The deployment of some intelligent components on the gateway inside the house considers privacy, reliability, efficiency and scalability.

Once the technological infrastructure within which the telepresence robot operates has been introduced, we can focus on the components that interest us most and increase the autonomy of the robotic telepresence platforms. First, note that these robots must operate within a home context, strongly unstructured and which evolves dynamically and in an unpredictable way due to the presence of the primary user. If, on the one side, indeed, robots are expected to implement in autonomy reactive and intelligent behaviours to assist the users, on the other, robots have to operate inside predefined boundaries to be acceptable and to adapt to the people needs. In other words, it emerges the necessity of planning the appropriate tasks involving the robot during the day, to schedule them by respecting a set of constraints (e.g., causal, temporal, related to people's preferences, etc.), and finally, to implement them exploiting the robot's capabilities. The pursued goal, in particular, is based on the integration of different AI technologies providing the capabilities to support humans in daily living scenarios fostering personalization and adaptation of the interaction [20,24].

An illustrative representation of the proposed architecture is shown in Fig. 2. The emotion detection module, in particular, is used to adapt the exercises starting from the camera images. The obstacle detection module and the skeleton recognition module are used to guarantee contextual navigation, supporting it both in the case of planned navigation and in the case of teleoperation. The skeleton detection module, additionally, is used for monitoring physical rehabilitation exercises. The speech to text and text to speech modules allow the robot, respectively, to recognize the user's sentences and pronounce sentences. The local task manager decides the low-level actions to be carried out based on the current state perceived by the robot's sensors, the commands coming from the operator during telepresence, and the activities planned autonomously by the deliberative layer, providing a feedback according to the emerging context. The videoconferencing module is used during telepresence to put the operator in communication with the user inside the house. During the autonomous interaction, the dialogue management module allows interpretation of the sentences pronounced by the users and to select, based on contextual information, the answers to be proposed to them. The physical and cognitive exercises modules deal with implementing the individual exercises, managing the information coming from the corresponding modules (e.g., emotion detection, skeleton detection), and providing feedback to the user (i.e., through dialogue or the tablet). Finally, the planning and execution modules, on the fog, are responsible for generating customized plans starting from the information provided by the local task manager, executing these plans and adapting them based on contextual information emerging from the environment.

It is worth mentioning that many of the components were built using off-the-shelf tools, requiring little or no integration effort. However, the components highlighted in red required more radical changes, and therefore, the implemented updates are detailed in the following sections. It is worth understanding how each component works at its own different "speeds" in this architecture. The on-fog tier, in particular, allows forms of semantic and causal reasoning that take into account all the possible activities that must be controlled inside the house. This tier chooses and organizes the tasks over time in order to respect the imposed causal and temporal constraints avoiding, if necessary, any overlaps between incompatible activities. The result consists of a personalized activity plan based on the characteristics of the primary user. Generating a plan that takes into account all constraints, however, can take a long time[1]. For this reason, when the current solutions are no longer compatible with the dynamic evolution of the environment, they should be adapted rather than regenerated from scratch. The on-board tier, on the other hand, by acting locally and in limited time windows, is more reactive and more easily adapts to the possible changes that may dynamically occur. However, this space-time locality does not allow the layer to have an overview of the various activities. Furthermore, the on-board reasoning must work smoothly on relatively cheap and, therefore, low-performing hardware.

3 The Deliberative Services for Personalization

The deliberative services, on the fog, integrate semantic and causal reasoning forms, allowing to generate a plan personalized on the user's characteristics, execute the plan over time, and adapt it according to the emerging context. The

[1] In its most general form, planning complexity is undecidable.

planned activities mainly concern personalized physical and cognitive rehabilitation, reminders on the medicines to be taken or on physiological measurements, as well as actions for the house's actuators. These services are triggered by the local task manager on the on-board tier and are carried out through an extension of timeline-based planning [21], which deals with managing, in an integrated and homogeneous way, the different forms of semantic and causal reasoning by the system's high-level tasks within a single house.

The basic building block of timeline-based planning is the *token* which, in its most general form, is described by an expression having the form $n\,(x_0,\ldots,x_i)_\chi$. In timeline-based planning tokens are used to represent the single unit of information. In particular, n is a *predicate* symbol, $x_0,\ldots,x_i$ are its *parameters* (i.e., constants, numeric variables or object variables) and $\chi \in \{f, g\}$ is a constant representing the class of the token (i.e., either a *fact*, inherently true, or a *goal*, which must be achieved). Starting from a set of tokens, declared and appropriately constrained in the planning problem, the resolution process applies a set of causal rules that introduce additional tokens and constraints that allow the achievement of the problem's goals. The resulting tokens are then projected onto timelines representing the temporal evolution of some relevant components of the modeled system, which can then be executed (refer to [9] for further details).

Given its general modeling flexibility, we have chosen to use the above technology at a deliberative tier, to generate personalised high-level plans. Within the proposed architecture, specifically, personalization concerns the planning of tasks over time (e.g., physical and cognitive rehabilitation exercises) personalised on the basis of the user's characteristics (i.e., any physical problems, the training degree, the level of perceived fatigue after a training session, etc.) and on her/his preferences (e.g., the preferred times to carry out such activities). In particular, by exploiting a combination of rules and constraints, and by using constants, whose value is established starting from the information stored in the database, to represent the user's status and her/his preferences, it is possible to generate a long-term plan containing several high-level interactions customized according to the user's needs.

Figure 3 describes how it is possible to exploit the application of the rules during the problem resolution process to generate personalised plans that aim to keep the user healthy. Suppose, for example, that from the interaction with an elderly user u it emerges that the person suffers from memory problems while is free of major physical problems. The deliberative tier could exploit this knowledge to plan some cognitive rehabilitation exercises to limit the person's further cognitive decline and some physical exercises to keep the person physically active. A hypothetical high-level goal could be, therefore, KEEPHEALTY. The rule that describes the requirements for the achievement of such a goal could contain, among other things, a conjunction of disjunctions like $(u.memory\_issues \wedge CognitiveExercize_g\,(\tau, s, e)) \vee \neg u.memory\_issues$ and $(\neg u.physical\_issues \wedge PhysicalExercize_g\,(\tau, s, e)) \vee u.physical\_issues$. In order to reach the KEEPHEALTY goal, specifically, the application of the rule, during the resolution process, will introduce a COGNITIVEEXERCIZE sub-goal (a goal

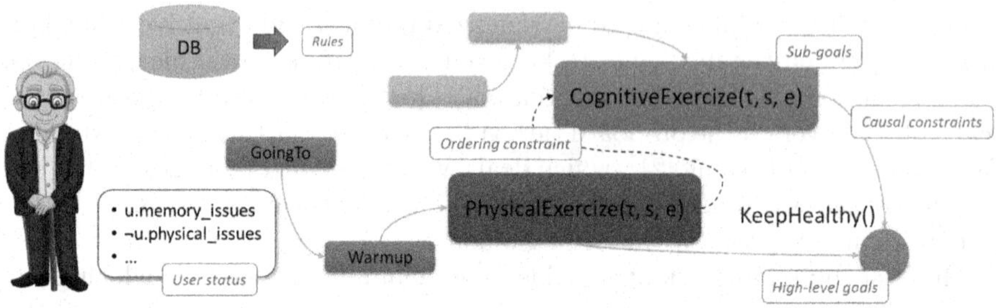

Fig. 3. Personalizing daily activities through integrated semantic and causal reasoning.

introduced by the application of a causal rule) within the partial plan if and only if the involved user has memory problems and a PHYSICALEXERCIZE sub-goal if and only if the involved user has no physical problems.

It is worth noting that the introduced tokens are endowed with the s and e numerical variables, representing the starting and the ending of the activities. Furthermore, the tokens are projected on the timeline represented by the object variable τ. In general, the planner decides the value of such variables, provided all the constraints defined in the problem and the applied rules are satisfied. Furthermore, to prevent temporal overlapping, the planner can add additional constraints if different tokens are projected on the same timeline (e.g., among physical and cognitive exercises). Finally, it is worth noticing that the sub-goals introduced by the reasoning process require, in turn, the application of their causal rules, possibly introducing additional constraints and further sub-goals, such as, in Fig. 3, a WARM-UP exercise preceding the PHYSICALEXERCIZE and, in turn, an autonomous navigation task preceding the WARM-UP.

3.1 Executing Plans and Adapting Them to the Reality

Generating a personalised plan that manages the coordination among the different activities that might take place within a house constitutes only part of the faced difficulties. The generated plan, in particular, must deal with the evolving reality of all the (often, unpredictable) events that can happen within a house. In other words, the plan must be *executed.* More than simply dispatching the planned activities, in particular, executing a plan means modifying it to make it fit the current reality. This is an open problem that is not yet fully solved except for particular cases typically limited to temporal adaptation.

For the simpler dispatching of activities, in particular, we adopt two (tasks, in general, can overlap in time) queues filled with the planned tasks and sorted, respectively, by the value of their start variable and by the value of their end variable (activities that must be carried out next can be found in the first positions). An internal *current-time* variable is incremented at each execution step (in our case, every second) and whenever its value exceeds the beginning (or the end) of a task, these are started (or ended). During the execution of a plan, however, various events can happen that require its adaptation (or, in some cases, its cancellation) depending on the fresh information that dynamically emerges from the environment. In its most general form, in particular, the types of adaptations we consider fall into four categories: 1) *freezing* the start or the end of a task (e.g., by introducing an equality constraint that forces a variable to assume a specific value); 2) *delaying* the start or the end of a task; 3) *failing* the execution of one (or more) tasks and 4) *adding* a new requirement to the problem.

It is worth underlying that each of the above adaptations can lead to potentially important consequences for the plan. For instance, in a navigation task, for which the duration is not known a priori, whenever the *current-time* value reaches the value of the start variable, the latter is frozen, and the start of the action is notified to the reactive tier. The end of the task, on the contrary, will be determined by a notification coming from the reactive tier. Whenever the *current-time* value reaches the end variable value, the latter increases by a time unit at each execution step, propagating all the plan constraints with possible consequences on other future tasks, until the executing task is notified as successful (or ruinous, whose management, which should keep the causal relations valid, is beyond the scope of this document).

4 Contextualized Navigation Services

One of the limitations of the current commercial robot is the absence of a robust navigation system. Indeed, in most cases, the current systems rely entirely on the remote users' ability to teleoperate the robot in the environment. The few experience of secondary users as well as the presence of possible delays in the transmission of the robot's camera streaming might make the task very complex. Given this premise, we are designing navigation services that contextualize the situations and activate specific behaviours performed by the robot in autonomy to facilitate the teleoperation operations and the interaction with the primary user. The robot can move by exploiting a priori knowledge about the environment (e.g., a map) and/or using the information derived by the robot's perception (see Fig. 4). For instance, initially the robot tries to move towards predefined positions where some activities are expected to be performed (e.g., during the cognitive and the physical exercises and when the robot needs charging). When changes happens (e.g., the person's walking in the environment during the interaction), the robot is authorized to start routines in autonomy. In these routines, the robot computes navigation goals that are updated while it is moving. In the examined example, the condition "the person is not present at the physical exercise session" triggers the "look for the person" routines where the robot explores the environment to search the primary user within a timeout. In other words, the navigation algorithm exploits the endowed perception capabilities to implement *obstacle-avoidance* and trigger social behaviours exploiting the joints detections from the skeleton tracker.

Moreover, to guarantee effective navigation, the robot's autonomy can vary over time by including the possibility of inserting the human operator in the loop. Specifically, the user can influence the robot's motion through directional

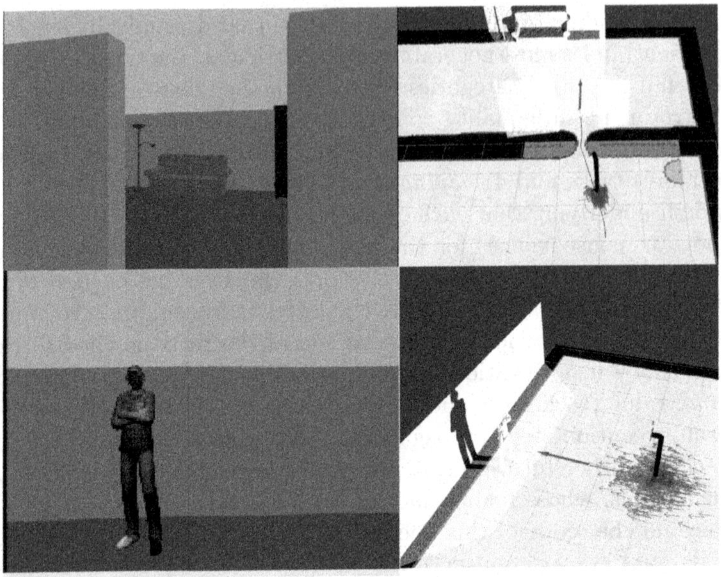

Fig. 4. An example of the robot's navigation service. In the top situation, the robot moves towards the goal chosen by the planner by computing the best trajectory towards that position. In the down pictures, the robot autonomously sets the navigation goal in the proximity of the detected person.

commands. The robot does not passively implement them, but it interprets with respect to the environment knowledge and avoids executing wrong commands like, for example, when such commands would cause collisions [2,3]. In details, the system treats the user's commands equally to the other sources of information (e.g., positions of the obstacle) that are mixed to determine the next most probable target positions for the robot through the definition of *policies*. In both cases, the navigation system optimizes the robot's trajectory by exploiting the local and global motion planner inside the ROS-Navigation Stack.

5 Advanced Perception

The robot's perception results from an RGBD camera, a 2D lidar and the microphone mounted on the robot. We have designed the services in charge of inferring the state of the environment and of the users on these inputs. Specifically, the robot sensing relies on the obstacle and skeleton tracking for managing the robot's movements and monitoring the user during the physical exercise, the speech to text for the natural interaction and the emotion detections for personalizing the robot's behaviors according to the user's emotional state. As we previously anticipated, the main barrier of building advancing sensing services is associated with the limited capabilities of the hardware. Since the robot is missing powerful resources, the execution of the fashionable and practical deep data-driven methods might be not straightforward. Regarding the skeleton tracking, in particular, we opted to wrap the *MediaPipe Pose* library inside ROS. Compared to more traditional algorithms typically used in robotics, such as the well-known *OpenPose*, indeed, *MediaPipe Pose* can achieve good real-time performance without requiring a GPU. As regards emotion detection, on the contrary, we designed and developed a custom real-time system based on the facial expressions considering this requirement. The most significant challenge has been the deployment of the trained DL model on a telepresence robot, which has limited hardware configuration in terms of memory and processing unit. Furthermore, the robot has to work with many other real-time integrated agents together for cognitive assistance approaches. The details of the pipeline underlying the developed light Deep learning model, specifically, are presented in the next subsections.

5.1 Emotion Detection

In the research community, most of the current emotion and facial expression recognition (FER) approaches are based on Deep Learning models. To achieve these models, a large quantity of data are needed to train the underlying deep neural networks. With this purpose, the first challenge consists of combining data from six available datasets – Ck+ [13,17], Jaffe [18], KDEF-DYN [4], KDEF-Session2 [5], Tfeid-High and Tfeid-slight [15] – to propose a new deep neural network architecture to address the FER problem across all of them. We assume that with the increasing of the size of training dataset, the model is expected to better generalise. Each dataset includes seven basic expressions (anger, fear, disgust, happiness, natural, sadness and surprise) which can define the richness and diversity of the human emotions. The majority of the current FER techniques extract facial features based on traditional feature extraction, ignoring the relative discriminant feature dependencies of facial expressions. Despite existing works performed in producing several techniques via deep learning algorithms for FER require real-time (Fast Response) generalizability when applied to unseen data or captured in a wild setting (i.e. the results may be significant

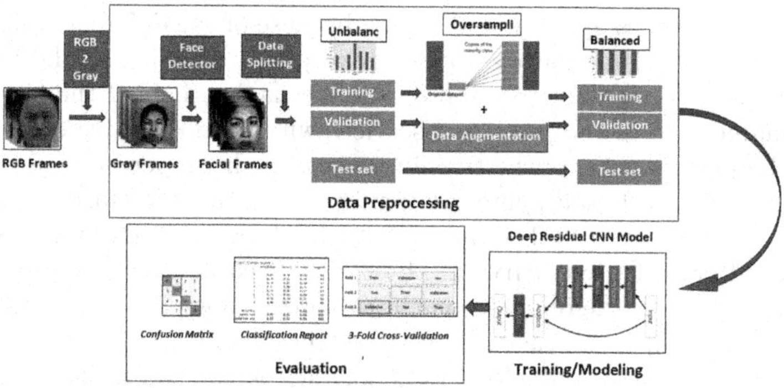

Fig. 5. Pipeline training phase

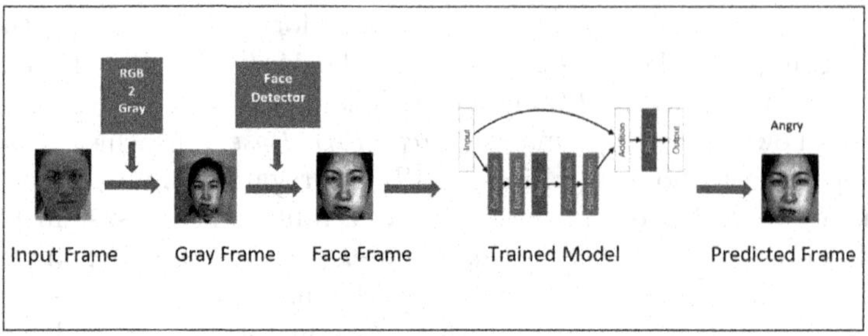

Fig. 6. Pipeline real-time testing phase

but having more computational complexity in terms of depth of the Artificial Neural Networks and trainable parameters).

We hence developed a Compact Deep Learning model considering the trade-off between the performance and computational complexity. The architecture is based on Residual Convolutional Neural Networks [11] with the combination of Dilation Convolution layers [10,28], Exponential Linear Unit (ELU) [8], Rectified Linear Unit (ReLU) [1] Activation Function, Stochastic Gradient Decent (SGD) loss function. In addition, ELU is integrated with the initial layers of the model, which preserve and pass information such as negative inputs [10] to forward layers which help to generalise the model through more information from input/initial layers, which improve the stability of the Network. The pipeline of the training and testing phases is shown respectively in Fig. 5 and in Fig. 6.

Our model contains only 3.9M parameters and achieves 87.71% on average accuracy on unseen data of a combination of the six datasets. Along with that, the average accuracy of individual test data is 82.07%, 77.53%, 99.52%, 72.18%, 88.03% and 61.5% on Ck+ [17], Jaffe [18], KDEF-DYN [4], KDEF-Session2 [5], Tfeid-High and Tfeid-slight [15] datasets respectively.

6 The Integrated System at Work

Given the heterogeneity of the services previously described, the holistic integration of the modules appears challenging because of the different technologies involved (e.g., robot's actuators, robot's perception, planning at the fog level) [6]. In this section, we want to dwell on the mechanism behind the functioning and communication of the presented services with an illustrative example. We suppose the planner returns the timeline shown in the upper part of Fig. 7. As mentioned in Sect. 3.1, the planner executor will notify the start of each task at specific time: first GoingTo, then LookForPerson, CognitiveExercise and finally, after some time, PhysicalExercise according to the selected timeline. Coherently with the observations in the previous work [6], once the scheduled task is known, it is crucial to manage the different levels of abstraction between the information provided by the planner on the fog, namely dependent from the domain, and the very specific and domain-independent local services.

To satisfy the dual necessity of being flexible in dispatching the current task and managing the heterogeneity of the on-board services, we include a reactive module, called *Local task manager*, in charge of determining the pipeline of reactive services needed to achieve the specific activity. The pairing between the task and the minimum set of reactive services to activate per task is established a priori and managed by a finite state machine. We represent such relations (e.g., the corresponding reactive services paired by color with each task) in the bottom part of the Fig. 7 (e.g., each reactive service is implemented inside a ROS node). For instance, the *Local task manager* has to enable the *Obstacle detections* and the *Contextualized navigation* service to implement the task GOINGTO. However, the occurrence of unexpected conditions can require the activation of services that are not predictable a priori. For instance, we are facing the current situation. We assume the robot has to keep its positions in front of the user during the execution of the *PhysicalExercise*. But, whether the person is walking, technically, this change leads to temporarily call the *Obstacle detections* and the *Contextualized navigation* services in parallel to make the robot move too. In this situation, the *Skeleton detections* service is used with a different functionality, namely to set a new navigation goal for the robot according to the estimated positions. Consequently, it emerges the central problem related to the composition of components to ensure their correct interoperation with both the fog and the on-board. Specifically, to maintain the execution of the plan in line with the evolution of the services, the *Local Task Manager* has also to communicate the start and the success or the failure of the execution of each task triggering the re-adaptation of the plan on the edge.

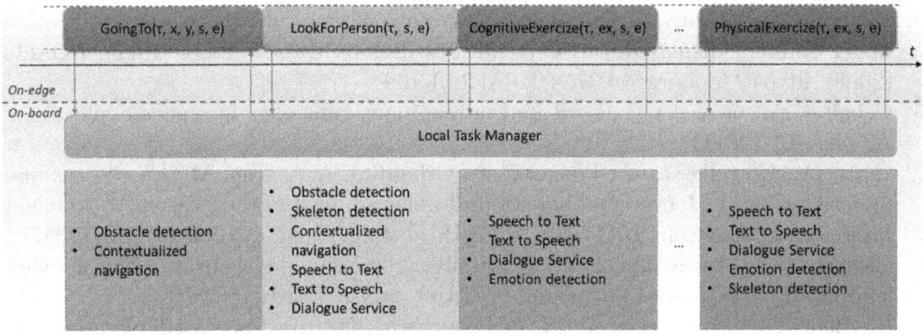

Fig. 7. An illustrative scheme of the flow of the system during the execution of the plan both at the *fog* and *on-board* levels.

7 Conclusions

This paper presents authors recent work to enrich a robotic platform for telepresence with additional services able to take advantage of: (a) the integration of

AI and robotics features, (b) the availability of AI advanced features for both model-based and data-intensive work. The overall goal aims at facilitating the life of older people at home with an artificial assistant that is closer to the current status of the technology and empower the mix of artificial and human assistance. This paper describes an architecture designed to control telepresence robots so as to enable personalized services for the users, as well as to capture and manage the uncertainty of the home environment, which dynamically and continuously evolves over time. It mostly describes the back-end services that are a seed for innovation, while further work is needed to develop front-ends for the heterogeneous users that are involved in the actual societal services supported by this technology.

References

1. Agarap, A.F.: Deep learning using rectified linear units (ReLU). CoRR abs/1803.08375 (2018)
2. Beraldo, G., Tonin, L., Cesta, A., Menegatti, E.: Brain-driven telepresence robots: a fusion of user's commands with robot's intelligence. In: Baldoni, M., Bandini, S. (eds.) AIxIA 2020. LNCS (LNAI), vol. 12414, pp. 235–248. Springer, Cham (2021). https://doi.org/10.1007/978-3-030-77091-4_15
3. Beraldo, G., Tonin, L., Menegatti, E.: Shared intelligence for user-supervised robots: from user's commands to robot's actions. In: Baldoni, M., Bandini, S. (eds.) AIxIA 2020. LNCS (LNAI), vol. 12414, pp. 457–465. Springer, Cham (2021). https://doi.org/10.1007/978-3-030-77091-4_27
4. Calvo, M.G., Fernández-Martín, A., Recio, G., Lundqvist, D.: Human observers and automated assessment of dynamic emotional facial expressions: KDEF-dyn database validation. Front. Psychol. **9**, 2052 (2018)
5. Calvo, M.G., Lundqvist, D.: Facial expressions of emotion (KDEF): identification under different display-duration conditions. Behav. Res. Methods **40**(1), 109–115 (2008). https://doi.org/10.3758/BRM.40.1.109
6. Ceballos, A., et al.: A goal-oriented autonomous controller for space exploration. ASTRA **11** (2011)
7. Cesta, A., Cortellessa, G., Fracasso, F., Orlandini, A., Turno, M.: User needs and preferences on AAL systems that support older adults and their carers. J. Ambient Intell. Smart Environ. **10**(1), 49–70 (2018). https://doi.org/10.3233/AIS-170471
8. Clevert, D.A., Unterthiner, T., Hochreiter, S.: Fast and accurate deep network learning by exponential linear units (ELUs). arXiv, Learning (2016)
9. De Benedictis, R., Cesta, A.: Lifted heuristics for timeline-based planning. In: 24th European Conference on Artificial Intelligence, ECAI 2020, Santiago de Compostela, Spain (2020)
10. Devaram, R.R., Allegra, D., Gallo, G., Stanco, F.: Hyperspectral image classification via convolutional neural network based on dilation layers. In: Ricci, E., Rota Bulò, S., Snoek, C., Lanz, O., Messelodi, S., Sebe, N. (eds.) ICIAP 2019. LNCS, vol. 11751, pp. 378–387. Springer, Cham (2019). https://doi.org/10.1007/978-3-030-30642-7_34
11. He, K., Zhang, X., Ren, S., Sun, J.: Deep residual learning for image recognition. In: Proceedings of the IEEE Conference on Computer Vision and Pattern Recognition (CVPR), June 2016

12. Isabet, B., Pino, M., Lewis, M., Benveniste, S., Rigaud, A.S.: Social telepresence robots: a narrative review of experiments involving older adults before and during the COVID-19 pandemic. Int. J. Environ. Res. Public Health **18**(7) (2021). https://www.mdpi.com/1660-4601/18/7/3597
13. Kanade, T., Cohn, J.F., Tian, Y.: Comprehensive database for facial expression analysis. In: Proceedings Fourth IEEE International Conference on Automatic Face and Gesture Recognition (Cat. No. PR00580), pp. 46–53. IEEE (2000)
14. Kristoffersson, A., Coradeschi, S., Loutfi, A.: A review of mobile robotic telepresence. Adv. Hum. Comput. Interact. **2013**, 1–17 (2013)
15. Chen, L.-F., Yen, Y.S.: Taiwanese facial expression image database. Brain Mapping Laboratory, Institute of Brain Science, National Yang-Ming University, Taipei, Taiwan (2007)
16. Laniel, S., Létourneau, D., Grondin, F., Labbé, M., Ferland, F., Michaud, F.: Toward enhancing the autonomy of a telepresence mobile robot for remote home care assistance. Paladyn J. Behav. Robot. **12**(1), 214–237 (2021)
17. Lucey, P., Cohn, J.F., Kanade, T., Saragih, J., Ambadar, Z., Matthews, I.: The extended Cohn-Kanade Dataset (CK+): a complete dataset for action unit and emotion-specified expression. In: 2010 IEEE Computer Society Conference on Computer Vision and Pattern Recognition - Workshops. IEEE, June 2010
18. Lyons, M., Akamatsu, S., Kamachi, M., Gyoba, J.: Coding facial expressions with gabor wavelets. In: Proceedings Third IEEE International Conference on Automatic Face and Gesture Recognition. IEEE Computer Society (1998)
19. Melendez-Fernandez, F., Galindo, C., Gonzalez-Jimenez, J.: A web-based solution for robotic telepresence. Int. J. Adv. Robot. Syst. **14**(6), 1729881417743738 (2017). https://doi.org/10.1177/1729881417743738
20. Moro, C., Nejat, G., Mihailidis, A.: Learning and personalizing socially assistive robot behaviors to aid with activities of daily living. ACM Trans. Hum. Robot Interact. **7**(2), 15:1–15:25 (2018)
21. Muscettola, N., Smith, S., Cesta, A., D'Aloisi, D.: Coordinating space telescope operations in an integrated planning and scheduling architecture. IEEE Control. Syst. **12**(1), 28–37 (1992)
22. Orlandini, A., et al.: ExCITE project: a review of forty-two months of robotic telepresence technology evolution. Presence **25**(3), 204–221 (2016)
23. Riano, L., Burbridge, C., Mc Ginnity, M.: A study of enhanced robot autonomy in telepresence. In: Proceedings of Artificial Intelligence and Cognitive Systems, AICS, Ireland, 31 August 2011, pp. 271–283. AICS (2011)
24. Rossi, S., Ferland, F., Tapus, A.: User profiling and behavioral adaptation for HRI: a survey. Pattern Recogn. Lett. **99**, 3–12 (2017)
25. Sheridan, T.B.: Musings on telepresence and virtual presence. Presence: Teleoper. Virtual Environ. **1**(1), 120–126 (1992). https://doi.org/10.1162/pres.1992.1.1.120
26. Tsui, K.M., Desai, M., Yanco, H.A., Uhlik, C.: Exploring use cases for telepresence robots. In: 2011 6th ACM/IEEE International Conference on Human-Robot Interaction (HRI), pp. 11–18 (2011). https://doi.org/10.1145/1957656.1957664
27. Umbrico, A., Cesta, A., Cortellessa, G., Orlandini, A.: A holistic approach to behavior adaptation for socially assistive robots. Int. J. Soc. Robot. **12**(3), 617–637 (2020). https://doi.org/10.1007/s12369-019-00617-9
28. Yu, F., Koltun, V.: Multi-scale context aggregation by dilated convolutions. In: Bengio, Y., LeCun, Y. (eds.) 4th International Conference on Learning Representations, ICLR 2016, San Juan, Puerto Rico, 2–4 May 2016, Conference Track Proceedings (2016)

Tafl-ES: Exploring Evolution Strategies for Asymmetrical Board Games

Roberto Gallotta[1(✉)] and Roberto Capobianco[1,2]

[1] Sapienza University of Rome, Rome, Italy
gallotta.1890251@studenti.uniroma1.it, capobianco@diag.uniroma1.it
[2] Sony AI, Tokyo, Japan

Abstract. NeuroEvolution Strategies (NES) are a subclass of Evolution Strategies (ES). While their application to games and board games have been studied in the past [11], current state of the art in most of the games is still held by classic RL models, such as AlphaGo Zero [16]. This is despite recent work showing their desirable properties [12].

In this paper we use NES applied to the board game Hnefatafl, a known hard environment given its asymmetrical nature. In the experiment we set up we coevolve two populations of intelligent agents. With results collected thus far we show the validity of this approach and useful techniques to overcome its large computation resource and time requirements.

Keywords: Hnefatafl · Reinforcement Learning · NeuroEvolution Strategies · Open-ended systems

1 Introduction

Prior to Reinforcement Learning, creating intelligent agents for board games usually required human expertise and crafting an *ad-hoc*, domain-specific algorithm. While some of these were incredibly well-performing (such as StockFish[1]), many others required too much computation power or time.

Reinforcement Learning (in particular the TD [20] family of algorithms) tried to remove most of the required expertise, producing very good results [1]. With the later surge of Deep Q-Learning, the improvement was constant over time, obtaining better and better agents. The turning point was the introduction of AlphaGo [15] which outperformed the best human player of Go in the world. The following improvements, [13] and [16], removed the reliance on human expertise of the domain and the knowledge of rules and then gave the ability to the model to generalize to unknown environments[2].

On the other hand, Evolution Strategies for board game have been investigated in either estimating states value [8] or actual game playing [21]. The generated agents however were only on par with their RL-based counterpart.

[1] https://stockfishchess.org/.
[2] We however agree with the remarks presented in [9] and the limitations of such statements.

S. Bandini et al. (Eds.): AIxIA 2021, LNAI 13196, pp. 46–58, 2022.
https://doi.org/10.1007/978-3-031-08421-8_4

Building on the previous work of [6] and inspired by the AlphaGo Zero approach to the problem, we test the feasibility of a competitive NES-based model in playing the board game Hnefatafl.

We chose Hnefatafl as the game for this project due to its goal-asymmetrical nature and its intrinsic complexity. As we discuss in Sect. 2.1, the game is more complex than it appears, with an effective branching factor that, in some variants, is much larger than Chess'. Additionally, the existence of a multitude of rules set and variants allows us to choose one such variant on which we can test our hypothesis without exceeding resources limits.

As we saw in AlphaGo [15], AlphaGo Zero [16] and, later, MuZero [13], a board game such as this could be solved by the same kind of algorithms. However, such a solution would only create a single highly-efficient player. Instead, by employing a NES algorithm we can evolve multiple different players with different play-styles that, even if not as efficient, are more interesting to play against. One key feature of ES systems is that individuals do not need to be "the best", but "good enough" to give interesting results. We discuss what we mean by "good enough" in Sect. 3.2.

In this paper we propose our approach to the problem and we release the required Gym [10] environment in [5]. Our approach is general enough to be applied to any 2-players fully-observable board game and the single modules it comprises can be easily further modified without breaking the system itself. The Gym environment, although specialised for Hnefatafl variants here, provides a solid blueprint for new implementations of different board games. We hope that our contribute will allow more people to effortlessly test new ideas in this field.

2 Background

In this section we give the necessary background knowledge on the Hnefatafl game itself and Evolution Strategies (ES).

2.1 Hnefatafl

The Story. Hnefatafl is a 2-player, zero-sum, asymmetrical board game supposedly originated in Scandinavia probably as a variant of Ludus Latronculorum and that lasted well into the 18th century, as Chess surged in popularity in the now-Christianized upper class families. The little we know about this game is derived from excerpts of poems and partial archaeological findings. Due to this, and taking into account the long time it has been played by many different cultures (thanks to the Viking invasions), it is no surprise that there is no standard way to play Hnefatafl and many variants have been theorized and some even modernized.

The board itself, along with the number of playing pieces, is different from variant to variant, ranging from a 7×7 grid to a 19×19 grid. The core gameplay, however, is the same. Two teams are placed on the board: the Defenders occupy the center of the board, protecting their King, whereas the Attackers are placed along the edges of the board. Each piece is allowed to move only orthogonally and cannot jump over any piece on its path (like a rook in Chess); capturing a piece is done by custodianship (surrounding the captured piece within two pieces of the opposite team).

The game is asymmetrical: the goal for the Defenders is to move their King to either a corner or an edge of the board (according to the variant rules) and the goal for the Attackers is to capture the King via enclosure, surrounding it with a certain number of pieces. This asymmetry in goals is balanced by numbers: the Attackers are in a 2:1 ratio with respect to the Defenders.

The Variant. We implement and release the TaflGym environment[3] to create a custom variant that would be as balanced as possible for novice players. This variant, later dubbed *Ard Sì* in the Discord Hnefatafl community, features the following rules:

- the board is a 7×7 grid;
- pieces count and arrangement follows the Lewis Cross disposition;
- the King is armed;
- the King is captured enclosing it with two pieces;
- there are no corners, therefore the Defenders win when the King reaches the edge of the board;
- the King can only move by one tile;
- a threefold repetition (repeating the same move three times in a row) leads to a draw.

The initial board setup is reported in Fig. 1.

Though the more balanced variants to date are *Sea Battle* 9×9, with a perfect averaged balance ratio of 1[4] and *Simple Tafl*, with a balance ratio of -1.03[5] (slightly favoring the Attacker), we implemented our own variant with a smaller board due to resource limits constraints.

2.2 State of the Art

Currently, board games are solvable with deep-RL techniques such as MuZero [13]. Such a model is able to predict internally at each time-step t the policy P_t to apply, the value function v_t, and the immediate reward r_t. These predictions are made by a model μ_θ, conditioned on past observations $o_1, ..., o_t$ and future actions $a_{t+1}, ..., a_{t+k}$. The model contains a semantic-detached internal state s that is used to align the representation function, the dynamics function, and the prediction function. The dynamics function mirrors an MDP but has no knowledge of the environment; it instead aims to accurately predict policies,

[3] *TaflGym* environment is available at https://github.com/gallorob/tafl-gym.
[4] Measure from Aage Nielsen webiste at http://aagenielsen.dk.
[5] Measure from Fellhuhn's Hnefatafl application at https://store.steampowered.com/app/1249510/Hnefatafl/.

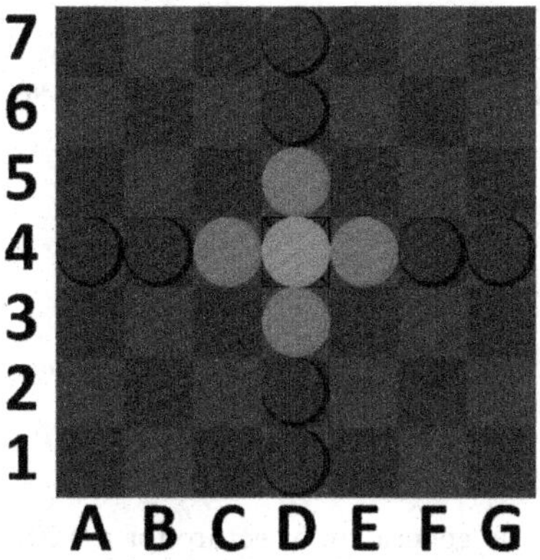

Fig. 1. The setup for *Ard Sì*

values, and rewards. It is then possible to search over hypothetical future trajectories to accurately predict a policy π_t and a value v_t (and, subsequently, apply the recommended action a_t. In the original paper, the search was based on a MCTS (Monte Carlo Tree Search), similarly to AlphaGo Zero [16]. Given its semantic agnosticism, the model can be applied to a multitude of environments (including board games such as Chess, Go, and Shogi), achieving superhuman performances.

While Hnefatafl is a valid candidate environment for MuZero, it has not yet been proven to be solvable (mainly due to the high computational costs a model such as MuZero requires). As of now, a program to play Hnefatafl at novice level is OpenTafl[6], which uses a Stockfish-like approach to explore the search tree. Using a tree-based search algorithm is extremely expensive when planning more than a few moves ahead, even when using optimization techniques such α-β pruning and transposition tables. Additionally, heuristics are all human-coded and may not be the best approximations of a true value function.

Unlike deep-RL, there is no "best" GA or ES method for game playing, as they both require domain knowledge to be embedded in the system itself [14]. On the other hand, NES systems can be applied to different domains easily but there are different types, each with its own advantages and disadvantages. For example, Conventional NeuroEvolution (CNE) evolves only the weights of an ANN and is able to find high-performing policies if they exist [3], whereas NEAT [17] and HyperNEAT [19], [18] also evolve the topology of the ANN along with its weights, increasing the complexity of the ANN according to the domain. Thus, while CNE may underperform compared to NEAT or HyperNEAT, the latter may suffer from bloating or risk being too task-specific. Performances also differ greatly on the environment. Thus, while these systems can be semantic-agnostic, it is not clear which model is *overall* superior to the others on all possible applications (Fig. 2).

[6] OpenTafl is available at https://github.com/jslater89/OpenTafl.

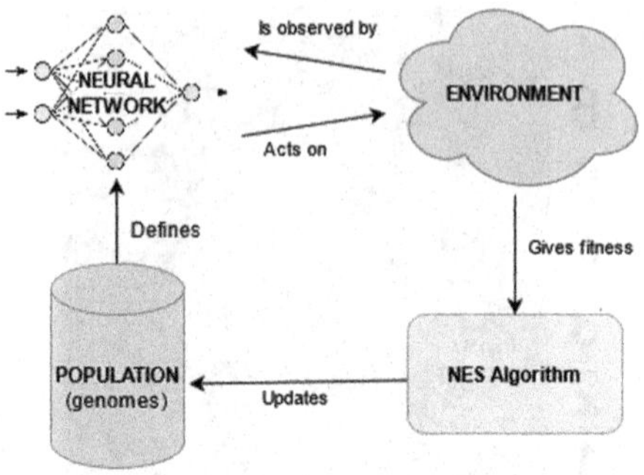

Fig. 2. The generic architecture for a NES system

2.3 Evolution Strategies

Evolution Strategies (ES) are a family of black-box optimization algorithms inspired by natural evolution. From a starting population of models, at every iteration each model is evaluated according to a predefined fitness function and the best performing model is then perturbed to generate the population for the following step. When the models are Artificial Neural Networks (ANNs), we apply NeuroEvolution Strategies (NES). The networks can be represented either explicitily (each model consisting of both architecture and parameters) or implicitly (each model consisting of parameters only or some different genotypic encoding). At its core, NES evolves a population of ANNs. Each network is evaluated on a task and its fitness is recorded. After all models are evaluated, fitter individuals are selected for reproduction in the next population. The reproduction can be obtained by perturbing the encoding genotypes of the network (or encoding the architecture of the network directly, as in [17]) or its parameters directly (in this case we would talk of *mutation*) or by recombining them with other individual's to generate new offsprings (generally identified with the name *crossover*). By repeating this evaluation-selection-reproduction cycle for many iterations, NES tries to find better and better ANNs for the task. A more complete overview of NES can be found at [4].

Using NE in Reinforcement Learning (RL) tasks has many advantages:

- higher performance on many domains;
- broader applicability, as NE can also be used in supervised or unsupervised learning;
- better scalability compared to TD algorithms;
- easy to obtain diverse solutions;
- broader search space makes it arguable that NE is an Open-Ended algorithm;
- can be easily applied to new kind of games.

One of the main drawbacks of using NE is, however, its lack of explainability, which would help a great deal in debugging the learned behavior.

3 Approach

3.1 Problem Formulation

In this section we characterize the main underlying mathematical properties of the problem.

We can define the game of Hnefatafl as a Markov Decision Process (MDP). An MDP is a discrete-time state-transition system characterized by a set of states S, a set of possible actions A, a reward function $R(s,a)$ with $s \in S$ and $a \in A$ and a descriptor function T for each action in each state. Formally, we define it as $MDP = \langle S, A, T, R \rangle$. The system is deterministic, so $T : S \times A \rightarrow S$ and fully observable. We note that we consider a possible state s to not be just the current board configuration but the current board configuration and the previous 7 configurations, so as to not break the Markov property. This is because, as in many other games such as Chess and Go, there exists the threefold repetition rule that leads either to a draw or a loss if the same move is applied three times in a row. The introduction of previous board configurations in the current state, as applied also in [15], instead allows the agent to consider enough past history to be able to learn not to play the same move thrice in a row.

The board is a 7×7 grid, in each cell there can be no piece, an Attacker, a Defender or a King. By applying one-hot encoding for each piece type, we can express a single state as a $3 \times 7 \times 7$ tensor. Hnefatafl has a rule about threefold repetition and we wanted to allow the model to take this into consideration. Since this rule can be checked on a series of just 8 states, we can stack the last 7 states onto the current one, obtaining a $24 \times 7 \times 7$ tensor. In the first few turns the missing states are $3 \times 7 \times 7$ empty tensors. We also allow to introduce the concept of current player by stacking an additional 7×7 array filled with 1s when the current player is the Attacker and 0s when it is the Defender, thus making the final sample a $25 \times 7 \times 7$ tensor.

The action space is defined as the discrete space of all valid moves for any piece. Given the board dimensions and considering that each piece moves orthogonally until it reaches the edge of the board (in the best case), we compute the number of all valid moves as the number of tuples

$$(tile_{i,j},\ tile_{x,y}),\quad 0 \leq i,j,x,y \leq 7,$$

that respect $i = x$ when $j \neq z$ and viceversa. By doing so, the action space has dimension 588.

The agent takes as input the $25 \times 7 \times 7$ tensor sample and outputs a vector of size 588. Each element of this vector is the probability associated to the possible move. By multiplying it by a mask vector we can then zero out the illegal moves. The move with the highest probability is the move that is played.

We evolve agents such that the move with the highest probability is the move that most likely leads to a victory. This is equivalent to having the agents find the policy π. An optimal policy would maximize the expected total reward of the match by selecting the action $a = \pi_{opt}(s)$. We can then define the Value

Algorithm 1. Overview of the evolution process

```
procedure EvolvePopulation(population, steps)
    i ← 0
    while i ≤ steps do
        matches ← play_matches(population)
        filtered_matches ← filter(matches)
        best_agent ← find_best(filtered_matches)
        population ← evolve_agent(best_agent)
        if has_good_score(best_agent) then:
            switch_evolving(population)
```

function $V_\pi = S \to \mathbb{R}$, which represents the expected objective value obtained following the policy π from each state $s \in S$.

The Value Network is used to estimate the value of the current state, i.e.: which player has more advantage. This network takes as input the same sample as the agent (a $25\times7\times7$ tensor) and predicts a real value $\in [-1, 1]$. The closer the value is to -1, the more advantage is estimated for the Attacker. The closer it is to 1, the more advantage is estimated for the Defender. Values closer to 0 signify instead a balanced board. The network is trained on a dataset of completed matches, as the true value of each state is unknown. We take advantage of the board symmetry to augment the dataset, adding at most 3 additional samples per board configuration (corresponding to rotating the board 3 times). The training takes place every few tournaments after the matches buffer has been filled in order to keep its predictions aligned.

The Filter Network is used to distinguish "interesting" matches from "unintersting" matches. It is a NN that takes the match history (in its entirety or the last n moves) and outputs a the probability that such match should be kept for evaluating the players or could be discarded. We train it on a dataset of matches that have been evaluated by the naive filter algorithm. The training takes place every few tournaments after the matches buffer has been filled in order to keep its predictions aligned.

3.2 Proposed Solution: Tafl-ES

Our proposed solution is Tafl-ES. In this ES, we coevolve two populations of agents: one population models the Defenders, the other the Attackers. The reason for this is the following: given the asymmetrical nature of Hnefatafl, we assume that the same model would under-perform if forced to play both sides, whereas having a separate model per team ensures a specialization in that team's tactics. Perhaps a more advanced model could overcome this possible limitation.

An overview of the Tafl-ES system is presented in Algorithm 1. The initial populations are populated with randomly initialized agents. Each agent is an ANN with the same structure as the one proposed in [15] for predicting actions given the current state and states history. Note that the initial populations do not have to respect any Minimal Criterion (MC) as there is no practical need here.[7]

We coevolve these populations for a fixed number of *tournaments*. During each tournament, one population is free to evolve, while the other is frozen. In a tournament, all the agents of one population play matches against a portion of the agents of the other population (in the first ever tournament, this chunk of agents is chosen at random and in subsequent tournaments it is comprised of the top k agents according to a predefined metric).

In order to save time and resources during tournaments, we randomly do not allow matches to be played to completion. We do this by implementing a constantly-updated NN similar to the value network first presented in [15]. As the NN becomes more accurate in the prediction over the matches dataset, we can cutoff matches earlier, safely assuming that the predicted outcome would coincide with the effective outcome of the match. Note that while in [15] and [16] a Monte Carlo Tree Search (MCTS) was implemented, here it is not needed, which saves additional time. The probability of using this network to cutoff a match increases as the NN is trained following the bounded monotonic positive function

$$p(t) = 2 \cdot \frac{\arctan(3 \cdot t \cdot \tau)}{\pi}$$

where t is the current training iteration and τ is the temperature value.

After all matches have been played, we first filter out "uninteresting" matches to keep only "interesting" agents. We can do this by either using an *ad-hoc* rule or by training a NN to filter out such matches by looking at the matches history.

Once all matches have been filtered, the agents of the evolvable population that played those matches are evaluated. Each agent has a personal ELO score that is updated as well as per-tournament points score. The ELO is a player's skill metric for zero-sum games invented by Arpad Elo. The points score instead is a value that we update whenever the agent wins or draws a game. In preliminary tests, we checked whether ELO score or point score was a better indicator for agent fitness and we found that point score was more reliable, as ELO score can flutter too much during the tournament. For this reason all experiments only take the agents' score into account.

The best performing agents are selected as parents for the next generation. Currently, only one best agent is chosen since we are not interested in creating diversity, though it is trivial to extend the procedure to include top-k agents instead of just one. The selected agent then produces n identical copies of itself and each of the offsprings is mutated. Mutation is applied by perturbation with Gaussian noise: given the θ vector of the agent's NN's parameters, we have

$$\theta_{k+1} \leftarrow \theta_k + \delta,$$

[7] If one wants to, however, it is possible to implement a Minimal Criterion Coevolution (MCC) system similar to the one presented by [2] by enforcing that the agent is able to win against a simple minimax algorithm.

Algorithm 2. Generation of population from single agent

```
procedure EvolveAgent(agent)
    new_population ← {agent}
    while size(new_population) < population_size do
        new_agent = copy(agent)
        θ ← get_parameters(new_agent)
        ϵ ∼ N(0, 1)
        θ' ← θ + μ · ϵ
        set_parameters(new_agent, θ')
    return new_population
```

where δ is the mutation vector of the same shape as θ. We compute δ as

$$\delta \leftarrow \mu \cdot \epsilon,$$

where $\epsilon \sim \mathcal{N}(0, 1)$ and μ is the mutation scale factor. An overview of the evolution process of an agent is given in Algorithm 2. We are aware that simply perturbing a Deep Neural Network (DNN) may result in a divergence in the current evolution trajectory, so a future improvement would be implementing Safe Mutations through Rescaling (SM-R) as proposed by [7] or some analogous technique to ensure we are not adding destructive noise.

We iterate the same tournament multiple times until the best agent for the evolving population reaches a desired score threshold, set to having won at least 75% of the matches, as it is "good enough" to let interesting behavior emerge and not simply optimize tactics. These optimization steps are required especially in asymmetrical games: one team always wins more easily than the other, thus making it extremely difficult for the other team to find an efficient policy to reduce this disparity. On the other hand, the favored team also has the drawback of not learning efficiently as random moves still lead to a victory in the earlier tournaments.

In order to ensure that we do not loose progress with each new generation we apply *elitism*, a common practice where we keep the parent agent unmodified in the population for the next generation. This also gives us the opportunity to reinitialize the entire population from it if needed.

Once the score threshold has been reached, the current population is frozen and the other is free to evolve in the next tournament.

4 Results

In preliminary results we found that agents evolved from random behavior to less-random behavior in just a few tournaments. By that we mean that, while they did not capture the gameplay logic in its entirety, they already started to show preference of certain moves (e.g.: a piece capturing another instead of moving past it).

We trained a population of 100 agents (50 agents per team) for 100 tournaments with a μ value of 0.1. The Value Network was trained for 15 epochs with a refresh rate of 3 tournaments and with an accuracy threshold of 75% for activation. We used Stochastic Gradient Descent (SGD) with momentum ($\mu = 0.9$, learning rate set to 0.001) as optimizer and MSE as loss. The Filter Networks were trained for 25 epochs with a refresh rate of 3 tournaments and an accuracy threshold of 75%. We used Adam (learning rate set to 0.01) as optimizer and L1 as loss. Both types of networks accepted batches of 64 samples from the matches buffer containing 1536 matches in total. As baseline we ran the tournaments without using the Value network nor the filters and picking a random agent as best agent at each iteration. The scores distributions for the baseline are reported in Fig. 3. It is clear that the attackers have a slight advantage over the defenders but the majority of the agents scores around 1 to 1.5 points.

We then tested all possible combinations of features: with and without value network and with naive or trainable filters. Due to the limitations on resources we could not run each test of combinations enough times to present a complete statistical analysis of the results; however all tests were ran with the same initial population (ensured by fixing the initial RNG seed) so the final results still have significance with respect to the effects of the components introduced in the system. The score distribution shows how many agents in the population scored a given number of points in the tournament. As agent's performance is measured by its score, this measure conveys the necessary information to assess the population performance. Since the evolution is halted each time a viable candidate solution is found, we will not see agents in the population converge to a specific policy; we are instead interested in whether the distributions with the different combinations of modules are comparable and are also different from the baseline.

As expected, the distribution of scores is more distributed, however we note that using the value network reduces the scores spread. Additionally, the effects of the trainable filters increase such effect. We report the scores distributions of the different combinations of features in Fig. 4, Fig. 5, Fig. 6 and Fig. 7. Unsurprisingly, the population of Defenders have been evolved for more iterations than the Attacker's due to the variant's imbalance. Additionally, these plots clearly show how the two populations are constantly improving from their previous tournaments and, even in iterations where the other population had the upper hand for multiple tournaments (e.g.: iterations 60 to 80 in Fig. 4 or around iterations 50 and 100 in Fig. 5) eventually a better strategy was found by a well-performing agent that generated an overall better population. Finally, we note that many agents performed poorly, though we argue that this is mainly due to the possible destructive noise we use to perturb the ANNs parameters vectors.

We report the metrics of the NNs in the different experiments at the end of the tournaments in Table 1.

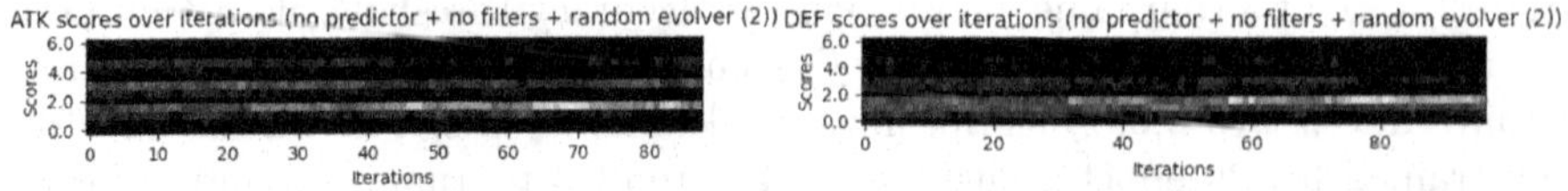

(a) Scores distributions for Attackers (b) Scores distributions for Defenders

Fig. 3. Scores distributions for attackers and defenders with no value network, no filter and random evolver.

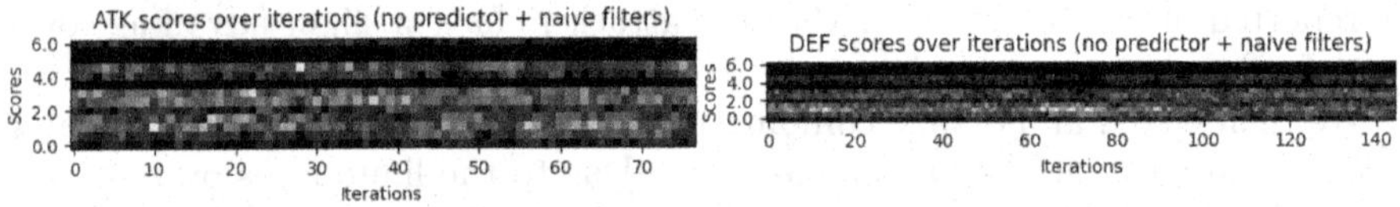

(a) Scores distributions for Attackers (b) Scores distributions for Defenders

Fig. 4. Scores distributions for attackers and defenders with no value network and using naïve filter.

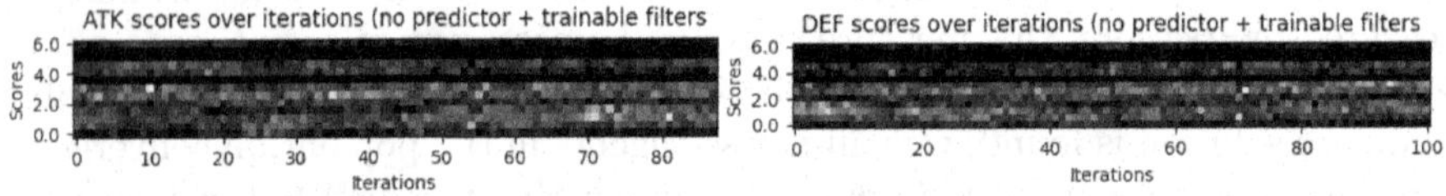

(a) Scores distributions for Attackers (b) Scores distributions for Defenders

Fig. 5. Scores distributions for attackers and defenders with no value network and using trainable filters.

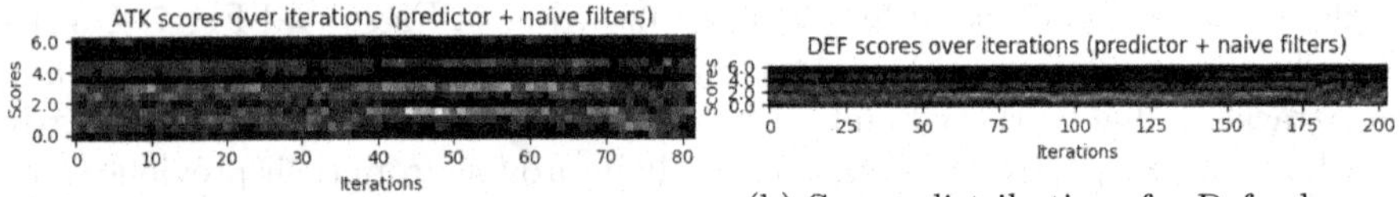

(a) Scores distributions for Attackers (b) Scores distributions for Defenders

Fig. 6. Scores distributions for attackers and defenders with value network and using naive filter.

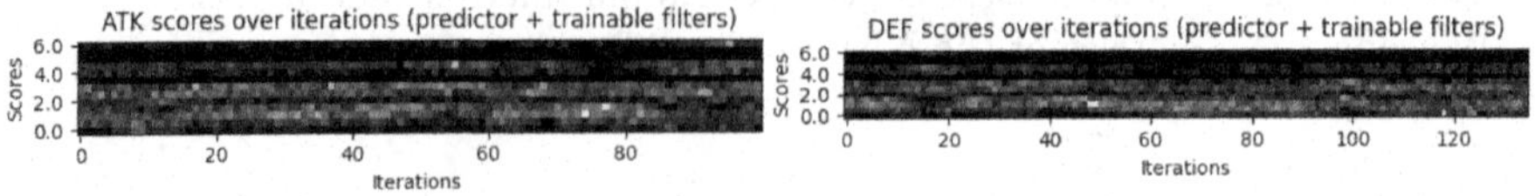

(a) Scores distributions for Attackers (b) Scores distributions for Defenders

Fig. 7. Scores distributions for attackers and defenders with value network and using trainable filters.

Table 1. Metrics comparison across experiments. Best values are in bold. Values with 1, 2 and 3 are for the value network, the filter network for the attackers and the filter network for the defenders respectively.

Experiment	Network	Train accuracy (%) ↑	Train loss ↓	Test accuracy (%) ↑	Test loss ↓
Value network only	Value network	81.25	0.5579	**81.9444**[1]	**0.4130**[1]
	ATK filter	–	–	–	–
	DEF filter	–	–	–	–
Value network + Trainable filters	Value network	**87.5**[1]	**0.2217**[1]	79.2968	0.5306
	ATK filter	87.5	0.7813	78.4482	1.279
	DEF filter	93.75	0.4061	**88.7019**[3]	0.6361
Trainable filters only	Value network	–	–	–	–
	ATK filter	**93.75**[2]	**0.098**[2]	**89.4531**[2]	**0.1401**[2]
	DEF filter	**98.4375**[3]	**0.0248**[3]	86.1607	**0.1833**[3]

5 Conclusions and Future Work

We found that evolving a population of agents with perturbation of their parameters and implementing both a Value network and trainable filters leads to constantly better populations. Additionally, the innate disadvantage of the chosen variant is still present but its effects are attenuated.

The experiments, while simplistic in many ways, yield promising results for more research: in particular, it would be interesting to see the benefits of a minimal criterion or the effects of applying safer mutations techniques that do not disrupt phenotypical behavior of the evolved agents. Other interesting additions regarding the tactics of the agents that could be explored are using a $k > 1$ when selecting the top-k agents and perhaps integrating human-in-the-loop controls during the filtering process.

References

1. Baxter, J., Tridgell, A., Weaver, L.: Reinforcement learning and chess, pp. 91–116, January 2001
2. Brant, J.C., Stanley, K.O.: Minimal criterion coevolution: a new approach to open-ended search. In: Proceedings of the Genetic and Evolutionary Computation Conference, GECCO 2017, pp. 67–74. Association for Computing Machinery, New York (2017). https://doi.org/10.1145/3071178.3071186
3. Clune, J., Stanley, K.O., Pennock, R.T., Ofria, C.: On the performance of indirect encoding across the continuum of regularity. IEEE Trans. Evol. Comput. **15**(3), 346–367 (2011). https://doi.org/10.1109/TEVC.2010.2104157
4. Floreano, D., Dürr, P., Mattiussi, C.: Neuroevolution: from architectures to learning. Evol. Intell. **1**(1), 47–62 (2008). https://doi.org/10.1007/s12065-007-0002-4
5. Gallotta, R.: OpenAI gym environment based on the Tafl board games for reinforcement learning (2021). https://github.com/gallorob/tafl-gym
6. Hingston, P.: Evolving players for an ancient game: Hnefatafl. In: 2007 IEEE Symposium on Computational Intelligence and Games, pp. 168–174 (2007). https://doi.org/10.1109/CIG.2007.368094

7. Lehman, J., Chen, J., Clune, J., Stanley, K.O.: Safe mutations for deep and recurrent neural networks through output gradients (2018)
8. Lucas, S.M., Runarsson, T.P.: Temporal difference learning versus co-evolution for acquiring Othello position evaluation. In: 2006 IEEE Symposium on Computational Intelligence and Games, pp. 52–59 (2006). https://doi.org/10.1109/CIG.2006.311681
9. Marcus, G.: Innateness, alphazero, and artificial intelligence (2018)
10. OpenAI: Gym, reinforcement learning toolkit. https://gym.openai.com/
11. Risi, S., Togelius, J.: Neuroevolution in games: state of the art and open challenges (2015)
12. Salimans, T., Ho, J., Chen, X., Sidor, S., Sutskever, I.: Evolution strategies as a scalable alternative to reinforcement learning (2017)
13. Schrittwieser, J., et al.: Mastering Atari, go, chess and shogi by planning with a learned model. Nature **588**(7839), 604–609 (2020). https://doi.org/10.1038/s41586-020-03051-4
14. Shah, S.M., Singh, D., Shah, J.: Using genetic algorithm to solve game of Go-Moku. IJCA Special Issue on Optimization and On-chip Communication (1), 28–31 (2012). Full text available
15. Silver, D., et al.: Mastering the game of go with deep neural networks and tree search. Nature **529**(7587), 484–489 (2016)
16. Silver, D., et al.: Mastering the game of go without human knowledge. Nature **550**(7676), 354–359 (2017)
17. Stanley, K.O., Miikkulainen, R.: Evolving neural networks through augmenting topologies. Evol. Comput. **10**(2), 99–127 (2002). https://doi.org/10.1162/106365602320169811
18. Stanley, K.O.: Compositional pattern producing networks: a novel abstraction of development. Genet. Program Evolvable Mach. **8**(2), 131–162 (2007)
19. Stanley, K.O., D'Ambrosio, D.B., Gauci, J.: A hypercube-based encoding for evolving large-scale neural networks. Artif. Life **15**(2), 185–212 (2009). https://doi.org/10.1162/artl.2009.15.2.15202
20. Sutton, R.S.: Learning to predict by the methods of temporal differences. Mach. Learn. **3**(1), 9–44 (1988)
21. Takahama, T., Sakai, S.: Learning game players by an evolutionary approach using pairwise comparison without prior knowledge. In: 2015 International Conference on Intelligent Informatics and Biomedical Sciences (ICIIBMS), pp. 121–127 (2015). https://doi.org/10.1109/ICIIBMS.2015.7439514

Constraints, Argumentation, and Logic Programming

Combining DCOP and MILP for Complex Local Optimization Problems

Fernanda N. T. Furukita, Fernando J. M. Marcellino(✉), and Jaime Sichman

Laboratório de Técnicas Inteligentes (LTI), Escola Politécnica (EP), Universidade de São Paulo (USP), Av. Prof. Luciano Gualberto 158 trav. 3, São Paulo, SP 05508-970, Brazil
{fernanda.namie,fmarcellino,jaime.sichman}@usp.br

Abstract. Supply chain management, which is composed of interdependent entities that have defined roles and responsibilities, shows several characteristics in common with Multi-Agent Systems (MAS). This type of problem may be divided into several local subproblems, which can be optimized separately. However, in general, the full problem cannot be solved in a centralized way due to its complexity or the need for information privacy. This work presents a distributed heuristic method which provides an acceptable optimization of this type of complex problem when compared to the centralized approach available for the considered instances, and better than a similar approach in the literature. It is based on modeling the considered problem first as a Distributed Constraint Optimization Problem (DCOP), and then by integrating it with Mixed-Integer Linear Programming (MILP) optimization models of its subproblems. We have obtained a value which is about 5% better than a similar distributed method in the literature and only about 7% worse than the actual optimum one. We consider a promising approach for increasingly real settings.

Keywords: Agent · Supply chain · Constraint programming · Optimization

1 Introduction

Supply chain management belongs to a problem category which is hard to be optimized. Traditionally, such problems are solved by a centralized algorithm. However, it is often inadequate or even impossible to have a centralized solution due to some reasons like the complexity of the whole chain integration [3]. On the other hand, supply chains and multi-agent systems show numerous intrinsic characteristics in common. Both own resources which are inherently distributed and they are naturally regarded as society of autonomous cooperating components. In fact, a supply chain consists of suppliers, factories, warehouses, distribution centers and retailers, working together to convert raw materials to products delivered to the customers. They cooperate with each other autonomously to

S. Bandini et al. (Eds.): AIxIA 2021, LNAI 13196, pp. 61–76, 2022.
https://doi.org/10.1007/978-3-031-08421-8_5

serve common goals but also have their own interests. However, there is lack of coordination and integration between these components. Agent technology therefore is very suitable to support collaboration in supply chain management. On the other hand, since there is no overall system controller, an agent-based solution may not be appropriate when global constraints are not maintained and decision-making based on local knowledge by individual agents may lead to globally sub-optimal decisions [18]. Therefore, our model uses the Constraint Programming approach, which provides a tight integration of the involved entities and may help to achieve a global optimization. Modeling a supply chain as a Distributed Constraint Optimization Problem (DCOP) [11] appears to be the best modeling choice. DCOP was defined as an extension of a Distributed Constraint Satisfaction Problem (DisCSP) [17]. In general, a DCOP is harder to solve than a DisCSP, since the goal is not just to find any solution, but the best one. In both paradigms, the problem is divided among a set of agents that communicate with each other to solve it. However, while DisCSP uses boolean constraints, DCOP uses valued constraints.

This work presents a distributed heuristic method which provides an acceptable optimization of this type of complex problem when compared to the centralized approach available for the considered instances, and better than a similar approach in the literature.

Section 2 makes a review about the employed techniques and related work, and discusses the adopted ideas and the motivations to develop our own approach, which is detailed in Sect. 3. Section 4 presents the performed experiments and their results, showing the viability and the advantages of the proposed method. Finally, Sect. 5 describes our conclusions and an outlook on future work.

2 Adopted Techniques and Related Work

To optimize the actions of all agents in the supply chain, it is often inadequate to have a centralized solution. According to Faltings and Yokoo [3], distributed methods are important mainly because of four reasons: (i) cost of creating a central authority when the problem is naturally distributed; (ii) knowledge transfer costs when constraints are internal to an agent and cannot easily be articulated to a central authority; (iii) privacy/security concerns, since agents' constraints may be strategic information that should not be revealed to competitors or even to a central authority; (iv) robustness against failure, since a failure of one agent does not necessarily compromise the system overall objective.

2.1 Distributed Constraint Optimization Problem

Distributed Constraint Optimization Problem (DCOP) is a formalism that generates distributed optimization models from those problems that are distributed in their very nature. In DCOP, agents try to find assignments to a set of variables that are subject to constraints. It is assumed that agents optimize the accumulated utility by the chosen solution. This is different from other related formalisms involving self-interested agents, which try to maximize their own utility individually. Thus, the agents can optimize a global function in a distributed fashion communicating only with neighbor agents, and even in an asynchronous way. A DCOP consists of a set of n variables $V = \{x_1, \ldots, x_n\}$, each assigned to an agent, where the values of the variables are taken from a set of finite and discrete domains $D = \{D_1, \ldots, D_n\}$, respectively. Only the agent who is assigned a variable has control on its value and knowledge of its domain. The agents' goal is to choose values for the variables such that a given global objective function is minimized (or maximized). The objective function is described as the sum of a set of cost functions, each one for a pair of variables x_i, x_j and defined as $f_{ij} : D_i \times D_j \rightarrow \mathbb{N}$. The cost functions in DCOP are the analogue of constraints from DisCSP, but they are referred to as valued or soft constraints [11]. Some examples of DCOP algorithms are ADOPT [11] and DPOP [12], among others.

2.2 DCOP with Complex Local Problems

The original DCOP definition assumes that each agent controls only a single variable. This limits the applicability of the algorithms to distributed practical applications and leaves some important open questions [1], such as how to solve complex local problems as part of a larger global problem and how to integrate the local solving process with the distributed search. Yokoo and Hirayama [16] have shown that any DCOP with complex local problems can be transformed to an original DCOP with exactly one variable per agent by problem reformulations. Therefore, a *DCOP with a Complex Local Problems* is defined by a tuple (A, V, D, F), where (i) $A = \{a_1, \ldots, a_n\}$ is a set of n agents; (ii) $V_i = \{v_{i\,1}, \ldots, v_{i\,m_i}\}$ is a set of variables which the agent a_i controls, such that $\forall i \neq j \; V_i \cap V_j = \emptyset$; $V = \cup V_i$ is the set of all the variables of the problem. The variables can be classified into 2 categories: *private* or *local* variables, which participate only in internal constraints of the corresponding agent (intra-agent constraints) and *public* variables, which also participate in external constraints with other agents (inter-agent constraints); (iii) $D = \{\ldots, D_{i\,j}, \ldots\}$ is a set of finite and discrete domains, where $D_{i\,j}$ is associated with the corresponding variable $v_{i\,j}$; and finally (iv) $F = \{f_1, \ldots, f_i, \ldots, f_k\}$ is a set of constraint functions, with $f_i : \prod_{i\,j} D_{i\,j} \rightarrow \mathbb{N}$. The goal is to find a complete instantiation V^* for all variables $v_{i\,j}$ that minimizes the global objective function $OF = \sum f_i$ [1,5].

2.3 Supply Chain Coordination Problem (SCC)

Burke et al. [2] proposed the Supply Chain Coordination (SCC) problem as a benchmark for Distributed Constraint Optimization in the supply chain management, as it involves planning and coordinating a range of activities relating to that area. The supply chain typically consists of several interdependent agents (organizations or business units), each holding the responsibility for provision of particular components that are combined in a final product. In order to reduce costs, each agent may try to optimize its internal processes. However, by making decisions locally and independently, the actions may lead to inefficiencies in the wider supply chain. The overall objective of the agents is to coordinate their production and delivery schedules such that the total costs (production, delivery, holding and penalty costs) in the supply chain network are minimized [6]. There are 3 types of agents in the SCC problem: **root agent** is one at the top of the supply chain and has a fixed demand for its products from customers; **leaf agents** are at the bottom of the supply chain and have fixed constraints on component availability and **intermediate agents**, which are both receiving components from agents and delivering products to other agents, which consider them as components. On account of Burke's work, the SCC benchmark was made available in CSPLib, which is a library of test problems for constraint solvers, distributed or not [6]. It includes the SCC problem formal specification, local models for each agent type, six problem instances and their respective best optimized solutions. They are shown in Fig. 1, where the root, intermediate and leaf agents are represented in red, blue and green, respectively.

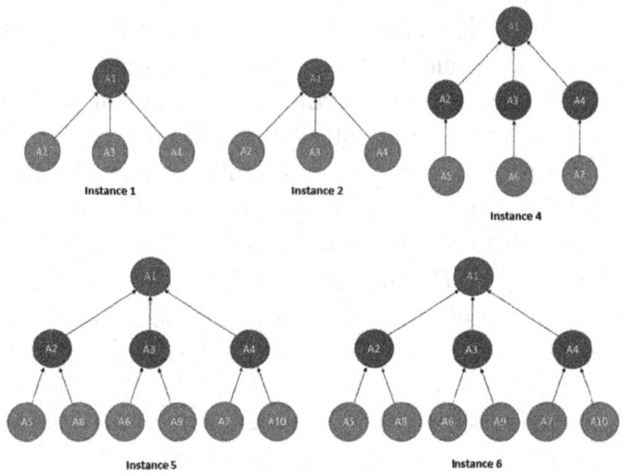

Fig. 1. Supply chain coordination problem benchmark in CSPLib [6] (Color figure online)

2.4 Attempts to Solve SCC with DCOP

The SCC benchmark problem considered the large internal problems of each agent via its corresponding model. A characteristic of this problem is that each agent has to solve a complex internal problem, which leads to a large, distributed search space and brings new challenges to the DCOP algorithms. In fact, conventional DCOP algorithms are not suitable to solve this class of problems by themselves. For this reason, Burke et al. [2] have also developed modeling techniques and search strategies to navigate this search space more efficiently. These improvements were included in the ADOPT algorithm, which has been extended for this purpose. However, a part of these changes is related to the aggregation process that has been applied to the planning horizon, number of components and number of batches per component, which simplified the model, moving it a little away from reality. Moreover, this approach does not allow a fair comparison of the performance of other DCOP algorithms to solve the supply chain problem, since it uses an improved version of ADOPT algorithm (ADOPT+).

Hence, our motivation was to propose a method that could use conventional DCOP algorithms to solve SCC problems. Our approach is to combine them with optimization models, which solve the internal complex subproblem of each agent, as detailed next.

3 Combining DCOP with MILP to Solve SCC

The hybrid method proposed in this work integrates a distributed search using traditional DCOP algorithms with a local optimization of the complex problem of each agent; in the SCC case, these problems can be modeled by mathematical programming, specifically Mixed-Integer Linear Programming (MILP), which, in general, is convenient for handling supply chain problems. Linear Programming (LP) maximizes (or minimizes) a linear objective function for a set of continuous variables subject to one or more constraints, while MILP adds one additional condition that at least one of these variables can only take on integer values [15]. Figure 2 illustrates the optimization method, which acts on a single root agent and the leaf agents, which are necessarily in the lowest layer. But it may also consider middle layers composed of intermediate agents, depending on the problem topology (see Fig. 1). The agents of each layer generate their own domains as partial solutions associated with the respective local problems, which are sent to the higher layer agents via models integration messages, which are represented in green dashed lines in Fig. 2. These latter agents use that information to generate their own domains in turn, up to the root agent, which does the same by creating its own domain. Finally, the distributed search starts and a particular DCOP algorithm can find the final global solution.

This method is based on the Constraint Programming (CP) paradigm, which allows a natural interconnection between existing submodels, aiming at the global best possible optimization. DCOP inherits the property of this paradigm, which requires that variables take values from discrete and finite domains. This is straightforward in the case of an integer variable, but for a continuous variable, such as cost, an adaptation is needed to associate it with a discrete domain, as shown in Sect. 3.2.

3.1 Formal Model

This work presents an alternative distributed model to optimize supply chain problems such as SCC. Its instances available in CSPLib were used as a benchmark for this new model, which is a subclass of DCOP, but integrated with complex local problem models. Thus, two more elements were included in its definition, which has become the tuple (A, V, D, X, O, U, F), where:

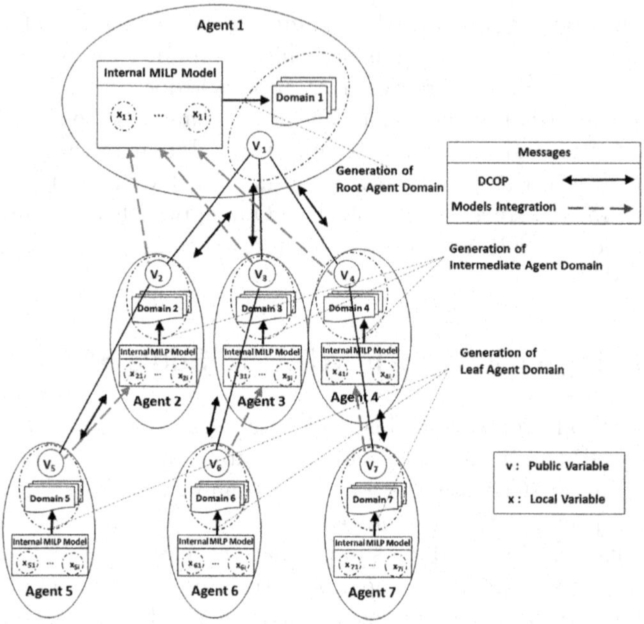

Fig. 2. Proposed method diagram

- $A = \{a_1, \ldots, a_i, \ldots, a_n\}$ is a set formed by a root and leaf agents necessarily, but possibly by intermediate agents as well;
- $V = \{V_1, \ldots, V_i, \ldots, V_n\}$ is a set of subsets, where $V_i = \{\ldots, v_{i\,j}, \ldots\}$ is a set of *public variables*, where each variable is associated with two neighboring agents a_i and a_j belonging to consecutive layers. However, only one of these agents is responsible for assigning a value to this variable. Each leaf agent is associated with a single public variable, whose value is assigned by that agent. On the other hand, each intermediate agent is associated with at least 2 variables, but it assigns the value just to one of them. The remaining variables are controlled by the neighboring agents of the lower layer. As for the root agent, it is also associated with one or more variables, but it assigns values to none of them. For supply chain problems in general, $v_{i\,j}$ belongs to a vector space. In the case of SCC, that space has the dimension defined by the number of time periods, where each element represents the number of batches delivered for a component in each time period by the respective agent to its neighbor. All instances in CSPLib consider 12 time periods. The values of these variables are defined by the distributed search;
- $D = \{\ldots, D_{i\,j}, \ldots\}$ is a set of *domains*, where each $D_{i\,j}$ is a finite and discrete set of elements, which is associated with the corresponding public variable $v_{i\,j}$. We consider that all the public variables have the same domain size;
- $X = \{X_1, \ldots, X_i, \ldots, X_n\}$ is a set of subsets, where $X_i = \{\ldots, x_{i\,j}, \ldots\}$ is a set of *local variables* associated with an agent a_i. These variables take part

only in the local optimization model of the respective agent, which defines the values of its local variables. They do not participate directly in the distributed search;
- $U = \{u_1, \ldots, u_i, \ldots, u_n\}$ is a set of valued functions, where u_i is the *utility* of agent a_i. It is a function of the public variables v_{ij}, but also of its local variables. In the SCC problem, it represents the agent's *cost*;
- $O = \{OM_1, \ldots, OM_i, \ldots, OM_n\}$ is a set of *local optimization models*, where OM_i models the local problem of the agent a_i. In the SCC problem, it represents the MILP model of that agent.

The goal is to find a complete instantiation V^* for all public variables v_{ij} and a complete instantiation X^* for all local variables x_{ij} as well, in order to minimize the *objective function* F, which corresponds to the sum of all utilities, as defined in Eq. 1.

$$F = \sum_{i=1}^{i=n} u_i \tag{1}$$

3.2 Algorithms

The optimization process is done by iterations with the gradual minimization of the value of F (total cost of all agents in Eq. 1). Thus, it converges to a final value, whose quality depends on the chosen domain size. In each iteration the domains of the public variables are generated by the MILP model of the associated agent (OM_i) (see Fig. 2). The algorithms to be shown underlie the proposed method. They use the following data structure:

- **idAg:** agent identifier[1];
- **domSize:** domain size used by the agent;
- **domain[i][j].value:** j-th value of the domain to be assigned to the public variable associated with the agent i;
- **domain[i][j].cost:** minimum cost associated with the respective domain[i][j]. value of the public variable controlled by the agent i. The exception is the root agent, which does not control any public variables. Its cost is defined by the public variables of its neighbor agents;
- **solution.index[i]:** index of the domain element associated with the current solution for agent i;
- **solution.totalCost:** best total cost associated with the current solution.

The main algorithm of the optimization method is described in Algorithm 1, which invokes three others, namely Algorithm 2 (line 9), Algorithm 3 (line 13) and Algorithm 4 (line 16), which are responsible for the domain generation of leaf, intermediate and root agents, respectively.

The domain generation of leaf agents (Algorithm 2) needs to call Algorithm 5 (line 18), which allows the adaptation of the continuous cost variable to a discrete

[1] (1...10 in CSPLib).

Algorithm 1. GlobalOptimization(domSize)

```
iteration ← 0
currentTotalCost ← ∞
newTotalCost ← currentTotalCost -1
solution ← empty
/* Iterations to find the lowest total cost */
while (newTotalCost < currentTotalCost) do
  currentTotalCost ← newTotalCost
  for (each Leaf Agent idAg) do
    domain[idAg] ← GenDomainLeaf(i, domSize, domain, solution, iteration)
  end for
  if (there are Intermediary Agents) then
    for (each Intermediary Agent idAg) do
      domain[idAg] ← GenDomainInterm(domain, domSize)
    end for
  end if
  domain[1] ← GenDomainRoot(domain, domSize)
  /* Execute the chosen DCOP algorithm */
  solution ← AlgorithmDCOP(domain)
  newTotalCost ← solution.totalCost
  iteration ← iteration + 1
end while
return currentTotalCost
```

Algorithm 2. GenDomainLeaf(idAg, domSize, domain, solution, iteration)

```
if (iteration == 0) then
  minCost ← LocalMilpMinLeaf(idAg)
  maxCost ← LocalMilpMaxLeaf(idAg)
  /* current solution is the first element of the domain */
else if (solution.index[idAg] == 1) then
  currentSolCost, minCost ← domain[idAg][1].cost
  maxCost ← domain[idAg][2].cost /* next element cost */
  /* current solution is the last element of the domain */
else if (solution.index[idAg] == domSize) then
  currentSolCost, maxCost ← domain[idAg][domSize].cost
  minCost ← domain[idAg][domSize-1].cost /* previous element cost */
else
  minCost ← domain[idAg][solution.index[idAg]-1].cost /*previous element cost*/
  maxCost ← domain[idAg][solution.index[idAg]+1].cost /* next element cost */
  currentSolCost ← solution.totalCost
end if
/* Homogeneous discretization of cost */
domain[idAg] ← DiscreteCostDomLeaf(idAg, domain[idAg], domSize, minCost,
  maxCost, currentSolCost)
return domain[idAg]
```

Algorithm 3. GenDomainInterm(idAgI, idAgA, [idAgB], domain, domSize)

```
/* Generation of Intermediate Agent Domain */
indexI ← 1 /* index of domain of intermediate agent */
/* All elements of domain of leaf agent A of lower layer */
for (indexA = 1 to domSize) do
   if (there is a second child leaf agent) then
      /* All elements of domain of leaf agent B of lower layer */
      for (indexB = 1 to domSize) do
         domain[idAgI][indexI] ← LocalMilpMinimizeIntermediate(idAgI, domain[idAgA][indexA].value, domain[idAgB][indexB].value)
         indexI ← indexI + 1
      end for
   else
      domain[idAgI][indexI] ← LocalMilpMinimizeIntermediate(idAgI, domain[idAgA][indexA].value)
      indexI ← indexI + 1
   end if
end for
domain[idAgI] ← ReduceDomainSize(domain[idAgI], domSize)
return domain[IdAgI]
```

Algorithm 4. GenDomainRoot(domSize, domain)

```
/* Generation of Root Agent Domain */
index1 ← 1/* index of domain of root agent 1 */
/* All elements of domain of agent 2 of lower layer */
for (index2 = 1 to domSize) do
   /* All elements of domain of agent 3 of lower layer */
   for (index3 = 1 to domSize) do
      /* All elements of domain of agent 4 of lower layer */
      for (index4 = 1 to domSize) do
         domain[1][index1] ← LocalMilpMinimizeRoot(domain[2][index2].value, domain[3][index3].value, domain[4][index4].value)
         index1 ← index1 + 1
      end for
   end for
end for
return domain[1]
```

domain, which changes as the solution evolves over the optimization improvement iterations.

For the domain generation, it is necessary to define the domain size, which is a relevant choice within the CP paradigm. In fact, it represents a trade off between the difficulty in finding the solution and its level of quality. In Sect. 4, the chosen domain sizes for the experiments are presented.

Algorithm 5 . DiscreteCostDomLeaf(idAg, domainLeaf, domSize, minCost, maxCost)

/* Homogeneous discretization of cost in the leaf domain */
stepCost ← (maxCost - minCost) / domSize
lowerCost ← minCost
for (index = 1 to domainSize) **do**
  domainLeaf[index] ← LocalMilpUpperLeaf(idAg, lowerCost)
  lowerCost ← lowerCost + stepCost
end for
return domainLeaf

In the case of intermediate agents, the domain generation (Algorithm 3) needs to call Algorithm 6 (line 16), which keeps the domainSize equals to the value of the agents in the lower layer.

Algorithm 6. ReduceDomainSize(domainInterm, domSize)

/* Reduce domain size to a common domSize */
currentDomSize ←| $domainIntern$ |
rateDomSize ← currentDomSize / domSize
for (index = 1 to currentDomSize step = rateDomSize) **do**
  newDomainItern[index] ← domainInterm[index*rateDomSize]
end for
return newDomainItern

Looking at the topology of CSPLib instances in Fig. 1, we conclude that the domain size of the intermediate agents should be $domSize^k$, where k is the number of its child leaf agents. Thus, in instance 5 as $k = 2$ the domain size of agent A2 would be 10^2 (100), since the domain size of the leaf agents (A5 and A8) is 10, as it will be shown in Sect. 4. But the domain size of A2 is constrained to 10 like the leaf agents. As stated in Sect. 3.1, the cost (utility) of each agent depends as much on its local variables as on its public variable. Thus, each of the values of A2 can be associated with different costs, keeping the range between its minimum and maximum cost over 10 domain elements. In addition, in order to reduce the entropy of the total number of combinations, for each value assignment of A2 it is chosen its associated lowest cost.

By the same reasoning, the domain size of the root agent should be equal to $domSize^k$, where k is the number of its lower layer neighbor agents. However, it does not control any public variables, and therefore this number does not need to be restricted. Thus, it is the result of the cartesian product of the k domains, which leads to the combination of possible costs of the root agent.

The remaining algorithms are statements rather than actually algorithms. Thus LocalMilpMinLeaf, LocalMilpMaxLeaf and LocalMilpUpperLeaf represent the call to the solver of the OM of leaf agents. The first two provide the minimum and maximum cost of these agents, while the last one returns the minimum, but imposing that it must be higher than a given value. On the other hand, LocalMilpMinimizeIntermediate provides the minimum cost from the OM associated with intermediate agents. Finally LocalMilpMinRoot provides the minimum cost from the OM associated with the root agent.

As already said, the proposed optimization method consists of two parts: the distributed search and the local optimization of all agents. In this work, this method has been implemented through a *compilation* process, which allows these two parts can execute independently. Thus, it is possible to realize in Algorithm 1 that Algorithm 2 is executed for all leaf agents (line 8), Algorithm 3 is executed for all intermediate agents (line 12) and Algorithm 4 is called in sequence (line 16), completing all local optimizations in that iteration. Finally, AlgorithmDCOP (line 18) transfers the control to the chosen DCOP algorithm, which starts the distributed search for the global solution using the domains compiled by the process previously accomplished (see Fig. 2). However, for the practical use of this method, these two parts must work synchronously, when the optimization process of each agent can be activated on demand of DCOP algorithm. For this to happen, it will be necessary to implement an interface for local optimization solvers within the distributed search platform in future.

4 Experiments

The FRODO 2 tool version 2.18.1 [9] is an open framework in Java for distributed combinatorial optimization. Among other reasons, it was chosen for the experiments in this work because it contains built-in DCOP algorithms. In addition, it uses XML files which represents the problem instances in a well-defined way. On the other hand, the local MILP model of each agent was developed in Optimization Programming Language (OPL), and solved by IBM ILOG CPLEX Optimization Studio version 12.2 [14]. The experiments were performed in a PC with a processor Intel Core i7 1.99 GHz and 16 GB RAM, whose results are presented in the following subsections. The algorithms available in FRODO can be classified as incomplete, when they produce only satisfactory solutions in return for reduced execution time, or complete, when they guarantee the best solution. The algorithms selected for the experiments are listed next by this criterion:

- Complete:
  - ADOPT (Asynchronous Distributed OPTimization) [11];
  - DPOP (Distributed Pseudo-tree Optimization Procedure) [12];
  - AFB (Asynchronous Forward Bounding) [7];
  - SynchBB (Synchronous Branch-and-Bound) [8];
- Incomplete:
  - DSA (Digital Stochastic Algorithm) [19];
  - Max-Sum [4];
  - MGM (Maximum Gain Message) [10];
  - MPC-DisCSP4 (Secure Multiparty Computations Distributed Constraint Satisfaction Problem 4) [13];

4.1 Description of Experiments

A series of experiments were executed to validate the proposed method using the benchmark with 6 instances of the SCC problem in CSPLib [6]. It considered all chosen DCOP algorithms and each of these experiments was performed 10 times. As to the domain size, in instances 1 and 2, which have no intermediate agents, we assumed the values 5 or 10 for the leaf agents, and 125 or 1000 ($5 \times 5 \times 5$ or $10 \times 10 \times 10$) for the root agent (see Sect. 3.2). For the remaining instances the domain size of all agents was kept at only 10, except the root with 1000. The choice of the value 10 was due to the search for the maximum possible value in order to increase the resulting quality, without making the experiment duration unacceptable. Instances 1 and 2 have the same topology with a root agent and 3 leaf agents, but each of these presents different total costs, since they are configured with specific parameters associated with the SCC problem. On the other hand, instance 4 has a different topology with a root agent, 3 intermediate agents and 3 leaf agents. Finally, instances 5 and 6 have a third topology with a root agent, 3 intermediate agents and 6 leaf agents. Instance 3 was discarded from the experiments of this work due to insufficient information in CSPLib.

Considering instance 1, for example, initially the domain sizes 5 for the leaf agents and 125 for the root agent were used to establish a first milestone. In the following experiments, the domain size has been enlarged to 10 for the leaf agents and 1000 for the root agent. It was possible to realize that the total cost decreases, confirming the forecast of solution quality improvement with the increase of the domain size. In the next step of the experiments, the result obtained using the domain size 10 defines the basic iteration of the optimization process (iteration 0). Hereafter it starts the application of the heuristic associated with the proposed method, which aims to improve the optimization, even maintaining the domain size. Thus, the next iteration (iteration 1) is obtained by zooming the current domain of leaf agents, selecting only the range defined by neighbors of the basic iteration partial solution. In this example, the partial solution is 47821, and its neighbours are 39203 and 56439, which respectively become the new upper and lower bounds of the next iteration. The same procedure has been applied again to generate the iteration 2, which led to a lower total cost. Finally the iteration 3 provided the lowest possible total cost and the optimization process terminated (see Algorithm 1). Figure 3 presents the process of solving instance 1, helping to visualize the proposed method. It highlights the best solution found in each iteration (darker shade of green cells) and the respective neighbours (less dark shade of green cells). This same method was applied to all other instances.

4.2 Results Analysis

Gathering the information collected from the experiments, it was possible to evaluate the DCOP algorithms performance in solving complex problems such as those in the supply chain, which were represented by the SCC benchmark, as well as the feasibility of the proposed optimization method. Considering instances 1 and 5, for example, the Fig. 4 shows the behaviour of DCOP algorithms with respect to the execution time. In this graph, which uses logarithmic scale, it is outstanding how efficient the algorithm DPOP has been during all phases of the experiments. This execution time is associated only with the distributed search, without considering the part related to the local optimization of each agent, which would depend on its computing resource. In addition, DPOP was the best with respect to the number of messages exchanged too, as shown in Fig. 5 for these 2 instances. In fact, DPOP was the best in both quantities for all instances.

It is interesting to note that DPOP scans agents in a tree structure, starting from the leaf agents, it aggregates the costs for the combination of variables values, which are propagated from children to their parents agents in the tree, up to the root agent, which selects the optimal value [12]. This behavior resembles the way the proposed method works by integrating the models from the leaf agent up to the root agent.

The left graph in Fig. 6 shows the optimization evolution of the method throughout the iterations for instance 1. The cost gradually moves away from the CSPLib value, approaching the centralized one, up to the iteration where the total cost stops decreasing. On the other hand, the right graph compares the method efficacy (the last iteration value) both with the Burke's method, which appears in CSPLib (see Sect. 2.4), and with the optimal value obtained by a centralized model, displaying the respective percent deviations. Thus, on average we have obtained a value which is 5.57% better than Burke's and only 7.06% worse than the actual optimum one. In real settings, where one doesn't know in advance the optimal values, this is a rather promising approach.

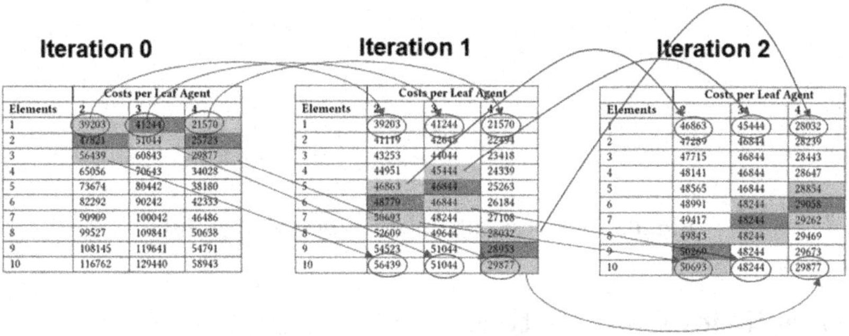

Fig. 3. Optimization process diagram

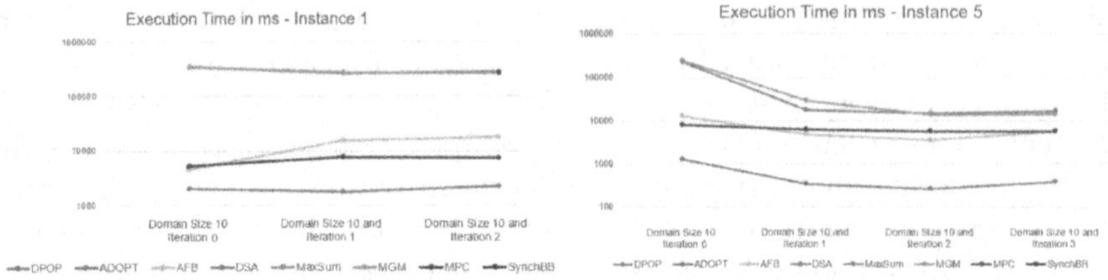

Fig. 4. Distributed execution time

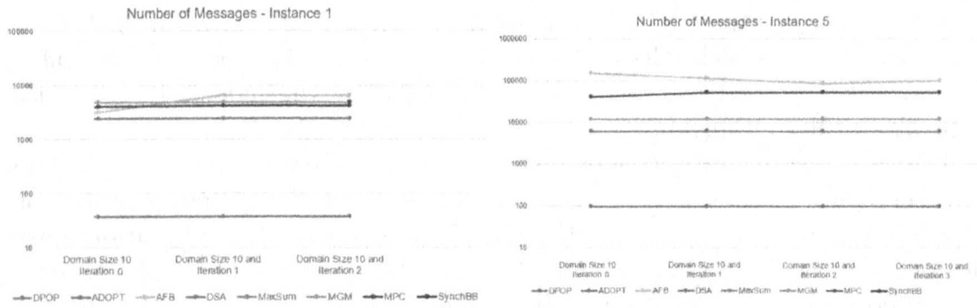

Fig. 5. Number of messages

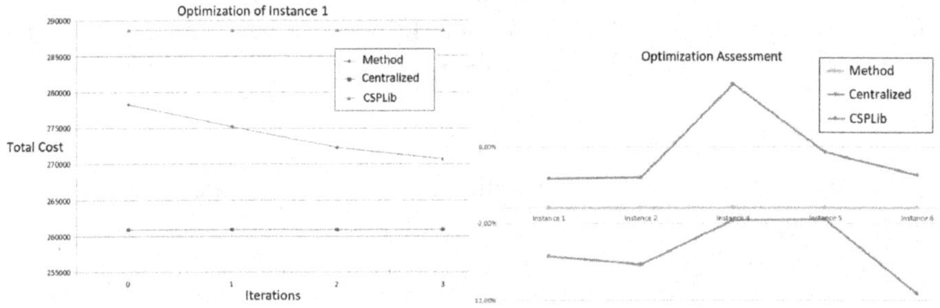

Fig. 6. Total cost optimization (domain size 10)

5 Conclusions and Future Work

In order to optimize large problems in a distributed way, it is possible to solve locally their complex subproblems. Since conventional DCOP algorithms can not face that challenge, a distributed method for that solution was created together with a benchmark for this type of problem (SCC). However, such a method does not allow the use of conventional DCOP algorithms, but only a special one which has been adapted with the inclusion of specific modeling techniques. Our approach accomplished this objective by allowing the use of any DCOP algorithm. It outperformed the original method in effectiveness and its best solution is not so different from the optimum value obtained by a centralized optimizer of the SCC problem, despite being a heuristic method. We selected the most relevant DCOP algorithms in the literature, whose performances were compared. In our experiments, DPOP was the best one to solve the SCC problem using our technique for all instances of CSPLib benchmark. In addition, it was possible to prove the proposed method effectiveness for that entire benchmark.

In the future, we intend to proceed with the experiments for new randomly generated instances of greater complexity than those of CSPLib with other topologies and more layers. The method will further improve so that its solution may be closer to the centralized ideal value, even for the most complex instances.

In addition, it is worth to provide an interface between the proposed method and DCOP distributed search platforms, such as FRODO, for example. Such an API would make it easier to integrate the method with MILP solvers.

Finally, taking into account the structural similarity between the proposed method and DPOP algorithm, it would be interesting to develop a DPOP version with the proposed heuristic method embedded using that previous API. That combination promises to be powerful if used in other problems even closer to reality.

Acknowledgments. This work has been supported by the National Agency for Petroleum, Natural Gas and Biofuels through the clauses for funding of Research, Development and Innovation investments established by the Resolution no. 50/2015 and by PETROBRAS under grant TC 5900.0112830.19.9. Fernanda N. T. Furukita was also supported by CNPq, Brazil, grant number 136228/2020-8.

References

1. Burke, D.A.: Exploiting problem structure in distributed constraint optimisation with complex local problems. Ph.D. thesis, Department of Computer Science, University College Cork, Ireland (2008)
2. Burke, D.A., Brown, K.N., Dogru, M., Lowe, B.: Supply chain coordination through distributed constraint optimization. In: 9th International Workshop on Distributed Constraint Reasoning (2007)
3. Faltings, B., Yokoo, M.: Introduction: special issue on distributed constraint satisfaction. Artif. Intell. **161**(1–2), 1–5 (2005)
4. Farinelli, A., Rogers, A., Petcu, A., Jennings, N.R.: Decentralised coordination of low-power embedded devices using the max-sum algorithm. In: Seventh International Conference on Autonomous Agents and Multi-Agent Systems, AAMAS 2008, 11–15 May 2008, pp. 639–646 (2008)
5. Fioretto, F., Pontelli, E., Yeoh, W.: Distributed constraint optimization problems and applications: a survey. J. Artif. Intell. Res. **61**, 623–698 (2018)
6. Gent, I.P., Walsh, T.: CSPlib: a benchmark library for constraints. In: Jaffar, J. (ed.) CP 1999. LNCS, vol. 1713, pp. 480–481. Springer, Heidelberg (1999). https://doi.org/10.1007/978-3-540-48085-3_36
7. Gershman, A., Meisels, A., Zivan, R.: Asynchronous forward bounding for distributed cops. J. Artif. Intell. Res. **34**, 61–88 (2009)
8. Hirayama, K., Yokoo, M.: Distributed partial constraint satisfaction problem. In: Smolka, G. (ed.) CP 1997. LNCS, vol. 1330, pp. 222–236. Springer, Heidelberg (1997). https://doi.org/10.1007/BFb0017442

9. Léauté, T., Ottens, B., Szymanek, R.: FRODO 2.0: an open-source framework for distributed constraint optimization. In: Proceedings of the IJCAI 2009 Distributed Constraint Reasoning Workshop (DCR 2009), Pasadena, California, USA, pp. 160–164 (2009). https://frodo-ai.tech
10. Maheswaran, R.T., Pearce, J.P., Tambe, M.: Distributed algorithms for DCOP: a graphical-game-based approach. In: ISCA PDCS, pp. 432–439 (2004)
11. Modi, P.J., Shen, W.M., Tambe, M., Yokoo, M.: An asynchronous complete method for distributed constraint optimization. In: Proceedings of the Second International Joint Conference on Autonomous Agents & Multiagent Systems, AAMAS 2003, Melbourne, Victoria, Australia, 14–18 July 2003, pp. 161–168. ACM (2003)
12. Petcu, A., Faltings, B.: DPOP: a scalable method for multiagent constraint optimization. In: IJCAI 2005, CONF, pp. 266–271 (2005)
13. Silaghi, M.C., Mitra, D.: Distributed constraint satisfaction and optimization with privacy enforcement. In: Proceedings of the IEEE/WIC/ACM International Conference on Intelligent Agent Technology, IAT 2004, pp. 531–535. IEEE (2004)
14. Studio IICO: OPL language user's manual version 12 release 7 (2017)
15. Williams, H.P.: Model Building in Mathematical Programming. Wiley, Hoboken (2013)
16. Yokoo, M., Hirayama, K.: Distributed constraint satisfaction algorithm for complex local problems. In: Proceedings International Conference on Multi Agent Systems (Cat. No. 98EX160), pp. 372–379. IEEE (1998)
17. Yokoo, M., Ishida, T., Durfee, E.H., Kuwabara, K.: Distributed constraint satisfaction for formalizing distributed problem solving. In: 1992 12th International Conference on Distributed Computing System, pp. 614–615. IEEE Computer Society (1992)
18. Yuan, Y., Liang, P., Zhang, J.J., et al.: Using agent technology to support supply chain management: potentials and challenges. Technical report. University Hamilton (2001)
19. Zhang, W., Wang, G., Xing, Z., Wittenburg, L.: Distributed stochastic search and distributed breakout: properties, comparison and applications to constraint optimization problems in sensor networks. Artif. Intell. **161**(1–2), 55–87 (2005)

Automated Design of Elevator Systems: Experimenting with Constraint-Based Approaches

Stefano Demarchi(✉), Marco Menapace, and Armando Tacchella

Università degli Studi di Genova, Viale Causa 13, 16145 Genova, Italy
{stefano.demarchi,marco.menapace}@edu.unige.it,
armando.tacchella@unige.it

Abstract. System configuration and design is a well-established topic in AI. While many successful applications exist, there are still areas of manufacturing where AI techniques find little or no application. We focus on one such area, namely building and installation of elevator systems, for which we are developing an automated design and configuration tool. The questions that we address in this paper are: (*i*) What are the best ways to encode some subtasks of elevator design into constraint-based representations? (*ii*) What are the best tools available to solve the encodings? We contribute an empirical analysis to address these questions in our domain of interest, as well as the complete set of benchmarks to foster further research.

1 Introduction

Context. The problem of automating product configuration and design has a long history in diverse application fields. In the late 1970s, possibly the first automated configuration program was developed at Digital Equipment Corporation to build computer systems meeting custom requirements [14]. Later on, approaches based on constraint programming [15,16] and extensions tackling a variable number of constraints [20,24] were presented. A relatively recent survey [25] mentions various product configuration tools and methods that have been reported in the literature. In spite of many success stories, product configuration and design remains still a manual endeavor in many, if not most, manufacturing areas. We argue that building and installation of elevator systems is one such area. Excluding two recent contributions of ours [1,9], to the best of our knowledge the only paper that tackles configuration of elevator systems dates back to [12].

Motivations. We are developing the tool LiftCreate to design elevator systems starting from a database of commercial components and some basic data, e.g., hoistway size, number of floors, and payload. LiftCreate guarantees feasibility of the design according to 2014/33/EU regulation within the framework of EN 81–20/81–50 norms. LiftCreate is built around special purpose heuristics to

S. Bandini et al. (Eds.): AIxIA 2021, LNAI 13196, pp. 77–90, 2022.
https://doi.org/10.1007/978-3-031-08421-8_6

handle most design subtasks, including choice and fitting of components and optimization of the design. Since LiftCreate is deployed as a web application, hard-coding of search and optimization subtasks allowed us to achieve the levels of efficiency and predictability required, but at the expense of flexibility as additions or modifications are now very time-consuming. This is why in previous works we started experimenting with Optimization Modulo Theories (OMT) solvers [22]. In our first attempts we focused on OMT techniques only, and we did not investigate different ways to encode elevator configuration as a constraint satisfaction problem.

Research Questions. Our first and foremost question is how to choose among different alternatives to encode design subtasks into sets of constraints. In particular, we consider alternative ways to (*i*) encode the choice of components, (*ii*) represent relevant quantities, (*iii*) encode functions and (*iv*) handle multiple cost functions. The second question relates to the constraint-based tools and techniques of choice. As shown in the literature, see, e.g., [2,5,8], there is some debate over using constraint-based technologies other than OMT solvers to tackle encodings involving a mixture of arithmetic constraints and cost functions. For this reason, here we compare the performances of two encodings, namely in the SMT-LIB [4] language and in the MiniZinc [18] language. We feed our SMT-LIB encoding to two OMT solvers, i.e., OptiMathSat [23] and z3 [17], and our MiniZinc encoding to a pool of constraint solvers, namely Chuffed [7], OR-Tools [19], $\mathrm{ECL}^i\mathrm{PS}^e$ [21], CPLEX [11] and Gurobi [10]. The ultimate goal is to understand how different encoding choices impact on different solvers in our context, but also to evaluate the best combination for LiftCreate.

Contribution. Our experiments involve a number of design scenarios characterized by different hoistway sizes and two different design targets: *baseline* and *full*. In the former we select, place and fit only two components, namely the car frame—the structure that supports the elevator car—and the doors. The full encoding includes also sizing of the hydraulic cylinder pushing the car frame, and minimization of the forces on the car frame rails. We provide empirical evidence that all the selected solvers can deal with the baseline integer-based encodings; on the other hand, the full encoding involves arithmetic over reals and thus only OMT solvers consistently provide results within the time limit of five CPU minutes. Most solvers show comparable performances on the baseline encoding, but only Chuffed seems to have an edge over the other solvers in this group, with only one exception on a scenario for which no feasible configuration exists; z3 is generally faster than OptiMathSat, but on integer-based encodings z3 must yield to Chuffed, albeit not substantially. Finally, we show that special purpose heuristics can still be faster than most combinations of solvers and encodings in the constraint-based approach; however, considering the gain in flexibility, some combinations of solvers and encodings are competitive enough to invest further development effort in them. Given our results, we believe that also our benchmarks make for a valuable contribution and we made them available at

https://github.com/sdemarch/AIxIA_2021_Benchmarks

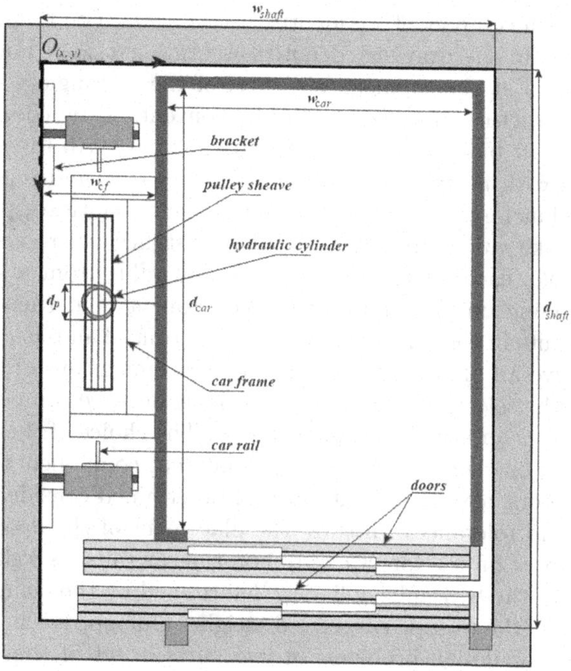

Fig. 1. Plan view of a configured RHE. The shaft is the gray box surrounding the other components, the car frame is on the left side of the drawing and the doors are at the bottom.

2 Design of Elevator Systems

In this paper we focus on Roped Hydraulic Elevators (RHEs) in which the lifting power is provided by hydraulics. In Fig. 1 we show the cross-section of a RHE with its main components to be described briefly in the following. The shaft (hoistway) is the outermost grey-filled rectangle: although it is not part of the elevator system per se, the shaft depth (d_{shaft}) and width (w_{shaft}) constrain the space available for installing the elevator. The main component of the elevator is the car for people transportation, represented as a rectangle with dark-grey borders (walls). The car is characterized by a depth (d_{car}) and a width (w_{car}). On the left side of Fig. 1, we can see the *car frame*, i.e., the structure that supports the car and connects it to the *hydraulic cylinder* providing the lifting power. The hydraulic cylinder is placed inside the car frame structure and it is depicted as two concentric circles below the *pulley sheave*. In the following, we consider the width of the car frame, denoted as w_{cf}, and the hydraulic cylinder barrel diameter, denoted as d_p. The car frame is fixed to the shaft walls via T-shaped *brackets* to support the *car rails* on which the car frame core gear slides. At the bottom of Fig. 1, we can see the doors, namely the *car door* and the *landing door*—three-paneled sliding doors in this case. The car door is only one and it is attached to the car, while there is one matching landing door for each floor. For each component we identify a *base point*, i.e., the insertion point of the component in the drawing, denoted as (x_{comp}, y_{comp}). Each component base point is found at the topmost left angle of the rectangle which envelopes the component structure, and we identify by convention the coordinate system origin with the shaft base point, shown in Fig. 1 as $\mathcal{O}_{x,y}$. All the named quantities are mapped with *decision variables* and *parameters*, and represent lengths measured in millimeters. As for the domain of such quantities, parameters are constrained to take values from the database instance where components are saved. In principle, each parameter can take any value from a set of discrete quantities depending on the choice of the component, and these numbers are treated as constants in the final encoding. On the other hand, decision variables are always positive and limited from above by the dimensions of the shaft.

We focus on the selection, placement and sizing of three components: the car frame, the car doors and the hydraulic cylinder. The choice of the doors and the car frame impacts on their placement, since different components have different sizes and parameters, and placement must be determined considering shaft size, encumbrances, and tolerances. In turn, the placement of the doors and the car frame has an impact on the forces exerted on the car rails, as well as the choice and verification of the hydraulic cylinder, determined by the compatibility with the car frame and the overall suspended weight. Our approach is to split the encoding of elevator design problems in two parts: a set of (hard) constraints to encode geometrical and dynamical aspects required to obtain *feasible* configurations, and a set of soft constraints, modeled as cost functions, to drive the search towards feasible configurations that are also *desirable* according to best practices in elevator design such as minimizing costs by choosing the smallest components that make the design feasible, while, at the same time, utilizing all the space available.

Considering geometrical and dynamical constraints first, we can observe that choosing and placing the car frame must take into account two main issues. First, given the shape of the brackets, it is not possible to model the car frame as a simple rectangle in order to fit it with the other components. Therefore the placement of the car frame is computed by subtracting residuals from the total shaft depth. Second, the placement of the car frame must take into account its maximum overhang, i.e., the car cannot "lean" too much outside the car frame core gear. The constraints to place the car-landing door pair should guarantee that both structures fit the shaft, that the actual opening fits the car and that the landing door frame does not exceed the shaft size. All these constraints are expressed through linear inequalities. In order to avoid collision of moving parts, there are two-dimensional non-overlapping constraints between the car door and both the car frame and the brackets, expressed with disjunctive constraints. Concerning the hydraulic cylinder, there are two main constraints to be respected. The first one is relative to the compatibility between the car frame and the cylinder, expressed through a car frame parameter which indicates the maximum diameter of a cylinder that can be inserted. The second constraint requires that the force on the piston, due to the overall suspended weight, does not exceed the critical force, i.e., the force which can make steel collapse, which also depends on the choice of car frame. The details related to geometrical and dynamical constraints corresponding to the informal description above are reported in [9].

To shape the cost functions, we consider four design objectives. The first is that the car frame should be aligned as much as possible to the center of the car on the y axis—i.e., considering Fig. 1, the car frame should appear vertically centered with respect to the car. The second objective regards doors positioning: in case of symmetric doors, i.e., the opening midpoint coincides with the door frame midpoint, the opening of the car door should be aligned as much as possible to the center of the car on the x axis; in case of asymmetric doors, then the opening should be as close as possible to the opposite side of the car frame in order to minimize the chance of interference. Notice that in Fig. 1 we have a non-symmetric door, which is aligned to the right car wall. As third objective we have that the car frame and the hydraulic cylinder should not be over-sized, and the opening of the car door should not be undersized. Finally, the fourth objective is that the force exerted on the car rails should be minimized.

3 Encoding Elevator Systems Design

Component Selection. The car frame, the cylinder and the doors are selected from a database of components. In order to automate the design of an elevator, we must consider that choosing different components yields different parameter values for each one. The relationship between the selection of a component and the assignment of the corresponding parameter values can be encoded via Boolean implications of the form

$$Id_x = i \Rightarrow x.p = v \tag{1}$$

where Id_x encodes the identifier of choice for component x (a decision variable), i is a specific identifier value, $x.p$ is some parameter of the component x and v is the value of $x.p$ given that the component x with identifier i was chosen—see, e.g., [3]. To encode constraints of the form (1) a combination of Boolean reasoning with integer arithmetic is sufficient. However, considering the way data sets are usually encoded in MiniZinc with arrays [13], we consider an alternative encoding where we associate an array to each component parameter. For example, if a component x has two parameters p_1 and p_2, we build two arrays P_1 and P_2 that will store the values of p_1 and p_2 for each instance of the component. The index of the arrays becomes a decision variable chosen by the solver to enforce the correct values of the parameters.

Look-Up Tables. Some parameters, e.g., the maximum number of passengers that the car may accommodate, are a function of others, e.g., the car surface. However, instead of expressing such constraints directly—which might involve the use of non-linear or transcendental functions—the correspondence between

Table 1. Look-up table to encode the number of passengers P with starting value P_0 as a function of the car surface A.

Surface (A)	Passengers (P)
$a1 < A \leq a2$	P_0
$a2 < A \leq a3$	$P_0 + 1$
$A > a3$	$P_0 + 2$

free parameters and derived ones is encoded with *look-up tables.* Table 1 exemplifies such a table assuming that the car surface A is contained within three ranges. The car payload is computed in a similar way, but, since the surface ranges are different, we need another set of constraints structured in the same way. These requirements can be easily modeled with implications in the same way as component selection: the surface A is a decision variable that implies the number of passengers or the payload. However, both SMT-LIB and MiniZinc allow users to define custom *functions.* In practice, functions are series of *if-then-else* statements about, e.g., the car surface, where each function returns, e.g., the corresponding number of passengers or the payload.

Integers vs. Reals. Most parameters involved in the design process are expressed in millimeters which suggests integer-based encodings. However, some parameters like the forces exerted on the car rails involve arithmetic over reals. This makes the corresponding constraint satisfaction problems members of the mixed-integer arithmetic family. In such encodings, the main disadvantage is that a large number of integer quantities may increase considerably the solution time. We try to improve on this by relaxing some of the integer quantities to reals. In particular, we consider component parameters since parameters are not *decided* but their value is only assigned based on the choice of a component. This means that the domain of the parameters is a finite set and we can relax the arithmetic encoding without producing invalid results. In this representation the only operation that could add decimal digits is division, but since in our encoding there are only a few such operations, boundary checking can be implemented easily. These considerations do not hold for some decision variables including, but not limited to, the index used to select components. Also, CP solvers like Chuffed are not affected by this choice due to the fact that they do not support floating-point arithmetic.

Single and Multi-objective Optimization. Here we describe alternative constructions of the cost functions, mentioning the details of the parameters involved when necessary. In particular, we encode the design objectives associating a cost to each one of them. The cost associated to car frame misalignment on the y axis is expressed by the absolute value of the distance between the car frame and the car axes. We define the car frame vertical axis $axisY_{cf}$ as the car frame vertical base point y_{cf} plus half of the distance between the car rails dcr

$$axisY_{cf} = y_{cf} + \frac{dcr}{2}. \tag{2}$$

The vertical car axis $axisY_{car}$ is defined as the car vertical base point y_{car} plus half of the car depth d_{car}:

$$axisY_{car} = y_{car} + \frac{d_{car}}{2}. \tag{3}$$

The difference between the terms (2) and (3) gives us the first contribution to the cost function c_{cf}:

$$c_{cf} = |axisY_{cf} - axisY_{car}| \tag{4}$$

The second objective we consider is related to doors. In this case we define the horizontal car axis $axisX_{car}$ as the horizontal car base point x_{car} plus half of the car width w_{car}:

$$axisX_{car} = x_{car} + \frac{w_{car}}{2} \tag{5}$$

The horizontal door axis $axisX_{door}$ is defined as the horizontal door base coordinate x_{cd} plus the length of its left axis la_{cd}:

$$axisX_{door} = x_{cd} + la_{cd} \tag{6}$$

In the case of symmetric doors, good design practices suggest that $axisX_{door}$ and $axisX_{car}$ should be aligned. In the case of non-symmetric doors, it is preferable to have the door *opening* as close as possible to the side of the car which is opposite to the car frame. In a configuration like the one in Fig. 1 we can define the base coordinate of such side as:

$$x_{wall} = x_{car} + w_{car} \tag{7}$$

To take into account the different arrangement of doors, we introduce a binary variable, δ_t, which is assigned to 1 if the current door is a non-symmetric door and to 0 otherwise. We can then summarize the contribution to the cost function as:

$$\begin{aligned} c_{door} =&((1 - \delta_t)|axisX_{car} - axisX_{door}|+ \\ &\delta_t(x_{wall} - (x_{cd} + la_{cd} + \frac{opening}{2}))) \end{aligned} \tag{8}$$

The first contribution of (8) is zero when $\delta_t = 1$, i.e., for non-symmetric doors we try to minimize the distance from the side of the elevator opposite to the car frame, whereas when $\delta_t = 0$ we try to align the door and the car axes. The third objective is related to the selection of the components, and gives the guidelines for sizing the car frame, the doors and the cylinder. The maximization of the door *opening* leads to accessible elevators which are always considered a plus, whenever feasible; the minimization of the car frame depth dcr and the barrel diameter d_p suggests components which are not over-sized, thus helping to keep costs at bay. These criteria can be translated into one additional contribution to the overall cost function defined as:

$$c_{size} = (dcr + d_p - opening) \tag{9}$$

Finally, the last term to minimize is the sum of F_{cr}^x and F_{cr}^y, i.e., the x and y components of the force exerted on the car rails F_{cr}:

$$c_{cr} = F_{cr}^x + F_{cr}^y \tag{10}$$

The computation of F_{cr} is non-trivial and requires additional equations and parameters that we briefly describe. The components of F_{cr} are obtained as

$$F_{cr}^x = k \cdot g \cdot \frac{Q_x(Q+75)+P_x \cdot car_W + cdP_x \cdot cd_W + cf_W \cdot CF_x}{2 \cdot h}$$
$$F_{cr}^y = k \cdot g \cdot \frac{Q_y(Q+75)+P_y \cdot car_W + cdP_y \cdot cd_W}{2 \cdot h}$$

where the parameters have the following meaning:

- k is a parameter depending on the kind of safety brakes installed;
- g is the standard acceleration due to gravity;
- Q is the car payload;
- P_x and P_y are the midpoint coordinates of the car;
- Q_x and Q_y are obtained through the equations

$$Q_x = max\{P_x + \frac{w_{car}}{8}, P_x - \frac{w_{car}}{8}\}$$
$$Q_y = max\{P_y + \frac{d_{car}}{8}, P_y - \frac{d_{car}}{8}\};$$

- car_W is the car weight;
- cdP_x, cdP_y are the coordinates of the center of gravity of the car door;
- cd_W is the car door weight and cf_W is the car frame weight;
- CF_x is a coefficient computed as

$$CF_x = 1.5 \cdot \frac{w_{cf}}{2}$$

  where w_{cf} is the distance from the car frame base point to the left car wall;
- h is the distance between guide shoes, i.e., the supports which slide on the car rails.

In previous works of ours we consider the weighted sum of the costs c_{cf}, c_{door} and c_{size} to obtain the overall cost function, but the contribution c_{cr} may conflict with the previous ones because the farthest is the door from the car frame, the greater is the force exerted on the car rails. Nevertheless, since the car rails can be chosen once the other components are fitted, this objective can be considered with a lower priority. If we follow a single-objective approach, we can weight the cost c_{cr} significantly less than the other three. The overall cost function $\mathcal{C}$ becomes

$$\mathcal{C} = \alpha_1 c_{cf} + \alpha_2 c_{door} + \alpha_3 c_{size} + \alpha_4 c_{cr} \tag{11}$$

with $\alpha_4 \ll \alpha_i$ for $i \neq 4$. Alternatively, we can exploit priorities among different cost functions by resorting to multi-objective optimization using, e.g., the lexicographic method whereby preferences are imposed by ordering the objective functions according to their significance—see [6] for details. Here we consider two cost functions:

$$\begin{aligned} \mathcal{C}_1 &= \alpha_1 c_{cf} + \alpha_2 c_{door} + \alpha_3 c_{size} \\ \mathcal{C}_2 &= c_{cr} \end{aligned} \tag{12}$$

where the objective function $\mathcal{C}_1$ is minimized first.

4 Experimental Results

To understand the impact of different choices for encoding our problem, we consider a pool of solvers from the SMT and CP communities. We test our SMT-LIB [4] encoding with two OMT solvers, namely z3 [17] by Microsoft Research and OptiMathSat [23] by FBK, and our MiniZinc [13] encoding with five different solvers. We use the lazy clause generation based solver Chuffed [7], the MiniZinc challenge winner Google OR-Tools [19], the CLP solver ECL^{i}PS^e [21] and the two MIP solvers CPLEX [11] and Gurobi [10]. With all these solvers we can observe how different approaches in solving combinatorial optimization problems behave with our encoding choices.[1] We consider the default configuration of every solver, even if we are aware that tuning each solver for the specific problem might yield better results. However, we do not wish to introduce bias in our experiments due to the fact that we may know a solver or a technique better than others and thus obtain effective configurations on specific solvers only.

All the results are obtained considering setups with shafts of varying sizes: we have a set of eight shafts with fixed width of 1300 mm and another set with 1500 mm width. In both cases, the depth goes from 800 to 1500 using a 100 mm step. Each experiment is subject to a timeout of 5 min of CPU time, and the times are expressed in milliseconds.[2] Since we evaluate diverse solvers, we consider run time as the only yardstick for comparison. Other measures, e.g., size of explored search space, number of sub-problems generated, might make sense only for specific solvers. Furthermore, our ultimate goal is to find an approach viable for practical applications where execution time is the most crucial aspect. We consider two different sets of experiments: a baseline encoding dealing with the configuration of the car frame and the door pair only, and a full encoding dealing also with the selection and sizing of the hydraulic cylinder as well as the minimization of forces on the car rails. In particular, in the baseline encoding we consider only the cost components related to car frame and doors, whereas the full encoding takes into account all the cost components. Overall, the baseline encoding features 29 parameters and 10 decision variables, whereas

[1] We run Chuffed v0.10.3, OR-Tools v7.8, ECL^{i}PS^e v7.0, CPLEX v12.7, Gurobi v9.0.1, z3 v4.8.7 and OptiMathSat v1.7.0.1. z3 and OptiMathSat do not generate proofs of their results in the (default) configuration that we tested.

[2] All tests run on a PC equipped with an Intel® Core^{TM} i7-6500U dual core CPU @ 2.50 GHz, featuring 8 GB of RAM and running Ubuntu Linux 16.04 LTS 64 bit.

Table 2. Comparison of solvers on the baseline encoding: the first column reports the setup and the other columns report the time (ms) taken to solve each setup by the solvers—best times appear in boldface.

Shaft	OR-Tools	Chuffed	ECL^iPS^e	CPLEX	Gurobi	z3	OptiMathSat
1300×800	662	200	924	856	886	**100**	254
1300×900	645	**198**	703	1020	1802	432	30680
1300×1000	674	**192**	1401	918	933	416	58066
1300×1100	659	**179**	1734	940	971	582	154739
1300×1200	655	**191**	1796	1056	1237	417	82698
1300×1300	661	**188**	1771	1090	1725	495	100822
1300×1400	637	**188**	1366	918	887*	435	79323
1300×1500	672	**206**	875	1118	925*	517	98355
1500×800	644	199	678	1023	824	**116**	247
1500×900	664	**179**	691	902	881	787	101458
1500×1000	673	**195**	1379	987	887*	619	70082
1500×1100	639	**206**	1942	971	903	682	105071
1500×1200	660	**264**	2024	1060	934	501	83719
1500×1300	636	**224**	2412	987	1018	417	121801
1500×1400	645	**192**	1509	871	919	470	97753
1500×1500	653	**216**	845	856	935	463	142557

the full encoding features 42 parameters and 17 decision variables. The number of constraints varies from a minimum of 30 for the baseline encoding considering arrays and functions to 401 for the full encoding with implications to represent parameters and look-up tables. Both the baseline and the full encodings are generated considering a database of 25 car frames, 236 doors and 47 hydraulic cylinders.

In Table 2 we show the results obtained on the baseline encoding by all the solvers we consider. For each solver we report the best time obtained on two variations: one in which the selection of components is based on arrays and another featuring Boolean implications. Both variations are integer-based because not all the solvers support arithmetic over reals, so we do not consider relaxations here; also, since the car surface computation involves a division, we omit the deduction of the car payload and passengers which are required for a complete design. All the solvers leveraging MiniZinc encodings fare the best runtime when the component parameters are encoded with arrays: CP solvers like Chuffed seem to make effective use of element constraints and MIP solvers appear to handle the translation of array constraints better than Boolean implications. On the other hand, OMT solvers run faster on the version based on Boolean implications, as the addition of arrays involves dealing with more theories at once and this inevitably hurts performances.

Table 3. Comparison of z3 and OptiMathSat on the full encoding: the first column reports each setup; the other columns, grouped by solver, report runtimes (ms) of different versions: integer-based "**I**", relaxed "**I + R**" and relaxed with functions "**I + R + F**", respectively. Subcolumns "**SO**" and "**MO**" refer to single objective and multiobjective optimization, respectively—best times among z3 and OptiMathSat appear in boldface. The last column reports LiftCreate heuristic engine runtimes.

Shaft	z3						OptiMathSat						Heuristic
	I		I + R		I + R + F		I		I + R		I + R + F		
	SO	MO	SO	MO	SO	MO	SO	MO	SO	MO	SO	MO	
1300 × 800	157	149	131	134	143	221	109	119	**100**	131	116	110	583
1300 × 900	8878	229522	1205	**844**	1978	2321	—	—	74960	53535	68215	52068	1784
1300 × 1000	36120	133325	2818	3362	4433	**2704**	156761	48328	136109	107356	132166	112379	921
1300 × 1100	36448	60589	3514	1967	2365	**1554**	192198	127753	160883	176491	199352	113889	2177
1300 × 1200	42328	5530	6876	3460	**2637**	4155	—	208852	276380	181817	193987	160401	6865
1300 × 1300	94325	8982	22279	**2521**	5294	5304	244973	129848	225067	165818	292777	197777	15278
1300 × 1400	30452	133087	7374	**1779**	11096	3707	259953	244078	—	256791	—	242488	11190
1300 × 1500	177355	25697	18810	4061	234235	**1998**	258119	213104	259693	172842	274986	222485	24380
1500 × 800	176	141	121	114	140	129	100	**85**	100	**85**	100	101	926
1500 × 900	25964	56674	1619	**1212**	3382	1876	141359	—	206751	95370	167671	100623	5215
1500 × 1000	91242	235192	2888	1803	5121	**1725**	—	118777	223241	93759	173623	187153	2952
1500 × 1100	—	18023	4977	7517	**3925**	4446	219596	187570	205041	179414	183862	156035	4875
1500 × 1200	139993	68562	7001	**1242**	7431	1571	251651	148664	231829	70431	254111	189705	6232
1500 × 1300	291712	—	26724	4895	20263	**4325**	—	225509	—	232735	—	255728	33785
1500 × 1400	—	6264	35073	3139	169215	**2675**	—	184555	271054	107886	—	180857	21910
1500 × 1500	—	17824	37722	2703	121472	**2528**	257242	222360	—	167762	—	251033	8699

As we can observe in Table 2, Chuffed is the one yielding the best runtimes, except for two setups where z3 is the fastest solver. Noticeably, these setups do not admit a feasible configuration given the shaft size and the components available. z3 and OR-Tools are second best, their runtimes being always less than one second; MIP solvers CPLEX and Gurobi seem slightly less effective than the leading pack. In some cases, marked with an asterisk in Table 2, Gurobi returned "*UNSAT or UNKNOWN*" as an answer even if a solution exists and the MiniZinc file is the same for all solvers, so we conjecture that numerical stability might be an issue in these cases, but we are investigating other potential causes. ECL^{i}PS^e results are mixed, i.e., some setups are solved faster than OR-Tools or z3, others take more than two seconds to solve. OptiMathSat is surprisingly slow on these encodings: if we exclude scenarios for which no feasible configuration exists, then OptiMathSat best result is 30 s to solve the 1300 × 900 setup.

When considering the full encoding, we limit our comparison to z3 and OptiMathSat, since they are the only ones that appear to handle encodings which contain a substantial part of arithmetic over reals involved in cylinder selection, sizing and computation of forces on the car rails. Among the MiniZinc-based tools, ECL^{i}PS^e is meant to support arithmetic over reals, but even the baseline encoding with relaxations resulted in a timeout for every setup other than the ones for which no feasible configuration exists. We experimented also with OR-Tools on an encoding obtained considering fixed-point arithmetic over 64 bit integers, but to no avail. We did not try the fixed-point encoding on other CP tools as they do not support 64 bit precision which is the least one required to avoid overflowing the calculations. In Table 3 we collect the results of the comparison between z3 and OptiMathSat, adding the runtime of the heuristic search performed by LiftCreate for reference. We focus on the implication-based encoding given the results with the baseline encoding. In the table, columns labeled "**I**" report runtimes on the integer-based versions, columns labeled "**I+R**" report runtimes on relaxed versions, and columns labeled "**I+R+F**" report runtimes on versions where look-up tables are represented as nested *if-then-else* functions rather than straight implications. The columns "**SO**" and "**MO**" report the results of single-objective and multi-objective optimization, respectively. In the single-objective case, considering equation (11), we set the free parameters α_1, α_2 and α_3 to 0.3 and α_4 to 0.1 in order to encode different priorities. In the multi-objective encoding, we set all weights to one. The choice of the weights reflects that the first three components of the cost function have the same priorities. Different weights could be chosen according to the user's preferences, and we know—from other experiments that we do not show here to save space—that different choices do not impact on performances.

Considering the results in Table 3, we see that the integer-based version of the full encoding is the least appealing option: while z3 performs slightly better than OptiMathSat on this version, other solutions yield faster runtimes. In particular, relaxing the encoding has a substantial impact both on z3 and OptiMathSat: solving time decreases by orders of magnitude in some cases with respect to the integer-based encoding. Finally, considering the addition of native SMT-LIB functions we see that the results are mixed, i.e., it is not so clear that choosing them improves the solving time. Noticeably, while OptiMathSat remains slower than z3, it never exceeds the time limit on this encoding. As for single vs. multi-objective encoding, we can see that the multi-objective approach performs better than the single-objective one. In spite of some exceptions, multi-objective optimization—specifically, with z3, relaxed encodings and native SMT-LIB functions—seems to be the winning option overall. When it comes to comparing the heuristic engine of LiftCreate with the best results of the constraint-based approach, we should take into account that the former deals with the *complete* design cycle and not just with some subtasks. Given this initial bias, that in some cases the heuristic engine outperforms most constraint-based solutions, but it is overall slower than the best ones, it is fair to say that OMT solvers with relaxed encodings and multi-objective optimization provide a feasible replacement to heuristic search in the design subtasks that we considered here.

5 Conclusions

In this paper we have considered the problem of solving some subtasks in automated design and configuration of elevator systems with a purely constraint-based approach. Elevator configuration is a seemingly neglected problem in the constraint programming literature, but we believe that it offers many interesting starting points for useful research that can spill over to other domains. We have shown that some combinations of encoding techniques like relaxations and multi-objective optimization together with specific solvers seem more promising than others, and that the best combination is competitive with special-purpose heuristics. Noticeably, this result has been obtained without tweaking the default configuration of the solvers to match the specific problem. While better results could be obtained for specific configurations we believe that an added value of a solver lies also in its ability to tackle problems effectively without undergoing extensive customization.

References

1. Annunziata, L., Menapace, M., Tacchella, A.: Computer intensive vs. heuristic methods in automated design of elevator systems. In: Proceedings of European Conference on Modelling and Simulation, ECMS 2017, Budapest, Hungary, 23–26 May 2017, pp. 543–549 (2017)
2. Ansótegui, C., Bofill, M., Palahí, M., Suy, J., Villaret, M.: Solving weighted CSPs with meta-constraints by reformulation into satisfiability modulo theories. Constraints Int. J. **18**(2), 236–268 (2013)
3. Bacchus, F.: GAC via unit propagation. In: Bessière, C. (ed.) CP 2007. LNCS, vol. 4741, pp. 133–147. Springer, Heidelberg (2007). https://doi.org/10.1007/978-3-540-74970-7_12
4. Barret, C., Fontaine, P., Tinelli, C.: The SMT-LIB standard - version 2.6 (2017). http://smtlib.cs.uiowa.edu/papers/smt-lib-reference-v2.6-r2017-07-18.pdf
5. Bofill, M., Palahí, M., Suy, J., Villaret, M.: Solving constraint satisfaction problems with SAT modulo theories. Constraints Int. J. **17**(3), 273–303 (2012)
6. Chang, K.H.: Multiobjective optimization and advanced topics, Chapter 19. In: Chang, K.H. (ed.) e-Design, pp. 1105–1173. Academic Press, Boston (2015)
7. Chu, G.: Improving combinatorial optimization. In: Twenty-Third International Joint Conference on Artificial Intelligence (2013)
8. Contaldo, F., Trentin, P., Sebastiani, R.: From MiniZinc to optimization modulo theories, and back. In: Hebrard, E., Musliu, N. (eds.) CPAIOR 2020. LNCS, vol. 12296, pp. 148–166. Springer, Cham (2020). https://doi.org/10.1007/978-3-030-58942-4_10
9. Demarchi, S., Menapace, M., Tacchella, A.: Automating elevator design with satisfiability modulo theories. In: 2019 IEEE 31st International Conference on Tools with Artificial Intelligence (ICTAI), pp. 26–33. IEEE (2019)
10. Gu, Z., Rothberg, E., Bixby, R.: Gurobi optimization (2019). http://www.gurobi.com/
11. IBM: IBM ILOG CPLEX optimization studio (2017) CPLEX users manual, version 12.7 (2017)
12. Marcus, S., Stout, J., McDermott, J.: VT: an expert elevator designer that uses knowledge-based backtracking. AI Mag. **8**(4), 41–41 (1987)
13. Marriott, K., Stuckey, P.J., Koninck, L., Samulowitz, H.: A minizinc tutorial (2014)
14. McDermott, J.: R1: the formative years. AI Mag. **2**(2), 21–21 (1981)
15. Mittal, S., Falkenhainer, B.: Dynamic constraint satisfaction. In: Proceedings Eighth National Conference on Artificial Intelligence, pp. 25–32 (1990)
16. Mittal, S., Frayman, F.: Towards a generic model of configuraton tasks. In: IJCAI, vol. 89, pp. 1395–1401 (1989)

17. de Moura, L., Bjørner, N.: Z3: an efficient SMT solver. In: Ramakrishnan, C.R., Rehof, J. (eds.) TACAS 2008. LNCS, vol. 4963, pp. 337–340. Springer, Heidelberg (2008). https://doi.org/10.1007/978-3-540-78800-3_24
18. Nethercote, N., Stuckey, P.J., Becket, R., Brand, S., Duck, G.J., Tack, G.: MiniZinc: towards a standard CP modelling language. In: Bessière, C. (ed.) CP 2007. LNCS, vol. 4741, pp. 529–543. Springer, Heidelberg (2007). https://doi.org/10.1007/978-3-540-74970-7_38
19. Perron, L., Furnon, V.: OR-Tools (2020). https://developers.google.com/optimization/
20. Quéva, M.: A Framework for constraint-programming based configuration. DTU Informatics (2011)
21. Schimpf, J., Shen, K.: ECLiPSe - from LP to CLP. Theory Pract. Logic Program. **12**(1–2), 127–156 (2012). https://doi.org/10.1017/S1471068411000469
22. Sebastiani, R., Trentin, P.: On optimization modulo theories, MaxSMT and sorting networks. In: Legay, A., Margaria, T. (eds.) TACAS 2017. LNCS, vol. 10206, pp. 231–248. Springer, Heidelberg (2017). https://doi.org/10.1007/978-3-662-54580-5_14
23. Sebastiani, R., Trentin, P.: OptiMathSAT: a tool for optimization modulo theories. J. Autom. Reason. **64**(3), 423–460 (2018). https://doi.org/10.1007/s10817-018-09508-6
24. Stumptner, M., Friedrich, G.E., Haselbok, A.: Generative constraint-based configuration of large technical systems. Artif. Intell. Eng. Des. Anal. Manuf. **12**(4), 307–320 (1998). https://doi.org/10.1017/S0890060498124046
25. Zhang, L.L.: Product configuration: a review of the state-of-the-art and future research. Int. J. Prod. Res. **52**(21), 6381–6398 (2014)

Modular Logic Argumentation in Arg-tuProlog

Roberta Calegari[1], Giuseppe Contissa[1], Giuseppe Pisano[1](✉), Galileo Sartor[2], and Giovanni Sartor[1]

[1] Alma AI – Alma Mater Research Institute for Human-Centered Artificial Intelligence, Alma Mater Studiorum—Università di Bologna, Bologna, Italy
{roberta.calegari,giuseppe.contissa,g.pisano,giovanni.sartor}@unibo.it
[2] University of Torino, Turin, Italy
galileo.sartor@unito.it

Abstract. A modular extension of Arg-tuProlog, a light-weight argumentation tool, is here presented and discussed, highlighting how it enables reasoning with rules and interpretations of multiple legal systems. Its effectiveness is demonstrated with examples from different national private international law (PIL) laws, running in Arg-tuProlog. PIL addresses overlaps and conflicts between legal systems by distributing cases between the authorities of such systems (jurisdiction) and establishing what rules these authorities have to apply to each case (choice of law).

Keywords: Modular argumentation · Private international law · Arg-tuProlog

1 Introduction

In our increasingly pervasive and interconnected world, the application and enforcement of the law make it necessary to take into account the interplay of multiple normative systems, especially when dealing with international contracts and other commercial and social interactions involving different countries. Moreover, normative systems may also interact or conflict on different levels: this is true of both national legal systems and of various transnational or international laws and conventions. All these sources of law need to be considered to properly reason about the law.

The research in this paper focuses on the field of private international law (PIL) – a growing and important domain of the law – which deals with the coexistence of multiple normative systems, having distinct and often contradictory rules, and the legal interaction of persons connected to different legal systems,

Roberta Calegari, Giuseppe Pisano and Giovanni Sartor have been supported by the H2020 ERC Project "CompuLaw" (G.A. 833647). Giuseppe Contissa and Galileo Sartor have been supported by the European Union's Justice programme under Grant Agreement No. 800839 for the project "InterLex: Advisory and Training System for Internet-related private International Law".

S. Bandini et al. (Eds.): AIxIA 2021, LNAI 13196, pp. 91–103, 2022.
https://doi.org/10.1007/978-3-031-08421-8_7

trying to establish priorities between them. Conflicts about competences and rules are addressed by identifying which authority is responsible for making a decision in each given case (jurisdiction), and which set of norms should be applied (applicable law).

A recent logical analysis of PIL has highlighted how this body of law can be suitably modelled by modular argumentation [8] so as to provide a formal model of the interaction among multiple legal systems. The model proceeds from the assumption that PIL is not concerned with specific inconsistencies between the rules of different legal systems, since only one system will be selected and applied, regardless of how the others would regulate the same case (choice of law). Thus, the law is modelled through sets of modules in which different legal systems are represented separately. Moreover, each legal-system module is further split into separate modules, each with a specific function: determining jurisdiction, establishing the law to be applied, and providing substantive legal outcomes. This formal model has not yet been captured and implemented in ready-to-use technology.

For this reason, we are here presenting an extension for the Arg-tuProlog framework [5,10] – a lightweight argumentation tool – enabling the exploitation of modular knowledge bases. In this work, previous works on Arg-tuProlog [3] are extended focusing on modularity issues and fully addressing a complete case study in the field of PIL and legal reasoning. Arg-tuProlog makes it possible to design and define knowledge organised in distinct and separate modules that can "call" one another. Such calls request skeptical or credulous reasoning. The final answers from the system are obtained by way of dialectical argumentation. In particular, a knowledge module – which may represent a legal system or parts of it – can be used by itself, or by referring to another module for specific issues. This second approach is done by directly calling and querying the relevant module.

In past years, research in either legal theory or AI and law has devoted little attention to the logical analysis of PIL. Only recently have several projects begun to fill this gap[1], providing computable representations of international and national PIL rules. This is an important development since private international law is an increasingly relevant domain of the law – and considering as well that legal relationships involving citizens of different countries are becoming increasingly frequent. The tool presented in this paper is a further advancement, for it can be used to expand existing projects (such as Interlex), and also as a basis for broader applications. Indeed, the model – and its technology – can also be useful for governing interactions and coordination between heterogeneous agents, belonging to different and differently regulated virtual societies, without recourse to a central regulatory agency [4].

[1] Among these is the European project Interlex, aimed at developing a consultative and training system for internet-related PIL, making it available as an online platform. The platform will be composed of three modules: a Decision Support Module (DSM), a Find Law Module (FLM), and a Training Module (TM). In this context, the core component of the Decision Support Module (DSM) lies in a set of logic representations in Prolog, providing basic legal reasoning capabilities.

Accordingly, the paper is organised as follows. Section 2 presents two examples in the PIL domain illustrating the interaction between national and international legislation. Section 3 then presents the Arg-tuProlog modular argumentation tool. In Sect. 4 the examples discussed in Sect. 2 are represented in the Arg-tuProlog framework. Section 5 discusses the results of the experiment and proposes future lines of research.

2 The Domain of Private International Law: Running Examples

In this section, we will provide two examples of a possible interaction between national and transnational normative systems. In particular, we will focus on one of the EU's main PIL instruments, the Brussels Regulation[2], providing common EU rules on jurisdiction and the recognition and enforcement of judgments. According to the Brussels Regulation, there are some cases where the regulation itself does not give an answer to the question of jurisdiction, pointing instead to national legislation for the relevant laws. This happens, for example, in the sections on consumer contracts (Sect. 4) and third-party proceedings (Sect. 5).

We have built two examples that set aside EU legislation and focus on the switch/conflict between national laws. In our examples, we focus in particular on two sets of national PIL laws: the Italian and the Bulgarian. The source texts presented here are extracted from then English translations of national laws available on the Interlex portal[3].

Example 1 (General jurisdiction rule)
In this example we consider article 3.1 of the Italian Law No. 218 of 31 May 1995 (Reform of the Italian System of Private International Law) and article 4 of the Bulgarian Law DB, bp. 42 ot 17.05.2005 r. (Private International Law Code).

> *Article 3 (Scope of jurisdiction)*
> *1. Italian courts shall have jurisdiction if the defendant is domiciled or resides in Italy or has a representative in this country who is enabled to appear in court pursuant to Article 77 of the Code of Civil Procedure, as well as in the other cases provided for by law. [...]]*

Thus Italian courts shall have jurisdiction if the defendant is domiciled or resides in Italy.

> *Article 4. General Jurisdiction*
> *(1) The Bulgarian courts and other authorities shall have international jurisdiction where: 1. the defendant has a habitual residence, statutory seat or principal place of business in the Republic of Bulgaria; [...]*

[2] Regulation (EU) No. 1215/2012 on jurisdiction and the recognition and enforcement of judgments in civil and commercial matters (recast) (the Brussels Regulation). The EU's two other main PIL instruments are Regulation (EC) No. 593/2008 on the law applicable to contractual obligations (Rome I) and Regulation (EC) No. 864/2007 on the law applicable to noncontractual obligations (Rome II).

[3] https://interlex-portal.eu/FindLaw/.

Thus Bulgarian courts shall have jurisdiction if the defendant has a habitual residence, statutory seat, or the principal place of business in Bulgaria.

Let us consider, as a first scenario, the case of Marius, an Italian citizen with his primary residence in the city of Rome. Marius is summoned to appear in front of a judge to answer a complaint brought against him. Based on this information we can determine that the Italian court of Rome should be assigned jurisdiction in this complaint.

In a second scenario, Marius is also the owner of a business in Bulgaria. In this case, the Bulgarian PIL law – called by the Brussels Regulation – would assign jurisdiction to a Bulgarian court. Since both rules are valid, the jurisdiction in Marius's case belongs to both the Italian and Bulgarian courts. If no priority was set, then a conflict of laws would arise, with two equally valid indications of jurisdiction.

Example 2 (Jurisdiction related to rights in rem)
In the second example we consider articles 5.1 of Italian PIL and article 12 of Bulgarian PIL.

> *Article 5 (Actions concerning rights in rem in immovables situated abroad)*
> *1. Italian courts shall have no jurisdiction over actions concerning rights in rem in immovables situated abroad.*

Thus, under Italian law, Italian Courts have no jurisdiction over actions concerning rights in rem in immovables (real property) situated outside Italy.

> *Article 12. Jurisdiction in Matters Relating to Rights in Rem*
> *(1) (Amended, SG No. 59/2007) The matters under Article 109 of the Code of Civil Procedure relating to immovable property situated in the Republic of Bulgaria, the matters relating to the enforcement or to security which such property constitutes, as well as the matters relating to transfer or establishment of rights in rem in such property, shall be exclusively cognizable in the Bulgarian courts and other authorities. [...]*

Thus, under Bulgarian law, Bulgarian Courts have jurisdiction for matters relating to the transfer or the establishment of rights in rem in immovable property situated in Bulgaria.

Let us consider Marius, an Italian citizen, owner of two houses, one in Italy (Milan) and the other in Bulgaria (Sofia). A claim is brought against Marius with an action concerning a right in rem over one of his immovable properties. Depending on which house is the object of the claim, Marius will be summoned in front of an Italian or Bulgarian judge respectively.

3 Modular Argumentation in Arg-tuProlog

Arg-tuProlog [5,13] is a lightweight modular argumentation tool that fruitfully combines modular logic programming and legal reasoning. It makes it possible to represent, reason, and carry out an argument on conditional norms featuring obligations, prohibitions, and (strong or weak) permissions – including under any burden-of-persuasion constraints that may apply – fully supporting the modular argumentation model, i.e., allowing theory fragmentation, thus enabling the coexistence of different modules.

The approach is based on common constructs in computational argumentation modules – rule-based arguments, argumentation graphs, and labelling semantics – laying their foundation on Dung's abstract argumentation [7] and structured argumentation [2]. Arguments are formed by chaining applications of inference rules into inference trees or graphs – i.e., arguments are constructed using deductive inference rules that license deductive inferences from premises to conclusions (cf. [9]).

The Arg-tuProlog-structured argumentation framework adopts an ASPIC$^+$-like syntax [11]: in a nutshell, arguments are produced from a set of defeasible rules, and attack relationships between arguments are drawn in argumentation graphs. The arguments in the graph are then labelled by applying an acceptance labelling semantics (namely, grounded semantics [1]) that takes burdens of persuasion into account. The framework addresses burdens of persuasion within an argumentation setting [6] (formal accounts of the adopted deontic extensions are discussed in detail in [12], while the implemented burden-of-persuasion model can be found in [6]). The argumentation model is then enhanced according to the concept of modularity [8], making it possible to separate knowledge as well as to create an internal structure of the knowledge (linked modules corresponding to knowledge organisation).

Being completely based on logic programming, the system makes possible a completely integrated cooperation between logic programming and argumentation, therefore – as in the following examples – the knowledge can contain strict rules on which basis to perform queries and reasoning.

3.1 Modular Logic: Architecture and Predicates

In the following, we will focus on deepening the discussion of the modular extension of Arg-tuProlog, being the core of this work and being functional to the appropriate design of private international law. Details on the argument model and its syntax and architecture can be found in [14].

The Arg-tuProlog framework leverages the underlying tuProlog engine and is freely available at [13]. The entire framework is a collection of tuProlog-compatible libraries, and all the required components exploit the tuProlog feature to allow the inclusion of external libraries during the evaluation process. The system's inner modular architecture greatly enhances the upgradability and flexibility of the entire system by making it possible to add new features or modify requirements.

As mentioned, the framework fully supports a modular argumentation model, i.e., it allows theory fragmentation and enables the coexistence and interaction of different modules. Different modules can be combined when querying the system, leading to different responses according to the modules considered. It is also possible to nest modules, thus establishing a hierarchy among the modules. These features make the system particularly suitable for designing and implementing complex scenarios such as the one relating to the PIL domain. Indeed, as discussed in Sect. 2, this legal domain is based on the coordination and cooperation of different legal systems, such as national law and international treaties. From a computational point of view, this mixture translates into a scenario where a logic theory (module) can query or consult a piece of information contained in another theory (module).

Modules are identified by distinct Prolog files (`.pl` files) and can be called and executed exploiting the predicate `module_call(+Modules, :Query)`, where `Modules` is an input parameter containing the list of the required modules – i.e., modules that need to be loaded to answer the query – and `Query` is the query that must be evaluated. In particular, the predicate: *i)* creates a new environment that contains *only* the required modules data, *ii)*, executes the query in the newly created environment, *iii)* and feeds the result to the caller—note that the original caller environment is not altered by the procedure.

The location of the modules must be included in the *root* theory (main module) through the predicate `modulesPath(++FileSystemPath)`, where the input parameter `FileSystemPath` denotes the full path file-system name. Note that in the case of nested calls, it is not necessary to re-specify the path in the submodules.

For example, consider the case in which there is a unique module in the modules folder (`systemPath/modules/moduleOne.pl`) containing the following theory:

```
legislation("italian legislation", moduleOne).
jurisdiction(C) :- legislation(C, ModuleName).
```

In order to use `moduleOne`, the root module needs to set the modules path as shown in the following. In order to better understand the system's functioning, we will add a fact `legislation` to the root module as well.

```
modulesPath(systemPath/modules).
legislation("root legislation", root).
jurisdiction(C):-modules_call([moduleOne], jurisdiction(C)).
```

Then, when calling the goal

```
:- jurisdiction(C)
```

the *module_call*/2 loads the required modules, in this case `moduleOne`; creates the new environment; and proceeds to the query evaluation. The result will be

```
C="italian legislation", ModuleName=moduleOne
```

highlighting that the root theory content is not considered during the query evaluation (i.e., `C="root legislation", ModuleName=root` is not a solution).

If we add a second module – *moduleTwo.pl* – containing the following theory:

```
legislation("bulgarian legislation", moduleTwo).
```

we can combine modules' content – and their solutions – writing the root module as follows:

```
modulesPath(systemPath/modules).
legislation("root legislation", root).
jurisdiction(C)  :- modules_call([moduleOne, moduleTwo],
                        jurisdiction(C)).
```

in such a case, the `legislation(L,X)` goal will provide the two distinct solutions

```
C="italian legislation", ModuleName=moduleOne

C="bulgarian legislation", ModuleName=moduleTwo
```

By exploiting the predicates just discussed, it is so possible to organize the knowledge into a series of distinct modules that may be dependent on and/or pertinent to a hierarchical structure. Accordingly, a dispatch of concerns and contents is possible while ensuring easy interaction and cooperation among distinct modules.

4 Running Examples in Arg-tuProlog

In the following, the examples discussed in Sect. 2 are reified in the Arg-tuProlog framework to show the technology's effectiveness and potential[4].

Both examples discussed in Sect. 2 can be mapped starting from the Brussels Regulation, the Italian national law, and the Bulgarian national law. For such a reason they have been mapped onto the Arg-tuProlog framework exploiting three distinct modules: one for the Brussels Regulation, one for the Italian national law, and one for the Bulgarian national law. In fact, the complexity of the scenario makes it necessary to take different bodies of law into account and to make them interact and interoperate, while also providing a tool for detecting possible conflicts and inconsistencies. For this reason, a modular approach is required.

In the following, we list an extract from the Brussels Regulation codification (*BrusselsRegulation.pl* module) that makes it possible to establish jurisdiction according to the content of the articles. In particular, the final choice on the complaint is referred to the national laws of the UE member states in question. This connection is modelled using the modularity feature of Arg-tuProlog and in particular the *call_module* predicate:

```
hasJurisdiction(Article, Country, Court, ClaimId):-
    personRole(PersonId, ClaimId, defendant),
    memberState(MemberLaw),
    call_module([MemberLaw, ClaimId],
        hasJurisdiction(Article, Country, Court, ClaimId)).
```

[4] The theories used in the examples can be found at https://github.com/tuProlog/arg2p/tree/master/example-theories/IPL-brussels.

```
hasJurisdiction(Article, Country, Court, ClaimId):-
    claimObject(ClaimId, rightsInRem),
    memberState(MemberLaw),
    call_module([MemberLaw, ClaimId],
        hasJurisdiction(Article, Country, Court, ClaimId)).
```

The Italian law module – *italy.pl* – is a simple theory that includes the Prolog translation of the articles from the Italian PIL law as described in Sect. 2. The articles may be represented in the Arg-tuProlog system as follows:

```
hasJurisdiction(art3_1, italy, Court, ClaimId) :-
    personRole(PersonId, ClaimId, defendant),
    personDomicile(PersonId, italy, Court).

hasJurisdiction(art3_1, italy, Court, ClaimId):-
    personRole(PersonId, ClaimId, defendant),
    personAgent(AgentId, PersonId),
    personDomicile(AgentId, italy, Court).

hasJurisdiction(art51, italy, Court, ClaimId):-
    claimObject(ClaimId, rightsInRem),
    immovableProperty(ClaimId, italy, Court).
```

The Bulgarian national law is represented by the *bulgaria.pl* module which contains the Prolog translation from the Bulgarian PIL law as described in Sect. 2. A possible Arg-tuProlog representation is as follows:

```
hasJurisdiction(art4_1, bulgaria, Court, ClaimId):-
    personRole(PersonId, ClaimId, defendant),
    personDomicile(PersonId, bulgaria, Court).

hasJurisdiction(art4_1, bulgaria, Court, ClaimId):-
    personRole(PersonId, ClaimId, defendant),
    personPlaceOfBusiness(PersonId, bulgaria, Court).

hasJurisdiction(art12, bulgaria, Court, ClaimId):-
    claimObject(ClaimId, rightsInRem),
    immovableProperty(ClaimId, bulgaria, Court).
```

Using this knowledge as our basis – the knowledge being split into the corresponding modules – let us discuss the resolution of some example complaints so as to illustrate the potential of using a modular argumentation framework.

Example 1 (General jurisdiction rule). Let us consider the case discussed in Example 2. The facts and details of the case are stored in a separate module (*claim1.pl*), listed in the following. In particular, we have facts establishing the role of Marius (i.e., defendant), his domicile (i.e., Italy), and his place of

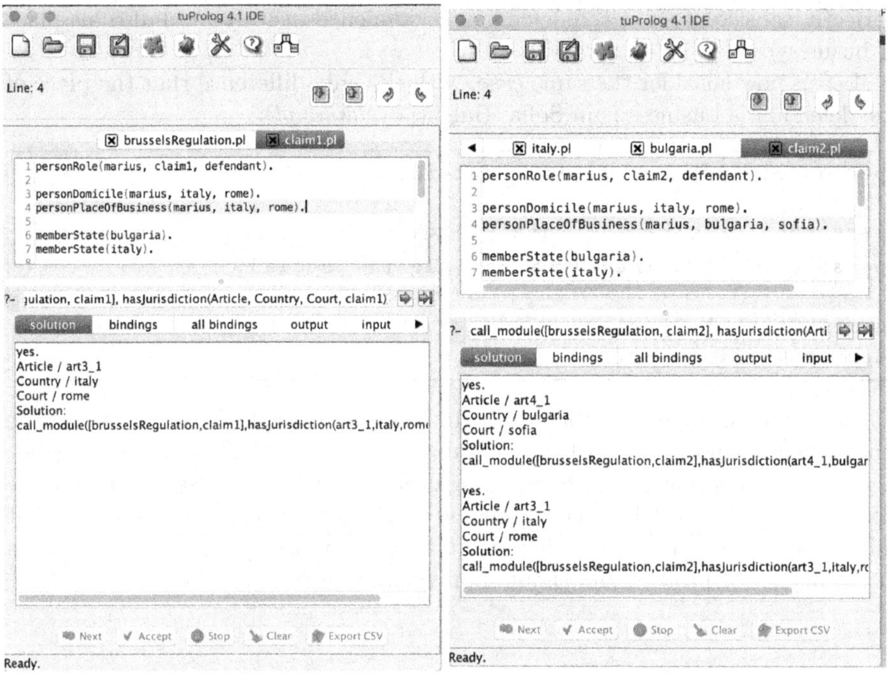

Fig. 1. Arg2p interface: result of claim1 (left) and claim2 (right).

business, which once again is Italy (respectively `personRole`, `personDomicile`, and `personPlaceOfBusiness` predicates). Finally, we have two facts establishing which states are EU member states (under the Brussels Regulation), which in our example are Italy and Bulgaria.

```
personRole(marius, claim1, defendant).

personDomicile(marius, italy, rome).
personPlaceOfBusiness(marius, italy, rome).

memberState(bulgaria).
memberState(italy).
```

To evaluate the case, we can select the jurisdiction simply by calling the following goal over the top module *brusselsRegulation.pl*:

```
call_module([brusselsRegulation, claim1],
    hasJurisdiction(Article, Country, Court, claim1)).
```

Figure 1 (left) shows the result, which is that under article 3.1 of the Italian law, the court to which the case is assigned is in Rome, Italy. The result is perfectly consistent since the defendant is domiciled in Italy (and also his place of business).

Let us now consider the same case, with the only difference that the place of the defendant's business is in Sofia, Bulgaria (*claim2.pl*).

```
personRole(marius, claim2, defendant).

personDomicile(marius, italy, rome).
personPlaceOfBusiness(marius,bulgaria,sofia).

memberState(bulgaria).
memberState(italy).
```

As shown in Fig. 1 (right), the answer in this case is twofold. Article 4.1 of the Bulgarian law and Article 3.1 of the Italian law should apply at the same time, assigning jurisdiction to the Sofia (Bulgarian) court in one case and the Rome (Italian) court in the other. The system makes it possible to detect and point out this inconsistency, indicating that two different articles, with different answers in the matter of jurisdiction, should apply simultaneously.

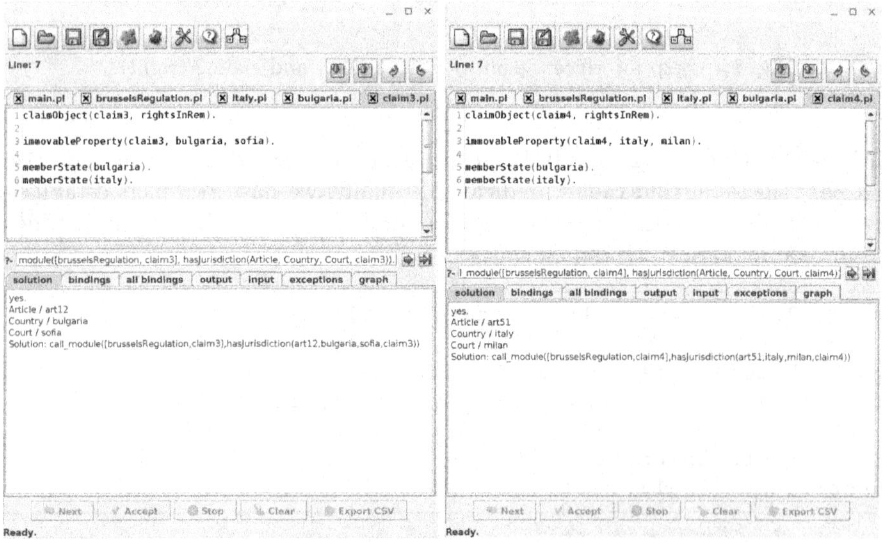

Fig. 2. Arg2p interface: result of claim3 (left) and claim4 (right).

Example 2 (Jurisdiction related to rights in rem). Let us now turn to the case discussed in Example 2. The facts of the case are stored in module *claim3.pl*. In particular, we have a fact establishing the object of the complaint (`claimObject`), in this case rights in rem. We then have a fact stating the place of the immovable property in case (`immovableProperty`), which in the case at hand is Sofia. Finally, as in the example before, we have facts establishing which states are members of the EU—in our examples, Italy and Bulgaria.

```
claimObject(claim3, rightsInRem).

immovableProperty(claim3, bulgaria, sofia).

memberState(bulgaria).
memberState(italy).
```

To evaluate the case, we can select the jurisdiction simply by calling the following goal over the top module *brusselsRegulation.pl*:

```
call_module([brusselsRegulation, claim3],
        hasJurisdiction(Article, Country, Court, claim3)).
```

The result is shown in Fig. 2 (left) and states that the jurisdiction and the court must be in Bulgaria. Once again, the system shows that the connection between different modules is a necessary feature. In fact, since the immovable property is in Bulgaria, the Brussels Regulation defers Bulgarian legislation to determine the jurisdiction. Bulgarian law confirms that if the property is in Bulgaria, the case must be brought before a Bulgarian court. It should be noted that in this case the Italian law only states that if the property is not in Italy, then it is not for an Italian court to take the case, but nowhere does the law state which court *should* do so. Therefore, without such a connection between the different bodies of law, there would be no answer that the Italian court could offer in deciding where the case should be heard.

If we change the fact concerning the property, indicating that it is in Italy, the system will respond, correctly, that the case must be adjudicated by an Italian court, and in particular the Milan court (Fig. 2 (right)).

```
claimObject(claim4, rightsInRem).

immovableProperty(claim4, italy, milan).

memberState(bulgaria).
memberState(italy).
```

5 Conclusion

In this paper we have shown how the domain of private international law can be suitably modelled by modular argumentation with the support of Arg-tuProlog, which provides a way to reason about a formal model of interaction among multiple legal systems.

Indeed, we were aware that the PIL domain is particularly difficult to formalize, especially by comparison with domains that are traditional fields where knowledge-based systems in law are applied, such as tax, administrative, and entitlement law.

In the future, we aim to extend the modular-argumentation approach supported by Arg-tuProlog so as to cover additional parts of the domain of EU PIL law. In particular, we aim to cover international and national rules dealing with laws that apply to both contracts and non-contractual obligations and to extend the set of modules so as to cover a broader range of national legal systems.

In addition, we think that the same approach, that combines modular argumentation and defeasible reasoning, can be used to further model legal domains presenting characteristics and issues similar to PIL law (e.g., multiple levels of conflicting/overlapping rules), such as internet and aviation law.

References

1. Baroni, P., Caminada, M., Giacomin, M.: An introduction to argumentation semantics. Knowl. Eng. Rev. **26**(4), 365–410 (2011). https://doi.org/10.1017/S0269888911000166
2. Besnard, P., et al.: Introduction to structured argumentation. Argument Comput. **5**(1), 1–4 (2014). https://doi.org/10.1080/19462166.2013.869764
3. Calegari, R., Contissa, G., Pisano, G., Sartor, G., Sartor, G.: Arg-tuProlog: a modular logic argumentation tool for PIL. In: Villata, S., Harašta, J., Křemen, P. (eds.) Legal Knowledge and Information Systems. JURIX 2020: The Thirty-third Annual Conference. Frontiers in Artificial Intelligence and Applications, vol. 334, pp. 265–268, 9–11 December 2020. https://doi.org/10.3233/FAIA200880
4. Calegari, R., Omicini, A., Sartor, G.: Computable law as argumentation-based mas. In: Proceedings of the 21th Workshop "From Objects to Agents", WOA (2020)
5. Calegari, R., Pisano, G., Omicini, A., Sartor, G.: Arg2P: an argumentation framework for explainable intelligent systems. J. Log. Comput. **32**, 369–401 (2022). https://doi.org/10.1093/logcom/exab089
6. Calegari, R., Sartor, G.: Burden of persuasion in argumentation. In: Proceedings 36th International Conference on Logic Programming (Technical Communications), ICLP 2020. EPTCS, 18–24 September 2020. Camera-ready sent
7. Dung, P.M.: On the acceptability of arguments and its fundamental role in nonmonotonic reasoning, logic programming and n-person games. Artif. Intell. **77**(2), 321–358 (1995). https://doi.org/10.1016/0004-3702(94)00041-X
8. Dung, P.M., Sartor, G.: The modular logic of private international law. Artif. Intell. Law **19**(2–3), 233–261 (2011). https://doi.org/10.1007/s10506-011-9112-5
9. Modgil, S., Prakken, H.: The ASPIC$^+$ framework for structured argumentation: a tutorial. Argument Comput. **5**(1), 31–62 (2014)
10. Pisano, G., Calegari, R., Omicini, A., Sartor, G.: A mechanism for reasoning over defeasible preferences in Arg2P. In: Monica, S., Bergenti, F. (eds.) CILC 2021 - Italian Conference on Computational Logic. Proceedings of the 36th Italian Conference on Computational Logic. CEUR Workshop Proceedings, vol. 3002, pp. 16–30. CEUR-WS, Parma, 7–9 September 2021. http://ceur-ws.org/Vol-3002/paper10.pdf

11. Prakken, H.: An abstract framework for argumentation with structured arguments. Argument Comput. **1**(2), 93–124 (2010). https://doi.org/10.1080/19462160903564592
12. Riveret, R., Rotolo, A., Sartor, G.: A deontic argumentation framework towards doctrine reification. J. Appl. Log.–IfCoLog J. Log. Their Appl. **6**(5), 903–940 (2019). https://collegepublications.co.uk/ifcolog/?00034
13. tuProlog: Arg-tuprolog repository. https://github.com/tuProlog/arg2p-kt
14. tuProlog: Arg-tuprolog website. https://pika-lab.gitlab.io/argumentation/arg2p-kt/

Burden of Persuasion in Meta-argumentation

Giuseppe Pisano[1(✉)], Roberta Calegari[1], Andrea Omicini[2], and Giovanni Sartor[1]

[1] Alma AI – Alma Mater Research Institute for Human-Centered Artificial Intelligence, Alma Mater Studiorum—Università di Bologna, Bologna, Italy
{g.pisano,roberta.calegari,giovanni.sartor}@unibo.it
[2] Dipartimento di Informatica – Scienza e Ingegneria (DISI), Alma Mater Studiorum—Università di Bologna, Cesena, Italy
andrea.omicini@unibo.it

Abstract. This work defines a burden of persuasion meta-argumentation model interpreting the burden as a set of meta-arguments. Bimodal graphs are exploited to define a *meta level* (dealing with the burden) and an *object level* (dealing with standard arguments). Finally, an example in the law domain addressing the problem of burden inversion is discussed in detail.

Keywords: Burdens of persuasion · Argumentation · Meta-argumentation

1 Introduction

In this work we discuss the model of the burden of persuasion in structured argumentation [2,3] under a meta-argumentative approach, which leads to *(i)* a clear separation of concerns in the model, *(ii)* a simpler and more efficient implementation of the corresponding argumentation tool, *(iii)* a natural model extension for dealing also with reasoning over the burden of persuasion concepts.

The work finds its foundation in the approaches of meta-argumentation that emphasize the inner nature of arguments and dialogues as inherently meta-logical [6,7]. Our approach relies on the works from [6,7] introducing only the required abstraction at the meta level. The proposed meta-argumentation framework for the burden of persuasion includes three ingredients: *(i) object-level argumentation* – to create arguments from defeasible and strict rules –, *(ii) meta-level argumentation* – to create arguments dealing with abstractions related to the burden concept using argument schemes (or meta-level rules) –, and *(iii) bimodal graphs* to define interaction between the object level and the meta level—following the account in [6].

Accordingly, Sect. 2 introduces basic elements of the meta-argumentation framework. Section 3 formally defines the framework for the burden of persuasion introducing related argument schemes and discusses its equivalence with the model

S. Bandini et al. (Eds.): AIxIA 2021, LNAI 13196, pp. 104–119, 2022.
https://doi.org/10.1007/978-3-031-08421-8_8

presented in [3]. Finally, Sect. 4 discuss a real case study in the law domain dealing with the problem of burden inversion. Conclusion are drawn in Sect. 5.

2 Meta-argumentation Framework

In this section, we introduce the meta-argumentation framework. For the sake of simplicity, we choose to model our meta-argumentation framework by exploiting bimodal graphs, which are often exploited both to define meta-level concepts and to understand the interactions of object-level and meta-level arguments [6,7]. Accordingly, Subsect. 2.1 presents the object-level argumentation language exploited by our model, leveraging on an ASPIC$^+$-like argumentation framework [9]. Then, Subsect. 2.2 introduces bimodal argumentation graphs main definitions. Finally, in Subsect. 2.3, the meta-level argumentation language based on the use of argument schemes [11] is introduced.

2.1 Structured Argumentation for Object-Level Argumentation

Let a literal be an atomic proposition or its negation.

Notation 1. *For any literal ϕ, its complement is denoted by $\bar{\phi}$. That is, if ϕ is a proposition p, then $\bar{\phi} = \neg p$, while if ϕ is $\neg p$, then $\bar{\phi}$ is p.*

Let us also identify burdens of persuasion, i.e., those literals the proof of which requires a convincing argument. We assume that such literals are consistent (it cannot be the case that there is a burden of persuasion both on ϕ and $\bar{\phi}$).

Definition 1 (Burdens of persuasion). *Burdens of persuasion are represented by predicates of the form bp(ϕ), stating the burden is allocated on the literal ϕ.*

Literals and *bp* predicates are brought into relation through defeasible rules.

Definition 2 (Defeasible rule). *A **defeasible rule** r has the following form: $\rho : \phi_1, ..., \phi_n, \sim \phi'_1, ..., \sim \phi'_m \Rightarrow \psi$ with $0 \leq n, m$, and where*

- *ρ is the unique identifier for r, denoted by $\mathsf{N}(r)$;*
- *each $\phi_1, \ldots, \phi_n, \phi'_1, \ldots, \phi'_m, \psi$ is a literal or a* bp *predicate;*
- *$\phi_1, \ldots \phi_n, \sim \phi'_1, ..., \sim \phi'_m$ are denoted by Antecedent(r) and ψ by Consequent(r);*
- *$\sim \phi$ denotes the weak negation (negation by failure) of ϕ—i.e., ϕ is an exception that would block the application of the rule whose antecedent includes $\sim \phi$.*

The unique identifier of a rule can be used as a literal to specify that the named rule is applicable, and its negation correspondingly to specify that the rule is inapplicable [5].

A superiority relation $\succ$ is defined over rules: $s \succ r$ states that rule s prevails over rule r.

Definition 3 (Superiority relation). *A **superiority relation** $\succ$ over a set of rules Rules is an antireflexive and antisymmetric binary relation over Rules.*

A defeasible theory consists of a set of rules and a superiority relation over the rules.

Definition 4 (Defeasible theory). *A **defeasible theory** is a tuple* $\langle Rules, \succ\rangle$ *where Rules is a set of rules, and* $\succ$ *is a superiority relation over Rules.*

Given a defeasible theory, by chaining rules from the theory, we can construct arguments [4,5,10].

Definition 5 (Argument). *An **argument** A constructed from a defeasible theory* $\langle Rules, \succ\rangle$ *is a finite construct of the form:* $A : A_1, \dots A_n \Rightarrow_r \phi$ *with* $0 \leq n$, *where*

- *A is the argument's unique identifier;*
- $A_1, \dots, A_n$ *are arguments constructed from the defeasible theory* $\langle Rules, \succ\rangle$;
- ϕ *is the* conclusion *of the argument, denoted by* $\mathsf{Conc}(A)$;
- $r : \mathsf{Conc}(A_1), \dots, \mathsf{Conc}(A_n) \Rightarrow \phi$ *is the top rule of A, denoted by* $\mathsf{TopRule}(A)$.

Notation 2. *Given an argument* $A : A_1, \dots A_n \Rightarrow_r \phi$ *as in Definition 5,* $\mathsf{Sub}(A)$ *denotes the set of subarguments of A, i.e.,* $\mathsf{Sub}(A) = \mathsf{Sub}(A_1) \cup \dots \cup \mathsf{Sub}(A_n) \cup \{A\}$. $\mathsf{DirectSub}(A)$ *denotes the direct subarguments of A, i.e.,* $\mathsf{DirectSub}(A) = \{A_1, \dots, A_n\}$.

Preferences over arguments are defined via a last-link ordering: an argument A is preferred over another argument B if the top rule of A is stronger than the top rule of B.

Definition 6 (Preference relation). *A **preference relation*** $\succ$ *is a binary relation over a set of arguments* $\mathcal{A}$*: an argument A is preferred to argument B, denoted by* $A \succ B$, *iff* $\mathsf{TopRule}(A) \succ \mathsf{TopRule}(B)$.

Arguments are put in relation according to the attack relation.

Definition 7 (Attack). *An argument A **attacks** argument B iff A undercuts or rebuts B, where*

- *A undercuts B (on B') iff* $\mathsf{Conc}(A) = \neg\mathsf{N}(\rho)$ *for some* $B' \in \mathsf{Sub}(B)$, *where* ρ *is* $\mathsf{TopRule}(B')$
- *A rebuts B (on B') iff*
  - $\mathsf{Conc}(A) = \bar{\phi}$ *for some* $B' \in \mathsf{Sub}(B)$ *of the form* $B''_1, ..., B''_M \Rightarrow \phi$ *and* $B' \nsucc A$, *or*
  - $\mathsf{Conc}(A) = \phi$ *for some* $B' \in \mathsf{Sub}(B)$ *such that* $\sim \phi \in Antecedent(\mathsf{TopRule}(B'))$

In short, arguments can be attacked on a conclusion of a defeasible inference (rebutting attack), or on a defeasible inference step itself (undercutting attack).

Definition 8 (Argumentation graph). *An **argumentation graph** is a tuple* $\langle \mathcal{A}, \rightsquigarrow\rangle$, *where* $\mathcal{A}$ *is the set of all arguments, and* $\rightsquigarrow$ *is* attack *relation over* $\mathcal{A}$.

Notation 3. *Given an argumentation graph $G = \langle \mathcal{A}, \rightsquigarrow \rangle$, we write $\mathcal{A}_G$, and $\rightsquigarrow_G$ to denote the graph's arguments and attacks respectively.*

Now, let us introduce the notion of the $\{\mathsf{IN}, \mathsf{OUT}, \mathsf{UND}\}$-labelling of an argumentation graph, where each argument in the graph is labelled IN, OUT,or UND, depending on whether it is accepted, rejected, or undecided, respectively.

Definition 9 (Labelling). *Let G be an argumentation graph. An $\{\mathsf{IN}, \mathsf{OUT}, \mathsf{UND}\}$-**labelling** L of G is a total function $\mathcal{A}_G \rightarrow \{\mathsf{IN}, \mathsf{OUT}, \mathsf{UND}\}$. The set of all $\{\mathsf{IN}, \mathsf{OUT}, \mathsf{UND}\}$-**labellings** of G will be denoted as $\mathcal{L}(\{\mathsf{IN}, \mathsf{OUT}, \mathsf{UND}\}, G)$.*

A labelling-based semantics prescribes a set of labellings for any argumentation graph according to some criterion embedded in its definition.

Definition 10 (Labelling-based semantic). *Let G be an argumentation graph. A labelling-based semantics S associates with G a subset of $\mathcal{L}(\{\mathsf{IN}, \mathsf{OUT}, \mathsf{UND}\}, G)$, denoted as $L_S(G)$.*

2.2 Object and Meta Level Connection: Bimodal Graphs

In this section we recall the main definitions of bimodal graphs as the model of interaction between object and meta level. Bimodal graphs allow capturing scenarios in which arguments are categorised in multiple levels—only two in our case, the object and the meta level. Accordingly, a bimodal graph is composed of two components: an argumentation graph for the meta level and an argumentation graph for the object level, along with a relation of support that originates from the meta level and targets attacks and arguments on the object level. Every object-level argument and every object-level attack is supported by at least one meta-level argument. Meta-level arguments can only attack meta-level arguments, and object-level arguments can only attack object-level arguments.

Definition 11 (Bimodal argumentation graph). *A **bimodal argumentation graph** is a tuple $\langle \mathcal{A}_O, \mathcal{A}_M, \mathcal{R}_O, \mathcal{R}_M, \mathcal{S}_A, \mathcal{S}_R \rangle$ where*

1. *$\mathcal{A}_O$ is the set of object-level arguments*
2. *$\mathcal{A}_M$ is the set of meta-level arguments*
3. *$\mathcal{R}_O \subseteq \mathcal{A}_O \times \mathcal{A}_O$, represents the set of object-level attacks*
4. *$\mathcal{R}_M \subseteq \mathcal{A}_M \times \mathcal{A}_M$, represents the set of meta-level attacks*
5. *$\mathcal{S}_A \subseteq \mathcal{A}_M \times \mathcal{A}_O$, represents the set of supports from meta-level arguments into object-level arguments*
6. *$\mathcal{S}_R \subseteq \mathcal{A}_M \times \mathcal{R}_O$, represents the set of supports from meta-level arguments into object-level attacks*
7. *$\mathcal{A}_O \cap \mathcal{A}_M = \emptyset$*
8. *$\forall A \in \mathcal{A}_O\ \exists\ B \in \mathcal{A}_M : (B, A) \in \mathcal{S}_A$*
9. *$\forall R \in \mathcal{R}_O\ \exists\ B \in \mathcal{A}_M : (B, R) \in \mathcal{S}_R$*

The object-level argument graph is represented by the couple $(\mathcal{A}_O, \mathcal{R}_O)$, while the meta-level argument graph is represented by the couple $(\mathcal{A}_M, \mathcal{R}_M)$. The two distinct components are connected by the support relations represented by $\mathcal{S}_A$ and $\mathcal{S}_R$. This supports are the only structural interaction between the meta and the object levels. Condition (8) in the above definition ensures that every object-level argument is supported by at least one meta-level argument, while condition (9) ensures that every object-level attack is supported by at least one meta-level argument. Perspectives of the object-level graph can be defined as:

Definition 12 (Perspective). *Let* $G = \langle \mathcal{A}_O, \mathcal{A}_M, \mathcal{R}_O, \mathcal{R}_M, \mathcal{S}_A, \mathcal{S}_R \rangle$ *be a bimodal argumentation graph and let* L_S *be a labelling semantics. A tuple* $\langle \mathcal{A}'_O, \mathcal{R}'_O \rangle$ *is an* L_S*-perspective of* G *if* $\exists\, l \in L_S(\langle \mathcal{A}_M, \mathcal{R}_M \rangle)$ *such that*

1. $\mathcal{A}'_O = \{\ A | \exists B \in \mathcal{A}_M \ \ s.t.\ l(B) = \mathsf{IN}, (B, A) \in \mathcal{S}_A\}$
2. $\mathcal{R}'_O = \{\ R | \exists B \in \mathcal{A}_M \ \ s.t.\ l(B) = \mathsf{IN}, (B, R) \in \mathcal{S}_R\}$

Consequently, an object argument may occur in one perspective and not in another according to the results yielded by the meta-level argumentation graph.

2.3 Argument Schemes for Meta-level Argumentation

A fundamental aspect to consider when dealing with a multi-level argumentation graph is how the higher-level graphs can be built starting from the object-level ones. At this purpose, in this work – following the example in [7] – we leverage on argument schemes [11]. In a few words, argumentation schemes are commonly used patterns of reasoning. They can be formalised in a rules-like form [8] where every argument scheme consists of a set of conditions and a conclusion. If the conditions are met, then the conclusion holds. Each scheme comes with a set of *critical questions* (CQ), identifying possible exceptions to the admissibility of arguments derived from the schemes.

Definition 13 (Meta-predicate). *A meta-predicate* P_M *is a symbol which represents a property or a relation between object-level arguments. Let be* $\mathcal{M}$ *the set of all* P_M.

Definition 14 (Object-relation meta-predicate). *An object-relation meta-predicate* O_M *is a predicate stating the existence of a relation at the object level— e.g., attacks, preferences, conclusions. Let be* $\mathcal{O}$ *the set of all* O_M.

Moving from the above definitions we can define an argument scheme as:

Definition 15 (Argument Scheme). *An* ***argument scheme*** s *has the form:* $s : P_1, ..., P_n, \sim P'_1, ..., \sim P'_m \Rightarrow Q$ *with* $0 \leq n, m$*, and where*

- *each* $P_1, \ldots, P_n, P'_1, \ldots, P'_m \in \mathcal{M} \cup \mathcal{O}$*, while* $Q \in \mathcal{M}$
- $\sim P$ *denotes weak negation (negation by failure) of* P*—i.e.,* P *is an exception that would block the application of the rule whose antecedent includes* $\sim P$
- *we denote with* CQ_s *the set of critical questions associated to scheme* s.

Using argument schemes we can build meta-arguments:

Definition 16 (Meta-Argument). *A* ***meta-argument*** *A constructed from a set of argument schemes S and an object-level argumentation graph G is a finite construct of the form:* $A: A_1, \ldots A_n \Rightarrow_s P$ *with* $0 \leq n$*, where*

- *A is the argument's unique identifier;*
- $s \in S$ *is the scheme used to build the argument;*
- $A_1, \ldots, A_n$ *are arguments constructed from S and G;*
- *P is the* conclusion *of the argument, denoted by* $\mathsf{Conc}(A)$*;*
- *we denote with* $CQ(A)$ *the critical questions associated to scheme s.*

The same notation introduced for standard arguments in Notation 2 applies also to meta-arguments. We can now define attacks over meta-arguments.

Definition 17 (Meta-Attack). *An argument A* ***attacks*** *argument B (on B′) iff*

- $\mathsf{Conc}(A) = \bar{P}$ *for some* $B' \in \mathsf{Sub}(B)$ *of the form* $B''_1, \ldots, B''_M \Rightarrow P$ *or*
- $\mathsf{Conc}(A) = P$ *for some* $B' \in \mathsf{Sub}(B)$ *such that* $\sim P \in$ *Antecedent* $(\mathsf{TopRule}(B'))$.

The same definition of *argumentation graph* and *labellings* introduced for standard argumentation in Definitions 8, 9, 10 also holds for meta-arguments and for the meta level.

3 Burden of Persuasion as Meta-argumentation

Informally, we can say that when we talk about the notion of the burden of persuasion concerning an argument, we intuitively argue over that argument according to a meta-argumentative approach.

Let us consider, for instance, an argument A: if we allocate the burden over it, we implicitly impose the duty to prove its admissibility on A. Thus, moving the analysis up to the meta level of the argumentation process, it is like having two arguments, let them be F_{BP} and S_{BP}, reflecting the burden of persuasion status. According to this perspective, F_{BP} states that "the burden is not satisfied if A *fails* to prove its admissibility" – i.e. A should be rejected or undefined – and, of course, F_{BP} is not compatible with A being accepted. Alongside, S_{BP} states that "A is admissible since it *satisfies* its burden". F_{BP} and S_{BP} have a contrasting conclusion and thus they attack each other.

Analysing the burden from this perspective makes immediately clear that the notions that the meta model should deal with are:

N.1 the notion of the burden itself expressing the possibility for an argument to be allocated with a burden of persuasion (i.e., *burdened argument*)
N.2 the possibility that this burden is satisfied (that is, a *burden met*) or not satisfied
N.3 the possibility of making *attacks* involving burdened arguments ineffective.

The outline of that multi-part evaluation scheme for burdens of persuasion in argumentation is now visible and can be formally designed. In the following, we formally define these concepts by exploiting bimodal argument graphs as techniques for expressing the two main levels of the model – meta level and object level – and the relationships between the two.

In particular, we are going to define each set of the bimodal argument graph tuple $\langle \mathcal{A}_O, \mathcal{A}_M, \mathcal{R}_O, \mathcal{R}_M, \mathcal{S}_A, \mathcal{S}_R \rangle$. With respect to $\mathcal{A}_O$ and $\mathcal{R}_O$, representing respectively the set of object-level arguments and attacks, they are built accordingly to the argumentation framework discussed in Subsect. 2.1. Hence, our analysis focuses on the meta-level graph $\langle \mathcal{A}_M, \mathcal{R}_M \rangle$ and on the support sets connecting the two levels ($\mathcal{S}_A$ and $\mathcal{S}_R$).

3.1 Meta-level Graph

We now proceed to detail all the argumentation schemes used to build arguments in the meta-level graph. Every scheme comes along with its critical questions.

Let us first introduce the basic argumentation scheme enabling the definition and representation of an argument with an allocation of the burden of persuasion (i.e., reifying **N.1**). We say that an object-level argument A has the burden of persuasion on it if exists an object-level argument B such that $\mathsf{Conc}(B) = bp(\mathsf{Conc}(A))$. This notion is modelled through the following argument scheme:

$$conclusion(A, \phi), conclusion(B, bp(\phi)) \Rightarrow burdened(A) \qquad (\mathsf{S0})$$

$$\textit{Are arguments } A \textit{ and } B \textit{ provable?} \qquad (\mathsf{CQ_{S0}})$$

where $bp(\phi)$ is a predicate stating ϕ is a literal with the allocation of the burden, $conclusion(A, \phi)$ is a structural meta-predicate stating that $\mathsf{Conc}(A) = \phi$ holds, and $burdened(A)$ is a meta-predicate representing the allocation of the burden on A. Of course an argument produced using this scheme holds only if both the arguments A and B on which the inference is based hold—critical question $\mathsf{CQ_{S0}}$.

Analogously, we introduce the scheme S1 representing the absence of such an allocation:

$$conclusion(A, \phi), \sim conclusion(B, bp(\phi)) \Rightarrow \neg burdened(A) \qquad (\mathsf{S1})$$

$$\textit{Is argument } A \textit{ provable? Is argument } B \textit{ really unprovable?} \qquad (\mathsf{CQ_{S1}})$$

Then, as informally introduced at the beginning of this section, we have two schemes reflecting the possibility for a burdened argument to meet or not the burden (**N.2**).

$$burdened(A) \Rightarrow bp\_met(A) \qquad (\mathsf{S2})$$

$$burdened(A) \Rightarrow \neg bp\_met(A) \qquad (\mathsf{S3})$$

$$\textit{Is argument } A \textit{ admissible?} \qquad (\mathsf{CQ_{S2}})$$

$$\textit{Is argument } A \textit{ refuted or undecidable?} \qquad (\mathsf{CQ_{S3}})$$

where *bp_met* is the meta-predicate stating the burden has been met. It is important to notice that these two schemes reach opposite conclusions from the same grounds—i.e., the presence of the burden on argument A. The discriminating elements are the critical questions they are accompanied by. In the case of S2, we have that only if exists a burden of persuasion on argument A, and A is admissible ($\mathsf{CQ}_{\mathsf{S3}}$), then the burden is satisfied. On the other side, the validity of S3 is linked to the missing admissibility of argument A. We will see in Sect. 3.3 how the meta-arguments and the associated questions concur to determine the model results.

Let us now consider attacks between arguments and their relation with the burden of persuasion allocation. When a burdened argument fails to meet the burden, the only thing affecting the argument acceptability is the burden itself—i.e., attacks from other arguments do not influence the burdened argument status that only depends on its inability to satisfy the burden. The same applies to attacks issued by an argument that fails to meet the burden: the failure implies the argument rejection and, as a direct consequence, the inability to effectively attack other arguments. In order to capture the nuance to differentiate among effective or ineffective object level attacks w.r.t the concept of burden of persuasion (**N.3**), we define the following scheme:

$$attack(B, A), \sim(\neg bp\_met(A)), \sim(\neg bp\_met(B)) \Rightarrow effectiveAttack(B, A) \qquad (\mathsf{S4})$$

Can we prove arguments A or B not fail to meet their burden? $(\mathsf{CQ}_{\mathsf{S4}})$

where *attack* is a structural meta-predicate stating an attack relation at the object level, while *effectiveAttack* is a meta-predicate expressing that an attack should be taken into consideration according to the burden of persuasion allocation. In other words, if an object-level attack involves burdened arguments, and one of these fail to satisfy the burden, then the attack is considered not effective w.r.t. the allocation of the burden.

Discussed schemes can be used to create a meta-level graph containing all the information concerning constraints related to the burden of persuasion concept thus leading to a clear separation of concerns, as demonstrated in the following example.

Example 1 (Base Example). Let us consider two object-level arguments A and B, concluding the literals a and $bp(a)$ respectively. Using the schemes in Subsect. 3.1 we can build the following meta-level arguments:

- A_{S0} representing the allocation of the burden on argument A.
- A_{S1} and B_{S1} standing for the absence of a burden on arguments A and B respectively. The scheme used to build those arguments exploits weak negation in order to cover those scenarios in which an argument concluding a *bp* literal exists at the object-level, but it is found not admissible.
- A_{S2} and A_{S3} sustaining that *i)* A was capable of meeting the burden on it, *ii)* A was not capable of meeting its burden.

The meta-level graph (Fig. 1) points out the relations actually implicit in the notion of burden of persuasion over an argument, where, intuitively, we argue over the consequences of A's possibly succeeding/failing to meet the burden. At the meta level, all the possible scenarios can be explored by applying different semantics over the meta-level graph.

Considering for instance the Dung's preferred semantics [1], we can obtain two distinct outcomes: the burden is not satisfied, i.e., argument A_{S3} is accepted, and consequently, A_{S2} is rejected, or we succeed in proving A_{S2}, i.e., the burden is met and A_{S3} is rejected (A_{S0}, A_{S1} are accepted and rejected accordingly). Although the discussed example is really simple – only basic schemes for reasoning on the burden are considered at the meta-level – it clearly demonstrates the possibility of reasoning over the burdens, i.e., establishes whether or not there is a burden on a literal ϕ – argument B in the example – and enables the evaluation of the consequences of a burdened argument to meet or not its burden.

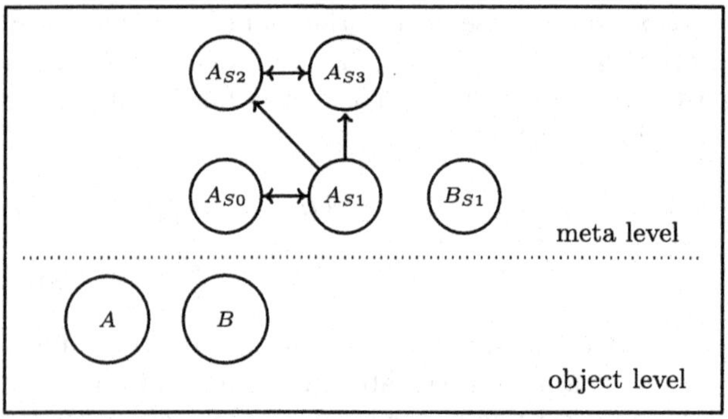

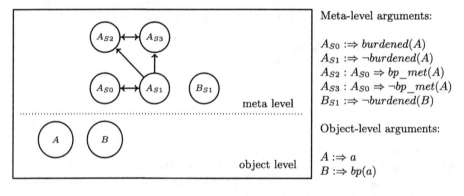

Meta-level arguments:

$A_{S0} :\Rightarrow burdened(A)$
$A_{S1} :\Rightarrow \neg burdened(A)$
$A_{S2} : A_{S0} \Rightarrow bp\_met(A)$
$A_{S3} : A_{S0} \Rightarrow \neg bp\_met(A)$
$B_{S1} :\Rightarrow \neg burdened(B)$

Object-level arguments:

$A :\Rightarrow a$
$B :\Rightarrow bp(a)$

Fig. 1. Argumentation graph (object- and meta-level) for Example 1

3.2 Object and Meta Level Connection: Supporting Sets

Let us now define how the meta level and the object level interact. Indeed, it is not enough to reason on the consequences of the burden of persuasion allocation only concerning the burdened argument, but the results of the argument satisfying or not such a burden constraint should affect the entire object-level graph. According to the standard bimodal graph theory, defining how the object level and the meta level interact is the role of the argument support relation $\mathcal{S}_A$ and of the attack support relation $\mathcal{S}_R$ respectively. According to Definition 11 (Subsect. 2.2), every node at level n is connected to an argument at level $n+1$ by a support edge in $\mathcal{S}_A$ or $\mathcal{S}_R$ depending on whether the node is an argument or an attack.

Let us define the support set $\mathcal{S}_A$ of meta arguments supporting object-level arguments as:

$$\begin{aligned} \mathcal{S}_A = &\{(Arg_1, Arg_2) \mid Arg_1 \in \mathcal{A}_M, Arg_2 \in \mathcal{A}_O, \\ &(\mathsf{Conc}(Arg_1) = bp\_met(Arg_2) \vee \mathsf{Conc}(Arg_1) = \neg burdened(Arg_2))\} \end{aligned}$$

Intuitively, an argument A at the object level is supported by arguments at the meta level claiming that the burden on A is satisfied (S2) or that there is no burden allocated on it (S1).

The set $\mathcal{S}_R$ of meta arguments supporting object-level attacks is defined as:

$$\mathcal{S}_R = \{(Arg_1, (B, A)) \mid Arg_1 \in \mathcal{A}_M, (B, A) \in \mathcal{R}_O, \mathsf{Conc}(Arg_1) = \mathit{effectiveAttack}(B, A)\}$$

In other words, an object-level attack is supported by arguments at the meta level claiming its effectiveness w.r.t. the burden of persuasion allocation (S4).

3.3 Equivalence with Burden of Persuasion Semantics

The defined meta-framework can be used to achieve the same results of the original burden of persuasion labelling semantics [3].

Let us first introduce the notion of *CQ-consistency* for a bimodal argumentation graph G.

Definition 18 (CQ-consistency). *Let $G = \langle \mathcal{A}_O, \mathcal{A}_M, \mathcal{R}_O, \mathcal{R}_M, \mathcal{S}_A, \mathcal{S}_R \rangle$ be a bimodal argumentation graph and let $L_S(G)$ be a labelling-based semantics. P is the set of corresponding L_S-perspectives. A perspective $p \in P$ is CQ-consistent if every* IN *argument A in the corresponding meta-level labelling satisfies its critical questions ($CQ(A)$).*

Using this new definition we can introduce the concept of *BP-perspective.*

Definition 19 (BP-perspective). *Let $G = \langle \mathcal{A}_O, \mathcal{A}_M, \mathcal{R}_O, \mathcal{R}_M, \mathcal{S}_A, \mathcal{S}_R \rangle$ be a bimodal argumentation graph, and P the set of its L_{stable}-perspectives* [1]. *We say that $p \in P$ is a BP-perspective of G iff w.r.t. the results given by the grounded evaluation of p, p is CQ-consistent.*

Proposition 1 *If $\nexists (A, B) \in \mathcal{R}_O$ such that both A and B have a burden of persuasion on them, the results yielded by the grounded evaluation of G's BP-perspectives are congruent with the evaluation of the object-level graph $\langle \mathcal{A}_O, \mathcal{R}_O \rangle$ under the grounded-bp semantics as presented in* [3].

Example 2 (Antidiscrimination law example). Let us consider a case in which a woman claims to have been discriminated against in her career on the basis of her sex, as she was passed over by male colleagues when promotions came available (`ev1`), and brings evidence showing that in her company all managerial positions are held by men (`ev3`), even though the company's personnel includes many equally qualified women, having worked for a long time in the company, and with equal or better performance (`ev2`). Assume that this practice is deemed to indicate the existence of gender-based discrimination and that the employer fails to provide prevailing evidence that the woman was not discriminated against. It seems that it may be concluded that the woman was indeed discriminated against on the basis of her sex.

Consider, for instance, the following formalisation of the European nondiscrimination law:

$$\begin{array}{lll} e1 : ev1 & e2 : ev2 & e3 : ev3 \\ er1 : ev1 \Rightarrow indiciaDiscrim & er2 : ev2 \Rightarrow \neg discrim & er3 : ev3 \Rightarrow discrim \\ r1 : indiciaDiscrim \Rightarrow bp(\neg discrim) & & \end{array}$$

We can then build the following object-level arguments:

$$\begin{array}{lll} A_0 :\Rightarrow ev1 & B_0 :\Rightarrow ev2 & C_0 :\Rightarrow ev3 \\ A_1 : A_0 \Rightarrow indiciaDiscrim & B_1 : B_0 \Rightarrow \neg discrim & C_1 : C_0 \Rightarrow discrim \\ A_2 : A_1 \Rightarrow bp(\neg discrim) & & \end{array}$$

and the following meta-level arguments:

$$\begin{array}{ll} A_{0_{S1}} :\Rightarrow -burdened(A_0) & B_{0}{}_{S1} :\Rightarrow -burdened(B_0) \\ A_{1_{S1}} :\Rightarrow -burdened(A_1) & B_{1_{S0}} :\Rightarrow burdened(B_1) \\ A_{2_{S1}} :\Rightarrow -burdened(A_2) & B_{1_{S1}} :\Rightarrow -burdened(B_1) \\ C_{0_{S1}} :\Rightarrow -burdened(C_0) & B_{1_{S2}} : B_{1_{S0}} \Rightarrow bp\_met(B_1) \\ C_{1_{S1}} :\Rightarrow -burdened(C_1) & B_{1_{S3}} : B_{1_{S0}} \Rightarrow \neg bp\_met(B_1) \\ C_1B_{1_{S4}} :\Rightarrow effectiveAttack(C_1, B_1) & B_1C_{1_{S4}} :\Rightarrow effectiveAttack(B_1, C_1) \end{array}$$

The resulting graph is depicted in Fig. 2. In this case, at the object-level, since there are indicia of discrimination (A_1), we can infer the allocation of the burden on non-discrimination (A_2). Moreover, we can build both arguments for discrimination (C_1) and non-discrimination (B_1), leading to a situation of undecidability.

At the meta level we can apply the rule S1 for every argument at the object level ($A_{0_{S1}}, A_{1_{S1}}, A_{2_{S1}}, B_{0}{}_{S1}, B_{1_{S0}}, C_{0_{S1}}, C_{1_{S1}}$) – where we can establish the absence of the burden for all of them –, and the rule S4 for every attack ($C_1B_{1_{S4}}, B_1C_{1_{S4}}$). By exploiting B_1 and A_2, we can also apply schema S0, and consequently rules S2 and S3. In a few words, we are concluding the meta argumentative structure given by the allocation of the burden of persuasion on argument B_1.

We can now apply the stable labelling to the meta-level graph, thus obtaining three distinct results. For clarity reasons, in the following we ignore the arguments that are admissible under every solution.

1. IN $= \{B_{1_{S1}}, C_1B_{1_{S4}}, B_1C_{1_{S4}}\}$, OUT $= \{B_{1_{S0}}, B_{1_{S2}}, B_{1_{S3}}\}$, UND $= \{\}$—i.e., B_1 is not burdened;
2. IN $= \{B_{1_{S0}}, B_{1_{S2}}, C_1B_{1_{S4}}, B_1C_{1_{S4}}\}$, OUT $= \{B_{1_{S1}}, B_{1_{S3}}\}$, UND $= \{\}$—i.e., B_1 is burdened and the burden is met;
3. IN $= \{B_{1_{S0}}, B_{1_{S3}}\}$, OUT $= \{B_{1_{S1}}, B_{1_{S2}}, C_1B_{1_{S4}}, B_1C_{1_{S4}}\}$, UND $= \{\}$—i.e., B_1 is burdened and the burden is not met.

Then, the meta-level results can be reified to the object-level perspectives taking into account the *CQ* we have to impose on the solutions and the results given by the perspective evaluation under the grounded semantics. Let us first consider solutions 1 and 2. They lead to the same perspective on the object-level graph—the graph remains unchanged w.r.t. the original graph. If we consider the critical questions attached to the IN arguments, both these solutions are not admissible. Indeed, according to solution 1 the burden is not allocated on argument B_1, but this is in contrast with argument A_2's conclusion (A_2 is IN under grounded labelling)—i.e., CQ_{S1} is not satisfied. Analogously, solution 2 concludes that B_1 is allocated with the burden and its success to meet the burden, but at the same time, argument B_1 is found undecidable at the object level (B_1 is UND under the grounded semantics)—i.e., CQ_{S2} is not satisfied.

The only acceptable result is the one given by solution 3. In this case, argument B_1 is not capable to meet the burden – ${B_1}_{S3}$ is IN – and, consequently, it is rejected and deleted from the perspective. Indeed, CQ_{S3} is satisfied. As a consequence, argument C_1 is labelled IN. In other words, the argument for non-discrimination fails and the argument for discrimination is accepted.

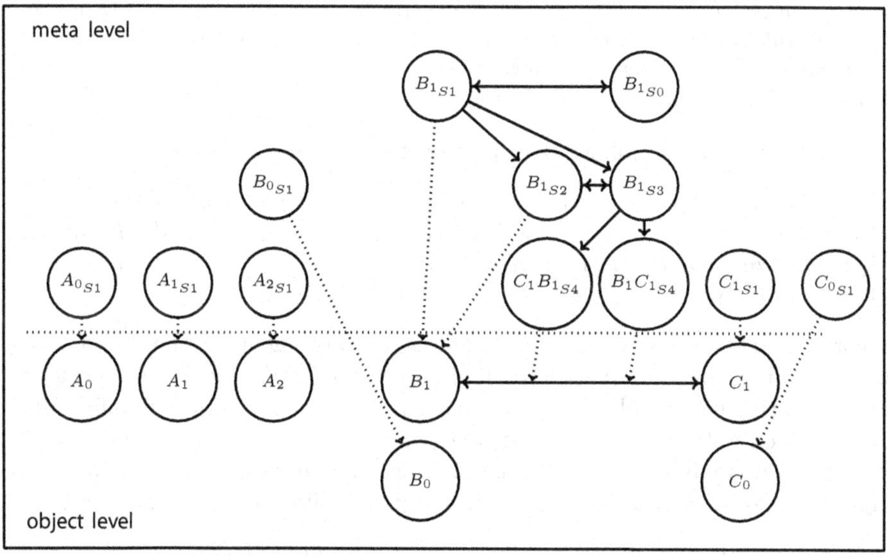

Fig. 2. Argumentation graph (object- and meta-level) for Example 2

4 Burden Inversion

Let us consider a situation in which one argument A is presented for a claim ϕ being burdened, and A (or one of its subarguments) is attacked by a counterargument B, of which the conclusion ψ is also burdened. Intuitively, if both arguments fail to satisfy the burden of persuasion, we would have to reject both of them. This is not the case if we take into account the inversion of the burden [2]—i.e., if no convincing argument for ψ is found, then the attack fails, and the uncertainty on ψ does not affect the status of A. Accordingly, B is rejected for failing to meet its burden, thus leaving A free to be accepted also if it was not able to satisfy the burden of persuasion in the beginning.

The model we propose in this work is able to correctly deal with the inversion of the proof, as we discuss in the next example adapted from [2].

Example 3 (Inversion of the burden of proof). Let us consider a case in which a doctor caused harm to a patient by misdiagnosing his case. Assume that there is no doubt that the doctor harmed the patient, but it is uncertain whether the doctor followed the guidelines governing this case. Assume that, under the applicable law, doctors are liable for any harm suffered by their patients, but they can avoid liability if they show that they exercised due care in treating the patient. Let also assume that a doctor is considered to be diligent if he/she follows the medical guidelines that govern the case. The doctor has to provide a convincing argument that he/she was diligent, and the patient has to provide a convincing argument for the doctor's liability.

We can formalise the case as follows:

$f1 : guidelines \quad f2 : \neg guidelines \quad f3 : harm$
$r1 : \neg guidelines \Rightarrow \neg dueDiligence \quad r2 : guidelines \Rightarrow \neg dueDiligence$
$r3 : harm, \sim dueDiligence \Rightarrow liable$
$bp1 : bp(dueDiligence) \quad bp2 : bp(liable)$

We can then build the following object-level arguments:

$A_0 :\Rightarrow bp(dueDiligence) \quad A_1 :\Rightarrow bp(liable) \quad A_2 :\Rightarrow guidelines$
$A_3 :\Rightarrow harm \quad A_4 :\Rightarrow \neg guidelines \quad A_5 : A_2 \Rightarrow dueDiligence$
$A_1 : A_0 \Rightarrow indiciaDiscrim \quad B_1 : B_0 \Rightarrow \neg discrim \quad C_1 : C_0 \Rightarrow discrim$
$A_6 : A_3 \Rightarrow liable \quad A_7 : A_4 \Rightarrow \neg dueDiligence$

According to the original burden semantics, the argument for the doctor's due diligence (A_5) fails to meet its burden of persuasion. Consequently, following the inversion principle, it fails to defeat the argument for the doctor's liability (A_6), which is then able to meet its burden of persuasion.

Let's now analyse the case under the meta-model perspective. Using argument schemes defined in Sect. 3 we can build the following meta-arguments:

$A_{0_{S1}} :\Rightarrow -burdened(A_0) \quad A_{1_{S1}} :\Rightarrow -burdened(A_1)$
$A_{2_{S1}} :\Rightarrow -burdened(A_2) \quad A_{3_{S1}} :\Rightarrow -burdened(A_3)$
$A_{4_{S1}} :\Rightarrow -burdened(A_4) \quad A_{7_{S1}} :\Rightarrow -burdened(A_7)$
$A_2A_{7_{S4}} :\Rightarrow effectiveAttack(A_2, A_7) \quad A_2A_{4_{S4}} :\Rightarrow effectiveAttack(A_2, A_4)$
$A_4A_{2_{S4}} :\Rightarrow effectiveAttack(A_4, A_2)$
$A_7A_{5_{S4}} :\Rightarrow effectiveAttack(A_7, A_5) \quad A_5A_{7_{S4}} :\Rightarrow effectiveAttack(A_5, A_7)$
$A_4A_{5_{S4}} :\Rightarrow effectiveAttack(A_4, A_5) \quad A_5A_{6_{S4}} :\Rightarrow effectiveAttack(A_5, A_6)$
$A_{5_{S0}} :\Rightarrow burdened(A_5) \quad A_{5_{S1}} :\Rightarrow -burdened(A_5)$
$A_{5_{S2}} : A_{5_{S0}} \Rightarrow bp\_met(A_5) \quad A_{5_{S3}} : A_{5_{S0}} \Rightarrow \neg bp\_met(A_5)$
$A_{6_{S0}} :\Rightarrow burdened(A_6) \quad A_{6_{S1}} :\Rightarrow -burdened(A_6)$
$A_{6_{S2}} : A_{6_{S0}} \Rightarrow bp\_met(A_6) \quad A_{6_{S3}} : A_{6_{S0}} \Rightarrow \neg bp\_met(A_6)$

Connecting the object- and meta- level arguments we obtain the graph in Fig. 3. Let us now consider the extensions obtained applying stable semantics to the meta-level graph:

1. $\{A_{6_{S0}}, A_{6_{S2}}, A_{5_{S0}}, A_{5_{S3}}\}$
2. $\{A_{6_{S0}}, A_{6_{S3}}, A_{5_{S0}}, A_{5_{S3}}\}$

3. $\{A6_{S0}, A6_{S2}, A5_{S0}, A5_{S2}, A_5A6_{S4}, A_5A7_{S4}, A_7A5_{S4}, A_4A5_{S4}\}$
4. $\{A6_{S0}, A6_{S3}, A5_{S0}, A5_{S2}, A_5A7_{S4}, A_7A5_{S4}, A_4A5_{S4}\}$
5. $\{A6_{S0}, A6_{S2}, A5_{S1}, A_5A6_{S4}, A_5A7_{S4}, A_7A5_{S4}, A_4A5_{S4}\}$
6. $\{A6_{S0}, A6_{S3}, A5_{S1}, A_5A7_{S4}, A_7A5_{S4}, A_4A5_{S4}\}$
7. $\{A6_{S1}, A5_{S0}, A5_{S2}, A_5A6_{S4}, A_5A7_{S4}, A_7A5_{S4}, A_4A5_{S4}\}$
8. $\{A6_{S1}, A5_{S1}, A_5A6_{S4}, A_5A7_{S4}, A_7A5_{S4}, A_4A5_{S4}\}$
9. $\{A6_{S1}, A5_{S0}, A5_{S3}\}$

The only extensions that produce a CQ-consistent perspective are the first and the second, all the others violate at least one of the constraints imposed by the critical questions—e.g. CQ_{S1} for $5, 6, 7, 8, 9$ and CQ_{S2} for $3, 4$. The first perspective acts exactly like the original semantics from [2]—i.e., the argument for the doctor's due diligence (A_5) fails to meet the burden ($A5_{S3}$), and consequently, the argument for doctor's liability (A_6) is able to satisfy its own burden ($A6_{S2}$). However, the model delivers a second result according to which both A_5 and A_6 fail to meet their burden of persuasion ($A6_{S3}$ and $A5_{S3}$). It is the result that we would have expected in absence of the inversion principle.

The example highlights the meta-argumentation model is able to provide both a solution that follows the inversion principle and the one not considering it. When the inversion principle is taken into account the number of burdened arguments are maximised in the final extension. Accordingly, we can provide a generalisation of Property 1:

Proposition 2. *Given the results yielded by the grounded evaluation of G's BP-perspectives, the results that maximise the number of burdened arguments in the* IN *set are congruent with the evaluation of the object-level graph $\langle \mathcal{A}_O, \mathcal{R}_O \rangle$ under the grounded-bp semantics as presented in* [3].

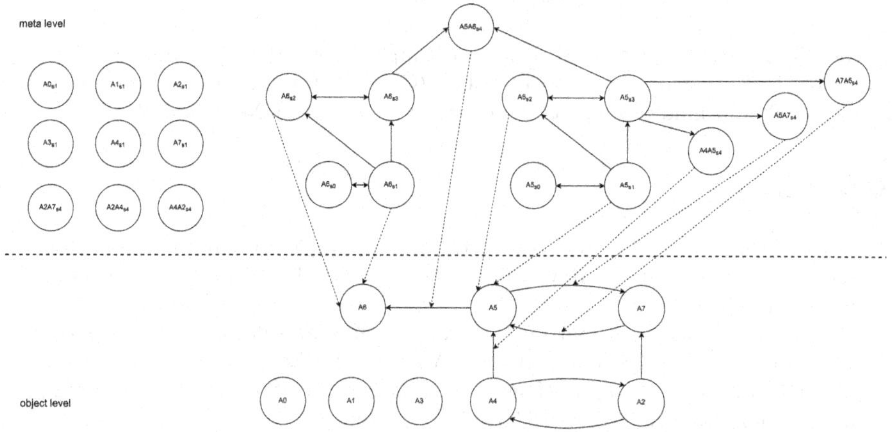

Fig. 3. Argumentation graph (object- and meta-level) for Example 3

5 Conclusions

In this paper we present a meta-argumentation approach for the burden of persuasion in argumentation. Our approach relies on the work from [6, 7] introducing the required abstraction at the meta level. In particular, [6] presents the first formalisation of meta-argumentation synthesising bimodal graphs, structured argumentation, and argument schemes in a unique framework. There, a formal definition of the meta-ASPIC framework is provided as a model for representing object arguments. Along the same line, [7] exploits bimodal graphs for dealing with arguments sources' trust. In [7] ASPIC+ is used instead of meta-ASPIC at the object level and on a set of meta-predicates related to the object level arguments and the schemes in the meta level, as in our approach. Both [6] and [7] use critical questions for managing attacks at the meta level.

Our framework and its model mix the two approaches exploiting bimodal graphs in ASPIC+ and defining all the burdens abstractions at the meta-level. The reification of the meta level at the object level allows the concept of burden of persuasion to be properly dealt with—i.e., arguments burdened with persuasion have to be rejected when there is uncertainty about them. As a consequence, those arguments become irrelevant to the argumentation framework including them: not only they fail to be included in the set of the accepted arguments, but they also are unable to affect the status of the arguments they attack.

We show how this model easily deals with all the nuances of burdens – e.g., reasoning over the concept of the burden itself –, thus leading to a full-fledged, interoperable framework open to further extensions. Moreover, the model correctly deals with the inversion of the burden of proof.

Future research will be devoted to study the properties of our meta framework and the connection of our framework with meta-ASPIC for argumentation. We also plan to investigate on the way our model fits into legal procedures and enables their rational reconstruction.

Acknowledgements. The work has been supported by the "CompuLaw" project, funded by the European Research Council (ERC) under the European Union's Horizon 2020 research and innovation programme (Grant Agreement No. 833647).

References

1. Baroni, P., Caminada, M., Giacomin, M.: An introduction to argumentation semantics. Knowl. Eng. Rev. **26**(4), 365–410 (2011). https://doi.org/10.1017/S0269888911000166
2. Calegari, R., Riveret, R., Sartor, G.: The burden of persuasion in structured argumentation. In: Maranhão, J., Wyner, A.Z. (eds.) 17th International Conference on Artificial Intelligence and Law (ICAIL 2021), pp. 180–184. ACM, June 2021. https://doi.org/10.1145/3462757.3466078
3. Calegari, R., Sartor, G.: A model for the burden of persuasion in argumentation. In: Villata, S., Harašta, J., Křemen, P. (eds.) Legal Knowledge and Information Systems, Frontiers in Artificial Intelligence and Applications, vol. 334, pp. 13–22. IOS Press, Brno (2020). https://doi.org/10.3233/FAIA200845

4. Caminada, M., Amgoud, L.: On the evaluation of argumentation formalisms. Artif. Intell. **171**(5–6), 286–310 (2007). https://doi.org/10.1016/j.artint.2007.02.003
5. Modgil, S., Prakken, H.: The ASPIC$^+$ framework for structured argumentation: a tutorial. Argument Comput. **5**(1), 31–62 (2014). https://doi.org/10.1080/19462166.2013.869766
6. Müller, J., Hunter, A., Taylor, P.: Meta-level argumentation with argument schemes. In: Liu, W., Subrahmanian, V.S., Wijsen, J. (eds.) SUM 2013. LNCS (LNAI), vol. 8078, pp. 92–105. Springer, Heidelberg (2013). https://doi.org/10.1007/978-3-642-40381-1_8
7. Ogunniye, G., Toniolo, A., Oren, N.: Meta-argumentation frameworks for multiparty dialogues. In: Miller, T., Oren, N., Sakurai, Y., Noda, I., Savarimuthu, B.T.R., Cao Son, T. (eds.) PRIMA 2018. LNCS (LNAI), vol. 11224, pp. 585–593. Springer, Cham (2018). https://doi.org/10.1007/978-3-030-03098-8_45
8. Prakken, H.: Ai & law, logic and argument schemes. Argumentation **19**(3), 303–320 (2005). https://doi.org/10.1007/s10503-005-4418-7
9. Prakken, H.: An abstract framework for argumentation with structured arguments. Argument Comput. **1**(2), 93–124 (2010). https://doi.org/10.1080/19462160903564592
10. Vreeswijk, G.: Abstract argumentation systems. Artif. Intell. **90**(1–2), 225–279 (1997). https://doi.org/10.1016/S0004-3702(96)00041-0
11. Walton, D., Reed, C., Macagno, F.: Argumentation Schemes. Cambridge University Press, UK (2008). https://doi.org/10.1017/CBO9780511802034

Knowledge Representation, Reasoning, and Learning

Reasoning About Smart Contracts Encoded in LTL

Valeria Fionda(✉), Gianluigi Greco, and Marco Antonio Mastratisi

DeMaCS, University of Calabria, Rende, Italy
{fionda,greco,mastratisi}@mat.unical.it

Abstract. Smart contracts are programs deployed on blockchains that automatically execute when some conditions are verified to satisfy the terms of an agreement. They are usually programmed in procedural languages even if some recent proposals use logic for their specification and verification. However, existing logic-based initiatives only enable the formal checking of properties of a single smart contract independently from the other smart contracts running on the same blockchain. This paper proposes a framework, called SCRea, that works on a set of smart contracts encoded in Linear Temporal Logics. SCRea can work offline or at runtime to verify whether the execution of each smart contract is compatible with the execution of the others and, in case, provides a particular order of execution ensuring that the preconditions of each smart contract are verified before its execution.

Keywords: Smart contracts · Linear temporal logic · Reasoning

1 Introduction

Distributed Ledger Technologies (DLT) [1] offers an infrastructure (technologies, processes and protocols) for the synchronized and shared management of data regulated via consensus algorithms. DLTs allow for the deployment and execution of smart contracts, that are programs stored within the distributed register of the DLT, that are automatically executed when certain conditions occur. The effect of the execution of a smart contract is, in general, the alteration of the state of the register corresponding to the addition of a new transaction. Some examples of smart contract application include banking functions (see e.g. Automated Escrow, Savings), decentralized markets (e.g. OpenBazaar, EtherMarket), prediction markets (Augur, Gnosis), distribution of music royalties (Ujo) and encoding of virtual property (Ascribe).

Smart contracts in blockchains are typically programmed in a procedural language (e.g., Solidity[1]) even if some initiatives exist in the literature for the formalization of smart contracts in logic (e.g., [2–4]). Formalizing a smart contract using a declarative language allows to specify what has to be done and

[1] https://docs.soliditylang.org/en/v0.8.7/.

S. Bandini et al. (Eds.): AIxIA 2021, LNAI 13196, pp. 123–136, 2022.
https://doi.org/10.1007/978-3-031-08421-8_9

how to do it, instead of specifying the exact sequence of steps to be followed. However, existing initiatives thag use logic to formalize smart contracts, only enable the formal checking of the correctness and some other properties of a single smart contract independently from the other smart contracts running on the same blockchain and the state of the blockchain itself.

In this paper we try to fill this gap by focusing on the application of linear temporal logic on finite traces (LTL_f) [23], with past operators, as a high-level logical tool for the formalization, validation and resolution of any conflicts in the execution of smart contracts running on the same blockchain infrastructure. In our framework, called SCREA, each smart contract is characterized by a set of preconditions and an effect obtained by the execution of the smart contract, where effects are visible on the blockchain immediately when the smart contract is activated or, at most, at the subsequent time instant. SCREA will enable, given a set of smart contracts, to verify whether the execution of each of them is compatible with the execution of the others. If so, the framework also allows to establish a particular order of execution that ensures that the preconditions of each smart contract are verified before its execution. Therefore, SCREA provides a useful tool to perform formal verification by demonstrating or refuting the compatibility of a set of smart contracts, and checking the formal (mathematical) model obtained against their formal specification in LTL_f.

Moreover, we also studied the applicability of SCREA for the identification of conflict situations at runtime. Verification at runtime checks the properties of a running system and deals with one execution trace at a time. In the domain of smart contracts, the term trace denotes a sequence of events executed by a blockchain or a sequence of function or event invocations issued by one or more smart contracts. The availability of information at runtime helps dynamic verification techniques to mitigate one of the main obstacles in the analysis of smart contracts: the need to model a complex blockchain execution environment.

The rest of the paper is organized as follows. In Sect. 2 we introduce some preliminary definitions. The encoding of smart contracts in linear temporal logic is discussed in Sect. 3 while Sect. 4 reports about reasoning problems that are enabled by our encoding. The SCREA framework is described in Sect. 5 and Sect. 6 will conclude the paper.

2 Preliminaries

2.1 Smart Contracts

Distributed Ledger Technologies (DLT) is a set of technologies, processes and protocols for the synchronized and shared management of a register by a network of nodes. In DLTs data is shared and controlled by several actors at the same time and the authorization to modify data is regulated via consensus algorithms.

The blockchain is a particular type of DLT in which new values of data are concatenated to those previously accepted thus forming a "chain of blocks". Each block contains the value and the respective alphanumeric sequence. There is the possibility that various participants propose different values at the same time instant, originating a double chain, called a fork, from a certain block onwards. In this case, through a distributed consensus algorithm, the community decides to eliminate one of the two branches. Examples of implementations of blockchain are Bitcoin [5] and Ethereum [6], that manage the exchange of cryptocurrency.

Smart contracts [7] are programs stored within the distributed register that automatically executed when certain conditions occur. In many cases, the effect of the execution of a smart contract is the alteration of the state of the register in terms of a new transaction. (e.g., transfer of cryptocurrency amounts or activation of other contracts). Once the contractual clauses have been correctly inserted in the code of a smart contract and this has been accepted by the contractors, the effects are no longer linked to their will or to the action of intermediaries. The DLT hosting the smart contract guarantees that the code is not modified and that the inputs come from identified sources. A smart contract can be implemented through specific languages of the host DLT platform, such as Solidity [8] for Ethereum, or in some cases using high-level languages such as Javascript, Java, Golang, and Python.

2.2 Linear Temporal Logic with Past Operators

Linear temporal logic, denoted by LTL, is a modal logic introduced in the 1970s as a formal tool for verifying the correctness of computer programs and reactive systems [9,10]. Since then, it has found applications in several fields of artificial intelligence and computer science, including planning [11–13], robotics and control theory [14,15], the management of business processes [16,17] and temporal querying of data [18]. LTL is a modal logic whose modalities are temporal operators related to events that occur at particular time instants on an ordered timeline. Classically, LTL formulas are interpreted on infinite traces, but there are some applications where is more appropriate to focus on interpretations on finite traces [20–22]. Indeed, a liner temporal logic endowed with this semantics, denoted by LTL_f, has been recently studied [19,23,24].

Syntax. In this section we discuss the syntax of a variant of LTL_f that allows for time operators looking both to the future and to the past, and that therefore allow to verify the validity of conditions expressed on time instants preceding or following the current one. For this purpose let's suppose that a universe V of propositional variables is given. An LTL_f formula φ is built on propositional variables in V using boolean connectives $\wedge$, $\vee$, $\neg$ as well as a number of time operators. Time operators can be divided into two categories: future temporal operators and past temporal operators. For the scope of this paper we will focus on a specific fragment of LTL_f which includes the future temporal operator X (next) and the past temporal operators Y (previous), H (always in the past), P (in the past), S (since). Moreover, we assume that the negation is atomic in φ in the sense that it is applied directly only to propositional variables (events). More formally, the formula φ is constructed according to the following grammar:

$$\varphi ::= x \mid \neg x \mid (\varphi \wedge \varphi) \mid (\varphi \vee \varphi) \mid X(\varphi) \mid Y(\varphi) \mid H(\varphi) \mid P(\varphi) \mid (\varphi \; S \; \varphi)$$

where x is any variable in V.

Semantics. A finite trace defined on the variables in V is a sequence $\pi = \pi_0, \pi_1, ...\pi_{n-1}$ that associates with each $i \in \{0, 1, ...n-1\}$ a state $\pi_i \subseteq V$ consisting of the set of all propositional variables that are assumed to be true in the time instant i. The number of time instants over which π is defined is its length, and it is denoted by $len(\pi)$.

Given a finite trace π, we define that an LTL_f formula φ evaluate true in π at the time instant $i \in \{0, 1, ...len(\pi)\text{-}1\}$ inductively as follows:

- $\pi, i| = x$ if and only if $x \in \pi_i$;
- $\pi, i| = \neg x$ if and only if $x \notin \pi_i$;
- $\pi, i| = (\varphi_1 \wedge \varphi_2)$ if and only if $\pi, i| = \varphi_1$ and $\pi, i| = \varphi_2$;
- $\pi, i| = (\varphi_1 \vee \varphi_2)$ if and only if $\pi, i| = \varphi_1$ or $\pi, i| = \varphi_2$;
- $\pi, i| = X(\varphi')$ if and only if $i < len(\pi) - 1$ and $\pi, i+1| = \varphi'$;
- $\pi, i| = Y(\varphi')$ if and only if $i > 0$ and $\pi, i-1| = \varphi'$;
- $\pi, i| = H(\varphi')$ if and only if for each j such that $0 \le j \le i$ it's true that $\pi, j| = \varphi'$;
- $\pi, i| = P(\varphi')$ if and only if exists j such that $0 \le j \le i$ and $\pi, j| = \varphi'$;
- $\pi, i| = (\varphi_1 \; S \; \varphi_2)$ if and only if exists j such that $0 \le j \le i$ and $\pi, j| = \varphi_2$ and for any k such that $j \le k \le i$ it's true that $\pi, k| = \varphi_1$.

When $\pi, n\text{-}1 \models \varphi$ we say that π is a model of φ and φ is satisfiable.

3 Encoding Smart Contracts in Linear Temporal Logic

Our goal is to use the fragment of linear time logic on finite traces with past operators described in the Sect. 2 to reason on smart contracts. From this perspective, the time operators are interpreted as reported in Table 1.

In our encoding, each smart contract is a pair $\langle p, e \rangle$, where: *(i)* p are the preconditions, i.e. an LTL_f formula using past operators only; *(ii)* e is the effect, i.e. a propositional formula or an LTL_f formula using future operators only. Since p are the preconditions that activate the smart contract and e the effect of its execution, the smart contract will be expressed by the LTL_f formula $\varphi = H(p \rightarrow e)$, i.e., every time the preconditions p occurs then the effect e must be visible since the smart contract must be executed. In the smart contracts domain, a trace π denotes a sequence of events executed by a blockchain platform or a sequence of function or event invocations issued by one or more smart contracts. If a trace π satisfies a smart contract $\langle p, e \rangle$ it means that it satisfies the LTL_f formula $\varphi = H(p \rightarrow e)$ encoding it.

Example 1. *Let's consider a simple smart contract within the sharing economy context to access multimedia contents. The contract consists of the following clause: if a user requests a content for which he has previously paid, that content must be transferred to him. The propositional variables encoding events are:*

1. *requireContent: the user requests the content;*

Table 1. Interpretation of temporal operators in the context of smart contracts and blockchains.

$x \in V$	The condition/action x occurs
$\neg x \mid x \in V$	The condition/action x does not occurs
$(x_1 \wedge x_2)$	The conditions/actions x_1 and x_2 occurs
$(x_1 \vee x_2)$	The conditions/actions x_1 or x_2 occurs
$X(x')$	In the next step the condition/action x' must apply/be executed
$Y(x')$	In the previous step the condition/action x' must be valid/have been executed
$P(x')$	In the past there must be an instant in which the condition/action x' was valid/was performed
$H(x')$	In the past the condition/action x' has been verified/has always been performed
$(x_1\ S\ x_2)$	In the past there is an instant in which x_2 has been verified/executed, and from that moment the condition/action x_1 has always been verified/executed

2. *payContent: the user pays for the content;*
3. *transmitContent: the content is transmitted to the user.*

The preconditions of the smart contract is $p = requireContent \wedge P(payContent)$, *that is when the user require a content it must be checked that s/he already payed for it. The effect is the transmission of the content to the user which is considered to be made in the time instant immediately following the request:* $e = X(transmitContent)$. *The smart contract will then be codified by the following formula:* $\varphi = H((requireContent \wedge P(payContent)) \rightarrow X(transmitContent))$.

4 Reasoning About Smart Contracts

Using LTL_f to encode smart contracts allows to reason over (group of) smart contracts by exploiting its reasoning capabilities. In this section we will discuss several reasoning problems on smart contracts that can be useful on a blockchain. Some of the reasoning problem discussed can be used before deploying a new smart contract to verify its compatibility to already running smart contracts. Other problems, instead, belong to the "reasoning at runtime" category and allows to investigate the behavior of a running blockchain system.

4.1 Reasoning Problems on a Single Smart Contract

By considering a single smart contract we can identify the following reasoning problems:

1. *Model checking*: the problem of checking if a trace π is a model of a given smart contract, i.e., the smart contract has been executed on the block chain every time its preconditions have been satisfied;

2. *Satisfiability*: deciding whether a given smart contract admits a model, i.e., establishing if it could be executed sometimes;
3. *Satisfiability at runtime*: given a partial trace π_p and a smart contract $\langle p, e\rangle$ we want to establish if there is a completion of π_p (a set of possible events on the blockchain) in which $\langle p, e\rangle$ will be executed.

Model Checking. A major issue when dealing with a smart contract is model verification or model checking. The goal is to verify if a given trace π, encoding the events registered by a blockchain, is a model of a given smart contract $\langle p, e\rangle$ encoded by the formula LTL$_f$ $\varphi = H(p \rightarrow e)$. This corresponds to check whether the smart contract has been executed (i.e., the effects of its execution are visible on the blockchain) every time its preconditions have been satisfyied. Checking if a trace is a model of a smart contract can be done in polynomial time w.r.t the length of the formula φ [19].

Example 2. *Let's consider the smart contract discussed in Example 1 and consisting in the following LTL$_f$ formula* $\varphi = H((requireContent \wedge P(payContent)) \rightarrow X(transmitContent))$ *that regulates the access to multimedia content and the trace* $\pi_1 = \{payContent\}\ \{requireContent\}\ \{transmit\ Content\}$*. It's easy to see that* π_1 *is a model of* φ*. Instead, the trace* $\pi_2 = \{payContent, requireContent\}$ *is not a model of* φ *since the precondition of the smart contract is satisfied but the content is not transmitted to the user.*

Satisfiability. Satisfiability is the problem of establishing whether a smart contract $\langle p, e\rangle$ encoded by the LTL$_f$ formula $\varphi = H(p \rightarrow e)$ admits a satisfying trace πin which it has been executed at least once. This corresponds to check whether the LTL$_f$ formula $P(p) \wedge H(p \rightarrow e)$ admits a model. In this regard, we note that in general, given an LTL$_f$ formula, establishing if there is a trace that satisfying it is a PSPACE-hard problem. However it is possible to use suitable techniques that mitigate the theoretical complexity and allow to obtain results in a reasonable time [19].

Example 3. *The smart contract discussed in Example 1 is satisfiable, and examples of traces that satisfy it are:*
$\pi_1 = \{payContent\}\ \{requireContent\}\ \{transmitContent\}$,
$\pi_2 = \{payContent, requireContent\}\ \{transmitContent\}$,
$\pi_3 = \{payContent\}\ \{requireContent\}\ \{transmitContent\}\ \{requireContent\}\ \{transmitContent\}$.

Satisfiability at Runtime. Satisfiability at runtime operates on a smart contract $\langle p, e\rangle$ encoded by the LTL$_f$ formula $\varphi = H(p \rightarrow e)$ and a partial trace π_p and it is the problem of verifying whether $\langle p, e\rangle$ is satisfiable given π_p. In particular, is the problem of verifying whether there exists a completion $\pi = \pi_p\pi_t$ of π_p (obtained by adding to π_p a subtrack π_t consisting of a certain number of states) such that the trace π obtained is a model of the LTL$_f$ formula $P(p) \wedge H(p \rightarrow e)$.

Example 4. *Consider again the smart contract discussed in Example 1 and the partial trace* $\pi_p = \{payContent\}\ \{requireContent\}$. *This smart contract can be satisfied at runtime starting from* π_p, *and examples of completions of* π_p *are:*
$\pi_1 = \{payContent\}\ \{requireContent\}\ \{transmitContent\}$
$\pi_2 = \{payContent\}\ \{requireContent\}\ \{transmitContent\}\ \{requireContent\}\ \{transmitContent\}$.

4.2 Reasoning Problems on a Set of Smart Contracts

The previous section considered reasoning problems defined on individual smart contracts. It is also interesting in the context of blockchains to consider problems defined on a set of smart contracts, which are supposed to operate and interact in the same blockchain infrastructure. In particular, we identified the following reasoning problems:

1. *Models checking*: the problem of checking whether a trace π is a model of a set of smart contracts, i.e., if no smart contract in the set is violated by π.
2. *Consistency*: deciding whether a given set of smart contracts admits a model in which all smart contracts have been executed or whether the execution of one of them prevents the execution of some other smart contract in the set.
3. *Consistency at runtime*: given a partial trace π_p and a set of smart contracts we want to establish if there is a completion of π_p that makes the set of smart contracts consistent.

Models Checking. Given a set of smart contracts $\{\langle p_1, e_1\rangle, \langle p_2, e_2\rangle, ..., \langle p_n, e_n\rangle\}$ encoded by the LTL_f formulas $\varphi_1 = H(p_1 \rightarrow e_1)$, $\varphi_2 = H(p_2 \rightarrow e_2)$,... , $\varphi_n = H(p_n \rightarrow e_n)$, the goal is to verify if a given trace π is a model of $\varphi_1, \varphi_2, ..., \varphi_n$. To this end, we can use the same approach used for the model checking of a single smart contract, but defining appropriately the LTL_f formula encoding the set. In particular, since no smart contract must be violated by the trace, such formula has to be defined as the conjunction of the formulas encoding the various smart contracts $\varphi = \varphi_1 \wedge \varphi_2 \wedge ... \wedge \varphi_n$.

Example 5. *Consider again the smart contract discussed in Example 1 consisting of the following* LTL_f *formula* $\varphi_1 = H((requireContent \wedge P(payContent)) \rightarrow X(transmitContent))$. *Let's consider another smart contract which consists of the following clause: if a user shares a content that has been previously transmitted to him, thus violating contractual terms, that user will be deleted from the system. In this case the propositional variables used for the encoding are:*

- *shareContent: the user shares the content;*
- *transmitContent: the content is transmitted to the user;*
- *deleteUser: the user is deleted from the system.*

The preconditions of the smart contract are $p = shareContent \wedge P(transmitContent)$. *The effect is the deletion of the user from the system which is considered to be made in the time instant immediately following the sharing*

$e = X(deleteUser)$. The smart contract is encoded by the following formula: $\varphi_2 = H((shareContent \wedge P(transmitContent)) \rightarrow X(deleteUser))$.

If φ_1 and φ_2 are running on the same blockchain, for model checking we can consider the LTL_f formula $\varphi = \varphi_1 \wedge \varphi_2 = H((requireContent \wedge P(payContent)) \rightarrow X(transmitContent)) \wedge H((shareContent \wedge P(transmit Content)) \rightarrow X(deleteUser))$.

Let's consider the following trace of events recorded on the blockchain:

$\pi = \{payContent\}\{requireContent\}\{transmitContent\}\{requireContent\}$ $\{transmitContent, shareContent\}, \{deleteUser\}$. It is easy to verify that π satisfies φ and it's compliant with the two smart contracts formalized by it.

Consistency of a Set of Smart Contracts. If we consider a set of smart contracts running on the same blockchain, another relevant problem is to verify their consistency, i.e. if it is possible that all smart contracts can sooner or later be executed or if they are incompatible with each other, meaning that the execution of one of them makes another smart contract never executable. The goal is to check if there is a trace π in which all the smart contracts in the set have been executed at least once.

Suppose that we have a set of smart contracts $\{\langle p_1, e_1\rangle, ..., \langle p_n, e_n\rangle\}$ encoded by the LTL_f formulas $\varphi_1 = H(p_1 \rightarrow e_1), \ldots, \varphi_n = H(p_n \rightarrow e_n)$. Then, the LTL_f formula allowing to check their consistency is the following: $\varphi = \bigwedge_{i\in\{1,\ldots,n\}}(H(p_i \rightarrow e_i) \wedge P(p_i))$, that is, the conjunction of the formulas encoding the individual smart contracts plus the check that the preconditions of each smart contract have been satisfied at least once (using the $P(p_i)$ subformulas).

Example 6. *Consider the set of smart contracts discussed in Example 5. This set of smart contracts is consistent, in fact we found a trace satisfying this set. Let: $\varphi_1'' = ((requiresContent \wedge P(paysContent)) \rightarrow X(transmitsContent)$ and $\varphi_2'' = ((sharesContent \wedge P(transmitContent)) \rightarrow X(deleteUser)$. The LTL_f formula allowing to check the consistency of the set is: $\varphi = H(\varphi_1'') \wedge H(\varphi_2'') \wedge P(requiresContent \wedge P(paysContent)) \wedge P(sharesContent \wedge P(transmitContent))$. A trace that satisfies φ is the following:*
$\pi = \{payContent\}$ $\{requestContent\}$ $\{transmitContent\}$ $\{requestContent\}$ $\{transmitContent, shareContent\}$ $\{deleteUser\}$.

Example 7. *Consider the two smart contracts within the sharing economy environment $\langle p_1 = (requestDeletion \wedge H(\neg notDeletable)), e_1 = deleteContent\rangle$ and $\langle p_2 = (requestPermanence \wedge H(\neg deleteContent)), e_2 = notDeletable\rangle$. The smart contract $\langle p_1, e_1\rangle$ establishes that if the owner of a content ask for its deletion (requestDeletion) and previously such content has not been declared not deletable ($H(\neg notDeletable)$), the content is deleted from the system. Instead, the smart contract $\langle p_2, e_2\rangle$ states that if a content is requested to be made permanent in the system (requestPermanence) and has not been previously deleted ($H(\neg deleteContent)$) then it is marked as not deletable. It is easy to see that the set of smart contracts is not consistent since the execution of one smart contract prevents the precondition of the other to be ever satisfied.*

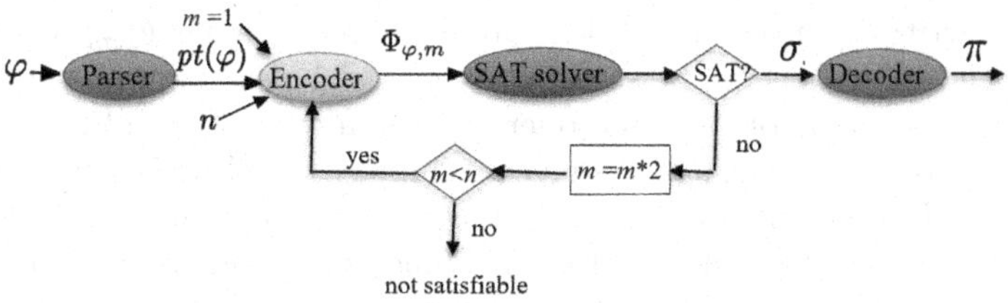

Fig. 1. SCREA conceptual architecture

Consistency at Runtime. Consistency at runtime operates on a set of smart contracts $\{\langle p_1, e_1\rangle, ..., \langle p_n, e_n\rangle\}$ and a partial trace π_p and corresponds to the problem of verifying whether $\langle p_1, e_1\rangle, ..., \langle p_n, e_n\rangle$ are satisfiable given π_p, that is to verify whether there exists a completion $\pi = \pi_p\pi_t$ of π_p (obtained by adding to π_p a subtrace π_t consisting of a certain number of states) such that all smart contracts in the set are executed at least once. To solve such a problem the encoding of the set of smart contracts in LTL_f is the same as discussed for the standard consistency checking. However, the partial trace π_p must be completed by adding indicator variables f_i to register the satisfaction of preconditions.

Example 8. *Consider again the set of smart contracts discussed in Example 6 and the partial trace* $\pi_p = \{payContent\}\{requireContent\}$*. The completion of* π_p *corresponds to the addition of the indicator variable* f_1 *in the last state, i.e.,* $\pi_p = \{payContent\}\{requireContent, f_1\}$*. The set of smart contracts is consistent at runtime starting from* π_p*, and examples of completions of* π_p *are:*
$\pi_1 = \{payContent\}$ $\{requireContent, f_1\}$ $\{transmitContent, shareContent, f_2\}$, $\{deleteUser\}$
$\pi_2 = \{payContent\}\{requireContent, f_1\}$ $\{transmitContent\}$ $\{requireContent, shareContent, f_1, f_2\}$ $\{transmitContent, deleteUser\}$

5 SCREA: Smart Contracts Reasoner

In this section we introduce the Smart Contracts Reasoner (SCREA) that works on smart contracts encoded in LTL_f and exploits boolean satisfiability for solving the reasoning tasks introduced in the previous section.

5.1 Conceptual Architecture

The proposed reasoner is based on a SAT (boolean satisfiability) rewrite technique that recalls the approach followed by (incremental) model checking methods for bounded LTL [25]. The conceptual architecture of SCREA is shown in Fig. 1. The input to the system is the LTL_f formula encoding a single smart contract or a group of smart contracts (see, Sect. 4).

The first component is the Parser which constructs the parse tree $pt(\varphi)$ associated with the input formula φ. Starting from the parse tree, the SAT rewriting technique rewrites φ into an equivalent propositional formula $\Phi_{\varphi,m}$ which is satisfiable if, and only if, φ can be satisfied by a model of maximum length m. To verify if $\Phi_{\varphi,m}$ is satisfiable, the reasoner can use any existing SAT solver (e.g., Glucose [26]). In particular, $pt(\varphi)$ is given as input to the Encoder module which produces a SAT translation of the formula by initially considering a model length m=1. Then, whenever no model of Φ_φ is found, m is doubled and the process is repeated until m exceeds the upper limit n given as input to the Encoder. If the SAT solver finds a model σ for a SAT formula $\Phi_{\varphi,m}$, the Decoder module translates σ into a trace π (having length at most m) which satisfies φ. Note that n is set by the user and could be less than the minimum length of any model of φ, so the reasoner acts as a correct, although not complete, solver.

5.2 Encoder and Decoder Modules

Given an LTL$_f$ formula representing one or a set of smart contracts, for its SAT encoding a crucial role is played by the parse tree of a formula $pt(\varphi) = (V, E, \lambda)$ that is a tree (V, E) with a node labeling function $\lambda : V \to \{\wedge, \vee, X, Y, P, H, S\} \cup \{x, \neg x | x \in V_\varphi\}$ inductively defined as follows:

- For any literal $l \in \{x, \neg x\}$ with $x \in V_\varphi$, $pt(l) = (\{r\}, \emptyset, \lambda)$ and $\lambda(r) = l$.
- If $pt(\varphi_i) = (V_i, E_i, \lambda_i)$, with $i \in \{1, 2\}$, it is an analysis tree having as root the vertex $r_i \in V_i$ and if $O \in \wedge, \vee$ is a boolean connective or $O = S$ then $pt(\varphi_1 O \varphi_2) = (\{r\} \cup V_1 \cup V_2, \{(r, r_1), (r, r_2)\} \cup E_1 \cup E_2, \lambda)$ is the analysis tree which has as roots the new node r, with r_1 and r_2 as its two children, and where λ is such that $\lambda(r) = O$ and its restriction on V_i coincides with λ_i.
- If $pt(\varphi') = (V', E', \lambda')$ is an analysis tree having the root r' and if $O \in \{X, Y, P, H\}$ is a time operator, then $pt(O(\varphi')) = (\{r\} \cup V', \{(r, r')\} \cup E', \lambda)$ is the tree rooted in the new node r whose only child is r' and where λ is such that $\lambda(r) = O$ and its restriction on V' coincides with λ.

To explain the encoding approach used by the reasoner to construct $\Phi_{\varphi,m}$, let us first note that, given a trace π, each node $v \in V$ of the parse tree $pt(\varphi) = (V, E, \lambda)$ can easily be equipped with a set $sat(v, \pi)$ of all time instants in which the sub-formula φ_v associated with vertex v holds in π. Formally, the set $sat(v, \pi)$ is inductively defined as follows:

- If $\lambda(v) = x$ or $\lambda(v) = \neg x$, then $sat(v, \pi) = \{i | \pi, i \models \lambda(v)\}$;
- If $\lambda(v) = \wedge$ (resp., $\lambda(v) = \vee$), then $sat(v, \pi) = sat(v_1, \pi) \cap sat(v_2, \pi)$ (resp., $sat(v, \pi)) = sat(v_1, \pi) \cup sat(v_2, \pi))$ where $v1$ and $v2$ are the two children of v in $pt(\varphi)$;
- If $\lambda(v) = X$, then $sat(v, \pi) = \{i - 1 | i > 0 \textit{ and } i \in sat(v', \pi)\}$ where v' is the only child of v in $pt(\varphi)$;
- If $\lambda(v) = Y$, then $sat(v, \pi) = \{i + 1 | i < len(\pi) \textit{ and } i \in sat(v', \pi)\}$ where v' is the only child of v in $pt(\varphi)$;
- If $\lambda(v) = P$, then $sat(v, \pi) = \{j | \in i \in sat(v', \pi) \textit{ such that } 0 \leq j \leq i\}$ where v' is the only child of v in $pt(\varphi)$;

- If $\lambda(v) = H$, then $sat(v, \pi) = \{j \in \{1, ..., len(\pi) - 1\} \mid \forall i \in \{0, ..., j\}, i \in sat(v', \pi)\}$ where v' is the only child of v in $pt(\varphi)$;
- If $\lambda(v) = S$, then $sat(v, \pi) = \{i \mid \exists\ j \in \{0, ..., i\}$ *such that* $j \in sat(v_2, \pi)$ *and* $k \in sat(v_1, \pi), \forall\ k \in \{j, ..., i\}\}$ where v_1 and v_2 are the two children of v in $pt(\varphi)$.

The basic idea we use to construct the formula $\Phi_{\varphi,m}$ is to imitate the construction of the sets $sat(v, \pi)$. Formally, we first define the variables $l[0], ..., l[m-1]$ that will be used to encode the last time instant of the model. Intuitively, $\Phi_{\varphi,m}$ will be defined in such a way that there exists an index $i \in \{0, ..., m-1\}$, such that $l[j]$ evaluates true (respectively, false) whenever $j \geq i$ (respectively, $j < i$). The instant i indicates the last time instant of a model of φ – more formally, whenever $\Phi_{\varphi,m}$ is satisfiable, there exists a model of φ of length $i \leq m$. Then, we associate the variables $sv[0], ..., sv[m-1]$ to each node v of $pt(\varphi)$. Intuitively, $sv[i]$ is meant to check if the formula encoded in the parse tree rooted at node v is satisfied at instant i. In the following expressions, we use two additional variables $sv[-1]$ and $sv[m]$, whose value will actually be a constant that will be fixed depending on the type of node v.

Then, the SAT encoding is the formula $\Phi_{\varphi,m} = \bigwedge_{v \in V}(\Phi_v \wedge sroot[m\text{-}1] \wedge l[m\text{-}1]) \wedge \bigwedge_{i=0}^{m-2}(l[i] \rightarrow l[i+1]) \wedge \bigwedge_{i=0}^{m-2}(l[i] \rightarrow \bigwedge_v (sv[i] \leftrightarrow sv[i+1]))$ and, for all $v \in V$, $\Phi_v = sv[0] \leftrightarrow \Phi_v^0 \bigwedge_{i=1}^{m-1}(\neg l[i\text{-}1] \rightarrow (sv[i] \leftrightarrow \Phi_v^i))$, where:

- if $\lambda(v) \in \{x, \neg x\}$, then $\Phi_v^i = \bigwedge_{v' \in V, \lambda(v') \equiv \neg\lambda(v)} \neg sv'[i] \wedge \bigwedge_{v' \in V, \lambda(v') \equiv \lambda(v)} sv'[i]$;
- if $\lambda(v) = \wedge$ or $\lambda(v) = \vee$, then $\Phi_v^i = sv_1[i]\lambda(v)sv_2[i]$, where v_1 and v_2 are the right and left children of v;
- if $\lambda(v) = X$ (respectively, $\lambda(v) = Xw$), then $\Phi_v^i = sv'[i+1] \wedge \neg l[i]$, where v' is the child of v and $sv[m]$ is the constant false (respectively, true);
- if $\lambda(v) = Y$ (respectively, $\lambda(v) = Yw$), then $\Phi_v^i = sv'[i-1]$, where v' is the child of v and $sv[-1]$ is the constant false (respectively, true);
- if $\lambda(v) = P$, then $\Phi_v^i = sv'[i] \vee sv[i-1]$, where v' is the child of v and $sv[-1]$ is the constant false;
- if $\lambda(v) = H$, then $\Phi_v^i = sv'[i] \wedge sv[i-1]$, where v' is the child of v and $sv[-1]$ is the constant true;
- if $\lambda(v) = S$, then $\Phi_v^i = (sv_2[i] \wedge sv_1[i]) \vee (sv_1[i] \wedge sv[i-1])$, where v_1 and v_2 are the left and right children of v and $sv[-1]$ is the constant false.

We note, for the sake of completeness, that $\Phi_{\varphi,m}$ is rewritten (in polynomial time) in conjunctive normal form, before being passed to the solver. Moreover, by construction, it is possible to establish that $\Phi_{\varphi,m}$ is satisfiable if, and only if, φ can be satisfied by a model π with $len(\pi) \leq m$.

When SCREA finds a model σ for a SAT formula $\Phi_{\varphi,m}$, the decoder module is responsible for the building of the trace π that satisfies the smart contract φ. In particular, starting from σ it is possible to construct the trace π satisfying φ by implementing the following steps:

- If $l[i] \in \sigma$ and there is no $l[j] \in \sigma$ with $j < i$ then the decoder constructs a trace π with i states.

- For every v such that $\lambda(v) = x$ and every i such that $sv[i] \in \sigma$ then the decoder adds x to $\pi[i]$.

5.3 SCREA at Runtime

In this section we will discuss how the reasoner can be applied to solve reasoning problems at runtime. To work a runtime it is necessary to slightly modify the architecture of SCREA. In particular, the Encoder module must also receive in input the partial trace π_p which contains the events recorded on the blockchain up to the current time instant. In this case, the parameter m concerns the additional number of states (i.e., sets of events) that can happen after those already present in π_p. The other modules remain unchanged with respect to the architecture already discussed. Moreover, if SCREA is meant to work on a set of smart contracts π_p must be preprocessed to add indicator variables.

Let φ be an LTL$_f$ formula encoding one o more smart contracts as discussed in Sect. 4, $pt(\varphi) = (V, E, \lambda)$ be its parse tree and π_p be the partial trace. Also in this case each node $v \in V$ of the parse tree $pt(\varphi) = (V, E, \lambda)$ is equipped with the set $sat(v, \pi)$. The variables $l[0], ..., l[len(\pi_p) + m - 1]$ encode the last instant of time of the model and, obviously, $l[0], \ldots l[len(\pi_p) - 2]$ will be set to false. Intuitively, $\Phi_{\varphi,m}$ will be defined in such a way that there exists an index $i \in \{len(\pi_p) - 1, ..., len(\pi_p) + m - 1\}$, such that $l[j]$ evaluates true (respectively, false) whenever $j \geq i$ (respectively, $j < i$). The instant i, also in this case, indicates the last time instant of a model of φ and clearly this cannot happen in the first $len(\pi_p) - 2$ time instants. As explained before, we associate the variables $sv[0], ..., sv[len(\pi_p) + m - 1]$ to each node v of $pt(\varphi)$, plus the two additional variables $sv[-1]$ and $sv[len(\pi_p) + m]$.

The final SAT formula is the same already discussed for the non-runtime case, with the difference that the variables $sv[i]$ relative to nodes v such that $\lambda(v) \in \{x, \neg x\}$ for the first $len(\pi_p)$-1 time instants will be set according to the partial track provided in input as follows:

- if $\lambda(v) = x$, then $sv[i] = true$ for all values $i \in [0, \ldots, len(\pi_p)\text{-}1]$ such that $x \in \pi_p[i]$;
- if $\lambda(v) = \neg x$, then $sv[i] = false$ for all values $i \in [0, \ldots, len(\pi_p)\text{-}1]$ such that $x \notin \pi_p[i]$.

We note, for the sake of completeness, that also in this case $\Phi_{\varphi,m}$ is rewritten (in polynomial time) in conjunctive normal form, before being passed to the solver.

6 Concluding Remarks

In this paper we proposed a framework, based on the encoding of smart contracts in Linear Temporal Logic on finite traces, that enables various reasoning tasks on a single and on a set of smart contracts running on the same blockchain. The proposed framework, called SCREA, is the first tool developed with the aim of checking the consistency of a set of smart contracts that are supposed to cooperate in same blockchain infrastructure and it is able to work at runtime on a running blockchain system. As a future work, we are planning to implement our framework on an existing blockchain infrastructure to test its effectiveness on a real system.

References

1. Douglis, F., Stavrou, A.: Distributed ledger technologies. IEEE Internet Comput. **24**(3) (2020)
2. Idelberger, F., Governatori, G., Riveret, R., Sartor, G.: Evaluation of logic-based smart contracts for blockchain systems. In: Alferes, J.J.J., Bertossi, L., Governatori, G., Fodor, P., Roman, D. (eds.) RuleML 2016. LNCS, vol. 9718, pp. 167–183. Springer, Cham (2016). https://doi.org/10.1007/978-3-319-42019-6_11
3. Hu, J., Zhong, Y.: A method of logic-based smart contracts for blockchain system. In: Proceedings of ICDPA, pp. 58–61 (2018)
4. Stancu, A., Dragan, M.: Logic-based smart contracts. In: Rocha, Á., Adeli, H., Reis, L.P., Costanzo, S., Orovic, I., Moreira, F. (eds.) WorldCIST 2020. AISC, vol. 1159, pp. 387–394. Springer, Cham (2020). https://doi.org/10.1007/978-3-030-45688-7_40
5. Nakamoto, S.: Bitcoin: a peer-to-peer electronic cash system (2008)
6. Wood, G.: Ethereum: a secure decentralised generalised transaction ledger. Ethereum Proj. Yellow Pap. **151**(2014), 1–32 (2014)
7. Szabo, N.: The idea of smart contracts. Nick Szabo's Papers and Concise Tutorials, 6 (1997)
8. Dannen, C.: Introducing Ethereum and Solidity, p. 185. Apress, Berkeley (2017)
9. Pnueli, A.: The Temporal logic of programs. In: Proceedings of FOCS, pp. 46–57 (1977)
10. Pnueli, A.: The temporal semantics of concurrent programs. Theoret. Comput. Sci. **13**, 45–60 (1981)
11. Bacchus, F., Kabanza, F.: Planning for temporally extended goals. Ann. Math. Artif. Intell. **22**(1–2), 5–27 (1998)
12. Calvanese, D., De Giacomo, G., Vardi, M.Y.: Reasoning about actions and planning in LTL action theories. In: Proceedings of KR, pp. 593–602 (2002)
13. Sohrabi, S., Baier, J.A., McIlraith, S.A.: Preferred explanations: theory and generation via planning. In Proceedings of AAAI, pp. 261–267 (2011)
14. Bobadilla, L., Sanchez, O., Czarnowski, J., Gossman, K., LaValle, S.: Controlling wild bodies using linear temporal logic. In: Proceedings of RSS, pp. 17–24 (2011)
15. Ding, X., Smith, S., Belta, C., Rus, D.: Optimal control of Markov decision processes with linear temporal logic constraints. IEEE Trans. Autom. Control **59**(5), 1244–1257 (2014)
16. Maggi, F.M., Montali, M., Westergaard, M., van der Aalst, W.M.P.: Monitoring business constraints with linear temporal logic: an approach based on colored automata. In: Rinderle-Ma, S., Toumani, F., Wolf, K. (eds.) BPM 2011. LNCS, vol. 6896, pp. 132–147. Springer, Heidelberg (2011). https://doi.org/10.1007/978-3-642-23059-2_13
17. Fionda, V., Guzzo, A.: Control-flow modeling with declare: behavioral properties, computational complexity, and tools. IEEE Trans. Knowl. Data Eng. **32**(5), 898–911 (2020)

18. Chekol, M.W., Fionda, V., Pirrò, G.: Time travel queries in RDF archives. In: Proceedings of MEPDaW, pp. 28–42 (2017)
19. Fionda, V., Greco, G.: LTL on finite and process traces: complexity results and a practical reasoner. J. Artif. Intell. Res. **63**, 557–623 (2018)
20. Pešić, M., Bošnački, D., van der Aalst, W.M.P.: Enacting declarative languages using LTL: avoiding errors and improving performance. In: van de Pol, J., Weber, M. (eds.) SPIN 2010. LNCS, vol. 6349, pp. 146–161. Springer, Heidelberg (2010). https://doi.org/10.1007/978-3-642-16164-3_11
21. Pesic, M., Schonenberg, H., Van der Aalst, W.: DECLARE: full support for loosely-structured processes. In: Proceedings of EDOC, pp. 287–298 (2007)
22. Van Der Aalst, W., Pesic, M., Schonenberg, H.: Declarative workflows: balancing between flexibility and support. Comput. Sci. Res. Dev. **23**(2), 99–113 (2009)
23. De Giacomo, G., Vardi, M.Y.: Linear temporal logic and linear dynamic logic on finite traces. In: Proceedings of IJCAI, pp. 854–860 (2013)
24. Li, J., Zhang, L., Pu, G., Vardi, M.Y., He, J.: LTLf satisfiability checking. In: Proceedings of ECAI, pp. 513–518 (2014)
25. Biere, A., Heljanko, K., Junttila, T., Latvala, T., Schuppan, V.: Linear encodings of bounded LTL model checking. Log. Methods Comput. Sci. **2**(5), 1–64 (2006)
26. Audemard, G., and Simon, L.: Predicting learnt clauses quality in modern SAT solvers. In: Proceedings of IJCAI, pp. 399–404 (2009)

A Combinatorial Approach to Weighted Model Counting in the Two-Variable Fragment with Cardinality Constraints

Sagar Malhotra[1,2(✉)] and Luciano Serafini[1]

[1] Fondazione Bruno Kessler, Povo, Italy
smalhotra@fbk.eu
[2] University of Trento, Trento, Italy

Abstract. Weighted First-Order Model Counting (WFOMC) computes the weighted sum of the models of a first-order logic theory on a given finite domain. First-Order Logic theories that admit polynomial-time WFOMC w.r.t domain cardinality are called domain liftable. In this paper, we reconstruct the closed-form formula for polynomial-time First Order Model Counting (FOMC) in the universally quantified fragment of FO^2, earlier proposed by Beame et al.. We then expand this closed-form to incorporate cardinality constraints and existential quantifiers. Our approach requires a constant time (w.r.t the previous linear time result) for handling equality and allows us to handle cardinality constraints in a completely combinatorial fashion. Finally, we show that the obtained closed-form motivates a natural definition of a family of weight functions strictly larger than symmetric weight functions.

First-Order Logic (FOL) allows specifying structural knowledge with formulas containing variables ranging over all the domain elements. Probabilistic inference in domains described in FOL requires grounding (aka instantiation) of all the individual variables with all the occurrences of the domain elements. This grounding leads to an exponential blow-up of the complexity of the model description and hence the probabilistic inference.

Lifted inference [13,15] aims at resolving this problem by exploiting symmetries inherent to the FOL structures. In recent years, *Weighted First-Order Model Counting* (WFOMC) has emerged as a useful formulation for probabilistic inference in Statistical Relational Learning (SRL) frameworks [6,14]. Formally, WFOMC [4] refers to the task of calculating the weighted sum of the models of a formula Φ over a domain of a given finite size $\text{WFOMC}(\Phi, w, n) = \sum_{\omega \models \Phi} w(\omega)$, where n is the cardinality of the domain and w is a *weight function* that associates a real number to each interpretation ω. An FOL theory Φ with weight function w which admit polynomial-time WFOMC w.r.t the domain cardinality is called *domain-liftable* [3]. In the past decade, multiple extensions of FO^2 (the fragment of FOL with two variables) have been proven to be domain-liftable [7,10,12].

S. Bandini et al. (Eds.): AIxIA 2021, LNAI 13196, pp. 137–152, 2022.
https://doi.org/10.1007/978-3-031-08421-8_10

In this paper, instead of relying on an algorithmic approach to WFOMC, as in [3], our objective is to find a closed-form for WFOMC in FO^2 that can be easily extended to larger classes of first-order formulas. To this aim, we introduce the novel notion of *lifted interpretation.* Lifted interpretations allow us to reconstruct the closed-form formula for First-Order Model Counting (FOMC) in the universally quantified fragment of FO^2 as proposed in [1] and to extend it to larger classes of FO formulas. We see the following key benefits of the presented formulation:

1. *The formulation is easily extended to* FO^2 *with Cardinality Constraints and Existential quantifiers.* A cardinality constraint on an interpretation is a constraint on the number of elements for which a certain predicate holds. Previous works have relied on Lagrange interpolation and Discrete Fourier Transform [12] for evaluating cardinality constraints. In this work, we deal with cardinality constraints in a completely combinatorial fashion. Furthermore, we provide a completely combinatorial proof for WFOMC with existential quantifiers which does not rely on the skolemization procedure as proposed in [2].
2. *Our approach requires a constant time overhead for dealing with equality.* In [1], the authors prove that WFOMC for a formula with equality can be performed with additional $n+1$ calls to the WFOMC oracle over an extended vocabulary. In this paper, we show that WFOMC for a formula with equality can be done in constant time w.r.t domain cardinality.
3. *The formula computes* WFOMC *for a class of weight functions strictly larger than symmetric weight functions.* This extended class of weight functions allow modelling the recently introduced count distributions [11].

Most of the paper focuses on First-Order Model Counting (FOMC) i.e. counting the number of models of a formula Φ over a finite domain of size n denoted by $\text{FOMC}(\Phi, n)$. We then show how WFOMC can be obtained by multiplying each term of the resulting formula for FOMC with the corresponding weight function. This allows us to separate the treatment of the counting part from the weighting part. The paper is therefore structured as follows: The next section describes the related work in the literature on WFOMC. We then present our formulation of the closed-form formula for FOMC given in [1] for the universally quantified fragment of FO^2. We then extend this formula to incorporate cardinality constraints and existential quantifiers dedicating one section to each of them respectively. The last part of the paper extends the formula for FOMC to WFOMC for the case of symmetric weight functions and for a larger class of weight functions that allow modeling count distributions [11].

1 Related Work

WFOMC was initially defined in [3]. The paper provides an algorithm for WFOMC over universally quantified theories based on *knowledge compilation* techniques. The notion of a *domain lifted theory* i.e. a first-order theory for which WFOMC can be computed in polynomial time w.r.t domain cardinality was first formalized in [8]. The same paper shows that a theory composed of a set of universally quantified clauses containing at most two variables is domain liftable. [2] extends this procedure to theories in full FO^2 (i.e. where existential quantification is allowed) by introducing a skolemization procedure for WFOMC. These results are theoretically analysed in [1], which provides a closed-form formula for WFOMC in the universally quantified fragment of FO^2. [10] extends the domain liftability results to FO^2 with a functionality axiom, and for sentences in *uniform one-dimensional fragment* U_1 [9]. It also proposes a closed-form formula for WFOMC in FO^2 with functionality constraints. [12] recently proposed a uniform treatment of WFOMC for FO^2 with cardinality constraints and counting quantifiers, proving these theories to be domain-liftable. With respect to the state-of-the-art approaches to WFOMC, we propose an approach that provides a closed-form for WFOMC with cardinality constraints, from which PTIME data complexity is immediately evident. Secondly, we provide an alternative approach to the skolemization procedure [2], providing an explicit use of inclusion-exclusion principle for dealing with existential quantifiers.

Finally, [11] introduces Complex Markov Logic Networks, which use complex-valued weights and allow for full expressivity over a class of distributions called *count distributions*. We show in the last section of the paper that our formalization is complete w.r.t. this class of distributions without using complex-valued weight functions.

2 FOMC for Universal Formulas

Let $\mathcal{L}$ be a first-order function free language with equality. A *pure universal formula* in $\mathcal{L}$ is a formula of the form $\forall x_1 \ldots \forall x_m.\Phi(x_1,\ldots,x_m)$, where $X = \{x_1,\ldots,x_m\}$ is a set of m distinct variables occurring in $\Phi(x_1,\ldots,x_m)$, and $\Phi(x_1,\ldots,x_m)$ is a quantifier free formula that does not contain any constant symbol. We use the compact notation $\Phi(\boldsymbol{x})$ for $\Phi(x_1,\ldots,x_m)$, where $\boldsymbol{x} = (x_1,\ldots,x_m)$. Notice that we distinguish between the m-tuple of variables $\boldsymbol{x}$ and the *set* of variables denoted by X. We use C to denote the set of domain constants. For every $\boldsymbol{\sigma} = (\sigma_1,\ldots,\sigma_m)$, m-tuple of constants or variables, $\Phi(\boldsymbol{\sigma})$ denotes the result of uniform substitution of x_i with σ_i in $\Phi(\boldsymbol{x})$. If $\Sigma \subseteq X \cup C$ is the set of constants or variables of $\mathcal{L}$ and $\forall \boldsymbol{x}\Phi(\boldsymbol{x})$ a pure universal formula then:

$$\Phi(\Sigma) = \bigwedge_{\boldsymbol{\sigma}\in\Sigma^m} \Phi(\boldsymbol{\sigma}) \tag{1}$$

$\Phi(\Sigma)$ is a very convenient notion, for instance, grounding of a pure universal formula $\forall \boldsymbol{x}.\Phi(\boldsymbol{x})$ over a set of domain constants C, can be simply denoted as $\Phi(C)$. Furthermore, $\Phi(X)$ and $\Phi(\boldsymbol{x})$ have the following useful relationship:

Lemma 1. *For any arbitrary pure universal formula $\forall \boldsymbol{x}\Phi(\boldsymbol{x})$, the following equivalence holds:*

$$\forall \boldsymbol{x}\Phi(\boldsymbol{x}) \leftrightarrow \forall \boldsymbol{x}\Phi(X) \tag{2}$$

Proof. For any $\boldsymbol{x}' \in X^m$, we have that $\forall \boldsymbol{x}\Phi(\boldsymbol{x}) \rightarrow \forall \boldsymbol{x}\Phi(\boldsymbol{x}')$ is valid. Which implies that $\forall \boldsymbol{x}\Phi(\boldsymbol{x}) \rightarrow \bigwedge_{\boldsymbol{x}' \in X^m} \forall \boldsymbol{x}\Phi(\boldsymbol{x}')$ is also valid. Since $\forall$ and $\wedge$ commute, we have that $\forall \boldsymbol{x}.\Phi(\boldsymbol{x}) \rightarrow \forall \boldsymbol{x}.\Phi(X)$. The viceversa is obvious since $\Phi(\boldsymbol{x})$ is one of the conjuncts in $\Phi(X)$.

Example 1. Let $\Phi(x, y) = A(x) \wedge R(x, y) \wedge x \neq y \rightarrow A(y)$, then $\Phi(X = \{x, y\})$ is the following formula

$$\begin{aligned} &(A(x) \wedge R(x,x) \wedge x \neq x \rightarrow A(x)) \\ \wedge\ &(A(x) \wedge R(x,y) \wedge x \neq y \rightarrow A(y)) \\ \wedge\ &(A(y) \wedge R(y,x) \wedge y \neq x \rightarrow A(x)) \\ \wedge\ &(A(y) \wedge R(y,y) \wedge y \neq y \rightarrow A(y)) \end{aligned} \tag{3}$$

Due to Lemma 1, we can assume that in any grounding of $\forall x \forall y.\Phi(X = \{x, y\})$, two distinct variables x and y, are always grounded to different domain elements. This is because the cases in which x and y are grounded to the same domain element are taken into account by the conjuncts $\Phi(x, x)$ and $\Phi(y, y)$ in $\Phi(X)$. See, for instance, the first and the last conjunct of (3).

Definition 1 (Lifted interpretation). *A* lifted interpretation τ *of a pure universal formula* $\forall \boldsymbol{x}\Phi(\boldsymbol{x})$ *is a function that assigns to each atom of* $\Phi(X)$ *either* 0 *or* 1 *(0 means false and, 1 means true) and assigns 1 to* $x_i = x_i$ *and 0 to* $x_i = x_j$ *if* $i \neq j$.

Lifted interpretations are different from FOL interpretations as they assign truth values to the atoms that contain free variables. Instead, lifted interpretations are similar to m-types [10] (we will later formalize this similarity), where m is the number of variables in the language $\mathcal{L}$. The *truth value* of a pure universal formula Φ under the lifted interpretation τ denoted by $\tau(\forall \boldsymbol{x}\Phi(\boldsymbol{x}))$, can be computed by applying the classical semantics for propositional connectives to the evaluations of the atoms in $\Phi(X)$. With abuse of notation, we sometimes write also $\tau(\Phi(X))$ instead of $\tau(\forall \boldsymbol{x}\Phi(\boldsymbol{x}))$.

Example 2. The following is an example of a lifted interpretation for the formula (3) of Example 1:

	$A(x)$	$R(x,x)$	$A(y)$	$R(y,y)$	$R(x,y)$	$R(y,x)$
τ	0	1	1	1	0	1
	τ_x		τ_y		τ_{xy}	

We omit the truth assignments of equality atoms since they are fixed for all lifted interpretations. We have that $\tau((3)) = 0$.

As highlighted in the previous example, any lifted interpretation τ can be decomposed into a set of partial lifted interpretations τ_Y where $Y \subseteq X$. Notice that τ_Y assigns truth value to all the atoms that contain *all* the variables Y. For instance, in Example 2, $\tau_{\{x,y\}}$ (denoted as τ_{xy} in the example) assigns to atoms $R(x, y)$ and $R(y, x)$ only and not to the atoms $R(x, x)$ and $A(x)$. In general, we will use the simpler notation τ_{xy} to denote the partial lifted interpretation $\tau_{\{x,y\}}$.

Example 3. Consider the assignment of Example 2 and the one obtained by the permutation π that exchanges x and y

	$A(x)$	$R(x,x)$	$A(y)$	$R(y,y)$	$R(x,y)$	$R(y,x)$
τ	0	1	1	1	0	1
τ_π	1	1	0	1	1	0

It is easy to see that $\tau((3)) = \tau_\pi((3))) = 0$. This is not a coincidence, it is actually a property that derives from the shape of $\Phi(X)$. This is stated in the following property.

[1] provides a mathematical formula for computing $\text{FOMC}(\Phi, n)$, where Φ is a pure universal formula in FO^2, i.e. sentences of the form $\forall xy.\Phi(x,y)$. In the following, we reconstruct this result using the notion of lifted interpretations. As it will be clearer later, using lifted interpretations allow us to seamlessly extend the result to larger extensions of FO^2 formulas.

Let $\forall xy.\Phi(x,y)$ be a pure universal formula. Let u be the number of atoms whose truth values are assigned by τ_x i.e. first-order atoms containing only the variable x. Let $P_1(x), \ldots, P_u(x)$ be an ordering of these atoms[1]. There are 2^u possible partial lifted interpretations τ_x which could assign truth values to these atoms. We assume that each such partial lifted interpretation τ_x is indexed by an integer i, where $0 \leq i \leq 2^u - 1$. Hence, the i-th partial lifted interpretation τ_x is defined as $\tau_x(P_j(x)) = bin(i)_j$, where $bin(i)_j$ represents the value of the jth bit in the binary encoding of i, for all $1 \leq j \leq u$. We use $i(x)$ to denote the conjunction of a maximally consistent set of literals (atoms and negated atoms) containing only the variable x which are satisfied by the i-th τ_x. For instance, in Example 1, $A(x)$ and $R(x,x)$ are the atoms assigned by τ_x. Assuming the order of atoms to be $(A(x), R(x,x))$, we have that $\tau_x = 1$ implies that $A(x)$ is interpreted to be false and $R(x,x)$ is interpreted to be true. Also, $i(x)$ denotes $\neg A(x) \wedge R(x,x)$ if $i = 1$ and $\neg A(x) \wedge \neg R(x,x)$ if $i = 0$. We use similar notation for atoms assigned by $\tau_y(y)$ i.e. atoms containing only the variable y. Furthermore, we use $i(c)$ to denote the conjunction of ground atoms containing only one constant c. In Example 1, $i(c)$ denotes $\neg A(c) \wedge R(c,c)$ if $i = 1$ and $\neg A(c) \wedge \neg R(c,c)$ if $i = 0$. Clearly, $i(x)$ exactly corresponds to 1-types. Furthermore, given an interpretation ω if $\omega \models i(c)$ then we say that c is of 1-type i.

For a pure universal formula Φ and $0 \leq i \leq j \leq 2^u - 1$, let n_{ij} be the number of lifted interpretations τ that satisfy Φ such that $\tau_x = i$ and $\tau_y = j$. Formally:

$$n_{ij} = |\{\tau \mid \tau \models \Phi(\{x,y\}) \wedge i(x) \wedge j(y)\}|$$

Example 4 (Example 1 cont'd). The set of atoms containing only x or only y in the formula (3) are $\{A(x), R(x,x)\}$ and $\{A(y), R(y,y)\}$ respectively. In this case $u = 2$. The partial lifted interpretations τ_x and τ_y corresponding to the lifted interpretation τ of Example 2 are: $\tau_x = 1$ and $\tau_y = 3$. n_{13} is the number of lifted interpretations satisfying (3) and agreeing with $\tau_x = 1$ and $\tau_y = 3$. In this case $n_{13} = 2$. The other cases are as follows:

[1] The list includes atoms of the form $P(x,x)$ for binary predicate P.

n_{00}	n_{01}	n_{02}	n_{03}	n_{11}	n_{12}	n_{13}	n_{22}	n_{23}	n_{33}
4	4	2	2	4	2	2	4	4	4

Theorem 1 (Beame et al.). *For any pure universal formula $\forall xy.\Phi(x,y)$*

$$\text{FOMC}(\forall xy.\Phi(x,y),n) = \sum_{\sum \boldsymbol{k}=n} \binom{n}{\boldsymbol{k}} \prod_{0\leq i\leq j\leq 2^u-1} n_{ij}^{\boldsymbol{k}(i,j)} \tag{4}$$

where $\boldsymbol{k} = (k_0, ..., k_{2^u-1})$ is a 2^u-tuple of non-negative integers, $\binom{n}{\boldsymbol{k}}$ is the multinomial coefficient and

$$\boldsymbol{k}(i,j) = \begin{cases} \frac{k_i(k_i-1)}{2} & if i = j \\ k_i k_j & otherwise \end{cases}$$

In order to prove Theorem 1, we first introduce the following notation and we also introduce Lemma 2 and Lemma 3.

For any set of constants C and any 2^u-tuple $\boldsymbol{k} = (k_0, \ldots, k_{2^u-1})$ such that $\sum \boldsymbol{k} = |C|$, let $\mathbb{C}_{\boldsymbol{k}}$ be any partition $(C_i)_{i=0}^{2^u-1}$ of C such that $|C_i| = k_i$. We define $\Phi(\mathbb{C}_{\boldsymbol{k}})$ as follows:

$$\Phi(\mathbb{C}_{\boldsymbol{k}}) = \Phi(C) \wedge \bigwedge_{i=0}^{2^u-1} \bigwedge_{c\in C_i} i(c) \tag{5}$$

Example 5. Examples of $\mathbb{C}_{(1,0,2,0)}$, on $C = \{a,b,c\}$ are $\{\{a\},\emptyset,\{b,c\},\emptyset\}$ and $\{\{b\},\emptyset,\{a,c\},\emptyset\}$.

$$\begin{aligned}\Phi(\{\{a\},\emptyset,\{b,c\},\emptyset\}) = \Phi(C) &\wedge \neg A(a) \wedge \neg R(a,a) \\ &\wedge A(b) \wedge \neg R(b,b) \\ &\wedge A(c) \wedge \neg R(c,c)\end{aligned}$$

Note there are $\binom{3}{1,0,2,0} = 3$ such partitions, and all the $\Phi(\mathbb{C}_{\boldsymbol{k}})$ for such partitions will have the same model count. These observations have been formalized in Lemma 2

Lemma 2. $\text{MC}(\Phi(C)) = \sum_{\boldsymbol{k}} \binom{n}{\boldsymbol{k}} \text{MC}(\Phi(\mathbb{C}_{\boldsymbol{k}}))$, *where* $\text{MC}(\alpha)$ *denotes the model count of an arbitrary propositional formula* α.

Proof. Let $\mathbb{C}_{\boldsymbol{k}}$ and $\mathbb{C}'_{\boldsymbol{k}}$, be two partitions with the same $\boldsymbol{k}$. Notice that $\mathbb{C}'_{\boldsymbol{k}}$ can be obtained by applying some permutation on C from $\mathbb{C}_{\boldsymbol{k}}$. Hence, $\Phi(\mathbb{C}_{\boldsymbol{k}}))$ and $(\Phi(\mathbb{C}'_{\boldsymbol{k}})$ are isomorphic to each other under some permutation of constants. Hence we have that:

$$\text{MC}(\Phi(\mathbb{C}_{\boldsymbol{k}})) = \text{MC}(\Phi(\mathbb{C}'_{\boldsymbol{k}}))$$

Furthermore notice that if $\mathbb{C}_{\boldsymbol{k}}$ is different from $\mathbb{C}'_{\boldsymbol{k}'}$ then $\Phi(\mathbb{C}_{\boldsymbol{k}})$ and $\Phi(\mathbb{C}'_{\boldsymbol{k}'})$ cannot be simultaneously satisfied. This implies that

$$\text{MC}(\Phi(C)) = \sum_{\boldsymbol{k}} \sum_{\mathbb{C}_{\boldsymbol{k}}} \text{MC}(\Phi(\mathbb{C}_{\boldsymbol{k}}))$$

Since there are $\binom{n}{\boldsymbol{k}}$ partitions of C, of the form $\mathbb{C}_{\boldsymbol{k}}$, then

$$\textsc{mc}(\Phi(C)) = \sum_{\boldsymbol{k}} \binom{n}{\boldsymbol{k}} \textsc{mc}(\Phi(\mathbb{C}_{\boldsymbol{k}}))$$

Lemma 3. *For any partition* $\mathbb{C}_{\boldsymbol{k}} = \{C_0, \ldots, C_{2^u-1})$

$$\textsc{mc}(\Phi(\mathbb{C}_{\boldsymbol{k}})) = \prod_{\substack{c \neq d \\ c,d \in C}} n_{i_c i_d}$$

where for all $c, d \in C$, $0 \leq i_c, i_d \leq 2^u - 1$ *are the indices such that* $c \in C_{i_c}$ *and* $d \in C_{i_d}$.

Proof. $\Phi(\mathbb{C}_{\boldsymbol{k}})$ can be rewritten in

$$\bigwedge_{\substack{\{c,d\} \subseteq C \\ c \neq d}} \Phi^{i_c, i_d}(\{c, d\})$$

$\Phi^{i_c,i_d}(\{c,d\}))$ is obtained by replacing each atom $P_j(c)$ with $\top$ if $bin(i_c)_j = 1$ and $\bot$ otherwise and each atom $P_j(d)$ with $\top$ if $bin(i_d)_j = 1$ and $\bot$ otherwise. Notice that all the atoms of $\Phi^{i_c,i_d}(\{c,d\})$ contain both c and d. Furthermore notice that if $\{c,d\} \neq \{e,f\}$ then $\Phi^{i_c,i_d}(\{c,d\}))$ and $\Phi^{i_e,i_f}(\{e,f\}))$ do not contain common atoms. Finally we have that $\textsc{mc}(\Phi^{i_c,i_d}(\{c,d\})) = n_{i_c i_d}$. Hence

$$\textsc{mc}\left(\bigwedge_{\substack{c,d \in C \\ c \neq d}} \Phi^{i_c,i_d}(\{c,d\}) \right) = \prod_{\substack{c \neq d \\ c,d \in C}} n_{i_c i_d}$$

Finally, we provide the following proof for Theorem 1.

Proof (Proof of Theorem 1*).* Notice that $\textsc{fomc}(\forall xy.\Phi(x,y), n) = \textsc{mc}(\Phi(C))$ for a set of constants C with $|C| = n$. Therefore, by Lemma 2, to prove the theorem it is enough to show that for all $\boldsymbol{k}$, $\textsc{mc}(\Phi(\mathbb{C}_{\boldsymbol{k}})) = \prod_{0 \leq i \leq j \leq 2^u-1} n_{ij}^{\boldsymbol{k}(i,j)}$. By the Lemma 3 we have that $\textsc{mc}(\Phi(\mathbb{C}_{\boldsymbol{k}})) = \prod_{c \neq d} n_{i_c i_d}$. Then:

$$\prod_{c \neq d} n_{i_c i_d} = \prod_i \prod_{\substack{c \neq d \\ c,d \in C_i}} n_{ii} \cdot \prod_{i<j} \prod_{\substack{c \in C_i \\ d \in C_j}} n_{ij}$$

$$= \prod_i n_{ii}^{\binom{k_i}{2}} \cdot \prod_{i<j} n_{ij}^{k_i k_j} = \prod_{0 \leq i \leq j < 2^u} n_{ij}^{\boldsymbol{k}(i,j)}$$

Notice that the method in [1] requires additional $n+1$ calls to a WFOMC oracle for dealing with equality. Lifted interpretations on the other hand allow us to fix the truth values of the equality atoms, by assuming (w.l.o.g.) that different variables are assigned to distinct domain elements in the grounding of $\forall \boldsymbol{x}.\Phi(X)$. The equality atoms then contribute to the model count only through n_{ij}, hence, allowing us to deal with equality in constant time w.r.t domain cardinality.

Example 6 (Example 1 continued). Consider a domain of 3 elements (i.e. $n = 3$). Each term of the summation (4) is of the form

$$\binom{3}{k_0, k_1, k_2, k_3} \prod_{i=0}^{3} n_{ii}^{\frac{k_i(k_i-1)}{2}} \prod_{\substack{i<j \\ i=0}}^{3} n_{ij}^{k_i k_j}$$

which is the number of models with k_0 elements for which $A(x)$ and $R(x, x)$ are both false; k_1 elements for which $A(x)$ is false and $R(x, x)$ true, k_2 elements for which $A(x)$ is true and $R(x, x)$ is false and k_3 elements for which $A(x)$ and $R(x, x)$ are both true. For instance: $\binom{3}{2,0,0,1} n_{00}^1 n_{03}^2 = \binom{3}{2,0,0,1} 4^1 \cdot 2^2 = 3 \cdot 16 = 48$ is the number of models in which 2 elements are such that $A(x)$ and $R(x, x)$ are false and 1 element such that $A(x)$ and $R(x, x)$ are both true.

As a final remark for this section, notice that the computational cost of computing n_{ij} is constant with respect to the domain cardinality. We assume the cost of multiplication to be constant. Hence, the computational complexity of computing (4) depends on the domain only through the multinomial coefficients $\binom{n}{\boldsymbol{k}}$ and the multiplications involved in $\prod_{ij} n^{\boldsymbol{k}(i,j)}$. The computational cost of computing $\binom{n}{\boldsymbol{k}}$ is polynomial in n and the total number of $\binom{n}{\boldsymbol{k}}$ are $\binom{n+2^u-1}{2^u-1}$, which has $\left(\frac{e\cdot(n+2^u-1)}{2^u-1}\right)^{2^u-1}$ as an upper-bound [5]. Also, the $\prod_{ij} n^{\boldsymbol{k}(i,j)}$ term has $O(n^2)$ multiplication operations. Hence, we can conclude that the formula (4) is computable in polynomial time with respect to the domain cardinality.

3 FOMC for Cardinality Constraints

Cardinality constraints are arithmetic expressions that impose restrictions on the number of times a certain predicate is interpreted to be true. A simple example of a cardinality constraint is $|A| = m$, for some unary predicate A and positive integer m. This cardinality constraint is satisfied by any interpretation in which $A(c)$ is interpreted to be true for exactly m distinct constants c in the domain C. A more complex example of a cardinality constraint could be: $|A|+|B| \leq |C|$, where A, B and C are some predicates in the language.

For every interpretation ω of the language $\mathcal{L}$ on a finite domain C, we define $A^\omega = \{c \in C \mid \omega \models A(c)\}$ if A is unary, and $A^\omega = \{(c, d) \in C \times C \mid \omega \models A(c, d)\}$ if A is binary. ω satisfies a cardinality constraint ρ, in symbols $\omega \models \rho$, if the arithmetic expression, obtained by replacing $|A|$ with $|A^\omega|$ for every predicate A in ρ, is satisfied.

If a cardinality constraint involves only unary predicates, then we can exploit Theorem 1 considering only a subset of $\boldsymbol{k}$'s. The multinomial coefficient $\binom{n}{\boldsymbol{k}}$ counts the models that contain exactly k_i elements of 1-type i, the cardinality of the unary predicates in these models are fully determined by $\boldsymbol{k}$.

To deal with cardinality constraints involving binary predicates, we have to expand the formula (4) by including also the assignments to binary predicates.

This implies extending the $\boldsymbol{k}$ vector in order to consider assignments to atoms that contain both variables x and y. Let $R_0(x,y), R_1(x,y), \ldots, R_b(x,y)$ be an enumeration of all the atoms in $\Phi(X)$ that contain both variables x and y. Notice that the order of variables leads to different atoms, for instance in Example 1, we have two binary atoms $R_1(x,y) = R(x,y)$ and $R_2(x,y) = R(y,x)$.

For every $0 \leq v \leq 2^b - 1$ let v denote the vth partial lifted interpretation τ_{xy}, such that τ_{xy} assigns $bin(v)_j$ to the j-th binary atom $R_j(x,y)$ for every $1 \leq j \leq b$. As for the unary case, $v(x,y)$ represents the conjunction of all the literals that are satisfied by v. For instance, in Example 1, $v(x,y)$ denotes $\neg R(x,y) \wedge R(y,x)$ if $v = 1$ and $R(x,y) \wedge \neg R(y,x)$ if $v = 3$. Clearly, the set of 2-types in the language of the formula Φ correspond to $i(x) \wedge j(x) \wedge v(x,y)$ .We define n_{ijv} as follows:

$$n_{ijv} = |\{\tau \mid \tau \models \Phi(\{x,y\}) \wedge i(x) \wedge j(y) \wedge v(x,y)\}|$$

Notice that $n_{ij} = \sum_{v=0}^{2^b-1} n_{ijv}$ and that n_{ijv} is either 0 or 1.

Example 7. For instance n_{13} introduced in Example 4 expands to $n_{130} + n_{131} + n_{132} + n_{133}$ where n_{13v} corresponds to the following assignments:

$A(x)$	$R(x,x)$	$A(y)$	$R(y,y)$	$R(x,y)$	$R(y,x)$	v	n_{13v}
0	1	1	1	0	0	0	$n_{130} = 1$
				0	1	1	$n_{131} = 0$
				1	0	2	$n_{132} = 1$
				1	1	3	$n_{133} = 0$
$\tau_x = 1$		$\tau_y = 3$		$\tau_{xy} = v$			

By replacing n_{ij} in Eq. (4) with its expansion $\sum_{v=0}^{2^b-1} n_{ijv}$ we obtain that $\text{FOMC}(\forall xy.\Phi(x,y), n)$ is equal to

$$\begin{aligned} &\sum_{\sum \boldsymbol{k}=n} \binom{n}{\boldsymbol{k}} \prod_{0 \leq i \leq j \leq 2^u-1} \left(\sum_{0 \leq v \leq 2^b-1} n_{ijv} \right)^{\boldsymbol{k}(i,j)} \\ &= \sum_{\boldsymbol{k},\boldsymbol{h}} \binom{n}{\boldsymbol{k}} \prod_{0 \leq i \leq j \leq 2^u-1} \binom{\boldsymbol{k}(i,j)}{\boldsymbol{h}^{ij}} \prod_{0 \leq v \leq 2^b-1} n_{ijv}^{h_v^{ij}} \end{aligned} \tag{6}$$

where, for every $0 \leq i \leq j \leq 2^u - 1$, $\boldsymbol{h}^{ij}$ is a vector of 2^b integers that sum up to $\boldsymbol{k}(i,j)$. To simplify the notation we define the function $F(\boldsymbol{k}, \boldsymbol{h}, \Phi)$ where Φ is a pure universal formula as follows

$$F(\boldsymbol{k}, \boldsymbol{h}, \Phi) = \binom{n}{\boldsymbol{k}} \prod_{0 \leq i \leq j \leq 2^u-1} \binom{\boldsymbol{k}(i,j)}{\boldsymbol{h}^{ij}} \prod_{0 \leq v \leq 2^b-1} n_{ijv}^{h_v^{ij}}$$

where h_v^{ij} is the v-th element of the vector $\boldsymbol{h}^{ij}$, which represents the number of pairs of constants of distinct elements that satisfy the 2-type $i(x) \wedge j(y) \wedge v(x,y)$.

We will now show that the $(\boldsymbol{k},\boldsymbol{h})$ vectors contain all the necessary information for determining the cardinality of the binary predicates.

For every $\mathcal{L}$-interpretation ω on the finite domain C, we define $(\boldsymbol{k},\boldsymbol{h})^{\omega} = (\boldsymbol{k}^{\omega},\boldsymbol{h}^{\omega})$ with $\boldsymbol{k}^{\omega} = \langle k_0^{\omega},\ldots,k_{2^u-1}^{\omega}\rangle$ such that k_i^{ω} is the number of constants $c \in C$ such that $\omega \models i(c)$. $\boldsymbol{h}^{\omega}$ is equal to $\{(\boldsymbol{h}^{ij})^{\omega}\}_{0\leq i\leq j\leq 2^b-1}$, where $(\boldsymbol{h}^{ij})^{\omega} = \langle (h_0^{ij})^{\omega},\ldots (h_{2^b-1}^{ij})^{\omega}\rangle$ such that $(h_v^{ij})^{\omega}$ is the number of pairs (c,d) with $c \neq d$ such that $\omega \models i(c)\wedge j(d)\wedge v(c,d)$ if $i<j$. When $i=j$, $(h_v^{ii})^{\omega}$ is equal to the count of the unordered pairs (c,d) (i.e. only one of the (c,d) and (d,c) is counted) for which $\omega \models i(c)\wedge i(d)\wedge v(c,d)$.

Lemma 4. *For every predicate P, and interpretations ω_1 and ω_2, $(\boldsymbol{k},\boldsymbol{h})^{\omega_1} = (\boldsymbol{k},\boldsymbol{h})^{\omega_2}$ implies $|P^{\omega_1}| = |P^{\omega_2}|$.*

Proof. Let $(\boldsymbol{k},\boldsymbol{h})$ be a vector such that $(\boldsymbol{k},\boldsymbol{h}) = (\boldsymbol{k},\boldsymbol{h})^{\omega}$. The Lemma is true iff $(\boldsymbol{k},\boldsymbol{h})$ uniquely determines the cardinality of P^{ω}. If P^{ω} is a unary predicate whose atom is indexed by s in the ordering of the unary atoms, then the cardinality of P^{ω} can be given as $\sum_{i=0}^{2^u-1} bin(i)_s \cdot k_i$. Similarly, if P is binary then in order to count P^{ω}, we need to take into account both $\boldsymbol{k}$ and $\boldsymbol{h}$. Let $P(x,x)$ be the atom indexed s i.e. P_s, let $P(x,y)$ be the atom indexed l i.e. P_l and let $P(y,x)$ be the atom indexed r i.e. P_r, then the cardinality of P if P is binary is given as $\sum_{i=0}^{2^u-1} bin(i)_s \cdot k_i + \sum_{i\leq j}\sum_{v=0}^{2^b-1}(bin(v)_l + bin(v)_r)\cdot h_v^{ij}$.

Example 8. Consider formula (3) with the additional conjunct $|A| = 2$ and $|R| = 2$. The constraint $|A| = 2$ implies that we have to consider $\boldsymbol{k}$ such that $k_2 + k_3 = 2$. $|R| = 2$ constraint translates to only considering $(\boldsymbol{k},\boldsymbol{h})$ with $k_1 + k_3 + \sum_{i\leq j}(h_1^{ij} + h_2^{ij} + 2h_3^{ij}) = 2$.

For a given $(\boldsymbol{k},\boldsymbol{h})$, we use the notation $\boldsymbol{k}(P)$ to denote cardinality of P if P is unary and $(\boldsymbol{k},\boldsymbol{h})(P)$ if P is binary. Using Lemma 4, we can conclude that FOMC$(\Phi \wedge \rho, n)$ where Φ is a pure universal formula with 2 variables can be computed by considering only the $(\boldsymbol{k},\boldsymbol{h})$'s that satisfy ρ, i.e. those $(\boldsymbol{k},\boldsymbol{h})'s$ where ρ evaluates to true, when $|P|$ is substituted with $(\boldsymbol{k},\boldsymbol{h})(P)$ when P is binary, and $\boldsymbol{k}(P)$ when P is unary.

Corollary 1 (of Theorem 1). *For every pure universal formula Φ and cardinality constraint ρ,* FOMC$(\Phi \wedge \rho, n) = \sum_{\boldsymbol{k},\boldsymbol{h}\models\rho} F(\boldsymbol{k},\boldsymbol{h},\Phi)$.

4 FOMC for Existential Quantifiers

In this section, we provide a proof for model counting in the presence of existential quantifiers. The key difference in our approach w.r.t [1] is that we make explicit use of the principle of inclusion-exclusion. We will first provide a corollary of the principle of inclusion-exclusion.

Corollary 2 ([17] Sect. 4.2). *Let Ω be a set of objects and let $\mathcal{S} = \{S_1,\ldots,S_m\}$ be a set of subsets of Ω. For every $\mathcal{Q} \subseteq \mathcal{S}$, let $N(\supseteq \mathcal{Q})$ be the count* *of objects in* Ω *that belong to all the subsets* $S_i \in \mathcal{Q}$, *i.e.* $N(\supseteq \mathcal{Q}) = \left|\{\bigcap_{S_i \in Q} S_i\}\right|$. *For every* $0 \leq l \leq m$, *let* $s_l = \sum_{|Q|=l} N(\supseteq \mathcal{Q})$ *and let* e_0 *be count of objects that do not belong to any of the* S_i *in* $\mathcal{S}$, *then*

$$e_0 = \sum_{l=0}^{m} (-1)^l s_l \tag{7}$$

Any arbitrary formula in FO^2 can be reduced to an equisatisfiable reduction called Scott's Normal Form (SNF) [16]. Moreover, SNF preserves FOMC as well as WFOMC if all the new predicates and there negation are assigned a unit weight [10]. A formula in SNF has the following form:

$$\forall x \forall y. \Phi(x,y) \land \bigwedge_{i=1}^{q} \forall x \exists y. \Psi_i(x,y) \tag{8}$$

where $\Phi(x,y)$ and $\Psi_i(x,y)$ are quantifier-free formulae.

Theorem 2. *For an FO*^{2} *formula in Scott's Normal Form as given in* (8), *let* $\Phi' = \forall xy.(\Phi(x,y) \land \bigwedge_{i=1}^{q} P_i(x) \rightarrow \neg\Psi_i(x,y))$ *where* P_i*'s are fresh unary predicates, then:*

$$\text{FOMC}((8), n) = \sum_{\boldsymbol{k},\boldsymbol{h}} (-1)^{\sum_i \boldsymbol{k}(P_i)} F(\boldsymbol{k}, \boldsymbol{h}, \Phi') \tag{9}$$

Proof. Let Ω be the set of models of $\forall xy.\Phi(x,y)$ over the language of Φ and $\{\Psi_i\}$ (i.e. the language of Φ' excluding the the predicates P_i) and on a domain C consisting of n elements. Let $\mathcal{S} = \{\Omega_{ci}\}_{c \in C,\ 1 \leq i \leq q}$ be the set of subsets of Ω where Ω_{ci} is the set of $\omega \in \Omega$, such that $\omega \models \forall y. \neg\Psi_i(c,y)$. Notice that for every model ω of (8) $\omega \not\models \forall y \neg\Psi_i(c,y)$, for any pair of i and c i.e. ω is not in any Ω_{ci}. Also, for every ω, if $\omega \in \Omega_{ci}$ then $\omega \not\models$ (8). Hence, $\omega \models$ (8) if and only if $\omega \notin \Omega_{ci}$ for all c and i. Therefore, the count of models of (8) is equal to the count of models in Ω which do not belong to any Ω_{ci}.

If we are able to compute s_l (as introduced in Corollary 2), then we could use Corollary 2 for computing cardinality of all the models which do not belong to any Ω_{ci} and hence $\text{FOMC}((8), n)$.

For every $0 \leq l \leq n \cdot q$, let us define

$$\Phi'_l = \Phi' \land \sum_{i=1}^{q} |P_i| = l \tag{10}$$

We will now show that s_l is exactly given by $\text{FOMC}((10), n)$.

Every model of Φ'_l is an extension of an $\omega \in \Omega$ that belongs to at least l elements in $\mathcal{S}$. In fact, for every model ω of $\forall xy.\Phi(x,y)$ i.e. $\omega \in \Omega$, if $\mathcal{Q}'$ is the set of elements of $\mathcal{S}$ that contain ω, then ω can be extended into a model of Φ'_l in $\binom{|Q'|}{l}$ ways. Each such model can be obtained by choosing l elements in Q' and interpreting $P_i(c)$ to be true in the extended model, for each of the l chosen elements $\Omega_{ci} \in \mathcal{Q}'$. On the other hand, recall that $s_l = \sum_{|\mathcal{Q}|=l} N(\supseteq Q)$. Hence, for any $\omega \in \Omega$ if $\mathcal{Q}'$ is the set of elements of $\mathcal{S}$ that contain ω, then there are $\binom{|\mathcal{Q}'|}{l}$ distinct subsets $\mathcal{Q} \subseteq \mathcal{Q}'$ such that $|\mathcal{Q}|= l$. Hence, we have that ω contributes $\binom{|\mathcal{Q}'|}{l}$ times to s_l. Therefore, we can conclude that

$$s_l = \text{FOMC}(\Phi'_l, n) = \sum_{|\mathcal{Q}|=l} N(\supseteq Q)$$

and by the principle of inclusion-exclusion as given in Corollary 2, we have that :

$$\begin{aligned}
\text{FOMC}((8), n) = e_0 &= \sum_{l=0}^{n \cdot q} (-1)^l s_l \\
&= \sum_{l=0}^{n \cdot q} (-1)^l \text{FOMC}(\Phi'_l, n) \\
&= \sum_{l=0}^{n \cdot q} (-1)^l \sum_{\boldsymbol{k},\boldsymbol{h} \models \sum_i |P_i|=l} F(\boldsymbol{k}, \boldsymbol{h}, \Phi') \\
&= \sum_{\boldsymbol{k},\boldsymbol{h}} (-1)^{\sum_i \boldsymbol{k}(P_i)} F(\boldsymbol{k}, \boldsymbol{h}, \Phi')
\end{aligned}$$

5 Weighted First-Order Model Counting

All the FOMC formulas introduced so far can be easily extended to weighted model counting by simply defining a positive real-valued weight function $w(\boldsymbol{k}, \boldsymbol{h})$ and adding it as a multiplicative factor to $F(\boldsymbol{k}, \boldsymbol{h}, \Phi)$ in all FOMC formulas. The case of Symmetric-WFOMC can be obtained by defining $w(\boldsymbol{k}, \boldsymbol{h})$ as follows:

$$w(\boldsymbol{k}, \boldsymbol{h}) = \prod_{P \in \mathcal{L}} w(P)^{(\boldsymbol{k},\boldsymbol{h})(P)} \cdot \bar{w}(P)^{(\boldsymbol{k},\boldsymbol{h})(\neg P)}$$

where $w(P)$ and $\bar{w}(P)$ associate positive real values to predicate P and it's negation respectively.

But symmetric-weight functions are clearly not the most general class of weight functions. [11] introduced a strictly more expressive class of weight functions which also preserves domain liftability. These weight functions can express count distributions, which are defined as follows:

Definition 2 (Count distribution [11]). *Let $\Phi = \{\alpha_i, w_i\}_{i=1}^m$ be a Markov Logic Network defining a distribution over a set of possible worlds (we call them assignments) of a formula Ω. The count distribution of Φ is the distribution over m-dimensional vectors of non-negative integers $\boldsymbol{n}$ given by*

$$q_\Phi(\Omega, \boldsymbol{n}) = \sum_{\omega \models \Omega,\ \boldsymbol{n} = \boldsymbol{N}(\Phi, \omega)} p_{\Phi,\Omega}(\omega) \tag{11}$$

where $\boldsymbol{N}(\Phi, \omega) = (n_1, \ldots, n_m)$, and n_i is the number of grounding of α_i that are true in ω.

[11] shows that count distributions can be modelled by Markov Logic Networks with complex weights. In the following, we prove that if α_i and Φ are in FO^2, then we can express count distributions with positive real valued counting weight functions.

Theorem 3. *Every count distribution over a set of possible worlds of a formula Ω definable in FO^2 can be modelled with a weight function on $(\boldsymbol{k}, \boldsymbol{h})$, by introducing m new predicates P_i and adding the axioms $P_i(x) \leftrightarrow \alpha_i(x)$ and $P_j(x, y) \leftrightarrow \alpha_j(x, y)$, if α_i and α_j has one and two free variables respectively, and by defining:*

$$q_\Phi(\Omega, \boldsymbol{n}) = \frac{1}{Z} \sum_{(\boldsymbol{k},\boldsymbol{h})(P_i)=n_i} w(\boldsymbol{k}, \boldsymbol{h}) \cdot F(\boldsymbol{k}, \boldsymbol{h}, \Omega) \tag{12}$$

where $Z = \mathrm{WFOMC}(\Omega, w, n)$ also known as partition function.

Proof (Proof of Theorem 3). Since Ω is a FO^2 formula, then we can compute FOMC as follows:

$$\mathrm{FOMC}(\Omega, n) = \sum_{\boldsymbol{k},\boldsymbol{h}} F(\boldsymbol{k}, \boldsymbol{h}, \Omega)$$

Let us define $w(\boldsymbol{k}, \boldsymbol{h})$ for each $\boldsymbol{k}, \boldsymbol{h}$ as follows:

$$w(\boldsymbol{k}, \boldsymbol{h}) = \frac{1}{F(\boldsymbol{k}, \boldsymbol{h}, \Omega)} \sum_{\substack{\omega \models \Omega \\ N(\alpha_1,\omega)_1 = (\boldsymbol{k},\boldsymbol{h})(P_1) \\ \cdots \\ N(\alpha_m,\omega)_m = (\boldsymbol{k},\boldsymbol{h})(P_m)}} p_{\Phi,\Omega}(\omega)$$

This definition implies that the partition function Z is equal to 1. Indeed:

$$\begin{aligned}
Z &= \mathrm{WFOMC}(\Omega, w, n) \\
&= \sum_{\boldsymbol{k},\boldsymbol{h}} w(\boldsymbol{k}, \boldsymbol{h}) \cdot F(\boldsymbol{k}, \boldsymbol{h}, \Omega) \\
&= \sum_{\boldsymbol{k},\boldsymbol{h}} \sum_{\substack{\omega \models \Omega \\ N(\alpha_1,\omega)_1 = (\boldsymbol{k},\boldsymbol{h})(P_1) \\ \cdots \\ N(\alpha_m,\omega)_m = (\boldsymbol{k},\boldsymbol{h})(P_m)}} p_{\Phi,\Omega}(\omega) \\
&= \sum_{\omega \models \Omega} \sum_{\substack{\boldsymbol{k},\boldsymbol{h} \\ N(\alpha_1,\omega)_1 = (\boldsymbol{k},\boldsymbol{h})(P_1) \\ \cdots \\ N(\alpha_m,\omega)_m = (\boldsymbol{k},\boldsymbol{h})(P_m)}} p_{\Phi,\Omega}(\omega) \\
&= \sum_{\omega \models \Omega} p_{\Phi,\Omega}(\omega) \\
&= 1
\end{aligned}$$

Hence,

$$
\begin{aligned}
q_\Phi(\Omega, \boldsymbol{n}) &= \sum_{(\boldsymbol{k},\boldsymbol{h})(P_i)=n_i} F(\boldsymbol{k}, \boldsymbol{h}, \Omega) \cdot w(\boldsymbol{k}, \boldsymbol{h}) \\
&= \sum_{(\boldsymbol{k},\boldsymbol{h})(P_i)=n_i} \sum_{\substack{\omega \models \Omega \\ N(\alpha_1,\omega)_1=(\boldsymbol{k},\boldsymbol{h})(P_1) \\ \dots \\ N(\alpha_m,\omega)_m=(\boldsymbol{k},\boldsymbol{h})(P_m)}} p_{\Phi,\Omega}(\omega) \\
&= \sum_{\substack{\omega \models \Omega \\ N(\alpha_1,\omega)_1=n_1 \\ \dots \\ N(\alpha_m,\omega)_m=n_m}} p_{\Phi,\Omega}(\omega)
\end{aligned}
$$

Example 9. In the example proposed in [11], they model the distribution of a sequence of 4 coin tosses such that the probability of getting odd number of heads is zero, and the probability of getting even number of heads is uniformly distributed. In order to model this distribution, we introduce a predicate $H(x)$ over a domain of 4 elements, we also define Ω as $\top$. This means that every model of this theory is a model of Ω. Notice that this distribution cannot be expressed using symmetric weights, as symmetric weights can only express binomial distribution for this language. But we can define weight function on $(\boldsymbol{k}, \boldsymbol{h})$ vector. In this case $\boldsymbol{k} = (k_0, k_1)$ such that $k_0 + k_1 = 4$. Since there are no binary predicates we can ignore $\boldsymbol{h}$. Intuitively, k_0 is the number of tosses which are not heads and k_1 is the number of tosses which are heads. If we define the weight function as $w(k_0, k_1) = 1 + (-1)^{k_1}$ by applying (12) we obtain the following probabilities:

$$
\begin{aligned}
q(\Omega, (4,0)) &= \frac{\binom{4}{4} \cdot (1+1)}{16} = \frac{1}{8} \\
q(\Omega, (3,1)) &= \frac{\binom{4}{3} \cdot (1-1)}{16} = 0 \\
q(\Omega, (2,2)) &= \frac{\binom{4}{2} \cdot (1+1)}{16} = \frac{3}{4} \\
q(\Omega, (1,3)) &= \frac{\binom{4}{1} \cdot (1-1)}{16} = 0 \\
q(\Omega, (0,4)) &= \frac{\binom{4}{0} \cdot (1+1)}{16} = \frac{1}{8}
\end{aligned}
$$

which coincides with the distribution obtained by [11]. Notice, that such a distribution cannot be expressed through symmetric weight functions and obligates the use of a strictly more expressive class of weight functions. In this example we are able to obtain this using real valued weight functions, whereas [11] relies on complex valued weight functions.

We are able to capture count distributions without loosing domain liftability. Furthermore, we do not introduce complex or even negative weights, making the relation between weight functions and probability rather intuitive.

6 Conclusion

In this paper, we have presented a closed-form formula for FOMC of universally quantified formulas in FO^2 that can be computed in polynomial time w.r.t. domain cardinality. From this, we are able to derive a closed-form expression for FOMC in FO^2 formulas in Scott's Normal Form, extended with cardinality constraints. These extended formulas are also computable in polynomial time, and therefore they constitute lifted inference algorithms. All the formulas are extended to cope with weighted model counting in a simple way, admitting a larger class of weight functions than symmetric weight functions. All the results have been obtained using combinatorial principles, providing a uniform treatment to all these fragments.

Acknowledgement. We thank Alessandro Daniele for the fruitful insights and for reviewing the proofs.

References

1. Beame, P., den Broeck, G.V., Gribkoff, E., Suciu, D.: Symmetric weighted first-order model counting. In: Milo, T., Calvanese, D. (eds.) Proceedings of the 34th ACM Symposium on Principles of Database Systems, PODS 2015, Melbourne, Victoria, Australia, 31 May–4 June 2015, pp. 313–328. ACM (2015). https://doi.org/10.1145/2745754.2745760
2. den Broeck, G.V., Meert, W., Darwiche, A.: Skolemization for weighted first-order model counting. In: Baral, C., Giacomo, G.D., Eiter, T. (eds.) Principles of Knowledge Representation and Reasoning: Proceedings of the Fourteenth International Conference, KR 2014, Vienna, Austria, 20–24 July 2014. AAAI Press (2014). http://www.aaai.org/ocs/index.php/KR/KR14/paper/view/8012
3. den Broeck, G.V., Taghipour, N., Meert, W., Davis, J., Raedt, L.D.: Lifted probabilistic inference by first-order knowledge compilation. In: Walsh, T. (ed.) IJCAI 2011, Proceedings of the 22nd International Joint Conference on Artificial Intelligence, Barcelona, Catalonia, Spain, 16–22 July 2011, pp. 2178–2185. IJCAI/AAAI (2011). https://doi.org/10.5591/978-1-57735-516-8/IJCAI11-363
4. Chavira, M., Darwiche, A.: On probabilistic inference by weighted model counting. Artif. Intell. **172**(6–7), 772–799 (2008). https://doi.org/10.1016/j.artint.2007.11.002
5. Das, S.: A brief note on estimates of binomial coefficients (2016). http://page.mi.fu-berlin.de/shagnik/notes/binomials.pdf
6. Getoor, L., Taskar, B.: Introduction to Statistical Relational Learning (Adaptive Computation and Machine Learning). The MIT Press (2007). https://mitpress.mit.edu/books/introduction-statistical-relational-learning
7. Kazemi, S.M., Kimmig, A., den Broeck, G.V., Poole, D.: New liftable classes for first-order probabilistic inference. In: Lee, D.D., Sugiyama, M., von Luxburg, U., Guyon, I., Garnett, R. (eds.) Advances in Neural Information Processing Systems 29: Annual Conference on Neural Information Processing Systems 2016, 5–10 December 2016, Barcelona, Spain, pp. 3117–3125 (2016). https://proceedings.neurips.cc/paper/2016/hash/c88d8d0a6097754525e02c2246d8d27f-Abstract.html

8. Kazemi, S.M., Kimmig, A., den Broeck, G.V., Poole, D.: Domain recursion for lifted inference with existential quantifiers. CoRR abs/1707.07763 (2017). http://arxiv.org/abs/1707.07763
9. Kuusisto, A.: On the uniform one-dimensional fragment. In: Lenzerini, M., Peñaloza, R. (eds.) Proceedings of the 29th International Workshop on Description Logics, Cape Town, South Africa, 22–25 April 2016. CEUR Workshop Proceedings, vol. 1577. CEUR-WS.org (2016). http://ceur-ws.org/Vol-1577/paper_16.pdf
10. Kuusisto, A., Lutz, C.: Weighted model counting beyond two-variable logic. In: Dawar, A., Grädel, E. (eds.) Proceedings of the 33rd Annual ACM/IEEE Symposium on Logic in Computer Science, LICS 2018, Oxford, UK, 09–12 July 2018, pp. 619–628. ACM (2018). https://doi.org/10.1145/3209108.3209168
11. Kuzelka, O.: Complex Markov logic networks: expressivity and liftability. In: Adams, R.P., Gogate, V. (eds.) Proceedings of the Thirty-Sixth Conference on Uncertainty in Artificial Intelligence, UAI 2020, virtual online, 3–6 August 2020. Proceedings of Machine Learning Research, vol. 124, pp. 729–738. AUAI Press (2020). http://proceedings.mlr.press/v124/kuzelka20a.html
12. Kuzelka, O.: Weighted first-order model counting in the two-variable fragment with counting quantifiers. J. Artif. Intell. Res. **70**, 1281–1307 (2021). https://doi.org/10.1613/jair.1.12320
13. Poole, D.: First-order probabilistic inference. In: Gottlob, G., Walsh, T. (eds.) IJCAI-03, Proceedings of the Eighteenth International Joint Conference on Artificial Intelligence, Acapulco, Mexico, 9–15 August 2003, pp. 985–991. Morgan Kaufmann (2003). http://ijcai.org/Proceedings/03/Papers/142.pdf
14. Raedt, L.D., Kersting, K., Natarajan, S., Poole, D.: Statistical Relational Artificial Intelligence: Logic, Probability, and Computation. Synthesis Lectures on Artificial Intelligence and Machine Learning, Morgan & Claypool Publishers (2016). https://doi.org/10.2200/S00692ED1V01Y201601AIM032
15. de Salvo Braz, R., Amir, E., Roth, D.: Lifted first-order probabilistic inference. In: Kaelbling, L.P., Saffiotti, A. (eds.) IJCAI-05, Proceedings of the Nineteenth International Joint Conference on Artificial Intelligence, Edinburgh, Scotland, UK, 30 July–5 August 2005, pp. 1319–1325. Professional Book Center (2005). http://ijcai.org/Proceedings/05/Papers/1548.pdf
16. Scott, D.: A decision method for validity of sentences in two variables. J. Symb. Log. **27**, 377 (1962)
17. Wilf, H.S.: Generatingfunctionology. CRC Press, Boca Raton (2005). https://doi.org/10.1016/C2009-0-02369-1

Option Discovery for Autonomous Generation of Symbolic Knowledge

Gabriele Sartor[1], Davide Zollo[2], Marta Cialdea Mayer[2], Angelo Oddi[3](✉), Riccardo Rasconi[3], and Vieri Giuliano Santucci[3]

[1] University of Turin, Turin, Italy
gabriele.sartor@unito.it
[2] Roma Tre University, Rome, Italy
cialdea@ing.uniroma3.it
[3] ISTC-CNR, Via San Martino della Battaglia, 44, 00185 Rome, Italy
{angelo.oddi,riccardo.rasconi,vieri.santucci}@istc.cnr.it

Abstract. In this work we present an empirical study where we demonstrate the possibility of developing an artificial agent that is capable to autonomously explore an experimental scenario. During the exploration, the agent is able to discover and learn interesting options allowing to interact with the environment without any assigned task, and then abstract and re-use the acquired knowledge to solve the assigned tasks. We test the system in the so-called Treasure Game domain described in the recent literature and we empirically demonstrate that the discovered options can be abstracted in an probabilistic symbolic planning model (using the PPDDL language), which allowed the agent to generate symbolic plans to achieve extrinsic goals.

1 Introduction

If we want robots to be able to interact with complex and unstructured environments like the real-life scenarios in which humans live, or if we want artificial agents to be able to explore and operate in unknown environments, a crucial feature is to give these robots the ability to autonomously acquire knowledge that can be used to solve human requests and adapt to unpredicted new contexts and situations. At the same time, these robots should be able to represent the acquired knowledge in structures that facilitate and speed up its reuse and eventually facilitate human-robot interactions [11].

The field of Intrinsically Motivated Open-ended Learning (IMOL, [30]) is showing promising results in the development of versatile and adaptive artificial agents. *Intrinsic Motivations* (IMs, [2,21]) are a class of self-generated signals that have been used, depending on different implementations, to provide robots with an autonomous guidance for several different processes, from state-and-action space exploration [14], to the autonomous discovery, selection and learning of multiple goals [3,8,29]. In general, IMs guide the agent in the acquisition of

S. Bandini et al. (Eds.): AIxIA 2021, LNAI 13196, pp. 153–167, 2022.
https://doi.org/10.1007/978-3-031-08421-8_11

new knowledge independently (or even in the absence) of any assigned task: this knowledge will then be available to the system to solve user-assigned tasks [31] or as a scaffolding to acquire new knowledge in a cumulative fashion [13,28] (similarly to what have been called curriculum learning [6]). Notwithstanding the advancements in this field, IMOL systems are still limited in acquiring long sequences of skills that can generate complex action plans. In addition to the specific complexity of the problem, this is also due to the fact that most of these systems store the acquired knowledge (e.g., contexts, actions, goals) in low-level representations that poorly support a higher-level reasoning that would guarantee a more effective reuse of such knowledge. Even if some works have shown interesting results with architectural solutions [13,25,27], the use of long-term memory [5], simplified planning [1], or representational redescription [10], the need to use constructs that ensure greater abstraction and thus higher-level reasoning still seems crucial to exploiting the full potential of autonomous learning.

Within reinforcement learning (RL, [35]) the *option framework* [36] implements temporally extended high-level actions (the options), defined as triplets composed of an initiation set (the low-level states from which the option can be executed), the actual policy, and the termination conditions (describing the probability of the option to end in specific low-level states). Options can be handled at a higher level with respect to classical RL policies and, as shown within hierarchical RL (HRL, [4]), they can be chunked together to form longer chains. Moreover, HRL has been combined with IMs to allow for different autonomous processes including, for example, the formation of skill sequences [38], the learning of sub-goals [24] and, together with deep RL techniques, to improve trajectories explorations [17]. However, despite the theoretical and operational power of this framework, options alone do not provide a complete abstraction of all the necessary elements to allow high-level reasoning and planning. Opposed to the low-level processes typical of IMOL and RL approaches, in classical planning frameworks [18] the states, actions and goals are represented as symbols that can be easily handled and composed to perform complex sequences of behaviours to solve assigned tasks. However, in symbolic planning systems, the knowledge on the domain is commonly fixed and provided by an expert at design time, thus preventing the possibility of exploiting this approach in truly autonomous systems.

Finding a bridge between autonomous learning approaches gathering low-level knowledge on the basis of IMs and high-level symbolic decision making is thus a crucial research topic towards the development of a new and more complete generation of artificial agents. In a seminal work, Konidaris and colleagues [16] presented an algorithm for the autonomous "translation" of low-level knowledge into symbols for a PPDDL domain and then used to solve complex high-level goal-achievement tasks such as the Treasure Game (see Fig. 2), by creating sequences of operators (or symbolic plans). However, in [16] the set of options to be abstracted into symbols is given to the system, thus lacking to "close the loop" between the first phase of autonomous exploration and learning, and the second phase of exploitation of the acquired knowledge.

In this work, we will present an empirical study in which we extend the results obtained in our previous research [19,20]. In particular, we deploy the data abstraction procedure on a more complex domain characterized by a higher number of variables, hence focusing on the probabilistic version of the PDDL (Probabilistic Planning Domain Definition Language - PPDDL [39]), demonstrating the possibility to develop an artificial agent that is capable to autonomously explore the experimental scenario, discover and learn interesting options allowing to interact with the environment without any pre-assigned task, and then abstract the acquired knowledge for potential re-utilization to reach high-level goals. In particular, we will test the system in the so-called Treasure Game domain described in [16], where the agent can move through corridors, climb up and down stairs, interact with handles, bolts, keys and a treasure. Two different results have been achieved by empirically following the proposed approach: on the one hand, we experimentally verified how the agent is able to find a set of options and generate symbolic plans to achieve high-level goals (e.g., open a door by using a key); on the other hand, we analyzed a number of technicalities inherently connected to the task of making explicit abstracted knowledge while directly exploring the environment (e.g., synthesizing the correct preconditions of a discovered option).

The paper is organized as follows: in Sect. 2 we introduce the problem faced by the research and the conceptual architecture of the solution proposed in this paper. In Sect. 3.1 we introduce the basic notation and the option framework and we describe our algorithm for automatically discovering options. Indeed, in this paper we describe a two-step learning phases: the first, to generate options from scratch and creating a preliminary action abstraction (Sect. 3.1), and the second, to produce a higher representation partitioning the options and highlighting their causal effects. The latter is described in Sect. 3.2, where we briefly describe the abstraction procedure introduced in [16]. Section 4 describes our empirical results for the Treasure Game domain; finally, in Sect. 5 we give some conclusions and discuss some possible directions of future work.

2 Problem Description

As described in the introduction, in this paper we want to show the possibility of developing an artificial system capable of "closing the loop" between low-level autonomous learning and high-level symbolic planning. Konidaris and colleagues [16] presented a promising approach, trying to combine learning in high-dimensional sensors and actuators spaces through the option framework with high-level, symbol-based, decision making through planning techniques. To do that, they proposed an algorithm able to abstract the knowledge of the system into symbols that can then be used to create sequences of operators to solve complex tasks in both simulated and real robotic scenarios. However, they assumed options where already given to the agent and then only tested the capability of their new algorithm to generate proper symbolic knowledge for a PDDL domain.

The general problem addressed in this paper is therefore to develop a system that effectively starts from learning options that can then be abstracted through the algorithm in [16] and used to solve through planning a task in which it is necessary to perform a sequence of different actions. Option learning has been thoroughly studied in the literature: in particular, when assigned with a goal, a system can leverage on this assigned task to discover or generate sub-goals that can be learnt and encapsulated into options [33]. In the Treasure Game example that we are considering here (see Fig. 2), given the assigned task of reaching for the treasure, the different passages of climbing up and down a ladder, pulling levers, picking keys, etc., can be identified as components of the sequence of actions needed to achieve the final goal, and thus learnt through any learning algorithm, described as options and chunked together in the proper sequence. Once these sub-goals and their related options are learnt, using the abstraction algorithm should be relatively easy, since we can be sure that all the options are actually useful to solve the task of the system.

However, the perspective we take in this work is that of an agent who has to learn autonomously to interact with the environment, without necessarily being aware of what tasks will be later assigned to it. We make this assumption because it forces us to develop versatile and adaptive agents that can be used in unknown and unstructured environments. In this perspective, the general problem described above becomes the more specific one of autonomously identifying which options to learn. Similarly to what done in [32], we need to provide the agent with a general criterion by which it can identify states and/or events in the world that can be the target of specific options: but whereas in that work each element in the grid world was actually connected to the sequence of interaction needed to achieve the most complex effects, our problem is that in an environment such as the one taken in consideration (as well as in real-world scenarios) there are many potentially interesting but "useless" interactions. As in theory we do not know what task the agent will be asked to perform, we will leverage intrinsic motivations to identify potentially interesting states and use them to build options (see Sec. 3.1).

To connect this process of autonomous option discovery with the generation of high-level planning procedures, following our preliminary works [19], we adopt a hierarchical approach aimed at developing a robotic architecture capable of holding together the different mechanisms needed to close the loop between low and high level learning and representations. In details, the idea depicted in Fig. 1, highlights the necessity of three different critical capabilities (or conceptual modules) that every robot must have in order to operate autonomously. The first one, the *option discovery* module combines primitives to create options and learns precondition and effect models. Then, these collected data are used by the *abstraction* module to generate a PPDDL domain containing operators following the *abstract sub-goal option* property. Finally, the PPDDL description can be used by an off-the-shelf planner to reach any sub-goal which can be described with the available high-level symbols. Potentially, the architecture can continue

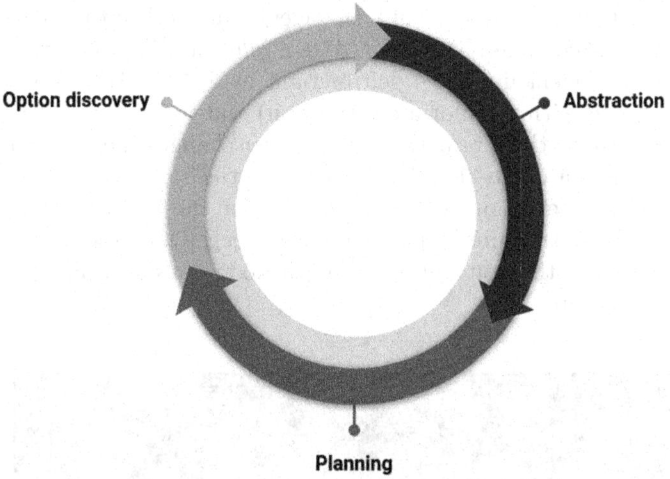

Fig. 1. The conceptual modules needed by the system: *1) Option discovery*, combining primitives to create options and learning precondition and effect models; *2) Abstraction*, translating models to a high-level planning representation; *3) Planning* using the description generated in the previous step.

to execute these steps in a loop extending its knowledge and capabilities over time, exploitable by the human who can ask to reach a certain goal expressed in automatically generated symbols.

3 Implementation

3.1 Option Discovery

Options are temporally-extended actions defined as $o(I, \pi, \beta)$ [34], in which π is the policy executed, I the set of states in which the policy can run and β the termination condition of the option. The option's framework revealed to be an effective tool to abstract actions and extend them with a temporal component. The use of this kind of actions demonstrated to improve significantly the performances of model-based Reinforcement Learning compared to older models, such as one-step models in which the actions employed are the primitives of the agent [37]. Intuitively, these low-level single-step actions, or *primitives*, can be repeatedly exploited to create more complex behaviours.

In this section, we describe a possible way to discover and build a set of options from scratch using the low-level actions available in the *Treasure Game* environment (see Fig. 2). In such environment, an agent starts from its initial position (home), moves through corridors and climbs ladders over different floors, while interacting with a series of objects (e.g., keys, bolts, and levers) to the goal of reaching a treasure placed in the bottom-right corner and bringing it back home.

In order to build new behaviours, the agent can execute the following primitives: 1) *go_up*, 2) *go_down*, 3) *go_left*, 4) *go_right*, and 5) *interact*, respectively used to move the agent up, down, left or right by 2–4 pixels (the exact value is randomly selected with a uniform distribution) and to interact with the closest object. In particular, the interaction with a lever changes the state (open/close) of the doors associated to that lever (both on the same floor or on different floors) while the interaction with the key and/or the treasure simply collects the key and/or the treasure inside the agent's bag. Once the key is collected, the interaction with the bolt unlocks the last door, thus granting the agent the access to the treasure.

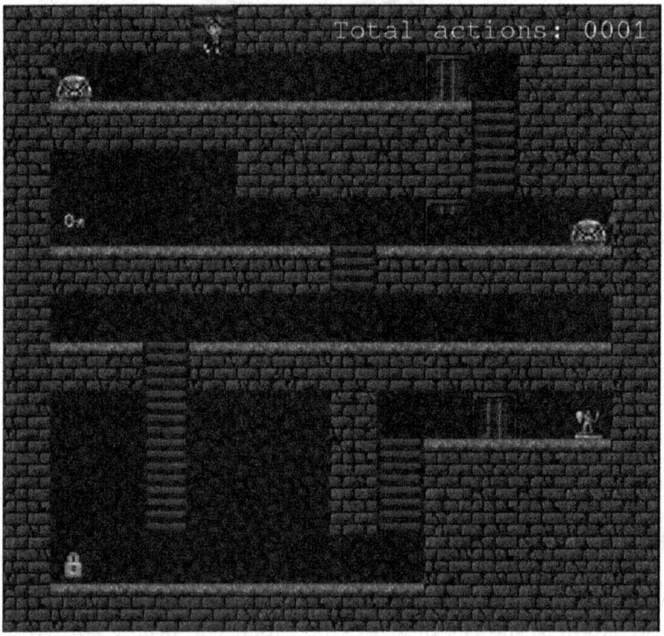

Fig. 2. The treasure game configuration used for the experimental analysis.

In our experiment, primitives are used as building blocks in the construction of the option, participating to the definition of π, I and β. In more details, we create new options from scratch, considering a slightly different definition of option $o(p, t, I, \pi, \beta)$ made up of the following components:

- p, the primitive used by the execution of π;
- t, the primitive which, when available, stops the execution of π;
- π, the policy applied by the option, consisting in repeatedly executing p until t is available or p can no longer be executed;

- I, the set of states from which p can run;
- β, the termination condition of the action, corresponding to the availability of the primitive t or to the impossibility of further executing p.

Consequently, this definition of option requires p, to describe the policy and where it can run, and t, to define the condition stopping its execution, maintaining its characteristic temporal abstraction. For the sake of simplicity, the option's definition will follow the more compact syntax $o(p, t)$ in the remainder of the paper. Algorithm 1 describes the process utilized to discover new options

Algorithm 1. Discovery option algorithm

```
 1: procedure DISCOVER(env, max_eps, max_steps)
 2:     options ← {}
 3:     ep ← 0
 4:     while ep < max_eps do
 5:         T ← 0
 6:         env.RESET_GAME()
 7:         while T < max_steps do
 8:             s ← env.GET_STATE()
 9:             p ← env.GET_AVAILABLE_PRIMITIVE()
10:             while env.IS_AVAILABLE(p) and not (env.NEW_AVAILABLE_PRIM())
    do
11:                 env.EXECUTE(p)
12:                 s' ← env.GET_STATE()
13:             if s ≠ s' then
14:                 if env.NEW_AVAILABLE_PRIM() then
15:                     t ← env.GET_NEW_AVAILABLE_PRIM()
16:                     op ← CREATE_NEW_OPTION(p, t)
17:                 else
18:                     op ← CREATE_NEW_OPTION(p, {})
19:                 options ← options ∪ op
20:     return options
```

autonomously inside the simulated environment. The procedure runs for a number of episodes *max_eps* and *max_steps* steps. Until the maximum of steps of the current episode is not reached, the function keeps track of the starting state s and randomly selects an available primitive p, such that p can be executed in s (line 7–9). Then, as long as p is available and there is no new available primitives (line 10), the option p is executed, and the final state s' of the current potential option is updated. The function *NEW_AVAILABLE_PRIM* returns **True** when a primitive which was not previously executable becomes available while executing p; the function returns **False** in all the other cases. For instance, if the agent finds out that there is a ladder over him while executing the *go_right* option, the primitive *go_up* gets available and the function returns **True**. In other words, *NEW_AVAILABLE_PRIM* detects the interesting event, thus implementing the surprise element that catches the agent's curiosity. For this reason, the primitive representing the exact reverse with respect to the one currently being executed is not interesting for the agent, i.e., the agent will not get interested in the *go_right* primitive while executing *go_left*. The same treatment applied to the (*go_left*, *go_right*) primitive pair is also used with the pair (*go_up*, *go_down*).

When the stopping condition of the most inner while is verified and $s \neq s'$, a new option can be generated according to the following rationale. In case the while exits because of the availability of a new primitive t in the new state s', a new option $o(p, t)$ is created (line 16); otherwise, if the while exits because the primitive under execution is no longer available, a new option $o(p, \{\})$ is created, meaning "*execute p while it is possible*" (line 18). In either case, the created option *op* is added to the list *options* (line 19), which is the output of the function.

In our test scenario, the algorithm generated 11 working options (see Sect. 4), suitable for solving the environment, and collected experience data to be abstracted in PPDDL [39] format successively. Consequently, as we introduced above, the agent performs two learning phases: the first, to generate options from scratch and creating a preliminary action abstraction, and the second, to produce a higher representation partitioning the options and highlighting their causal effects. The latter phase, producing a symbolic representation suitable for planning, is analyzed in the next section.

3.2 Abstracting Options in PPDDL

In this section we provide a summary description of the knowledge abstraction procedure, in order to allow the reader to get a grasp of the rationale behind the synthesis of the PPDDL domain. A thorough description of the abstraction algorithm is beyond the scope of this paper; for further details, the reader is referred to [16].

The procedure basically executes the following five steps:

1. **Data collection:** during this step, the options learned according to Sect. 3.1 are repeatedly executed in the environment and the information about the initial and final state (respectively before and after the execution of each option) are collected. Such data are successively aggregated, and two data structures are returned from the *Data collection* phase: the *initiation data* and the *transition data*, both to be used in the following steps.
2. **Option partition:** this step is dedicated to partitioning the learned options in terms of *abstract subgoal options*. This operation is necessary as the (P)PDDL operators are characterized by a single precondition set and a single effect set; therefore, options that have multiple termination conditions starting from the same initiation set cannot be correctly captured in terms of (P)PDDL operators. As a consequence, before launching the abstraction procedure it is necessary to generate a set of options each of which is guaranteed to produce a single effect (*partial subgoal option*). This operation utilizes the *transition data* set computed in Step 1, as they capture the information about the domain segment the option modifies. Option partition is ultimately

obtained by properly clustering the *transition data* through the DBSCAN algorithm [12] present in the scikit-learn toolkit [23].
3. **Precondition estimation:** this step is dedicated to learning the symbols that will constitute the *preconditions* of the PPDDL operators associated to all the options. This operation utilizes the *initiation data* set computed in Step 1, and is performed utilizing the support vector machine [9] classifier implementation in scikit-learn.
4. **Effect estimation:** analogously, this step is dedicated to learning the symbols that will constitute the *effects* of the PPDDL operators. The effect distribution was modelled through the Kernel density estimation [22,26].
5. **PPDDL Domain synthesis:** finally, this step is dedicated to the synthesis of the PPDDL domain, characterized by the complete definition of all the operators associated to the learned options, in terms of preconditions and effect symbols.

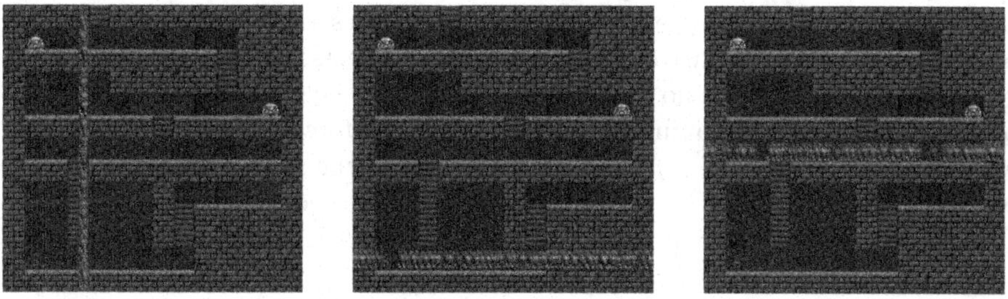

(a) *Symbol_19*. (b) *Symbol_29*. (c) *Symbol_30*.

Fig. 3. Graphical representation of the symbols used in the *option-0* operator. *Symbol_19* represents the agent's x position; *Symbol_29* represents the agent's y position before the operator's execution, while *Symbol_30* represents the agent's y position after the operator's execution.

For instance, Fig. 4 depicts an example operator (`option-0`) whose action corresponds to modifying the agent's position as it has to climb up a stair to reach a new location. The operator's formalization follows the standard Probabilistic PDDL (PPDDL)[1], where the precondition set is composed of the symbols {*Symbol_19*, *Symbol_29*}, the effect set is composed of the symbol {*Symbol_30*}, and the negative effect set contains the symbol {*Symbol_29*} (note that the name of the symbols is automatically generated). The reader should also consider that the PPDDL operators returned by the abstraction procedure are *grounded*; automatically abstracting parametric PPDDL representations is beyond the scope of this work and will be the object of future work. Finally, each PPDDL operator is associated to a reward (17.60 in this case).

[1] Despite the operator selected in this particular example does not make use of probabilities, it has been chosen due to its simplicity to exemplify the utilization of the automatically generated symbols.

```
(:action option-0
    :parameters ()
    :precondition (and (symbol_19) (symbol_29))
    :effect (and (symbol_30) (not (symbol_29)) (decrease (reward) 17.60))
)
```

Fig. 4. Example of autonomously produced PPDDL operator whose semantics is "climb the stairs from the 1st to the 2nd floor".

In order to provide the reader with some information about the meaning of the symbols that populate the previous operator, the semantics of all symbols is graphically presented in Fig. 3. In particular, *Symbol_19* proposition in the operator's preconditions has the following semantics: "*the agent's x coordinate is vertically aligned with the stairs*", while the semantics of *Symbol_29* proposition is "*the agent's y coordinate positions it at a level equivalent to being at the bottom of the stairs*". From the description above, it is clear that the intersection (i.e., the logical *AND*) of the previous two symbols places the agent exactly at the bottom of the stairs. Relatively to the operator's effects, we see that *Symbol_29* gets negated (the agent is no longer at the bottom of the stairs) and it is replaced by *Symbol_30* whose meaning is "*the agent's y coordinate positions it at a level equivalent to being at the top of the stairs*". Lastly, the reader should note that *Symbol_19* remains valid throughout the whole execution of the operator, and that the logical intersection of *Symbol_19* and *Symbol_30* clearly describes the situation where the agent has climbed the stairs.

4 Empirical Analysis

In this section we describe the results obtained from a preliminary empirical study, carried out by testing the Algorithm 1 in the context of the Treasure Game domain [16]. The algorithm was implemented in Python 3.7 under Linux Ubuntu 16.04 as an additional module of the *Skill to Symbols* software[2], using the *Treasure Game* Python package. As previously stated, the Treasure Game domain defines an environment that can be explored by the agent by moving through corridors and doors, climbing stairs, interacting with handles (necessary to open/close the doors), bolts, keys (necessary to unlock the bolts) and a treasure.

In our experimentation, the agent starts endowed with no previous knowledge about the possible actions that can be executed in the environment; the agent is only aware of the basic motion primitives at his disposal, as described in Sect. 3.1. The goal of the analysis is to assess the correctness, usability and quality of the abstract knowledge of the environment autonomously obtained by the agent.

[2] We thank George Konidaris and Steve James for making both the Skills to Symbols and the Treasure Game software available.

The experiment starts by using Algorithm 1, whose application endows the agent with the following set of learned options (11 in total):

$$O = \{(go\_up, \{\}), (go\_down, \{\}), (go\_left, \{\}), (go\_left, go\_up), (go\_left, go\_down), (go\_left, interact), (go\_right, \{\}), (go\_right, go\_up), (go\_right, go\_down), (go\_right, interact), (go\_right, interact), (interact, \{\})\} \quad (1)$$

The test has been run on an Intel I7, 3.4 GHz machine, and the whole process took 30 minutes. All the options are expressed in the compact syntax (p, t) described in Sect. 3.1, where p represents the primitive action corresponding to the action's behavior, and t represents the option's stop condition (i.e., the new primitive action discovered, or an empty set).

Once the set of learned options has been obtained, the test proceeds by applying the knowledge abstraction procedure described in the previous Sect. 3.2. In our specific case, the procedure eventually generated a final PPDDL domain composed by a set of 1528 operators. In order to empirically verify the correctness of the obtained PPDDL domain, we tested the domain with the off-the-shelf mGPT probabilistic planner [7]. The selected planning goal was to find the treasure, located in a hidden position of the environment (i.e., behind a locked door that could be opened only by operating on a bolt with a key) and bring it back to the agent's starting position, in the upper part of the Treasure Game environment. The agent's initial position is by the small stairs located on the environment's 5th floor (up left).

The symbolic plan depicted in Fig. 4 was successfully generated and, as readily observable, reaches the previous goal. The plan is composed of 33 actions, which confirmed the correctness of the proposed methodology (note that the PPDDL operators are named after their exact semantics manually, in order to facilitate their interpretation for the reader.). We also discovered a number of difficulties inherently connected to the task of explicitly abstracting the knowledge by means of a direct exploration of the environment. One consequence of such difficulties is evident from the quality of the plan outlined above. In fact, it is clear that the plan is not optimal, as the agent performs sometime useless actions, such as going left to the bolt and then right to the stairs (22. *go_left[to bolt]* and 23. *go_right[to stairs]*, respectively) instead of directly executing a *go_left[to stairs]*. Another example of redundant actions is the pair 25. *go_right[to wall]*, 26. *go_left[to stairs]* instead of directly executing a *go_right[to stairs]*. It can be easily seen that the optimal plan is composed of 31 actions.

The previous analysis is still ongoing work. In this paper, we are presenting the encouraging results obtained so far, though we have observed that a number of improvements are worth being studied. One observation can be made about the quality of the obtained PPDDL domain; despite we have demonstrated that such domain can be successfully used for automated planning, we have also observed that it contains a number of infeasible operators (i.e., characterized by mutually conflicting preconditions) as well as operators characterized by a high failure probability. Of course, the presence of such operators does not hinder

```
1. go_down [to 5th floor]; 2. go_left [to handle];
3. interact(handle); 4. go_right [to wall];
5. go_down [to 4th floor]; 6. go_right [to handle];
7. interact(handle); 8. go_left [to key]; 9. interact(key);
10. go_right [to stairs]; 11. go_down [to 3rd floor];
12. go_left [to stairs]; 13. go_down [to 1st floor];
14. go_left [to bolt]; 15. interact(bolt, key);
16. go_right [to wall]; 17. go_up [to 2nd floor];
18. go_right [to treasure]; 19. interact(treasure);
20. go_left [to stairs]; 21. go_down [to 1st floor];
22. go_left [to bolt]; 23. go_right [to stairs];
24. go_up [to 3rd floor]; 25. go_right [to wall];
26. go_left [to stairs]; 27. go_up [to 4th floor];
28. go_right [to handle]; 29. interact(handle)
30. go_left [to stairs]; 31. go_up [to 5th floor];
32. go_left [to stairs]; 33. go_up [home];
```

Fig. 5. Plan generated by the mGPT planner with our autonomously synthesized PPDDL domain. The goal of the plan is to (i) find the treasure located behind a closed door that can only be opened by finding a key and then using it to unlock a bolt, and (ii) bringing it to the agent's initial position.

the feasibility of the produced plan (i.e., the former operators will always be discarded by the planner, while the latter will at most make the planning process more demanding, thus decreasing the probability of obtaining an optimal solution) yet, further work must be done to arrive to "crisper" domain representations.

In this respect, there are at least two research lines to investigate. The first line entails the study of different fine-tuning strategies of all the parameters utilized in the previously mentioned Machine Learning tools (such as DBSCAN, SVM, Kernel Density Estimator) involved in the knowledge-abstraction process. The second line is about analyzing the most efficient environment exploration strategy used to collect all the transition data that will be used for the classification tasks that are part of the abstraction procedure, as both the quantity and the quality of the collected data may be essential at this stage.

5 Conclusions and Future Work

In this paper we tested an option discovery algorithm driven by *intrinsic motivations* for an agent operating in the Treasure Game domain [16]. We experimentally demonstrated that the discovered options can be abstracted in an probabilistic symbolic planning model (using the PPDDL language), which allowed the agent to generate symbolic plans to achieve extrinsic goals. One of the possible direction of future work will be the exploration of innovative iterative procedures to incrementally refine [15] the generated PPDDL model.

References

1. Baldassarre, G., Lord, W., Granato, G., Santucci, V.G.: An embodied agent learning affordances with intrinsic motivations and solving extrinsic tasks with attention and one-step planning. Front. Neurorobot. **13**, 45 (2019)
2. Baldassarre, G., Mirolli, M. (eds.): Intrinsically Motivated Learning in Natural and Artificial Systems. Springer, Heidelberg (2013). https://doi.org/10.1007/978-3-642-32375-1
3. Barancs, A., Oudeyer, P.Y.: Active learning of inverse models with intrinsically motivated goal exploration in robots. Robot. Auton. Syst. **61**(1), 49–73 (2013)
4. Barto, A.G., Mahadevan, S.: Recent advances in hierarchical reinforcement learning. Disc. Event Dyn. Syst. **13**(1), 41–77 (2003)
5. Becerra, J.A., Romero, A., Bellas, F., Duro, R.J.: Motivational engine and long-term memory coupling within a cognitive architecture for lifelong open-ended learning. Neurocomputing **452**, 341–354 (2021)
6. Bengio, Y., Louradour, J., Collobert, R., Weston, J.: Curriculum learning. In: Proceedings of the 26th Annual International Conference on Machine Learning, pp. 41–48 (2009)
7. Bonet, B., Geffner, H.: mGPT: a probabilistic planner based on heuristic search. J. Artif. Int. Res. **24**(1), 933–944 (2005)
8. Colas, C., Fournier, P., Chetouani, M., Sigaud, O., Oudeyer, P.Y.: CURIOUS: intrinsically motivated modular multi-goal reinforcement learning. In: International Conference on Machine Learning, pp. 1331–1340. PMLR (2019)
9. Cortes, C., Vapnik, V.: Support-vector networks. Mach. Learn. **20**(3), 273–297 (1995). https://doi.org/10.1023/A:1022627411411
10. Doncieux, S., et al.: Open-ended learning: a conceptual framework based on representational redescription. Front. Neurorobot. **12**, 59 (2018)
11. Ebrahimi, M., Eberhart, A., Bianchi, F., Hitzler, P.: Towards bridging the neuro-symbolic gap: deep deductive reasoners. Appl. Intell. **51**, 1–23 (2021)
12. Ester, M., Kriegel, H.P., Sander, J., Xu, X.: A density-based algorithm for discovering clusters in large spatial databases with noise. In: Proceedings of the Second International Conference on Knowledge Discovery and Data Mining, KDD 1996, pp. 226–231. AAAI Press (1996)
13. Forestier, S., Portelas, R., Mollard, Y., Oudeyer, P.Y.: Intrinsically motivated goal exploration processes with automatic curriculum learning. arXiv preprint arXiv:1708.02190 (2017)
14. Frank, M., Leitner, J., Stollenga, M., Förster, A., Schmidhuber, J.: Curiosity driven reinforcement learning for motion planning on humanoids. Front. Neurorobot. **7**, 25 (2014)
15. Hayamizu, Y., Amiri, S., Chandan, K., Takadama, K., Zhang, S.: Guiding robot exploration in reinforcement learning via automated planning. In: Proceedings of the International Conference on Automated Planning and Scheduling, vol. 31, no. 1, pp. 625–633 (2021), https://ojs.aaai.org/index.php/ICAPS/article/view/16011
16. Konidaris, G., Kaelbling, L.P., Lozano-Perez, T.: From skills to symbols: learning symbolic representations for abstract high-level planning. J. Artif. Intell. Res. **61**, 215–289 (2018). http://lis.csail.mit.edu/pubs/konidaris-jair18.pdf
17. Kulkarni, T.D., Narasimhan, K., Saeedi, A., Tenenbaum, J.: Hierarchical deep reinforcement learning: integrating temporal abstraction and intrinsic motivation. Adv. Neural. Inf. Process. Syst. **29**, 3675–3683 (2016)

18. Nau, D., Ghallab, M., Traverso, P.: Automated Planning: Theory & Practice. Morgan Kaufmann Publishers Inc., San Francisco (2004)
19. Oddi, A., et al.: Integrating open-ended learning in the sense-plan-act robot control paradigm. In: ECAI 2020, the 24th European Conference on Artificial Intelligence (2020)
20. Oddi, A., et al.: An intrinsically motivated planning architecture for curiosity-driven robots. In: 6th Italian Workshop on Artificial Intelligence and Robotics, AIRO 2019, vol. 2594, pp. 19–24. CEUR-WS (2020)
21. Oudeyer, P.Y., Kaplan, F., Hafner, V.: Intrinsic motivation systems for autonomous mental development. IEEE Trans. Evol. Comput. **11**(2), 265–286 (2007)
22. Parzen, E.: On estimation of a probability density function and mode. Ann. Math. Stat. **33**(3), 1065–1076 (1962). http://www.jstor.org/stable/2237880
23. Pedregosa, F., et al.: Scikit-learn: machine learning in python. J. Mach. Learn. Res. **12**(null), 2825–2830 (2011)
24. Rafati, J., Noelle, D.C.: Learning representations in model-free hierarchical reinforcement learning. In: Proceedings of the AAAI Conference on Artificial Intelligence. vol. 33, pp. 10009–10010 (2019)
25. Romero, A., Baldassarre, G., Duro, R.J., Santucci, V.G.: Analysing autonomous open-ended learning of skills with different interdependent subgoals in robots. In: 2021 20th International Conference on Advanced Robotics (ICAR), pp. 646–651. IEEE (2021)
26. Rosenblatt, M.: Remarks on some nonparametric estimates of a density function. Ann. Math. Stat. **27**(3), 832–837 (1956). http://www.jstor.org/stable/2237390
27. Santucci, V.G., Baldassarre, G., Cartoni, E.: Autonomous reinforcement learning of multiple interrelated tasks. In: 2019 Joint IEEE 9th International Conference on Development and Learning and Epigenetic Robotics (ICDL-EpiRob), pp. 221–227. IEEE (2019)
28. Santucci, V.G., Baldassarre, G., Mirolli, M.: Biological cumulative learning through intrinsic motivations: a simulated robotic study on development of visually-guided reaching. In: Proceedings of the Tenth International Conference on Epigenetic Robotics (EpiRob2010), pp. 121–128 (2010)
29. Santucci, V.G., Baldassarre, G., Mirolli, M.: Grail: a goal-discovering robotic architecture for intrinsically-motivated learning. IEEE Trans. Cognitive Dev. Syst. **8**(3), 214–231 (2016)
30. Santucci, V.G., Oudeyer, P.Y., Barto, A., Baldassarre, G.: Intrinsically motivated open-ended learning in autonomous robots. Front. Neurorobot. **13**, 115 (2020)
31. Seepanomwan, K., Santucci, V.G., Baldassarre, G.: Intrinsically motivated discovered outcomes boost user's goals achievement in a humanoid robot. In: 2017 Joint IEEE International Conference on Development and Learning and Epigenetic Robotics (ICDL-EpiRob), pp. 178–183 (2017)
32. Singh, S., Barto, A.G., Chentanez, N.: Intrinsically motivated reinforcement learning. In: Proceedings of the 17th International Conference on Neural Information Processing Systems, NIPS 2004, pp. 1281–1288. MIT Press, Cambridge (2004)
33. Stolle, M., Precup, D.: Learning options in reinforcement learning. In: Koenig, S., Holte, R.C. (eds.) SARA 2002. LNCS (LNAI), vol. 2371, pp. 212–223. Springer, Heidelberg (2002). https://doi.org/10.1007/3-540-45622-8_16
34. Sutton, R.S., Barto, A.G.: Reinforcement Learning: An Introduction. MIT Press, Cambridge (1998)
35. Sutton, R.S., Barto, A.G.: Reinforcement Learning: An Introduction. MIT Press, Cambridge (2018)

36. Sutton, R.S., Precup, D., Singh, S.: Intra-option learning about temporally abstract actions. In: Proceedings of 15th International Conference on Machine Learning, pp. 556–564. Morgan Kaufmann, San Francisco (1998)
37. Sutton, R.S., Precup, D., Singh, S.: Between mdps and semi-mdps: a framework for temporal abstraction in reinforcement learning. Artif. Intell. **112**(1-2), 181–211 (1999). https://doi.org/10.1016/S0004-3702(99)00052-1
38. Vigorito, C.M., Barto, A.G.: Intrinsically motivated hierarchical skill learning in structured environments. IEEE Trans. Auton. Ment. Dev. **2**(2), 132–143 (2010). https://doi.org/10.1109/TAMD.2010.2050205
39. Younes, H., Littman, M.: PPDDL1.0: an extension to PDDL for expressiong planning domains with probabilistic effects. Technical report, Carnegie Mellon University (2004). CMU-CS-04-167

Natural Language Processing

A Neural-Machine-Translation System Resilient to Out of Vocabulary Words for Translating Natural Language to SPARQL

Manuel Borroto(✉), Francesco Ricca, and Bernardo Cuteri

University of Calabria, 87036 Rende, CS, Italy
{manuel.borroto,francesco.ricca,bernardo.cuteri}@unical.it
https://informatica.unical.it

Abstract. The development and diffusion of ontologies allowed the creation of large banks of information regarding multiple domains known as knowledge bases. Ontologies propose a way to represent information providing semantic meaning that allows the data to be machine-interpretable. However, enjoying such rich knowledge is a difficult task for the majority of potential users who do not know either the knowledge-base definition or how to write queries with SPARQL. Systems able to translate natural language questions into SPARQL queries have the potential to overcome this problem. In this paper, we propose an approach that combines the Named Entity Recognition and Neural Machine Translation tasks to perform an automatic translation of natural language questions into executables SPARQL queries. The resulting approach provides robustness to the presence of terms that do not occur in the training set. We evaluate the potential of our approach by using Monument and QALD-9, which are well-known datasets for Question Answering over the DBpedia ontology.

Keywords: Natural Language Processing · Question answering · Knowledge base · Neural machine translation

1 Introduction

Today we have large and complex knowledge bases (KB) created by the integration of thousands of repositories that contain data referring to a wide variety of domains, providing users with access to an unbelievable amount of information in what is known as Linked Data. Ontologies played a crucial role in this scenario by proposing a new way of modeling, storing, and sharing data so that machines can interpret it. As a relevant example, one can consider the DBpedia project, which constitutes one of the most popular and richest knowledge bases nowadays. However, enjoying such rich knowledge is a difficult task for most of the potential users who do not know either the KB definition or how to write queries with the technical language SPARQL, forcing them to have limited access to the knowledge bases as it is provided by predefined interfaces.

S. Bandini et al. (Eds.): AIxIA 2021, LNAI 13196, pp. 171–184, 2022.
https://doi.org/10.1007/978-3-031-08421-8_12

Systems able to translate questions posed in natural language in SPARQL queries have the potential of overcoming this problem because they can remove all technical complexity to the final users. Thus, natural language Question Answering (QA) is gaining importance in the area of the Semantic Web.

The most advanced QA approaches over knowledge bases [3,17,19] propose systems for translating automatically natural language questions into SPARQL queries. These are mostly based on deep neural networks to tackle the problem and exploit the great development achieved by Deep Learning in the last few years. However, existing approaches do not consider explicitly the problem of handling the presence of terms that do not occur in the training set, known as *out-of-vocabulary* (OOV) words. A feature particularly useful when dealing with evolving ontologies that are continuously enriched with new individuals.

In this paper, we introduce *sparql-qa*, a system for performing automatic translation of natural language questions in SPARQL queries based on Neural Machine Translation. Our system was built to mitigate the impact caused by (OOV) words.

We achieve this result with a novel architecture based on a Neural Machine Translation (NMT) [1] module and a Named Entity Recognition (NER) module both based on *Bidirectional Recurrent Neural Networks* (BRNN) [10,21]. The NMT module translates the input NL question into a SPARQL template, whereas the NER module extracts the entities from the question. The combination of the results of the two modules results in a SPARQL query ready to be executed. Importantly, we introduce a formal definition of a training set format that reduces the output space and is essential for the proper functioning of the system and also allows us to tackle the problem with out-of-vocabulary words, a major weakness of the majority of the related approaches today. We empirically test the system on the Monument [8] and QALD-9 [16] datasets, which are benchmarks for Question Answering on the well-known DBpedia ontology.

This paper is structured as follows. In Sect. 2, we talk briefly about some preliminary concepts mentioned during the reading. Section 3 goes into the particular details of our approach. Section 4 focuses on the discussion of experiments and results. Then in Sect. 5, we talk about related works, and finally, we provide some conclusions and aspects for future work.

2 Preliminaries

This section provides a gentle introduction to the basic notions mentioned in this paper, with the goal of making it broadly accessible to readers from different areas of AI.

2.1 Knowledge Bases and SPARQL

Knowledge Bases. Informally, a knowledge-base is a formal description of a domain of interest that is suitable to be managed by an engine reasoning about the facts modeled in the knowledge base itself, e.g., query existing knowledge or obtain new knowledge. A formal description of knowledge as a set of concepts within a domain and the relationships that hold between them is called *ontology* [7].

In a KB, resources can be defined through URIs, which allows reference to non-local resources. This property permits the interaction among various KBs, making the information that can be accessed grow considerably, not only in volume but also in the diversity of domains. To access the information, given an ontology, one has to resort to a proper *query language*. In our context, the de-facto standard for this type of task is SPARQL [22].

SPARQL is an SQL-like language to query RDF-graphs. The syntax and semantics of the language are defined by the fact that RDF is represented as a directed labeled graph, written through triples, so to write a query it is necessary to define triples looking for a match with *subject-predicate-object* patterns within the graph [22]. The following is an example of a SPARQL query:

```
PREFIX dbo: <http://dbpedia.org/ontology/>
PREFIX dbr: <http://dbpedia.org/resource/>
SELECT ?place WHERE { dbr:Hillary_Clinton  dbo:birthPlace ?place }
```

The first and second lines (PREFIX) defines the prefix namespace, which is used to disambiguate concepts with the same name, the third line (SELECT) returns a list with the values of the variable *?place*. The *WHERE* clause contains the triples to match against the RDF graph, where *dbr:Hillary_Clinton* identifies the KB resource, and the identifiers that begin with "?" are considered variables. This example query models the answer to the question "Where was Hillary Clinton born?".

The full language allows to express complex queries, for more details we refer the reader to [22].

2.2 Recurrent Neural Networks

The models proposed in this paper rely heavily on Recurrent Neural Networks (RNN), a special type of neural network. RNNs work by iterating over the elements of a sequence S and keeping a state h that contains information relative to what was already processed so that the result of processing the element at time t is also conditioned by the previous information $t-1$ [5]. In our case, we used two variants known as Long short-term memory (LSTM) and Bidirectional LSTM (BiLSTM).

Long Short-Term Memory. In 1997, [9] proposed a particular type of RNN called *Long short-term memory* (LSTM), aiming to address a common phenomenon known as Vanishing Gradient Descent [9], that affects the standards RNNs. To achieve this, the LSTMs employ a mechanism called Gates when computing the hidden states. The gating mechanism can regulate the flow of information and decide what information is important to keep or throw away. This is done by mean of:

$$i = \sigma(x_t U^i + s_{t-1} W^i) \qquad f = \sigma(x_t U^f + s_{t-1} W^f)$$
$$o = \sigma(x_t U^o + s_{t-1} W^o) \qquad g = \tanh(x_t U^g + s_{t-1} W^g)$$
$$c_t = c_{t-1} \circ f + g \circ i \qquad s_t = \tanh(c_t) \circ o$$

where the input i, forget f, and output o represent gates that are squashed by the sigmoid into vectors of values between 0 and 1. Multiplying the vectors determines how much of the other vectors to let into the current input state. g is a candidate hidden state that is computed based on the current input and the previous hidden state. c_t is used as the internal memory, which is a combination of the previous memory c_{t-1} multiplied by the input gate, and the hidden state s_t is a combination of the internal memory and the output gate.

Bidirectional RNNs. A BRNN network usually consists of using two RNNs in any variant (naive RNN, LSTM, or GRU [4]), each of which processes the sequence in one direction and then merging their outputs. In this way, it is possible to capture patterns that may not be seen by a unidirectional RNN. The one using LSTM is called BiLSTM.

Conditional Random Fields. [13] are a probabilistic framework for labeling and segmenting sequential data. They use contextual information from previous labels to increase the amount of information available to make a good prediction. CRFs rely on Feature Functions to express some characteristic of the sequence that the data point represents. Feature Functions could take several input values like the set of input vectors X, the position i of the data point being labeled, the label of data point $i-1$ in X, and the label of data point i in X. To build the conditional field, it is necessary to assign to each feature function a set of weights λ that the algorithm will learn by applying Gradient Descent iteratively until the parameter values converge. A sequence is tagged by mean of:

$$p(y|X,\lambda) = \frac{1}{Z(X)} exp\{\sum_{i=1}^{n} \sum_{j} \lambda_j f_j(X, i, y_{i-1}, y_i)\} \qquad (1)$$

where Z(X) is the normalization to [0, 1] since the output is expected to be a probability, and f_j is the feature function. For more details about CRFs, the readers can refer to [12,13].

3 From Natural Language Questions to SPARQL

Knowledge bases are a rich source of information related to a great variety of domains, which can be accessed by experts of formal query languages. The potential of exploiting knowledge bases can be greatly increased by allowing any user to query the ontology by posing questions in natural language.

In this paper, this problem is seen as the following Natural Language Processing task: Given an RDF knowledge base O and a question Q_{nat} in natural language (to be answered using O), translate Q into a SPARQL query $S_{Q_{nat}}$ such that the answer to Q_{nat} can be obtained by running $S_{Q_{nat}}$ on the underlying ontology O.

The starting point is training set containing a number of pairs $\langle Q_{nat}, G_{Q_{nat}} \rangle$, where Q_{nat} is a natural language question, and $G_{Q_{nat}}$ is a SPARQL query, called the *gold query*. The gold query is a SPARQL query that models (i.e., allows to retrieve from O) the answers to Q_{nat}. The training set has to be used to learn how to answer questions posed in natural language using O, so that, given a question in natural language Q_{nat}, the QA system can generate a query $S'_{Q_{nat}}$ that is equivalent to the gold query $G_{Q_{nat}}$ for Q_{nat}, i.e., such that $answers(S'_{Q_{nat}}) = answers(G_{Q_{nat}})$.[1] In particular, we approach this problem as a machine translation task, that is we compute $S'_{Q_{nat}}$ as $S'_{Q_{nat}} = Translate(Q_{nat})$, where $Translate$ is the translation function implemented by our QA System, called *sparql-qa*.

Most of the solutions currently proposed to convert from natural language to SPARQL language make use of various techniques, either using patterns or deep neural networks. In any machine translation technique, the definition of input and output vocabularies is necessary, which, working with natural language, can become large enough to be a real problem when undertaking the translation task. This large size directly affects systems based on neural networks because they depend on a training set that allows networks to generalize a given domain. Obtaining a good dataset that includes all the words and names in the English language and includes all DBpedia resources is a task with a high level of difficulty. The datasets currently available comprise only a part of the vocabulary, generating a problem of *Words Out Of Vocabulary* (WOOV) that affects both the input and the output.

Systems affected by the WOOV problem have difficulty dealing with words not seen during the training phase because they do not know how to map those words to the output vocabulary. For example, let's assume we have a training set containing the "*Abraham Lincoln*" words and a system trained on it. If we want to translate the question *When Abraham Lincoln was born?*; the system will be able to identify the right KB resource, but on the other hand, the system will fail to translate a question using the same pattern, but changing "*Abraham Lincoln*" by something not present in the vocabulary, let say "*Barack Obama*".

To reduce the impact of the WOOV and to boost the training time of the entire process, we will introduce in the next subsection a suitable format to represent an NL to SPARQL datasets that we call *QQT* format.

[1] Note that we are interested in computing the answers, and not in reproducing syntactically the gold query.

Table 1. $\langle Question, Query \rangle$ pair for *Who painted the Mona Lisa?*

Question	Query
Who painted the Mona Lisa?	select ?a where {dbr:Mona_Lisa dbo:author ?a.}

Table 2. $\langle Question, QueryTemplate, Tagging \rangle$ pair for *Who painted the Mona Lisa?*

Question	QueryTemplate	Tagging
Who painted the Mona Lisa?	select ?a where {?w dbo:author ?a. ?w rdfs:label $1}	O O O B I O

3.1 Mitigating the WOOV Problem

In general, NL to SPARQL datasets are composed of a set of pairs $\langle Q_{nat}, G_{Q_{nat}} \rangle$. In such a common type of representation, the named entities found in the question are typically represented directly by their URIs in the SPARQL query, but this transformation is hard to learn from mere examples, and the trained system would fail if the transformation can not be described as simple rules. This is an issue, especially in large ontologies, where there is a huge number of resources.

A dataset in QQT is composed of a set of triples in the form $\langle Question, QueryTemplate, Tagging \rangle$, where *Question* is a natural language question, and *Tagging* marks which parts of *Question* are entities, and *QueryTemplate* is a SPARQL query template with the following modifications: (*i*) The KB resources are replaced by one or more variables; (*ii*) A new triple is added for each variable in the form "*?var rdfs:label placeholder*". *Placeholders* are meant to be replaced by substrings of *Question* depending on *Tagging*.

In Table 1 we show an example of a $\langle Q_{nat}, Q_{sparql} \rangle$ pair for the question *Who painted the Mona Lisa?*, while Table 2 shows the corresponding $\langle Question, QueryTemplate, Tagging \rangle$ triple in the QQT format.

In Table 2 the term $1 denotes a placeholder, where 1 means that it has to be replaced by the first entity occurring in the question, that is *Mona Lisa* as represented by *B* and *I* in *Tagging*. Note that, in the QQT format, the query template does not contain any DBpedia resource, thus the learning model (which is the neural network in our case) does not need to understand that Mona Lisa stands for the *dbr:Mona_Lisa* resource and the *QueryTemplate* is exactly the same for all questions asking the author of a given artwork. For the scope of our work, we automatically transform the considered datasets to a QQT format by looking for the KB resources (dbr) occurrences in the queries and replacing them with the corresponding QTT syntax.

3.2 Out-of-Vocabulary Words in NL Questions

Although we can reduce the size of the output vocabulary by creating a QQT dataset, there is still a problem with the input vocabulary because there may be many absent words. This problem causes the model not to learn how to translate those OOV words because they were not seen during the training process. To address this problem, we used the pre-trained word embeddings provided by the FastText [2] library, allowing us to have access to thousands of embeddings vectors learned over millions of words, becoming a positive aspect because to obtain something similar, it is necessary a lot of time and computational resources. FastText can provide a word-embedding of a token even if it was not part of the vocabulary used to train the vectors, making it possible to manipulate OOV words.

3.3 The Model

Our approach consists of two deep neural networks, the first one specialized in Neural Machine Translation (NMT) based on the well-known Seq2Seq [21] model and the second one used for extracting the entities from the question using the Named Entity Recognition (NER) technique.

Neural Machine Translation. The network focused on NMT is used to translate the question into a SPARQL *QueryTemplate*. The network is based on an Encoder-Decoder model with *Luong's attention* [14], in which the Encoder extracts semantic content from the question in natural language and encodes it into a fixed-dimensional vector representation V. Instead, the Decoder tries to decode V into a sequence in the output language (*QueryTemplate*).

The Encoder is composed of an input layer that receives a question in natural language converted into a sequence of word-embeddings obtained by mean of FastText, in the form $\{x_1, x_2, ..., x_t\}$, where x_t is the vector representation of the word t in the sentence. Next, we use a Bidirectional LSTM (BiLSTM) to summarize $\{x_1, x_2, ..., x_t\}$ into V, in forward and reverse orders. V is formed by concatenating the last hidden states in the two directions.

On the other hand, during the training process, the Decoder is responsible for calculating the word-embeddings of the output language tokens (SPARQL), which is used together with the vector V, provided by the Encoder, as input to a Luong-Decoder layer. This layer is responsible for decoding the sentence supported by the attention mechanism. Finally, the values are feed to a Fully Connected Network with a Softmax activation function that predicts the output sequence by calculating the conditional probability over the output vocabulary. Figure 1 shows the described network architecture.

Named Entity Recognition. To perform the entity recognition, we created a BiLSTM-CRF [10] network that constitutes state-of-the-art for this type of task. In this case, we again used FastText to obtain the word-embeddings and deal with OOV words. The model is composed of an input layer that receives the sequences of embeddings, followed by a BiLSTM connected to a Fully Connected layer. Finally, the information flows through a Conditional Random Fields (CRF) layer that calculates the probabilities of tagging a word from the input sequence

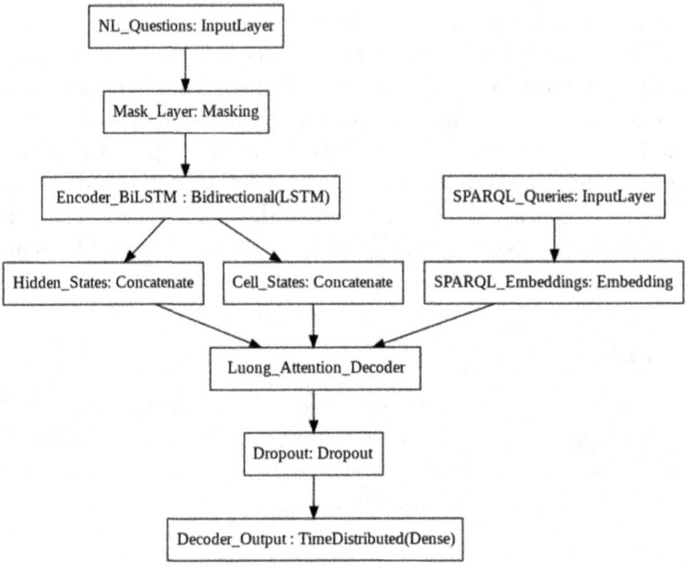

Fig. 1. NMT neural network architecture

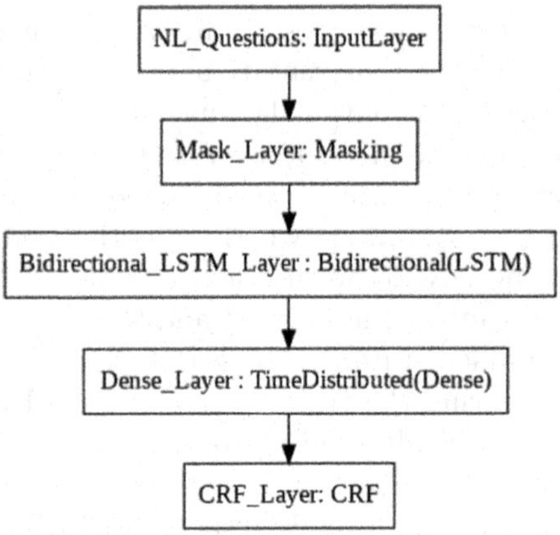

Fig. 2. NER neural network architecture

with the tokens contained in the tagging vocabulary. Figure 2 shows the described network architecture.

The final step of our system mixes the results of both networks to obtain the query $S'_{Q_{nat}}$. Here, the placeholders in the *QueryTemplate* are replaced by the corresponding entities obtained with the NER network.

Table 3. Comparison on monument datasets.

	Mon300			Mon600		
	P	R	F1	P	R	F1
NSpM	0.860	0.861	0.852	0.929	0.945	0.932
sparql-qa	0.78	0.78	0.78	0.791	0.791	0.791

4 Experiments

We report here an empirical assessment of our approach.

Experiment Setup. We have implemented our models by using Keras, a well-known framework for machine learning, on top of TensorFlow. We trained the networks by using Google Collaboratory, which is a virtual machine environment hosted in the cloud and based on Jupyter Notebooks. The environment provides 12GB of RAM and connects to Google Drive. We considered two well-known publicly available datasets for QA over the DBpedia ontology: Monument and QALD-9. To assess the systems, we adopted the macro precision (**P**), recall (**R**), and F1-score measures, which are the most used ones to assess this kind of system.

4.1 Evaluation on Monument Dataset

The Monument dataset was proposed as part of the Neural SPARQL Machines (NSpM) [19] research. It contains 14,778 question-query pairs about the instances of type monument present in DBpedia.

For the sake of comparison with the state-of-the-art, we have trained the Learner Module of NSpM as it was done in [19], where the authors proposed two instances of the Monument dataset that we will denote by Monumet300 and Monument600 containing 8,544 and 14,788 pairs, respectively. In both cases, the dataset split fixes 100 pairs for both validation and test set and keeps the rest for the training set. All the data is publicly available in the NSpM GitHub project.[2] To train our system, we first performed hyperparameter tuning focused on three metrics: embedding-size of the target language, batch size, and LSTM hidden units. The task was performed by using a grid search method. We set the number of epochs to 5, shuffling the dataset at the end of each one. After tuning, we set the hyperparameters of the two networks as follows: embedding-size is set to 300, LSTM hidden units are set to 96, and batch size is set to 64. From the results of the execution reported in Table 3, we can see that our system performs reasonably well, reaching F1-score values greater than 0.7. On the other hand, NSpM achieves better results.

We have investigated the cases in which our system could not provide an optimal answer, and we discovered that the performance of our approach is mainly affected by problems in the dataset. We found a set of questions that lacks context to determine specific expected URIs. For example, for the question "What is

[2] https://github.com/LiberAI/NSpM/tree/master/data.

Table 4. Comparison with OOV entities on Monument datasets.

	Mon300			Mon600		
	P	R	F1	P	R	F1
NSpM	0.097	0.123	0.101	0.11	0.11	0.11
sparql-qa	0.795	0.795	0.795	0.785	0.785	0.785

Washington Monument related to?" our system uses "Washington Monument", but the gold query uses the specific URI: *Washington_Monument_(Baltimore)*. Note that there is no reference to Baltimore in the question text, and there are Washington Monuments also in Milwaukee and Philadelphia, according to DBPedia. Surprisingly, NSpM can often use the specific URI of the gold query. Thus, we decided to devise a tougher experiment to better understand the issue. We used the templates provided by NSpM and a randomly selected set of unseen monument entities extracted from DBpedia to create a new test set of 200 pairs. The results reported in Table 4 show that our approach confirms the same good performance (F1 score greater than 0.78), demonstrate to be capable of better generalizing power being basically resilient to the presence of unseen entities and also performs better than NSpM.

4.2 Evaluation on QALD-9

The *Question Answering over Linked Data* (QALD) is a series of challenges that aim to provide benchmarks for assessing and comparing QA systems on DBpedia [16]. We considered the benchmark proposed as part of the ninth edition of QALD, known as QALD-9.[3] The dataset contains 558 question-query pairs in 11 different languages. The data is split into 408 training and 150 testing questions, and we focus on the ones expressed in English. It is important to note that this dataset is very challenging to be approached using learning techniques given the very small training set not covering all questions types of the test set. We reproduced the original QALD-9 setting to compare our system with the systems that participated in the competition. To train our network, we performed a cross-validation process to adjust the model parameters, motivated by the small number of examples in the training set. We use the same settings as with the Monument dataset and set the epochs to 45.

Table 5 shows the performance of the QALD-9 challengers and the *NSQA* [11] system proposed by the IBM research group, demonstrating that our model was able to learn from small data, ranking virtually in the third position.

Given the very small set of questions, we decided to expand the training set to further improve our system and better understand its behavior. Thus, we created templates from the gold questions by annotating all the named entities with spaCy and checked them manually; then, we generated new questions by replacing the annotated entities with others randomly selected up to creating a total of 1816 pairs. This is the *expanded* training set. Further, we applied the same query

[3] https://github.com/ag-sc/QALD/tree/master/9/data.

Table 5. Comparison on QALD-9.

	P	R	F1	F1 QALD
Elon	0.049	0.053	0.050	0.100
QASystem	0.097	0.116	0.098	0.200
TeBaQA	0.129	0.134	0.130	0.222
wdaqua-core1	0.261	0.267	0.250	0.289
gAnswer	0.293	0.327	0.298	0.430
NSQA	0.314	0.321	0.308	0.453
sparql-qa	0.279	0.277	0.273	0.410

generation process to the pairs of the test set and added additional pairs to the expanded training set. No pair or gold query from the original test set was added. In this way, we created a new benchmark (labeled *expanded w/test*) containing 2331 examples. As we can see in Table 6, expanding the dataset with the same question types (*expanded dataset*) does not improve the results too much, rather it could be harmful because there is more repeatability in a training set that is not representative of the test set, conducting to less generalization. Moreover, when the training set is expanded with patterns from the original test set (see the expanded w/test row), our system reaches very good performance (F1 QALD of 0,75). This latter experience confirms that the training set of QALD-9 is not fully representative of the test set. This explains why our system does not perform in an optimal way in this benchmark. Nonetheless, the performance of our system is not that far from NSQA and can be better once a more representative training set is considered.

5 Related Work

Pattern-Based. The idea of employing query patterns for mapping questions to SPARQL-queries was already exploited in the literature [18,20]. The approach presented by Pradel and Ollivier [18] also adopts named entity recognition but applies a set of predefined rules to obtain all the query elements and their relationships. The approach by Steinmetz et al. [20] has 4 phases, firstly, the question is parsed and the main focus is extracted, then general queries are generated from the phrases in natural language according to predefined patterns and finally make a subject-predicate-object mapping of the general question to triples in RDF. Despite both of the above-mentioned approaches performed well

Table 6. *sparql-qa* on QALD-9 expanded.

	P	R	F1	F1 QALD
Expanded	0.288	0.288	0.285	0.423
Expanded w/test	0.633	0.634	0.628	0.751

in selected benchmarks, they rely on patterns and rules defined manually for all existing types of questions. A limit that is not present in our proposal.

Deep Learning-Based. In the Seq2SQL approach [26] an LSTM Seq2Seq model is used to translate from natural language to SQL queries. The interesting thing about this approach is that they use *Reinforcement Learning* to guide the learning. The usage Encoder-Decoder model based in LSTM with an attention mechanism to associate a vocabulary mapping between natural language and SPARQL was proposed also in the literature [15] obtaining good results.

The *Neural SPARQL Machines (NSpM)* [19] approach is based on the idea of modifying the SPARQL queries to treat them as a foreign language. To achieve this, they encoded the brackets, URIs, operators, and other symbols, making the tokenization process easier. The resulting dataset was introduced in a Seq2Seq model responsible for performing the question-query mapping. The same authors created the *DBNQA dataset* [8], and their model was tested on a subdomain referring to monuments and evaluated using the purely syntactic BLEU score [19]. As a consequence, it performs well in reproducing the syntax of the gold query but is less able to generalize to unseen natural language questions and OOV words when compared with our approach.

The query building approach by Chen et al. [3] features two stages. The first stage consists of predicting the query structure of the question and leverages the structure to constrain the generation of the candidate queries. The second stage performs a candidate query rank. As in our approach, Chen et al. [3] uses BiLSTM networks, but query representation is based on abstract query graphs.

Kapanipathi et al. [11] proposed an interesting system called NSQA that performs several steps to obtain the final query. First, the question is semantically parsed to an Abstract Meaning Representation (AMR). Next, they align the AMR with the KB by applying entity linking followed by a path-based algorithm to generate triples that have a one-to-one correspondence to the triples in the final SPARQL query. Finally, the triples are converted to a first-order logic representation to be used by a Logical Neural Networks responsible to performs the reasoning to generate the SPARQL query. This system does not require end-to-end training data and has been demonstrated to work well on QALD9 and LC-QuAD 1.0 datasets. We wanted to compare NSQA with our system using the Monument dataset, but it is not an open-source project. Then, we asked the authors for help to obtain the necessary data for performing the comparison, but finally, we did not receive the information.

Also, we report that eight different models based on RNNs and CNNs were compared by Yin and colleagues [23]. In this large experiment, the ConvS2S [6] model proved to be the best.

For completeness, we studied another related line of work that aims to translate the natural language questions into SQL queries. The work proposed by Yu et al. [24] introduces a large-scale, complex, and cross-domain semantic parsing and text-to-SQL dataset. To validate the work contribution, they used the proposed dataset to train different models to convert text to SQL queries. Most of the models were based on a Seq2Seq architecture with attention, demonstrating an adequate performance. Another interesting case of study is the editing-based approach for text-to-SQL generation introduced by Zhang et al. [25]. They implement a Seq2Seq model with Luong's attention, using BiLSTMs and BERT embeddings. The approach demonstrates to perform well on SParC and Spider datasets, outperforming the related work in some cases.

Our architecture addresses many of the issues connected with the translation resorting to specific tools, an aspect that is not present in mentioned works. Moreover, existing approaches based on NMT do nothing special to deal with OOV words.

6 Conclusions and Future Work

The paper presents an approach based on deep neural networks to query knowledge bases by using natural language. We exploit the strength of several well-known NLP tools and pose a special focus on reducing the target vocabulary of the NMT task and attenuating the impact of the OOV words, an important issue that is not well considered in existing approaches. Our system showed competitive results on Monument and QALD-9 datasets and demonstrated a more general and robust behavior on unseen questions among the compared systems.

In future work, we plan to extend our system to improve translation performance by integrating other NLP tools, such as Named Entity Linking and BERT contextual word embeddings. We also plan to extend our experiments considering other recently-developed QA benchmarks.

References

1. Bahdanau, D., Cho, K., Bengio, Y.: Neural machine translation by jointly learning to align and translate. arXiv preprint arXiv:1409.0473 (2014)
2. Bojanowski, P., Grave, E., Joulin, A., Mikolov, T.: Enriching word vectors with subword information. TACL **5**, 135–146 (2017)
3. Chen, Y., Li, H., Hua, Y., Qi, G.: Formal query building with query structure prediction for complex question answering over knowledge base. In: IJCAI (2020)
4. Cho, K., et al.: Learning phrase representations using RNN encoder-decoder for statistical machine translation. arXiv:1406.1078 (2014)
5. Francois, C.: Deep Learning with Python. Manning Publications Company (2017)
6. Gehring, J., Auli, M., Grangier, D., Yarats, D., Dauphin, Y.N.: Convolutional sequence to sequence learning. In: ICML. Proceedings of ML Research, vol. 70, pp. 1243–1252. PMLR (2017)
7. Gruber, T.R.: Toward principles for the design of ontologies used for knowledge sharing? Int. J. Hum.-Comput. Stud. **43**(5–6), 907–928 (1995)
8. Hartmann, A., Marx, E., Soru, T.: Generating a large dataset for neural question answering over the DBpedia knowledge base (2018)
9. Hochreiter, S.: Recurrent neural net learning and vanishing gradient. Int. J. Uncert. Fuzz. KB Syst. **6**(2), 107–116 (1998)
10. Huang, Z., Xu, W., Yu, K.: Bidirectional LSTM-CRF models for sequence tagging. CoRR abs/1508.01991 (2015)

11. Kapanipathi, et al.: Question answering over knowledge bases by leveraging semantic parsing and neuro-symbolic reasoning. arXiv preprint arXiv:2012.01707 (2020)
12. Klinger, R., Tomanek, K.: Classical probabilistic models and conditional random fields. Citeseer (2007)
13. Lafferty, J., McCallum, A., Pereira, F.C.: Conditional random fields: probabilistic models for segmenting and labeling sequence data (2001)
14. Luong, M., Pham, H., Manning, C.D.: Effective approaches to attention-based neural machine translation. arXiv preprint arXiv:1508.04025 (2015)
15. Luz, F.F., Finger, M.: Semantic parsing natural language into SPARQL: improving target language representation with neural attention. CoRR abs/1803.04329 (2018)
16. Ngomo, N.: 9th challenge on question answering over linked data (QALD-9). Language **7**(1) (2018)
17. Panchbhai, A., Soru, T., Marx, E.: Exploring sequence-to-sequence models for SPARQL pattern composition. In: Villazón-Terrazas, B., Ortiz-Rodríguez, F., Tiwari, S.M., Shandilya, S.K. (eds.) KGSWC 2020. CCIS, vol. 1232, pp. 158–165. Springer, Cham (2020). https://doi.org/10.1007/978-3-030-65384-2_12
18. Pradel, C., Haemmerlé, O., Hernandez, N.: Natural language query interpretation into SPARQL using patterns (2013)
19. Soru, T., et al.: SPARQL as a foreign language. SEMANTiCS 2017 - Posters and Demos (2017). https://arxiv.org/abs/1708.07624
20. Steinmetz, N., Arning, A., Sattler, K.: From natural language questions to SPARQL queries: a pattern-based approach. In: BTW. LNI, vol. P-289, pp. 289–308. Gesellschaft für Informatik, Bonn (2019)
21. Sutskever, I., Vinyals, O., Le, Q.V.: Sequence to sequence learning with neural networks. In: NIPS, pp. 3104–3112 (2014)
22. W3C: Semantic web standards (2014). https://www.w3.org
23. Yin, X., Gromann, D., Rudolph, S.: Neural machine translating from natural language to SPARQL. CoRR abs/1906.09302 (2019)
24. Yu, T., et al.: Spider: a large-scale human-labeled dataset for complex and cross-domain semantic parsing and text-to-SQL task. arXiv preprint arXiv:1809.08887 (2018)
25. Zhang, R., et al.: Editing-based SQL query generation for cross-domain context-dependent questions. arXiv preprint arXiv:1909.00786 (2019)
26. Zhong, V., Xiong, C., Socher, R.: Seq2SQL: generating structured queries from natural language using reinforcement learning. CoRR abs/1709.00103 (2017)

Exploiting Textual Similarity Techniques in Harmonization of Laws

Emilio Sulis(✉), Llio Bryn Humphreys, Davide Audrito, and Luigi Di Caro

Computer Science Department, University of Torino, Corso Svizzera 185, Turin, Italy
{emilio.sulis,lliobryn.humphreys,davide.audrito,luigi.dicaro}@unito.it

Abstract. This paper describes an application of textual similarity techniques in the Legal Informatics domain. In European law, a relevant interest relates to the transposition of EU directives by the Member States, which can be complete, partial, or eventually absent. As part of an European project, legal experts annotated transpositions of six directives on a per-article basis. Following an established NLP pipeline, we explore a similarity-based technique to identify correspondences between transpositions of national implementations. Early results are promising and show the role that Artificial Intelligence may play within the process of harmonization and standardization of domestic legal systems as a result of the adoption of EU legislation.

Keywords: Legal informatics · Text similarity · Harmonization of laws · Natural language processing

1 Introduction

Computational text analysis is an important research area with many practical applications in a variety of research areas, e.g. sentiment analysis [19], marketing [16], education [1], business process management [3]. Typically, text mining techniques concern unstructured text, such as reviews, social media posts, and online comments [28,40]. The goal of these analyses mostly involves identifying patterns and extracting knowledge through supervised or unsupervised mechanisms [15]. Law represents a rapidly-growing area of application of Natural Language Processing (NLP) [30], and Legal Informatics is a particular research area which concerns the application of Information and Communication Technologies (ICT) in the legal domain [13,22]. Legislative documents are usually formally structured and contain special features such as preambles, citations, recurring phrases, and references [7].

This contribution concerns European Law, focusing on the *approximation of laws* and *harmonization*, i.e. the alignment of domestic legal frameworks in light of the EU legislation. In the EU, legislative harmonization has two important functions: first, it reduces legal differences between Member States, with a view to foster economic, social and cultural exchanges. Moreover, it aims to achieve

S. Bandini et al. (Eds.): AIxIA 2021, LNAI 13196, pp. 185–197, 2022.
https://doi.org/10.1007/978-3-031-08421-8_13

a variety of political results, e.g. the establishment of a European single market, the achievement of common minimum standards regarding social protection, the establishment of rules concerning the rights of suspects and accused persons in criminal proceedings. This concept finds practical application in the analysis of national implementations (NIMs) of European directives, i.e., the *transposition* of European law in each Member State legislation. In particular, we describe the results of a legal experts' effort aiming at identifying and labeling NIMs. In general, "a directive shall be binding, as to the result to be achieved, upon each Member State to which it is addressed, but shall leave to the national authorities the choice of form and methods" (Article 288(3), Treaty on the Functioning of the European Union). As such, although national legislators have a certain margin of discretion in the choice of methods and forms for implementation, a certain degree of similarity of NIMs is expected. By comparing the English versions of the different implementations, this type of legal text can be explored using computational methods to assess the similarity of legal texts [5].

As a case study, we based on a research project in which "transpositions" of six EU directives were assessed "manually" by legal experts. Two main methods have been used for transposing EU law into national law: i. *Copy-out*: implementing legislation adopts the same, or mirrors as closely as possible the original wording of the directive; ii. *Elaboration*: choosing a particular meaning according to what the draftsperson believes the provision to mean, with the aim of working a provision into something clearer (this is an UK practice). The typical method for transpositions is *copy-out* [12]. In this respect, texts of NIMs are expected to be similar.

As main objective, we investigate the impact and efficacy of standard text analysis techniques applied to NIMs, focusing on the following research questions:

i Can we compare the implementations of EU directives in different countries by using NLP techniques?
ii By focusing on "Explicitly Transposed" articles for each directive in TT, can we adopt some meaningful metrics (e.g., similarity or network measures) to compare (pairs of) NIMs? Are these metrics significant at the article's granularity level?

In this paper we describe an essential application of NLP for legal texts by taking advantage of the initial results of an ongoing EU research project, *CrossJustice*. We first introduce some related work (Sect. 2), and the dataset of the case study (Sect. 3). Then, we report a possible solution to investigate the harmonization with similarity of NIMs (Sect. 4). We conclude the paper in Sect. 5.

2 Related Work

Legal research has seen an increased focus on the use of Artificial Intelligence (AI) techniques to the law [8–10, 17, 21, 33, 45, 46]. In a critical area of AI, machine learning techniques include similarity measures [31] as an essential analysis in a NLP pipeline [14]. Existing methodologies for finding similar legal documents can be classified into two main categories [6,25]: (i) network-based methods, which rely on citations to prior case documents [43]; (ii) text-based methods, which use the content/textual information of the documents [24]. We explore (ii), whereas recent works on 'similarity' in legal informatics concern the comparison between the EU directive and the transposition into the national law [18,20].

Text mining and NLP techniques have been explored to assist the Commission and legal professionals in studying and evaluating the transposition of directives at a fine-grained provision level [29]. Some approaches adopted embeddings models [26] to represent legal texts in a semantic vector space, by applying the method of cosine similarity (CS) [32]. Recent work addressed the task of identifying similarities among court rulings by adopting a graph-based method, to identify prominent concepts present in a ruling by extracting representative sentences [44]. Some experiments on legal judgments [25] explored CS by considering the document vector, where each term score is calculated with Term frequency - Inverse document frequency method (Tf-Idf) [34]. They performed well by considering only legal terms in the document vector, instead of using all terms or co-citations. In previous work, a pipeline with Tf-Idf, stemming, and co-occurrence networks has been shown to be significant in the automatic analysis of legal texts [38].

Finally, a recent work has measured the similarity between two court case documents, observing how "the more traditional methods (such as the Tf-Idf and LDA) that rely on a bag-of-words representation performs better than the more advanced context-aware methods (like BERT and Law2Vec) for computing document-level similarity" [27].

Harmonization. The effective protection of fundamental rights throughout the EU is heavily affected by the highly varying legal frameworks which characterize Member States regulation on procedural rights [4,42]. Legal actors often struggle to identify which legislation and therefore which procedural rights are applicable to persons accused or suspected of a crime in specific cases, due to both language barriers and the peculiarities of different national legal systems [35,36]. This situation persists also after the introduction of the EU directives derived from the Stockholm Programme, aiming at creating a certain level of harmonized rules on the matter [23]. A directive comes into effect only after it has been transposed into national law by the Member States, via the so-called NIMs [37].

3 Case Study

3.1 CrossJustice Project

The CrossJustice (CJ) project[1] on which this work is based concerns the compliance of national instruments implementing EU directives with the *acquis communautaire*, in the protection of fundamental rights for persons accused or suspected of a crime (one of the main objectives of EU policy in the field of justice).

[1] https://www.crossjustice.eu.

Legal experts have been involved to assess the compatibility between national frameworks as a result of the implementation of six EU directives. The output concerns the creation of a web platform to support and disseminate the results.

CJ aims to tackle the issues described above by identifying critical gaps and solutions in a comparative perspective, to improve the efficiency of judicial systems and their cooperation, thanks to information and communication technology. The online platform contains advice and support on the effectiveness of procedural rights providing a free service, mainly directed to legal professionals, but accessible to law students, NGOs and all EU citizens.

The CJ platform[2] addresses information pertaining to procedural rights, by delivering: i) A free of charge and updated information and advisory service directed to legal professionals (lawyers, magistrates, and public servants), but also accessible to law students and citizens. ii) Capacity building for legal professionals and law students.

3.2 Types of Annotations

The annotation process from the legal experts used the following four labels to distinguish the four types of national implementations:

1. Explicitly transposed - either via new legislation or via amendments to existing legislation.
2. De facto/indirectly implemented - transposition unnecessary because the right already existed in previous legislation.
3. No national implementation (either explicitly or de facto/indirectly) - lack of transposing national norm or non-conformity of the national norm with the requirements of the EU provision.
4. Specific transposition is not required - transposition may be unnecessary because: i) The legal provision lacks deontic or constitutive value e.g. articles 1 and 2 of directives usually only define the scope of the directive; ii) Member states may derogate from a particular provision (e.g. Article 6(3) of directive 2016/800).

3.3 Dataset Overview

The six EU directives under consideration (2010/64, 2012/13, 2013/48, 2016/343, 2016/800, 2016/1919) obtain different transpositions in the laws of different Member States. Legal experts involved in CJ annotated each part (e.g., an article or a paragraph) of a directive with both the above mentioned labels and the text of transposing legal provisions with a commentary in the so-called Transposition Table (TT). The CJ platform includes 3,458 annotations in the TT - as extracted on 1st June 2021 - and the distribution is represented in Table 1. The TT contains several differences among the Member States in terms of the number of annotations. For instance, the Member State with the lowest

[2] https://www.crossjustice.eu/en/index.html#crossjustice-platform.

number of TT annotations is Bulgaria (223), the highest is Portugal (375). In particular, the number of explicitly transposed (ET) parts of EU directives in the TT varies depending on the Member State. Croatia and the Netherlands have the highest value of "explicit" transpositions, while Portugal and Sweden have the lowest number of ETs according to the CJ table.

Table 1. Number of NIMs of the considered EU directives by Member States and by four types: Explicitly transposed (Explicit), De facto/indirectly implemented (Indirect), No national implementation (NoImpl), Specific transposition is not required (NotReq)

Member state	Explicit	Indirect	NoImpl	NotReq	Total
Bulgaria	40	151	17	15	223
Croatia	146	81	24	0	251
France	49	153	41	0	243
Germany	99	234	11	0	344
Italy	65	221	32	0	318
Netherlands	150	146	57	16	369
Poland	32	154	86	0	272
Portugal	0	353	22	0	375
Romania	85	239	50	0	374
Spain	91	135	89	0	315
Sweden	8	325	0	41	374
Total	**765**	**2,192**	**429**	**72**	**3,458**

4 Methodology

4.1 Text Processing

We adopted a quite established NLP pipeline with preprocessing, stemming, and calculating n-grams. The processed data needed to be converted into a numerical format, where each text is represented by an array (vectors). In natural language processing, the assumption about vectorization is that similar texts must result in nearest-neighbor vectors (i.e., vectors derived from textual data to reflect various linguistic properties of the text).

In particular, the here proposed methodological framework includes the analysis of legal texts of the TT by using both *bag-of-ngrams* and the frequency of terms with Tf-Idf.

NIMs have been processed with the following four main phases:

- *Preprocessing and POS tagging.* We processed texts according to the following steps: lower case reduction, stop words and punctuation removal, pos-tagging (to consider only nouns, verbs, and adjectives).

- *Stemming.* Stemming further reduces the variability of the text. The root form of terms is computed according to Porter stemming algorithm [41]. Finally, we removed all the *stems* of one single char length.
- *Modeling text.* The automatic analysis of legal text requires a numerical text representation (model). A typical computational approach in NLP and IR represents text in vectors of frequency of terms (bag-of-words). Another typical approach considers the aggregations of a certain number of letters (n) which appear contiguous in the given text or speech (*n-grams*). In particular, *bigrams* are sequences of two consecutive terms, while *trigrams* are three consecutive terms. With *bag-of-ngrams* models, by considering *n-grams*, instead of individual words (*stems*), we obtain different more effective representation of the same text. Furthermore, most frequent features can be selected to reduce sparsity. Finally, the corresponding vector of numbers counts the occurrences of terms in the document.
- *Tf-Idf transform.* A typical automatic text analysis pipeline involves transforming each piece of text (i.e., legal provisions) into a vector, where each word is replaced by significant numbers. Such numbers can be mere counts or frequency of occurrences, as well as more sophisticated measures such as Tf-Idf. This scoring measure is widely used in NLP based on the complete collection of terms from the transpositions of each directive (each directive therefore has a *corpus* of variable dimension). Term frequency-inverse document frequency (Tf-Idf) is a numerical statistic for reflecting how important a word is to a document in our collection. The measure implies two parts: Term Frequent (Tf) simply describes how frequently a term (t) appears in each document (d). Inverse Document Frequency (Idf) computes the importance of the term in the complete collection.
- *Document-Term Matrix.* For each individual NIMs we obtain a vector in the corresponding Document-Term Matrix (DTM). In the resulting matrix, every row is a NIM (here, a single TT part/article) and every column is a term/stem/n-gram. The values in the matrix are the frequencies of each term in a document. As the columns are too many, we considered the application of a dimensionality reduction strategy, e.g. Principal Component Analysis (PCA) or Multidimentional Scaling (MDS) [11]. We opted to reduce the number of features with MDS, which improves similarity measure by exploiting the latent semantics of co-occurrences between words.

4.2 Similarity Measure

To investigate text similarity with the above mentioned research objectives, we adopted CS as an established similarity metrics in this kind of research. Mathematically, CS represents the cosine of the angle between two vectors projected in a multi-dimensional space. In particular, CS between the vectors of two NIMs (A and B) is computed as follows:

$$CS(A,B) = \frac{V1V2}{||V1||||V2||}$$

The numerator is the dot product of the vectors V1 and V2, representing A and B respectively. The denominator is the product of their Euclidean norms, which normalizes the similarity value. The range of values that the CS can vary is -1, 1. The CS values have been computed between the NIMs at the level of each part/article considered in the TT[3]. For instance, in an EU directive, by considering two Member States (e.g., Italy and Bulgaria), we compare the corresponding "Explicit transpositions" of Article 1 both in Italy and in Bulgaria. Finally, we obtain the most similar NIMs for each EU directive.

5 Output

5.1 Text Representation

We summarize here the transformation of each text (corresponding to *Explicit transpositions*) to a fixed-length vector of integer values by describing the *bag-of-ngrams* output, and dimensionality reduction, as better detailed in the following paragraphs.

Explicit Transpositions. We focused on the annotation effort of CJ's legal experts, who indicated in the TTs the parts (at the level of Article or Sub-Article) of the EU directives that were explicitly transposed in Member States legislation. For instance, the case of EU directive 2012/13 has 563 different implementations of different types, of these the ET implementations are 245. In particular, Article 2 has only 7 ET cases concerning 2 Member States, i.e. Croatia (4) and Spain (3), according to the complete database (a view in Fig. 1). Next, we considered merging the contents of all implementations regarding the same part of the EU directive, for each Member State.

ID	EUdir	State	NumArt	Label	Text
2039	0013	Croatia	art_2	Exp	summon suspect must specifi suspect suspect theins...
2040	0013	Croatia	art_2	Exp	upon arrest arrest person must immedi provid writt...
2041	0013	Croatia	art_2	Exp	letter right must deliv accus person search warran...
2043	0013	Spain	art_2	Exp	ani person punish act attribut may exercis right d...
2044	0013	Spain	art_2	Exp	admiss complaint suit ani procedur action imput cr...
2045	0013	Spain	art_2	Exp	right defens shall exercis without limit expressli...
2050	0013	Croatia	art_2	Exp	prior file indict compet court bodi proceed perpet...

Fig. 1. A view of Explicitly Transposed (ET) legal provisions for each parts of Article 2 of the European directive n.2012/13.

Bag-of-Words and n-Grams. We considered ET of NIMs as our *corpus*, for each EU directive. With the bag-of-words technique we represented the text of each

[3] From the *scikit-learn* python library *sklearn.metrics.pairwise* we adopted cosine_similarity method.

document in numbers, based on a vocabulary from all the unique *stems*. As mentioned, we obtained the *bag-of-ngrams* of our *corpus*, as a more sophisticated approach based on a vocabulary of grouped *stems* of length n (i.e., *n-grams*). We computed the *stems* for 1,714 individual parts of our ET implementations for the considered EU directives. In particular, we obtained a median value of 105 *stems*, as well as a maximum of 1,365 *stems* (for EU directive 2013/48, art_10 paragraph_3).

Dimensionality Reduction. The definitive *corpus* includes the vectors for each article which has been explicitly transposed in TT, where the 'columns' are the terms (or the n-grams considered). In the case of bigrams, the number of features is 4,549. In the case of trigrams, the features are 6,213. We reduced the dimension of the problem with multidimensional scaling of different size, e.g. 100 or 200 features.

Similarity. The CS between two implementations of each pair of Member States describes the degree of similarity between the vector representations of the text. For instance, we mention here the simple case of the "Annex 1" of the 2012/13 European directive which has been explicitly implemented by three States (France, Spain, Romania). A "manual" inspection of the three corresponding NIMs describes a certain similarity only between France and Spain, and not in the other pairs. This is also true after observing the CS measures, both using top 100 more frequent terms (Vect100) or MDS method with 100 or 200 features (MDS100, MDS200), as described in Table 2.

Table 2. An example of similarity scores concerning the Article "Ann_1" of the European directive n.2012/13 for three pairs of States.

Member states		Vect100	MDS100	MDS200
France	Romania	0.376	0.055	0.056
France	Spain	0.581	0.206	0.205
Romania	Spain	0.460	0.079	0.084

5.2 Heat Maps Visualization

To facilitate the understanding of the results, we considered heat maps describing the degree of similarity between pairs of Member States, for each parts of NIMs. Darker colors (e.g., blue or green) imply no similarity, while lighter colors (e.g., white/yellow) indicate a certain degree of text similarity. For the sake of clarity, Fig. 2 is an example of a heat map concerning a NIM of EU directive n. 2012/13. This type of visualization clearly describes how France and Sweden have more similar text (lighter color) than other States. The diagonal is null (dark color, in our case), because the relationship between the text of a State and itself is not considered. This type of visualization allows an immediate understanding of the similarity among NIMs. As part of the project, legal experts have confirmed that the heat maps are meaningful. Therefore, the tool appears to be useful in helping analysts to detect/suggest the degree of harmonization of national laws.

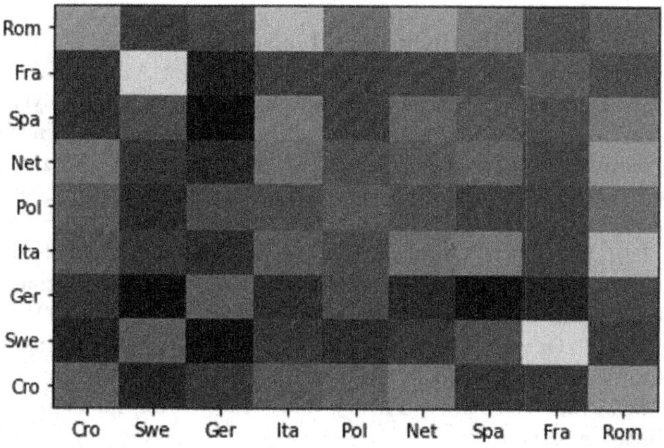

Fig. 2. A heat map representation of similarity metrics for NIMs (Color figure online)

6 Conclusions

This paper discussed the first outcome of an ongoing research project involving NLP and Law, focusing on the key concept of Harmonization in EU Law. We investigate computational text similarity technique to the idea of making identical rules in more areas of governance. We performed similarity metrics computation, analysis of results, and visualisation to demonstrate how an established NLP pipeline for preprocessing text and similarity metrics can be applied to support legal harmonization purposes.

As a future work, we aim to explore network analysis techniques with co-occurrence of terms or *stems*. The approach already provided meaningful results [38,39] in modeling inter-relationships between norms [2]. We plan to investigate different similarity techniques and hybrid approaches, including embedding methods (e.g., Node2Vec for graph embedding approach or Word2Vec implementation). Finally, we plan to extend the evaluation with a "user study" and at the same time propose an extension of the technology used in the CJ project.

Acknowledgement. This work has been supported by the European Union's Justice Programme (Grant Agreement No. 847346) for the project "Knowledge, Advisory and Capacity Building Information Tool for Criminal Procedural Rights in Judicial Cooperation".

References

1. Amado, A., Cortez, P., Rita, P., Moro, S.: Research trends on big data in marketing: a text mining and topic modeling based literature analysis. Eur. Res. Manag. Bus. Econ. **24**(1), 1–7 (2018)
2. Amantea, I.A., Caro, L.D., Humphreys, L., Nanda, R., Sulis, E.: Modelling norm types and their inter-relationships in EU directives. In: Ashley, K.D., et al. (eds.) Proceedings of the Third Workshop on Automated Semantic Analysis of Information in Legal Texts co-located with the 17th International Conference on Artificial Intelligence and Law (ICAIL 2019), Montreal, QC, Canada, 21 June 2019. CEUR Workshop Proceedings, vol. 2385. CEUR-WS.org (2019). http://ceur-ws.org/Vol-2385/paper8.pdf
3. Amantea, I.A., Robaldo, L., Sulis, E., Boella, G., Governatori, G.: Semi-automated checking for regulatory compliance in e-health. In: 25th International Enterprise Distributed Object Computing Workshop, EDOC Workshop 2021, Gold Coast, Australia, 25–29 October 2021, pp. 318–325. IEEE (2021). https://doi.org/10.1109/EDOCW52865.2021.00063
4. Andenas, M., Andersen, C.B.: Theory and Practice of Harmonisation. Edward Elgar Publishing (2012)
5. Ashley, K.D.: Artificial Intelligence and Legal Analytics: New Tools for Law Practice in the Digital Age. Cambridge University Press, Cambridge (2017)
6. Bhattacharya, P., Ghosh, K., Pal, A., Ghosh, S.: Methods for computing legal document similarity: a comparative study. CoRR abs/2004.12307 (2020). https://arxiv.org/abs/2004.12307
7. Biasiotti, M., Francesconi, E., Palmirani, M., Sartor, G., Vitali, F.: Legal informatics and management of legislative documents. Global Center for ICT in Parliament Working Paper 2 (2008)
8. Boella, G., Di Caro, L., Humphreys, L., Robaldo, L., Rossi, P., van der Torre, L.: Eunomos, a legal document and knowledge management system for the web to provide relevant, reliable and up-to-date information on the law. Artif. Intell. Law **24**(3), 245–283 (2016)
9. Boella, G., Di Caro, L., Leone, V.: Semi-automatic knowledge population in a legal document management system. Artif. Intell. Law **27**(2), 227–251 (2018). https://doi.org/10.1007/s10506-018-9239-8
10. Boella, G., Di Caro, L., Rispoli, D., Robaldo, L.: A system for classifying multi-label text into EuroVoc. In: Proceedings of the Fourteenth International Conference on Artificial Intelligence and Law, pp. 239–240 (2013)
11. Cox, M.A., Cox, T.F.: Multidimensional scaling. In: Chen, C., Härdle, W., Unwin, A. (eds.) Handbook of Data Visualization, pp. 315–347. Springer, Heidelberg (2008). https://doi.org/10.1007/978-3-540-33037-0_14
12. Dimitrakopoulos, D.G.: The transposition of EU law:'post-decisional politics' and institutional autonomy. Eur. Law J. **7**(4), 442–458 (2001)
13. Durante, M.: Computational Power: The Impact of ICT on Law, Society and Knowledge, Routledge (2021)
14. Elekes, Á., Schäler, M., Böhm, K.: On the various semantics of similarity in word embedding models. In: 2017 ACM/IEEE Joint Conference on Digital Libraries, JCDL 2017, Toronto, ON, Canada, 19–23 June 2017, pp. 139–148. IEEE Computer Society (2017). https://doi.org/10.1109/JCDL.2017.7991568
15. Feldman, R., Sanger, J.: The Text Mining Handbook - Advanced Approaches in Analyzing Unstructured Data. Cambridge University Press, Cambridge (2007)

16. Ferreira-Mello, R., André, M., Pinheiro, A., Costa, E., Romero, C.: Text mining in education. Wiley Interdisc. Rev.: Data Min. Knowl. Discov. **9**(6), e1332 (2019)
17. Friedrich, R., Luzzatto, M., Ash, E.: Entropy in legal language. In: Aletras, N., Androutsopoulos, I., Barrett, L., Meyers, A., Preotiuc-Pietro, D. (eds.) Proceedings of the Natural Legal Language Processing Workshop 2020 co-located with the 26th ACM SIGKDD International Conference on Knowledge Discovery & Data Mining (KDD 2020), Virtual Workshop, 24 August 2020. CEUR Workshop Proceedings, vol. 2645, pp. 25–30. CEUR-WS.org (2020). http://ceur-ws.org/Vol-2645/paper4.pdf
18. Haverland, M., Steunenberg, B., Van Waarden, F.: Sectors at different speeds: analysing transposition deficits in the European union. JCMS: J. Common Mark. Stud. **49**(2), 265–291 (2011)
19. Hu, M., Liu, B.: Mining and summarizing customer reviews. In: Proceedings of the Tenth ACM SIGKDD International Conference on Knowledge Discovery and Data Mining, pp. 168–177 (2004)
20. Humphreys, L., Santos, C., Di Caro, L., Boella, G., Van Der Torre, L., Robaldo, L.: Mapping recitals to normative provisions in EU legislation to assist legal interpretation. In: JURIX, pp. 41–49 (2015)
21. John, A.K., Di Caro, L., Robaldo, L., Boella, G.: Legalbot: a deep learning-based conversational agent in the legal domain. In: Frasincar, F., Ittoo, A., Nguyen, L.M., Métais, E. (eds.) NLDB 2017. LNCS, vol. 10260, pp. 267–273. Springer, Cham (2017). https://doi.org/10.1007/978-3-319-59569-6_32
22. Katz, D.M., Dolin, R., Bommarito, M.J.: Legal Informatics. Cambridge University Press, Cambridge (2021)
23. Kaunert, C., Occhipinti, J.D., Léonard, S.: Introduction: supranational governance in the area of freedom, security and justice after the stockholm programme (2014)
24. Kim, M.-Y., Xu, Y., Goebel, R.: Legal question answering using ranking SVM and syntactic/semantic similarity. In: Murata, T., Mineshima, K., Bekki, D. (eds.) JSAI-isAI 2014. LNCS (LNAI), vol. 9067, pp. 244–258. Springer, Heidelberg (2015). https://doi.org/10.1007/978-3-662-48119-6_18
25. Kumar, S., Reddy, P.K., Reddy, V.B., Suri, M.: Finding similar legal judgements under common law system. In: Madaan, A., Kikuchi, S., Bhalla, S. (eds.) DNIS 2013. LNCS, vol. 7813, pp. 103–116. Springer, Heidelberg (2013). https://doi.org/10.1007/978-3-642-37134-9_9
26. Levy, O., Goldberg, Y., Dagan, I.: Improving distributional similarity with lessons learned from word embeddings. Trans. Assoc. Comput. Linguist. **3**, 211–225 (2015). https://doi.org/10.1162/tacl_a_00134
27. Mandal, A., Ghosh, K., Ghosh, S., Mandal, S.: Unsupervised approaches for measuring textual similarity between legal court case reports. Artif. Intell. Law **29**(3), 417–451 (2021). https://doi.org/10.1007/s10506-020-09280-2
28. Meo, R., Sulis, E.: Processing affect in social media: a comparison of methods to distinguish emotions in tweets. ACM Trans. Internet Techn. **17**(1), 7:1–7:25 (2017). https://doi.org/10.1145/2996187
29. Nanda, R., et al.: Unsupervised and supervised text similarity systems for automated identification of national implementing measures of European directives. Artif. Intell. Law **27**(2), 199–225 (2018). https://doi.org/10.1007/s10506-018-9236-y
30. Nay, J.J.: Natural Language Processing for Legal Texts, pp. 99–113. Cambridge University Press, Cambridge (2021). https://doi.org/10.1017/9781316529683.011

31. Ontañón, S.: An overview of distance and similarity functions for structured data. Artif. Intell. Rev. **53**(7), 5309–5351 (2020). https://doi.org/10.1007/s10462-020-09821-w
32. Renjit, S., Idicula, S.M.: CUSAT nlp@aila-fire2019: similarity in legal texts using document level embeddings. In: Mehta, P., Rosso, P., Majumder, P., Mitra, M. (eds.) Working Notes of FIRE 2019 - Forum for Information Retrieval Evaluation, Kolkata, India, 12–15 December 2019. CEUR Workshop Proceedings, vol. 2517, pp. 25–30. CEUR-WS.org (2019). http://ceur-ws.org/Vol-2517/T1-4.pdf
33. Robaldo, L., Villata, S., Wyner, A., Grabmair, M.: Introduction for artificial intelligence and law: special issue "natural language processing for legal texts" (2019). https://doi.org/10.1007/s10506-019-09251-2
34. Salton, G., Buckley, C.: Term-weighting approaches in automatic text retrieval. Inf. Process. Manage. **24**(5), 513–523 (1988)
35. Satzger, H.: The harmonisation of criminal sanctions in the European union - a new approach. Eucrim (2019). https://doi.org/10.30709/eucrim-2019-007
36. Schroeder, W.: Limits to European harmonisation of criminal law. Eucrim (2020). https://doi.org/10.30709/eucrim-2020-008
37. Steunenberg, B., Rhinard, M.: The transposition of European law in EU member states: between process and politics. Eur. Polit. Sci. Rev. **2**, 495–520 (2010). https://doi.org/10.1017/S1755773910000196
38. Sulis, E., Humphreys, L., Vernero, F., Amantea, I.A., Audrito, D., Di Caro, L.: Exploiting co-occurrence networks for classification of implicit inter-relationships in legal texts. Inf. Syst. 101821 (2021). https://doi.org/10.1016/j.is.2021.101821
39. Sulis, E., et al.: Exploring network analysis in a corpus-based approach to legal texts: a case study. In: Tagarelli, A., Zumpano, E., Latific, A.K., Calì, A. (eds.) Proceedings of the First International Workshop "CAiSE for Legal Documents" (COUrT 2020) Co-located with the 32nd International Conference on Advanced Information Systems Engineering (CAiSE 2020), Grenoble, France, 9 June 2020. CEUR Workshop Proceedings, vol. 2690, pp. 27–38. CEUR-WS.org (2020). http://ceur-ws.org/Vol-2690/COUrT-paper3.pdf
40. Sulis, E., Lai, M., Vinai, M., Sanguinetti, M.: Exploring sentiment in social media and official statistics: a general framework. In: Bosco, C., Cambria, E., Damiano, R., Patti, V., Rosso, P. (eds.) Proceedings of the 2nd International Workshop on Emotion and Sentiment in Social and Expressive Media: Opportunities and Challenges for Emotion-Aware Multiagent Systems Co-located with 14th International Conference on Autonomous Agents and Multiagent Systems (AAMAS 2015), Istanbul, Turkey, 5 May 2015. CEUR Workshop Proceedings, vol. 1351, pp. 96–105. CEUR-WS.org (2015). http://ceur-ws.org/Vol-1351/paper8.pdf
41. Van Rijsbergen, C.J., Robertson, S.E., Porter, M.F.: New models in probabilistic information retrieval, vol. 5587. British Library Research and Development Department London (1980)
42. Vogenauer, S., Weatherill, S.: The Harmonisation of European Contract Law: Implications for European Private Laws, Business and Legal Practice. Bloomsbury Publishing (2006). https://doi.org/10.1111/j.1468-0386.2007.00376_4.x
43. Wagh, R., Anand, D.: Application of citation network analysis for improved similarity index estimation of legal case documents: a study. In: 2017 IEEE International Conference on Current Trends in Advanced Computing (ICCTAC), pp. 1–5 (2017). https://doi.org/10.1109/ICCTAC.2017.8249996
44. Wagh, R.S., Anand, D.: Legal document similarity: a multi-criteria decision-making perspective. PeerJ Comput. Sci. **6**, e262 (2020). https://doi.org/10.7717/peerj-cs.262

45. Wyner, A., Mochales-Palau, R., Moens, M.-F., Milward, D.: Approaches to text mining arguments from legal cases. In: Francesconi, E., Montemagni, S., Peters, W., Tiscornia, D. (eds.) Semantic Processing of Legal Texts. LNCS (LNAI), vol. 6036, pp. 60–79. Springer, Heidelberg (2010). https://doi.org/10.1007/978-3-642-12837-0_4
46. Zhong, H., Xiao, C., Tu, C., Zhang, T., Liu, Z., Sun, M.: How does NLP benefit legal system: a summary of legal artificial intelligence. In: Jurafsky, D., Chai, J., Schluter, N., Tetreault, J.R. (eds.) Proceedings of the 58th Annual Meeting of the Association for Computational Linguistics, ACL 2020, Online, 5–10 July 2020, pp. 5218–5230. Association for Computational Linguistics (2020). https://doi.org/10.18653/v1/2020.acl-main.466

Easy Semantification of Bioassays

Marco Anteghini[1,2](✉), Jennifer D'Souza[3], Vitor A. P. Martins dos Santos[1,2], and Sören Auer[3]

[1] Lifeglimmer GmbH, Markelstr. 38, 12163 Berlin, Germany
{anteghini,vds}@lifeglimmer.com
[2] Wageningen University and Research, Laboratory of Systems and Synthetic Biology, Stippeneng 4, 6708 WE Wageningen, The Netherlands
[3] TIB Leibniz Information Centre for Science and Technology, Hannover, Germany
{jennifer.dsouza,auer}@tib.eu

Abstract. Biological data and knowledge bases increasingly rely on Semantic Web technologies and the use of knowledge graphs for data integration, retrieval and federated queries. We propose a solution for automatically *semantifying biological assays*. Our solution contrasts the problem of automated semantification as labeling versus clustering where the two methods are on opposite ends of the method complexity spectrum. Characteristically modeling our problem, we find the clustering solution significantly outperforms a deep neural network state-of-the-art labeling approach. This novel contribution is based on two factors: 1) a learning objective closely modeled after the data outperforms an alternative approach with sophisticated semantic modeling; 2) automatically *semantifying biological assays* achieves a high performance $F1$ of nearly 83%, which to our knowledge is the first reported standardized evaluation of the task offering a strong benchmark model.

Keywords: Open Research Knowledge Graph · Open science graphs · Unsupervised learning · Clustering · Supervised learning · Labeling · Automatic semantification · Bioassays

1 Introduction

Semantifying scholarly communication within the next-generation Knowledge-Graph-based Scholarly Digital Libraries, such as the Open Research Knowledge Graph[1] (ORKG) [5], relies on core semantic techniques such as ontologized formalizations and Web resource identifiers [8]. This supports the mainstream *Knowledge representation and reasoning* vision in AI. Further, semantified data can enable knowledge-based interoperability between multiple databases simply

[1] https://www.orkg.org/.

Supported by TIB Leibniz Information Centre for Science and Technology, the EU H2020 ERC project ScienceGRaph (GA ID: 819536) and the ITN PERICO (GA ID: 812968).

S. Bandini et al. (Eds.): AIxIA 2021, LNAI 13196, pp. 198–212, 2022.
https://doi.org/10.1007/978-3-031-08421-8_14

by reusing identifiers and utilizing no-SQL query languages such as SPARQL [33] that can perform distributed queries over the various data sources. Obtaining improved machine interpretability of scientific findings has seen keen interest in the Life Sciences [23] domain. Many major bioinformatics databases such as UniProt [11], KEGG [22], REACTOME [20] and the NCBI database [35] which includes the PubChem BioAssay database now make their data available as Linked Data in which both biological entities and connections between them are ontologized with standardized relations and are identified through a unique identifier (an Internationalized Resource Identifier or IRI). In a parallel Computational Linguistics ecosphere, many recent interdisciplinary data collection and annotation efforts [24–26,31] are focused on the shallow semantic structuring of unstructured text based on the Life Sciences ontologies. E.g., instructional content in lab protocols, descriptions of chemical synthesis reactions, or bioassays. Thus information described otherwise in *ad hoc* ways within scholarly documents attain machine-actionable, structured representations. Such datasets inadvertently facilitate the development of automated machine readers.

In this work, we take up the problem of the automated semantification of Biological Assays (Bioassays). This problem has both Life Science-specific solutions as the Bioassay Ontology [43] and Computational Linguistics-based semantified unstructured text annotations [10,37,42]. A bioassay is, by definition, a standard biochemical test procedure used to determine the concentration or potency of a stimulus (physical, chemical, or biological) by its effect on living cells or tissues [18,19]. It is described with relevant information on basic procedures such as determining the signal that indicates biological activity, determining doses used during the test, calculation methods etc. Also, bioassays are always qualified and validated [41] to highlight their accuracy, repeatability, and adequacy for use in the measurement of relative potency. Thus, a semantic description of the assay represented as logical annotations consisting of property and value pairs is the semantic equivalent of the unstructured bioassay text. They would enable their large-scale analysis in diverse systems. Bioassay texts are semantified based on the BioAssay Ontology (BAO) [1,43]. The BAO describes chemical and biological screening assays and their related results to facilitate their categorization and data analysis. On the BioPortal[2] where the BAO is hosted, the BAO showed 7513 classes and 227 properties dated June 3, 2021. Thus the semantification of an assay is a tedious human annotation task since they have to: 1) decide which ontologized class relation pair applies to a biossay; and 2) given a sentence from the bioassay text, decide whether it is expressible as a logical statement by the BAO. This results in a large decision space for the human annotator making it a time-consuming endeavor. Computational techniques fitted appropriately with the problem semantics can fully alleviate the tedious human annotation task.

In this paper, we examine the computational aspects of the automated semantification of biological assays (bioassays) in light of two different approaches and their evaluations. We first formulate a labeling objective for bioassay semantification. This we recently proposed as a work-in-progress idea leveraging a

[2] https://bioportal.bioontology.org/.

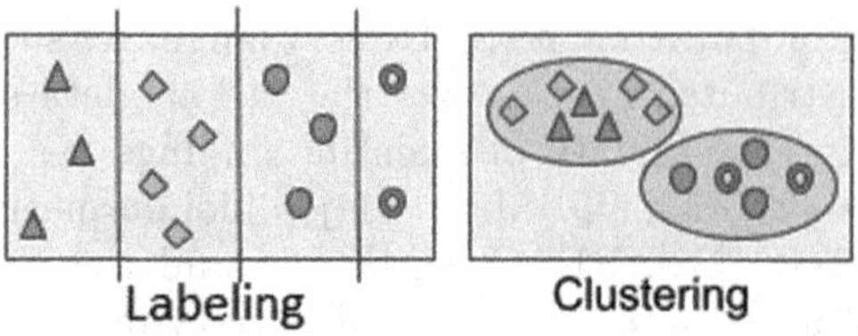

Fig. 1. Illustration of labeling versus clustering to aggregate data points

transformer-based supervised classifier [3,4]. Herein, we carry out in detail the experiments we began and further examine a novel clustering objective to bioassays semantification. Labeling and clustering are two methods of pattern identification used in machine learning. Although both techniques have certain similarities, the difference lies in the fact that labeling relies on a predefined set of labels assigned to objects, while clustering identifies similarities between objects, which it groups according to those characteristics in common and which differentiate them from other groups of objects. This is illustrated in Fig. 1. On the one hand, we identify each logical statement of a semantified bioassay as a potential label. On the other hand, we observed that bioassays with similar text descriptions also had similar semantic representations. Thus a fine-grained clustering of the assays themselves could mean a cluster as a whole can be semantified by a standard set of labels. If it takes a classifier multiple passes to fully label an assay, it takes a clustering model just one pass over the data to semantify clusters. Via our experiments, we observed that labeling and clustering have contrasting score and time footprints. As a surprising result, the powerful transformer-based labeling method proves to be less accurate than a clustering solution at 54% F1 vs. 83% F1; and labeling with a large labels set has a significantly longer prediction time accounting for per-label classifications.

In summary, the contributions of our work are:

1. We formalize two machine learning objectives, i.e. labels classification and clustering, for the automated semantification of bioassays. Relatedly, we discuss the dataset characteristics and its adaptations. To our knowledge, these standardized machine learning tasks over a corpus of bioassays are discussed for the first time.
2. We empirically evaluate the approaches and report unconventional findings that favor k-means clustering over the more resource-intensive transformers;
3. We present an application of bioassay semantification within the Open Research Knowledge Graph scholarly contributions knowledge digitalization platform. The workflow allows scientists to upload bioassays, obtain automated semantified bioassays as results, and curate the semantic annotations.

2 A Motivating Example for Bioassay Semantification

Assay ID 1960. An example sentence from the assay is 'Finally, fluorescence polarization can be used to effectively monitor the in vitro RNA-binding activity of both proteins using a standard fluorescence plate reader.' This sentence as it is is not computable. In other words, the terms 'fluorescence polarization', 'in vitro RNA-binding activity' or 'standard fluorescence plate reader' in the unstructured text have no semantic interpretation to a computer. However, in the context of the standardized Bioassay terminology, the sentence is annotated with the following logical statement: 'has detection method' → 'fluorescence polarization' from the BioAssay ontology [43] grounded to the identifiers (bao:BAO_0000207, bao:BAO_0000003). This semantic annotation is now computable by machines, e.g., within reasoning tasks. But these annotations need to be manually curated by an expert who reads from context information in the phrase 'Finally, fluorescence polarization can be used to effectively monitor' and is also familiar with the experimental setting of the assay. To semantify the above statement, the expert deduces that 'high polarization' in 'protein-probe complex' was detected by the method 'fluorescence polarization.' However, making such decisions is an expensive human annotation task and nearly impossible at scale. Nevertheless, if such logical statements are annotated for a small set of bioassays, they can be easily annotated at scale via machine learning which is the focus of this work. Another motivating example is available in Supplementary Materials (SM)[3].

3 Related Work

3.1 Corpora of Semantified Life Science Publications

Increasingly, text mining initiatives are seeking out recipes or formulaic semantic patterns to automatically mine machine-actionable information from scholarly articles [24–26,31]. In [25], they annotate wet lab protocols, covering a large spectrum of experimental biology, including neurology, epigenetics, metabolomics, cancer and stem cell biology, with actions corresponding to lab procedures and their attributes including materials, instruments and devices used to perform specific actions. Thereby the protocols then constituted a prespecified machine-readable format as opposed to the ad hoc documentation norm. Kulkarni et al. [25] release a large human-annotated corpus of semantified wet lab protocols to facilitate machine learning of such shallow semantic parsing over natural language instructions. Within scholarly articles, such instructions are typically published in the Materials and Method section in Biology and Chemistry fields. Along similar lines, inorganic materials synthesis reactions and procedures continue to reside as natural language descriptions in the text of journal articles. There is a growing need in such fields to find ways to systematically reduce the time and effort required to synthesize novel materials that presently remains one of the grand challenges in the field. In [24,31], to facilitate machine learning models for automatic extraction of materials syntheses from text, they present datasets of synthesis procedures annotated with semantic structure by domain experts in Materials Science. The types of information captured include synthesis operations (i.e. predicates), and the materials, conditions, apparatus and other entities participating in each synthesis step.

[3] https://github.com/MarcoAnteghini/Easy-Semantification-of-Bioassays-SM.

In this work, we leverage a similar semantically annotated corpus in the Life Science domain, but the knowledge theme tackled in our corpus is that of semantifying bioassays [43]. Normally, bioassays can be stored and accessed on PubChem [45,46] which now contains more than 1.3M bioassays (22-06-2021). Only considering the period between 2015 and 2021, 389,835 new bioassays have been added to PubChem. To semantify a single bioassay is expert-specific and time-consuming. However, the process is not scalable for large-scale analyses, e.g. searching databases for related assays and comparisons or clustering similar entries. This requires the creation of new approaches to favor bioassays semantification, analysis, comparison and facilitate knowledge sharing. The ultimate goal would be to obtain a fully-automated software that can easily transform a human-friendly unstructured bioassay text report to a computer-friendly version as their semantic equivalent in the form of a set of logical statements.

3.2 AI-Based Scholarly Knowledge Graph Construction

Early scholarly knowledge graph (SKG) construction initiatives were based on the sentences' information granularity. For this, ontologies and vocabularies were created [12,32,38,40] from diverse aspects of the publication including discourse and specific themes as experiments; corpora were annotated [16,28], and symbolic features-based ML techniques were implemented [27]. Recent scientific search technology led to new annotated corpora focusing on phrases with three or six types of generic scientific concepts in articles across up to ten different scholarly disciplines [15,30,34], for which neural systems were developed [2,9,13]. In SKG creation, relation extraction has also raised keen interest, thanks also to community challenges such as ScienceIE 2017 [6], SemEval 2018 Task 7 [17] and NlpContributionGraph 2021 [14], where participants tackled the problem of detecting semantic relations; newer advanced methods employed attention-based bidirectional long short-term memory networks (BiLSTM) [47] or used dynamic span graph framework based on BiLSTMs [44]. Recently, strategically designed neural-symbolic hybrid approaches have proven effective [29].

For the scholarly knowledge theme of structuring Bioassays, specifically, the only prior machine learning approach was a morpho-syntactic features-based Bayes classifier [10]. This early system, however, had unreplicable human-engineered aspects and non-standard evaluations. We focus on machine learning that entails no additional hand-engineering and report standardized evaluations.

4 Materials and Methods

4.1 An Expert-Annotated Semantified Bioassays Corpus

To develop our automated semantifiers, we leverage a corpus comprising an expert-annotated collection of 983 semantified bioassays [37,42]. In Table 1, we

Table 1. Four example logical statements (from 50 total) for the semantified PubChem Assay with ID 360 (https://pubchem.ncbi.nlm.nih.gov/bioassay/360). Note, these statements are triples with subject 'Bioassay.'

HAS PARTICIPANT → DMSO
HAS ASSAY PHASE CHARACTERISTIC → HOMOGENEOUS PHASE
HAS TEMPERATURE VALUE → 25 °C
HAS INCUBATION TIME VALUE → 20 MIN

show four logical statements of a semantified bioassay (ID 360 in PubChem) as an example. Each logical statement is expressed as a predicate and value pair. In the chosen example, the first two statements are *ontologized* statements, i.e. the predicate and value pair are in the Bioassay Ontology (BAO) [43]. These annotations are made by a domain expert based on comprehensive knowledge of the BAO which contains thousands of predicate value pairs as semantification candidates. The next two statements are *partially ontologized*, i.e. their predicates can be found in the BAO but the values are directly from the bioassay text description and hence are bioassay-specific. These statements report the various specific measurements made in the course of the bioassay. Semantified Bioassays contain both *ontologized* and *partially ontologized* statements. For the semantification task addressed in this paper, we restrict ourselves only to the *ontologized* statements of each semantified bioassay. For this, we prune all *partially ontologized* statements from each semantified assay. In Table 2, we summarize the dataset statistics for the original corpus with all the statements and the corpus we use after pruning. We can see that prior to pruning, the original corpus had 5524 total unique statements overall, which after pruning are reduced to 1906 statements. In the pruned corpus, bioassays have between 2 minimum and 87 maximum statements at an average of 37 statements. Considering only the predicates in these 1906 total statements, some predicates apply to semantify a bioassay more commonly than others. This is shown via the predicates statistics reported in Table 3. In particular, 94% of the semantic statements comprise only the 40 most commonly occurring predicates from a total of 80 unique predicates. Note this labels repetition detail of the corpus is critical since the labeling of bioassays with semantic statements are only among those observed in the data. In our preavius works [3,4] we adopted different pruning strategies. A comparison with this final version is available in SM.

Corpus Formalization. Let B be the overall semantified bioassays collection. A bioassay b from B is semantified with a set of *ontologized* logical statements sls (or semantic statements) which is $sls = \{ls_1, ls_2, ls_3, ..., ls_k\}$ where ls_x is a logical statement $\in LS$ such that LS is the collection of all the distinct *ontologized* logical statements used for semantification seen in the training data. And sls has k different statements when taken together form the semantic equivalent

Table 2. Semantified bioassays corpus statistics shown before ('original' row) and after ('pruned' row) pruning its *partially ontologized* statements. Note the corpus used for the work in this paper is the 'pruned' version.

	Average	Minimum	Maximum	Total
Original	56	7	162	5524
Pruned	37	2	87	1906

Table 3. Fine-grained pruned semantified corpus statistics in terms of the top 10, 20, 30, etc., most common predicates seen in the statements. E.g., the top 10 column contains the ten most frequently occurring predicates in the 1906 statements. Note the last column ('top 80') reflects the total unique predicates in the corpus. The rows show the number of the unique statements with the corresponding frequent predicates. The parenthesized numbers show the statements' proportion in the overall corpus.

Top 10	Top 20	Top 30	Top 40	Top 50	Top 60	Top 70	Top 80
795	959	1492	1804	1866	1879	1896	1906
(41.7)	(50.3)	(78.3)	(94.6)	(97.9)	(98.6)	(99.5)	(100.0)

of bioassay b. Across bioassays, their corresponding sls sizes vary. As shown in Table 2, the corpus we use has $|LS| = 1906$ unique statements (after pruning the *partially ontologized* statements).

Two semantification machine learning objectives are contrasted next.

4.2 *Labeling* Task Definition for Bioassay Semantification

Bioassays semantification can be addressed as a labeling problem. In this scenario, each logical statement can be treated within a binary classification task as applicable or not. On average in our data, a bioassay could then have around 37 applicable logical statements from LS. The task can be formalized as follows.

Task Formalism. Each input data instance is the pair $(b, ls; c)$ where $c \in \{true, false\}$ is the classification of the label ls. Thus, specifically, our semantification problem entails classifying labels: (b, ls) is $true$ if $ls \in$ logical statements set of b, else $false$. The $false$ instances are formed by pairing b with any other label not in the logical statements set sls of b.

Intuitively, this task formulation is meaningful because it emulates the way the human expert annotates the data. Basically, the expert, from their memory of all logical statements LS, simply assigns ls to a given b if they deem it as $true$; irrelevant statements are not considered, thus implicitly deemed $false$.

Task Model. Our machine learning system is the state-of-the-art, bidirectional transformer-based SciBERT [7], pre-trained on millions of scientific articles. For bioassay semantification, we use the SciBERT classification architecture. In each data instance $(b, ls; c)$, the classifier input representation for the pair 'b, ls' is the standard SciBERT format, treating them as sentence pairs separated by the special [SEP] token; the special classification token ([CLS]) remains the first token of every instance. Its final hidden state is used as the aggregate sequence representation for classification and is fed into a linear classification layer.

4.3 *Clustering* Task Definition for Bioassay Semantification

We define clustering as the second machine learning strategy. This is from corpus observations wherein bioassays with similar text descriptions were semantified with similar sets of logical statements. Thus, bioassays could be clustered based on their text descriptions into semantic groups and each cluster group could be collectively semantified for its bioassays. This task formalism is as follows.

Task Formalism. Let K be the total number of clusters of bioassays represented by the set $C = \{c_1, c_2, ..., c_K\}$. $B_{train} = \{b_1, b_2, ..., b_n\}$ corresponds to the total bioassays in the training set used to obtain optimal cluster centroids; and $V_{train} = \{v_1, v_2, ..., v_n\}$ is the vectorized representation of each bioassay to fit the clustering model. Note, $K < n$. Further, each cluster c_x is associated with all the distinct logical statements of the bioassays in the respective cluster group. If cluster c_x is fitted with two bioassays b_p and b_q in the training set, then c_x is associated with $sls_{c_x} = sls_{b_p} \cap sls_{b_q}$. Thus, new logical statements sets are formed as $\{ls_{c_1}, ls_{c_2}, ..., ls_{c_K}\}$ associated with the K clusters. After the clustering semantification model is fitted with V_{train}, semantification is performed. Each new bioassay b_{test} is assigned based on v_{test} to its closest cluster and semantified with the logical statements set of that cluster.

Clustering has the following alternative semantification task intuition. The domain expert tries to repeat their semantification decisions as much as possible based on similar bioassays they already annotated. In other words, for a new bioassay, they would copy as many logical statements from a similar already semantified bioassay and then decide if additional logical statements were needed. While this latter aspect is not modeled within the clustering problem, our results show that just copying the logical statements between similar bioassays is a significantly accurate automatic semantification strategy.

Task Model. Each bioassay text is represented based on the TF-IDF [36] vectorized format. The clustering approach we employ is the K-means algorithm [21]. To determine the optimal clusters K, we employ the elbow optimization strategy that tries to select the smallest number of clusters accounting for the largest amount of variation in the data [39][4].

[4] https://scikit-learn.org/stable/modules/generated/sklearn.cluster.KMeans.html.

Table 4. Bioassay semantification results by SciBERT-based labels classification. The first column shows the number of *false* statements (RF) that each bioassay was labeled with—the rows report 3 different experiments (170RF as optimal).

	P	R	F1
160RF	0.33	0.94	0.49
170RF	**0.37**	**0.94**	**0.54**
180RF	0.35	0.94	0.51

Table 5. Rate of semantifying bioassays on various corpus subsets using SciBERT

	Top 10	Top 20	Top 30	Top 40	Top 50	Top 60	Top 70	Full
TPU	34 s	38 s	42 s	1 m 10 s	1 m 24 s	1 m 22 s	1 m 12 s	1 m 20 s
CPU	28 m 10 s	29 m 15 s	34 m 7 s	58 m 3 s	1 h 6 m	1 h 6 m 14 s	1 h 6 m 4 s	1 h 6 m 8 s

Table 6. SciBERT-based bioassay semantification on corpus subsets starting with only the statements containing the 10 most common predicates (*top 10* row) until the full corpus (*all 80* row). In these experiments, the optimal 170RF was used.

Predicates	P	R	F1	Predicates	P	R	F1
top 10	0.53	0.94	0.67	*top 50*	0.36	0.95	0.52
top 20	0.50	0.89	0.64	*top 60*	0.41	0.92	0.57
top 30	0.45	0.95	0.61	*top 70*	0.32	0.95	0.48
top 40	0.37	0.94	0.52	*all 80*	**0.37**	**0.94**	**0.54**

5 Bioassay Semantification Experiments

5.1 Experimental Setup

1. Labeling Task-Specific Settings. Unlike clustering, the labeling task entails defining *false* logical statement semantification candidates as well. Since each assay had on average 37 *true* logical statements, we experimented with a random set of *false* (RF) statements in the range between 100 and 200 in increments of 10. The values were set to avoid biasing the classifier on only *false* inferences but also to be sufficiently representative. **2. Three-Fold Cross Validation.** For both labeling and clustering, we performed 3-fold cross validation experiments with a training/test set distribution of 600 and 300 assays, respectively. The test set assays were selected such that they were unique between the folds. **3. Evaluation Metrics.** We measure the standard precision, recall, and F1 scores for bioassay semantification per fold experiment. The final scores are then averaged over the three folds.

Table 7. Bioassay semantification results by K-means clustering

Num. of clusters	Labels freq ≥ 5			Labels freq ≥ 4			Labels freq ≥ 3			Labels freq ≥ 2			Labels freq ≥ 1		
	P	R	F1	P	R	F1	P	R	F1	P	R	F1	P	R	F1
50	0.54	**0.75**	**0.63**	0.48	**0.80**	0.60	0.40	**0.84**	0.54	0.32	**0.89**	0.47	0.19	**0.94**	0.31
100	0.69	0.59	0.63	0.66	0.66	**0.66** ↑	0.62	0.76	0.68 ↑	0.53	0.85	0.66 ↑	0.32	0.92	0.47 ↑
150	0.83	0.40	0.54 ↓	0.80	0.49	0.61 ↓	0.76	0.63	**0.69** ↑	0.70	0.79	**0.74** ↑	0.54	0.90	0.68 ↑
200	0.86	0.34	0.49 ↓	0.83	0.43	0.56 ↓	0.80	0.56	0.66 ↓	0.76	0.72	0.74	0.66	0.89	0.75 ↑
250	0.88	0.22	0.36 ↓	0.86	0.31	0.45 ↓	0.85	0.44	0.58 ↓	0.79	0.65	0.72 ↓	0.71	0.88	0.79 ↑
300	0.91	0.18	0.30 ↓	0.88	0.24	0.37 ↓	0.86	0.35	0.50 ↓	0.81	0.56	0.66 ↓	0.75	0.86	0.80 ↑
350	0.94	0.10	0.17 ↓	0.90	0.15	0.25 ↓	0.88	0.27	0.41 ↓	0.84	0.47	0.60 ↓	0.78	0.86	0.82 ↑
400	0.93	0.06	0.11 ↓	0.93	0.09	0.17 ↓	0.91	0.20	0.32 ↓	0.86	0.38	0.53 ↓	0.80	0.85	0.82
450	0.95	0.05	0.10 ↓	0.94	0.08	0.14 ↓	0.93	0.12	0.22 ↓	0.86	0.27	0.41 ↓	0.81	0.85	**0.83** ↑
500	0.95	0.03	0.06 ↓	0.94	0.05	0.09 ↓	0.93	0.08	0.15 ↓	0.88	0.17	0.28 ↓	0.82	0.85	0.83
550	0.95	0.03	0.06 ↓	0.95	0.03	0.06 ↓	0.94	0.04	0.08 ↓	0.89	0.09	0.17 ↓	0.82	0.84	0.83
600	**1.0**	0.02	0.05 ↓	**0.95**	0.02	0.05 ↓	**0.96**	0.03	0.06 ↓	**0.94**	0.04	0.07 ↓	**0.83**	0.84	0.83

5.2 Experimental Results

SciBERT-Based Semantification. Given the results in Table 4, we examine the ***RQ***: *is the proposed transformer-based neural method effective at semantifying bioassays?* A score of 0.54 $F1$ tells us, suprisingly, that our attempted neural-based method is not an effective solution to the problem which is a surprising result since it is the state-of-the-art in classification tasks over scientific data [7]. Further, it proves practically inefficient, since, given the full corpus of statements, each test assay is semantified at a rate of 1 h on the CPU (see Table 5). On smaller subsets of the statement labels, the time is indeed faster and the scores are better (see Table 6), however, time performance rate of 28 min on the smallest subset is still impractical.

K-Means Clustering-Based Semantification. Detailed results with their performance rise and fall trends are shown in Table 7 for different cluster sizes and labels frequency thresholds within the clusters. E.g., the 'Labels freq $\geq$ 5' column evaluates only the statements that appeared 5 or more times within the cluster groups when the semantic statements from the various bioassays were aggregated. As the labels frequency threshold is lowered, the semantification score rises. The best scores are obtained when all the statements are considered (the 'Labels freq $\geq$ 1' column). This method obtains a high semantification score of 0.83 F1. This result when compared with the SciBERT-based neural model frustrates common expectations. Furthermore, this method is effective even w.r.t. the rate of semantification, since bioassays can be semantified in microseconds.

6 Digital Library Bioassay Semantification Workflows

We now describe the bioassay semantifier as an AI service application powering the structuring of scholarly knowledge in a real-world digital library (DL). The semantifier is importable within any DL that aim to establish knowledge-based information flows as the standard format for reporting and publishing research

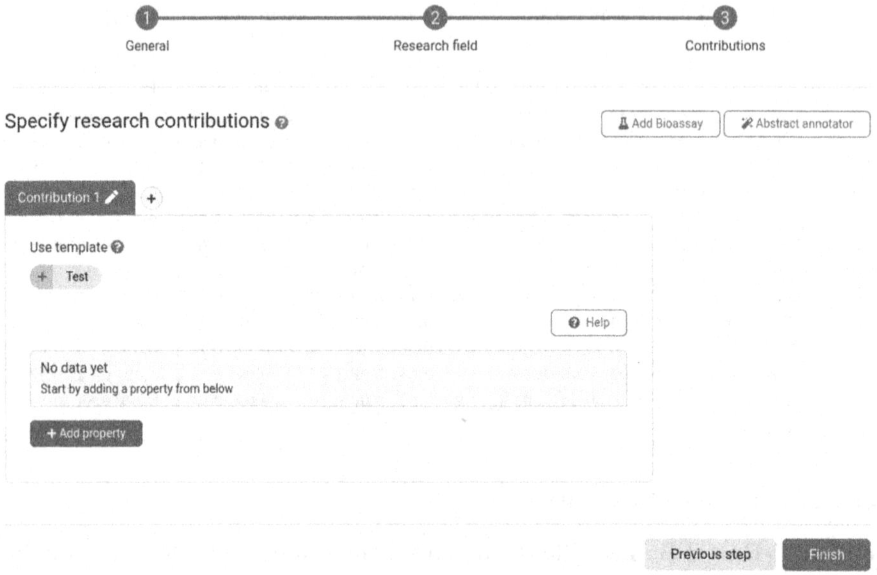

Fig. 2. (1) General - add publication metadata; (2) Research field - select a research field from a taxonomy https://gitlab.com/TIBHannover/orkg/orkg-backend/-/blob/master/scripts/ResearchFields.json; and (3) Contributions - either structure an articles' contribution as *method*, *material* and *results*, or add a bioassay text description by clicking 'Add Bioassay.' Note the 'Add Bioassay' button is activated only for some research fields in the Life Sciences.

findings, aka contributions. The high-level workflow is a distributed, decentralized, and collaborative creation and development model comprising information templates, vocabularies, and ontologies (e.g., OBO foundry, Medline, MESH taxonomies, BAO in the Biomedical/Life Sciences domains). We discuss the service as implemented in TIB's Open Research Knowledge Graph (ORKG) platform (https://www.orkg.org/) [5]. The online semantification workflow will be a synergistic combination of automated and manual processes involving the extraction of new ontologized entity types from literature (e.g., target, assay type, experimental conditions in bioassays publications), open access data generation in accord with the FAIR principles thus easily reusable by anyone, and curation support tools for semantified data curation. Figures 2, 3, and 4 depict the workflow. It is pragmatically designed as a hybrid of automatic semantification linked to the BAO (http://bioassayontology.org/) and a simplified user interface to help scientists curate their data with minimum effort. This offers a highly accurate semantification model without placing unrealistic expectations on scientists to semantify their assays from scratch. In general, by thus drastically reducing the time required for scientists to annotate their contributions, we can realistically advocate for semantified contributions to become a standard part of the publication process. On such digitalized data, the ORKG additionally supports advanced data interlinking, integration, visualization, and search.

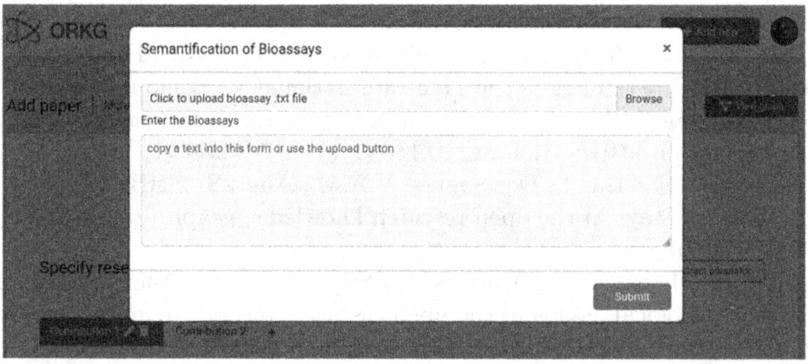

Fig. 3. A popup pane to either upload or copy-paste a bioassay text description

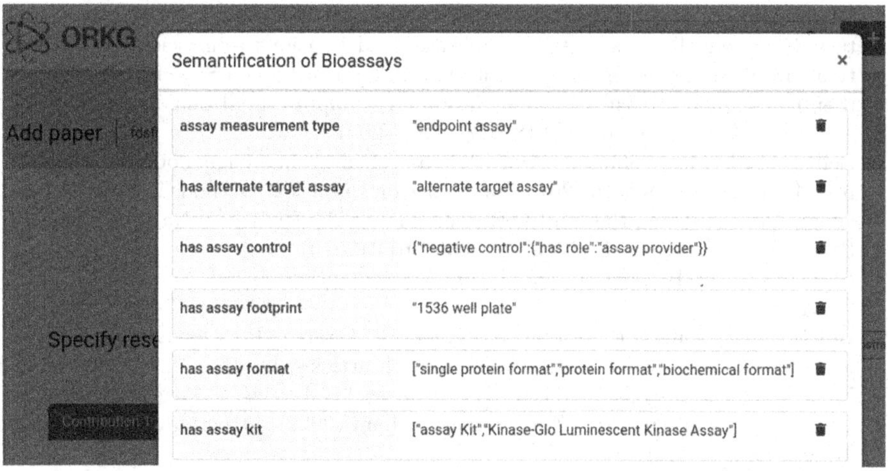

Fig. 4. An automatically semantified bioassay based on submitted text with an interaction button to delete statements that the domain expert judges invalid

7 Conclusion

In this work, we have presented an end-to-end model to semantify bioassays descriptions in the context of knowledge-based digital libraries as the ORKG. As a result, we have implemented a highly accurate semantification machine learning method based on clustering. Our code is open source https://gitlab.com/TIBHannover/orkg/orkg-bioassays-semantification. Finally, we report an unconventional finding that resource-light clustering problem formulation can better support bioassay semantification than a state-of-the-art neural approach.

References

1. Abeyruwan, S., et al.: Evolving BioAssay ontology (BAO): modularization, integration and applications. J. Biomed. Semantics **5**(Suppl 1), S5 (2014)

2. Ammar, W., Peters, M.E., Bhagavatula, C., Power, R.: The AI2 system at SemEval-2017 task 10 (ScienceIE): semi-supervised end-to-end entity and relation extraction. In: Proceedings of the 11th International Workshop on Semantic Evaluation (SemEval-2017), pp. 592–596. Association for Computational Linguistics, Vancouver (2017). https://doi.org/10.18653/v1/S17-2097
3. Anteghini, M., D'Souza, J., Dos Santos, V.A.M., Auer, S.: SciBERT-based semantification of bioassays in the open research knowledge graph. In: EKAW-PD 2020, pp. 22–30 (2020)
4. Anteghini, M., D'Souza, J., Martins dos Santos, V.A.P., Auer, S.: Representing semantified biological assays in the open research knowledge graph. In: Ishita, E., Pang, N.L.S., Zhou, L. (eds.) ICADL 2020. LNCS, vol. 12504, pp. 89–98. Springer, Cham (2020). https://doi.org/10.1007/978-3-030-64452-9_8
5. Auer, S.: Towards an open research knowledge graph (2018). https://doi.org/10.5281/zenodo.1157185
6. Augenstein, I., Das, M., Riedel, S., Vikraman, L., McCallum, A.: SemEval 2017 task 10: ScienceIE - extracting keyphrases and relations from scientific publications. In: Proceedings of the 11th International Workshop on Semantic Evaluation (SemEval-2017), pp. 546–555. Association for Computational Linguistics, Vancouver (2017). https://doi.org/10.18653/v1/S17-2091
7. Beltagy, I., Lo, K., Cohan, A.: SciBERT: a pretrained language model for scientific text. In: Proceedings of the 2019 Conference on Empirical Methods in Natural Language Processing and the 9th International Joint Conference on Natural Language Processing (EMNLP-IJCNLP), pp. 3606–3611 (2019)
8. Berners-Lee, T., Hendler, J., Lassila, O.: The semantic web. Sci. Am. **284**(5), 34–43 (2001)
9. Brack, A., D'Souza, J., Hoppe, A., Auer, S., Ewerth, R.: Domain-independent extraction of scientific concepts from research articles. In: Jose, J.M., Yilmaz, E., Magalhães, J., Castells, P., Ferro, N., Silva, M.J., Martins, F. (eds.) ECIR 2020. LNCS, vol. 12035, pp. 251–266. Springer, Cham (2020). https://doi.org/10.1007/978-3-030-45439-5_17
10. Clark, A.M., Bunin, B.A., Litterman, N.K., Schürer, S.C., Visser, U.: Fast and accurate semantic annotation of bioassays exploiting a hybrid of machine learning and user confirmation. PeerJ **2**, e524 (2014)
11. The UniProt Consortium: UniProt: the universal protein knowledgebase in 2021. Nucleic Acids Res. **49**(D1), D480–D489 (2020). https://doi.org/10.1093/nar/gkaa1100
12. Constantin, A., Peroni, S., Pettifer, S., Shotton, D., Vitali, F.: The document components ontology (DoCo). Semantic Web **7**(2), 167–181 (2016). https://doi.org/10.3233/SW-150177
13. Dessì, D., Osborne, F., Reforgiato Recupero, D., Buscaldi, D., Motta, E., Sack, H.: AI-KG: an automatically generated knowledge graph of artificial intelligence. In: Pan, J.Z., et al. (eds.) ISWC 2020. LNCS, vol. 12507, pp. 127–143. Springer, Cham (2020). https://doi.org/10.1007/978-3-030-62466-8_9
14. D'Souza, J., Auer, S., Pedersen, T.: SemEval-2021 Task 11: NLPContributionGraph - structuring scholarly NLP contributions for a research knowledge graph. In: Proceedings of the 15th International Workshop on Semantic Evaluation (SemEval-2021), pp. 364–376. Association for Computational Linguistics, Online (2021). https://doi.org/10.18653/v1/2021.semeval-1.44

15. D'Souza, J., Hoppe, A., Brack, A., Jaradeh, M.Y., Auer, S., Ewerth, R.: The STEM-ECR dataset: grounding scientific entity references in STEM scholarly content to authoritative encyclopedic and lexicographic sources. In: Proceedings of the 12th Language Resources and Evaluation Conference, pp. 2192–2203. European Language Resources Association, Marseille (2020). https://aclanthology.org/2020.lrec-1.268
16. Fisas, B., Ronzano, F., Saggion, H.: A multi-layered annotated corpus of scientific papers. In: LREC (2016)
17. Gábor, K., Buscaldi, D., Schumann, A.K., QasemiZadeh, B., Zargayouna, H., Charnois, T.: SemEval-2018 task 7: semantic relation extraction and classification in scientific papers. In: Proceedings of The 12th International Workshop on Semantic Evaluation, pp. 679–688. Association for Computational Linguistics, New Orleans (2018). https://doi.org/10.18653/v1/S18-1111
18. Hoskins, W.M., Craig, R.: Uses of bioassay in entomology. Annu. Rev. Entomol. **7**(1), 437–464 (1962)
19. Irwin, J.: Statistical method in biological assay. Nature **172**(4386), 925–926 (1953)
20. Jassal, B., et al.: The reactome pathway knowledgebase. Nucleic Acids Res. (2019). https://doi.org/10.1093/nar/gkz1031
21. Jin, X., Han, J.: K-means clustering. In: Sammut, C., Webb, G.I. (eds) Encyclopedia of Machine Learning. Springer, Boston (2011). https://doi.org/10.1007/978-0-387-30164-8_425
22. Kanehisa, M., Goto, S.: KEGG: Kyoto encyclopedia of genes and genomes. Nucleic Acids Res. **28**(1), 27–30 (2000). https://doi.org/10.1093/nar/28.1.27
23. Katayama, T., et al.: Biohackathon series in 2011 and 2012: penetration of ontology and linked data in life science domains. J. Biomed. Semantics **5**(1), 1–13 (2014)
24. Kononova, O., et al.: Text-mined dataset of inorganic materials synthesis recipes. Sci. Data **6**(1), 1–11 (2019)
25. Kulkarni, C., Xu, W., Ritter, A., Machiraju, R.: An annotated corpus for machine reading of instructions in wet lab protocols. In: NAACL: HLT, vol. 2, pp. 97–106 (Short Papers). New Orleans (2018). https://doi.org/10.18653/v1/N18-2016
26. Kuniyoshi, F., Makino, K., Ozawa, J., Miwa, M.: Annotating and extracting synthesis process of all-solid-state batteries from scientific literature. In: LREC, pp. 1941–1950 (2020)
27. Liakata, M., Saha, S., Dobnik, S., Batchelor, C., Rebholz-Schuhmann, D.: Automatic recognition of conceptualization zones in scientific articles and two life science applications. Bioinformatics **28**(7), 991–1000 (2012). https://doi.org/10.1093/bioinformatics/bts071
28. Liakata, M., Teufel, S., Siddharthan, A., Batchelor, C.: Corpora for the conceptualisation and zoning of scientific papers. In: Proceedings of the Seventh International Conference on Language Resources and Evaluation (LREC 2010). European Language Resources Association (ELRA), Valletta (2010)
29. Liu, H., Sarol, M.J., Kilicoglu, H.: UIUC_BioNLP at SemEval-2021 task 11: a cascade of neural models for structuring scholarly NLP contributions. In: Proceedings of the 15th International Workshop on Semantic Evaluation (SemEval-2021), pp. 377–386. Association for Computational Linguistics, Online (2021). https://doi.org/10.18653/v1/2021.semeval-1.45
30. Luan, Y., He, L., Ostendorf, M., Hajishirzi, H.: Multi-task identification of entities, relations, and coreference for scientific knowledge graph construction. In: Proceedings of the 2018 Conference on Empirical Methods in Natural Language Processing, pp. 3219–3232. Association for Computational Linguistics, Brussels (2018). https://doi.org/10.18653/v1/D18-1360

31. Mysore, S., et al.: The materials science procedural text corpus: annotating materials synthesis procedures with shallow semantic structures. In: Proceedings of the 13th Linguistic Annotation Workshop, pp. 56–64 (2019)
32. Pertsas, V., Constantopoulos, P.: Scholarly ontology: modelling scholarly practices. Int. J. Digit. Libr. **18**(3), 173–190 (2017)
33. Prud'hommeaux, E., Seaborne, A.: SPARQL query language for RDF. w3c recommendation (2008)
34. QasemiZadeh, B., Handschuh, S.: The ACL RD-TEC: a dataset for benchmarking terminology extraction and classification in computational linguistics. In: Proceedings of the 4th International Workshop on Computational Terminology (Computerm), pp. 52–63. Association for Computational Linguistics and Dublin City University, Dublin (2014). https://doi.org/10.3115/v1/W14-4807
35. Wheeler, D.L., et al.: Database resources of the national center for biotechnology information. Nucleic Acids Res. **46**(D1), D8–D13 (2017). https://doi.org/10.1093/nar/gkx1095
36. Sammut, C., Webb, G.I. (eds.): TF-IDF, pp. 986–987. Springer, Boston (2010)
37. Schürer, S.C., Vempati, U., Smith, R., Southern, M., Lemmon, V.: Bioassay ontology annotations facilitate cross-analysis of diverse high-throughput screening data sets. J. Biomol. Screen. **16**(4), 415–426 (2011)
38. Soldatova, L.N., King, R.D.: An ontology of scientific experiments. J. R. Soc. Interface **3**(11), 795–803 (2006). https://doi.org/10.1098/rsif.2006.0134
39. Syakur, M., Khotimah, B., Rochman, E., Satoto, B.D.: Integration k-means clustering method and elbow method for identification of the best customer profile cluster. In: IOP Conference Series: Materials Science and Engineering, vol. 336, p. 012017. IOP Publishing (2018)
40. Teufel, S., Carletta, J., Moens, M.: An annotation scheme for discourse-level argumentation in research articles. In: Ninth Conference of the European Chapter of the Association for Computational Linguistics, pp. 110–117. Association for Computational Linguistics, Bergen (1999). https://aclanthology.org/E99-1015
41. Thomas, A.L.: Essentials in bioassay development. BioPharm Int. **32**(11), 42–45 (2019)
42. Vempati, U.D., et al.: Formalization, annotation and analysis of diverse drug and probe screening assay datasets using the BioAssay Ontology (BAO). PLoS ONE **7**(11), e49198 (2012)
43. Visser, U., Abeyruwan, S., Vempati, U., Smith, R.P., Lemmon, V., Schürer, S.C.: BioAssay Ontology (BAO): a semantic description of bioassays and high-throughput screening results. BMC Bioinform. **12**(1), 257 (2011)
44. Wadden, D., Wennberg, U., Luan, Y., Hajishirzi, H.: Entity, relation, and event extraction with contextualized span representations. arXiv preprint arXiv:1909.03546 (2019)
45. Wang, Y., et al.: PubChem BioAssay: 2017 update. Nucleic Acids Res. **45**(D1), D955–D963 (2016)
46. Wang, Y., et al.: PubChem's BioAssay database. Nucleic Acids Res. **40**(D1), D400–D412 (2011)
47. Zhou, P., et al.: Attention-based bidirectional long short-term memory networks for relation classification. In: Proceedings of the 54th Annual Meeting of the Association for Computational Linguistics (vol. 2: Short Papers), pp. 207–212. Association for Computational Linguistics, Berlin (2016). https://doi.org/10.18653/v1/P16-2034

Pruned Graph Neural Network for Short Story Ordering

Melika Golestani[1(✉)], Zeinab Borhanifard[1], Farnaz Tahmasebian[1,2], and Heshaam Faili[1]

[1] School of Electrical and Computer Engineering, College of Engineering, University of Tehran, Tehran, Iran
{melika.golestani,borhanifardz,hfaili}@ut.ac.ir
[2] Alumni of Emory University, Atlanta, GA, USA

Abstract. Text coherence is a fundamental problem in natural language generation and understanding. Organizing sentences into an order that maximizes coherence is known as sentence ordering. This paper is proposing a new approach based on the graph neural network approach to encode a set of sentences and learn orderings of short stories. We propose a new method for constructing sentence-entity graphs of short stories to create the edges between sentences and reduce noise in our graph by replacing the pronouns with their referring entities. We improve the sentence ordering by introducing an aggregation method based on majority voting of state-of-the-art methods and our proposed one. Our approach employs a BERT-based model to learn semantic representations of the sentences. The results demonstrate that the proposed method significantly outperforms existing baselines on a corpus of short stories with a new state-of-the-art performance in terms of Perfect Match Ratio (PMR) and Kendall's Tau (τ) metrics. More precisely, our method increases PMR and τ criteria by more than 5% and 4.3%, respectively. These outcomes highlight the benefit of forming the edges between sentences based on their cosine similarity. We also observe that replacing pronouns with their referring entities effectively encodes sentences in sentence-entity graphs.

1 Introduction

Text coherence is a fundamental problem in natural language generation and understanding. A coherent text adheres to a logical order of events which facilitates better understanding. One of the subtasks in coherence modeling, called sentence ordering, refers to organizing shuffled sentences into an order that maximizes coherence [4]. Several downstream applications benefit from this task to assemble sound and easy-to-understand texts, such as extraction-based multi-document summarization [3,13,29,34], natural language generation [38], retrieval-based question answering [28,48], concept-to-text generation [21], storytelling [12,18,51], opinion generation [44], conversational analysis [49], image captioning [2], recipe generation [7], and discourse coherence [4,11,16].

In early studies, researchers modeled sentence structure using hand-crafted linguistic features [4,5,11,23], nonetheless, these features are domain-specific.

S. Bandini et al. (Eds.): AIxIA 2021, LNAI 13196, pp. 213–227, 2022.
https://doi.org/10.1007/978-3-031-08421-8_15

Therefore recent studies employed deep learning techniques to solve sentence ordering tasks [8, 14, 15, 27, 29].

[10] used graph neural networks, called ATTOrderNet, to accomplish this task. They used a self-attention mechanism combined with LSTMs to encode input sentences. Their method could get a reliable representation of the set of sentences regardless of their input order. In this representation, an ordered sequence is generated using a pointer network. Since ATTOrderNet is based on fully connected graph representations, it causes to build an association among some irrelevant sentences, which introduces massive noise into the network. Furthermore, since a self-attention mechanism only uses the information at the sentence level, other potentially helpful information such as entity information is missed.

To overcome these drawbacks, [47] developed the Sentence-Entity Graph (SE-Graph), which adds entities to the graph. While in the ATTOrderNet, every node is a sentence representation, SE-Graph consists of two types of nodes: sentence and entity[1]. Moreover, the edges come in two forms called SS and SE:

- SS: this edge is between sentence nodes that share a common entity,
- SE: this edge connects a sentence and an entity within the sentence labeled with the entity's role.

However, the introduced methods perform poorly for short story reordering tasks. The SE-graph solution seems effective for long texts but not for short stories. In this paper, we suggest modifications to the introduced graph methods to improve the performance for short story reordering tasks. Some issues arise in short stories: First, entities are often not repeated in multiple sentences in a short story or text; instead, pronouns refer to an entity. To address this problem, we improve the semantic graph by replacing the pronouns with their corresponding entities. Another issue is a high correlation between the sentences in a short story along with a high commonality of entities across sentences, which leads us to end up with a complete graph in most cases. Our solution is moving towards a Pruned Graph (PG).

As with the ATTOrderNet and SE-Graph networks, the PG architecture consists of three components: 1. Sentence encoder based on SBERT-WK model [41], 2. Graph-based neural story encoder, and 3. Pointer network based decoder.

With PG, the network nodes and SE edges are created based on SE-Graph, in a way that the first and third components are the same. However, in the story encoding phase, after generating the nodes and SE edges based on SE-Graph method, the pruning phase is started on SS edges. This pruning process is defined as follow: each sentence edged out its neighbors with the first and second most cosine similarities [37]. This method alleviates some problems of the previous two methods in the case of organizing short story sentences. It is noteworthy that pronouns are replaced with entities during pre-processing.

Finally, we present a method based on majority voting to combine our proposed graph network-based method with the state-of-art methods to benefit from each. Contributions of this study are as follows:

[1] The entity should be common to at least two sentences.

1. Proposing a new method based on graph networks to order sentences of a short stories corpus by:
   (a) Suggesting a new method for creating the edges between sentences,
   (b) Creating a better sentence-entity graph for short stories by replacing pronouns in sentences with entities,
   (c) Moreover, taking advantage of BERT-based sentence encoder.
2. Using majority voting to combine sentence ordering methods.

2 Related Work

2.1 Sentence Ordering

In early studies on sentence ordering, the structure of the document is modeled using hand-crafted linguistic features [4,5,11,23]. [23] encoded sentences as vectors of linguistic features and used data to train a probabilistic transition model. [5] developed the content model in which topics in a specific domain are represented as states in an HMM. Some other like [4] utilize the entity-based approach, which captures local coherence by modeling patterns of entity distributions. Other approaches used a combination of the entity grid and the content model [11] or employed syntactic features [30] in order to improve the model.

However, linguistic features are incredibly domain-specific, so applying these methods across different domains can decrease the performance. To overcome this limitation, recent works have used deep learning-based approaches. [26] proposes a neural model of distribution of sentence representations based on recurrent neural networks. In [27], graph-based neural models are used to generate a domain-independent neural model. [1] introduced a method that involves combining two points elicited from the unary and pairwise model of sentences. [8] used an LSTM encoder and beam search to construct a pairwise model. Based on a pointer network that provides advantages in capturing global coherence, [15] developed an end-to-end approach that predicts order of sentences. In another work, by applying an encoder-decoder architecture based on LSTMs and attention mechanisms, [29] suggested a pairwise model and established the gold order by beam search. In [35], we presented a method that does not require any training corpus due to not having a training phase. We also developed a framework based on a sentence-level language model to solve the sentence ordering problem in [14]. Moreover, in several other studies, including [10] and [47], graph neural networks are used to accomplish this task, as explained in the following.

2.2 Graph Neural Networks in NLP

Graph neural networks (GNN) have shown to be effective in NLP applications, including syntactic dependency trees [31], neural machine translation [6], knowledge graphs [43], semantic graphs [39], sequence-to-graph learning [19], graph-to-sequence learning [6], sentence ordering [47], and multi-document summarization [9,45].

In particular, text classification is a common application of GNNs in natural language processing. A GNN infers document labels based on the relationships among documents or words [17]. [9] used a GNN in multi-document summarization. They create multi-document graphs which determine pairwise ordering constraints of sentences based on the discourse relationship between them. [20] proposed Graph Convolutional Networks (GCN), which is used in [45] to generate sentence relation graphs. The final sentence embeddings indicate the graph representation and are utilized as inputs to achieve satisfactory results on multi-document summarization.

Another method is presented in [31] where a syntactic GCN is developed with a CNN/RNN as sentence encoder. The GCN indicates syntactic relations between words in a sentence. In a more recent work, [47] proposed a graph-based neural network for sentence ordering, in which paragraphs are modeled as graphs where sentences and entities are the nodes. The method showed improvement in evaluation metrics for sentence ordering task. In this work, we explore the use of GRN for NLP tasks, especially to perform sentence-ordering on a corpus of short stories.

3 Baselines

This section introduces ATTOrderNet [10] and SE-Graph [47], which achieve state-of-the-art performances and serve as baseline for our work.

3.1 ATTOrderNet

ATTOrderNet introduced in [10] is a model using graph neural networks for sentence ordering. The model includes three components as follows: a sentence encoder based on Bi-LSTM, a paragraph encoder based on self-attention, and a pointer network-based decoder. In the sentence encoder, sentences are translated into distributional representations with a word embedding matrix. Then a sentence-level representation using the Bi-LSTM is learned. An average pooling layer follows multiple self-attention layers in the paragraph encoder. The paragraph encoder computes the attention scores for all pairs of sentences at different positions in the paragraph. Therefore, each sentence node is connected to all others where the encoder exploits latent dependency relations among sentences independent of their input order.

Having an input set of sentences, the decoder aims to predict a coherent order, identical to the original order. In this method, LSTM-based pointer networks are used to predict the correct sentence ordering from the final paragraph representation. Based on the sequence-to-sequence model, the pointer network-based decoders predict the correct sentence sequence [40]. Specifically, input tokens are encoded using the pointer network as summary vectors[2], and the next token vector is decoded repeatedly. Finally, the output token sequence is derived from the output token vector.

3.2 SE-Graph

SE-Graph, similarly to ATTOrderNet, consists of three components: 1. a sentence encoder based on Bi-LSTM, 2. a paragraph encoder, 3. a pointer network based decoder

[2] The paragraph vector is nonetheless influenced by the permutations of input sentences.

Nevertheless, the difference between SE-Graph and ATTOrderNet is only in the encoder paragraph component, described in the following. In contrast to the fully connected graph representations explored by ATTOrderNet, [47] represented input paragraphs as sentence-entity graphs. The SE-Graph includes two types of nodes: sentence and entity. The entity should be common to at least two sentences to be considered as a node of the graph. There are also two types of edges: SS edges that connect sentence nodes with at least a common entity, and SE edges that link a sentence with an entity within that and with a label of the entity's role. SE edges are labeled based on the syntactic role of the entity in the sentence, such as a subject, an object, or other. When an entity appears multiple times in a sentence with different roles, the role that has the highest rank is considered. The highest rank of roles is the subject role; after that are the object roles. SE-Graph framework utilizes a GRN-based paragraph encoder that integrates the paragraph-level state along with the sentence-level state.

4 Methodology

In this section, first, the problem is formulated, second the dataset is introduced and explains why this dataset is suitable for the sentence ordering task. Then two methodologies are proposed. The first proposed method, called Pruned Graph, is based on graph networks, and the second is based on the majority voting to combine the outputs of three different models.

4.1 Problem Formulation

Consider $S(O)$ is a set of n unordered sentences taken from a coherent text:
$O = s_1, s_2, \dots, s_n$,

$$s(o_1) > s(o_2) > \cdots > s(o_n) \tag{1}$$

The goal of sentence ordering is to find a permutation of sentences of O like $S(o')$,

$$s(o_1{}') > s(o_2{}') > \ldots > s(o_n{}') \tag{2}$$

that corresponds to the gold data arrangement. In other words, sentence ordering aims to restore the original orders:

$$s(o_1{}^*) > s(o_2{}^*) > \ldots > s(o_n{}^*) \tag{3}$$

where $S(o^*)$ represents the original or gold order. As a result a correct output leads to $S(o') = S(o^*)$. Based on the above definition and notions we propose our sentence ordering method.

4.2 Dataset

In this paper, we used a corpus of short stories, called ROCStories [32]. It contains 98,162 commonsense stories, each with exactly five sentences and an average word count of 50. [33] created ROCStories corpus for a shared task called LSDSem, in which models are supposed to predict the correct ending to short stories. 3,742 of the stories have two options for the final sentence. It is worth noting that humans generated all of the stories and options.

We can learn sequences of daily events from this dataset because it contains some essential characteristics: The stories are **rich with causal and temporal relations among events**, which makes this dataset a highly useful resource for learning narrative structure across a wide range of events. The dataset consists of a **comprehensive collection of daily and non-fictional short stories** useful for modeling the coherence of a text [32].

Due to these features, ROCStories can be used to learn sequences of sentences. Thus, the corpus is useful for organizing sentences in a text.

4.3 Pruned Graph Sentence Ordering (PG)

We propose a neural network based on the pruned graph for arranging the sentences of short stories, a modified version of the ATTOrderNet [10] and Sentence-Entity Graph [47]. The PG method consists of three components: **sentence encoder**, **story encoder**, and **decoder**. In order to be a fair comparison, we used the same decoder as ATTOrderNet and SE-Graph. Due to space limitations, here we explain our sentence encoder and our story encoder. The Sentence encoder uses BERT encoding to encode sentences, while Story encoder uses a graph neural network for encoding stories.

Sentence Encoder: SBERT-WK. We use fine-tuned pre-trained SBERT-WK model to encode sentences. BERT contains several layers, each of which captures a different linguistic characteristic. SBERT-WK found better sentence representations by fusing information from different layers, [41]. The system geometrically analyzes space using a deep contextual model that is trained on both word-level and sentence-level, without further training. For each word in a sentence, it determines a unified word representation then computes the final sentence embedding vector based on the weighted average based on the word importance of the word representations. Even with a small embedding size of 768, SBERT-WK outperforms other methods by a significant margin on textual similarity tasks [41].

Story Encoder. To use graph neural networks for encoding stories, input stories should be represented as graphs. We propose a pruned graph (PG) representation instead of SE-Graph [47] for encoding short stories. Nodes in PG are composed of sentences and entities. We replace pronouns with the entities they refer to since entities are not often repeated from one sentence to another during a short story[3], we will go into more detail in the experiments. We consider all nouns of an input story as entities at first. After that, we eliminate entities that do not occur more than once in the story.

We can formalize our undirected pruned graphs as G = (V_s, V_e, E), where V_s indicates the sentence-level nodes, V_e denotes the entity-level nodes, and E represents edges. Edges in PG graphs are divided into two types: SS and SE. The SS type links two

[3] We use the Stanford's tool [25].

sentences in a story that have the highest or second-highest value of cosine similarity with each other; and the SE type links a sentence with an entity within that with a label of the entity's role. Equation 4 shows the formula for calculating the cosine similarity, where CosSim is cosine similarity and Emb_{s_i} represents vector of sentence i.

$$CosSim(Emb_{s_i}, Emb_{s_j}) = \frac{Emb_{s_i} * Emb_{s_j}}{||Emb_{s_i}||||Emb_{s_j}||} \tag{4}$$

SE edges are labeled according to the syntactic role of the entity in the sentence, such as a subject, an object, or other. The role that has the highest rank in an instance of an entity appearing multiple times is considered. The ranking is as follows: subject role, object roles, and other. The use of referring entities rather than pronouns is crucial.

Thus, sentence nodes are linked to both sentence and entity nodes, whereas an entity node is not connected to any other entity nodes. For graph encoding, we use GRN [50], which has been found effective for various kinds of graph encoding tasks. GRN used in our PG is the same as GRN in [47], so we do not explain it.

4.4 Majority Voting

We combine the output of three methods to achieve better results in majority voting. Since the stories in Rocstories all have five sentences, there are 20 possible pair sentence orderings as follow:

1. s_1s_2 or 2. s_2s_1, 3. s_1s_3 or 4. s_3s_1, 5. s_1s_4 or 6. s_4s_1, 7. s_1s_5 or 8. s_5s_1, 9. s_2s_3 or 10. s_3s_2, 11. s_2s_4 or 12. s_4s_2, 13. s_2s_5 or 14. s_5s_2, 15. s_3s_4 or 16. s_4s_3, 17. s_3s_5 or 18. s_5s_3, 19. s_4s_5 or 20. s_5s_4

Each suggested order for a story includes 10 of the above pair orderings, either of the two pair orderings that have an "or" between them. Through majority voting[4], we can combine the outputs of three separate methods to generate a final order.

According to the number of occurrences in each of the three output arrangements, we assign scores to each of the 20 possible pairings. As a result, each of these possible pairings is scored between 0 and 3. 0 indicates that this pairing does not appear in any of the three methods' outputs, while 3 indicates that it appears in all of them. In the end, all pairs with a greater score of 1 occur in the final orderings[5]. Indeed, these are ten pairs[6], and with the chosen pairs, the sentences of the story are arranged uniquely.

In the following subsection, we are proving that majority voting is a valid way to combine the outputs generated from three different methods for arranging sentences. By using contradiction, we demonstrate the validity of the majority voting method for combining three distinct methods of sentence ordering to arrange two sentences.

---

[4] For example, either s_1s_2 or s_2s_1 occurs, and without a doubt, the co-occurrence of these is a vast and impossible contradiction.

[5] Suppose the outputs of the three methods for arranging $sentence_1$ (s_1) and $sentence_2$ (s_2) are: Method 1: s_1s_2, Method 2: s_1s_2, and Method 3: s_2s_1. Therefore, the order s_1s_2 gets two points and the order s_2s_1 gets one, so s_1s_2 applies to the final output.

[6] Either of the two pair orderings that have an "or" between them.

Assuming the majority voting of three methods fails to create an unique order, then two orders are possible, s_1s_2, and s_2s_1. In the first case, s_1 appears before s_2 in two or more outputs of the methods, and in the second case, s_2 appears before s_1 in two or more outputs. Due to the three methods, this assumption causes a contradiction. To ordering more than two sentences, it can be proved by induction.

5 Experiment

5.1 Evaluation Metrics

We use two standard metrics to evaluate the proposed model outputs that are commonly used in previous work: Kendall's tau and perfect match ratio, as described below.

- **Kendall's Tau** (τ)
  Kendal's Tau [24] measures the quality of the output's ordering, computed as follows:
$$\tau = 1 - \frac{(2 * \#\ of\ Inversions)}{N * (N-1)/2} \tag{5}$$
  where N represents the sequence length (i.e. the number of sentences of a story, which is always equal to 5 for ROCStories), and the inversions return the number of exchanges of the predicted order with the gold order for reconstructing the correct order. τ is always between -1 and 1, where the upper bound indicates that the predicted order is exactly the same as the gold order. This metric correlates reliably with human judgments, according to [24].
- **Perfect Match Ratio (PMR)**
  According to this ratio, each story is considered as a single unit, and a ratio of the number of correct orders is calculated. Therefore no penalties are given for incorrect permutations [15]. PMR is formulated mathematically as follows:
$$PMR = 1/N \sum_{1}^{N} o'_i = o^*_i \tag{6}$$
  where o'_i represents the output order and o^*_i indicates the gold order. N specifies the sequence length. Since the length of all the stories of ROCStories is equal to 5, N in this study is always equal to 5. PMR values range from 0 to 1, with a higher value indicating better performance.

5.2 Contrast Models

We compare our PG to the state of the arts, namely the following: 1. LSTM + PtrNet [15], 2. LSTM + Set2Seq [29], 3. ATTOrderNet [10], 4. SE-Graph [47], 5. HAN [42], 6. SLM [14], 7. RankTxNet ListMLE [22], 8. Enhancing PtrNet + Pairwise [46], 9. B-TSort [36]. We teach LSTM + PtrNet, ATTOrderNet, SE-Graph, and B-TSort on the ROCStories. The following is a brief description of the mentioned methods, but We refer to Sect. 3 to explain ATTOrderNet and SE-Graph.

[15] proposes LSTM + PtrNet as a method for ordering sentences. In this end-to-end method, pointer networks sort encrypted sentences after decoding them by LSTM. [29] recommended LSTM + Set2Seq. Their method encodes sentences, learns context representation by LSTM and attention mechanisms, and utilizes a pointer network-based decoder to predict sentences' order. A transformer followed by an LSTM was added to the sentence encoder in [42] to capture word clues and dependencies between sentences; and so on, HAN is developed.

In [14], we developed the Sentence-level Language Model (SLM) for Sentence Ordering, consisting of a Sentence Encoder, a Story Encoder, and a Sentence Organizer. The sentence encoder encodes sentences into a vector using a fine-tuned pre-trained BERT. Hence, the embedding pays more attention to the sentence's crucial parts. Afterward, the story encoder uses a decoder-encoder architecture to learn the sentence-level language model. The learned vector from the hidden state is decoded, and this decoded vector is utilized to indicate the following sentence's candidate. Finally, the sentence organizer uses the cosine similarity as the scoring function in order to sort the sentences.

An attention-based ranking framework is presented in [22] to address the task. The model uses a bidirectional sentence encoder and a self-attention-based transformer network to endcode paragraphs. In [46], an enhancing pointer network based on two pairwise ordering prediction modules, The FUTURE and HISTORY module, is employed to decode paragraphs. Based on the candidate sentence, the FUTURE module predicts the relative positions of other unordered sentences. Although, the HISTORY module determines the coherency between the candidate and previously ordered sentences. And lastly, [36] designed B-TSort, a pairwise ordering method, which is the current state-of-the-art method for sentence ordering. This method benefits from BERT and graph-based networks. Based on the relative pairwise ordering, graphs are constructed. Finally, the global order is derived by a topological sort algorithm on the graph.

5.3 Setting

For a fair comparison, we follow [47]'s settings. Nevertheless, we use SBERT-WK's 768-dimension vectors for sentence embedding. Furthermore, the state sizes for sentence nodes are set to 768 in the GRN; The Batch size is 32. In preprocessing, we use Stanford's tool [25] to replace pronouns with the referring entities.

5.4 Results

In this paper, we propose a new method based on graph networks for sentences ordering short stories called Pruned Graph (PG). In order to achieve this, we propose a new method for creating edges between sentences (by calculating the cosine similarity between sentences), and we create a better sentence-entity graph for short stories by replacing pronouns with the relevant entities. Besides, to make a better comparison, we also teach the following cases:

1. All nodes in the graph are of the sentence type, and the graph is fully connected. In other words, we train ATTOrderNet on ROCStories[7].

[7] [10] did not train ATTOrderNet on the ROCStories dataset.

2. The nodes include sentence and entity nodes, and each sentence's node has the edge over all other sentences' nodes (semi fully connected SE-Graph[8]).
3. The network comprises sentence and entity nodes, and every two sentences with at least one entity in common are connected (SE-Graph[9]).
4. Replacing pronouns with the relevant entities in SE-Graph (SE-Graph + Co-referencing).
5. Similar to PG, but each sentence is connected to a sentence with the highest cosine similarity (semi PG_1).
6. Similar to PG; however, each sentence is connected to three other sentences based on their cosine similarity (semi PG_3).
7. Pruned Graph with a Bi-LSTM based sentence encoder[10] (PG').

Note that in the above methods, where the graph also contains the nodes of the entity, there is an edge between a sentence and an entity within it[11]. Table 1 reports the results of Pruned Graph (PG) and the above seven methods.

To get the training, validation, and testing datasets, we randomly split ROCStories into 8:1:1. Therefore, the training set includes 78,529 stories, the validation set contains 9,816 stories, and the testing set consists of 9,817 stories.

As shown in Table 1, our PG beats all seven other methods. The results show that all three of our innovations to the graph-based method have improved the performance. Based on our analysis, the SBERT-WK sentence encoder is more beneficial than the Bi-LSTM. Our experiences also find that using referring entities instead of pronouns is helpful to create a more effective sentence-entity graph. Additionally, it indicates connecting each sentence to two others using cosine similarity is efficient to encode a story.

Table 1. Reporting the results of the proposed network called Pruned Graph in comparison with the seven methods mentioned above

Method	τ	PMR
ATTOrderNet	0.7364	0.4030
Fully connected SE-Graph	0.7300	0.3927
SE-Graph	0.7133	0.3687
SE-Graph + Co-ref	0.7301	0.3981
PG + 1 SS	0.7534	0.4349
PG + 3 SS	0.7379	0.4100
PG + Bi-LSTM-based sentence encoder	0.7852	0.4769
Pruned Graph	0.8220	0.5373

[8] Entity nodes are not connected to all nodes.

[9] We train SE-Graph on ROCStories since [47] did not.

[10] To demonstrate the advantages of the PG's BERT-based sentence encoder, this component is considered exactly like the sentence encoder of SE-Graph and ATTOrderNet.

[11] Entity nodes can only have a link to sentence nodes.

Table 2 reports the results of the proposed method of this paper in comparison with competitors. When compared with ATTOrdeNet, PG improved the Tau by over 8.5% as well as PMR by 13.5%. Furthermore, the Tau is increased by 10.8% and the PMR by more than 16.8% compared to SE-Graph. PG outperforms the state-of-the-art on ROCStories with a more tthan 1.8% increase in pmr and a more than 3.9% improvement in τ.

Table 2. Results of our PG compared to baselines and competitors

Model	τ	PMR
LSTM+PtrNet	0.7230	0.3647
LSTM+Set2Seq	0.7112	0.3581
ATTOrderNet	0.7364	0.4030
SE-Graph	0.7133	0.3687
HAN	0.7322	0.3962
SLM	0.7547	0.4064
RankTxNet ListMLE	0.7602	0.3602
Enhancing PtrNet + Pairwise	0.7681	0.4600
B-TSort	0.8039	0.4980
Our Pruned Graph	0.8220	0.5373

Finally, we merged the outputs of the three methods using the majority voting method, including Enhancing PtrNet, B-TSort, and Our Pruned Graph. Table 3 shows the results of the combination, which improves the PMR and τ criteria by more than 5% and 4.3% on ROCStories, respectively.

Table 3. Results of combining of Enhancing PtrNet, B-TSort, and Pruned Graph using majority voting

Method	τ	PMR
Combination	0.8470	0.5488

6 Conclusion

This paper introduced a graph-based neural framework to solve the sentence ordering task. This framework takes a set of randomly ordered sentences and outputs a coherent order of the sentences. The results demonstrate that SBERT-WK is a reliable model to encode sentences. Our analysis examined how the method is affected by using a Bi-LSTM model in the sentence encoder component. In addition, we found that replacing pronouns with their referring entities supplies a more informative sentence-entity graph to encode a story. The experimental results indicate that our proposed graph-based neural model significantly outperforms on ROCStories dataset. Furthermore, we recommend a method for combining different methods of sentence ordering based on majority voting that achieves state-of-the-art performance in PMR and τ scores. In future, we plan to apply the trained model on sentence ordering task to tackle other tasks including text generation, dialogue generation, text completion, retrieval-based QA, and extractive text summarization.

References

1. Agrawal, H., Chandrasekaran, A., Batra, D., Parikh, D., Bansal, M.: Sort story: sorting jumbled images and captions into stories. In: Proceedings of the 2016 Conference on Empirical Methods in Natural Language Processing, pp. 925–931. Association for Computational Linguistics, Austin (2016). https://doi.org/10.18653/v1/D16-1091
2. Anderson, P., et al.: Bottom-up and top-down attention for image captioning and visual question answering. In: Proceedings of the IEEE Conference on Computer Vision and Pattern Recognition, pp. 6077–6086 (2018)
3. Barzilay, R., Elhadad, N.: Inferring strategies for sentence ordering in multidocument news summarization. J. Artif. Intell. Res. **17**, 35–55 (2002)
4. Barzilay, R., Lapata, M.: Modeling local coherence: an entity-based approach. Comput. Linguist. **34**(1), 1–34 (2008)
5. Barzilay, R., Lee, L.: Catching the drift: probabilistic content models, with applications to generation and summarization. In: Proceedings of the Human Language Technology Conference of the North American Chapter of the Association for Computational Linguistics: HLT-NAACL 2004, pp. 113–120 (2004)
6. Beck, D., Haffari, G., Cohn, T.: Graph-to-sequence learning using gated graph neural networks. In: Proceedings of the 56th Annual Meeting of the Association for Computational Linguistics (vol. 1: Long Papers), pp. 273–283. Association for Computational Linguistics, Melbourne (2018). https://doi.org/10.18653/v1/P18-1026
7. Chandu, K., Nyberg, E., Black, A.W.: Storyboarding of recipes: grounded contextual generation. In: Proceedings of the 57th Annual Meeting of the Association for Computational Linguistics, pp. 6040–6046 (2019)
8. Chen, X., Qiu, X., Huang, X.: Neural sentence ordering. arXiv preprint arXiv:1607.06952 (2016)
9. Christensen, J., Soderland, S., Etzioni, O.: Towards coherent multi-document summarization. In: Proceedings of the 2013 Conference of the North American Chapter of the Association for Computational Linguistics: Human Language Technologies, pp. 1163–1173. Association for Computational Linguistics, Atlanta (2013). https://www.aclweb.org/anthology/N13-1136
10. Cui, B., Li, Y., Chen, M., Zhang, Z.: Deep attentive sentence ordering network. In: Proceedings of the 2018 Conference on Empirical Methods in Natural Language Processing, pp. 4340–4349 (2018)
11. Elsner, M., Austerweil, J., Charniak, E.: A unified local and global model for discourse coherence. In: Human Language Technologies 2007: The Conference of the North American Chapter of the Association for Computational Linguistics, Proceedings of the Main Conference, pp. 436–443 (2007)
12. Fan, A., Lewis, M., Dauphin, Y.: Strategies for structuring story generation. In: Proceedings of the 57th Annual Meeting of the Association for Computational Linguistics, pp. 2650–2660. Association for Computational Linguistics, Florence (2019). https://doi.org/10.18653/v1/P19-1254

13. Galanis, D., Lampouras, G., Androutsopoulos, I.: Extractive multi-document summarization with integer linear programming and support vector regression. In: Proceedings of COLING 2012, pp. 911–926 (2012)
14. Golestani, M., Razavi, S.Z., Borhanifard, Z., Tahmasebian, F., Faili, H.: Using BERT encoding and sentence-level language model for sentence ordering. In: Ekštein, K., Pártl, F., Konopík, M. (eds.) Text, Speech, and Dialogue, pp. 318–330. Springer International Publishing, Cham (2021)
15. Gong, J., Chen, X., Qiu, X., Huang, X.: End-to-end neural sentence ordering using pointer network. arXiv preprint arXiv:1611.04953 (2016)
16. Guinaudeau, C., Strube, M.: Graph-based local coherence modeling. In: Proceedings of the 51st Annual Meeting of the Association for Computational Linguistics (vol. 1: Long Papers), pp. 93–103 (2013)
17. Hamilton, W.L., Ying, R., Leskovec, J.: Inductive representation learning on large graphs. In: Proceedings of the 31st International Conference on Neural Information Processing Systems, pp. 1025–1035. NIPS 2017, Curran Associates Inc., Red Hook, NY (2017)
18. Hu, J., Cheng, Y., Gan, Z., Liu, J., Gao, J., Neubig, G.: What makes a good story? Designing composite rewards for visual storytelling. In: Proceedings of the AAAI Conference on Artificial Intelligence, vol. 34, pp. 7969–7976 (2020)
19. Johnson, D.: Learning graphical state transitions. In: ICLR (2017)
20. Kipf, T.N., Welling, M.: Semi-supervised classification with graph convolutional networks. arXiv preprint arXiv:1609.02907 (2017)
21. Konstas, I., Lapata, M.: Concept-to-text generation via discriminative reranking. In: Proceedings of the 50th Annual Meeting of the Association for Computational Linguistics (vol. 1: Long Papers), pp. 369–378 (2012)
22. Kumar, P., Brahma, D., Karnick, H., Rai, P.: Deep attentive ranking networks for learning to order sentences. In: Proceedings of the AAAI Conference on Artificial Intelligence, vol. 34, pp. 8115–8122 (2020)
23. Lapata, M.: Probabilistic text structuring: experiments with sentence ordering. In: Proceedings of the 41st Annual Meeting of the Association for Computational Linguistics, pp. 545–552 (2003)
24. Lapata, M.: Automatic evaluation of information ordering: Kendall's tau. Comput. Linguist. **32**(4), 471–484 (2006). https://doi.org/10.1162/coli.2006.32.4.471
25. Lee, H., Peirsman, Y., Chang, A., Chambers, N., Surdeanu, M., Jurafsky, D.: Stanford's multi-pass sieve coreference resolution system at the CoNLL-2011 shared task. In: Proceedings of the 15th Conference on Computational Natural Language Learning: Shared Task, pp. 28–34. Association for Computational Linguistics (2011)
26. Li, J., Hovy, E.: A model of coherence based on distributed sentence representation. In: Proceedings of the 2014 Conference on Empirical Methods in Natural Language Processing (EMNLP), pp. 2039–2048 (2014)
27. Li, J., Jurafsky, D.: Neural net models of open-domain discourse coherence. In: Proceedings of the 2017 Conference on Empirical Methods in Natural Language Processing, pp. 198–209. Association for Computational Linguistics, Copenhagen (2017). https://doi.org/10.18653/v1/D17-1019
28. Liu, X., Shen, Y., Duh, K., Gao, J.: Stochastic answer networks for machine reading comprehension. In: Proceedings of the 56th Annual Meeting of the Association for Computational Linguistics (vol. 1: Long Papers), pp. 1694–1704. Association for Computational Linguistics, Melbourne (2018). https://doi.org/10.18653/v1/P18-1157
29. Logeswaran, L., Lee, H., Radev, D.: Sentence ordering and coherence modeling using recurrent neural networks. In: Proceedings of the AAAI Conference on Artificial Intelligence, vol. 32 (2018)

30. Louis, A., Nenkova, A.: A coherence model based on syntactic patterns. In: Proceedings of the 2012 Joint Conference on Empirical Methods in Natural Language Processing and Computational Natural Language Learning, pp. 1157–1168 (2012)
31. Marcheggiani, D., Titov, I.: Encoding sentences with graph convolutional networks for semantic role labeling. In: Proceedings of the 2017 Conference on Empirical Methods in Natural Language Processing, pp. 1506–1515. Association for Computational Linguistics, Copenhagen (2017). https://doi.org/10.18653/v1/D17-1159
32. Mostafazadeh, N., et al.: A corpus and cloze evaluation for deeper understanding of commonsense stories. In: Proceedings of the 2016 Conference of the North American Chapter of the Association for Computational Linguistics: Human Language Technologies, pp. 839–849. Association for Computational Linguistics, San Diego (2016). https://doi.org/10.18653/v1/N16-1098
33. Mostafazadeh, N., Roth, M., Louis, A., Chambers, N., Allen, J.: LSDSem 2017 shared task: the story cloze test. In: Proceedings of the 2nd Workshop on Linking Models of Lexical, Sentential and Discourse-level Semantics, pp. 46–51. Association for Computational Linguistics, Valencia (2017). https://doi.org/10.18653/v1/W17-0906
34. Nallapati, R., Zhai, F., Zhou, B.: SummaRuNNer: a recurrent neural network based sequence model for extractive summarization of documents. In: Proceedings of the AAAI Conference on Artificial Intelligence, vol. 31 (2017)
35. Pour, M.G., Razavi, S.Z., Faili, H.: A new sentence ordering method using BERT pretrained model. In: 2020 11th International Conference on Information and Knowledge Technology (IKT), pp. 132–138. IEEE (2020)
36. Prabhumoye, S., Salakhutdinov, R., Black, A.W.: Topological sort for sentence ordering. In: Proceedings of the 58th Annual Meeting of the Association for Computational Linguistics, pp. 2783–2792. Association for Computational Linguistics, Online (2020). https://doi.org/10.18653/v1/2020.acl-main.248
37. Rahutomo, F., Kitasuka, T., Aritsugi, M.: Semantic cosine similarity. In: The 7th International Student Conference on Advanced Science and Technology ICAST, vol. 4, p. 1 (2012)
38. Reiter, E., Dale, R.: Building applied natural language generation systems. Nat. Lang. Eng. **3**(1), 57–87 (1997)
39. Song, L., Zhang, Y., Wang, Z., Gildea, D.: N-ary relation extraction using graph-state LSTM. In: Proceedings of the 2018 Conference on Empirical Methods in Natural Language Processing, pp. 2226–2235. Association for Computational Linguistics, Brussels (2018). https://doi.org/10.18653/v1/D18-1246
40. Sutskever, I., Vinyals, O., Le, Q.V.: Sequence to sequence learning with neural networks. In: Proceedings of the 27th International Conference on Neural Information Processing Systems, vol. 2, pp. 3104–3112. NIPS 2014, MIT Press, Cambridge (2014)
41. Wang, B., Kuo, C.C.J.: SBERT-WK: a sentence embedding method by dissecting BERT-based word models. IEEE/ACM Trans. Audio Speech Lang. Process. **28**, 2146–2157 (2020)
42. Wang, T., Wan, X.: Hierarchical attention networks for sentence ordering. In: Proceedings of the AAAI Conference on Artificial Intelligence, vol. 33, pp. 7184–7191 (2019)
43. Wang, Z., Lv, Q., Lan, X., Zhang, Y.: Cross-lingual knowledge graph alignment via graph convolutional networks. In: Proceedings of the 2018 Conference on Empirical Methods in Natural Language Processing, pp. 349–357. Association for Computational Linguistics, Brussels (2018). https://doi.org/10.18653/v1/D18-1032
44. Yanase, T., et al.: Learning sentence ordering for opinion generation of debate. In: Proceedings of the 2nd Workshop on Argumentation Mining, pp. 94–103 (2015)
45. Yasunaga, M., Zhang, R., Meelu, K., Pareek, A., Srinivasan, K., Radev, D.: Graph-based neural multi-document summarization. In: Proceedings of the 21st Conference on Computational Natural Language Learning (CoNLL 2017), pp. 452–462. Association for Computational Linguistics, Vancouver (2017). https://doi.org/10.18653/v1/K17-1045

46. Yin, Y., et al.: Enhancing pointer network for sentence ordering with pairwise ordering predictions. In: Proceedings of the AAAI Conference on Artificial Intelligence, vol. 34, pp. 9482–9489 (2020)
47. Yin, Y., Song, L., Su, J., Zeng, J., Zhou, C., Luo, J.: Graph-based neural sentence ordering. In: Proceedings of the Twenty-Eighth International Joint Conference on Artificial Intelligence, IJCAI 2019, pp. 5387–5393. International Joint Conferences on Artificial Intelligence Organization (2019). https://doi.org/10.24963/ijcai.2019/748
48. Yu, A.W., et al.: QANet: combining local convolution with global self-attention for reading comprehension. arXiv preprint arXiv:1804.09541 (2018)
49. Zeng, X., Li, J., Wang, L., Beauchamp, N., Shugars, S., Wong, K.F.: Microblog conversation recommendation via joint modeling of topics and discourse. In: Proceedings of the 2018 Conference of the North American Chapter of the Association for Computational Linguistics: Human Language Technologies, vol. 1 (Long Papers), pp. 375–385 (2018)
50. Zhang, Y., Liu, Q., Song, L.: Sentence-state LSTM for text representation. In: Proceedings of the 56th Annual Meeting of the Association for Computational Linguistics (vol. 1: Long Papers), pp. 317–327. Association for Computational Linguistics, Melbourne (2018). https://doi.org/10.18653/v1/P18-1030
51. Zhu, Y., Song, R., Dou, Z., Nie, J.Y., Zhou, J.: ScriptWriter: narrative-guided script generation. In: Proceedings of the 58th Annual Meeting of the Association for Computational Linguistics, pp. 8647–8657. Association for Computational Linguistics, Online (2020). https://doi.org/10.18653/v1/2020.acl-main.765

Multi-task and Generative Adversarial Learning for Robust and Sustainable Text Classification

Claudia Breazzano, Danilo Croce(✉), and Roberto Basili(✉)

Department of Enterprise Engineering, University of Roma, Tor Vergata, Roma, Italy
{croce,basili}@info.uniroma2.it

Abstract. Modern neural networks are quite demanding regarding the size and coverage of adequate training evidences, as far as complex inferences are involved. This is the case of offensive language detection that focuses on a phenomenon, the recognition of offensive uses of language, that is elusive and multifaceted. In this scenarios gathering training data can be prohibitively expensive and the dynamics and multidimensional nature of the abusive language phenomena are also demanding of timely and evolving evidence for training in a continuous fashion.

The `MT-GAN-BERT` approach proposed here aims to reduce the requirements of neural approaches both in terms of the amount of annotated data and the computational cost required at classification time. It focuses corresponds to a general BERT-based architecture for multi faceted text classification tasks. On the one side, `MT-GAN-BERT` enables semi-supervised learning for Transformers based on the Generative Adversarial Learning paradigm. It also implements a Multi-task Learning approach able to train over and solve multiple tasks, simultaneously. A single BERT-based model is used to encode the input examples, while multiple linear layers are used to implement the classification steps, with a significant reduction of the computational costs. In the experimental evaluations we studied six classification tasks related to the detection of abusive uses of language in Italian. Outcomes suggest that `MT-GAN-BERT` is sustainable and generally improves the raw adoption of multiple BERT-based models, with much lighter requirements in terms of annotated data and computational costs.

Keywords: Sustainable NLP · BERT · Semi supervised learning · Generative Adversarial Learning · Multi-task learning

1 Introduction

In recent years, Deep Learning methods have become very popular in Natural Language Processing (NLP), e.g., they reach high performances by relying on very simple input representations (for example, in [7,10,11]). In particular, Transformer-based architectures, e.g., BERT [4], provide representations of their inputs as a result of a pre-training stage. These are, in fact, trained over

S. Bandini et al. (Eds.): AIxIA 2021, LNAI 13196, pp. 228–244, 2022.
https://doi.org/10.1007/978-3-031-08421-8_16

large scale corpora and then effectively fine-tuned over a targeted task achieving state-of-the-art results in different and heterogeneous NLP tasks. However, several critical aspects tend to critically limit the impact of such Transformer-based architectures on sustainable real-word applications. First of all, they have been generally shown to achieve state-of-the-art results when trained using very large-scale datasets but significant performance drops have been observed when annotated material of limited size is adopted [3]. Unfortunately, obtaining annotated data is a time-consuming and costly process. In addition, Transformer-based solutions are characterized by complex architectures, with a large number of parameters and therefore have huge computational costs [22]. Several works proposed solutions devoted to the reduction of such computational complexity [21,23,25]. However, whenever the problem at hand requires decomposing the decision process into a (possibly large) set of decision steps, the overall computational cost is likely to grow rapidly. In fact, entire workflow generally corresponds to the sum of the (millions) of parameters of the individual architectures. Let us consider the adoption of Language Technologies against Offensive Language on the Web and Social Networks. Offensive language (also called "abusive language") refers to any insult or vulgarity that demeans a target [16,24].

The NLP community has worked on methods to mitigate this phenomenon by developing technologies to automatically detect abuse in texts. However, some of these methods largely focused on a limited definition of abuse, i.e. detecting hateful comments against only certain communities, such as comments referring to ethnic minorities, and marginalizing other types of communities, such as hateful comments towards women [18]. For this reason, abusive behavior is considered a problem with many "faces", as it involves cases of hate speech, offensive language, sexism and racism but also aggression, cyberbullying, harassment or trolling. Each form of abusive behavior has its own characteristics and manifests itself differently [6]. As a result, several datasets exist [24] but they are focused on specific aspects of abusive language. We speculate here that a solution consisting of several classifiers (each specialized on a dataset) is not completely sustainable, especially when the cost of adopting multiple architectures to classify large amounts of data may not be sustainable. Furthermore, we hypothesize that training each classifier separately on a different dataset might lead to sub-optimal quality compared to a classifier trained on a dataset where each instance is labeled with respect to each phenomenon of interest. Unfortunately, accessing datasets where individual instances are labeled for all the different aspects of the abusive language is not always possible.

In this paper, we propose a methodology to handle multifaceted problems, in this case, language abuse recognition, but keeping the final solution sustainable in terms of both: *i*) the amount of annotated data required to train the final model an *ii*) the computational cost characterizing the classification stage. In order to address the issue *i*) we propose the adoption of semi-supervised methods, such as in [2,12,26,28] to improve the generalization capability when few annotated data is available, while the acquisition of unlabeled sources is possible. In particular we will adopt `GAN-BERT` [3], a recently proposed method that enables semi-supervised learning in BERT-based architectures based on

Generative Adversarial Learning [8]. Moreover, we will mitigate the issue *ii*) by adopting the Multi-task learning approach proposed in [13], a specific formulation of BERT-based architectures that solve multiple tasks simultaneously. Instead of using a different BERT architecture for each task (each composed of hundreds of millions of parameters), a single BERT model is used to encode the input examples, but multiple classifiers (each composed of a negligible number of parameters) are used to implement the classification steps. This significantly reduces the overall cost and, in addition, allows the final architecture to be trained using disjoint datasets. Finally, we will introduce the combination of both of the above approaches in `MT-GAN-BERT`, a new architecture that extends BERT-based models with semi-supervised learning while using a single encoder when applied to multiple tasks[1]. Experimental evaluations against six classification tasks involved in detecting abusive languages in Italian suggests: the beneficial impact of `GAN-BERT` when trained on a reduced labeled dataset (e.g., 200 labeled vs. thousands of unlabeled examples); the high accuracy of a unified Multi-task model that achieves results comparable to those of multiple models, trained on a disjoint datasets; the reduced requirements posed to the size of annotated data and the computational costs implied by `MT-GAN-BERT` that thus represents a sustainable solution with respect to the raw adoption of multiple BERT-based models.

In the rest of this paper, Sect. 2 discusses the adopted architectures and presents `MT-GAN-BERT`. Section 3 reports the experimental evaluation while Sect. 4 derives the conclusions.

2 Multi-task and Generative Adversarial Learning in `MT-GAN-BERT`

Multi-task Learning in Transformer-Based Architectures. Multi-task learning (MTL) is a paradigm useful for multiple (related) tasks to be learned jointly so that the knowledge learned in one task can support other tasks [29]. Hard parameter sharing is the most commonly used approach of MTL with neural networks and it is generally applied by sharing hidden layers between all tasks, while maintaining different task-specific output levels. Sharing hard parameters greatly reduces the risk of over-fitting. Recently, there is a growing interest in applying MTL to representation learning using deep neural networks (DNNs) for two reasons. First, supervised learning of DNNs requires large

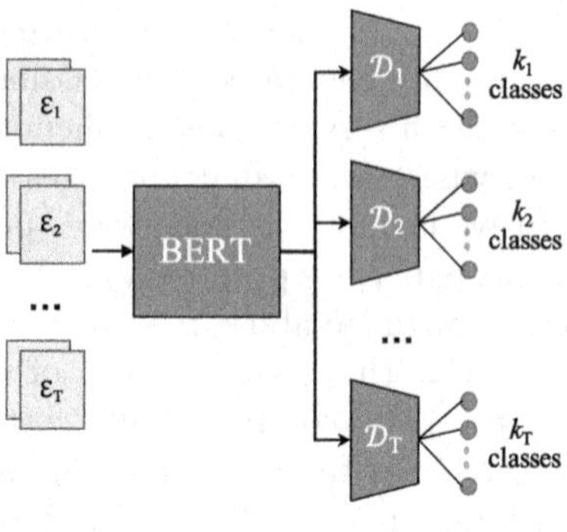

Fig. 1. `MT-DNN` architecture

[1] `MT-GAN-BERT` is publicly available at: https://github.com/crux82/mt-ganbert.

amounts of task-specific labeled data, which is not always available. MTL provides an effective way of leveraging supervised data from many related tasks. Second, the use of multi-task learning profits from a regularization effect via alleviating over-fitting to a specific task, thus making the learned representations universal across tasks. [13] proposed Multi-Task Deep Neural Network (MT-DNN) to incorporate a single pre-trained BERT model [4] to be applied at the same time to several NLI tasks involving single-sentence classification, pairwise text classification, text similarity scoring, and relevance ranking. The architecture of the MT-DNN model is shown in Fig. 1 and adhere to the approach proposed in [13] in a scenario involving only classification tasks. A BERT-based encoder represents the shared layers across all T tasks, while the output layers $\mathcal{D}_1, \ldots, \mathcal{D}_T$ implement the specific classification tasks. For each input example (either a sentence or a pair of sentences packed together) composed of n word-pieces, BERT captures the contextual information for each word via self-attention, generating a sequence of contextual embeddings: these are $n+2$ vector representations in R^d, i.e., $(h_{CLS}, h_{w_1}, ..., h_{w_n}, h_{SEP})$. As suggested in [4], h_{CLS} corresponds to the d-dimensional representation of the entire input sequence, while $h_{w_1}, ..., h_{w_n}$ represent the d-dimensional embeddings for the individual word-pieces. As we are interested in sentence based classification tasks, only the h_{CLS} is retained[2] and it is given as input to the D_t layer to classify the input sentence w.r.t. the task $t = 1, ..., T$.

Algorithm 1. Training of a MT-DNN model Θ

Load the BERT parameters acquired during the pre-training stage as in [4]
Initialize $D_1, \ldots, D_T$ randomly
for t in $1, \ldots, T$ **do** *//Prepare the data for T tasks.*
    Divide data $\mathcal{E}_t$ of the t-th task into mini-batches $\mathcal{B}_j^t$ so that $\mathcal{E}_t = \bigcup_j \mathcal{B}_j^t$
end for
for *epoch* in $1, ..., epoch_{max}$ **do**
    Merge datasets: $\mathcal{E} = \mathcal{E}_1 \cup \cdots \cup \mathcal{E}_T$
    Shuffle $\mathcal{E}$
    for $\mathcal{B}^t$ in $\mathcal{E}$ **do** *//$\mathcal{B}^t$ is a mini-batch of the task t.*
        1. Use the shared BERT to encode $h_{CLS}^{\mathcal{B}^t}$
        2. Classify $h_{CLS}^{\mathcal{B}^t}$ using D_t against the k_t classes
        3. Compute L_t loss as the Cross-entropy w.r.t. the k_t classes
        4. Compute gradient: $\nabla(\Theta)$ using L_t
        5. Update the entire model: $\Theta = \Theta - \nu\nabla(\Theta)$
    end for
end for

The training procedure of MT-DNN is reported in the Algorithm 1. Input examples generally belong to datasets $\mathcal{E}_1, \ldots, \mathcal{E}_T$ that are specific for each task and they do not share the same labels. As a consequence, MT-DNN requires that each dataset is shuttered in mini-batches $\mathcal{B}_j^t$, each containing valid examples for the same task t. In each epoch, a random mini-batch $\mathcal{B}_j^t$ is selected, all examples

[2] The remaining h_{w_k} embeddings can be used for other tasks, such as sequence labeling tasks, not considered in this work.

are encoded using the same BERT and the generated $h^{\mathcal{B}^t}_{CLS}$ are classified by the D_t. This allows estimating a loss L_t that is task-specific but used to update the entire model via back-propagation. In this way, the output layer D_t is fine-tuned with respect to the t-th task but, most importantly, BERT encodings are at the same time optimized in *all* tasks. In addition to the benefits associated with regularization and the reduction in over-fitting discussed in [13], `MT-DNN` shows a significant reduction of the computational costs at classification time. In fact, each example is encoded only once by BERT (which is composed of hundreds of millions of parameters [4]) and then classified by each classifier D_t which is significantly smaller and composed of about one thousand parameters for each of the k_t classes. Moreover, whenever the tasks are related to each other, such as Sentiment Classification or Hate Speech Detection, the multi-task training procedure is also expected to improve the final classification accuracy.

`GAN-BERT` and Semi-Supervised Learning. Recent Transformer-based architectures, e.g., BERT, provide impressive results in many Natural Language Processing tasks. However, most of the adopted benchmarks are made of (sometimes hundreds of) thousands of examples. In many real scenarios, obtaining high-quality annotated data is expensive and time consuming; in contrast, unlabeled examples characterizing the target task can be, in general, easily collected. `GAN-BERT` [3] enables semi-supervised learning in BERT-based architectures, by implementing a Semi-Supervised Generative Adversarial Learning technique. In general, SS-GANs [19] enable semi-supervised learning in a GAN framework. A network (called discriminator) is trained over a $(k+1)$-class objective: "true" examples are classified in one of the target $(1, ..., k)$ classes, while the generated samples are classified into the $k+1$ class. More formally, let $\mathcal{D}$ and $\mathcal{G}$ denote the discriminator and generator, and p_d and $p_{\mathcal{G}}$ denote the real data distribution and the generated examples, respectively. In order to train a semi-supervised k-class classifier, the objective of $\mathcal{D}$ is extended as follows. Let us define $p_m(\hat{y} = y|x, y = k+1)$ the probability provided by the model m that a generic example x is associated with the fake class and $p_m(\hat{y} = y|x, y \in (1, ..., k))$ that x is considered real, thus belonging to one of the target classes. The loss function of $\mathcal{D}$ is $L_{\mathcal{D}} = L_{\mathcal{D}_{\text{sup.}}} + L_{\mathcal{D}_{\text{unsup.}}}$ where:

$$
\begin{aligned}
L_{\mathcal{D}_{\text{sup.}}} &= -\mathbb{E}_{x,y\sim p_d} \log[p_{\text{m}}(\hat{y} = y|x, y \in (1, ..., k))] \\
L_{\mathcal{D}_{\text{unsup.}}} &= -\mathbb{E}_{x\sim p_d} \log[1 - p_{\text{m}}(\hat{y} = y|x, y = k+1)] \\
&\quad - \mathbb{E}_{x\sim\mathcal{G}} \log[p_{\text{m}}(\hat{y} = y|x, y = k+1)]
\end{aligned}
$$

$L_{\mathcal{D}_{\text{sup.}}}$ measures the error in assigning the wrong class to a real example among the original k categories. $L_{\mathcal{D}_{\text{unsup.}}}$ measures the error in incorrectly recognizing a real (unlabeled) example as fake and not recognizing a fake example.

At the same time, $\mathcal{G}$ is expected to generate examples that are similar to the ones sampled from the real distribution p_d. As suggested in [19], $\mathcal{G}$ should generate data approximating the statistics of real data as much as possible. In other words, the *average* example generated in a batch by $\mathcal{G}$ should be similar to the real *prototypical* one. Formally, let $f(x)$ denote the activation on an intermediate layer of $\mathcal{D}$. The *feature matching* loss of $\mathcal{G}$ is then defined as:

$$L_{\mathcal{G}_{\text{feature matching}}} = \left\| \mathbb{E}_{x \quad sim\ p_d} f(x) - \mathbb{E}_{x \sim \mathcal{G}} f(x) \right\|_2^2$$

that is, the generator should produce examples whose intermediate representations provided in input to $\mathcal{D}$ are very similar to the real ones. The $\mathcal{G}$ loss also considers the error induced by fake examples correctly identified by $\mathcal{D}$, i.e.,

$$L_{\mathcal{G}_{unsup.}} = -\mathbb{E}_{x \sim \mathcal{G}} \log[1 - p_m(\hat{y} = y | x, y = k+1)]$$

The $\mathcal{G}$ loss is $L_{\mathcal{G}} = L_{\mathcal{G}_{\text{feature matching}}} + L_{\mathcal{G}_{unsup.}}$. `GAN-BERT` [3] is based on the already pre-trained BERT model and adapts the fine-tuning by adding two components: i) task-specific layers, as in the usual BERT fine-tuning; ii) SS-GAN layers to enable semi-supervised learning.

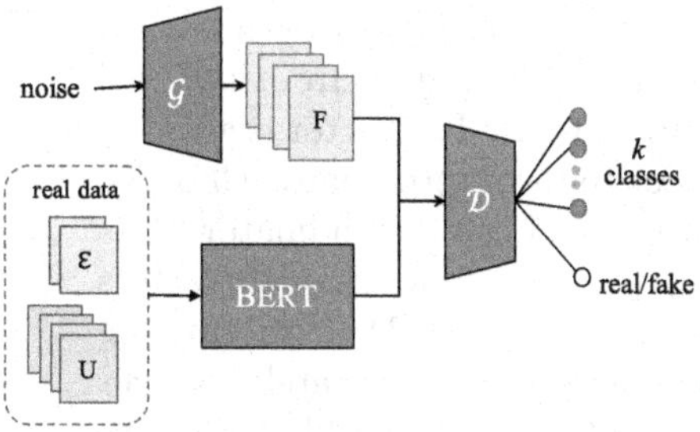

Fig. 2. `GAN-BERT` architecture

Without loss of generality, let us assume we are facing a sentence classification task over k categories. As in the previous `MT-DNN` architecture, given an input text, we select the h_{CLS} representation as a sentence embedding for the target tasks. As shown in Fig. 2, the SS-GAN architecture introduces on top of BERT two components: i) a discriminator $\mathcal{D}$ for classifying examples, and ii) a generator $\mathcal{G}$ acting adversarially. In particular, $\mathcal{G}$ is a Multi Layer Perceptron (MLP) that takes in input a 100-dimensional noise vector drawn from $N(\mu, \sigma^2)$ and produces in output a vector h_{fake} of the same dimension of h_{CLS}. The discriminator is another MLP that receives in input a vector h_*: this can be either h_{fake} produced by the generator or h_{CLS} for unlabeled or labeled examples from the real distribution. The last layer of $\mathcal{D}$ is a softmax-activated layer, whose output is a $k+1$ vector of logits.

During the forward step, when real instances are sampled (i.e., $h_* = h_{CLS}$), $\mathcal{D}$ should classify them in one of the k categories; when $h_* = h_{fake}$, it should classify each example in the $k+1$ category. The training process of `GAN-BERT` tries to optimize two competing losses, i.e., L_D and L_G. During back-propagation, the unlabeled examples contribute only to $L_{D_{unsup.}}$, i.e., they are considered in the loss computation only if they are erroneously classified into the $k+1$ category. In all other cases, their contribution to the loss is masked out. The labeled examples thus contribute to the supervised loss $L_{D_{sup.}}$. Finally, the examples generated by $\mathcal{G}$ contribute to both L_D and L_G, i.e., $\mathcal{D}$ is penalized when not finding examples generated by $\mathcal{G}$ and vice-versa. When updating $\mathcal{D}$, BERT weights are changed in order to fine-tune its inner representations, so accounting for both labeled and unlabeled data.

`MT-GAN-BERT`: Combining Multi-task and Adversarial Learning. In order to take advantage of both Multi-task learning and Adversarial learning and also try to reduce the computational cost, using few labeled data, this paper proposes the `MT-GAN-BERT` architecture. The `MT-GAN-BERT` model combines `GAN-BERT` and

MT-DNN, by relying on a shared Transformer, i.e. BERT, and applying as many Generators and Discriminators as the number of the targeted tasks. As shown in Fig. 3, BERT represents the shared layers across all tasks as suggested by MT-DNN and takes labeled and unlabeled data as input, as proposed in GAN-BERT. In this case, no overall Discriminator and Generator are foreseen, but for each t-th task that you want to (simultaneously) solve we extend BERT with: i) a Discriminator $\mathcal{D}_t$ for classifying examples, and ii) a Generator $\mathcal{G}_t$ acting adversely.

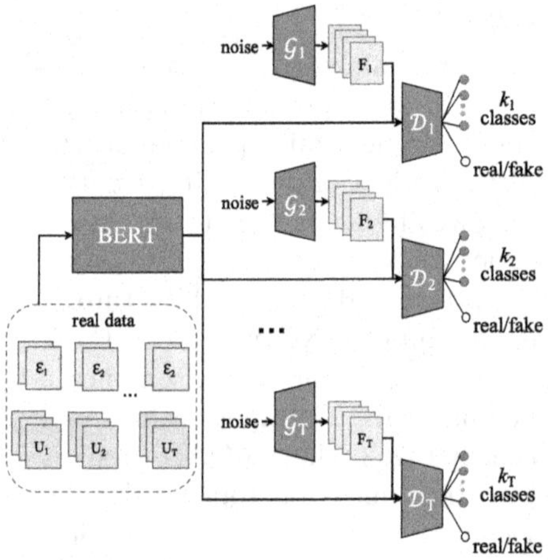

Fig. 3. MT-GAN-BERT architecture

During the forward step, a batch $\mathcal{B}_t$ belonging to a t-th task is randomly selected. Therefore, each sentence of the selected batch is given as input to BERT, which outputs the vector h_{CLS} (for unlabeled or labeled examples from the real distribution). The vector is given as input to the discriminator D_t of the t-th task. Each discriminator $\mathcal{D}_t$ is a MLP and, in addition to vectors produced by BERT over training sentences, it also separately receives in input h^t_{fake} produced by the generator $\mathcal{G}_t$, of the t-th task. Each Generator is also a Multi Layer Perceptron (MLP), that behaves in the same way as described above: so, it takes as input a 100-dimensional noise vector drawn from $N(\mu, \sigma^2)$ and outputs a vector $h^t_{fake} \in R^d$. The last layer of $\mathcal{D}_t$ is a softmax-activated layer and, when real instances are sampled (i.e., $h_* = h_{CLS}$), $\mathcal{D}_t$ should classify them in one of the k_t categories specific to the t-th task; when $h_* = h^t_{fake}$, it should classify each example in the "fake" k_t+1 category. The losses of $\mathcal{D}_t$ and $\mathcal{G}_t$ are computed as in GAN-BERT, and the back-propagation applies to the MLP as well as on the underlying BERT pre-trained model that is also modified. Changing weights in BERT during the training batch $\mathcal{B}_t$ of a particular task t allows to specialize BERT on that task t. By cycling and alternating forward and back-propagation steps to all the different tasks, BERT is asked to cross-generalize and learn from all of them. Moreover, the capability of individual generators $\mathcal{G}_t$ for each task, that generate task-specific fake examples, further improves the learning of the individual discriminator $\mathcal{D}_t$ for each task t, even when few labeled data are used. MT-GAN-BERT correspondingly improves the sustainability of the overall learning approach.

3 Experimental Evaluation

In this section, we assess the impact of the MT-DNN model, the GAN-BERT model and MT-GAN-BERT over different sentence classification tasks characterized by different training conditions, i.e., number of examples and number of categories. In particular, the objectives of this experimentation are three-fold. First, we aim at demonstrating that the existing `MT-DNN` model allows to share a single Transformer (BERT) in the training for multiple classification tasks at the same time, by preserving or improving performances against a model trained specifically on one task at a time (a standard BERT model). Second, we show that `GAN-BERT` trained over few annotated data, supports more accurate classification against the standard BERT model. In particular, the results of the BERT and `GAN-BERT` models are compared on specific training data of different sizes for each task: 100, 200 and 500 annotated examples. Finally, we show that `MT-GAN-BERT` further improves performance, compared to applying as many BERT models as there are tasks involved.

In this work we focus on several classification tasks involved in the recognition of Abusive language, a complicated task due to the multifaceted nature of its target [24]. In fact, detecting abusive language involves knowledge about specific and heterogeneous bad linguistic behaviors manifested by Social Web data. For this reason, experiments across different tasks each involving a specific form of abuse are useful to assess the impact of the `MT-GAN-BERT` paradigm on the overall phenomena. We report measures of our approach over the following tasks. First, we considered *Hate Speech Recognition* over two datasets, HaSpeeDe and DANKMEMEs. HaSpeeDe, proposed in the 2018 EVALITA Competition, is a corpus that includes Twitter posts, in Italian [17,20], that do or do not express hate. The hateful tweets are mainly addressed to minorities and social groups, which are potential targets of hate speech in Italy, such as immigrants, Muslims and Rom. An example of a message expressing hate against immigrants is: "*Altro che profughi? Sono zavorre e tutti uomini!*" (in English: "*Are these the refugees? They are ballast and all men!*"); instead, a message still referring to a group of people but not expressing hate is: "*Corriere: Mafia Capitale, 4 patteggiamenti. Gli appalti truccati dei campi rom*" (in English: "*Corriere: Mafia Capitale, 4 settlements. The rigged contracts of the rom camps*"). In the latter message, people are mentioned without any hate or subjectivity, while in the former one the writer is hatefully judging immigrants as *ballast.*

DANKMEMES (multimoDal Artefacts recogNition Knowledge for MEMES) [15] is the first EVALITA task for the recognition of MEMEs and the identification of hateful events or hate speech in them. A MEME is a multi-modal artifact, manipulated by users, which combines textual and visual elements to convey a message. The DANKMEMES task foresees three subtasks, which involve both images and sentences. However, in this work, we will focus only on the dataset used within the Hate Speech Detection task, only referring to the textual parts. Again, individual instances are annotated to discriminate sentences that are hateful from those that are not.

Then, we considered *Misogyny Identification* experimenting over the dataset of the Automatic Misogyny Identification (AMI) task of the 2018 EVALITA competition [5]. AMI consists of two subtasks. In this work, tweets from the two subtasks are used to create two different datasets, AMI subtask A and AMI subtask B. In the first subtask, tweets are classified as misogynous or not. A misogynous message is "*Beh se Asia Argento é una donna allora...*" (in English: "*Well if Asia Argento is a woman then ...*") while a not misogynous one is "*Prima ancora Asia Argento... e la Oxa... Sotto a chi tocca!?*" ("*Before Asia Argento ... and Oxa ... whose turn is it?!*"). While the second message refers to two women, Asia Argento and Anna Oxa, without insulting them, in the first sentence the fact that a woman like Asia Argento is actually a woman is questioned, thus demeaning her figure; in AMI subtask, misogynous tweets are further classified into specific categories: "STEREOTYPE", i.e., tweets expressing a widely diffused but fixed and simplified image of a woman, like in the tweet "*Il problema è sorto da quando il premier francese fece assassinare Gheddafi in combutta con il presidente USA e la culona tedesca.*" (in English: "*The problem arose since the the French premier had Gaddafi assassinated in cahoots with the US president and the German fat ass.*"). In this sentence, the writer refers to the ex-Chancellor of Germany Angela Merkel as "German fat as", so emphasizing female characteristics, rather than referring to her exclusively by her name or her title, as was done with the president of the USA. In this way, the figure of Angela Merkel is diminished, as she is chancellor, but also as a woman, due to the hate that the interlocutor wants to express towards her; tweets expressing "SEXUAL HARASSMENT" contain sexual advances, but also the intent to physically assert power over women, through threats of violence. An example of such messages is "*Non puoi immaginare cosa posso fare sul tuo corpo...*" (in English: "*You can't imagine what I can do on your body ...*"), where the writer is making sexual advances towards a woman; the last class "DISCREDIT" refers to messages that are bad at women with no other specific focus, like in the tweet "*@lauraboldrini oh!! ma sta a vedere che era un androide e non una donna comune!!#mavaiacagaretuequellascrofaacida!*" (in English: "*@lauraboldrini oh!! but it turns out that she was an android and not an ordinary woman!! #butgotohellyouandthatsoursow!*"). In this tweet, the interlocutor is insulting the Italian politician, Laura Boldrini without a precise reason by associating her with an android, therefore probably suggesting that she is not human and has no feelings and also with the "#" continues to insult her, together with another woman, who is also insulted.

Finally, we considered *Sentiment Analysis* over the dataset of SENTIment POLarity Classification (SENTIPOLC) task of the 2016 EVALITA competition [1], whose goal is sentiment analysis (SA). Although SENTIPOLC is divided into three subtasks, we only focused on the first two tasks: these are the *subjectivity classification* task and the *polarity recognition* task, respectively. In this way, we obtained two independent datasets, SENTIPOLC subtask 1 and SENTIPOLC subtask 2. In the first binary subtask, tweets are classified as subjective or objective. An example of subjective tweet: "*Primo passaggio alla #strabrollo ma secondo me non era un iscritto*" (in English: "*First step to #strabrollo but in my opinion he was not a member*"); instead, an example of an objective message, i.e., without any subjectivity is: "*L'articolo di Roberto Ciccarelli dal manifesto di oggi*" ("*Roberto Ciccarelli's article from today's manifesto*"). The first tweet

Table 1. List of dataset considered in the evaluation. For each dataset, the list of available class and corresponding number of examples are reported.

Task	Classes	#examples per class
HaSpeeDe	Hate, not hate	972, 2028
AMI A	Misogynous, not misogynous	1828, 2172
AMI B	Stereotype, sexual harassment, discredit	668 , 431, 634
DankMEMEs	Hate, not hate	395, 405
SENTIPOLC 1	Subj, obj	5098, 2312
SENTIPOLC 2	Positive, negative, neutral	1611, 2543, 2816

is subjective as suggested by the expression "*in my opinion*", as opposed to the second one which does not express feelings. In subtask 2, tweets are classified into positive, negative, neutral ones. An example of a message expressing a positive feeling is: "*Splendida foto di Fabrizio, pluri cliccata nei siti internazionali di Photo Natura*" (in English: "*Wonderful photo of Fabrizio, multiple clicks on the international sites of Photo Natura*"). On the contrary, a negative message is: "*Monti, ripensaci: l'inutile Torino-Lione inguaia l'Italia: Tav, appello a Mario Monti da Mercalli, Cicconi*" (in English: "*Monti, reconsider it: the useless Turin-Lyon troubles Italy: Tav, appeal to Mario Monti from Mercalli, Cicconi*"), in which adjectives such as "useless" are used, the verb "think again" suggests that the speaker is not satisfied with the work of the Italian politician Monti; and finally an example of a neutral message is: "*Arriva il governo monti?*" (in English: "*Does the Monti government come?*"). This is a question, which does not express any subjectivity, neither positive nor negative.

Even though different and specific classification tasks are considered in the above datasets, input texts are mostly Twitter posts. Opinions and subjective positions are thus mainly expressed in an immediate and direct style: a post consists of a few words, exploiting at most 280 bytes. In the case of the DANKMEMEs dataset, the sentences have a typical structure of MEMEs and they express concepts in a very direct way, which are sometimes understandable not only by reading the text, but also by observing the image. In other words, most datasets (i.e., HaSpeeDee, AMI and SENTIPOLC all from Twitter) are made of messages almost having the same linguistic complexity, with an average length of 35 tokens per message, typical of tweets in Italian. On the contrary, DankMEMEs is a dataset made of shorter texts (on average made of 7 tokens), most of them lacking explicit main verbs. For each task, performances are reported through two metrics: Accuracy and Macro F-measure, the harmonic mean of the Precision and the Recall. As a comparison, we report the performances of the basic BERT model that is independently fine-tuned on the training material of each task.

Experimental Setup. The MT-DNN and GAN-BERT implementations are based on the code made available[3] in support of [13] and [3], respectively. The MT-GAN-BERT combines the above models and it is entirely written in PyTorch, based on the HuggingFace framework [27]. All the models are based on BERT and, in particular, UmBERTo[4], that is a BERT model for the Italian language, based on Roberta [14] and trained on large Italian Corpora. While GAN-BERT is trained individually on each task, MT-DNN and MT-GAN-BERT are trained on all tasks, simultaneously. In the MT-DNN model, the last layers, those specific to individual tasks, are single-level linear classifiers. 10 epochs are used to carry out the training, with a batch size of 16 and a learning rate of $5 \cdot 10^{-5}$. The adopted Loss function is the Cross Entropy Loss. For the GAN-BERT and MT-GAN-BERT models, the Generator components are implemented as MLPs, with one hidden layer activated by a GELU [9] function and dropout set to 0.1 after a hidden layer. Generator inputs consist of noise vectors drawn from a normal distribution $N(0,1)$: they pass through the MLP and finally result in 768-dimensional vectors, that are used as fake examples. The Discriminator components are also MLP with only a softmax layer for the final prediction. In the training phase of GAN-BERT and MT-GAN-BERT the batch size chosen is 64, the loss function is again the Cross Entropy Loss. The GAN-BERT model is used in comparison with the basic BERT model: 25 epochs are used to carry out the training and the adopted learning rate is 10^{-5}. In MT-GAN-BERT the adopted loss functions are the loss of the discriminator $\mathcal{D}_t$ and of the generator $\mathcal{G}_t$ of each t-th task. To overcome the scarcity of data of some datasets, in the models that apply multi-task learning, a balancing technique is applied: examples are replicated for smaller training datasets of some tasks, until the number of samples in the largest training dataset is reached. During the training of each model, the best model is established, taking the model at the time when the average Accuracy (or Macro F-Measure) between the Accuracy (or Macro F-Measure) of each task, is the highest on the Validation set. The best model is then applied to the Test set to establish the reported Accuracy and Macro F-Measure. In order to obtain stable results and overcome the variable performance of model runs caused by the small size of some datasets, more executions (in particular 3) were carried out for each model: the average of the resulting measurement is then reported.

BERT-Based Model vs MT-DNN. This section shows the performance of the experiments carried out to compare the results obtained with the MT-DNN model, with the results obtained with the BERT-based model. The MT-DNN model is trained over all the tasks simultaneously, while the BERT-based model is trained individually on each task. In particular, Table 2 shows the results of the BERT-based model with Macro F-measure (second column) and Accuracy (third column), while the results of the Multi-task Model (MT-DNN) are reported in the fourth and fifth column. Finally, the last two columns reports the absolute differences between MT-DNN and the original BERT. If considering the computational

[3] The original code repositories are available at https://github.com/namisan/mt-dnn and https://github.com/crux82/ganbert.

[4] https://huggingface.co/Musixmatch/umberto-wikipedia-uncased-v1.

Table 2. Results BERT-based model vs MT-DNN in Macro F-measure e Accuracy

Task	BERT model		MT-DNN		Difference	
	MF1	ACC	MF1	ACC	MF1	ACC
HaSpeeDe	**77.79%**	80.13%	77.73%	**80.67%**	−0.06	+0.53
AMI A	83.70%	83.87%	**84.70%**	**84.93%**	+1.01	+1.07
AMI B	80.41%	80.64%	**84.97%**	**85.13%**	+4.56	+4.48
DANKMEMES	72.96%	73.17%	**74.77%**	**74.83%**	+1.81	+1.67
SENTIPOLC 1	**73.35%**	**73.03%**	72.04%	72.55%	−1.30	−0.48
SENTIPOLC 2	**63.85%**	**67.84%**	59.91%	64.34%	−3.94	−3.50

costs, when applying both solutions on unseen data, the MT-DNN allows reducing about the 80% of parameters: in fact MT-DNN use only one encoder (made of 125M millions of parameters, as based on RoBERTa) while the baseline adopts 6 encoders, one per task[5]. Results show that a monolithic architecture trained on multiple tasks maintains the same performance as a model trained individually on the same tasks. In particular, it can be noted how the AMI B task is able to benefit from the data of the other tasks. In contrast, the polarity dataset (SENTIPOLC 2) loses performance points, probably because it is one of the two largest datasets among tasks and benefits less from other sentence polarity recognition tasks.

BERT-Based Model vs GAN-BERT. This section shows the performances of the experiments carried out to compare the results obtained with the BERT-based model with those obtained with the GAN-BERT model. In particular, three results are shown in Table 3, as the training procedure was applied to labeled datasets of increasing sizes, i.e., 100, 200 and 500 labeled examples, respectively. The results obtained show that GAN-BERT obtains better performances than the BERT-based model with 100 and 200 labeled data, while with 500 examples in some tasks the performances are stable compared to those of the BERT-based models. It is clear that with GAN-BERT there is the possibility to generalize when there are little data. There are more differences when there are more data and therefore more contribution. Thus, the more unlabeled data, the more GAN-BERT benefits from the contribution of adversarial learning.

BERT-Based Model vs MT-GAN-BERT. This section shows the performances of the experiments carried out to compare the results obtained with the BERT-based model with those obtained with the MT-GAN-BERT model. Two results are shown in Table 4, where the results of the two models are compared, being trained respectively with 200 and 500 data labeled.

From the results, it can be seen that MT-GAN-BERT model, trained on 200 labeled examples, improves learning, except in the AMI B and DANKMEMEs tasks. By training the model with 500 examples, the tasks that suffered a wors-

[5] The number of parameters of $\mathcal{D}$ are negligible if compared to the encoder.

Table 3. Results BERT-based model vs GAN-BERT, with 100, 200 and 500 labeled examples

Task	$BERT_{100}$		$GANBERT_{100}$		Difference	
	MF1	ACC	MF1	ACC	MF1	ACC
HaSpeeDe	56.20%	67.03%	**61.77%**	**68.17%**	+5.57	+1.13
AMI A	66.03%	65.20%	**69.94%**	**71.90%**	+3.91	+6.70
AMI B	43.85%	44.92%	**46.65%**	**47.01%**	+2.80	+2.09
DANKMEMES	49.81%	50.00%	**53.62%**	**54.00%**	+3.81	+4.00
SENTIPOLC 1	58.94%	65.22%	**61.43%**	**67.17%**	+2.49	+1.95
SENTIPOLC 2	37.57%	47.95%	**44.74%**	**50.75%**	+7.17	+2.80
Task	$BERT_{200}$		$GAN\text{-}BERT_{200}$		**Difference**	
	MF1	**ACC**	**MF1**	**ACC**	**MF1**	**ACC**
HaSpeeDe	61.62%	67.23%	**62.70%**	**67.97%**	+1.08	+0.73
AMI A	64.34%	65.53%	**69.03%**	**69.03%**	+4.69	+3.50
AMI B	52.80%	51.94%	**56.09%**	**55.98%**	+3.29	+4.04
DANKMEMES	53.38%	53.00%	**56.42%**	**56.67%**	+3.03	+3.67
SENTIPOLC 1	61.23%	65.70%	**63.62%**	**67.97%**	+2.39	+2.27
SENTIPOLC 2	41.42%	49.66%	**48.69%**	**54.18%**	+7.27	+4.51
Task	$BERT_{500}$		$GAN\text{-}BERT_{500}$		**Difference**	
	MF1	**ACC**	**MF1**	**ACC**	**MF1**	**ACC**
HaSpeeDe	**63.50%**	68.93%	63.33%	**69.30%**	−0.18	+0.37
AMI A	70.24%	71.17%	**72.48%**	**72.60%**	+2.24	+1.43
AMI B	56.70%	56.65%	**60.71%**	**58.52%**	+4.01	+1.87
DANKMEMES	56.58%	**57.00%**	**58.43%**	56.17%	+1.85	−0.83
SENTIPOLC 1	58.94%	66.87%	**63.02%**	**66.88%**	+4.08	+0.01
SENTIPOLC 2	43.12%	51.92%	**48.67%**	**54.89%**	+5.55	+2.97

ening with 200 examples, obtain performance similar to that of the BERT-based model. In conclusion, from the experiments can be seen that MT-DNN, trained simultaneously on different tasks, is able to maintain the performance of the BERT-based model, trained individually on each task. By introducing Adversarial Semi-Supervised learning, the experiments obtained notable results and for this reason it was decided to implement a model (MT-GAN-BERT) that combined the GAN-BERT and MT-DNN model. The resulting model achieves overall equivalent or better results, although not in all tasks. This limitation is evident for small datasets, such as in DANKMEMES, where the size of the labeled dataset almost corresponds to the size of the original material.

Analysis Across Tasks. The results obtained across tasks are summarized in Figs. 4 and 5, where the average accuracy and F1 across the six investigated tasks are reported, correspondingly. For each model (reported below the group

Table 4. Results BERT-Based model vs MT-GAN-BERT with 200 e 500 labeled examples

Task	$\mathbf{BERT}_{200}$		$\mathbf{MT\text{-}GAN\text{-}BERT}_{200}$		Difference	
	MF1	**ACC**	**MF1**	**ACC**	**MF1**	**ACC**
HaSpeeDe	61.62%	**67.23%**	**63.22%**	64.17%	+1.60	−3.07
AMI A	64.34%	65.53%	**69.10%**	**68.70%**	+4.76	+3.17
AMI B	**52.80%**	**51.94%**	48.76%	48.28%	−4.04	−3.66
DANKMEMES	**53.38%**	**53.00%**	51.34%	52.67%	−2.04	−0.33
SENTIPOLC 1	61.23%	65.70%	**63.56%**	**66.58%**	+2.33	+0.88
SENTIPOLC 2	41.42%	49.66%	**45.45%**	**52.09%**	+4.03	+2.43
Task	$\mathbf{BERT}_{500}$		$\mathbf{MT\text{-}GAN\text{-}BERT}_{500}$		**Difference**	
	MF1	**ACC**	**MF1**	**ACC**	**MF1**	**ACC**
HaSpeeDe	**63.50%**	**68.93%**	62.83%	67.93%	−0.67	−1.00
AMI A	70.24%	71.17%	**71.81%**	**73.83%**	+1.57	+2.67
AMI B	56.70%	**56.65%**	**58.48%**	55.46%	+1.78	−1.20
DANKMEMES	**56.58%**	**57.00%**	54.64%	55.00%	−1.94	−2.00
SENTIPOLC 1	58.94%	66.88%	**65.29%**	**70.48%**	+6.35	+3.60
SENTIPOLC 2	43.12%	51.92%	**49.79%**	**56.18%**	+6.67	+4.26

of bars), the results were obtained incrementally using 100, 200, and 500 labeled examples. It is clear that, on average, the reduced computational complexity obtained through the straight adoption of MT-DNN leads to lower performances. This is even more evident with smaller sets of labeled datasets, in particular with 100 examples. This drop is highly compensated by the adoption of GAN-BERT with systematic improvements with respect to BERT and MT-DNN. It is also worth noting that GAN-BERT compensates for the differences in terms of accuracy and F1 especially between the setting 100, 200 with respect to 500. When using MT-GAN-BERT, the computational saving obtained by using a shared encoder, still induces a performance drop with respect to GAN-BERT when using a smaller set of labeled data (i.e., 100 and 200). However, the overall process clearly improves with respect to the simple adoption of MT-DNN and, in particular, it improves the original BERT (where multiple encoders are used, with a clearly higher computational cost).

This improvement is straightforward if considering the computational costs required to apply such methods at classification time in real scenarios. If considering that a model like BERT requires 110 million parameters, its application to 6 tasks would require an ensemble model made of 660 million parameters. The application of MT-DNN allows reducing this complexity back to 110 million parameters, being the encoder (that actually "costs" all these parameters, as the classifier is negligible) is shared across tasks. GAN-BERT has the same computational costs as BERT [3], so again 660 million parameters. Finally, MT-GAN-BERT mitigates this cost using only one shared encoder, made of 110 million parameters.

Overall, Figs. 4 and 5 shows that MT-GAN-BERT achieves the same or better results with respect to the original BERT at $\frac{1}{6}$ sixth of the computational cost (where 6 is the number of tasks).

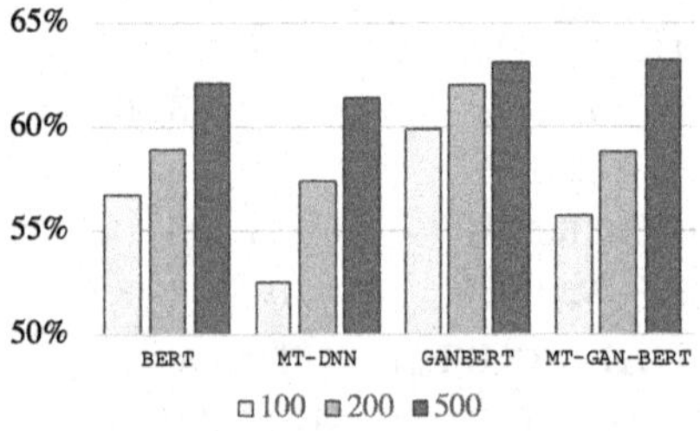

Fig. 4. Average accuracy across tasks

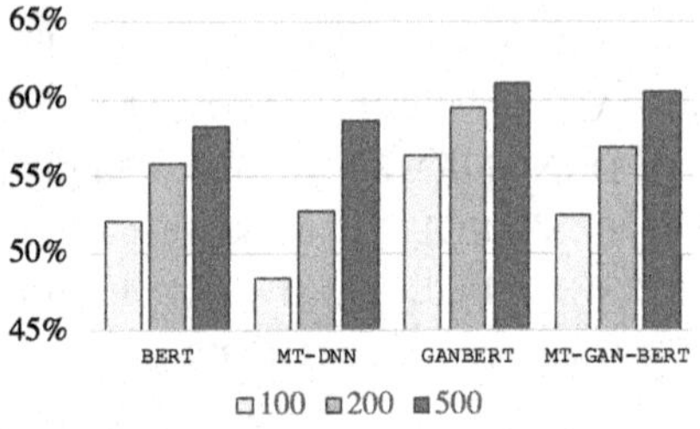

Fig. 5. Average F1 across tasks

4 Conclusion

This paper presents MT-GAN-BERT, a Transformer-based architecture for multi-faceted classification problems. The proposed solution represents a sustainable way that generally improves the adoption of multiple BERT-based models with less stringent requirements in terms of annotated training data. Results in a problem involving 6 tasks suggest that an 80% reduction in computational costs can be achieved without a significant reduction in prediction quality. In contrast, it shows improvements in datasets where only a few examples are manually annotated while larger sets of unlabeled material exist.

This is the first result that needs to be confirmed on other tasks and languages. In addition, we will study the adoption of structured losses in order to make stronger dependencies between classification results in the multi-task setting, to impose consistencies w.r.t. to outputs in strictly related tasks.

References

1. Barbieri, F., Basile, V., Croce, D., Nissim, M., Novielli, N., Patti, V.: Overview of the Evalita 2016 sentiment polarity classification task. In: Proceedings of EVALITA 2016, Napoli, CEUR Workshop Proceedings, vol. 1749 (2016)
2. Chapelle, O., Schlkopf, B., Zien, A.: Semi-Supervised Learning. The MIT Press, 1st edn. (2010)
3. Croce, D., Castellucci, G., Basili, R.: GAN-BERT: generative adversarial learning for robust text classification with a bunch of labeled examples. In: Proceedings of the 58th Annual Meeting of the Association for Computational Linguistics, ACL 2020, Online, 5–10 July 2020, pp. 2114–2119. Association for Computational Linguistics (2020)

4. Devlin, J., Chang, M.W., Lee, K., Toutanova, K.: BERT: pre-training of deep bidirectional transformers for language understanding. In: Proceedings of the 2019 Conference of the North American Chapter of the Association for Computational Linguistics: Human Language Technologies, vol. 1 (Long and Short Papers), pp. 4171–4186. Minneapolis, Minnesota (2019)
5. Fersini, E., Nozza, D., Rosso, P.: Overview of the Evalita 2018 task on automatic misogyny identification (AMI). In: Proceedings of EVALITA 2018, Turin, 12–13 December 2018. CEUR Workshop Proceedings, vol. 2263. CEUR-WS.org (2018). http://ceur-ws.org/Vol-2263/paper009.pdf
6. Founta, A., Chatzakou, D., Kourtellis, N., Blackburn, J., Vakali, A., Leontiadis, I.: A unified deep learning architecture for abuse detection. arXiv preprint arXiv:1802.00385 (2018)
7. Goldberg, Y.: A primer on neural network models for natural language processing. J. Artif. Int. Res. **57**(1), 345–420 (2016)
8. Goodfellow, I.J.: NIPS 2016 tutorial: generative adversarial networks. arXiv preprint arXiv:1701.00160 (2017)
9. Hendrycks, D., Gimpel, K.: Bridging nonlinearities and stochastic regularizers with Gaussian error linear units. arXiv preprint arXiv:1606.08415 (2016)
10. Kim, Y.: Convolutional neural networks for sentence classification. In: Proceedings of the 2014 Conference on Empirical Methods in Natural Language Processing, EMNLP 2014, 25–29 October 2014, Doha, Qatar, A meeting of SIGDAT, a Special Interest Group of the ACL, pp. 1746–1751 (2014)
11. Kim, Y., Jernite, Y., Sontag, D., Rush, A.M.: Character-aware neural language models. In: Proceedings of the Thirtieth AAAI Conference on Artificial Intelligence, 12–17 February 2016, Phoenix, Arizona, pp. 2741–2749 (2016)
12. Kipf, T.N., Welling, M.: Semi-supervised classification with graph convolutional networks. arXiv preprint arXiv:1609.02907 (2016)
13. Liu, X., He, P., Chen, W., Gao, J.: Multi-task deep neural networks for natural language understanding. arXiv preprint arXiv:1901.11504 (2019)
14. Liu, Y., et al.: RoBERTa: a robustly optimized BERT pretraining approach. arXiv preprint arXiv:1907.11692 (2019)
15. Miliani, M., Giorgi, G., Rama, I., Anselmi, G., Lebani, G.E.: Dankmemes @ Evalita2020: The memeing of life: memes, multimodality and politics. In: Basile, V., Croce, D., Di Maro, M., Passaro, L.C. (eds.) Proceedings of Seventh Evaluation Campaign of Natural Language Processing and Speech Tools for Italian. Final Workshop (EVALITA 2020). CEUR.org, Online (2020)
16. Mishra, P., Yannakoudakis, H., Shutova, E.: Tackling online abuse: a survey of automated abuse detection methods. arXiv preprint arXiv:1908.06024 (2019)
17. Poletto, F., Stranisci, M., Sanguinetti, M., Patti, V., Bosco, C.: Hate speech annotation: analysis of an Italian Twitter corpus. In: CLiC-it (2017)
18. Rajamanickam, S., Mishra, P., Yannakoudakis, H., Shutova, E.: Joint modelling of emotion and abusive language detection. arXiv preprint arXiv:2005.14028 (2020)
19. Salimans, T., et al.: Improved techniques for training gans. In: Lee, D.D., Sugiyama, M., Luxburg, U.V., Guyon, I., Garnett, R. (eds.) Advances in Neural Information Processing Systems 29, pp. 2234–2242. Curran Associates, Inc. (2016)
20. Sanguinetti, M., Poletto, F., Bosco, C., Patti, V., Stranisci, M.: An Italian Twitter corpus of hate speech against immigrants. In: LREC (2018)
21. Sanh, V., Debut, L., Chaumond, J., Wolf, T.: DistilBERT, a distilled version of BERT: smaller, faster, cheaper and lighter. arXiv preprint arXiv:1910.01108 (2019)
22. Sharir, O., Peleg, B., Shoham, Y.: The cost of training NLP models: a concise overview. arXiv preprint arXiv:2004.08900 (2020)

23. Shen, S., et al.: Q-BERT: hessian based ultra low precision quantization of BERT. arXiv preprint arXiv:1909.05840 (2019)
24. Vidgen, B., Derczynski, L.: Directions in abusive language training data, a systematic review: garbage in, garbage out. PLOS ONE **15**(12), 1–32 (2021). https://doi.org/10.1371/journal.pone.0243300
25. Voita, E., Talbot, D., Moiseev, F., Sennrich, R., Titov, I.: Analyzing multi-head self-attention: specialized heads do the heavy lifting, the rest can be pruned. arXiv preprint arXiv:1905.09418 (2019)
26. Weston, J., Ratle, F., Collobert, R.: Deep learning via semi-supervised embedding. In: Proceedings of the 25th International Conference on Machine Learning, pp. 1168–1175. ICML 2008, ACM, NY (2008)
27. Wolf, T., et al.: Huggingface's transformers: state-of-the-art natural language processing. arXiv preprint arXiv:1910.03771 (2019)
28. Yang, Z., Cohen, W.W., Salakhutdinov, R.: Revisiting semi-supervised learning with graph embeddings. In: Proceedings of the 33rd International Conference on International Conference on Machine Learning, vol. 48, pp. 40–48. ICML 2016, JMLR.org (2016). http://dl.acm.org/citation.cfm?id=3045390.3045396
29. Zhang, Y., Yang, Q.: A survey on multi-task learning. arXiv preprint arXiv:1707.08114 (2017)

Punctuation Restoration in Spoken Italian Transcripts with Transformers

Alessio Miaschi[1,2], Andrea Amelio Ravelli[2(✉)], and Felice Dell'Orletta[2]

[1] Department of Computer Science, Università di Pisa, Pisa, Italy
alessio.miaschi@phd.unipi.it
[2] Istituto di Linguistica Computazionale "Antonio Zampolli" (ILC–CNR), ItaliaNLP Lab, Pisa, Italy
{andreaamelio.ravelli,felice.dellorletta}@ilc.cnr.it

Abstract. In this paper, we propose an evaluation of a Transformer-based punctuation restoration model for the Italian language. Experimenting with a BERT-base model, we perform several fine-tuning with different training data and sizes and tested them in an in- and cross-domain scenario. Moreover, we conducted an error analysis of the main weaknesses of the model related to specific punctuation marks. Finally, we test our system either quantitatively and qualitatively, by offering a typical task-oriented and a perception-based acceptability evaluation.

Keywords: Punctuation restoration · Transformers · Speech transcription

1 Introduction

Nowadays, Automatic Speech Recognition (ASR) and Speech-to-Text technologies and services have reached an incredible level of accuracy in transcribing recorded (or live) speech audio streams. A simple but effective test can be run by using the dictation feature, from any modern smartphone, to write a text message.[1] However, we can immediately notice that the audio stream is transcribed as a word stream, lacking any punctuation or sentence segmentation, and sometimes pieces of text are difficult to understand without some attempts to mentally insert punctuation marks in the flow of words[2].

Lack of punctuation may be a minor problem in everyday short-text messaging, but correctly inserted punctuation is crucial in many tasks, such as long speech transcription or live subtitling, and it is absolutely necessary in any NLP processing of speech data, especially for downstream processes such as parsing, information extraction, dialog modeling. Many major commercial services

[1] Obviously, the speech must have a close-to-standard accent without using dialectal or slang words.

[2] Other than difficult, unpunctuated text can be also ambiguous. Here is an amusing example of two completely different letters, with the same words but different punctuation: https://www.nationalpunctuationday.com/dearjohn.html.

S. Bandini et al. (Eds.): AIxIA 2021, LNAI 13196, pp. 245–260, 2022.
https://doi.org/10.1007/978-3-031-08421-8_17

such as Google Cloud[3] or Microsoft Azure[4] offer the option of including automatically generated punctuation. As well, it is possible to train a public ASR model, such as wav2vec [28] or Vosk,[5] and then apply a common technique of Punctuation Restoration on the output of the first. Both alternatives come at a cost: on one side, commercial services requires a payment fee; on the other, training a model to restore/generate punctuation requires computational power, time and, above all, good and enough training data in the form of aligned audio sources, transcriptions and phonetic annotations. By assuming of working on already transcribed data, recent Transformers models could be a convenient way of tackling punctuation restoration in transcriptions of standard language, as they can be easily fine-tuned on many tasks, including the insertion of commas, periods and question marks. The objective of this paper is to verify if it could be possible to obtain good results in transcription by post-processing raw text from everyday Speech-to-Text technologies (e.g. dictation on a smartphone) with a Transformers model fine-tuned for Punctuation Restoration. More specifically, we set our experiments on Italian language and we verify the impact of different domains and sizes of fine-tuning data on the performance of a Transformer-based punctuation restoration model. Then, we tested its performances on an in- and cross-domain scenario, and we verified the acceptability of the resulting punctuated texts through human judgements.

The rest of the paper is organized as follows: in Sect. 2 we present related works; in Sect. 3 we introduce the setting, models and data used for the experiments; in Sect. 4 we discuss the obtained results, for which we offer an error analysis in Sect. 5; in Sect. 6 we describe the evaluation based on the acceptability of the resulting texts and compare them with the gold standard and an alternative manually punctuated version of the same texts; in Sect. 7 we conclude the work by exposing our final thoughts[6].

Contributions. In this paper we: i) investigate the impact of different training sizes on the performance of a punctuation restoration model based on the Transformer architecture; ii) we test the performance of the model in different scenarios (in- and cross-domain); iii) we inspect the most common errors emerged during the experiments; iv)we evaluate quantitatively the best model on a standard dataset; v) we design a qualitative evaluation in comparison with human produced punctuation.

2 Related Work

Punctuation restoration is a well known task, especially in Speech Processing and Machine Translation, where many approaches have been tested to tackle

[3] https://cloud.google.com/speech-to-text/.
[4] https://azure.microsoft.com/en-us/services/cognitive-services/speech-to-text/.
[5] https://alphacephei.com/vosk/.
[6] This paper is a slightly revised version, updated and integrated with an extensive evaluation, of our previous contribution [21] to the NL4AI Workshop at AI*IA2021 conference.

the problem in the past decades. In early attempts, acoustic features has been exploited to train finite-states or Hidden Markov Models [7,12,14]: the basic idea was to model prosody from speech data and use pauses as cues for sentence boundary, thus as signal of full stop punctuation marks. While prosody is useful in some cases, most of the time cannot be used to place punctuation in an ASR output because speakers use pauses in speech not only to shape the rhythm of their communication, but also for physical needs (e.g. breathing) or hesitations.

To solve this problem, multimodal models have been proposed, making use of parallel audio and transcripts as training [13,29]. Most of these approaches take Language Models scores, tokens or POS tags of a huge amount of continuous words as the textual features, and exploit pause, pitch contour, energy and prosody as principal acoustic features [18]. With the rise of Deep Learning techniques, many works reported good performances by training Deep Neural Networks with parallel acoustic and textual features [6,16,17,32].

Obviously, multimodal approaches can obtain better results if compared to unimodal ones (i.e. text-only data), but such models need a discrete amount of parallel audios and texts, and outside the English World it is not trivial at all to find such data. For this reason, many works have focused on textual-only approaches [15,33,37] and, more recently, the potential of Transformer-based Neural Language Models (NLMs) have been exploited in several studies [22,35,36]. For instance, [20] used a pre-trained BERT model [9] with bidirectional LSTM and a CRF layer to achieve state-of-the-art results on the reference transcriptions of the IWSLT2012 dataset.[7] [36], instead, proposed an adversarial multitask learning approach with auxiliary part-of-speech tagging using a pre-trained BERT model.

While the vast majority of such researches are focused on the English language, relatively little work has been done to inspect the potential of these models on other languages. [11] proposed a method based on Chinese punctuation prediction by combining the BERT model with a BiLSTM that outperformed the baseline by up to 31% absolute in overall micro-F1 on a Chinese news dataset. The study by [1], from which we built our experiments for the Italian language, explored different Transformer-based models and propose an augmentation strategy for the punctuation restoration task both on high- and low-resource languages, namely English and Bangla.

3 Experimental Setting

We explored the potential of transformer based language models for the punctuation restoration task on the Italian language. Specifically, we defined two sets of experiments. The first consists in evaluating the impact of the fine-tuning set size on the task performances. For that purpose, we tested the performance of a state-of-the-art transformer based architecture for punctuation restoration [1] with incremental fine-tuning sizes.

[7] http://hltc.cs.ust.hk/iwslt/index.php/evaluation-campaign/ted-task.html.

In the second set of experiments, we compared the performances of two differently fine-tuned models on 4 test datasets, as explained in Sect. 3.2. Moreover, we proposed an error analysis in order to investigate strength and weakness of the proposed methodology. Model and datasets used for the experiments are described below.

3.1 Model

We relied on the architecture previously defined in [1]. The architecture is based on a Transformer model from which the internal representations are then used as input for a BiLSTM layer, consisting of 768 hidden units. The outputs of the BiLSTM layer are then concatenated at each time step to a fully connected layer with four output neurons: one for the O (Other) class and three for the punctuation marks of Comma (C), Period (P) and Question (Q). Thus, this model casts the punctuation restoration problem as a classification problem: the output is basically a class assigned to each token.

The pre-trained Transformer used in our experiments is the XXL uncased version of the BERT model for the Italian language developed by the MDZ Digital Library Team and available trough the Huggingface's *Transformers* library [34][8]. The model was trained on Italian Wikipedia and texts from the OPUS [31] and OSCAR [30] corpora. We will refer to the model as BERT-BiLSTM.

3.2 Data

The model has been fine-tuned on two corpora, in order to evaluate divergences in the results with respect to the domain variation deriving from different data. The first corpus is a large collection of authentic contemporary texts in Italian derived from the web, and it is the *de-facto* reference corpus for Italian in many NLP applications: the Italian Web as Corpus (ItWaC) [3]. It counts 2 billion words and it has been built from the Web by limiting the crawl to the *.it* domain, and using as seeds medium-frequency words from La Repubblica journalistic corpus [2] and *Il Nuovo Vocabolario di Base* (NVdB - list of basic words of Italian) [8]. Given the extension and the origin, the ItWaC corpus spans across many domains. It contains texts with registries that vary from colloquial (i.e. texts derived from forums and social media) to highly formal (i.e. official documents, newspapers, technical descriptions), and the use of punctuation varies accordingly.

The second corpus used for the fine-tuning is the Italian sub-corpus of the Opensubtitles Multilingual Corpus [19].[9] This huge corpus has been compiled from a large database of movie and TV subtitles collected from the Opensubtitles website,[10] and includes a total of 1,689 bi-texts spanning 2.6 billion sentences

[8] https://huggingface.co/dbmdz/bert-base-italian-xxl-cased.

[9] https://opus.nlpl.eu/OpenSubtitles-v2018.php.

[10] http://www.opensubtitles.org.

Table 1. Statistics on the datasets used for fine-tuning and test. In parenthesis, the average distribution per sentence.

Dataset	Sentences	Tokens	Commas	Periods	Questions
ItWaC	765,491	19,226,715 (25.12)	1,403,527 (1.83)	729,806 (0.95)	35,685 (0.05)
Opensubtitles_it	1505279	14,468,346 (9.61)	754,951 (0.5)	1,265,306 (0.84)	239,973 (0.16)
ParlaMint_it	134,887	3,203,374 (23.75)	238,960 (1.77)	130,386 (0.97)	4,501 (0.03)
TEDx_it	1,139	21,667 (19.02)	1,823 (1.6)	1,070 (0.94)	69 (0.06)

across 60 languages. The Italian-only subcorpus consists of a total of 769.5 millions of words. Language of movies and television has been often defined as *broadcast-spoken* [23,25], that is a variety of language that sits in the middle between written and spoken. More specifically, broadcast-spoken is characterised by the fact that it is a well programmed language, based on pre-written texts, and performed to mimic spoken variety. Obviously, it lacks features specific of the spontaneous speech, such as hesitations, retracting and fillers, and it shows high regularity, especially in the use punctuation as marks of pauses in the transcription.

By creating two fine-tuned models, we want to investigate if the language diversity observable in the two corpora (i.e. average written language and multi-registry from ItWaC, close-to-spoken but highly regular from Opensubtitles) is reflected in the way the models handle punctuation.

Moreover, we considered other two resources for the purpose of evaluating the two models performances in a cross-domain scenario. The first resource is the Italian part of the ParlaMint Comparable Corpora [10], which contains transcriptions of parliamentary debates from 2015 to mid-2020, counting about 20 millions of words.[11] Given the context of the texts, language is highly formal, and thus also the use of punctuation in the transcripts is precise and regular.

As a second *test-only* resource we used the Italian part of the Multilingual TEDx Dataset [26,27],[12] which is a collection of audio recordings from TEDx talks in 8 source languages aligned with transcriptions produced by volunteers transcribers. The TEDx Italian subset derives from transcriptions of Italian TEDx speeches and it counts about 18 thousands words.

Table 1 reports some numbers about the datasets herein described. These statistics refer to the whole set of texts processed, and for all the experiments conducted with different size of fine-tuning a random selection of sentences has been collected.

Data Pre-processing. The model implemented in our experiments is trained on a classification of tokens on the basis of the presence or absence of a punctuation mark immediately after the target token. It is important to remember

[11] The complete collection of comparable corpora in 17 languages is available at: https://www.clarin.si/repository/xmlui/handle/11356/1432.

[12] The full dataset is available at: http://www.openslr.org/100/.

that punctuation is a feature of the written language modality, and it is used to mimic oral pauses in the transcription of speech: commas are used for short pauses, periods for long pauses at the end of an utterance and question marks for questions. For this reason, we collapsed all the possible punctuation marks to these 3 classes, reducing the complexity of the fine-tuning data.

Table 2. Mapping of punctuation marks to reduced classes for model fine-tuning.

Class	Punctuation marks
COMMA	, ; — - ( )
PERIOD	. : !
QUESTION	?

Table 2 shows how each punctuation mark has been mapped to the corresponding class. The majority of the symbols have been mapped to COMMA because normally they are used to signal parenthetical clauses and do not interrupt the sentence, while exclamation mark and suspension points, which signals sentence boundaries, are assimilated to the PERIOD class, but question marks have been considered as a separate class (QUESTION), in order to keep the distinction between questions and assertions. Along with these 3 classes, the class OTHER have been used to annotate tokens not followed by a punctuation mark. We are aware that this mapping and reduction could be simplistic, but, again, we are targeting our experiments towards speech transcription, where no punctuation at all exists, and we need to account for all possible punctuation found in the training data.

To feed the model with data in the correct format, we previously pos-tagged all the corpora with Stanza [24] in order to easily recognise punctuation marks and thus label correctly tokens followed by them. To better explain, consider the following sentence: *During my career, I had responsibilities and many satisfactions.*. This sentence needs to be converted as shown in Table 3. During the process, we also lower-cased all tokens to avoid the possibility of predicting full stops (such as periods, exclamation marks and suspension points) on the basis of the casing of the next token.

Table 3. Example of a pre-processed sentence for the fine-tuning.

During my career, I had responsibilities and many satisfactions								
during	my	career	i	had	responsibilities	and	many	satisfactions
O	O	COMMA	O	O	O	O	O	PERIOD

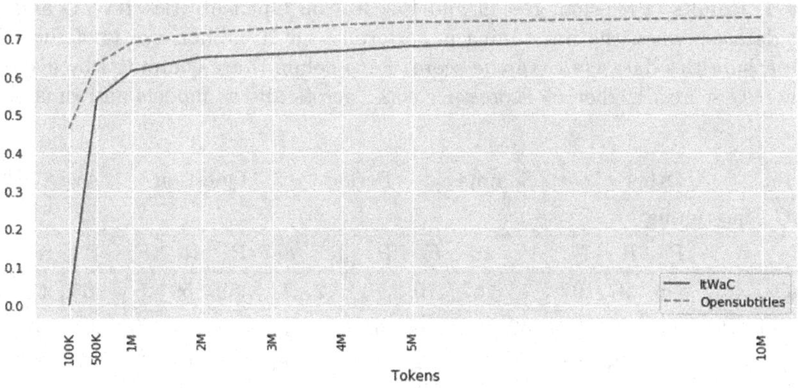

Fig. 1. Average micro F-scores obtained with increasing ItWaC and Opensubtitles dataset sizes.

4 Results

We first investigate the impact of different training sizes on the performance of BERT-BiLSTM. In order to do so, we fine-tuned our punctuation restoration models in parallel, with increasingly large portions of the two corpora, from 100k to 10 million tokens, and then tested them on a previously unseen portion of the two datasets consisting of 200k words. Results (in terms of micro F-score) are reported in Fig. 1. As a general remark, we found that, for both models, the curve tends to flatten out when the fine-tuning process is performed with portions larger than 2 million tokens. As regards the differences between the two datasets, we can notice that the model fine-tuned on Opensubtitles performed slightly better than the one trained on ItWac. For instance, focusing on the results obtained in the last run (10 million tokens) we can observe that the difference between the two models in terms of F-score is about 0.05 points (0.75 vs. 0.70). Moreover, it is interesting to note that while the Opensubtitles model obtained quite good results even with very small portions of the dataset (e.g. 100K), the itWac model requires at least one million words to achieve comparable results. This behaviour is quite predictable due to the fact that Opensubtitles texts are extremely regular and minimum variation is appreciable through the whole set of data. On the contrary, using ItWaC that is more heterogeneous, the system need more data to start correctly modelling the distribution of punctuation marks.

To better investigate their performances, we report in Table 4 the results obtained by the two models fine-tuned with 10 millions words from Opensubtitles/ItWac and tested in two different scenarios: i) in-domain, i.e. testing on the same dataset; ii) cross domain, i.e. testing on the other domain. Moreover, in order to provide a direct comparison between the two models, we tested both their performance on the Parlamint datasets.

As it can bee seen by looking at the average scores (column *Avg*), the in-domain configuration always achieves the best results (ItWaC: 0.65; Opensub-

Table 4. Results (Precision, Recall and F-score) on Opensubtitles/ItWaC and Parlamint datasets when the fine-tuning is performed on 10 million words of the ItWac and Opensubtitles datasets. Average scores (*Avg* column) are computed by averaging *C*, *P* and *Q* scores. Higher F_1 scores per class, across all the models and runs, are in bold.

Test set	Other			Comma			Period			Question			Avg (CPQ)		
ItWaC Fine-tuning															
	P	R	F_1	P	R	F_1	P	R	F_1	P	R	F_1	P	R	F_1
ItWaC	.96	.97	.97	.73	.67	.70	.70	.72	.71	.52	.59	.55	.65	.66	.65
Opensubtitles	.96	.98	.97	.62	.36	.46	.68	.74	.71	.54	.61	.58	.61	.57	.58
ParlaMint	.97	.98	**.98**	.80	.70	**.74**	.77	.83	**.80**	.54	.63	.58	.70	.72	.70
Opensubtitles Fine-tuning															
	P	R	F_1	P	R	F_1	P	R	F_1	P	R	F_1	P	R	F_1
Opensubtitles	.97	.98	**.98**	.74	.64	.69	.80	.80	**.80**	.75	.69	**.72**	.76	.71	**.73**
ItWaC	.95	.96	.96	.62	.45	.52	.50	.67	.57	.56	.45	.50	.56	.52	.53
ParlaMint	.97	.98	**.98**	.75	.59	.66	.65	.80	.72	.48	.55	.51	.63	.64	.63

titles: 0.73). By focusing on the cross-domain configurations, it is interesting to notice that the high variability of ItWaC texts strengthens the model and enables it to handle punctuation with better performances with respect to the model fine-tuned on Opensubtitles. Specifically, observing the performances of ItWaC model on Opensubtitles testset and viceversa, we notice a difference of 0.05 points. While, looking at both models (ItWaC and Opensubtitles) tested on ParlaMint, the gap increases to 0.07 points in favour of the ItWaC model. We can explain this behaviour on the basis of the nature of the ParlaMint dataset, where regularity and formality leads to longer sentences with punctuation usage closer to average written texts. Thus, ItWaC model, which is based on an heterogeneous collection of texts larger than Opensubtitles, is capable of predicting punctuation in a more robust way.

Looking at per-class scores, it is possible to notice that all systems perform better in predicting the PERIOD class: with exclusion of the Opensubtitles model tested on ItWaC, all scores are above 0.70. This result is encouraging because periods, exclamation marks and other full stops are used to signal the end of a sentence, thus a similar model can be effectively exploited to tackle the task of segmenting the continuous flow of speech transcription, enabling better subsequent sentence-based methods of analysis (e.g. part-of-speech tagging, dependency parsing and so on).

We register lower figures on the QUESTION class. It is probably due to the unpredictability of these in Italian only on the basis of transcribed text, without considering intonation. We further investigate this problem in Sect. 5.

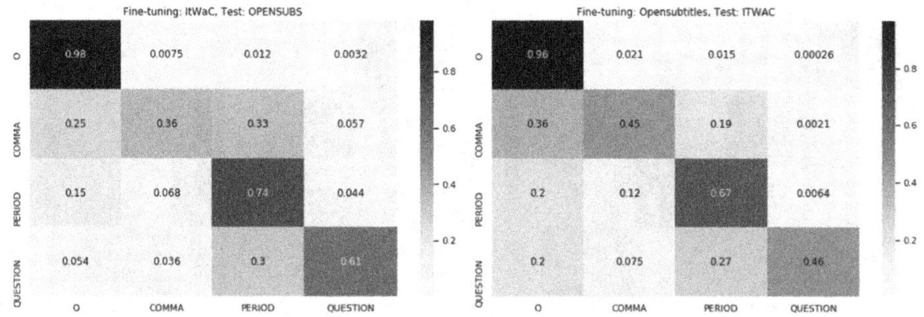

Fig. 2. Confusion matrices of the results obtained by the model fine-tuned on ItWaC and tested on Opensubtitles (*Fine-tuning: ItWaC, Test: OPENSUBS*) and vice-versa (*Fine-tuning: Opensubtitles, Test: ITWAC*).

5 Error Analysis

In order to further deepen our analysis, in this section we investigate in more detail the main errors made by the two models when predicting the different punctuation marks. In Fig. 2 we report the confusion matrices (in terms of accuracy) of the results obtained by the model fine-tuned on ItWaC and tested on Opensubtitles and vice-versa. As a general remark, we can highlight that the COMMA class is the most confused in both models. Due to the unbalanced distribution of the O (Other) class with respect to the punctuation classes, the high confusion of every class with this one is easily predictable. Thus, if we exclude the O class from the figure, we can notice that the class with which the COMMA is often confused is PERIOD, for both models tested on the opposite dataset (e.g. model fine-tuned on ItWaC and tested on Opensubtitles and vice versa). We can ascribe this problem to the average length of sentences, that diverges between the two: in ItWaC, the average sentence counts 25.12 tokens with about 1.83 commas per sentence; in Opensubtitles, the average sentence is 9.61 tokens long, with a distribution of commas of 0.5. For this reason, we can assume that the Opensubtitles model tends to create shorter sentences, thus using the full stop mark more frequently than the ItWaC one.

Figure 3 reports instead the confusion matrices of the results obtained by the two fine-tuned models (ItWaC and Opensubtitles) on ParlaMint test data. As we have seen previously, the model fine-tuned on ItWaC is the one that achieved better results regardless of the class taken into account. In fact, with the exception of *Other* (*O*), in all the other classes we observe a performance gap that goes from 0.2 (*PERIOD*) to 0.11 (*COMMA*) accuracy points. The system also shows a certain difficulty in correctly classifying question marks (QUESTION), and it is probably due to the fact that Italian language have no many cues to identify a question beside the possible presence of an interrogative pronoun (such as "what" or "who") and the pronunciation, with the latter being accessible only from the acoustic realisation of a sentence and not available in the written modality. Notwithstanding this, it is important to highlight that

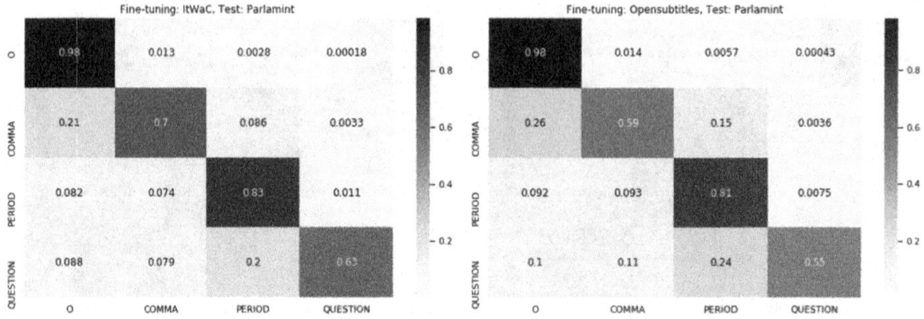

Fig. 3. Confusion matrices of the results obtained by the models fine-tuned on ItWac/Opensubtitles and tested on ParlaMint.

the most common mistake made by the system is to classify QUESTION as PERIOD, which is still a full stop mark, thus having a divergent semantic but the same syntactic function in the writing.

Focusing on the mismatched classes, we can see once again that commas are often mistaken as other tokens (O), as in the following example:

> **Original:** Vorrei ricordarvi i fallimenti ai quali siete andati incontro e state continuamente andando incontro con i bonus. Devo ricordarvi, forse il bonus vacanze? [en. *I would like to remind you of the failures you have experienced and you are continually experiencing with the bonuses. Should I remind you the holiday bonus?*]
> **ItWaC/Opensubtitles:** Vorrei ricordarvi i fallimenti ai quali siete andati incontro e state continuamente andando incontro con i bonus. devo ricordarvi, forse il bonus vacanze.

If we look at the differences between the two models, we can clearly notice that the one fine-tuned on Opensubtitles tends to wrongly classify in 0.15 of the cases a comma also as a full stop, as in the following example:

> **Original:** Scusate la digressione: pure io sono un mancato operaio, due braccia rubate all'agricoltura - allora lo si diceva in senso denigratorio, mentre oggi tale definizione si è qualificata un po' di più - e ho potuto permettermi di studiare e di laurearmi. [en. *Sorry for the digression: I am too a non-working class person, two arms stolen from agriculture - at the time this was said in a derogatory sense, whereas today this definition has been requalified - and I was able to afford my studies and my degree.*]
> **ItWaC:** Scusate la digressione, pure io sono un mancato operaio, due braccia rubate all'agricoltura, allora lo si diceva in senso denigratorio, mentre oggi tale definizione si è qualificata un po' di più e ho potuto permettermi di studiare e di laurearmi

Opensubtitles: Scusate la digressione. pure io sono un mancato operaio. due braccia rubate all'agricoltura. allora lo si diceva in senso denigratorio, mentre oggi tale definizione si è qualificata un po' di più e ho potuto permettermi di studiare e di laurearmi

From the previous example, we can also highlight that the hyphens were correctly classified as COMMA by the ItWaC model (punctuation marks to class mapping in Table 2), while they were identified as full stops by the Opensubtitles one. This could be due to the fact that since the Opensubtites dataset is composed of shorter sentences (derived from transcribed dialogic turns), the model tends to extend this behaviour on its inferences. Conversely, the colon were correctly identified as PERIOD by the Opensubtitles models.

6 Extended Evaluation

In this section we describe an extensive evaluation of our fine-tuned punctuation restoration model, by comparing its performances quantitatively, in terms of Precision, Recall and F-measure, with those obtained by expert annotators on the same dataset of unpunctuated texts. Nevertheless, the use of punctuation can be considered as an aspect of writing pertaining to the personal style of the writer, thus it is not something that can be purely evaluated through quantitative metrics. In other words, by evaluating our system against a dataset, we are measuring how precise the model is in mimicking a specific writer/set of writers, but we cannot be sure on the quality of the resulting texts. In order to overcome this issue and to propose a qualitative evaluation, we also designed a test based on the perceived acceptability of the use of punctuation.

We extracted 100 small textual fragments from the TEDx Italian dataset, removed punctuation and casing and processed them with our model trained with the ItWaC corpus; in parallel, we asked expert annotators[13] to add commas, periods and question marks to the same 100 punctuation-purged texts. The text fragment we used for this evaluation have been randomly extracted by considering a window of 70 tokens and without considering the begin or end of sentences, in order to not introduce a bias due to the fact that, for sure, there would have been at least one or two known bounds to mark with a period or question mark. We are confident that a window of 70 tokens can ensure from 2 to 4 full sentences, considering that the average Italian sentence length, computed on the ISDT-UD TreeBank[14] [4,5], is of 19,65 tokens.

In Table 5 we report the quantitative evaluation based on the classification results computed with the predictions made by our BERT-based model and the ones obtained with expert annotators. As we can notice, the average scores (column *Avg*) are quite similar, thus suggesting that, at least in a task-oriented scenario, the BERT model can achieve results comparable to those obtained by expert annotators. Focusing instead on per-class results, it is possible to observe

[13] We recruited 10 volunteer linguists among the staff of our Institute, ILC-CNR.

[14] https://universaldependencies.org/treebanks/it_isdt/.

Table 5. Results (Precision, Recall and F-score) obtained with the predictions made by our model (BERT-BiLSTM) fine tuned on ItWaC corpus and by expert annotators on TEDx transcriptions.

Test set	Other			Comma			Period			Question			Avg (CPQ)		
	P	R	F_1	P	R	F_1	P	R	F_1	P	R	F_1	P	R	F_1
BERT-BiLSTM (ItWaC)	.94	.98	.96	.76	.48	.59	.71	.68	.70	.47	.61	.53	.73	.55	.63
Expert Annotators	.94	.98	.96	.71	.51	.60	.71	.70	.70	.80	.54	.65	.72	.58	.64

that the main difference between the two scoring system is due to the classification of question marks, for which expert annotators outperformed BERT by .12 F_1 points.

As a qualitative evaluation, we asked Italian mother tongue speakers to express a judgment about the use of punctuation on a 1–7 scale, where 1 stands for "absolutely unacceptable" and 7 for "absolutely acceptable", for all the 100 textual fragments, in the three versions of the original, the one punctuated by our system and the one punctuated by expert annotators. In this way, we not only tested the quality of the output of our model, but we also compare it to the original data and to a second round of manually reproduced punctuation on the basis of the acceptability of the result.

We recruited a total of 200 Italian mother tongue speakers as raters through the Prolific crowd-sourcing platform.[15] We selected exclusively annotators born in Italy, actually living in Italy, having Italian as first language and having never been diagnosed any language disorder. A total of 200 raters have been involved in our study, and the sample have been balanced on the basis of sex (101 female and 99 male participants). Each participant have been presented with a total of 31 stimuli: 10 derived from the pool of original fragments, 10 among the texts punctuated by the expert annotators, 10 among the others punctuated by our system, plus an on purpose wrongly punctuated textual fragment to be used as attention check.[16]

As a first analysis, we computed the Spearman ρ correlation between the acceptability judgements given to fragments as annotated by BERT-BiLSTM, expert and original (gold) annotators. Interestingly enough, we noticed that all acceptability scores exhibit moderate and quite similar correlations, with values that ranges from 0.54 (expert annotators vs. BERT) to 0.61 (original annotators vs. BERT). This suggests that there is a relationship between the process of punctuation restoring as performed by a Transformer model and human annotators, despite of being experts or not.

Moving instead to the acceptability scores, in Table 6 we report average results (with standard deviation) assigned by human raters to the fragments

[15] https://www.prolific.co.

[16] We inserted an absolutely unreadable text (with periods between auxiliar and main verb, commas in the middle of multiwords and so on) in order to highlight bad raters and exclude them from the evaluation.

Table 6. Average acceptability scores (with standard deviation) assigned by human raters to the fragments annotated by our model (BERT-BiLSTM), expert and original annotators (Gold).

Annotator	Mean	StDev
BERT-BiLSTM	4.60	1.48
Expert	4.80	1.45
Gold	4.53	1.55

restored by BERT and expert annotators, and also to the original texts. Predictably, the fragments annotated by expert annotators were judged, on average, to be more acceptable than the others. Nevertheless, we can notice that the three average scores present rather similar values, thus suggesting that human raters did not perceive a significant variation in the acceptability of punctuation marks when restored by a human annotator or a NLM. Moreover, it is interesting to notice that the fragments punctuated by our model achieved a slightly higher score, on average, than the original ones. This result seems to confirm the potential of using a system based on the Transformer architecture for the punctuation restoration task.

7 Conclusions

In this paper we verified if it could be possible to obtain good results in restoring punctuation in raw transcription texts by means of a fine-tuned Transformers model. We chose to exploit 2 corpora as fine-tuning, namely ItWaC and Opensubtitles, in order to observe the differences emerging from domain variety and their projection on performances.

First, we evaluated the impact of different sizes of fine-tuning datasets, and we observed that the model fine-tuned on highly regular data (i.e. Opensubtitles) need less information to start modelling punctuation with regards to the model fine-tuned on more heterogeneous data (i.e. ItWaC); for both models, the curve tends to flatten out with fine-tuning portions larger than 2 million tokens. Moreover, the model fine-tuned on ItWaC obtains the best results when tested cross-domain on ParlaMint dataset, which is used as neutral testing field for both models.

Lately, we offered both a quantitative and a qualitative evaluation: first, we created a dataset of randomly selected textual fragments and evaluated our system performance in a classic task-oriented scenario, obtaining scores extremely close to those from expert annotators; then, we evaluated the acceptability of three versions of the same texts (the original ones, the output produced by our system and the version of them punctuated by expert annotators), showing that our system is able to add punctuation in texts in a way that is absolutely comparable to humans, with a mean acceptability score on the use of punctuation that sits in the middle between volunteer transcribers and expert linguists.

With this findings, we can draw the conclusion that it is possible to obtain good quality speech-to-text transcripts with added punctuation without the need of paying for a professional service (either automatic or manual), by just quickly post-processing automatic transcriptions, obtained with any Speech-to-Text enabled device, with a system similar the one proposed herein.

References

1. Alam, T., Khan, A., Alam, F.: Punctuation restoration using transformer models for high-and low-resource languages. In: Proceedings of the Sixth Workshop on Noisy User-Generated Text (W-NUT 2020), pp. 132–142. Association for Computational Linguistics (2020). https://doi.org/10.18653/v1/2020.wnut-1.18. https://aclanthology.org/2020.wnut-1.18
2. Baroni, M., et al.: Introducing the La Repubblica Corpus: a large, annotated, TEI (XML)-compliant Corpus of Newspaper Italian. In: LREC (2004)
3. Baroni, M., Bernardini, S., Ferraresi, A., Zanchetta, E.: The WaCky wide web: a collection of very large linguistically processed web-crawled corpora. Lang. Resour. Eval. **43**(3), 209–226 (2009). https://doi.org/10.1007/s10579-009-9081-4
4. Bosco, C., Simonetta, M., Maria, S.: Converting Italian treebanks: towards an Italian stanford dependency treebank. In: 7th Linguistic Annotation Workshop and Interoperability with Discourse, pp. 61–69. The Association for Computational Linguistics (2013)
5. Bosco, C., Simonetta, M., Maria, S., et al.: Harmonization and merging of two Italian dependency treebanks. In: LREC 2012 Workshop on Language Resource Merging, pp. 23–30. ELRA (2012)
6. Che, X., Luo, S., Yang, H., Meinel, C.: Sentence boundary detection based on parallel lexical and acoustic models. In: INTERSPEECH, pp. 2528–2532 (2016)
7. Christensen, H., Gotoh, Y., Renals, S.: Punctuation annotation using statistical prosody models (2001)
8. De Mauro, T.: Il Nuovo vocabolario di base della lingua italiana. In: Guida all'uso delle parole. Editori Riuniti (1980)
9. Devlin, J., Chang, M.W., Lee, K., Toutanova, K.: BERT: pre-training of deep bidirectional transformers for language understanding. In: Proceedings of the 2019 Conference of the North American Chapter of the Association for Computational Linguistics: Human Language Technologies, Minneapolis, Minnesota (Long and Short Papers), vol. 1, pp. 4171–4186. Association for Computational Linguistics, June 2019. https://doi.org/10.18653/v1/N19-1423. https://aclanthology.org/N19-1423
10. Erjavec, T., et al.: Multilingual comparable corpora of parliamentary debates ParlaMint 2.1 (2021). http://hdl.handle.net/11356/1432, Slovenian language resource repository CLARIN.SI
11. Fang, M., Zhao, H., Song, X., Wang, X., Huang, S.: Using bidirectional LSTM with BERT for Chinese punctuation prediction. In: 2019 IEEE International Conference on Signal, Information and Data Processing (ICSIDP), pp. 1–5 (2019). https://doi.org/10.1109/ICSIDP47821.2019.9172986
12. Gotoh, Y., Renals, S.: Sentence boundary detection in broadcast speech transcripts. In: Automatic Speech Recognition: Challenges for the New Millenium ISCA Tutorial and Research Workshop (ITRW), ASR 2000 (2000)

13. Gravano, A., Jansche, M., Bacchiani, M.: Restoring punctuation and capitalization in transcribed speech. In: 2009 IEEE International Conference on Acoustics, Speech and Signal Processing, pp. 4741–4744. IEEE (2009)
14. Kim, J.H., Woodland, P.C.: A combined punctuation generation and speech recognition system and its performance enhancement using prosody. Speech Commun. **41**(4), 563–577 (2003)
15. Kim, S.: Deep recurrent neural networks with layer-wise multi-head attentions for punctuation restoration. In: 2019 IEEE International Conference on Acoustics, Speech and Signal Processing (ICASSP), ICASSP 2019, pp. 7280–7284. IEEE (2019)
16. Klejch, O., Bell, P., Renals, S.: Punctuated transcription of multi-genre broadcasts using acoustic and lexical approaches. In: 2016 IEEE Spoken Language Technology Workshop (SLT), pp. 433–440. IEEE (2016)
17. Klejch, O., Bell, P., Renals, S.: Sequence-to-sequence models for punctuated transcription combining lexical and acoustic features. In: 2017 IEEE International Conference on Acoustics, Speech and Signal Processing (ICASSP), pp. 5700–5704. IEEE (2017)
18. Levy, T., Silber-Varod, V., Moyal, A.: The effect of pitch, intensity and pause duration in punctuation detection. In: 2012 IEEE 27th Convention of Electrical and Electronics Engineers in Israel, pp. 1–4. IEEE (2012)
19. Lison, P., Tiedemann, J.: OpenSubtitles 2016: extracting large parallel corpora from movie and TV subtitles (2016)
20. Makhija, K., Ho, T.N., Chng, E.S.: Transfer learning for punctuation prediction. In: 2019 Asia-Pacific Signal and Information Processing Association Annual Summit and Conference (APSIPA ASC), pp. 268–273. IEEE (2019)
21. Miaschi, A., Ravelli, A.A., Dell'Orletta, F.: Evaluating transformer models for punctuation restoration in Italian. In: Proceedings of the Fifth Workshop on Natural Language for Artificial Intelligence (NL4AI 2021). CEUR Workshop Proceedings, vol. 3015. CEUR-WS.org (2021)
22. Nagy, A., Bial, B., Ács, J.: Automatic punctuation restoration with BERT models. arXiv preprint arXiv:2101.07343 (2021)
23. Nencioni, G.: Parlato-parlato, parlato-scritto, parlato-recitato. Strumenti critici **29** (1976)
24. Qi, P., Zhang, Y., Zhang, Y., Bolton, J., Manning, C.D.: Stanza: a python natural language processing toolkit for many human languages. In: Proceedings of the 58th Annual Meeting of the Association for Computational Linguistics: System Demonstrations, pp. 101–108 (2020)
25. Sabatini, F.: La comunicazione orale, scritta e trasmessa. In: Boccafurni, A.M., Serromani, S. (eds.) Educazione linguistica nella scuola superiore: sei argomenti per un curricolo, pp. 105–127 (1982)
26. Salesky, E., et al.: Multilingual TEDx corpus for speech recognition and translation. In: Proceedings of INTERSPEECH (2021)
27. Salesky, E., et al.: The multilingual TEDx corpus for speech recognition and translation. arXiv:2102.01757 (2021)
28. Schneider, S., Baevski, A., Collobert, R., Auli, M.: wav2vec: unsupervised pretraining for speech recognition. arXiv preprint arXiv:1904.05862 (2019)
29. Stolcke, A., et al.: Automatic detection of sentence boundaries and disfluencies based on recognized words. In: ICSLP, vol. 2, pp. 2247–2250. Citeseer (1998)
30. Suárez, P.J.O., Sagot, B., Romary, L.: Asynchronous pipeline for processing huge corpora on medium to low resource infrastructures. In: Challenges in the Management of Large Corpora (CMLC-7), p. 9 (2019)

31. Tiedemann, J., Nygaard, L.: The OPUS corpus-parallel and free. Citeseer (2004). http://logos.uio.no/opus
32. Tilk, O., Alumäe, T.: LSTM for punctuation restoration in speech transcripts. In: Sixteenth Annual Conference of the International Speech Communication Association (2015)
33. Tilk, O., Alumäe, T.: Bidirectional recurrent neural network with attention mechanism for punctuation restoration. In: INTERSPEECH, pp. 3047–3051 (2016)
34. Wolf, T., et al.: Transformers: state-of-the-art natural language processing. In: Proceedings of the 2020 Conference on Empirical Methods in Natural Language Processing: System Demonstrations, pp. 38–45. Association for Computational Linguistics, October 2020. https://doi.org/10.18653/v1/2020.emnlp-demos.6. https://www.aclweb.org/anthology/2020.emnlp-demos.6
35. Yi, J., Tao, J.: Self-attention based model for punctuation prediction using word and speech embeddings. In: 2019 IEEE International Conference on Acoustics, Speech and Signal Processing (ICASSP), ICASSP 2019, pp. 7270–7274. IEEE (2019)
36. Yi, J., Tao, J., Bai, Y., Tian, Z., Fan, C.: Adversarial transfer learning for punctuation restoration. arXiv preprint arXiv:2004.00248 (2020)
37. Yi, J., Tao, J., Wen, Z., Li, Y., et al.: Distilling knowledge from an ensemble of models for punctuation prediction. In: INTERSPEECH, pp. 2779–2783 (2017)

AI for Content and Social Media Analysis

On the Impact of Social Media Recommendations on Opinion Consensus

Vincenzo Auletta, Antonio Coppola(✉), and Diodato Ferraioli

Università degli Studi di Salerno, Salerno, Italy
{auletta,ancoppola,dferraioli}@unisa.it

Abstract. We consider a discrete opinion formation problem in a setting where agents are influenced by both information diffused by their social relations and from recommendations received directly from the social media manager. We study how the "strength" of the influence of the social media and the homophily ratio affect the probability of the agents of reaching a consensus and how they can determine the type of consensus reached.

In a simple 2-symmetric block model we prove that agents converge either to a consensus or to a persistent disagreement. In particular, we show that when the homophily ratio is large, the social media has a very low capacity of determining the outcome of the opinion dynamics. On the other hand, when the homophily ratio is low, the social media influence can have an important role on the dynamics, either by making harder to reach a consensus or inducing it on extreme opinions.

Finally, in order to extend our analysis to more general and realistic settings we give some experimental evidences that our results still hold on general networks.

1 Introduction

Over the last years, we witnessed a rapid rise of social networking platforms, such as Facebook or Twitter, and as a consequence, individuals increasingly rely on them to get news and form their opinions. E.g., according to Pew Research Center survey in 2018 [46] 68% of American adults get news on social media, a significant rise from 49% of 2012. Moreover, it has been observed that social media may have a relevant effect in many real-world critical settings, such as in electoral campaigns [3,30]. For example, some studies showed that the social media may lead to extremism [14] and polarization in individuals' opinions [2].

Hence, it urges to understand how the social media may affect the opinions of their users. To this aim, several models have been introduced to describe how the opinions of agents evolve as effect of the social influence. The first such model, due to DeGrooot, states that each agent adopts an opinion that averages among the ones of individuals which she interacts with [23]. One of the most relevant

Partially supported by GNCS-INdAM and by the Italian MIUR PRIN 2017 Project ALGADIMAR "Algorithms, Games, and Digital Markets".

S. Bandini et al. (Eds.): AIxIA 2021, LNAI 13196, pp. 263–278, 2022.
https://doi.org/10.1007/978-3-031-08421-8_18

extensions of this model is, undoubtedly, the dynamics described by Friedkin-Johnsen [17,29], that limits the effects of social influence by holding agents close to their original ideology. These models assume that opinions may take values in a continuous space. However, in several real settings, i.e., electoral contexts, the number of candidates around which opinions should converge are limited, and thus these continuous models turn out to be scarcely representative. For this reason, discrete versions of these models have been proposed in which agents' opinions must belong to a discrete set [20,25].

However, it is not sufficient to take into account only the social influence among agents, but we have also to understand how the social media may influence the opinion formation process, and whether and how it is necessary to mitigate in some way the effects it provokes. There has been recently an increasing interest on these questions. In particular, most of the recent literature in the social choice area focuses on the opportunity for the social media to manipulate the opinion formation process in order to support a target opinion. Different forms of manipulations have been studied, such as seeding, edge addition/deletion, and alteration of the order of changes (c.f. Related Works).

In this work, we deviate from this approach, and we do not consider the social media as a manipulator. That is, the social media does not have a target that should be promoted, but it only acts as a platform for sharing information. However, social media's goal is to maximize the activity of the agents on the platform and it acts policy about which, when, and to whom information are shared, in order to maximize engagement of users to their service. Although the actual implementation of these policies is private, it is evident that users are more likely to be exposed to information closer to their own opinion [13,38]: it has been indeed proved that agents have larger probability of interacting (by viewing, liking, or re-sharing) with this kind of information [32], witnessing in this way their major engagement with the social media.

In this paper we want to answer to the following question: how much a social media implementing these policies can influence the opinion formation process? This problem has been recently addressed in [4] in the context of continuous opinion formation processes. Their answer depends on the strength of the influence of the social media platform on individuals: if this is high, then agents' opinions tend to extremes; if low, agents' opinion tend to converge; in the middle, instead, some non-extreme disagreement can occur.

However, the continuous approach adopted by [4] does not fit with many real world critical contexts, such as in voting, in which we usually have a discrete and limited number of candidates around which opinions should converge. For this reason, in this work, we will depart from the work of [4], by focusing on the discrete opinion formation process, as defined in [25].

Our Contribution. In this work, we evaluate the impact of social media recommendations with respect to their influence on the ability of users to reach a consensus. Indeed, the likelihood that a consensus is reached has been widely adopted for comparing different opinion models, and for evaluating the impact that variations on the model may have on opinion formation [9,23,33] (c.f.,

Related Works). Note also that consensus is a required goal in many practical settings: from the analysis of collective behaviour of flocks and swarms [42,45], to sensor fusion [43], to formation control for multi-robot systems [39,48].

In this work we first focus on a very simple class of networks, namely *symmetric two-block model* [4], in which agents are separated in two components, and agents from the same component have the same initial opinion and receive the same influence from individuals inside and outside their component. Despite of the simplicity of this network, it highlights a very important difference with respect to the results given in [4]: namely, the impact of social media not only depends on the strength of social media influence, but also on the *homophily ratio*, that is how much individuals weight their similar with respect to others. This measure has been often showed to be a key attribute in opinion formation dynamics (see, e.g., [22]). Hence, our results show a better alignment with respect to the previous literature than the one given in [4].

Specifically, we will show that whenever the homophily ratio or the strength of the social media influence is large, consensus is essentially impossible to achieve whenever the initial opinions of the two groups are far from each other. Interestingly, for these initial opinions, consensus is also impossible to achieve when the homophily ratio is large, but the strength of the social media is very small. We also show how the chance of reaching a consensus changes with respect to how extreme are the initial opinions in the two groups. Finally, when initial opinions are instead close to each other, we show that consensus is always possible, but the likelihood of consensus increases when the homophily ratio is large or the strength of the social media is low.

We conjecture that these findings hold not only for the simple symmetric two-block model, but also for more complex networks whenever initial opinions can be partitioned in two macro-blocks. As an evidence of this conjecture, we provide a massive set of experiments both on synthetic and on real networks: all our experiments show that the dynamics essentially follows the behaviour prescribed by results on the symmetric two-block model as the strength of the social media, the homophily ratio, and the value of initial opinions change.

Related Works. Several extensions have been recently proposed to the seminal models by DeGroot and by Friedkin and Johnsen (and their discrete counterparts), by considering only limited interaction by agents [27,28], or an evolving environment [9,15,16,26,33], or both repulsive and attractive interaction [1,6]. Despite their larger adherence with many real world aspects, however none of these variants has received the same level of interest as the models by DeGroot and by Friedkin and Johnsen. Moreover, the simplicity of the latter models allows a more clear analysis of the influence of social media, by untying it from the complexities of the former models.

Consensus in opinion formation has been object of intense research since the seminal work of [23]. Indeed, most works aim to evaluate opinion formation models based on their ability to reach a consensus [9,33]. Many other works try to characterize the parameters that enable a given dynamics to reach consensus [10,24,41]. In this work we pursue both approaches: on one side, we investigate on how the social media recommendations may vary the probability that a consensus is reached; on the other side, we identify the settings, in terms of homophily ratio, strength of the social media influence, and initial agents' opinions, where the probability of consensus is larger.

The study of the influence of a (non-manipulating) social media on the opinion formation process has been initiated in [4], where, as described above, the focus is on continuous opinions, while we here consider discrete opinions.

Many works instead focus on manipulation of the opinion formation process in social networks, in particular in the framework of election manipulation. The first and most studied manipulation technique is *seeding*, that consists in selecting a set of sources of news from which to start a successful viral campaign in favour of a designed candidate or against her competitors [18,19,21,34,50].

Another kind of manipulation that received large interest consists in adding or deleting links [12,18,19,47]: these may be implemented by social media by hiding the content of a "friend" or "neighbour" in the social network, or promoting the content of non-friends (e.g., as advertised content or through the mechanism of friend suggestion).

A last kind of manipulation that recently received a lot of interest consists in guiding the dynamics by influencing the order in which agents are prompted to update their opinion (e.g., by delaying the visualization of a news) so that they will update their opinion only when there are enough friends to push them towards the desired candidate [5,7,8,10,11]. We note that, as described above, our work differs from these works, since we are not considering a social media operating with the goal of promoting a specific candidate.

2 The Model

We consider $n \geq 2$ agents whose relationships are embedded into a social network modelled as an undirected weighted graph $G = (V, E, w)$, where each vertex of the graph represents an agent. Each agent i keeps an opinion $x_i^0 \in \Theta = \{-1, -1+\delta, \dots, -\delta, 0, \delta, \dots, 1-\delta, 1\}$ for some $0 < \delta \leq \frac{1}{2}$. Observe that $|\Theta| = 2\left\lceil\frac{1}{\delta}\right\rceil + 1$. Let $\mathbf{x} = (x_1, \dots, x_n)$ be a profile of opinions held by players, where x_i is the opinion kept of player i. The opinions of agents are influenced by their social relationships. Specifically, we assume that, for each edge $(i, j) \in E$, opinions of agents i and j are mutually influenced and the weight $w_{ij} > 0$ of the edge models the strength of this influence.

Moreover, we assume that the opinion of an agent can be also influenced by recommendations received directly from the social media and not diffused through their own neighbours. We assume that the social media can present to the agents different recommendations, tailoring them on their interests. In particular, we assume that the social media has a discrete subset Ω of $[-1, 1]$, representing the available information, and it decides to present to an agent with opinion x the information $s(x) \in \Omega$, where the function $s\colon \Theta \to \Omega$ models the recommendation procedure adopted by the media. Clearly, since the social media is interested in increasing the engagement of their users to the platform, it is interested in advertising to users information that best matches their profile.

Thus, at each time step t agents update their opinions depending on the opinions held by their social relations and the recommendations received by the social media. We denote by $\mathbf{x}^t$ the profile of opinions held by agents at time t.

In this work, following [4], we will consider a specific choice for Ω and s: in particular, we assume $\Omega = \{-1, 0, 1\}$ (we will sometimes refer to the elements of Ω as "extreme left", "extreme moderate", and "extreme right" information or opinions), and assume s being a symmetric threshold function such that $s(x) = -1$ if $x < -\lambda$, $s(x) = 1$ if $x > \lambda$, and $s(x) = 0$ otherwise, for some $0 < \lambda < 1$. While this choice is clearly simplifying the model, it still leads to interesting results about how these social media recommendations may affect the chance that agents may reach a consensus. Moreover, w.l.o.g., we will assume that $\lambda = 1/2$. This essentially means that the social media shows to each agent the information that is closest to her opinion (by breaking ties in favour of the "moderate" information). We remark that all our results about the impact of social media recommendations may be easily extended to arbitrary values of λ.

The combined influence of neighbours and social media recommendations may lead an agent to update her opinion. In this work, we follow the principles of the DeGroot model [23] to represent how the opinion is updated. Specifically, since our focus is on a setting with discrete opinions, we will adapt to our model the discrete generalization of the DeGroot model defined in [25]: at each step $t \geq 1$, agent i will choose the opinion x that minimizes $c_i(x, \mathbf{x}^{t-1}) = b(x - s(x_i^{t-1}))^2 + \sum_{j:\,(i,j)\in E} w_{ij}(x - x_j^{t-1})^2$, where $b > 0$ is the weight of the influence of the social media on agents, and $\mathbf{x}^{t-1} = (x_1^{t-1}, \ldots, x_n^{t-1})$ is the opinion profile at the previous time step. We notice that this setting can be equivalently described as a game: agents are the players, opinions are their strategies, and the function c_i is the cost function of player i. According to this game-theoretic viewpoint, the opinion update consists essentially of selecting the *best-response* strategy, i.e. the one that minimizes the cost of the player given the strategies currently selected by other players and the social media.

We say that an opinion profile $\mathbf{x}^t = (x_1^t, \ldots, x_n^t)$ is a *consensus* (on opinion $\overline{x}$) if $x_i^t = \overline{x}$ for every i. Moreover, we say that an opinion profile $\mathbf{x}^t = (x_1^t, \ldots, x_n^t)$ is *stable* if it is a Nash equilibrium of the corresponding game, i.e. x_i^t minimizes $c_i(x, \mathbf{x}^t)$ for every agent i. Next theorem states that a stable profile always exists. We achieved this result by proving that the proposed game is a generalized ordinal potential game but due to the lack of space, this and the following proofs are omitted or only sketched.

Theorem 1. *For every $G = (V, E, w)$ and every $b \geq 0$, there is an opinion profile $\mathbf{x}$ that is stable.*

In the literature the DeGroot model was studied associated to different update rules, depending on how it is selected the set of agents that at time t is allowed to change their opinions. In this paper we will focus on *synchronous* update, where at each time step t all the agents update their opinions.

3 Symmetric Two-Block Model

We will start our study by focusing on a simple setting: an $(a_{\text{in}}, a_{\text{out}})$-*symmetric two-block model*. This is defined as follows: given an undirected graph $G = (V, E)$ and a value $b \geq 0$, we partition the set V of agents in two subsets, L and R such that, for each agent $u \in P$ with $P \in \{L, R\}$, we set $x_u^0 = x_P^0$. Moreover, we set weights w_{ij} for each edge $(i, j) \in E$, such that for each agent $i \in P$, we have that $\sum_{\substack{j \in P \\ (i,j) \in E}} w_{ij} = a_{\text{in}}$ and $\sum_{\substack{j \in \overline{P} \\ (i,j) \in E}} w_{ij} = a_{\text{out}}$, where $\overline{P} = \{L, R\} \setminus P$, and $a_{\text{in}}, a_{\text{out}} > 0$. Roughly speaking, in a symmetric two-block model we assume that agents held only two opinions and we can partitionate them in two symmetric communities depending on their opinion. Moreover, the cumulative influence that an agent receives from members of her own community is the same for each agent, namely a_{in}. Similarly, the influence that the agent receives from members of the opposite community is the same for each agent, namely a_{out}. The ratio $h = \frac{a_{\text{in}}}{a_{\text{out}}}$ is sometimes termed *homophily ratio* [22], and the ratio $\tilde{b} = \frac{b}{a_{\text{out}}}$ is termed the *relative amount of media influence*. They will play an important role in our analysis.

We will investigate on how the influence b of the social network and the homophily ratio h affect the probability of reaching a consensus in this setting and the type of the consensus obtained. In particular, we will show that if either the homophily ratio h or the media influence b are very large, consensus is very hard to achieve when the initial opinions in the communities are divergent, i.e., $x_i^0 < 0$ for each $i \in P$, and $x_j^0 > 0$ for each $j \in \overline{P}$. This result follows from the fact that both homophily and media influence tend to extremize the opinions of the two groups, by leading them to diverge.

Moreover, we will show that, if the homophily ratio is large, then convergence to consensus becomes hard even for low values of media influence. Interestingly, this latter holds regardless of the number of opinions in Θ: in particular, it holds even if this number is very large (and thus the parameter δ is very small). However, for small values of δ and b our model resembles the DeGroot model, for which it is known that a consensus is always reached. In other words, our results prove that the consensus property of DeGroot model is not robust even to a small discretization of the opinion space.

Moreover, we also study the type of the consensus reached by the players. In particular, we show that when b is great, consensus is only possible on extreme opinions, namely -1, 0 and 1, even for small values of h, and even for non-diverging initial opinion profiles.

In conclusion, our results show that in the two-block model the effect of the social media influence is limited on communities with a large homophily ratio. However, when agents becomes more prone to heterogeneous influence, then the social media may play an important role, by making consensus either harder to reach, or reachable only on extreme opinions.

3.1 Characterization

In this subsection, we will study which type of consensus can be achieved, depending on the the homophily ratio and the social media influence. We will distinguish different cases, depending on the initial opinions held by the players in the two blocks. To this aim let us define the following quantities that will play a fundamental role in our characterization: $\tau_1(h) = \frac{2+2\lambda+\delta-\delta h}{2-2\lambda-\delta}$, $\tau_2(h) = \left(\frac{2}{\delta}-1\right)-h$, $\tau_3(h) = \frac{2-\delta-(2\lambda+3\delta)h}{2+\delta}$, $\tau_4(h) = h-\left(\frac{2}{\delta}+1\right)$, and $\tau_5(h) = \frac{2+\delta-(2\lambda+\delta)h}{2-\delta}$.
Divergent and Extreme Initial Opinions. We start by considering the case where the two initial opinions diverge (i.e., one is positive and the other is negative) and are both far away from 0.

Theorem 2. *Given an (a_{in}, a_{out})-symmetric two-block model $G = (L \cup R, E, w)$ and a social media influence b, if $|x_L^0| > \lambda$ and $|x_R^0| > \lambda$ and $x_L^0 \cdot x_R^0 < 0$, then*

$$\begin{cases} \text{if } \tilde{b} > \tau_1(h), & \text{no consensus can be stable;} \\ \text{if } \max\{0, \tau_2(h), \tau_3(h), \tau_4(h)\} < \tilde{b} \le \tau_1(h), & \text{only consensus on } 0 \text{ can be stable;} \\ \text{if } \max\{0, \tau_4(h)\} < \tilde{b} \le \max\{\tau_2(h), \tau_3(h)\}, & \text{non-extreme consensus can be stable;} \\ \text{if } 0 < \tilde{b} \le \max\{0, \tau_4(h)\}, & \text{no consensus can be stable.} \end{cases} \tag{1}$$

Proof (Sketch). Suppose first that $\tilde{b} > \tau_1(h)$. Then, it may be showed that no agent $i \in L$ can take an opinion x_L^1 such that $|x_L^1| \le \lambda$, and no agent $j \in R$ can take an opinion x_R^1 such that $|x_L^1| \le \lambda$. Hence, after the first time step $|x_L^1| > \lambda$ and $|x_R^1| > \lambda$ and $x_L^1 \cdot x_R^1 < 0$. Then, we can iteratively apply the same argument to conclude that the opinions of the two blocks never converge to consensus.

Suppose now that $\max\{0, \tau_2(h), \tau_3(h), \tau_4(h)\} < \tilde{b} \le \tau_1(h)$. W.l.o.g., suppose that $x_L^0 \le 0$ and $x_R^0 \ge 0$. Since $\tilde{b} > \max\{\tau_2(h), \tau_3(h)\}$, then, it may be showed that no agent $i \in L$ can take an opinion $x_L^1 > 0$, and no agent $j \in R$ can take an opinion $x_R^1 < 0$. Hence, after the first time step $x_L^1 \le 0$ and $x_R^1 \ge 0$. Then, we can iteratively apply the same argument above to conclude that the unique opinion on which the two blocks can converge is 0.

Finally, suppose that $0 < \tilde{b} \le \max\{0, \tau_4(h)\}$. As above, it may be showed that no agent $i \in L$ can take an opinion $x_L^1 \ge 0$, and no agent $j \in R$ can take an opinion $x_R^1 \le 0$. Hence, after the first time step $x_L^1 < 0$ and $x_R^1 > 0$. Then, we can iteratively apply the same argument above to conclude that the two blocks never converge to a consensus. □

Remark 1. We observe that it is impossible that the interval corresponding to last two cases of (1) are both non-empty. Indeed, if the last interval is non-empty, then $\tau_4(h) > 0$ and thus $h > \frac{2}{\delta} + 1$. It is not hard to check that this implies that $\max\{\tau_2(h), \tau_3(h)\} < \tau_4(h) = \max\{0, \tau_4(h)\}$. Hence for $\tilde{b} \le \max\{0, \tau_2(h), \tau_3(h), \tau_4(h)\}$, either no consensus can be stable, or it is possible to achieve consensus also on non-extreme opinions.

Roughly speaking, Theorem 2 shows that if we have initial opinions that are divergent and far away from 0, consensus is impossible to achieve for high values of the media influence b, while it can be achieved on non-extremal opinions only for small values of b and under opportune conditions. Remark 1 also shows that the outcome also depends on the value of h. Specifically, for small values of h, the chance of having a consensus decreases as $\tilde{b}$ increases, since we go from a range in which non-extreme consensus can be stable to a range in which only consensus on 0 is stable, and finally to a range in which consensus is impossible. Instead, for large h the behaviour is less "monotone": indeed, we go from no consensus to possible consensus (on opinion 0) and again to no consensus.

Divergent Initial Opinion: Only One is Extreme. Consider now the case of divergent initial opinions, but we assume that only one of them is far from 0. It will turn out that, as above, consensus is impossible whenever either the social media influence or the homophily ratio is large, and it is possible on non-extreme opinions only for small values of b and under opportune conditions on h.

Theorem 3. *Given an (a_{in}, a_{out})-symmetric two-block model $G = (L \cup R, E, w)$ and a social media influence b, if $|x_L^0| > \lambda$ or $|x_R^0| > \lambda$ and $x_L^0 \cdot x_R^0 < 0$, then*

$$\begin{cases} \text{if } \tilde{b} > \tau^*(h), & \text{no consensus can be stable;} \\ \text{if } \max\{0, \tau_2(h), \tau_3(h), \tau_4(h)\} < \tilde{b} \le \tau^*(h), & \text{only consensus on 0 can be stable;} \\ \text{if } \max\{0, \tau_4(h)\} < \tilde{b} \le \max\{\tau_2(h), \tau_3(h)\}, & \text{non-extreme consensus can be stable;} \\ \text{if } 0 < \tilde{b} \le \max\{0, \tau_4(h)\}, & \text{no consensus can be stable,} \end{cases}$$

where $\tau^*(h) = \max\{\tau_1(h), \tau_2(h)\}$.

Next corollary stresses that, when the homophily ratio is large, convergence to consensus is impossible, regardless of the strength of the social media influence.

Corollary 1. *Given an (a_{in}, a_{out})-symmetric two-block model $G = (L \cup R, E, w)$ and a social media influence b, if $|x_L^0| > \lambda$ or $|x_R^0| > \lambda$ and $x_L^0 \cdot x_R^0 < 0$, then no consensus opinion profile can be stable if $h \ge \frac{2}{\delta} + \frac{1}{1-\lambda}$, regardless of the value of the social media influence b. Moreover, consensus can be stable on non-extreme opinions only if $h < \max\left\{\frac{2}{\delta} - 1, \frac{2-\delta}{2\lambda+3\delta}\right\}$.*

Divergent Initial Opinion: Both are Moderate. Consider now the case that initial opinions of the two blocks are still divergent but both close to opinion 0. Clearly, in this case, large values of the social influence would push these opinions to 0, thus leading to a consensus on this opinion. However, we show that this is the only possible consensus in this setting when b is large.

Theorem 4. *Given an (a_{in}, a_{out})-symmetric two-block model $G = (L \cup R, E, w)$ and a social media influence b, if $|x_L^0| \le \lambda$ and $|x_R^0| \le \lambda$ and $x_L^0 \cdot x_R^0 < 0$, then*

$$\begin{cases} \text{if } \tilde{b} > \max\{\tau_2(h), \tau_3(h)\}, & \text{only consensus on 0 can be stable;} \\ \text{if } \max\{0, \tau_4(h)\} < \tilde{b} \le \max\{\tau_2(h), \tau_3(h)\}, & \text{non-extreme consensus can be stable;} \\ \text{if } 0 < \tilde{b} \le \max\{0, \tau_4(h)\}, & \text{no consensus can be stable.} \end{cases}$$

Convergent Initial Opinions. We conclude this section by considering the case that initial opinions do not diverge. We observe that, in this case, a large influence of the social media (with respect to homophily ratio) may lead only to consensus on extreme opinions, namely $-1, 0, 1$.

Theorem 5. *Given an* (a_{in}, a_{out})*-symmetric two-block model* $G = (L \cup R, E, w)$ *and a social media influence* b*, if* $x_L^0 \cdot x_R^0 \geq 0$*, then consensus on opinions different from* $-1, 0, 1$ *can be stable only if* $\tilde{b} \leq h + 1$*.*

Next corollary highlights a fundamental difference between the discrete and the continuous setting. Indeed, stable profiles that are non-extreme consensus are feasible in the discrete case while they are not in the continuous case [4].

Corollary 2. *Given an* (a_{in}, a_{out})*-symmetric two-block model* $G = (L \cup R, E, w)$ *and a social media influence* b*, if* $\delta \to 0$*, then consensus on opinions different from* $-1, 0, 1$ *can not be stable.*

4 General Networks

In previous section we presented some results related to the two-block model of a social network. We conjecture that our results hold in more general settings under the hypothesis that it is possible to distinguish in the network two well separated sets of similar agents. In this section we present some experimental evidences to support our conjecture. In particular, we run our experiments on stochastic two-block model graphs, random graphs and on real graphs. In the latter two cases we use algorithmic techniques to separate nodes in two components and then we define weights of the edges in order to define the influence coming on an agent from her own component and from the other component.

Observe that in a symmetric two-block model network, for each agent i, $\sum_{\substack{j \in P \\ (i,j) \in E}} w_{ij}$, that is the influence that she receives from the other agents in the same component, is equal to a constant a_{in}. At the same time, for each agent i, $\sum_{\substack{j \in \overline{P} \\ (i,j) \in E}} w_{ij}$, that is the influence that she receives from the other agents in the same component, is equal to a constant a_{out}. Moreover, agents in the same component have the same initial opinion. In our first experiment we extend this model by relaxing these assumptions. In particular, the set of vertices is $V = L \cup R$, where $|L| = |R| = N$, and each edge between two agents in the same component exists with probability p_{in} and each edge between agents in different components exist with probability p_{out}. However, all edges have the same weight. Thus, two agents may receive different influences, even if they are equal in expectation. Indeed, the expected influence received by her component is $(N-1)p_{in}$ and the expected influence that an agent receive from her opposite component is Np_{out}. Furthermore, agents in the same component can have different initial opinions.

We set $N = 50$ and simulate our opinion dynamics with different values of p_{in}, p_{out}, δ, and b. For each setting we run $n_p = 1000$ simulations. For each simulation, given the two blocks, say L and R, we assume that for each agent in L, the initial opinion x_i^0 is drawn at random in the interval $[l_L, h_L]$, and for each agent in R the choice is drawn at random in the interval $[l_R, h_R]$, where h_L and l_R are set respectively to $-\xi$ and ξ, ξ is drawn uniformly at random in the interval $[0, \lambda + \delta]$, l_L is drawn at random in the interval $[-1, h_L]$, and h_R

is drawn at random in the interval $[l_R, 1]$. Let m the number of runs in which the dynamic converges to consensus, we measure the consensus probability as $p_c = m/n_p$ and the 95% confidence interval as $p_c \pm 2\sqrt{p_c(1-p_c)/n_p}$.

Next we consider networks generated to three well-known network formation models: the Random Graphs model [31], the Watts-Strogatz model [49] and the Hyperbolic Random Graph model [36]. We remark that the Random Graph model is generally used to generate random networks. The other two graphs models are known to generate networks enjoying properties usually satisfied by real social networks. In particular, the Watts-Strogatz model is known to generate smallworld networks (i.e., network with small diameter and a large clustering index). In [36] it has been showed that the Hyperbolic Random Graph model, for a special choice of parameters, generate networks that are smallworlds with a degree distribution that is a power law, a characteristic that is shown by several real-life social networks.

In the Random Graphs model, for each pair of vertices u and v the edge (u, v) is created with probability p. Notice that, in general, the random graph $G = (V, E)$ generated in this way cannot be separated in well-defined components of the same size. However, we can partition the set of vertices in two components, L and R, achieved by running the well-known Kernighan-Lin algorithm [35], that returns the partition generated by the sparsest cut. We then assign weight w_{in} to edges among nodes in the same component, and w_{out} to the remaining edges. Note that, as in the two block model, each node has a different social influence from nodes within the same component and from nodes of the opposite component. However, in this case even the expected influences received by agents of the same component may be different. Indeed, for each node $i \in P$, with $P \in \{L, R\}$, we set $a_{\text{in}}(i) = w_{\text{in}}|\{j \in P\colon (i,j) \in E\}|$ and $a_{\text{out}}(i) = w_{\text{out}}|\{j \notin P\colon (i,j) \in E\}|$, and it is not hard to build a graph such that $a_{\text{in}}(i) \neq a_{\text{in}}(j)$ or $a_{\text{out}}(i) \neq a_{\text{out}}(j)$ for a pair of nodes i, j. Nevertheless, we can define, even in this setting, the homophily ratio as $h = \frac{a^*_{\text{in}}}{a^*_{\text{out}}}$, where $a^*_{\text{in}} = \frac{1}{|V|}\sum_{v \in V} a_{\text{in}}(v)$ and $a^*_{\text{out}} = \frac{1}{|V|}\sum_{v \in V} a_{\text{out}}(v)$. We use a similar approach for Watts-Strogatz and Hyperbolic Random Graphs.

For each of these three classes of graphs we set the number of agents to be 100 and we run our opinion dynamics for different values of w_{in}, w_{out}, δ, and b. For each setting, we run 1000 simulations and we measure the consensus probability and the confidence interval as stated before. For Random Graph networks, for each simulation we draw the value of p uniformly at random in the interval $[0.3, 0.7]$ and select the initial opinions of each node as described above.

Finally, we considered two samples of real social networks that are freely available in the SNAP library [37]. The first one, `ego-Facebook`, is a sample of 4039 nodes and 88234 edges retrieved from Facebook network [40]. The second one, `feather-lastfm-social` consists in a less dense network of 7624 nodes and 27806 edges [44]. In order to run multiple simulations on these networks we do not use a deterministic partitioning algorithm to retrieve communities, but for each simulation an agent is assigned to cluster L with a probability p_L drawn uniformly at random in $[0.4, 0.6]$, and to cluster R otherwise. We will show below that, despite this random choice of the partitions, we still are able to achieve results that are similar to previous more regular networks. Weights, homophily ratio, the influence, the social media, initial opinions, consensus probability and the confidence interval are then computed as described above (but mediated over only 500 simulations, due to the larger size of these networks).

We observe that numerical oscillations can make impossible to reach consensus even if opinions of agents are very close to each other. For this reason, in the following we consider a relaxed definition of *consensus*. In particular, following [4] we will focus on the average opinion $\overline{x}_P = \frac{\sum_{i \in P} x_i}{|P|}$ for each partition P, and on its projection $\underline{x}_P$ on Θ, being the opinion in Θ closest to $\overline{x}_P$. Then, a stable opinion profile $x = (x_1, x_2, \ldots, x_n)$ is a consensus if $\underline{x}_L = \underline{x}_R$.

Our Experimental Results. Our experiments highlight that the consensus probability essentially depends only on the relative social media influence $\tilde{b}$ and the homophily ratio h, and not on the absolute values of the media influence b, the inter-cluster influence a_{out}, and the intra-cluster influence a_{in}. Indeed, Fig. 1[1] shows that the probability of reaching a consensus is essentially the same when $\tilde{b}$ and h are unchanged, even if we change the values of $b, a_{\text{out}}, a_{\text{in}}$.

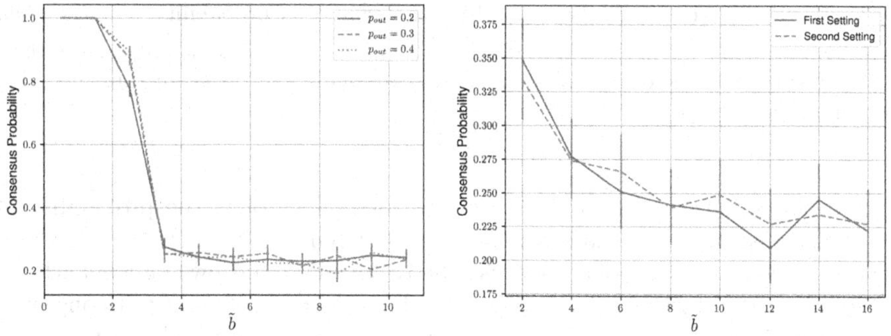

(a) Two Block Model (b) `ego-Facebook`

Fig. 1. In Fig. 1a we show how the consensus probability changes when $\delta = 0.25$, $p_{\text{in}} = \frac{100 p_{\text{out}}}{49}$ (so h is always 2) and $b \in \{25p_{\text{out}}, 25p_{\text{out}} + 50p_{\text{out}}, \ldots, 525p_{\text{out}})\}$ (so $\tilde{b} \in \{0.5, 0.5 + 1, \ldots, 10.5\}$). In Fig. 1b we show the consensus probability for $\tilde{b} \in \{0.5, 2.5, \ldots, 14.5\}$, and for each of these value, we evaluate this probability on two different settings. In the first,$w_{\text{in}} = w_{\text{out}} = 1$ (from which the homophily ratio is h_1) and b such that $ba^*_{\text{out}} = \tilde{b}$; in the second, with different blocks,we set $w_{\text{in}} = 1$, w_{out} is such that the homophily ratio is is equal to h_1, and $\tilde{b}$ is as in the first setting. In this and the next pictures, the confidence intervals are shown as error bars.

The analysis of the symmetric two-block model also highlights that the probability of consensus usually decreases when either $\tilde{b}$ or h increases. This behaviour

[1] Figures only shows experimental results only for some of the considered networks. Similar results have been obtained for the other network models.

is confirmed in all our experiments, even for the more complex networks. Specifically, Fig. 2 shows how the probability of consensus changes as $\tilde{b}$ increases for different values of h.

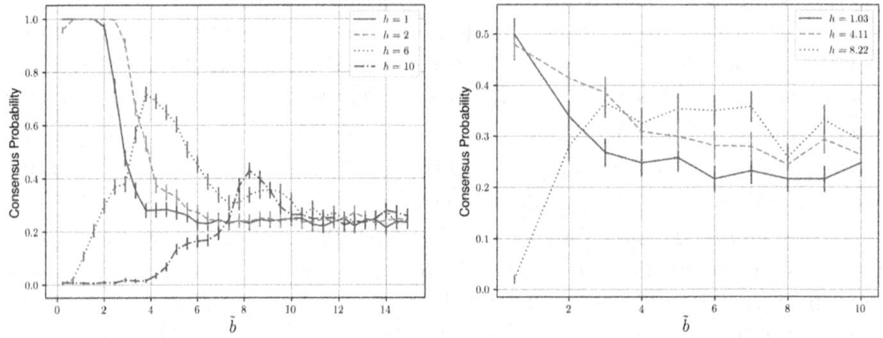

(a) Two Block Model (b) ego-Facebook

Fig. 2. In Fig. 2a we show how the consensus probability changes when $\delta = 0.25$, $p_{\text{out}} = 0.09$, p_{in} is set in order to have the desired h, and b is set to have $\tilde{b} \in \{0.3, 0.3 + \frac{1}{25 p_{\text{out}}}, \ldots, 14.88\}$). In Fig. 2b we show how the consensus probability changes when $\delta = 0.25$, $w_{\text{out}} = 1$, $w_{\text{in}} \in \{1, 4, 8\}$, and b is set to have $\tilde{b} \in \{1, 2, 3, \ldots, 10\}$). Note that, in this setting, h is the expected value of the homophily ratio over all runs involving the same value for w_{in}.

It is immediate to see that, except for low values of $\tilde{b}$, the probability of consensus effectively decreases with $\tilde{b}$. Moreover, our results show that, for each value of $\tilde{b}$, the probability of consensus usually appears to be lower when h is large (notice that, due to the fact that for very large $\tilde{b}$ the probability of consensus is very small, in this range the results showed in Fig. 2 are highly affected by statistical noise, as it is also highlighted by the fact that the 95% confidence interval are much larger in this range). An apparently strange behaviour occurs for low values of $\tilde{b}$. Indeed, in this range we have that the consensus probability increases. However, this behaviour is still in line with the results achieved for the symmetric two-block model. Indeed, as observed above, for large values of h, the probability of consensus is expected to have this non-monotone behaviour: it first increases (by going from no consensus to possible consensus on 0), and then decreases (by going from possible consensus on 0 to no consensus again).

Results in Sect. 3 show that convergence to consensus is affected by the initial opinions of agents: indeed conditions for non-consensus in case both initial opinions are larger than λ in absolute value are stricter than in the case of a single initial opinion far from 0, and the latter are much more stricter in the case of both initial opinion are close to zero. This behaviour still holds even in more complex graph structures. Specifically, Fig. 3 shows that the consensus probability decreases as the average opinion of agents in a component goes to

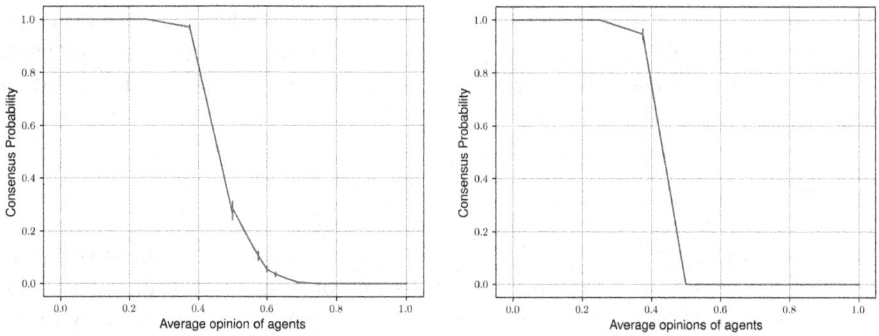

(a) Two Block Model (b) `ego-facebook`

Fig. 3. In Fig. 3a we show how the consensus probability changes when $\delta = 0.25$, $p_{\text{out}} = 0.2$, $p_{\text{in}} = 0.4$, and b is set to have $\tilde{b} = 1.2 \cdot \tau_1(h)$. In Fig. 3b we show how the consensus probability changes when $\delta = 0.25$, $w_{\text{in}} = 1$, w_{out} is drawn at each simulation uniformly at random in $[0.3, 4]$, and b is set to have $\tilde{b} = 1.2 \cdot \tau_1(h)$. Note that in this experiment the initial opinions are still drawn uniformly at random in intervals $[l_L, h_L]$ and $[l_R, h_R]$, but these interval are fixed (they are chosen to be the same interval but with opposite sign) to have that the average opinions of agents in each component has absolute value $x\delta$, with $x \in \{0, 0.6, 0.8, 1, 1.5, 2, 3, 4\}$.

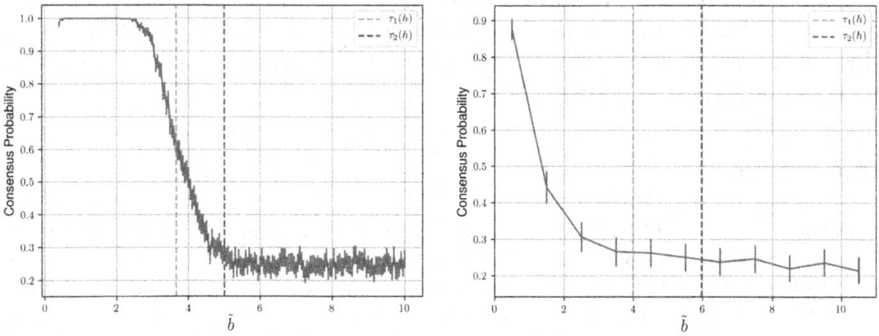

(a) Two Block Model (b) `ego-facebook`

Fig. 4. In Fig. 4a we show how the consensus probability changes when $\delta = 0.25$, $p_{\text{out}} = 0.2$, $p_{\text{in}} = 0.4$, and b is set to have $\tilde{b} \in \{0.4, 0.405, 0.41, \ldots, 10\}$. In Fig. 4b we show how the consensus probability changes when $\delta = 0.25$, $w_{\text{in}} = w_{\text{out}} = 1$, and b is set to have $\tilde{b} \in \{0.5, 1.5, \ldots, 10.5\}$.

1. Interestingly, the figure highlights that a sharp change of probability occurs exactly around $\lambda = 0.5$, by confirming our findings.

We observe that the behaviour on complex networks is very close to the one described for the simple symmetric two-block model. Specifically, in Fig. 4 we show that the trend of the consensus probability confirms our findings. Here, there are three possible phases: when $\tilde{b}$ is small, we have high probability of consensus; for intermediate values, the probability is smaller, but still far away from zero; finally, for large $\tilde{b}$, the probability of consensus get close to zero. Interestingly, the phases changes occurs, as indicated by results described in Sect. 3, around $\tau_1(h)$ and $\tau_2(h)$.

5 Conclusions

In this work we analyzed the impact of social media recommendations on opinion formation processes, when opinions may assume only discrete values, as is the case in many electoral environments. We focused mainly on how and how much the social media may influence the likelihood that agents converge to a consensus. Clearly, it would be interesting also to deepen our analysis by evaluating how the social media influences, not only the probability of consensus, but also the kind of equilibria that can be reached by the opinion formation process.

In this work we focused on a classical opinion formation model. However, we believe that it would be undoubtedly interesting to analyze whether our results extend to more complex (but more realistic) opinion formation model.

Even if, our experimental results highlight a large adherence to the theoretical findings about the symmetric two-block model, some small differences exist among the results for different network structures (mainly, in the case that initial opinions are convergent). It would be then interesting to understand whether and how these difference may be motivated through a detailed study of the relationship among the impact of the social influence and the structural and topological properties of the social network.

References

1. Acar, E., Greco, G., Manna, M.: Group reasoning in social environments. In: AAMAS. pp. 1296–1304 (2017)
2. Allcott, H., Braghieri, L., Eichmeyer, S., Gentzkow, M.: The welfare effects of social media. Am. Econ. Rev. **110**(3), 629–76 (2020)
3. Androniciuc, A.I.: Using social media in political campaigns. Evidence from Romania. SEA-Pract. Appl. Sci. **4**(10), 51–57 (2016)
4. Anunrojwong, J., Candogan, O., Immorlica, N.: Social learning under platform influence: extreme consensus and persistent disagreement. In: SSRN (2020)
5. Auletta, V., Caragiannis, I., Ferraioli, D., Galdi, C., Persiano, G.: Minority becomes majority in social networks. In: Markakis, E., Schäfer, G. (eds.) WINE 2015. LNCS, vol. 9470, pp. 74–88. Springer, Heidelberg (2015). https://doi.org/10.1007/978-3-662-48995-6_6
6. Auletta, V., Caragiannis, I., Ferraioli, D., Galdi, C., Persiano, G.: Generalized discrete preference games. In: IJCAI, pp. 53–59 (2016)
7. Auletta, V., Caragiannis, I., Ferraioli, D., Galdi, C., Persiano, G.: Information retention in heterogeneous majority dynamics. In: Devanur, N.R., Lu, P. (eds.) WINE 2017. LNCS, vol. 10660, pp. 30–43. Springer, Cham (2017). https://doi.org/10.1007/978-3-319-71924-5_3
8. Auletta, V., Caragiannis, I., Ferraioli, D., Galdi, C., Persiano, G.: Robustness in discrete preference games. In: AAMAS, pp. 1314–1322 (2017)

9. Auletta, V., Fanelli, A., Ferraioli, D.: Consensus in opinion formation processes in fully evolving environments. In: AAAI, pp. 6022–6029 (2019)
10. Auletta, V., Ferraioli, D., Greco, G.: On the complexity of reasoning about opinion diffusion under majority dynamics. Artif. Intell. **284**, 103288 (2020)
11. Auletta, V., Ferraioli, D., Greco, G.: Optimal majority dynamics for the diffusion of an opinion when multiple alternatives are available. Theoret. Comput. Sci. **869**, 156–180 (2021)
12. Auletta, V., Ferraioli, D., Savarese, V.: Manipulating an election in social networks through edge addition. In: Alviano, M., Greco, G., Scarcello, F. (eds.) AI*IA 2019. LNCS (LNAI), vol. 11946, pp. 495–510. Springer, Cham (2019). https://doi.org/10.1007/978-3-030-35166-3_35
13. Bakshy, E., Messing, S., Adamic, L.A.: Exposure to ideologically diverse news and opinion on Facebook. Science **348**(6239), 1130–1132 (2015)
14. Benigni, M.C., Joseph, K., Carley, K.M.: Online extremism and the communities that sustain it: detecting the ISIS supporting community on Twitter. PLoS ONE **12**, 1–23 (2017)
15. Bhawalkar, K., Gollapudi, S., Munagala, K.: Coevolutionary opinion formation games. In: STOC, pp. 41–50 (2013)
16. Bilò, V., Fanelli, A., Moscardelli, L.: Opinion formation games with dynamic social influences. Theoret. Comput. Sci. **746**, 444–458 (2018)
17. Bindel, D., Kleinberg, J.M., Oren, S.: How bad is forming your own opinion? Games Econom. Behav. **92**, 248–265 (2015)
18. Bredereck, R., Elkind, E.: Manipulating opinion diffusion in social networks. In: IJCAI, pp. 894–900 (2017)
19. Castiglioni, M., Ferraioli, D., Gatti, N., Landriani, G.: Election manipulation on social networks: seeding, edge removal, edge addition. J. Artif. Intell. Res. **71**, 1049–1090 (2021)
20. Chierichetti, F., Kleinberg, J., Oren, S.: On discrete preferences and coordination. J. Comput. Syst. Sci. **93**, 11–29 (2018)
21. Corò, F., Cruciani, E., D'Angelo, G., Ponziani, S.: Exploiting social influence to control elections based on scoring rules. In: IJCAI, pp. 201–207 (2019)
22. Dandekar, P., Goel, A., Lee, D.T.: Biased assimilation, homophily, and the dynamics of polarization. Proc. Natl. Acad. Sci. **110**(15), 5791–5796 (2013)
23. DeGroot, M.: Reaching a consensus. J. Am. Stat. Assoc. **69**(345), 118–121 (1974)
24. Feldman, M., Immorlica, N., Lucier, B., Weinberg, S.M.: Reaching consensus via non-Bayesian asynchronous learning in social networks. In: APPROX/RANDOM, pp. 192–208 (2014)
25. Ferraioli, D., Goldberg, P., Ventre, C.: Decentralized dynamics for finite opinion games. Theoret. Comput. Sci. **648**, 96–115 (2016)
26. Ferraioli, D., Ventre, C.: Social pressure in opinion games. In: IJCAI, pp. 3661–3667 (2017)
27. Fotakis, D., Kandiros, V., Kontonis, V., Skoulakis, S.: Opinion dynamics with limited information. In: Christodoulou, G., Harks, T. (eds.) WINE 2018. LNCS, vol. 11316, pp. 282–296. Springer, Cham (2018). https://doi.org/10.1007/978-3-030-04612-5_19
28. Fotakis, D., Palyvos-Giannas, D., Skoulakis, S.: Opinion dynamics with local interactions. In: IJCAI, pp. 279–285 (2016)
29. Friedkin, N., Johnsen, E.: Social influence and opinions. J. Math. Sociol. **15**(3–4), 193–206 (1990)

30. Fujiwara, T., Müller, K., Schwarz, C.: The effect of social media on elections: Evidence from the united states. Tech. rep, National Bureau of Economic Research (2021)
31. Gilbert, E.N.: Random graphs. Ann. Math. Stat. **30**(4), 1141–1144 (1959)
32. Halberstam, Y., Knight, B.: Homophily, group size, and the diffusion of political information in social networks: evidence from Twitter. J. Public Econ. **143**, 73–88 (2016)
33. Hegselmann, R., Krause, U.: Opinion dynamics and bounded confidence: models, analysis and simulation. J. Artif. Soc. Soc. Simul. **5**, 1–24 (2002)
34. Kempe, D., Kleinberg, J., Tardos, E.: Maximizing the spread of influence through a social network. In: KDD, pp. 137–146 (2003)
35. Kernighan, B.W., Lin, S.: An efficient heuristic procedure for partitioning graphs. Bell Syst. Tech. J. **49**(2), 291–307 (1970)
36. Krioukov, D., Papadopoulos, F., Kitsak, M., Vahdat, A., Boguná, M.: Hyperbolic geometry of complex networks. Phys. Rev. E **82**(3), 036106 (2010)
37. Leskovec, J., Krevl, A.: SNAP datasets: Stanford large network dataset collection (2014). http://snap.stanford.edu/data
38. Levy, R.: Social media, news consumption, and polarization: evidence from a field experiment. Am. Econ. Rev. **111**(3), 831–70 (2021)
39. Lin, Z., Francis, B., Maggiore, M.: Necessary and sufficient graphical conditions for formation control of unicycles. IEEE Trans. Autom. Control **50**(1), 121–127 (2005)
40. McAuley, J.J., Leskovec, J.: Learning to discover social circles in ego networks. In: NIPS, vol. 2012, pp. 548–556 (2012)
41. Mossel, E., Neeman, J., Tamuz, O.: Majority dynamics and aggregation of information in social networks. Auton. Agent. Multi-Agent Syst. **28**(3), 408–429 (2013). https://doi.org/10.1007/s10458-013-9230-4
42. Olfati-Saber, R.: Flocking for multi-agent dynamic systems: algorithms and theory. IEEE Trans. Autom. Control **51**(3), 401–420 (2006)
43. Olfati-Saber, R., Shamma, J.S.: Consensus filters for sensor networks and distributed sensor fusion. In: CDC, pp. 6698–6703 (2005)
44. Rozemberczki, B., Sarkar, R.: Characteristic functions on graphs: birds of a feather, from statistical descriptors to parametric models. In: CIKM, pp. 1325–1334 (2020)
45. Savkin, A.V.: Coordinated collective motion of groups of autonomous mobile robots: analysis of Vicsek's model. IEEE Trans. Autom. Control **49**(6), 981–982 (2004)
46. Shearer, E., Matsa, K.E.: News use across social media platforms 2018 (2018). https://www.pewresearch.org
47. Sina, S., Hazon, N., Hassidim, A., Kraus, S.: Adapting the social network to affect elections. In: AAMAS, pp. 705–713 (2015)
48. Tanner, H.G., Pappas, G.J., Kumar, V.: Leader-to-formation stability. IEEE Trans. Robot. Autom. **20**(3), 443–455 (2004)
49. Watts, D.J., Strogatz, S.H.: Collective dynamics of 'small-world' networks. Nature **393**(6684), 440–442 (1998)
50. Wilder, B., Vorobeychik, Y.: Controlling elections through social influence. In: AAMAS, pp. 265–273 (2018)

Misogynous MEME Recognition: A Preliminary Study

Elisabetta Fersini, Giulia Rizzi, Aurora Saibene, and Francesca Gasparini(✉)

Department of Informatics, Systems and Communication, University of Milano-Bicocca, Milano, Italy
{elisabetta.fersini,francesca.gasparini}@unimib.it, {g.rizzi10,a.saibene2}@campus.unimib.it

Abstract. Misogyny is a form of hate against women and has been spreading exponentially through the Web, especially in social media platforms. Hateful contents may be expressed through popular communication tools, like memes. A meme is an image characterised by a pictorial content with an overlaying text introduced a posteriori, and its main aim is originally to be funny and/or ironic. However, the use of memes to convey misogynous messages has increased and thus an automatic detection of these contents seems to be necessary to counteract this phenomenon. This task is particularly challenging, having that (1) different memes can present the same image, but different texts and vice versa, (2) two memes with the same image but different texts can convey a misogynous and not misogynous message, respectively, (3) misogyny can be expressed by image alone, text alone or their combination. In this paper both unimodal and multimodal approaches are investigated whose classifiers are trained and tested on a dataset of in the wild memes, which present both experts and perceived labels. The proposed multimodal approach provides better results compared to the unimodal ones and the VisualBERT state-of-the-art benchmark.

Keywords: Misogyny detection · Multimodal classifier · Memes · Image processing · Natural language processing

1 Introduction

In our society, social media platforms can potentially influence people's opinions and convey any type of message, from positive to hateful ones. A popular communication tool employed on these platforms are memes [31]. A meme can be defined as an image presenting a pictorial content with a superimposed text, which is introduced in a second moment by a human. The meme should also be funny and/or ironic [31]. Although most of the memes are created with the intent of making funny jokes, in a short time people started to use them as a form of hate against diversity, minorities, gender identities. Among these hateful contents, the ones targeting women may land to sexist and aggressive messages

S. Bandini et al. (Eds.): AIxIA 2021, LNAI 13196, pp. 279–293, 2022.
https://doi.org/10.1007/978-3-031-08421-8_19

in online environments [23], that may translate in the offline world into sexual stereotyping and gender inequality [12]. Moreover, hateful contents seem to be less offensive when conveyed by irony and funny jokes [32], but it has been proved that regular exposure to hateful humor allows people to voluntarily express hate without the fear of possible consequences [11]. These could also lead to dangerous behaviours. Several authors [26,27,35] found that enjoying sexist humor increases the levels of men rape attitude and increases sexual aggression. In order to counteract this phenomenon, online platforms, ranging from social networks to online communities, should automatically identify abusive candidate content against the female gender. In this paper, we investigate the specific task of automatically detecting misogynous memes by modelling the problem at unimodal and multimodal levels.

The main contribution of this work can be summarised as follows:

- Unimodal and multimodal classifiers are trained and tested on a dataset of memes collected in the wild. The dataset peculiarities are represented by the real-world memes downloaded from the Web and the inclusion of images with different qualities.
- We consider two different labels, one obtained involving subjects through a crowdsourcing platform (called perceived labelling) and a second one obtained by three domain experts (experts labelling), to underline differences between labels with a different level of noise.
- We perform an error analysis to deepen the weaknesses of the most promising models, highlighting the necessity to address the problem of biased training.

The rest of the paper is organised as follows. In Sect. 2, the state of the art in the context of automatic recognition of hateful contents on the Web and in particular misogyny is outlined. In Sect. 3, the *Misogynistic-MEME* dataset of *in the wild memes* is presented and compared with other datasets available in the literature. In Sect. 4 the unimodal and multimodal models are presented and compared with VisualBERT [20] that is considered one of the multimodal benchmark in the state of the art. Finally, in Sect. 5 conclusions and features work are detailed.

2 State of the Art

As a consequence of the *Hateful Memes (HM) Challenge: Detecting Hate Speech in Multimodal Memes* promoted by Facebook [17], the natural language processing and computer vision communities found an increased interest in the automatic detection of hateful comments conveyed through memes. Meme classification is a multimodal problem, due to the intrinsic nature of the memes. However, compared to other multimedia classification tasks that involve both text and visual content [5,25], it is more challenging. A meme can have a pleasant caption and a non-offensive visual content, but the same text can become extremely offensive when combined with another image, as well as a nice or non-offensive image can be associated with hateful text. Moreover, the hateful message can be expressed by image alone, text alone or by a combination of both. For this reason, unimodal classifiers are usually not able to perform adequately and models that learn multimodal aspects are required [1]. Contemporary to their challenge proposal, *Kiela et al.* have shown that state-of-the-art methods (both unimodal and multimodal) perform poorly compared to humans, underlying the difficulty of this particular classification task and the need of developing new machine learning models to solve this issue. The best multimodal approaches in the state of the art combine textual and visual features extending the architecture of the unimodal textual model BERT [6] to incorporate visual information. Among these models, the best-performing multimodal ones are ViLBERT [22], pretrained on the Conceptual Caption (CC) dataset [30], and VisualBERT [20] pretrained on the Common Objects in Context (COCO) dataset [21].

Focusing on the specific topic of this paper, and thus considering only a form of hatred against women, there has been surprisingly little work related to misogyny detection, with only a few papers including both text and image modality. From a linguistic perspective, few studies have been focused on detecting hate speech against women. A first attempt was conducted in [2], where a collection of misogynous tweets were selected from twitter and classified using Support Vector Machine, Naive Bayes, Multi-Layer Perceptron Neural Network and Random Forest. During the Automatic Misogyny Identification tasks organised at *Evalita* [8,9] and *IberEval* [10], several additional approaches based on natural language processing techniques have been proposed. Recently in [16,24,28], violence on Twitter has been explored applying a deep learning approach, while in [15], the authors faced the problem of discrimination of sexual minorities. From a visual point of view, the main research slightly related to this topic concerns sexual and pornographic content detection, exploiting skin detectors [3] to automatically identify naked persons in images [19] or other deep learning approaches such as in [34]. A preliminary attempt to perform the automatic detection of misogyny with a multimodal point of view has been proposed in [13] where the authors performed an analysis of sexist advertisements, merging visual and textual information. Specifically focusing on memes, the same authors [7] gave a first insight in the field of automatic detection of misogynous contents, by investigating both unimodal and multimodal approaches to understand the contribution of textual and visual cues.

3 The MEME Dataset

The *Misogynistic-MEME* (MM) dataset [7,14] has been employed to perform the proposed classification strategies. This dataset presents 800 memes collected from popular social media platforms (e.g., Facebook, Twitter, Instagram, and Reddit), which should be representative of the real world, without being affected by the possible bias introduced by synthetic meme generation. Moreover, the collection criteria were based on different manifestations of hate against women and thus targeting misogyny with a broad spectrum. These misogynous manifestations may be divided into four main categories, depicted in Fig. 1:

- *Shaming*, which expresses disapproval of women's behaviours and physical appearances compared to a given type of expectation, e.g. body shaming.
- *Stereotype*, which expresses a generalised belief concerning women in different contexts, e.g., societal role, personality and behaviours.
- *Objectification*, which consists in considering and/or treating women as objects.
- *Violence*, which may instigate or express violence against women.

(a) Shaming (b) Stereotype

(c) Objectification (d) Violence

Fig. 1. Graphical examples of misogynous memes.

Having that the misogyny can be expressed by the text/image only or by the entire meme contents and that the misogyny perception is subjective, this dataset presents (i) the meme with both the textual and pictorial information, (ii) the transcribed text of the meme, and (iii) the labelling regarding the presence/absence of misogyny given by both field experts and annotators of a crowdsourcing platform. Therefore, analyses can be conducted by considering the expert labels (50.00% misogynous memes) and the general public perceived misogyny ones (46.13% misogynous memes). Notice that for the expert labels a 100% agreement was considered and a consistency between similar meme labelling required. On the contrary, the perceived labels required at least a 2 out of 3 agreement and may present discordant labels on similar memes.

Significant differences can be underlined comparing the MM dataset with the HM challenge one. The data collection for the MM dataset considers a real-world scenario by browsing social media platform, while in HM the memes are synthetic. Consequently, the MM collected memes have different data quality (in terms of resolution, compression and in general noise), while in HM memes are provided with a high quality only. Regarding the meme messages, the MM dataset only considers misogyny, while the HM one presents memes that could be considered generically hateful (thus including misogyny). Notice that *Kirk et al.* have recently demonstrated that models trained on the HM dataset achieve lower performance when applied to real-world Pinterest memes. Therefore, the MM dataset can be considered as an *in the wild* dataset, which should be able to avoid the classification problems deriving from synthetic ones and that could be used as a gold standard to collect and label new misogynous memes.

The MM dataset is available at https://github.com/MIND-Lab/MEME. For more details, please refer to [14].

4 Models and Results

According to the state of the art, we decided to investigate sub-symbolic approaches to address this task. As far as we know, no pure symbolic approaches have been adopted in this area of research. The majority of proposed works in hate detection field adopt a pure sub-symbolic or a hybrid approach to cope with the continuous growth and evolution of language. Especially in hate speech, a commonly used word with a harmless meaning can be harmless if used in a certain way and in a specific context. This phenomenon is even more evident in memes because they often report slang or dialect expressions.

In order to face the problem of recognising misogynous memes, several strategies have been investigated, experimenting both unimodal and multimodal approaches. Each model subsequently introduced has been trained and validated using a 10-fold cross validation both on expert and perceived labels available in the dataset.

4.1 Unimodal Classifiers

Visual Based Models. We performed two different experiments, based on the pretrained VGG16 classification model [33]. For both of them the following layers have been introduced to have a fine-tuning according to the misogynous and not misogynous labels:

- Flatten layer
- Dense layer of 256 output nodes, ReLu activation and L2 regularisation
- Dropout layer with dropout rate of 0.2
- Dense layer of 64 output nodes, ReLu activation and L2 regularisation
- Dense layer - output with sigmoid activation

The objective function minimises the *binary crossentropy loss*, and is optimised with *adam* [18], with a training phase of 30 epochs and a batch size of 64 instances. The raw based input model is depicted in Fig. 2. The first experimented approach considers the memes as images, without distinguishing the two sources of information. Therefore, the text is also considered as part of the pictorial information. We call this model *Raw Input based model.* The results are reported in the confusion matrices in Table 1, where NM means *Not Misogynous* and M means *Misogynous.*

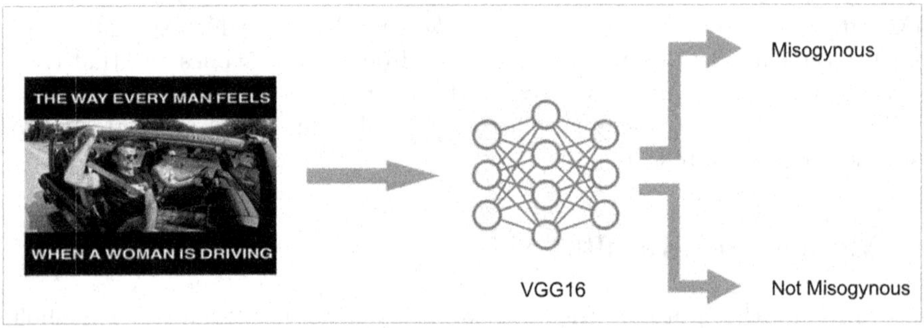

Fig. 2. Raw input based model.

Table 1. Confusion matrices of the raw input based model.

	Expert			Perceived	
	Predicted			Predicted	
Actual	NM	M	Actual	NM	M
NM	186	214	NM	231	200
M	199	201	M	201	168

Considering the reported confusion matrices, as expected, the task seems to be very challenging for both label sets. Table 2 summarises the achieved results in terms of Precision, Recall, Accuracy, F1-Measure and AUC. It can be easily noticed that, considering the meme as a raw image, there are no sufficient information to distinguish properly the misogynous content from the non misogynous one. In fact, the obtained classification performance are comparable with the output of a random classifier.

Table 2. Performance of the raw input based model.

Label	Recall	Precision	Accuracy	F1-Measure	AUC
Expert	0.483	0.465	0.484	0.474	0.494
Perceived	0.535	0.536	0.499	0.535	0.517

The second approach that has been considered adopts as input the pictorial component of the memes only, thus without considering the text. To this end, each meme has been preprocessed using the OpenCV[1] functions to remove the text. In particular, the bounding box of the characters have been identified and deleted. The image was then properly restored by using the inpainting or cropping the meme (in case the text was present only in the boarders).

The resulting image was given as input to the VGG16 pretrained Convolutional Neural Network, as in the previous experiment. An overview of the *Picture based model* is depicted in Fig. 3.

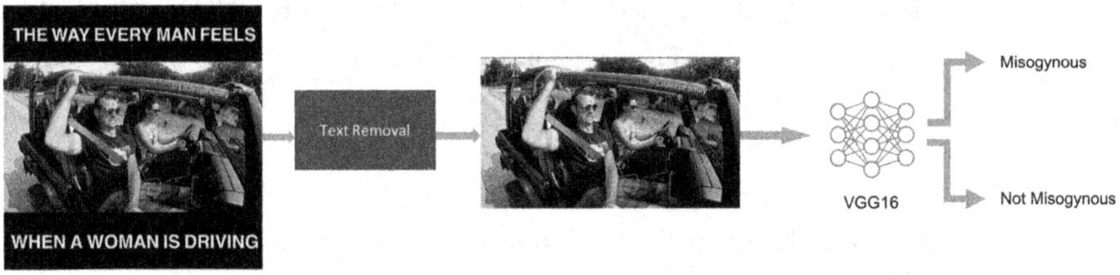

Fig. 3. Picture based model.

The model has been evaluated again on both labels (expert and perceived). The corresponding confusion matrices and performance measures are reported in Tables 3 and 4, respectively.

Table 3. Confusion matrices of the picture based model.

	Expert			Perceived	
	Predicted			Predicted	
	NM	M		NM	M
Actual NM	286	114	Actual NM	272	159
Actual M	149	251	Actual M	146	223

It can be observed that the Picture based model has better prediction capabilities (with an increase of more than 10%) compared with the Raw Input based one, although it does not yet achieve optimal results.

Removing the text from the pictorial content resulted in the removal of confounding visual features related to characters (e.g., texture, edges and contrast), which are obviously not related to the misogynous content. As a further remark, it can be said that the visual component within a meme has a significant correlation with the misogynous content, thus it should be taken into account. Moreover, given that the same visual content associated with different texts can

[1] https://opencv.org.

convey both a misogynous and a not misogynous message, the necessity of having a multimodal approach arises.

Comparing the differences between expert and perceived labels, recall that the perceived ones are noisier than the expert ones. Also, a 100% agreement was considered for the expert labels, which present consistent labels for similar memes, while a 2 out of 3 agreement was considered for the perceived ones, which seem to present contrasting opinion on similar memes.

Table 4. Performance of the picture based model.

Label	Recall	Precision	Accuracy	F1-Measure	AUC
Expert	0.657	0.715	0.671	0.685	0.657
Perceived	0.651	0.631	0.619	0.641	0.623

Text Based Model. The third considered approach uses as input the textual component of the memes, thus providing only the textual contents as training samples. In particular, the transcription of the text enclosed in the meme has been taken as input to derive the corresponding embeddings and train a subsequent neural model based on Long Short Term Memory (LSTM) [29]. More specifically, once the embedding of the text is derived by means of the Universal Sentence Enconder (USE) [4], it is provided as input to the neural model with the following architecture:

- Input layer
- LSTM layer of 32 output nodes, 0.2 dropout rate
- Dense layer of 10 output nodes, ReLu activation
- Dropout layer of 0.2 dropout rate
- Dense layer - output with sigmoid activation

A summary of the model is depicted in Fig. 4.

Tables 5 and 6 report the corresponding confusion matrices and performance measures. The prediction capabilities of the *Text based Model* have a further improvement compared with the previous visual ones, indicating that the textual component plays an import role to detect misogynous content. In fact, we notice that specific words, such as keywords denoting a discredit towards a woman (e.g., *bi*ch*), are a strong discriminant while training a model.

Regarding the performance of the model, the results show a remarkable improvement both on expert and perceived annotations, achieving respectively an F1-Measure equal to 0.908 and 0.860. The model obtains a balanced compromise between precision and recall, performing well on both misogynous and not misogynous labels.

However, the considerations given for the Picture based model hold for the Text based one. In fact, although the performance achieved by considering only the textual component seems more than encouraging, considering only the text enclosed

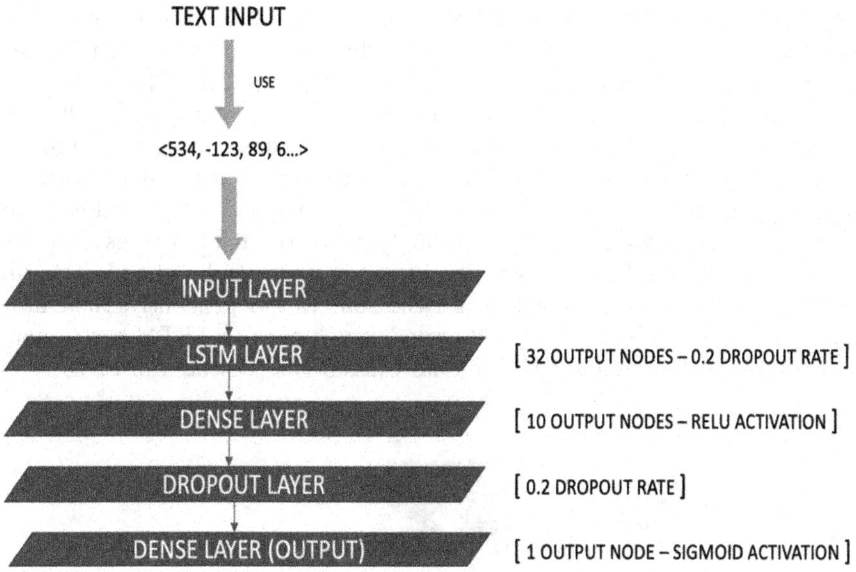

Fig. 4. Text based model.

Table 5. Confusion matrices of the text based model.

Expert

		Predicted	
		NM	M
Actual	NM	370	30
	M	45	355

Perceived

		Predicted	
		NM	M
Actual	NM	364	67
	M	52	317

in a meme could lead to poor results when the misogynous message is conveyed by the image itself or by the interaction between visual and textual components.

Therefore, since the nature of the memes is definitely multimodal, it is mandatory to explore a solution that combines both the available sources of information.

4.2 Multimodal Classifier

In order to address the above mentioned issues, a multimodal approach has been designed. Firstly, this model deals with each source independently, combining them to train the final model. In particular, the textual source is embedded using

Table 6. Performance of the text based model.

Label	Recall	Precision	Accuracy	F1-Measure	AUC
Expert	0.892	0.925	0.906	0.908	0.908
Perceived	0.875	0.845	0.851	0.860	0.848

the previously introduced USE model, while the visual component is analysed to extract the objects/subjects contained within the meme. In order to identify what is contained in each meme from a visual perspective, the Clarifai tool[2] has been used. Clarifai is based on Convolutional Neural Networks and offers the possibility of extracting subjects/objects contained in an image according to a set of 11 K available tags. To our purposes, 14 tags of particular interest for the misogyny identification problem (e.g., man, woman, kitchen, and car) were selected and each meme tagged accordingly. Once the relevant tags have been extracted using Clarifai, they are considered as texts and embedded through the USE model. Having embedded all the sources independently, their latent representation are concatenated and provided as input to a LSTM based model. An overview of the proposed Multimodal Classifier is presented in Fig. 5.

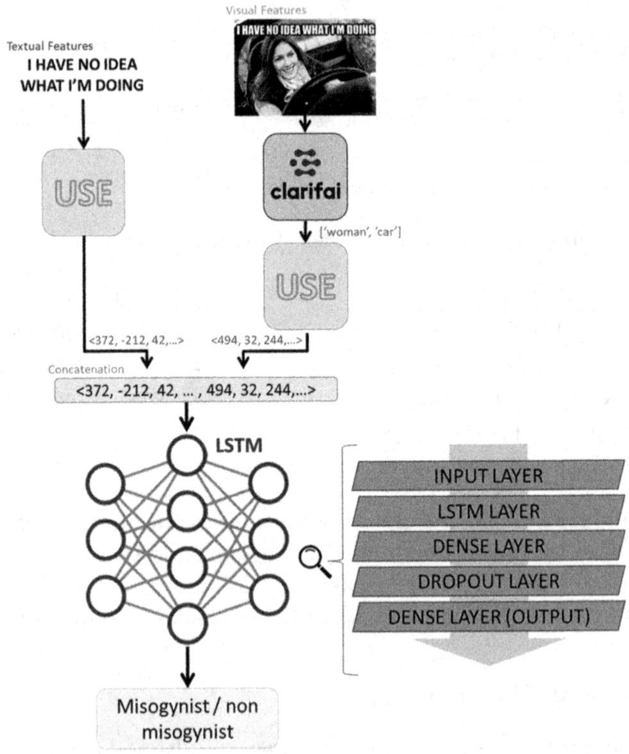

Fig. 5. Multimodal classifier.

Regarding the results of the model, as can be derived by looking at Tables 7 and 8, it emerges that the multiple information provided by the available

[2] https://docs.clarifai.com.

sources allow the Multimodal Classifier to outperform the previously experimented solutions.

Table 7. Confusion matrices of the multimodal classifier.

Expert			
		Predicted	
		NM	M
Actual	NM	373	27
	M	41	359

Perceived			
		Predicted	
		NM	M
Actual	NM	367	64
	M	46	323

Moreover, the Multimodal Classifier not only has remarkable recognition performance for both the expert and perceived label cases, but it is able to learn more accurately on the expert annotations.

Table 8. Performance of the multimodal classifier.

Label	Recall	Precision	Accuracy	F1-Measure	AUC
Expert	0.901	0.933	0.915	0.916	0.914
Perceived	0.889	0.852	0.863	0.870	0.869

Finally a comparison between the considered unimodal classifiers, the proposed multimodal one and the benchmarking technique represented by VisualBERT, is reported in Table 9.

Table 9. Summary of the results achieved on the expert labelled data.

Approach	Classifier	Recall	Precision	Accuracy	F1-Measure	AUC
Unimodal	Raw input visual based	0.483	0.465	0.484	0.474	0.494
	Picture based	0.657	0.715	0.671	0.685	0.657
	Text based	0.892	0.925	0.906	0.908	0.908
Multimodal	VisualBERT	0.888	0.892	0.890	0.891	0.890
	Our proposal	0.901	0.933	0.915	0.916	0.914

Comparing unimodal classifiers, the one that relies on textual data outperforms the visual based ones. However, visual contents are significant to detect misogyny especially when only the pictorial component is considered (Visual based only Classifier). Finally, as expected, the multimodal classifiers outperform the unimodal ones, and our proposal with respect to VisualBERT is able to achieve better results.

In order to understand the main weaknesses of the multimodal classifiers, an error analysis has been performed. Regarding the misclassified memes, the error is almost balanced: around 8.75% of memes are wrongly classified, where half of the memes are actually misogynous erroneously predicted as not misogynous, and vice-versa. Among the misogynous memes that are wrongly classified as not misogynous, the most common error relates to those memes that are not explicitly misogynous, but their interpretation (with additional knowledge about the context) implies a hateful content towards women (see Fig. 6(a)). Regarding the errors performed on not misogynous memes that are wrongly classified as misogynous, we can highlight that in the majority of the cases the misclassification can be traced back to the presence of words strongly related to typical misogynous terms (e.g. fat) or the presence of an neutral text but depicting a woman as main subject of the meme (see Fig. 6(b)). This means that, the models could be biased by those memes in the training data that visually or textually denote misogynous content.

(a) (b)

Fig. 6. Examples of misclassified memes.

5 Conclusions

In this paper we focused on the problem of automatic detection of misogynous content on memes belonging to an in the wild collection. A multimodal approach that considers both visual and textual information allows better classification results compared to both unimodal classifiers and the VisualBERT model considered as a multimodal state-of-the-art benchmark. As a final consideration, we want to notice that even if the results achieved so far seem to be promising, the recognition of misogynous memes is still in its infancy. What has been designed in this paper is just a preliminary study that needs to be further investigated. In particular, what is called an *unintended bias* could have been introduced and could affect the real performance of the models. In this research area, metrics to estimate the bias of a misogyny recognition model and techniques to mitigate it are still missing. Finally, from the preliminary results of this work it also emerges that multimodal approaches are mandatory to solve this classification task and that huge in the wild datasets are required to permit proper investigations.

Future developments could include an analysis of irony, a fundamental intrinsic component of memes, in order to identify significant elements to enrich the input of the model and better understand the meaning of the meme itself, for instance to distinguish benevolent sexist memes from the abusive ones [36]. Another area of study concerns the perception of misogyny itself. Misogyny is currently represented based on annotations obtained from experts or the crowdsourcing platform. Instead, it should be modeled taking into account all the different typologies with which it manifests itself, to obtain a representation that does not represent only the perception of the majority, but that takes into account all the individual evaluations.

References

1. Afridi, T.H., Alam, A., Khan, M.N., Khan, J., Lee, Y.K.: A multimodal memes classification: A survey and open research issues. In: The Proceedings of the Third International Conference on Smart City Applications, pp. 1451–1466. Springer (2020). https://doi.org/10.1007/978-3-030-66840-2_109
2. Anzovino, M., Fersini, E., Rosso, P.: Automatic identification and classification of misogynistic language on twitter. In: Silberztein, M., Atigui, F., Kornyshova, E., Métais, E., Meziane, F. (eds.) NLDB 2018. LNCS, vol. 10859, pp. 57–64. Springer, Cham (2018). https://doi.org/10.1007/978-3-319-91947-8_6
3. Bianco, S., Gasparini, F., Schettini, R.: Adaptive skin classification using face and body detection. IEEE Trans. Image Process. **24**(12), 4756–4765 (2015)
4. Cer, D., et al.: Universal sentence encoder for english. In: Proceedings of the 2018 Conference on Empirical Methods in Natural Language Processing: System Demonstrations, pp. 169–174 (2018)
5. Corchs, S., Fersini, E., Gasparini, F.: Ensemble learning on visual and textual data for social image emotion classification. Int. J. Mach. Learn. Cybern. **10**(8), 2057–2070 (2017). https://doi.org/10.1007/s13042-017-0734-0
6. Devlin, J., Chang, M.W., Lee, K., Toutanova, K.: Bert: Pre-training of deep bidirectional transformers for language understanding. arXiv preprint arXiv:1810.04805 (2018)
7. Fersini, E., Gasparini, F., Corchs, S.: Detecting sexist meme on the web: a study on textual and visual cues. In: 2019 8th International Conference on Affective Computing and Intelligent Interaction Workshops and Demos (ACIIW), pp. 226–231. IEEE (2019)
8. Fersini, E., Nozza, D., Rosso, P.: Overview of the evalita 2018 task on automatic misogyny identification (ami). EVALITA Eval. NLP Speech Tools Italian **12**, 59 (2018)
9. Fersini, E., Nozza, D., Rosso, P.: Ami@ evalita2020: automatic misogyny identification. In: EVALITA (2020)
10. Fersini, E., Rosso, P., Anzovino, M.: Overview of the task on automatic misogyny identification at ibereval 2018. IberEval@ SEPLN, vol. 2150, pp. 214–228 (2018)
11. Ford, T.E., Boxer, C.F., Armstrong, J., Edel, J.R.: More than "just a joke": the prejudice-releasing function of sexist humor. Pers. Soc. Psychol. Bull. **34**(2), 159–170 (2008)
12. Franks, M.A.: Unwilling avatars: idealism and discrimination in cyberspace. Colum. J. Gender L. **20**, 224 (2011)

13. Gasparini, F., Erba, I., Fersini, E., Corchs, S.: Multimodal classification of sexist advertisements. In: ICETE (1), pp. 565–572 (2018)
14. Gasparini, F., Rizzi, G., Saibene, A., Fersini, E.: Benchmark dataset of memes with text transcriptions for automatic detection of multi-modal misogynistic content. arXiv preprint arXiv:2106.08409 (2021)
15. Khatua, A., Cambria, E., Ghosh, K., Chaki, N., Khatua, A.: Tweeting in support of lgbt? a deep learning approach. In: Proceedings of the ACM India Joint International Conference on Data Science and Management of Data, pp. 342–345 (2019)
16. Khatua, A., Cambria, E., Khatua, A.: Sounds of silence breakers: exploring sexual violence on twitter. In: 2018 IEEE/ACM International Conference on Advances in Social Networks Analysis and Mining (ASONAM), pp. 397–400. IEEE (2018)
17. Kiela, D., et al.: The hateful memes challenge: detecting hate speech in multimodal memes (2021)
18. Kingma, D.P., Ba, J.: Adam: a method for stochastic optimization. arXiv preprint arXiv:1412.6980 (2014)
19. Lee, J.S., Kuo, Y.M., Chung, P.C., Chen, E.L.: Naked image detection based on adaptive and extensible skin color model. Pattern Recogn. **40**(8), 2261–2270 (2007)
20. Li, L.H., Yatskar, M., Yin, D., Hsieh, C.J., Chang, K.W.: Visualbert: a simple and performant baseline for vision and language. arXiv preprint arXiv:1908.03557 (2019)
21. Lin, T.-Y., et al.: Microsoft COCO: common objects in context. In: Fleet, D., Pajdla, T., Schiele, B., Tuytelaars, T. (eds.) ECCV 2014. LNCS, vol. 8693, pp. 740–755. Springer, Cham (2014). https://doi.org/10.1007/978-3-319-10602-1_48
22. Lu, J., Batra, D., Parikh, D., Lee, S.: Vilbert: pretraining task-agnostic visiolinguistic representations for vision-and-language tasks. arXiv preprint arXiv:1908.02265 (2019)
23. Paciello, M., D'Errico, F., Saleri, G., Lamponi, E.: Online sexist meme and its effects on moral and emotional processes in social media. Comput. Hum. Behav. **116**, 106655 (2021)
24. Parikh, P., Abburi, H., Chhaya, N., Gupta, M., Varma, V.: Categorizing sexism and misogyny through neural approaches. ACM Trans. Web (TWEB) **15**(4), 1–31 (2021)
25. Poria, S., Cambria, E., Bajpai, R., Hussain, A.: A review of affective computing: from unimodal analysis to multimodal fusion. Inf. Fusion **37**, 98–125 (2017)
26. Romero-Sánchez, M., Durán, M., Carretero-Dios, H., Megías, J.L., Moya, M.: Exposure to sexist humor and rape proclivity: the moderator effect of aversiveness ratings. J. Interpersonal Violence **25**(12), 2339–2350 (2010)
27. Ryan, K.M., Kanjorski, J.: The enjoyment of sexist humor, rape attitudes, and relationship aggression in college students. Sex Roles **38**(9), 743–756 (1998). https://doi.org/10.1023/A:1018868913615
28. Safi Samghabadi, N., Patwa, P., PYKL, S., Mukherjee, P., Das, A., Solorio, T.: Aggression and misogyny detection using BERT: a multi-task approach. In: Proceedings of the Second Workshop on Trolling, Aggression and Cyberbullying, pp. 126–131. European Language Resources Association (ELRA), Marseille, France (2020)
29. Schmidhuber, J., Hochreiter, S., et al.: Long short-term memory. Neural Comput. **9**(8), 1735–1780 (1997)
30. Sharma, P., Ding, N., Goodman, S., Soricut, R.: Conceptual captions: a cleaned, hypernymed, image alt-text dataset for automatic image captioning. In: Proceed-

ings of the 56th Annual Meeting of the Association for Computational Linguistics (Volume 1: Long Papers), pp. 2556–2565 (2018)
31. Shifman, L.: Memes in a digital world: reconciling with a conceptual troublemaker. J. Comput.-Mediated Commun. **18**(3), 362–377 (2013). https://doi.org/10.1111/jcc4.12013
32. Siddiqi, N., Bains, A., Mushtaq, A., Aleem, S.: Analysing threads of sexism in new age humour: a content analysis of internet memes. Indian J. Soci. Res. **59**(3), 355–367 (2018)
33. Simonyan, K., Zisserman, A.: Very deep convolutional networks for large-scale image recognition. arXiv preprint arXiv:1409.1556 (2014)
34. Tabone, A., Camilleri, K., Bonnici, A., Cristina, S., Farrugia, R., Borg, M.: Pornographic content classification using deep-learning. In: Proceedings of the 21st ACM Symposium on Document Engineering, pp. 1–10 (2021)
35. Thomae, M., Viki, G.T.: Why did the woman cross the road? the effect of sexist humor on men's rape proclivity. J. Soci. Evol. Cult. Psychol. **7**(3), 250 (2013)
36. Zeinert, P., Inie, N., Derczynski, L.: Annotating online misogyny. In: Proceedings of the 59th Annual Meeting of the Association for Computational Linguistics and the 11th International Joint Conference on Natural Language Processing (Volume 1: Long Papers), pp. 3181–3197. Association for Computational Linguistics (2021). https://doi.org/10.18653/v1/2021.acl-long.247, https://aclanthology.org/2021.acl-long.247

Signal Processing: Images, Videos and Speech

A Relevance-Based CNN Trimming Method for Low-Resources Embedded Vision

Dalila Ressi(✉), Mara Pistellato, Andrea Albarelli, and Filippo Bergamasco

DAIS, Università Ca'Foscari Venezia, 155, via Torino, Venice, Italy
{dalila.ressi,mara.pistellato,albarelli,filippo.bergamasco}@unive.it

Abstract. A significant amount of Deep Learning research deals with the reduction of network complexity. In most scenarios the preservation of very high performance has priority over size reduction. However, when dealing with embedded systems, the limited amount of resources forces a switch in perspective. In fact, being able to dramatically reduce complexity could be a stronger requisite for overall feasibility than excellent performance. In this paper we propose a simple to implement yet effective method to largely reduce the size of Convolutional Neural Networks with minimal impact on their performance. The key idea is to assess the relevance of each kernel with respect to a representative dataset by computing the output of its activation function and to trim them accordingly. The resulting network becomes small enough to be adopted on embedded hardware, such as smart cameras or lightweight edge processing units. In order to assess the capability of our method with respect to real-world scenarios, we adopted it to shrink two different pre-trained networks to be hosted on general purpose low-end FPGA hardware to be found in embedded cameras. Our experiments demonstrated both the overall feasibility of the method and its superior performance when compared with similar size-reducing techniques introduced in recent literature.

Keywords: Computer Vision · CNN · Industrial application · Compression · Filter pruning

1 Introduction

Over the past few years industrial applications have been exploiting extensively the advantages coming from Deep Learning, in particular when using Convolutional Neural Networks (CNNs). The intrinsic flexibility of these networks makes them widely adopted in a variety of practical applications, from medical to industrial. In particular, image and signal processing tasks are well-suited for the convolutional architecture, therefore a huge number of Computer Vision solutions have been proposed in the literature. Deploying a large and accurate model to perform a certain task takes considerable energy and space. Even if

S. Bandini et al. (Eds.): AIxIA 2021, LNAI 13196, pp. 297–309, 2022.
https://doi.org/10.1007/978-3-031-08421-8_20

this might not be a problem during the training phase, it becomes a big issue at inference time, especially if the model has to run on devices with reduced computational resources or small storage space.

This is the case with many modern applications, including IoT devices, smart cameras, drones, smartphones or any other kind of device characterized by limited resources and low energy consumption requirements. For this reason, the adaptation of inference networks to embedded systems has been covered by many researchers [5,27], devising solutions ranging from architectures specially crafted for Field Programmable Gate Arrays (FPGAs) [13,23] to techniques focused on low consumption for wireless and mobile devices [28]. Indeed, according to the type of task to perform, two main approaches are to be found in literature. The choice is between training from scratch a smaller specialized network, or compressing a large pre-trained network and adapting it for the task (pruning).

In this paper we introduce a pruning technique that, while of general application, has been developed to address a specific vision task. Namely, our goal was to synthesize on FPGA hardware, available on commercial smart cameras, a lightweight CNN to locate both 1D and 2D signal peaks respectively in line scan and area scan images. To this end, we started from full-size networks and we made them tiny by means of a novel pruning algorithm which does not require manual tuning of parameters and allows to greatly reduce the number of floating point operations (FLOPs) computed. In a throughout experimental section we show that the trimmed network achieves better results with respect to a network with the pruned architecture that is trained starting from random weights. Moreover, the resulting performance is better than the one obtainable with other state-of-the-art trimming methods. Finally, by using other compression techniques such as quantization of the weights [3,24] the resulting model can even be further reduced.

2 Related Work

Fitting large inference networks to embedded systems is a topic that attracted the attention of many researchers in the recent past. A typical solution consists to re-design network components to achieve similar results with smaller resources. It is the case of MobileNets [10] and ThinNet [2], where the authors substitute classical convolutions with depthwise separable convolutions. Another example is SqueezeNet [12], achieving the same accuracy of AlexNet with 50 times less parameters. It uses multiple strategies to reduce each layer complexity, like design space exploration and the introduction of new modules. Such solutions are usually targeted for mobile devices [14,29] but can also be implemented in large networks to reduce their size. Another interesting approach, called distillation [9], consists in using a larger network to teach the same task to a smaller network. However, it can only be used for classification.

Great effort has also been put on techniques to compress existing networks by reducing the number and/or precision of each weight. The former is usually referred as *Pruning* [1] and the latter as *Quantization* [3,6,24]. Pruning comes in a lot of different flavours, and sometimes it is difficult to actually understand which method is the best [30] considering the high inconstancy of performance for different application scenarios [20]. Weight pruning techniques [7] remove single connections by setting some weights to zero, but the resulting sparse matrices cannot exploit BLAS libraries and are hard to implement on FPGA [6]. A simpler and more structured manner is to prune whole *kernels* from a Convolutional Neural Network. This procedure is often referred as *filter pruning* or *trimming* [11]. Our work belongs to this category.

As discussed in [17], filter pruning techniques can be further categorized into two groups: methods focusing on *property importance* and others concentrating on *adaptive importance*. In the first group we find methods which prune filters according to intrinsic properties of the networks, and do not modify the training loss. In 2016, Hu et al. [11] proposed a layer-wise method which analyses the neuron outputs to compute the *Average Percentage of Zero (APoZ)* activations after the ReLU mapping. The idea is to remove neurons with an APoZ larger than one standard deviation from the average APoZ of the target trimming layer. Instead of looking at the outputs, the method proposed by Li et al. [16] measures the relative importance of a filter in each layer by computing the sum of its absolute weights (i.e. its *L1-Norm*). A more recent approach has been suggested by He et al. [8]. It expands the norm-based filter criterion by computing the Geometric Median (*GM*) of the filters within the same layer. The idea is that filters close to the GM can be represented by the other filters, and therefore are good candidates to be pruned. The authors illustrate how the smallest norm filters can be very important, as they could actually be larger than zero or they can have a small norm deviation. In 2020 Lin et al. [17] proposed a method called Filter Pruning using High-Rank Feature Maps (*HRank*). They claim that average rank of multiple feature maps generated by a single filter is independent from the distribution of the images. Filters which generate lower-rank feature maps are less important and can be removed first in a one-shot manner, requiring only a few fine-tuning epochs after the pruning phase.

Adaptive importance methods like [18,19] usually achieve better compression and speed-up than property importance based ones. On the other hand, these techniques change the loss function up to the point that retraining becomes a separated problem, usually requiring to search again a new best set of hyper-parameters.

There is a last class of filter pruning algorithms that deserves to be mentioned. Sometimes filter pruning is exploited to find the best sub-network from an original one. It is the case of [4] and [26] where they use PCA to compressing both length and width of the network. Our goal however is to compress an existing network without the need to retrain it completely. For this reason, we focus on *Property Importance* algorithms.

Methods aiming to remove parameters from the network, regardless where the connections or the filters are, can be considered *global*. Usually there is only one threshold to be set, such as the number of filters or the compression rate to achieve. Some methods focus on specific layers, usually relying on certain statistics to pick the most promising ones. Rather than global methods, these *layer-wise* pruning algorithms require more than one threshold or other parameters to be set, making them less robust.

Finally, pruning is usually performed in three stages: (i) preparation of an appropriately large network either by training it from scratch or by adapting an existing trained network using transfer learning; (ii) removal of superfluous parameters and (iii) fine-tuning to recover the loss of accuracy. The second and third stages are often repeated until the network reaches the desired level of compression. Some methods, however, perform pruning in a *one-shot* fashion by removing a chosen set of weights in a single pass [17].

3 The Pruning Method

We propose a global filter pruning method based on the idea that kernels can be ranked by means of a *relevance metric* computed according to the output after the activation function. Less relevant filters are iteratively removed in a *prune one and re-train* fashion, to allow the network to adjust to the reduced channel. Conforming with this process, we call our method ReFT (Relevance-based Filter Trimming).

More formally, given a convolutional layer, its input can be represented as a 2D tensor $I \times H$ containing a signal of I single $H-$dimensional feature vectors[1]. The convolutional layer contains K different $S \times H$ kernels that are convolved with the input to produce an $I \times K$ output tensor. This operation requires approximately $S \times H$ multiply-add operations for I filter shift for a total of $SHIK$ operations. Our goal is to define a *relevance function* to be computed over the K kernels in order to iteratively remove the kernel with smaller relevance. Each kernel removal will result in a reduction of the multiply-add operation in the order of SHI. Furthermore, it will reduce the size of the output of the layer of a factor proportional to the input I.

In detail, the ReFT iterative reduction process is performed according to the pseudo-code described in Algorithm . Here, $Kernels$ is the full set of kernels in the network, $Kernels(i)$ is the subset of kernels at layer i and $Kernels(i, c)$ points to a specific kernel. The value $output(i, c, s)$ refers to the output of the activation function after $Kernels(i, c)$ for data point s.

The network reduction stops when either the number of kernels left is below a given threshold t or the performance of the network (measured by the function $perfMetric$) is less than minimum acceptable value ϵ. The actual characteristic measured by $perfMetric$ could change according to the application scenario. For instance it could be a function of the average loss with respect to a validation set or a specific metric over the confusion matrix.

During its main iteration the ReFT algorithm selects the least relevant kernel, removes it from the network and performs a partial retrain if the removed kernel was not negligible (i.e. exhibiting an output value of 0 for all the samples in $\mathcal{S}$.

[1] this is actually the case for 1D convolutional layers, but the extension to 2D layers is straightforward.

Algorithm: ReFT network reduction

```
Choose a representative dataset S;
while |Kernels| > t and perfMetric > ε do
    for s ∈ S do
        for i ∈ Layers do
            for c ∈ Kernels(i) do
                O_c^i(s) ← output(i, c, s)
            end
        end
    end
    (α, β) = argmin_{i,c}(relevance(i, c));
    Remove Kernels(α, β) from the network;
    if Σ_{s∈S} O_β^α(s) ≠ 0 then
        Retrain a few epochs to adapt model;
    end
end
```

Of course, key to the effectiveness of the ReFT reduction is the choice of a suitable *relevance* function. As anticipated when introducing the method, the main idea is to account for the output distribution of the kernel with respect to real data, rather than for its input weight (which is much more common in literature). The rationale is to look at the *actual* effect of the kernel, rather than at its *potential* impact expressed in an implicit way by its input weights. To this end, we define a *span* function as:

$$span(i, c, \gamma) = q_{100-\gamma}(O_c^i) - q_\gamma(O_c^i)$$

That is the difference between percentile $100 - \gamma$ and percentile γ in the distribution O_c^i over all the data points s in the dataset $\mathcal{S}$. Thus, we have that $span(i, c, 0)$ represents the distance between the maximum and the minimum output for $Kernels(i, c)$ over the dataset $\mathcal{S}$.

In principle, the *span* function could be directly adopted to define relevance by choosing a specific value for γ. However, in order to mitigate the effect of outliers, we would like to use the full span only to disambiguate between kernels with similar output distributions, while adopting more conservative percentiles most of the time.

To obtain this result, we define *relevance* as an implicit metric by defining this pairwise partial ordering function:

$$\begin{aligned} relevance(j, k) < relevance(l, m) \iff \\ span(j, k, 2) < span(l, m, 2) \quad \lor \\ span(j, k, 2) = span(l, m, 2) \quad \land \\ span(j, k, 0) < span(l, m, 0)) \end{aligned}$$

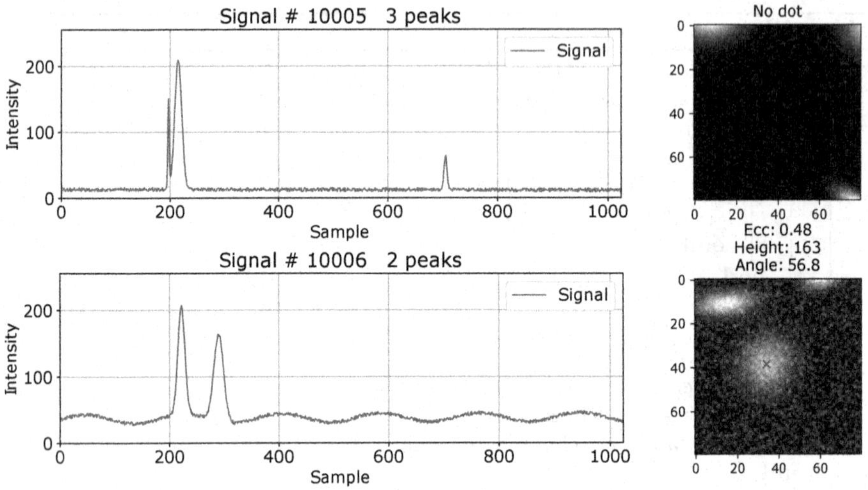

Fig. 1. Left: two scanlines acquired by the camera for the peak detection task. Multiple or no peaks can be present in the same scanline, sometimes very close to each other. Right: two samples from the *Dots* dataset. Also in this case there might not be any dot present or multiple ones. In the bottom right picture the detected dot center is highlighted by a red cross. (Color figure online)

In practice, this means that filter j, k is less relevant than filter n, m if the distance between the 98th and the 2nd percentile is lower or, if they are equal, the full span is lower. While it could seem counter-intuitive that the 98th and the 2nd can be frequently equal, this actually happens a lot due to the behaviour of clamping functions such as ReLU.

4 Applications and Experimental Evaluation

In this section we compare our method to other similar recent pruning algorithms introduced in Sect. 2. In order to have a fair comparison, we selected *property importance* methods focusing on the L1-norm of the filters [16], rank of the feature maps (HRank [8]), and layers' outputs like Apoz [11] and GM [17]. We first analyse the performances of the proposed technique (ReFT) for specific camera tasks, designed to be carried out in relatively small embedded devices. After that, we apply our pruning to VGG16 on Cifar10 to show that the proposed method is effective also when applied to more complex architectures.

4.1 Pruning CNNs for Camera Tasks

As already discussed, image processing for quality inspection in an industrial environment often involves strict requirements. For this reason, smart cameras that can pre-process frames during acquisition (for example by feeding images to

Table 1. Average accuracy, average peak position error, average height error, number of parameters and compression ratio for Peak network with 34 pruned kernels (out of the 40 available distributed across 3 conv layers). Pruning methods have been repeated 20 times. ReFT-S is the training of Peak-ReFT with random weights. See Fig. 2 for standard deviation.

Model	Acc	Pos err	Height err	Params	Flops	Ratio
Peaks	0.999	0.342	0.0149	2.22 K	2.412 M	1.00
Peaks-ReFT	**0.993**	**0.644**	**0.0471**	0.936 K	0.290 M	0.42
Peaks-APoZ	0.988	0.717	0.0566	0.885 K	0.295 M	0.42
Peaks-L1-norm	0.984	0.806	0.0635	0.936 K	0.290 M	0.42
Peaks-GM	0.965	1.04	0.0784	0.936 K	0.290 M	0.42
Peaks-ReFT-S	0.989	1.1400	0.0578	0.936 K	0.290 M	0.42

Table 2. Average accuracy, average dot position error, average eccentricity error, number of parameters and compression ratio with 34 pruned kernels (out of 40) in the first three convolutional layers. Pruning methods have been repeated 20 times. Dot-ReFT-S is the training of Dot-ReFT with random weights. See Fig. 2 for standard deviation.

Model	Acc	Pos err	Ecc err	Params	Flops	Ratio
Dots	1.000	1.11	0.073	14.2 K	10.537 M	1.00
Dots-ReFT	**0.999**	**3.21**	**0.073**	10.3 K	0.332 M	0.73
Dots-APoZ	0.997	3.73	0.137	10.2 K	0.711 M	0.71
Dots-L1-norm	0.791	5.91	0.153	10.3 K	0.332 M	0.73
Dots-GM	0.745	5.61	0.158	10.3K	0.332 M	0.73
Dots-HRank	0.953	4.57	0.156	10.3 K	0.332 M	0.73
Dots-ReFT-S	0.994	1.25	0.101	10.3 K	0.332 M	0.73

a built-in CNN) may offer a substantial advantage over classical image processing solutions [21,22]. Usually, such setups require extreme and specialised network pruning approaches, in order to improve both time and memory efficiency. As a case study, we show two practical applications which significantly benefit from the proposed pruning method, especially when implemented on a FPGA device.

The first is realized by a CNN to detect peaks in a one-dimensional light intensity timeserie. This is a typical scenario in 3D reconstruction in which planar laser beams are projected onto the object under study and observed by one or more cameras geometrically calibrated with the laser. The intersection of each laser plane with the object results in a line, usually orthogonal with the pixel arrangement of the linear camera. Therefore, each line produces a spike, or peak, whose position can be easily related with the depth of the object 3D point illuminated by the laser (See for example the signal plotted in the left column

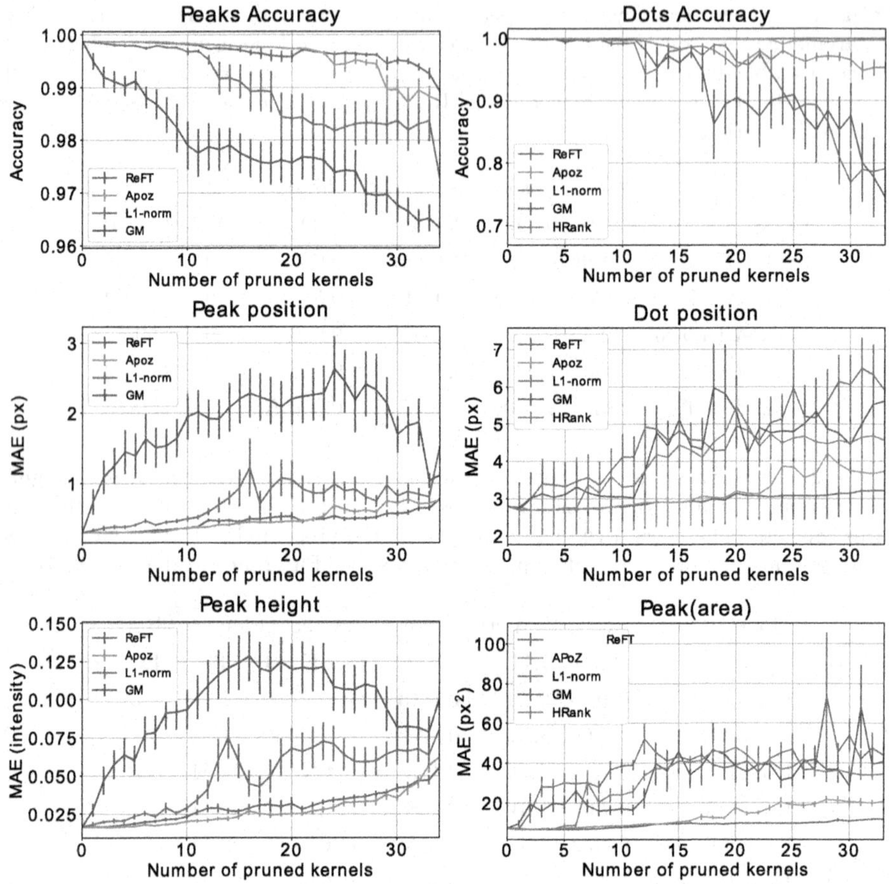

Fig. 2. Comparison of different pruning techniques for peak and dot detection networks (1st and 2nd columns respectively). For each task we report accuracy, MAE of position error and MAE of height and area.

of Fig. 1). Our tested model is a relatively simple feed-forward Convolutional Neural Network taking in input a vector of 1024 intensity values and producing a vector of N output bins, each one containing peak probability, height, location and width of detected peaks. The network is made of 4 convolutional blocks (interleaved by ReLU activations and maxpooling) and then it splits to compute the different losses.

The second case study is the 2-dimensional extension of the linear peak detection network to detect dots in image data (see the right column of Fig. 1 for some examples). The network architecture is essentially equal to the corresponding 1-dimensional case, except for it takes a 2D images as input and 1-dimensional convolutions are replaced with their 2D counterparts.

Both networks provide multiple outputs, namely: the probability of the presence of a peak or dot, the information about peak position, and its height. In the 2D case, we also consider dot area and eccentricity.

Synthetic Datasets. Our *Peaks* dataset contains 100000 line scan acquisitions divided into training, validation and test set with ratio 80:10:10. Intensity ranges from 0 to 255 in vectors of 1024 values representing a line-camera image. *Dots* dataset was generated by approximating the intensity response with a bivariate Normal function characterized by a certain height (the intensity of the dot), eccentricity (how much the dot deviates from being circular) and angle (the major axis orientation). Signals are assumed to be acquired 80 scanlines at a time and multiple dots can be simultaneously present in each image. It consists of 100000 acquisitions with separated test and validation set of 10000 samples each.

Network Training and Pruning. Both the networks were trained with a learning rate (lr) of $1E-5$, decreased by a factor of 0.1 if the loss does not improve for 3 consecutive epochs. The validation set is used to stop before over-fitting. Fine tuning after pruning is performed with $lr = 1E-5$ for a fixed number of epochs = 3. We pruned both the *Peaks* and *Dots* networks only from the first 3 blocks, which contain 16, 16 and 8 kernels respectively, leaving at least 1 kernel per block.

Results. Fig. 2 shows how the performance of the 1D peak detection (top) and 2D dot detection (bottom) networks are affected by the pruning process. Our method lead to a good prediction accuracy even if a severe number of kernels are removed. L1-norm tend to perform worst, with the accuracy dropping significantly especially for the 2D dot detection network. Together with the detection accuracy, position and height are better estimated when the network is pruned with our proposed method. Apoz shows similar performance but higher standard deviation. Tables 1 and 2 summarize the performance of the two networks while pruning an optimal number of kernels (33 in this case). It is interesting to notice that both the models pruned with our method (Peak-ReFT and Dots-ReFT) perform better than a model with the same number of kernels trained from scratch (Peak-ReFT-S and Dots-ReFT-S). In other words, it is better to trim a complex network than training a simpler network from the start.

4.2 VGG16 on Cifar10

To demonstrate that our method is valid also on more complex CNNs we used VGG16 [25] network on Cifar10 dataset [15]. Cifar10 contains 60000 RGB images belonging to 10 classes and it is often used together with VGG16 to assess the efficiency of compressing methods. VGG16 is a large convolutional network trained on the ILSVR2012 dataset. The network contains 13 convolutional layers with

3 fully connected on top and the activation function for each layer is a ReLU, except for the final softmax. In order to perform classification on a dataset different from the one the network has been trained on, we need to use *transfer learning.* We exploited the pretrained 13 convolutional layers, to which we attached two more fully connected layers with a small dropout rate and ReLU activations. Finally, we added one last fully connected layer to reduce the output to the correct number of classes. The images are resized from their 32×32 original shape to 48×48, which is the smallest input size required to be able to use all VGG16 convolutional layers. We split the images into 3 separated datasets for train, validation and test with a 60:20:20 ratio. A fast training with learning rate $3E-5$ is performed on Cifar10 dataset, using the validation set to stop the training at a proper time. Every time the pruning algorithm removes a filter we performed a fine tuning step with 5 epochs and a small learning rate set to $1E-6$, followed by another 5 epochs with the same learning rate divided by 10, to recover any loss in accuracy. We tested HRank with the same parameters except for one during the recovery stage, as the pruned kernels are removed in a single pass, and the authors suggest a higher number of epochs (50) to recover the accuracy. The convolutional layers are frozen both at training and pruning time, such that the network can only modify the fully connected weights.

Figure 3 shows the top1 accuracy varying the number of pruned kernels. Our method outperforms the others, with a particularly remarkable difference when more than 300 kernels are removed. Even though ReFT algorithm achieved fair superior performances, some credit has to be given to the other methods. In general, methods that are limited to compute metrics on the filter values (like L1-norm and GM) perform worse than ones analyzing the output of the layers (our method and Apoz). However, the latter are more computational intensive and require a representative dataset to be used, something particularly noticeable when working with images on large networks, such as Cifar10 on VGG16. HRank mitigated this problem by requiring only a small set of images to compute the output responses, but in our tests consistently performed worse than others. HRank, anyway, needs to be run only once, drastically decreasing the computing time during the pruning phase.

Table 3. Comparison of top1 accuracy, top5 accuracy, number of parameters, FLOPs and compression ratio achieved by filter pruning on VGG16 and Cifar10 after pruning 460 filters.

Model	Top1	Top5	Params	Flops	Ratio
VGG16	0.801	0.988	15.1 M	1.41 G	1.000
VGG16-ReFT	**0.780**	**0.986**	11.9 M	1.15 G	0.789
VGG16-APoZ	0.761	0.983	11.5 M	1.23 G	0.762
VGG16-L1-norm	0.731	0.979	11.9 M	1.15 G	0.789
VGG16-GM	0.581	0.944	11.9 M	1.15G	0.789

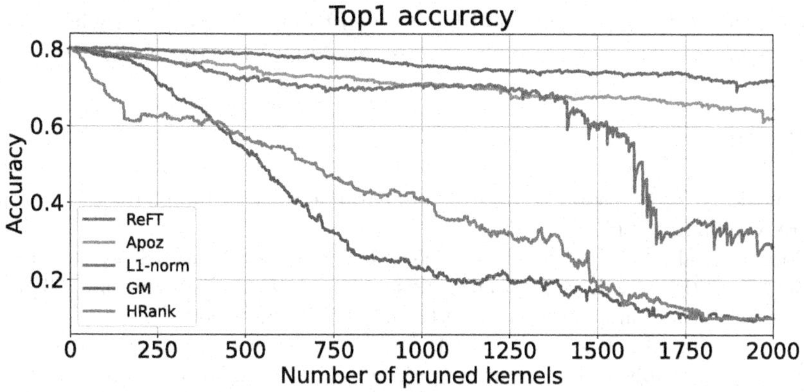

(a) Top1 accuracy of VGG16 on Cifar10 with different pruning methods.

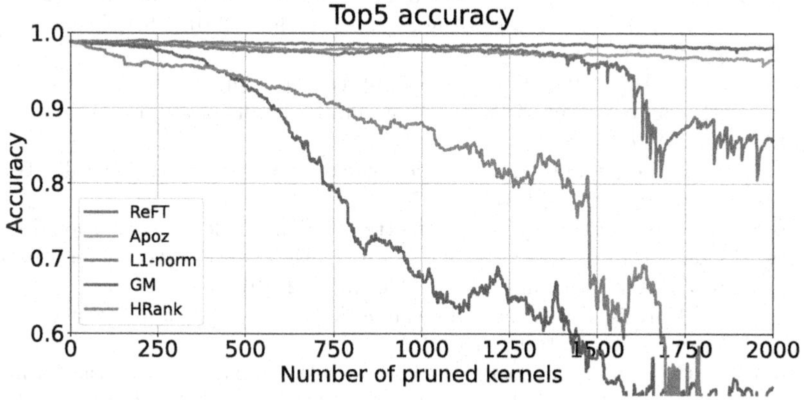

(b) Top5 accuracy of VGG16 on Cifar10 with different pruning methods.

Fig. 3. Accuracy loss as the number of pruned filter increases for the different methods analysed. The speed in performance degradation is connect to the experimental setup, as the fine-tuning phase does not take into consideration the validation loss for a proper stopping condition, but rather it runs for a fixed number of epochs.

5 Conclusions

We presented a simple CNN pruning method working by ranking the relevance of each convolutional kernel according to the output produced on a representative dataset. Our heuristic is simple to implement but it better preserves the network predicting power compared to similar state-of-the-art approaches while pruning a large amount of kernels.

We analysed two practical case study: peak detection in both 1 and 2 dimensional intensity signals to assess the feasibility on simple networks designed for FPGA hardware. In our tests, we almost halved the number of weights without a noticeable decrease of prediction accuracy. Even if developed to implement low-level vision tasks, our method has proven to be effective even when applied on classical datasets and network architectures like VGG16 on Cifar10.

References

1. Blalock, D., et al.: What is the state of neural network pruning? In: arXiv preprint arXiv:2003.03033 (2020)
2. Cao, S., et al.: ThinNet: an efficient convolutional neural network for object detection. In: 2018 24th International Conference on Pattern Recognition (ICPR), pp. 836–841 (2018). https://doi.org/10.1109/ICPR.2018.8545809
3. Courbariaux, M., Bengio, Y., David, J.P.: Training deep neural networks with low precision multiplications. In: arXiv preprint arXiv:1412.7024 (2014)
4. Garg, I., Panda, P., Roy, K.: A low effort approach to structured CNN design using PCA. IEEE Access **8**, 1347–1360 (2019)
5. Gasparetto, A. et al.: Cross-dataset data augmentation for convolutional neural networks training. In: vol. 2018-August, pp. 910–915 (2018). https://doi.org/10.1109/ICPR.2018.8545812
6. Han, S., Mao, H., Dally, W.J.: Deep compression: compressing deep neural networks with pruning, trained quantization and huffman coding. In: arXiv preprint arXiv:1510.00149 (2015)
7. Han, S., et al.: Learning both weights and connections for efficient neural networks. arXiv preprint arXiv:1506.02626 (2015)
8. He, Y., et al.: Filter pruning via geometric median for deep convolutional neural networks acceleration. In: Proceedings of the IEEE/CVF Conference on Computer Vision and Pattern Recognition, pp. 4340–4349 (2019)
9. Hinton, G., Vinyals, O., Dean, J.: Distilling the knowledge in a neural network. In: arXiv preprint arXiv:1503.02531 (2015)
10. Howard, A.G., et al.: Mobilenets: Efficient convolutional neural networks for mobile vision applications. In: arXiv preprint arXiv:1704.04861 (2017)
11. Hu, H., et al.: Network trimming: a data-driven neuron pruning approach towards efficient deep architectures. In: arXiv preprint arXiv:1607.03250 (2016)
12. Iandola, F.N., et al.: SqueezeNet: AlexNet-level accuracy with 50x fewer parameters and $<$ 0.5 MB model size (2016)
13. Jahanshahi, A.: TinyCNN: a tiny modular CNN accelerator for embedded FPGA. In: arXiv preprint arXiv:1911.06777 (2019)
14. Jin, J., Dundar, A., Culurciello, E.: Flattened convolutional neural networks for feedforward acceleration. In: arXiv preprint arXiv:1412.5474 (2014)
15. Krizhevsky, A., Nair, V., Hinton, G.: CIFAR-10 (Canadian Institute for Advanced Research). http://www.cs.toronto.edu/~kriz/cifar.html
16. Li, H., et al.: Pruning filters for efficient convnets. In: arXiv preprint arXiv:1608.08710 (2016)
17. Lin, M., et al.: Hrank: Filter pruning using high-rank feature map. In: Proceedings of the IEEE/CVF Conference on Computer Vision and Pattern Recognition, pp. 1529–1538 (2020)
18. Lin, S., et al.: Towards optimal structured cnn pruning via generative adversarial learning (2019)
19. Liu, Z., et al.: Learning efficient convolutional networks through network slimming. In: Proceedings of the IEEE International Conference on Computer Vision, pp. 2736–2744 (2017)

20. Liu, Z., et al.: Rethinking the value of network pruning. In: arXiv preprint arXiv:1810.05270 (2018)
21. Pistellato, M., Bergamasco, F., Albarelli, A., Torsello, A.: Dynamic optimal path selection for 3D triangulation with multiple cameras. In: Murino, V., Puppo, E. (eds.) ICIAP 2015. LNCS, vol. 9279, pp. 468–479. Springer, Cham (2015). https://doi.org/10.1007/978-3-319-23231-7_42
22. Pistellato, M., et al.: Robust joint selection of camera orientations and feature projections over multiple views, pp. 3703–3708 (2016). https://doi.org/10.1109/ICPR.2016.7900210
23. Qiu, J., et al.: Going deeper with embedded fpga platform for convolutional neural network. In: Proceedings of the 2016 ACM/SIGDA International Symposium on Field-Programmable Gate Arrays (2016)
24. Rastegari, M., Ordonez, V., Redmon, J., Farhadi, A.: XNOR-Net: Imagenet classification using binary convolutional neural networks. In: Leibe, B., Matas, J., Sebe, N., Welling, M. (eds.) ECCV 2016. LNCS, vol. 9908, pp. 525–542. Springer, Cham (2016). https://doi.org/10.1007/978-3-319-46493-0_32
25. Simonyan, K., Zisserman, A.: Very deep convolutional networks for large-scale image recognition (2014). CoRR abs/1409.1556
26. Suau, X., Apostoloff, N., et al.: Filter distillation for network compression. In: 2020 IEEE Winter Conference on Applications of Computer Vision (WACV). IEEE, pp. 3129–3138 (2020)
27. Sze, V., et al.: Efficient processing of deep neural networks: a tutorial and survey. In: Proceedings of the IEEE, vol. 105(12) (2017)
28. Zhang, C., Patras, P., Haddadi, H.: Deep learning in mobile and wireless networking: a survey. In: IEEE Communications surveys & tutorials, vol. 21 no. 3, pp. 2224–2287 (2019)
29. Zhang, X., et al.: Shuffenet: an extremely efficient convolutional neural network for mobile devices. In: Proceedings of the IEEE Conference on Computer Vision and Pattern Recognition, pp. 848–6856 (2018)
30. Zhu, M., Gupta, S.: To prune, or not to prune: exploring the efficacy of pruning for model compression. In: arXiv preprint arXiv:1710.01878 (2017)

Vision-Based Holistic Scene Understanding for Context-Aware Human-Robot Interaction

Giorgio De Magistris[1], Riccardo Caprari[1,2], Giulia Castro[1,2], Samuele Russo[2], Luca Iocchi[1], Daniele Nardi[1], and Christian Napoli[1](✉)

[1] Department of Computer, Automation and Management Engineering, Sapienza University of Rome, Via Ariosto 25, 00185 Rome, Italy
{demagistris,iocchi,nardi,cnapoli}@diag.uniroma1.it

[2] Department of Psychology, Sapienza University of Rome, Via dei Marsi 78, 00185 Rome, Italy
samuele.russo@uniroma1.it

Abstract. Human activity recognition systems from static images or video sequences are becoming more and more present in our life. Most computer vision applications such as human-computer interaction, virtual reality, public security, smart home monitoring, or autonomous robotics, to name a few, highly rely on human activity recognition. Of course, basic human activities, such as "walking" and "running", are relatively easy to recognize. On the other hand, identifying more complex activities is still a challenging task that could be solved by retrieving contextual information from the scene, such as objects, events, or concepts. Indeed, a careful analysis of the scene can help to recognize human activities taking place. In this work, we address a holistic video understanding task to provide a complete semantic level description of the scene. Our solution can bring significant improvements in human activity recognition tasks. Besides, it may allow equipping a robotic and autonomous system with contextual knowledge of the environment. In particular, we want to show how this vision module can be integrated into a social robot to build a more natural and realistic context-based Human-Robot Interaction. We think that social robots must be aware of the surrounding environment to react in a proper and socially acceptable way, according to the different scenarios.

Keywords: Human activity recognition · Human-robot interaction · Computer vision · Image understanding · Neural Networks

1 Introduction

Human activity recognition (HAR) has the aim of identifying human actions from the most simple ones such as gestures or atomic actions like "walking" or "sitting" to the most complex ones like behaviors or events, using sensory data

S. Bandini et al. (Eds.): AIxIA 2021, LNAI 13196, pp. 310–325, 2022.
https://doi.org/10.1007/978-3-031-08421-8_21

information. On the field of robotics and human-robot interaction, especially when elderly people are involved, HAR can represent an important moment that produces a feeling of comfort and reassurance. This can in turn: reduce the risk factors connected to the feeling of being "useless" and "incapable", increasing, instead, the positive feelings of self-efficacy, since the person can feel dependent on other humans. Moreover also a sense of empowerment can follow and allow the elderly person to feel more understood and at the same time less dependent on caregivers. On some occasions this interaction can also constitute a moment perceived as "company" that can reduce the feeling of loneliness, real or fantasized, which often accompanies the elderly person's experience. HAR from static images or video sequences has experienced significant growth over the last decade in the scientific areas of computer vision. As a consequence, a lot of applications in a wide spectrum of domains greatly rely on HAR systems. Few examples are human-computer interaction, augmented reality, intelligent home monitoring, or also video assistance and surveillance in public security, where crowds movements are tracked to detect violent or criminal situations. More complex applications also concern advanced robotics, including mobile robot navigation or human-robot cooperation, and it also touches the medical environment to ensure surgical operations or continuous patient monitoring. Of course basic human activities, such as "walking" and "running," are quite easy to recognize, but identifying more complex activities is still a challenging task, due to intraclass and interclass similarities problems. Namely, the same action can be expressed differently by diverse body movements of different users, and on the contrary different types of actions may show the same information or very similar features. Other common problems when dealing with HAR tasks are also related to complex background, lightness, scaling, and point of view that may represent significant limitations as well. In all these cases, only the contextual information extracted from the background and the detection of objects in the same scene may help to better understand the ongoing event and then the ongoing human activity. For this reason, in this work, we want to address a holistic video understanding (HVU) task, which is a multi-label and multi-task learning problem introduced in [1]. First of all, *Holism* is a theoretical position according to which the properties of a system cannot be explained just by its singular components, but capturing also their relative overall connections. It is a very common theory and widely used approach when we need to describe real-world phenomena, just look at the fundamental sciences of medicine or physics. Following this new current of thought, the aim of the holistic video understanding is not only to recognize specific and individual actions but also to provide a semantic level description of the scene describing the higher level connections among objects. Of course, the HVU task we propose includes human activity recognition and, at the same time, it provides valuable information on other multiple semantic categories. To naturally capture contextual information from dynamic real-world scenarios it's reasonable to use objects, scenes, attributes, concepts, actions, and events. First of all, the fact that we can identify together multiple semantic categories from the scene may be very useful for the recognition of specific and advanced actions, even in complex or cluttered background, or in a crowded environment with multiple subjects and actions, that is one of the biggest challenges in HAR. At the same time, this new holistic approach will allow capturing the contextual knowledge of the environment, not only to acquire information about the ongoing action but also to know where, why, and how that particular action is performed. In this way, for example, a robot could infer also the reasons and causes, which are hidden inside the scene, that led to perform a specific action. The ability to fast recognizing contextual information is a very strong and highly desirable feature for any intelligent robotic system that needs to react online to the dynamic situation evolving in time. Particularly, for social and assisting robots in public and private environments, the use of contextual knowledge can be a key factor for achieving higher flexibility and adaptability to environmental conditions.

The remainder of this paper is structured as follows. Section 2 analyzes existing literature and discusses the state-of-the-art in human activity recognition, holistic video understanding, and context-aware robots. Section 3 reviews some of the most influential HAR datasets over the last decade. Section 4 formalizes the problem statement and explains our proposed system architecture and methodology with particular attention to Convolutional Neural Networks and Recurrent Neural Networks. Section 5 presents experiments, implementation details, and their relative results. Section 6 shows how this vision-based holistic scene understanding module can be integrated to build an efficient context-aware human-robot interaction and possible application scenarios. Finally, in Sect. 7, we discuss conclusions and future directions.

2 Related Work

Human activity recognition has been widely explored in the last decade, given the growing technological progress in the field. Several methods and approaches have been studied in literature starting from a multi-modal human action analysis from gestures poses, facial expressions, and signals in general [2,3]. More advanced human activity recognition systems use depth cameras to create a more informative 3D representation of the human body as in [4,5] or also human body parts motion analysis from skeletal poses as in [6,7]. Only in the very recent years, research has focused on how HAR tasks can be expanded from single-label classification problems towards a more comprehensive understanding of image and video sequences. A first attempt was provided with the SOA dataset (Scene-Object-Actions) in [8], that first analyzed the possibility of applying the information learned from one task to improve the others. Only the last year, the authors of [1] provided a public available multi-label and multi-task video dataset intending to promote new research ideas and further works in the field of the holistic video understanding (HVU). This dataset strongly differs from the most influential ones in the HAR field, since it provides a significant increase both in the number of semantic categories (Scene-Object-Actions-Attribute-Concept-Event) and both in the corresponding number of labels per category. Indeed, the most common HAR video datasets, from the earliest ones such as UCF101 [9] and HMDB [23] to more recent and largest works such as ActivityNet [10] and Kinetics [11] are targeting human action or sport recognition in non complex background which makes them non-applicable in real-world applications. HVU dataset, instead, contains about 572K videos with approximately 9 million annotations spanning over 3142 labels among 6 different semantic categories. Given the significant improvements and the great potential of this very innovative dataset, the main goal of this work is to contribute and enlarge research in the holistic video understanding field by proposing a new model able to capture the whole information of a video. Our work is based on the idea proposed in [1] but it differentiates by introducing a new spatio-temporal network architecture: a Convolutional Neural Network (CNN) is used to acquire spatial information, combined with a Recurrent Neural Network (RNN) for capturing temporal relationships. Moreover, differently from previous works that just analyze possible solutions for recognizing human activities or the whole video content, our project wants to show how the holistic video understanding task can be successfully exploited to build a more natural context-aware human-robot interaction. Indeed it is another area that still needs to be explored to let many intelligent and robotic systems be operational in many advanced application domains. The necessity of having complementary holistic learning is also validated in [12], in which the authors show the substantial importance of having contextual knowledge as "the information that surrounds a situation of interest in the world", as anticipated in [13,14]. They identified 3 main benefits an intelligent system can acquire from the ability to quickly recognize the context: *(i)* robustness to complete the required tasks, namely the performance of the systems, as well as its sake of applicability *(ii)* adaptability to multiple operational conditions and application domains *(iii)* flexibility in tackling the main goal of a robot. In the last years, many approaches have just proven the benefits of using contextual information for solving robot navigation problems. For example, the authors of [26] develop an intelligent mobile robot system that understands the semantics of human environments and the spatial relationships with and between humans. Context-awareness for person following is considered in [27], while in [28] the robot's speed is adjusted when it is in a hallway setting. To the best of our knowledge, instead, very few experiments have been conducted in the field of context-aware human-robot interaction [29]. Even fewer works have shown how crucial contextual information can be leveraged to make the robot aware of the environment, and also reactive to various situations when interacting with real people. For this reason, the main goal of our work is not only to promote new ideas in the field of human activity recognition and holistic video understanding but also to demonstrate how they can be exploited to provide key information for the development of active and assistive social robots. This will allow not only to make the robot operative in variable conditions but also to avoid prefixed models that may result in non-natural robot behaviors and interactions, since models that are based solely on predefined user scenarios and action scripts may not be able to take into account the uncertainty introduced by variations in the environment or unclear expectations from the user [29].

3 Datasets

The most popular and commonly used video datasets in the field of human activity recognition are strictly targeting highly specific human actions or sports recognition. Early datasets in the HAR field like Hollywood [15] and UCF101 [9] were simple and were completely scripted datasets filmed in very ideal and fully controlled conditions. Moreover, they include very little variation in the ambiance parameters such as lighting, occlusion, and viewpoints. In most cases, the non-complex backgrounds and the non-intraclass variations in human movements make these datasets non-applicable for real-world applications. More recent datasets like Something-Something [16], ActvityNet [10] and Kinetics [11] typically consider unconstrained videos, which emulate real environments. Concurrently, being datasets with million-scale samples, they provide a great increase in the number of labels and videos. However, they are always limited to a single semantic category, allowing to recognize human actions only, while leaving a significant gap towards describing the overall content of a video. This holistic spirit is first observable in the SOA dataset [8] and YouTube-8 M [17] that is the largest multi-label video classification dataset, composed of ∼8 million videos to recognize several visual concepts. Above all, the HVU dataset [1] has brought in last year more attention to holistic video understanding as a comprehensive and multi-faceted problem, as it encompasses the largest and most comprehensive list of semantic categories. HVU consists of 572 k real-world trimmed video clips whose duration can vary from a minimum of 2 s length to a maximum of 10 s. Each video sample is associated with a set of labels (or tags). Each one of the tags can belong to 6 main semantic categories: scene, object, action, event, attribute, and concept, that are able to naturally capture real-world scenarios. There are in total 3142 labels with, on average, ∼2112 annotations per label between training, validation, and test set. The dataset is not manually annotated since it would require a vast amount of time due to the considerable number of labels and videos. The automatic annotation mechanism uses the Google Vision API [19] and Sensifai Video Tagging API [18], providing relatively coarse and approximate results and allowing to select exactly 30 tags for each video. Then the tags are adjusted and arranged manually to remove amiss labels. For a better understanding of the dataset.

4 Methodology

In this section, we first introduce the concept of Convolutional Neural Networks (CNNs) and how they work with data of different dimensionality. Next, we proceed by explaining the idea behind Recurrent Neural Networks (RNNs) and by reviewing the state of the art of this class of Artificial Neural Networks (ANNs).

Finally, our model architecture is introduced to tackle the problem of classification while satisfying its requirements. We model the problem of HAR as a Supervised Learning (SL) classification task over the labels of different categories C_i with $i \in [1,6]$, more precisely, $C \in$ {object, action, concept, scene, attribute, event}. For each category i, we assume there is a set of binary labels L_i with a cardinality that is category-dependent. In particular, a value $y \in L_i$, $i \in [1,6]$, is equal to 1 if the corresponding label appears in the video, 0 otherwise. In the training phase, the vision-based system receives, as input, an unordered set of N videos $\{v_n\}_{n=0}^{N}$ of dimension $[H \times W \times C]$, with C fixed to 3 as we work with RGB data and H, W, the height and width of the videos, respectively. The length of the videos can be variable and depends on the specific dataset. Assigning a set of binary labels for each video and setting $L = \sum_{i=0}^{6} L_i$, we can write the dataset as $D = \{(v_n, L_n)_{n=0}^{N}\}$. In the test phase, given a set of videos, we want to classify each video with its labels accordingly. Finally, the vision module is exploited in a HRI setting to detect which scenario is more plausible in a real-world designed application and how the robot should act in line with the visual context.

4.1 Convolutional Neural Network

Convolutional Neural Network is a deep learning model for processing image data in grid-shape matrices, with the primary goal of identifying features and extracting specific and even complex patterns from an image. A CNN can successfully capture the pixel spatial dependencies and recognize more sophisticated feature schemes to achieve effective results in classification and object recognition tasks than a simple feed-forward network. A CNN architecture comprises multiple convolution layers, followed by pooling layers and fully connected layers. This connectivity structure reduces the size of the image and thus the number of parameters to be optimized during the training process, still keeping salient features crucial to accomplish the intended visual task. The core layer of a CNN is the convolutional one. In order to capture salient information, the image, i.e., a tensor, is convolved with a set of learnable filters, also known as kernels or weights. The filters are stacked together as multiple stages of feature extractor: earlier stages compute basic features, higher stages focus on more global and invariant features [30]. Given an input image I of dimension $H \times W$, and a squared filter K of dimension $F \times F$, a 2D convolution operation can be mathematically formalized as:

$$O[i,j] = \sum_{m=-\infty}^{\infty} \sum_{n=-\infty}^{\infty} K[m,n] \cdot I[i-m, j-n] \quad (1)$$

where O is the output feature map, and each pixel location $O[i,j]$ is computed as the weighted sum of the original pixel and the eight nearby ones.

4.2 Recurrent Neural Network

Recurrent Neural Network (RNN) is introduced in [31]. This type of neural network is commonly used to process sequential data that show a temporal correlation. Its functioning consists of maintaining internal memory states, called *hidden states*, while handling data sequences of variable length, just like videos. The process of a Recurrent Neural Network carrying memory can be written as:

$$h_t = \phi(Kx_t + Th_{t-1}) \tag{2}$$

The formula states that the hidden state at time t depends on the previous hidden state at $t-1$ multiplied by a transition matrix T and the input at time step t multiplied by a weight matrix K. This sum is then given as input to an activation function ϕ that is typical $tanh$ or $ReLU$. Equation 2 can be seen as a loop in which each hidden state h_t maintain the memory of the state up to $t-1$, as long as this can be traced. Indeed, some of the drawbacks of RNNs are the vanishing and exploding gradient problems, resulting in major difficulties in keeping track of long-term dependencies. Most of the RNN disadvantages have been solved with the introduction of a variation called Long Short-Term Memory (LSTM) [32]. This neural network, in fact, is capable of capturing long-term dependencies. LSTMs present a different and more sophisticated structure, starting from the addition of the cell states C_t. Moreover, an LSTM regulate its information flow using three different gates:

- Input gate

$$i_t = \sigma(W_i\,[h_{t-1}, x_t] + b_i)\tilde{C_t} = tanh(W_c\,[h_{t-1}, x_t] + b_c) \tag{3}$$

- Forget gate

$$f_t = \sigma(W_f\,[h_{t-1}, x_t] + b_f) \tag{4}$$

- Output gate

$$C_t = f_t\,C_{t-1} + i_t\,\tilde{C}_t o_t = \sigma(W_o\,[h_{t-1}, x_t] + b_o)h_t = o_t\,tanh(C_t) \tag{5}$$

These gates together completely solve the vanishing gradient problem that occurs in the vanilla RNNs. While LSTMs are well suited for capturing temporal correlations along an input sequence, they require much memory and may take longer to train. In the last years, a new class of RNN has been introduced in [33], namely, Gated Recurrent Unit (GRU). GRUs inherits LSTMs structure with the difference that the output gate is discarded. Indeed, the hidden state is completely exposed, without any control, while the cell state C is not used anymore. In this way, the structure of GRUs results less complex and so computationally more efficient than LSTMs. Another note in favor of GRUs is that they perform better on smaller datasets and almost equal to LSTMs on bigger amounts of data [34].

4.3 CNN + RNN Architecture

While CNNs are powerful feed-forward artificial neural networks suitable for spatial data, on the other side, sequential data like videos represent temporal information of arbitrary length which is better handled by Recurrent Neural Networks. However, the authors of [1] show how Convolutional Neural Networks that work in 3 dimensions (3D CNNs), in combination with 2D CNNs, can capture both spatial and temporal details from sequential data. Moreover, previous works like [35] and [36], already proposed the use of 3D ConvNets in HAR achieving promising outcomes. This simple architecture consists of expanding the 2D Convolution explained in Sect. 4.1 with a third dimension that represents the time steps. In this way, videos can be processed as a series of 3D volumes. Furthermore, recent works have reached state-of-the-art results combining 3D CNNs with RRNs ([37–39]) in human activity recognition and prediction tasks. Although higher dimension ConvNets help to catch richer motion information, they bring a substantial number of parameters that make the computation more complex. In addition, the purpose of this work is to design a robotics application that most likely has limited computational resources which are in contrast with 3D CNNs characteristics. A reasonable architecture that meets the requirements of our application can be a simple concatenation of 2D Convolutional layers with an RNN module. In particular, as mentioned in Sect. 4.2, GRUs are, in terms of performance, comparable to LSTMs while also exploiting a much lighter structure. For this reason, we propose the use of a CNN-GRU architecture to solve the first task of video labels classification problem. Our model architecture is composed of several layers. The input of the network is a batch of videos that can be seen as a set of images (frames) sequences or, formally, as a tensor of dimension (b, t, h, w, c) where: b is the batch size, t the time steps, h and w respectively the height and width of the images, and c its channels. Input data flows into a CNN block made of groups of 2D Convolutional layers and 2D Max Pooling operations. As explained in Subsect. 4.1, this process reduces input size while expanding its depth in terms of feature extraction. Afterward, the data tensor dimension is reduced using a 2D Global Max Pooling operation and its shape becomes (b, t, f) with f the final number of features, in this case, 64. The three-dimension CNN output is straightly given as input to the GRU block. This latter looks for temporal correlations in the features of the videos and returns a matrix of dimension (b, u) which are the hidden states of each video at their last timestep. In fact, u is the number of units of the GRU which also corresponds to hidden states length. A set of fully-connected layers is then placed after the recurrent action. In particular, we use a *Sigmoid* activation function for the very last *Dense* layer, in order to predict a set of probabilities in the [0,1] range for each label in all categories. Therefore, the number of units of this last layer depends on the total number of labels in the dataset.

5 Experiments

The model architecture introduced in the previous section is evaluated with a subset of the HVU [1] dataset. We first introduce how we select a portion of the data and which metrics are used to carry out this task. We proceed by listing some of the implementation details of our work. In the end, we analyze and discuss the training and test phases of our model.

5.1 Dataset

We collected part of the data from the Large Scale holistic video understanding dataset instead of using it entirely. Indeed, two strong reasons led us not to use the entire dataset. The first motivation is that the HVU dataset has more than 3k labels and not all of them might be of interest in designing an HRI application. Selecting a subset of labels, consequently, reduces the number of annotations, and so videos. The second reason is that a large dataset of 572k videos requires a model with many parameters and, in consequence, a huge number of computational resources. The first metric we adopt to lighten the dataset is to re-order the labels of each category by the number of their annotations in the videos. In this way, we have a clear view of the most frequent labels. Next, we pick a subset of labels for each category from the ordered list. Moreover, we manually add some labels which we think to be helpful in an HRI scenario. These two actions lead us to a total number of 80 selected labels, about 13 per category. After an initial screening of the labels, we select the videos to be used in the training and test steps. To accomplish the task, we use an effective metric, which we name discard factor (d_f). This parameter has the task of discarding videos that contain a low number of activations, i.e., the number of 1s in the binary vector of labels describing the video, as explained in section ??. Given a video, we compare the discard factor with the ratio between the number of labels present in the video that belong to our 80 selected labels and the number of its total annotations. If this ratio is below d_f then the video is discarded. Next, we drop from the video the labels different from the selected ones and ensure each video to have at least 3 activations. In this manner, we get many samples with multiple labels present at the same time, ensuring the model recognizes multiple entities together. This is also done to increase as much as possible the ratio between 1 s and 0 s in the binary vectors of labels. Indeed, using a really small number of non-weighted activations could lead the model to always predict zeros. The other important reason we use the discard factor is to obtain a set of videos that don't refer to an excessively complex context that differs too much from the background areas described by the selected labels. In terms of our implementation, we have set $d_f = 0.68$. Finally, we further limit the number of annotations for each of the 80 selected labels to be 4000. In this manner, we reduce the imbalance of video annotations among the selected labels, avoiding too many activations for a set of them. In particular, given the annotations of a video, if a label has reached its limit and is among them, we discard the entire video. We prefer to have a balanced number of labels for each category instead of an equal number of annotations for each label. In this way, we show the model's fair ability to recognize different labels from different categories. An alternative would be to balance both things setting this up an optimization problem. This, however, could result in a long and complex procedure. This problem can be resumed as a choice between innovation and performance. In the first case, we push the model to recognize diverse categories of entities. In the second, we aim at a balanced number of annotations and so enough data for each label not to compromise the model's capability while renouncing on recognizing different context areas. After these preprocessing steps, we obtain a dataset of ~10k videos. Since the original HVU dataset is composed of videos of different aspect ratios, including vertical videos, we decide to apply a center cropping to obtain a fixed aspect ratio. During the experiments, this operation doesn't show notable disadvantages in model performance. In particular, we use 0.66 as aspect ratio and resize the videos to be $(vid_w, vid_h, vid_c) = (150, 100, 3)$. Finally, we discard videos having less than 60 frames, which corresponds to 2 s if the video is recorded at 30 fps (like the majority of the videos from the HVU dataset), because during training each sample is clipped at 60 frames from the start in order to have sequences with the same length inside a batch. Thereby, we obtain a final dataset of 8k videos.

5.2 Implementation Details

For the implementation, we highly rely on TensorFlow 2.4 framework. In particular, we build an efficient data pipeline to process videos as a set of images using *TFRecords* format [20] and *tf.data* API [21]. This significantly increases performance during the training process. We train the network from scratch using mini-batch gradient descent with a batch size of $b = 32$. We normalize the dataset dividing each video frame by 255 to transform values in [0, 1] range and help the convergence of the model. Moreover, we cut videos from the start to have exactly 60 frames and process simultaneously multiple batches (batch, frames, height, width, channels). However, we would like to point out that, at inference time, the model is still capable of classifying videos of variable length. The validation set is composed of the 20% of the dataset, and we use Adam optimizer with learning rate $lr = 1e{-}4$, and decay equal to 0.9. We decide to fix the number of GRU units to 64 and use a dropout value of 0.2 to prevent overfitting. All these values come from a fine-tuning procedure. For the loss, we use binary cross-entropy (BCE) since our ground truth labels are either zeros or ones. In particular, we implement a modified version of BCE, which weighs the values 1 in the labels 2.5 times more than the zeros. In this way, we adjust the balance of annotations in the videos. The evaluation metrics that we use are binary accuracy, precision, and recall, all with a threshold of 0.5. Our network has 11 layers for a total number of 77k parameters, which makes it pretty light. To accomplish our experiments we make use of an NVIDIA RTX 3060 12 GB GPU, while the mean training time for one epoch (validation step included) is about 270 s.

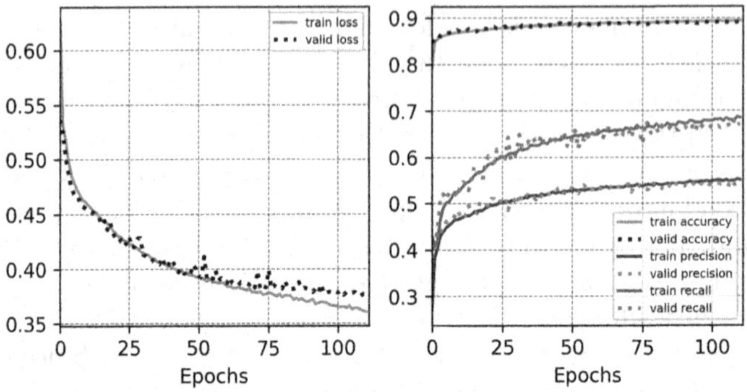

Fig. 1. (Left) Training and validation curves for weighted binary cross-entropy loss. (Right) Training and validation curves for accuracy, precision, and recall.

5.3 Result Analysis

The performance results of our model on the parsed dataset are shown in Fig. 1. We do not report HATNet [1] as a baseline since no source code has been made available by the authors. Moreover, not enough implementation details were provided to reproduce the network and use it on our dataset. The presented results refer to a training procedure of 110 epochs. The left plot shows the loss curve, which is a weighted binary cross-entropy. As evidenced by the trend, the network presents minor issues of underfitting in the first part caused by the small dropout in the GRU layer. In the end, there is a small gap of overfitting between the training and validation losses. Instead, the accuracy on the right plot presents a stable and slowly-growing behavior and reaches, at the last epoch, a score of 0.89. Conversely, the precision reaches a lower value of $\sim$0.55 while also showing no overfitting tendency. The highlighted difference between accuracy and precision could be due to the unbalanced distribution of the labels' video annotations. The recall, instead, reaches a value of $\sim$0.68 both for training and validation. In summary, the network can recognize the labels in the video and perceive many true positives. Instead, it suffers from false positives due to the missing labels of the HVU dataset. This can also be noticed by the recall being higher than the precision. These results confirm that the model can capture the spatial and temporal information in the videos and predict in a good way ground truth labels.

6 Context-Aware Human-Robot Interaction

In this chapter, we discuss and analyze a possible HRI application that exploits the holistic scene understanding vision module. The aim is to elaborate on how the robot's interaction performance can be improved when contextual knowledge is provided to the embedding system. Indeed, human-robot interaction can take several advantages from being context-aware [29]. First of all, the ability

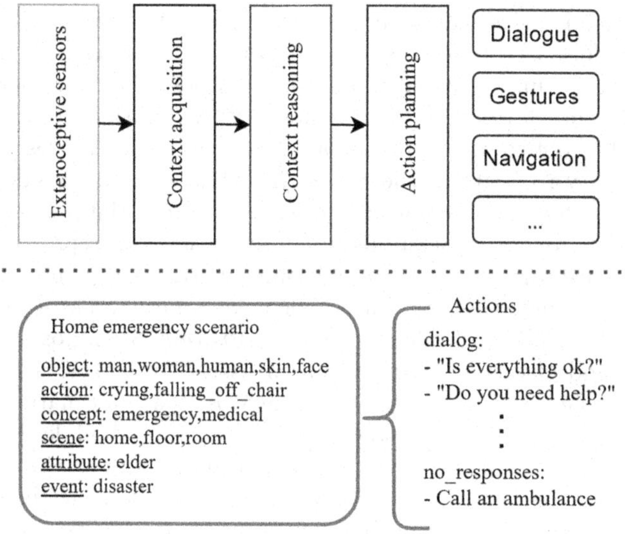

Fig. 2. (Up) A robot framework in an HRI setting. (Down) Example of context scenario.

to be operative and deployable in different application domains, and adaptable to multiple operational conditions, which is a key factor for achieving precision and robustness when accomplishing the desired task. Secondly, the information extracted from the context can be extremely useful to control the interaction so that it appears much more natural according to the particular situation. Moreover, this induced behavior could also be an important milestone in terms of the robot's social acceptance. We propose a complete architectural framework for developing a context-based human-robot interaction. It includes three main components: (*i*) a vision-based context acquisition module with the aim of extracting contextual information labels from the environment by using a holistic scene understanding; (*ii*) a context reasoning module for translating contextual knowledge into agent's behaviors; (*iii*) an action planner module to control the interaction employing motion, gestures, communication, and other means. A complete sketch of the framework is shown in the upper part of Fig. 2.

6.1 Application

We present a proof of concept on a possible application that makes use of the holistic scene understanding capabilities. In its general form, an HRI framework should be able to perceive environmental information. In particular, we require the robot to possess a vision system, such as an accessible low-resolution RGB camera. For the moment, we exclude the use of advanced and expensive sensors like LiDARs. Since we are in a HRI setting, the robot must have means of communication, such as automatic speech recognition and Text-To-Speech (TTS). This is necessary to expose a realistic behavior to the user while not making him disdain the technological capabilities of the robot. Another attribute of interest, especially for social robots, is to be capable of gesturing and, eventually, to move in the environment. When a robot approaches a human, it needs to have some sort of context reasoning and context representation. Specifically, when we refer to the context we point out a set of high-level features that improve robots' capability to adapt in the real world while standing beside humans. In our application, we use different categories labels from the real world as high-level features for robots' understanding. Once we have the representation of the context, we move forward with the reasoning part. As a result, we introduce the concept of context scenario which is defined as *an unordered set of category labels that, put together, refer to a particular situation*. Scenarios are, in general, hand-crafted and customizable by the final user. The aim of the context reasoning part in the framework is to select the Most Likely Scenario (MLS) using the probabilities of the labels extracted from the vision module. In this way, is possible to link a set of actions to the various scenarios and let the robot plan an action, based also on humans' requests and needs. As shown in the bottom part of Fig. 2, we provide an example of context scenario. In the first part, we select a set of the proposed labels which comes divided into 6 categories. Subsequently, a group of possible actions is linked to the scenario, letting the robot plan among them. For this purpose many types of planning can be used, like the one based on user interactions as proposed before. Among the possible test cases, one of the most interesting that could happen and has to be analyzed is when multiple scenarios occur. To solve this issue we propose priority-level context scenarios. As said before, a scenario takes place when it's considered the most likely one. This imposes the check of scenario's labels probabilities and a threshold value that establishes when a particular situation is happening. However, this doesn't guarantee the recognition of a single scenario, especially in a wide multi-tasking environment. Apart from the likelihood, we consider also a priority level which makes the difference in multiple-scenarios settings. In this way, urgent scenarios can take place safely while same-priority scenarios can be selected randomly when overlapping happens.

7 Conclusion and Further Work

In this work, we address the problem of Human Action Recognition (HAR) and expand its horizon presenting holistic approach for video understanding in Human-Robot Interaction (HRI). This new perspective consists of recognizing human activities while also considering other key factors like the scene, the objects, or the concept. We propose a CNN-RNN architecture to solve the problem of multi-labeled video classification. The results show that the proposed methodologies can be well suited to a medium-sized dataset. We further design an HRI scenario-based application showing its possible benefits and test cases. In the future, we want to focus on different application fields suitable for our conceptual HRI pipeline. In the first place, the development of a scenario-based application in a social robot like Pepper from SoftBank Robotics [42]. This, together with human questionnaire analysis [41], would show the effects of context acquisition on robot behaviors, which we think could be particularly beneficial. In certain circumstances, such as in a nursing home, the constant presence of the operator is not always possible and this can result in possible episodes or moments in which the elderly person remains alone when he decides to take an action. The presence of the robot would therefore allow to offer a logistic support and perform functions in order to help the elder. For example, when an elder is alone and wants to reach an object far from his reach, the robot recognizing the action of the person can help the elderly in carrying at the end of his behavior aimed at a purpose. The same scenario can be applied for youngsters and children, enforcing a list of allowed and forbidden objects to make reachable. In facts, this same principle can be extended into other contexts where there are different types of frailty. In this way the fragile individual could enjoy a moment in which his request is listened to and welcomed, giving the child a feeling of gratification and interaction. A further improvement for the HRI system could also include more advanced forms of automatic reasoning. As already done in [29] and [40], robot's interaction behaviors can be modeled using, specific to a given context, a Partially Observable Markov Decision Process (POMDP). This will allow us to condition on the observations, that is the contextual information, the future actions of the robot. Another possible direction of future work could explore a similar strategy for developing a visual context-aware Automatic Speech Recognition system (VC-ASR). The basic idea is exploiting visual signals and contextual knowledge to improve the robustness and reliability of ASR, with particular attention to grounding and re-ranking. Indeed, we can leverage the acquired visual context to re-rank the lists of transcriptions, and to ground text hypothesis from the first pass of ASR.

Acknowledgments. This research was supported supported by the HERMES (WIRED) project within Sapienza University of Rome Big Research Projects Grant Framework 2020.

References

1. Diba, A., et al.: Large scale holistic video understanding. In: Vedaldi, A., Bischof, H., Brox, T., Frahm, J.-M. (eds.) ECCV 2020. LNCS, vol. 12350, pp. 593–610. Springer, Cham (2020). https://doi.org/10.1007/978-3-030-58558-7_35
2. Jaimes, A., Sebe, N.: Multimodal human-computer interaction: a survey. Comput. Vis. Image Underst. **108**(1–2), 116–134 (2007)
3. Bonanno, F., Capizzi, G., Coco, S., Napoli, C., Laudani, A., Sciuto, G.L.: Optimal thicknesses determination in a multilayer structure to improve the SPP efficiency for photovoltaic devices by an hybrid FEM - Cascade Neural Network based approach. In: 2014 International Symposium on Power Electronics. Electrical Drives, Automation and Motion, SPEEDAM, vol. 2014, pp. 355–362 (2014)
4. Aggarwal, J.K., Xia, L.: Human activity recognition from 3D data: a review. Pattern Recogn. Lett. **48**, 70–80 (2014)
5. Li, W., Zhang, Z., Liu, Z.: Action recognition based on a bag of 3D points, Computer Vision and Pattern Recognition (CVPR) (2010)

6. Chen, L., Wei, H., Ferryman, J.: Tracking-based 3D human skeleton extraction from stereo video camera toward an on-site safety and ergonomic analysis. Computational Vision Group. School of Systems Engineering, University of Reading, UK (2013)
7. Liu, M., Han, S., Lee, S.: A survey of human motion analysis using depth imagery. Constr. Innov. **16**(3), 348–367 (2016)
8. Ray, J., et al.: Scenes-objects-actions: a multi-task, multi-label video dataset. In: European Conference on Computer Vision (ECCV) (2018)
9. Soomro, K., Zamir, A.R., Shah, M.: UCF101: a dataset of 101 human actions classes from videos in the wild. Center for Research in Computer Vision (CRCV) (2012)
10. Heilbron, F.C., Escorcia, V., Ghanem, B., Niebles, J.C.: ActivityNet: a large-scale video benchmark for human activity understanding. In: IEEE Conference on Computer Vision and Pattern Recognition (CVPR) (2015)
11. Kay, W., et al.: The kinetics human action video dataset. In: IEEE Conference on Computer Vision and Pattern Recognition (CVPR) (2017)
12. Bloisi, D.D., Nardi, D., Riccio, F., Trapani, F.: Context in robotics and information fusion. In: Snidaro, L., García, J., Llinas, J., Blasch, E. (eds.) Context-Enhanced Information Fusion. ACVPR, pp. 675–699. Springer, Cham (2016). https://doi.org/10.1007/978-3-319-28971-7_25
13. Snidaro, L., García, J., Llinas, J.: Context-based information fusion: a survey and discussion. Inf. Fusion **25**, 16–31 (2015)
14. Nowak, B.A., Nowicki, R.K., Woźniak, M., Napoli, C.: Multi-class nearest neighbour classifier for incomplete data handling. In: Rutkowski, L., Korytkowski, M., Scherer, R., Tadeusiewicz, R., Zadeh, L.A., Zurada, J.M. (eds.) ICAISC 2015. LNCS (LNAI), vol. 9119, pp. 469–480. Springer, Cham (2015). https://doi.org/10.1007/978-3-319-19324-3_42
15. Laptev, I., Marszałek, M., Schmid, C., Rozenfeld, B.: Learning realistic human actions from movies. In: 26th IEEE Conference Computer Vision Pattern Recognition (CVPR) , pp. 1–8 (2008)
16. Goyal, R., et al.: The "something something" video database for learning and evaluating visual common sense. In: IEEE International Conference of Computer Vision (ICCV) (2017)
17. Abu-El-Haija, S., et al.: Youtube-8m: a large-scale video classification benchmark. CoRR, abs/1609.08675 (2016)
18. Sensifai video tagging API. www.sensifai.com
19. Google vision AI API. https://cloud.google.com/vision
20. TFRecord TensorFlow Tutorial. www.tensorflow.org/tutorials/load_data/tfrecord
21. tf.data TensorFlow API. www.tensorflow.org/api_docs/python/tf/data
22. Beddiar, D.R., Nini, B., Sabokrou, M., Hadid, A.: Vision-based human activity recognition: a survey. Multimedia Tools Appl. **79**(41), 30509–30555 (2020). https://doi.org/10.1007/s11042-020-09004-3
23. Kuehne, H., Jhuang, H., Garrote, E., Poggio, T., Serre, T.: HMDB: a large video database for human motion recognition. In: Proceedings of the IEEE International Conference on Computer Vision, pp. 2556–2563 (2011)
24. Karpathy, A. et al.: Large-scale video classification with convolutional neural networks (2014)
25. Sigurdsson, G.A., Varol, G., Wang, X., Farhadi, A., Laptev, I., Gupta, A.: Hollywood in homes: crowdsourcing data collection for activity understanding. In: Leibe, B., Matas, J., Sebe, N., Welling, M. (eds.) ECCV 2016. LNCS, vol. 9905, pp. 510–526. Springer, Cham (2016). https://doi.org/10.1007/978-3-319-46448-0_31

26. Cosgun, A., Christensen, H.I.: Context-aware robot navigation using interactively built semantic maps. Paladyn Journal of Behavioral Robotics (2018)
27. Zender, H., Jensfelt, P., Kruijff, G.: Human-and situation-aware people following. In: 16th IEEE International Symposium on Robot and Human interactive Communication (RO-MAN), pp. 1131–1136 (2007)
28. Pacchierotti, E., Christensen, H.I., Jensfelt, P.: Human-robot embodied interaction in hallway settings: a pilot user study. In: IEEE International Workshop on Robot and Human Interactive Communication (ROMAN), pp. 164–171 (2005)
29. Quintas, J., Martins, G.S., Santos, L., Menezes, P., Dias, J.: Toward a context-aware human-robot interaction framework based on cognitive development. IEEE Trans. Syst. Man Syst. Cybern. **49**(1), 227–237 (2018)
30. Capizzi, G., Coco, S., Sciuto, G.L., Napoli, C.: A new iterative FIR filter design approach using a gaussian approximation. IEEE Sign. Process. Lett. **25**(11), 1615–1619 (2018)
31. Rumelhart, D., Hinton, G., Williams, R.: Learning representations by back-propagating errors. Nature **323**(6088), 533–536 (1986)
32. Hochreiter, S., Schmidhuber, J.: Long short-term memory. Neural Comput. **9**(8), 1735–80 (1997)
33. Cho, K., et al.:Learning phrase representations using RNN encoder-decoder for statistical machine translation. arXiv preprint arXiv:1406.1078 (2014)
34. Chung, J., Gulcehre, C., Cho, K., and Bengio, Y.: Empirical evaluation of gated recurrent neural networks on sequence modeling. arXiv preprint arXiv:1412.3555 (2014)
35. Tran, D., Bourdev, L., Fergus, R., Torresani, L., and Paluri, M.: Learning spatiotemporal features with 3D convolutional networks. In: IEEE International Conference on Computer Vision (ICCV), pp. 4489–4497 (2015)
36. Ji, S., Xu, W., Yang, M., Yu, K.: 3D convolutional neural networks for human action recognition. IEEE TPAMI **35**(1), 221–231 (2013)
37. Yao, L., Qian, Y.: DT-3DResNet-LSTM: an architecture for temporal activity recognition in videos. In: Hong, R., Cheng, W.-H., Yamasaki, T., Wang, M., Ngo, C.-W. (eds.) PCM 2018. LNCS, vol. 11164, pp. 622–632. Springer, Cham (2018). https://doi.org/10.1007/978-3-030-00776-8_57
38. Umamakeswari, A., Angelus, J., Kannan, M., Bragadeesh, S. A.: Action recognition using 3D CNN and LSTM for video analytics. In: International Conference on Intelligent Computing and Communication. Springer, Singapore (2020). https://doi.org/10.1007/978-981-15-1084-7_51
39. Alfaifi, R., Artoli, A.M.: Human action prediction with 3D-CNN. SN Comput. Sci. **1**(5), 1–15 (2020). https://doi.org/10.1007/s42979-020-00293-x
40. Kim, J.: POMDP-based human-robot interaction behavior model. J. Inst. Control **20**(6), 599–605 (2014)
41. Bartneck, C., Croft, E., Kulic, D., Zoghbi, S.: Measurement instruments for the anthropomorphism, animacy, likeability, perceived intelligence, and perceived safety of robots. Int. J. Soc. Robot. **1**(1), 71–81 (2009). https://doi.org/10.1007/s12369-008-0001-3
42. Pandey, A. K., and Gelin, R.: A mass-produced sociable humanoid robot: pepper: the first machine of its kind. In: IEEE Robotics & Automation Magazine (2018)

Human Detection in Drone Images Using YOLO for Search-and-Rescue Operations

Sergio Caputo, Giovanna Castellano, Francesco Greco, Corrado Mencar, Niccolò Petti, and Gennaro Vessio(✉)

Department of Computer Science, University of Bari Aldo Moro, Bari, Italy
{giovanna.castellano,corrado.mencar,gennaro.vessio}@uniba.it

Abstract. Today, unmanned aerial vehicles, more commonly known as drones, can be equipped with high-resolution cameras and embedded GPUs powerful enough to provide effective and efficient aid to Search-and-Rescue (SAR) operations in remote and hostile environments. Locating victims, who may be unconscious or injured, as quickly as possible is critical to improving their chance of survival. Therefore, using drones as flying machines for computer vision can increase the detection rate while reducing rescue time. In this paper, we present the results of an experimental evaluation in which we used the latest, lightweight version of the YOLO detection algorithm, namely YOLOv5, to detect humans in danger using two new benchmark datasets specifically designed for SAR with drones. The results obtained are encouraging, as they are competitive with respect to the state-of-the-art in terms of detection accuracy, but with much faster detection time.

Keywords: Drones · Search-and-Rescue · Computer vision · YOLOv5

1 Introduction

Search-and-Rescue (SAR) is the search for people in danger or imminent danger to rescue them. Rescue operations must be performed quickly, as any delay can potentially cause injury or even human loss. Furthermore, the environments in which they are performed are often hostile, such as in the case of post-disaster scenes, low light situations, inaccessible areas, etc. [6].

In this context, unmanned aerial vehicles (UAVs), commonly known as drones, are increasingly used as technological support tools [10,23]. In fact, once equipped with high-resolution cameras, drones can provide cost-effective help to emergency rescue operations for several reasons. Swarms of aerial vehicles can quickly spread across a disaster area by providing mobile ad-hoc networks [1]. They can quickly fly over and traverse hard-to-reach regions, such as mountains, islands, deserts, etc., covering large areas with sparse human distribution. They can deliver rescue equipment, such as drugs, much faster than rescue teams. Furthermore, compared to classic helicopters used for these purposes, drones can fly below the normal altitude of air traffic, have lower costs and faster responses, and can get closer to the area of interest.

S. Bandini et al. (Eds.): AIxIA 2021, LNAI 13196, pp. 326–337, 2022.
https://doi.org/10.1007/978-3-031-08421-8_22

The literature is already populated with many use cases where drones have been successfully used in humanitarian settings, e.g. [7,19]. However, detecting people in online SAR images during inspection flights is still not a trivial task for human operators. First, it requires a long concentration to perform the flight operation and the search task at the same time. Secondly, operators may work in poor conditions, mainly due to the small size of the monitor they are equipped with, as well as the brightness of the screen monitored by the operator outdoors. Therefore, it would be helpful if the visual inspection process were somehow automated using visual patterns that suggest or detect potential humans in the image. Such a system can prove extremely beneficial for SAR operations, mainly because, as previously mentioned, locating victims, who may be unconscious or injured, as quickly as possible, is critical to improving their chances of survival.

This goal motivated research efforts to develop intelligent real-time decision support tools to be mounted directly on board drones, leveraging the integrated yet powerful GPUs available for UAVs. Unfortunately, there is currently still a small body of knowledge on applying pattern recognition and computer vision strategies to this type of problem, e.g. [15,21]. The large-scale variation and dense distribution of objects characteristic of UAV images pose challenges to human detection due to different heights, perspectives, poses of the human body, presence of many objects in the scene or very small objects to be detected, etc. Furthermore, most of the state-of-the-art computer vision algorithms for people detection in images and videos (e.g., [13,25]), which leverage convolutional neural network (CNN) models, while effective, are usually very expensive from a computational point of view, making their use on flying drones impractical. In fact, despite being equipped with powerful GPUs, a drone still needs fast solutions, given the limited battery it is equipped with as well as the limited bandwidth to communicate with the operator or the ground station [5].

In light of this, in this paper we investigate how recently proposed lighter versions of the popular YOLO detection algorithm [20], fine-tuned on new datasets specifically designed to help the community focused on this task, can provide an effective and at the same time efficient solution to aid SAR operations with drones. This experimental effort promises to better guide further research towards an acceptable trade-off between accuracy and speed of detection, which is crucial and still missing in this particular domain.

The rest of this paper is organized as follows. Section 2 reviews related work. Section 3 describes the datasets used and the proposed method. Section 4 presents the experimental results obtained. Section 5 concludes the paper and depicts future developments of our research.

2 Related Work

The use of drones to support SAR operations is becoming increasingly popular. However, there are currently few noteworthy works in the literature that explicitly make use of computer vision techniques to provide a drone with automatic image processing capabilities.

In an early work [16], Martins et al. used traditional Histogram of Oriented Gradient features and a Support Vector Machine classifier to classify frames as containing or not containing people and distinguish between safe and dangerous landing sites. While this approach provides promising prediction results, one of its main drawbacks is detection time.

Thanks to the success of deep learning in many areas, including classification and detection tasks in aerial images [4], research in this direction has rapidly moved towards an end-to-end pipeline. Kashihara et al. [11] proposed using a fast object detection model like YOLO to detect people in drone videos. Interestingly, to improve performance time, they did not feed the model with the overall video stream, but proposed to extract snapshots at periodic time intervals. Unfortunately the video frames they collected are very few and this penalizes the generalizability of the results obtained. Mishra et al. [18] have recently proposed a large dataset for human action recognition from drones, whose main goal is to provide support for SAR. The proposed dataset is characterized by a rich variety in terms of colors, heights, poses and background. However, the dataset was collected in and out of a campus, making the depicted scenes less realistic for a typical SAR scenario, which includes remote and hostile environments.

Similar to us, Lygouras et al. [15] used a lightweight version of YOLO, TinyYOLOv3 in their case, to aid SAR operations with drones. In particular, they proposed a system to detect swimmers in danger. The novelty of the proposed method is the combination of computer vision with a global satellite navigation system both for the precise detection of people and for the release of the rescue apparatus. The sea background provides a completely different background from other SAR scenarios, which we are interested in, with its specificities.

Two new datasets for SAR with drones have recently been released that offer the community new benchmarks to advance research in this field. HERIDAL focuses on Mediterranean and sub-Mediterranean landscapes [3]. The authors have proposed a method that works quite well on these data, which begins by reducing the search space through a visual attention algorithm that detects the salient or most prominent segments in the image; then, the regions most likely to contain a person are selected using a pre-trained and fine-tuned CNN for detection. Similarly, the SARD database has been created to detect victims and people in SAR scenarios in drone images and videos [22]. Actors were involved, who were asked to simulate tired and injured people and classic types of movement of people in nature, such as running and walking. Several state-of-the-art detectors have been used, including YOLOv4, which obtained very promising results. In this paper, we look at how newer algorithms for detecting people in images and videos, especially the lightweight versions of YOLOv5, can further improve detection performance.

Many other works, such as [17] and [21], have used thermal imaging to develop real-time people detection systems. However, it should be noted that in certain circumstances they have not proved to be a good solution, for example when the scanned areas reach very high temperatures, as the temperature of the environment can emit thermal radiation higher than the heat emanating from a human body. These situations limit the use of thermal imaging cameras during the day; however, fusion methods, based on the combination of thermal and optical imaging, appear to be a candidate solution.

3 Materials and Methods

The goal of our research is to provide a model for people detection that could potentially work on a drone, therefore with limited hardware resources. For this reason, we focused on lightweight versions of YOLO, that was chosen for its known speed and accuracy. YOLO ("You Look Only Once") is an open source model, initially introduced in 2016 by Joseph Redmon et al. [20], which is capable of doing object detection at very high speed, thus making it suitable as a real-time system. In our study we leverage YOLOv5, which is the latest version of YOLO, and also the lightest. Two new datasets available in the literature have been considered, namely the HERIDAL dataset and the SARD dataset. In the following we provide details on the datasets and the YOLO model adopted.

3.1 HERIDAL Dataset

The HERIDAL dataset contains approximately 1700 images of wildlife in various locations captured from an aerial perspective with drones equipped with a high-definition camera. In particular, images were captured by various UAVs from custom solutions to popular solutions such as DJI Phantom 3 or Mavic Pro, at altitudes from 30 m to 60 m. HERIDAL contains 4000 × 3000 full-size, labeled real images, split into 1583 training and 101 testing images. The images consist of realistic scenes of mountains, wilderness or remote places in non-urban areas. Since most research is conducted in remote locations outside of urban areas, the emphasis is on land and natural environments. In particular, the images were collected in various locations in Croatia and Bosnia-Herzegovina during mountain hikes, nature trips or during mountain rescue exercises. Most of them have more than one person, on average 3.38 people. In order to compile a dataset that would be a realistic representation of a real SAR operation, the authors used statistical data and specialist knowledge on SAR operations. In fact, there are many variations of the positions (standing, lying, squatting, etc.) in which a lost person can be found. Nevertheless, this specific information is not labeled, so the training and testing was done for human detection only.

3.2 SARD Dataset

To develop the SARD dataset, the authors involved actors, who simulated exhausted and injured people and classic types of movement. The images were sampled at a rate of 50 frames per second from a video recorded with an FHD resolution of 1920 × 1080 pixels with a high-performance camera on the DJI Phantom 4A drone. All the videos were shot in the Moslavacka Gora area, Croatia, outside the urban area. The positions of the people in the images vary from the standard ones (standing, sitting, lying, walking, running) to typical positions of tired or injured people reconstructed by the actors at their discretion. The actors were nine people of different ages and genders, ages 7 to 55, to include differences in movement and posture associated with age and body constitutions. As different terrains and backgrounds determine possible events and scenarios in the captured images and videos, the actors are located in various places, from those clearly visible (to the naked eye) to those in the woods, tall grass, shade and the like, which further complicates the detection. From the total length of approximately 35 min recordings, 1981 individual frames with people on them were identified. In the selected images, people have been manually labeled with the bounding boxes typically used to annotate objects. The training set contains 1189 images, in which 3921 people are marked, while the test set contains 792 images, in which 2611 people are marked. Furthermore, each person was labeled as belonging to one of the 6 classes corresponding to the different human movements, although some of them are under-represented.

3.3 YOLOv5

YOLO is a regression-based method and is in fact much faster than region proposal-based methods (such as R-CNN [8]), although it is not as accurate. The idea behind YOLO is to realize object detection by considering it as a regression and classification problem: the first is used to find the bounding box coordinates for the objects in the image, while the second is used to classify the objects found in an object class. This is done in a single step by first dividing the input image into a grid of cells, and then calculating, for each cell, the bounding box and the relative confidence score for the object in that cell.

Although the latest stable version of YOLO is YOLOv4 [2], we used YOLOv5 [9], which is still in development. The latest version of YOLO was chosen because several empirical results showed how it can work accurately, compared to YOLOv4, but with an extremely smaller model size[1]. Many controversies about YOLOv5 have been raised by the community[2]. These controversies are mainly caused by the fact that YOLOv5 does not even (yet) have a published paper; nevertheless, we have preferred to use the latter version to obtain experimental results that could be a valid reference for future work, as other projects, such as [24], have done. In some experiments on the well-known COCO dataset [14], YOLOv5s showed much lower training time and model storage size than the custom YOLOv4 model. Also, YOLOv5 takes less inference time, making it faster than YOLOv4.

The original YOLO architecture features 24 convolutional layers followed by 2 fully connected layers. More generally, a YOLO network is made up of three main parts: a CNN that aggregates image characteristics at different granularities; a series of layers that combine the extracted features; an output head whose goal is to regress bounding box coordinates and classify objects. YOLOv5 is

[1] https://blog.roboflow.com/yolov5-is-here/.
[2] https://blog.roboflow.com/yolov4-versus-yolov5/.

different from all other previous versions; in particular, the major improvements introduced include mosaic data augmentation and the ability to autonomously learn bounding box anchors, i.e. the set of predefined bounding boxes of a certain height and width used to detect objects.

In order to evaluate the best human detection model in SAR operations using the integrated resources available on drones, as mentioned above we have tested different architectures based on different versions of YOLOv5. In particular, we considered the less expensive models YOLOv5s and YOLOv5m, respectively acronym for "small" and "medium" size models. In fact, YOLOv5s is the smallest model available among those provided by the Ultralytics repository [9]; YOLOv5m is the medium model available among those provided. The two models differ in size, speed and mAP (mean average precision) achieved. The size of YOLOv5 is only 14 MB compared to YOLOv5m, for which it is 41 MB; moreover, the former is faster in detection but tends to exhibit a lower mAP.

4 Experiment

4.1 Setting

As a programming environment, we used Google Colaboratory (Colab). Colab provides a code environment like Jupyter Notebook and it is free to use a Graphic Processing Unit (GPU) or a Tensor Processing Unit (TPU). Colab has pre-installed popular libraries in deep learning research such as PyTorch, TensorFlow, Keras, and OpenCV. Since machine learning/deep learning algorithms require a system to have high speed and processing power (usually GPU-based), normal computers are not equipped with high performance GPUs. Therefore, Colab supplies GPUs such as the Tesla K80 manufactured by NVIDIA. To optimize the use of the datasets, we used the increasingly popular Roboflow platform[3]. It is very useful for computer vision tasks, as it provides tools for label annotation, dataset organization, image preprocessing, image augmentation, and training. For example, we used Roboflow to convert the originally provided Pascal VOC annotations to the supported YOLOv5 PyTorch format. Additionally, storing the dataset on Roboflow offers practical benefits for training models, as it avoids some additional steps usually required to load large datasets to Colab.

In our experiments we conducted transfer learning with weights pre-trained on the COCO dataset, running the small size model for 200 epochs and the medium size model for 100 epochs, when a plateau was reached on a held-out validation set. As an optimization algorithm, we experimented with the traditional stochastic gradient descent, using a learning rate of 0.01. To make training feasible, the high resolution input images were resized to 800×800 and the mini-batch size was set to 32 for the small and 16 for the medium size model.

[3] https://roboflow.com/.

4.2 Metrics

To properly evaluate the detection model on both datasets, standard object detection metrics, specifically precision and recall, were calculated. Precision represents the percentage of people correctly detected out of the total number of proposed objects classified as people. Recall measures the percentage of missing persons who have been correctly detected among all those labeled in the dataset. We also used average precision (AP) to evaluate the differences between the trained models, which calculates the average precision value for recall values from 0 to 1.

Finally, it is worth noting that a true positive detection is provided when the intersection over union (IoU) between the ground truth and the predicted bounding box is greater than or equal to a fixed threshold; as a common choice, we used a threshold of 50%.

4.3 Results

Table 1 reports the results obtained with the models experimented on the testing sets of the HERIDAL and SARD dataset. The results of the state-of-the-art on these data are also reported, for a comparison with the current literature. On HERIDAL, YOLOv5s achieved 0.753 precision, 0.694 recall and an AP of 0.731. Detecting an image took an extremely short time of ~0.015 s. Slightly better results are obtained with YOLOv5m, which achieved a precision of 0.797, a recall of 0.812 and an AP of 0.810. This gain in accuracy has doubled the detection time, although it is still an extremely fast time of 0.030 s per image. Currently, the state-of-the-art results on this dataset have been obtained by the multi-modal region-proposal CNN proposed in [12], in which a precision of 0.689 and a recall of 0.946 are reported. Our results are much better in terms of precision, at the expense of less recall. However, it should be noted that the state-of-the-art model takes around 15 s to process every single image, even on the powerful NVIDIA GeForce GTX 1080Ti Turbo. This implies that our proposed models are not only much faster, but can also mitigate the lower recall, as, given the very high frame rate, a missed detection can be recovered in a next frame in a very short time.

Regarding the SARD dataset, we observed an opposite behavior where, with the same ensemble of hyperparameters of the previous experiment, the medium size model performs worst than the small one. In fact, YOLOv5s achieved very good precision, recall and AP of 0.940, 0.917 and 0.933, respectively. In contrast, YOLOv5m achieved a performance of around 0.77 for all three metrics. This may be explained by the fact that the medium size model is an over-parameterized model compared to the small one, so it may have been overfitted this different dataset. On the same computational platform, and with the same input image resolution, detection time remains unchanged. The previous YOLOv4 model, experimented in [22], maintains the state-of-the-art on the SARD dataset. However, the single AP reported is only 0.03 better than our best model, and the detection time, while pretty short, is still an order of magnitude higher. Again,

Table 1. Detection performance and comparison with the state-of-the-art ("-" means "not provided").

Model	Precision	Recall	Avg. Precision	Secs per image
HERIDAL				
Region-proposal CNN [12]	0.689	0.946	-	~15
YOLOv5s (*this work*)	0.753	0.694	0.731	~0.015
YOLOv5m (*this work*)	0.797	0.812	0.810	~0.030
SARD				
YOLOv4 [22]	-	-	0.960	~0.27
YOLOv5s (*this work*)	0.940	0.917	0.933	~0.015
YOLOv5m (*this work*)	0.775	0.767	0.762	~0.030

Fig. 1. Examples of human detection on the HERIDAL dataset.

the state-of-the-art model was not tested on one of the embedded GPUs typically mounted on drones, but on a laptop with a GeForce GTX 1660Ti.

Examples of human detection on both datasets are shown in Fig. 1 and 2. It can be seen that in the case of the HERIDAL dataset, we can only detect

Fig. 2. Examples of human detection on the SARD dataset.

objects as containing humans. In the case of SARD, we can also classify the type of pose/movement exhibited by the detected person. It is worth noting that, especially in the HERIDAL images, we have high-altitude scenes where it is sometimes difficult to detect people even with the naked eye. Instead, the computer vision model proved very effective in this challenging task.

Since SARD is also provided with human pose labels, in Fig. 3 we report the confusion matrix for the task of classifying people's posture (i.e., "running", "walking", etc.), obtained on this dataset. Due to the data imbalance, our model performed worse on the under-represented target class "running": in fact, it can be seen that the latter is often (∼33%) confused with the "walking" class, which is represented in the dataset substantially more, while only ∼56% of the times is correctly predicted. As for the other classes, we can see how the model can achieve really good results, with an accuracy, on average, of ∼84%.

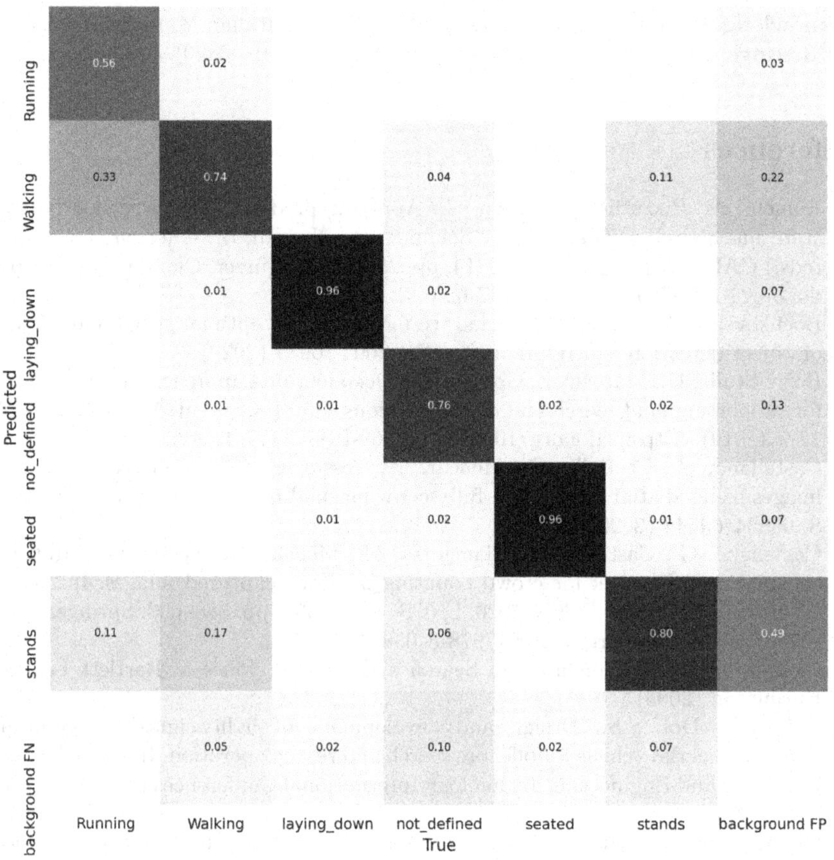

Fig. 3. Normalized confusion matrix obtained from the classification of people's posture on the SARD dataset (darker means better).

5 Conclusion

In this paper, we have demonstrated promising human detection performance using several approaches based on the latest YOLOv5 detection algorithm. Experimental results conducted on two new benchmark datasets showed that such a computer vision approach can provide an effective support tool to aid Search-and-Rescue operations with drones. Furthermore, the detection speed achieved allows people to be detected in a very short period of time, thus ensuring a rapid organization of the rescue.

As a future work, we want to combine optical and thermal imaging technology to further improve detection accuracy. Furthermore, we want to improve the results obtained on the multi-class classification based on human pose by properly augmenting the under-represented classes.

Acknowledgements. This work was supported by the Italian Ministry of University and Research within the RPASInAir project (PON ARS01_00820).

References

1. Bianchi, A., Pizzutilo, S., Vessio, G.: Applying predicate abstraction to abstract state machines. In: Gaaloul, K., Schmidt, R., Nurcan, S., Guerreiro, S., Ma, Q. (eds.) CAISE 2015. LNBIP, vol. 214, pp. 283–292. Springer, Cham (2015). https://doi.org/10.1007/978-3-319-19237-6_18
2. Bochkovskiy, A., Wang, C.Y., Liao, H.Y.M.: Yolov4: optimal speed and accuracy of object detection. arXiv preprint arXiv:2004.10934 (2020)
3. Božić-Štulić, D., Marušić, Ž, Gotovac, S.: Deep learning approach in aerial imagery for supporting land search and rescue missions. Int. J. Comput. Vis. **127**(9), 1256–1278 (2019). https://doi.org/10.1007/s11263-019-01177-1
4. Castellano, G., Castiello, C., Mencar, C., Vessio, G.: Crowd detection in aerial images using spatial graphs and fully-convolutional neural networks. IEEE Access **8**, 64534–64544 (2020)
5. Castellano, G., Castiello, C., Cianciotta, M., Mencar, C., Vessio, G.: Multi-view convolutional network for crowd counting in drone-captured images. In: Bartoli, A., Fusiello, A. (eds.) ECCV 2020. LNCS, vol. 12538, pp. 588–603. Springer, Cham (2020). https://doi.org/10.1007/978-3-030-66823-5_35
6. Cooper, D.C.: Fundamentals of Search and Rescue. Jones & Bartlett Learning, Burlington (2005)
7. Eid, S.E., Dol, S.S.: Design and development of lightweight-high endurance unmanned aerial vehicle for offshore search and rescue operation. In: 2019 Advances in Science and Engineering Technology International Conferences (ASET), pp. 1–5. IEEE (2019)
8. Girshick, R., Donahue, J., Darrell, T., Malik, J.: Rich feature hierarchies for accurate object detection and semantic segmentation. In: Proceedings of the IEEE conference on computer vision and pattern recognition, pp. 580–587 (2014)
9. Jocher, G., et al.: ultralytics/yolov5: v5.0 - YOLOv5-P6 1280 models, AWS, Supervise.ly and YouTube integrations (2021). https://doi.org/10.5281/zenodo.4679653
10. Karaca, Y., Cicek, M., Tatli, O., Sahin, A., Pasli, S., Beser, M.F., Turedi, S.: The potential use of unmanned aircraft systems (drones) in mountain search and rescue operations. Am. J. Emerg. Med. **36**(4), 583–588 (2018)
11. Kashihara, S., Wicaksono, M.A., Fall, D., Niswar, M.: Supportive information to find victims from aerial video in search and rescue operation. In: 2019 IEEE International Conference on Internet of Things and Intelligence System (IoTaIS), pp. 56–61. IEEE (2019)
12. Kundid Vasić, M., Papić, V.: Multimodel deep learning for person detection in aerial images. Electronics **9**(9), 1459 (2020)
13. Li, W.H., Hong, F.T., Zheng, W.S.: Learning to learn relation for important people detection in still images. In: Proceedings of the IEEE/CVF Conference on Computer Vision and Pattern Recognition, pp. 5003–5011 (2019)
14. Lin, T.-Y., et al.: Microsoft COCO: common objects in context. In: Fleet, D., Pajdla, T., Schiele, B., Tuytelaars, T. (eds.) ECCV 2014. LNCS, vol. 8693, pp. 740–755. Springer, Cham (2014). https://doi.org/10.1007/978-3-319-10602-1_48

15. Lygouras, E., Santavas, N., Taitzoglou, A., Tarchanidis, K., Mitropoulos, A., Gasteratos, A.: Unsupervised human detection with an embedded vision system on a fully autonomous uav for search and rescue operations. Sensors **19**(16), 3542 (2019)
16. Martins, F., de Groot, M., Stokkel, X., Wiering, M.A.: Human detection and classification of landing sites for search and rescue drones. In: ESANN (2016)
17. McGee, J., Mathew, S.J., Gonzalez, F.: Unmanned aerial vehicle and artificial intelligence for thermal target detection in search and rescue applications. In: 2020 International Conference on Unmanned Aircraft Systems (ICUAS), pp. 883–891. IEEE (2020)
18. Mishra, B., Garg, D., Narang, P., Mishra, V.: Drone-surveillance for search and rescue in natural disaster. Comput. Commun. **156**, 1–10 (2020)
19. Murphy, S.O., Sreenan, C., Brown, K.N.: Autonomous unmanned aerial vehicle for search and rescue using software defined radio. In: 2019 IEEE 89th vehicular technology conference (VTC2019-Spring), pp. 1–6. IEEE (2019)
20. Redmon, J., Divvala, S., Girshick, R., Farhadi, A.: You only look once: unified, real-time object detection. In: Proceedings of the IEEE Conference on Computer Vision and Pattern Recognition, pp. 779–788 (2016)
21. Rodin, C.D., de Lima, L.N., de Alcantara Andrade, F.A., Haddad, D.B., Johansen, T.A., Storvold, R.: Object classification in thermal images using convolutional neural networks for search and rescue missions with unmanned aerial systems. In: 2018 International Joint Conference on Neural Networks (IJCNN), pp. 1–8. IEEE (2018)
22. Sambolek, S., Ivasic-Kos, M.: Automatic person detection in search and rescue operations using deep cnn detectors. IEEE Access **9**, 37905–37922 (2021)
23. Waharte, S., Trigoni, N.: Supporting search and rescue operations with UAVs. In: 2010 International Conference on Emerging Security Technologies, pp. 142–147. IEEE (2010)
24. Xu, R., Lin, H., Lu, K., Cao, L., Liu, Y.: A forest fire detection system based on ensemble learning. Forests **12**(2), 217 (2021)
25. Zheng, Y., Zhang, X., Wang, F., Cao, T., Sun, M., Wang, X.: Detection of people with camouflage pattern via dense deconvolution network. IEEE Sig. Process. Lett. **26**(1), 29–33 (2018)

ArabCeleb: Speaker Recognition in Arabic

Simone Bianco[1], Luigi Celona[1(✉)], Intissar Khalifa[2], Paolo Napoletano[1], Alexey Petrovsky[3], Flavio Piccoli[1], Raimondo Schettini[1], and Ivan Shanin[3]

[1] University of Milano-Bicocca, Milan, Italy
{simone.bianco,luigi.celona,paolo.napoletano,flavio.piccoli, raimondo.schettini}@unimib.it

[2] Research Team in Intelligent Machines, National Engineering School of Gabes, Gabes, Tunisia

[3] Moscow Research Center, Huawei Technologies Co. Ltd., Moscow, Russia

Abstract. Due to the growing interest in speech recognition technologies, several datasets of speech acquired under uncontrolled conditions have been proposed in recent years. The majority of the datasets available to the community are in English, which reduces the possibility of developing and evaluating recognition technologies in languages other than English. In this paper we try to reduce this language-related gap by proposing a dataset for Arabic language speech recognition. The dataset is made available to the community and contains 100 speakers of both genders. Experiments with some of the latest speaker recognition approaches have been performed both with and without a suitable training on the Arabic language. Results suggest that, to effectively develop recognition technologies in other languages, suitable data for that language are necessary to allow at least a transfer learning approach. In particular, such data is crucial when short utterances are considered.

Keywords: Speaker recognition · Arabic language · Dataset

1 Introduction

Speaker recognition aims to recognize claimed identities of speakers, and includes identification and verification tasks. Nowadays the number of applications of speaker recognition continues to grow, ranging from biometric authentication to forensic tests, from interaction with smart devices to speaker diarization [7,8, 13,17,21].

This increasing number of successful applications has been made possible by the substantial improvements that deep Convolutional Neural Networks (CNNs) have given in speech recognition [10] as well as in computer vision [1] and related fields. CNNs showed in fact to be able to deal with data collected in the wild

This work has been done when I.K. was at the University of Milano-Bicocca.

S. Bandini et al. (Eds.): AIxIA 2021, LNAI 13196, pp. 338–347, 2022.
https://doi.org/10.1007/978-3-031-08421-8_23

without the need of handcrafted features. Fundamental for the success of these methods is the availability of large datasets.

Unfortunately, the performance of speaker recognition systems often degrades significantly when they are tested on data coming from a different language with respect to the one used for training.

A great effort has been made in recent years in collecting audio data under uncontrolled acquisition conditions and different languages. Nagrani *et al.* [14] propose VoxCeleb, a large-scale benchmark for speaker identification. This dataset is text-independent and collected in the wild. Together with the description of the collection protocol they provide a baseline with the state of the art methods for both speaker identification and verification. Chung *et al.* [4] using the protocol defined by [14] propose VoxCeleb2, a bigger dataset which pairs the audio with the visual information. Both benchmarks [14] and [4] are of native American English speakers. Zeinali *et al.* [20] propose DeepMine, a large scale speaker database in Persian and English. Unfortunately this dataset is not publicly available. Later on, in 2020, Fan *et al.* [5], taking inspiration from the VoxCeleb dataset, collected a Chinese speaker dataset named CN-Celeb. Differently from the VoxCeleb which contains mainly speeches taken from interviews, CN-Celeb covers more genres of speech ranging from entertainment, interview to drama and recitation. A summary of the aforementioned datasets and their main characteristics is shown in Table 1.

Unsurprisingly, the largest datasets available in the state of the art are in English, with limited data for other languages. Furthermore, most existing datasets for speaker recognition are collected under constrained conditions, where the acoustic environment, channel and speaking style or sentences do not change significantly for each speaker (e.g. [6,12,16]). These datasets are not suitable for the development and validation of speaker recognition systems in the real-world scenario and thus under unconstrained conditions.

Trying to address this lack of appropriate data for languages different from English, in this paper we present *ArabCeleb*, a dataset collected in the wild that specifically focuses on Arabic language. The proposed dataset contains utterances from 100 celebrities taken from videos on YouTube.com. The dataset might be used for several speaker recognition tasks: identification, verification, gender recognition as well as multimodal recognition tasks thus integrating audio and video tracks. All the audio tracks of the *ArabCeleb* dataset as well as the urls of the YouTube videos can be downloaded here http://www.ivl.disco.unimib.it/activities/ArabCeleb/.

The rest of the paper is organized as follows. Section 2 details the *ArabCeleb* dataset, and Sect. 3 reports on benchmark achieved by using the most recent state-of-the-art speaker recognition algorithms. Finally, Sect. 4 concludes the paper with a brief discussion on future works.

Table 1. Statistics of the most commonly known datasets for speaker recognition. POI: Person of Interest.

Dataset	VoxCeleb1 [14]	VoxCeleb2 [4]	DeepMine [20]	CN-Celeb [5]	ArabCeleb
Language	English	English	English/Persian	Chinese	Arabic
# of POIs	1251	6112	1355	1000	100
# of male speakers	690	3761	775	N/A	71
# of videos	22,496	150,480	N/A	N/A	118
# of hours	3,521,930	2442	N/A	274	3
# of utterances	153,516	1,128,246	370,000	130,109	1930
Avg # of videos per speaker	18	25	N/A	N/A	1
Avg # of utterances per speaker	116	185	N/A	130	19
Avg length of utterances (s)	8.2	7.8	N/A	7.6	5.2
Public Available	Yes	Yes	No	Yes	Yes

2 The ArabCeleb Dataset

The ArabCeleb dataset has been created with the intent of gapping the lack of a benchmark for arab speakers. This dataset can be used for many purposes. In plain audio configuration can be used both for speaker identification and verification. For research lines gathering multimodal information it is possible to use the ArabCeleb for head tracking from audio-visual signals. The dataset contains the proper information for accomplishing each one of these tasks.

2.1 Description

The ArabCeleb dataset is composed by 100 Tunisian subjects, 71 males and 29 females (pie chart on the left of the bottom row of Fig. 1). All subjects of which is known the birthday were born between 1917 and 2000 (bar chart in the middle of the bottom row of Fig. 1 shows the number of subjects for each year). Each subject is represented from 10 to 60 audio tracks, with an average of 19.3 tracks per subject. In total there are 1930 samples with an average length of 5.20 s. The smallest and the biggest audio samples have respectively a length of 2.96 s and 9.45 s (see Fig. 1 (bottom, right) for the histogram of lengths). The majority of the audio samples is stereo (97.82%) while the rest is mono channel (2.18%). All audios have been sampled at a sampling rate of 44, 100 samples per second.

The dataset contains both development and test sets for speaker verification. To allow the training of methods for speaker identification that can then be reused for speaker verification, we randomly generate the development and test sets making sure that there is no overlap between the speakers of the development and test sets. The test set contains a total of 443 utterances from 20 speakers while the development set contains a total of 1487 utterances from 80 speakers. The characteristics of the generated splits are provided in Table 2. The development set is further divided into training, validation, and test sets for speaker identification.

Table 2. Development and test set statistics for verification.

Set	# POIs	# Videos	# Utterances
Dev	80	98	1487
Test	20	20	443
Total	100	118	1930

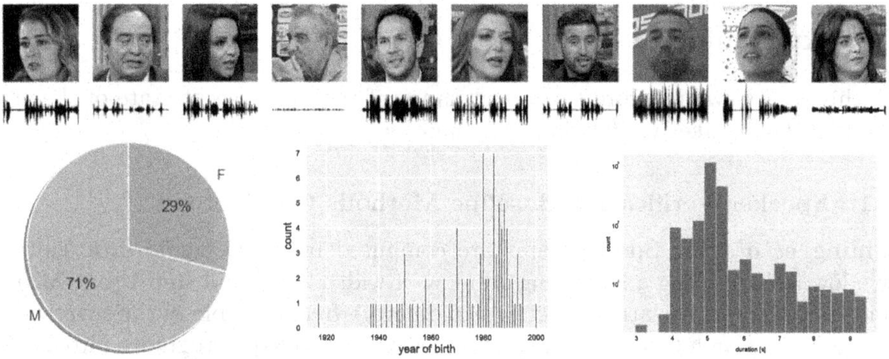

Fig. 1. Top row: Examples from the ArabCeleb dataset. For some of the speakers in the dataset, the cropped face from a sampled frame and the audio are shown. **Bottom row:** (left) Gender distribution of the celebrities included in our dataset; (middle) Frequency of samples by year of birth for the celebrities included in the ArabCeleb dataset; (right) Histogram of the lengths of the utterance in the ArabCeleb dataset. All utterances have a length included between 2.96 and 9.45 s with an average length of 5.20 s.

2.2 Collection Pipeline

The pipeline adopted for the collection of the dataset is as described as follows:

Stage 1. Candidate list of Persons of Interest (POIs). The candidates were chosen among the most famous personalities in Tunisia. The rationale behind this choice is that it's easy to find audio-video material of famous persons and this material is usually of high quality as it is acquired by professionals such as journalists or streamers with high-grade acquisition devices. All candidates speak modern standard Arabic as native language, which is the official language of Tunisia.

Stage 2. Downloading videos. The list of videos has been manually choosen. Each video has been automatically collected from YouTube.com and cropped so that each crop contains the subject talking in front of the camera with the face totally visible and without scene cuts or changes. In this way, it's possible to use the facial information to accomplish multimodal tasks.

Stage 3. Face tracking, face verification and active speaker verification. To make sure that the face is visible in the entire crop of the video, that there is no scene-cut or change and that the face detected always corresponds to the

right celebrity, a manual check of all videos is performed. Given the reduced cardinality of the dataset, this check is done by three people who determines the active speaker basing on the audio-visual match.
Stage 4. Obtaining demographic information. For each subject, the year of birth and gender have been manually searched and annotated. For nine subjects out of 100 it was not possible to retrieve the year of birth, as this information was not present on internet.

3 Experiments

In this section we measure the performance of the most recent state-of-the-art methods for speaker verification on *Arabceleb*.

3.1 Speaker Verification Baseline Methods Considered

Chung *et al.* [4][1]**.** Spectrograms are computed from raw audio in a sliding window fashion using a Hamming window of width 25 ms and step 10 ms. Mean and variance normalization is performed on every frequency bin of the spectrum. A ResNet-50 architecture [9] is then used to encode spectrograms into 2048 feature vectors. The model is trained from scratch by randomly sampling 3-s segments from each utterance using cross-entropy loss to discriminate the 5994 speakers of VoxCeleb2. The classification layer is then replaced with a fully connected layer of output dimension 512 and the whole model is further trained using a contrastive loss.

Xie *et al.* [19][2]**.** A fixed size spectrogram is generated in a sliding window fashion using a Hamming window of width 25 ms and step 10 ms. A 512 point FFT, is then use to provide 256 frequency components, which together with the DC component of each frame gives a short-time Fourier transform (STFT) of size 257×250 (frequency $\times$ temporal) for a utterance of 2.5 s. The obtained spectrogram is normalised by subtracting the mean and dividing by the standard deviation of all frequency components in a single time step. A Thin-ResNet architecture extracts frame-level features that are then aggregated into a single utterance-level descriptor of length 512 in the second part of the network using GhostVLAD [22]. During training, 2.5 s temporal segment are randomly extracted from each utterance and the additive margin softmax (AM-Softmax) [18] loss is used to measure the speaker identification error.

Chung *et al.* [3][3]**.** A Fast ResNet encodes 40-dimensional Mel filterbanks that are firstly normalized by applying instance normalization [15]. The network is a much more efficient and lightweight version of the traditional ResNet-34 [9]. Self-attentive pooling (SAP) [2] is used to aggregate frame-level features into utterance-level representation while paying attention to the frames that are more informative for utterance-level speaker recognition. The network is trained using the angular prototypical loss on VoxCeleb2.

[1] Source code available at: https://github.com/a-nagrani/VGGVox.
[2] Source code available at: https://github.com/WeidiXie/VGG-Speaker-Recognition.
[3] Source code available at: https://github.com/clovaai/voxceleb_trainer.

3.2 Results

In this Section we report the performance of the previously described methods in different experiments conducted on the proposed dataset. For all the experiments we report the performance in terms of Equal Error Rate (EER) which is the rate at which both acceptance and rejection errors are equal.

Verification on ArabCeleb. Table 3 compares the performance of the considered speaker verification baseline methods on ArabCeleb test set. From the results it is possible to see that when the whole utterance is considered, the results obtained by all methods are comparable to their performance on the training set.

Table 3. Results for verification on the ArabCeleb test set (lower is better).

Models	Trained on	EER (%)
Chung *et al.* [4]	VoxCeleb2	1.92
Xie *et al.* [19]	VoxCeleb2	1.41
Chung *et al.* [3]	VoxCeleb2	1.69

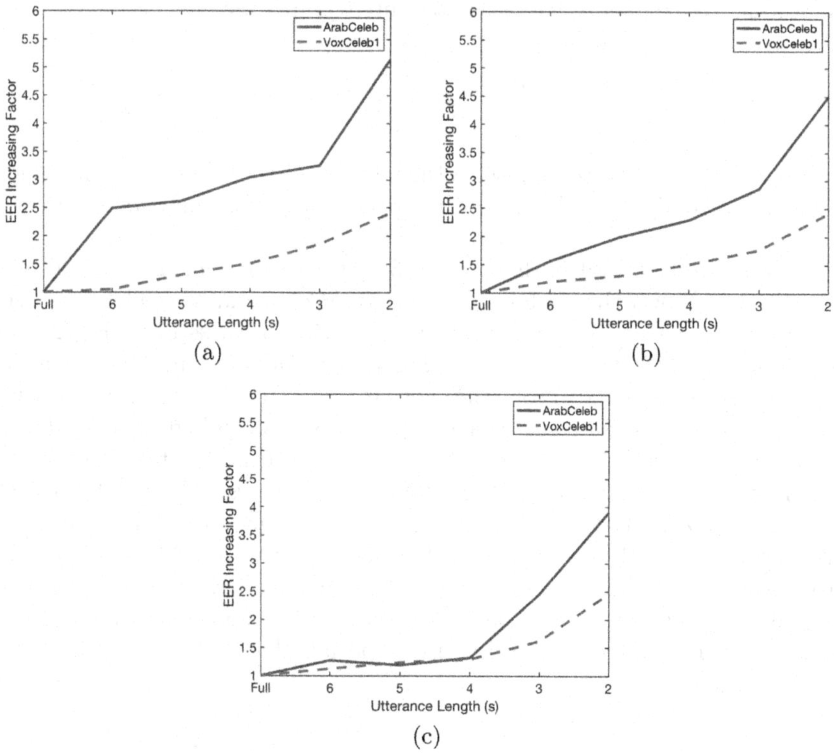

Fig. 2. EER increasing factor as the length in seconds of the utterance decreases. (a) Chung *et al.* [4]; (b) Xie *et al.* [19]; (c) Chung *et al.* [3].

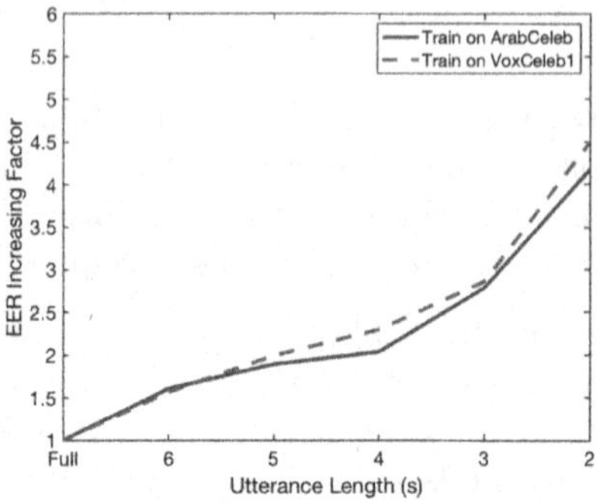

Fig. 3. EER increasing factor for Xie *et al.* [19] after fine-tuning as the length in seconds of the utterance decreases.

Probing Verification Based on Length. In this experiment we measure the impact of utterance length on performance. For this evaluation, to get segments with relevant speech activity, that is segments without silent, an energy-based voice activity detector (VAD) is used [11]. Each utterance has been divided into windows of T seconds with an overlap of half window length. For each of these windows the signal energy has been computed as follows:

$$E_w = \frac{1}{N} \sum_{i=1}^{N} |x(i)|^2, \tag{1}$$

where $N = T \cdot sample\_rate$ represents the total number of samples in the window of length T seconds. We select the window w that scored the maximum energy E_w.

We crop segments of length $T = \{2\,\text{s}, 3\,\text{s}, 4\,\text{s}, 5\,\text{s}, 6\,\text{s}\}$ from the original utterances. Table 4 shows the performance on *ArabCeleb* and VoxCeleb1 test sets. In order to have a more meaningful representation of these data, Fig. 2 shows the relation between the EER increasing factor and the length in seconds of the utterances considered. From the plots it is possible to see how the performance degradation when using shorter utterances is much higher on *ArabCeleb*: considering the method by Chung *et al.* [4] moving from the full utterances to utterances with a length of 2 s on *ArabCeleb* increases the EER by a 5.14× factor, while on VoxCeleb1 EER increases by a 2.40× factor. The same happens with the method by Xie *et al.* [19]: EER increases by a 4.50× and a 2.41× factor respectively, and for Chung *et al.* [3], where the EER increases by 3.90× and 2.46× respectively. This experiment suggest the importance of appropriate data for languages different from English, especially for applications where short utterances are considered.

Table 4. Performance on ArabCeleb and VoxCeleb1 tests at varying utterance lengths (in seconds).

	Models	EER (%)				
		2 s	3 s	4 s	5 s	6 s
Arab	Chung *et al.* [4]	9.86	6.26	5.85	5.03	4.79
	Xie *et al.* [19]	6.34	4.03	3.24	2.81	2.21
	Chung *et al.* [3]	6.59	4.15	2.23	2.01	2.15
Vox1	Chung *et al.* [4]	9.49	7.34	5.96	5.17	4.15
	Xie *et al.* [19]	7.77	5.70	4.87	4.20	3.87
	Chung *et al.* [3]	5.45	3.59	2.87	2.75	2.50

Fine-Tuning. In this section we show the advantage of adapting a pre-trained method on the English language considering the speakers contained in the large VoxCeleb2, to the proposed ArabCeleb. To this end we fine-tuned the method proposed by Xie *et al.* [19]. During fine-tuning, we randomly extract a 2.5 s temporal segment from each utterance without applying any voice activity detection (VAD), or automatic silence removal. We then generate the corresponding spectrogram in a sliding window fashion using a Hamming window of width 25 ms and step 10 ms. We use a 512 point FFT, giving us 256 frequency components, which together with the DC component of each frame gives a STFT of size 257×250 (frequency $\times$ time) out of every 2.5 s crop. The normalized spectrogram is obtained by subtracting the mean and dividing by the standard deviation of all frequency components in a single time step.

We initialize the model with the parameters learned on VoxCeleb2, while for the classification layer we use the random orthogonal initialization. We freeze the backbone parameters and we fine-tune the model for 10 epochs using the Adam optimizer with a fixed learning rate of $5e-5$. We fine-tune the model for identifying the 80 speakers of the development set of ArabCeleb using the Cross-entropy loss function.

On the full length utterances, the EER obtained with the fine-tuned method corresponds to 1.30, which is better than the performance obtained both by the one trained on VoxCeleb2 and by the other two methods evaluated, i.e. Chung *et al.* [4] and Chung *et al.* [3]. Table 5 reports the EER as the length of the sampled sequence from the entire utterance is reduces. As it is possible to see, the fine-tuned model outperforms the one pre-trained on VoxCeleb2 for all the sequence lengths. We also highlight that the fine-tuned model achieves better performance than the other considered methods on the shortest sequences considered (i.e. 2 and 3 s). Finally, in Fig. 3 we report the relation between the EER increasing factor and the length in seconds of the utterances considered, where it is possible to see that after fine-tuning the EER increasing factor is similar for both datasets.

Table 5. EER of Xie *et al.* [19] fine-tuned on ArabCeleb.

Model	EER (%)				
	2 s	3 s	4 s	5 s	6 s
Xie *et al.* [19]	5.43	3.62	2.65	2.46	2.09

4 Conclusions

In this paper we introduce ArabCeleb, a new dataset for speaker recognition in Arabic language. The dataset contains utterances of 100 celebrities of both genders taken from YouTube.com videos. Utterances as well as video urls are made publicly available. We evaluated the most recent state-of-the-art methods for speaker recognition by measuring robustness as the length of the utterances increases. Results show that methods trained on the English language do not generalize on the Arabic language especially on short utterances and can be improved by fine-tuning them on the target language, highlighting the importance of having appropriate data.

References

1. Bianco, S., Cadene, R., Celona, L., Napoletano, P.: Benchmark analysis of representative deep neural network architectures. IEEE Access **6**, 64270–64277 (2018)
2. Cai, W., Chen, J., Li, M.: Exploring the encoding layer and loss function in end-to-end speaker and language recognition system. In: Odyssey 2018 the Speaker and Language Recognition Workshop, pp. 74–81 (2018)
3. Chung, J.S., et al.: In defence of metric learning for speaker recognition. In: Interspeech, pp. 2977–2981 (2020)
4. Chung, J.S., Nagrani, A., Zisserman, A.: Voxceleb2: deep speaker recognition. In: Interspeech, pp. 1086–1090 (2018)
5. Fan, Y., et al.: Cn-celeb: a challenging chinese speaker recognition dataset. In: International Conference on Acoustics, Speech and Signal Processing (ICASSP), pp. 7604–7608. IEEE (2020)
6. Garofolo, J.S., Lamel, L.F., Fisher, W.M., Fiscus, J.G., Pallett, D.S.: Darpa timit acoustic-phonetic continous speech corpus cd-rom. nist speech disc 1–1.1. NASA STI/Recon Technical report n 93, 27403 (1993)
7. Hanifa, R.M., Isa, K., Mohamad, S.: A review on speaker recognition: Technology and challenges. Computers & Electrical Engineering **90**, 107005 (2021)
8. Hansen, J.H., Hasan, T.: Speaker recognition by machines and humans: a tutorial review. IEEE Sign. Process. Mag. **32**(6), 74–99 (2015)
9. He, K., Zhang, X., Ren, S., Sun, J.: Deep residual learning for image recognition. In: Conference on Computer Vision and Pattern Recognition (CVPR). pp. 770–778. IEEE (2016)
10. Hinton, G., et al.: Deep neural networks for acoustic modeling in speech recognition: the shared views of four research groups. IEEE Sign. Process. Mag. **29**(6), 82–97 (2012)

11. May, T., Van de Par, S., Kohlrausch, A.: Noise-robust speaker recognition combining missing data techniques and universal background modeling. IEEE Trans. Audio Speech Lang. Process. **20**(1), 108–121 (2011)
12. Millar, J.B., Vonwiller, J.P., Harrington, J.M., Dermody, P.J.: The australian national database of spoken language. In: International Conference on Acoustics, Speech and Signal Processing (ICASSP), vol. 1, pp. I-97. IEEE (1994)
13. Minaee, S., Abdolrashidi, A., Su, H., Bennamoun, M., Zhang, D.: Biometric recognition using deep learning: A survey. arXiv preprint arXiv:1912.00271 (2019)
14. Nagrani, A., Chung, J.S., Zisserman, A.: Voxceleb: a large-scale speaker identification dataset. In: Interspeech, pp. 2616–2620 (2017)
15. Ulyanov, D., Vedaldi, A., Lempitsky, V.: Instance normalization: the missing ingredient for fast stylization. arXiv preprint arXiv:1607.08022 (2016)
16. Vloed, D., Bouten, J., van Leeuwen, D.: Nfi-frits: a forensic speaker recognition database and some first experiments. In: Odyssey Speaker and Language Recognition Workshop, pp. 6–13. [Sl]: ISCA Speaker and Language Characterization special interest group (2014)
17. Wan, L., Wang, Q., Papir, A., Moreno, I.L.: Generalized end-to-end loss for speaker verification. In: International Conference on Acoustics, Speech and Signal Processing (ICASSP), pp. 4879–4883. IEEE (2018)
18. Wang, F., Cheng, J., Liu, W., Liu, H.: Additive margin softmax for face verification. IEEE Sign. Process. Lett. **25**(7), 926–930 (2018)
19. Xie, W., Nagrani, A., Chung, J.S., Zisserman, A.: Utterance-level aggregation for speaker recognition in the wild. In: International Conference on Acoustics, Speech and Signal Processing (ICASSP), pp. 5791–5795. IEEE (2019)
20. Zeinali, H., Sameti, H., Stafylakis, T.: Deepmine speech processing database: text-dependent and independent speaker verification and speech recognition in Persian and English. In: Odyssey. pp. 386–392 (2018)
21. Zhang, A., Wang, Q., Zhu, Z., Paisley, J., Wang, C.: Fully supervised speaker diarization. In: International Conference on Acoustics, Speech and Signal Processing (ICASSP), pp. 6301–6305. IEEE (2019)
22. Zhong, Y., Arandjelović, R., Zisserman, A.: GhostVLAD for set-based face recognition. In: Jawahar, C.V., Li, H., Mori, G., Schindler, K. (eds.) ACCV 2018. LNCS, vol. 11362, pp. 35–50. Springer, Cham (2019). https://doi.org/10.1007/978-3-030-20890-5_3

Static, Dynamic and Acceleration Features for CNN-Based Speech Emotion Recognition

Intissar Khalifa[1,2], Ridha Ejbali[1,2], Paolo Napoletano[1,2(✉)], Raimondo Schettini[1,2], and Mourad Zaied[1,2]

[1] Department of Informatics, System and Communication, University of Milan-Bicocca, Milan, Italy
{intissar.khalifa,ridha.ejbali,paolo.napoletano,raimondo.schettini, mourad.zaied}@unimib.it, i.khalifa@campus.unimib.it

[2] Research Team on Intelligent Machines, National Engineering School of Gabes, University of Gabes, Gabes, Tunisia

Abstract. Speech emotion recognition is a significant source of information especially when other channels, like face or body, are hidden. The shape of the vocal tract, tone of the voice, pitch and other characteristics are influenced by human emotions. In this paper, we propose the use of static, dynamic and acceleration features which are very effective in encoding those characteristics of the speech that are influenced by human emotions. These features are based on the concatenation of three global measures of Mel-frequency Cepstral Coefficients (MFCCs) (the static part) and the first (the dynamic part) and second derivatives (the acceleration part) of MFCCs. The features are processed with a custom 1-D CNN suitable designed by the authors for emotion recognition.

Experiments are performed on two publicly available speech datasets containing audio files from different people and language and several emotions. Our approach on average overcomes the state of the art on both datasets.

Keywords: Speech emotion recognition · Spectral features · Static, dynamic and acceleration features · CNNs

1 Introduction and Related Work

Nonverbal behavior expresses and reveals human emotions and represents, according to social psychologists, the 93% of our interactions with others [18]. Nonverbal behavior can be divided into four categories [8]: proxemics, haptics, kinesics and vocalics. Proxemics is related to how a person uses the space around his/her body in human interactions. Haptics refers to how a person communicates with others via the sense of touch. Kinesics is related to body motions such as gestures [12,20] and facial expressions [32]. Vocalics, or paralanguage, refers to how speakers express their emotions through voice [30]. In this paper

S. Bandini et al. (Eds.): AIxIA 2021, LNAI 13196, pp. 348–358, 2022.
https://doi.org/10.1007/978-3-031-08421-8_24

we focus on Speech Emotion Recognition (SER) which can be largely employed in several application domains like: human computer interface, robotics, audio surveillance, e-learning, computer games, decisional system for job interview, etc. [1].

Human speech is influenced by the physiology of the speaker, shape of vocal tract, tone of the voice and the phonetic content such as pitch, intensity, energy and duration [30]. Since these characteristics are influenced by emotions, the selection of the right speech descriptors is fundamental to achieve an automatic discrimination and recognition of distinct emotions such as: neutral, calm, happy, sad, angry, fearful, disgust and surprised. Following the categorization proposed by Ayadi et al. [4,29], the most used features for SER are grouped into four categories: (1) Continuous - such as pitch, energy, and formants; (2) Qualitative - such as voice quality, harshness, breathy; (3) Spectral - such as Linear Predictive Coding (LPC), Mel-Frequency Cepstral Coefficients (MFCC) (4) Teager Energy Operator (TEO)-based - such as TEO-FM-Var, TEO-CB-Auto-Env. In SER, features have been experimented in combination with several classification methods, such as: Hidden Markov Model (HMM) [11], Support Vector Machine (SVM) [27], Gaussian mixture model (GMM) [31], Neural Networks (NN) [23], brain emotional learning model (BEL) [19], Voiced Segment Selection (VSS) [7] and and very recently Deep Learning (DL) architectures [1].

In this paper, we propose the exploitation of static, dynamic and acceleration spectral features for speech emotion recognition based on MFCC [10,17,24,26]. We exploit the features with a standard Random Forest Classifier, and with a 1-D Convolutional Neural Network (CNN) suitable designed by the authors. Experiments are carried out on two publicily available datasets. Results show that the use of the proposed features with our custom 1-CNN outperforms on average the state of the art on both datasets.

2 Proposed Method

An overview of the proposed method is showed in Fig. 1. Before feature extraction, the audio sample is pre-processed as follows:

- *Silence trimming*: we trim silence in each audio clip using a 30 dB threshold.
- *Windowing*: the input audio signal is divided into segments of 20 ms with a step of 10 ms. The Hamming window is applied to each segment in order to decrease the edge effects due to the window cutting.

After pre-processing and segmentation, Mel-frequency Cepstral Coefficients (MFCCs) are generated since they proved to be robust in different speech recognition applications [5,17,26]. MFCCs are computed as follows [24]:

- *Spectrogram computation and normalization*: given an audio sample (Fig. 2(a)), we calculate, for each segment, the magnitute of the Fast Fourier Transform (FFT). These are then concatenated in order to obtain a the spectrogram. Each frequency bin of the spectrum is normalized by using the mean and standard deviation of the sample (see Fig. 2(b)).

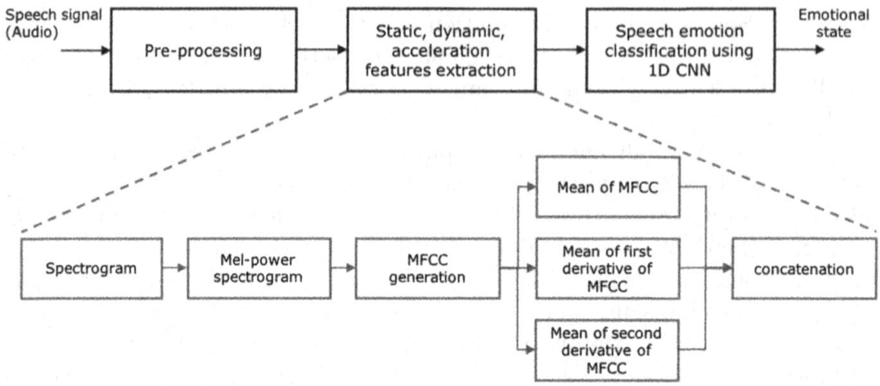

Fig. 1. Pipeline of the proposed method. The audio sample is initially pre-processed by removing silence and by separating it into windows of 20 ms with a step of 10 ms. For each segment of the audio sample the Fast Fourier Transform (FFT) is applied to compute the sample spectrogram. The power of the spectrogram is mapped into the *mel* scale. The MFCCs are the amplitudes of the resulting spectrum. Mean of the MFCCs, of their first and second derivatives are concatenated to obtain the final feature vector. The feature vector is the input of the 1-D CNN. The output of the network is one of the possible emotion states, i.e. neutral, calm, happy, sad, angry, fearful, disgust and surprised.

- *Mel-power spectrum computation*: The spectrogram power is processed with a filter bank made of triangular band pass filters. This operation maps the power of the spectrogram onto the *mel* scale. The Mel-spectrum is the log of the output of the filters (see Fig. 2(c)).
- *MFCCs computation:* The Discrete Cosine Transform (DCT) is applied to the Mel-power spectrum. The MFCCs are the first 40 coefficients of the DCT (see Fig. 2(d)).

2.1 Static, Dynamic and Acceleration Features

The static part of our features is represented by the MFCCs (see Figs. Fig. 2(d)) while the dynamic and acceleration parts are represented by the first (see Fig. 2(e)) and the second derivatives (see Fig. 2(f)) of the MFCCs. The rationale behind the use of the first and second derivatives of the MFCCs is that derivatives are very effective to catch the main characteristics of the human voices that are modified by emotions, such as the shape of the vocal tract, tone of the voice, pitch etc. [9].

For each frame t, the first derivative (Δ_t) and the second derivative (Δ_t^2) of the MFCCs are calculated as follows:

$$\Delta_t = \frac{\sum_{n=1}^{N} n(C_{t+n} - C_{t-n})}{2\sum_{n=1}^{N} n^2}$$

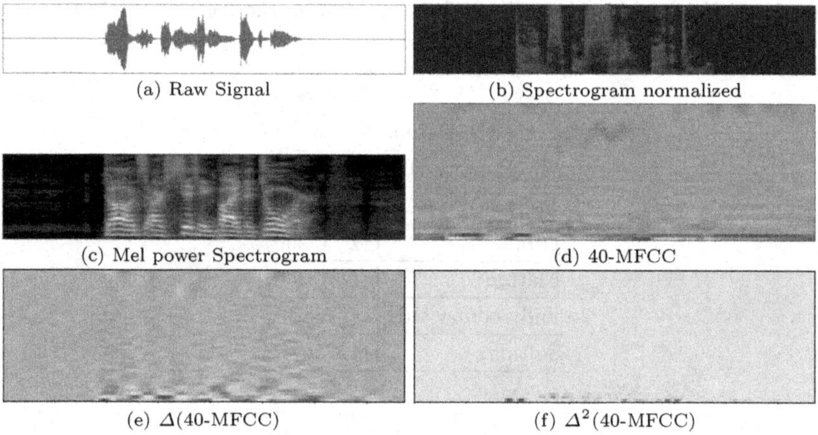

Fig. 2. From the input signal to the MFCCs and their derivatives generation: (a) Input audio clip, (b) Normalized spectrogram, (c) Mel-power spectrogram, (d) 40 MFCCs. (e) First derivative of the 40 MFCCs(f) Second derivative of 40 MFCCs.

$$\Delta_t^2 = \frac{\sum_{n=1}^{N} n(\Delta_{t+n} - \Delta_{t-n})}{2\sum_{n=1}^{N} n^2}$$

where N is equals to 2 and represents the number of samples considered in the calculation of the derivatives, while $\mathcal{C}_t$ is the static coefficient of the frame t of the MFCC.

2.2 Global Features

Global features, such as minimum, maximum, mean, standard deviation, kurtosis, etc., have been proved to be more effective than local features in speech recognition and analysis [6]. In this paper, for each sample, we consider the mean of the MFCCs, the mean of Δ(MFCCs) and the mean of Δ^2(MFCCs). The final feature vector is the concatenation of these three components, thus obtaining a 120-dimensional feature vector.

2.3 Proposed 1-D Convolutional Neural Network

Deep learning techniques have been successfully applied to many domains of affective computing [2,13,16]. We design a 1-Dimensional (1-D) Convolutional Neural Network (CNN). Our static, dynamic and acceleration feature vector is the input of the CNN while the output of the network is one of the possible emotion states, i.e. neutral, calm, happy, sad, angry, fearful, disgust and surprised. The designed network is described in Table 1. It is composed of 1 convolutional layer with 512 filters having a kernel of size 5×1, stride 1 and padding 4. After a Relu and a pooling layer with kernel 4×1 we have another convolutional

Table 1. CNN-1D architecture. L can be 40 or 120 on the basis of the feature vector used.

Layer	Input size
Conv-1D + Relu	$(1, L)$
MaxPooling-1D	$(L, 512)$
Conv-1D + Relu	$(L/4, 512)$
Dropout	$(L/4, 256)$
Flatten	$(L/4, 256)$
Fully connected	$(1, 7680)$
Softmax	$(1, 256)$

layer which has 256 filters. A flatten layer prepares the input for a fully connected layer which is followed by a softmax. The output of the network is a vector $(1, K)$ where K is the number of emotions to be predicted. The categorical cross-entropy is applied as loss function and Adam optimizer is used with a learning rate of $1e - 3$ to minimize the loss function over mini batches of 64 speech segments of the training data.

3 Experiments

3.1 Datasets

To evaluate the performance of our proposed method we employ two public datasets:

- RAVDESS [15] The Ryerson Audio-Visua Emotional Speech and Song dataset is composed by 7356 recordings in English with an average duration of 3 s. Audio clips with 8 emotions with normal and strong intensity are recorded by 24 professional actors (12 male, 12 female). The emotions are: emotions: neutral, calm, happy, sad, angry, fearful, disgust and surprised. All actors produced 104 distinct vocalizations that have been extracted to create three separate modality conditions: audio-only (48 kHz .wav), audio-video (48 kHz, .mp4), and video-only (no sound). In our experiments we use the 4784 recordings from the two modalities (audio-only and audio-video).
- EMODB [3] The Berlin Database of Emotional Speech is a public German dataset composed of 535 recording files spoken by 10 actors (5 male and 5 female). It is popular in the domain of emotion recognition due to the good quality of its recording. The average duration of the audio files is 3 s with sampling rate of 16 kHz. The speakers produced 7 emotions: neutral, happy, sad, angry, fearful, disgust and bored speech utterances.

We employ the five-fold cross validation for all the experiments.

Table 2. Comparison between RF and CNN using Mean MFCC (40) on the RAVDESS dataset

	Metric	Neutral	Calm	Happy	Sad	Angry	Fearful	Disgust	Surprised
RF	Precision	0.83	0.86	0.78	0.77	0.82	0.76	0.73	0.86
	F-score	0.89	0.91	0.82	0.79	0.77	0.80	0.67	0.71
	Recall	0.86	0.88	0.80	0.78	0.79	0.78	0.70	0.78
	Accuracy	80.24%							
CNN	Precision	0.92	0.90	0.89	0.85	0.95	0.95	0.96	0.95
	F-score	0.92	0.97	0.92	0.91	0.91	0.93	0.83	0.87
	Recall	0.92	0.93	0.90	0.88	0.93	0.94	0.89	0.91
	Accuracy	91.38%							

Table 3. Comparison between RF and CNN using Mean MFCC (40) + Mean Δ(MFCC) (40) + Δ^2(MFCC) (40) on the RAVDESS dataset

	Metric	Neutral	Calm	Happy	Sad	Angry	Fearful	Disgust	Surprised
RF	Precision	0.82	0.89	0.93	0.84	0.89	0.83	0.77	0.88
	F-score	0.91	0.93	0.89	0.86	0.89	0.88	0.69	0.75
	Recall	0.86	0.91	0.91	0.85	0.89	0.85	0.72	0.81
	Accuracy	86.40%							
CNN	Precision	0.95	0.96	0.90	0.90	0.98	0.93	0.92	0.95
	F-score	0.89	0.96	0.94	0.95	0.93	0.96	0.91	0.88
	Recall	0.92	0.96	0.92	0.92	0.95	0.95	0.92	0.91
	Accuracy	93.41%							

3.2 Comparison with the State of the Art

The following methods are considered for comparison:

- Shegokar et al. [25] Select features based on continuous wavelet transform (CWT) and prosodic coefficients combined using a SVM with a Quadratic kernel (Q-SVM).
- Lampropoulos and Tsihrintzis [14] use MPEG-7- low level audio descriptors combined with a Radial Basis Function SVM (RBF-SVM). the Basic spectral and Timbral (spectral and temporal).
- Tanmoy et al. [29] use features based on Discrete Wavelet Transform (DWT) combined with three methods: Support Vector Classifier (SVC), Gaussian Naive Bayes (GNB) and K-Nearest Neighbour (KNN).
- Zamil et al. [33] use 13-dimensional MFCC features as input to the Logistic Model Tree (LMT) classifier with linear regression.
- Parry et al. [21] use spectrograms as input of a combination of both a Convolutional Neural Network (CNN) and a Long-Term Short-Term network (LSTM).
- Popova et al. [22] also use spectrograms as input of a pre-trained VGG-16.

Table 4. Comparison between RF and CNN using Mean MFCC (40) on the EMODB dataset

	Metric	Neutral	Happy	Sad	Angry	Fearful	Disgust	Bored
RF	Precision	0.74	0.80	0.80	0.83	0.84	0.61	0.62
	F-score	0.91	0.74	0.80	0.82	0.79	0.50	0.59
	Recall	0.82	0.77	0.80	0.83	0.81	0.55	0.61
	Accuracy	76.50%						
CNN	Precision	0.82	0.76	0.96	0.87	0.95	0.86	0.70
	F-score	0.85	0.97	0.74	0.71	0.91	0.86	0.93
	Recall	0.84	0.86	0.83	0.78	0.93	0.86	0.80
	Accuracy	84.75%						

- Badshah et al. [1] use a spectrogram as input of a 2-D CNN with a rectangular kernels of varying shapes and sizes, along with max pooling in rectangular neighborhoods.
- For sake of completeness we have also processed our proposed features using a Random Forest (RF) classifier with 60 trees of depth 10.

3.3 Result

We measure the performance of our method in terms of precision (Pr), recall (Re), F1 measure and Accuracy. The comparison with the state of the art is made only in terms of accuracy since only this metric is reported in the corresponding publications.

Tables 2 and 4 show the results achieved using the simplified version of our features (mean of the 40 MFCCs) combined with the RF and 1-D CNN classifiers on RAVDESS and EMODB datasets respectively. It can be noticed that the use of our 1-D CNN increases the overall accuracy of about 10% on both datasets with respect to the use of RF.

Tables 3 and 5 show the results achieved using the 120-dimensional feature vector composed of the mean of 40 MFCC + 40 Δ(MFCC) + 40 Δ^2(MFCC) combined with RF and 1-D CNN on RAVDESS and EMODB datasets respectively. Also in this case, the 1-D CNN increases performance with respect RF.

Most important, the use of our 120-dimensional feature vector increases the accuracy of about 6% and 2%, in the case of RF and 1-D CNN respectively, with respect to the use of the 40-dimensional feature vector. This proves that the use of dynamic and acceleration features increase performance with respect to the use of only static features. This improvement related to the 1-D CNN could be likely much higher by modifying the network architecture. We did not do that since we mainly wanted to investigate the effectiveness of the designed features.

Table 5. Comparison between RF and CNN using Mean MFCC (40) + Mean Δ(MFCC) (40) + Δ^2(MFCC) (40) on the EMODB dataset

	Metric	Neutral	Happy	Sad	Angry	Fearful	Disgust	Bored
RF	Precision	0.78	0.87	0.82	0.90	0.87	0.67	0.76
	F-score	0.91	0.76	0.84	0.87	0.86	0.65	0.72
	Recall	0.84	0.81	0.83	0.89	0.87	0.66	0.74
	Accuracy	82.37%						
CNN	Precision	0.91	0.93	0.82	0.92	0.85	0.70	0.87
	F-score	0.91	0.78	0.86	0.92	0.89	0.78	0.84
	Recall	0.91	0.84	0.84	0.92	0.87	0.74	0.85
	Accuracy	86.48%						

Table 6. Comparison between our method and state-of-the-art methods using RAVDESS dataset

Method	Features	Classifier	Accuracy (%)
Shegocar et al. [25]	278 pros. features	Q-SVM	60.10
Popova et al. [22]	Spectrogram	VGG-16	71.00
Tanmoy et al. [29]	DWT	SVM	73.67
Tanmoy et al. [29]	DWT	GNB	77.71
Tanmoy et al. [29]	DWT	KNN	69.41
Parry et al. [21]	Spectrogram	CNN-LSTM	65.67
Zamil et al. [33]	13-dimensional MFCC	LMT	70.00
Our	40-dim MFCC	RF	80.24
Our	40-dim MFCC	1-D CNN	91.38
Our	120-dim MFCC	RF	86.40
Our	120-dim MFCC	1-D CNN	**93.41**

Finally, the comparison of our methods with the state of the art is reported in Tables 6 and 7. In this case, it could be noticed that for RAVDESS dataset the improvement in accuracy with respect to the best method in the state of the art is about 15%. Concerning the EMODB dataset, the improvement in accuracy with respect to the best method in the state of the art is much smaller and it is of about 5%.

Table 7. Comparison between our method and state-of-the-art methods using EMODB dataset

Method	Features	Classifier	Accuracy (%)
Lampropoulos et al. [14]	MPEG-7 descriptors	RBF-SVM	77.88
Tanmoy et al. [29]	DWT	SVM	73.74
Tanmoy et al. [29]	DWT	GNB	80.88
Tanmoy et al. [29]	DWT	KNN	72.75
Zamil et al. [33]	13-dimentional MFCC	LMT	64.51
Parry et al. [21]	Spectrogram	LSTM	69.72
Badshah et al. [1]	Spectrogram	2-D CNN	80.97
Our	40-dim MFCC	RF	76.50
Our	40-dim MFCC	1-D CNN	84.75
Our	120-dim MFCC	RF	82.37
Our	120-dim MFCC	1-D CNN	**86.48**

4 Conclusion

In this paper, we exploited static, dynamic and acceleration spectral features for recognizing emotions such as happiness, sadness, surprise, etc. from audio clips. We experimentally proved that the proposed method improves the state of the art being able to better modeling those characteristics of the human speech which are influenced by emotions. From a computational point of view there is room for further improvements in performance by better investigating the length and composition of the global feature vector and the architecture of the CNN-based classifier that has been ad-hoc defined here. This type of investigation can be approached by exploiting, for example, genetic programming [28]. As a future work, we want to exploit multi-modality. The use of vocalics combined with other cues like facial expressions or body language could increase emotion recognition rate.

References

1. Badshah, A.M., Rahim, N., Ullah, N., Ahmad, J., Muhammad, K., Lee, M.Y., Kwon, S., Baik, S.W.: Deep features-based speech emotion recognition for smart affective services. Multimedia Tools Appl. **78**(5), 5571–5589 (2017). https://doi.org/10.1007/s11042-017-5292-7
2. Barros, P., Parisi, G.I., Weber, C., Wermter, S.: Emotion-modulated attention improves expression recognition: a deep learning model. Neurocomputing **253**, 104–114 (2017)
3. Burkhardt, F., Paeschke, A., Rolfes, M., Sendlmeier, W.F., Weiss, B.: A database of German emotional speech. In: Ninth European Conference on Speech Communication and Technology (2005)

4. El Ayadi, M., Kamel, M.S., Karray, F.: Survey on speech emotion recognition: features, classification schemes, and databases. Pattern Recognit. **44**(3), 572–587 (2011)
5. Ganchev, T., Fakotakis, N., Kokkinakis, G.: Comparative evaluation of various MFCC implementations on the speaker verification task. In: Proceedings of the SPECOM, vol. 1, pp. 191–194 (2005)
6. Gao, Y., Li, B., Wang, N., Zhu, T.: Speech emotion recognition using local and global features. In: Zeng, Y., et al. (eds.) BI 2017. LNCS (LNAI), vol. 10654, pp. 3–13. Springer, Cham (2017). https://doi.org/10.1007/978-3-319-70772-3_1
7. Gu, Y., Postma, E., Lin, H.X., Herik, J.V.D.: Speech emotion recognition using voiced segment selection algorithm. In: Proceedings of the Twenty-second European Conference on Artificial Intelligence, pp. 1682–1683. IOS Press (2016)
8. Hans, A., Hans, E.: Kinesics haptics, and proxemics: aspects of non-verbal communication. IOSR J. Humanit. Soc. Sci. (IOSR-JHSS) **20**(2), 47–52 (2015)
9. Hanson, B.A., Applebaum, T.H.: Robust speaker-independent word recognition using static, dynamic and acceleration features: experiments with Lombard and noisy speech. In: International Conference on Acoustics, Speech, and Signal Processing, pp. 857–860. IEEE (1990)
10. Hasan, M.R., Jamil, M., Rahman, M., et al.: Speaker identification using mel frequency cepstral coefficients. Variations **1**(4), 565–568 (2004)
11. Ingale, A.B., Chaudhari, D., Ingale Ashish, B., et al.: Speech emotion recognition using hidden Markov model and support vector machine (2012)
12. Khalifa, I., Ejbali, R., Zaied, M.: Body gesture modeling for psychology analysis in job interview based on deep spatio-temporal approach. In: Park, J.H., Shen, H., Sung, Y., Tian, H. (eds.) PDCAT 2018. CCIS, vol. 931, pp. 274–284. Springer, Singapore (2019). https://doi.org/10.1007/978-981-13-5907-1_29
13. Khan, A., Sohail, A., Zahoora, U., Qureshi, A.S.: A survey of the recent architectures of deep convolutional neural networks. Artif. Intell. Rev. **53**(8), 5455–5516 (2020). https://doi.org/10.1007/s10462-020-09825-6
14. Lampropoulos, A.S., Tsihrintzis, G.A.: Evaluation of mpeg-7 descriptors for speech emotional recognition. In: 2012 Eighth International Conference on Intelligent Information Hiding and Multimedia Signal Processing, pp. 98–101. IEEE (2012)
15. Livingstone, S.R., Russo, F.A.: The Ryerson audio-visual database of emotional speech and song (RAVDESS): a dynamic, multimodal set of facial and vocal expressions in north American English. PloS One **13**(5), e0196391 (2018)
16. Ly, S.T., Lee, G.S., Kim, S.H., Yang, H.J.: Emotion recognition via body gesture: deep learning model coupled with keyframe selection. In: Proceedings of the 2018 International Conference on Machine Learning and Machine Intelligence, pp. 27–31 (2018)
17. Majeed, S.A., Husain, H., Samad, S.A., Idbeaa, T.F.: Mel frequency cepstral coefficients (MFCC) feature extraction enhancement in the application of speech recognition: a comparison study. J. Theor. Appl. Inf. Technol. **79**(1) (2015)
18. Mehrabian, A.: Communication without words. Psychol. Today, **2**(4) (1968)
19. Motamed, S., Setayeshi, S., Rabiee, A.: Speech emotion recognition based on a modified brain emotional learning model. Biologically Inspired Cognitive Architectures **19**, 32–38 (2017)
20. Noroozi, F., Kaminska, D., Corneanu, C., Sapinski, T., Escalera, S., Anbarjafari, G.: Survey on emotional body gesture recognition. IEEE Trans. Affect. Comput. **12**(2), 505–523 (2018)
21. Parry, J., et al.: Analysis of deep learning architectures for cross-corpus speech emotion recognition. In: Proceedings Interspeech, vol. 2019, 1656–1660 (2019)

22. Popova, A.S., Rassadin, A.G., Ponomarenko, A.A.: Emotion recognition in sound. In: Kryzhanovsky, B., Dunin-Barkowski, W., Redko, V. (eds.) NEUROINFORMATICS 2017. SCI, vol. 736, pp. 117–124. Springer, Cham (2018). https://doi.org/10.1007/978-3-319-66604-4_18
23. Prasomphan, S.: Improvement of speech emotion recognition with neural network classifier by using speech spectrogram. In: 2015 International Conference on Systems, Signals and Image Processing (IWSSIP), pp. 73–76. IEEE (2015)
24. Rabiner, L.: Fundamentals of speech recognition (1993)
25. Shegokar, P., Sircar, P.: Continuous wavelet transform based speech emotion recognition. In: 2016 10th International Conference on Signal Processing and Communication Systems (ICSPCS), pp. 1–8. IEEE (2016)
26. Singh, N., Khan, R., Shree, R.: MFCC and prosodic feature extraction techniques: a comparative study. Int. J. Comput. Appl. **54**(1) (2012)
27. Sree, G.D., Chandrasekhar, P., Venkatesshulu, B.: SVM based speech emotion recognition compared with GMM-UBM and NN. IJESC **6**(11), 3293–3298 (2016)
28. Sun, Y., Xue, B., Zhang, M., Yen, G.G.: Automatically designing CNN architectures using genetic algorithm for image classification. arXiv preprint arXiv:1808.03818 (2018)
29. Tanmoy, R., Snehashish, C., Tshilidzi, M., Paul, S.: Introducing new feature set based on wavelets for speech emotion classification. In: 2018 IEEE Applied Signal Processing Conference (ASPCON), pp. 124–128. IEEE (2018)
30. Vogt, T., André, E., Wagner, J.: Automatic recognition of emotions from speech: a review of the literature and recommendations for practical realisation. In: Peter, C., Beale, R. (eds.) Affect and Emotion in Human-Computer Interaction. LNCS, vol. 4868, pp. 75–91. Springer, Heidelberg (2008). https://doi.org/10.1007/978-3-540-85099-1_7
31. Vondra, M., Vích, R.: Recognition of emotions in German speech using gaussian mixture models. In: Esposito, A., Hussain, A., Marinaro, M., Martone, R. (eds.) Multimodal Signals: Cognitive and Algorithmic Issues. LNCS (LNAI), vol. 5398, pp. 256–263. Springer, Heidelberg (2009). https://doi.org/10.1007/978-3-642-00525-1_26
32. Witkower, Z., Tracy, J.L.: Bodily communication of emotion: evidence for extrafacial behavioral expressions and available coding systems. Emot. Rev. **11**(2), 184–193 (2019)
33. Zamil, A.A.A., Hasan, S., Baki, S.M.J., Adam, J.M., Zaman, I.: Emotion detection from speech signals using voting mechanism on classified frames. In: 2019 International Conference on Robotics, Electrical and Signal Processing Techniques (ICREST), pp. 281–285. IEEE (2019)

EEG-Based BCIs for Elderly Rehabilitation Enhancement Exploiting Artificial Data

Aurora Saibene[1,2](✉), Francesca Gasparini[1,2](✉), and Jordi Solé-Casals[3](✉)

[1] University of Milano-Bicocca, Viale Sarca 336, 20126 Milan, Italy
a.saibene2@campus.unimib.it, francesca.gasparini@unimib.it
[2] NeuroMI, Milan Center for Neuroscience, University of Milano-Bicocca, Piazza dell'Ateneo Nuovo 1, 20126 Milan, Italy
[3] University of Vic-Central University of Catalonia, C de la Laura 13, 08500 Vic, Barcelona, Spain
jordi.sole@uvic.cat

Abstract. The ageing process may lead to cognitive and physical impairments, which may affect elderly everyday life. In recent years, the use of Brain Computer Interfaces (BCIs) based on Electroencephalography (EEG) has revealed to be particularly effective to promote and enhance rehabilitation procedures, especially by exploiting motor imagery experimental paradigms. Moreover, BCIs seem to increase patients' engagement and have proved to be reliable tools for elderly overall wellness improvement. However, EEG signals usually present a low signal-to-noise ratio and can be recorded for a limited time. Thus, irrelevant information and faulty or insufficient samples could affect the BCI performance. Introducing a methodology that allows the extraction of informative components from the EEG signal while maintaining its intrinsic characteristics, may provide a solution to the described issues: noisy data may be avoided by having only relevant components and combining relevant components may represent a good strategy to substitute or augment the data without requiring long or repeated EEG recordings. To this end, in this work the EEG signal decomposition by means of multivariate empirical mode decomposition is proposed to obtain its oscillatory modes, called Intrinsic Mode Functions (IMFs). Subsequently, a novel procedure for relevant IMF selection based on the IMF time-frequency representation and entropy is provided. After having verified the reliability of the EEG signal reconstruction with the relevant IMFs only, the relevant IMFs are combined to produce new artificial data and provide new samples to use for BCI training.

Keywords: BCI · Data augmentation · EEG · Entropy · MEMD

1 Introduction

In the last years, the global growth of the elderly population [33,40] and the increased life expectancy [34] have been determining factors to increase the

S. Bandini et al. (Eds.): AIxIA 2021, LNAI 13196, pp. 359–374, 2022.
https://doi.org/10.1007/978-3-031-08421-8_25

awareness on the impact that ageing has on elderly people in their everyday life [40]. In fact, the ageing process may subjectively affect elderly cognitive abilities and introduce motor control impairments [1], which could require the intervention of caretakers and rehabilitation procedures, limiting an elderly person autonomy. Assistive technologies have become particularly attractive to enhance elderly people overall wellbeing, to allow them a certain independence and maintain their social connections [33,34,40].

Among the various technological innovations, the Brain Computer Interfaces (BCIs) have proved to be particularly apt to these tasks and found their application in cognitive and motor rehabilitation systems [1,4,12,22,24]. In fact, BCIs allow the decoding of brain dynamics in an on-line configuration [42] and can be exploited to control heterogeneous systems (e.g., wheelchairs [15]), and provide an instantaneous feedback to their users [24].

The most popular method to allow the recording of the BCI input brain signals is electroencephalography (EEG), which provides multivariate time series collected by placing electrodes on the scalp of a subject. Therefore, the EEG signals have proved to be particularly efficient in accessing brain activities and functions by bringing time, space (electrodes) and frequency information of the neuronal signals [20] in a non-invasive way. Regarding the frequency information, the EEG signal is characterized by different frequency bands (or rhythms) that are representative of specific brain dynamics [39,41]. We are particularly interested in the α and β frequency bands that can be specifically associated to different cognitive and motor functions and thus their dynamic changes can be widely exploited in rehabilitation systems based on motor imagery (MI) tasks [12,38]. An MI task consists of the imagination of a real movement, like imaging the opening and closing of a hand, and it has been proved that MI practice improve real movements during a rehabilitation process [22,24].

However, controlling a BCI system with MI is difficult and the ability to perform this task varies from person to person. A good control of a BCI is usually achieved when a user reaches the 70% accuracy in the MI paradigm [18]. Reaching this level of accuracy may require a long time, however MI tasks usually enhance brain plasticity and providing a feedback to their users could further improve the cognitive, motor and intellectual functions of elderly users, who are particularly affected by brain dynamic changes due to the ageing process [12].

Even though MI-BCI systems based on EEG signals seem to be promising tools for rehabilitation purposes, there are many challenges that should be considered and that can affect the overall BCI performance. In fact, the EEG signals, that are at the core of these systems, are extremely heterogeneous and easily affected by noise [31]. Moreover, collecting an adequate quantity of reliable data to perform the classification tasks involved in the BCI control system is difficult, due to the lack of sufficient time for recording, the possible poor number of subjects and the difficulty of the experimental tasks [45]. These issues may lead to a general classification deterioration and thus affect machine learning model performances [23].

In the EEG domain, attempts to solve the problem of generating new artificial signals have been provided by the data augmentation literature [20,23,45].

Many data augmentation approaches have been proposed in the literature [20]: additive noise, generative adversarial networks, sliding or overlapping windows, different sampling methods, EEG segment recombination and so on. However, the coherence between these artificial data and the brain dynamics recorded by the EEG should be considered and verified.

Dinarès-Ferran et al. [7] proposed an interesting data substitution approach[1]. They exploit the recombination of the oscillatory modes, called Intrinsic Mode Functions (IMFs), obtained through Empirical Mode Decomposition (EMD) [17] of the EEG signals to maintain the EEG time and frequency information even in the artificially produced portions of signals.

Motivated by this work and wanting to provide consistent artificial data to be employed in BCI systems without requiring elderly people to sit over long experimental sessions, we propose a novel processing of EEG data for BCI rehabilitation systems. Therefore, the present paper extends *Dinarès-Ferran et al.* [7] work and focuses on finding significant IMFs for portions of MI signals presenting tasks of interest, from now on called trials. The IMFs are computed with a multivariate extension of the EMD algorithm [29], wanting to maintain the cross-channel interdependence typical of EEG data [5]. The IMFs are then selected and recombined in order to obtain an unbiased data substitution or augmentation. Therefore, our main contributions are (i) the time-frequency representation of the IMFs, on which (ii) the entropy is computed to define the most informative (relevant) IMFs and (iii) the reconstruction of artificial trials by significant IMF combination. These steps should provide artificial EEG signals presenting coherent brain dynamics and thus exploitable in a BCI paradigm.

The work is then organized as follows. Section 2 provides a brief literature review on EMD and its multivariate extension, when exploited for IMF selection or data substitution/augmentation. Section 3 presents the datasets and literature methods employed. Section 4 describes our proposed approach for relevant IMF selection and artificial data generation. Section 5 discusses the obtained results and Sect. 6 concludes the work.

2 Related Works

As introduced in Sect. 1 and starting from [7], this work will focus on the use of the Multivariate Empirical Mode Decomposition (MEMD) [29] to select relevant IMFs and recombine them to produce new trials. In this section a brief overview of the works presenting some solutions for relevant, redundant, or noisy IMF selection will be provided.

In the EMD literature, some authors [2,25] have focused on finding redundant IMFs by exploiting the Minkowski distance and the Jensen-Rènyi divergence [28] to track the differences between the original signals and the IMFs. Instead, *Bueno et al.* [3] selected the IMFs if their entropy was greater than a specifically defined threshold $(\max \boldsymbol{e} - \min \boldsymbol{e})/2 + \min \boldsymbol{e}$, where $\boldsymbol{e}$ is the vector containing the entropy of all the IMFs.

[1] The original code is available at https://github.com/ffbear1993/DR-EMD.

Considering the MEMD literature, the IMF selection has been performed (i) empirically by retaining the IMFs whose combination provides the best classification performance [26], (ii) by comparing through the Wasserstein distance [32] the IMFs obtained by decomposing the EEG data against the IMFs coming from reference electrodes [16], or (iii) by using a measure of similarity between IMFs and reference noise [14,19]. Instead, in [10,27] the authors found the α and β rhythm contributions by computing the median frequency values of each IMF, or obtained consistent IMFs between subjects and selected the first 2 IMFs retaining δ rhythm information. Similarly, our IMF selection is based on choosing the frequency ranges characterizing EEG rhythms of interest.

Besides IMF selection or noise removal, EMD and some of its variations have been exploited for artificial data generation. Considering the reference work, *Dinarès-Ferran et al.* [7] employed EMD and obtained IMFs for each trial. Afterwards, they generated artificial data by combining 15 IMFs of different trials and used them to substitute certain percentages of the data, finding that the efficacy of these substitutions varies from subject to subject. A similar strategy has been presented by *Lee et al.* [21], who decomposed the signals with the ensemble variation of the EMD [43], instead of using the original EMD. Instead, *Zhang et al.* [46] directly exploited the strategy defined by *Dinarès-Ferran et al.* and used it for data augmentation by obtaining a significant improvement of their neural network results. Similarly, *Zhao et al.* [47] achieved better performances on their deep learning model, by recombining the signals transformed in the frequency domain through discrete cosine transform.

As a final remark, notice that the majority of the described methodologies set the maximum number of IMFs to combine to a specific and unchanged number (during computation), and when producing artificial data, all the IMFs are considered.

3 Methods

3.1 Datasets

The following procedures have been tested on 3 datasets: (i) the *EEG Simulated* (ES) dataset [8,9], (ii) the *EEG Motor Imagery BCI* (MIB) dataset [7], and (iii) the *EEG Motor Movement/Imagery Dataset* (MMI) [11,37].

The choice of the ES dataset was driven by the necessity of assessing the efficacy of the proposed relevant IMF selection on controlled data. In fact, it presents clean and raw (noise affected with signal-to-noise ratio from −20 dB to 20 dB and adding ocular artifacts) simulated EEG signals on 19 electrodes, i.e., $C\{3,4,z\}$, $F\{3,4,7,8,z\}$, $Fp\{1,2\}$, $O\{1,2\}$, $P\{3,4,z\}$, $T\{3,4,5,6\}$, and considering the α, β, and γ rhythms. 10 trials of 10 s each have been generated. For further details, please refer to [8,9].

Instead, the MIB dataset was chosen due to the fact that it has been employed by the reference work on artificial trial substitution for a BCI paradigm [7]. 7 healthy males were asked to perform a MI task consisting of left/right wrist dorsiflexion imagined movements. Each subject participated to 2 experimental runs, during each of which 40 tasks of left and 40 tasks of right wrist MI were randomly performed. A trial consisted of 2 s of resting time, an acoustic cue for task preparation and 5 s of motor imagination. The recorded electrodes were $C\{1, 2, 3, 4, 5, 6, z\}$, $Cp\{1, 2, 5, 6\}$, $Fc\{1, 2, 5, 6, z\}$. Notice that the dataset has been pre-processed by the authors, who used a bandpass ($0.5 - 30$ Hz) and a notch (50 Hz) filter. For more details, please refer to [7].

Lastly, to confirm the results obtained on the MIB dataset, the MMI dataset has been chosen, presenting runs of left/right fist MI and thus with experimental conditions similar to the MIB ones. In fact, 109 subjects were asked to perform 3 runs of left/right hand motor imagery tasks, according to a visual cue. Between each task (4.1 s), a resting phase (4.2 s) was always presented. In the present work, of the 64 recorded electrodes, 27 have been used for our procedure testing, i.e., $C\{1, 2, 3, 4, 5, 6, z\}$, $F\{1, 2, 3, 4, z\}$, $Fp\{1, 2, z\}$, $P\{1, 2, 3, 4, z\}$, $O\{1, 2, z\}$, $T\{7, 8, 9, 10\}$. 3 subjects were excluded due to technical issues present on the recordings. Find more details on the dataset repository[2].

3.2 Multivariate Empirical Mode Decomposition

The Empirical Mode Decomposition (EMD) [17] is a signal processing technique that allows the decomposition of a time series into oscillatory modes (the IMFs), with a completely data-driven approach and avoiding the loss or distortion of the data [44]. In fact, considering a signal $x(t)$, it (i) finds the signal local maxima and minima, (ii) defines $x(t)$ upper and lower envelopes, (iii) computes their mean envelope and (iv) subtracts it from $x(t)$, obtaining the detail $d(t)$. The computation is repeated assigning $d(t)$ to $x(t)$, until $d(t)$ satisfies the IMFs conditions, i.e., its number of zero-crossings and extrema are equal or differ by a unit and its mean envelope is zero. Thus, $d(t)$ is considered as an IMF and $x(t)$ can be reconstructed by summing the obtained I IMFs and a residuum $\epsilon(t)$: $x(t) = \sum_{i=1}^{I} IMF_i(t) + \epsilon_I(t)$. Therefore, EMD seems to be suitable to deal with non-stationary and non-linear signals [8], like the EEG ones. However, it works on multivariate signals with a channel-by-channel approach, thus ignoring the cross-channel interdependence which characterizes the EEG signals [5].

To address this issue, *Rehman and Mandic* proposed an EMD variation, i.e., the Multivariate Empirical Mode Decomposition (MEMD) [29]. MEMD provides IMFs with the same number of oscillations for each channel by exploiting different projections of the n-channel signal into a n-dimensional space. Thus, given a multivariate signal $\{\boldsymbol{x}(t)\}_{t=1}^{T} = \{x_1(t), x_2(t), ..., x_n(t)\}$, MEMD:

1. Chooses a suitable direction vector $\boldsymbol{v}^{\theta_k} = \{v_1^k, v_2^k, ..., v_n^k\}$, where $k = 1, 2, ..., K$ and K is the total number of direction vectors and $\boldsymbol{\theta}_k = \{\theta_1^k, \theta_2^k, ..., \theta_l^k\}$ are the angles on a $(n-1)$ sphere along which are defined the direction vectors.
2. Computes the kth projection of $\{\boldsymbol{x}(t)\}_{t=1}^{T}$ along $\boldsymbol{v}^{\theta_k}$, obtaining $\{\boldsymbol{p}^{\theta_k}(t)\}_{k=1}^{K}$ for all k.

[2] https://physionet.org/content/eegmmidb/1.0.0/.

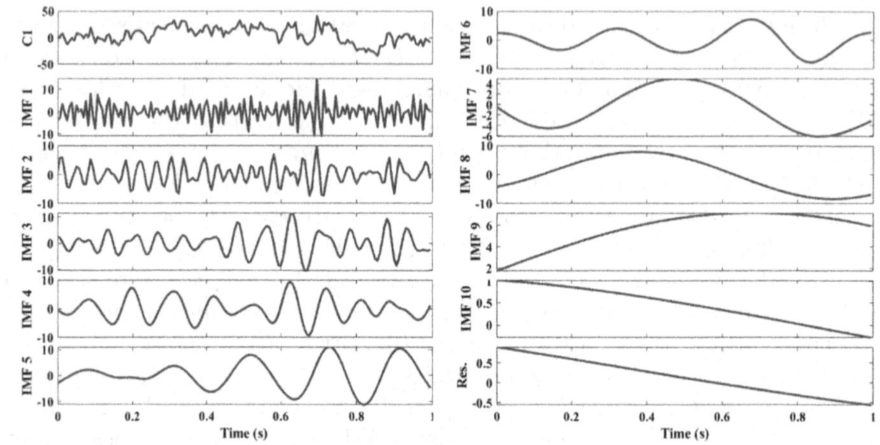

Fig. 1. Example of IMFs obtained by applying MEMD to electrode *C1*. The last oscillatory mode corresponds to the residuum.

3. Finds $\{\boldsymbol{t}_i^{\theta_k}\}_{k=1}^{K}$ time instants, which correspond to the $\{\boldsymbol{p}^{\theta_k}(t)\}_{k=1}^{K}$ maxima.
4. Interpolates $[\boldsymbol{t}_i^{\theta_k}, \boldsymbol{x}(\boldsymbol{t}_i^{\theta_k})]$ to obtain $\{\boldsymbol{e}^{\theta_k}(t)\}_{k=1}^{K}$ for all k.
5. Estimates the mean envelope for a set of K direction vectors: $\boldsymbol{m}(t) = \frac{1}{K}\sum_{k=1}^{K}\boldsymbol{e}^{\theta_k}(t)$.
6. Extracts the detail $\boldsymbol{d}_j(t) = \boldsymbol{x}(t) - \boldsymbol{m}(t)$, where $j = 1, 2, ..., J$ and J is the maximum number of decomposition scales. If $\boldsymbol{d}_j(t)$ meets the IMF conditions, point 1–3 are applied to $\boldsymbol{x}(t) - \boldsymbol{d}_j(t)$, otherwise to $\boldsymbol{d}_j(t)$.

In this work, MEMD is used to decompose the data of each subject and trial. Figure 1 shows an example of the IMFs obtained by applying MEMD on the electrode *C1* of a specific subject and trial. The x axis corresponds to the time (s) and the y axis to the signal amplitude (μV).

4 Our Proposal

After having obtained the same number of IMFs for each electrode of a specific subject and trial, the IMFs are used as inputs to the proposed procedure, which consists of 4 main steps: (i) generation of the time-frequency images for each IMF, (ii) entropy computation on the time-frequency images, (iii) significant IMF selection criterion, and (iv) data substitution/augmentation.

Firstly, the time-frequency image generation requires the choice of a frequency range of interest and its time-frequency resolution. Having as targets MI tasks, the chosen frequency range spans from 8 to 30 Hz. In fact, this range includes the α (8–13 Hz) and β (13–30 Hz) frequency bands, which are involved in the motor tasks [38] (Sect. 1). Also, a trade-off between the time and frequency resolution [35] is preferred for image reconstruction. Then, the procedure loops on the frequency range and starts with the generation of a complex Morlet

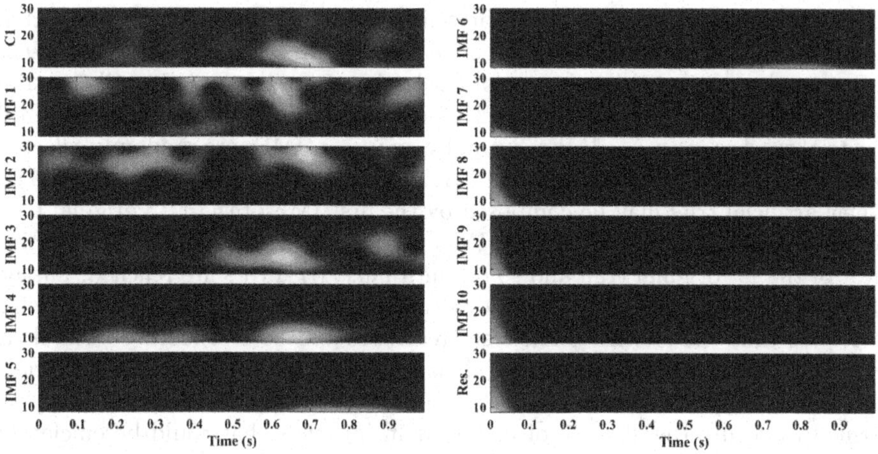

Fig. 2. Example of the time-frequency images obtained by applying Morlet wavelet convolution on each of the IMFs presented in Fig. 1.

wavelet [6] exploiting the described parameters. Subsequently, it proceeds with the application of the fast Fourier transform on both the wavelet and the original signal. Afterwards, the inverse fast Fourier transform is applied to the wavelet convolved on the signal. Finally, the power data of the convolution is computed and thus the time-frequency image obtained.

Figure 2 presents a colored example of the time-frequency images obtained by computing this procedure on each subject, trial, electrode and relative IMFs (presented in Fig. 1). The x axis corresponds to the time (s) and the y axis to the frequency range (Hz). From the provided example, some clear differences in the IMFs can be observed and we can hypothesize that the IMFs containing more information are the ones which present a more complex texture. Entropy [13] can be used to characterize the texture of an image and thus is employed to find the IMFs having more variability. Here the entropy is computed on the time-frequency gray scale image and is equal to $-\sum(p \times \log_2(p))$, where p presents the normalized histogram counts of the time-frequency image.

Considering the entropy obtained on all the IMFs of all the electrodes of a specific trial, the IMFs having entropy greater than the mean entropy are selected as the most significant ones. A more conservative approach is preferred to the elimination of a greater number of IMFs in order to avoid the exclusion of effective neurophysiological signals. The same number of IMFs are selected for all the electrodes of the same trial.

Finally, the last step of our proposal is the artificial data generation, which is performed on each subject by randomly combining the entropy-selected IMFs of different trials of the same task, using a scheme similar to the one described in [7,46]. For each subject, a specific number of artificial trials balanced between the tasks of interest are produced following 3 main steps. Firstly, the maximum number of entropy-selected IMFs max_{IMF} is found to have the same number of

IMFs for each trial. In case a trial presents a lesser number of entropy-selected IMFs if it was decomposed in at least max_{IMF}-IMFs, the corresponding oscillation modes discarded by the entropy selection are reintegrated until the trial reaches max_{IMF}-IMFs, otherwise IMFs equal to a null vector are added until the trial reaches max_{IMF}-IMFs. Secondly, max_{IMF}-IMFs are randomly selected from the IMFs of max_{IMF} different original trials for each artificial trial. E.g., a new artificial trial may be composed by the first IMF of the 17th original trial (of the same task), by the second IMF of the 5th original trial, by the third IMF of the 1st original trial and so on until max_{IMF}-IMFs are reached. Lastly, the artificial trials are reconstructed according to the IMFs obtained at point 2. Notice that the original trials were reconstructed by considering both their max_{IMF}-IMFs to provide coherent signals to compare with the artificial trials and the entropy-selected IMFs. Also, analyses on the trial similarity are performed to ensure the absence of biased artificial trials that could be efficiently used in BCI rehabilitation systems.

5 Results and Discussion

To better understand the reliability of the proposed relevant IMF selection, a preliminary experiment has been conducted on the *EEG Simulated* (ES) dataset.

MEMD has been applied for each trial of the clean and raw data, considering all the signal-to-noise ratio realizations (from -20 dB to 20 dB). Subsequently, the time-frequency images of the obtained IMFs have been generated considering the $8-30$ Hz frequency range. Finally, the entropy selection criterion has been applied and the entropy-selected IMFs summed up to obtain the reconstructed EEG signal.

The assessment of the proposed method reliability has been performed by computing the similarity between the clean and raw/entropy-reconstructed data by means of Pearson correlation coefficient. The similarity check has been applied to each signal-to-noise ratio realization, trial, and electrode.

We found that for low signal-to-noise ratios (about -20 dB to -17 dB), the Pearson correlation coefficient obtained by comparing the clean data versus the entropy-reconstructed ones do not deviate from the results obtained by applying it on the clean data versus the raw ones. However, a significant increase of the Pearson correlation coefficient is present for the clean versus entropy-reconstructed signal case with signal-to-noise ratio greater or equal to -12 dB. Even though the similarity between the clean and entropy-reconstructed signals increases with higher values of signal-to-noise ratio, it seems that for the electrodes that are usually affected by ocular artifacts the Pearson correlation coefficient remains generally low. For all the clean versus raw data cases, the mean similarity remains always lower than 0.9 and for the majority of the electrodes remains under 0.6.

Therefore, the proposed strategy is considered sufficiently reliable for relevant IMF selection and signal reconstruction, having that its results do not deviate from the raw data or that are sufficiently similar to the clean ones.

Having obtained a reliable method for relevant IMF selection, it is hypothesized that the entropy-selected IMFs could be efficiently used to reconstruct simulated trials while sufficiently maintaining the intrinsic EEG brain dynamics. As previously introduced, having that the proposed strategy is modeled on the one described by *Dinarès-Ferran et al.* [7] and that considers a BCI experiment, the *EEG Motor Imagery BCI* (MIB) dataset has been used for testing.

The procedure has been computed on each subject and again the MEMD has been applied for each trial separately. Notice that the final goal is to discriminate the left (LW) from the right (RW) wrist MI, which could be applied to control a rehabilitation system. Firstly, random trials were substituted by artificial ones. These trials were obtained by unique combinations of max_{IMF} relevant IMFs selected through the entropy criterion and belonging to max_{IMF} different original trials. Remind that max_{IMF} corresponds to the overall *maximum number of IMFs* selected by the entropy criterion. The artificial trials were then reconstructed by summing the selected IMFs.

To reproduce *Dinarès-Ferran et al.* [7] testing, 2.5, 5.0, 7.5, 10.0, 12.5, 25.0, 37.5, 50.0% of trial substitutions were performed.

The power spectral density was extracted for each electrode through Morlet wavelet convolution [36]. This feature extraction follows the time-frequency image representation computation, but as a final step, the power data is integrated in the frequency range of interest. Two rhythms were considered separately, i.e., the α and β frequency bands, obtaining a total of 38 features. These rhythms have been chosen, due to the presence of MI tasks (Sect. 1). The feature extraction has been restricted on the signal portion during which the MI task is performed to mimic *Dinarès-Ferran et al.* [7] experimental setting.

Finally, a Linear Discriminant Analysis (LDA) classifier has been applied. For each subject the first run has been used as the training set and the second run as the test set.

As a first analysis, Table 1 reports the median error rates, i.e., the percentages of predicted values that have been wrongly classified for each class [7], for both the RW and LW conditions after having applied LDA 100 times on the original and reconstructed data. The results obtained by *Dinarès-Ferran et al.* [7] (row *DF* of Table 1) have been reported for completeness, however notice that their error rate evaluation is based on all the signal samples and that the features are extracted through common spatial pattern application.

The remaining table rows present the results obtained by considering the runs in their original form (row *OO*), and the entropy-reconstructed data of run 1 as the training set and the original data of run 2 as the test set (row *RO*). This last test has been conducted trying to mimic a real-time scenario, during which previously analysed data (e.g., BCI training phase) may be exploited to predict new unseen data (e.g., BCI translation phase).

Firstly, notice that the results obtained by the proposed strategy seem to be more balanced compared to the ones reported in [7] (DF). Secondly, the *RO* results have been used for comparison with the artificial trial substitution results, which are reported in Table 2, having that their values are comparable

Table 1. Median error rates (%) obtained by applying 100 times the LDA classifier on the right (RW) and left wrist (LW) motor imagery.

	S01		S02		S03		S04		S05		S06		S07	
	RW	LW	RW	LW	RW	LW	RW	LW	RW	LW	RW	LW	RW	LW
DF	5.50	6.68	11.20	66.67	29.83	20.39	42.67	32.96	36.24	35.79	27.27	39.60	58.34	22.74
OO	0.00	0.00	35.00	60.00	57.50	55.00	45.00	42.50	45.00	35.00	45.00	45.00	35.00	35.00
RO	0.00	2.50	35.00	57.50	52.50	57.50	32.50	40.00	45.00	37.50	45.00	45.00	35.00	37.50

to the ones obtained for the *OO* test. Notice that the field *AT (%)* refers to the percentage of trial substitutions balanced between the RW and LW conditions. Therefore, row 1 (*0.0%*) corresponds to the *RO* results presented in the last row of Table 1.

It can be observed that the results vary from subject to subject. In fact, subject *S01* may be considered a good MI task performer, having that in the RO case the error rates are 2.50 and 0.00 for the RW and LW task, respectively and thus complying with what has been stated in Sect. 1: a person is good in performing MI tasks when he/she can accurately imagine the movement for at least the 70% of the task repetitions. Considering a less stringent constraint, *S07* may be also considered good in the MI experiment. Instead, the remaining subjects seem to have some difficulties performing the MI tasks. Analysing *S01* and *S07*, besides the 37.5% and 50.0% substitutions performed on *S01*'s trial, it can be noticed that the error rates remain stable or improve. Concerning the remaining subjects, the error rates are generally not improved. However, these error rates become more balanced between the conditions and for *S03* and *S04* there seem to be a decrease in the error rate values for some substitution percentages.

Therefore, to ensure that the results obtained with the trial substitutions are coherent with the original results, a double Median Absolute Deviation (MAD) [30] has been applied to detect if the median results obtained on the original trials could be considered outliers in respect to all the 100 results obtained for each trial substitution. Notice that if more than the 50% of the classification results are equal, the MAD is 0. Table 3 reports the outliers detected by double MAD application, with the following interpretation: (i) if a cell contains *0M*, it means that the MAD is 0, (ii) if a cell contains *o*, it means that the result obtained on the original trial is considered an outlier in respect to the results obtained on the artificial trial substitution, and (iii) if a cell contains a non-zero number, it means that the double MAD detected that specific number of outliers.

Analysing Table 3, the original trial result seems to appear as an outlier in a sufficiently limited number of cases. The proposed strategy results unreliable for *S02*'s RW condition, otherwise it results efficient especially when making few substitutions (2.5 to 5.0%) or a greater number of substitutions (25.0 to 50.0%). The overall number of outliers seems also to be fairly low.

Therefore, the artificial trial generation is subsequently exploited for data augmentation, obtaining the median error rates reported in Table 4. The *AT (%)* field refers to the percentage of augmented trials, balanced between RW

Table 2. Median error rates (%) obtained by applying 100 times the artificial trial generation and the LDA classifier on the right (RW) and left wrist (LW) dorsiflexion for the trial substitution experiment.

AT	S01		S02		S03		S04		S05		S06		S07	
(%)	RW	LW	RW	LW	RW	LW	RW	LW	RW	LW	RW	LW	RW	LW
0.0	0.00	2.50	35.00	57.50	52.50	57.50	32.50	40.00	45.00	37.50	45.00	45.00	35.00	37.50
2.5	0.00	2.50	37.50	57.50	52.50	52.50	32.50	40.00	45.00	45.00	45.00	45.00	27.50	30.00
5.0	0.00	2.50	37.50	55.00	47.50	47.50	32.50	37.50	45.00	47.50	42.50	47.50	27.50	27.50
7.5	0.00	2.50	40.00	52.50	45.00	47.50	32.50	37.50	45.00	50.00	42.50	50.00	27.50	30.00
10.0	0.00	2.50	42.50	52.50	45.00	50.00	32.50	37.50	45.00	50.00	42.50	50.00	30.00	30.00
12.5	0.00	2.50	42.50	52.50	45.00	47.50	32.50	37.50	45.00	50.00	40.00	50.00	30.00	30.00
25.0	2.50	5.00	47.50	50.00	42.50	45.00	32.50	37.50	45.00	50.00	40.00	50.00	32.50	32.50
37.5	5.00	7.50	47.50	47.50	42.50	45.00	37.50	40.00	47.50	47.50	42.50	50.00	32.50	35.00
50.0	7.50	10.00	47.50	45.00	45.00	45.00	40.00	42.50	50.00	47.50	45.00	52.50	37.50	37.50

Table 3. Outlier detection performed through double MAD computation on the original and trial substitution results for the trial substitution experiment.

AT	S01		S02		S03		S04		S05		S06		S07	
(%)	RW	LW	RW	LW	RW	LW	RW	LW	RW	LW	RW	LW	RW	LW
2.5	0M	0M	0M	0M	28	9	15	0M	6	17	0M	0M	9	0M
5.0	0M	0M	0M - o	11	17	18	0M	1	6	9	9	9	9	9
7.5	0M	0M	20	4	1	7	9	0M - o	10	3 - o	28	0M	10 - o	10
10.0	0M	0M	17 - o	8	8	4	16	2	17	4 - o	28	13	0M - o	9
12.5	0M	0M	14 - o	20	7	4	11	0M - o	13	7 - o	0M	0M	0M - o	3
25.0	0M	0M	17 - o	1	8	5	3	3	23	1	21	19	4	19
37.5	22	0M - o	15 - o	8	32	5	4	12	9	1	11	9	12	1
50.0	22 - o	8	13 - o	1	4	3	20	10	9	2	2	6	14	11

and LW conditions. Notice that the observations given for the trial substitution case hold, with an ulterior improvement of the error rates for subject *S01*, *S07*, *S03* and *S04*. For the other subjects, the error rates do not improve, but are again more balanced between conditions and do not increase significantly.

Making a final evaluation of the results achieved by the trial substitution through the proposed artificial trial generation, the observation given by *Dinarès-Ferran et al.* [7] is confirmed: for subjects that naturally perform better the MI tasks, the strategy is generally more effective. Moreover, the proposed methodology seems to be not extremely faulty when dealing with possibly unskilled subjects. Thus, the performed data augmentation may represent a good solution to the EEG data dimensionality problem, providing improved results that do not deviate excessively from the original ones to train a BCI system.

To have a further assessment on these last observations, the proposed trial simulation for data augmentation has been tested on the left (LH) and right hand

Table 4. Median error rates (%) obtained by applying 100 times the artificial trial generation and the LDA classifier on the right (RW) and left wrist (LW) dorsiflexion for the trial augmentation experiment.

AT	S01		S02		S03		S04		S05		S06		S07	
(%)	RW	LW	RW	LW	RW	LW	RW	LW	RW	LW	RW	LW	RW	LW
0.0	0.00	2.50	35.00	57.50	52.50	57.50	32.50	40.00	45.00	37.50	45.00	45.00	35.00	37.50
2.5	0.00	0.00	37.50	57.50	52.50	52.50	32.50	40.00	45.00	45.00	45.00	45.00	27.50	32.50
5.0	0.00	0.00	37.50	55.00	50.00	50.00	32.50	37.50	45.00	47.50	42.50	50.00	25.00	30.00
7.5	0.00	2.50	40.00	55.00	47.50	47.50	32.50	37.50	45.00	47.50	42.50	50.00	27.50	27.50
10.0	0.00	2.50	40.00	52.50	47.50	47.50	30.00	37.50	42.50	47.50	40.00	50.00	27.50	27.50
12.5	0.00	2.50	42.50	52.50	45.00	47.50	30.00	37.50	45.00	50.00	40.00	52.50	30.00	27.50
25.0	0.00	5.00	45.00	52.50	42.50	47.50	30.00	37.50	45.00	50.00	40.00	55.00	30.00	30.00
37.5	0.00	5.00	47.50	52.50	42.50	47.50	30.00	37.50	45.00	47.50	37.50	55.00	30.00	30.00
50.0	0.00	5.00	47.50	50.00	40.00	47.50	30.00	37.50	45.00	47.50	37.50	55.00	30.00	30.00

(RH) MI tasks present in the *EEG Motor Movement/Imagery Dataset* (MMI). In fact, these conditions are similar to the MIB dataset ones and could be easily exploited to control a BCI system.

Firstly, the data have been bandpass (0.5 – 100 Hz) and notch (50 Hz) filtered. Then, the decomposition through MEMD application has been performed on each subject and trial. Afterwards, the time-frequency images of the obtained IMFs have been generated considering the frequency range of interest (8 – 30 Hz) as in MIB testing. Subsequently, the relevant IMFs have been selected through the entropy criterion. The signal has been reconstructed and the data augmented 100 times differently for each added trial set. Notice that each run contains 45 tasks of LH and RH MI. The conditions are sufficiently balanced, having their number differing of at most a unit. Therefore, the added trials per condition are 3 (∼10%), 6 (∼25%), 9 (∼40%), 12 (∼50%), 15 (∼65%), 18 (∼80%), and 21 (∼90%). For each filtered original, reconstructed and data augmented obtained set, the power spectral density has been extracted through Morlet wavelet convolution on electrodes $C\{1, 2, 3, 4, z\}$, considering the α and β frequency bands, and a trade-off between the time and frequency precision. Therefore, 10 features have been extracted. The electrode subset was chosen to avoid curse of dimensionality while performing the classification on the original set and maintained to have comparable results. The choice of the central electrodes is also justified by the MI literature, which states that the motor rhythms are activated in the central brain area [12]. Afterwards, the LDA classifier has been applied with a 5-fold cross validation.

Classifying all the original data (106 subjects) with the LDA model, we noticed that only 24 subjects could be considered sufficiently good MI performers. Therefore, the procedure has been performed on these 24 subjects and on 24 other random subjects that seem to have some difficulties in completing the

MI tasks[3]. Subsequently, median error rates (%) have been obtained (i) for the 100 repetitions of the LDA classification on the original and reconstructed data, and (ii) by applying the same classifier to the 100 repetitions of the data augmentation strategy.

The results on the original and reconstructed data are comparable as in the MIB test for all the subjects. Moreover, the error rates decrease significantly compared to the original and reconstructed results, while for the other subjects, the error rate generally increases. This effect could be due not only to the difficulties a subject may face in performing the MI task which could lead to unreliable trials for a control system, but also to the presence of noisy data. Therefore, a further development of the trial simulation could be represented by the identification of faulty trials in respect to the experiment of interest. In fact, these trials could deteriorate the overall classification performances and by removing them the trial recombination could benefit the data generation procedure. Moreover, a BCI system could benefit from the faulty trial detection not only intended as noisy trials but also as unreliable trials. In fact, understanding immediately if an elderly person has some difficulties in performing the MI task could provide a better BCI training phase by giving preciser feedback to the subject him/herself and thus increase the task success and decrease subjects' possible frustration.

As a final remark, the proposed methodology seems however to be not extremely faulty when dealing with possibly unskilled subjects. Thus, the performed data substitution may represent a good solution to the EEG data dimensionality problem, providing results that do not deviate excessively from the original ones to train a BCI system.

6 Conclusions

This work has provided a brief overview of BCI systems based on motor imagery and electroencephalography to enhance elderly people rehabilitation procedures.

A novel strategy to process the EEG signals before inputting them to the BCI system has been proposed to provide more reliable data without requiring long experimental sessions.

In fact, having the possibility of producing artificial trials that are coherent with the natural brain dynamics can benefit the training phase of a BCI, which usually requires a long time to have a precise subject profile and thus guarantee a correct control of the system. By decreasing the training time, the BCI tasks should also become less demanding both physically and mentally for an elderly patient, who could feel more engaged and less stressed by the training procedure.

Therefore, the EEG signal decomposition by means of MEMD and the relevant IMFs selection through a newly defined entropy criterion have been applied to 3 datasets. The proposed approach testing revealed that the signal reconstruction by using only the relevant IMFs is reliable and that the recombination of the relevant IMFs can be efficiently used for artificial trial generation. However,

[3] The detailed results and relative tables are available at https://github.com/asaibn/AIxIA2021.

we have noticed that the proposed strategy is particularly suitable for trial substitution of signals recorded from good MI performers (as in [7]). Therefore, we hypothesize that detecting faulty trials in terms of noise and unsuccessful MI performing, may benefit the artificial trial generation as well as the BCI training phase during which an elderly user may effectively improve his/her brain plasticity.

Future works will focus on these directions and on exploiting the trial generation strategy on datasets outside the field of motor imagery, wanting to address a broader spectrum of elderly-related impairments, like the cognitive ones.

References

1. Belkacem, A.N., Jamil, N., Palmer, J.A., Ouhbi, S., Chen, C.: Brain computer interfaces for improving the quality of life of older adults and elderly patients. Front. Neurosci. **14**, 692 (2020)
2. Boutana, D., Benidir, M., Barkat, B.: On the selection of intrinsic mode function in emd method: application on heart sound signal. In: 2010 3rd International Symposium on Applied Sciences in Biomedical and Communication Technologies (ISABEL 2010), pp. 1–5. IEEE (2010)
3. Bueno-López, M., Muñoz-Gutiérrez, P.A., Giraldo, E., Molinas, M.: Analysis of epileptic activity based on brain mapping of EEG adaptive time-frequency decomposition. In: Wang, S., Yamamoto, V., Su, J., Yang, Y., Jones, E., Iasemidis, L., Mitchell, T. (eds.) BI 2018. LNCS (LNAI), vol. 11309, pp. 319–328. Springer, Cham (2018). https://doi.org/10.1007/978-3-030-05587-5_30
4. Carelli, L., et al.: Brain-computer interface for clinical purposes: cognitive assessment and rehabilitation. BioMed Res. Int. **2017** (2017)
5. Chen, X., Xu, X., Liu, A., McKeown, M.J., Wang, Z.J.: The use of multivariate EMD and CCA for denoising muscle artifacts from few-channel EEG recordings. IEEE Trans. Instrum. Meas. **67**(2), 359–370 (2017)
6. Cohen, M.X.: A better way to define and describe Morlet wavelets for time-frequency analysis. NeuroImage **199**, 81–86 (2019)
7. Dinarès-Ferran, J., Ortner, R., Guger, C., Solé-Casals, J.: A new method to generate artificial frames using the empirical mode decomposition for an EEG-based motor imagery BCI. Front. Neurosci. **12**, 308 (2018)
8. Gallego-Jutglà, E., Solé-Casals, J., Rutkowski, T.M., Cichocki, A.: Application of Multivariate Empirical Mode Decomposition for Cleaning Eye Blinks Artifacts from EEG Signals. In: IJCCI (NCTA), pp. 455–460 (2011)
9. Gallego Jutglà, E., et al.: New signal processing and machine learning methods for EEG data analysis of patients with Alzheimer's disease. Ph.D. thesis, Universitat de Vic-Universitat Central de Catalunya (2015)
10. Gaur, P., Pachori, R.B., Wang, H., Prasad, G.: An automatic subject specific intrinsic mode function selection for enhancing two-class EEG-based motor imagery-brain computer interface. IEEE Sens. J. **19**(16), 6938–6947 (2019)
11. Goldberger, A.L., et al.: PhysioBank, PhysioToolkit, and PhysioNet: components of a new research resource for complex physiologic signals. Circulation **101**(23), e215–e220 (2000)
12. Gomez-Pilar, J., Corralejo, R., Nicolas-Alonso, L.F., Álvarez, D., Hornero, R.: Neurofeedback training with a motor imagery-based BCI: neurocognitive improvements and EEG changes in the elderly. Med. Biol. Eng. Comput. **54**(11), 1655–1666 (2016). https://doi.org/10.1007/s11517-016-1454-4

13. Gonzalez, R.: Digital image processing using Matlab-Gonzalez Woods & Eddins. pdf. Education (2004)
14. Hao, H., Wang, H., Rehman, N.: A joint framework for multivariate signal denoising using multivariate empirical mode decomposition. Signal Process. **135**, 263–273 (2017)
15. Herweg, A., Gutzeit, J., Kleih, S., Kübler, A.: Wheelchair control by elderly participants in a virtual environment with a brain-computer interface (BCI) and tactile stimulation. Biol. Psychol. **121**, 117–124 (2016)
16. Hu, M., Liang, H.: Search for information-bearing components in neural data. PLoS One **9**(6), e99793 (2014)
17. Huang, N.E., et al.: The empirical mode decomposition and the Hilbert spectrum for nonlinear and non-stationary time series analysis. Proc. R. Soc. Lond. A: Math. Phys. Eng. Sci. **454**(1971), 903–995 (1998)
18. Kaiser, V., Bauernfeind, G., Kreilinger, A., Kaufmann, T., Kübler, A., Neuper, C., Müller-Putz, G.R.: Cortical effects of user training in a motor imagery based brain-computer interface measured by fNIRS and EEG. Neuroimage **85**, 432–444 (2014)
19. Komaty, A., Boudraa, A., Dare, D.: EMD-based filtering using the Hausdorff distance. In: 2012 IEEE International Symposium on Signal Processing and Information Technology (ISSPIT), pp. 000292–000297. IEEE (2012)
20. Lashgari, E., Liang, D., Maoz, U.: Data augmentation for deep-learning-based electroencephalography. J. Neurosci. Methods **346**, 108885 (2020)
21. Lee, H.K., Lee, J.H., Park, J.O., Choi, Y.S.: Data-driven data augmentation for motor imagery brain-computer interface. In: 2021 International Conference on Information Networking (ICOIN), pp. 683–686. IEEE (2021)
22. Liu, Y., et al.: A tensor-based scheme for stroke patients' motor imagery EEG analysis in BCI-FES rehabilitation training. J. Neurosci. Methods **222**, 238–249 (2014)
23. Luo, Y., Lu, B.L.: EEG data augmentation for emotion recognition using a conditional Wasserstein GAN. In: 2018 40th Annual International Conference of the IEEE Engineering in Medicine and Biology Society (EMBC), pp. 2535–2538. IEEE (2018)
24. Mane, R., Chouhan, T., Guan, C.: BCI for stroke rehabilitation: motor and beyond. J. Neural Eng. **17**(4), 041001 (2020)
25. Moctezuma, L.A., Molinas, M.: EEG-based subjects identification based on biometrics of imagined speech using EMD. In: Wang, S., et al. (eds.) BI 2018. LNCS (LNAI), vol. 11309, pp. 458–467. Springer, Cham (2018). https://doi.org/10.1007/978-3-030-05587-5_43
26. Park, C., Looney, D., ur Rehman, N., Ahrabian, A., Mandic, D.P.: Classification of motor imagery BCI using multivariate empirical mode decomposition. IEEE Trans. Neural Syst. Rehabil. Eng. **21**(1), 10–22 (2012)
27. Piper, D., Schiecke, K., Pester, B., Benninger, F., Feucht, M., Witte, H.: Time-variant coherence between heart rate variability and EEG activity in epileptic patients: an advanced coupling analysis between physiological networks. New J. Phys. **16**(11), 115012 (2014)
28. Rato, R., Ortigueira, M.D., Batista, A.: On the HHT, its problems, and some solutions. Mech. Syst. Signal Process. **22**(6), 1374–1394 (2008)
29. Rehman, N., Mandic, D.P.: Multivariate empirical mode decomposition. Proc. R. Soc. A: Math. Phys. Eng. Sci. **466**(2117), 1291–1302 (2010)
30. Rosenmai, P.: Using the median absolute deviation to find outliers. Eureka Stat. **25**(11) (2013)

31. Roy, Y., Banville, H., Albuquerque, I., Gramfort, A., Falk, T.H., Faubert, J.: Deep learning-based electroencephalography analysis: a systematic review. J. Neural Eng. **16**(5), 051001 (2019)
32. Rüschendorf, L.: The Wasserstein distance and approximation theorems. Probab. Theory Relat. Fields **70**(1), 117–129 (1985)
33. Saibene, A., Assale, M., Giltri, M.: Addressing digital divide and elderly acceptance of medical expert systems for healthy ageing. In: AIxAS@ AI* IA, pp. 14–24 (2020)
34. Saibene, A., Gasparini, F.: Cognitive and physiological response for health monitoring in an ageing population: a multi-modal System. In: El Yacoubi, S., Bagnoli, F., Pacini, G. (eds.) INSCI 2019. LNCS, vol. 11938, pp. 341–347. Springer, Cham (2019). https://doi.org/10.1007/978-3-030-34770-3_29
35. Saibene, A., Gasparini, F.: Human-machine interaction: EEG electrode and feature selection exploiting evolutionary algorithms in motor imagery tasks. In: CENTRIC 2020 : The Thirteenth International Conference on Advances in Human-oriented and Personalized Mechanisms, Technologies, and Services. pp. 8–14. IARIA, Think-Mind (2020)
36. Saibene, A., Gasparini, F.: GA for feature selection of EEG heterogeneous data. arXiv preprint arXiv:2103.07117 (2021)
37. Schalk, G., McFarland, D.J., Hinterberger, T., Birbaumer, N., Wolpaw, J.R.: BCI2000: a general-purpose brain-computer interface (BCI) system. IEEE Trans. Biomed. Eng. **51**(6), 1034–1043 (2004)
38. Szczuko, P., Lech, M., Czyżewski, A.: Comparison of classification methods for EEG signals of real and imaginary motion. In: Stańczyk, U., Zielosko, B., Jain, L.C. (eds.) Advances in Feature Selection for Data and Pattern Recognition. ISRL, vol. 138, pp. 227–239. Springer, Cham (2018). https://doi.org/10.1007/978-3-319-67588-6_12
39. Vaid, S., Singh, P., Kaur, C.: EEG signal analysis for BCI interface: a review. In: 2015 fifth international conference on advanced computing & communication technologies, pp. 143–147. IEEE (2015)
40. Vancea, M., Solé-Casals, J.: Population aging in the European information societies: towards a comprehensive research Agenda in eHealth innovations for elderly. Aging Dis. **7**(4), 526 (2016)
41. Wan, X., Zhang, K., Ramkumar, S., Deny, J., Emayavaramban, G., Ramkumar, M.S., Hussein, A.F.: A review on electroencephalogram based brain computer interface for elderly disabled. IEEE Access **7**, 36380–36387 (2019)
42. Wolpaw, J.R., Birbaumer, N., McFarland, D.J., Pfurtscheller, G., Vaughan, T.M.: Brain-computer interfaces for communication and control. Clin. Neurophysiol. **113**(6), 767–791 (2002)
43. Wu, Z., Huang, N.E.: Ensemble empirical mode decomposition: a noise-assisted data analysis method. Adv. Adapt. Data Anal. **1**(01), 1–41 (2009)
44. Zeiler, A., Faltermeier, R., Keck, I.R., Tomé, A.M., Puntonet, C.G., Lang, E.W.: Empirical mode decomposition-an introduction. In: The 2010 International Joint Conference on Neural Networks (IJCNN), pp. 1–8. IEEE (2010)
45. Zhang, K., et al.: Data augmentation for motor imagery signal classification based on a hybrid neural network. Sensors **20**(16), 4485 (2020)
46. Zhang, Z., et al.: A novel deep learning approach with data augmentation to classify motor imagery signals. IEEE Access **7**, 15945–15954 (2019)
47. Zhao, X., et al.: Classification of epileptic IEEG signals by CNN and data augmentation. In: ICASSP 2020–2020 IEEE International Conference on Acoustics, Speech and Signal Processing (ICASSP), pp. 926–930. IEEE (2020)

Machine Learning for Argumentation, Explanation, and Exploration

Supporting Trustworthy Artificial Intelligence via Bayesian Argumentation

Federico Cerutti[1,2(✉)]

[1] Department of Information Engineering, University of Brescia, via Branze 38, 25123 Brescia, Italy
federico.cerutti@unibs.it
[2] School of Computer Science, Cardiff University, 5 The Parade, Cardiff CF24 3AA, UK

Abstract. This paper introduces argumentative-generative models for statistical learning—i.e., generative statistical models seen from a Bayesian argumentation perspective—and shows how they support trustworthy artificial intelligence (AI). Generative Bayesian approaches are already very promising for achieving robustness against adversarial attacks, a fundamental component of trustworthy AI. This paper shows how Bayesian argumentation can help us achieve transparent assessments of epistemic uncertainty and testability of models, two necessary ingredients for trustworthy AI. We also discuss the limitations of this approach, notably those traditionally linked to Bayesian methods.

Keywords: Statistical learning · Argumentation · Generative models

1 Introduction

Successful human-AI (Artificial Intelligence) teaming hinges on the human correctly deciding when to follow the recommendations of the AI system and when to override them [3]. If the human mistakenly trusts the AI system in regions where it is likely to err, catastrophic failures may occur. The interaction improves when it is clear what the system can do and how well it performs [2, 16] as summarised by recent guidelines [1] recommending to *Make clear what the system can do* (**G1**), and to *Make clear how well the system can do what it can do* (**G2**).

To satisfy such guidelines, we must equip AI—notably machine learning (ML)—systems with the ability to *honestly* answer critical questions posed by the different human actors involved in the machine learning ecosystem, see Fig. 1 and [26]. *Honest*, and not *persuasive*, answers require to look at human-AI argumentation through a critical perspective [21, 30], viz. as a process of trying to unseat conjectures that have been surmised, rather than from the standpoint of providing palatable *post hoc* justification or explanation of existing models.

For instance, *Operators*—e.g. analysts informing for example decision makers or other *Executors*, see Fig. 1—must create a mental model that helps them assess what the system can do (**G1**) and how well it operates (**G2**). Hence, these two guidelines designed to increase the trust in AI systems can give rise to *questions* that must be

S. Bandini et al. (Eds.): AIxIA 2021, LNAI 13196, pp. 377–388, 2022.
https://doi.org/10.1007/978-3-031-08421-8_26

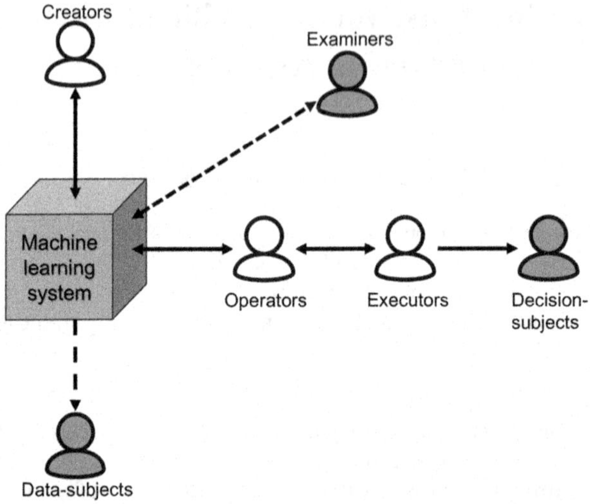

Fig. 1. Illustration of a machine learning ecosystem and interactors. The direction of arrow indicates the direction of interaction (e.g., data-subjects do not interact with the system, but the system has their data) [26, Figure 1, reproduced with permission of the authors].

critically evaluated to help operators formulate their mental model. To answer such questions, we need to distinguish between (at least) two different sources of uncertainty: *aleatory*, and *epistemic* uncertainty [13,14]. Aleatory uncertainty refers to the variability in the outcome of an experiment, which is due to inherently random effects (e.g., flipping a fair coin): no additional source of information but Laplace's daemon[1] can reduce such a variability. Epistemic uncertainty refers to the epistemic state of the agent using the model, hence its lack of knowledge that—in principle—can be reduced based on additional data samples. Not only we need to distinguish between different types of uncertainty, but we also need to take into consideration other factors, such as the provenance of training data or model choices.

In Sect. 4 we unveil the first proposal of a normative Bayesian framework—the *argumentative-generative framework*—for trustworthy human-AI teaming, enabling AI systems to answer critical questions and handle epistemic uncertainty. To this end, we build upon the proposal for Bayesian argumentation (Sect. 3), which is closer to statistics than other approaches to argumentation. We ground our analysis on elementary generative models (Sect. 2), leaving some further discussions—including a benefit-drawback assessment of the argumentative-generative framework—to Sect. 5.

[1] "An intelligence that, at a given instant, could comprehend all the forces by which nature is animated and the respective situation of the beings that make it up" [17, p.2].

2 A Primer in Statistical Learning

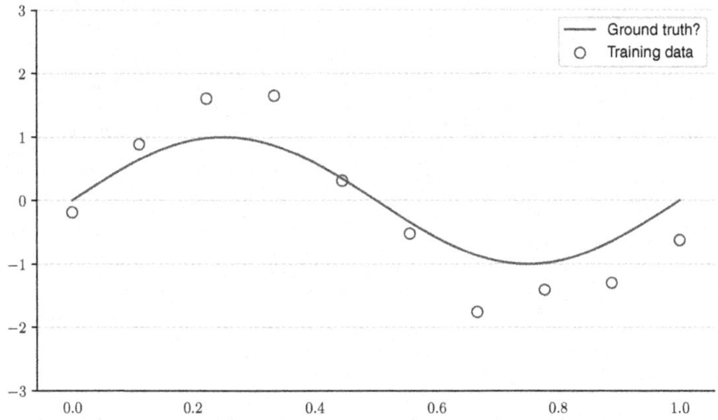

Fig. 2. Ten datapoints (blue circle), allegedly generated from $\sin(2\pi x) + \varepsilon$, with $\varepsilon \sim \mathcal{N}(\mu, \sigma^2)$ with μ and σ unknown.

Let us consider one of the simplest, yet not simplistic, textbook statistical learning tasks: the curve fitting problem, e.g. [4]. Indeed, this task is at the basis of a vast set of research in the social sciences, where relatively simple regression models are adopted for analysing complex societal problems, from plastic surgeon hiring practices factors [6], to CO_2 emission drivers [32], to the role of vitamin C in supporting intensive-care unit patients [12].

While regression analyses—and more articulated techniques such as structural equation modelling [18]—require additional statistical tools, in the interest of simplicity and clarity, in this paper we will focus on the simplest of such cases. The goal is to be able to make predictions for the target variable t given some new value of the input variable x on the basis of a set of training data—assumed to be representative of the underlying ground truth—comprising N input values $\mathsf{x} = (x_1, \ldots, x_N)^{\mathrm{T}}$ and their corresponding target values $\mathsf{t} = (t_1, \ldots, t_N)^{\mathrm{T}}$, cf. Fig. 2. A test set of 100 samples is used for assessing how well the model generalises.

Let us choose to fit the data using a polynomial function of the form

$$y(x, \mathbf{w}) = \sum_{j=0}^{M} w_j x^j \tag{1}$$

This model has M parameters $\mathbf{w}$ that can be determined by minimising an error function, for instance the root mean square error between the predictions and the target values:

$$E_{\mathrm{RMS}} = \sqrt{\frac{1}{N} \sum_{n=1}^{N} (y(x, \mathbf{w}) - t_n)^2}. \tag{2}$$

Figure 3 illustrates polynomials with degree $M = 3$ and $M = 9$ that minimise their E_{RMS} from the training data. It is evident that $M = 9$ is a textbook case of overfitting, i.e., it perfectly fits the training data, but it does not generalise well.

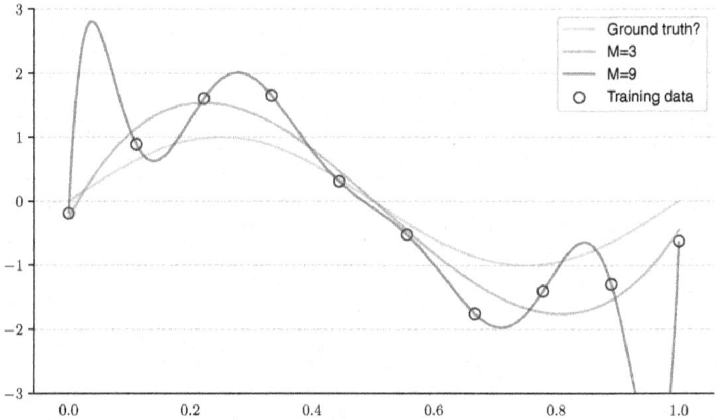

Fig. 3. Polynomials with $M = 3$ (red) and $M = 9$ (purple) minimising their E_{RMS} from the training data in circled blue. In green the alleged ground truth. (Color figure online)

Let us now start considering our epistemic uncertainty: a natural way of doing it is to express our lack of knowledge over the true value of the target variable. One of the simplest assumptions we can make is that it is affected by normally distributed noise with $\mu = 0$ and $\sigma^2 = \frac{1}{\beta}$ and that samples are independent and identically distributed random variables (i.i.d.). The likelihood function—assessing the goodness of fit of $y(\mathsf{x}, \mathbf{w})$ to our samples t—is thus:

$$p(\mathsf{t}|\mathsf{x}, \mathbf{w}, \beta) = \prod_{n=1}^{N} \mathcal{N}(t_n | y(x_n, \mathbf{w}), \beta^{-1}) \tag{3}$$

Let us add a Gaussian prior over the polynomial coefficients $\mathbf{w}$ with $\boldsymbol{\mu} = \mathbf{0}$ and $\boldsymbol{\Sigma} = \alpha^{-1}\mathbf{I}$, α being the precision of the distribution:

$$p(\mathbf{w}|\alpha) = \mathcal{N}(\mathbf{w}|\mathbf{0}, \alpha^{-1}\mathbf{I}) = \left(\frac{\alpha}{2\pi}\right)^{(M+1)/2} \exp\left\{-\frac{\alpha}{2}\mathbf{w}^{\mathrm{T}}\mathbf{w}\right\} \tag{4}$$

In this way, the posterior assessment of the parameters $\mathbf{w}$, calculated using the Bayes' theorem,

$$p(\mathbf{w}|\mathsf{x}, \mathsf{t}, \alpha, \beta) \propto p(\mathsf{t}|\mathsf{x}, \mathbf{w}, \beta) p(\mathbf{w}|\alpha) \tag{5}$$

is also normally distributed. Figure 4 thus depicts the *generative model*—i.e. the model that captures a causal representation of a process that could have generated the observed data—for our example: nodes are random variables, and edges represent causal links.

Assuming α and β arbitrary but fixed,

$$p(t|x, \mathsf{x}, \mathsf{t}) = \int p(t|x, \mathbf{w}) p(\mathbf{w}|\mathsf{x}, \mathsf{t}) \mathrm{d}\mathbf{w} \tag{6}$$

is also normally distributed. Figure 5 depicts our $\mu \pm \sigma$ confidence region, i.e., there is a 68% chance that the ground truth belongs to that region.

This helps to assess the aleatory uncertainty: with more training data, the $\mu \pm \sigma$ region would become narrower and narrower. However, that is not enough for answering in full the critical questions associated with guidelines [1, **G1**] and [1, **G2**] (Sect. 1). For that, we need to look at Bayesian argumentation.

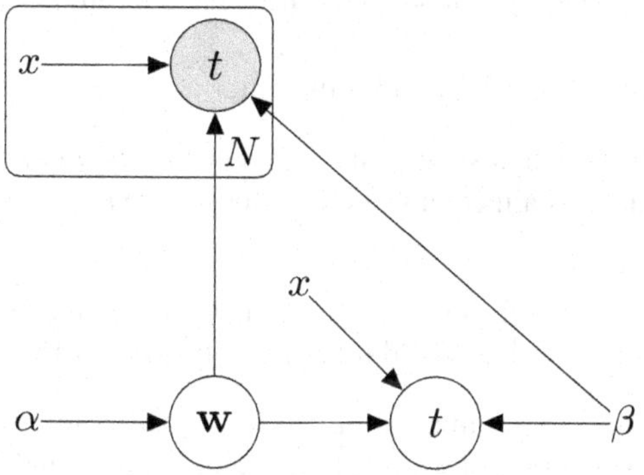

Fig. 4. Bayesian generative model for the curve fitting analysis.

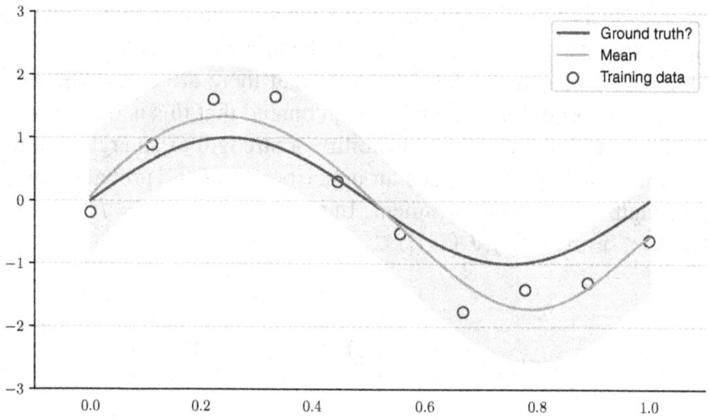

Fig. 5. Predictive distribution using an $M = 9$, $\alpha = 2 \times 10^{-3}$ and $\beta = 2$. The pink region corresponds to $\mu \pm \sigma$. (Color figure online)

3 A Primer in Bayesian Argumentation

Argumentation schemes [30] provide the fundamental stepping stone towards achieving trustworthy AI. They are reasoning patterns providing structures for conjectures, typically formed by a set of premises tentatively (defeasibly) supporting a given conclusion, and the means for refutation, namely *critical questions*. Their use in systems based on formal argumentation already provides evidence that they support critical discourse by mitigating the effects of cognitive biases [27].

One of the simplest examples of an argumentation scheme is the *argument from sign*:

Major premise: $\mathfrak{X}$ (a finding) is true in this situation
Minor premise: $\mathfrak{Y}$ is generally indicated as true when its sign $\mathfrak{X}$ is true in this kind of situation
Conclusion: Therefore $\mathfrak{Y}$ is true in this situation

where $\mathfrak{X}$ and $\mathfrak{Y}$ are unspecified statements. Associated *critical questions* (CQs) can be used to generate arguments aimed at refuting a conjecture surmised using an argument from sign:

CQ1: What is the strength of the correlation of the sign with the event signified?
CQ2: Are there other events that would more reliably account for the sign?

Bayesian approaches to argumentation [9] is a reaction to the MAXMIN rule for argumentation when combining linked and convergent arguments. When two or more independent arguments all support the same claim, we are in presence of *convergent arguments*. Linked arguments instead form a chain of dependencies, thus providing support for a claim only in combination.

For convergent arguments, Walton [31] argues in favour of the MAX rule, i.e. the overall strength or plausibility of the argument is determined by the maximum of the independent arguments converging to the same claim. For linked arguments, researchers [20,31] propose that the overall plausibility of the argument is determined by its weakest link. While some researchers [31] concede that there are cases where plausibility and probability are closely linked, others [11] contend that this is true in several cases. A probabilistic interpretation of the plausibility or strength of an argument leads to the conclusion that the MIN rule provides an upper bound of the probabilistic interpretation of the strength of a linked argument. Indeed, $P(A \wedge B) = P(A) \cdot P(A|B) = P(B) \cdot P(B|A) \leq \min\{P(A), P(B)\}$.

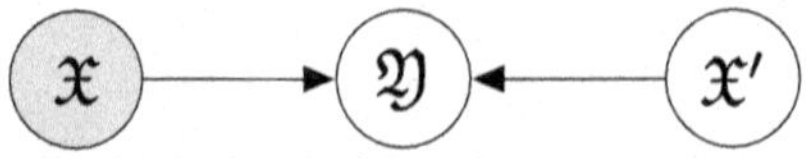

Fig. 6. Simple belief network representing the *argument from sign* according to [9]

Arguments, for their defeasible nature, can be represented by a network of random variables connected in a belief network, i.e. a directed graph where nodes are random variables, and edges represent causal links. Hahn et al. [9] provide a Bayesian account of the *argument from sign* (cf. Fig. 6), showing how belief networks can be used to *quantify* the effect of critical questions. For instance, answers to **CQ1** are provided by $p(\mathfrak{Y} \mid \mathfrak{X})$ and $p(\mathfrak{Y} \mid \overline{\mathfrak{X}})$ (cf. Fig. 6), while **CQ2** is linked to the exploration of other events, e.g. $\mathfrak{X}'$, that have a higher correlation with $\mathfrak{Y}$. This modelling has been used to test the strength of various argumentation schemes, and experimental studies such as [10] detail how the Bayesian framework is operationalised for obtaining qualitative and quantitative predictions of lay people's perception of arguments strength.

4 Argumentative-Generative Framework

Argumentative-generative models merge Bayesian generative models with Bayesian argumentation to equip the learning system with the ability to *honestly* answer critical questions, hence satisfying the two guidelines illustrated in Sect. 1, [1, **G1**] and [1, **G2**]. Figure 7 shows an argumentative-generative model for our curve-fitting problem.

First of all, expressing what the system can do [1, **G1**] is a much stronger version of the critical question **CQ1** associated to the *argument for sign* as discussed by [9]. It can be answered by quantifying $p(\mathsf{t} \mid \mathsf{x})$ and $p(\mathsf{t} \mid \overline{\mathsf{x}})$. Both the generative-only model (Fig. 4), and the argumentative-generative model (Fig. 7) can do it.

Let us consider how well the system does what it does, cf. [1, **G2**]. Looking at Fig. 7, two major components have been added compared to the generative-only model (Fig. 4): (1) hyper-parameters on the training data, i.e. Trustworthiness, Expertise, and Provenance; and (2) a hyper-parameter ξ on the variables of the model.

Let us begin with the hyper-parameters on the training data, and let us ponder: what if the training set is not representative of the underlying ground truth? For instance, the same samples could have been generated by a completely different phenomenon, cf. Figure 8. While more data would be beneficial here to reduce epistemic uncertainty, generative-only models can help only up to a point. Indeed, if the alternative ground truth is—as it indeed is in our running example—the real ground truth, for values around 0.8, the prediction stops being accurate (Fig. 9). This is a case of what some researchers call *selection bias* [28] and occurs when parts of the input space are unrepresented, like when sampling without considering the Nyquist-Shannon theorem [25] as in our case. Other examples of selection bias have been uncovered by the controversy associated with the use of ImageNet [7] for general purposes. Among the geographically identifiable images of the ImageNet dataset of 2011, China and India were represented with 1% and 2.1% of the images, respectively [24] despite hosting 20% and 18% of the world population.

The only countermeasure we have here is to question whether the *Creators* (cf. Figure 1) of the machine learning systems identified the right *Data-subjects* representative of the domain. This might be assessed based on Trustworthiness and the Expertise of the *Creators* and the Provenance of data (cf. Figure 7). All of this affects the *reputation* H_{rep} of the *Creators*—cf. also the analysis of *argument from expert opinion* in [9]—and, in turn, the adequacy τ of the training (and testing) set, which should also be taken into consideration when assessing β.

Finally, ξ is a hyper-parameter that controls the model choices, and we can use it to compare them, thus answering **CQ2** associated with *argument from sign*. The selection

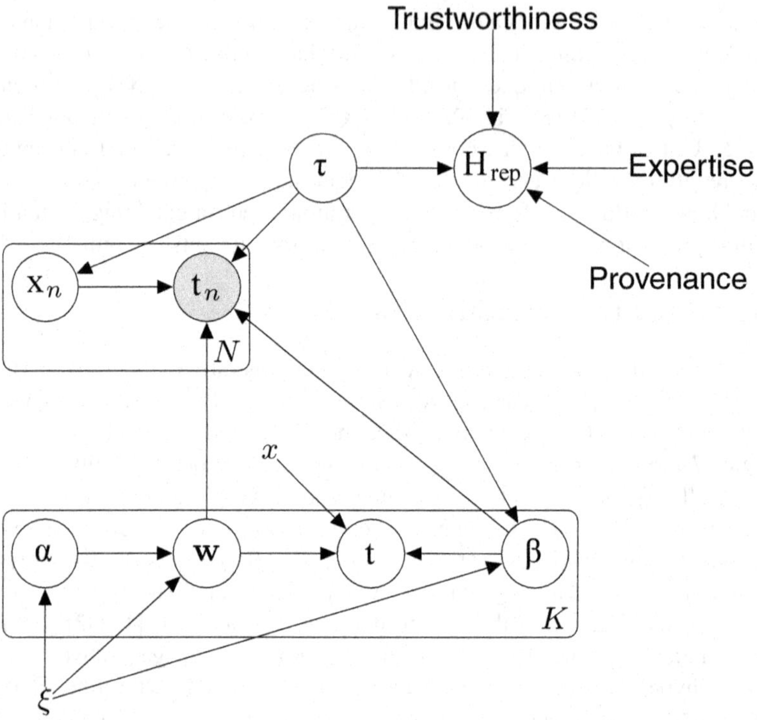

Fig. 7. Bayesian argumentative-generative model for the curve fitting analysis.

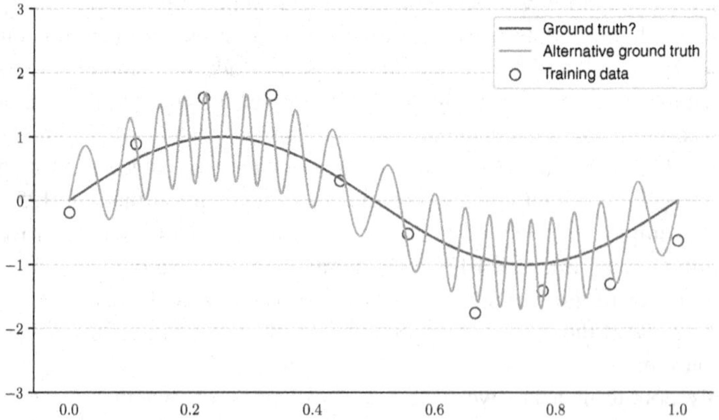

Fig. 8. Ten datapoints (blue circle) generated either from $\sin(2\pi x) + \epsilon$ (green line) or from $\sin(2\pi x) + 0.7 \sin\{20 \cdot 2\pi x + 5 \sin(2 \cdot 2\pi(x + 0.25)\} + \varepsilon$ (grey line and the actual ground truth used for generating this example, with $\varepsilon \sim \mathcal{N}(\mu, \sigma^2)$, $\mu = 0$ and $\sigma = 0.4$). (Color figure online)

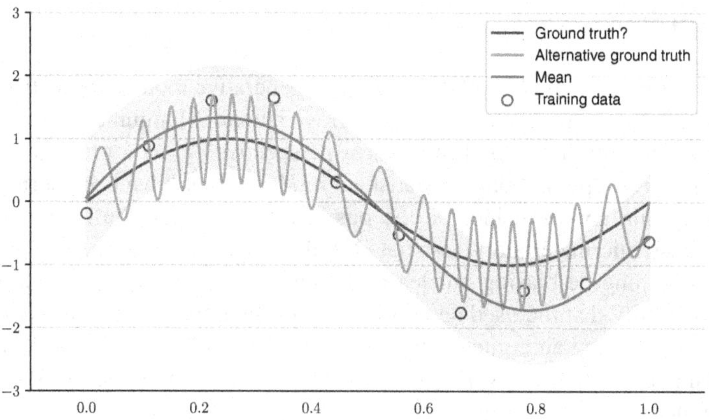

Fig. 9. Predictive distribution using an $M = 9$, $\alpha = 2 \times 10^{-3}$ and $\beta = 2$. The pink region corresponds to $\mu \pm \sigma$. (Color figure online)

of M, as well as of α and β are discretionary to the *Creator* of the machine learning system, and we have an example in Fig. 3 of their potential impact. Varying ξ can be for machine learning what mutation testing is for computer security [19]: a principled, powerful tool for testing variations of the same model.

In this way, the argumentative-generative model helps to address [1, **G1**] and [1, **G2**], and brings us closer to trustworthy AI by providing a computational framework to test the robustness of assumptions and design choices.

By framing a Bayesian analysis inside an argumentation procedure, we provide a formal machinery for assessing the quality of the analysis itself in a way remarkably close to current best-practices such as the WAMBS-checklist [8]. In their seminal paper, Depaoli and van de Schoot introduce a checklist for improving transparency and replication of Bayesian statistics analyses that—in argumentation terms—is a list of 10 critical questions, including *Do you understand the priors?* and *Is there a notable effect of the prior when compared with non-informative priors?* The WAMBS-checklist is mostly focused in the parameter ξ: in this paper we refrained to expand the model illustrated in Fig. 7 further to encompass the entire checklist. Our intention is to illustrate the flexibility of the Bayesian argumentation paradigm in accommodating complex scientific enquiries.

It is also worth remarking how the WAMBS-checklist does not consider at all the τ parameter, as it is beyond the scope of Bayesian analysis. However, in the current socio-political context where we as researchers in AI have the duty to foster trustworthy artificial intelligence systems, it becomes of paramount importance being able to raise critical questions linked to the provenance of data, trustworthiness in the collection and management, and expertise of the data managers. In this respect, our proposal of a Bayesian argumentative model is a first step towards forcing researchers in at least questioning the quality of the data they are using in their analyses, thus not only encompassing but also enriching existing best-practices for ensuring high-quality scientific outputs.

5 Conclusions

This paper introduces the idea of argumentative-generative models for statistical learning as a stepping stone towards trustworthy AI via human-AI argumentation. This argumentation is seen through a narrow, critical perspective, so as a process of trying to unseat conjectures—predictions by statistical models—that have been surmised. Benefits of using this approach include the possibility to deepen the assessment of the inevitable epistemic uncertainty associated with statistical learning. This goes in the direction of helping de-biasing our learnt system and quantifying the risk associated with the possibility that the used dataset is not representative of the underlying ground truth. Finally, adopting an argumentative-generative model for statistical learning provides a computational framework for ensuring robustness and critical assessment of competing models.

Like any other generative approach, producing an argumentative-generative model requires a substantial knowledge engineering effort. The two research communities in formal argumentation and machine learning should jointly identify stereotypical patterns that can form the basis of future recommendations, in the same way scholars in informal argumentation identified a large set of argumentation schemes. Once the model is produced, quantifying answers to critical questions is an expensive computational task, as it is for the vast majority of Bayesian approaches. Heuristics and better engineering can help reduce the search space of random variables values. Moreover, for some cases, approximate procedures, such as [5,15,22,23], already provide excellent results without a substantial increase in the requested computational power.

Finally, in this paper we focus on generative models. Argumentative-discriminative models can also be derived in the same fashion, as the main difference between them is linked to the computation of $p(y \mid x)$ without the need to estimate $p(x, y)$. However, the effect of using argumentative-discriminative models for evaluating epistemic uncertainty—necessary for trustworthy learning—will be severely reduced compared to the use of argumentative-generative models.

This paper is a first step towards trustworthy statistical learning. Many more lie ahead of us from both statistical learning and Bayesian argumentation perspectives. In particular, we will study which questions the argumentative-generative framework can effectively answer. We will also compare our framework with other approaches aimed at demystifying machine learning models using non-Bayesian argumentation [29].

Acknowledgments. This research was sponsored by the Italian Ministry of Research through a Rita Levi-Montalcini Personal Fellowship (D.M. n. 285, 29/03/2019) and by the U.S. Army Research Laboratory and the U.K. Ministry of Defence under Agreement Number W911NF-16-3-0001. The views and conclusions contained in this document are those of the authors and should not be interpreted as representing the official policies, either expressed or implied, of the U.S. Army Research Laboratory, the U.S. Government, the U.K. Ministry of Defence or the U.K. Government. The U.S. and U.K. Governments are authorized to reproduce and distribute reprints for Government purposes notwithstanding any copyright notation hereon.

References

1. Amershi, S., et al.: Guidelines for human-AI interaction. In: Conference on Human Factors in Computing Systems - Proceedings, pp. 1–13. Association for Computing Machinery, New York, USA (2019)
2. Bansal, G., Nushi, B., Kamar, E., Lasecki, W., Weld, D., Horvitz, E.: Beyond accuracy: the role of mental models in human-AI team performance. In: HCOMP. AAAI (2019)
3. Bansal, G., Nushi, B., Kamar, E., Weld, D.S., Lasecki, W.S., Horvitz, E.: Updates in human-AI teams: understanding and addressing the performance/compatibility tradeoff. In: AAAI, pp. 2429–2437 (2019)
4. Bishop, C. M., Nasrabadi, N.M.: Pattern Recognition and Machine Learning. ISS, Springer, New York (2006). https://doi.org/10.1007/978-0-387-45528-0_9
5. Cerutti, F., Kaplan, L.M., Kimmig, A., Sensoy, M.: Probabilistic logic programming with beta-distributed random variables. In: The Thirty-Third AAAI Conference on Artificial Intelligence, AAAI 2019, pp. 7769–7776 (2019)
6. Copeland, A.E., et al.: What does it take to become an academic plastic surgeon in Canada: hiring trends over the last 50 years. Plastic Surgery (to appear)
7. Deng, J., Dong, W., Socher, R., Li, L.J., Li, K., Fei-Fei, L.: ImageNet: a Large-Scale Hierarchical Image Database. In: CVPR09 (2009)
8. Depaoli, S., Van de Schoot, R.: Improving transparency and replication in Bayesian statistics: the WAMBS-checklist. Psychol. Methods **22**(2), 240 (2017)
9. Hahn, U., Hornikx, J.: A normative framework for argument quality: argumentation schemes with a Bayesian foundation. Synthese **193**(6), 1833–1873 (2015). https://doi.org/10.1007/s11229-015-0815-0
10. Hahn, U., Oaksford, M.: The rationality of informal argumentation: a Bayesian approach to reasoning fallacies. Psychol. Rev. **114**(3), 704–732 (2007)
11. Hahn, U., Oaksford, M., Harris, A.J.L.: Testimony and argument: a Bayesian perspective. In: Zenker, F. (ed.) Bayesian Argumentation. SL, vol. 362, pp. 15–38. Springer, Dordrecht (2013). https://doi.org/10.1007/978-94-007-5357-0_2
12. Hemilä, H., Chalker, E.: Vitamin C may reduce the duration of mechanical ventilation in critically ill patients: a meta-regression analysis. J. Intensive Care **8**(1), 15 (2020)
13. Hora, S.C.: Aleatory and epistemic uncertainty in probability elicitation with an example from hazardous waste management. Reliab. Eng. Syst. Saf. **54**(2), 217–223 (1996)
14. Hüllermeier, E., Waegeman, W.: Aleatoric and epistemic uncertainty in machine learning: a tutorial introduction (2019)
15. Kaplan, L.M., Ivanovska, M.: Efficient belief propagation in second-order Bayesian networks for singly-connected graphs. Int. J. Approximate Reasoning **93**, 132–152 (2018)
16. Kocielnik, R., Amershi, S., Bennett, P.N.: Will you accept an imperfect AI? exploring designs for adjusting end-user expectations of AI systems. In: Conference on Human Factors in Computing Systems - Proceedings, pp. 1–14. Association for Computing Machinery, New York, USA (2019)
17. Laplace, P.S.: A Philosophical Essay on Probabilities. Springer, Heidelberg (1825). Translator: Dale, A.I. (1995)
18. Mehmetoglu, M., Venturini, S.: Structural Equation Modelling with Partial Least Squares Using Stata and R. CRC Press, Boca Raton (2021)
19. Mohammadian, M., Javed, Z.: Intelligent evaluation of test suites for developing efficient and reliable software. Int. J. Parallel, Emergent Distrib. Syst. 1–30 (2019)
20. Pollock, J.L.: Defeasible reasoning with variable degrees of justification. Artif. Intell. **133**(1–2), 233–282 (2001)

21. Popper, K.R.: Conjectures and Refutations: The Growth of Scientific Knowledge. Routledge, 5th edn. (1989)
22. Sensoy, M., Kaplan, L., Cerutti, F., Saleki, M.: Uncertainty-aware deep classifiers using generative models. In: The Thirty-Forth AAAI Conference on Artificial Intelligence, AAAI 2020 (2020)
23. Sensoy, M., Kaplan, L.M., Kandemir, M.: Evidential deep learning to quantify classification uncertainty. In: Advances in Neural Information Processing Systems 31: Annual Conference on Neural Information Processing Systems 2018, NeurIPS 2018, 3–8 Dec 2018, Montréal, Canada, pp. 3183–3193 (2018)
24. Shankar, S., Halpern, Y., Breck, E., Atwood, J., Wilson, J., Sculley, D.: No classification without representation: assessing geodiversity issues in open data sets for the developing world. In: NIPS 2017 Workshop on Machine Learning for the Developing World (2017)
25. Shannon, C.E.: Communication in the presence of noise. Proceed. IRE **37**(1), 10–21 (1949)
26. Tomsett, R., Braines, D., Harborne, D., Preece, A.D., Chakraborty, S.: Interpretable to whom? a role-based model for analyzing interpretable machine learning systems. In: 2018 ICML Workshop on Human Interpretability in Machine Learning (WHI 2018) (2018)
27. Toniolo, A., et al.: Supporting reasoning with different types of evidence in intelligence analysis. In: Proceedings of the International Joint Conference on Autonomous Agents and Multiagent Systems, AAMAS, vol. 2 (2015)
28. Torralba, A., Efros, A.A.: Unbiased look at dataset bias. In: CVPR 2011, pp. 1521–1528 (2011)
29. Vassiliades, A., Bassiliades, N., Patkos, T.: Argumentation and explainable artificial intelligence: a survey. Knowl. Eng. Rev. **36**, e5 (2021)
30. Walton, D., Reed, C., Macagno, F.: Argumentation Schemes. Cambridge University Press, NY (2008)
31. Walton, D.: Rules for plausible reasoning. Informal Logic, **14**(1) (1992)
32. Xu, B., Lin, B.: Investigating drivers of CO2 emission in China's heavy industry: a quantile regression analysis. Energy **206**, 118159 (2020)

Logic Constraints to Feature Importance

Nicola Picchiotti[1,2(✉)] and Marco Gori[1,3]

[1] SAILAB, University of Siena, Siena, Italy
[2] University of Pavia, Pavia, Italy
nicola.picchiotti01@universitadipavia.it
[3] MAASAI, Universitè Côte d'Azur, Nice, France
marco@diism.unisi.it
http://sailab.diism.unisi.it

Abstract. In recent years, Artificial Intelligence (AI) algorithms have been proven to outperform traditional statistical methods in terms of predictivity, especially when a large amount of data was available. Nevertheless, the "black box" nature of AI models is often a limit for a reliable application in high-stakes fields like diagnostic techniques, autonomous guide, etc. Recent works have shown that an adequate level of interpretability could enforce the more general concept of model trustworthiness [7]. The basic idea of this paper is to exploit the human prior knowledge of the features' importance for a specific task, in order to coherently aid the phase of the model's fitting. This sort of "weighted" AI is obtained by extending the empirical loss with a regularization term encouraging the importance of the features to follow predetermined constraints. This procedure relies on local methods for the feature importance computation, e.g. LRP, LIME, etc. that are the link between the model weights to be optimized and the user-defined constraints on feature importance. In the fairness area, promising experimental results have been obtained for the Adult dataset. Many other possible applications of this model agnostic theoretical framework are described.

Keywords: Feature importance · Explainability · Logic constraints · Fairness · Reliability

1 Introduction

Trustworthiness of an Artificial Intelligence (AI) model, i.e. the stability of the performances under many possible future scenarios, is a fundamental requirement for the real world applications. The topic has became particularly relevant in the last decades, since technology development and data availability led the adoption of models more and more complex, widen the gap between performances on train/test data and reliability of the models.

Model trustworthiness is usually linked to other factors, including the interpretability of the algorithm, the stationary of data, the possible bias in the data, etc. [16,23]. Especially in the field of interpretability, many work has been done

S. Bandini et al. (Eds.): AIxIA 2021, LNAI 13196, pp. 389–402, 2022.
https://doi.org/10.1007/978-3-031-08421-8_27

in order to explain and interpret the models developed by AI in a human comprehensible manner. The main reason behind these effort is that the human experience and its capacity for abstraction allow to monitor the process of the model decisions in a sound way, trying to mitigate the risk of data-driven models.

Anyway, an effective interaction between the model and the human is still lacking and mostly of the current machine learning approaches tends to rely too heavily on training/testing data. On the other hand, sources of knowledge like domain knowledge, expert opinions, understanding from related problem etc. could be very important for a better definition of the model.

Here we present a novel framework trying to bridge the gap between data-driven optimization and human high-level domain knowledge. The approach provides for the inclusion of the human understanding of the importance of the input features. The basic idea is to extend the empirical loss with a regularization term depending on the constraints defined by the apriori knowledge on the importance of the features. We provide experimental results on the fairness topic.

2 Bibliographic Review

There are few existing feature weighting approaches aimed at improving the performances of machine learning models. In [1] the author exploits weak domain knowledge in the form of feature importance to help the learning of Importance-Aided Neural Networks (IANN). The feature importance is based on the absolute weight of the first hidden layer neurons of the network. IANN is successfully applied in [6]. In [29] an ontology-based clustering algorithm is introduced along with a feature weights mechanism able to reflect the different features' importance. [21] uses both correlation and mutual information to weight the features for the algorithms SVM, KNN, and Naive Bayes. Instead, in order to accelerate the learning process, in [12] the algorithm is required to match the correlation between the features and the predictive function with the empirical correlation.

Anyway, none of the previous works define a general framework including the knowledge on the importance of the input features in the framework of explainable machine learning models.

3 Mathematical Setting of Feature Importance

In this section, we review the existing approaches aimed at assigning an importance score for each feature of a given input example in relation to the task of the model, i.e. the so-called local explainable methodologies. It is worth mentioning that the importance of a feature is one of the most used strategies to gain local explainability from an opaque machine learning model.

Let us consider a *predictor function* $\tilde{f}$ going from the d-dim feature space $\mathcal{X} = \mathcal{X}_1 \times \mathcal{X}_2 ... \times \mathcal{X}_d$ to the 1-dim target space $\mathcal{Y}$:

$$\tilde{f} : \mathcal{X} \to \mathcal{Y}.$$

Such a predictor function is the output of a learner:

$$\mathcal{L} : (\mathcal{X}^n \times \mathcal{Y}^n) \to (\mathcal{X} \to \mathcal{Y}),$$

able to process a supervised dataset $\mathcal{D} = \{X, Y\}$ where $X \in \mathcal{X}^n$ and $Y \in \mathcal{Y}^n$ with n instances. In order to fix the idea, we can think of $\mathcal{L}$ as a Deep Neural Network providing the predictor function $\tilde{f}$.

Definition 1 (Local feature importance). *The local feature importance is a function mapping a predictor $\tilde{f}$ and a single instance $\boldsymbol{x} \in \mathcal{X}$ to a d-dim vector of real values in the range* $[0, 1]$*:*

$$\boldsymbol{I}(\tilde{f}, \boldsymbol{x}) : (\mathcal{X} \to \mathcal{Y}) \times \mathcal{X} \to [0, 1]^d$$

The local feature importance is a measure of how much the model relies on each feature for the prediction $\tilde{f}(\boldsymbol{x})$ made by $\tilde{f}$ on the particular pattern $\boldsymbol{x}$. Basically, the quantity $I_i(\tilde{f}, \boldsymbol{x})$ tells us how much the i-th feature contributes with respect to the others for a specific prediction. In the limit cases of $I_i(\boldsymbol{x}) = 0$ or $I_i(\boldsymbol{x}) = 1$ the feature i can be considered respectively useless or the most important one for the prediction done by the predictor on the pattern $\boldsymbol{x}$.

Example. Given a linear predictor $\tilde{f}(\boldsymbol{x}) = \sum_{i=1}^{d} w_i x_i$, the function

$$\boldsymbol{I}(\tilde{f}, \boldsymbol{x}) = \frac{|\boldsymbol{w}|}{max_{i \in [1,d]} |w_i|}$$

is a local feature importance function.

Definition 2 (Local feature importance methods). *Local feature importance methods are methods that given a predictor $\tilde{f}$, with its learner and the dataset, computes a local feature importance function $\boldsymbol{I}(\tilde{f}, \boldsymbol{x})$.*

The existing methodologies for the computation of feature importance are reviewed in [10] and [2]. *Permutation feature importance* methods quantify the feature importance through the variation of a loss metric by perturbing the values of a selected feature on a set of instances in the training or validation set. The approach is firstly introduced in [4] for random forest and in [22] for Neural Network. Other methods, such as *class model visualization* [25], compute the partial derivative of the score function with respect to the input, and [20] introduce expert distribution for the input giving *activation maximization*. In the paper [24] the author introduces *deep lift* and computes the discrete gradients with respect to a baseline point, by backpropagating the scoring difference through each unit. Instead, integrated gradients [28] cumulates the gradients with respect to inputs along the path from a given baseline to the instance.

A set of well known methods called *Additive Feature Attribution Methods* (AFAM) defined in [19] rely on the redistribution of the predicted value $\hat{f}(\boldsymbol{x})$ over the input features. They are designed to mimic the behaviour of a predictive function $\tilde{f}$ with a surrogate Boolean linear function g. This surrogate function takes values in a space of the transformed vector of the input features: $\boldsymbol{x}' = h(\boldsymbol{x}) \in [0, 1]^d$:

$$\hat{f}(\boldsymbol{x}) \approx g(\boldsymbol{x}') = \phi_0 + \sum_{i=1}^{d} \phi_i x'_i.$$

Keeping the notation introduced above, by defining

$$\boldsymbol{I}(\hat{f}, \boldsymbol{x}) = \frac{|\boldsymbol{\phi}|}{max_{i \in [1,d]} |\phi_i|},$$

we have a local feature importance method.

Among the additive feature attribution methods, the popular *LIME* (Local Interpretable Model-agnostic Explanations) [23] builds the linear approximated model with a sampling procedure in the neighborhood of the specific point. By considering proper weights to the linear coefficients of LIME, the author in [19] demostrated that *SHAP* (SHapley Additive exPlanation) is the unique solution of additive feature attribution methods granting a set of desirable properties (local accuracy, missingness and consistency). This last method lays the foundation on the *Shapley* method introduced in [26] and [27] for solving the problem of redistributing a reward (prediction) to a set of player (features) in coalitional game theory framework. Finally, *Layer-wise Relevance Propagation* (LRP) in [3] backpropagates the prediction along the network, by fixing a redistribution rule based on the weights among the neurons.

The set of feature importance methods, along with the data type and the model to which the method is referred are reported in Table 1. For a tabular dataset, the feature importances are usually represented as a rank reported in a histogram. For images or texts, the subset of the input which is mostly in charge of the predictions gives rise to saliency masks; for example, they can be parts of the image or a sentence of a text.

4 Constraints to Feature Importance

The overall goal of the present work is to define a framework where the local importance of the model's features can be constrained to specific intervals. We introduce a novel regularization loss term L_I, related to the not fulfillment of the feature importance's constraints:

$$L_r(\boldsymbol{x}, \boldsymbol{w}) + L_I(\boldsymbol{I}(\tilde{f}(\boldsymbol{w}, \cdot), \boldsymbol{x})), \tag{1}$$

where L_r is the usual empirical risk loss and $\boldsymbol{I}$ the d-dim vector of importances. It is worth observing that in Eq. (1) we explicated the dependence of the importance on the structure of the black box model via the weights of the model $\boldsymbol{w}$.

Let us suppose a First Order Logic (FOL) formula $E(\boldsymbol{I}(\tilde{f}, \boldsymbol{x}))$ with variable $\boldsymbol{x} = [x_1, x_2 ..., x_d]$ containing an apriori statement with inequalities on the features' importances. For example, we could require that, for every $\boldsymbol{x}$, both the

Table 1. Review of the most known feature importance methods in explainability. TAB: Tabular dataset, IMG: Images, AGN: Model agnostic methodology, NN: Neural Network, TE: Tree Ensemble, AFAM: Additive Feature Attribution Methods.

Method	Data Type	Model	Reference	AFAM
SHAP	ANY	AGN	[19]	v
LIME	ANY	AGN	[23]	v
Shapley value	TAB	AGN	[26,27]	v
Permutation feature importance	ANY	NN/TE	[4,22]	–
Class model visualization	IMG	NN	[25]	–
Activation maximization	IMG	NN	[20]	–
LRP	ANY	NN	[3]	v
Taylor Decomposition	ANY	NN	[3]	–
DeepLift	ANY	NN	[24]	v
Integrated Gradients	ANY	NN	[28]	–
GAM	ANY	AGN	[17,18]	–

feature 1 and the feature 2 should not be important for the prediction function to properly work:

$$\forall \boldsymbol{x}: \; I_1(\tilde{f}, \boldsymbol{x}) < c_1 \wedge I_2(\tilde{f}, \boldsymbol{x}) < c_2, \tag{2}$$

with $c_1 \in [0,1]$ and $c_2 \in [0,1]$.

In order to treat the logic formula with real value functions, each inequality of the FOL formula can be transformed into a new variable $l_{i,c_i} \in [0,1]$ through the following transformation:

$$I_i(\tilde{f}, \boldsymbol{x}) < c_i \;\; \longrightarrow \;\; l_{i,c_i}(\boldsymbol{x}) = \frac{\max(I_i(\tilde{f}, \boldsymbol{x}) - c_i, 0)}{1 - c_i}. \tag{3}$$

Although Eq. (3) is a quite natural choice for an increasing function from 0 to 1, other choices are possible. In Fig. 1 we represent the variable $l_{i,c_i}(\boldsymbol{x})$ of Eq. (3) for the case $c_i = 0.1$ of a generic feature.

So, thanks to Eq. (3), the aforementioned FOL formula Eq. (2) can be written as:

$$\forall \boldsymbol{x}: \; l_{1,c_1}(\tilde{f}, \boldsymbol{x}) \wedge l_{2,c_2}(\tilde{f}, \boldsymbol{x}).$$

Then, we exploit the framework of t-norm fuzzy logic that generalizes Boolean logic to variables assuming values in $[0,1]$. We can convert the formula depending on the losses $E(\boldsymbol{l}(\tilde{f}, \boldsymbol{x}))$ by exploiting a T-norm t in the following:

$$\Phi_\forall(\boldsymbol{l}(\tilde{f}, \mathcal{X})) = \frac{1}{|\mathcal{X}|} \sum_{\boldsymbol{x} \in \mathcal{X}} t_E\left(\boldsymbol{l}\left(\tilde{f}, \boldsymbol{x}\right)\right),$$

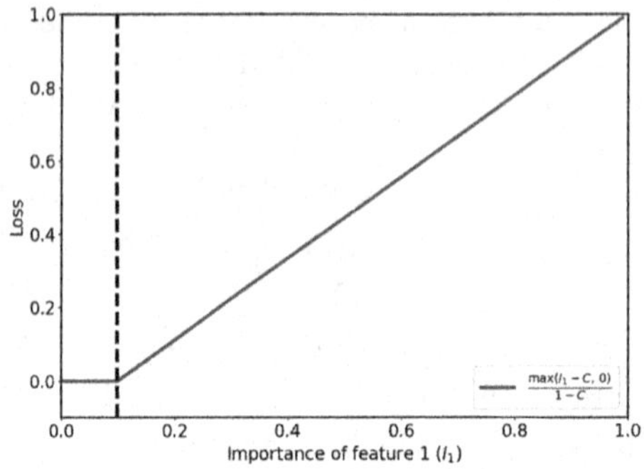

Fig. 1. Example of loss as for the inequality on the importance of the constrained feature for $I_i < 0.1$.

that is an average over the t-norm of the truth degree when grounded $\boldsymbol{x}$ over its domain. Then, a loss term can be defined by exploiting the logic constraints, e.g.

$$L_I(\boldsymbol{I}(\tilde{f}, \mathcal{X})) = \lambda(1 - \Phi_\forall(\boldsymbol{I}(\tilde{f}, \mathcal{X}))),$$

where λ is the strength of the regularization.

Finally, the partial derivative of the logic part of the loss L_I with respect to the j-th weight of the i-th importance loss function is

$$\frac{\partial L_I}{\partial w_{i,j}} = \sum_k \frac{\partial L_I}{\partial \Phi_k} \frac{\partial \Phi_k}{\partial l_i} \frac{\partial l_i}{\partial w_{i,j}},$$

and the derivative to being evaluated is: $\frac{\partial l_i}{\partial w_{i,j}}$. By resuming, the scheme is the following:

1. write the FOL formula depending on the feature importance, in turn, depending on the model weights through the chosen feature importance method;
2. convert the inequality terms $I_i < c_i$ into loss terms l_{i,c_i};
3. convert the FOL formula with the t-norm into an overall loss term;
4. the loss term is optimized in an iterative process by computing the importance at each step of the algorithm.

5 Fairness Through Feature Importance Constraints

Fairness is a natural field where the constraints to feature importance can be applied. In the following, we resume the principal fairness measures and we discuss how they can be translated by using our proposed scheme based on Constraints to Feature Importance, denoted hereafter as CTFI.

The *Demographic Parity* (DP) fairness metric is satisfied when, given the random variable $\tilde{Y}$ representing the binary predictor $\tilde{f}$ and a protected Boolean feature X_s we have:

$$P(\tilde{Y} = 1 | X_s = 0) = P(\tilde{Y} = 1 | X_s = 1).$$

DP is a very strong requirement: groups based on a sensitive feature, e.g. black and white, should have the same rate of positive prediction, even if differences are present.

DP can be translated into a constraint, where the importance of the protected feature s needs to be lower than a given threshold $c \in [0, 1]$:

$$\forall \boldsymbol{x} \;\; I_s(\boldsymbol{x}) < c. \tag{4}$$

The possible well-known issue of *unfairness due to correlated features* (see for instance [5]) can be tackled by setting a constraint also for the features that are correlated with the protected one. Obviously, the regularization strength λ_i of the i-th correlated feature should be lower with respect to λ_s, for instance given by the product of λ_i and the Pearson correlation between the s-th and i-th feature, i.e., $\rho_{s,i}$:

$$\lambda_i = \lambda_s \cdot \rho_{s,i}. \tag{5}$$

The advantage of this formulation is that the constraints are smooth between 0 and 1, and can be used both with binary and continuous features.

A measure of discrepancy from DP, which will be useful for the experimental part, is the *Disparate impact* (DI):

$$\text{DI} = \frac{P(\tilde{Y} = 1 | X_s = 0)}{P(\tilde{Y} = 1 | X_s = 1)}. \tag{6}$$

A possible relaxation of DP is where we grant that the protected attribute x_s can be used to discriminate among groups that are actually different in the ground truth label y, i.e., between $y = 0$ and $y = 1$, but not within each one. This is called *Equalized odd* (EOD) and is described in paper [11]. We say that a predictor $\tilde{Y}$ satisfies EOD if $\tilde{Y}$ and X_s are independent, conditional on Y:

$$P(\tilde{Y} = 1 | X_s = 0; Y = 1) = P(\tilde{Y} = 1 | X_s = 1; Y = 1),$$
$$P(\tilde{Y} = 1 | X_s = 0; Y = 0) = P(\tilde{Y} = 1 | X_s = 1; Y = 0).$$

A quite natural measure of discrepancy from EOD is the *average equality of odds difference* (EO):

$$\begin{aligned} \text{EO} = & \frac{P(\tilde{Y} = 1 | X_s = 0; Y = 1) - P(\tilde{Y} = 1 | X_s = 1; Y = 1)}{2} \\ & + \frac{P(\tilde{Y} = 1 | X_s = 0; Y = 0) - P(\tilde{Y} = 1 | X_s = 1; Y = 0)}{2}. \end{aligned} \tag{7}$$

Finally, another measure of fairness discrepancy defined in [15] is *counterfactual fairness difference* (CF):

$$\text{CF} = P(\tilde{Y}_{x_s \leftarrow 0} = 1 | X_s = 1) - P(\tilde{Y} = 1 | X_s = 1), \tag{8}$$

where the idea is to evaluate the differences of the prediction's probabilities by changing the protected feature of the patterns from 1 to 0.

6 Toy Example: Constraint of the Form $I_i(x) < c$

As a toy example useful to test the effectiveness of the proposed scheme, we used the German credit risk dataset (1000 instances), available in [8], containing information about bank account holders and a binary target variable denoting the credit risk. The considered features are reported in Table 2.

Table 2. Features for the German credit risk dataset.

Feature	Description	Range
Age	Age of the costumer	Numerical [19, 74]
Job	Job qualification	Ordinal [0, 3]
Amount	Credit amount (€) of the loan	Numerical
Duration	Duration (year) of the loan	Numerical [4, 72]
Gender	Male (1) Vs Female (0)	Boolean

We exploited a neural network with one hidden layer and 16 neurons. The learning rate of SGD is 0.01 with 10 epochs. The activation function is ReLU and the loss is given by the binary cross-entropy.

After the training phase, the Layer-wise Relevance Propagation method has been applied to the instances of the testing set (50% of the overall samples) for computing the feature importances. The black line in Fig. 2 reports the average feature importance computed with LRP. We observe that the most relevant feature is the *duration* of the loan, followed by the *amount* and the *gender*.

Let us introduce a constraint to the importance of *gender* feature that we want to be less-equal than zero (see Eq. (4)), with a regularization $\lambda = 0.05$. As expected, we observe (green line in Fig. 2) that the *gender* feature has become useless for the model predictions. Basically, the model found another solution, by giving more importance to other features, e.g. the *job*.

Furthermore, we computed the correlation matrix between the different features and we found out that, for instance, the *age* feature is correlated with the *gender* (with a Pearson correlation coefficient of $\rho_{\text{gender,age}} = 16\%$). So, in the third experiment we constrained also the other features, by using different regularization strength given by:

$$\lambda_i = \lambda \cdot \rho_{\text{gender},\, i}$$

for the i-th feature (see Eq. (5)). We note from the results reported in Fig. 2 with a red line, that the correlated *age* feature decreases its importance, coherently with the expectation.

7 Fairness Through Constraints to Feature Importance

In this section we report the results of the experimental part related to fairness. We tested the CTFI scheme proposed in the previous section to the *Adult income*

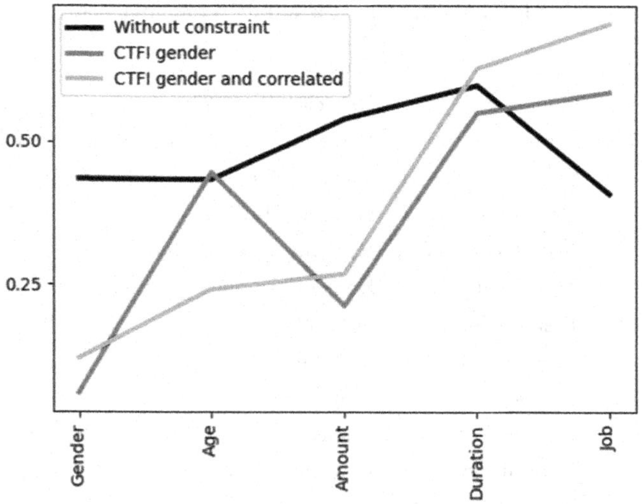

Fig. 2. Feature importance (LRP) for the original model (black line), for the model with the constraints on the *gender* feature (green line) and that constraining also the correlated features (red line).

data set, also considered by [14]. It contains 48,842 instances with 12 attributes (see Table 3 for the description) and a binary classification task for people earning more or less than $50,000 per year. The protected attribute we will examine is the *race*, categorized as white and non-white. In order to better evaluate the fairness metrics with a uniform test set, the dataset has been balanced and the chosen split of training/test is 50%. The model is a Neural Network with one hidden layer and 4 neurons. The learning rate is 0.1, the number of epochs is 10 and the batch size is fixed to 1 in order to compute the local feature importance for each analyzed pattern. The activation function is the ReLU function and the loss is given by the binary cross-entropy.

We used the constraint defined in Eq. (4) with $c = 0$ for the *race* feature; whereas as a fairness metric we consider both the disparate impact (DI) defined in Eq. (6), the average equality of odds difference (EO) in Eq. (7) and counterfactual fairness (CF) reported in Eq. (8). For the accuracy, we calculate the Area under the ROC curve (ROC-AUC).

Firstly, we evaluated the different fairness metrics in the testing set, with an increasing level of the regularization strength λ (10 values from 0 to 0.5). In Fig. 3 we report the accuracy metric (ROC-AUC in the lower plot) and the three measures of fairness: disparate impact (DI), average equality of odds difference (EO), and counterfactual fairness (CF) as a function of the regularization strength.

Table 3. Features for the adult income dataset.

Feature	Range
Age	Numerical [19, 74]
Race	Boolean: white Vs non-white
Sex	Boolean: female Vs male
Education	Ordinal: [1, 5]
Native-country	Boolean: US Vs other
Marital-status	Boolean: single Vs couple
Relationship	Ordinal: [1, 5]
Employment type	Ordinal: [1, 5]
Fnlwgt	Continuous
Capital loss	Boolean: Yes Vs NO
Capital gain	Boolean: Yes Vs NO
Hours-per-week	Continuous

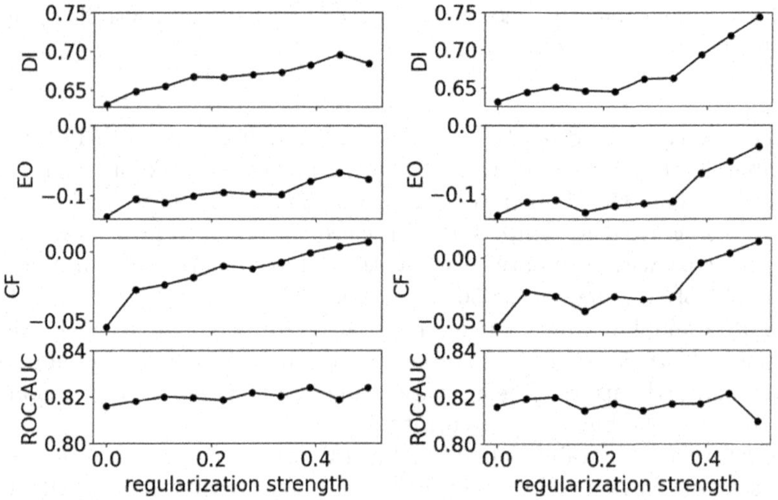

Fig. 3. Accuracy (ROC-AUC); and fairness measured as: disparate impact (DI), average equality of odds difference (EO) and counterfactual fairness (CF) (for each measure, the higher the values the higher the fairness levels), by constraining only the *race* feature (left Panel) and by constraining both *race* and the correlated ones (right Panel), as a function of the regularization strength.

In Fig. 3 we observe that, while the level of the ROC-AUC score practically remains the same, both DI, EO, and CF grow as the regularization strength augments, denoting an increased level of all the fairness measures. In particular, the CF measure reaches the value of 0, meaning that the protected feature no longer affects the predictions. The other two measures, DI and EO, do not reach the maximum level (1 and 0 respectively) because of the issue of correlated features. However, when also the correlated features are constrained through Eq. (5), we note that the increase of fairness is more pronounced (right panel of Fig. 3).

Then, as a further analysis we compared the fairness/accuracy levels obtained with the CTFI methodology[1] to the following benchmark methodologies:

1. the *unawareness* method [9], avoiding to use the *race* feature during the training phase;
2. a pre-processing method based on the *undersampling* of the samples with protected attribute;
3. the pre-processing method called *reweighing* [13] that assigns weights to the samples in the training dataset to reduce bias.

The AIF-360 library was used to apply the benchmark methodologies and the fairness metrics. The models are coded in the Pytorch environment and available at the Github repository https://github.com/nicolapicchiotti/ctfi.

In Fig. 4 we report the results of the accuracy measure given by the ROC-AUC (x-axis) and fairness metric EO (y-axis) for the different methodologies (unawareness, undersampling, reweighting) and the CFTI. The values are reported in Table 4.

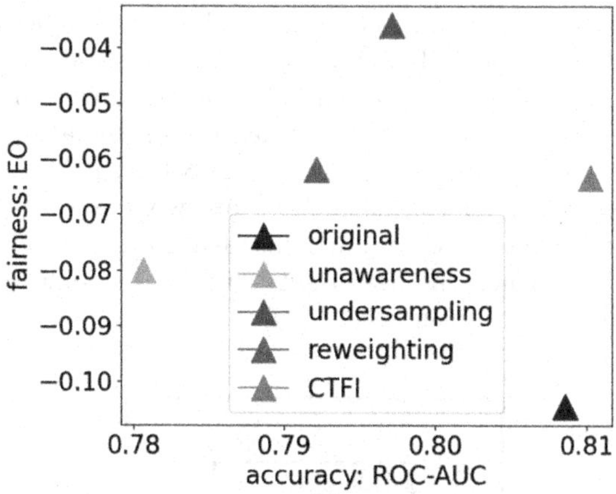

Fig. 4. Results of accuracy (ROC-AUC) and fairness (EO) for the different methodologies: original, unawareness, undersampling, reweighting and CTFI.

[1] With regularization chosen to be 0.1 and constraining also the other features, by using regularization strengths given by $\lambda \cdot \rho_{\text{gender},i}$ (see Eq. (5)).

Table 4. Results of the trade-off between accuracy (ROC-AUC) and fairness (EO) for the different methodologies: original, unawareness, undersampling, reweighting and CTFI.

Method	ROC-AUC	EO
Original	0.809	−0.104
Unawareness	0.781	−0.080
Undersampling	0.797	−0.036
Reweighting	0.792	−0.062
CTFI	0.810	−0.063

We note that, with respect to the original model, the unawareness, the undersampling, and the reweighting methodologies grant a high level of fairness at the expense of accuracy. On the other side, the CTFI methodology provides higher fairness metrics with a similar level of accuracy.

8 Conclusion and Future Work

In this work we have presented a novel model agnostic framework able to inject the apriori knowledge on the relevance of the input features into a machine learning model. This "weighted" approach can contribute to bridge the gap between the fully data-driven models and the human-guided ones. The advantage of the proposed method is the flexibility: the logic constraints are fully customizable and do not depend neither on the nature of input features (numerical, categorical etc.) nor on the architecture of the model, nor on the algorithms chosen for the computation of the feature importance, e.g. SHAP, LIME, LRP, etc.

A further application of the proposed framework is to enforce an apriori selective attention of the model on particular features, e.g. $I_i(\boldsymbol{x}) > c_i$. This can be useful for example when the user wants to focus on some relevant words in the text, or a region of an image (see Fig. 5).

Fig. 5. The middle part of an image may be subject to an apriori focus.

Furthermore, there could be many cases where the users want to inject prior knowledge in the form of feature importance in the model. For example, from experience, one could know that one feature should be less important than another for the business of the company, e.g. the age, the gender in a particular financial context. Also in the medical field, the a priori knowledge of the input features' importance can improve model performances where the sample sizes are limited. Another possibility is when we apriori know which feature is less reliable e.g. less stationary with respect to the others.[2] It is worth noting that the constraints can be settled for just a portion of the dataset.

As future work we are interested in providing a software solution for the integration of the proposed framework within the popular machine learning software. Another future work is to apply the logic constraints to other contexts, in terms of both dataset, e.g. images, text etc. and models (random forest, SVM etc.). Finally, the usage of other measures based on information entropy can be explored in order to take into account the problem of correlation between features.

References

1. Al Iqbal, R.: Empirical learning aided by weak domain knowledge in the form of feature importance. In: 2011 International Conference on Multimedia and Signal Processing, vol. 1, pp. 126–130. IEEE (2011)
2. Arrieta, A.B., et al.: Explainable artificial intelligence (XAI): Concepts, taxonomies, opportunities and challenges toward responsible AI. Inf. Fusion **58**, 82–115 (2020)
3. Bach, S., Binder, A., Montavon, G., Klauschen, F., Müller, K.R., Samek, W.: On pixel-wise explanations for non-linear classifier decisions by layer-wise relevance propagation. PLoS One **10**(7), e0130140 (2015)
4. Breiman, L.: Random forests. Mach. Learn. **45**(1), 5–32 (2001). https://doi.org/10.1023/a:1010933404324
5. Calders, T., Žliobaitė, I.: Why unbiased computational processes can lead to discriminative decision procedures. In: Custers, B., Calders, T., Schermer, B., Zarsky, T. (eds.) Discrimination and Privacy in the Information Society, pp. 43–57. Springer, Heidelberg (2013). https://doi.org/10.1007/978-3-642-30487-3_3
6. Diersen, S., Lee, E.J., Spears, D., Chen, P., Wang, L.: Classification of seismic windows using artificial neural networks. Procedia Comput. Sci. **4**, 1572–1581 (2011)
7. Doshi-Velez, F., Kim, B.: Towards a rigorous science of interpretable machine learning. arXiv preprint. arXiv:1702.08608 (2017)
8. Dua, D., Graff, C.: UCI machine learning repository (2017). http://archive.ics.uci.edu/ml
9. Grgic-Hlaca, N., Zafar, M.B., Gummadi, K.P., Weller, A.: The case for process fairness in learning: feature selection for fair decision making. In: NIPS Symposium on Machine Learning and the Law, vol. 1, p. 2 (2016)
10. Guidotti, R., Monreale, A., Ruggieri, S., Turini, F., Giannotti, F., Pedreschi, D.: A survey of methods for explaining black box models. ACM Comput. Surv. (CSUR) **51**(5), 1–42 (2018)

[2] In linear regression a similar problem is called attenuation bias, where errors in the input features cause the weights going toward zero.

11. Hardt, M., Price, E., Srebro, N.: Equality of opportunity in supervised learning. Adv. Neural Inf. Process. Syst. **29**, 3315–3323 (2016)
12. Iqbal, R.A.: Using feature weights to improve performance of neural networks. arXiv preprint. arXiv:1101.4918 (2011)
13. Kamiran, F., Calders, T.: Data preprocessing techniques for classification without discrimination. Knowl. Inf. Syst. **33**(1), 1–33 (2012). https://doi.org/10.1007/s10115-011-0463-8
14. Kamishima, T., Akaho, S., Sakuma, J.: Fairness-aware learning through regularization approach. In: 2011 IEEE 11th International Conference on Data Mining Workshops, pp. 643–650. IEEE (2011)
15. Kusner, M.J., Loftus, J.R., Russell, C., Silva, R.: Counterfactual fairness. arXiv preprint. arXiv:1703.06856 (2017)
16. Lipton, Z.C.: The mythos of model interpretability: In machine learning, the concept of interpretability is both important and slippery. Queue **16**(3), 31–57 (2018)
17. Lou, Y., Caruana, R., Gehrke, J.: Intelligible models for classification and regression. In: Proceedings of the 18th ACM SIGKDD International Conference on Knowledge Discovery and Data Mining, pp. 150–158 (2012)
18. Lou, Y., Caruana, R., Gehrke, J., Hooker, G.: Accurate intelligible models with pairwise interactions. In: Proceedings of the 19th ACM SIGKDD International Conference on Knowledge Discovery and Data Mining, pp. 623–631 (2013)
19. Lundberg, S., Lee, S.I.: A unified approach to interpreting model predictions. arXiv preprint. arXiv:1705.07874 (2017)
20. Montavon, G., Samek, W., Müller, K.R.: Methods for interpreting and understanding deep neural networks. Digital Signal Process. **73**, 1–15 (2018)
21. Peng, X., Zhu, Y.: A novel feature weighted strategy on data classification. In: 2018 IEEE 3rd International Conference on Cloud Computing and Internet of Things (CCIOT), pp. 589–594. IEEE (2018)
22. Recknagel, F., French, M., Harkonen, P., Yabunaka, K.I.: Artificial neural network approach for modelling and prediction of algal blooms. Ecol. Model. **96**(1–3), 11–28 (1997)
23. Ribeiro, M.T., Singh, S., Guestrin, C.: "why should i trust you?" explaining the predictions of any classifier. In: Proceedings of the 22nd ACM SIGKDD International Conference on Knowledge Discovery and Data Mining, pp. 1135–1144 (2016)
24. Shrikumar, A., Greenside, P., Kundaje, A.: Learning important features through propagating activation differences. In: International Conference on Machine Learning, pp. 3145–3153. PMLR (2017)
25. Simonyan, K., Vedaldi, A., Zisserman, A.: Deep inside convolutional networks: visualising image classification models and saliency maps. arXiv preprint. arXiv:1312.6034 (2013)
26. Strumbelj, E., Kononenko, I.: An efficient explanation of individual classifications using game theory. J. Mach. Learn. Res. **11**, 1–18 (2010)
27. Štrumbelj, E., Kononenko, I.: Explaining prediction models and individual predictions with feature contributions. Knowl. Inf. Syst. **41**(3), 647–665 (2013). https://doi.org/10.1007/s10115-013-0679-x
28. Sundararajan, M., Taly, A., Yan, Q.: Gradients of counterfactuals. arXiv preprint. arXiv:1611.02639 (2016)
29. Zhang, L., Wang, Z.: Ontology-based clustering algorithm with feature weights. J. Comput. Inf. Syst. **6**(9), 2959–2966 (2010)

Clustering-Based Interpretation of Deep ReLU Network

Nicola Picchiotti[1,2(✉)] and Marco Gori[1,3]

[1] SAILAB, University of Siena, Siena, Italy
marco@diism.unisi.it
[2] University of Pavia, Pavia, Italy
nicola.picchiotti01@universitadipavia.it
[3] MAASAI, Universitè Côte d'Azur, Nice, France
http://sailab.diism.unisi.it

Abstract. Amongst others, the adoption of Rectified Linear Units (ReLUs) is regarded as one of the ingredients of the success of deep learning. ReLU activation has been shown to mitigate the vanishing gradient issue, to encourage sparsity in the learned parameters, and to allow for efficient backpropagation. In this paper, we recognize that the non-linear behavior of the ReLU function gives rise to a natural clustering of the input space when the pattern of network's active neurons is considered. This observation helps to deepen the learning mechanism of the network; in fact, we demonstrate that, within each cluster, the network can be fully represented as an affine map. The consequence is that we are able to recover an explanation, in the form of feature importance, for the predictions done by the network to the instances belonging to a specific cluster. The methodology we propose is able to increase the level of interpretability of a fully connected feedforward ReLU neural network, downstream from the fitting phase of the model, without altering the structure of the network. A simulation study and the empirical application to the Titanic dataset, show the capability of the method to bridge the gap between the algorithm optimization and the human understandability of the black box deep ReLU networks.

Keywords: ReLU · Clustering · Explainability · Linearity · Feature importance

1 Introduction

The recent developments of deep neural networks offer enormous progress in artificial intelligence in various sectors. In particular, the ReLU functions have been shown to mitigate the vanishing gradient issue, encourage sparsity in the learned parameters and allow for efficient backpropagation [12]. On the other hand, the "black box" nature of deep neural network models is often a limit for high-stakes applications like diagnostic techniques, autonomous guide etc. since the reliability of the model predictions can be affected by the incompleteness in the optimization problem formalization [9].

S. Bandini et al. (Eds.): AIxIA 2021, LNAI 13196, pp. 403–412, 2022.
https://doi.org/10.1007/978-3-031-08421-8_28

Recent works have shown that an adequate level of interpretability could enforce the neural network trustworthiness (see [4]). Thus, much work has been done in order to explain and interpret the models developed by AI in a human comprehensible manner. The main reason behind these effort is that the human experience and capacity for abstraction allow to monitor the process of the model decisions in a sound way, trying to mitigate the risks of data-driven models. However, this is generally difficult to achieve without alter the mechanism of deep learning [14]. The topic has became particularly relevant in the last decades, since technology development and data availability led to the adoption of more and more complex models, and widened the gap between performances on train/test data and interpretability.

In this paper, we tackle the explainability problem of deep ReLU networks, by characterizing the natural predisposition of the network to partition the input dataset in different clusters. The direct consequence of the clustering process is that, within each cluster, the network can be simplified and represented as an affine map. Surprisingly, the deep network provides a notion of cluster-specific importance for each feature.

2 Bibliographic Review

Despite the benefits and the expressiveness of Rectifier Networks have been widely investigated, e.g. in [12], the cluster analysis and the consequent interpretation of the network via the modeling of the pattern of active neurons have not been discussed in the literature, to our knowledge.

On the other hand, many model-specific methodologies can be applied for gaining interpretability in neural network models (see [1] and [6] for a review). The importance of a feature is one of the most used strategies to gain local explainability from an opaque machine learning model. *Permutation feature importance* methods evaluate the feature importance through the variation of a loss metric by permuting the feature's values on a set of instances in the training or validation set. The approach is introduced for random forest in [3] and for neural network in [13]. Other methods, such as *class model visualization* [16], compute the partial derivative of the score function with respect to the input, and [11] introduces expert distribution for the input giving *activation maximization*. In [15] the author introduces *deep lift* and computes the discrete gradients with respect to a baseline point, by backpropagating the scoring difference through each unit. *Integrated gradients* [17] cumulates the gradients with respect to inputs along the path from a given baseline to the instance. Finally, a set of well known methods called *additive feature attribution methods* defined in [10] rely on the redistribution of the predicted value $\hat{f}(\boldsymbol{x})$ over the input features. They are designed to mimic the behaviour of a predictive function $\hat{f}$ with a surrogate Boolean linear function g.

Relevant to our work are explorations of the roles of semantic concepts inside neural networks. In fact, the methodology we are here presenting is linked to other lines of research exploiting the connectionist paradigm, where the goal is to evaluate whether the network's structure is able to represent, within itself, a set of semantic concepts. For example, in [19] the authors demonstrate that, in a network specifically designed for classifying scenes, individual units behave as object detectors without being explicitly trained with the notion of objects. In a similar way, in [18] the authors show that in a convolutional neural network the filters represent patterns that make sense to us visually, and help us to insect the input images.

Among the strategies aiming at extracting information from the network's structure, in [2] the authors quantify the interpretability of latent representations of CNNs, by exploiting a set of concepts drawn from a broad and dense segmentation dataset (*Network Dissection*). Similarly, [7] tries to interpret high-dimensional internal state of a neural network in terms of human-friendly concepts, by using the directional derivatives to quantify the degree to which a user-defined concept is important to a classification result. So, for instance, a typical problem is to assess how sensitive a prediction of an animal is to the presence of a particular texture, e.g. the stripes. Anyway, we underlying that the cited approaches need a predetermined set of semantic concepts; for instance giving labels across a range of objects, scenes, textures, colors, etc. Instead, the methodology we are proposing does not require to introduce apriori knowledge on the semantic concepts and the arising clusters can be seen as novel concepts.

3 Deep ReLU Networks for the Partition of the Input Space

In this section, we demonstrate that a deep ReLU neural network gives rise to a partition of the input dataset into a set of clusters, each one characterized by an affine map.

Let us denote by $W_i,\ \ i \in [1, \ldots, p]$ the weight matrices associated with the p layers of a given multilayer network with predictor $\tilde{f}$ (of a q-dim target variable) and collect[1] $\hat{W}_i$ in $\hat{W} = [\hat{W}_1, \ldots, \hat{W}_p]$. For any input $\boldsymbol{u} \in \mathbb{R}^d$, the initial Directed Acyclic Graph (DAG) $\mathcal{G}$ of the deep network is reduced to $\mathcal{G}_{\boldsymbol{u}}$ which only keeps the units corresponding to active neurons[2] and the corresponding arcs. This DAG is clearly associated with a given set of weights $\hat{W}$. We can formally state this pruning for the given neural network, characterized by $\mathcal{G}$, paired with input $\boldsymbol{u}$ with weights $\hat{W}$ by

$$\mathcal{G}_{\boldsymbol{u}} = \gamma(\mathcal{G}, \hat{W}, \boldsymbol{u}),$$

where, since all neurons operate in "linear regime" (affine functions), as stated in the following, the output, the composition of affine functions, is in fact an affine function itself.

Theorem 1. *Let $\mathscr{X}_i \subset \mathbb{R}^{d_i},\ \ i \in [1, \ldots, p]$ be, where $d_1 = d$. Let $\{h_1, \ldots, h_p\}$ be a collection of affine functions, where*

$$h_i : \mathscr{X}_i \mapsto \mathscr{Y}_i : x \mapsto W_i x + \boldsymbol{b}_i = \hat{W}_i \hat{x},$$

[1] The ˆ in the notation means that the bias term is incorporated in the variable.

[2] A neuron is considered active for a particular pattern if the input falls in the right linear part of the domain's function.

and assume that $\mathscr{Y}_i$ *is chosen in such a way that* $\forall i = 1, \ldots, p-1: \quad \mathscr{X}_{i+1} \subset \mathscr{Y}_i$, *whereas* $\mathscr{Y}_p \subset \mathbb{R}^{d_q}$. *Then we have that*

$$\tilde{f}(\hat{W}, \boldsymbol{u}) = h_p \circ h_{p-1} \circ \cdots \circ h_2 \circ h_1(\boldsymbol{u})$$

is affine and we have $\tilde{f}(W, \boldsymbol{u}) = f(\hat{\Omega}, \hat{\boldsymbol{u}}) = \Omega\, \boldsymbol{u} + \boldsymbol{b}$, *where*[3]

$$\hat{\Omega} := [\Omega, \boldsymbol{b}] \tag{1}$$

$$\Omega(p) = \prod_{i=p}^{1} W_i \tag{2}$$

$$\boldsymbol{b}(p) = \sum_{i=1}^{p} \left(\prod_{t=p+1}^{i+1} W_t \right) \cdot \boldsymbol{b}_i \tag{3}$$

being $W_{p+1} := \mathbb{I}$.

Proof. The proof is given by induction on p.

- *Basis*: For $p = 1$ we have $\tilde{f} = W_1\, \boldsymbol{u} + \boldsymbol{b}_1$ and $\Omega(1) = W_1$ which confirms (2), and when considering $W_2 := \mathbb{I}$, we have

$$\boldsymbol{b}(1) = W_2 \cdot \boldsymbol{b}_1 = \boldsymbol{b}_1,$$

  in according to (3).
- *Induction step*: By induction, a network with $p-1$ layers is defined by an affine transformation that is

$$y(p-1) = \Omega(p-1)\, \boldsymbol{u} + \boldsymbol{b}(p-1).$$

  Hence

$$\begin{aligned}
y(p) &= W_p\, y(p-1) + \boldsymbol{b}_p \\
&= W_p(\Omega(p-1)\, \boldsymbol{u} + \boldsymbol{b}(p-1)) + \boldsymbol{b}_p \\
&= W_p\Big(\prod_{i=p-1}^{1} W_i\, \boldsymbol{u} + \sum_{i=1}^{p-1} \Big(\prod_{t=p}^{i+1} W_t \Big) \cdot \boldsymbol{b}_i \Big) + \boldsymbol{b}_p \\
&= W_p\Big(\prod_{i=p-1}^{1} W_i\, \boldsymbol{u} + \sum_{i=1}^{p-2} \Big(\prod_{t=p-1}^{i+1} W_t \Big) \cdot \boldsymbol{b}_i + \mathbb{I} \cdot \boldsymbol{b}_{p-1} \Big) + \boldsymbol{b}_p \\
&= \prod_{i=p}^{1} W_i\, \boldsymbol{u} + \sum_{i=1}^{p-2} \Big(\prod_{t=p}^{i+1} W_t \Big) \cdot \boldsymbol{b}_i + W_p\, \boldsymbol{b}_{p-1} + \boldsymbol{b}_p \\
&= \prod_{i=p}^{1} W_i\, \boldsymbol{u} + \sum_{i=1}^{p-1} \Big(\prod_{t=p}^{i+1} W_t \Big) \cdot \boldsymbol{b}_i + \mathbb{I} \cdot \boldsymbol{b}_p \\
&= \Big(\prod_{i=p}^{1} W_i \Big) \boldsymbol{u} + \sum_{i=1}^{p} \Big(\prod_{t=p+1}^{i+1} W_t \Big) \cdot \boldsymbol{b}_i
\end{aligned} \tag{4}$$

[3] We stress the dependence of Ω and $\boldsymbol{b}$ from the number of layer (p) since it will be useful for the proof.

Now let $\mathscr{U} \subset \mathbb{R}^d$ the input space. The given deep net yields a partition on $\mathscr{U}$ which is associated with the following equivalence relation:

$$\boldsymbol{u}_1 \sim \boldsymbol{u}_2 \leftrightarrow \mathcal{G}_{\boldsymbol{u}_1} = \mathcal{G}_{\boldsymbol{u}_2}$$

We denote[4] by $[\boldsymbol{u}]_\sim = \{\boldsymbol{v} \in \mathscr{U} : \boldsymbol{v} \sim \boldsymbol{u}\}$ and by $\mathscr{U}/\sim$ the corresponding quotient set. Hence, $[\boldsymbol{u}]_\sim$ is the equivalent class associated with representer $\boldsymbol{u}$ which, in turn, corresponds with $\mathcal{G}_{\boldsymbol{u}}$. Notice that, as a consequence, $[\boldsymbol{u}]_\sim$ is fully defined by the set of neurons of the active neural network.

Feature Importance Explanation The characterization done above allows to assigning a matrix $\hat{\Omega}$ to each cluster of the network. In this way, the matrix is able to represent the network for the patterns of the specific cluster as an affine map.

For simplicity, if we consider a problem where the output of the network is scalar, the matrix Ω reduces to a d-dimensional effective vector $\boldsymbol{\omega}$ whose components can be interpreted as the *feature importance of the cluster's solution.*

4 Simulation Study

In this section, we report the simulation studies carried out on the ReLU network architecture applied to a Boolean artificial dataset, in order to assess the power of the clustering-based interpretation.

We consider a set of 10 Boolean feature variables $v_{i \in [1,\ldots,10]}$. The first 3 features determine the target variable through the following relation:

$$t = (v_1 \wedge v_3) \vee (v_2 \wedge \neg v_3) \tag{5}$$

whereas the other 7 features introduce noise. The rationale of the formula is that the feature v_3 splits the data set in two groups (v_3 and $\neg v_3$), each ruled by a different term of the Boolean formula involving either v_1 or v_2 respectively. In the following, we investigate whether the network clustering is able to recognize the different terms of the formula.

We simulated $100,000$ samples, and we exploited a two-hidden-layer Multilayer Perceptron (MLP) with 4 and 2 neurons characterized by ReLU activation function and an output neuron with a sigmoid activation function. The cross-entropy loss is minimized via the Adam stochastic optimizer with a step size of 0.01 for 10 epochs, and a batch size of 100. An activity regularizer with 0.02 is added to the empirical loss. At the end of the training, the network solves the problem with an accuracy of 100%. The experiments are implemented with Keras in the Python environment on a regular CPU.

The analysis of the network, by considering the possible patterns of the active neurons, originates three clusters.

[4] In this work $[\cdot]$ is the Iverson's notation, whereas $[\cdot]_\sim$ is reserved to the equivalent class induced by equivalence relation $\sim$.

1. A trivial cluster characterized by all non-active neurons including all the patterns predicted as 0.

Instead, the other two clusters activate the two neurons of the last layer but a different neuron of the first hidden layer. In Fig. 1 we report the table resuming the 8 possibilities of the Boolean function restricted to the first 3 features, as well as the bar plot for the importance of the features for the two non-trivial clusters. As explained above, the importance of the feature is computed by the specific coefficient of the effective vector for that cluster.

2. The second cluster, represented by the blue bars in Fig. 1, includes patterns predicted as 1 and characterized either by $v_1 = v_2 = v_3 = 1$ or by $v_1 = 1$, $v_2 = 0$, $v_3 = 1$. We can argue that this cluster takes in charge the patterns predicted as 1 due to the first term of Eq. (5), i.e. $v_1 \wedge v_3$. Coherently with this setting, the feature importance given by the effective vector is zero for the feature v_2 that does not appear in the first term of Eq. (5). On the other side, the coefficient of the effective vector is positive for the feature v_1.
3. In a similar way, the third cluster (orange color), represents the term $v_2 \wedge \neg v_3$ of Eq. (5) since the patterns belonging to it are predicted as 1 and are characterized either by $v_1 = v_2 = 1, v_3 = 0$ or by $v_1 = 0, v_2 = 1, v_3 = 0$. As expected, the feature importance of v_1 is zero, whereas for v_2 the feature importance is positive.

Features			Target value	Feature Importance		
v_1	v_2	v_3	$(v_1 \wedge v_3) \vee (v_2 \wedge \neg v_3)$	I_1	I_2	I_3
1	1	1	1	>0	0	>0
1	0	1	1			
0	1	1	0			
0	0	1	0			
1	1	0	1	0	>0	<0
1	0	0	0			
0	1	0	1	0	>0	<0
0	0	0	0			

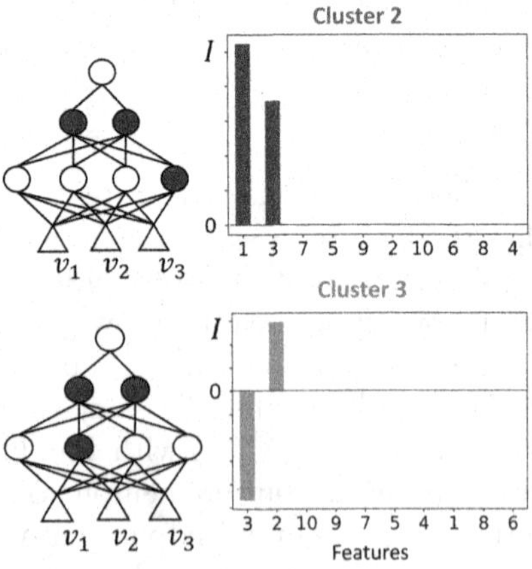

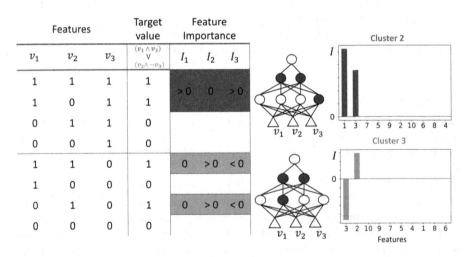

Fig. 1. Possible results of the simulated task (8 combinations) and representation of the actual clusters provided by the cluster-based interpretation of the ReLU network.

From the simulation study, we note that the clustering-based interpretation of the ReLU network helps to achieve a more profound understanding of the solution meaning. In particular, the methodology tries to disentangle the complexity of the solutions into a set of more comprehensible linear solutions within a specific cluster.

As a further confirmation of the usefulness of cluster-based interpretation, when the activity regularizer is removed, the network keeps solving the task giving rise to 8 clusters, each one specific for each combination of the first three features. Based on the cluster interpretation, we conclude that the network has chosen in this case a less abstract way to solve the problem.

5 Titanic Dataset

In this section, we report the experimental analysis performed on the well-known Titanic dataset[5]. Each sample represents a passenger with specific features, and the binary target variable indicates if the person survived the Titanic disaster. A standard data cleaning and feature selection procedure[6] are implemented. In Table 1 we report a brief description of the features of the dataset.

Table 1. Features for the Titanic dataset

Feature	Description	Range
Age	Age of the passenger discretized in 5 bins	$[0, 4]$
Gender	1 if the passenger is female	$\{0, 1\}$
PClass	Travel class: first, second, third	$[1, 3]$
Fare	Ticket fare discretized in 3 bins	$[0, 3]$
Embarked	Location for the embarked	$[0, 2]$
Title	Title of the passenger: Mr, Miss, Mrs, Master, Rare	$[1, 5]$
Is Alone	1 if the passenger has not relatives	$\{0, 1\}$

Similar to the previous experiment, we exploit a two-hidden-layer MLP with 4 and 2 neurons characterized by ReLU activation function and an output neuron with a sigmoid activation function. The cross-entropy loss is minimized via the Adam stochastic optimizer with a step size of 0.01 for 10 epochs and a batch size of 100. An activity regularizer with 0.02 is added to the empirical loss. The experiments are implemented with Keras in the Python environment. The code is freely available at https://github.com/nicolapicchiotti/relu_nn_clustering.

The accuracy of the network is 77% (see [8]) and the study of the active neurons patterns provides a partition of the dataset into three clusters, as shown in Fig. 2.

(a) The first cluster a) includes passengers with mixed features and a percentage of survived ones equal to 38%. As expected from the univariate exploratory analyses, *gender* and *class* had the most significant relationship for survival rate.

[5] https://www.kaggle.com/c/titanic.
[6] https://www.kaggle.com/startupsci/titanic-data-science-solutions.

(b) The cluster b) instead, includes only males belonging to the third class (4% of the overall): the prediction for these passengers is always 0. This cluster confirms the expectation on the male gender and third class as relevant features for not survive. We observe that the feature importance is quite similar to the one of cluster a) except for the fact that the "age" feature assumes slightly more relevance. Finally,
(c) in the cluster c) the passengers are females and belonging to the first class (16% of the overall), the predicted value is always 1. The feature importance, in this case, shows that the high value of the *title*, *age*, and the other features contribute to survival, in addition to being female. This cluster helps us to understand the solution provided by the network. For instance, we note that the "age" feature has an opposite behavior with respect to the other two clusters: in this cluster the older the women, the higher the survival probability.

In this experiment, we have shown that the ReLU network can be disentangled into a set of clusters that can be analyzed individually. The clusters have a practical meaning helping the human to interpret the mechanism of prediction of the network.

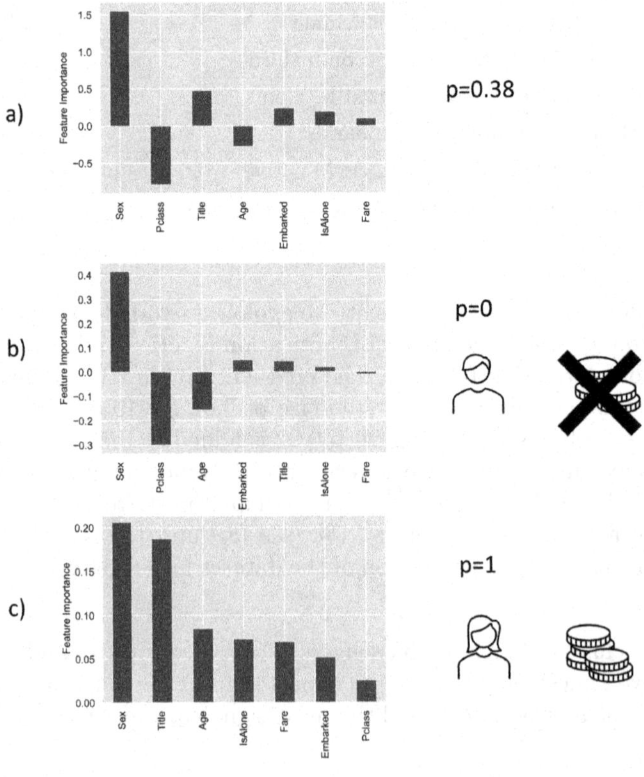

Fig. 2. Bar plot with the feature importance for each of the three clusters originated by the ReLU neural network.

6 Conclusions and Limitations

This paper proposes a methodology for increasing the level of interpretability of a fully connected feedforward neural network with ReLU activation functions, downstream from the fitting phase of the model. It is worth noting that the introduced methodology does not alter neither the structure nor the performance of the network, and can be easily applied after the training of the model since it relies on the clustering that naturally arises from the binary status of the different neurons of the network (in turn, related to the two regimes of the ReLU function).

Then, the existence of a feature importance explanation based on an affine map for each cluster has been proved, and the empirical application to the Titanic dataset showed the capability of the method to bridge the gap between the algorithm optimization and human understandability. Our results are encouraging and should be validated by a larger set of datasets, possibly with more complex networks in terms of number of layers and tasks to be solved.

A limitation of the work is related to the potential high number of clusters that the networks could generates. Further ways should be explored in order to grant a parsimonious principle of the clustering process, such as exploiting the hierarchy of the layers, the principle of minimum entropy or the orthogonality of the hyperplanes representing the clusters. Finally, it is worth mentioning that, if the input variables are highly correlated or belong to a very high-dimensional spaces, the weights of the affine map cannot be trivially interpreted as the features importance, see for instance [5].

References

1. Arrieta, A.B.: Explainable artificial intelligence (XAI): Concepts, taxonomies, opportunities and challenges toward responsible AI. Inf. Fusion **58**, 82–115 (2020)
2. Bau, D., Zhou, B., Khosla, A., Oliva, A., Torralba, A.: Network dissection: quantifying interpretability of deep visual representations. In: Proceedings of the IEEE Conference on Computer Vision and Pattern Recognition, pp. 6541–6549 (2017)
3. Breiman, L.: Random forests. Mach. Learn. **45**(1), 5–32 (2001). https://doi.org/10.1023/a:1010933404324
4. Doshi-Velez, F., Kim, B.: Towards a rigorous science of interpretable machine learning. arXiv preprint. arXiv:1702.08608 (2017)
5. Fránay, B., Hofmann, D., Schulz, A., Biehl, M., Hammer, B.: Valid interpretation of feature relevance for linear data mappings. In: 2014 IEEE Symposium on Computational Intelligence and Data Mining (CIDM), pp. 149–156. IEEE (2014)
6. Guidotti, R., Monreale, A., Ruggieri, S., Turini, F., Giannotti, F., Pedreschi, D.: A survey of methods for explaining black box models. ACM Comput. Surv. (CSUR) **51**(5), 1–42 (2018)
7. Kim, B., Wattenberg, M., Gilmer, J., Cai, C., Wexler, J., Viegas, F., et al.: Interpretability beyond feature attribution: Quantitative testing with concept activation vectors (tcav). In: International conference on machine learning, pp. 2668–2677. PMLR (2018)
8. Lam, E., Tang, C.: Cs229 titanic - machine learning from disaster (2012)

9. Lipton, Z.C.: The mythos of model interpretability: in machine learning, the concept of interpretability is both important and slippery. Queue **16**(3), 31–57 (2018)
10. Lundberg, S.M., Lee, S.I.: A unified approach to interpreting model predictions. In: Proceedings of the 31st International Conference on Neural Information Processing Systems, pp. 4768–4777 (2017)
11. Montavon, G., Samek, W., Müller, K.R.: Methods for interpreting and understanding deep neural networks. Dig. Signal Process. **73**, 1–15 (2018)
12. Pan, X., Srikumar, V.: Expressiveness of rectifier networks. In: International Conference on Machine Learning, pp. 2427–2435. PMLR (2016)
13. Recknagel, F., French, M., Harkonen, P., Yabunaka, K.I.: Artificial neural network approach for modelling and prediction of algal blooms. Ecol. Model. **96**(1–3), 11–28 (1997)
14. Ribeiro, M.T., Singh, S., Guestrin, C.: "Why should i trust you?" explaining the predictions of any classifier. In: Proceedings of the 22nd ACM SIGKDD International Conference on Knowledge Discovery and Data Mining, pp. 1135–1144 (2016)
15. Shrikumar, A., Greenside, P., Kundaje, A.: Learning important features through propagating activation differences. In: International Conference on Machine Learning, pp. 3145–3153. PMLR (2017)
16. Simonyan, K., Vedaldi, A., Zisserman, A.: Deep inside convolutional networks: visualising image classification models and saliency maps. In: In Workshop at International Conference on Learning Representations. Citeseer (2014)
17. Sundararajan, M., Taly, A., Yan, Q.: Gradients of counterfactuals. arXiv preprint. arXiv:1611.02639 (2016)
18. Zeiler, M.D., Fergus, R.: Visualizing and understanding convolutional networks. In: Fleet, D., Pajdla, T., Schiele, B., Tuytelaars, T. (eds.) ECCV 2014. LNCS, vol. 8689, pp. 818–833. Springer, Cham (2014). https://doi.org/10.1007/978-3-319-10590-1_53
19. Zhou, B., Khosla, A., Lapedriza, A., Oliva, A., Torralba, A.: Object detectors emerge in deep scene cnns. arXiv preprint. arXiv:1412.6856 (2014)

Exploration-Intensive Distractors: Two Environment Proposals and a Benchmarking

Jim Martin Catacora Ocana[1(✉)], Roberto Capobianco[1,2], and Daniele Nardi[1]

[1] Department of Computer, Control and Management Engineering, Sapienza University, Rome, Italy
catacora@diag.uniroma1.it
[2] Sony AI, Zürich, Switzerland

Abstract. Sparse-reward environments are famously challenging for deep reinforcement learning (DRL) algorithms. Yet, the prospect of solving tasks with intrinsically sparse rewards in an end-to-end fashion and without any extra reward engineering is highly appealing. Such aspiration has recently led to the development of numerous DRL algorithms able to handle reward sparsity to some extent. Some methods have even gone one step further and have tackled sparse-reward tasks involving different kinds of distractors (e.g., a broken TV, a self-moving phantom object and many more). In this work, we put forward two motivating new sparse-reward environments containing the so-far largely overlooked class of exploration-intensive distractors. Furthermore, we conduct a benchmarking that reveals that state-of-the-art algorithms are not yet all-around suitable for solving our proposed environments.

Keywords: Reinforcement learning · Sparse rewards · Benchmarking

1 Introduction

In recent years, deep reinforcement learning has achieved remarkable results in a number of domains, such as: learning to play Go at a superhuman level only from self-play [32], reaching Grandmaster level in Starcraft II [37], surpassing the scores of non-expert human players in all 57 games of the Atari 2600 suite [2], as well as performing complex robotic tasks [12,13,21].

In spite of this success, DRL still struggles to perform competently in various settings. One of them corresponds to sparse-reward environments, i.e., domains where rewards are zero everywhere except in few special states. A well-known example is the Atari game Montezuma's revenge. Strikingly, several general-purpose DRL algorithms have notoriously failed to score higher than an average human player in such a game despite achieving superhuman performances in many other Atari scenarios [8,14–16,23,29]. In response to this challenge, over

We acknowledge the CINECA award under the ISCRA initiative, for the availability of high performance computing resources and support.

S. Bandini et al. (Eds.): AIxIA 2021, LNAI 13196, pp. 413–428, 2022.
https://doi.org/10.1007/978-3-031-08421-8_29

the years researchers have developed numerous DRL algorithms to specifically address tasks with sparse rewards [1,4,7,9,22,24,26,31,34–36]. And significant progress has been made; for instance, RND [6] more than doubles the score of a human player on Montezuma's revenge. Likewise, NGU [3] and Agent57 [2], while being general methods, have recently reached similar results in this game.

Nevertheless, these state-of-the-art algorithms are not yet the definitive solution to every sparse-reward problem. For example, RND has been shown to fundamentally fail in the presence of pixel-level noise [18,33]. Such noise is more generally referred to as a distractor, i.e., a dynamic element that can be observed by the learning agent and is irrelevant to the resolution of the task at hand. Distractors have also taken the form of: a broken TV [28], a remote-controlled noisy TV [5] or a self-moving phantom ball [19]. Crucially, the previous distractors share one commonality, their dynamics are easily distinguishable from those of most DRL benchmark environments. In particular, they possess at least one of the following three perverse properties. 1) They are uncontrollable; i.e., agents are conferred no actions that alter the state of these distractors. 2) They are highly unpredictable; i.e., their transition probabilities tend to adopt a uniform distribution, and hence, numerous and widely different states are equally likely to follow any given state. 3) They demand a low transitioning effort [28]; that is, moving between any two states requires a minimum of one time step or less. Unsurprisingly, previous works have leveraged these visible differences to formulate rather successful algorithms that first detect and then ignore elements whose dynamics display one of the former properties [27,28].

Unfortunately, there exist distractors that have none of said three properties, and thus, they blend perfectly within any interesting environment. These pose an intriguing new problem since a detect-neglect strategy is no longer viable for dealing with them. And consequently, they can also be expected to push learners to explore their pointless state spaces in the same way as they would do with other relevant elements of an environment. For that reason, we name them exploration-intensive distractors. The archetypal example is a Rubik's cube, which is controllable, deterministic (though exploration-intensive distractors can exhibit stochastic dynamics as well), and is known to have pairs of configurations such that the minimum number of moves needed to transition from one to the other is 20. Moreover, its state space being virtually infinite is the cherry on top that makes this distractor overly perplexing, as that may sway some learners to play endlessly with the cube.

The current literature reveals no major studies focusing on exploration-intensive distractors, and neither is there a well-known benchmark environment showcasing them. In light of this, as first contribution, we have developed two new environments displaying this class of distractors, which we have made open to the community[1]. Our second contribution is a benchmarking covering these two environments and three accomplished algorithms, namely RND [6], ICM [27] and ECO [28]. Results from this benchmarking demonstrate that none of these methods manages to solve both scenarios and, more importantly, they do not exhibit an exploration policy fitting for this kind of domain.

[1] https://github.com/JimCatacora/bespa.

2 Related Work

2.1 Approaches to Sparsity

DRL researchers have followed a wide range of avenues to find satisfactory solutions to the problem of sparse rewards. Some of these miscellaneous ideas include: intrinsic motivation arising from dense interestingness measures such as novelty, curiosity, empowerment, compressiveness and many others [4,6,18,27,28,34]; optimizing a set of exploration policies to cover the state space [20]; approximations to Bayesian uncertainty as guidance for deep exploration [24,26,31]; exploitation of behavioral diversity [9]; leveraging hindsight to learn from mistakes in multi-goal scenarios [1]; imitating an agent's own past successful or unfamiliar trajectories [25], automatically generating a curriculum of subtasks whose difficulty increases to match the agent's current expertise [10,11,35]; imposing a hierarchy of learners that communicates via acquired subgoals [36].

2.2 Distractors

In [19], the authors present an environment comprising a robotic arm and two balls. One ball can be grasped by the manipulator, while the other takes the role of a distractor. The arm can see this second ball moving around in a random walk, but it cannot touch it. Essentially, it acts as a phantom object. In [18,33], pixel-level white noise is applied to various environments. It is added probabilistically both to chosen image observations and to chosen regions within those images. The agent has no control over this noise; it cannot influence its magnitude or its occurrence. In [28], a 3D maze is augmented with a broken TV that covers a quarter of the agent's view at all times. The TV shows only static, whose pattern invariably changes at each time step. In [5], a noisy TV is also introduced into a 3D maze. In this case, the agent is endowed with a special action that allows it to change the TV station. Importantly, every next station is drawn at random. A similar implementation is found in [28].

3 Environment Design

This section provides detailed specifications of our two proposed sparse-reward environments, which showcase exploration-intensive distractors fashioned as TVs.

3.1 Base Environment

Following in the footsteps of [27,28], our environments too are built upon the very sparse version of the MyWayHome task of ViZDoom [17]. This a visual navigation task that compels an agent to traverse a maze of corridors and rooms of varying textures (see Fig. 1). The agent's start location remains constant across episodes, though its orientation varies randomly between them. Its goal is to get a green armor, found always furthest from its initial location. Reaching this armor is a terminal event that yields the only positive reward of the environment.

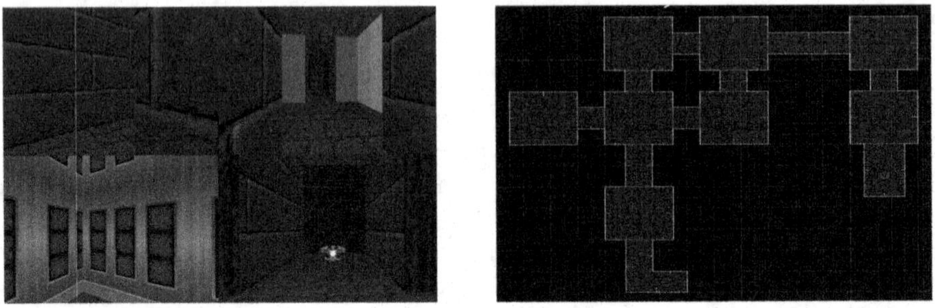

Fig. 1. Miscellaneous views of MyWayHome. Green circles in the layout indicate start (left) and goal (right) locations. (Color figure online)

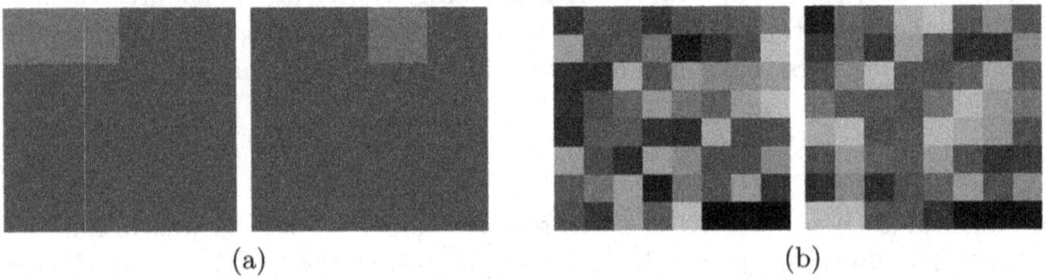

Fig. 2. (a) State transition from 3 (left) to 4 (right) in SASR TV. (b) State transition from 0 (left) to 1 (right) in MADR TV.

In terms of observations, this environment generates first-person view images of the world, whose resolution and color format can be specified by the researcher. Concerning resolution, there are plenty of options ranging from 160×120 to 1920×1080. As for color format, it is possible to choose between RGB, RGBA, grayscale and Doom's 2 original palette. With regard to the agent's action set, ViZDoom offers up to 43 actions. Nevertheless, we have constrained this set to three actions: turn right, turn left and move forward; in accordance with [28].

3.2 Single-Action Static-Rendering (SASR) TV

Our first TV distractor allows an agent to change the station with just one action. The internal state of this TV is an L-digit base-b number, where L and b are set by the researcher. In particular, to define L, we must first configure the desired number of rows (r) and columns (c) into which the TV is to be partitioned; then $L = r \cdot c$. Nonetheless, in all experiments conducted here, we have used $p = 2$ and $r = c = 4$ for this distractor. In other words, its internal state is a 16-digit binary number. Such a state is set to zero at the beginning of every episode. Then, it is updated by incrementing it by one whenever the agent requests to change the station.

Eventually, this internal state is converted into an image observation that can be perceived by the agent (see Fig. 2a). Such rendering is accomplished in a straightforward manner, with the help of a constant colormap that assigns a unique color to each symbol used in base-b. This means that the same symbol always encodes the same color. Note that the color format of this TV is another configurable feature that can be set to either RGB or grayscale. To summarize, a TV station is visualized as an r by c grid. There, each cell is linked to a specific digit of the internal state and the cell's color is determined by the current symbol (value) of that digit via the constant colormap.

3.3 Multi-Action Dynamic-Rendering (MADR) TV

The construction of this second TV distractor follows many of the same considerations as the previous one. Just as before, the researcher is free to pick the color format, as well as parameters b, r and c. Likewise, these parameters shape the representation of the TV's internal state. In this case, we have set $b = 16$ and $r = c = 8$ in all related experiments. This gives a 64-digit hexadecimal number as the internal state, which again starts at zero in every episode.

However, this distractor has three key differences. First, an agent is endowed with four actions for switching the station. Each action updates the internal state by adding or subtracting b^E from it, where E is an integer exponent initialized to zero at every episode. Having multiple actions grants the agent the chance to travel anywhere in the vast space of the TV; something impossible with a single action. The exact action set and corresponding transitions are as follows (the notation $\langle$internal state-exponent$\rangle$ is used in the examples):

- Station up: Increases the internal state by b^E. E.g., $\langle 36_{16}, 1_5\rangle \rightarrow \langle 46_{16}, 1_5\rangle$
- Station down: Decreases the internal state by b^E. E.g., $\langle 36_{16}, 1_5\rangle \rightarrow \langle 26_{16}, 1_5\rangle$
- Exponent up: Increments E by one, then increases the internal state by b^E. E.g., $\langle 36_{16}, 1_5\rangle \rightarrow \langle 136_{16}, 2_5\rangle$
- Exponent down: Decreases the internal state by b^E, then decrements E by one. E.g., $\langle 36_{16}, 1_5\rangle \rightarrow \langle 26_{16}, 0_5\rangle$

The second difference refers to the rendering of the exponent along with the station. Since the exponent plays a vital role in the TV's dynamics, we augment the agent's observations with it to ensure that our distractor is predictable. With this intent, we split the internal state into two separate fields, one for the station and one for the exponent. Specifically, the size of the exponent field is given by the minimum number of digits needed to encode the size of the station field in base-5 (arbitrary choice). In this way, a 64-digit internal state comprises 3 exponent digits and 61 station digits. The rendering of exponent digits always occupies the bottom right corner of the TV grid. Moreover, it is only available as grayscale and it relies simply on a constant colormap for its implementation.

The third adjustment involves the dynamic rendering of station digits. Here, by dynamic we imply that a symbol in the internal state can be translated into any out of b colors depending on the present value of the state. In detail, we first define a constant matrix of size $b \times M$ ($M = 10^6$), whose elements are integers uniformly distributed between 0 and $b-1$. Next, a symbol $s \in [0, b-1]$ is mapped

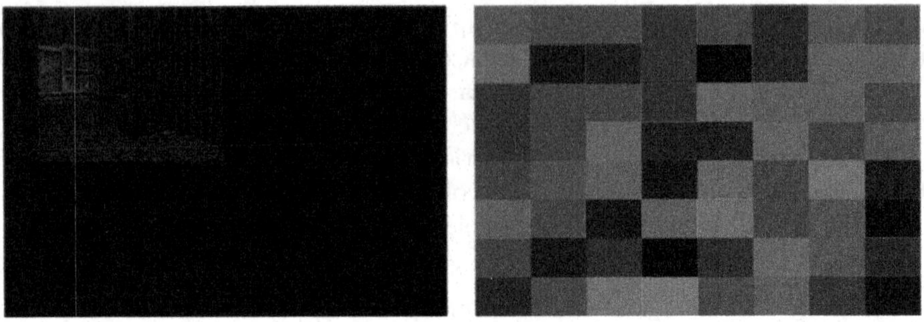

Fig. 3. Side-by-side of maze and TV views.

to a color by following 3 steps. 1) We count the number of appearances of that symbol in all base-b numbers between zero and the state's value (station digits only). 2) We extract from the former matrix the element at row index s and column index equal to the modulo of the previous count with respect to M. 3) We pass this element through a constant colormap to get the final rendering color. Figure 2b depicts a transition in this TV. The main advantage of such dynamic rendering is that it virtually removes the possibility of generalizing the prediction of the forward dynamics from an understanding of basic arithmetic. A prospect that could conceivably lessen the curiosity of an agent towards this distractor.

3.4 ViZDoom-TV Integration

As a final step, we integrate the MyWayHome task with our TV distractors. Unlike [28], where an agent simultaneously observes the maze and the TV at all times, we grant the agent an extra action that switches between the maze and TV full-screens. Therefore, the tasks resulting from consolidating the SASR and MADR TV distractors into MyWayHome have a total of 5 and 8 actions, respectively. A detail worth mentioning is that TV actions are inconsequential in the maze view (stations do not change), whereas navigation actions maintain their expected effects in the TV view (the agent moves regardless).

Having a view-switching action takes away any limitation on the relative size of the TV. In fact, with the help of a black background, we arrange that the area containing meaningful information is four times larger in the TV view than in the maze view (see Fig. 3). Overall, magnifying the size of the distractor is anticipated to make the problem harder as it makes it less likely to be overlooked.

4 Benchmarking

This section elaborates on our benchmarking effort, in which the two previously described environments are confronted with three influential DRL algorithms.

4.1 Covered Algorithms

The algorithms taking part in this benchmarking are: Random network distillation (RND) [6], Intrinsic curiosity module (ICM) [27] and Episodic curiosity (EC) [28]. Coincidentally, all three approaches utilize Proximal policy optimization (PPO) [30] to learn a policy that maximizes intrinsic and extrinsic rewards.

As already stated in Sect. 1, RND marked a performance milestone in Montezuma's revenge. And even today, its achieved score stands as one of the highest for an end-to-end DRL solution. In RND, exploration is driven by novelty, that is, this learner rewards itself for seeing new or rare observations. Specifically, RND keeps a fixed randomly-initialized network that generates embeddings from observations and trains a second network to predict those embeddings. Afterwards, intrinsic rewards are computed as the Euclidean distance between random and predicted embeddings; thus, they are smaller for observations perceived more often. Given this formulation, sources of never-ending novel observations; for instance, pixel-level noise, a broken/noisy TV or a Rubik's cube, present a potential problem for an RND agent as it could become fixated on them.

ICM is another greatly influential approach. Insomuch that it has been assimilated by NGU to produce an impressive general-purpose algorithm. The behavior of ICM is grounded on curiosity. In particular, this method relies on the prediction error stemming from a trained one-step forward dynamics model to quantify curiosity, which is then used as an intrinsic reward that guides exploration towards not yet well-predicted transitions. Critically, ICM also trains an inverse dynamics model that shares a representation with the forward one, and this has the benefit of keeping out from the computation of curiosity elements unaffected by the actions of the interacting agent. All in all, ICM tends to be resilient against uncontrollable distractors (e.g., phantom objects, pixel-level noise), but it can fall victim to unpredictable ones (e.g., a noisy TV).

EC made a breakthrough in the field by solving the noisy TV problem. In a nutshell, an EC agent awards itself a high intrinsic reward every time it visits a hard-to-reach state. By continuously adding such states to an episodic memory, any future state is labeled as hard-to-reach only if it requires at least k actions to get to from any state already in the memory. To compute reachability, EC trains a neural classifier from pairs of states that were less or more than k-steps apart in past trajectories. In the standard version of EC, this classifier is pretrained thanks to a random policy; while in the online version, called ECO by its authors, the reachability network is learned concurrently with the agent's policy. By construction, EC is expected to ignore any distractor that demands a low transitioning effort; such as: pixel-level noise or a broken/noisy TV.

4.2 Training Details

In terms of preprocessing, we enforce a frame skip of 4 steps in every tested environment, where only the last frame is passed through without any max pooling. We additionally set a timeout of 2100 steps at the engine's level, which translates to 525 steps at the agent's level (because of the frame skip). Moreover, we have run all three algorithms using observation formats comparable to the ones found in their original papers. Hence, for RND and ICM, each observation is put together as a stack of 4 consecutive 84×84 grayscale game frames. Meanwhile, ECO receives as input a single 84×84 RGB image.

Regarding neural architectures, an identical multi-head policy-value network is employed by all methods. Such a network consists first of a stack of 4 convolutional layers with 32 filters each, kernel size of 3, stride of 2 and same padding. Then, the output of this convolutional module is flattened and passed through 2 dense hidden layers with 2048 units each, before going to the output policy and value heads. RELU activation is employed in every convolutional and hidden layer, while linear activation is applied to all outputs. RND's random and predictor networks each use a convolutional module with the aforementioned topology, but instead their activations are ELU and leaky RELU, respectively. Both modules are fed only the last frame of each observation as input. The random network's module is then connected to an output linear layer with a representation size of 256. In turn, the output of the predictor's module goes through 2 dense hidden layers with 512 units each and RELU activation. ICM also adopts the previous 4-layer convolutional assembly for the encoder of its curiosity module, except that it replaces the activations with ELU. Its forward and inverse models are each built with a single dense hidden layer containing 1024 RELU units; plus, the former model has a linear output layer whose dimensionality is 1152. For its reachability classifier, ECO builds a siamese network where each of its two branches has a replica of the convolutional module used by its policy. These branches are followed by a stack of 4 dense hidden layers with 512 RELU units each and, subsequently, by a softmax layer with 2 neurons.

Table 1 gathers the remaining hyperparameters used in this benchmarking.

4.3 Results and Discussion

We evaluated RND, ICM and ECO three-ways on the very sparse MyWayHome environment: without any TV (baseline), with a SASR TV and with a MADR TV. In all cases, a black background covered 75% of each ViZDoom frame, as explained in Sect. 3.4. The baseline experiments were stopped after 10 million frames, while the others went on for 10 million more to account for the added difficulty of facing distractors. For reference, regardless of the algorithm, a single run of 20 million frames takes about 1 to 2 d to complete using an NVIDIA A100 GPU together with an 8-core 16-thread processor. Each experiment was repeated with three different seeds. The following graphs report simple averages across runs that, except the historical station count, are derived from cumulative averages taken along each run.

Baseline experiments: Fig. 4 demonstrates that all three approaches are capable of solving the baseline task. In particular, every solution converges to a policy that on average travels 14 sectors per episode (rooms & corridors), which is the minimum necessary to reach the goal (as seen in Fig. 1).

Table 1. Overview of applied hyperparameters

Hyperparameter	RND	ICM	ECO
Number of workers	32	16	16
Rollout length	128	80	256
Number of optimization epochs	4	4	4
Learning rate	1.0e–4	2.5e–3	2.5e–4
Learning rate decay	None	Linear	Linear
Entropy coefficient	0.01	0.01	0.01
PPO (λ)	1.0	1.0	0.95
Coefficient of extrinsic rewards	500	1.0	1.0
Coefficient of intrinsic rewards	1	0.01	0.03
Extrinsic discount factor (γ_E)	0.99	0.99	0.99
Intrinsic discount factor (γ_I)	0.99	–	–
RND experience fraction used by the predictor	1.0	–	–
ICM curiosity loss strength (λ)	–	0.1	–
ICM forward inverse ratio (β)	–	0.2	–
ECO episodic memory size	–	–	200
ECO action distance threshold	–	–	5
ECO negative sample multiplier	–	–	5
ECO reward shift (β)	–	–	0.5
ECO novelty threshold ($b_{novelty}$)	–	–	0.5
ECO aggregation function (F)	–	–	P_{90}
ECO reachability training learning rate	–	–	1.0e–4
ECO reachability training history size	–	–	16K

SASR experiments: Only ICM manages to solve this problem satisfactorily on most occasions (see Fig. 5). This result is not unexpected given that in practice this TV distractor conveys an ordered sequence of just 525 predictable transitions. With such a few TV transitions, an ICM agent is bound to experience them more frequently than those relative to the maze, especially the ones closer to the initial station. Consequently, its curiosity remains constantly lower for the TV than for the maze (see Fig. 7), which pushes the agent to prioritize the exploration of the latter over the former. The same line of reasoning applies to an RND learner. It should quickly get bored with a TV that has few stations (merely 525) and switch its attention to the maze. However, much to our surprise, this is not what happens. Instead, we have identified that its policy swiftly converges to a uniform distribution across the entire action set. As a result, what we observe in the graphs is an agent that keeps the TV on exactly half of the time and makes no significant exploration of neither the maze nor the TV. On the other hand, ECO is the single method that becomes obsessed with this TV.

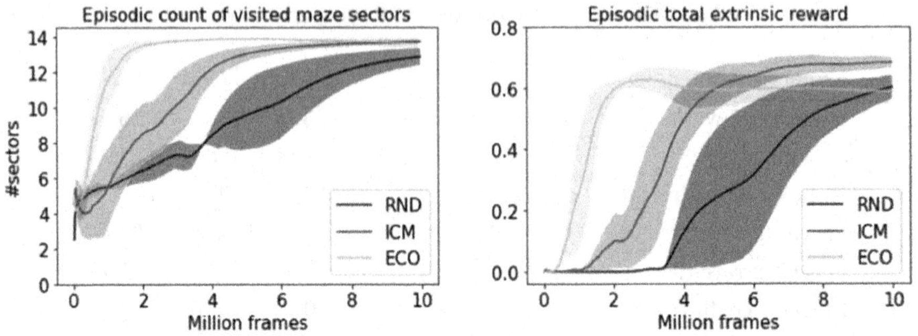

Fig. 4. Baseline results.

Running its final policies on testing mode reveals that ECO learns the trivial strategy of always changing the station. A policy that is optimal for collecting intrinsic rewards since it guarantees maximizing the action distance between final and initial stations within an episode. As to why this method completely ignores the maze; we presume it is because of the low complexity of the SASR TV, which makes it possible to learn an effective far-reaching policy much faster in the TV than in the maze. Once found, such policy denotes a global maximum of the intrinsic return and, as such, seriously hinders the exploration of other parts of the environment.

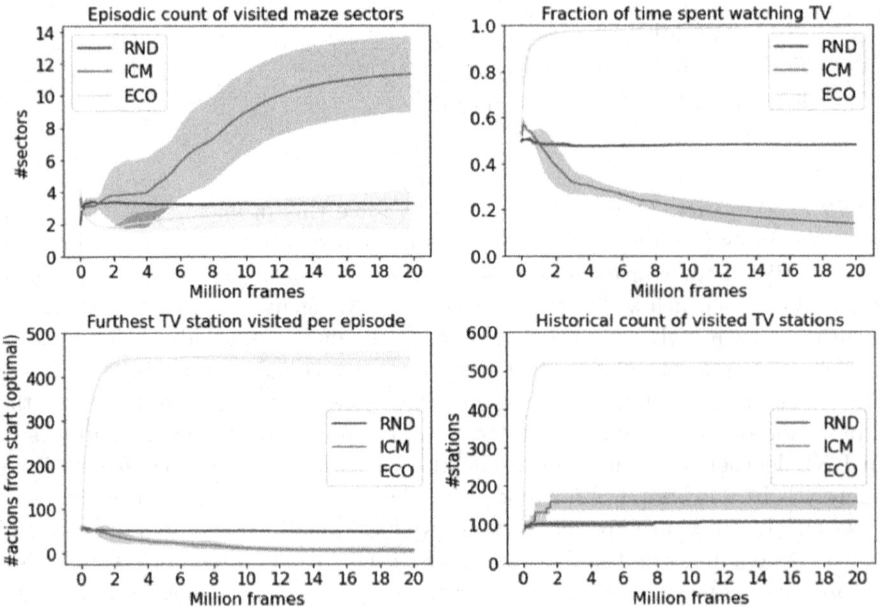

Fig. 5. SASR results.

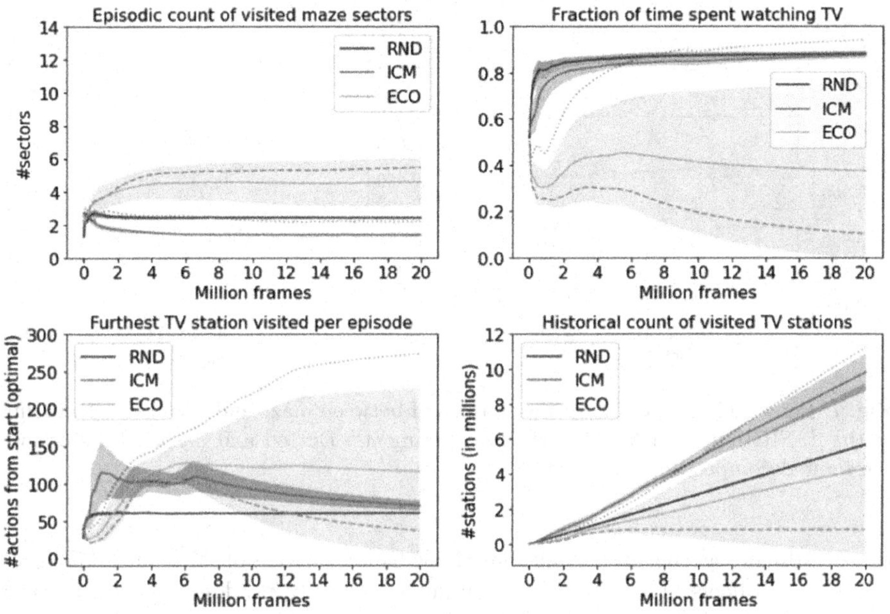

Fig. 6. MADR results. Just for ECO, these results are further disaggregated into two averages condensing the runs where the learner gets captivated (dotted lines) or not (dashed lines) by the TV.

MADR experiments: As shown in Fig. 6, none of the three benchmarked methods solves this environment. RND and ICM consistently get fairly fixated on this TV, i.e., the fraction of time they have the TV on is well above 0.8. Furthermore, they essentially do not explore the maze seeing that they never visit more than about 2 sectors on average per episode. Looking also into the historical number of stations visited by these two algorithms, we notice that this count grows linearly, which is evidence that they continuously discover new stations and transitions throughout a run. A behavior that is perfectly aligned with their theoretical motivations for novelty and curiosity. To figure out why this happens concretely, we run the final policies of RND and ICM on testing mode (frozen policies) for a few extra million frames and each time we collected the historical count of visited stations. These additional results indicate that for both approaches the slopes during training and during testing of such a count are almost identical to each other. This suggests that these methods learn high-entropy stochastic policies that work everywhere in the MADR TV. Such solutions are additionally rather trivial given the extremely large state space of this distractor and its chaotic dynamics, i.e., two very similar sequences of actions will produce two greatly different sequences of states. Indeed, it is easy to see that because of those qualities, even a random policy over the 4 TV actions will reproduce the previous slopes, since during an entire run it will hardly perceive twice states or transitions occurring a couple dozen actions after the beginning of an episode. Putting all

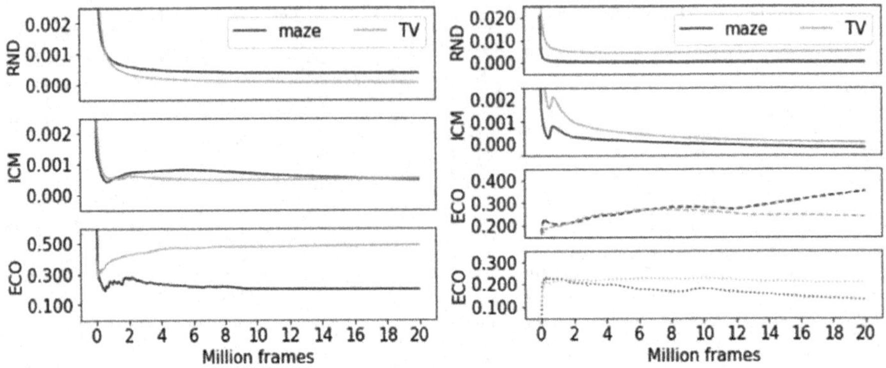

Fig. 7. Per-step intrinsic reward disaggregated between maze and TV states occurring in the SASR (left) and MADR (right) experiments. Dotted and dashed lines denote the same decomposition as in Fig. 6.

these findings together, we argue that the learning process of RND and ICM goes roughly as follows. They quickly learn such primarily random policies; as seen in the historical station count graph where their linear tendency is visible from the very beginning. These policies gather a meaningful episodic intrinsic return that does not wither down significantly over time considering they mostly observe novel states and transitions from start to finish of the training. Ultimately, those policies constitute hard and permanent local minima of the PPO optimization objective, as getting a return of the same order of magnitude while exploring the maze requires vastly more effort and experiences.

Moving on to ECO, we note that its learning evolution varies drastically across runs. In one run, its full attention is drawn to the TV as it also exhibits a will to reach increasingly remote stations, settling in at an average distance of over 250 actions from the start. Whereas, in the other two runs, it steadily loses interest in the TV; eventually having it off most of the time. To better understand this contradiction, we inspected the accuracy of the reachability networks emerging during these runs. This examination reports that ECO consistently (in all 3 runs) converges to an erroneous generalization regarding the reachability landscape arising from the MADR TV. One in which two TV stations are close to or far from each other depending on whether the difference between their exponents is respectively below or above a threshold of around 5 units. This mistake is not truly shocking; two stations many exponents apart will always be distant from each other and this concept is surely faster to grasp than the true action distance function. Still, it is relevant to wonder why ECO never evolves beyond this error. We posit this is due to the astronomical number of stations and the even larger number of pairings between them originating from this TV, as well as the lack of helpful clues for the generalization of distances contained in individual observations. In the end, it seems unrealistic that any practical neural architecture would have enough capacity and would see enough examples to learn that much information. In any case, to maximize the intrinsic return stemming from this TV under the previous faulty reachability model, our inspection exposes that ECO always acquires one simple but effective policy. It almost exclusively enacts either exponent up or exponent down. However, since such strategy stops seeing hard-to-reach states after the first 60 steps of an episode (this TV has only 61 exponents), its associated intrinsic return ends up being merely a local maximum. We then hypothesize this to be the primary reason leading to the disparate results shown by ECO. On some runs, due to their random seeds, the learner finds the local maximum lurking in the TV so fast that it thereafter diverts all attention away from any other less rewarded search effort. Other times, the maze and the TV are explored more in unison until the return associated with the latter hits its limit. From that moment onward, the agent receives higher returns by focusing purely on the maze, prompting its progressive neglect of the TV.

Some final remarks before closing this section. This benchmarking reveals that ICM and ECO, two algorithms designed to handle distractors by ignoring them, do not fundamentally dismiss both our exploration-intensive distractors, which validates their research relevancy. Furthermore, it is a little unsatisfying that we were not able to construct a solo distractor that impairs all 3 benchmarked approaches. Nonetheless, to make this happen, a simple idea is to merge our two distractors; for instance, by allowing the view-switching action to cycle between the maze, the SASR TV and the MADR TV. In such an environment, every algorithm that has been hypnotized by a distractor in this benchmarking should succumb to the exact same fate. Lastly, we would like to answer one pending concern. Is there a principled way to deal with exploration-intensive distractors? In fact, we envision a learner that through experience becomes aware of which elements with recognizable local dynamics exist in its world, e.g., a TV or a Rubik's cube. Having identified these, a sensible solution is to concurrently learn an array of exploration policies where each one focuses on an imaginary world in which a particular set of dynamic elements has been abstracted away. For example, with reference to our TV distractors, we would need a policy that ignores the TV, one that ignores the maze and another that ignores neither. Provided the learner also guarantees allocating sufficient exploration resources to each policy, then we are certain that at least one will crack the problem while paying no attention to the distractor. Needless to say, none of the algorithms included in this benchmarking displays this insight.

5 Conclusions

In this work, we have proposed two new sparse-reward environments, each displaying an exploration-intensive distractor modeled as a TV. In addition, we have performed a benchmarking that tested three relevant algorithms on said environments. Findings from this benchmarking show that our tasks were challenging enough for these methods. In particular, all of them remained permanently mesmerized by the existence of a TV in at least one of our environments. And as a consequence, their exploration of the main task was severely hindered, to the point that they were no longer able to solve it. All of this leads us to conclude that current algorithms, by and large, are not yet sufficiently competent to handle exploration-intensive distractors in a comprehensive and principled manner. Finally, by making these environments open-source, we hope that they serve as a helpful reference for advancing the research in this topic.

References

1. Andrychowicz, M., et al.: Hindsight experience replay. In: Proceedings of the 31st International Conference on Neural Information Processing Systems, NIPS'17, Red Hook, NY, USA, pp. 5055–5065. Curran Associates Inc. (2017)
2. Badia, A.P., et al.: Agent57: outperforming the atari human benchmark. In: Proceedings of the 37th International Conference on Machine Learning, ICML 2020, 13–18 July 2020, Virtual Event. Machine Learning Research, vol. 119, pp. 507–517. PMLR (2020). http://proceedings.mlr.press/v119/badia20a.html
3. Badia, A.P., et al.: Never give up: learning directed exploration strategies. In: International Conference on Learning Representations (2020). https://openreview.net/forum?id=Sye57xStvB
4. Bellemare, M.G., Srinivasan, S., Ostrovski, G., Schaul, T., Saxton, D., Munos, R.: Unifying count-based exploration and intrinsic motivation. In: Proceedings of the 30th International Conference on Neural Information Processing Systems, NIPS'16, Red Hook, NY, USA, pp. 1479–1487. Curran Associates Inc. (2016)
5. Burda, Y., Edwards, H., Pathak, D., Storkey, A.J., Darrell, T., Efros, A.A.: Large-scale study of curiosity-driven learning. In: 7th International Conference on Learning Representations, ICLR 2019, New Orleans, LA, USA, 6–9 May 2019. OpenReview.net (2019). https://openreview.net/forum?id=rJNwDjAqYX
6. Burda, Y., Edwards, H., Storkey, A.J., Klimov, O.: Exploration by random network distillation. In: 7th International Conference on Learning Representations, ICLR 2019, New Orleans, LA, USA, 6–9 May 2019. OpenReview.net (2019). https://openreview.net/forum?id=H1lJJnR5Ym
7. Choi, J., et al.: Contingency-aware exploration in reinforcement learning. In: International Conference on Learning Representations (2019). https://openreview.net/forum?id=HyxGB2AcY7
8. Espeholt, L., et al.: IMPALA: scalable distributed deep-RL with importance weighted actor-learner architectures. In: Dy, J., Krause, A. (eds.) Proceedings of the 35th International Conference on Machine Learning. Machine Learning Research, 10–15 Jul 2018, vol. 80, pp. 1407–1416. PMLR (2018). http://proceedings.mlr.press/v80/espeholt18a.html
9. Eysenbach, B., Gupta, A., Ibarz, J., Levine, S.: Diversity is all you need: learning skills without a reward function. In: International Conference on Learning Representations (2019). https://openreview.net/forum?id=SJx63jRqFm
10. Florensa, C., Held, D., Geng, X., Abbeel, P.: Automatic goal generation for reinforcement learning agents. In: Dy, J., Krause, A. (eds.) Proceedings of the 35th International Conference on Machine Learning. Machine Learning Research, 10–15 July 2018, vol. 80, pp. 1515–1528. PMLR (2018). http://proceedings.mlr.press/v80/florensa18a.html

11. Florensa, C., Held, D., Wulfmeier, M., Zhang, M., Abbeel, P.: Reverse curriculum generation for reinforcement learning. In: Levine, S., Vanhoucke, V., Goldberg, K. (eds.) Proceedings of the 1st Annual Conference on Robot Learning. Machine Learning Research, 13–15 November 2017, vol. 78, pp. 482–495. PMLR (2017). http://proceedings.mlr.press/v78/florensa17a.html
12. Gu, S., Holly, E., Lillicrap, T.P., Levine, S.: Deep reinforcement learning for robotic manipulation with asynchronous off-policy updates. In: 2017 IEEE International Conference on Robotics and Automation (ICRA), pp. 3389–3396 (2016)
13. Haarnoja, T., Ha, S., Zhou, A., Tan, J., Tucker, G., Levine, S.: Learning to walk via deep reinforcement learning. In: Robotics: Science and Systems (2019). https://doi.org/10.15607/RSS.2019.XV.011
14. Hessel, M., et al.: Rainbow: combining improvements in deep reinforcement learning. In: McIlraith, S.A., Weinberger, K.Q. (eds.) AAAI, pp. 3215–3222. AAAI Press (2018). http://dblp.uni-trier.de/db/conf/aaai/aaai2018.html#HesselMHSODHPAS18
15. Horgan, D., et al.: Distributed prioritized experience replay. In: International Conference on Learning Representations (2018). https://openreview.net/forum?id=H1Dy---0Z
16. Kapturowski, S., Ostrovski, G., Dabney, W., Quan, J., Munos, R.: Recurrent experience replay in distributed reinforcement learning. In: International Conference on Learning Representations (2019). https://openreview.net/forum?id=r1lyTjAqYX
17. Kempka, M., Wydmuch, M., Runc, G., Toczek, J., Jaśkowski, W.: ViZDoom: a doom-based AI research platform for visual reinforcement learning. In: IEEE Conference on Computational Intelligence and Games, Santorini, Greece, pp. 341–348. IEEE, September 2016. http://arxiv.org/abs/1605.02097. The best paper award
18. Kim, Y., Nam, W., Kim, H., Kim, J.H., Kim, G.: Curiosity-bottleneck: exploration by distilling task-specific novelty. In: Chaudhuri, K., Salakhutdinov, R. (eds.) Proceedings of the 36th International Conference on Machine Learning. Machine Learning Research, 09–15 June 2019, vol. 97, pp. 3379–3388. PMLR (2019). http://proceedings.mlr.press/v97/kim19c.html
19. Laversanne-Finot, A., Péré, A., Oudeyer, P.: Curiosity driven exploration of learned disentangled goal spaces. In: Proceedings of the 2nd Annual Conference on Robot Learning, CoRL 2018, Zürich, Switzerland, 29–31 October 2018. Machine Learning Research, vol. 87, pp. 487–504. PMLR (2018). http://proceedings.mlr.press/v87/laversanne-finot18a.html
20. Lee, L., Eysenbach, B., Parisotto, E., Xing, E.P., Levine, S., Salakhutdinov, R.: Efficient exploration via state marginal matching. CoRR abs/1906.05274 (2019). http://arxiv.org/abs/1906.05274
21. Levine, S., Finn, C., Darrell, T., Abbeel, P.: End-to-end training of deep visuomotor policies. J. Mach. Learn. Res. **17**, 39:1–39:40 (2015)
22. Machado, M.C., Bellemare, M.G., Bowling, M.: A laplacian framework for option discovery in reinforcement learning. In: Proceedings of the 34th International Conference on Machine Learning, ICML'17, vol. 70, pp. 2295–2304. JMLR.org (2017)
23. Mnih, V., et al.: Human-level control through deep reinforcement learning. Nature **518**, 529–533 (2015)
24. O'Donoghue, B., Osband, I., Munos, R., Mnih, V.: The uncertainty bellman equation and exploration. In: Dy, J.G., Krause, A. (eds.) Proceedings of the 35th International Conference on Machine Learning, ICML 2018, Stockholmsmässan, Stockholm, Sweden, 10–15 July 2018. Machine Learning Research, vol. 80, pp. 3836–3845. PMLR (2018). http://proceedings.mlr.press/v80/o-donoghue18a.html

25. Oh, J., Guo, Y., Singh, S., Lee, H.: Self-imitation learning. In: Dy, J., Krause, A. (eds.) Proceedings of the 35th International Conference on Machine Learning. Machine Learning Research, 10–15 July 2018, vol. 80, pp. 3878–3887. PMLR (2018). http://proceedings.mlr.press/v80/oh18b.html
26. Osband, I., Blundell, C., Pritzel, A., Roy, B.V.: Deep exploration via bootstrapped DQN. In: Proceedings of the 30th International Conference on Neural Information Processing Systems, NIPS'16, Red Hook, NY, USA, pp. 4033–4041. Curran Associates Inc. (2016)
27. Pathak, D., Agrawal, P., Efros, A.A., Darrell, T.: Curiosity-driven exploration by self-supervised prediction. In: 2017 IEEE Conference on Computer Vision and Pattern Recognition Workshops (CVPRW), pp. 488–489 (2017)
28. Savinov, N., et al.: Episodic curiosity through reachability. In: International Conference on Learning Representations (2019). https://openreview.net/forum?id=SkeK3s0qKQ
29. Schrittwieser, J., et al.: Mastering Atari, Go, chess and shogi by planning with a learned model. Nature **588**(7839), 604–609 (2020). https://doi.org/10.1038/s41586-020-03051-4
30. Schulman, J., Wolski, F., Dhariwal, P., Radford, A., Klimov, O.: Proximal policy optimization algorithms. CoRR abs/1707.06347 (2017). http://arxiv.org/abs/1707.06347
31. Sekar, R., Rybkin, O., Daniilidis, K., Abbeel, P., Hafner, D., Pathak, D.: Planning to explore via self-supervised world models. In: International Conference on Machine Learning (2020)
32. Silver, D., et al.: Mastering the game of go without human knowledge. Nat. **550**, 354–359 (2017)
33. Song, Y., et al.: Mega-reward: achieving human-level play without extrinsic rewards. In: Proceedings of the AAAI Conference on Artificial Intelligence, vol. 34, no. 04, pp. 5826–5833, April 2020. https://doi.org/10.1609/aaai.v34i04.6040. https://ojs.aaai.org/index.php/AAAI/article/view/6040
34. Stanton, C., Clune, J.: Deep curiosity search: intra-life exploration improves performance on challenging deep reinforcement learning problems. CoRR abs/1806.00553 (2018). http://arxiv.org/abs/1806.00553
35. Sukhbaatar, S., Lin, Z., Kostrikov, I., Synnaeve, G., Szlam, A., Fergus, R.: Intrinsic motivation and automatic curricula via asymmetric self-play. In: 6th International Conference on Learning Representations, ICLR 2018, Vancouver, BC, Canada, 30 April–3 May 2018, Conference Track Proceedings. OpenReview.net (2018). https://openreview.net/forum?id=SkT5Yg-RZ
36. Vezhnevets, A.S., et al.: Feudal networks for hierarchical reinforcement learning. In: Proceedings of the 34th International Conference on Machine Learning, ICML'17, vol. 70, pp. 3540–3549. JMLR.org (2017)
37. Vinyals, O., et al.: Grandmaster level in StarCraft II using multi-agent reinforcement learning. Nature **575**(7782), 350–354 (2019). https://doi.org/10.1038/s41586-019-1724-z

Neural QBAFs: Explaining Neural Networks Under LRP-Based Argumentation Frameworks

Purin Sukpanichnant(✉), Antonio Rago, Piyawat Lertvittayakumjorn, and Francesca Toni

Imperial College London, London, UK
{ps1620,a.rago,pl1515,ft}@imperial.ac.uk

Abstract. In recent years, there have been many attempts to combine XAI with the field of symbolic AI in order to generate explanations for neural networks that are more interpretable and better align with human reasoning, with one prominent candidate for this synergy being the subfield of computational argumentation. One method is to represent neural networks with quantitative bipolar argumentation frameworks (QBAFs) equipped with a particular semantics. The resulting QBAF can then be viewed as an explanation for the associated neural network. In this paper, we explore a novel LRP-based semantics under a new QBAF variant, namely *neural QBAFs* (nQBAFs). Since an nQBAF of a neural network is typically large, the nQBAF must be simplified before being used as an explanation. Our empirical evaluation indicates that the manner of this simplification is all important for the quality of the resulting explanation.

Keywords: Neural networks · Computational argumentation · Image classification

1 Introduction

Several attempts have been made to improve explainability of AI systems. One prominent research area of XAI is devoted to explaining black-box methods such as deep learning. A popular method from this area is *Layer-wise Relevance Propagation* (LRP) [11]. This method determines how relevant nodes in a neural network are towards the neural network output. However, LRP does not explicitly indicate the relationship between each node. To address this issue, we combine this method with computational argumentation. This is a field of study about how knowledge can be represented as relationships between arguments. Each complete set of relationship(s) is referred to as an Argumentation Framework (AF) [6]. There are several types of AF, depending on types of relationships. In this paper, we consider a type of AF known as Quantitative Bipolar Argumentation Frameworks (QBAFs) [2], which is a form of knowledge representation displaying relationships between arguments in forms of support and

S. Bandini et al. (Eds.): AIxIA 2021, LNAI 13196, pp. 429–444, 2022.
https://doi.org/10.1007/978-3-031-08421-8_30

attack. These attacks and supports lend themselves well to represent negative and positive influences from input features as obtained using LRP.

QBAFs are interpreted by *semantics* which, in a nutshell, determine the arguments' dialectical strengths, taking into account (the dialectical strength of) their attackers and supporters.

As QBAFs illustrate how arguments relate to one another, they can be applied to reflect the relationship between nodes of a neural network, which can be viewed as an explanation. However, to do this, one needs to match the neural network functioning and the QBAF semantics. In this paper, we focus on LRP as a semantics for suitable forms of the QBAFs that we introduce. QBAFs derived by an LRP-based semantics may be very large and too complicated for human cognition in the context of explanation. Hence a new variant of QBAF is needed. To address this issue, we introduce a new variant of QBAF, namely neural QBAFs (nQBAFs), under LRP-based semantics for generating argumentative explanations from neural networks and prove their dialectical properties. Finally, we conduct some preliminary experiments by applying our LRP-based semantics to the Deep Argumentative Explanation (DAX) method from [1] and the method from [13] in order to show practical issues with nQBAFs as explanations. This is work in progress, on exploring the use of LRP, in combination with other techniques, in visualisation for image classification: we leave a comparison with visualisations drawn from nQBAFs as future work.

2 Background

We start by defining relevant concepts for our setting. These amount to multi-layer perceptrons (MLPs), Layer-wise Relevance Propagation (LRP) and Quantitative Bipolar Argumentation Frameworks (QBAFs).

2.1 MLP Basics

A MLP is a form of feed-forward neural network where all neurons in one layer are connected to all neurons in the next layer. We follow [14] for background on MLPs, captured by Definitions 1 and 2 below.

Definition 1. *A Multi-layer Perceptron (MLP) is a tuple* $\langle V, E, B, \theta \rangle$ *where*

- $\langle V, E \rangle$ *is an acyclic directed graph.*
- $V = \uplus_0^{d+1} V_i$ *is the disjoint union of sets of nodes* V_i;
- *We call* V_0 *the input layer,* V_{d+1} *the output layer and* V_i *the i-th hidden layer for* $1 \leq i \leq d$;
- $E \subseteq \bigcup_{i=0}^{d} (V_i \times V_{i+1})$ *is a set of edges between subsequent layers;*
- $B : (V \setminus V_0) \to \mathbb{R}$ *assigns a bias to every non-input node;*
- $\theta : E \to \mathbb{R}$ *assigns a weight to every edge.*

Figure 1 (left) visualises a fragment of an MLP with at least two hidden layers. Note that any MLP referred to afterwards only has one output node. This may be obtained by extracting all nodes and the edges between these nodes from another MLP that have paths[1] to the chosen output node, including the output node itself.

MLPs typically result from training with sample data. Since this training is not a focus of this paper, we will simply assume that a trained MLP is available. For example, in Sect. 5, we will conduct experiments with a pre-trained MLP for image classification.

The next definition explains how we obtain an activation value for each node.

Definition 2. *For any* $j \in V_0$*, the* activation $x_j \in \mathbb{R}$ *of node* j *is an input value for* j*. For any* k *such that* $1 \leq k \leq d+1$*, the* activation *of node* $i \in V_k$ *is* $x_i = act(B(i) + \Sigma_{n \in V_{k-1}} x_n \theta(n,i))$ *where act:* $\mathbb{R} \to \mathbb{R}$ *is an activation function.*[2]

Activations are a fundamental component of a neural network. They are involved in the calculation process of a neural network from a given input towards the output layer. An activation of each node can also be used to explain what the neural network is emphasising, as we discuss in the next section.

2.2 LRP Basics

Layer-Wise Relevance Propagation (LRP) [11] is a method for obtaining explanations, for outputs of MLPs in particular. Intuitively, with LRP, each node of the MLP is given a relevance score, showing how this node contributes to the node of interest in the output layer. Starting from the output layer, the node we want to explain has its relevance score equal to its activation while other nodes of the output layer (if any) have zero relevance score. Then we can calculate the relevance score for each non-output node using Definition 3, adapted from the presentation of LRP in [9].

Definition 3. *Let* $\langle V, E, B, \theta \rangle$ *be an MLP, and* $i \in V_k$*, and* $j \in V_{k+1}$ *where* $0 \leq k \leq d$*, and the layer* k *has* n *nodes. Then the* relevance score *the node* i *receives from the node* j *is* $R_{i \leftarrow j}$ *such that* $R_{i \leftarrow j} = \frac{z_{ij}}{\Sigma_{l=1}^{n} z_{lj}} R_j$ *where* z_{ij} *is the contribution from* i *to* j *during the forward pass, i.e.,* $z_{ij} = x_i \theta(i,j) + \frac{B(j)}{n} + \frac{\epsilon}{n}$ *where* $\epsilon \in \mathbb{R}$ *is a small positive stabiliser.*

Note that this definition assumes that ϵ is distributed equally to the n nodes: we adopt this assumption from [9]. To calculate the relevance score node i has towards the output node of interest, i.e. R_i, we simply sum all the relevance scores it receives from all the nodes of the layer $k+1$. In other words, $R_i = \Sigma_j R_{i \leftarrow j}$.

From Definition 3, we obtain also that LRP has *conservative properties* (for $i \in V_k$, and $j \in V_{k+1}$), i.e., $R_j = \Sigma_i R_{i \leftarrow j}$ and $\Sigma_i R_i = \Sigma_j R_j$.

[1] The definition of *path* is adopted from [1], where there exists a *path* via E (set of edges) from n_a to n_b (from a node to another) iff $\exists n_1, ..., n_t$ with $n_1 = n_a$ and $n_t = n_b$ such that $(n_1, n_2), ..., (n_{t-1}, n_t) \in E$.

[2] Note that, with an abuse of notation, $\theta(n,i)$ stands for $\theta((n,i))$, for simplicity. Unless explicitly stated, this notation is used throughout the rest of the paper.

2.3 QBAF Basics

QBAFs [2] are abstractions of debates between arguments, where arguments may attack or support one another and are equipped with a base score, which reflects the arguments' intrinsic, initial dialectical strength. We adopt the formal definition of QBAFs from [2].

Definition 4. *A* QBAF *is a tuple* $\langle A, Att, Supp, \gamma \rangle$ *where*

- A *is a set (whose elements are referred to as* arguments*);*
- $Att \subseteq A \times A$ *is the* attack *relation;*
- $Supp \subseteq A \times A$ *is the* support *relation;*
- $\gamma : A \rightarrow D$ *is a function that maps every argument to its* base score *(from some set* D *of a given set of values).*[3]

A QBAF may be equipped with a notion of dialectical strength, given by a *strength function* $\sigma : A \rightarrow D$, indicating a dialectical strength value (again from D) for each argument, taking into account the strength of the attacking and supporting arguments within the debate represented by the QBAF, as well as the argument's intrinsic strength given by γ. Several notions of σ (called *semantics* in the literature on computational argumentation) have been given in the literature (e.g. see [3]) but their formal definitions are outside the scope of this paper. Various *dialectical properties* for semantics σ have been studied in the literature (e.g. see [3]) as a way to validate their use in concrete settings and to compare across different semantics. We will follow this approach in this paper.

Variants of QBAFs can be extracted from neural networks, e.g. as in [1,14]. An example of the structure underpinning these QBAFs is given in Fig. 1 (centre, for the MLP on the left): here, the nodes represent the arguments and the edges represent the union of the attack and support relations. In these works, the extracted QBAF can be seen as indicating how some nodes in the neural network relate to others, and hence can be viewed as an explanation of that neural network. We follow this approach in this paper, but using a variant of QBAFs, defined next.

3 nQBAFS and LRP-Based Argumentation Semantics

We study LRP as a semantics σ for novel forms of QBAFs extracted from MLPs. We aim to prove that this LRP-based semantics satisfies multiple dialectical properties, which we believe are intuitive when QBAFs are used as the basis for explanations of MLPs.

The novel QBAFs take into account the structure of MLPs. As of Definition 3, a non-output node in an MLP may contribute to several nodes of the next layer, as in Fig. 1 (left). For any non-output node i, if we consider each edge from i to a node of the next layer and represent the node i with a unique argument for every

[3] In this paper, we will choose $D = \mathbb{R}$.

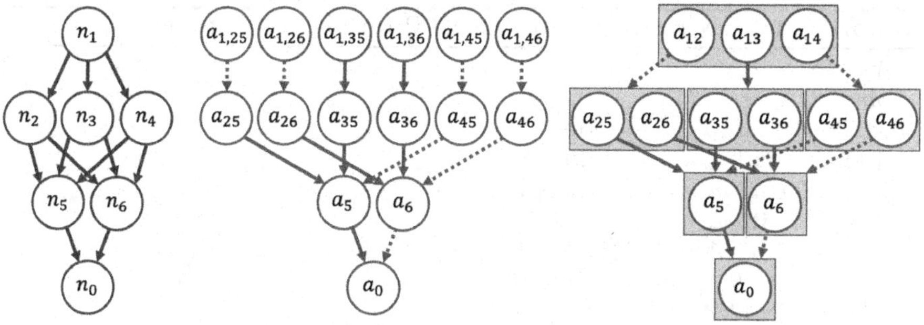

Fig. 1. Example of an MLP (left), a standard QBAF (centre) and the associated nQBAF (right). Each box refers to a group of arguments. In the QBAF and the nQBAF, dashed lines represent attacks and solid lines represent supports.

edge (as in [4,14]), there would be several arguments representing that node i. This method would also be non-scalable since the relation between arguments in the resulting QBAF would become too complex to analyse as more layers are considered. To avoid this, we define a new, leaner form of QBAFs, where arguments referring to the same node are grouped together.

Definition 5. *A* neural quantitative bipolar argumentation framework *(nQBAF) is a tuple* $\langle A, Att, Supp, \gamma \rangle$ *where*

- A *is a set (of* arguments*);*
- $Att \subseteq A \times \mathcal{P}(A)$[4] *is the* attack *relation;*
- $Supp \subseteq A \times \mathcal{P}(A)$ *is the* support *relation;*
- $\gamma : A \cup \mathcal{P}(A) \rightarrow \{0\}$ *is a function that maps every argument and set of arguments to a fixed base score of zero.*

Thus, attack and support relations may exist not just between arguments, as in standard QBAFs, but also between arguments and sets thereof. Given that we choose $D = \mathbb{R}$ as the set of values that could be used as base score and strength of arguments, the choice of γ indicates that each argument and set of arguments starts with a "neutral" base score of zero.

We first need to relate arguments of an nQBAF and nodes of a given MLP $\langle V, E, B, \theta \rangle$. Each argument represents only one node but a node can be represented by several arguments. Accordingly, we assume a function $\rho : A \cup \mathcal{P}(A) \rightarrow V \cup \{\perp\}$ mapping each argument/set of arguments to a node of the MLP, if one exists (or mapping to $\perp$ otherwise). We omit the formal definition of ρ for lack of space. As an illustration, for the MLP in Fig. 1 (left), in the derived nQBAF (right), $n_1 = \rho(\alpha_{12}) = \rho(\alpha_{13}) = \rho(\alpha_{14}) = \rho(\{\alpha_{12}, \alpha_{13}, \alpha_{14}\})$, $n_2 = \rho(\alpha_{25}) = \rho(\alpha_{26}) = \rho(\{\alpha_{25}, \alpha_{26}\})$, $n_3 = \rho(\alpha_{35}) = \rho(\alpha_{36}) = \rho(\{\alpha_{35}, \alpha_{36}\})$, $n_4 = \rho(\alpha_{45}) = \rho(\alpha_{46}) = \rho(\{\alpha_{45}, \alpha_{46}\})$, $n_5 = \rho(\alpha_5) = \rho(\{\alpha_5\})$, $n_6 = \rho(\alpha_6) = \rho(\{\alpha_6\})$, $n_0 = \rho(\alpha_0) = \rho(\{\alpha_0\})$ and, for any other set S of arguments, $\rho(S) = \perp$.

[4] Note that $\mathcal{P}(A)$ is the power set of a set A.

Algorithm 1: Extracting A from an MLP with the output node α_0

```
A ← {α_0};
currentLayer ← d;
while currentLayer >= 0 do
    for n_i in V_currentLayer do
        for n_j in V_currentLayer+1 do
            if (n_i, n_j) in E then
                A ← A ∪ {α_ij}
    currentLayer ← currentLayer − 1
for α_mn in A do
    if ρ(α_mn) in V_0 then
        A ← A ∪ {α_(mn)'mn}
```

We then have to determine which pairs (i.e. edges as shown in Fig. 1 (right)) belong to the attack or support relations. This is done using two *relation characterisations*, inspired by those in [1]: $c_+, c_- : A \times \mathcal{P}(A) \rightarrow \{true, false\}$ where, for any argument i and group of arguments j such that $\rho(i) \neq \perp$ and $\rho(j) \neq \perp$ are in adjacent layers (i.e. $(\rho(i), \rho(j)) \in E$):

- $c_+(i, j)$ is true iff $R_{\rho(i) \leftarrow \rho(j)} > 0$, and
- $c_-(i, j)$ is true iff $R_{\rho(i) \leftarrow \rho(j)} < 0$.

With c_+ and c_-, we can formally define our *Att* and *Supp* relations and the nQBAF derived from an MLP, as follows:

Definition 6. *The* nQBAF derived from $\langle V, E, B, \theta \rangle$ *is* $\langle A, Att, Supp, \gamma \rangle$ *where*

- *A is defined according to Algorithm 1;*
- $Att = \{(i, j) \in A \times \mathcal{P}(A) \mid c_-(i, j) \text{ is true}\}$;
- $Supp = \{(i, j) \in A \times \mathcal{P}(A) \mid c_+(i, j) \text{ is true}\}$;
- $\gamma : A \cup \mathcal{P}(A) \rightarrow \{0\}$.

Algorithm 1 extracts the set of arguments by iterating backwards from the last hidden layer to the input layer. It also add imaginary arguments to the set of arguments for input nodes, for the reason discussed in the next section.

Before we define our strength function , let us introduce some notation:

- $Att(x) = \{a \in A \mid (a, x) \in Att\}$ for all $x \in \mathcal{P}(A)$;
- $Supp(x) = \{s \in A \mid (s, x) \in Supp\}$ for all $x \in \mathcal{P}(A)$;
- $\mathcal{G} = \{g \in \mathcal{P}(A) \mid \exists a \in A[(a, g) \in Att \vee (a, g) \in Supp]\}$.

Now we define the LRP-based semantics for our nQBAF as follows:

Definition 7. *The* LRP-based semantics *of the nQBAF derived from an MLP* $\langle V, E, B, \theta \rangle$ *is* $\sigma : A \cup \mathcal{G} \rightarrow \mathbb{R}$ *such that*

$$\sigma(x) = \begin{cases} x_i & \textit{if } \rho(x) \in V_{d+1} \textit{ with final activation } x_i \\ R_{m \leftarrow \rho(y)} & \textit{if } x = \alpha_{(mn)'mn}, z = \alpha_{mn} \textit{ and } \exists!(z, y) \in \textit{Att} \cup \textit{Supp} \\ R_{\rho(x) \leftarrow \rho(y)} & \textit{if } \exists!(x, y) \in \textit{Att} \cup \textit{Supp} \\ \Sigma_{a \in x} \sigma(a) & \textit{if } x \in \mathcal{G} \\ 0 & \textit{otherwise} \end{cases}$$

Now we are able to conceive the relations between arguments, and to what amount each argument supports or attacks a group of arguments, but how natural is it? Does it follow the way humans naturally debate? To answer these questions, we have to consider whether our nQBAFs satisfy dialectical properties.

4 Properties for nQBAFS Under LRP Semantics

We now consider dialectical properties that determine how natural the argumentation is for any argumentation framework, i.e. how similar it is to human reasoning and debate. Our dialectical properties, as shown in Table 1, are based on those in [1] and [2] but are adapted specifically for nQBAFs. In the table, we associate these properties with names, mostly borrowing from the literature, where, however, they have been used for other types of argumentation frameworks.

Before defining the properties, we first make an addition regarding the input layer. Every dialectical property which follows considers the strength of a group of arguments based on its attackers and supporters. As of now, there are no attackers or supporters for groups of arguments representing nodes of the input layer, so it is likely most properties will not be satisfied here. To resolve this issue, we add imaginary arguments to target the input nodes. These added arguments are not considered as part of the set of all groups of arguments $\mathcal{G}$. Formally, for any $g \in \mathcal{G}$ such that $\rho(g) \in V_0$, $\textit{Att}(g) = \{x \in A \mid \rho(x) = \bot \wedge \exists a \in g[\sigma(x) = \sigma(a) \wedge \sigma(x) < 0]\}$ and $\textit{Supp}(g) = \{x \in A \mid \rho(x) = \bot \wedge \exists a \in g[\sigma(x) = \sigma(a) \wedge \sigma(x) > 0]\}$ and $|\textit{Att}(g) \cup \textit{Supp}(g)| = |g|$. For example, a given input node may be represented by a group of arguments $\{\alpha_i, \ldots, \alpha_n\}$ and has a set of supporting/attacking arguments $\{\alpha_{ci}, \ldots, \alpha_{cn}\}$ corresponding to each argument of the group.

According to Table 1, to explain, Additive Monotonicity requires that the strength of a group of arguments is the sum of that of its supporters and attackers. Balance requires that the strength of a group of arguments differs from the sum of base scores of that group only if such a group is a target of other arguments. Weakening requires that when there are no supporters but at least one attacker, the strength of a group of arguments is lower than the total sum of base scores of that group. Conversely, Strengthening considers the situation when there are no attackers but at least one supporter instead. Weakening Soundness is loosely the opposite direction of Weakening, requiring that if the strength of a group of arguments is lower than the sum of base scores of that group, then the group must have at least one attacker. Similarly, Strengthening Soundness is loosely the opposite direction of Strengthening. Equivalence states that groups of arguments with equal conditions in terms of attackers, supporters and the sum of base scores within a group have the same strength. Attack Counting

Table 1. Dialectical properties for nQBAFs adapted from [1] and [2] where $\mathcal{G}$ represents the set of all groups of arguments in the argumentation framework.

#	Property	Name
1	$\forall g \in \mathcal{G}, \sigma(g) = \Sigma_{x \in Att(g)} \rho(x) + \Sigma_{x \in Supp(g)} \rho(x)$	Additive Monotonicity
2	$\forall g \in \mathcal{G}, Att(g) = \emptyset \wedge Supp(g) = \emptyset \rightarrow \sigma(g) = \Sigma_{x \in g} \gamma(x)$	Balance
3	$\forall g \in \mathcal{G}, Att(g) \neq \emptyset \wedge Supp(g) = \emptyset \rightarrow \sigma(g) < \Sigma_{x \in g} \gamma(x)$	Weakening
4	$\forall g \in \mathcal{G}, Att(g) = \emptyset \wedge Supp(g) \neq \emptyset \rightarrow \sigma(g) > \Sigma_{x \in g} \gamma(x)$	Strengthening
5	$\forall g \in \mathcal{G}, \sigma(g) < \Sigma_{x \in g} \gamma(x) \rightarrow Att(g) \neq \emptyset$	Weakening Soundness
6	$\forall g \in \mathcal{G}, \sigma(g) > \Sigma_{x \in g} \gamma(x) \rightarrow Supp(g) \neq \emptyset$	Strengthening Soundness
7	$\forall g_1, g_2 \in \mathcal{G}, Att(g_1) = Att(g_2) \wedge Supp(g_1) = Supp(g_2) \wedge \Sigma_{x \in g_1} \gamma(x) = \Sigma_{x \in g_2} \gamma(x) \rightarrow \sigma(g_1) = \sigma(g_2)$	Equivalence
8	$\forall g_1, g_2 \in \mathcal{G}, Att(g_1) \subset Att(g_2) \wedge Supp(g_1) = Supp(g_2) \wedge \Sigma_{x \in g_1} \gamma(x) = \Sigma_{x \in g_2} \gamma(x) \rightarrow \sigma(g_2) < \sigma(g_1)$	Attack Counting
9	$\forall g_1, g_2 \in \mathcal{G}, Supp(g_1) \subset Supp(g_2) \wedge Att(g_1) = Att(g_2) \wedge \Sigma_{x \in g_1} \gamma(x) = \Sigma_{x \in g_2} \gamma(x) \rightarrow \sigma(g_1) < \sigma(g_2)$	Support Counting
10	$\forall g_1, g_2 \in \mathcal{G}, Att(g_1) = Att(g_2) \wedge Supp(g_1) = Supp(g_2) \wedge \Sigma_{x \in g_1} \gamma(x) > \Sigma_{x \in g_2} \gamma(x) \rightarrow \sigma(g_1) > \sigma(g_2)$	Base Score Reinforcement
11	$\forall g_1, g_2 \in \mathcal{G}, g_1 <_a g_2 \wedge Supp(g_1) = Supp(g_2) \wedge \Sigma_{x \in g_1} \gamma(x) = \Sigma_{x \in g_2} \gamma(x) \rightarrow \sigma(g_1) > \sigma(g_2)$	Attack Reinforcement
12	$\forall g_1, g_2 \in \mathcal{G},\ Att(g_1) = Att(g_2) \wedge g_1 >_s g_2 \wedge \Sigma_{x \in g_1} \gamma(x) = \Sigma_{x \in g_2} \gamma(x) \rightarrow \sigma(g_1) > \sigma(g_2)$	Support Reinforcement

(Support Counting) requires that a strictly larger set of attackers (supporters, respectively) determines a lower (higher, respectively) strength. Base Score Reinforcement requires that a higher sum of base scores gives a higher strength. For the last two properties, we have to define the notion of weaker and stronger attack/support relations between sets.

Definition 8. *For any set* $A, B \in \mathcal{G}$*:*
$A <_a B$ *iff* $\Sigma_{x \in Att(A)} \sigma(x) > \Sigma_{x \in Att(B)} \sigma(x)$*;*
$A <_s B$ *iff* $\Sigma_{x \in Supp(A)} \sigma(x) < \Sigma_{x \in Supp(B)} \sigma(x)$*;*
$A >_a B$ *iff* $B <_a A$*;* $\quad A >_s B$ *iff* $B <_s A$*.*

Then, Attack Reinforcement states that a weaker set of attackers determines a higher strength whereas Support Reinforcement states that a stronger set of supporters determines a higher strength.

Any nQBAF satisfies all given properties. This indicates that our LRP-based nQBAFs may align with human reasoning.

Proposition 1. *nQBAFs under LRP-based semantics satisfy Properties 1–12.*

Proof. We will make use of Lemmas 1-3 in the Appendix.

Property 1. Any group of arguments in $\mathcal{G}$ represents a single node. From Definition 7, the strength of this group is the sum of that of its members. We can view members as contributions this node receives from all nodes in the next layer. So overall, the total sum is the relevance score of this node. This also holds for the output node of interest by Definition 7 and our choice of LRP. By conservative properties of LRP, this sum is equal to the sum of contributions this node gives to all the nodes in the previous layer. Since Algorithm 1 constructs a set of arguments A by considering all the pairs of nodes in adjacent layers, each contribution must be the strength of a unique argument in the previous layer. From Lemma 3, any non-attacking and non-supporting argument that does not represent an output node has zero strength, so the sum can be calculated from adding strengths of attacking and supporting arguments from the previous layer altogether. Hence this property is satisfied. □

Property 2. For an arbitrary group $g \in \mathcal{G}$, if $Att(g) = Supp(g) = \emptyset$ then by Property 1 we have $\sigma(g) = 0 + 0 = 0$. As γ gives all arguments a base score of zero, then $\Sigma_{x \in g}\gamma(x) = 0$. So $\sigma(g) = \Sigma_{x \in g}\gamma(x)$. As g is arbitrary, this is true for all $g \in \mathcal{G}$. □

Property 3. From Lemmas 1 and 2, any attacker has a negative strength while any supporter has a positive strength. For any group $g \in \mathcal{G}$, if $Att(g) \neq \emptyset$ and $Supp(g) = \emptyset$ then by Property 1 the strength $\sigma(g)$ must be negative. As γ gives all arguments a base score of zero, then $\Sigma_{x \in g}\gamma(x) = 0$. Hence $\sigma(g) < \Sigma_{x \in g}\gamma(x)$. □

Property 4. Similar to the proof of Property 3 above, any group $g \in \mathcal{G}$ that only has supporters has a positive strength by Property 1, which is more than $\Sigma_{x \in g}\gamma(x) = 0$. □

Property 5. Take arbitrary $g \in \mathcal{G}$ and assume $\sigma(g) < \Sigma_{x \in g}\gamma(x)$. We have to show that $Att(g) \neq \emptyset$. Assume $Att(g) = \emptyset$. There are two cases: $Supp(g) = \emptyset$ or $Supp(g) \neq \emptyset$. The first case leads to $\sigma(g) = \Sigma_{x \in g}\gamma(x)$ by Property 2, and the second case leads to $\sigma(g) > \Sigma_{x \in g}\gamma(x)$ by Property 4, both of which are contradictions. Hence $Att(g) \neq \emptyset$. □

Property 6. Take arbitrary $g \in \mathcal{G}$ and assume $\sigma(g) > \Sigma_{x \in g}\gamma(x)$. We have to show that $Supp(g) \neq \emptyset$. Assume $Supp(g) = \emptyset$. There are two cases: $Att(g) = \emptyset$ or $Att(g) \neq \emptyset$. The first case leads to $\sigma(g) = \Sigma_{x \in g}\gamma(x)$ by Property 2, and the second case leads to $\sigma(g) < \Sigma_{x \in g}\gamma(x)$ by Property 3, both of which are contradictions. Hence $Supp(g) \neq \emptyset$. □

Property 7. By Property 1, any group with similar attackers and supporters must have the same strength so this property is satisfied. □

Property 8. Assume we have two groups with similar sets of attackers and supporters. By Property 7, both groups have the same strength. Since any attacker has a negative strength (by Lemma 1), adding it to any group reduces the group strength by Property 1. Hence the property follows. □

Property 9. Assume we have two groups with similar sets of attackers and supporters. By Property 7, both groups have the same strength. Since any supporter has a positive strength (by Lemma 2), adding it to any group increases the group strength by Property 1. Hence the property follows. □

Property 10. Since every argument has a base score of zero (by our choice of γ), every group's sum of base scores is zero so the antecedent is always false. This property is therefore satisfied. □

Property 11. Take two arbitrary groups $g_1, g_2 \in \mathcal{G}$. Assume $g_1 <_a g_2$ and $Supp(g_1) = Supp(g_2)$. We have to show that $\sigma(g_1) > \sigma(g_2)$. Since g_1 and g_2 have the same supporters, $\Sigma_{x \in Supp(g_1)}\sigma(x) = \Sigma_{x \in Supp(g_2)}\sigma(x)$. As $g_1 <_a g_2$, then $\Sigma_{x \in Att(g_1)}\sigma(x) > \Sigma_{x \in Att(g_2)}\sigma(x)$. By Property 1, $\sigma(g_1) > \sigma(g_2)$ and this property is satisfied. □

Property 12. Take two arbitrary groups $g_1, g_2 \in \mathcal{G}$. Assume $Att(g_1) = Att(g_2)$ and $g_1 >_s g_2$. We have to show that $\sigma(g_1) > \sigma(g_2)$. Since g_1 and g_2 have the same attackers, $\Sigma_{x \in Att(g_1)}\sigma(x) = \Sigma_{x \in Att(g_2)}\sigma(x)$. As $g_1 >_s g_2$, then $\Sigma_{x \in Supp(g_1)}\sigma(x) > \Sigma_{x \in Supp(g_2)}\sigma(x)$. By Property 1, $\sigma(g_1) > \sigma(g_2)$ and this property is satisfied. □

5 Empirical Study

We apply our nQBAF variant as an underpinning argumentation framework for explaining a neural network-based image classifier. However, the network consists of several layers of multiple nodes, so the resulting argumentation framework will be too large to comprehend. To resolve this issue, we simplify the nQBAF variant further by grouping groups of arguments together. As each group of arguments has its well-defined strength, it can be treated as another type of argument that can be grouped together in a manner similar to its underlying arguments. Accordingly, all the dialectical properties are still satisfied by this additional layer of grouping. This double-layer grouping idea is, in essence, equivalent to grouping nodes of a neural network together. This idea is also exhibited in two approaches, namely *deep argumentative explanation* (DAX) [1] and the approach in [13] by Google. In this paper, we apply the LRP-based semantics on both approaches, each of which generates a separate set of explanations. We then analyse the obtained explanations qualitatively.

5.1 DAX Basics

DAX [1] is a general methodology for building local explanations (i.e. input-based explanations) for a neural network outputs. Unlike other explanation methods which are only based on inputs (and thus can be deemed to be flat), DAX takes account of the hidden layers too. DAX is based on extracting an argumentation framework from a neural network; explanations are then drawn from the framework, represented in a comprehensible format to humans. The extraction of the argumentation framework requires the choice of a semantics (for determining the strength of arguments) directly matching the behaviour of the neural network.

Here we apply DAX using our LRP semantics at its core. Also, we choose nQBAFs as the argumentation framework underpinning DAXs. We may theoretically achieve a full (local) explanation by viewing the entire nQBAF extracted from a neural network. However, the explanation would be too large for complex networks, therefore too complicated for humans to comprehend. To make things human-scale, we only consider a fragment of the nQBAF, in the spirit of [1], as well as grouping groups of arguments representing a single node (i.e. grouping nodes) together, and visualise the grouping as an explanation.

5.2 The Basics of Google's Method

Google's method [13] combines *feature visualisation* (i.e. what is a neuron looking for?, see [12]) with *attribution* (i.e. how does a specific node contributes to the output?) to generate a local explanation for a neural network output. We use the implementation of this method available at [7], changing the attribution method from a linear correlation to LRP. We leverage on the existing implementation's choices for visualisation.

5.3 Settings

For both methods, we aim to explain a Keras VGG16 model [16] (with linear activation function for the output layer) pretrained on the ImageNet dataset [5]. Since the whole model is too large, we only consider the last convolutional layer, explaining what the layer prioritises in a given image. We test our method in combination with DAX, comparing it to Google's method, on three images: a police van from [19], a barbell from [18], and a diaper from [20]. In all cases, we use the output node with maximum activation as the output class, with such an activation referred to as the output prediction.

To generate explanations using DAX, we modify the code from the ArgFlow library [4] and apply to each of the three images. For each explanation, the size of each image illustrates the attribution thereof towards the output class, with red and green arrows depicting attacking and supporting the output class prediction respectively.

For Google's approach, we modify the code from [7] which is one of the Colaboratory notebooks in [13]. We then apply the code to the three images, each results in the set of images indicating parts of the original image. Each number below each factor refers to how much attribution each component has towards the output prediction. The arrow sizes also reflect these attributions.

5.4 DAX Vs Google Comparisons

Image 1: Police Van. Explanations from both methods (as shown in Fig. 2) indicate that the model focuses mostly on the background and the red stripe of the van. There are some subtle differences between them mainly with the strength for each factor, but their factors are quite similar. However, an interesting point is that DAX considers the siren light of the van as one of the top six factors contributing to the output class prediction (according to the rightmost image of Fig. 2a) while Google's approach does not present this (arguably important) factor.

Image 2: Barbell. According to Fig. 3, both methods explain that the model focuses on the plates and the background. However, DAX considers the plates to contribute to the prediction more than the background, while it is the opposite for the Google's explanation. Somewhat counter-intuitively though, DAX considers the plates to both attack (the fourth image from the right of Fig. 3a) and support (the rightmost image from the right of Fig. 3a) the class prediction, even

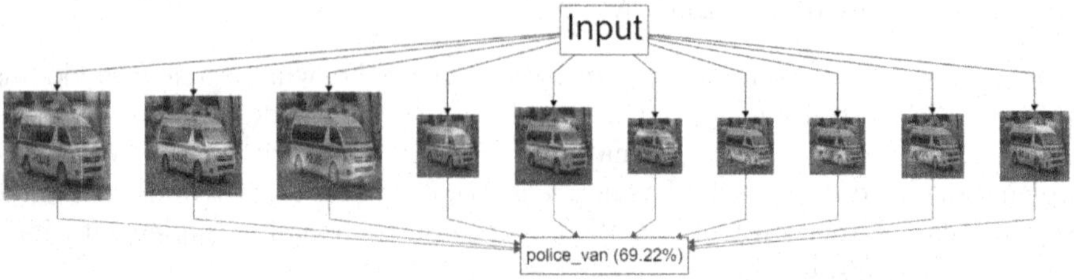

(a) The DAX approach

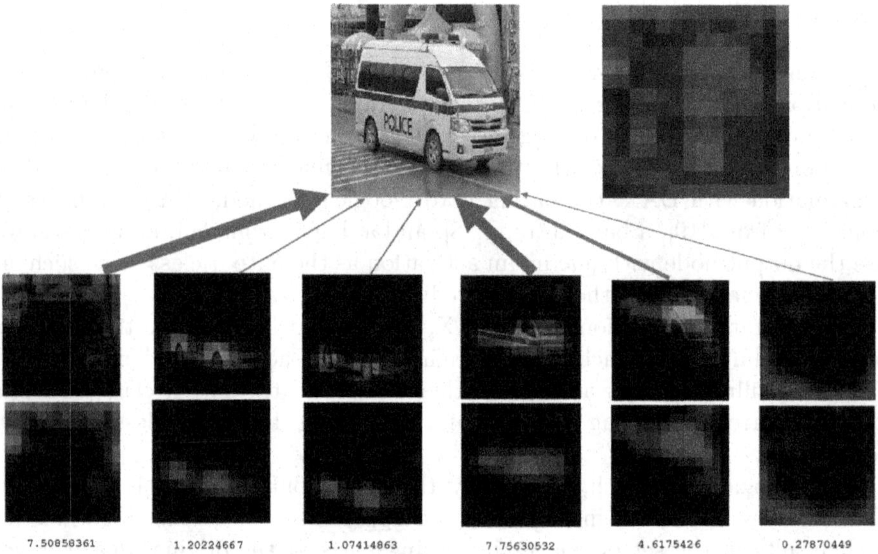

(b) Google's approach

Fig. 2. Explanations given using (a) the DAX approach (with attacks in red and supports in green, either indicated in the filters or as arrows, and the size of arguments for the filters indicating their dialectical strength, see [1] for details) and (b) Google's approach for the police van image with the predicted class *police_van* (with arrows indicating support, and the size of arrows representing the LRP values). The police van image source is (https://bit.ly/3Fi1oqx). (Color figure online)

though the attacking argument (the fourth image from the right) is much less strong. If the DAX is faithful to the model, then this incongruence may result from an incongruence in the model.

Image 3: Diaper. From Fig. 4, both methods indicate that the model focuses on other things instead of the diaper. The DAX in Fig. 4a shows that the model focuses on the baby instead of the diaper. It even indicates that the diaper attacks the prediction of the class itself. In contrast, Google's explanation (Fig. 4b) indicates that the model focuses on the background and the diaper, giving the baby lower attributions.

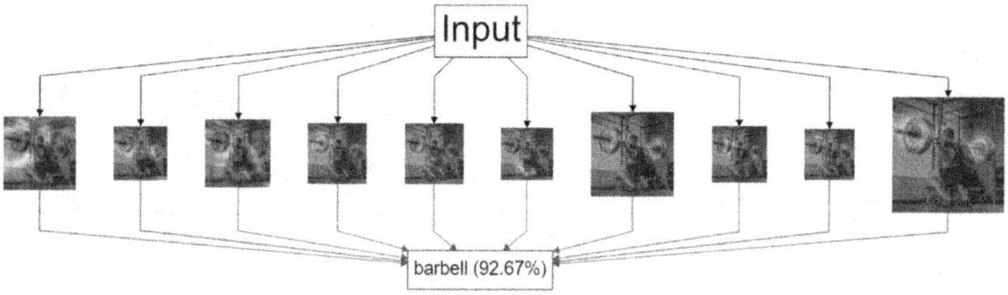

(a) The DAX approach

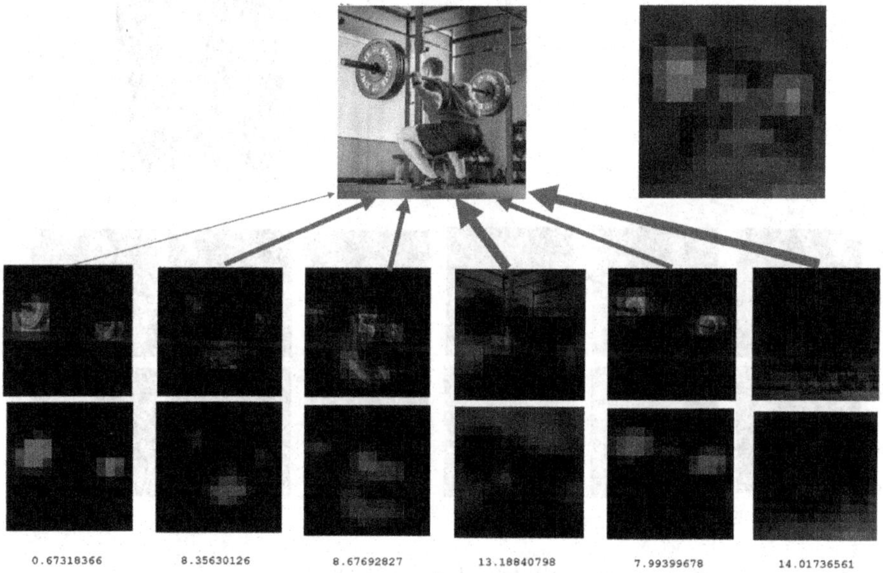

(b) Google's approach

Fig. 3. Explanations given using (a) the DAX approach and (b) Google's approach for the barbell image with the predicted class *barbell*. The barbell image source is (https://amzn.to/3Db2xOQ). (Color figure online)

5.5 Discussion

The comparisons above clearly indicate that even with similar semantics (LRP), for the same model, explanations vary depending on how the grouping (of argument groups) is done. Google's approach seems to take account of the fact that concepts are usually recognised around particular positions of an image, whereas DAX only focuses on the concepts. DAX seems to unearth conflicts, with the same feature both attacking and supporting a prediction. Overall, more experimentation is needed to understand which explanation method is more "faithful" to the underlying model.

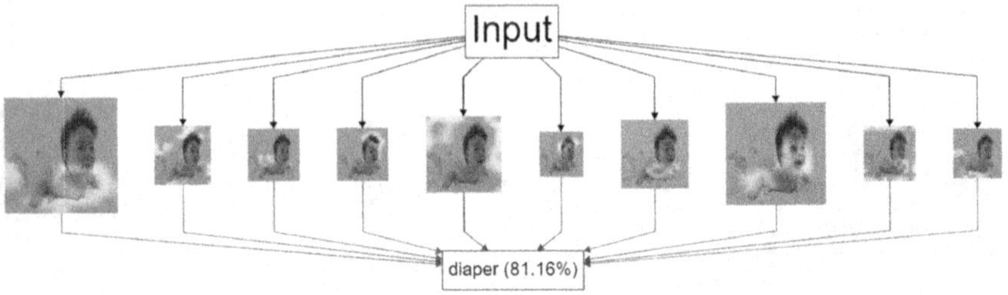

(a) The DAX approach

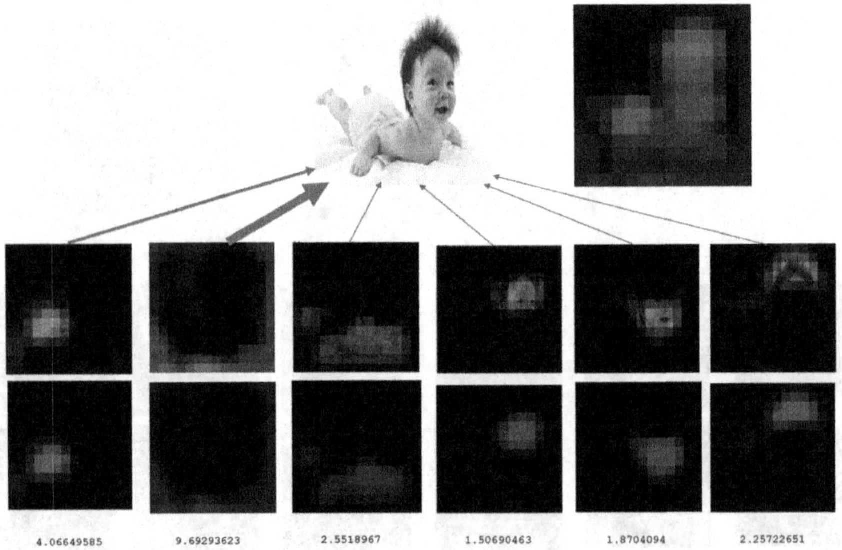

(b) Google's approach

Fig. 4. Explanations given using (a) the DAX approach and (b) Google's approach for the baby image with the predicted class *diaper*. The diaper image source is (https://bit.ly/3D8FZya). (Color figure online)

6 Conclusions

We presented a variant of Quantitative Bipolar Argumentation Frameworks (QBAFs) called neural QBAFs (nQBAFs) and considered how the LRP-based semantics satisfies the modified dialectical properties for nQBAFs. We also conducted preliminary experiments explaining an image classifier, by applying the LRP-based semantics to two approaches: Deep Argumentative Explanation (DAX) and Google's approach, and comparing both sets of explanations. DAX groups argument groups (i.e. nodes) in the same filter together, while Google's approach groups them by means of matrix factorisation optimising for activations. The comparison shows that how argument groups (each representing a node) are grouped can affect the resulting explanations. As future work, we plan to conduct experiments with using nQBAFs for visualisation for text classification, in comparison with DAX and Google's approaches with LRP as well as other methods, such as smoothgrad [17], deeplift [10], gradcam [15] and TCAV [8]. Finally, it would be interesting to conduct experiments to assess demands on the cognitive load for end-users using different (instantiations of) visualisations.

Acknowledgements. The first author was funded in part by Imperial College London under UROP (Undergraduate Research Opportunities Programme). The last author was partially funded by the European Research Council (ERC) under the European Union's Horizon 2020 research and innovation programme (grant agreement No. 101020934). Finally, Rago and Toni were partially funded by J.P. Morgan and by the Royal Academy of Engineering under the Research Chairs and Senior Research Fellowships scheme. Any views or opinions expressed herein are solely those of the authors listed.

Appendix: Lemmas for Dialectical Properties Proofs

Lemma 1. *Any attacking argument has a negative strength.*
$\forall a \in A[\exists x \in \mathcal{P}(A)[a \in Att(x)] \rightarrow \sigma(a) < 0]$

Proof. Take arbitrary $a \in A$. Assume there exists some $x \in \mathcal{P}(A)$ such that $a \in Att(x)$. Since $a \in Att(x)$, $(a, x) \in Att$ so $c_-(a, x)$ is true, meaning $R_{\rho(a) \leftarrow \rho(x)} < 0$. As $\sigma(a) = R_{\rho(a) \leftarrow \rho(x)}$ by Definition 7, then $\sigma(a) < 0$. □

Lemma 2. *Any supporting argument has a positive strength.*
$\forall a \in A[\exists x \in \mathcal{P}(A)[a \in Supp(x)] \rightarrow \sigma(a) > 0]$

Proof. Take arbitrary $a \in A$. Assume there exists some $x \in \mathcal{P}(A)$ such that $a \in Supp(x)$. Since $a \in Supp(x)$, $(a, x) \in Supp$ so $c_+(a, x)$ is true, meaning $R_{\rho(a) \leftarrow \rho(x)} > 0$. As $\sigma(a) = R_{\rho(a) \leftarrow \rho(x)}$ by Definition 7, then $\sigma(a) > 0$. □

Lemma 3. *Any argument that neither supports nor attacks any group and does not represent an output node has zero strength.*
$\forall a \in A[\forall x \in \mathcal{P}(A)[(a, x) \notin Supp \wedge (a, x) \notin Att] \wedge \rho(a) \notin V_{d+1} \rightarrow \sigma(a) = 0]$

Proof. This proposition follows immediately from Definition 7. □

References

1. Albini, E., Lertvittayakumjorn, P., Rago, A., Toni, F.: Deep argumentative explanations (2021). https://arxiv.org/abs/2012.05766
2. Baroni, P., Rago, A., Toni, F.: How many properties do we need for gradual argumentation?. In: AAAI (2018)
3. Baroni, P., Rago, A., Toni, F.: From fine-grained properties to broad principles for gradual argumentation: a principled spectrum. Int. J. Approx. Reason. **105**, 252–286 (2019). https://doi.org/10.1016/j.ijar.2018.11.019

4. Dejl, A., et al.: Argflow: a toolkit for deep argumentative explanations for neural networks. In: International Foundation for Autonomous Agents and Multiagent Systems, Richland, SC, pp. 1761–1763 (2021)
5. Deng, J., Dong, W., Socher, R., Li, L.J., Li, K., Fei-Fei, L.: Imagenet: a large-scale hierarchical image database. In: 2009 IEEE Conference on Computer Vision and Pattern Recognition, pp. 248–255 (2009). https://doi.org/10.1109/CVPR.2009.5206848
6. Dung, P.M.: On the acceptability of arguments and its fundamental role in non-monotonic reasoning, logic programming and n-person games. Artif. Intell. **77**(2), 321–357 (1995). https://doi.org/10.1016/0004-3702(94)00041-X
7. Google, L.: Neuron groups - building blocks of interpretability (2018). https://bit.ly/3a483Xc
8. Kim, B., et al.: Interpretability beyond feature attribution: auantitative testing with concept activation vectors (TCAV). In: Dy, J., Krause, A. (eds.) Proceedings of the 35th International Conference on Machine Learning. Proceedings of Machine Learning Research, 10–15 July 2018, vol. 80, pp. 2668–2677. PMLR (2018). https://proceedings.mlr.press/v80/kim18d.html
9. Lertvittayakumjorn, P., Specia, L., Toni, F.: FIND: human-in-the-loop debugging deep text classifiers. In: Proceedings of the 2020 Conference on Empirical Methods in Natural Language Processing (EMNLP), pp. 332–348. Association for Computational Linguistics, November 2020. https://doi.org/10.18653/v1/2020.emnlp-main.24
10. Li, J., Zhang, C., Zhou, J.T., Fu, H., Xia, S., Hu, Q.: Deep-lift: deep label-specific feature learning for image annotation. IEEE Trans. Cybern. 1–10 (2021). https://doi.org/10.1109/TCYB.2021.3049630
11. Montavon, G., Binder, A., Lapuschkin, S., Samek, W., Müller, K.-R.: Layer-wise relevance propagation: an overview. In: Samek, W., Montavon, G., Vedaldi, A., Hansen, L.K., Müller, K.-R. (eds.) Explainable AI: Interpreting, Explaining and Visualizing Deep Learning. LNCS (LNAI), vol. 11700, pp. 193–209. Springer, Cham (2019). https://doi.org/10.1007/978-3-030-28954-6_10
12. Olah, C., Mordvintsev, A., Schubert, L.: Feature visualization. Distill **2**(11), e7 (2017). https://doi.org/10.23915/distill.00007
13. Olah, C., et al.: The building blocks of interpretability. Distill **3**(03), e10 (2018). https://doi.org/10.23915/distill.00010
14. Potyka, N.: Interpreting neural networks as quantitative argumentation frameworks. In: Proceedings of the AAAI Conference on Artificial Intelligence, vol. 35, no. 7, pp. 6463–6470, May 2021. https://ojs.aaai.org/index.php/AAAI/article/view/16801
15. Selvaraju, R.R., Cogswell, M., Das, A., Vedantam, R., Parikh, D., Batra, D.: Grad-cam: visual explanations from deep networks via gradient-based localization. In: Proceedings of the IEEE International Conference on Computer Vision (ICCV), October 2017
16. Simonyan, K., Zisserman, A.: Very deep convolutional networks for large-scale image recognition. In: International Conference on Learning Representations (2015)
17. Smilkov, D., Thorat, N., Kim, B., Viégas, F., Wattenberg, M.: Smoothgrad: removing noise by adding noise (2017)
18. Synergee Fitness Worldwide, I.: (2019). https://amzn.to/3Db2xOQ
19. Wataree: Police van Thailand (2019). https://bit.ly/3Fi1oqx
20. websubstance: Baby tummy time (nd). https://bit.ly/3D8FZya

Machine Learning and Applications

Domino Saliency Metrics: Improving Existing Channel Saliency Metrics with Structural Information

Kaveena Persand(✉), Andrew Anderson, and David Gregg

Trinity College Dublin, Dublin 2, Ireland
{persandk,aanderso}@tcd.ie, david.gregg@cs.tcd.ie

Abstract. Channel pruning is used to reduce the number of weights in a Convolutional Neural Network (CNN). Channel pruning removes slices of the weight tensor so that the convolution layer remains dense. The removal of these weight slices from a single layer causes mismatching number of feature maps between layers of the network. A simple solution is to force the number of feature map between layers to match through the removal of weight slices from subsequent layers. This additional constraint becomes more apparent in DNNs with branches where multiple channels need to be pruned together to keep the network dense. Popular pruning saliency metrics do not factor in the structural dependencies that arise in DNNs with branches. We propose Domino metrics (built on existing channel saliency metrics) to reflect these structural constraints. We test Domino saliency metrics against the baseline channel saliency metrics on multiple networks with branches. Domino saliency metrics improved pruning rates in most tested networks and up to 25% in AlexNet on CIFAR-10.

Keywords: Convolutional Neural Networks · Pruning · Machine learning

1 Introduction

Deep neural networks can reach human level accuracy for many classification problems [31], but they have huge memory and computation cost. Pruning reduces the size of neural networks via the removal of unnecessary weights [9,27]. Channel pruning removes weights corresponding to an entire channel in the output of a layer. When the weights of the entire channel are set to zero, the corresponding output feature map of the channel becomes zero. This zero output feature map feeds into subsequent layers which may allow the corresponding channel to be removed from these subsequent layers in a *domino effect.*

In a network architecture where each layer has exactly one output and one input layer, the removal of an output feature map leads to the following layer's input feature map no longer contributing to the network. This scenario is illustrated in Fig. 4 where the consumer layer is a convolution or fully-connected

S. Bandini et al. (Eds.): AIxIA 2021, LNAI 13196, pp. 447–461, 2022.
https://doi.org/10.1007/978-3-031-08421-8_31

layer, the resulting zero input channel allows the corresponding weights from the consumer layer to be pruned.

In networks with branches/splits, the output feature map from one layer may feed into multiple others. With joins, feature maps from different layers feed into a single layer. A common occurence of split and join connections in CNNs is due to skip connections, which were first pioneered in ResNet architectures. The common structure of a ResNet block containing join and split connections is shown in Fig. 1. The presence of these joins allows multiple output feature maps to be removed together when one feature map is considered for removal. Networks that offer state-of-the-art accuracy for image classification often contain skip connections [1,23,32,35,36]. ResNet architectures are also more difficult to prune for their lower redundancy [5,14,21]. Hence, improving pruning rates for networks containing skip connections can be very advantageous.

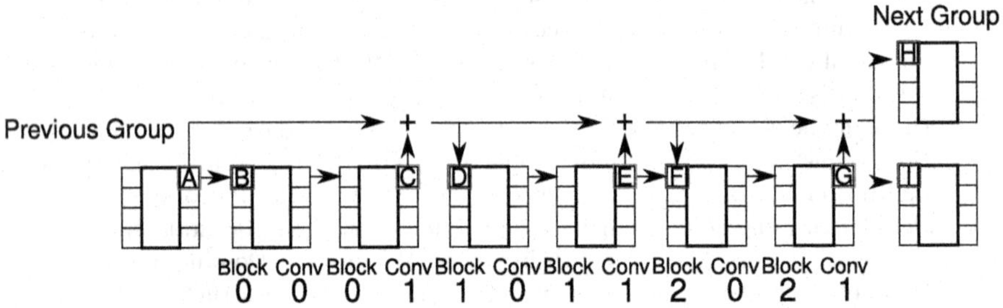

Fig. 1. Structure of a block in ResNet-20. The direction of arrows show the direction in which data flows.

Another common occurence of joins is group convolution. Group convolution was originally used in the AlexNet architecture [16] to parallelise convolution on multiple GPUs. Since, it has also been used in state of the art architectures [1,35].

Most approaches do not factor in the removal of different feature maps when computing the saliency metric used for pruning. We propose using *Domino saliency metrics* to factor in the saliency of feature maps and weights that need to removed together. We make the following contributions: (1) We propose Domino saliency metrics, where existing saliency metrics are combined together depending on the set of channels that need to be removed together. (2) Combining channel saliency metrics to obtain Domino saliency metrics, has a negligible computational cost to computing channel saliency metrics and requires very little modification to existing pruning strategies. (3) We experimentally evaluate two variants of Domino saliency metrics: $Domino-o$ and $Domino-io$, and find that they significantly improve pruning.

2 Data Flow Graph for Pruning

2.1 Background

Pruning is the removal of weights from the network. The pruned weights are set to zero. Pruning can be done in an unstructured or structured way. Unstructured pruning removes weights from the network without any given constraint in pattern. On the other hand, structured pruning removes weights in a chosen pattern. Common patterns for structured pruning are (in increasing size of pattern): intra-kernel, kernel, and channels (or filters).

Channel pruning removes entire channels from convolution layers of the network. By removing entire channels, the weight tensor remains dense, so existing DNN dense libraries can be used. The removal of an entire channel of convolution weights leads to the removal of its subsequent feature map. Removing a feature map may allow corresponding weights from subsequent layers to be removed. In a network where each layer has at most one input layer and output layer, this relationship is obvious.

2.2 Channel Pruning Networks with Splits and Joins

While simpler neural networks are often linear and acyclic [15,18], modern networks often contain join nodes and split nodes [11,16].

It is obvious which weights need to be removed when applying channel pruning to a network where each layer is fed to only one successor. However in networks with branches, feature maps are used by more than one layer. A layer can have multiple successors due to skip connections. Skip connections are element-wise additions between output feature maps of different convolutions to produce the input feature map of the following layer.

In networks with branches, applying a reachability analysis such as is performed by a compiler on a more traditional computational structure, the control-flow graph, to uncover the weights that need to be pruned together to keep the network dense. The basic intuition here is that if the definition of some feature map *reaches* a layer, the pruning of that feature map may also imply the removal of more feature maps which are computed from it. While this seems trivial for linear networks, the introduction of splits and joins in the graph mean that extra care must be taken in order to exploit the dependence relationship to achieve better pruning results.

2.3 Data Flow Graph

Neural networks form a directed graph structure where simple input-output dependence exists between producer and consumer layers in the network (i.e. the network forms a *data flow graph*). When representing the data flow graph, we can make abstraction of activation layers (see Sect. 2.6). Hence, we only need to represent the data flow between a convolution or fully-connected layer to other convolution or fully-connected layers.

We introduce some notation to facilitate the description of the data flow graph. A layer l has a set of 3-dimensional input feature maps $I(l)$, a set of 3-dimensional output feature maps $O(l)$ and weights W^l (with shape $m_{out}^l \times m_{in}^l \times k^l \times k^l$). $O_i(l)$ and $I_i(l)$ refer to the ith 2-dimensional feature map of $O(l)$ and $I(l)$ respectively. We can describe the flow of information between layers with a successor relation $O(l) = I(succ(l))$. Intuitively, the *data flow successors* $succ(l)$ of a layer l are those layers whose input is the output of layer l.

When a layer in a neural network joins the output of multiple producer channels, we write $O(l) \subset I(succ(l))$ i.e. the successor relation extends to any channel which consumes the output of l. If $I(l+1)$ is the input feature map of the following, then it is the direct successor of $O(l)$.

2.4 Join and Split Nodes

$I(l+1)$ is not necessarily the only successor of $O(l)$. For example, in Fig. 2a the elementwise sum of two layers l and l' is fed to layer $l+1$. $l+1$ satisfies $O(l) \subset I(l+1) \wedge O(l') \subset I(l+1)$. We can also consider data dependencies for a single channel, C_i^l, instead of an entire layer, l, with $O(C_i^l) = O_i(l)$. So we would say that both $succ(C_i^l) = \{C_i^{l+1}\}$ and $succ(C_i^{l'}) = \{C_i^{l+1}\}$. Split, or broadcast relationships also exist, where the output of a layer is used by multiple consumers. An example of split in the data flow graph is seen in Fig. 2b where $succ(C_i^l) = \{C_i^{l+1}, C_i^{l+2}\}$.

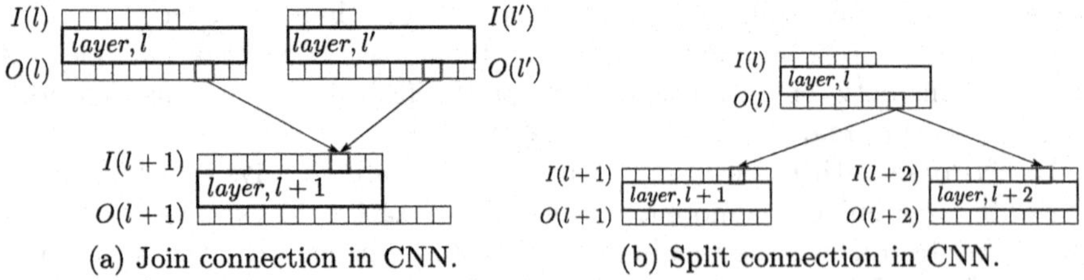

Fig. 2. Data dependencies with join and split connections in CNNs. The arrows are in the direction of data flow.

2.5 Group Convolution

Data dependencies at the entrance of group convolutions can be modeled using a simple convolution layer that has g sets of input feature maps that result in g sets of partial output feature maps. These partial output feature maps are then added together to create the final output feature map of the layer. We have $m_{in}^{l+1} = \frac{m_{out}^l}{g^l}$ with the group size, $g^l > 1$. Figure 3 illustrates a group convolution with a group size of 2.

Hence, $O(C_i^{l-1}) \subset I(C_i^l) \wedge O(C_{i+g^l}^{l-1}) \subset I(C_i^l)$. In Fig. 3b, $succ(C_i^{l-1}) = \{C_i^l, C_{i+2}^l\}$.

Considering a neural network graph with G channels, we can define the successor relation as:

$$\forall c \in G, \exists x \in G : O(c) \subset I(x) \Rightarrow x \in succ(c) \qquad \text{(SUCCESSOR)}$$

Let the predicate $P(c)$ be true where a feature map c is being pruned, and false otherwise. The truth of $P(c)$ is determined locally for the input or output feature maps of a specific layer by the pruning process.

We are interested in how the truth of $P(c)$ locally in any single layer may influence the truth of $P(c)$ for connected layers in the network, or more informally, how pruning some feature maps may imply the pruning of other feature maps.

$$\forall c \in G, \forall x \in succ(c) : P(O(c)) \Leftrightarrow P(I(x)) \qquad \text{(CHANNEL PRUNING)}$$

Equation CHANNEL PRUNING states that the pruning an output feature map $O(c)$ is materially equivalent to pruning the input feature map $I(x)$, with x a successor of c. This predicate is valid for all the channels in the network. Hence, in a typical ResNet style block this leads to the simultaneous pruning of multiple channels. In Fig. 1, feature maps A-I need to be removed simultaneously.

Equation CHANNEL PRUNING is used to propagate pruning of feature maps. However, for channel pruning we need to remove weights from the network. To prune an output channel, $c = C_i^l$, from the network, weights $W^l[i, :, :, :]$ are removed from network with ":" representing all valid indices. Hence, when a feature map $O(C_i^l)$ is pruned, $W^l[i, :, :, :]$ is pruned and when a feature map $I(C_i^l)$ is pruned, $W^l[:, i, :, :]$ is pruned.

2.6 How to Prune Biases and Activation Layers

The output of a convolution is not often fed directly to the next convolution or fully-connected layer. Instead, at least one activation function is applied to the feature map before being fed to the next layer. Hence, the output feature map produced by a layer is not directly equivalent to the input feature map of the following layer.

For most activation functions, applying them to a zero feature map results in a zero feature map. ReLU, GELU, and max/average pooling layers, are examples of activation functions that output zero for a zero input. When these activation functions are used, a pruned output feature map results in pruned input feature maps of the subsequent layers. However, in the case of activation functions with biases such as Batch Norm or bias layers, a zero input does not always result into a zero output unless the biases are also set to zero. Hence, the pruned feature map and the pruned weights cannot be removed from the network. However, if the corresponding biases are set to zero, the weights can then be removed from the network.

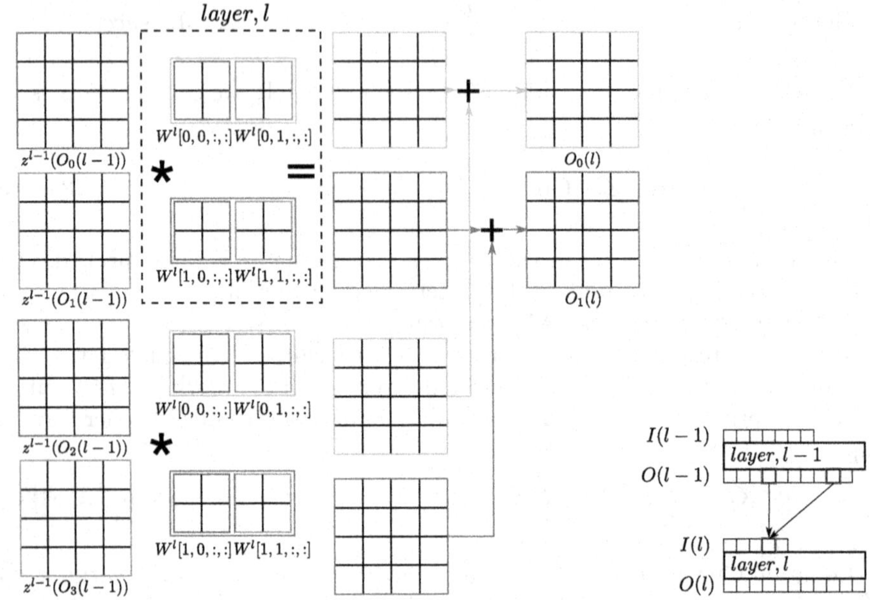

(a) Group convolution with $g^l = 2, m_{in}^l = 2, m_{out}^{l-1} = 4$.

(b) Group convolution data dependency.

Fig. 3. Data flow with group convolutions in CNNs. The arrows are in the direction of data flow.

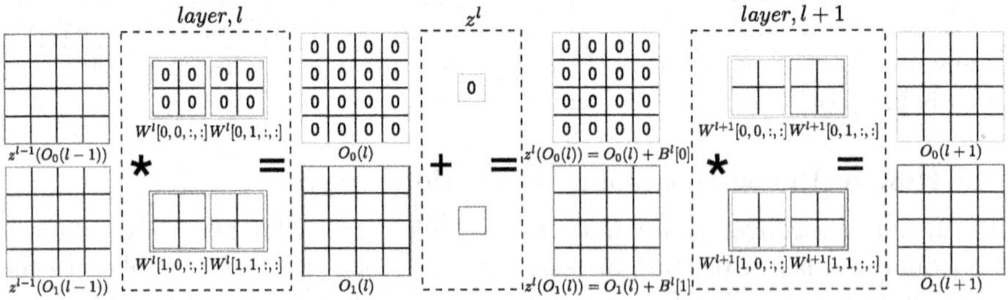

Fig. 4. Channel pruning where the outputs of convolution l are fed into an activation layer (with bias), z^l before being fed to the successor $l + 1$.

A simple channel pruning case is shown in Fig. 4, For the convolution layer l, to produce a single $O_i(l)$ each jth input feature map is convolved with its corresponding 2D filter $W^l[i, j, :, :]$ and summed together. In Fig. 4, $O_0(l) = z^{l-1}(O_0(l-1)) * W^l[0, 0, :, :] + z^{l-1}(O_1(l-1)) * W^l[0, 1, :, :]$ and $O_1(l) = z^{l-1}(O_0(l-1)) * W^l[1, 0, :, :] + z^{l-1}(O_1(l-1)) * W^l[1, 1, :, :]$. To prune the output channel C_0^l, $W^l[0, 0, :, :]$ and $W^l[0, 1, :, :]$ are set to zero. If the corresponding bias in the activation layer z^l (B_0^l), is set to zero, then the input feature map $z^l(O_0(l))$ is also zero. Since convolution with a zero feature map results into a zero feature map, the values of $W^{l+1}[0,0,:,:]$ and $W^{l+1}[1,0,:,:]$ no longer influence feature maps $O_0(l+1)$ and $O_1(l+1)$. Hence, $W^l[0,0,:,:]$, $W^l[0,1,:,:]$, B^l_0, $W^{l+1}[0,0,:,:]$, and $W^{l+1}[1,0,:,:]$, can be set to zero and removed.

If the biases are not set to zero, then feature maps filled with zeroes still need to be stored to keep the network dense. In practice, output feature maps filled with zeroes are removed from the network to increase memory savings. Hence, biases of activation functions are also set to zero and the obsolete parameters are removed to keep the network dense. Hence, to simplify the data flow graph, we can make abstraction of activation functions even if they contain biases. We can also assume that when a channel is pruned, weights, feature maps and activation layer parameters of that channel are set to zero.

3 Domino Pruning

When pruning neural networks with skip or group connections, most approaches use the same saliency metrics as for simple forward feed neural networks without any modification. The construction of these saliency metrics do not take into account the structural dependencies that may to be satisfied between layers to keep the network dense.

We argue that a more straightforward inspection of the data dependence structure may be more prudent. Using a reachability analysis such as may be performed by a compiler, we show how the removal of one set of parameter may be used to heuristically perform a cascade of removals of other reachable parameters. We refer to this technique as "Domino" saliency metrics. Any saliency metric that has been formulated to give each channel a saliency measure can be used with Domino saliency metrics.

$$\forall x \in succ(c), \exists y : x \in succ(y) \Rightarrow y \in coparent(c) \qquad \text{(COPARENT)}$$

$$\forall x \in succ(c), \exists y : y \in succ(c) \Rightarrow y \in sibling(x) \qquad \text{(SIBLING)}$$

With Domino pruning, the output channels that are considered coparents are considered as a single pruning choice. Hence, they cannot be removed without the other coparent output channels. Output channels are considered coparent if they share a common successor as shown in Equation COPARENT. Similarly Equation SIBLING is used to find siblings of direct successors. We consider the *coparent* and *sibling* relationships to be birectional and transitive, i.e., if $A \in coparent(B)$ then $B \in coparent(A)$ and if, $C \in coparent(B)$ then $C \in coparent(A)$. $coparents^+$ and $siblings^+$ are the transitive closure of the *coparent* and *sibling* relationships. When c is an output channel, then $siblings^+(c)$ represents the transitive closure of any of c's successors and when c is an input channel, $coparents^+(c)$ represents the transitive closure of any output channel that is used to produce c. The feature maps and weights removed when one output channel is removed is given by Equation CHANNEL PRUNING. The set of parameters $coparents^+(c) \cup siblings^+(c)$ is pruned when the output channel c is pruned. In the case of a network with no joins and no splits $coparents^+(c) = \{c\}$ and $siblings^+ = succ(c)$.

Saliency metrics are traditionally computed for a single output channel. This is also true for networks with skip connections (ResNets). With Domino metrics we combine the channel saliency of channels that are removed together.

We propose two variants of Domino saliency: $Domino - o$ and $Domino - io$.

$Domino - o$ adds the saliency of all output channels that are removed together. Since most channel pruning algorithms use the channel saliency of output channels, $Domino - o$ has negligible cost and require minimal change to the pruning algorithm. Equation 1 decribes how to compute $Domino - o$ for a channel using $coparents^+$ and their channel saliency S.

$$Domino(c) = \sum_{x \in coparents^+(c)} S(x) \tag{1}$$

As illustrated in Fig. 4, the output feature produced by a convolution channel ultimately becomes the input feature map for the following layer. Few approaches apart from feature reconstruction based metrics, exploit this relationship for saliency computation. With $Domino - io$, we add the saliency of all the weights or feature maps that are removed when a channel is removed to get the saliency of the channel to be pruned. Equation 2 shows how to compute $Domino - io$ using the channel saliency of $coparents^+$ (output feature maps or weights) and $siblings^+$ (input feature maps or weights) using a channel saliency S.

$$Domino - io(c) = \sum_{x \in coparents^+(c)} S(x) + \sum_{x \in siblings^+(c)} S(x) \tag{2}$$

4 Experimental Evaluation

Channel saliency is the use of the saliency metric of a single output channel to prune all the dependent weights and feature maps. This is the common strategy when pruning networks. In practice, this leads to the lowest saliency of the output channels that are pruned together to be used as saliency metric of the set of weights or feature maps to be pruned. This baseline is denoted S.

We compare Domino saliency metrics constructed using a channel saliency against the use of the base channel saliency.

A Domino saliency metric is built using a baseline channel saliency metric. If the saliency of all channels are roughly of the same order and positive, their addition is of greater order than channels that are not part of split or join nodes. We use an average of the number of weights or output points to avoid favoring isolated channels for pruning. Saliency metrics that use feature maps are scaled using the number of pixels in the feature maps. For example, if two saliency $S(c)$ and $S(z)$ are computed using N_c and N_z weights then, the Domino-scaled metric is $\frac{S(c)+S(z)}{N_c+N_z}$ instead of $S(c) + S(z)$. The scaled channel metrics are $\frac{S(c)}{N_c}$ and $\frac{S(z)}{N_z}$. Metric with this average is suffixed with -avg.

4.1 Pruning Algorithm

The saliency metric is one component of the pruning algorithm. We choose a pruning algorithm that heavily relies on the choices of the saliency metric to determine the improvement brought by changing the saliency metric. Since our aim is to find better saliency metrics, we avoid obfuscating the contribution of the saliency metric by not retraining after each pruning step. If a saliency metric is able to achieve higher pruning rates without retraining, then it can also be used to reduce the cost of retraining [29].

For each pruning iteration we compute the saliency of every output channel. The lowest saliency channel is then pruned according to Equation CHANNEL PRUNING. This process is repeated until the test accuracy falls under 5% of its initial value.

4.2 Networks

We evaluate Domino saliency metrics on popular architectures with split and join nodes. We evaluate the original ResNet architecture [11] and a state-of-the-art ResNet-inspired architecture, NFNET-F0 [1]. We also evaluate Domino saliency metrics on AlexNet [16]. The join and split connections in ResNet arise due to skip connections. The join connections in AlexNet arise due to group convolutions. NFNET-F0 contain both skip connections and group convolutions.

We use the CIFAR-10 [15], CIFAR-100 [15], ImageNet-32 [2] (a downsized ImageNet variant), and ImageNet [3] datasets. ResNet-20[1] on ImageNet, ResNet-50 [30] on ImageNet and NFNET-F0 [1] on ImageNet are pretrained networks. The remaining networks are trained from scratch.

4.3 Saliency Metrics

The most popular pruning saliency metrics are either a derivative of the L1 or L2 norm of weights [6–9,12,13,17,20,24,33] or Taylor expansions [4,10,19,25, 26,28]. With channel pruning, Taylor Taylor expansions can be applied to either weights or feature maps.

The channel saliency metrics that we evaluate are: Taylor expansion using weights, Taylor expansion using feature maps, and L1 norm of weights.

5 Results

We measure the improvement of Domino saliency metrics by comparing the percentage of convolution weights removed for a drop of 5% in test accuracy. The results are an average from 4 runs.

Figures 5, 6, and 7 show the percentage of convolution weights removed. In most cases, we observe an improvement by using the Domino saliency metrics. $Domino - io$ significantly improves the pruning rates for AlexNet on CIFAR-10,

[1] https://github.com/HolmesShuan/ResNet-18-Caffemodel-on-ImageNet.

AlexNet on ImageNet-32 and ResNet-20 on CIFAR-10. *Domino* − *io* includes the saliency of input feature maps or input channel weights in addition to *Domino* − *o*. The larger improvement brought by *Domino* − *io* suggests that the saliency of input feature maps or input channel weights contain relevant information for pruning.

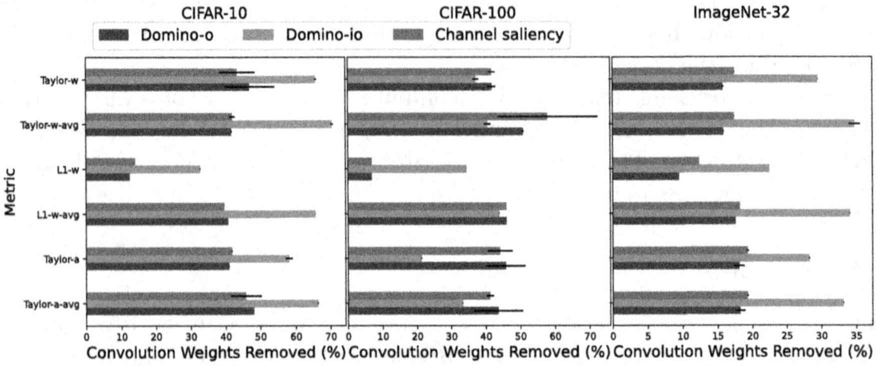

Fig. 5. AlexNet

From Fig. 5, we see that using *Domino* − *io* on AlexNet for CIFAR-10 and ImageNet greatly improves the base saliency metric. A notable result is the L1 norm of weights (with averaging) which can match the pruning rates of Taylor expansion based methods with *Domino* − *io*. The L1 norm of weights is a very popular metric for pruning for its low computational cost and good pruning rates. *Domino* − *io* has a negligible cost overhead while greatly improving the L1 norm of weights (with averaging).

From Fig. 6, we observe a similar trend where the L1 norm of weights (with averaging) can be improved to match and exceed the pruning rates of Taylor based method on ResNet-20 on ImageNet.

Figure 7 shows that the improvement of Domino saliency metrics are marginal on NFNET-F0. However since the pruning rates are also extremely low, the results are inconclusive for this network. On the other hand, ResNet-50 benefits from the additional structural information used by Domino saliency metrics. The pruning rates on ResNet-50 can be improved by a few percentage points with either *Domino* − *o* or *Domino* − *io*.

The average improvement of using Domino metrics over channel metrics for each network, is shown in Fig. 8a. On all the networks, except AlexNet on CIFAR-100, *Domino* − *io* on average improves the baseline channel metric. *Domino* − *io* can be used to push the pruning rate of a network farther. The improvement shown in Fig. 8b corresponds to the difference between the maximum percentage of weights removed between the best Domino metric and the best channel metric for a given network. With *Domino* − *io*, up to 25% and 15% more weights can be respectively removed from AlexNet on the CIFAR-10 dataset and the ImageNet-32 dataset.

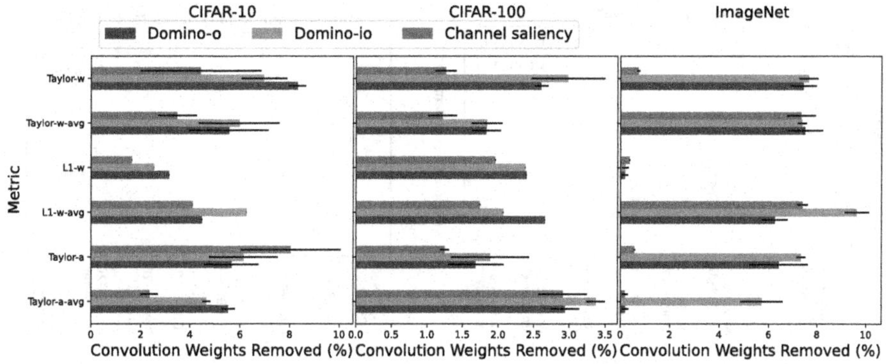

Fig. 6. ResNet-20

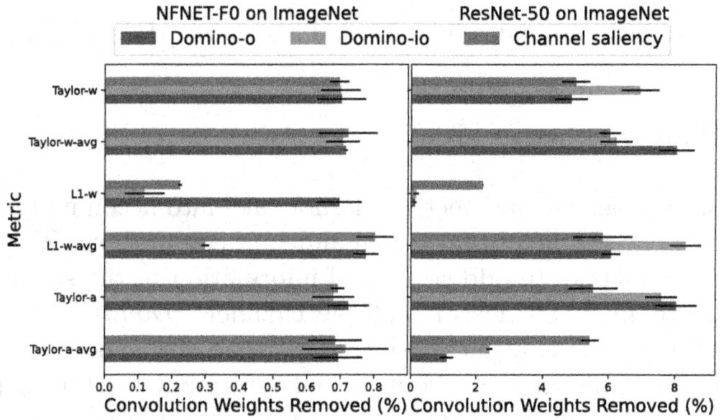

Fig. 7. NFNET-F0 and ResNet-50

6 Related Work

When pruning networks with branch connections, multiple channels are removed to keep the network dense. However, most channel pruning approaches use the same saliency metric [24,25] as for simple forward feed networks. These saliency metrics do not factor in the other output channels that need to be removed when one channel is removed. Some pruning approaches that are based on feature-map reconstruction [14,22] explicitly describe how branches are taken in account. He et al. [14] and Thinet [22] remove output channels by considering the effect on the next layer's input feature map. For the ResNet architecture, He et al. [14] consider the input feature map after the skip connection. ThiNet [22] avoid pruning layers that could result in mismatching number of feature maps in the network. Feature maps reconstruction-based approaches are computationally expensive. They are poor candidates for elaborate pruning schemes [12,13,34] that rely on computationally cost effective saliency metrics.

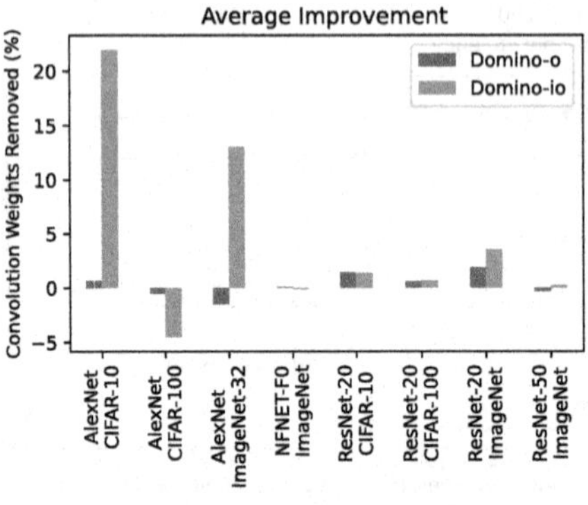

(a) Average improvement.

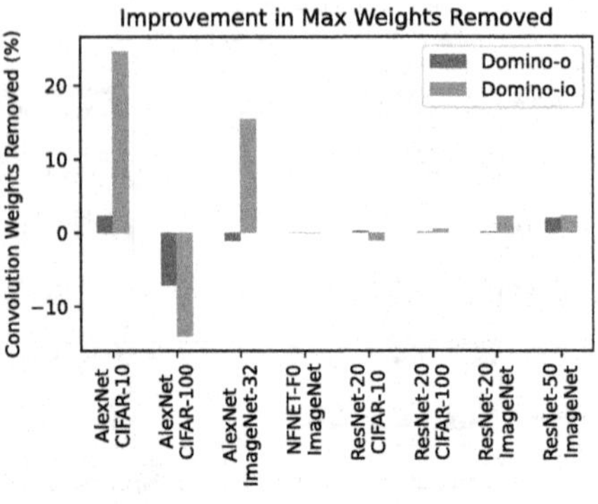

(b) Improvement in maximum weights removed.

Fig. 8. The improvement of domino saliency metrics over the base channel metric.

7 Conclusion

Most popular channel saliency metrics do not take into account structural constraints that can arise when pruning join and split connections. We propose two Domino saliency metrics to add structural information to the saliency measure by combining channel saliency of multiple channels. $Domino - o$ adds information about the other output feature maps that are removed together and $Domino - io$ adds information about output and input feature maps that are removed together. We observe a small improvement when using $Domino - o$ over the baseline channel saliency metric and a significant improvement when using $Domino - io$. $Domino - io$ can be use to improve the pruning rates by 25% and 15% for AlexNet on CIFAR-10 and ImageNet-32. In conclusion, the use of $Domino - io$ can significantly improve pruning rates for networks with join/split connections. This suggests that, in addition to output feature maps or weights, information about input feature maps or weights is relevant for pruning.

References

1. Brock, A., De, S., Smith, S.L., Simonyan, K.: High-performance large-scale image recognition without normalization. CoRR abs/2102.06171 (2021). https://arxiv.org/abs/2102.06171
2. Chrabaszcz, P., Loshchilov, I., Hutter, F.: A downsampled variant of ImageNet as an alternative to the CIFAR datasets. CoRR abs/1707.08819 (2017). http://arxiv.org/abs/1707.08819
3. Deng, J., Dong, W., Socher, R., Li, L.J., Li, K., Li, F.F.: ImageNet: a large-scale hierarchical image database. In: Proceedings of IEEE Conference on Computer Vision and Pattern Recognition (CVPR 2009), 20–25 June 2009, Miami, Florida, USA, pp. 248–255 (2009). https://doi.org/10.1109/CVPR.2009.5206848

4. Ding, X., Ding, G., Zhou, X., Guo, Y., Han, J., Liu, J.: Global sparse momentum SGD for pruning very deep neural networks. In: Proceedings of Conference on Neural Information Processing Systems (NeurIPS 2019), Vancouver, BC, Canada, 8–14 December 2019, pp. 6379–6391 (2019). http://papers.nips.cc/paper/8867-global-sparse-momentum-sgd-for-pruning-very-deep-neural-networks
5. Dong, X., Huang, J., Yang, Y., Yan, S.: More is less: a more complicated network with less inference complexity. In: Proceedings of IEEE Conference on Computer Vision and Pattern Recognition (CVPR 2017), Honolulu, HI, USA, 21–26 July 2017, pp. 1895–1903 (2017). https://doi.org/10.1109/CVPR.2017.205
6. Frankle, J., Carbin, M.: The lottery ticket hypothesis: finding sparse, trainable neural networks. In: Proceedings of International Conference on Learning Representations (ICLR 2019), New Orleans, LA, USA, 6–9 May 2019 (2019). https://openreview.net/forum?id=rJl-b3RcF7
7. Guo, Y., Yao, A., Chen, Y.: Dynamic network surgery for efficient DNNs. In: Proceedings of Conference on Neural Information Processing Systems (NeurIPS 2016), Barcelona, Spain, 5–10 December 2016, pp. 1379–1387 (2016). http://papers.nips.cc/paper/6165-dynamic-network-surgery-for-efficient-dnns
8. Han, S., et al.: DSD: dense-sparse-dense training for deep neural networks. In: Proceedings of International Conference on Learning Representations (ICLR 2017), Toulon, France, 24–26 April 2017 (2017). https://openreview.net/forum?id=HyoST_9xl
9. Han, S., Pool, J., Tran, J., Dally, W.J.: Learning both weights and connections for efficient neural network. In: Proceedings of Conference on Neural Information Processing Systems (NeurIPS 2015), Montreal, Quebec, Canada, 7–12 December 2015, pp. 1135–1143 (2015). http://papers.nips.cc/paper/5784-learning-both-weights-and-connections-for-efficient-neural-network
10. Hassibi, B., Stork, D.G.: Second order derivatives for network pruning: optimal brain surgeon. In: Proceedings of Conference on Neural Information Processing Systems (NeurIPS 1992), Denver, Colorado, USA, 30 November–3 December 1992, pp. 164–171 (1992). http://papers.nips.cc/paper/647-second-order-derivatives-for-network-pruning-optimal-brain-surgeon
11. He, K., Zhang, X., Ren, S., Sun, J.: Deep residual learning for image recognition. In: Proc. IEEE Conference on Computer Vision and Pattern Recognition (CVPR 2016), Las Vegas, NV, USA, 27–30 June 2016, pp. 770–778 (2016). https://doi.org/10.1109/CVPR.2016.90
12. He, Y., Kang, G., Dong, X., Fu, Y., Yang, Y.: Soft filter pruning for accelerating deep convolutional neural networks. In: Proceedings of International Joint Conference on Artificial Intelligence (IJCAI 2018), Stockholm, Sweden, 13–19 July 2018, pp. 2234–2240 (2018). https://doi.org/10.24963/ijcai.2018/309
13. He, Y., Lin, J., Liu, Z., Wang, H., Li, L.-J., Han, S.: AMC: AutoML for model compression and acceleration on mobile devices. In: Ferrari, V., Hebert, M., Sminchisescu, C., Weiss, Y. (eds.) ECCV 2018. LNCS, vol. 11211, pp. 815–832. Springer, Cham (2018). https://doi.org/10.1007/978-3-030-01234-2_48
14. He, Y., Zhang, X., Sun, J.: Channel pruning for accelerating very deep neural networks. In: Proceedings of International Conference on Computer Vision (ICCV 2017), Venice, Italy, 22–29 October 2017, pp. 1398–1406 (2017). https://doi.org/10.1109/ICCV.2017.155
15. Krizhevsky, A.: Learning multiple layers of features from tiny images (2009). https://www.cs.toronto.edu/~kriz/cifar.html

16. Krizhevsky, A., Sutskever, I., Hinton, G.E.: ImageNet classification with deep convolutional neural networks. Commun. ACM **60**(6), 84–90 (2017). https://doi.org/10.1145/3065386, https://doi.acm.org/10.1145/3065386
17. Lebedev, V., Lempitsky, V.S.: Fast convnets using group-wise brain damage. In: Proceedings of IEEE Conference on Computer Vision and Pattern Recognition (CVPR 2016), Las Vegas, NV, USA, 27–30 June 2016, pp. 2554–2564 (2016). https://doi.org/10.1109/CVPR.2016.280
18. Lecun, Y., Bottou, L., Bengio, Y., Haffner, P.: Gradient-based learning applied to document recognition, vol. 86, pp. 2278–2324. IEEE (1998). https://doi.org/10.1109/5.726791
19. LeCun, Y., Denker, J.S., Solla, S.A.: Optimal brain damage. In: Proceedings of Conference on Neural Information Processing Systems (NeurIPS 1989), Denver, Colorado, USA, 27–30 November 1989, pp. 598–605 (1989). http://papers.nips.cc/paper/250-optimal-brain-damage
20. Li, H., Kadav, A., Durdanovic, I., Samet, H., Graf, H.P.: Pruning filters for efficient convnets. In: Proceedings of International Conference on Learning Representations (ICLR 2017), Toulon, France, 24–26 April 2017 (2017). https://openreview.net/forum?id=rJqFGTslg
21. Luo, J., Wu, J., Lin, W.: ThiNet: a filter level pruning method for deep neural network compression. In: Proceedings of International Conference on Computer Vision (ICCV 2017), Venice, Italy, 22–29 October 2017, pp. 5068–5076 (2017). https://doi.org/10.1109/ICCV.2017.541
22. Luo, J.H., Zhang, H., Zhou, H.Y., Xie, C.W., Wu, J., Lin, W.: ThiNet: pruning CNN filters for a thinner net. IEEE Trans. Pattern Anal. Mach. Intell. **41**(10), 2525–2538 (2019). https://doi.org/10.1109/TPAMI.2018.2858232
23. Mahajan, D., et al.: Exploring the limits of weakly supervised pretraining. In: Ferrari, V., Hebert, M., Sminchisescu, C., Weiss, Y. (eds.) ECCV 2018. LNCS, vol. 11206, pp. 185–201. Springer, Cham (2018). https://doi.org/10.1007/978-3-030-01216-8_12
24. Mao, H., et al.: Exploring the granularity of sparsity in convolutional neural networks. In: Proceedings of IEEE Conference on Computer Vision and Pattern Recognition (CVPR 2017), Honolulu, HI, USA, 21–26 July 2017, pp. 1927–1934 (2017). https://doi.org/10.1109/CVPRW.2017.241
25. Molchanov, P., Mallya, A., Tyree, S., Frosio, I., Kautz, J.: Importance estimation for neural network pruning. In: Proceedings of IEEE Conference on Computer Vision and Pattern Recognition (CVPR 2019), Long Beach, CA, USA, 16–20 June 2019, pp. 11264–11272 (2019). https://doi.org/10.1109/CVPR.2019.01152, http://openaccess.thecvf.com/content_CVPR_2019/html/Molchanov_Importance_Estimation_for_Neural_Network_Pruning_CVPR_2019_paper.html
26. Molchanov, P., Tyree, S., Karras, T., Aila, T., Kautz, J.: Pruning convolutional neural networks for resource efficient inference. In: Proceedings of International Conference on Learning Representations (ICLR 2017), Toulon, France, 24–26 April 2017 (2017). https://openreview.net/forum?id=SJGCiw5gl
27. Mozer, M., Smolensky, P.: Skeletonization: a technique for trimming the fat from a network via relevance assessment. In: 1988 Proceedings of Conference on Neural Information Processing Systems (NeurIPS), Denver, Colorado, USA, pp. 107–115 (1988). http://papers.nips.cc/paper/119-skeletonization-a-technique-for-trimming-the-fat-from-a-network-via-relevance-assessment

28. Peng, H., Wu, J., Chen, S., Huang, J.: Collaborative channel pruning for deep networks. In: Proceedings of International Conference on Machine Learning (ICML 2019), Long Beach, California, USA, 9–15 June 2019. Proceedings of Machine Learning Research, vol. 97, pp. 5113–5122 (2019). http://proceedings.mlr.press/v97/peng19c.html
29. Persand, K., Anderson, A., Gregg, D.: Taxonomy of saliency metrics for channel pruning. IEEE Access **9**, 120110–120126 (2021). https://doi.org/10.1109/ACCESS.2021.3108545
30. Simon, M., Rodner, E., Denzler, J.: ImageNet pre-trained models with batch normalization. CoRR abs/1612.01452 (2016). http://arxiv.org/abs/1612.01452
31. Taigman, Y., Yang, M., Ranzato, M., Wolf, L.: DeepFace: closing the gap to human-level performance in face verification. In: Proceedings of IEEE Conference on Computer Vision and Pattern Recognition (CVPR 2014), Columbus, OH, USA, 23–28 June 2014, pp. 1701–1708 (2014). https://doi.org/10.1109/CVPR.2014.220
32. Touvron, H., Vedaldi, A., Douze, M., Jégou, H.: Fixing the train-test resolution discrepancy. In: Proceedings of Conference on Neural Information Processing Systems (NeurIPS 2019), Vancouver, BC, Canada, 8–14 December 2019, pp. 8250–8260 (2019). https://proceedings.neurips.cc/paper/2019/hash/d03a857a23b5285736c4d55e0bb067c8-Abstract.html
33. Wang, H., Zhang, Q., Wang, Y., Hu, H.: Structured probabilistic pruning for convolutional neural network acceleration. In: Proceedings of British Machine Vision Conference (BMVC 2018), Newcastle, UK, 3–6 September 2018, p. 149 (2018). http://bmvc2018.org/contents/papers/0870.pdf
34. Wang, Z., Li, F., Shi, G., Xie, X., Wang, F.: Network pruning using sparse learning and genetic algorithm. Neurocomputing **404**, 247–256 (2020). https://doi.org/10.1016/j.neucom.2020.03.082
35. Xie, S., Girshick, R.B., Dollár, P., Tu, Z., He, K.: Aggregated residual transformations for deep neural networks. CoRR abs/1611.05431 (2016). http://arxiv.org/abs/1611.05431
36. Zhang, H., et al.: ResNeSt: split-attention networks. CoRR abs/2004.08955 (2020). https://arxiv.org/abs/2004.08955

Learned Sorted Table Search and Static Indexes in Small Model Space

Domenico Amato, Giosué Lo Bosco(✉), and Raffaele Giancarlo

Dipartimento di Matematica e Informatica, Universitá degli Studi di Palermo, Palermo, Italy
giosue.lobosco@unipa.it

Abstract. Machine Learning Techniques, properly combined with Data Structures, have resulted in Learned Static Indexes, innovative and powerful tools that speed-up Binary Search, with the use of additional space with respect to the table being searched into. Such space is devoted to the ML model. Although in their infancy, they are methodologically and practically important, due to the pervasiveness of Sorted Table Search procedures. In modern applications, model space is a key factor and, in fact, a major open question concerning this area is to assess to what extent one can enjoy the speed-up of Learned Indexes while using constant or nearly constant space models. We address it here by (a) introducing two new models, i.e., denoted **KO-BFS** and **SY-RMI**, respectively; (b) by systematically exploring, for the first time, the time-space trade-offs of a hierarchy of existing models, i.e., the ones in **SOSD**, together with the new ones. We document a novel and rather complex time-space trade-off picture, which is very informative for users. We experimentally show that the **KO-BFS** can speed-up Interpolation Search and Uniform Binary Search in constant space. For other versions of Binary Search, our second model, together with the bi-criteria **PGM** index, can achieve a speed-up with a model space of 0.05% more than the one taken by the table, being competitive in terms of time-space trade-off with existing proposals. The **SY-RMI** and the bi-criteria **PGM** complement each other quite well across the various levels of the internal memory hierarchy. Finally, our findings are of interest to designers, since they highlight the need of further studies regarding the time-space relation in Learned Indexes.

1 Introduction

With the aim of obtaining time/space improvements in classic Data Structures, an emerging trend is to combine Machine Learning techniques with the ones

This research is funded in part by MIUR Project of National Relevance 2017WR7SHH "Multicriteria Data Structures and Algorithms: from compressed to learned indexes, and beyond". We also acknowledge an NVIDIA Higher Education and Research Grant (donation of a Titan V GPU). Additional support to RG has been granted by INdAM - GNCS Project 2020 "Algorithms, Methods and Software Tools for Knowledge Discovery in the Context of Precision Medicine".

S. Bandini et al. (Eds.): AIxIA 2021, LNAI 13196, pp. 462–477, 2022.
https://doi.org/10.1007/978-3-031-08421-8_32

proper of Data Structures. This new area goes under the name of Learned Data Structures. It was initiated by [15], it has grown very rapidly [8] and now it has been extended to include also Learned Algorithms [20], while the number of Learned Data Structures grows [4]. In particular, the theme common to those new approaches to Data Structures Design and Engineering is that a query to a data structure is either intermixed with or preceded by a query to a Classifier [6] or a Regression Model [10], those two being the learned part of the data structure. Learned Bloom Filters [15,19] are an example of the first type, while Learned Indexes are examples of the second one [8,15]. Those latter are also the object of this research.

1.1 Learned Searching in Sorted Sets

With reference to Fig. 1, a generic paradigm for learned searching in sorted sets consists of a model, trained over the data in a sorted table. As described in Sect. 3.2, such a model may be as simple as a straight line or more complex, with a tree-like structure. It is used to make a prediction regarding where a query element may be in the sorted table. Then, the search is limited to the interval so identified and, for the sake of exposition, performed via Binary Search.

All of the available current contributions to this area have provided Learned Indexes, i.e., models more complex than straight lines and that occupy space in addition to the one taken by table. Such a space occupancy cannot be considered a constant, since it depends on various parameters characterizing the model.

But the use of more space to speed-up Binary Search in important Data Base tasks is not new, e.g., [22]. Consider the mapping of elements in the table to their relative position within the table. Since such a function is reminiscent the of Cumulative Ditribution Function over the universe U of elements from which the ones in the table are drawn, as pointed out by Markus et al. [17], we refer to it as CDF. Now, for the same speed-up task, the fact that one can derive a CDF from the table and approximate that curve via a regression line to make a prediction is not new, e.g., [3].

It is quite remarkable then that the novel model proposals, sustaining Learned Indexes, are quite effective at speeding up Binary Search at an unprecedented scale and be competitive with respect to even more complex indexing structures, i.e., B^+**-Tree** [5]. Indeed, a recent benchmarking study [17] (see also [12]) shows quite well how competitive those Learned Data Structures are, in addition to providing an entire experimental environment designed to be useful for the consistent evaluation of current Learned Indexes proposals and hopefully future ones. Another, more recent, study offers an in-depth analysis of Learned Indexes and provides recommendations on when to use them as opposed to other data structures [16]. Relevant for the research presented here are the Recursive Model Index paradigm (**RMI**, for short) [15], the Radix-Spline index (**RS**, for short) [13], and the Piecewise Geometric Model index (**PGM**, for short) [7,9]. For the convenience of the reader, they are briefly described in Sect. 3.2.

As already mentioned, all those models use non-constant additional space with respect to the original table. In fact, experimental studies show a time-space trade-off, which has not been investigated consistently and coherently with respect to the time-honored methodology coming from Classic Data Structures [14]. Moreover, it is missing an assessment of how good would be constant space models at speeding-up classic Sorted Table Search Procedures, i.e., Binary, Interpolation Search and their variants.

Indeed, two related fundamental questions have been overlooked. The first consists of assessing to what extend one can enjoy the speed-up of Binary Search provided by Learned Indexes with respect to the additional space one needs to use. The second consists of assessing how space-demanding should be a predictive model in order to speed-up Sorted Table Search Procedures, In particular, a constant space model would yield Learned Sorted Table Search Procedures, rather than indexes: a point of methodological importance and that has been overlooked so far. Indeed, answer to this question would put the Learned Searching in Sorted Sets Methodology at a par with respect to the classic purely Algorithmic Methodology: first, constant space algorithms and then more space demanding data structures, such as Search Trees (see [14]).

1.2 Our Contributions

To shed light on the posed related questions, we systematically analyse a hierarchy of representative models, without the pretence to be exhaustive. They range from very simple ones to State of the Art ones. We consider two scenarios. The simple one, which can be referred to as "textbook code", that uses nearly standard implementations of search methods and models. The second, much more advanced, uses the Learned Indexing methods and the highly tuned software supporting their execution, i.e. **CDFShop** [18] and Search on Sorted Data (**SOSD** for short) [17] (see also [12]). For our experimental evaluation, we generalize the one adopted in the benchmarking study, by extending the sizes of the datasets to fit in all the internal memory levels (see Sect. 3.4). Other than that, we adhere completely to the mentioned study.

Our findings, outlined in Sects. 4, 5 and 6, and in full in [2], reveal a rather complex scenario, in which it is possible to obtain speed-ups of Sorted Table Search procedures via Learned procedures that use small space, but the achievement of such a methodologically and practically important result is not so immediate from the State of the Art. Indeed, we need to introduce two new models.

- the **KO-BFS**, which is a constant space model and that can be used, in the simple scenario, to consistently speed-up Interpolation Search and Uniform Binary Search [14], this latter also referred to as branch-free Binary Search [11].
- The **SY-RMI**, which is a parametric space model that succinctly represents a set of models in the **RMI** family. In the second scenario, with as little as 0.05% additional space, it can speed-up branchy Binary Search, Eyzinger layout Binary Search [11] and be competitive in query time with respect to more space demanding Learned Indexes instances.

Finally, as a whole, our investigation systematically highlights, for the first time, the time-space trade-offs involved in the use of Learned Searching in Sorted Data, including indexes, which can be of use to users and stimulating for designers. Indeed, our findings call for further study of the time-space relation of Learned Indexes. In order to make our results replicable, we provide datasets and software used for this research in [1], in addition to the already available **CDFShop** and **SOSD**.

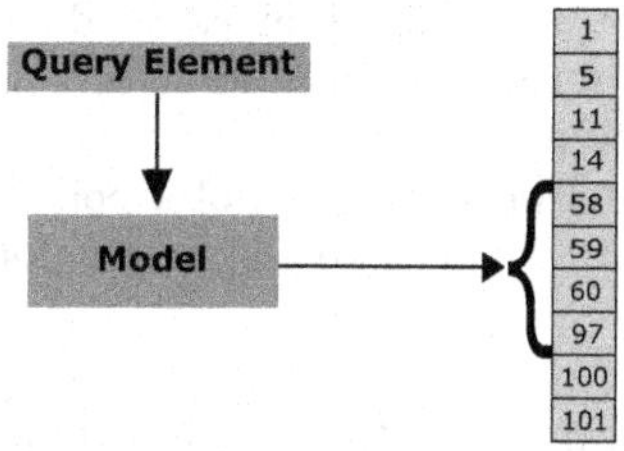

Fig. 1. A general paradigm of Learned Searching in a Sorted Set [17]. The model is trained on the data in the table. Then, given a query element, it is used to predict the interval in the table where to search (included in brackets in the figure).

2 A Simple View of Learned Searching in Sorted Sets

Consider a sorted table A of n keys, taken from a universe U. It is well known that Sorted Table Search can be phrased as the Predecessor Search Problem: for a given query element x, return the $A[j]$ such that $A[j] \leq x < A[j+1]$. Kraska et al. [15] have proposed an approach that transforms such a problem into a learning-prediction one. With reference to Fig. 1, the model learned from the data is used as a predictor of where a query element may be in the table. To fix ideas, Binary Search is then performed only on the interval returned by the model.

We now outline the basic technique that one can use to build a model for A. It relies on Linear Regression, with Mean Square Error Minimization [10]. With reference to the example in Fig. 2, and assuming that one wants a linear model, i.e., $F(x) = ax + b$, Kraska et al. note that they can fit a straight line to the CDF and then use it to predict where a point x may fall in terms of rank and accounting also for approximation errors. More in general, in order to perform a query, the model is consulted and an interval in which to search for is returned. Then, to fix ideas, Binary Search on that interval is performed. Different models may use different schemes to determine the required range, as outlined in Sect. 3.2. The reader interested in a rigorous presentation of those ideas can consult Markus et al.

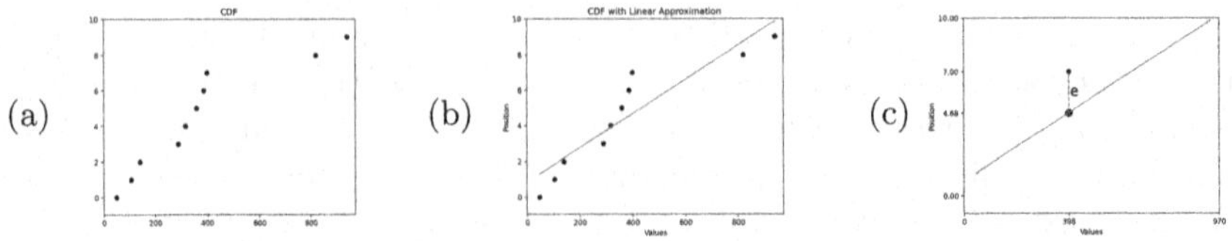

Fig. 2. The process of learning a simple model via linear regression. Let A be $[47, 105, 140, 289, 316, 358, 386, 398, 819, 939]$. (a) The CDF of A. In the diagram, the abscissa indicates the value of an element in the table, while the ordinate is its rank. (b) The straight line $F(x) = ax + b$ is obtained by determining a and b via Linear Regression, with Mean Square Error Minimization. (c) The maximum error ϵ one can incur in using F is also important. In this case, it is $\epsilon = 3$, i.e., accounting for rounding, it is the maximum distance between the rank of a point in the table and its rank as predicted by F. In this case, the interval to search into, for a given query element x, is given by $[F(x) - \epsilon, F(x) + \epsilon]$.

For this research, it is important to know how much of the table is discarded once the model makes a prediction on a query element. For instance, Binary Search, after the first test, discards 50% of the table. Because of the diversity across models to determine the search interval, and in order to place all models on a par, we estimate the reduction factor of a model, i.e., the percentage of the table that is no longer considered for searching after a prediction, empirically. That is, with the use of the model and over a batch of queries, we determine the length of the interval to search into for each query. Based on it, it is immediate to compute the reduction factor for that query. Then, we take the average of those reduction factors over the entire set of queries as the reduction factor of the model for the given table.

3 Experimental Methodology

Our experimental set-up follows closely the one outlined in the already mentioned benchmarking study by Marcus et al. regarding Learned Indexes, with some variations. Namely, in agreement with the main intent of our study, we concentrate on Sorted Table Search methods that use $O(1)$ additional space with respect to the table size. We also include the three Learned Indexes that have been extensively benchmarked in [17], in order to possibly derive versions of them that use only a fraction of additional space, granting better query times with respect to the basic Sorted Table Search procedures query times. Moreover, since an additional intent of this study is to gain deeper insights regarding the circumstances in which Learned versions of the Sorted Table Search procedure and Indexes are profitable, as a function of the main memory hierarchy and in small space, we derive our own benchmark datasets from the ones in [17].

3.1 Sorted Table Search and Classic Indexes

For this research, we use the methods and relative implementations listed and outlined below (additional technical details, as well as more literature references, are provided in [2]). The setting we consider is static, i.e., the sorted table is not modified during its lifetime.

- **Binary Search.** In addition to a standard Binary Search method, we use the best ones that come out of the work by Khuong and Morin [11] and by Shutz et al. [23]. As for terminology, we follow the one in [11]. Indeed, we refer to standard Binary Search as Branchy Binary Search (**BBS**, for short). Moreover, we refer to Uniform Binary Search [14] and its homologous routines as branch-free. Those routines differentiate themselves from the standard one because there is no test for exit within the main loop and the remaining test is transformed into a conditional move at compile time (see [11] for details). We also include in this research, a branch-free version of Binary Search (**BFS**, for short), the branch-free Eytzinger layout (**BFE**, for short) from the study in [11], branch-free k-ary search (**K-BFS**, for short) and its branchy version (**K-BBS**, for short). We use k in $[3, 20]$, although the recommendation in that study is to use $k = 3$.
- **Interpolation Search.** As a baseline of this method, introduced by Peterson [21], we use our own textbook implementation (denoted **IBS**, for short) and **TIP** by VanSandt et al. [24]. However, we do not report results regarding this procedure due to its poor performance.
- **Classic Indexes:B-Trees** [5], in particular B^+**-Tree** [15].

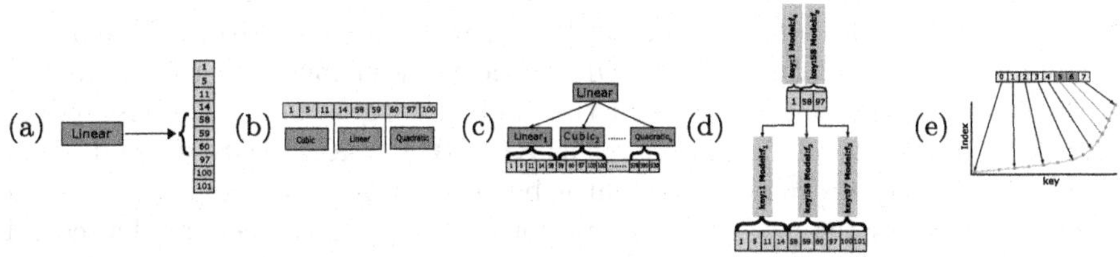

Fig. 3. Examples of various Learned Indexes (see also [17]). (a) an Atomic Model, where the box linear means that the CDF of the entire dataset is estimated by a linear function via Regression, as exemplified in Fig. 2. (b) An example of a **KO-BFS**, with $k = 3$. The top part divides the table into three segments and it is used to determine the model to pick at the second stage. Each box indicates which Atomic Model is used for prediction on the relevant portion of the table. (c) An example of an **RMI** with two layers and branching factor equal to b. The top box indicates that the lower models are selected via a linear function. As for the leaf boxes, each indicates which Atomic Model is used for prediction on the relevant portion of the table. (d) An example of a **PGM** Index. At the bottom, the table is divided into three parts. A new table is so constructed and the process is iterated. (e) An example of an **RS** Index. At the top, the buckets where elements fall, based on their three most significant digits. At the bottom, a linear spline approximating the CDF of the data, with suitably chosen spline points. Each bucket points to a spline point so that, if a query element falls in a bucket (say six), the search interval is limited by the spline points pointed to by that bucket and the one preceding it (five in our case).

3.2 Model Classes Characterizing Model Space

With the exception of the ones operating on table layouts different than sorted and the **B-Trees**, all procedures mentioned in Sect. 3.1 have a natural Learned version. For each, its time and space performances depend critically on the model used to predict the interval to search into. Here we consider four classes of models. The first two classes consist of models that use constant space, while the other two consist of models that use space as a function of some model parameters. For each of those models, the reduction factor is determined as described in Sect. 2. Moreover, as already pointed out, the **KO-BFS** and the **SY-RMI** models are new and fit quite naturally in the hierarchy that we present.

Atomic Models: One Level and no Branching Factor

- **Simple Regression** [10]. We use linear, quadratic and cubic regression models. Each can be thought of as an atomic model in the sense that it cannot be divided into "sub-models". Figure 3(a) provides an example. In particular, The corresponding learned methods are prefixed by **L, Q,** or **C**. That is, **L-BFS** denotes the branch-free version of branch-free Binary Search with a linear model to restrict the search interval.

A Two-Level Hybrid Model, with Constant Branching Factor

- **A Natural Generalization of K-BFS and K-BBS.** This model partitions the table into a fixed number of segments. For each, Atomic Models are computed to approximate the CDF of the table elements in that segment. Finally, we assign to each segment the model that guarantees the best reduction factor. We denote such a model as **KO-BFS** or **KO-BBS**, depending on the base Binary Search routine that is being used. An example is provided in Fig. 3(b). As for the prediction, we perform a sequential search for the second level segment to pick and use the corresponding model for the prediction, followed by Binary Search. The number of segments is independent of the input and bounded by a small constant, i.e., at most 20 in this study.

Two-Level RMIs with Parametric Branching Factor

- **Heuristically Optimized RMIs.** Informally, an **RMI** is a multi-level, directed graph, with Atomic Models at its nodes. When searching for a given key and starting with the first level, a prediction at each level identifies the model of the next level to use for the next prediction. This process continues until a final level model is reached. This latter is used to predict the interval to search into. As pointed out in the benchmarking study, in most applications, a generic **RMI** with two layers, a tree-like structure and a branching factor b suffices. An example is provided in Fig. 3(c). It is to be noted that Atomic Models are **RMIs**. Moreover, the difference between **KO-BFS** and **RMIs** is that the first level in the former partitions the table, while that same level in the latter partitions the Universe of the elements. Following the benchmarking study, we use two-layers **RMIs** and verbatim the optimization software provided in **CDFShop** to obtain up to ten versions of the generic model, for a given table. That is, for each model, the optimization software picks an appropriate branching factor and the type of regression to use within each part of the model, those latter quantities being the parameters that control the precision of the prediction as well as its space occupancy. It is also to be remarked, as pointed out in [18], that the optimization process provides only approximations to the real optimum and it is heuristic in nature, with no theoretic approximation performance guarantees. The problem of finding an optimal model in polynomial time is open.

- **Synoptic RMI.** For a given set of tables of approximately the same size, we use **CDFShop** as above to obtain a set of models (at most 10 for each table). For the entire set of models so obtained and each model in it, we compute the ratio (branching factor)/(model space) and we take the median of those ratios as a measure of branching factor *per unit* of model space, denoted UB. Among the **RMIs** returned by **CDFShop**, we pick the relative majority winner, i.e., the one that provides the best query time, averaged over a set of simulations. When one uses such a model on tables of approximately the same size as the ones used as input to **CDFShop**, we set the branching factor to be a multiple of UB, that depends on how much space the model is expected to use relative to the input table size. Since this model can be intuitively considered as the one that best summarizes the output of **CDFShop** in terms of query time, for the given set of tables, we refer to it as *synoptic* and denote it as **SY-RMI**.

CDF Approximation-Controlled Models

- **PGM** [9]. It is also a multi-stage model, built bottom-up and queried top down. It uses a user-defined approximation parameter ϵ, that controls the prediction error at each stage. With reference to Fig. 3(d), the table is subdivided into three pieces. A prediction in each piece can be done via a linear model guaranteeing an error of ϵ. A new table is formed by selecting the minimum values in each of the three pieces. This new table is possibly again partitioned into pieces, in which a linear model can make a prediction within the given error. The process is iterated until only one linear model suffices, as in the case in the Figure. A query is processed via a series of predictions, starting at the root of the tree. Also in this case, for a given table, we have built models, i.e., ten, as prescribed in the benchmarking study and with the use of the parameters, software and methods provided there, i.e., **SOSD**. It is to be noted that the **PGM** index, in its bi-criteria version, is able to return the best query time index, within a given amount of space the model is supposed to use. We refer to this version of **PGM** as **PGM_M**.
- **RS** [13]. It is a two-stage model. It also uses a user-defined approximation parameter ϵ. With reference to Fig. 3(e), a spline curve approximating the

CDF of the data is built. Then, the radix table is used to identify spline points to use to refine the search interval. Also in this case, we have performed the training as described in the benchmarking study.

In what follows, for ease of reference, we refer to the models in the first two classes as constant space models, while to the ones in the remaining classes as parametric space models.

3.3 Hardware

All the experiments have been performed on a workstation equipped with an Intel Core i7-8700 3.2 GHz CPU with three levels of cache memory: (a) 64 kb of L1 cache; (b) 256 kb of L2 cache; (c) 12 Mb of shared L3 cache. The total amount of system memory is 32 Gbyte of DDR4. The operating system is Ubuntu LTS 20.04.

3.4 Datasets

We use the same real datasets of the benchmarking study. In particular, we restrict attention to integers only, each represented with 64 bits unless otherwise specified. For the convenience of the reader, a list of those datasets, with an outline of their content, is provided next.

- **amzn:** book popularity data from Amazon. Each key represents the popularity of a particular book. We have two versions of this dataset, one where each item is represented with 64 and another with 32 bits, respectively.
- **face:** randomly sampled Facebook user IDs. Each key uniquely identifies a user.
- **osm:** cell IDs from Open Street Map. Each key represents an embedded location.
- **wiki:** timestamps of edits from Wikipedia. Each key represents the time an edit was committed.

Moreover, we adapt those datasets for our research, as follows. Starting from them, we produce sorted tables of varying sizes and that preserve the CDF of the original dataset, so that each fits in a level of the internal memory hierarchy. Our choice provides a wider spectrum of experimentation with respect to the one provided in all of the Learned Indexes studies, including the benchmarking one. Given the four level memory hierarchy, each table is referred to with the suffix of that level, i.e. **amzn-L1** refers to the **L1** level cache. As for query dataset generation, for each of the tables built as described above, we extract uniformly and at random (with replacement) one million elements.

4 Learning the CDF of a Sorted Table and Mining SODS Output for the Synoptic RMI: Outline of Experiments and Findings

Models need to learn the CDF function of the table to be searched into. Regarding this point, the full set of experiments, across tables, memory levels and models, are reported in full in Section 4 of the main manuscript [2]. Due to space constraints, here we limit ourselves to report only the time required to obtain the synoptic **RMI** from the output of **CDFShop** (see Fig. 4). Such a construction is performed as described in Sect. 3.2. The simulation to identify the relative majority **RMIs** is performed on query datasets extracted as described in the previous section, but using only 1% of the number of query elements specified there.

A full discussion of our experiments is available in Section 4 of the main manuscript [2]. Here we limit ourselves to report that the construction of the **SY-RMI** is in line with the **CDFShop** training and therefore can be profitably used as a post-processor to it. Moreover, regarding the Learning time of the **RS** and **PGM** indexes, they can be both built in one pass, which is important for Database applications [13]. According to the study just mentioned and results in [17], the **RS** is faster to build than the **PGM** index for tables fitting in main memory. Our experiments show that the **PGM** is faster to build for tables fitting each level of the cache. This is an important addition to the current State of the Art.

5 Constant Space Models: Outline of Query Experiments

This is the elementary scenario, in which we use nearly standard textbook code. In particular, the models considered in this section use constant space. The full set of experiments regarding the procedures described in Sects. 3.1 and 3.2 (constant space models) have been performed on all tables considered for this research and reported in Sect. 5 of the main manuscript [2], where a detailed discussion is also present. Among all the figures documenting our query experiments, here we provide only one representative case, i.e., Fig. 5.

The learned versions of Interpolation Search, together with the variants considered here, can profitably use constant space models to consistently obtain a speed-up with respect to the standard counterparts, across memory levels, and in particular with the simple models based on simple linear regression (see Sect. 2). As for branch-free Uniform Binary Search [11,14] and the corresponding variant of k-ary Search [23], the speed-up can be achieved in constant space with a slightly more complex model, i.e., the **KO-BFS** introduced here (see Sect. 3.2). As for classic branchy Binary Search, speed-up with constant space seems to be problematic with simple regression models.

In summary, Learned Searching in a Sorted Set, with Interpolation Search or Uniform Binary Search, is fully analogous to the classic approach, with benefits in the practical performance of the former over the latter.

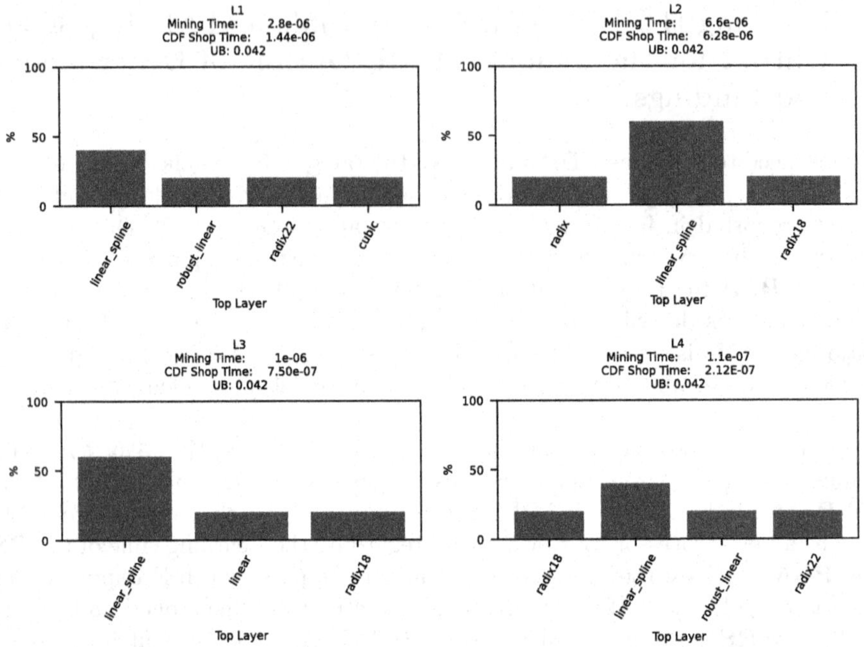

Fig. 4. Time and UB for the identification of SY-RMIs. For each memory level, only the top layer of the various models is indicated in the abscissa, while the ordinate indicates the number of times, in percentage, the given model is the best in terms of query performance on a table. The branching factor per unit of space as well as the time it took to identify the proper **SY-RMI** (average time per element, over all **RMIs** returned by **CDFShop**) are reported on top of each figure. For comparison, we also report the same time for the output of **CDFShop.**

We also consider array layouts other than sorted, a point completely overlooked in the research conducted in Learned Indexes. Quite surprisingly, our experiments show that none of the constant space models used in this research is able to "beat" Binary Search with an Eytzinger layout [11]. This finding has important methodological implications: it points out the need to devise Models able to speed up Binary Search with array layouts other than sorted.

6 Parametric Space Models: Outline of Query Experiments

This is the advanced scenario. In particular, the models considered here have a space occupancy that depends on parameters specific to the models. Moreover, all the experiments are supported by a highly effective software environment such as **SOSD**.

The full set of experiments is described in Section 6 of the main manuscript [2]. For the bi-criteria **PGM** and for **SY-RMI**, we have considered three

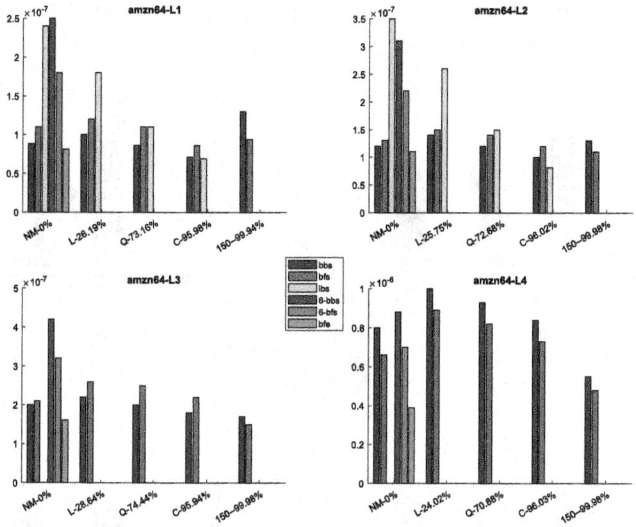

Fig. 5. Query times for the amzn64 dataset on Sorted Table Search procedures. The methods are the ones in the legend (middle of the four panels, the notation is as in the main text and each method has a distinct colour). For each memory level, the abscissa reports methods are grouped by model. From left to right, no model, linear, quadratic, cubic and **KO-**, with $k = 15$, and with **BFS** and **BBS** as search methods. **K-BFS** is reported with $k = 6$. For each model, the reduction factor corresponding to the table is also reported on the abscissa. On the ordinate, it is reported the average query time, in seconds. For memory level **L4**, **IBS**, **L-IBS** and **Q-IBS** have been excluded, since inclusion of their query time values (3.1e−06, 2.1e−06, 1.2e−06, respectively) would make the histograms poorly legible.

space-bound: $0.05\%, 0.7\%, 2\%$. For each percentage, this is the amount of additional space the model can use with respect to the table size. As for the remaining models, including the **PGM**, we use the output of **SODS**. However, we do not consider models that use a percentage of space higher than 10% of each table size. For the remaining models, we report the one with the best query time. Moreover, we take as a baseline the **SOSD** version of **BBS**, which is implemented via vectors rather than arrays (as in the elementary case). All models use that version of **BBS** and, for consistency with the benchmarking study, we use those "branchy" models. For completeness and as a further baseline, we also include our own vector implementation of **BFS**, executed within the **SOSD** software.

The full set of results are reported in Sect. 6 of the main manuscript [2]. For completeness, we report in Fig. 6 the same representative dataset, as for the constant space case. Query times are again averages over one million queries. Moreover, in order to gain a synoptic quantitative evaluation of the relationships among space, query time and prediction accuracy, Table 6 in the Supplementary Material of [2] (omitted here for brevity) reports the average space, query time and reduction factor computed on all experiments performed in this study, normalized with respect to the best query time model coming out of **SOSD**.

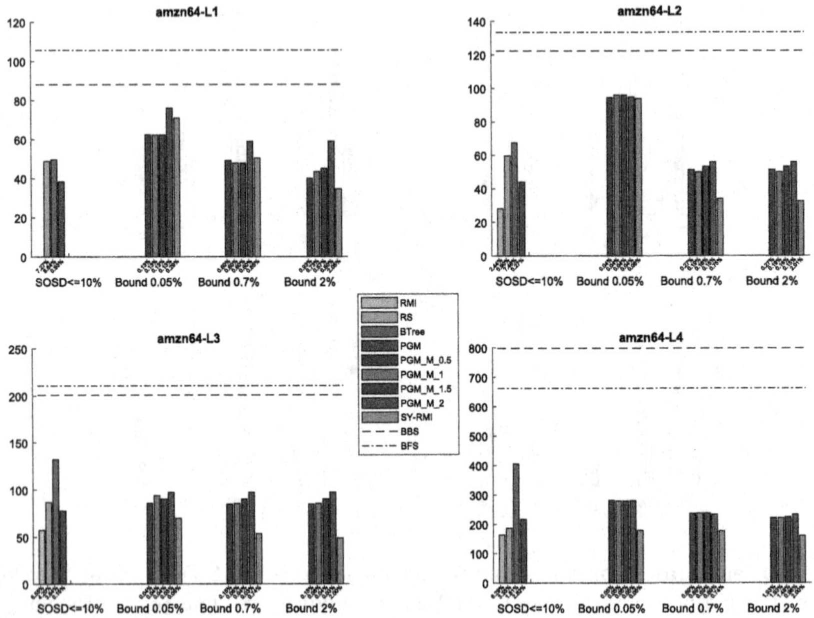

Fig. 6. Query times for the amzn64 dataset on Learned Indexes in Small Space. The methods are the ones in the legend (middle of the four panels, the notation is as in the main text and each method has a distinct color). For each memory level, the abscissa reports methods grouped by space occupancy, as specified in the main text. When no model in a class output by **SOSD** takes at most 10% of additional space, that class is absent. The ordinate reports the average query time, with **BBS** and **BFS** executed in **SOSD** as baseline (horizontal lines).

Our experiments show that both **SY-RMI** and the bi-criteria **PGM** are able to perform better than **BBS** and **BFS** across datasets and memory levels, with very little additional space.

That is, as far those two Binary Search Routines are concerned and within the **SOSD** software environment, one can enjoy the speed of Learned Indexes with very little of a space penalty.

Our study also provides additional useful insights into the relation time-space in Learned Indexes.

- **The Models Provided by SOSD with at Most** 10% **of Additional Space.** Both the **RS** and the **B-tree** are not competitive with respect to the other Learned Indexes. Those latter consistently use less space and time, across datasets and memory levels. As for the **RMIs** coming out of **SOSD**, they are not able to operate in small space at the **L1** memory level. On the other memory levels, they are competitive with respect to **PGM_M** and **SY-RMI**, but seem to require more space compared to them.

- The **PGM_M** and **SY-RMI**. Except for the **L1** memory level, it is possible to obtain models that take space very close to a user-defined bound. The **L1** memory level is an exception since the table size is really small. As for query time, the **PGM_M** performs better on the **L1** and **L4** memory levels, while the **SY-RMI** on the remaining two. This complementarity and good control of space make those two models quite useful in practice.
- **Space, Time, Accuracy of Models.** The benchmarking study provides evidence that a small model with good accuracy may not provide the best query time. Table 6 in the Supplementary Material of [2] provides a more detailed and somewhat more articulate picture. It reports the average space, query time and reduction factor computed on all experiments performed in this study, normalized with respect to the best query time model coming out of **SOSD**. First, it can be observed that, even in small space, it is possible to obtain very good, if not nearly perfect, prediction. However, prediction power is somewhat marginal to assess performance. Indeed, across memory levels, we see a space hierarchy of model configurations. The most striking feature of this hierarchy is that the gain in query time between the best model and the others is within small constant factors, while the difference in space occupancy may be several orders of magnitude. That is, space is the key to efficiency.

7 Conclusions and Future Directions

In this research, we have provided a systematic experimental analysis regarding the ability of Learned Model Indexes to perform better than Binary and Interpolation Search in small space. Although not as simple as it seems, we show that this is indeed possible. However, our results also indicate that there is a big gap between the best performing methods and the others we have considered and that operate in small space. Indeed, the query time performance of the latter with respect to the former is bounded by small constants, while the space usage may differ even by five orders of magnitude. This brings to light the acute need to investigate the existence of "small space" models that should close the time gap mentioned earlier. Another important aspect, with potential practical impact, is to devise models that can work on layouts other than Sorted, i.e., Eytzinger. Finally, given that **BFE** within **SOSD** is consistently faster than **BBS** for datasets fitting in main memory, an investigation of **SOSD** "branchy" models (the actual ones) with respect to "branch-free" new models also deserves to be investigated.

References

1. https://github.com/globosco/A-learned-sorted-table-search-library
2. Amato, D., Lo Bosco, G., Giancarlo, R.: Learned sorted table search and static indexes in small model space. CoRR, abs/2107.09480 (2021)

3. Ao, N., et al.: Efficient parallel lists intersection and index compression algorithms using graphics processing units. Proc. VLDB Endow. **4**(8), 470–481 (2011)
4. Boffa, A., Ferragina, P., Vinciguerra, G.: A "learned" approach to quicken and compress rank/select dictionaries. In: Proceedings of the SIAM Symposium on Algorithm Engineering and Experiments (ALENEX) (2021)
5. Comer, D.: Ubiquitous B-tree. ACM Comput. Surv. (CSUR) **11**(2), 121–137 (1979)
6. Duda, R.O., Hart, P.E., Stork, D.G.: Pattern Classification, 2nd edn. Wiley, Hoboken (2000)
7. Ferragina, P., Lillo, F., Vinciguerra, G.: On the performance of learned data structures. Theoret. Comput. Sci. **871**, 107–120 (2021)
8. Ferragina, P., Vinciguerra, G.: Learned data structures. In: Oneto, L., Navarin, N., Sperduti, A., Anguita, D. (eds.) Recent Trends in Learning From Data. SCI, vol. 896, pp. 5–41. Springer, Cham (2020). https://doi.org/10.1007/978-3-030-43883-8_2
9. Ferragina, P., Vinciguerra, G.: The PGM-index: a fully-dynamic compressed learned index with provable worst-case bounds. PVLDB **13**(8), 1162–1175 (2020)
10. Freedman, D.: Statistical Models: Theory and Practice. Cambridge University Press, Cambridge (2005)
11. Khuong, P.V., Morin, P.: Array layouts for comparison-based searching. J. Exp. Algorithmics **22**, 1.3:1–1.3:39 (2017)
12. Kipf, A., et al.: SOSD: a benchmark for learned indexes. In: ML for Systems at NeurIPS, MLForSystems @ NeurIPS 2019 (2019)
13. Kipf, A., et al.: RadixSpline: a single-pass learned index. In: Proceedings of the Third International Workshop on Exploiting Artificial Intelligence Techniques for Data Management, aiDM 2020, pp. 1–5. Association for Computing Machinery (2020)
14. Knuth, D.E.: The Art of Computer Programming. Sorting and Searching, vol. 3 (1973)
15. Kraska, T., Beutel, A., Chi, E.H., Dean, J., Polyzotis, N.: The case for learned index structures. In: Proceedings of the 2018 International Conference on Management of Data, pp. 489–504. ACM (2018)
16. Maltry, M., Dittrich, J.: A critical analysis of recursive model indexes. CoRR, abs/2106.16166 (2021)
17. Marcus, R., et al.: Benchmarking learned indexes. **14**, 1–13 (2020)
18. Marcus, R., Zhang, E., Kraska, T.: CDFShop: exploring and optimizing learned index structures. In: Proceedings of the 2020 ACM SIGMOD International Conference on Management of Data, SIGMOD 2020, pp. 2789–2792 (2020)
19. Mitzenmacher, M.: A model for learned bloom filters and optimizing by sandwiching. In: Bengio, S., Wallach, H., Larochelle, H., Grauman, K., Cesa-Bianchi, N., Garnett, R. (eds.) Advances in Neural Information Processing Systems, vol. 31. Curran Associates Inc. (2018)
20. Mitzenmacher, M., Vassilvitskii, S.: Algorithms with predictions. CoRR, abs/2006.09123 (2020)
21. Peterson, W.W.: Addressing for random-access storage. IBM J. Res. Dev. **1**(2), 130–146 (1957)
22. Rao, J., Ross, K.A.: Cache conscious indexing for decision-support in main memory. In: Proceedings of the 25th International Conference on Very Large Data Bases, pp. 78–89. Morgan Kaufmann Publishers Inc. (1999)

23. Schulz, L.-C., Broneske, D., Saake, G.: An eight-dimensional systematic evaluation of optimized search algorithms on modern processors. Proc. VLDB Endow. **11**, 1550–1562 (2018)
24. Van Sandt, P., Chronis, Y., Patel, J.M.: Efficiently searching in-memory sorted arrays: revenge of the interpolation search?. In: Proceedings of the 2019 International Conference on Management of Data, SIGMOD 2019, pp. 36–53. ACM, New York (2019)

Siamese Networks with Transfer Learning for Change Detection in Sentinel-2 Images

Giuseppina Andresini[1(✉)], Annalisa Appice[1,2], Domenico Dell'Olio[1], and Donato Malerba[1,2]

[1] Department of Computer Science, University of Bari "Aldo Moro", Bari, Italy
{giuseppina.andresini,annalisa.appice,donato.malerba}@uniba.it, d.dellolio8@studenti.uniba.it
[2] CINI - Consorzio Interuniversitario Nazionale per l'Informatica, Bari, Italy

Abstract. The Earth's surface is constantly changing due to various anthropogenic and natural causes. Leveraging machine learning to monitor land cover changes over time may provide valuable information on the transformation of the Earth's environment. This study focuses on the discovery of land cover changes in bi-temporal, Sentinel-2 images. In particular, we rely on a Siamese network trained with labelled, imagery data of the same Earth's scene acquired with Sentinel-2 at different times. Subsequently, we adopt a transfer learning strategy to adapt the Siamese network to Sentinel-2 data acquired in any new unlabeled scene. To deal with the lack of change labels in the new scene, transfer learning is performed with change pseudo-labels estimated in the new scene in unsupervised manner. We assess the effectiveness of the proposed change detection method in two couples of images acquired with Sentinel-2, at different times, in the urban areas of Cupertino and Las Vegas.

Keywords: Siamese network · Transfer learning · Change detection · Earth observation · Sentinel-2 images

1 Introduction

Copernicus is the European Union's Earth observation programme that looks at our planet and its environment to benefit all European citizens. It has allowed a frequent revisit time of Earth by making available an unprecedented volume of optical images of various Earth's scenes [8]. For example, the Copernicus Sentinel-2 mission has involved a constellation of two satellites with a spatial resolution of 10 and 20/60 m and a targeted revisit time of 5 days supplying optical information ranging from visible to near and shortwave infrared. The recent volume of optical images acquired with Sentinel-2 has unleashed the potential of change detection (CD) methods in a wide range of remote sensing applications ranging from urban planning, environmental monitoring, agriculture investigation, disaster assessment and map revision [11].

Existing CD methods commonly resort to machine learning [20] to compare optical data of a scene acquired at distinct time points and delineate changes

S. Bandini et al. (Eds.): AIxIA 2021, LNAI 13196, pp. 478–489, 2022.
https://doi.org/10.1007/978-3-031-08421-8_33

at either pixel or object level of the observed scene. These methods are mainly classified into supervised and unsupervised approaches regarding the learning paradigm they adopt [20]. In particular, supervised CD methods [12,19,24,26] rely on prior information about the ground changes. So, their accuracy depends on the availability and quality of the ground truth that is commonly based on human intervention and tends to be generated object-wise, rather than pixel-by-pixel, since it is costly in terms of time and effort. A poor-quality ground truth map may prevent even a good supervised learning method from highlighting its quality by producing contradictory results. On the other hand, unsupervised CD methods [4,7,10], in general, base on a reliable measure of distance (or similarity) computed between the two optical images of the same scene. They commonly resort to the Change Vector Analysis (CVA) strategy that always determines a threshold to separate the changed pixels from the unchanged background.

In this paper, we present a semi-supervised CD method, named ATLANTIS (siAmese Network with Transfer Learning for chANge detection in saTellite ImageS), that cascades a supervised learning step and an unsupervised learning step. In the supervised learning step, a Siamese network [6]—a deep metric learning (DML) architecture—is learned to detect changes from labelled, bi-temporal, Sentinel-2 images of some Earth's scene. Labels describe ground changes occurred in the scene. In the unsupervised step, a fine tuning strategy [21]—an application of transfer learning principle in deep learning—is performed, in order to accommodate the Siamese network learned in the supervised step to the unlabeled, bi-temporal, Sentinel-2 images of a new scene. The updated Siamese network can then be used to identify the changes in the new scene. In principle, the unsupervised step may be also repeated on multiple scenes, in order to transfer the same Siamese network to the unknown changes occurring in various scenes.

The Siamese network is widely used in computer vision for entities' comparison. It learns hierarchical non-linear transformations to map data sample pairs into a new feature space that is more suitable for comparing or matching operations. This is done by exploiting deep neural network architectures that minimise a loss function related to a sample distance and unify deep learning and metric learning into a joint learning framework [14]. In CD, Siamese networks have been recently investigated in [22]. This study trains a Siamese network from a selection of labeled pixels of a scene. Subsequently, it has used the Siamese network to annotate the change information of the pixels previously unlabeled the same scene. The fine-tuning strategy allows us to adapt the pre-trained Siamese network to new change events without retraining from scratch, which would incur significant overhead. In [12], a fine-tuning strategy has been recently used for CD with Convolution neural networks. However, this study uses a selection of ground truth labels acquired in the new scene to complete fine-tuning. Differently, in our study, fine-tuning is fully unsupervised. In fact, we leverage a simple CVA method to produce change estimates in the new scene. We process these estimates (in absence of labels of ground change) to adapt the Siamese network to the signature of possible, new change categories. Note that the proposed unsupervised fine-tuning strategy allows us to restrict the cost of the manual labelling operation to the single couple of images that are used to supervise the training of the original Siamese network. In fact, the proposed unsupervised fine tuning strategy allows us to avoid any manual labelling effort spent in adapting this network to any new couple of unlabelled images. This may be helpful in a scenario with a huge amount of unlabelled data.

We evaluate both the accuracy and efficiency of the proposed CD method in two datasets of bi-temporal, optical images acquired with Sentinel-2 in the urban areas of Las Vegas and Cupertino. As the change information is available on both these datasets, the empirical study can verify the gain in accuracy of ATLANTIS compared to both the Siamese network trained in the purely supervised setting and the CVA method operating in the purely unsupervised setting.

The paper is organised as follows. The related works are presented in Sect. 2. The proposed CD method is illustrated in Sect. 3 and the implementation is described in Sect. 4. The findings in the evaluation of the proposed approach with Sentinel-2 are discussed in Sect. 5. Finally, Sect. 6 draws conclusions and proposes future developments.

2 Related Work

Unsupervised CD methods are commonly based on the CVA strategy that computes a measure of similarity (or distance) between co-located pixels of a couple of images and uses a threshold-based approach to identify a distance threshold to separate changed pixels from the unchanged background. Various similarity (or distance) measures have been investigated for CVA methods [4,15,19,25], while the threshold to detect the changes has been commonly estimated in a data-driven manner. A well-known approach often used for the threshold determination is the Otsu's algorithm [16]. In [15], the Otsu's algorithm is evaluated in combination with the Spectral Angle Mapper (SAM) distance. Clustering algorithms have been also studied [3,4] to separate distances (or similarities) of changed pixels from the unchanged background.

Supervised CD methods are based on the availability of ground change information (often acquired by human intervention) and use a classification framework, in which the ground truth is used to learn a classifier. In [23], changes are identified by using a trained classifier to directly classify data from multiple periods (i.e., multi-date classification or direct classification) and comparing multiple classification maps (i.e., post-classification comparison). In [17], a logistic regression layer is trained to perform supervised fine-tuning and classification on the autoencoder denoised representation of image time series feature extracted within tunable Q discrete wavelet transform. In [18], a fully Convolutional neural network is combined with Long short-term network for land cover supervised CD. Finally, transfer learning strategies have been recently investigated to alleviate the lack of training samples and optimise the training process in a semi-supervised scenario. In any case, existing studies perform transfer learning requiring a few labelled samples for the CD model fine-tuning [12].

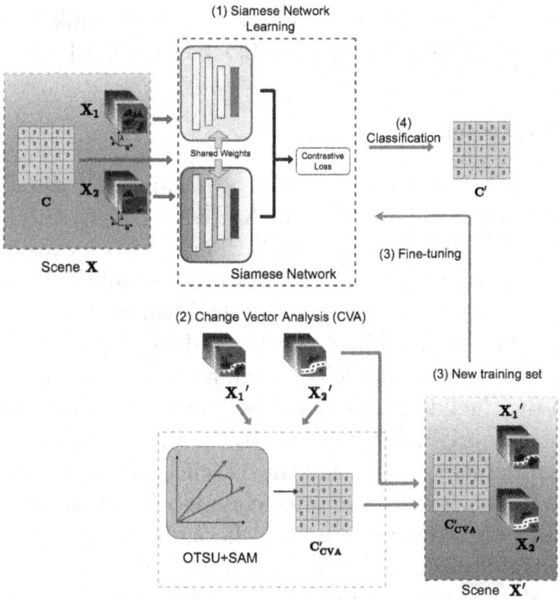

Fig. 1. ATLANTIS methodology

3 The Proposed Approach

Let us consider two Earth's scenes $\mathbf{X}$ and $\mathbf{X}'$ and an optical camera to acquire optical images of both scenes. $\mathbf{X}$ is a grid of $m \times n$ pixels and $\mathbf{X}'$ is a grid of $m' \times n'$ pixels, respectively. Every pixel of both scenes is a region of around a few square meters of the Earth's surface, which is a function of the sensor spatial resolution. The optical camera covers h spectral bands (spectral feature vector) ranging from Visible and Near-Infrared (VNIR) to Shortwave Infrared (SWIR) wavelengths.[1] This camera is used to acquire optical images $\mathbf{X_1}$, $\mathbf{X_2}$, $\mathbf{X_1'}$ and $\mathbf{X_2'}$. In particular, $\mathbf{X_1}$ and $\mathbf{X_2}$ are bi-temporal, optical images of scene $\mathbf{X}$ acquired at times t_1 and t_2 with $t_1 \neq t_2$. They are hypercubes with size $m \times n \times h$. $\mathbf{X_1'}$ and $\mathbf{X_2'}$ are bi-temporal, optical images of scene $\mathbf{X}'$ acquired at times t_1' and t_2' with $t_1' \neq t_2'$. They are hypercubes with size $m' \times n' \times h$. In addition, let us also consider the binary matrix $\mathbf{C}$ that conveys the $m \times n$ prior ground change information available for pixels of scene $\mathbf{X}$. In particular, $\mathbf{C}(i,j) = 1$ if the annotator knows that a change occurred at pixel (i,j) of $\mathbf{X}$ from time t_1 to time t_2. $\mathbf{C}(i,j) = 0$, otherwise. ATLANTIS is a two-stepped, semi-supervised CD method that takes as input $\mathbf{X_1}$, $\mathbf{X_2}$, $\mathbf{X_1'}$, $\mathbf{X_2'}$ and $\mathbf{C}$ and determines the binary matrix $\mathbf{C}'$ that conveys the $m' \times n'$ estimates of the change information about the pixels of scene $\mathbf{X}'$. In the first step, it trains a Siamese network for CD from $\mathbf{X_1}$ and $\mathbf{X_2}$ and $\mathbf{C}$. In the second step, it transfers this Siamese network to $\mathbf{X_1'}$

[1] In Sentinel-2, the optical camera covers 13 bands.

and $\mathbf{X}_2'$ and uses the updated network to estimate the unknown change labels of $\mathbf{C}'$ about scene $\mathbf{X}'$. Figure 1 shows the block diagram of ATLANTIS.

3.1 Siamese Network

A Siamese network is trained with the $m \times n$ pairs of h-dimensional spectral feature vectors conveyed in both $\mathbf{X}_1$ and $\mathbf{X}_2$, respectively, and labeled with the corresponding change labels conveyed in $\mathbf{C}$. This network consists of two identical supervised artificial neural networks that are capable of learning the hidden representation of the input bi-temporal, spectral feature vectors. The two neural networks are both feed-forward perceptrons, and employ error back-propagation during training. They work parallelly in tandem and compare their outputs at the end through the Euclidean distance. The Siamese network optimizes the contrastive loss that was originally proposed in [9]. In the original formulation, the contrastive loss minimises the Euclidean distance between the feature embeddings of samples that belong to the same class label and maximises the distance between samples with different labels in the embedding space. In this paper, bi-temporal spectral vectors of changed pixels are dealt as pairs of samples with different labels, while bi-temporal spectral vectors of unchanged pixels are dealt as pairs of samples labeled with the same class. Through the predicted distance measure, the Siamese network states that the two spectral feature vectors acquired on the same pixels at different times are different (distance greater than a threshold $\theta_{Siamese}$) or similar (distance lower than a threshold $\theta_{Siamese}$). The algorithm then labels the pixel as 1 (changed) if in the former case, or as 0 (unchanged) if in the latter case. To automatically determine $\theta_{Siamese}$, we use the Otsu method [16]. This adaptive threshold algorithm is commonly used in image binarization problems. It determines $\theta_{Siamese}$ by minimising the intra-class intensity variance defined as a weighted sum of variances of the distances on the two classes.

3.2 Fine-tuning

In the fine-tuning strategy, a deep neural network is trained on data from the target distribution, but rather than the weights being randomly initialized, they are those pretrained on data from a different—but related—distribution. In this paper, the fine-tuning strategy is applied starting with the weights of the Siamese network that is initially trained to fit the spectral feature vectors of both $\mathbf{X}_1$ and $\mathbf{X}_2$ to the ground change labels of $\mathbf{C}$. Subsequently, these weights are updated accommodating the Siamese network to fit the spectral feature vectors of $\mathbf{X}_1'$ and $\mathbf{X}_2'$ to the estimates of the corresponding change labels conveyed in $\mathbf{C}'_{\mathbf{CVA}}$. This allows us to adapt the pre-trained Siamese network to the hypothetical new changing events without retraining from scratch with class estimates only, which would incur significant overhead and cause artefacts. Finally, we use the fine-tuned Siamese network to yield the final estimates of change information $\mathbf{C}'$ about scene $\mathbf{X}'$.

The original formulation of the fine-tuning strategy requires the availability of class labels about new scene $\mathbf{X}'$. In our formulation, we do not rely on any prior ground change information about $\mathbf{X}'$. So, we apply a simple CVA method [15] to determine $\mathbf{C}'_{\mathbf{CVA}}$ and leverage $\mathbf{C}'_{\mathbf{CVA}}$ for fine-tuning. In this way, the adopted fine-tuning strategy founds on the exchange of information between two CD methods (Siamese network and CVA). The diversity of the two CD methods provides arguments to their different predictive capabilities and supports the idea of generating independent estimates through CVA to better accommodate the Siamese network to the new scene. We investigate the effectiveness of this hypothesis in the empirical study.

To build $\mathbf{C}'_{\mathbf{CVA}}$, we first compute pixelwise the distance between $\mathbf{X_1}'$ and $\mathbf{X_2}'$ by resorting to the algorithm SAM that is commonly used in CVA methods [3,4,13]. Let us consider pixel (i,j), $SAM(i,j)$ measures the angle between the bi-temporal, spectral feature vectors associated with (i,j) in both $\mathbf{X_1}'$ and $\mathbf{X_2}'$. This angle is computed as follows:

$$SAM(i,j) = \arccos \frac{\mathbf{X_1}'(i,j) \cdot \mathbf{X_2}'(i,j)}{||\mathbf{X_1}'(i,j)||\ ||\mathbf{X_2}'(i,j)||}. \tag{1}$$

Subsequently, we use the Otsu's algorithm to determine the upper threshold θ_{SAM} of SAM distances for separating pixels of $\mathbf{X}'$ into foreground and background. Therefore, we build the binary $m' \times n'$ matrix $\mathbf{C}'_{\mathbf{CVA}}$ such that $\mathbf{C}'_{\mathbf{CVA}}(i,j) = 1$ if $SAM(i,j)$ is greater than θ_{SAM}, $\mathbf{C}'_{\mathbf{CVA}}(i,j) = 0$, otherwise.

Further considerations concern the direct application of both the CVA method and the Siamese network for change labelling will neglect the spatial arrangement of pixels. It may occasionally yield spurious assignments of pixels to classes. To avoid this issue, we may apply the principle of local auto-correlation congruence of objects [2,4], according to which detected clusters, comprising changed objects, generally expand across contiguous areas. Based on this principle, we may decide to change the assignment of pixels that strongly disagree with surrounding assignments. This mainly corresponds to performing a spatial-aware correction of the change assignment. This correction assigns each pixel to the class that originally groups the majority of its neighbouring pixels. As a neighbourhood, we consider a square-shaped neighbourhood with radius R.

4 Implementation Details

ATLANTIS has been implemented in Python 3.8, with the Siamese architecture implemented using Keras 2.4—a high-level neural network API with TensorFlow as the backend. The Siamese network is implemented with two base feed-forward networks with shared weights. Each base network is a deep neural network with three layers with 224 × 128 × 64 neurons and two dropout layers. We apply the *ReLu* activation to each layer and the contrastive function [9] as loss function. In the supervised inialization step, the weights are initialises following the Xavier scheme, while in the fine-tuning step, the weights saved from the previous network are used as a starting point. For each dataset, we have conducted a

Table 1. Hyperparameter search space for the siamese model.

Hyperparameter	Values
Batch size	$\{2^5, 2^6, 2^7, 2^8, 2^9\}$
Learning rate	[0.0001, 0.01]
Dropout	[0, 0.5]

Table 2. Cupertino and Las Vergas description: scene size (column 2), data acquisition timestamps (columns 3 and 4), number of changed pixels in the ground truth (GT) change map (column 5), number of unchanged pixels in the change map (column 6).

Dataset	Size (pixels)	Time (pre)	Time (post)	♯ changed	♯ unchanged
Cupertino	788 × 1015	Sep 18, 2015	Mar 26, 2018	18942 (2.43%)	780878 (97.57%)
Las Vegas	824 × 716	Aug 20, 2015	Feb 05, 2018	45270 (7.67%)	544714 (92.33%)

hyper-parameter optimization using the tree-structured Parzen estimator algorithm as implemented in the Hyperopt library [5], by using 20% of the training set as the validation set. We choose the configuration of the parameter that achieved the best validation loss. The hyper-parameters and their corresponding possible values are reported in Table 1. Data have been scaled using the Min-Max scaler. Finally, the threshold-based step is performed using the implementation of Otsu's algorithm from scikit-image library.[2]

5 Experimental Evaluation

The empirical study is performed to investigate the accuracy performance of ATLANTIS in transferring a Siamese network trained for CD from a labeled dataset to an unlabeled dataset. The two datasets comprise bi-temporal, optical images acquired with Sentinel-2 in the urban areas of Las Vegas and Cupertino, respectively. Before illustrating the results, we describe the datasets, the experimental setting and the evaluation metrics.

5.1 Datasets, Experimental Setting and Evaluation Metrics

We consider two pairs of 13-band, bi-temporal images taken in the urban area of Cupertino and Las Vegas, respectively [8].[3] Each pair of images is acquired with spatial resolution of 10 mt from the Sentinel-2 satellites on 2015 and 2018, respectively. For both pairs of images, the ground truth change information is available to validate the accuracy of the produced change maps. A summary of the characteristics of both datasets is reported in Table 2. We evaluate the performance of ATLANTIS in two experiments:

[2] https://scikit-image.org/docs/dev/api/skimage.filters.html#skimage.filters.threshold_otsu.

[3] https://rcdaudt.github.io/oscd/.

Table 3. Accuracy performance: OA, MAR, FAR F-score(C) and F-score(U) of OTSU+SAM, SIAMESE and ATLANTIS. All results are achieved with spatial correction ($R = 3$). For each experiment, for each metric, the best result is in bold.

Dataset	Algorithm	OA	MAR	FAR	F-score(C)	F-score(U)
Cupertino ↦ *Las Vegas*	OTSU+SAM	94.8%	**29.1%**	3.2%	67.5%	97.2%
	SIAMESE	82.8%	33.0%	15.9%	37.4%	90.0%
	ATLANTIS	**95.6%**	37.7%	**1.6%**	**68.7%**	**97.7%**
Las Vegas ↦ *Cupertino*	OTSU+SAM	95.5%	**16.4%**	4.2 %	46.6%	97.6%
	SIAMESE	83.7%	47.5%	15.6%	13.2%	91.0%
	ATLANTIS	**97.4%**	32.1%	**1.9%**	**55.1%**	**98.6%**

- *Cupertino* ↦ *Las Vegas*: we train the Siamese network on the labeled pixels of the Cupertino dataset and transfer this network to the unlabeled pixels of the Las Vegas dataset to generate the change map of Las Vegas.
- *Las Vegas* ↦ *Cupertino*: we train the Siamese network on the labelled pixels of the Las Vegas dataset and transfer this network to the unlabelled pixels of the Cupertino dataset to generate the change map of Cupertino.

In both experiments, we compare the accuracy of the change maps generated with ATLANTIS against the accuracy of the change maps generated with the original Siamese network without fine tuning (SIAMESE) and the change maps generated with the CVA method that applies the Otsu's algorithm to the SAM distances (OTSU+SAM). Note that OTSU+SAM is a related CD method adopted in several CVA studies (e.g. [1,15]). In this comparative study, it represents a baseline as ATLANTIS incorporates OTSU+SAM to generate the pseudo-labels processed in the fine tuning stage of the Siamese network. To evaluate the accuracy performance, we measure the Overall Accuracy (OA) – percentage of pixels correctly classified, the Missed Alarm Rate (MAR– percentage of changed pixels assigned to the unchanged background) and False Alarm Rate (FAR) – percentage of unchanged pixels labelled as changed). These metrics are commonly considered in remote sensing for the evaluation of change detection methods. In addition, we measure F-score(C)– f-score of the class "changed" and F-score(U)– f-score of the class "unchanged". Finally, we analyse the time spent in seconds performing the learning process and generating the change maps. For context, the experiments are executed using a CPU Ryzen 5 3600 3.60Ghz and memory RAM DDR of 16 GB.

5.2 Results

We start evaluating the effectiveness of the transfer learning strategy of ATLANTIS in the two experiments. To this aim, we compare the accuracy of ATLANTIS against that of its baselines OTSU+SAM and SIAMESE. Table 3 displays the OA, MAR, FAR, F-score(C) and F-score(U) of OTSU+SAM, SIAMESE

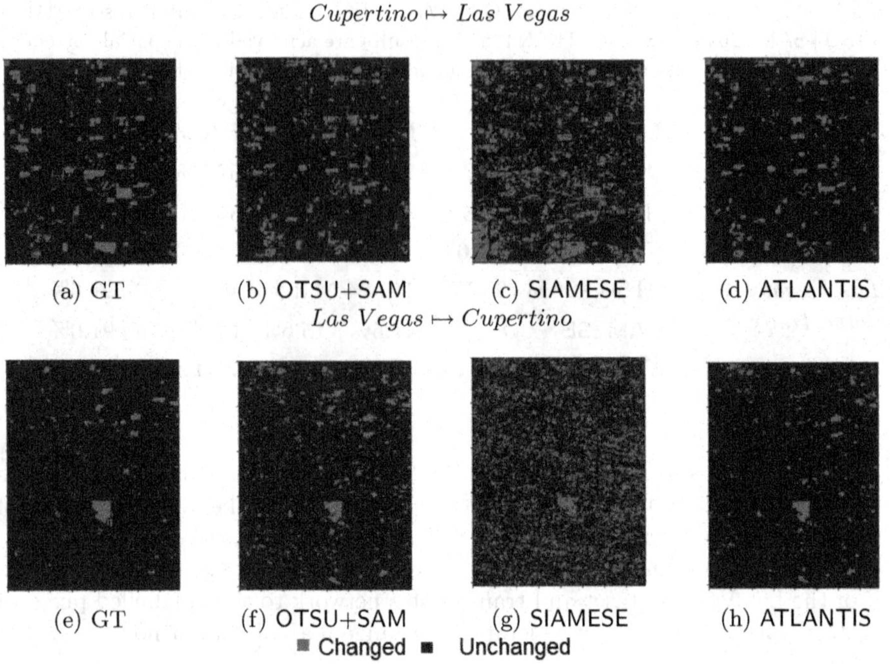

Fig. 2. Change maps of Las Vegas (*Cupertino* ↦ *Las Vegas* in Figs. 2a–2d) and Cupertino (*Las Vegas* ↦ *Cupertino* in Figs. 2e–2h) generated with OTSU+SAM, SIAMESE and ATLANTIS

and ATLANTIS. Figure 2 displays the changes maps generated by the compared algorithms. All the results are collected with spatial correction applied with $R = 3$. The results show that ATLANTIS outperforms both baselines in all the metrics with the exception of MAR. This means that ATLANTIS reduces the number of false change events raised compared to its baselines, but at the cost of an increase in the number of changed areas that are wrongly assigned to the unchanged background. In particular, these results show that the fine-tuning strategy with the pseudo-labels generated through the Otsu's algorithm is an effective strategy to generate an accurate change map of a scene by taking advantage of the Siamese network trained in a different scene. In addition, ATLANTIS gains accuracy compared to the traditional CVA method OTSU+SAM that is commonly used for unsupervised change detection in satellite images.

We proceed analysing the effect of the spatial correction on the compared algorithms. Figure 3 compares the OA achieved with OTSU+SAM, SIAMESE and ATLANTIS with spatial correction ($R = 3$) against the OA achieved disabling the spatial correction. We note that, although the spatial correction is beneficial in all the algorithms, the gain in accuracy is lower in ATLANTIS, where the most of the improvement is actually achieved with the fine-tuning strategy.

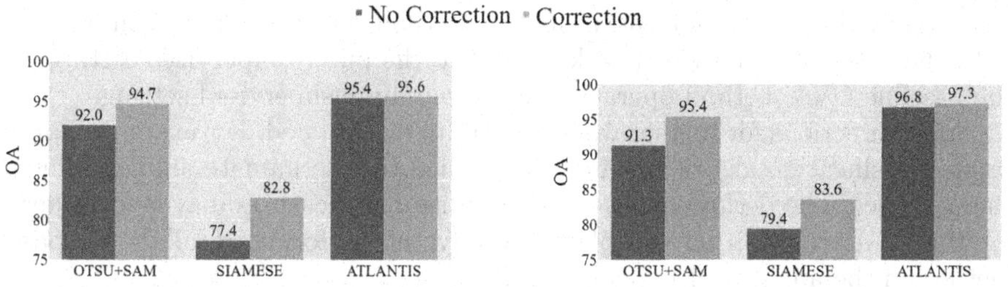

(a) *Cupertino* $\mapsto$ *Las Vegas* (b) *Las Vegas* $\mapsto$ *Cupertino*

Fig. 3. Spatial correction analysis: OA of OTSU+SAM, SIAMESE and ATLANTIS without spatial correction and with spatial correction ($R = 3$)

Table 4. Computation time spent in seconds generating the change maps with OTSU+SAM, SIAMESE and ATLANTIS.

Dataset	OTSU+SAM	SIAMESE	ATLANTIS
Cupertino $\mapsto$ *Las Vegas*	7.87	9114	9249.96
Las Vegas $\mapsto$ *Cupertino*	7.55	7216.16	7442.03

We complete this study comparing the computation time spent in seconds generating the change maps. Table 4 reports the computation time of OTSU+SAM, SIAMESE and ATLANTIS. These results show that training a Siamese network is very time consuming in both SIAMESE and ATLANTIS, especially compared to using a simple, unsupervised CVA method as OTSU+SAM. The higher computation time of ATLANTIS is due to the time spent completing the fine tuning. However, the time that ATLANTIS spends completing the fine-tuning of a Siamese network is negligible compared to the time spent training the original Siamese network. As a Siamese network, once trained with the labelled data of a scene, may be potentially fine-tuned to several unlabelled scenes with a limited computation burden, we may consider acceptable the more computation effort requested by ATLANTIS to generate change maps that are more accurate than the maps generated with OTSU+SAM and ATLANTIS.

6 Conclusion

This papers describes a semi-supervised method for CD in Sentinel-2, bi-temporal images of Earth's scenes. It bases on a Siamese network and integrates the fine-tuning strategy to transfer the Siamese network trained in a labeled scene to any new unlabeled scene. Fine-tuning is performed with change pseudo-labels estimated in the new scene using a simple CVA method.

The empirical study is performed by processing two datasets of Sentinel-2, bi-temporal images acquired in the urban areas of Las Vegas and Cupertino, respectively. It shows that the proposed method gains accuracy compared to both the baseline Siamese network trained in the purely supervised setting and the baseline CVA method operating in the purely unsupervised setting.

Some directions for further work are still to be explored. For example, appropriate classification algorithms may be studied to discriminate among different change types. The performances of various distance measures may be considered for the CVA. In addition, we plan to study the performance of the proposed method in the analysis of hyperspectral data.

Acknowledgements. This work fulfills the research objectives of the PON "Ricerca e Innovazione" 2014–2020 project "CLOSE – Close to the Earth" (ARS01_00141), funded by the Italian Ministry for Universities and Research (MIUR).

References

1. Andresini, G., Appice, A., Iaia, D., Malerba, D., Taggio, N., Aiello, A.: Leveraging autoencoders in change vector analysis of optical satellite images. J. Intell. Inf. Sys. **58**, 1–20 (2021). https://doi.org/10.1007/s10844-021-00670-9
2. Appice, A., Ciampi, A., Malerba, D.: Summarizing numeric spatial data streams by trend cluster discovery. Data Min. Knowl. Discov. **29**(1), 84–136 (2013). https://doi.org/10.1007/s10618-013-0337-7
3. Appice, A., Di Mauro, N., Lomuscio, F., Malerba, D.: Empowering change vector analysis with autoencoding in bi-temporal hyperspectral images. In: MACLEANECMLPKDD Workshop, vol. 2466, pp. 1–10. CEUR Workshop Proceedings (2019)
4. Appice, A., Guccione, P., Acciaro, E., Malerba, D.: Detecting salient regions in a bi-temporal hyperspectral scene by iterating clustering and classification. Appl. Intell. **50**(10), 3179–3200 (2020). https://doi.org/10.1007/s10489-020-01701-8
5. Bergstra, J., Yamins, D., Cox, D.D.: Making a science of model search: hyperparameter optimization in hundreds of dimensions for vision architectures. In: ICML, pp. 115–123 (2013)
6. Bromley, J., Guyon, I., Lecun, Y., Säckinger, E., Shah, R.: Signature verification using a siamese time delay neural network. Int. J. Pattern Recogn. Artif. Intell. - IJPRAI **7**(04), 669–688 (1993)
7. Bruzzone, L., Prieto, D.F.: Automatic analysis of the difference image for unsupervised change detection. IEEE Trans. Geosci. Remote Sens. **38**(2), 1171–1182 (2000)
8. Caye Daudt, R., Le Saux, B., Boulch, A., Gousseau, Y.: Urban change detection for multispectral earth observation using convolutional neural networks. In: IEEE International Geoscience and Remote Sensing Symposium (IGARSS) (2018)
9. Hadsell, R., Chopra, S., LeCun, Y.: Dimensionality reduction by learning an invariant mapping. In: 2006 IEEE Computer Society Conference on Computer Vision and Pattern Recognition (CVPR'06), vol. 2, pp. 1735–1742 (2006)
10. Hussain, M., Chen, D., Cheng, A., Wei, H., Stanley, D.: Change detection from remotely sensed images: from pixel-based to object-based approaches. ISPRS J. Photogrammetry Remote Sens. **80**, 91–106 (2013)
11. Kwan, C.: Methods and challenges using multispectral and hyperspectral images for practical change detection applications. Information **10**(11), 353 (2019)

12. Larabi, M., Souleyman, C., Bakhti, K., Kamel, H., Amine, B.: High-resolution optical remote sensing imagery change detection through deep transfer learning. J. Appl. Remote Sens. **13**(11), 046512 (2019)
13. Lopez-Fandino, J., Garea, A.S., Heras, D.B., Argüello, F.: Stacked autoencoders for multiclass change detection in hyperspectral images. In: 2018 IEEE International Geoscience and Remote Sensing Symposium, IGARSS 2018, pp. 1906–1909. IEEE (2018)
14. Lu, J., Hu, J., Zhou, J.: Deep metric learning for visual understanding: an overview of recent advances. IEEE Signal Process. Mag. **34**(6), 76–84 (2017)
15. López-Fandiño, J., B. Heras, D., Argüello, F., Dalla Mura, M.: GPU framework for change detection in multitemporal hyperspectral images. Int. J. Parallel Program. **47**(2), 272–292 (2017). https://doi.org/10.1007/s10766-017-0547-5
16. Otsu, N.: A threshold selection method from gray-level histograms. IEEE Trans. Geosci. Remote Sens. **9**(1), 62–66 (1972)
17. Planinšič, P., Gleich, D.: Temporal change detection in SAR images using log cumulants and stacked autoencoder. IEEE Geosci. Remote Sens. Lett. **15**(2), 297–301 (2018)
18. Sefrin, O., Riese, F.M., Keller, S.: Deep learning for land cover change detection. Remote Sens. **13**(1), 78 (2021)
19. Seydi, S.T., Hasanlou, M.: A new land-cover match-based change detection for hyperspectral imagery. Eur. J. Remote Sens. **50**(1), 517–533 (2017)
20. Shi, W., Zhang, M., Zhang, R., Chen, S., Zhan, Z.: Change detection based on artificial intelligence: state-of-the-art and challenges. Remote Sens. **12**(10), 1688 (2020)
21. Tan, C., Sun, F., Kong, T., Zhang, W., Yang, C., Liu, C.: A survey on deep transfer learning. In: Kůrková, V., Manolopoulos, Y., Hammer, B., Iliadis, L., Maglogiannis, I. (eds.) ICANN 2018. LNCS, vol. 11141, pp. 270–279. Springer, Cham (2018). https://doi.org/10.1007/978-3-030-01424-7_27
22. Wang, M., Tan, K., Jia, X., Wang, X., Chen, Y.: A deep siamese network with hybrid convolutional feature extraction module for change detection based on multi-sensor remote sensing images. Remote Sens. **12**(01), 205 (2020)
23. Wu, C., Du, B., Cui, X., Zhang, L.: A post-classification change detection method based on iterative slow feature analysis and Bayesian soft fusion. Remote Sens. Environ. **199**, 241–255 (2017)
24. Wu, K., Du, Q., Wang, Y., Yang, Y.: Supervised sub-pixel mapping for change detection from remotely sensed images with different resolutions. Remote Sens. **9**(3), 284 (2017)
25. Yang, Z., Mueller, R.: Spatial-spectral cross-correlation for change detection: a case study for citrus coverage change detection. In: ASPRS 2007 Annual Conference, vol. 2, no. 01, pp. 767–777 (2007)
26. Yuan, F., Sawaya, K.E., Loeffelholz, B.C., Bauer, M.E.: Land cover classification and change analysis of the twin cities (Minnesota) metropolitan area by multitemporal landsat remote sensing. Remote Sens. Environ. **98**(2), 317–328 (2005)

Adversarial Machine Learning in e-Health: Attacking a Smart Prescription System

Salvatore Gaglio[1,2], Andrea Giammanco[2], Giuseppe Lo Re[1,2], and Marco Morana[1,2(✉)]

[1] Smart Cities and Communities National Lab CINI - Consorzio Interuniversitario Nazionale per l'Informatica, Rome, Italy
{salvatore.gaglio,giuseppe.lore,marco.morana}@unipa.it
[2] Department of Engineering, University of Palermo, Palermo, Italy
andrea.giammanco@unipa.it

Abstract. Machine learning (ML) algorithms are the basis of many services we rely on in our everyday life. For this reason, a new research line has recently emerged with the aim of investigating how ML can be misled by adversarial examples. In this paper we address an e-health scenario in which an automatic system for prescriptions can be deceived by inputs forged to subvert the model's prediction. In particular, we present an algorithm capable of generating a precise sequence of moves that the adversary has to take in order to elude the automatic prescription service. Experimental analyses performed on a real dataset of patients' clinical records show that a minimal alteration of the clinical records can subvert predictions with high probability.

Keywords: Adversarial Machine Learning · Healthcare · Evasion attacks

1 Introduction

Machine learning algorithms are extensively adopted in scenarios where the analysis of large amounts of data is mandatory [28]. Typically, the higher the confidence of the automatic learning algorithm on its predictions, the higher the trust that the practitioner has towards the model, orienting his decisions accordingly. In recent years, a novel research line, named Adversarial Machine Learning (AML), is studying how to exploit the same optimization mechanism at the core of ML algorithms with an opposite intent: to let the model be sure, with high confidence, about an erroneous prediction. In particular, *Adversarial examples* are defined as "those that change the verdicts of machine learning systems but not those of humans" [7]. Because of the immediateness for a human to verify the appearance of a certain image and evaluate the correctness of the classifier, image processing has been for several years the most common scenario in which the effectiveness of adversarial examples can be demonstrated. In this context, the attacks are aimed at creating noise patterns [29] that exhibit two

S. Bandini et al. (Eds.): AIxIA 2021, LNAI 13196, pp. 490–502, 2022.
https://doi.org/10.1007/978-3-031-08421-8_34

main characteristics: their superimposition over the original image is invisible to the human eye, and they cause an error in the classification algorithm. Moreover, algorithms for adversarial images corruption can heavily exploit the very large number of features (i.e., all the pixels of the image), as well as their scale of variability depending on the adopted encoding, so that the ascent along the gradient can proceed simultaneously in multiple directions at the same time. In other application domains, understanding the best way to corrupt the input with adversarial noise can be very challenging. For instance, considering a malware detection algorithm based on the API calls made by a software [15], one possible adversarial noise may consist in adding innocuous calls [5], while preserving the malicious behavior of the software. In an ambient intelligence scenario [4], sensors' raw data can be altered through a vector of carefully selected real values, in order to let a smart anomaly detection system [12] raise false irregularity alerts regarding users' behaviors, or interrupt the operation of an intelligent energy-saving system [13]. Assuming the presence of a Reputation Management System capable of identifying malicious entities in a sharing environment [2,3], changing the released feedback patterns can refresh the bad reputation of an adversary. Conjugated in Online Social Networks, slight modifications in spammers behavior (e.g., inflating the number of innocuous tweets) can hide their malicious intent to an intelligent detector [11]. Systems relying on smartphones sensors to recognize the activities carried out by users [9,10], may be trained on corrupted labeled data and fail in their identification task worsening the end services provided. In other domains, guaranteeing that the final verdict of the human remains unchanged is not straightforward. In a *healthcare* scenario, for example, it would mean that an expert clinician should not alter his judgment in the face of an altered clinical record. However, if the adversary's move consists in altering the patient's record, it is highly likely that the final decision made by the clinician will change. Nonetheless, perturbed clinical records may still be regarded as adversarial examples, as they share both the final goal to fool a machine learning algorithm, and the methodology used to get to the specific noise through the formulation of an optimization problem. In this paper, we address this issue and show how an adversary may alter binary entries in the clinical record of a patient in order to elude a smart prescription system. In this scenario, given that economic return is one of the most common motivations to conduct adversarial attacks in the healthcare domain [17], we can imagine as adversary an agent of a pharmaceutical company that produces a particular active ingredient, and wants to increase the sales by artificially inflate the number of prescriptions. In order to elude the smart prescription system, we propose an algorithm capable of generating the precise sequence of moves that the adversary has to take, i.e., which binary entries on the clinical record of the patient need to be flipped. In particular, we assume that the target model to evade is a neural network, whose parameters can be reasonably emulated by probing the smart prescription service as a black box [6]. The remainder of the paper is organized as follows. Section 2 discusses recent studies in the field of *AML*. Section 3 outlines the *healthcare* scenario considered as case study. Section 4 formalizes the model of the adversary. Section 5 describes the algorithm to generate the adversarial perturbation for the clinical records of the patients. Section 6 presents the experimental analysis to validate our proposal. Section 7 draws the conclusions.

2 Related Work

In recent years, *AML* has been the subject of studies from multiple fields of inquiry [6]. These are spearheaded by the image processing field, given the easy demonstrability of how well-designed adversarial examples are potentially lethal. In [29] for example, the authors formulate a method to create a perturbation which is strictly constrained in space, in order to craft a sort of sticker that is similar to real-world noise. By applying such stickers to danger road signs, state-of-art object detectors are led to completely different predictions, which can be fatal for self-driving cars. Considering the speech recognition field, in [21] multiple denoising strategies are leveraged to defend against attempts of altering the semantics of the sentences. These attempts reveal their full malevolent potential when cast on popular systems (e.g., Alexa), in order to redirect users to fraudulent sites instead of performing their intended requests. The problem of malware detection is studied in [24], where a set of instructions are injected after the *return* statement of ActionScript programs in order to inflate the detection of false negatives (i.e., malicious applications classified as benign) without altering the behavior of the code. In [5] is presented a similar approach, where the malevolent behavior in terms of Windows API calls is kept fixed, while the addition of benign calls serves the purpose to inflate the recognition of false negatives. The security of machine learning algorithms in mobile edge computing scenarios is addressed in [30], where false data are injected in the training set of the models in order to alter the aggregated results computed by the server, and in turn, the service offered to end users. The authors propose a graph matching algorithm to filter outliers according to the distance between the graph inferred from data, and the graph extracted from popular location based social networks. Network intrusion detection systems are examined in [8], where an autoencoder is employed to generate features resembling the benign class, which an attacker can use to circumvent automatic detectors. With regard to the *healthcare* domain, in [26] the authors evaluated the impact of several attack algorithms against models trained on a dataset containing ten vital signs of patients, showing how both attacks during training and test phase can have perilous implications. However, it is not formulated a precise sequence of steps the adversary has to make in order to achieve his goal, given that the perturbation is a real number which is difficult to interpret, and thus, inject into the data in a realistic scenario.

3 Case Study

Electronic healthcare represents an ideal scenario to describe an adversary attack because of the strong economic interests that move the pharmaceutical production. In this paper we consider a typical scenario, schematically represented in Fig. 1, where Alice and Bob are the doctor and the patient respectively. Bob

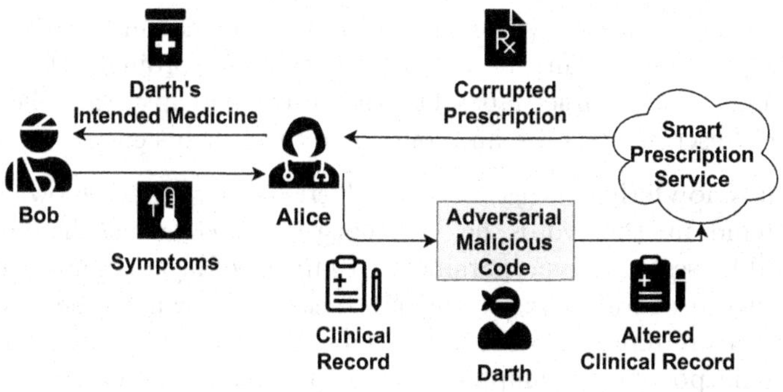

Fig. 1. A smart prescription system with adversary.

reports his symptoms to Alice, who compiles a medical record also including his personal information, so that a decision about which treatment to prescribe can be made. In order to refine her decision, Alice relies on a trusted *Smart Prescription Service* on cloud, which is able to reason about the information in the medical record and suggest appropriate treatment. It is assumed that the model beneath this service is a neural network. In this context, a pharmaceutical company infiltrator named Darth, gains an economic return when a drug of its corporation is prescribed. Darth suggests Alice to install a software in the host that will interact with the cloud service, whose stated purpose is to optimize response times and effectiveness of the prescription system. Actually, this program performs an *AML* algorithm able to elude the *Smart Prescription Service* and induce the prescription of Darth's intended treatment. In particular, this middleware software identifies a restricted set of features which have to be altered in order to deceive the predictor in the cloud. Altering just a few features is a characteristic of the utmost importance in this scenario, since the *Smart Prescription Service* may return a detailed report including the altered clinical record received as input, which therefore needs to contain no striking changes in order not to make any doctor suspicious. Finally, Alice will weigh her judgment based on the response of the intelligent service, resulting in the prescription of Darth's intended drug with high probability. The following subsections describe the attack.

4 Threat Model

Following the guidelines proposed in [6], in this section we frame the model of the adversary according to three main aspects: what is the pursued security breach (attacker's goal); what is the degree of acquired knowledge on the problem domain (attacker's knowledge); what are the concrete viable actions to achieve the malevolent intent (attacker's capability).

Attacker's Goal: the adversary carries out an *integrity* violation of the predictive algorithm in order to flip its belief without disrupting the system in the whole, thus protecting himself from the risk of being caught. The attack specificity is *indiscriminate*, since the adversary does not make any distinction between the patients he wants to fool at his benefit. Accordingly, the error specificity is *specific*, as the target label, i.e., the active principle, that the adversary wants to be prescribed to raise an economic return for his company, is prefixed.

Attacker's Knowledge: we assume the adversary has perfect knowledge on the domain at hand, in other words, he conducts a *white-box* attack. The parameters (weights and biases) and hyperparameters (number of layers, number of neurons per layer) of the neural network under attack are known to the adversary, as well as the feature representation of the data. What needs not to be necessarily known are the portion of samples being part of the training set, and certain hyperparameters of the training process such as the batch size, the number of epochs, the learning rate, the weight decay factor adopted as regularizer, and the momentum coefficient for gradient descent. Although these assumptions may seem highly unlikely, it is common practice to test the strength of a machine learning model against the worst case scenario, so that under real and softer conditions the security of the system should not decrease. Moreover, in light of the transferability property of adversarial attacks [16], the model's parameters can be estimated by querying repeatedly, until a surrogate model capable of providing the same answers as the target model can be built.

Attacker's Capability: the attack influence is *exploratory*, as the adversary has no access to the training data, and can only corrupt data belonging to the test set. The data manipulation constraints strongly depend on the particular scenario we are addressing in this study, where data are in the form of binary feature vectors. It is thus clear that the adversary has to respect the range of allowed values in the clinical records of the patients, i.e., values either of 0 or 1.

5 Methodology

The target *Smart Prescription Service* is a neural network, whose structure will be further investigated in Sect. 6.1. The pseudocode for the proposed strategy to create an effective perturbation against this model is provided in Algorithm 1. Our approach leverages the logic behind the Fast Gradient Sign Method (FGSM) [20], by first computing the gradient of the model's loss function $L(\theta, x, y)$ with respect to the input vector x, ground truth label y, and trained parameters θ. It then selects the least amount of features whose perturbation leads to the most precipitous step taken along the direction of the gradient. In what follows we retrace the complete logical flow of the proposed algorithm.

This algorithm is executed by the malicious code injected by Darth into Alice's PC. The first step of the attack consists in computing the forward pass of the neural network w.r.t. the input vector x Darth wants to perturb. If the hypothesis of the model $\hat{y}$ is different from the target label y_{target}, Darth's objective is to flip the predicted label for the input vector x to the intended one. In other terms, the goal of the attack is to find the perturbation δ such that $h_\theta(x + \delta) \neq \hat{y}$. First, Darth puts in place a revised version of FGSM [20]. The

Algorithm 1. Binary Adversarial Perturbation

Input:

x: the input binary feature vector to perturb;
y: the ground truth label for x;
$mask$: a binary indicator of alterable features;
θ: trained parameters of the neural network;
ψ: number of binary features the adversary may perturb;
y_{target}: the desired output label.

Output:

δ: perturbation to add to the input sample such that: $h_\theta(x + \delta) = y_{target} \neq \hat{y}$.

$\hat{y} \leftarrow h_\theta(x)$
$\delta \leftarrow zeros\_like(x)$
if $\hat{y} == y_{target}$ **then**
    return δ
$\xi \leftarrow \nabla_x L(\theta, x, y)$
$\xi_{ranked} \leftarrow sort\_descending(\xi,\ key = abs)$
$flippable \leftarrow mask\ \&\ (x \oplus sign(\xi))$
$counter \leftarrow 0$
for $value \in \xi_{ranked}$ **do**
    if $counter == \psi$ **then**
        break
    $idx \leftarrow \xi.index(value)$
    if $flippable[idx] == 1$ **then**
        if $x[idx] == 0$ **then**
            $\delta[idx] \leftarrow +1$
        else if $x[idx] == 1$ **then**
            $\delta[idx] \leftarrow -1$
        $counter \leftarrow counter + 1$
return δ

traditional approach aims at climbing up the gradient by adding the perturbation $\xi = \epsilon \cdot sign(\nabla_x L(\theta, x, y))$, for a given $\epsilon > 0$, so that the perturbation vector ξ is composed by values equal to $\pm\epsilon$. ∇_x symbolizes the gradient taken w.r.t. the input vector. In this paper we decided to consider only the term $\xi = \nabla_x L(\theta, x, y)$, so that each single $\xi_i \in \mathbb{R}$. The reason lies in the need to select only a small subset of the input features to perturb. Opposed to the image processing domain, where each pixel may be perturbed with a small step in its scale of representation, in different domains where the features may assume a limited set of values (in this case, binary values), each single perturbation added to the input features has to be selected with care. Therefore, from the real-valued perturbations vector ξ, Darth has to craft a binary perturbation mask to add to the input sample in order to flip the neural network's prediction. Initially, Darth sorts the perturbation vector ξ according to the absolute values of its components. The higher the value in ξ for a specific feature, the higher the contribute along the error that its perturbation will induce, thus becoming the optimum target. Let us now suppose that the application domain imposes some constraints on the features that may be altered; we represent these constraints in the form of a binary *mask* as input to our algorithm, where the presence of a 1 indicates that the related feature may be perturbed. This *mask* explicates those features whose alteration is risky, because they can easily lead to the possibility of being disclosed during the attack. Another input parameter to the attack algorithm is the maximum number of features ψ that Darth may alter from the input vector. A single input feature x_i may be altered in two cases:

1. $x_i == 1$ and the perturbation which results from ascending along the gradient of the loss function has negative sign, i.e. $sign(\xi_i) = -$, so that x_i may be flipped by adding $\delta_i = -1$. In other words, a feature value of 1 can be altered to 0 only if the sign of the gradient along that feature is negative;
2. $x_i == 0$ and the perturbation has positive sign instead, i.e. $sign(\xi_i) = +$, so that in order to flip x_i, $\delta_i = +1$ may be added.

To achieve this aim, we first take the sign of the perturbation vector ξ, $sign(\xi)$, which is then XORed with the input vector x: $x \oplus sign(\xi)$, so as to obtain a True value only when the input feature is 1 and the perturbation has negative sign, and vice versa. We represent $sign(\xi)$ as a binary vector where 1 stands for the sign '+' and 0 for '−'. The result of this operation is then processed with a bit-wise AND with the input *mask*: $flippable = mask \ \& \ (x \oplus sign(\xi))$. This operation results in a binary vector, *flippable*, which signals all those features that, if altered, make the neural network increase the error, because their alteration is concordant with the direction of the loss's gradient. Finally, having the list of features he may alter to deceive the neural network, Darth chooses the ψ features with maximum absolute value, in order to take the gradient's sharpest stride.

In order to achieve the attack, Darth must have a deep knowledge of the medical domain he is going to infiltrate. This implies the awareness of both the set of alterable features to compose the *mask* and, most importantly, the parameters θ of the model beneath the smart prescription service. The latter can be achieved by probing the service as a black box, and building a surrogate model which responds in the most similar manner to the smart prescription service [6]. This approach finds his justification in the demonstrated transferability property of adversarial attacks [16]. When Alice provides Bob's clinical record to Darth, he first decides a threshold ψ of maximum binary feature values to perturb. He computes the loss' gradient ∇_x of the surrogate model's parameters with respect to Bob's record. The most proficient features to alter are those which posses three properties: they do not appear in the *mask* of inconvenient features; they have the highest correspondent module in ∇_x; their alteration is concordant with the respective sign of ∇_x. The perturbed clinical record is then provided to the smart prescription service, which will return, with high probability, a report to Alice containing Darth's intended medicine as the suggested prescription. It is Darth's concern to select ψ as a good trade-off between an higher probability of subverting the smart prescriber prediction, and a lower probability of raising Alice's doubts towards the model's outcome.

6 Experimental Analysis

In order to validate our proposal, we adopted the AMR-UTI dataset[1] [18,23,27], which contains electronic health records of patients with urinary tract infections. Each record consists of demographic information, past clinical data such as previous antibiotic exposure or resistance, and the antibiotic prescription chosen by a clinician to treat the patient. This dataset, allows to train a model able to prescribe the so-called "empiric antibiotic treatment", which the patient should take while waiting the necessary three days for the accurate response from his urinal specimen analysis. In our scenario, the interest of the adversary lies in altering the treatment chosen by the model, simultaneously respecting any contraindications w.r.t. the patient's clinical status. In particular, we considered the patients who were treated with a first-line antibiotic, which is one of two classes: nitrofurantoin (NIT) and trimethoprim-sulfamethoxazole (SXT). The authors of the dataset provided a train/test division based on the years: specimen samples of the train set have been collected during the years 2007–2013, whereas the specimen in the test set refers to the period 2014–2016. Respecting this original division, the train set of first-line prescriptions contains 6815 samples, while the test set contains 2618 samples. Among the train set, 1892 samples received an empirical prescription of nitrofurantoin (NIT), and 4923 the trimethoprim-sulfamethoxazole (SXT). In the test set, 1358 samples where prescribed nitrofurantoin (NIT), the remaining 1260 trimethoprim-sulfamethoxazole (SXT).

Among the features exposed in the AMR-UTI dataset, we considered the patients' demographic information as *"not-corruptible"* (which we model through the input *mask* in Algorithm 1), in the sense that the adversary has no interest in altering these information in the clinical record of the patient, because of their ease of counter-proofing with reality. By performing other preprocessing steps which are released as part of the source code[2], we resort to a set of 564 binary features which are represented with different time granularities. In this paper, we restrict the analysis to the features registered within 180 days, also because this is the time window most commonly shared between all the features, for a total amount of 135. Finally, we select the κ best features according to the chi-square independence test [25], where κ is considered as one of the hyperparameters whose exploration will be further described in the next subsection. Having fixed a specific value for κ, we remove all those samples with equal binary features values but different label.

6.1 The Classification Network

Experiments were performed starting from an existing neural network[3], which we extended by adding the cross entropy loss function, the softmax activation layer, the momentum gradient descent, the regularization through weight decay,

[1] https://www.physionet.org/content/antimicrobial-resistance-uti/1.0.0/.
[2] https://github.com/agiammanco94/AIxIA2021.
[3] https://github.com/RafayAK/NothingButNumPy.

Table 1. Ranges of values for the hyperparameters explored with Random Search.

Category	Hyperparameter	Min	Max
Network	Number of layers	2	7
	Number of neurons in 1st layer	50	500
Dataset	Number of κ features	20	70
Training	Learning rate α	$1e^{-4}$	$1e^{-3}$
	Weight decay λ	$1e^{-5}$	$1e^{-3}$
	Momentum ν	$1e^{-3}$	$8e^{-1}$

the random search algorithm for hyperparameters tuning [19], the FGSM [20], and the attack algorithm proposed in this work. We employ the random search approach [19] to explore different structures for the neural network (in terms of number of layers, and number of neurons per layer) and different configurations of the training phase (the learning rate, weight decay, and momentum factors for the gradient descent algorithm). Table 1 shows the range of values explored for each of the hyperparameters: in each experiment, a uniform probability with Min and Max as extremes is sampled for every hyperparameter. In particular, once the number of neurons for the first layer had been selected, the neurons for the subsequent layers are halved, given that a preliminary experimental evaluation proved this architectural choice to be more effective. The number of neurons in the last layer is equal to 2, since there are two classes (NIT and SXT) in the problem we are addressing. The activation functions employed are the ReLU for all the intermediate layers, and the Softmax for the output layer. This choice led to the adoption of the weights initialization procedure described in [22], which has been proved to be the optimal choice to combine with ReLU layers.

The *f-score* measure [19] has been employed to evaluate the effectiveness of the neural network classification; to be more specific, *f-score* values have been computed for each of the two classes separately, thus by assuming NIT and SXT as the positive class in turn. Then, in order to evaluate the effectiveness of the attack algorithm, the analysis was restricted to the portion of samples of the test set that the neural network identifies correctly, and we measured the error percentage of the model w.r.t. the corrupted input samples of a specific class as:

$$error\ {<}class{>} = \frac{|h_\theta(x+\delta) \neq class\ \&\ h_\theta(x) = class = y|}{|h_\theta(x) = class = y|},$$

where h_θ is the hypothesis of the model with the trained parameters θ, x is the set of samples in the test set, δ is the perturbation created with the attack algorithm, and y is the ground truth class.

6.2 Results and Discussion

We ran 50 batches of experiments where the neural network architecture hyperparameters are sampled from ranges shown in Table 1. For each batch, 50 dif-

Table 2. F-score and errors of the best performing experiment in each group.

Exp.	f-score NIT	f-score SXT	Error NIT					Error SXT				
			$\psi = 1$	$\psi = 2$	$\psi = 3$	$\psi = 4$	$\psi = 5$	$\psi = 1$	$\psi = 2$	$\psi = 3$	$\psi = 4$	$\psi = 5$
1	0.80	0.72	0.74	1.00	1.00	1.00	1.00	0.71	0.96	1.00	1.00	1.00
2	0.73	0.70	0.58	0.87	0.97	1.00	1.00	0.78	1.00	1.00	1.00	1.00
3	0.64	0.67	0.31	0.70	0.89	0.96	1.00	0.29	0.60	0.84	0.95	1.00

Table 3. Hyperparameters of the most significant experiments.

Experiment	Neurons	κ	α	λ	ν
1	$145, 2$	29	$6.70e^{-4}$	$1.71e^{-4}$	$4.38e^{-1}$
2	$177, 2$	42	$5.40e^{-4}$	$1.36e^{-4}$	$7.49e^{-3}$
3	$215, 2$	59	$5.18e^{-4}$	$3.25e^{-5}$	$7.65e^{-1}$

ferent samplings of training hyperparameters have been explored while keeping fixed the network structure sharing such values in all neurons, so resulting in a total number of 2500 configurations. Results have been analyzed according to the value of κ; in particular we considered three ranges of values, i.e., κ in $[20; 30]$, $[31; 50]$, and $[51; 70]$. For the sake of clarity, in Table 2 we present the most significant results from each group, while the corresponding hyperparameters are reported in Table 3. In particular, Table 2 shows the *f-scores* of the selected models w.r.t. the two classes, as well as the error percentage due to the injection of $\psi \in [1, 2, 3, 4, 5]$ binary feature values into the test data with our attack algorithm. When the dataset is preprocessed in order to select only the $\kappa = 29$ most meaningful features (first row), our attack procedure with $\psi = 3$ allowed to completely mislead the neural network for all the test data. This result can be due to the extreme sparsity of the AMR-UTI dataset, in which the vast majority of the binary features have value 0. For such a reason, when a binary feature value is flipped from 0 to 1 in the direction of the loss' gradient, it is extremely likely that the new feature becomes "characteristic" for the target class, thus flipping the label with high probability. As the number of features considered increases, an higher quantity of features needs to be perturbed in order to completely subvert the predictions, in particular, for $\kappa = 42$ and $\kappa = 59$ (second and third row of Table 2), the best performances of the algorithm are achieved by altering 4 and 5 features respectively.

In order to provide a more in-depth analysis of the features that have actually been altered in the experiments carried out, Fig. 2 shows the percentage of times that a given feature has been chosen by our algorithm, and the corresponding success rate in deceiving the model. The two heatmaps are computed aggregating the results of the three experiments reported in Table 2. It is important to note that the percentages of feature selections depicted in the first heatmap have unitary sum for a fixed value of ψ, meaning that the shown set of features contains all the perturbed ones. Instead, the percentages of success due

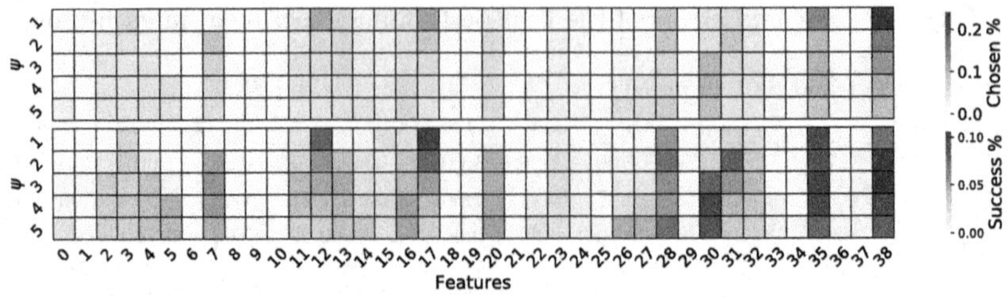

Fig. 2. Heatmaps of the perturbed features by our attack algorithm, and the respective success percentage in changing the prediction of the model.

to feature perturbations represented in the second heatmap sum to the error rate of the model, e.g., when $\psi = 5$ the percentages of success add up to 1, since results shown full model deception in all the experiments by altering 5 features. The most selected feature (38) is related to breathing difficulties, and it has been chosen for the 13.67% of times across both all the experiments and ψ values, leading to success in 8.89% of cases w.r.t. the total of all other perturbation attempts. The motivation behind this fact can be traced back to the adverse effects of the two active principles. Indeed, among the side effects of nitrofurantoin assumption[4] there is pulmonary toxicity, which is instead absent in trimethoprim-sulfamethoxazole's side effects[5]. In light of this consideration, our approach realized the shrewd behavior of the doctor prescribing SXT treatment for patients who have recently experienced breathing complications.

7 Conclusions

In this paper, we proposed an algorithm for the generation of adversarial examples in scenarios with electronic health records in the form of binary data. In particular, we studied how an adversary may alter the medical record of a patient in order to fool an intelligent system for antibiotic prescription. The experimental results showed that even only modifying three fields in the patient record, a trained neural network can almost always be induced into suggesting a prearranged treatment. As part of our future works, we want to eliminate the time granularity as input parameter to filter the dataset. For example, if the adversarial noise produced by an attack algorithm suggests to modify a feature with time granularity equal to 14 days from 0 to 1, then, all the features falling in the same category and with a granularity > 14 should be set to 1. Moreover, we plan to define an automatic strategy for dynamically choosing the number of ψ features to perturb based on the magnitude of the gradient, so that ψ does not need to be specified as input to the approach. Finally, we want to investigate the

[4] https://www.msdmanuals.com/professional/infectious-diseases/bacteria-and-antibacterial-drugs/nitrofurantoin.

[5] https://www.msdmanuals.com/professional/infectious-diseases/bacteria-and-antibacterial-drugs/trimethoprim-and-sulfamethoxazole.

feasibility of our approach in other smart environments such as university campuses [1], where adversarial attacks aim at disrupting the provision of intelligent services to users [14].

References

1. Agate, V., Concone, F., Ferraro, P.: WIP: smart services for an augmented campus. In: 2018 IEEE International Conference on Smart Computing, pp. 276–278 (2018)
2. Agate, V., De Paola, A., Gaglio, S., Lo Re, G., Morana, M.: A framework for parallel assessment of reputation management systems. In: 17th International Conference on Computer Systems and Technologies, pp. 121–128 (2016)
3. Agate, V., De Paola, A., Lo Re, G., Morana, M.: A simulation software for the evaluation of vulnerabilities in reputation management systems. ACM Trans. Comput. Syst. (TOCS) **37**(1–4), 1–30 (2021)
4. Agate, V., Ferraro, P., Gaglio, S.: A cognitive architecture for ambient intelligence systems. In: AIC, pp. 52–58 (2018)
5. Al-Dujaili, A., Huang, A., Hemberg, E., O'Reilly, U.M.: Adversarial deep learning for robust detection of binary encoded malware. In: 2018 IEEE Security and Privacy Workshops (SPW), pp. 76–82 (2018)
6. Biggio, B., Roli, F.: Wild patterns: ten years after the rise of adversarial machine learning. Pattern Recogn. **84**, 317–331 (2018)
7. Buckner, C.: Understanding adversarial examples requires a theory of artefacts for deep learning. Nat. Mach. Intell. **2**, 731–736 (2020)
8. Chen, J., Wu, D., Zhao, Y., Sharma, N., Blumenstein, M., Yu, S.: Fooling intrusion detection systems using adversarially autoencoder. Digit. Commun. Netw. **7**, 453–460 (2020)
9. Concone, F., Gaglio, S., Lo Re, G., Morana, M.: Smartphone data analysis for human activity recognition. In: Esposito, F., Basili, R., Ferilli, S., Lisi, F. (eds.) AI*IA 2017. LNCS, vol. 10640, pp. 58–71. Springer, Cham (2017). https://doi.org/10.1007/978-3-319-70169-1_5
10. Concone, F., Lo Re, G., Morana, M.: A fog-based application for human activity recognition using personal smart devices. ACM Trans. Internet Technol. (TOIT) **19**(2), 1–20 (2019)
11. Concone, F., Lo Re, G., Morana, M., Ruocco, C.: Twitter spam account detection by effective labeling. In: ITASEC (2019)
12. De Paola, A., et al.: A context-aware system for ambient assisted living. In: Ochoa, S.F., Singh, P., Bravo, J. (eds.) UCAmI 2017. LNCS, vol. 10586, pp. 426–438. Springer, Cham (2017). https://doi.org/10.1007/978-3-319-67585-5_44
13. De Paola, A., Ferraro, P., Lo Re, G., Morana, M., Ortolani, M.: A fog-based hybrid intelligent system for energy saving in smart buildings. J. Ambient. Intell. Humaniz. Comput. **11**(7), 2793–2807 (2019). https://doi.org/10.1007/s12652-019-01375-2
14. De Paola, A., Gaglio, S., Giammanco, A., Lo Re, G., Morana, M.: A multi-agent system for itinerary suggestion in smart environments. In: CAAI Transactions on Intelligence Technology (2021)
15. De Paola, A., Gaglio, S., Lo Re, G., Morana, M.: A hybrid system for malware detection on big data. In: IEEE INFOCOM 2018 - IEEE Conference on Computer Communications Workshops (INFOCOM WKSHPS), pp. 45–50 (2018)
16. Demontis, A., et al.: Why do adversarial attacks transfer? Explaining transferability of evasion and poisoning attacks. In: 28th USENIX Security Symposium (USENIX Security 2019), pp. 321–338 (2019)

17. Finlayson, S.G., Bowers, J.D., Ito, J., Zittrain, J.L., Beam, A.L., Kohane, I.S.: Adversarial attacks on medical machine learning. Science **363**(6433), 1287–1289 (2019)
18. Goldberger, A.L., et al.: PhysioBank, PhysioToolkit, and PhysioNet: components of a new research resource for complex physiologic signals. Circulation **101**(23), e215–e220 (2000)
19. Goodfellow, I., Bengio, Y., Courville, A.: Deep Learning. MIT Press, Cambridge (2016)
20. Goodfellow, I., Shlens, J., Szegedy, C.: Explaining and harnessing adversarial examples. In: International Conference on Learning Representations (2015)
21. Guo, Q., et al.: INOR-an intelligent noise reduction method to defend against adversarial audio examples. Neurocomputing **401**, 160–172 (2020)
22. He, K., Zhang, X., Ren, S., Sun, J.: Delving deep into rectifiers: surpassing human-level performance on ImageNet classification. In: Proceedings of the IEEE International Conference on Computer Vision (ICCV) (2015)
23. Kanjilal, S., Oberst, M., Boominathan, S., Zhou, H., Hooper, D.C., Sontag, D.: A decision algorithm to promote outpatient antimicrobial stewardship for uncomplicated urinary tract infection. Science Transl. Med. **12**(568) (2020)
24. Maiorca, D., Demontis, A., Biggio, B., Roli, F., Giacinto, G.: Adversarial detection of flash malware: limitations and open issues. Comput. Secur. **96** (2020)
25. McHugh, M.L.: The chi-square test of independence. Biochemia medica **23**(2), 143–149 (2013)
26. Newaz, A.I., Haque, N.I., Sikder, A.K., Rahman, M.A., Uluagac, A.S.: Adversarial attacks to machine learning-based smart healthcare systems. In: 2020 IEEE Global Communications Conference, GLOBECOM 2020, pp. 1–6 (2020)
27. Oberst, M., Boominathan, S., Zhou, H., Kanjilal, S., Sontag, D.: AMR-UTI: antimicrobial resistance in urinary tract infections (version 1.0.0). Physionet (2020)
28. Verbraeken, J., Wolting, M., Katzy, J., Kloppenburg, J., Verbelen, T., Rellermeyer, J.S.: A survey on distributed machine learning. ACM Comput. Surv. (CSUR) **53**(2), 1–33 (2020)
29. Xue, M., Yuan, C., He, C., Wang, J., Liu, W.: NaturalAE: natural and robust physical adversarial examples for object detectors. J. Inf. Secur. Appl. **57**, 102694 (2021)
30. Zhao, P., Huang, H., Zhao, X., Huang, D.: P^3: privacy-preserving scheme against poisoning attacks in mobile-edge computing. IEEE Trans. Comput. Soc. Syst. **7**, 818–826 (2020)

Deep Learning of Recurrence Texture in Physiological Signals

Tuan D. Pham(✉)

Center for Artificial Intelligence, Prince Mohammad Bin Fahd University, Khobar 31952, Saudi Arabia
tpham@pmu.edu.sa

Abstract. The concept of recurrence in nonlinear dynamics has been found useful for discovering patterns in complex time series of natural, physical, and biological processes. The method of fuzzy recurrence plots has recently been developed for studying patterns of recurrent behaviors in dynamical systems. Analysis of physiological time series has increasingly become important for medical research, and deep learning is reported in literature as the most advanced approach in artificial intelligence for classification of time series. For the first time, this paper presents the idea of computing texture properties of fuzzy recurrence of physiological time series to be used as input data for classification of physiological time series with deep recurrent neural networks. A public gait in Parkinson's disease database was used to test the performance of the proposed approach. The deep learning of texture can significantly increase improvements in classification accuracy over some existing deep-learning models.

Keywords: Deep learning · Texture · Fuzzy recurrence plots · Physiological signals · Classification

1 Introduction

Artificial intelligence (AI) methods for analysis of physiological time series have been recognized to be useful for gaining insights into biomedical patterns and discovering latent information embedded in complex data, where conventional statistical techniques may not provide good solutions [1,2]. Advances in time series analysis offer the potential for facilitating better understanding of the dynamics underlying experimental or observational data in medicine and biology. The application of AI for discovering such dynamical behaviors associated with medical sensor-based data is critical for forecasting and prediction of future outcome [3]. In fact, the use of deep learning in AI for pattern recognition using sensor-based data is an area of research attracting increasing interest in recent years [4]. The need for mathematical time-series analysis in medicine has been well recognized because it can help medical researchers timely understand differences between normal and disordered physiology, study the development of

S. Bandini et al. (Eds.): AIxIA 2021, LNAI 13196, pp. 503–514, 2022.
https://doi.org/10.1007/978-3-031-08421-8_35

disease processes, be useful for monitoring response to drugs and interventions, and investigate transient behaviors in the data associated with many complex human diseases [5–8].

In nonlinear dynamics, an approach for visualization and analysis of nonlinear time series is the method of recurrence plots [9]. Recurrence plots have been found useful for discovering hidden patterns in nonlinear data [10]. A recurrence plot is a two-dimensional graphical representation of times at which a phase space trajectory visits the same area in the phase space. Its visual appearance can discover several useful properties of structural changes of the dynamical system under study. However, a reliable construction of a recurrence plot critically depends on the selection of a similarity threshold, which can be very sensitive in many applications and therefore requires special attention [11]. To overcome the difficulty in the definition of similarity for the inclusion of a revisit in a recurrence plot, the concept of a fuzzy recurrence plot has recently been introduced to address this issue as an advanced method for nonlinear time-series analysis [12]. Furthermore, while a recurrence plot displays recurrences as a binary image, a fuzzy recurrence plot is a grayscale image of recurrences and therefore much richer in texture.

Because texture is well known as an effective feature for image classification, this study presents a new way for a recurrent neural network in learning sequential data with textural features. In contrast to the model reported in [13], which proposed no more than the use of a fuzzy recurrence plot as the input into the long short-term memory (LSTM) neural network, the model presented in this study has the different key feature: Constructing textural images of recurrence from time series by means of the method of fuzzy recurrence plots, and temporal texture features are extracted from local regions of these images of time series and used as input into an LSTM neural network for the classification of physiological time series.

2 Methods

2.1 Texture of Recurrence Dynamics

Let $X = (\mathbf{x}_1, \dots, \mathbf{x}_N)$ be a collection of phase-space vectors, in which $\mathbf{x}_i$ is the state of a dynamical system at time i in m-dimensional space. A fuzzy recurrence plot (FRP) represents the recurrences of $\{\mathbf{x}\}$, which visits the same area in the phase space, as a grayscale image whose intensity distribution takes values in $[0, 1]$ [12].

In mathematical terms, let $\mathbf{V} = \{\mathbf{v}\}$ be the set of fuzzy clusters of the phase-space vectors. A binary relation $\tilde{\mathbf{R}}$ from $\mathbf{X}$ to $\mathbf{V}$ is a fuzzy subset of $\mathbf{X} \times \mathbf{V}$ characterized by a fuzzy membership function $\mu \in [0, 1]$. This fuzzy membership grade is the degree of relation of each pair $(\mathbf{x}_i, \mathbf{v}_j)$, $i = 1, \dots, N$, $j = 1, \dots, c$, where c is the number of clusters, which has the following properties [12]:

1. Reflexivity: $\mu(\mathbf{x}_i, \mathbf{x}_i) = 1$, $\forall \mathbf{x} \in \mathbf{X}$,
2. Symmetry: $\mu(\mathbf{x}_i, \mathbf{v}_j) = \mu(\mathbf{v}_j, \mathbf{x}_i)$, $\forall \mathbf{x} \in \mathbf{X}, \forall \mathbf{v} \in \mathbf{V}$, and
3. Transitivity: $\mu(\mathbf{x}_i, \mathbf{x}_k) = \vee_{\mathbf{v}}[\mu(\mathbf{x}_i, \mathbf{v}_j) \wedge \mu(\mathbf{v}_j, \mathbf{x}_k)]$, $\forall \mathbf{x} \in \mathbf{X}$, which is called the max-min composition, where the symbols $\vee$ and $\wedge$ stand for max and min, respectively.

If the fuzzy membership function that indicates the similarity between the phase space trajectory at two different times (visiting the same area in the phase space) can be obtained, then the above three properties of an FRP can be readily constructed. A solution for computing the fuzzy membership function is by using the fuzzy *c*-means algorithm [14]. To be consistent with the definition of a recurrence plot, where black and white dots indicate recurring and non-recurring events, respectively; the complement of the fuzzy membership function of an FRP is therefore used to display the recurrences of the phase-space vectors as a grayscale image of texture [12]. More detailed description of the construction of FRPs and available Matlab codes can be found in [12,15].

Figure 1 shows the FRPs of a sinc function, white Gaussian noise, and z-component of the Lorenz system time series of 1000 points in length, constructed with embedding dimension = 3, time delay = 1, and the number of fuzzy clusters = 3. The FRPs of the three time series exhibit different patterns of texture: homogeneous distribution of points for the random data, checkerboard structure for the sinc function, and gray bands for the chaotic signal.

2.2 Deep Learning of Texture of Recurrence in Time Series

An LSTM network is a popular type of recurrent neural networks (RNNs) in state-of-the-art AI [16,17]. The network can learn long-term dependencies between time steps of sequential data [18]. Unlike conventional feedforward neural networks, an LSTM model has feedback loops that allow information of previous events to be carried on in the sequential learning process. The difference between an LSTM neural network and a conventional RNN is the use of memory blocks for the former network instead of hidden units for the latter [19].

The new architecture for an LSTM block is graphically described in Fig. 2. This figure illustrates the flow of a time series $\mathbf{u}$ with M features of length N through an LSTM layer. These features are texture properties extracted from an FRP and are used as input values that play the role in creating multiple dimensions for the time series to enhance the LSTM-network training. Furthermore, the original time points of the time series are now replaced with reduced time points on the transformed multidimensional data. Thus, instead of learning from the direct input of time series, the LSTM is fed with temporal texture features of multiple dimensions.

The learnable weights of an LSTM layer are the input weights, denoted as $\mathbf{a}$, recurrent weights, denoted as $\mathbf{r}$, and bias, denoted as b. The matrices $\mathbf{A}$, $\mathbf{R}$, and vector $\mathbf{b}$ are the concatenations of the input weights, recurrent weights, and bias of each component, respectively. The concatenations are expressed as [8]

$$\mathbf{A} = [\mathbf{a}_i, \mathbf{a}_f, \mathbf{a}_g, \mathbf{a}_o]^T, \quad (1)$$

$$\mathbf{R} = [\mathbf{r}_i, \mathbf{r}_f, \mathbf{r}_g, \mathbf{r}_o]^T, \quad (2)$$

$$\mathbf{b} = [b_i, b_f, b_g, b_o]^T, \quad (3)$$

where i, f, g, and o denote the input gate, forget gate, cell candidate, and outputgate, respectively.

The cell state at time step t is defined as

$$\mathbf{c}_t = f_t \circ \mathbf{c}_{t-1} + i_t \circ g_t, \quad (4)$$

where $\circ$ is the Hadamard product.

The hidden state at time step t is given by

$$\mathbf{h}_t = o_t \circ \sigma_c(\mathbf{c}_t), \quad (5)$$

where σ_c is the state activation function that is usually computed as the hyperbolic tangent function (tanh).

At time step t, the input gate (i_t), forget gate (f_t), cell candidate (g_t), and output gate (o_t) are defined as

$$i_t = \sigma_g(\mathbf{a}_i \mathbf{u}_t + \mathbf{r}_i \mathbf{h}_{t-1} + b_i), \quad (6)$$

$$g_t = \sigma_c(\mathbf{a}_g \mathbf{u}_t + \mathbf{r}_g \mathbf{h}_{t-1} + b_g), \quad (7)$$

$$o_t = \sigma_g(\mathbf{a}_o \mathbf{u}_t + \mathbf{r}_o \mathbf{h}_{t-1} + b_o), \quad (8)$$

where σ_g denotes the gate activation function that usually adopts the sigmoid function.

The extraction of temporal texture features from an FRP for the LSTM learning is carried out by dividing the FRP into subimages having a width $w < N$ pixels. The process is done on either the top row, which is FRP(1,:), or far left column, which is FRP(:,1), of the FRP. Consider that the width w is taken along the top row of the FRP. Subimages of size N-by-w are therefore created out of the FRP for the timewise extraction of texture features. The N-by-w subimages are constructed by starting at the first column of the FRP and sequentially dividing it into smaller images with a non-overlapping interval of w pixels until the last column of the FRP is included. The width of the last subimage can be smaller than w if the ratio of N to w is a non-integer. Figure 3 illustrates the construction of the subimages of an FRP for texture extraction.

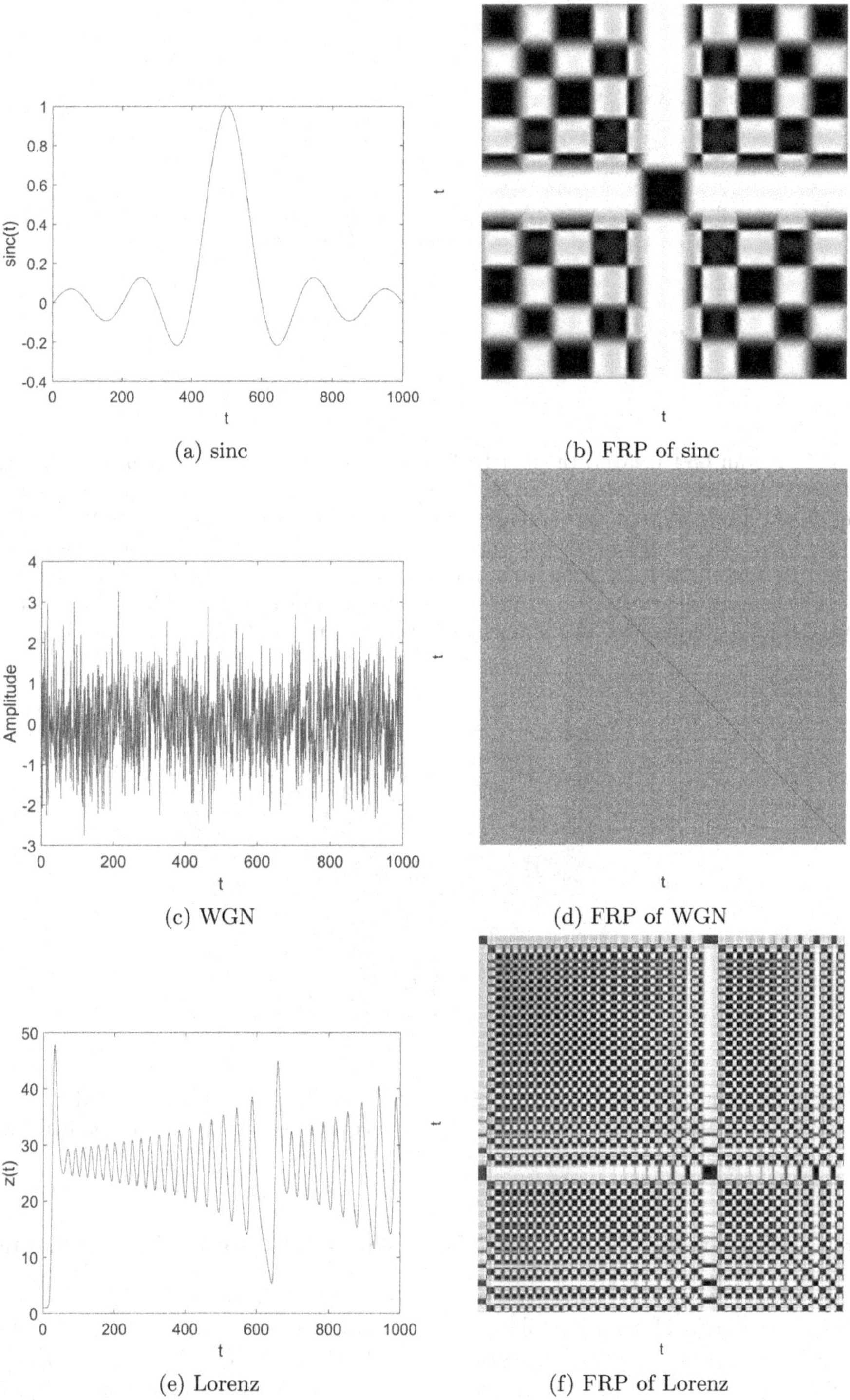

Fig. 1. Time series and FRPs of sinc function, white Gaussian noise (WGN), and z-component of the Lorenz system.

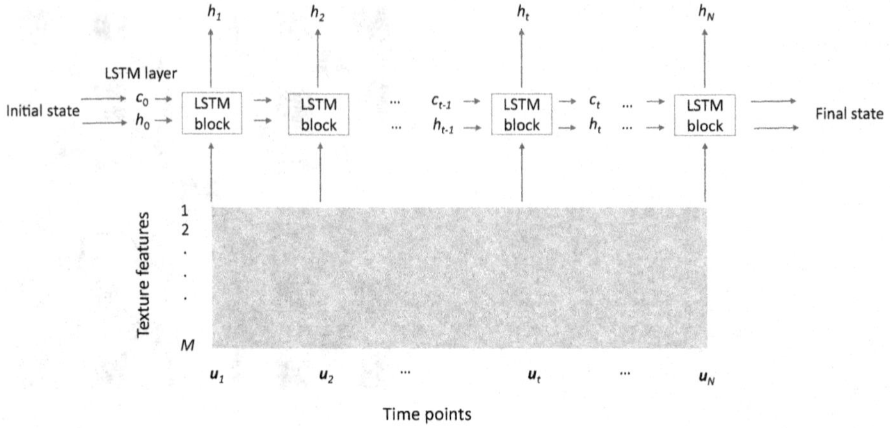

Fig. 2. For an LSTM layer, the first LSTM block takes the initial state of the network and the first time point of the $M \times N$ temporal texture data ($\mathbf{u}_1$), and then computes the first output h_1 and the updated cell state c_1, then at time step t, the LSTM block takes the current state of the network c_{t-1}, h_{t-1} and the next time point of the temporal texture at t, and then computes the output h_t and the updated cell state c_t. Texture-feature dimensions and time points are not drawn to scale. The texture image is a virtual representation of the texture features extracted from the associated FRP.

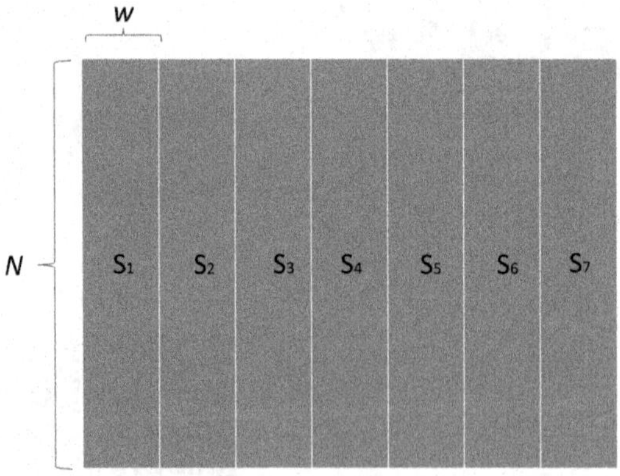

Fig. 3. Example of seven subimages ($S_1, \ldots, S_7$), each of size N-by-w, created from an FRP for temporal texture extraction, where the column size of S_7 can be smaller than w, depending on the column size of the FRP.

2.3 Simulation of Texture for Data Augmentation in Deep Learning

An advantage of the transformation of time series into an FRP is that the grayscale image of an FRP allows data augmentation by geostatistical simulation for improving the training of the LSTM network described earlier. Based on simulated FRPs, more texture features can be extracted for training the network. The sequential Gaussian simulation (SGS) is a geostatistical method for stochastic simulation, which can generate equiprobable maps of the spatial distribution of the original data [20]. Therefore, using SGS, numerous simulated copies of an original image can be produced for training deep neural networks [21]. The simulation process is mainly carried out using a kriging method, which is a local spatial estimator and described as follows.

Let $Z(x)$ be a random function. Assuming that the kriging error produced by kriging estimate of the random function at location x_0, denoted as $\hat{Z}(x_0)$, is normally distributed, the probability distribution for the actual value is $N(\hat{z}(x_0), \sigma^2(x_0))$. Based on this assumption, the SGS can be performed using kriging estimates, where each simulated value is a realization of a multivariate normal process. In addition, for the conditional SGS, which is specified with a percentage of unchanged (hard) data, the kriging variance at these locations is zero. This condition is set to ensure that only possible drawings are those of the observed values.

The simple kriging estimator is applied to estimate the value at location x_0 by a linear combination of its neighboring values as [20]

$$\hat{Z}(x_0) = m + \sum_{i=1}^{k} w_i[Z(x_i) - m], \tag{9}$$

where $\hat{Z}(x_0)$ is the estimated value, m is the mean of the random function $Z(x)$, w_i are kriging weights, and k is the number of neighbors of x_0.

The kriging weights can be computed as

$$\sum_{i=1}^{k} w_i C(x_i, x_j) = C(x_0, x_j), j = 1, \ldots, k. \tag{10}$$

where $C(\cdot)$ is the covariance of the random function of interest, which is usually replaced with a model of theoretical semi-variograms such as the Gaussian semi-variogram or experimental semi-variogram [20]. The use of the semi-variogram function is often adopted because the random function $Z(x)$ can be intrinsic and the covariance function does not exist [22].

Using the computed simple kriging weights, the minimized mean square error for the simple kriging, denoted as $\sigma^2_{SK}(x_0)$, can be determined as

$$\sigma^2_{SK}(x_0) = C(x_0, x_0) - \sum_{i=1}^{k} w_i C(x_0, x_i), \tag{11}$$

where $C(x_0, x_0)$ is called the nugget effect in geostatistics.

The steps for carrying out the SGS are outlined as follows:

1. Transform the original data into normal scores, if the data are not univariate normal.
2. Select randomly a node at location x_i that is not yet simulated.

3. Estimate $Z(x_i)$ using Eq. (9) and compute kriging variance $\sigma^2_{SK}(x_i)$ using Eq. (11).
4. The simulated value is the one randomly drawn from the normal distribution $N(\hat{Z}(x_i), \sigma^2_{SK}(x_i))$.
5. Include the simulated value in the conditional or unconditional data.
6. If x_i is not the last node to be simulated, go back to Step 2.
7. If the original data were transformed, then back transform all the values to the original data range.

2.4 Procedure of Proposed Method

The procedure for the proposed LSTM-based classification of time series can be outlined as follows.

1. Given a time series, generating phase-space vectors from the data in which each vector is a state of a dynamical system in time.
2. Transform the phase-space vectors into a grayscale texture image (FRP) representing recurrences of a state-space vector in the same area of the phase space using FRP.
3. Generate texture augmentation using SGS.
4. For every pixel of the grayscale texture image, selecting a local window, where the pixel is at the center.
5. Extract temporal texture features of each window to obtain a multi-dimensional time series of corresponding multiple texture features.
6. Input the time series of multidimensional texture to an LSTM network for deep learning and classification.

3 Results and Discussion

The Gait in Parkinson's Disease Database [23,24] was used in this study to test and compare the LSTM learning of texture of time series, denoted as LSTM-Texture, with existing state-of-the-art methods for time-series classification. The database contains measures of gait dynamics from 93 patients with idiopathic PD, and 72 healthy controls. The database includes the vertical ground reaction force (VGRF) records of subjects as they walked at their usual, self-selected pace for approximately 2 min on level ground. Underneath each foot were 8 sensors that measure force (in Newtons) as a function of time. VGRF data recorded from a sensor located under the right foot of each subject were used. To balance the sample sizes of the two cohorts, 72 patients with PD and 72 healthy controls were selected in this study. The time-series length of 2000 was chosen by taking the time points from the beginning of the signals. Figure 4 shows time series of the gait dynamics and the corresponding FRPs of a healthy and a PD subjects.

The deep LSTM network was configured with the number of hidden layers = 100, maximum number of epochs = 200, and learning rate = 0.001. The FRPs were constructed with the embedding dimension = 1, time delay = 1, number

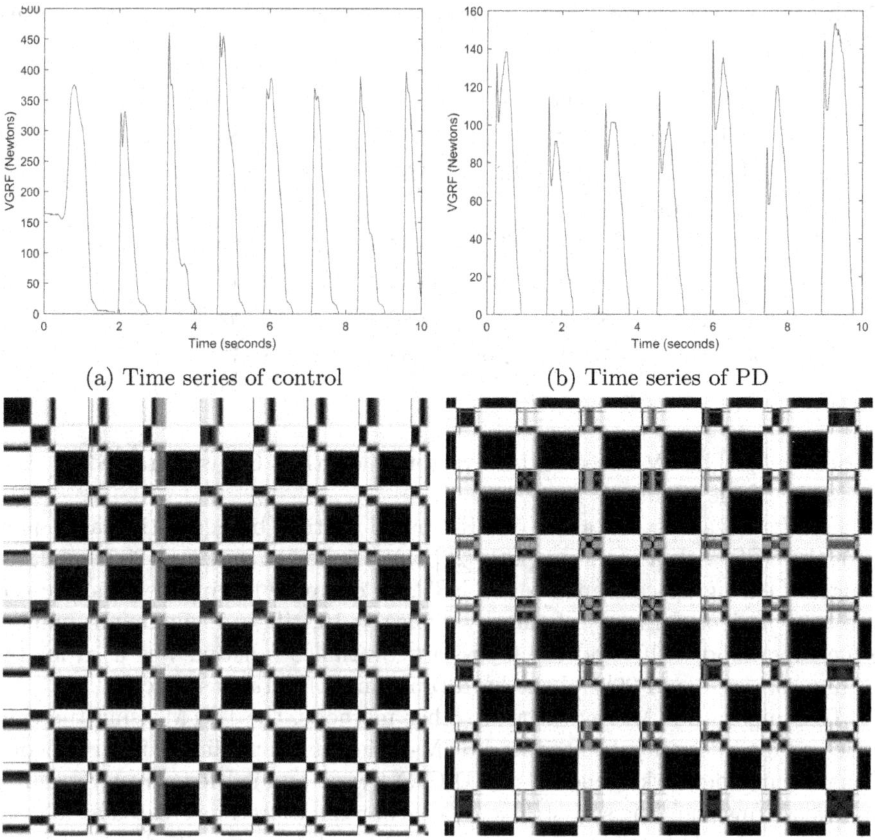

(a) Time series of control (b) Time series of PD

(c) FRP of Control (d) FRP of PD

Fig. 4. Time series and FRPs of control and PD subjects.

of clusters = 3, and fuzzy weighting exponent $q = 2$. To extract texture from an FRP, $w = 15$, 20, 25, and 30 were specified at each time point of the time series.

Gray-level co-occurrence matrix (GLCM) [25], local binary pattern (LBP) [26], and semi-variogram (SV) [27] features were extracted from the subimages of each FRP. The GLCM-based texture includes 19 features described in [28], including entropy, energy, correlation, contrast, sum of squares (variance), sum average, sum variance, sum entropy, difference variance, difference entropy, information measures of correlation, autocorrelation, dissimilarity, homogeneity, cluster prominence, cluster shade, maximum probability, inverse difference, and inverse difference moment normalized. For the extraction of the LBP-based texture, the algorithm parameters were chosen as follows: number of neighbors = 8, radius = 1, and nearest interpolation method was used to compute pixel neighbors; the histogram parameters: cell size = 2-element vector, and normal-

Table 1. Average ten-fold cross-validations of classification of gait-dynamics time series.

Feature	Accuracy (%)	Sensitivity (%)	Specificity (%)
LSTM-series	43.62 ± 11.42	18.93 ± 17.66	67.86 ± 11.22
1D-CNN	46.79 ± 12.38	43.57 ± 15.27	50.00 ± 10.48
LSTM-Texture			
$w = 15$	76.93 ± 10.39	79.57 ± 14.75	74.29 ± 13.94
$w = 20$	81.79 ± 9.03	86.43 ± 18.50	77.14 ± 8.25
$w = 25$	**82.64** ± 13.02	92.86 ± 17.29	72.43 ± 6.52
$w = 30$	76.21 ± 12.49	71.69 ± 13.47	80.73 ± 7.43

ization = L_2. The SV-based texture vector of length = 6 was extracted for each subimage of the FRPs.

For the data augmentation of FRP-based texture by geostatistical simulation, the SGS with a constant path [29] was applied to generate 200 simulated images of each grayscale image of an FRP. To compute kriging weights, the vertical and horizonal ranges of the covariance = 10, sill = 1, maximum number of neighborhood = 10, and the Gaussian covariance function was used for the kriging estimate, and 90% of the hard (unchanged) data was specified.

To compare LSTM-Texture with other methods, the LSTM using the time series as direct input, denoted as LSTM-Series, and one-dimensional convolutional neural network, denoted as 1D-CNN, were applied for directly training and classifying the time series. The 1D-CNN architecture was created as follows. The input size of the time series to the CNN model was specified as $L \times 1 \times 1$, where L is the length of the time series. A convolutional layer was constructed with 16 filters that have the height and width of 3. Padding was applied to the input along the edges. Padding was set so that the output size was the same as the input size where the stride is 1. A fully connected layer with an output size of 384 in the hidden layer and 2 as the output classes were specified.

Average results of five 10-fold cross-validations in terms of accuracy, sensitivity, and specificity obtained from the LSTM by directly using the time series and by learning FRP-based texture of the time series are given in Table 1. In similarity to the study of the voice data, the use of texture extracted from the VGRF time series (LSTM-Texture) outperforms the direct use of the VGRF time series (LSTM-Series) and 1D-CNN in terms of accuracy, sensitivity, and specificity in all values specified for w, where again $w = 25$ achieves the best accuracy. The results shown in Table 1 indicate that the classification of this dataset is a challenge for LSTM-series and 1D-CNN that provided very low accuracy rates. LSTM-Series yields the sensitivity much lower than the specificity. Sensitivity rates are higher than specificity for the three best results provided by the proposed LSTM-Texture with $w = 15$, 20, and 25. Regarding the classification accuracy, the LSTM-Texture can improve the result over the LSTM-Series by 89% ($(83 - 44)/44 \times 100$) and 1D-CNN by 77% ($(83 - 47)/47 \times 100$).

A most recent study on the classification of gait dynamics in PD patients and control subjects using the same dataset [30] took the advantage of multivariate data recorded from all 8 sensors for both left and right feet, i.e., 16 time series for each of 93 PD and 72 subjects, and the accuracy rate obtained from the method of tensor decomposition and least-squares support vector machines = 100%. However, it should be pointed out that the proposed LSTM network learning of texture of time series is a univariate-based method, which involves the analysis of a single variable, i.e., only one time series recorded from a single sensor placed under the right foot of each subject used for classification, but the results using balanced data (72 PD patients and 72 controls) is as high as 83%, thus suggesting the high performance of the proposed approach.

4 Conclusion

A new concept of transforming time series into texture for deep learning with the LSTM neural network has been presented and discussed. The results obtained using the gate dynamics database show that the texture-based deep learning provides significant improvements over other time-series-based deep learning models. The combination of nonlinear time-series analysis in physics, texture in image processing, and machine learning in AI is a powerful tool for the analysis and classification of physiological signals, particularly where medical data for machine learning is limited [31].

References

1. Topol, E.: Deep Medicine: How Artificial Intelligence Can Make Healthcare Human Again. Basic Books, New York (2019)
2. Rieke, N., Hancox, J., Li, W., et al.: The future of digital health with federated learning. NPJ Digit. Med. **3**, 119 (2020)
3. Jebb, A.T., Tay, L., Wang, W., Huang, Q.: Time series analysis for psychological research: examining and forecasting change. Front. Psychol. **6**, 727 (2015)
4. Wang, J., Chen, Y., Hao, S., Peng, X., et al.: Deep learning for sensor-based activity recognition: a survey. Pattern Recogn. Lett. **119**, 3–11 (2019)
5. Sinha, A., Lutter, R., Xu, B., et al.: Loss of adaptive capacity in asthmatic patients revealed by biomarker fluctuation dynamics after rhinovirus challenge. Elife **8**, e47969 (2019)
6. Li, P.: EZ entropy: a software application for the entropy analysis of physiological time-series. Biomed. Eng. Online **18**, 30 (2019)
7. Olsavszky, V., Dosius, M., Vladescu, C., Benecke, J.: Time series analysis and forecasting with automated machine learning on a national ICD-10 Database. Int. J. Environ. Res. Public Health **17**, 4979 (2020)
8. Pham, T.D.: Time-frequency time-space LSTM for robust classification of physiological signals. Sci. Rep. **11**, 6936 (2021)
9. Eckmann, J.P., Kamphorst, S.O., Ruelle, D.: Recurrence plots of dynamical systems. Europhys. Lett. **5**, 973–977 (1987)
10. Marwan, N., Romano, M.C., Thiel, M., Kurths, J.: Recurrence plots for the analysis of complex systems. Phys. Rep. **438**, 237–329 (2007)

11. Facchini, A., Mocenni, C., Vicino, A.: Generalized recurrence plots for the analysis of images from spatially distributed systems. Phys. D **238**, 162–169 (2009)
12. Pham, T.D.: Fuzzy recurrence plots. EPL **116**, 50008 (2016)
13. Pham, T.D., Wardell, K., Eklund, A., et al.: Classification of short time series in early Parkinson's disease with deep learning of fuzzy recurrence plots, IEEE/CAA. J. Autom. Sin. **6**, 1306–1317 (2019)
14. Bezdek, J.C.: Pattern Recognition with Fuzzy Objective Function Algorithms. Plenum Press, New York (1981)
15. Pham, T.D.: Fuzzy Recurrence Plots and Networks with Applications in Biomedicine. Springer, Cham (2020). https://doi.org/10.1007/978-3-030-37530-0
16. Van Houdt, G., Mosquera, C., Nápoles, G.: A review on the long short-term memory model. Artif. Intell. Rev. **53**(8), 5929–5955 (2020). https://doi.org/10.1007/s10462-020-09838-1
17. Sherstinsky, A.: Fundamentals of recurrent neural network (RNN) and long short-term memory (LSTM) network. Phys. D **404**, 132306 (2020)
18. Hochreiter, S., Schmidhuber, J.: Long short-term memory. Neural Comput. **9**, 1735–1780 (1997)
19. Greff, K., Srivastava, R.K., Koutnik, J., et al.: LSTM: a search space odyssey. EEE Trans. Neural Netw. Learn. Syst. **28**, 2222–2232 (2017)
20. Olea, R.A.: Geostatistics for Engineers and Earth Scientists. Kluwer Academic Publishers, Boston (1999)
21. Pham, T.D.: Geostatistical simulation of medical images for data augmentation in deep learning. IEEE Access **7**, 68752–68763 (2019)
22. Journel, A.G., Huijbregts, C.J.: Mining Geostatistics. Blackburn Press, New Jersey (2003)
23. PhysioNet. https://physionet.org/content/gaitpdb/1.0.0/
24. Goldberger, A., Amaral, L., Glass, L., et al.: PhysioBank, PhysioToolkit, and PhysioNet: components of a new research resource for complex physiologic signals. Circulation **101**, e215 (2000)
25. Haralick, R.M., Shanmugam, K., Dinstein, I.: Textural features for image classification. IEEE Trans. Syst. Man Cybern. Syst. **3**, 610–621 (1973)
26. Ojala, T., Pietikainen, M., Maenpaa, T.: Multiresolution gray-scale and rotation invariant texture classification with local binary patterns. IEEE Trans. Pattern Anal. Mach. Intell. **24**, 971–987 (2002)
27. Pham, T.D.: The semi-variogram and spectral distortion measures for image texture retrieval. IEEE Trans. Image Process. **25**, 1556–1565 (2016)
28. Pham, T.D., Watanabe, Y., Higuchi, M., et al.: Texture analysis and synthesis of malignant and benign mediastinal lymph nodes in patients with lung cancer on computed tomography. Sci. Rep. **7**, 43209 (2017)
29. Nussbaumer, R., Mariethoz, G., Gravey, M., et al.: Accelerating sequential Gaussian simulation with a constant path. Comput. Geosci. **112**, 121–132 (2018)
30. Pham, T.D., Yan, H.: Tensor decomposition of gait dynamics in Parkinson's disease. IEEE Trans. Biomed. Eng. **65**, 1820–1827 (2018)
31. Gavrishchaka, V., Senyukova, O., Koepke, M.: Synergy of physics-based reasoning and machine learning in biomedical applications: towards unlimited deep learning with limited data. Adv. Phys. X **4**, 1582361 (2019)

Highlighting the Importance of Reducing Research Bias and Carbon Emissions in CNNs

Ahmed Badar(✉), Arnav Varma, Adrian Staniec, Mahmoud Gamal, Omar Magdy, Haris Iqbal, Elahe Arani, and Bahram Zonooz

Advanced Research Lab, NavInfo Europe, Eindhoven, The Netherlands
ahmed.badar@navinfo.eu

Abstract. Convolutional neural networks (CNNs) have become commonplace in addressing major challenges in computer vision. Researchers are not only coming up with new CNN architectures but are also researching different techniques to improve the performance of existing architectures. However, there is a tendency to over-emphasize performance improvement while neglecting certain important variables such as simplicity, versatility, the fairness of comparisons, and energy efficiency. Overlooking these variables in architectural design and evaluation has led to research bias and a significantly negative environmental impact. Furthermore, this can undermine the positive impact of research in using deep learning models to tackle climate change. Here, we perform an extensive and fair empirical study of a number of proposed techniques to gauge the utility of each technique for segmentation and classification. Our findings restate the importance of favoring simplicity over complexity in model design (Occam's Razor). Furthermore, our results indicate that simple standardized practices can lead to a significant reduction in environmental impact with little drop in performance. We highlight that there is a need to rethink the design and evaluation of CNNs to alleviate the issue of research bias and carbon emissions.

Keywords: Sustainability · Green AI · Convolutional neural networks

1 Introduction

Deep neural networks (DNNs) have achieved remarkable results in recent years [1], in applications such as image classification [2,3], speech recognition [4] and automation [5]. A number of techniques have been proposed to further improve the performance of the networks which target different aspects of the learning and inference process. This has led to development of techniques including different learning rate schedulers [6–9], loss functions [10,11], optimizers [12,13] and other network customizations [14–18]. On the other hand, larger networks are being designed with increased depth and width to improve accuracy.

To further optimize these networks, there is an overemphasis on adding more complexity to either the network architecture or to the training procedure which

S. Bandini et al. (Eds.): AIxIA 2021, LNAI 13196, pp. 515–531, 2022.
https://doi.org/10.1007/978-3-031-08421-8_36

can come at the cost of simplicity, explainability, inference time and energy efficiency. Moreover due to the energy inefficiency, the overall carbon footprint of the model increases significantly which has an adverse environmental impact [19], for instance, training a common deep learning model can have a larger carbon footprint than half the life cycle of a car [20]. In an effort to create a low carbon society to tackle climate change which is one of the major challenges faced by humanity today, researchers recently proposed using machine learning to decarbonize major pollution contributors such as the transport and the industrial sector [21]. Paradoxically, this approach itself is becoming a major contributor to CO_2 emissions. Thus, addressing the energy efficiency and decarbonization of deep learning models during design and evaluation is vital.

In conjunction with the aforementioned issues, the lack of a standardized methodology for experimentation has led to a non-rigorous evaluation of the utility of the different techniques. The importance of this issue is also underscored by *Bouthillier et al.*, [22] *"Reproducibility is not only about code sharing, but most importantly about experiment design"*. Furthermore, the lack of a standardized pipeline resulting in unfair comparisons and the neglect of important variables such as energy consumption, design simplicity and evaluation of neural networks can play important roles in reinforcing "research bias", i.e. the process where scientists overlook or influence certain observations to report results in order to portray a certain outcome.

In this paper, we conduct an exhaustive and fair empirical study to evaluate architectural design and a wide spectrum of techniques that have been proposed to improve neural networks performance. Our findings echo the importance of the Occam's Razor principle and further demonstrate that following simple standardized practices can curtail the environmental impact with little to no drop in performance. We conclude that it is crucial to rethink the design and evaluation of neural networks to ameliorate the problem of research bias. Our main contributions are as follows:

- We assess the performance of a diverse set of techniques on different datasets and tasks under common settings.
- We evaluate the effect of each technique on energy consumption and carbon emissions to estimate its environmental impact.
- We address the relationship between computational cost, energy efficiency, and performance gain.
- We highlight the necessity of a standard pipeline for neural network design and evaluation, and to curtail their carbon footprint.
- We show that following simple standardized practices can help in fair comparison of various techniques, thereby mitigating research bias.

2 Related Work

As a consequence of the increasing need for computational resources for deep learning methods, some researchers are now interested in studying and documenting the effect of the carbon footprint of these techniques. Strubell et al. [20]

study the energy consumption of different DL models during training. They conclude that the energy required for training models has increased significantly in recent years to a point where the large carbon footprint is becoming a major concern, i.e. energy consumption of the average deep learning model training can produce more than half the carbon emissions of the entire life cycle of an automobile. Schwartz et al. [19] argue that energy efficiency of DL models is as important as the accuracy and put forward multiple methods to estimate the carbon emissions of AI models. The authors contend that researchers should report energy consumption and floating point operations per model as an evaluation metric. Following this recommendation, we report these metrics in our study.

Inference, in general, contributes more towards the carbon footprint of a model during its life cycle compared to the training. To this end, a number of studies have proposed to optimize the inference process. Wang et al. [23] provide a general framework to optimize inference on mainstream integrated GPUs. Moons et al. [24] suggest the use of precision scaling for CNNs to reduce the overall energy consumption. By representing weights and values that are least affected by quantization with a lower precision, they reduce the energy consumption. Dami et al. [25] introduce the idea of "Data Echoing" whereby they optimize the pre-optimizer steps by reusing the idle upstream times of the GPUs to speed up training. However, the focus of all the aforementioned methods is on hardware optimization and they do not investigate how the deep learning architectures themselves affect environment and performance related metrics. After completion of this work, we became aware of the paper by Musgrave et al. [26] where they too emphasize fair comparisons and highlight flaws in experimental setups. However, the scope of their study is metric learning. In this study, we focus on weighing the utility of different recent methods for classification and segmentation tasks on both the training and inference efficiency in terms of overall performance and the energy expended.

3 Methodology

Our methodology is designed to ensure that the DL algorithms are evaluated with minimal effect of the hardware and software used for training, testing and inference. First, we use identical computing environment for all our experiments (Intel 8700 and NVIDIA RTX 2080 Ti). Second, we check all the techniques for each task (segmentation and classification) on the same network that performs competitively on well-known public datasets. Third, we provide a comprehensive analysis by not only reporting performance, but also energy consumption and inference time. For segmentation, we report the mean intersection over union (mIoU) on training and validation sets, overall energy consumed, the total number of parameters, floating point operations (FLOPs), inference time and energy per image are provided. For classification tasks, we report the same metrics as above with the exception of mIoUs, where classification accuracy is reported instead. In case of multiple possible hyperparameter settings, we report the best results for each technique.

3.1 Base Network Selection

Segmentation. BiSeNet [27] (with a ResNet-18 backbone pretrained on ImageNet [2]) is selected for the segmentation task. We use two datasets for segmentation training and inference, Cityscapes [28] and COCO-Stuff [29]. For both datasets, we use a poly learning rate decay with a decay rate of 0.9, stochastic gradient descent (SGD) as optimizer and cross-entropy (CE) as the loss function. For Cityscapes, we train for 1000epochs with an initial lr of 0.025, batch size 16, and random rescaling between 0.5 to 2 with a base size of 1024, followed by randomly cropped windows of size 512 $\times$ 512. For COCO-Stuff on the other hand, we train for 60 epochs with an initial lr of 0.01, batch size 12, and random rescaling between 0.5 to 2 with a base size of 640, followed by randomly cropped windows of size 640 $\times$ 640.

Classification. ResNet-50 with no pre-training is chosen for the classification task. We train and test the network on CIFAR-100 [30] and Tiny-ImageNet [31] datasets. We use an initial lr of 0.1 with a step-wise lr decay, batch size 128, SGD optimizer and CE as the loss function with maximum number of epoch set to 200.

These networks are selected as they are well-studied and known to perform well in their respective domains. Moreover, we are interested in real-time applications and want to reduce the time spent on multiple training runs. The hyperparameter values for baseline experiments are the same as in the original publications. Unless otherwise stated, we follow the standard training scheme given above.

3.2 Categories for Experimentation

We divide the experiments into several subcategories. Grouping similar categories allows for a concrete comparison of different techniques based on the multiple reported metrics. A summary of our grouping is provided below:

- Architecture Modification
- Learning Rate Scheduler
- Data Augmentation
- Optimizer
- Loss Function
- Custom Nodes and Layer

3.3 How do we Measure Energy Consumption?

We spawn a new thread running parallel to training or inference code. In this thread, we poll GPU power usage (using NVIDIA Management Library [32]) and integrate it over time, similar to the method described in [33]. However, we only sample the power every 10ms as it was the shortest time giving consistent results. Since we use the same data pipeline and dataloader, the CPU power remains same throughout the experiments, making it essentially an offset that we exclude from our reports. To measure training energy, we run all experiments on the same machine for 10 epochs and scale it up to 1000 epochs. The only exception is the progressive resizing technique, where we run the measurement for all epochs as the number of computations varies during the run. To measure inference energy, we run 10000 forward passes with batch size 1 of randomly generated "images". We repeat this procedure three times and report the average energy per image. Lacoste et al. [34] is used to calculate the CO_2 emissions in kg per week (kg/wk) with an RTX 2080 Ti. The CO_2 emissions are calculated for the models on 168 h of video (1 week) recorded at 2048 × 1024 and 30 FPS.

4 Experimental Evaluation

We perform systematic experimentation to test each technique with all the major metrics in perspective. Each section is organized as follows: we first describe the relevant techniques, we then report a summary of the results. For techniques that do not modify the network architecture we do not report the inference metrics as they are same as the baseline.

4.1 Architecture Modification

Spatial Branch Ablation (One-Branch). Many recent CNNs use a multi-branch architecture for learning the spatial details and global context separately and then fusing these features to segment the images [27,35,36]. In such networks, the context branch is deep (including many layers), and usually performs calculations on an image that is scaled down by a certain factor either via strided convolutions or bilinear resizing, while the spatial branch consists of fewer layers to preserve the spatial detail. Yu et al. [27] show that adding the spatial branch has a very small yet positive effect on mIoU and negligibly effects the inference time. However, no tests are conducted on how this branch can affect energy consumption. Here, we consider the effect of the spatial branch on the energy consumption.

Table 1 shows that there is a negligible difference between the full model (baseline) and the One-Branch in terms of mIoU. The validation mIoU is 0.7 percentage points (pp) and 0.5 pp below the baseline for Cityscapes (CS) and COCO-Stuff respectively, while both the required training energy and inference time (Table 3) are significantly reduced. This highlights the importance of the trade-off between energy consumption and the performance, questioning the utility of such architectural complexity at the cost of energy and computational efficiency.

Table 1. Effect of different techniques on mIoU calculated for both training and validation sets, and total GPU energy used for training per run for segmentation on Cityscapes (with image size of 512 × 512) and COCO-Stuff (with image size of 640 × 640). All values that are same or better than the baseline are in bold and the best results are highlighted.

Method	Cityscapes			COCO-Stuff		
	mIoU train.	mIoU valid.	Energy train.	mIoU train.	mIoU valid.	Energy train.
Baseline	84.4%	69.3%	19.6 MJ	35.4%	27.1%	65.8 MJ
One-Branch	83.5%	68.6%	**17.1 MJ**	34.48%	26.6%	**64.1 MJ**
Random Grad.	**85.1%**	**69.7%**	19.7 MJ	**38.13%**	22.6%	68.9 MJ
Cyclic LR	80.5%	67.6%	**19.5 MJ**	35.13%	**27.2%**	**65.3 MJ**
Poly LR 1/2 epochs	82.3%	**69.3%**	**9.8 MJ**	31.51%	26.2%	**35.6 MJ**
Prog. resize	80.3%	64.5%	**8.0 MJ**	29.08%	24.3%	**30.3 MJ**
Mixup	41.8%	68.1%	20.3 MJ	16.19%	25.5%	84.5 MJ
RAdam	82.5%	67.8%	20.1 MJ	26.79%	21.9%	73.1 MJ
LookAhead	**84.9%**	68.8%	**19.5 MJ**	**39.82%**	**27.4%**	71.6 MJ
Label relaxation	81.6%	67.4%	33.7 MJ	32.22%	24.9%	95.2 MJ
Dice loss	**85.6%**	68.5%	25.7 MJ	**36.67%**	26.7%	77.5 MJ
Focal loss	83.5%	68.5%	20.8 MJ	**36.01%**	**27.6%**	82.7 MJ
BlurPool	**84.6%**	67.3%	26.2 MJ	**36.96%**	**27.4%**	91.1 MJ
SwitchNorm	84.3%	68.7%	19.7 MJ	**36.23%**	**27.3%**	76.8 MJ
Sp. bottleneck	79.8%	66.0%	20.8 MJ	31.38%	24.9%	71.5 MJ
GE-θ	84.3%	68.7%	**19.6 MJ**	32.15%	24.9%	72.2 MJ
GE-θ^-	84.4%	68.3%	**18.8 MJ**	32.39%	25.2%	71.0 MJ
CoordConv	83.1%	69.0%	24.3 MJ	32.29%	25.3%	83.1 MJ

4.2 Learning Rate Scheduler

A number of learning rate manipulation techniques have been suggested over the years to improve training and inference for CNNs. Below we introduce and analyze the effect of a number of learning rate optimization techniques.

Random Gradient. Random gradient [9] multiplies the learning rate for each mini-batch by a random number sampled from $U([0,1])$. The authors claim this minimizes fluctuations in the optimization process. This technique has been shown to perform well in many fields.

Cyclic Learning Rate. Cyclic learning rate (CLR) [8], developed to remove the need for a learning rate hyperparameter, is based on cyclically changing the learning rate throughout the training. The variant giving the best result is named *triangular2*, which varies the learning rate linearly and halves the upper limit every cycle. The authors show that it can improve the training and overall accuracy of different types of neural networks. For segmentation,

Table 2. Effect of different techniques on accuracy calculated for both training and validation/test sets, and total GPU energy used for training per run for classification on CIFAR-100 and Tiny-ImageNet. All values that are same or better than the baseline are in bold and the best results are highlighted.

Method	CIFAR-100			Tiny-ImageNet		
	Accuracy train.	Accuracy test	Energy train.	Accuracy train.	Accuracy valid.	Energy train.
Baseline	99.96%	78.65%	2.40 MJ	99.95%	87.15%	6.89 MJ
Random Grad.	99.93%	78.07%	2.43 MJ	98.76%	86.36%	8.16 MJ
Cyclic LR	99.92%	74.08%	**2.35 MJ**	82.46%	74.65%	8.86 MJ
Poly LR 1/2 eochs	99.89%	77.26%	**1.36 MJ**	99.95%	86.49%	**3.47 MJ**
Mixup	99.35%	**80.65%**	2.62 MJ	96.6%	**87.27%**	7.81 MJ
RAdam	99.50%	73.65%	4.31 MJ	**99.99%**	83.48%	8.91 MJ
LookAhead	**99.97%**	**79.10%**	2.45 MJ	**99.99%**	**88.03%**	9.51 MJ
Focal loss	99.60%	78.16%	2.41 MJ	98.60%	86.55%	7.68 MJ
BlurPool	99.93%	**79.44%**	3.18 MJ	**99.97%**	86.73%	12.11 MJ
SwitchNorm	99.50%	77.12%	4.63 MJ	99.92%	86.36%	17.14 MJ
Sp. bottleneck	99.93%	72.76%	4.25 MJ	97.02%	85.22%	11.67 MJ
GE-θ	99.94%	**78.98%**	3.37 MJ	**99.97%**	**87.43%**	22.24 MJ
GE-θ^-	99.93%	78.57%	2.70 MJ	99.95%	87.08%	7.01 MJ
CoordConv	99.95%	**78.82%**	2.79 MJ	99.91%	86.61%	9.12 MJ

we tried multiple hyperparameter settings and report the best results achieved with `base_lr`=0.0001 and `base_lr`=0.00004, `max_lr`=0.01 and `max_lr`=0.004, and `stepsize`=50 and `stepsize`=3 for Cityscapes and COCO-Stuff respectively. For classification, we set a `base_lr`=0.0001, `max_lr`=0.01 and a `stepsize`=20 epochs for both datasets.

Poly LR with $\frac{1}{2}$ Maximum Epochs. In our base experiment, learning rate follows a polynomial curve. This means that the rate at which the learning rate decreases with each epoch is inversely proportional to maximum number of epochs. We test how having a smaller number of maximum epochs affects training and validation. To ensure that this result is not due to the variability in experiments we run three experiments and report the average mIoU.

Results. In Table 1, we show that for segmentation compared to the baseline, random gradient experiments yield an improvement in mIoU for CS, but a decrease in COCO-Stuff mIoU at the cost of a small increase in energy. On the other hand, for cyclic learning rate, a significant drop in mIoU is observed for CS, whereas a minor increase in mIoU is observed for COCO-Stuff. Running the network for half the number of epochs with a poly lr reduces the energy consumption (19.6 MJ to 9.8 MJ for CS and 65.8 MJ to 35.6 MJ for COCO) with little to no drop in validation mIoU. This emphasizes that proper experimental design can play an important role in environmental impact.

Table 3. Per image inference metrics for segmentation (Cityscapes 512 × 512) and (COCO-Stuff 640 × 640). All values that are same or better than the baseline are in bold and the best results are highlighted. The CO_2 emissions are calculated for full resolution 2048 × 1024 images.

	Cityscapes					COCO-Stuff				
Method	Params	FLOPs	Time	Energy	CO_2	Params	FLOPs	Time	Energy	CO_2
Baseline	14.01 M	25.93 G	6.51 ms	1.57 J	28.6 kg/wk	14.01 M	36.3 G	7.81 ms	4.41 J	34.3 kg/wk
One-Branch	**13.88 M**	**22.85 G**	**5.07 ms**	**1.26 J**	**22.2 kg/wk**	**13.88 M**	**32.0 G**	**6.52 ms**	**3.8 J**	**28.6 kg/wk**
BlurPool	**14.01 M**	34.16 G	11.7 ms	2.892 J	51.4 kg/wk	14.01 M	47.8 G	13.9 ms	6.6 J	61.1 kg/wk
SwitchNorm	**14.01 M**	25.93 G	7.25 ms	1.589 J	31.9 kg/wk	14.01 M	36.3 G	8.68 ms	4.8 J	38.2 kg/wk
Sp. bottleneck	**14.01 M**	**15.36 G**	**6.51 ms**	1.608 J	**28.6 kg/wk**	14.01 M	**21.5 G**	**7.76 ms**	**4.35 J**	**34.1 kg/wk**
GE-θ	21.88 M	**25.93 G**	6.73 ms	1.635 J	29.5 kg/wk	25.05 M	36.3 G	8.06 ms	**4.40 J**	35.4 kg/wk
GE-θ^-	**14.01 M**	**25.93 G**	6.71 ms	1.711 J	29.5 kg/wk	14.01 M	36.3 G	8.04 ms	**4.39 J**	35.3 kg/wk
CoordConv	14.02 M	27.16 G	8.10 ms	2.009 J	35.6 kg/wk	14.02 M	38.0 G	9.71 ms	4.79 J	42.7 kg/wk

Table 4. Classification CIFAR-100 and Tiny-ImageNet. All values that are same or better than the baseline are in bold and the best results are highlighted. The CO_2 emissions are calculated for resolution 64 × 64 images.

	CIFAR-100					Tiny-ImageNet				
Method	Params	FLOPs	Time	Energy	CO_2	Params	FLOPs	Time	Energy	CO_2
Baseline	2.37 M	1.3 G	**6.6 ms**	0.98 J	29.0 kg/wk	2.39 M	1.3 G	**6.6 ms**	**0.92 J**	29.0 kg/wk
BlurPool	**2.37 M**	1.93 G	6.7 ms	1.0 J	29.4 kg/wk	**2.39 M**	1.93 G	6.7 ms	0.94 J	29.4 kg/wk
SwitchNorm	**2.37 M**	**1.3 G**	23.1 ms	2.4 J	101.5 kg/wk	**2.39 M**	**1.3 G**	22.9 ms	2.2 J	100.7 kg/wk
Sp. bottleneck	**2.37 M**	**0.86 G**	7.32 ms	1.1 J	32.1 kg/wk	**2.39 M**	**0.86 G**	7.21 ms	1.0 J	31.7 kg/wk
GE-θ	2.42 M	**1.3 G**	6.97 ms	1.0 J	30.6 kg/wk	2.59 M	**1.3 G**	6.9 ms	1.0 J	30.3 kg/wk
GE-θ^-	**2.37 M**	**1.3 G**	6.96 ms	1.0 J	30.6 kg/wk	**2.39 M**	**1.3 G**	6.9 ms	0.98 J	30.3 kg/wk
CoordConv	2.42 M	**1.3 G**	6.66 ms	**0.97 J**	29.2 kg/wk	2.43 M	**1.3 G**	6.7 ms	0.94 J	29.4 kg/wk

For classification, we observe that neither CLR nor random gradient affect the energy consumption significantly for CIFAR-100 while for the larger training run with Tiny-ImageNet the training energies go up from the baseline. The overall test/validation accuracy with random gradient is slightly lower, while CLR reports considerably lower accuracy than the baseline. For half the number of maximum epochs with poly lr, we observe that the energy consumption is almost halved while the test/validation accuracy is 1.39 pp and 0.66 pp lower than the baseline for CIFAR-100 and Tiny-ImageNet respectively. However, we noted that our evaluation matches that of the original CLR publication, the only difference being that they use a constant lr for the base experiment.

4.3 Data Augmentation

Different types of data augmentation techniques have been applied to neural networks to deal with the scarcity of training data. These techniques reuse data after applying image processing techniques., such as random crops, random flipping, resizing, brightness and contrast modification. They have, in several cases, shown to improve the robustness of CNNs [37]. We run our baseline experiment with the aforementioned techniques.

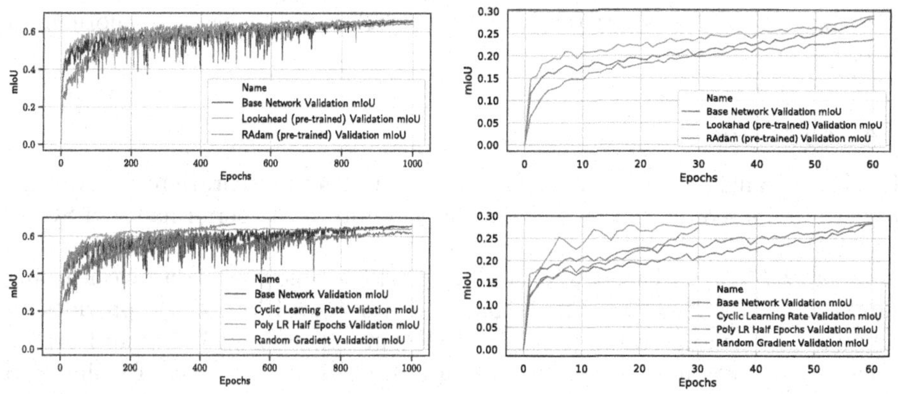

Fig. 1. **(Top)** the validation mIoU (calculated on square center crops) profiles for different optimizers (Cityscapes on **Left** and COCO-Stuff on **Right**) indicate that LookAhead optimizer has a better convergence than the baseline while the convergence for RAdam is slower than the baseline. **(Bottom)** The validation mIoU for different learning rate modifications(Cityscapes on **Left** and COCO-Stuff on **Right**). Poly LR with half epochs still gives competent results, even outperforming the remaining methods on Cityscapes. Cycles are visible for CLR. Values don't exactly match the Table as mIoU was calculated only on the square center crops.

Progressive Resizing. Progressive resizing is a technique where the training is sped up by training on downsized images for a given number of epochs, followed by training progressively on relatively larger images until the point where final epochs are done on images of original size [38,39]. This has been shown to reduce training times significantly. We run our experiment with image size $\frac{1}{8}$ of the original image, and upscale the image by a factor of 2 after every 250 epochs for Cityscapes, and 15 epochs for COCO-Stuff. This is done until we get the original image size, which is kept constant for the rest of the training.

Mixup. Mixup [17] is a simple data augmentation scheme, which trains the network on convex combinations of pairs of data points and the corresponding one-hot representations of their labels, to improve generalization of deep neural networks. We use $\tilde{x} = \lambda x_i + (1-\lambda)x_j$ and $\tilde{y} = \lambda y_i + (1-\lambda)y_j$. Where $0 \leq \lambda \leq 1$, x_i, x_j are raw input vectors, and y_i, y_j are one-hot label encodings. Here, we evaluate how the mixup affects the overall training process.

Results. For segmentation, progressive resizing results in an inferior mIoU but considerably better training energy (see Table 1), while for mixup the negative effect on mIoU is less pronounced with a slight increase in energy consumption for both datasets. For classification, we observe that mixup leads to a significant improvement in test/validation accuracy with almost identical energy consumption for CIFAR-100 and increased consumption for Tiny-ImageNet. We do not employ progressive resizing for classification as the CIFAR-100 and

Tiny-ImageNet images are too small (32×32) to retain enough information after resizing.

4.4 Optimizer

DNNs are trained using variants of stochastic gradient descent. Here, we evaluate recently proposed optimizers which claim to improve the performance of SGD.

RAdam Optimizer. The RAdam optimizer [12] employs an adaptive learning rate which is rectified to ensure a consistent variance. It effectively provides an automated warm-up custom tailored to the current dataset. Warm-up learning rate strategy sets up a small learning rate in the starting phase of training to cater for the undesirably large variance. After a specific number of epochs, the learning rate is stepped up to a larger value.

$$lr = \begin{cases} x_e \cdot lr_0 \; e < n \\ x_n \cdot lr_0 \; e \geq n \end{cases} \tag{1}$$

where n is the number of threshold epochs for the warm-up, x_i is the learning rate modifier for ith epoch, e is the current epoch, and lr_0 denotes the base learning rate. In case of the spiking learning rate warm-up we have,

$$lr = \begin{cases} x \cdot lr_0 \; e \; mod \; n = 0 \\ lr_0 \quad\; else \end{cases} \tag{2}$$

RAdam was run with default hyperparameters used by Liu et al. [12] while keeping all other settings of the optimizer same as the baseline.

LookAhead Optimizer. LookAhead optimizer uses "fast weights" multiple times using another standard optimizer before updating the "slow weights" in the direction of the final fast weights [13] and has been shown to reduce the variance, resulting in better convergence and versatility with little hyperparameter tuning. We run LookAhead with outer optimizer looking ahead every 5 iterations and interpolation coefficient $\alpha = 0.5$. Inner optimizer has the same optimization routine and learning rate schedule as the baseline. Same hyperparameters for LookAhead were chosen as those by Zhang et al. [13] for ImageNet data.

Results. For segmentation, Table 1 shows that RAdam produces an mIoU that is 1.5 pp and 5.1 pp lower than the baseline on Cityscapes and COCO-Stuff respectively. On the other hand, it consumes around 0.5 MJ more energy on Cityscapes, and 7.3 MJ more energy on COCO-Stuff. LookAhead optimizer performs relatively better with the reported mIoU only 0.5 pp below the Cityscapes baseline with similar energy consumption, and 0.3 pp above the COCO-Stuff baseline with 5.8 MJ more energy consumption. Figure 1 shows that lookahead optimizer improves the convergence over the baseline (SGD). For classification, in Table 2 we observe a test accuracy drop of 5.0 pp for RAdam and an increase of 0.45 pp for lookahead on CIFAR-100, and a validation accuracy drop of 3.67 pp for

RAdam and an increase of 0.88 pp for lookahead on Tiny-ImageNet, indicating that the former reduces accuracy while the latter improves it. Lookahead has almost the same energy as the CIFAR-100 baseline but consumes more energy on Tiny-ImageNet, while the RAdam optimizer consumes significantly more energy on both datasets.

4.5 Loss Function

Boundary Label Relaxation. The boundary label relaxation [11] leverages the idea that segmentation boundaries close to one another can easily be classified as one or the other with minor effect on segmentation quality. It calculates a soft cross-entropy loss value, where the summation of the probabilities of all the neighbouring classes at a given pixel is used as the final class probability for that pixel. If $P(C) = P(A \cup B) = P(A) + P(B)$ then $L_{Relax} = -log \sum_{C \in N} P(C)$ where A and B are the mutually exclusive classes and $P(.)$ represents the softmax class probability. We perform the experiment with label relaxation where a 3×3 kernel is used to check for neighbouring pixels.

Soft Dice Loss. The dice coefficient gives a measure of overlap between two sample sets. Dice loss applies the dice coefficient to measure the overlap between the softmax output and the ground-truth [40,41]. If $L_{Dice}(p, \hat{p}) = 1 - \frac{2\sum_{pixels} p\hat{p}}{\sum_{pixels} p + \sum_{pixels} \hat{p}}$ then we use $L_{SoftDice} = L_{CE} + \gamma L_{Dice}$, where $L_{SoftDice} =$ Total loss, $L_{CE} =$ cross-entropy loss, $L_{Dice} =$ dice loss, and γ is a scaling factor for the dice loss. When the network is trained with dice loss alone, significantly lower performance is observed. Therefore, we tested with multiple values of γ and got the best performance with $\gamma = 1$.

Focal Loss. Lin *et al.* [42] introduced focal loss after observing that two stage detectors are more accurate because of the inherent extreme foreground-background class imbalance. They introduce focal loss to address this class imbalance by focusing more on hard negatives and down-weighing the easier samples. In this study, we adapt the focal loss for segmentation by treating each pixel as a separate sample. We use $L_{Focal}(p, \hat{p}) = -\sum_{pixels}[((1 - \hat{p})^{\gamma} \log(\hat{p})) \cdot p]$ where $\hat{p}$ is softmax output vector, $\cdot$ is a dot product, and p is a one-hot label vector. We train with $\gamma = 2$ as according to author it yields the best results.

Results. For segmentation, the boundary label relaxation lowers the mIoU by 1.9 pp and 2.2 pp for CS and COCO-Stuff respectively while consuming significantly more energy. For dice loss, we get a lower mIoU (-0.8 pp for CS and -0.4 pp for COCO-Stuff) relative to the baseline and 6.1 MJ and 11.7 MJ increase in energy consumption. Additionally, an improvement (1.2 pp for both datasets) in training mIoU is observed. For the focal loss, we observe a drop of 0.8 pp and an increase of 0.5 pp in validation mIoU with more energy consumption for CS and COCO-Stuff respectively. For classification, we test only focal loss and observe that it marginally reduces the test/validation accuracy (0.49 pp and 0.60 pp for CIFAR-100 and Tiny-ImageNet respectively).

4.6 Custom Nodes and Layers

A number of studies have been carried out to improve the neural networks performance by introducing new custom nodes and layers.

BlurPool (Shift-Invariant Pooling). Zhang [18] introduced a new way to perform the pooling operation for resizing features, called BlurPool. This challenges the common assumption that CNNs are inherently shift-invariant. This is evident from the fact that even small translational perturbations (e.g. due to max pooling, resizing etc.) of an image can produce a drastically erroneous result. To counter the effect of this uncertainty, anti-aliasing is used in conventional image processing. The study uses the same idea for neural networks by adding anti-aliasing filters prior to downsampling. We run the BlurPool experiment by modifying all downsampling operations with BlurPool layers of kernel size 5×5 while keeping the strides same as the original downsampling operation.

Switchable Normalization. A number of normalization techniques have been put forward in recent years, such as batch normalization (BN) [43], instance normalization (IN) [44] and layer normalization (LN) [45]. The relative performance of each technique depends on the task at hand. Switchable Normalization (SN) [46] learns to combine different normalization techniques. This experiment is carried out with all the batch normalization layers replaced by switchable normalization layers. For segmentation, we use switchable normalization everywhere except the backbone. We report these results in Table 1 and 3.

Spatial Bottleneck. Spatial bottlenecks [47] decomposes convolutions into two stages for computational efficiency. The first stage reduces the spatial computation using stride k for the convolution layer. The second stage uses transposed convolution layer with the same stride k to recover the original size. According to authors, this reduces computations by a factor of $2/k^2$, and can hence be used to reduce computation with a tolerable reduction in accuracy. The spatial bottleneck experiments are run with the ResNet18 backbone modified to include the ResBlocks with spatial bottleneck modules instead of the standard convolution and deconvolution.

Gather-Excite Operators. Hu et al. [15] introduced gather-excite (GE) operators to better capture long range dependencies and interactions across an image. Gather operator aggregates features with a large receptive field and the excite operator redistributes the condensed information to the local features without adding much to the computational overhead. We refer to the GE modules with trainable parameters as GE-θ and the non-trainable modules as GE-θ^-. Both experiments are also carried out by attaching these modules to the outputs of each of the ResBlocks in the ResNet18 backbone.

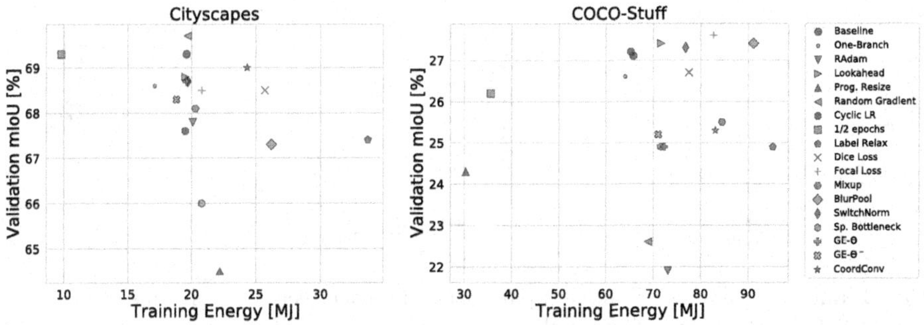

Fig. 2. Validation mIoU vs. training energy for each technique on Cityscapes (left) and COCO-Stuff (right): no correlation between the training energy and validation mIoU is observed.

Coordinate Convolution. The Coordinate Convolution (CoordConv), introduced by Liu et al. [16], concatenates pixel coordinates to the input tensor before a convolution. The coordinates are added as additional channels having x, y and radial coordinates correspondingly. The authors claim that the technique improves localization accuracy for GANs and classification tasks. We apply CoordConv to the first layer of the spatial path.

Results. Unless otherwise stated, the pp comparison is relative to the baseline. For Cityscapes, we observe that Random Gradient yields the best training and validation mIoU, that is 0.7 pp and 0.4 pp higher, respectively. This improvement could be attributed to the lower lr for training as Random Gradient multiplies the lr with $0 < \alpha < 1$. Another result of note is that for 1/2 the number of epochs, we get the same validation mIoU, indicating that training for more epochs leads to overfitting. For COCO-Stuff, we observe that focal loss yields the best result as the data balancing from focal loss plays a greater role for the larger and more imbalanced dataset. The most notable results for training energy are on progressive resizing and 1/2 epoch run for both the datasets. Even though progressive resizing runs for twice the number of epochs, it consumes less energy than the 1/2 epoch run, indicating that image size has a greater impact on training energy than epochs.

For both the classification datasets, most of the train accuracy values are over 99% with much lower test accuracy, indicating overfitting on the training set. For test accuracy, we observe that methods such as Mixup and Lookahead yield the best results. Lookahead optimizer performs well as it reduces the variance of the gradients of randomly picked batch sizes, while Mixup improves performance because of the strong regularization it provides. In terms of training energy, as expected, running half the number of epochs leads to lowest consumption.

For segmentation inference, we observed that the inference speed is not directly proportional to FLOPs as variables such as data parallelism and memory transfer can play a role in overall inference speed. Additionally, note that the difference in inference times observed for COCO-Stuff and Cityscapes is because

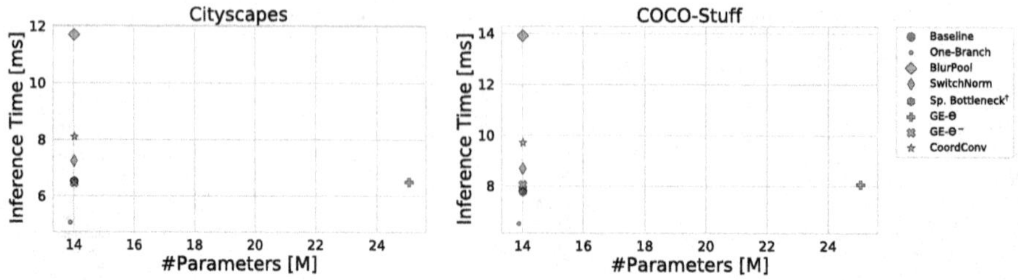

Fig. 3. Inference time vs. Number of parameters for each technique on Cityscapes (left) and COCO-Stuff (right): The number of parameters is not the only determinant for inference time.

we report the results for them at different resolutions (640×640 and 512×512 respectively). In case of classification inference, we observe that all the methods are slower than the baseline and thus possess a larger carbon footprint than the baseline.

5 Discussion

This study empirically evaluated architectural design and a broad spectrum of methods proposed to improve CNNs performance to highlight the issue of research bias in deep learning. Training an average deep learning model can have an immense impact on the environment. For instance, a model can have as much as more than half the carbon footprint of a car's entire life-cycle [20]. On the other hand, researchers have recently proposed the use of machine learning models to tackle climate change [21]. Paradoxically, these models themselves can have a considerable environmental impact. We therefore perform an extensive evaluation in order to assess the suitability of different techniques for distinct tasks. We used BiSeNet(ResNet-18 backbone) as our baseline for segmentation task, and observed that removing the spatial branch had a modest impact on the accuracy but considerably improved the carbon footprint and inference time. This again emphasizes the importance of model simplicity in addition to the overall performance during the design process. On the other hand, for training, we also showed that by simply reducing the maximum number of epochs, we can get the same accuracy at half the carbon cost. We evaluated a wide variety of other techniques, such as CoordConv, anti-aliasing for shift-invariance, optimizers such as LookAhead, RAdam, and loss functions such as Focal Loss, Dice Loss, and observe that a majority of these techniques have a negligible effect on the overall network performance. Moreover, some of these techniques considerably increased the complexity, carbon footprint and inference times. From the results in Fig. 2, we could not observe a clear trade-off between accuracy and energy savings. In addition, Fig. 3 illustrated that the number of parameters is not the only determinant of the inference time. While machine learning competitions such as Kaggle have been a great boon towards advancing research, they have exacerbated the issue of research bias by causing researchers to overlook several important variables such as environmental impact, and versatility. This appears to be a good example of Goodhart's Law which states that "When a measure becomes a target it ceases to be a good one" [48]. While we report our results on vision based applications, the same conclusions may extend to other DL intensive applications such as NLP [49,50]. In this study, we call the community's attention to these important variables, and ask them to rethink the experimental design for deep learning; first by taking these important variables into account, and second by following a standard pipeline. Simple standardized practices can lead to significant reduction in environmental impact, as evidenced by Sect. 4.2. We also suggest the research community to take a step back and focus on the bigger picture when designing the networks, instead of targeting minute improvements with narrow applicability at the cost of simplicity, versatility, and energy.

References

1. LeCun, Y., Bengio, Y., Hinton, G.: Deep learning. Nature **521**(7553), 436 (2015)
2. He, K., Zhang, X., Ren, S., Sun, J.: Deep residual learning for image recognition. In: Proceedings of the IEEE Conference on Computer Vision and Pattern Recognition, pp. 770–778 (2016)
3. Krizhevsky, A., Sutskever, I., Hinton, G.E.: ImageNet classification with deep convolutional neural networks. In: Pereira, F., Burges, C.J.C., Bottou, L., Weinberger, K.Q. (eds.) Advances in Neural Information Processing Systems 25, pp. 1097–1105. Curran Associates Inc (2012). http://papers.nips.cc/paper/4824-imagenet-classification-with-deep-convolutional-neural-networks.pdf
4. Deng, L., Hinton, G., Kingsbury, B.: New types of deep neural network learning for speech recognition and related applications: an overview. In: 2013 IEEE International Conference on Acoustics, Speech and Signal Processing, pp. 8599–8603. IEEE (2013)
5. Bojarski, M., et al.: End to end learning for self-driving cars. arXiv preprint arXiv:1604.07316 (2016)
6. Hazan, E., Klivans, A.R., Yuan, Y.: Hyperparameter optimization: a spectral approach (2017). http://arxiv.org/abs/1706.00764
7. Loshchilov, I., Hutter, F.: SGDR: Stochastic Gradient Descent with Restarts (2016). http://arxiv.org/abs/1608.03983
8. Smith, L.N.: No more pesky learning rate guessing games (2015). http://arxiv.org/abs/1506.01186
9. Wei, J.: Fast, better training trick - random gradient (2018). http://arxiv.org/abs/1808.04293
10. Lin, T.-Y., Goyal, P., Girshick, R.B., He, K., Dollár, P.: Focal loss for dense object detection (2017). http://arxiv.org/abs/1708.02002
11. Zhu, Y., et al.: Improving semantic segmentation via video propagation and label relaxation (2018). http://arxiv.org/abs/1812.01593
12. Liu, L., et al.: On the variance of the adaptive learning rate and beyond. arXiv preprint arXiv:1908.03265 (2019)
13. Zhang, M.R., Lucas, J., Hinton, G.E., Ba, J.: Lookahead optimizer: k steps forward, 1 step back (2019). http://arxiv.org/abs/1907.08610

14. He, K., Zhang, X., Ren, S., Sun, J.: Spatial pyramid pooling in deep convolutional networks for visual recognition. IEEE Trans. Pattern Anal. Mach. Intell. 37(9), 1904–1916 (2015). https://doi.org/10.1109/TPAMI.2015.2389824. ISSN 0162–8828
15. Hu, J., Shen, L., Albanie, S., Sun, G., Andrea Vedaldi. Gather-excite: exploiting feature context in convolutional neural networks. Adv. Neural Inf. Proc. Syst. 9401–9411 (2018)
16. Liu, R., et al.: An intriguing failing of convolutional neural networks and the coordconv solution (2018). http://arxiv.org/abs/1807.03247
17. Zhang, H., Cisse, M., Dauphin, Y.N., Lopez-Paz, D.: Mixup: beyond empirical risk minimization. arXiv preprint arXiv:1710.09412 (2017)
18. Zhang, R.: Making convolutional networks shift-invariant again. arXiv preprint arXiv:1904.11486 (2019)
19. Schwartz, R., Dodge, J., Smith, N.A., Etzioni, O.: Green AI. arXiv preprint arXiv:1907.10597 (2019)
20. Strubell, E., Ganesh, A., McCallum, A.: Energy and policy considerations for deep learning in NLP. arXiv preprint arXiv:1906.02243 (2019)
21. Rolnick, D., et al.: Tackling climate change with machine learning. arXiv preprint arXiv:1906.05433 (2019)
22. Bouthillier, X., Laurent, C., Vincent, P.: Unreproducible research is reproducible. In: Chaudhuri, K., Salakhutdinov, R. (eds.) Proceedings of the 36th International Conference on Machine Learning, volume 97 of Proceedings of Machine Learning Research, Long Beach, California, USA, 09–15 June 2019, pp. 725–734. PMLR (2019). http://proceedings.mlr.press/v97/bouthillier19a.html
23. Wang, L., et al.: A unified optimization approach for CNN model inference on integrated GPUS (2019). URL http://arxiv.org/abs/1907.02154
24. Moons, B., De Brabandere, B., Van Gool, L., Verhelst, M.: Energy-efficient convnets through approximate computing. In: 2016 IEEE Winter Conference on Applications of Computer Vision (WACV), pp. 1–8. IEEE (2016)
25. Choi, D., Passos, A., Shallue, C.J., Dahl, G.E.: Faster neural network training with data echoing (2019). http://arxiv.org/abs/1907.05550
26. Musgrave, K., Belongie, S., Lim, S.-N.: A metric learning reality check. In: Vedaldi, A., Bischof, H., Brox, T., Frahm, J.-M. (eds.) ECCV 2020. LNCS, vol. 12370, pp. 681–699. Springer, Cham (2020). https://doi.org/10.1007/978-3-030-58595-2_41
27. Yu, C., Wang, J., Peng, C., Gao, C., Yu, G., Sang, N.: BiSeNet: bilateral segmentation network for real-time semantic segmentation (2018). http://arxiv.org/abs/1808.00897
28. Cordts, M., et al.: The cityscapes dataset for semantic urban scene understanding. In: Proceedings of the IEEE Conference on Computer Vision and Pattern Recognition (CVPR) (2016)
29. Caesar, H., Uijlings, J., Ferrari, V.: Coco-stuff: thing and stuff classes in context. In: Proceedings of the IEEE Conference on Computer Vision and Pattern Recognition, pp. 1209–1218 (2018)
30. Krizhevsky, A.: Learning multiple layers of features from tiny images. University of Toronto, 05 2012
31. Pouransari, H., Ghili, S.: Tiny imagenet visual recognition challenge (2014)
32. NVDIA. pyNVML: Python bindings to the NVIDIA Management Library (NVML) (2019). https://pypi.org/project/pynvml/
33. Puig, M.P., De Giusti, L.C., Naiouf, M., De Giusti, A.E.: GPU performance and power consumption analysis: a DCT based denoising application. In: XXIII Congreso Argentino de Ciencias de la Computación (La Plata, 2017) (2017)

34. Lacoste, A., Luccioni, A., Schmidt, V., Dandres, T.: Quantifying the carbon emissions of machine learning. arXiv preprint arXiv:1910.09700 (2019)
35. Poudel, R.P.K., Bonde, U., Liwicki, S., Zach, C.: ContextNet: exploring context and detail for semantic segmentation in real-time (2018). http://arxiv.org/abs/1805.04554
36. Poudel, R.P.K., Liwicki, S., Cipolla, R.: Fast-SCNN: fast semantic segmentation network (2019). http://arxiv.org/abs/1902.04502
37. Cubuk, E.D., Zoph, B., Mane, D., Vasudevan, V., Le, Q.V.: Autoaugment: learning augmentation policies from data. arXiv preprint arXiv:1805.09501 (2018)
38. Arani, E., Marzban, S., Pata, A., Zonooz, B.: RGPNet: a real-time general purpose semantic segmentation. arXiv preprint arXiv:1912.01394 (2019)
39. Howard, J., et al.: Fast.AI (2018). https://github.com/fastai/fastai
40. Milletari, F., Navab, N., Ahmadi, S.-A.: V-net: fully convolutional neural networks for volumetric medical image segmentation. In: 2016 Fourth International Conference on 3D Vision (3DV), pp. 565–571. IEEE (2016)
41. Sudre, C.H., Li, W., Vercauteren, T., Ourselin, S., Jorge Cardoso, M.: Generalised dice overlap as a deep learning loss function for highly unbalanced segmentations. In: Cardoso, M.J., et al. (eds.) DLMIA/ML-CDS -2017. LNCS, vol. 10553, pp. 240–248. Springer, Cham (2017). https://doi.org/10.1007/978-3-319-67558-9_28
42. Lin, T.-Y., Goyal, P., Girshick, R., He, K., Dollár, P.: Focal loss for dense object detection. In: Proceedings of the IEEE International Conference on Computer Vision, pp. 2980–2988 (2017)
43. Ioffe, S., Szegedy, C.: Batch normalization: accelerating deep network training by reducing internal covariate shift (2015)
44. Ulyanov, D., Vedaldi, A., Lempitsky, V.: The missing ingredient for fast stylization, instance normalization (2016)
45. Ba, J.L., Kiros, J.R., Hinton, G.E.: Layer normalization. arXiv preprint arXiv:1607.06450 (2016)
46. Luo, P., Ren, J., Peng, Z., Zhang, R., Li, J.: Differentiable learning-to-normalize via switchable normalization (2018)
47. Peng, J., Xie, L., Zhang, Z., Tan, T., Wang, J.: Accelerating deep neural networks with spatial bottleneck modules (2018)
48. Strathern, M.: 'improving ratings': audit in the British University system. Eur. Rev. **5**(3), 305–321 (1997). https://doi.org/10.1002/(SICI)1234-981X(199707)5:3⟨305::AID-EURO184⟩3.0.CO;2-4
49. Bender, E.M., Gebru, T., McMillan-Major, A., Shmitchell, S.: On the dangers of stochastic parrots: can language models be too big. In: Proceedings of the 2020 Conference on Fairness, Accountability, and Transparency. Association for Computing Machinery, New York (2021)
50. Ethayarajh, K., Jurafsky, D.: Utility is in the eye of the user: a critique of NLP leaderboards (2020)

Generating Local Textual Explanations for CNNs: A Semantic Approach Based on Knowledge Graphs

Vitor A. C. Horta(✉) and Alessandra Mileo

Insight Centre for Data Analytics, Dublin City University, Dublin, Ireland
{vitor.horta,alessandra.mileo}@insight-centre.org

Abstract. Explainable Artificial Intelligence (XAI) has recently become an active research field due to the need for transparency and accountability when deploying AI models for high-stake decision making. In Computer Vision, despite state-of-the-art Convolutional Neural Networks (CNNs) have achieved great performance, understanding their decision processes, especially when a mistake occur, is still a known challenge. Current XAI methods for explaining CNNs mostly rely on visually highlighting parts of the image that contributed the most to the outcome. Although helpful, such visual clues do not provide a deeper understanding of the neural representation and need to be interpreted by humans. This limits scalability and possibly adds bias to the explainability process, in particular when the outcome is not the one expected. In this paper, we propose a method that provides textual explanations for CNNs in image classification tasks. The explanations generated by our approach can be easily understood by humans, which makes our method more scalable and less dependent on human interpretation. In addition, our approach gives the opportunity to link neural representations with knowledge. In the proposed approach we extend our notion of co-activation graph to include input data and we use such graph to connect neural representations from trained CNNs with external knowledge. Then, we use link prediction algorithms to predict semantic attributes of unseen input data. Finally, we use the results of these predictions to generate factual and counterfactual textual explanations of classification mistakes. Preliminary results show that when the link prediction accuracy is high, our method can generate good textual factual and counterfactual explanations that do not need human interpretation. Despite a more extensive evaluation is still ongoing, this indicates the potential of our approach in combining neural representations and knowledge graphs to generate explanations for mistakes in semantic terms.

Keywords: Explainable AI · Knowledge graphs · Deep representation learning · Computer vision

S. Bandini et al. (Eds.): AIxIA 2021, LNAI 13196, pp. 532–549, 2022.
https://doi.org/10.1007/978-3-031-08421-8_37

1 Introduction

Explainable Artificial Intelligence (XAI) is the research field that focuses on bringing more transparency to the decision making process of AI systems [11]. With the success of Convolutional Neural Networks (CNNs), and the desire to deploy these models in high-stake decision making, researchers in XAI are focusing on the need to be able to explain the decisions made by CNNs [1]. Providing such explanations is crucial to guarantee their reliability [23], and to ensure compliance with the EU's new AI regulation[1]. However, given their black box nature, deriving explanations for CNNs is not trivial, especially when mistakes happen [22].

In image classification, where CNNs are known to achieve start-of-the-art performance, the model needs to solve complex tasks using highly unstructured data, such as raw images, which increases even more the challenge for explainability. Current methods commonly use visual approaches, such as saliency maps, to highlight parts of the input image that has mostly influenced a given outcome [25]. Such visual clues can be misleading and make human interpretation particularly difficult, especially when trying to explain unexpected outcomes [16,19].

In this paper, our goal is to provide easy-to-understand textual explanations that do not need to be visually interpreted. We specifically focus on explaining mistakes as these can be particularly challenging to interpret, and we generate both factual and counterfactual explanations as known concepts in cognitive science [24] and widely used in the XAI community [3]. The factual explanations produced by our approach indicate in human terms what made the model classify an instance i as class c_{wrong} instead of $c_{correct}$. The counterfactuals indicate what could help the model to correctly classify i as $c_{correct}$ instead of c_{wrong}.

In our approach, we follow the idea that combining knowledge and deep representations can be the key to more transparent decision making [7,16]. If we consider knowledge graphs, for example, the benefits of combining the learning capabilities from CNNs and the explicit and structured representation from knowledge graphs is extensively discussed by [16]. Unlike CNN representation, knowledge graphs represent information explicitly so that each decision taken can be explained in semantic terms. Also, the knowledge represented by such graphs can be automatically analysed using a variety of well studied graph analysis methods. Combining the two approaches, however, is not trivial due to the opaque nature of neural networks and the difficulty in integrating semantics to their hidden neurons [16].

As a first step towards enabling this combination, in previous work we proposed and validated the notion of co-activation graph [14], which connects neurons from a trained deep learning model based on their mutual activity. Using graph analysis methods such as community detection and centrality analysis on such graph, we have been able to provide a global interpretation for a trained CNN. Building upon that work, in this paper we first augment co-activation

[1] https://ec.europa.eu/commission/presscorner/detail/en/IP_21_1682).

graphs to link with input data and external knowledge. We then use link prediction to predict attributes of unseen data and use such predictions to generate factual and counterfactual explanations of mistakes in image classification.

The potential of our method is demonstrated in an experiment on CUB200 birds dataset [27], used for fine-grained classification of birds images among very similar classes. We fine tune a VGG-16 model [20], construct the proposed knowledge graph form VGG-16 and use link prediction to derive explanations for classification mistakes in terms of semantic properties and their values, such as *"This bird was misclassified as Blue Jay instead of Black Footed Albatross because the model has identified blue as value for primary_color instead of brown."*

Our evaluation points to the feasibility of our solution and shows that, by using link prediction over the proposed knowledge graph, it is possible to predict the semantic attributes of unseen data with a high accuracy. Moreover, a visual analysis indicates that the factual and counterfactual explanations produced by our method are visibly appropriate, and they help explaining why a given image was wrongly classified and what would the neural representation need to learn to invert the classification.

The rest of this paper is organised as follows: in Sect. 2 we present related work on explaining mistakes from CNNs. Section 3 describes our method for automatically generating easy-to-understand explanations. In Sect. 4 an experiment is conducted to evaluate the outcome of our method. Section 5 presents final remarks and what we envision for future work.

2 Related Work

When it comes to supporting explanation of the outcomes of a CNN, a common practice is to use visualisation techniques to highlight parts of the image that contributed the most for that outcome. There is an extensive number of works around visualisation techniques, as well as several surveys that summarise the main approaches in this category [4,10,18]. Despite their popularity, visual explanations, need to be interpreted by a human case by case, which limits the scalability and can add human bias to the process. Saliency maps, for example, do not reveal the model's inference process, making them hard to interpret or misleading, expecially when they refer to a mistake such as a misclassified input [26].

A more flexible way to analyse the outcome of a Deep Neural Network is by using case-based approaches, which have been widely used also to interpret the network's mistake. In this type of techniques, an explanation can be derived by comparing the mistaken input data with its closest neighbors. Case-based approaches have been used to generate factual and counterfactual explanations on both tabular data [21] as well as for image classification [15], but their explanations is solely based on the input feature space. In addition, case-based explanations also require human interpretation especially when dealing with highly unstructured data such as raw images, thus being time-consuming and prone to misinterpretation and human bias.

By using a phrase-critic model, authors in [12] provide a method to extract factual and counterfactual explanations for image classification models. Their method however makes use of auxiliary black box models, like LSTMs, adding an additional level of opacity in the explainability process.

In [2], network dissection is introduced and used to identify neurons that are responsible for detecting semantic concepts for object detection tasks. After mapping neurons to semantic concepts, they show that explanations around such concepts can be achieved by analysing the behaviour of the respective neurons for a new image. In [6] this idea is extended, and instead of mapping individual neurons to semantic concepts authors relate them with patterns of filter activities. The main difference between these works and the one we proposed in this paper is that they rely on pixel-level segmented datasets, such as BRODEN, and their ability to produce meaningful explanations is limited to the concepts existing in the dataset. Although the BRODEN dataset contains a variety of concepts, it mainly contains information about objects and it is not suitable for supporting explanations based on semantic attributes of such objects.

We show that our method works even for fine-grained image classification tasks, in which the amount of annotated data is limited and an auxiliary dataset such as BRODEN is not available. In addition, although [2,6] make use of semantic annotations, none of the above methods is able to leverage external knowledge bases to generate explanations that are easily understandable in human terms. Our main contributions are: i) the extension of the co-activation graph to include input data and external knowledge bases, ii) a graph-based approach to identify semantic attributes that might be responsible for a mistake using link prediction, and iii) an algorithm for the automatic generation of easy-to-understand factual and counterfactual textual explanation for mistakes based on the results of link prediction.

3 Methodology

Our approach focuses on providing textual post-hoc factual and counterfactual explanations in image classification, and we specifically focus on explaining mistakes as they are harder to explain.

In classification models whenever a mistake happens it involves two classes, the ground truth class $c_{correct}$ and the wrongly predicted class c_{wrong}. A factual explanation describes what influenced the model to classify a given input i as of class c_{wrong}, while a counterfactual explanation tells what changes to the input i could invert a wrong prediction from c_{wrong} to $c_{correct}$.

Our approach to generate these textual explanations is to first define and construct a knowledge graph that extends the co-activation graph proposed in [13,14] by including input data and external knowledge bases, so that knowledge about such input (in terms of its properties) can be added to the graph. On such extended graph, we then apply link prediction to generate the explanations. In what follows we are going to provide details of each step.

3.1 The Knowledge Graph Model

Since our Knowledge Graph Model extends the notion of co-activation graph, we first provide some preliminaries on co-activation graphs and then indicate how we extend their definition in this paper to connect them with input data as well as external knowledge bases.

Preliminaries on Co-activation Graphs. In co-activation graphs, nodes represent neurons from a given trained CNN and edges connect pairs of nodes that tend to be activated together. We can represent neurons from both dense and convolutional layers as detailed in [13,14]. The nodes are instantiated by extracting the neurons from the model and the edges can be created for each pair of nodes by calculating a statistical correlation on their respective neurons' activation values following the three-steps process detailed in [13,14]: first, the testing set is passed through the network and, for each data point, the activation value of each neuron is stored; second, given that each neuron is associated to a list of activation values, a statistical correlation is calculated for every possible pair of neurons; third a threshold is used to discard the non relevant statistical correlations. As a result of this process, in the co-activation graph nodes are neurons and edges represent statistical correlations between their activation values. If a neuron belongs to the output layer, it is represented using a node of type *class*, otherwise, we represent it using a node of type *Neuron*, as shown in Fig. 1.

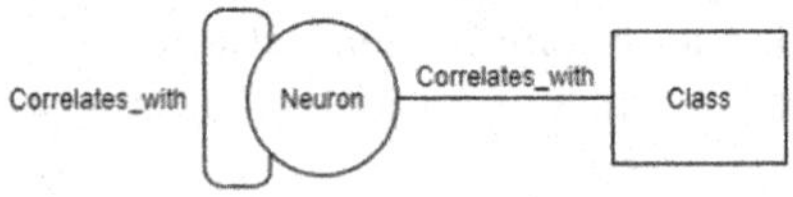

Fig. 1. Co-activation graph diagram.

We have already demonstrated in [13,14] how co-activation graphs provide a suitable representation for the knowledge embedded in a trained CNN, which can be used to generate global insights about the inner workings of the network using graph analysis. In this paper, we extend this representation by integrating input data and external knowledge to the graph in order to provide local explanations by means of link prediction algorithms.

Connecting the Input Data. In order to represent the input data in co-activation graphs, we create a new type of node, called *Input* node. An *Input* node i can be connected to both *Neuron* nodes and *Class* nodes. The connection between i and a *Class* node c can be created in two ways:

- if the deep learning model predicted c when classifying i, an edge of type *has_prediction* is created between i and c;
- if c is the ground truth for i, an edge of type *has_ground_truth* is created between i and c.

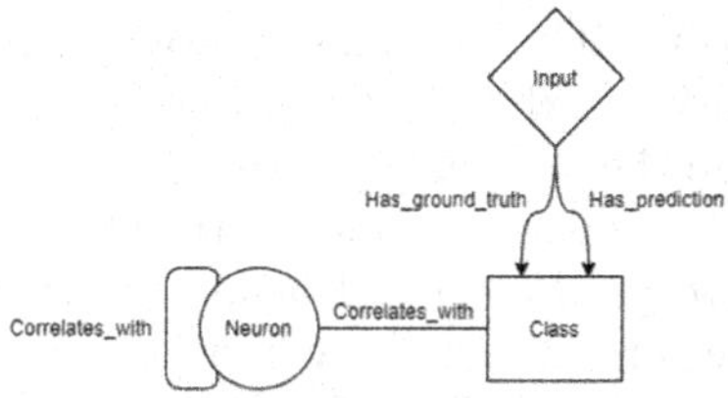

Fig. 2. Diagram after connecting inputs to classes.

The resulting model can be seen in Fig. 2. To create connections between *Input* and *Neuron* nodes we measure the relevance of the activation caused by each input to each neuron. When one input is passed through a CNN, neurons in dense layers will output an activation value and filters in convolutional layers will output an activation map. As discussed in [13,14], it is possible to apply a global pooling to reduce an activation map into a single activation value. Considering that an activation value is accessible for each neuron, our goal is to be able to connect the respective input data to the generated graph.

A naive approach would be to create a link between the *Input* node and every *Neuron* node and to use the activation value as the edge weight. One issue with this approach is that it would generate a huge number of connections, which increases quadratically with respect to the number of neurons and data points. A second issue is that neurons at different layers activate with different magnitude and the different scales in the edge weight distribution could lead to biases when applying graph algorithms.

To address these two issues, we normalise and discretise the neuron activations. After extracting the activation values, we first calculate how relevant was the activation of each neuron for a given input data as proposed in [9]. To calculate the activation relevance we first compute the *zscore* of each activation, which gives the distance between each activation and the mean. We can then apply a threshold to the *zscores*, as explained by the same authors in [8], so that the final relevance score will assume the values of -1, 0 or 1. This eliminates the side-effects of variability of the activation values. If the final score is 1 we consider that the neuron activation was relevant to the input, otherwise we discard it. This way we do not have to deal with a quadratic number of generated connections, since we only connect inputs to neurons that were activated in relation to that input. After calculating the scores, we can extend the graph by creating a new edge of type *Activated*, denoted with $e_{in} = (i, n)$ where i is the input data and n is a neuron. The resulting model is illustrated in Fig. 3.

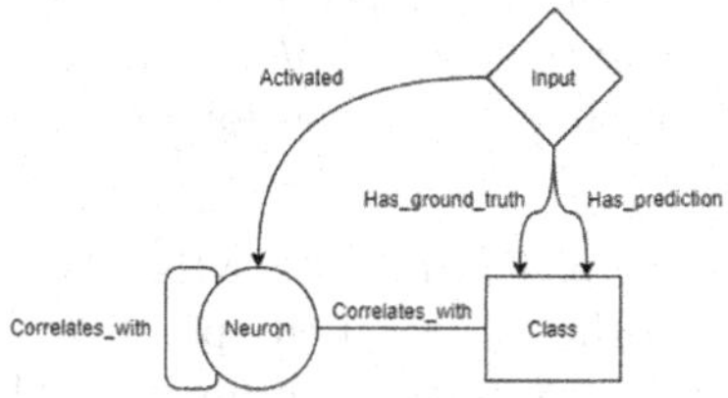

Fig. 3. Diagram after connecting inputs to neurons.

Connecting the Graph with External Knowledge Bases. In this phase of the approach, we consider external knowledge bases that contain real world entities (e.g. animals) and their semantic attributes (e.g. body shape and colors). We incorporate these entities and semantic attributes in our graph by creating two new node types: *External Entity* and *Semantic Attribute.*

External Entity nodes are the semantic entities corresponding to the output classes in the deep neural network. They can be easily connected to *Class* nodes when classes which are neurons in the output layer represent entities in the real world. In this case, we create unweighted edges of type *Refers_to* between a *Class* node in the co-activation graphs and their respective entities in the external knowledge base. When *External Entities* are related to *Semantic Attributes* in the external knowledge base, we can create an edge of type *Has_attribute* between the *External Entity* and each of its *Semantic Attribute.* Since modern datasets, like CUB200 birds, provide annotated data, we can create *Has_attribute* edges between *Input* nodes and *Semantic Attribute* nodes. This concludes the step of connecting co-activation graphs with external knowledge bases and the final diagram is illustrated by Fig. 4.

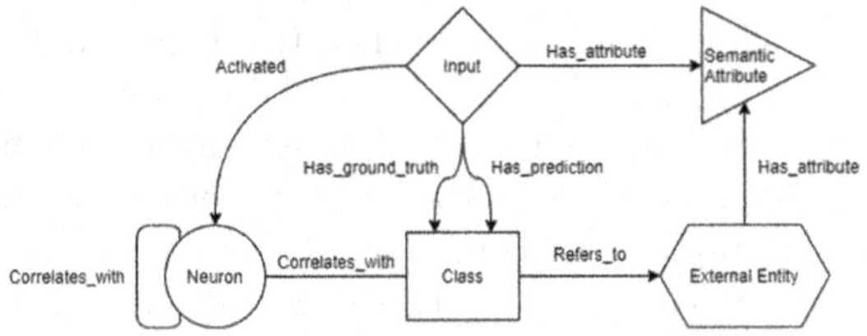

Fig. 4. Diagram after connecting inputs and classes to entities in external knowledge bases.

3.2 Generation of Textual Factual and Counterfactual Explanations for Mistakes

We can now leverage the knowledge graph constructed in the previous section to generate textual factual and counterfactual explanations for mistakes in image classification.

Our method is divided in three phases: first, we generate hypotheses around possible semantic attributes that could have caused the mistake; second, each hypothesis is either accepted or rejected based on link prediction; third, textual explanations are automatically generated based on the accepted hypotheses. After describing each phase in details, we provide an example using real data from the CUB200 dataset and the *WhatBird* external knowledge base containing semantic information about the bird species found in the CUB200 dataset.

Generating Hypotheses for Explaining Mistakes. The first phase in our method is to generate hypotheses for all the possible semantic attributes that could have caused a mistake. Consider each image in the dataset as annotated with a set of attributes A, and each attribute $a \in A$ can assume different values $V_a = \{V_{a_1}, V_{a_2}, ..., V_{a_n}\}$, where n is the number of possible values for a. Given an output class c, the knowledge graph in Fig. 4 can be queried to find $V_a(c)$, which is the value attribute a assumes for class c. Given a misclassified input i, the ground truth class $c_{correct}$, the wrongly predicted class c_{wrong} and an attribute a, we consider that a may have caused the mistake if a assumes different values for $c_{correct}$ and c_{wrong}, i.e. $V_a(c_{correct}) \neq V_a(c_{wrong})$.

A hypothesis $h(a, i)$ can now be defined as follows:

$h(a, i)$: since attribute a assumes different values for classes $c_{correct}$ and c_{wrong}, a **has influenced** input i to be misclassified as belonging to class c_{wrong} instead of class $c_{correct}$

For each mistake made by the CNN, a list of hypotheses can be generated by querying the graph to obtain the semantic attributes that assume different values between $c_{correct}$ and c_{wrong}. Note that such query is possible given the edges linking *Class*, *External Entity* and *Semantic Attribute* nodes, which gives all the information needed to compare $V_a(c_{correct})$ with $V_a(c_{wrong})$ for each attribute of each entity. Each hypothesis generated is then either accepted or rejected as detailed in the next phase.

From Hypotheses to Relevant Features Through Link Prediction. In this second phase, we take as input a list of hypothesis on attributes that might have caused the mistake, and accept or discard them based on the semantic attributes of the misclassified input i.

A hypothesis $h(a, i)$ is accepted if the attribute a assumes the same value for input i and class c_{wrong}, i.e. $V_a(i) = V_a(c_{wrong})$. The intuition behind this is that when a has the same value for i and c_{wrong}, the model may have classified i as c_{wrong} because of a. As discussed previously, $V_a(c_{wrong})$ can be obtained by querying the graph. However, when i is an unseen input data, $V_a(i)$ is not directly available in the graph as we do not have information about its attributes. Our method leverage the connection between input i and the *Neuron* nodes in our knowledge graph and uses link prediction to discover its attributes.

Given the proposed knowledge graph contains seen input data from the training set, we can predict semantic attributes for unseen data using link prediction. The rationale of using a link prediction algorithm is to predict the semantic attributes of unseen input i based only on the behaviour of the neurons in the deep learning model. To guarantee that the link prediction is not biased by the connections between classes and external entities, an alternative graph is created which contains only the connections between neurons, inputs and semantic attributes. This alternative graph used only for the link prediction and illustrated in Fig. 5a, can be easily derived from the original knowledge graph by removing *Class* nodes, *External Entity* nodes and their respective relationships. Figure 5b shows the resulting graph, in which the dashed connection results from the link prediction method.

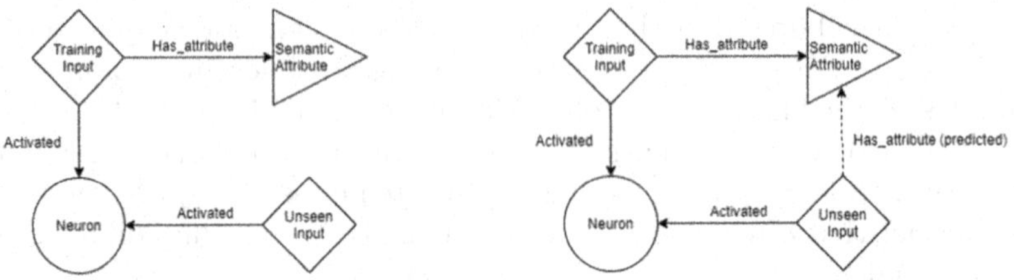

(a) (b)

Fig. 5. (a) Alternative graph used for link prediction. (b) Resulting graph after applying link prediction.

Consider that $V_a(c_{correct})$ and $V_a(c_{wrong})$ are the values that a assumes for $c_{correct}$ and c_{wrong} respectively. The procedure for accepting or discarding a hypothesis $h(a, i)$ around an attribute a and a misclassified input i is described in Algorithm 1, where $h(a, i)$ is denoted as h for simplicity. In the algorithm, line 2 uses link prediction to calculate the probability $P_{correct}$ of input i having the attribute value $V_a(c_{correct})$. Line 3 predicts the probability P_{wrong} of input i having the attribute value $V_a(c_{wrong})$. Line 4 compares these two probabilities: if the condition is true, it means that $V_a(i) = V_a(c_{correct})$, so we discard this hypothesis because $V_a(c_{correct})$ is already the attribute of the ground truth class; if the condition is false it indicates that $V_a(i) = V_a(c_{wrong})$ and we accept this hypothesis in Line 8, because $V_a(c_{wrong})$ is the attribute of the wrongly predicted class and thus it could be the cause of the mistake. After applying Algorithm 1 to every hypothesis generated in the previous phase, the output of this phase is a list of accepted or discarded hypotheses as well as the predicted attributes values for input i.

Algorithm 1

1: **procedure** EVALUATE_HYPOTHESIS(h, $graph$, i, a, V_a, $c_{correct}$, c_{wrong})
2: $P_{correct} \leftarrow$ LinkPrediction($graph$, i, $V_a(c_{correct})$)
3: $P_{wrong} \leftarrow$ LinkPrediction($graph$, i, $V_a(c_{wrong})$)
4: **if** $P_{correct} > P_{wrong}$ **then**
5: discard(h)
6: **else**
7: accept(h)
8: **end if**
9: **end procedure**

Generating Factual and Counterfactual Explanations. After evaluating the hypotheses, the third and final phase is used to generate the explanations. Given an accepted hypothesis $h(a, i)$, a factual statement can be automatically generated as:

> The input i was misclassified as c_{wrong} instead of $c_{correct}$ because the model has identified $V_a(c_{wrong})$ as value for a in i instead of $V_a(c_{correct})$.

It is important to note that, when multiple hypotheses are accepted, the final factual explanation will consist of multiple factual statements. Following the same logic, a counter factual statement can be automatically generated as:

If the attribute a of input i assumed the value $V_a(c_{correct})$ instead of $V_a(c_{wrong})$, input i would more likely be classified as $c_{correct}$ instead of c_{wrong}

Note that a final counterfactual explanation will consist of multiple counterfactual statements in case of more than one hypothesis is accepted.

Example Using Real Data. To illustrate the three phases of our method, consider an input data sample $i = img001$ extracted from the CUB200 dataset and the attribute $a = primary\_color$. For this data sample, $c_{correct} = Black\ Footed\ Albatross$ and $c_{wrong} = Blue\ Jay$. According to *WhatBird*, used as a knowledge base, we have that:

$$V_{primary\_color}(Black\ Footed\ Albatross) = brown$$

$$V_{primary\_color}(Blue\ Jay) = blue$$

Since the attribute *primary_color* assumes different values for the two classes, a hypothesis $h(primary\_color, img001)$ can be created as follows:

$h(primary\_color, img001)$: since *primary_color* assumes different values for *Black Footed Albatross* and *Blue Jay*, *primary_color* **has influenced** $img001$ to be misclassified as *Blue Jay* instead of *Black Footed Albatross.*

In the second phase, we evaluate $h(primary\_color, img001)$ using Algorithm 1. If the algorithm finds that $P_{correct} > P_{wrong}$, our method would assumes that $img001$ has brown as *primary_color*, which is the expected value for a *Black Footed Albatross.* In this case we have that $V_a(i) = V_a(c_{correct})$ and we reject $h(primary\_color, img001)$. If $P_{wrong} > P_{correct}$ instead, we consider that $img001$ has blue as *primary_color* and we accept $h(primary\_color, i)$, since $V_a(i) = V_a(c_{wrong})$.

If the hypothesis is accepted, the third phase generates the factual and counterfactual explanations that can be written as follows:

- **Factual explanation**: "The input $img001$ was misclassified as *Blue Jay* instead of *Black Footed Albatross* because the model has identified *blue* as value for *primary_color* in $img001$ instead of the expected value *brown.*
- **Counterfactual explanation**: "If the attribute *primary_color* of input $img001$ assumed the value *brown*, input $img001$ would more likely be classified as a *Black Footed Albatross* instead of *Blue Jay*".

In this example, we illustrated the three phases using only a single attribute. However, as it will be shown in the next section, our explanations may contain more than one attribute if multiple hypotheses are accepted simultaneously.

In the next section we evaluate our method in two ways. First, we perform a quantitative evaluation over the link prediction method to analyse whether it is possible to predict the semantic attribute for a given input with reasonable accuracy. Then, we provide a visual qualitative evaluation to demonstrate how the automatically generated explanations can help understand the model's decisions.

4 Experimental Evaluation

Our experiment is based on fine-grained image classification using the CUB200 dataset. The dataset contains 200 classes of bird species and 11,788 input images in total. Each image is annotated with a set of attributes A. In our experiment, specifically, we use five attributes such that $A = \{primary\_color, underparts\_color, upperparts\_color, nape\_color, bill\_shape\}$. Each attribute $a \in A$ can assume different values V_a. For example, for $a = underparts\_color$, we have $V_{underparts\_color} = \{blue, brown, iridescent, purple, rufous, grey, yellow, olive, green, pink, orange, black, white, red, buff\}$. The experiment was conducted as follows:

- A VGG-16 network pretrained over ImageNet was fine-tuned to achieve 86% accuracy in the classification task.
- The knowledge graph was created for the model, following the steps described in Sect. 3.1.
- For each misclassified input, we have generated the hypotheses and performed link prediction as described in Sect. 3.2.
- Factual and counterfactual explanations were generated for the accepted hypothesis as described in Sect. 3.2.

Our knowledge graph was implemented in Neo4j[2], which facilitates reproducibility and provides access to many graph analysis algorithms. To predict links between *Input* and *Semantic Attribute* nodes we used the Personalised PageRank algorithm [17] implemented on Neo4j.

One issue that could affect the outcome of our link prediction algorithm is that the CUB200 dataset is not well balanced in terms of the semantic attributes. For example, there are 1443 birds with brown primary_color but only 27 with pink primary_color. To avoid link prediction to always output the most frequent attribute in the dataset, we normalised the Personalised PageRank score by the Global PageRank score.

The PageRank algorithm, also called Global PageRank, calculates a score that can be interpreted as the importance of each node in a graph by performing random walks in such a graph. Its variant, the Personalised PageRank, calculates

[2] https://neo4j.com.

the probability of a link between a source and a target node in the graph. In our experiments, the probability of a link between a source *Input* node i and a target *Semantic Attribute* node a, denoted $Link(i, a)$, was calculated as shown in Eq. 1.

$$Link(i, a) = \frac{PersonalisedPageRank(i, a)}{GlobalPageRank(a)} \quad (1)$$

Since our method relies heavily on link prediction, in our experimental evaluation we first perform a quantitative analysis of the accuracy of the link prediction algorithm used to discover the attributes of unseen inputs from the testing set. Then, we visually evaluate the quality of the factual and counterfactual explanations for some of these inputs.

4.1 Evaluating Link Prediction for Semantic Attributes

The first part of our evaluation focuses on verifying how accurately we can predict semantic attributes for unseen inputs using link prediction over our knowledge graph. For this, we used the alternative graph described in Sect. 3.1 containing only *Input*, *Neuron* and *Semantic Attribute* nodes. As already mentioned, this approach guarantees that the prediction of attributes relies only on the interactions between a given input and the neurons in the hidden layer of a deep learning model and is not biased by any external information.

In our approach we focus on classification mistakes between two classes. For each attribute $a \in A$ we evaluate the link prediction between pairs of attribute values in V_a. For this, we first remove the ground truth connections between inputs in testing set and *Semantic Attribute* nodes. Then, we calculate the link prediction using Eq. 1 to obtain a score for each link between an input data and a semantic attribute. Finally, the link with the higher score is taken as the predicted one, which can be checked against the ground truth since the CUB200 dataset provides such annotations.

On average, the link prediction accuracies over all possible pairs of values for the attributes *underparts_color*, *upperparts_color* and *bill_shape* are: 83.4%, 82.54% and 77.4% respectively. There was however some variability in that the method is much more accurate for some pairs of attribute values than some others. For example, as shown in Table 1, the method obtained 99% accuracy when distinguishing between the values *pink* and *white* for the attribute *underparts_color*, which means that the model is almost perfect in detecting the *underparts color* of a bird if it considers in advance that the bird is either *pink* or *white*. Other very high accuracy values can be seen for the attribute *upperparts_color* between *black* and *purple*, as well as between *hooked* and *all-purpose* for the attribute *bill_shape*.

We can also observe that for some pairs of very similar attribute values our method does not perform so well, which is the case for *purple* and *pink* in attribute *underparts_color* and other pairs as shown in Table 2. But considering that classes in fine-grained image classification are already similar, it is expected that the method would produce lower accuracy for similar attributes. Looking into using more sophisticated link prediction strategies is something worth exploring in future work.

Table 1. Examples of pairs of attributes that can be well distinguishable by the proposed method.

Top predictions								
Underparts color			Upperparts color			Bill shape		
Value one	Value two	Acc	Value one	Value two	Acc	Value one	Value two	Acc
Pink	White	99%	Purple	Black	99%	Hooked	All-purpose	95%
Grey	Green	94%	Pink	White	98%	Needle	All-purpose	93%
Iriscident	Black	94%	Orange	Black	96%	Hooked	Cone	93%
Orange	White	92%	Iriscident	Black	96%	Curved	Cone	90%
Blue	White	92%	Grey	Orange	94%	Cone	Specialized	89%

Table 2. Examples of pairs of attributes that are not well distinguishable by the proposed method.

Lowest predictions								
Underparts color			Upperparts color			Bill shape		
Value one	Value two	Acc	Value one	Value two	Acc	Value one	Value two	Acc
Purple	Pink	45%	Purple	Pink	55%	Curved	Hooked	58%
Orange	Red	64%	Orange	Red	60%	All-purpose	Cone	62%
Olive	Green	64%	Green	Orange	64%	Hooked	Needle	64%
Grey	Buff	66%	Iriscident	Orange	65%	Hooked	Specialised	64%
Grey	Black	66%	Grey	Black	66%	Dagger	All-purpose	65%

4.2 A Visual Evaluation for Factual and Counterfactual Explanations

Now that we have provided a quantitative analysis of the performance of our link prediction approach, we proceed by visually analysing some of the factual and counterfactual explanations generated by our method. The explanations within this section were generated by considering only the pairs of attribute values in which our link prediction performs with accuracy higher than 80%.

Since there is no ground truth for such textual explanations, and a user evaluation is beyond the scope of this paper, we provide visual evaluations based on randomly selected examples. Visual evaluations are used to check if the attributes used in our textual explanations are in fact present in the images. Note that in order to generate an explanation we first identify all attributes that could have caused a given mistake as hypothesis, and then we use link prediction to accept or deny each individual hypothesis, as explained in Sect. 3.

The first example of explanation presented below refers to the data sample used in the previous section and the hypotheses are shown in Table 3. Figure 6 shows the image for this data and the respective factual and counterfactual explanations.

Table 3. Predicted attributes for the data sample *img*001. Bold rows indicate accepted hypotheses.

	Black footed albatross	Blue jay	Predicted for i
Bill shape	Hooked-seabird	All-purpose	Hooked-seabird
Primary color	**Brown**	**Blue**	**Blue**
Underparts color	**Brown**	**White**	**White**
Upperparts color	**Brown**	**Blue**	**Blue**
Nape color	Brown	Blue	Brown

Fig. 6. Misclassification involving Black Footed Albatross (ground truth class) and Blue Jay (wrong predicted class). (Color figure online)

- **Factual explanation**: "The input *img001* was misclassified as *Blue Jay* instead of *Black Footed Albatross* because the model has identified *blue* as value for *primary_color* in *img001* instead of *brown* and *blue* as value for *upperparts_color* instead of *brown* and *white* as value for *underparts_color* instead of *brown*.
- **Counterfactual explanation**: "If the attribute *primary_color* of input *img*001 assumed the value *brown* and *underparts_color* assumed the value *brown* and *upperparts_color* assumed the value *brown*, input *img*001 would more likely be classified as a *Black Footed Albatross* instead of *Blue Jay*".

According to our method, this first mistake was caused by the presence of blue and white colors, which are characteristic of the Blue Jay species. It is worth noting that, if the bird in the image had the value *brown* for its *underparts_color*, *upperparts_color* and *primary_color*, it would likely be classified as the correct class. In addition, our method discarded hypotheses around attributes *bill_shape* and *nape_color*. This happened because, according to our link predictions, this bird image has *hooked-seabird* as a value for attribute *bill_shape* and *brown* as a value for attribute *nape_color*, which are already the values for the correct class and thus are not likely to have caused the mistake.

In the second mistake, shown in Fig. 7, our factual explanation tells that the detection of white colors are the causes of the misclassification. The counterfactual explanation indicates that if the bird was more black, it would likely be classified correctly. In this case we discard any hypotheses around the *bill_shape*, the *nape_color* and the *upperparts_color*.

It can be seen that in both cases the factual explanations are visually compatible with the real images. In the first case, the *blue primary_color*, *blue upperparts_color* and the *white underparts_color* are in fact visible. In the second, except for a small part in its wings, the bird is visibly more white than black. Although the known limitation of such visual evaluations in terms of scaling, these examples give an indication that our method generates reasonable factual explanations.

Fig. 7. Misclassification involving Black Tern (ground truth class) and Elegant Tern (wrong predicted class)

- **Factual explanation**: "The input *img*002 was misclassified as *Elegant Tern* instead of *Black Tern* because the model has identified *white* as value for *underparts_color* in *img002* instead of *black* and *white* as value for *primary_color* instead of *black*.
- **Counterfactual explanation**: "If the attribute *underparts_color* of input *img*002 assumed the value *black* and *primary_color* assumed the value *black*, input *img*002 would more likely be classified as a *Black Tern* instead of *Elegant Tern*".

The counterfactuals generated by our approach also provide interesting insights about why the mistakes happened and what could invert the classifications. If we look back into Fig. 6, it is intuitive that if the bird had brown colors instead of blue and white, this would probably change the classificaton to the correct class. A similar intuition is present in the second case, in Fig. 7, in the sense that if the bird were black it would probably be correctly classified.

As discussed in the first part of our evaluation, currently the quality of our explanations is mainly associated with the accuracy of the link prediction algorithm used. More experiments are required to explore under which conditions we can guarantee sufficiently high accuracy and what adjustments can be made for cases in which the link prediction does not work as expected. Another point worth noting is that when generating counterfactuals with the current approach we cannot quantify the exact contribution of each attribute. This is another area of current investigation.

5 Conclusions and Future Work

In this paper, we propose an approach for generating factual and counterfactual explanations of mistakes made by deep learning models in classification tasks.

In our method, we first construct a knowledge graph that connects the components of deep learning models (the neurons) with input data as well as external knowledge. Once created, the knowledge graph can be queried to generate hypotheses around semantic attributes that have potentially caused a given mistake. In order to accept or discard each hypothesis, a link prediction algorithm is used to predict the semantic attributes of unseen data based on the behaviour of the neurons in the deep learning model, as represented in the knowledge graph. Accepted hypotheses based on the results of link prediction are used to generate factual and counterfactual explanations.

Our evaluation on fine-grained image classification was conducted over the CUB200 dataset and using a VGG-16 pretrained on ImageNet and fine-tuned on CUB200. The results obtained show that, by applying the link prediction algorithm over our knowledge graph it is possible to identify semantic attributes of unseen data for different pairs of attribute values. This result is valuable especially if we consider the case of fine-grained image classification, where subtle differences among the classes contribute to make disambiguation a challenging task.

After evaluating the suitability of the approach for discovering attributes through link prediction, we present a visual inspection over selected mistakes in the dataset. The investigation showed that the factual explanations generated by our approach which are automatically generated can help understanding why a mistake happened in an easy-to-understand way and with no need for interpretation. The visual inspection also gave a first indication that the counterfactuals can indicate what semantic attribute would need to be learned differently to possibly correct the mistake.

The proposed approach assumes we have a dataset annotated with semantic attributes and an external knowledge base describing the relations between those attributes and real world entities. Given both, the approach is flexible in that it can be applied to any CNN.

This work paves the way for several interesting lines of investigation we are planning to explore. First of all, a more formal evaluation of the counterfactual explanations needs to be conducted to verify that the actions automatically suggested by our approach have in fact the potential of inverting the classification. Another key aspect is the investigation of link prediction algorithms, their performance and the condition under which they can be used to generate explanations in semantic terms. This also includes considering different architectures to explore how well our knowledge graph can capture and augment their representation. For the CUB200 dataset for example, a promising alternative could be the one presented in [5]. The ability to test our approach over more challenging benchmark datasets is also underway, and we plan to consider how a similar way of combining neural and semantic representation via knowledge graphs can be generalised to other problems such as object detection and image segmentation, as well as beyond computer vision tasks in other domains such as text classification and named-entity linking.

References

1. Arrieta, A.B., et al.: Explainable artificial intelligence (XAI): concepts, taxonomies, opportunities and challenges toward responsible AI. Inf. Fusion **58**, 82–115 (2020). https://doi.org/10.1016/j.inffus.2019.12.012, https://www.sciencedirect.com/science/article/pii/S1566253519308103
2. Bau, D., Zhou, B., Khosla, A., Oliva, A., Torralba, A.: Network dissection: quantifying interpretability of deep visual representations. In: Computer Vision and Pattern Recognition (2017)
3. Byrne, R.M.J.: Counterfactuals in explainable artificial intelligence (XAI): evidence from human reasoning. In: Proceedings of the Twenty-Eighth International Joint Conference on Artificial Intelligence, IJCAI-19. International Joint Conferences on Artificial Intelligence Organization, pp. 6276–6282 (2019). https://doi.org/10.24963/ijcai.2019/876
4. Chatzimparmpas, A., Martins, R.M., Jusufi, I., Kerren, A.: A survey of surveys on the use of visualization for interpreting machine learning models. Inf. Visual. 147387162090467 (2020). https://doi.org/10.1177/1473871620904671
5. Cui, Y., Song, Y., Sun, C., Howard, A., Belongie, S.: Large scale fine-grained categorization and domain-specific transfer learning. In: Proceedings of the IEEE Conference on Computer Vision and Pattern Recognition (CVPR), June 2018
6. Fong, R., Vedaldi, A.: Net2vec: quantifying and explaining how concepts are encoded by filters in deep neural networks (2018). http://arxiv.org/abs/1801.03454
7. Futia, G., Vetrò, A.: On the integration of knowledge graphs into deep learning models for a more comprehensible AI-Three challenges for future research. Information **11**(2) (2020). https://doi.org/10.3390/info11020122
8. Garcia-Gasulla, D., et al.: On the behavior of convolutional nets for feature extraction (2017). http://arxiv.org/abs/1703.01127
9. Garcia-Gasulla, D., et al.: An out-of-the-box full-network embedding for convolutional neural networks. In: 2018 IEEE International Conference on Big Knowledge (ICBK), pp. 168–175 (2018). https://doi.org/10.1109/ICBK.2018.00030
10. Grün, F., Rupprecht, C., Navab, N., Tombari, F.: A taxonomy and library for visualizing learned features in convolutional neural networks. arXiv preprint arXiv:1606.07757 (2016)
11. Gunning, D., Stefik, M., Choi, J., Miller, T., Stumpf, S., Yang, G.Z.: XAI-explainable artificial intelligence. Sci. Robot. **4**(37), eaay7120 (2019). https://doi.org/10.1126/scirobotics.aay7120, https://openaccess.city.ac.uk/id/eprint/23405/, this is the author's version of the work. It is posted here by permission of the AAAS for personal use, not for redistribution. The definitive version was published in Science Robotics 4(37) (2019). https://doi.org/10.1126/scirobotics.aay7120
12. Hendricks, L.A., Hu, R., Darrell, T., Akata, Z.: Grounding visual explanations (2018)
13. Horta, V.A.C., Mileo, A.: Towards explaining deep neural networks through graph analysis. In: Anderst-Kotsis, G., et al. (eds.) Database and Expert Systems Applications, pp. 155–165. Springer International Publishing, Cham (2019)
14. Horta, V.A., Tiddi, I., Little, S., Mileo, A.: Extracting knowledge from deep neural networks through graph analysis. Future Gener. Comput. Syst. **120**, 109–118 (2021). https://doi.org/10.1016/j.future.2021.02.009, https://www.sciencedirect.com/science/article/pii/S0167739X21000613

15. Kenny, E.M., Keane, M.T.: On generating plausible counterfactual and semi-factual explanations for deep learning. In: Thirty-Fifth AAAI Conference on Artificial Intelligence, AAAI 2021, Thirty-Third Conference on Innovative Applications of Artificial Intelligence, IAAI 2021, The Eleventh Symposium on Educational Advances in Artificial Intelligence, EAAI 2021, Virtual Event, 2–9 February 2021, pp. 11575–11585. AAAI Press (2021). https://ojs.aaai.org/index.php/AAAI/article/view/17377
16. Lecue, F.: On the role of knowledge graphs in explainable AI. Semant. Web **11**(1), 41–51 (2019). https://doi.org/10.3233/SW-190374
17. Page, L., Brin, S., Motwani, R., Winograd, T.: The PageRank citation ranking: bringing order to the web. Tech. Rep. 1999–66, Stanford InfoLab, November 1999, http://ilpubs.stanford.edu:8090/422/previousnumber=SIDL-WP-1999-0120
18. Qin, Z., Yu, F., Liu, C., Chen, X.: How convolutional neural network see the world - a survey of convolutional neural network visualization methods (2018)
19. Rudin, C.: Stop explaining black box machine learning models for high stakes decisions and use interpretable models instead. Nature Mach. Intell. **1**(5), 206–215 (2019). https://doi.org/10.1038/s42256-019-0048-x
20. Simonyan, K., Zisserman, A.: Very deep convolutional networks for large-scale image recognition (2014). http://arxiv.org/abs/1409.1556
21. Smyth, B., Keane, M.T.: A few good counterfactuals: generating interpretable, plausible and diverse counterfactual explanations (2021). https://arxiv.org/abs/2101.09056
22. Suzuki, M., Kamcya, Y., Kutsuna, T., Mitsumoto, N.: Understanding the reason for misclassification by generating counterfactual images. In: 2021 17th International Conference on Machine Vision and Applications (MVA), pp. 1–5 (2021). https://doi.org/10.23919/MVA51890.2021.9511352
23. Tjoa, E., Guan, C.: A survey on explainable artificial intelligence (XAI): towards medical XAI (2019). http://arxiv.org/abs/1907.07374
24. Van Hoeck, N., Watson, P.D., Barbey, A.K.: Cognitive neuroscience of human counterfactual reasoning. Front. Hum. Neurosci. **9**, 420 (2015). https://doi.org/10.3389/fnhum.2015.00420
25. Vilone, G., Longo, L.: Classification of explainable artificial intelligence methods through their output formats. Mach. Learn. Knowl. Extr. **3**(3), 615–661 (2021). https://doi.org/10.3390/make3030032
26. Wan, A., et al.: NBDT: neural-backed decision trees (2020). https://arxiv.org/abs/2004.00221
27. Welinder, P., et al.: Caltech-UCSD birds 200. Technical report CNS-TR-2010-001, California Institute of Technology (2010)

Detection Accuracy for Evaluating Compositional Explanations of Units

Sayo M. Makinwa[1], Biagio La Rosa[1(✉)], and Roberto Capobianco[1,2]

[1] Sapienza University of Rome, Rome, Italy
{larosa,capobianco}@diag.uniroma1.it
[2] Sony AI, Zurich, Switzerland

Abstract. The recent success of deep learning models in solving complex problems and in different domains has increased interest in understanding what they learn. Therefore, different approaches have been employed to explain these models, one of which uses human-understandable concepts as explanations. Two examples of methods that use this approach are Network Dissection [5] and Compositional explanations [23]. The former explains units using atomic concepts, while the latter makes explanations more expressive, replacing atomic concepts with logical forms. While intuitively, logical forms are more informative than atomic concepts, it is not clear how to quantify this improvement, and their evaluation is often based on the same metric that is optimized during the search-process and on the usage of hyper-parameters to be tuned. In this paper, we propose to use as evaluation metric the Detection Accuracy, which measures units' *consistency of detection* of their assigned explanations. We show that this metric (1) evaluates explanations of different lengths effectively, (2) can be used as a stopping criterion for the compositional explanation search, eliminating the explanation length hyper-parameter, and (3) exposes new specialized units whose length 1 explanations are the perceptual abstractions of their longer explanations. Code available at https://github.com/KRLGroup/detacc-compexp.

Keywords: Explainable AI · Explainability · Deep learning · Machine learning · Metrics

1 Introduction

In the last decade, the interest on explaining what *complex* deep learning models learn has grown due to the success of these models and the will to apply them on critical domains, like healthcare, where their decision process could improve our daily life. Recent works show that units of models trained for a variety of tasks learn to detect human-understandable concepts, despite the fact that they are not trained to do it [9,30,37]. This observation allows researchers to propose concept-based methods to provide explanations about the learned behavior of these models [5,8,14,23]. An example of such a work is the framework of Network Dissection proposed by Bau et al. [5]. Starting from the assumption that

S. Bandini et al. (Eds.): AIxIA 2021, LNAI 13196, pp. 550–563, 2022.
https://doi.org/10.1007/978-3-031-08421-8_38

Unit 25 Explanations

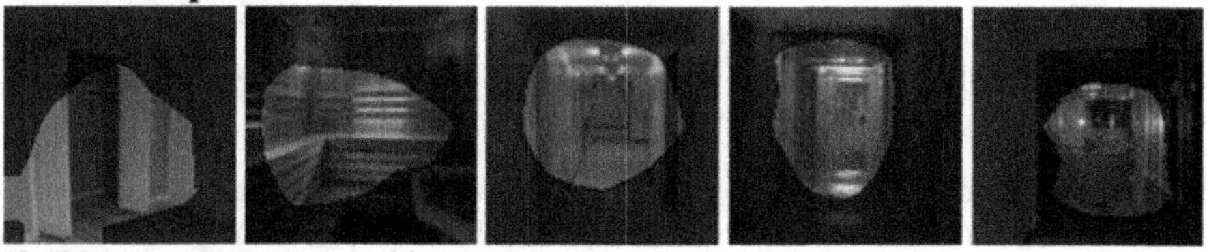

NetDissect: (IoU 0.0670) corridor
Comp Len2: (IoU 0.0791) corridor OR sauna
Comp Len3: (IoU 0.0827) corridor OR sauna OR elevator
Comp Len5: (IoU 0.0857) corridor OR sauna OR elevator OR basement OR fire escape
Comp Len10: (IoU 0.0871) corridor OR sauna OR elevator OR basement OR fire escape OR cargo container OR elevator door OR freight elevator AND (NOT door frame) OR corridor

Fig. 1. An example showing the activations of Unit 25 from ResNet model on some images, the Network Dissection [5] and Compositional explanations [23] of length 3, 5, and 10 for the unit, generated using existing methods, and the corresponding IoU scores for each explanation. While the compositional explanations are more expressive, their IoU evaluation rates endlessly long explanations better.

explanations should be understandable to humans [20,22,28], it proposes to associate a human-understandable concept to each unit using a probing dataset. This method focuses on explaining the internal representation of a model, therefore explanations are generated for the units of the model and not the predictions of the model. Noting that assigning a single concept to each unit may be too simplistic to properly capture the units behavior, Mu and Andreas [23] extend the framework associating logical forms of concepts to units, calling these forms *compositional explanations.*

In both Network Dissection and compositional explanations, the same metric is used to generate explanations and to evaluate them (i.e. Intersection over Union score). This means that by design, the compositional explanations always score higher, because the score increases with the number of concepts in the explanation (Fig. 1). Hence, longer explanations are always deemed better than more precise ones. This is in contrast to the literature on explanations, which state that human-understandable explanations should be selected and precise [11,20–22,35]. Our hypothesis is that we need a different metric to compare concept-based methods and to properly assess when units are better explained by a method or another.

We propose to use Detection Accuracy for this purpose, which measures the *consistency of detection* of the explanations by the concerned units. We test the metric comparing Network Dissection and compositional explanation, obtaining a more balanced evaluation. Additionally, we show that Detection accuracy

1. holds more information about the association between the concepts learned by units and the predictions of the model;

2. can replace the maximum length hyper-parameter in the compositional search to generate variable length unit-optimal explanations;
3. reveals new specialized units whose length 1 explanations are the perceptual abstractions of their longer explanations.

Note that the goal of this work is not to associate unit explanations to predictions, but rather to evaluate the extent to which the explanations explain their associated units. The remaining sections are organized as follows; we briefly discuss existing work in concept explanations and evaluations in Sect. 2, we present our approach in Sect. 3 and then discuss our experiments and results in Sects. 4. In Sect. 5, we present the conclusion and future work.

2 Related Work

Explanation Methods. Deep networks are complex models for which various class of explanation methods have been developed [4,7,31]. One such class of methods deals with the visualization of units, either by finding the most activated input image [6,36,37], by synthesizing an input using generative approaches [16,24], or by generating saliency maps from gradients [19,27]. The extracted concepts by these methods can be exploited in several ways to obtain explanations. Kim et al. [14] propose to generate concept-based explanations by computing directional derivatives on a linear classifier to measure the importance of a concept from a user-defined dataset, to a class prediction. Ghorbani et al. [8] suggests to segment concepts, group these segmentations, and evaluate them against classes to know which concepts are more important for which class. These two approaches explain the *local* behaviour around a particular prediction. Conversely, Bau et al. [5] propose to generate *global* explanations by explaining each unit in the model, using a framework called Network Dissection. This method extracts unit activation above a threshold on a large dataset, and computes the overlap with the concepts in the dataset. Mu and Andreas [23] then extends Network Dissection by producing explanations that are logical compositions of concepts from the dataset.

Evaluation of Explanations. Extensive work has been done to establish general guidelines for assessing explanations [11,20,25,32,35], which has now formed a basis for evaluation of explanations and explanation methods. The majority of the current approaches measure how generated explanations change in response to perturbations in the input data, either as a result of completely removing a feature [3,18], or just some modifications of the feature [18,26,29,33]. Alternative approaches are the sanity checks [1] that randomize the weights of the layers and inspect how the generated explanations change, or the method of Lin et al. [17], which create a backdoor in the model, adding a trigger on the data for a specific prediction, and observing how explanations detect this attack. Finally, Kim et al. [13] propose to evaluate example-based explanations by generating criticisms to the explanations, in addition to the positive examples. Kim et al. [14] is the closest to our work; it explains a class prediction of a model by measuring how consistently a concept influences the class prediction, using a user-defined concept dataset. It is however local to a particular prediction, and it is also embedded within an explanation method. Our work evaluates the global relationship of concept explanations to the units they explain, does not require users to build and annotate their own concept dataset, and is separate from the explanation method.

3 Methodology

This section describes the Network Dissection framework and the procedure to generate compositional explanations, and then the proposed explanation evaluation metric, Detection Accuracy.

3.1 Network Dissection and Compositional Explanations

Network Dissection [5] explains a unit by measuring the alignment between the unit and semantic concepts from a probing dataset. First, we collect the unit's activation $A_u(X)$ on the images in the dataset and compute its distribution a_u, then we determine the top quantile level T_u for this unit such that $P(a_u > T_u) = 0.005$. We then scale $A_u(X)$ up to the dimension of concepts' annotation mask and convert $A_u(X)$ to a binary form where $M_u(X) \equiv A_u(X) \geq T_u$. Finally, we compute the Intersection over Union (IoU) score as follows:

$$IoU_{u,E} = \frac{\sum|M_u(X) \cap G_E(X)|}{\sum|M_u(X) \cup G_E(X)|} \tag{1}$$

where $G_E(X)$ is the binary annotation mask for a concept explanation E, and $|.|$ is the set cardinality. The IoU score is computed for each concept explanation and the one that maximizes the IoU is assigned to the unit:

$$\overline{E}_u = \underset{E \in \mathcal{L}(\mathcal{C})^1}{\operatorname{argmax}} IoU_{u,E} \tag{2}$$

where $\mathcal{L}(\mathcal{C})^1$ is the set of all the atomic concepts in the dataset.

Compositional explanations [23] replace the set of atomic concepts $\mathcal{L}(\mathcal{C})^1$ with a set of n-ary logical forms $\mathcal{L}(\mathcal{C})^n$ composed of up to length n concepts. We build the set of logical forms incrementally using *beam search*, which takes as input the set of atomic concepts, computes their IoU, and initializes the beam with the explanations with the top B IoU. B is the beam size. It then combines each explanation in the beam with each atomic concept, it merges the resulting set with the set in the beam to create the next length set of logical forms, and computes the IoU of all the explanations in this new set, keeping only the explanations with the top B IoU in the beam. The search returns the explanation with the highest IoU as the explanation for the unit:

$$\overline{E}_u = \underset{E \in \mathcal{L}(\mathcal{C})^n_B}{\operatorname{argmax}} IoU_{u,E} \tag{3}$$

3.2 Detection Accuracy

The intuition behind the Detection Accuracy score is that an explanation is associated to a unit to the degree of how consistently the unit *detects* it. To measure the Detection Accuracy score of a unit u on an explanation E that is composed of n concepts c_{1-n} over a dataset X of images, we evaluate the following equation:

$$DetAcc_{u,E} = \frac{\sum_{imgs} M_u(X) \cap G_E(X)}{\sum_{imgs} G_E(X)} \tag{4}$$

where G_E is the gold binary mask of explanation E in the dataset, and M_u is unit u's binary activation map described in Sect. 3.1. We compute $M_u(X) \cap G_E(X)$ over binary pixels while $\sum_{imgs}$ represents an image-wise summation. In particular, for every image in the dataset that contains the given explanation, we compare the pixels of the image to the pixels of the unit activation on the image via a pixel-wise binary operation, to find out if the unit activates on the image and if this activation overlaps the explanation. After this, we count the total number of images where the unit activates on the explanation and compute the ratio of this number to the number of images where the explanation exists. The idea is to measure how consistently the unit *sees* the explanation, not minding how well it covers the explanation each time. A high Detection Accuracy score of a unit on an explanation corresponds to a high consistency in the unit's detection of the explanation. Therefore, if multiple explanations are given for a unit, we consider the explanation with the highest Detection Accuracy score as the one that better explains the unit.

4 Experiments

This section describes the dataset and models used for our experiments. Then, it presents and analyzes the results on the quality of Detection Accuracy's evaluations, showing its properties.

4.1 Setup

As dataset, we use the ADE20K [38] scene parsing dataset. It is contains 22,210 densely annotated images on the pixel level with human-understandable concepts from the Broden Dataset [5], categorized into classes of scenes (468), colors (11), parts (96), and objects (518). We consider only concepts with at least 5 samples, leaving only 1093 of the 1,105 concepts. Following Mu and Andreas [23], the experiments are conducted on the units of the final layer of ResNet-18 [10], AlexNet [15], DenseNet-161 [12], and ResNet-50 [10], trained on the Places365 dataset [39].

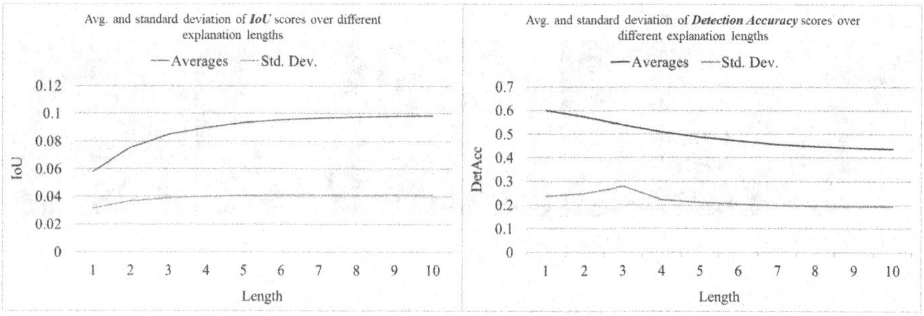

Fig. 2. Plots of averages and standard deviation of IoU (L) and Detection Accuracy (R) scores over all the units of ResNet-18 for explanation lengths 1 to 10. The plots show how the IoU scores generally increase as explanation length increases, while the Detection Accuracy scores generally reduce.

4.2 Detection Accuracy as Evaluation Metric

First, we test Detection Accuracy as an evaluation metric against the IoU, comparing their evaluation on Network Dissection and compositional explanations. We fix the length of compositional explanations to 3 as in Mu and Andreas [23]. The results (Table 1) show that the IoU scores of the compositional explanations are higher for nearly 100% of the units across different models. The Detection Accuracy's evaluation on the other hand is more distributed, rating the Network Dissection explanations higher for approximately half the number of units, and the compositional explanations higher for the other units across all the models. To observe the behaviour of the scores as maximum explanation length increases, we further generate explanations of lengths up to 10. We see that the Detection Accuracy penalizes verbose explanations while the IoU rewards them (Fig. 2), which establishes that when Detection Accuracy scores a longer explanation higher, it has merely rated the actual value of the explanation rather than rewarding the length. See an example in Fig. 3.

Proceeding to inspect how valuable the Detection Accuracy evaluation is, we measure the correlation between the IoU score and the prediction accuracy of

Table 1. Evaluation results of IoU and Detection Accuracy on Network Dissection explanations and length 3 composition explanations for all the units in ResNet-18, AlexNet, ResNet-50, and DenseNet-161 models. Each percentage represents the percentage of units in the model that have the corresponding *higher* score for the explanation. Note that the scores do not necessarily add up to 100% for each model because a few compositional explanations have exactly the same scores.

	ResNet-18 (512 units)		AlexNet (256 units)		ResNet-50 (2048 units)		DenseNet-161 (2208 units)	
	NetDis.	Comp.	NetDis.	Comp.	NetDis.	Comp.	NetDis.	Comp.
IoU	0.2%	99.8%	0%	100%	0.05%	99.95%	0.05%	99.95%
DetAcc	56.45%	43.16%	37.89%	60.94%	53.76%	45.31%	56.46%	42.82%

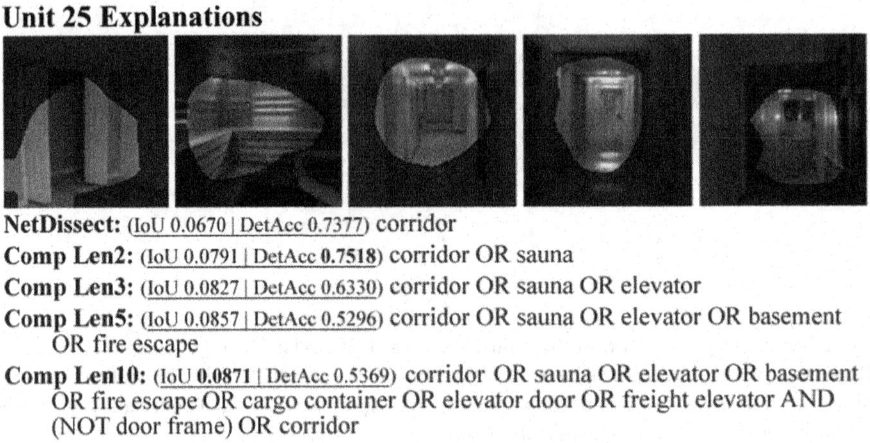
Unit 25 Explanations
NetDissect: (IoU 0.0670 | DetAcc 0.7377) corridor
Comp Len2: (IoU 0.0791 | DetAcc 0.7518) corridor OR sauna
Comp Len3: (IoU 0.0827 | DetAcc 0.6330) corridor OR sauna OR elevator
Comp Len5: (IoU 0.0857 | DetAcc 0.5296) corridor OR sauna OR elevator OR basement OR fire escape
Comp Len10: (IoU 0.0871 | DetAcc 0.5369) corridor OR sauna OR elevator OR basement OR fire escape OR cargo container OR elevator door OR freight elevator AND (NOT door frame) OR corridor

Fig. 3. The explanations generated for Unit 25 in Fig. 1 are now evaluated with Detection Accuracy. The Detection Accuracy score for the length 2 explanation is the highest, while the IoU score is highest for the longest explanation.

the model, and the correlation between the Detection Accuracy score and the prediction accuracy of the model. To do this, we take each unit and its explanation, we select images from the dataset on which the unit fires and those on which the explanation is present, then we combine both sets by finding the union and the intersection to create two new sets. We then measure the model prediction accuracy on these sets and compute correlation of these accuracy scores with the IoU and Detection Accuracy of the explanations. Results show that the Detection Accuracy positively correlates to model prediction accuracy on both Network Dissection and compositional explanations, and these correlation scores are higher the than IoU's correlation scores (Table 2). This means that the Detection Accuracy scores better reflect how the concepts in the input images contribute to the correctness of the model predictions.

Additionally, we can observe that the correlation for Network Dissection explanations are higher for the Detection Accuracy, while the correlation for compositional explanations are higher for the IoU. This suggests a behaviour where the Detection Accuracy's correlation prefers precise explanations, while

Table 2. Correlation scores of all units in the last layer of the ResNet-18 model over images associated to each unit and its Network Dissection or compositional explanations. The best scores are marked in bold.

	Union Corr.		Intersection Corr.	
	IoU	DetAcc	IoU	DetAcc
NetDissect	0.2224	**0.3615**	0.0365	**0.5799**
Comp.	0.2733	**0.3294**	0.1158	**0.4876**

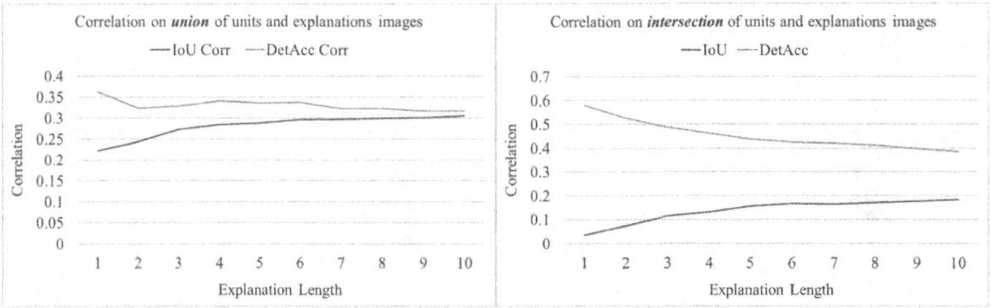

Fig. 4. Plots of IoU and Detection Accuracy correlation scores for explanation lengths 1 to 10 over all the units in the last layer of ResNet-18 model, computed over the *union* [L] and *intersection* [R] of images associated with each unit and its explanation. The plots show how the Detection Accuracy score is consistently more correlated to model accuracy than the IoU score. We also see how the IoU correlation scores increase with explanation length.

the IoU's correlation prefers verbose explanations. We test this further by computing correlation for explanations of lengths up to 10, since Mu and Andreas [23] showed that the increase in the IoU of explanation lengths greater than 10 is not substantial. Results show that the Detection Accuracy's correlation scores generally decrease as explanation length increases, while that of the IoU generally increases (Fig. 4). From the Detection Accuracy's perspective, the precise explanations sufficiently capture the concepts that are important to the model predictions, while the extra concepts added in the verbose explanations rewarded by IoU do not have the same level of importance.

4.3 Detection Accuracy as Optimization Metric

In this test we investigate if it is possible to use the Detection Accuracy also for optimizing explanations. First, we insert Detection Accuracy into the beam search by selecting the explanation with the highest Detection Accuracy from the beam at each step of the search. Note that since the beam has a size B, the explanations in the beam are ones with the top IoU scores. The best explanation at each step is therefore the one with the best Detection Accuracy from the set of top B IoU explanations. Equation 3 then becomes:

$$\overline{E}_u = \underset{E \in \mathcal{L}(C)^n_B}{\operatorname{argmax}}\, DetAcc_{u,E} \tag{5}$$

In addition to using Detection Accuracy to select the best explanation from the beam, we also allow the search to continue to run until the Detection Accuracy score for the unit can no longer be improved.

Figure 5 shows that ∼85.5% of the units (438 of 512) are assigned explanations of length 1. This is because the most frequently detected explanations are greedily selected early in the search. We then proceed to inspect how valuable the explanations are using the correlation of the model accuracy to their IoU

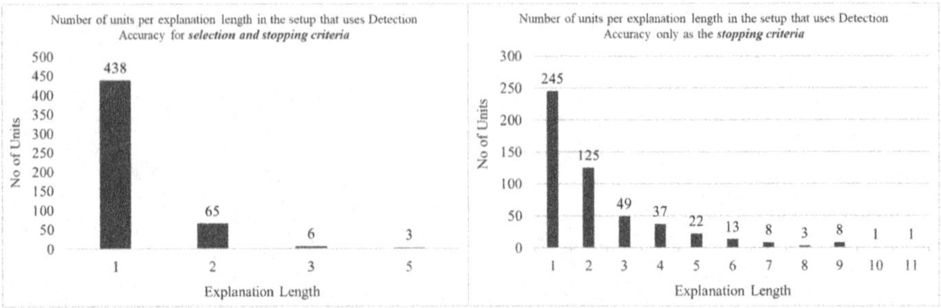

Fig. 5. Summary of explanation lengths across units of the last layer of ResNet-18 model from two modified compositional methods; where best explanations are chosen from the beam using their Detection Accuracy scores [L], and where Detection Accuracy is used only as a stopping criterion [R]. The setup in [L] returns mostly length 1 explanations for units, while the lengths of the explanations returned for units by the setup in [R] are more spread.

and Detection Accuracy scores. Both correlation scores dropped compared to the regular compositional explanations method (Table 3). This means that the concepts in these explanations have a weaker relationship to the model predictions and therefore, the Detection Accuracy cannot be exploited in generating explanations as described in this experiment.

At this point we question if it is possible to use Detection Accuracy only to stop the beam search, removing the maximum explanation length hyper-parameter and letting the search run until the best Detection Accuracy score so far is no longer improved. In this case, we find that the explanation lengths become more varying than before, while not losing the preference for precision in the explanations (Fig. 5). In probing how valuable these new explanations are, we also compute the correlation of the model accuracy to the IoU and Detection Accuracy scores (Table 4). We find that for the Detection Accuracy, not only are the correlation scores better than the scores from the previous experiment, they also improve on the correlation scores from the regular compositional method. The IoU correlation scores however did not improve, further establishing that the IoU prefers longer explanations. We argue that these varying length explanations allow units to be described with explanations of lengths that are optimal for

Table 3. Correlation scores of the regular compositional method and the modified compositional method where best explanations are *selected* from the beam using their Detection Accuracy scores.

	Union Corr.		Intersection Corr.	
	IoU	DetAcc	IoU	DetAcc
Len3 Comp. Expl	0.2733	0.3294	0.1158	0.4876
Comp.+Select	0.2341	0.2247	0.0368	0.3603

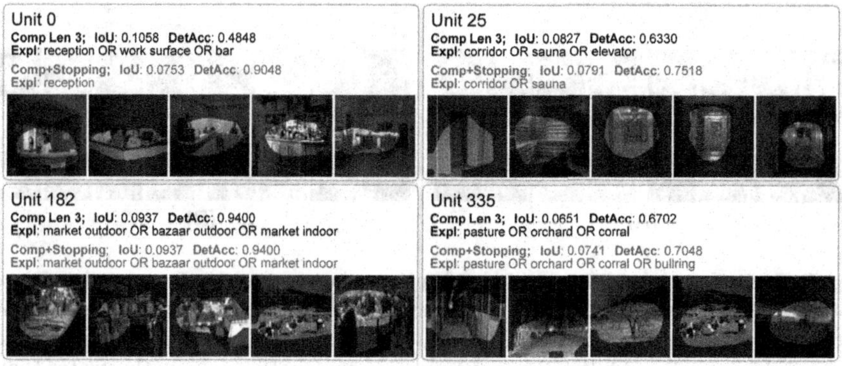

Fig. 6. Examples of explanations from the modified compositional explanations method where Detection Accuracy is used *only* to stop the search. The examples contain Unit 25 from Fig. 1 and Fig. 3, and other units. The new method is now able to determine the best length for the explanation of each of the units. The explanations are compared to fixed length 3 compositional explanations from Mu and Andreas [23].

them, as opposed to *forcing* them shorter or longer like in the regular setup with the maximum explanation length hyper-parameter (See examples in Fig. 6).

New Specialized Units. Querying further the results from the last setup where we use the Detection Accuracy only as a stopping criterion, we find that the Detection Accuracy score exposes a new set of specialized units, keeping their explanations to length 1. These new length 1 explanations correspond to the perceptual abstractions described by their *longer* explanations from the regular compositional setup (Fig. 7 (A)). They are also different from the L_1 AND NOT L_2 form described in Mu and Andreas [23]. It is important to note that not all the units with length 1 explanations in this setup are in this category. A manual inspection of the explanations of the units shows that from the 245 in 512 units with length 1 explanations, only 179 (~73%) of them fall in this category. The other 66 units (~27%) have explanations where the longer explanations failed to improve the Detection Accuracy during the explanation search (Fig. 8). Additionally, units with explanation lengths greater than 1 in this setup have the

Table 4. Comparison of correlation scores among the compositional methods on the ResNet-18 model.

	Union Corr.		Intersection Corr.	
	IoU	DetAcc	IoU	DetAcc
Len3 Comp. Expl	0.2733	0.3294	0.1158	0.4876
Comp.+Select	0.2341	0.2247	0.0368	0.3603
Comp.+Stopping	0.2007	0.3409	−0.0546	0.5331

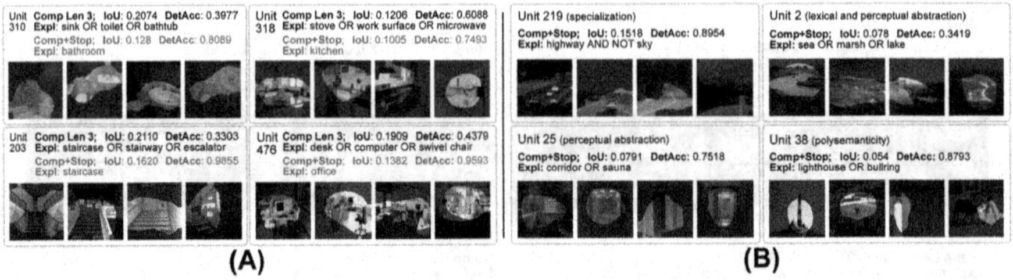

Fig. 7. Examples of the different kinds of units in the compositional setup where Detection Accuracy is used only to stop the search. (A) are examples where the these new explanations are perceptual abstractions of the regular compositional explanations from Mu and Andreas [23], while (B) are examples of explanations of length greater than 1 and their groupings, similar to Mu and Andreas [23].

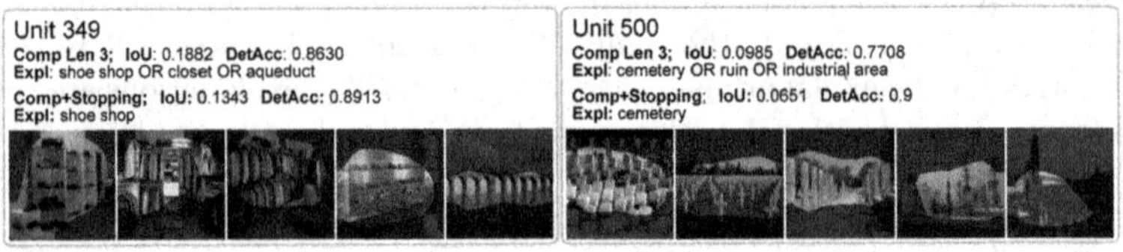

Fig. 8. Examples of exceptions to the examples described in Fig. 7 (A).

same behaviour noted in Mu and Andreas [23]; they have either learned lexically coherent or incoherent perceptual abstractions, or they are polysemantic. See Fig. 7 (B) for examples.

5 Conclusion and Future Work

In this work, we proposed an evaluation of compositional explanations of CNN units using Detection Accuracy. By evaluating Network Dissection and compositional explanations of different lengths, we showed that Detection Accuracy's evaluation of explanations is more objective and that it encodes the relationship between the concepts units learn and the predictions of the model. We further presented a modified algorithm for compositional explanations where the maximum explanation length hyper-parameter is removed using Detection Accuracy. We established that the results from this modified procedure are a better reflection of what units learn, while also showing how a new set of specialized units are exposed. Finally, we showed how that Detection Accuracy is more valuable as an evaluation method than an explanation method.

Following these results, our suggestions for future work as are follows:

1. Past work [2,34] showed that pruning of CNNs can be informed using feature importance scores from explanations. Can Detection Accuracy scores achieve a better pruning of units?

2. In the setup of Detection Accuracy as stopping criterion for the compositional search, we noted that the setup strictly sticks to the shorter explanation if the Detection Accuracy of the next length explanation is not better. Would introducing an adaptive or decaying tolerance term produce better results?
3. Finally, can these internal representation explanations be translated to explain the predictions of the model?

References

1. Adebayo, J., Gilmer, J., Muelly, M. Goodfellow, I., Hardt, M., Kim, B.: Sanity checks for saliency maps (2018). http://arxiv.org/abs/1810.03292
2. Alqahtani, A., Xie, X., Jones, M.W., Essa, E.: Pruning CNN filters via quantifying the importance of deep visual representations. Comput. Vis. Image Underst. **208**, 103220 (2021). ISSN 1077–3142. https://doi.org/10.1016/j.cviu.2021.103220, https://www.sciencedirect.com/science/article/pii/S1077314221000643
3. Ancona, M., Ceolini, E., Öztireli, A.C., Gross, M.H.: A unified view of gradient-based attribution methods for deep neural networks (2017). http://arxiv.org/abs/1711.06104
4. Arrieta, A.B., et al.: Explainable artificial intelligence (XAI): concepts, taxonomies, opportunities and challenges toward responsible AI. Inf. Fusion **58**, 82–115 (2020). ISSN 1566–2535. https://doi.org/10.1016/j.inffus.2019.12.012, https://www.sciencedirect.com/science/article/pii/S1566253519308103
5. Bau, D., Zhou, B., Khosla, A., Oliva, A., Torralba, A.: Network dissection: quantifying interpretability of deep visual representations (2017). http://arxiv.org/abs/1704.05796
6. Dalvi, F., et al.: Neurox: a toolkit for analyzing individual neurons in neural networks. In: Proceedings of the AAAI Conference on Artificial Intelligence, **33**(01), 9851–9852 (2019). https://doi.org/10.1609/aaai.v33i01.33019851, https://ojs.aaai.org/index.php/AAAI/article/view/5063
7. Došilović, F.K., Brčić, M., Hlupić, N.: Explainable artificial intelligence: a survey. In: 2018 41st International Convention on Information and Communication Technology, Electronics and Microelectronics (MIPRO), pp. 0210–0215 (2018). https://doi.org/10.23919/MIPRO.2018.8400040
8. Ghorbani, A., Wexler, J., Zou, J., Kim, B.: Towards automatic concept-based explanations (2019)
9. Gonzalez-Garcia, A., Modolo, D., Ferrari, V.: Do semantic parts emerge in convolutional neural networks? (2016). http://arxiv.org/abs/1607.03738
10. He, K., Zhang, X., Ren, S., Sun, J.: Deep residual learning for image recognition. In: 2016 IEEE Conference on Computer Vision and Pattern Recognition (CVPR), pp. 770–778 (2016). https://doi.org/10.1109/CVPR.2016.90
11. Hilton, D.J.: Mental models and causal explanation: judgements of probable cause and explanatory relevance. Thinking Reasoning **2**(4), 273–308 (1996)
12. Huang, G., Liu, Z., Weinberger, K.Q.: Densely connected convolutional networks (2016). http://arxiv.org/abs/1608.06993
13. Kim, B., Koyejo, O., Khanna, R.: Examples are not enough, learn to criticize! criticism for interpretability. In: Lee, D.D., Sugiyama, M., von Luxburg, U., Guyon, I., Garnett, R. (eds.) Advances in Neural Information Processing Systems 29: Annual Conference on Neural Information Processing Systems 2016, 5–10 December 2016, Barcelona, Spain, pp. 2280–2288 (2016). https://proceedings.neurips.cc/paper/2016/hash/5680522b8e2bb01943234bce7bf84534-Abstract.html

14. Kim, B., et al.: Interpretability beyond feature attribution: quantitative Testing with Concept Activation Vectors (TCAV) (2018)
15. Krizhevsky, A., Sutskever, I., Hinton, G.E.: Imagenet classification with deep convolutional neural networks. In: Pereira, F., Burges, C.J.C., Bottou, L., Weinberger, K.Q. (eds.) Advances in Neural Information Processing Systems, vol. 25. Curran Associates Inc (2012). https://proceedings.neurips.cc/paper/2012/file/c399862d3b9d6b76c8436e924a68c45b-Paper.pdf
16. Le, Q.V., et al.: Building high-level features using large scale unsupervised learning (2011). http://arxiv.org/abs/1112.6209
17. Lin, Y., Lee, W., Celik, Z.B.: What do you see? evaluation of explainable artificial intelligence (XAI) interpretability through neural backdoors (2020). https://arxiv.org/abs/2009.10639
18. Lundberg, S.M., Lee, S.-I.: A unified approach to interpreting model predictions. In: Guyon, I., Luxburg, U.V., Bengio, S., Wallach, H., Fergus, R., Vishwanathan, S., Garnett, R. (eds.) Advances in Neural Information Processing Systems, vol. 30. Curran Associates Inc (2017). https://proceedings.neurips.cc/paper/2017/file/8a20a8621978632d76c43dfd28b67767-Paper.pdf
19. Mahendran, A., Vedaldi, A.: Understanding deep image representations by inverting them (2014). http://arxiv.org/abs/1412.0035
20. Miller, T.: Explanation in artificial intelligence: insights from the social sciences (2017). http://arxiv.org/abs/1706.07269
21. Mittelstadt, B.D., Russell, C., Wachter, S.: Explaining explanations in AI (2018). http://arxiv.org/abs/1811.01439
22. Molnar, C.: Interpretable machine learning (2019). https://christophm.github.io/interpretable-ml-book/
23. Mu, J., Andreas, J.: Compositional explanations of neurons (2020). https://arxiv.org/abs/2006.14032
24. Nguyen, A.M., Dosovitskiy, A., Yosinski, J., Brox, T., Clune, J.: Synthesizing the preferred inputs for neurons in neural networks via deep generator networks (2016). http://arxiv.org/abs/1605.09304
25. Rosenfeld, A.: Better metrics for evaluating explainable artificial intelligence. In: International Foundation for Autonomous Agents and Multiagent Systems, Richland, SC, pp. 45–50 (2021). 9781450383073
26. Samek, W., Binder, A., Montavon, G., Lapuschkin, S., Müller, K.-R.: Evaluating the visualization of what a deep neural network has learned. IEEE Trans. Neural Networks Learn. Syst. **28**(11), 2660–2673 (2017). https://doi.org/10.1109/TNNLS.2016.2599820
27. Simonyan, K., Vedaldi, A., Zisserman, A.: Deep inside convolutional networks: visualising image classification models and saliency maps (2014)
28. Slugoski, B.R., Lalljee, M., Lamb, R., Ginsburg, G.P.: Attribution in conversational context: effect of mutual knowledge on explanation-giving. Eur. J. Soc. Psychol. **23**(3), 219–238 (1993)
29. Sundararajan, M., Taly, A., Yan, Q.: Axiomatic attribution for deep networks. In: Precup, D., Teh, Y.W. (eds.) Proceedings of the 34th International Conference on Machine Learning, Proceedings of Machine Learning Research, vol. 70, pp. 3319–3328. PMLR (2017). http://proceedings.mlr.press/v70/sundararajan17a.html
30. Vondrick, C., Pirsiavash, H., Torralba, A.: Generating videos with scene dynamics (2016). http://arxiv.org/abs/1609.02612

31. Xu, F., Uszkoreit, H., Du, Y., Fan, W., Zhao, D., Zhu, J.: Explainable AI: a brief survey on history, research areas, approaches and challenges. In: Tang, J., Kan, M.-Y., Zhao, D., Li, S., Zan, H. (eds.) Natural Language Processing and Chinese Computing, pp. 563–574 (2019). Springer International Publishing, Cham. ISBN 978-3-030-32236-6
32. Yang, F., Du, M., Hu, X.: Evaluating explanation without ground truth in interpretable machine learning (2019) http://arxiv.org/abs/1907.06831
33. Yeh, C., Hsieh, C., Suggala, A.S., Inouye, D.I., Ravikumar, P.: How sensitive are sensitivity-based explanations? (2019). http://arxiv.org/abs/1901.09392
34. Yeom, S., Seegerer, P., Lapuschkin, S., Wiedemann, S., Müller, K., Samek, W.: Pruning by explaining: a novel criterion for deep neural network pruning (2019). http://arxiv.org/abs/1912.08881
35. Ylikoski, P.: Causal and constitutive explanation compared. Erkenntnis **78**(2), 277–297 (2013). https://doi.org/10.1007/s10670-013-9513-9
36. Zeiler, M.D., Fergus, R.: Visualizing and understanding convolutional networks (2013). http://arxiv.org/abs/1311.2901
37. Zhou, B., Khosla, A., Lapedriza, A., Oliva, A., Torralba, A.: Object detectors emerge in deep scene CNNS (2015)
38. Zhou, B., Zhao, H., Puig, X., Fidler, S., Barriuso, A., Torralba, A.: Scene parsing through ADE20K dataset. In: 2017 IEEE Conference on Computer Vision and Pattern Recognition (CVPR), pp. 5122–5130 (2017). https://doi.org/10.1109/CVPR.2017.544
39. Zhou, B., Lapedriza, A., Khosla, A., Oliva, A., Torralba, A.: Places: a 10 million image database for scene recognition. IEEE Trans. Pattern Anal. Mach. Intell. **40**(6), 1452–1464 (2018). https://doi.org/10.1109/TPAMI.2017.2723009

Knowledge-Based Neural Pre-training for Intelligent Document Management

Daniele Margiotta[1], Danilo Croce[1(✉)], Marco Rotoloni[2], Barbara Cacciamani[2], and Roberto Basili[1(✉)]

[1] University of Roma Tor Vergata, Rome, Italy
{croce,basili}@info.uniroma2.it
[2] ABI Lab, Rome, Italy
{m.rotoloni,b.cacciamani}@abilab.it

Abstract. Banks are usually large and complex companies that face a number of challenges to support the rapid and effective sharing of information and content across their organizations. Extracting complex metadata from raw bank documents is therefore central to support intelligent data indexing, information circulation and to promote more complex predictive capabilities, e.g., compliance assessment problems. In this paper, we present a weakly-supervised neural methodology for creating semantic metadata from bank documents. It exploits a neural pre-training method optimized against legacy semantic resources able to minimize the training effort. We studied an application to business process design and management in banks and tested the method on documents from the Italian banking community. The measured impact of the proposed training approach to process-related metadata creation confirms its applicability.

Keywords: Domain-specific neural learning · Domain knowledge modeling · Zero-shot learning in NLP · Bert-based NL inference

1 Introduction

Traditional information technologies in banking are primarily oriented to transaction processing and data analysis. Artificial Intelligence pushes for the adoption of data-driven methods able to induce expert rules and accurate prediction capabilities to be applied in typical financial forecasting tasks, such as estimation of future values for bonds and equities, identification of market opportunities as well as anti-money laundering decisions. In [4] financial time-series mapped into images encoded as candlestick, charts are used to induce trade strategies. There, unrelated areas of quantitative finance and neural computer vision are integrated, as neural image classifiers are adopted to derive financial trading rules combining typical patterns regarding traders' intuition, skill, and experience. A similar path is followed in [3] for applying CNNs to induce trade predictions.

However, inherent shortcomings are met with non-numerical data, especially when dealing with massive unstructured information. In response, one strategy adopted by financial information management applications is transforming

S. Bandini et al. (Eds.): AIxIA 2021, LNAI 13196, pp. 564–579, 2022.
https://doi.org/10.1007/978-3-031-08421-8_39

unstructured data into structured data, to better support information labeling, searching, and effectively promote industry development. In [10], a graph neural network method is suggested to deal with highly interconnected but poorly structured financial data for improving explainability aspects of different detection tasks. Neural entity labeling for networks representing financial organizations and interactions is proposed based on graph neural networks. Graph feature explanation methods for the predictions over graph-structured financial data are proposed. In [1] a classification-based methodology is applied over specific relational representation in the context of Anti-Money Laundering. Authors propose a novel behavior-based model to infer the goals of activities by classifying the behavior into money laundering or standard behavior.

The complex nature of unstructured data is particularly evident in organization and logistic information in the financial and banking domain [11]. In this case, the internal documentation of a bank includes all the reference texts needed to share information and norms. As such, texts are used to record, regulate (i.e., constrain) and to document the decisions, the processes, and the organizational units of the bank through general regulatory documents, reference models (e.g., organization taxonomies), or terminologies, as well as daily service orders. The overall corpus of texts produced by a bank is a valuable repository of the core data and information needed to systematically support business analysis as well as strategic planning.

Organizational regulations, such as norms or process descriptions, are always expressed in semi-formal, or sometimes textual, i.e. strongly qualitative, ways. This is the perfect domain for application of natural language processing (NLP) approaches whereas data-driven technologies have shown great value since the '90s. Although general purpose tools are easily available and neural techniques demonstrated very accurate language modeling and inference capabilities (e.g., BERT [6] or GPT-3 [2]), straightforward applications of such neural methods in business process mining scenarios are still limited. Structured representations of legacy models such as terminologies or ontological resources, e.g., Process Hierarchies, are not directly exploitable in supervised learning tools, as they are difficult to integrate with the unstructured information counterparts, e.g. linguistic concept descriptions, defined informally. Most importantly, the application of state-of-the-art NLP models still requires the availability of manually annotated examples in the target domain. As an example, organizations are generally required to make explicit connections between normative documentation and ontological models, such as Process Trees (PTs). Machine learning approaches, e.g., BERT or similar neural models, are particularly appealing to discover and classify such many-to-many associations among hundreds of nodes in a PT and thousands of documents produced daily by the organization. Unfortunately, the effort required by experts to provide examples of such complex associations is significant, making complete coverage of possibly large trees uneconomic.

In this work, we investigate the application of a *zero-shot learning* approach [2] based on the (re-)use of complex predictive NLP models, even in scenarios where manually labeled datasets are limited (or even absent). In particular, we propose to exploit a semantic model, e.g., a knowledge graph (KG) in form of a process tree (PTs), as a linguistically augmented information source, where domain-specific relations between concepts are made explicit. In the suggested augmentation, we map individual relations into short texts, able to make semantic evidence about the domain (e.g., definitions or hierarchical relations) available since the early phases of the training of a Transformer-based architecture. The suggested approach allows to pre-train a BERT-based model [6] through a large-scale domain-specific training dataset (up to 1.2M controlled sentences), which can be easily extracted from the semantic resource, including concept definitions and ontological relations within a taxonomy (i.e., the PT). As a result, the pre-trained model allows i) text classification by associating raw texts to (possibly multiple) nodes of the KG and ii) supporting more complex natural language inference tasks in the domain, e.g., by predicting properties of the process described in the PT taxonomy. The experimental results over the pre-training stage and the automatic acquisition of process-related metadata suggest the feasibility of the approach at the industry level.

In the following part of document, Sect. 2 introduces the Transformer-based approach. Section 3 and 4 present the proposed method for knowledge-based pre-training and metadata creation. Section 5 reports the experimental evaluations while Sect. 6 draws some conclusion.

2 Transformers for Robust NL Inferences

In the field of computer vision, researchers have repeatedly shown the beneficial contribution of pre-training a neural network model on a known task and then fine-tuning it to a different, but related task, e.g., [8]. The approach proposed in [6], namely Bidirectional Encoder Representations from Transformers (BERT), provides a very effective model to pre-train a deep and complex neural network over a very large scale non-annotated text collection and apply it to a large variety of linguistic inference tasks, by simply extending it through fine-tuning towards new problems. The building block of BERT is the *Transformer* element [16], an attention-based mechanism that learns contextual relations between words (or sub-words, i.e., word pieces, [14]) in a text. In line with [13], BERT aims at providing a sentence embedding (as well as the contextualized embeddings of each word composing the sentence) where the pre-training stage is used to acquire an expressive and robust language model, targeted by the encoder. The encoder reads once the entire word sequence and can reconstruct the original sentence through the optimization of a language model. It applies different general tasks, such as the MLM (*masked language model*) pre-training target: in MLM, randomly some of the tokens are masked from the input, with the encoding objective of predicting the original word according to its context. In addition, BERT also applies the *next sentence prediction* task, which is jointly optimized on text pairs extracted from the corpus. This last objective is specifically important to improve the network capability of modeling relational information between sentence pairs, obtaining state-of-the-art results in semantic processing tasks such as Textual Entailment or NL Inference [7,15].

After the above two pre-training stages are applied against a generic document collection, the resulting BERT model allows encoding an entire sentence in form of the leftmost output vector corresponding to the so-called fake `[CLS]` token. These encodings can be used as input to further layers of a neural architecture to train task-specific models, such as sentence classification, sequence labeling, or relation extraction learning tasks: the simple stacking of further neural layers on top of the BERT encoder allows to fine-tune the entire architecture for such specific new tasks. *Fine-tuning* is thus applied by adding task-specific and simple layers on top of the acquired BERT language model. The straightforward application of BERT has shown better results than previous state-of-the-art models on a wide spectrum of natural language processing tasks. BERT is pre-trained over text in English, and it can capture language models for this natural language, as the captured linguistic information strictly depends on the language of the pre-training texts. As we target documents and semantic resources in Italian, we adopted GilBERTo[1], a BERT-based model pre-trained with the Italian Wikipedia.

Finally, despite the huge impact of the pre-training stage, BERT-based architectures depend from (possibly large-scale) annotated datasets for fine-tuning. In line with existing *zero-shot learning* approaches [2], the next section presents a methodology to extend pre-training and adapting BERT to a new domain, by exploiting the linguistic information provided by legacy semantic resources. This enables the applicability of BERT-based classifiers in the bank domain without resorting to manually annotated examples.

3 ABILaBERT: Injecting Domain Knowledge in BERT

Business-related problems in banks, such as Financial Planning, Risk assessment, or Anti-Money Laundering, involve a large part of the entire organization, therefore, the correct and continuous sharing of timely and precise information is crucial. The governance of this complex information eco-system, needed for fast and effective strategic planning and decision making, is usually ensured through rigorous process frameworks that design, monitor, and finally document, also for legal purposes, all the stages of the involved organizational steps. As a consequence, bank governance produces information about processes shared in a semi-formal manner, mainly through documents, i.e., unstructured or semi-structured data. The banking processes are defined by specialists, consultants, and banking leaders, such as the set of actions that support a given activity life-cycle with its expected performance. For example, the *"Services for the Acquisition of new customers"* (*"Servizi di acquisizione di nuovi clienti"*) is a complex set of processes including: telemarketing activities, user application processing, underwriting, customer/merchant credit evaluation and verification, credit approval, document processing, account opening as well as customer care and *on-boarding*.

The design and maintenance of a suitable process system is a stable activity for a bank. Usually, machine-readable forms of the processes are first obtained

[1] https://huggingface.co/idb-ita/gilberto-uncased-from-camembert.

through semi-formal specification (e.g., through Business Process Modeling Languages, e.g., [12]) and then documented in automatic manners in Process management platforms. However, once the processes are identified, they need to become operational. This means that bank analysts are using process-related information (e.g., norms or activity obligations) in their document and information management processes. Employees are usually exposed to processes and hierarchies, whose different abstraction levels formalize tasks and obligations. More general processes (i.e., *"Analysis of the company positioning"*) are higher in the hierarchy with respect to more focused process specifications (i.e., *"Definition of reference financial markets"*). It is worth noting that the specification of the bank processes provided by the whole hierarchy is by no means connected explicitly to individual documents.

In this work, we will consider the ABILab Process Tree Taxonomy[2] as a general, i.e., bank-independent, formalization of the processes currently active in the Italian bank eco-system. The objective of this taxonomy is to achieve a complete and shared mapping of the bank's processes, covering all areas of activity at a level of detail that can be considered common across different banks and financial organizations, without explicit reference to existing organizational structures, products offered or delivery channels. The process naming and descriptions are in Italian, even though all examples will be reported through their English translations in the rest of the paper.

More formally, the process taxonomy $\mathcal{P}$ defines conceptualized process types, i.e., taxonomy nodes $p \in \mathcal{P}$, and a subsumption relation $\sqsubset$ in $\mathcal{P} \times \mathcal{P}$. Specific properties of a process p include at least the label, i.e., the process naming term $\text{LABEL}(p)$, and its textual description, namely $\text{DESC}(p)$. As an example, a process p has $\text{LABEL}(p)$: *"Definition of the Company Vision"*, while its description $\text{DESC}(p)$: "*The process of Defining, at an abstract level, some company objectives towards the different stakeholder, the expected company positioning and the policies to be adopted to achieve them*". Each process $p \in \mathcal{P}$ is thus defined by at least the following properties:

- **Term**, $\text{LABEL}(p)$, the term that names the process, such as *"Definition of the company budget"*;
- **Description**, $\text{DESC}(p)$, the text that defines p, such as "*The process of management of the budget plan, through the definition of the configuration rules, their application, and the monitoring of the compliance to them.*";
- **Parent**, $\text{FATHER}(p)$, the process of a single higher-level that expresses concept p in a more general way, defined as: $\text{FATHER}(p) = q \in P$ such that $p \sqsubset q$, e.g., as $\text{LABEL}(\text{FATHER}(p))$=$\text{LABEL}(q)$="*Resource allocation and budgeting*";
- **Sub-processes**, $\text{CH}(p)$, as the subset of $\mathcal{P}$ expressing the concept p in a more specific way, i.e., $\text{CH}(p) = \{q \in \mathcal{P} |\ q \sqsubset p\}$, with, for the example $\text{LABEL}(q)$="*Budget rule definition*";
- **Siblings**, $\text{SIB}(p)$, the subset of $\mathcal{P}$ characterized by nodes sharing a common direct *parent process* with p, i.e., $\text{SIB}(p) = \{q \in \mathcal{P} \mid \text{FATHER}(p) = \text{FATHER}(q)\}$,

[2] It is available at: https://www.abilab.it/tassonomia-processi-bancari.

such as $q \in \text{SIB}(p)$ with $\text{LABEL}(q)=$ "*Definition of business objectives at operational level*", i.e., a direct specialization of $\text{FATHER}(p)$.

3.1 Injecting Process Knowledge as Auxiliary Tasks

Language modeling has been largely used as an effective pre-training method of large-scale neural networks. However, the auxiliary tasks adopted (such as *language masking*) just emphasize language general properties, and models *de facto*, task- and, more importantly, domain-independent information. Domain knowledge seems instead particularly relevant in several inferences, such as entity recognition: it is even more influential on tasks such as metadata creation process in the financial domain.

Without in-depth knowledge about the process tree, no target category would be even available to an inductive metadata creation method. The idea is to avoid the manual labeling stage characterizing the training resources for a supervised approach to metadata creation, and to instead foster auxiliary tasks sensitive to the knowledge implicit in the process tree.

The good news about using the process tree as a source for pre-training is that all its nodes and properties have a linguistic nature, which can be used to model some textual inference task.

A knowledge-driven auxiliary task for our metadata creation problem is a text classification task, whose positive (as well as negative) examples can be automatically derived from the taxonomy and its related textual properties. For example, the **subsumption recognition** $f(p, q)$ task that given two processes, p and q, establishes the validity of the subsumption relation between them, i.e., $f(p, q) = true$ iff $q \sqsubset p$ can be easily mapped into a text classification inference: in fact, for every $p, q \in \mathcal{P}$ it can be easily seen that $f(p, q) \Leftrightarrow$ "$\text{DESC}(q)$ *describes a process more specific than* $\text{DESC}(p)$" is a valid sentence. $f(p, q)$ is in fact true if and only if the sentence derived from the two descriptions, i.e., $\text{DESC}(p)$ and $\text{DESC}(q)$, is also accepted as true. Notice how examples of true (and false) statements can be easily derived from the taxonomy, by sampling different (p, q) pairs with $q \in \text{CH}(p)$ and $q \notin \text{CH}(p)$. More importantly, other auxiliary tasks can be derived from $\mathcal{P}$. Other properties of $\mathcal{P}$ can be mapped into language expressions with analogous logical valence, such as definitions of the form "$\text{LABEL}(p)$ *is defined by* $\text{DESC}(p)$".

Given the process taxonomy, each node can give rise to one or more potential examples for the target auxiliary tasks. They can be used as auxiliary tasks for a Transformer-based approach to metadata creation. They allow learning the main aspects of the taxonomy: definitions of individual processes and relations between node pairs.

While the Transformer is auxiliary trained to understand how processes are defined and how they subsume other processes, linguistic information derived implicitly from definitions encode the domain knowledge embodied by the taxonomy. In this way, domain-specific pretraining is empowered and made available for a zero-shot learning approach to specific tasks (e.g. document classification).

3.2 Auxiliary Tasks for Domain Specific Pre-training

The auxiliary tasks aim at acquiring domain knowledge implicitly from definitions and from relational texts, i.e., statements about direct subsumption relationships between nodes of different levels in the taxonomy. The general assumption here is that every process $p \in \mathcal{P}$ can give rise to base sentences corresponding to its description, denoted by $S_{\mathcal{P}}^{\text{DESC}}$, or to its name, denoted by $S_{\mathcal{P}}^{\text{LABEL}}$. A composite sentence is obtained by applying templates to individual sentence pairs in $S_{\mathcal{P}}^{\text{DESC}} \times S_{\mathcal{P}}^{\text{LABEL}}$ or $S_{\mathcal{P}}^{\text{DESC}} \times S_{\mathcal{P}}^{\text{DESC}}$. For example,

$$\text{“}\textsc{label}(p) \;\; \textit{is defined as} \;\; \textsc{desc}(p)\text{”}$$

is one such composed sentence in $S_{\mathcal{P}}^{\text{DESC}} \times S_{\mathcal{P}}^{\text{LABEL}}$. An instance of a composite sentence is: *Definition of the company budget is defined as “The process of management of the budget plan, through the definition of the configuration rules, their application and the monitoring of the compliance to them.”*. Every such composite statement can be used to train a Transformer based language modeling process to recognize its logical status according to the knowledge embodied by $\mathcal{P}$. The following auxiliary tasks can be thus defined.

Definition Recognition. In this task, the model description and the term of a node in the taxonomy are related and the model is thus expected to recognize $f_{desc} : S_{\mathcal{P}}^{\text{DESC}} \times S_{\mathcal{P}}^{\text{LABEL}} \longrightarrow \{\text{TRUE}, \text{FALSE}\}$, i.e., if that association is true or false. Notice that the inductive task can be modeled as the regression of the probability function $p(f_{desc}(s) = \text{TRUE})$ whereas s derives from an input space $S_{\mathcal{P}}^{\text{DESC}} \times S_{\mathcal{P}}^{\text{LABEL}}$ through the template derived from definitions shown above. The probability scores are of course such that $p(f_{desc}(s) = \text{TRUE}) = 1 - p(f_{desc}(s) = \text{FALSE})$.

Subsumption Recognition. In this task, hierarchical relations are mapped into composite sentences declaring the property over two nodes, $q, p \in \mathcal{P}$. The nodes descriptions are here combined through a template over $S_{\mathcal{P}}^{\text{DESC}} \times S_{\mathcal{P}}^{\text{DESC}}$. One such template can be “$\textsc{desc}(p)$ *is a more general process than* $\textsc{desc}(q)$”. Notice that the template expresses a correct sentences only when $q \sqsubset p$ in $\mathcal{P}$. Directionality can also be captured by alternative templates that can be applied to get more examples, such that “$\textsc{desc}(q)$ *is a process more specific than* $\textsc{desc}(p)$”. As a consequence $f_{hie} : S_{\mathcal{P}}^{\text{DESC}} \times S_{\mathcal{P}}^{\text{DESC}} \longrightarrow \{\text{TRUE}, \text{FALSE}\}$ defines a logical function whose role is to provide the inductive auxiliary task to estimate the probability $p(f_{hie}(s) = \text{TRUE})$ given a sentence s derived through the application of the templates involved in the Subsumption Recognition task to pairs $(p, q) \in S_{\mathcal{P}}^{\text{DESC}} \times S_{\mathcal{P}}^{\text{DESC}}$. Obviously, s expresses a correct sentences only when $q \sqsubset p$ in $\mathcal{P}$. Moreover, $\forall s \;\; p(f_{hie}(s) = \text{TRUE}) = 1 - p(f_{hie}(s) = \text{FALSE})$.

Sibling Recognition. In this task, we can build a sentence involving three process descriptions $f, c_1, c_2 \in \mathcal{P}$: the node f is the direct ancestor of both c_1 and c_2, i.e., $c_1 \sqsubset f \wedge c_2 \sqsubset f$ so that the last two nodes are siblings, i.e., $c_1 \in \textsc{sib}(c_2)$ as well as $c_2 \in \textsc{sib}(c_1)$. A possible template for declaring linguistically such a ternary relationship is “$\textsc{desc}(c_1)$ *is a sibling of* $\textsc{desc}(c_2)$, *as both are specialization of* $\textsc{desc}(f)$”. The model can be also pre-trained over the recognition of $f_{sib} : S_{\mathcal{P}}^{\text{DESC}} \times S_{\mathcal{P}}^{\text{DESC}} \times S_{\mathcal{P}}^{\text{DESC}} \longrightarrow \{\text{TRUE}, \text{FALSE}\}$ whose role is to provide the auxiliary task of estimating the probability $p(f_{sib}(s) = \text{TRUE})$ given a sentence s derived through the application of template from the current task to triples $(c_1, c_2, f) \in S_{\mathcal{P}}^{\text{DESC}} \times S_{\mathcal{P}}^{\text{DESC}} \times S_{\mathcal{P}}^{\text{DESC}}$. Obviously s expresses a correct sentences only when $c_1 \sqsubset f \wedge c_2 \sqsubset f$. In addition, it is strictly required that $\forall s \quad p(f_{sib}(s) = \text{TRUE}) = 1 - p(f_{sib}(s) = \text{FALSE})$.

Negation and directionality. Each of the above relational auxiliary tasks can be further enriched through the application of some linguistic counterparts of the logical *negation* and *inversion* operators. For example, the first template from the Subsumption Recognition task can be modified as "DESC(p) *is not more general than* DESC(q)" with a logical switch from TRUE to FALSE. Even in Definition Recognition, one such switching is possible and a negated template can be used to gather more examples. Inverting the direction of a statement is also possible, with a larger variety of statements used to capture the process taxonomy logics. An example of inverted template of f_{desc} is "*The term for* DESC(p) *is* LABEL(p)". As a consequence, we can add further auxiliary tasks, such as from f_{desc} can be extended with f_{desc}^{neg} (when negation is applied), f_{desc}^{inv} (with inversion applied) and $f_{desc}^{neg/inv}$ when both are applied.

4 Using ABILaBERT for Text-Driven Process Mining

The above methods for pre-training the BERT model allow optimizing the language modeling capability in the target financial domain. The objective is to allow the system to encode free sentences from domain documents in an informed manner and support classification, i.e. the association of the proper processes from $\mathcal{P}$ to input texts. The resulting model is called ABILaBERT and, given an incoming sentence s exploits the Transformer-based architecture to generate an embedding for s (contained in the vector in the first position `[CLS]`) and make it available to fine-tuning for classification. It is worth noting that during the encoding of a sentence s the system is also able to estimate several properties of s through the solution of one or more auxiliary tasks, as described in the previous section. For example for every sentence s and process $p \in \mathcal{P}$ the system can estimate functions such as $f_{desc}(s, \text{LABEL}(p))$, which states if a sentence s is a valid process description. These promote the node p as a good candidate to represent the semantics of a sentence s with respect to the process taxonomy $\mathcal{P}$. The more precise is the promotion of nodes p, the faster will be the identification of the candidate process for the incoming s. Note that a document is usually made of complex textual units (e.g., paragraphs) made of more than one sentence.

As a consequence, ABILaBERT can be used to automatically extract metadata from a document by adapting it to the individual sentences. Short, by applying the different templates introduced in Sect. 3.2, each sentence s generates several examples to be classified by ABILaBERT with respect to individual processes p according to one or more auxiliary tasks f. Each time s is positively classified with respect to f, it provides a vote, within a voting strategy for the final process assignment.

Algorithm 1. Candidate Selection

1: **procedure** SELECT_CANDIDATE_PROCESSES(*input text s, process tree $\mathcal{P}$, filter threshold k*)
2: ▷ $\vec{w}$ *contains the cumulative similarity for each p against the input text s*
3: $\vec{w} = [w_1, \ldots, w_{\|\mathcal{P}\|}] = \vec{0}$
4: ▷ *Get the [CLS] embedding for s by ABILaBert*
5: $\texttt{cls}_s$ = GET_ABILABERT_EMBEDDING(s)
6: **for** $p \in P$ **do**
7: $\vec{z}_p = \vec{0} \in \mathbb{R}^4$
8: ▷ *Scan the Auxiliary Task sentences as defined in Section 3.2*
9: **for** $t \in \{$LABEL(p), DESC(p), $f_{desc}, f_{desc}^{inv}\}$ **do**
10: s_p^t = GENERATE_AUXILIARY_TEXT_EXAMPLES(t, p)
11: ▷ *Get the CLS embedding for the sentence* s_p^t
12: $\texttt{cls}_p^t$ = GET_ABILABERT_EMBEDDING(s_p^t)
13: $\vec{z}_p[t]$ = COSINE_SIMILARITY$(\texttt{cls}_s, \texttt{cls}_p^t)$
14: ▷ *p is scored as the average similarity across the tasks.*
15: $\vec{w}[p] = \mu(\vec{z}_p)$
16: ▷ *Rank the processes using the accumulated similarities and select the top k*
17: C = RANK_AND_TRIM$(\mathcal{P}, \vec{w}, k)$
18: **return** C

The application of ABILaBERT to the metadata creation task over entire paragraphs of a bank document is made of 2 phases.

Candidate Selection. It is important to highlight that evaluating ABILaBERT over all possible combinations of sentences and processes risks to be computational expensive and pruning some of the processes $p \in \mathcal{P}$ is useful to reduce the overall complexity of the actual classification stage. In Algorithm 1 the input is an individual sentence s of the document paragraph. At first, the embedding of the first `[CLS]` token is acquired through ABILaBERT (line 5). Then, for each process node $p \in \mathcal{P}$, 4 different textual representations are made available: the term, LABEL(p) of the process, the description of the process, i.e., DESC(p), and two sentences corresponding to the f_{desc} and f_{desc}^{inv} from the Definition Recognition task of Sect. 3.1 (line 9). These different tasks t are thus characterized by different sentences s_p^t that provide four embeddings $\texttt{cls}_p^t$. Their cosine similarity with the input sentence s embedding $\texttt{cls}_s$ correspond to four independent confidence scores (line 13). The average of the 2 highest of such scores (line 10) is used to rank across all processes (line 15). Finally, the top k processes are returned (line 17).

Paragraph Classification. The objective of this phase is to assign one or more processes $p \in \mathcal{P}$ as semantic metadata to entire paragraphs of an input bank document. In Algorithm 2, the input is a paragraph extracted from a bank document, possibly split into a sequence of sentences, also seen as adjacent pairs or triples. After that, for each sentence in the paragraph, the Candidate selection function of Algorithm 1 returns a limited list of k processes that are"candidate" metadata. Then, all examples are classified by the ABILaBERT model with

Algorithm 2. Classification phase

```
1: procedure CLASSIFY(text TXT, process tree 𝒫, filter threshold k, process Size l,
   process threshold τ)
2:     ▷ v⃗ contains as many numerical scores as processes in P, initialized to 0
3:     v⃗ = [v_1, ..., v_||P||] = 0⃗
4:     ▷ the input text TXT is split in singles, pairs and triples of sentences
5:     S = SPLIT_IN_SENTENCES(TXT)
6:     S = S ∪ GET_SENT_PAIRS(S) ∪ GET_SENT_TRIPLES(S)
7:     ▷ for each piece of TXT
8:     for s ∈ S do
9:         v⃗^s = [v^s_1, ..., v^s_||𝒫||] = 1⃗          ▷ a vector of specific votes for s is initialized
10:        ▷ returns k candidate processes semantically related to the input text s
11:        C = SELECT_CANDIDATE_PROCESSES(s, P, k)          ▷ See Algorithm 1
12:        for p ∈ C do
13:            for f ∈ F = {f_desc, f^neg_desc, f^inv_desc, ...} do ▷ Auxiliary Tasks of Section 3.2
14:                v⃗^s[p] += 𝟙(f(s, p) = TRUE)          ▷ 𝟙(TRUE) = 1 while 𝟙(FALSE) = 0
15:            v[p] += log(v⃗^s[p]) ▷ Accumulate votes across different pieces from TXT
16:    ▷ Rank the processes according to the accumulated votes and select the top l
17:    R = ORDER_BY_AND_TRIM(P, v⃗, l)
18:    for p ∉ R do                                     ▷ Remove from v⃗ all processes not in R
19:        v⃗[p] = 0
20:    ▷ Apply a softmax so that the final score resembles a probability distribution
21:    v⃗_SOFT = SOFTMAX(v⃗)
22:    ▷ Remove processes whose final score does not exceed the threshold τ
23:    for p ∈ R do
24:        if v⃗_SOFT[p] < τ then
25:            R = R / p
26:    return R
```

respect to a set of auxiliary tasks F selected through cross-validation (line 13) and the estimated probability is cumulated on a logarithmic base (line 14/15). These (logarithmic) votes are used to select the l most voted processes (line 17). For these processes the corresponding votes are converted in a probability distribution using the Softmax function over their scores (line 18–21). A final pruning is applied to remove processes with a probability score lower than τ.

The Classification and Pruning algorithms establish an unsupervised meta-data creation method that assigns one or more processes to any paragraph of an incoming bank document. It is sensitive to the domain knowledge about the process hierarchy $\mathcal{P}$ through the pre-training operating on different dedicated auxiliary semantic tasks. The method is largely applicable, with many examples and variants derived from nodes of the hierarchy and textual templates.

5 Experimental Evaluation

The following evaluations aims to confirm that the proposed methodology can: (1) solve the auxiliary tasks in a highly efficient and effective manner (2) support an accurate process labeling, and (3) be consistent with the process that would be assigned by real analysts. The targeted ABI Lab taxonomy includes 459 processes organized across 4 granularity levels. We selected processes up to the third level that amounts to 168 different nodes. They are suited to represent the metadata category for banking documents. The targeted portion of the taxonomy $\mathcal{P}$ has a branching factor of 2.5 children per node, an average number of the sibling of 5.5, while the average length of $\text{DESC}(p)$ is about 40 tokens.

Evaluating ABILaBERT Against the Auxiliary Tasks. To pre-train ABI-LaBERT, we generated a set of about 1,25 Million examples across all tasks introduced in Sect. 3.2, whose details are shown in Table 1: rows refers to specific tasks, while columns contain the number of examples whereas negation and directionality criteria are applied. Processes were randomly selected from $\mathcal{P}$ with the only constraint that a ratio of 1 : 5 between positive and negative examples is guaranteed. About 150 sentence templates are used to generate examples for each auxiliary task. Only siblings at levels 2 and 3 were targeted by our tests.

The GilBERTo model, introduced in Sect. 2, was fine-tuned over the dataset obtained in the pre-training phase subjected to parameter tuning through a 10-cross fold validation. Moreover, for any task, the sentences associated with any of the processes used in the test set were removed from the training material. The GilBERTo model, implemented through the Huggingface library [17], was trained on a total of 10 epochs with a batch size of 16, a maximum length of 256 word pieces, using the AdamW optimizer with a learning rate of $1e^{-5}$. Given the unbalanced nature of the dataset, we measured the performances in terms of Precision and Recall for the binary label of the examples as in Table 2.

Table 1. Number of artificial sentences uses to pre-train ABILaBERT

	Positive examples				Negative examples			
	negation/directional				negation/directional			
	yes/no	no/yes	no/no	yes/yes	yes/no	no/yes	no/no	yes/yes
Definition Recog.	25,187	19,450	19,372	25,199	43,140	124,980	125,099	42,561
Subsumption Recog.	32,666	30,508	30,863	32,875	96,670	151,130	152,401	95,103
Sibling Recog.	9,996	10,773	10,833	10,758	44,696	44,728	44,440	44,657
Total	258,480				1,009,605			

The achieved F1 values in such a large-scale test set clearly suggest that the resulting ABILaBERT model almost perfectly discriminates process definitions (F1 = 0.93) and is also highly stable in recognizing siblings (with F1 = 0.99). The Subsumption recognition task appears more complex as the lower scores (F1 = 0.86): this suggests that descriptions of sibling nodes are more consistent and process descriptions are less textually related to their direct parent ones. However, although more focused tests are needed, ABILaBERT seems overall quite robust to bridge linguistic information with knowledge about the target financial domain.

Table 2. Results of ABILaBERT within the auxiliary tasks

	Prec.	Rec.	F1
Defin. Rec.	0.94	0.92	0.93
Subs. Rec.	0.91	0.86	0.86
Sibl. Rec.	0.98	0.99	0.99

Table 3. Results of ABILaBERT in the automatic metadata extraction

	Prec.	Rec.	F1
Baseline	0.15	0.10	0.12
GilBERTo	0.18	0.94	0.30
ABILaBERT	0.43	0.84	0.56

Automatic metadata acquisition. In order to validate applicability to the metadata creation tasks, we randomly selected 62 paragraphs from financial documents expressing bank processes across different Italian Organisations. To reduce any bias in the test, we provided to the annotators exactly 10 processes/paragraphs pairs (p, t) for each paragraph t. When ABILaBERT provided less than 10 processes, the missing ones were alternately selected through random selection by $\mathcal{P}$. Overall, in these experiments, 135 different processes were involved in at least one pair (p, t). The overall 620 assignments were thus submitted to ABI Lab analysts, asking to decide among the following labels to: `accept` whenever p was clearly associated to the text t, `neutral` whenever t just references activities partially connected to p and `reject` whenever t clearly refers to activities completely indifferent to p. ABILaBERT assigned with a confidence higher than τ about 2 process per paragraph, on average.

We measured the quality of this assignment through Precision (the percentage of correctly proposed processes by ABILaBERT), Recall (the percentage of correct processes among the 10 suggested processes), and the F1 (the harmonic mean between Precision and Recall). An ABILaBERT decision p is considered correct for t only whenever the analyst assigns `accept` or `neutral` to the (p, t) pair, as such p's are considered consistent with t by the analyst.

Results are in Table 3: the first row shows the results of a Baseline system based on random sampling 10 processes among the targeted 168 ones and promoting 2 of such processes as accepted by the baseline system in order to be consistent with the generative power of the ABILaBERT approach. The low accuracy of the baseline method is also a measure of the task complexity, against 168 possible (and not mutually exclusive) target choices. The second row shows the application of the Algorithm 2 only driven by the original domain-independent GilBERTo transformer, useful to validate the effectiveness of the proposed knowledge-based pre-training stage.

Finally, the last row shows the result of ABILaBERT, whose tuning over 5 held-out paragraphs suggested the following parameters: i) the μ function that rank the candidate processes (see row 15 from Algorithm 1) only considers the two most valuable candidate; ii) the filter threshold $k = 5$ in Algorithm 1; iii) the set of tasks that we use to vote individual nodes is $F = \{f_{desc}, f_{desc}^{neg}, f_{desc}^{inv}, f_{desc}^{neg/inv}\}$[3] (see row 13 in Algorithm 2). Results clearly show a significant

[3] Decision functions f other than f_{desc} and the adoption of the Sibling Recognition task had no significant impact on performances. Also negation provided little improvement of Recall (0.83 wrt 0.84).

improvement of ABILaBERT ($F1 = 0.56$) wrt the baseline ($F1 = 0.12$) as well as the straight application of GilBERTo ($F1 = 0.30$) confirming the beneficial impact of the proposed unsupervised pre-training strategy. Moreover, ABILaBERT, i.e., as an unsupervised classifier, has already a high Recall, i.e., it can recover almost all correct processes ($Recall = 0.84$), even at the expense of some noise ($Precision = 0.43$).

Assessing the quality of ABILaBERT. We also compared the behavior of ABILaBERT against a pool of 9 bank analysts, required to annotate a subset of the same 10 paragraphs of the test set. We considered ABILaBERT as the tenth annotator and compared every annotator with all the others (considered as the gold standard each time). On average, ABILaBERT obtained an average of $F1 = 0.597$ (with a standard deviation of 0.17). Considered that human analysts obtained an average of $F1 = 0.601$, with a standard deviation of 0.08, this is very encouraging as the proposed weakly supervised method is very close to human performance. A matrix containing individual comparisons across all annotators is reported in the Appendix for further observations that cannot be here expended for limitation in the paper space.

6 Conclusion

This paper presented a weakly supervised methodology for training a neural model for process mining and meta-data acquisition in the bank and financial domain. The proposed methodology exploits the linguistic information from an existing knowledge graph to fine-tune a state-of-the-art Transformer-based model on the target domain. As a result, ABILaBERT is an information extraction system capable of dealing with complex classifications of banking documents against a process tree with 168 classes. The experimental results are very encouraging especially considering that ABILaBERT was trained without any manually annotated example and our proposed zero-shot learning technique enabled the creation of a first dataset that can be easily validated by the analysts.

Future evaluations will be carried out to improve the above results also using annotated material, implementing completely supervised or semi-supervised learning schema, e.g., [5]. Moreover, we will consider additional frameworks (such as [9]) to add additional constraints in the process taxonomy modeling.

Acknowledgment. This research was developed in the context of H2020 INFINITECH project (EC grant agreement number 856632). We would like to thank the "Istituto di Analisi dei Sistemi ed Informatica - Antonio Ruberti" (IASI) for supporting the experimentations through access to dedicated computing esources.

Appendix

This appendix reports the result of the assessment analysis from Sect. 5. Each cell of the matrices contains the comparison between the pool of analysts $A1 - A9$ (where also ABILaBERT is considered). As an example, in Table 4 the value in the fourth row and the first column contains the $Precision = 0.52$ obtained by the analyst $A4$ when compared with the "gold-standard" annotation of $A1$. As another example, in Table 6 the element from the first row and the third column contains $F1 = 0.82$ of ABILaBERT when compared with the annotations of $A3$.

Table 4. Precision of the assessment analysis.

	Precision									
	A1	A2	A3	A4	A5	A6	A7	A8	A9	Avg
ABILaBERT	0.75	0.58	0.75	0.25	0.42	0.67	0.50	0.50	0.33	0.528
A1		0.70	0.57	0.52	0.48	0.70	0.52	0.52	0.61	0.595
A2	0.70		0.41	0.47	0.32	0.53	0.47	0.56	0.38	0.491
A3	0.57	0.41		0.63	0.69	0.88	0.69	0.88	0.63	0.678
A4	0.52	0.47	0.63		0.50	0.65	0.55	0.55	0.45	0.507
A5	0.48	0.32	0.69	0.50		0.73	0.67	0.67	0.67	0.571
A6	0.70	0.53	0.88	0.65	0.73		0.74	0.74	0.57	0.688
A7	0.52	0.47	0.69	0.55	0.67	0.74		0.84	0.53	0.611
A8	0.52	0.56	0.88	0.55	0.67	0.74	0.84		0.40	0.628
A9	0.61	0.38	0.63	0.45	0.67	0.57	0.53	0.40		0.506

Table 5. Recall of the assessment analysis.

	Recall									
	A1	A2	A3	A4	A5	A6	A7	A8	A9	Avg
ABILaBERT	0.90	0.41	0.90	0.43	0.83	0.80	1,00	0.67	0.57	0.723
A1		0.47	0.81	0.60	0.73	0.70	0.63	0.71	0.56	0.678
A2	0.47		0.88	0.80	0.73	0.78	0.84	0.76	0.76	0.715
A3	0.81	0.88		0.50	0.73	0.61	0.58	0.56	0.59	0.684
A4	0.60	0.80	0.50		0.67	0.57	0.58	0.44	0.53	0.567
A5	0.73	0.73	0.73	0.67		0.48	0.53	0.40	0.59	0.632
A6	0.70	0.78	0.61	0.57	0.48		0.89	0.68	0.76	0.696
A7	0.63	0.84	0.58	0.58	0.53	0.89		0.64	0.59	0.697
A8	0.71	0.76	0.56	0.44	0.40	0.68	0.64		0.59	0.604
A9	0.56	0.76	0.59	0.53	0.59	0.76	0.59	0.59		0.616

Table 6. F1 of the assessment analysis.

	F1									
	A1	A2	A3	A4	A5	A6	A7	A8	A9	Avg
ABILaBERT	0.82	0.48	0.82	0.32	0.56	0.73	0.67	0.57	0.42	0.597
A1		0.56	0.67	0.56	0.58	0.70	0.57	0.60	0.58	0.626
A2	0.56		0.56	0.59	0.45	0.63	0.60	0.64	0.51	0.559
A3	0.67	0.56		0.56	0.71	0.72	0.63	0.68	0.60	0.659
A4	0.56	0.59	0.56		0.57	0.60	0.56	0.49	0.49	0.526
A5	0.58	0.45	0.71	0.57		0.58	0.59	0.50	0.63	0.572
A6	0.70	0.63	0.72	0.60	0.58		0.81	0.71	0.65	0.680
A7	0.57	0.60	0.63	0.56	0.59	0.81		0.73	0.56	0.635
A8	0.60	0.64	0.68	0.49	0.50	0.71	0.73		0.48	0.600
A9	0.58	0.51	0.60	0.49	0.63	0.65	0.56	0.48		0.545

References

1. Borrajo, D., Veloso, M., Shah, S.: Simulating and classifying behavior in adversarial environments based on action-state traces: an application to money laundering. CoRR abs/2011.01826 (2020). https://arxiv.org/abs/2011.01826
2. Brown, T.B., et al.: Language models are few-shot learners. CoRR abs/2005.14165 (2020). https://arxiv.org/abs/2005.14165
3. Chen, J.-H., Tsai, Y.-C.: Encoding candlesticks as images for pattern classification using convolutional neural networks. Financ. Innov. **6**(1), 1–19 (2020). https://doi.org/10.1186/s40854-020-00187-0
4. Cohen, N., Balch, T., Veloso, M.: Trading via image classification. CoRR abs/1907.10046 (2019). http://arxiv.org/abs/1907.10046
5. Croce, D., Castellucci, G., Basili, R.: GAN-BERT: generative adversarial learning for robust text classification with a bunch of labeled examples. In: Proceedings of the 58th Annual Meeting of the Association for Computational Linguistics, pp. 2114–2119. Association for Computational Linguistics, July 2020. https://doi.org/10.18653/v1/2020.acl-main.191, https://aclanthology.org/2020.acl-main.191
6. Devlin, J., Chang, M., Lee, K., Toutanova, K.: BERT: pre-training of deep bidirectional transformers for language understanding. CoRR abs/1810.04805 (2018). http://arxiv.org/abs/1810.04805
7. Geiger, A., Richardson, K., Potts, C.: Neural natural language inference models partially embed theories of lexical entailment and negation. arXiv preprint. arXiv:2004.14623 (2020)
8. Girshick, R.B., Donahue, J., Darrell, T., Malik, J.: Rich feature hierarchies for accurate object detection and semantic segmentation. CoRR abs/1311.2524 (2013)
9. Li, X., Vilnis, L., Zhang, D., Boratko, M., McCallum, A.: Smoothing the geometry of probabilistic box embeddings. In: International Conference on Learning Representations (2019). https://openreview.net/forum?id=H1xSNiRcF7
10. Li, X., Saúde, J., Reddy, P., Veloso, M.: Classifying and understanding financial data using graph neural network. In: AAAI-20 Workshop on Knowledge Discovery from Unstructured Data in Financial Services (2020)

11. Pejić Bach, M., Krstic, Z., Seljan, S., Turulja, L.: Text mining for big data analysis in financial sector: a literature review. Sustainability, **11**(5) (2019). https://doi.org/10.3390/su11051277, https://www.mdpi.com/2071-1050/11/5/1277
12. Pereira, J.L., Silva, D.: Business process modeling languages: a comparative framework. In: New Advances in Information Systems and Technologies. AISC, vol. 444, pp. 619–628. Springer, Cham (2016). https://doi.org/10.1007/978-3-319-31232-3_58
13. Peters, M., et al.: Deep contextualized word representations. In: Proceedings of the 2018 Conference of the North American Chapter of the Association for Computational Linguistics: Human Language Technologies, vol. 1 (Long Papers), pp. 2227–2237. Association for Computational Linguistics, New Orleans, Louisiana, June 2018. https://doi.org/10.18653/v1/N18-1202, https://www.aclweb.org/anthology/N18-1202
14. Schuster, M., Nakajima, K.: Japanese and Korean voice search. In: International Conference on Acoustics, Speech and Signal Processing, pp. 5149–5152 (2012)
15. Talman, A., Chatzikyriakidis, S.: Neural network models for natural language inference fail to capture the semantics of inference. CoRR abs/1810.09774 (2018). http://arxiv.org/abs/1810.09774
16. Vaswani, A., et al.: Attention is all you need. In: Guyon, I., et al. (eds.) Advances in Neural Information Processing Systems, vol. 30, pp. 5998–6008. Curran Associates, Inc. (2017). http://papers.nips.cc/paper/7181-attention-is-all-you-need.pdf
17. Wolf, T., et al.: Huggingface's transformers: state-of-the-art natural language processing. CoRR abs/1910.03771 (2019). http://arxiv.org/abs/1910.03771

Improving Machine Translation of Arabic Dialects Through Multi-task Learning

Youness Moukafih[1,2(✉)], Nada Sbihi[1], Mounir Ghogho[1], and Kamel Smaili[2]

[1] TICLab, College of Engineering and Architecture, Université Internationale de Rabat, Rabat, Morocco
{youness.moukafih,nada.sbihi,mounir.ghogho}@uir.ac.ma
[2] LORIA/INRIA-Lorraine, 615 rue du Jardin Botanique, BP 101, 54600 Villers-16s-Nancy, France
{youness.moukafih,kamel.smaili}@loria.fr

Abstract. Neural Machine Translation (NMT) systems have been shown to perform impressively on many language pairs compared to Statistical Machine Translation (SMT). However, these systems are data-intensive, which is problematic for the majority of language pairs, and especially for low-resource languages. In this work, we address this issue in the case of certain Arabic dialects, those variants of Modern Standard Arabic (MSA) that are spelling non-standard, morphologically rich, and yet resource-poor variants. Here, we have experimented with several multitasking learning strategies to take advantage of the relationships between these dialects. Despite the simplicity of this idea, empirical results show that several multitasking learning strategies are capable of achieving remarkable performance compared to statistical machine translation. For instance, we obtained the BLUE scores for the Algerian → Modern-Standard-Arabic and the Moroccan → Palestinian of 35.06 and 27.55, respectively, while the scores obtained with a statistical method are 15.1 and 18.91 respectively. We show that on 42 machine translation experiments, and despite the use of a small corpus, multitasking learning achieves better performance than statistical machine translation in 88% of cases.

Keywords: Neural network · Machine translation · Multitask learning · Low-resource languages · Arabic dialects

1 Introduction

Arabic dialects are morphologically rich vernaculars, just like Modern Standard Arabic (MSA), this leads to some challenges in automatic language processing in general and in machine translation in particular. In the Arab world, at least two languages coexist in a single country, one of which is MSA. This phenomenon of coexistence of languages used by the same linguistic community is known, in linguistics, under the name of diglossia [11]. The modern standard Arabic is unique, has a standard orthography and is used in formal settings such as broadcast news, religious speeches, governmental documents, and other printed material, while Arabic dialects are several, they are considered as the mother tongues of the population that depend on the their born regions.

S. Bandini et al. (Eds.): AIxIA 2021, LNAI 13196, pp. 580–590, 2022.
https://doi.org/10.1007/978-3-031-08421-8_40

These latter have no standard written form and are used mostly for verbal communication [17]. Arabic dialects can be clustered in two groups: the Mashriqi (eastern) dialects group, which includes dialects of Arabian Peninsula, Mesopotamia, Levant, Egypt and Sudan, and the Maghrebi (western) dialects group, which are characterized by a high level of code-switching in the daily communication. While mutual intelligibility within each group is high, it is not so between the two groups, e.g., Moroccan and Palestinian. This reason could justify the development of Machine translation among these dialects. [5] studied the linguistic variation among Arabic dialects to that among Romance languages, indicating the need for machine translation between these dialects. However, while most machine translation systems have been conducted for rich-resource language pairs, [1,20], only very limited number of works tackled the issue of Dialect-to-dialect pairs due to the problem of parallel data sparsity [2,10,16,18]. Arabic dialects are under-resourced languages, in addition, they face two other issues: *morphological richness*, *orthographic ambiguity*. None of these issues are unique to Arabic dialect, but their combination makes DA processing particularly challenging.

Morphological Richness: Arabic (MSA and Arabic dialects) is a morphologically complex language which includes rich inflectional morphology and a high number of clitics. For instance, the Moroccan dialect word "وَغَايْكَتْبُوهَا" correspond to the English phrase "and they will write it". This phenomenon leads to a higher number of unique words compared to English, which has the consequence to increase the number of entries in the vocabulary and therefore necessitates a bigger parallel corpus for the training that are not available for Arabic dialects.

Orthographic Ambiguity: The Arabic script uses optional diacritical marks to represent short vowels and other phonological information that are useful for removing the ambiguity [13]. For instance, the word كتبت (without diacritics) could correspond to several other words, among them: كَتَبَتْ (*she wrote*), كَتَبْتُ (*I wrote*. Arab speakers do not generally have a problem with reading undiacritized text, they use the context in order to remove the ambiguity depending on the position of the no-vowled word. However, for computers or beginners in Arabic, this task is very challenging.

Many attempts were proposed to handle the issue of translating these dialects to each other or from or into MSA. However, most of these system are based on either rule-based approach or a statistical machine translation approach. This last one used to dominate MT research for decades. For instance, in [16,18], the authors developed statistical machine translation systems between several Arabic dialects using Parallel Arabic DIalect Corpus (PADIC)[1].

Another work, based on neural network approach, proposed by [2], in which the authors proposed a multi-task learning method for translating dialectal Arabic to MSA by leveraging a pivot Language (English). However, due to the aforementioned problems of Arabic dialects, adding English or any other structured language do not help the model due to the gap between the different data distributions of these different languages.

In this paper, we adopt a different approach where we leverage the closeness between Arabic dialects and perform simultaneous translations of multiple dialect pairs

[1] https://smart.loria.fr/corpora/.

using a neural multi-task learning framework. This alleviates the issue of parallel data sparsity. To the best of our knowledge, our work is the first to use the translations of multiple Arabic dialect pairs as related tasks in a multi-task learning setup. Our approach outperformed previous statistical machine translation and achieved state-of-the-art result on 88% of the translation directions of the pairs of languages of PADIC corpus.

The remainder of this paper is structured as follows. In the next section, we discuss related work. Section 3 provides a detailed description of PADIC dataset. Section 4 describes the proposed method. In Sect. 5, we present the results of the proposed machine translation approach using several language pairs, and compare these results with those of other learning strategies. Finally, conclusions are drawn in Sect. 6.

2 Related Work

Sequence to sequence models are the common choice for machine translation systems in most language pairs. However, these models are rarely used in Arabic dialects due to scarcity of parallel corpora. A lot of work on the translation from Arabic dialects to MSA, based on rule-based methods, has been carried out. For example, [21] proposed a rule-based approach that relies on language modeling to translate from Moroccan dialect to MSA by adapting many tools such as Alkhalil morphological analyzer [4], which was initially developed for MSA. In [9], the authors used a rule-based method to improve Egyptian-English translation by identifying a mapping from Egyptian dialect to MSA to reduce the out-of-vocabulary rate. [12] proposed a machine translation system for both TUN to MSA and MSA to TUN based on deep morphological representations of roots and patterns' features. The system reached about 80% recall in the TUN to MSA direction and 84% recall in the opposite direction. All the methods used in the above-mentioned papers focused on a rue-based approach which requires enormous amount and linguistic resources.

[3] tackled the challenge of translating from Arabic dialects (Levantine dialects and Maghrebi dialects) to MSA by using a neural machine translation system. In that work, the authors used a multi-task learning paradigm by sharing one decoder between two target languages (MSA and English) and each source language has an encoder (the sources languages were Arabic dialects and MSA). Another interesting work was presented in [2] which proposed a unified multitask neural machine translation model where an encoder is shared between two tasks, the first task being Arabic Dialect to MSA translation and the second task being segment-level Part-Of-Speech (POS) tagging. The model achieved a definite improvement of the translation performance, and a good performance on the test set for the POS tagging task.

[16, 18] presented the PADIC dataset which consists of parallel sentences in Levantine dialects (Syrian and Palestinian), Maghrebi dialects (Moroccan, two dialects from Algeria and Tunisian) and MSA. The authors proposed a statistical machine translation method by employing different smoothing techniques for the language model to translate not only from Arabic dialects to MSA but also between all language pairs within PADIC dataset. The obtained results were relatively good given the size of the training corpus, especially for similar languages.

3 Dataset

It is well known that parallel corpora are the foundation stone of several natural language processing tasks, particularly cross-language applications such as machine translation, bilingual lexicon extraction and multilingual information retrieval. Building this kind of resources is a challenging task especially when it deals with under-resourced languages. Arabic dialects are among those languages for which the parallel corpora are scarce.

In this paper, we use The Parallel Arabic DIalect Corpus (PADIC) [16]. The corpus (containing 273k words) has been built from scratch because there are no standard resources. Indeed, Arabic dialects are only used in daily oral communication and social networks and not for formal writing. PADIC contains six dialects from both the Maghreb and the Middle-East as well as MSA. The dialects are: Annaba's dialect (ANB) and Algiers's dialect (ALG) which are Algerian dialects, Moroccan dialect (MAR), Sfax's dialect (TUN) used in the south of Tunisia, Syrian dialect (SYR) and Palestinian dialect (PAL) which are spoken in Damascus and Gaza respectively.

4 Methodology

4.1 Sequence-to-Sequence Learning

Here, we describe briefly the underlying framework, called Encoder-Decoder architecture. The encoder-decoder with recurrent neural networks has two components:

An encoder reads the input sentence, a sequence of words (x_1,x_2,...,x_T), where x_t is the tth word, and produces a context vector c_i which encodes sentence information with strong focus on the parts surrounding the ith word, as shown in Eq. 1 :

$$c_i = \sum_{j=1}^{T} \alpha_{ij} h_j \tag{1}$$

where $h_t = f(x_t, h_{t-1})$, with:

- $h_t \in \mathcal{R}^d$ being the hidden state at time t, and d is the the dimension of the hidden state vector.
- f being a nonlinear activation function (LSTM or GRU).
- α_{ij} being the so-called energy, computed by:

$$\alpha_{ij} = \frac{\exp{(e_{ij})}}{\sum_{k=1}^{T} \exp{(e_{ik})}} \tag{2}$$

where

$$e_{ij} = a(s_{i-1}, h_j) \tag{3}$$

with a being a feed-forward neural network trained jointly with all the other components of the model that scores how well the inputs around the position j and the output at position i match, and s_{i-1} being the previous hidden state of the decoder.

On the other hand, a decoder takes as inputs the context vector c_i and all the previously predicted words (y_1,...,y_{i-1}) trained to predict the next word y_i as in Eq. 4

$$p(\mathbf{y}) = \prod_{i=1}^{T_y} p(y_i | \{y_1, ..., y_{i-1}\}, c_i) \tag{4}$$

where $\mathbf{y} = \{y_1,...,y_{T_y}\}$. With an RNN, each conditional probability is modeled as follows:

$$p(y_i | \{y_1, ..., y_{i-1}\}, c_i) = g(y_{i-1}, s_i, c_i) \tag{5}$$

where g is a nonlinear, potentially multi-layered, function that outputs the probability of y_i, and s_i is an RNN hidden state for time i, computed as in Eq. 6.

$$s_i = f(s_{i-1}, y_{i-1}, c_i) \tag{6}$$

4.2 Multi-task Sequence-to-Sequence Learning

Multi-Task Learning (MTL) has been used successfully in many domains such as natural language processing [7], speech recognition [8], and computer vision [15].

The use of multi-task learning in this work is motivated by the relatively small size of PADIC corpus and also by the idea that learning one encoder across multiple language pairs jointly may result in a better generalization because of the similarities between the languages considered here.

Learning multiple tasks simultaneously can be applied in different ways such as periodic task alternations training with a ratio for each task based on the size of the task's data-set. In this work, we used the simplest approach to train these multiple tasks jointly by taking a mini-batch of data per task for each training iteration and update the model's parameters for every mini-batch. Figure 1 illustrate an example where the model takes first as input MSA-to-MAR mini-batch data; the encoder encodes the MSA sentences and the decoder takes the encoded vector and produces the Moroccan translation sentences, then the model takes the second mini-batch (ALG-to-MAR) and so on.

4.3 Model Training

In this work, the translation model is composed of one encoder, shared among several translation directions, and a decoder for each target language. The main objective is to develop a model which is able to map an input sentence from a chosen language ℓ_k in $\{\ell_1, \ell_2, ...\ell_L\}$ to a target language ℓ_t, where L is the number of input languages we use for our encoder. Mathematically, given a sentence $S_k \sim \mathcal{D}_{\ell_k}$ of m words $x = (x_1,x_2,...,x_m)$ an encoder E (x, ℓ_k, θ_E) produces a representation vector $h_k \in \mathbf{R}^n$ where θ_E are weights shared across all input languages and n is the dimension of the hidden states, then a decoder D(h_k, ℓ_t, θ_D) takes as input the vector representation and generates an output sentence $y = (y_1,y_2,...,y_q)$. The objective function is defined as follows:

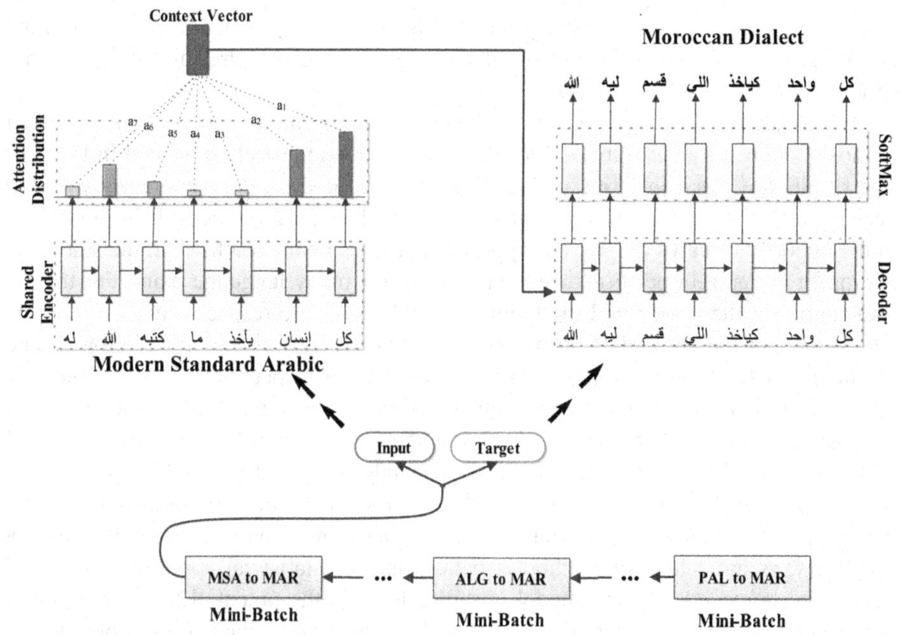

Fig. 1. Illustration of the architecture of the used multitask sequence-to-sequence learning with an attention mechanism. The model takes a mini-batch of data from each language pair.

$$\mathcal{L}(\theta_E, \theta_D, \mathbb{Z}, \ell_{in}, \ell_o) = \mathbb{E}_{x \sim \mathcal{D}_{\ell_{in}}, y \sim \mathcal{D}_{\ell_o}}[\Delta(y, \hat{y})] \tag{7}$$

where Z is the set of word embeddings, ℓ_{in} is the input languages, ℓ_{ou} is the output language, $\hat{y}$ is the predicted sentence, and Δ is the sum of token-level cross-entropy losses.

5 Experimental Results and Discussion

5.1 Experiment Settings

We use Pytorch [19] library to implement all our experiments. We set the size of the embedding vectors to 256 for all languages. The embedding vectors are initialized randomly. Each mini-batch used in the training consists of 32 sentences randomly selected from each translation direction with equal ratios for each language pair. In each mini-batch, we trained the encoder-decoder model using GRUs [6], each having 256 hidden units, to minimize the sum of token-level cross-entropy losses provided in Eq. 7 using Adam optimizer [14] with a learning rate of $\alpha = 0.003$.

Performance of the Many-to-One Multi-task Learning Approach. We recall that we opted for one shared encoder that encodes several dialects and one decoder for the target language. In other words, any target language among the languages used in the encoding step could be decoded by one decoder. We will refer to this multi-task learning strategy as Many-to-One (M-2-O).

Table 4 shows the results of this Multi-task learning model and we compare them to those obtained by the statistical machine translation approach presented in [16, 18]. The results are given in terms of BLEU score measured on the same corpus of 500 unseen parallel sentences. In bold, we reported the best performances. It is shown that in the majority of cases (88%), our approach achieves better results than the statistical approach; the gain in performance is significant for many language pairs. For the M-2-O approach, the lowest and the highest BLEU scores are respectively 22.75 for the pair Moroccan-Syrian, and 35.96 for the pair Algiers-Palestinian, while the lowest and the highest BLEU scores for the statistical model are respectively 7.29 for the pair Algiers-Syrian and 61.06 for the pair Annaba-Algiers. The latter result is due to the fact that the corresponding dialects are from the same country; 60% of words are shared between the two dialects in accordance to the study presented in [16, 18]. The method that we propose here has not achieved this high score because the aim is to learn a general-purpose sentence representations across all translation directions. But, except few cases, as indicated our method is better than the statistical approach in 88% of cases. The proposed learning model is shown to have the potential to learn sentence representations across all language pairs and produce non-trivial translations, which confirms the effectiveness and the robustness of the approach.

Table 1. Comparison of the performance of the M-2-0 Multi-task learning model and the statistical model of [16]

	Target													
	MSA		ALG		ANB		TUN		PAL		SYR		MAR	
Source	M-2-O	SMT	M-2-O	SMT	M-2-O	SMT	M-2-O	SMT	M-2-O	SMT	M-2-O	SMT	M-2-O	SMT
MSA	——	——	**27.71**	13.55	**27.27**	12.54	**27.96**	20.03	30.79	**42.46**	**26.55**	21.38	**28.45**	20.02
ALG	**35.06**	15.1	——	——	30.41	**61.06**	**32.39**	09.67	**35.96**	10.61	**32.64**	07.29	**33.23**	10.22
ANB	**30.81**	14.44	27.55	**67.31**	——	——	**29.56**	09.08	**31.63**	10.12	**31.82**	07.52	**33.38**	10.00
TUN	25.42	**25.99**	**24.61**	09.89	**25.04**	09.34	——	——	**27.88**	22.55	**25.95**	13.05	**25.29**	14.37
PAL	34.50	**40.48**	**33.61**	11.28	**33.39**	09.53	**34.64**	17.93	——	——	**32.46**	23.29	**33.86**	16.08
SYR	**27.85**	24.14	**26.94**	07.57	**25.05**	07.50	**24.98**	13.67	**27.88**	26.60	——	——	**26.73**	09.93
MAR	**26.18**	24.93	**24.01**	10.13	**23.33**	10.16	**23.82**	14.68	**27.55**	18.91	**22.75**	09.68	——	——

It is evident from Table 4 that the results achieved by our proposed multi-task learning approach are significantly better than those obtained with the statistical model [16]. This could be attributed to the fact the architecture of the proposed multi-task learning model is, thanks to its sophistication, capable of capturing more relationships between the source and the target sentences, and also by the fact that this model benefits from more data since all the entire corpus has been used to train one neural network model, whereas in the statistical model, only data corresponding to a pair of languages is used in the training. In addition, our proposed system address one of the weakness in conventional NMT systems which is their inability to correctly translate very rare words. Table 2 summarises the improvement in performance achieved by the proposed model over the statistical one. The first column indicates the average BLEU corresponding to the translation of any language to a specific target language. For instance, the first line corresponds to the average performance achieved from any dialect to the the Moroccan dialect. In our experiments, the best performance is achieved for pairs of dialects where the target language is the Moroccan dialect (an improvement of 124.49%).

Table 2. A summary of the results of different machine translation methods for several pairs of dialects

	Many-to-One	Statistical	Rate (%)
Any-to-MAR	30.15	13,43	124,49
Any-to-ALG	27,40	19,95	37,34
Any-to-ANB	27,41	18,35	49,37
Any-to-TUN	28,89	14,17	103,88
Any-to-PAL	30,27	21,87	38,40
Any-to-SYR	28,69	13,70	109,41
Any-to-MSA	29,97	24,18	23,94

Performance of Single-Task Neural Network. We have carried out other experiments based on a simple sequence-to sequence neural network in order to determine the impact of using neural network machine translation when using a small training corpus. The single task model (S-task), used in this paper, has one encoder and one decoder and it is trained only in one translation direction. For instance, from Moroccan dialect to Algerian dialect the encoder will take as input the Moroccan sentence and the decoder will produce the Algerian dialect sentence. The results are given in the Table 3, unlike the results given by the Multi-task learning (One-To-Many) approach, the results in this case are mixed, we only have 50% of cases where the sequence to sequence approach achieves better results than those given by the statistical machine translation approach. This could be explained by the lack of data necessary for learning a sequence-to-sequence neural network, while in MTL (M-2-0), the model benefited from the entire corpus for training the encoder.

Performance of the One-To-Many Multi-task Learning Approach. In this experiment, we test an end-to-end architecture with one encoder, and one decoder for each target language. It is worth pointing out that the authors of [16] trained one statistical model, and then translated all the other dialects with the learnt translation model. From this point of view, the One-To-Many (O-2-M) multitask learning approach is thus somehow similar to the method in [16]. In Table 4, we report the results of the 0-2-M architecture and we compare them to those given by the statistical approach. We notice that the One-To-Many model is more efficient than the statistical model in 62% of cases. We can in particular notice that the Algerian dialect is better translated by the O-2-M

Table 3. Comparison of the performance of the S-task learning model and the statistical model of [16]

	Target													
	MSA		ALG		ANB		TUN		PAL		SYR		MAR	
Source	S-Task	SMT	S-Task	SMT	S-Task	SMT	S-Task	SMT	S-Task	SMT	S-Task	SMT	S-Task	SMT
MSA	——	——	14.45	13.55	12.22	12.54	14.55	20.03	21.96	42.46	18.94	21.38	15.56	20.02
ALG	15.83	15.51	——	——	20.89	61.31	11.23	09.67	16.06	10.61	10.92	7.29	12.94	10.22
ANB	13.97	14.44	22.08	76.31	——	——	12.42	09.08	11.63	10.12	15.27	07.52	14.71	10.00
TUN	18.65	25.99	14.42	09.89	12.32	09.34	——	——	18.24	22.55	17.83	13.52	13.76	14.37
PAL	20.13	40.48	13.31	11.28	13.45	09.53	15.49	17.93	——	——	20.14	23.29	14.98	16.08
SYR	19.17	24.14	14.23	07.57	14.66	07.50	12.43	13.67	17.36	26.60	——	——	14.22	09.93
MAR	15.32	24.93	15.43	10.13	15.76	10.16	14.77	14.68	18.19	18.91	17.01	09.68	——	——

approach than by the statistical approach with the exception of the couple of dialects Algiers-Annaba, two dialects of the same country and sharing more than 60% of words.

Table 4. Comparison of the performance of the O-2-M Multi-task learning model and the statistical model of [16]

	Target													
	MSA		ALG		ANB		TUN		PAL		SYR		MAR	
Source	O-2-M	SMT	O-2-M	SMT	O-2-M	SMT	O-2-M	SMT	O-2-M	SMT	O-2-M	SMT	O-2-M	SMT
MSA	——	——	16.07	13.55	16.31	12.54	15.59	20.03	23.66	42.46	17.60	21.38	17.19	20.02
ALG	17.05	13.55	——	——	21.70	61.06	13.87	09.67	16.75	10.61	15.42	07.29	16.30	10.22
ANB	14.96	14.44	21.82	67.31	——	——	14.06	09.08	16.94	10.12	14.12	07.52	14.27	10.00
TUN	17.64	25.99	13.66	09.89	14.75	09.34	——	——	18.69	22.55	15.84	13.05	15.95	14.37
PAL	21.60	40.48	15.16	11.28	14.75	09.53	16.85	17.93	——	——	18.79	23.29	16.54	16.08
SYR	18.20	24.14	13.84	07.57	14.50	07.50	14.70	13.67	19.71	26.60	——	——	15.29	09.93
MAR	18.21	24.93	16.48	10.13	13.85	10.16	13.75	14.68	18.02	18.91	15.61	09.68	——	——

In order to go beyond the BLEU score, we give in Table 5 an example of translations from Algiers dialect to Annaba dialect using single task, One-to-Many and Many-to-One models. We can remark that the quality of the proposed MTL (M-2-0) translation approach is much better than the other models and this the case of all the majority of the examples we examined. Note that, in order to understand the the weakness and the mistakes carried out by the different approaches for non-Arabic speakers, we provide a word-by-word translation to English language for the source and the model's outputs.

Table 5. An example of translations produced by different model architecture alongside the ground truth translation

Source (ALG)	انا البارح سمعت عبدو يهدر قال لي يديكوديو ليميساج لي يجيو للوالي حوايج كيما هاكا
Reference(ANB)	انا لبارح تسمع في عبدو يهدر قال لي يديكوديو ليميساج لي يجيو للوالي حوايج كيما اك
English translation	I yesterday heard Abdou talking he said those who are decoding the messages received by the governor something like that
Translation(S-task)	انا البارح راح يجي خلاه قال لي في اديكا لي لي دايما لي كيما
Translation	I yesterday will be a disaster, he said that that as usual
Translation(One-to-Many)	انا البارح يجي خلاه عبدو قال لي في اديكا لي لي كيما هاكا
Translation	I yesterday will be a disaster Abdou said in that that like
Translation(Many-to-One)	انا لبارح نسمع عبدو يهدر قال ليميساج لي يجيو للوالي حوايج كيما
Translation	I yesterday am hearing Abdou talking he said the messages received by governor things like

6 Conclusion

In this article, we used a neural machine translation system for six Arabic dialects using a multitasking learning approach to tackle the problem of parallel data scarcity. The problem for Arabic dialects is the unavailability of parallel corpora for these vernacular languages. All the models we have presented are trained on a small corpus (PADIC) which is composed of only 6400 parallel sentences. The multitasking learning approach makes it possible by taking advantage of the similarity between Arabic dialects. One-to-many and many-to-one multitasking learning strategies were investigated and compared to single-task learning and statistical machine translation methods. Single-task learning and statistical methods achieved globally similar results, while One-to-many performs better in 61% of the cases in comparison to statistical approach and Many-to-one provides good quality translations and performs better in 88% of the cases. We showed, in this article that even with a small parallel corpus, it is possible to develop neural machine translation for difficult "languages" like Arabic dialects.

References

1. Bahdanau, D., Cho, K., Bengio, Y.: Neural machine translation by jointly learning to align and translate. arXiv preprint arXiv:1409.0473 (2014)
2. Baniata, L.H., Park, S., Park, S.B.: A multitask-based neural machine translation model with part-of-speech tags integration for Arabic dialects. Appl. Sci. **8**(12), 2502 (2018)
3. Baniata, L.H., Park, S., Park, S.B.: A neural machine translation model for Arabic dialects that utilizes multitask learning (MTL). Comput. Intell. Neurosci. (2018)
4. Boudlal, A., Lakhouaja, A., Mazroui, A., Meziane, A., Bebah, M., Shoul, M.: Alkhalil morpho Sys1: a morphosyntactic analysis system for Arabic texts. In: International Arab Conference on Information Technology, pp. 1–6. Elsevier Science, NY (2010)

5. Chiang, D., Diab, M., Habash, N., Rambow, O., Shareef, S.: Parsing Arabic dialects. In: 11th Conference of the European Chapter of the Association for Computational Linguistics (2006)
6. Cho, K., et al.: Learning phrase representations using RNN encoder-decoder for statistical machine translation. arXiv preprint arXiv:1406.1078 (2014)
7. Collobert, R., Weston, J.: A unified architecture for natural language processing: deep neural networks with multitask learning. In: Proceedings of the 25th International Conference on Machine Learning, pp. 160–167 (2008)
8. Deng, L., Hinton, G., Kingsbury, B.: New types of deep neural network learning for speech recognition and related applications: an overview. In: 2013 IEEE International Conference on Acoustics, Speech and Signal Processing, pp. 8599–8603. IEEE (2013)
9. Durrani, N., Koehn, P.: Improving machine translation via triangulation and transliteration. In: Proceedings of the 17th Annual Conference of the European Association for Machine Translation, pp. 71–78 (2014)
10. Erdmann, A., Habash, N., Taji, D., Bouamor, H.: Low resourced machine translation via morpho-syntactic modeling: the case of dialectal Arabic. arXiv preprint arXiv:1712.06273 (2017)
11. Ferguson, C.A.: Diglossia. Word **15**(2), 325–340 (1959)
12. Hamdi, A., Boujelbane, R., Habash, N., Nasr, A.: The effects of factorizing root and pattern mapping in bidirectional Tunisian-standard Arabic machine translation (2013)
13. Harrat, S., Meftouh, K., Abbas, M., Smaïli, K.: Grapheme to phoneme conversion - an Arabic dialect case. In: Spoken Language Technologies for Under-Resourced Languages. Saint Petesbourg, Russia (2014)
14. Kingma, D.P., Ba, J.: Adam: a method for stochastic optimization. arXiv preprint arXiv:1412.6980 (2014)
15. Long, M., Wang, J.: Learning multiple tasks with deep relationship networks. arXiv preprint arXiv:1506.02117 (2015)
16. Meftouh, K., Harrat, S., Smaïli, K.: PADIC: extension and new experiments. In: 7th International Conference on Advanced Technologies ICAT. Antalya, Turkey (2018)
17. Meftouh, K., Bouchemal, N., Smaïli, K.: A study of a non-resourced language: the case of one of the Algerian dialects. In: The Third International Workshop on Spoken Languages Technologies for Under-Resourced Languages-SLTU 2012, pp. 1–7 (2012)
18. Meftouh, K., Harrat, S., Jamoussi, S., Abbas, M., Smaili, K.: Machine translation experiments on PADIC: a parallel Arabic dialect corpus. In: The 29th Pacific Asia Conference on Language, Information And Computation (2015)
19. Paszke, A., et al.: Pytorch: an imperative style, high-performance deep learning library. In: Advances in Neural Information Processing Systems, pp. 8026–8037 (2019)
20. Sutskever, I., Vinyals, O., Le, Q.V.: Sequence to sequence learning with neural networks. In: Advances in Neural Information Processing Systems, pp. 3104–3112 (2014)
21. Tachicart, R., Bouzoubaa, K.: A hybrid approach to translate Moroccan Arabic dialect. In: 2014 9th International Conference on Intelligent Systems: Theories and Applications (SITA 2014), pp. 1–5. IEEE (2014)

Continuous Defect Prediction in CI/CD Pipelines: A Machine Learning-Based Framework

Lazzarinetti Giorgio(✉), Massarenti Nicola, Sgrò Fabio, and Salafia Andrea

Noovle S.p.A, Milan, Italy
giorgio.lazzarinetti@gmail.com
https://www.noovle.com/en/

Abstract. Recent advances in information technology has led to an increasing number of applications to be developed and maintained daily by product teams. Ensuring that a software application works as expected and that it is absent of bugs requires a lot of time and resources. Thanks to the recent adoption of DevOps methodologies, it is often the case where code commits and application builds are centralized and standardized. Thanks to this new approach, it is now possible to retrieve log and build data to ease the development and management operations of product teams. However, even if such approaches include code control to detect unit or integration errors, they do not check for the presence of logical bugs that can raise after code builds. For such reasons in this work we propose a framework for continuous defect prediction based on machine learning algorithms trained on a publicly available dataset. The framework is composed of a machine learning model for detecting the presence of logical bugs in code on the basis of the available data generated by DevOps tools and a dashboard to monitor the software projects status. We also describe the serverless architecture we designed for hosting the aforementioned framework.

Keywords: Continuous defect prediction · Machine learning · DevOps · Continuous integration

1 Overview

In the context of the italian Fondo per la Crescita Sostenibile, Bando "Agenda Digitale", D.M. Oct. 15th, 2014, funded by "Ministero dello Sviluppo Economico", a lot of teams manage and contribute to different software projects daily. Given the high number of activities that must be taken into account, such

Activities were partially funded by Italian "Ministero dello Sviluppo Economico", Fondo per la Crescita Sostenibile, Bando "Agenda Digitale", D.M. Oct. 15th, 2014 - Project n. F/020012/02/X27 - "Smart District 4.0".

S. Bandini et al. (Eds.): AIxIA 2021, LNAI 13196, pp. 591–606, 2022.
https://doi.org/10.1007/978-3-031-08421-8_41

as managing branches (development, stage, production, features), architecting software applications, coordinating the developers and interacting with project managers, it's useful to have some automatic tools that alert the developers in case bugs are detected in code. For such a reason, we propose a framework that aims at easing the management and development activities and that integrates with DevOps methodologies, with a focus on Continuous Integration (CI) and Continuous Delivery (CD) operations. With CI/CD operations, thanks to analysis tools such as Jenkins [35], it is possible to detect and avoid unit or integration errors before shipping applications to production environments. However, such tools are not able to detect logical bugs and therefore to block builds triggered from commits. For this reason we decided to develop a methodology based on machine learning techniques to detect if a commit could contain a logical bug. The final goal is that of using the proposed methodology to build a monitoring framework integrated with CI/CD operations that allows a visual exploration of the status of each software project, in order to evaluate the quality of the software produced and, in case the machine learning model detects issues, automatically raise alerts to fix the bug before it reaches production environments.

The rest of this paper is organized as follows: Sect. 2 describes the state of the art for continuous defect prediction, whereas Sect. 3 describes the dataset, the preprocessing operations, the models used and the developed dashboard. In Sect. 4 some infrastructural considerations are described and, finally, Sect. 5 draws some conclusions and some future works.

2 State of the Art

DevOps is a software development methodology used in computer science that aims at enhancing communication, collaboration and integration between developers and information technology operations [1]. DevOps wants to respond to the interdependence between software development and IT operations, aiming to help an organization to develop software products and services more quickly and efficiently [2]. DevOps automated analysis systems generate huge amounts of data that can be used to detect unnecessary processes, monitor production and predict bugs. Server logs can reach hundreds of megabytes in a short time while additional monitoring tools, like Jenkins [35] or SonarQube [36] can generate gigabytes of data. Quantities force developers to set up automatic checks with the use of thresholds for identifying problems. However, the thresholds are not optimal in this context, given the scarce generalization of the parameters and the zero adaptation to the infrastructure over time [3]. Moreover, generally, the systems used in projects that adopt DevOps are many and of different nature. Each system monitors the health and performance of applications in different ways. It is therefore difficult to find relationships between different data sources. Thus, a better approach to analyze this data in real time is through the application of machine learning techniques, which allow to give a new vision of the metrics collected with the DevOps tools. Machine learning techniques applied in this context allow to monitor the progress of deliveries and the presence of bugs using data collected by continuous integration systems. Machine learning systems can also use input data of a different nature to produce a more robust view of the applications on which they are used [4].

When it comes to software bugs, they usually appear during the software development process and are difficult to detect or identify, thus developers spend a large amount of time locating and fixing them. In order to detect them, many machine learning algorithms have been developed and tested [11]. Indeed, machine learning algorithms can be applied to analyze data from different perspectives and can benefit from the large amount of code production metrics that are also used by developers to obtain useful information. Many examples of machine learning solutions for detecting software bugs have been implemented. For example in [13] a combination approach of contexts and Artificial Neural Network (ANN) is proposed. In [14] three algorithms are compared, namely Naive Bayes (NB), Decision Tree (DT) and ANN, showing that DT has the best results over the others. In [15] Bayesian Network (BN) and Random Forest (RF) are compared, showing that BN can outperform RF. Differently, in [16] NB, RF and ANN are compared, showing that RF is better than the others. In [17] also deep learning techniques are proposed, showing good performance.

From all these studies emerge that, apart from the choice of the algorithm that varies according to the used dataset, software metrics are extremely important for fault prediction in quality assurance, hence, identification of proper metrics is essential in all software projects [9]. D'Ambros et al. [5] proposed a benchmark to compare prediction techniques on five publicly available datasets focusing on the different metrics related to code production, such as line of code, code complexity [6], number of changes [7] or previous fault [8].

In the context of DevOps CI builds, software bug detection plays an extremely important role, particularly at change-level. Change-level defect prediction, also known as *just-in-time* defect prediction, aims at predicting defective changes (i.e. commits to a version control system) and is more practical because it can not only ensure software quality in the development process, but also make the developers check and fix the defects just at the time they are introduced. There are a lot of studies about this. For example, in [12] the authors propose a deep learning based approach over six different datasets, showing good results in this kind of task. Indeed, their framework relies on a preprocessing and feature engineering step and on the definition of the deep neural network classifier. The chosen model differs from the proposal of [10], that relies on Logistic Regression (LR), because LR considers the contribution of each feature independently and performs well only when input features and output labels are linearly correlated. For such reasons, in [12] the authors propose a Deep Belief Network (DBN) which has the advantage of generating new non-linear combinations features given the initial set of features.

Scientific community also proposed several datasets related to continuous defect prediction. In [3] the authors make available 11 million data rows retrieved from CI builds that embrace 1265 software projects, 30022 distinct commit authors and several software process metrics. Another well known dataset for continuous defect prediction is the Technical Debt Dataset [18], a curated set of project metrics data from 33 Java projects from the Apache Software Foundation. It has been produced using four tools, i.e. PyDriller [24], Ptidej [37], Refactoring Miner [25] and SonarQube. The Technical Debt Dataset includes information at commit granularity, such as the commit hash, the date, the message, on the refactoring list applied in each commit, on the code quality, such as the list of detected issues related to a commit, the style violations, the detected anti-patterns and the code smells. Other included information are the Jira [27] issues retrieved from the project's issue tracker as well as the fault-inducing and the fault-fixing commits, that are the association for each fixed fault of the commit where the fault was created and where the fault was fixed.

3 The Framework

The objective of this research is to develop a framework capable of identifying bugs from committed code in order to provide from the one hand a synoptic point of view of the status of software projects and from the other hand alerting if some inconsistencies and logical bugs are detected.

The goal is that of using such framework trained on a publicly available dataset in a real case scenario.

The proposed framework consists of three main components: a data processing pipeline, a machine learning model for classification and a monitoring dashboard. In the following sections we will described all these components in details, by focusing on the publicly available dataset used for training the model, the preprocessing operations executed to make the dataset compliant with data from the production environment (since data collected from the real case infrastructure has a different granularity with respect to those coming from the publicly available dataset because of system constraints), the machine learning models tested that follows the trend of the state of the art and the implemented dashboard with the way of using and the kinds of analysis performed over it.

3.1 The Dataset

The dataset used for model training is the Technical Debt Dataset [18]. It contains information at the granularity level of the commits organized in nine different tables:

- **Projects:** contains the links to the GitHub repository and the associated Jira issue tracker.
- **Sonar measures:** contains the SonarQube measures such as number of code lines in the commit, the code complexity and the number of functions.
- **Commits:** contains the information retrieved from the git log including the commit hash, the message, the author, the date and timezone and the list of branches.

- **Commit changes:** contains the changes contained in each commit, including the old path of the file, the new path, the type of change (added, deleted, modified or renamed), the diff, the number of lines added.
- **Jira issues:** contains Jira issues for each project with information such that the key, the creation and resolution dates and the priority.
- **Fault inducing commits:** reports the results from the execution of the SZZ [20] algorithm.
- **Refactoring miner:** contains the list of refactoring activities applied in the repository. The table contains the project, commit hash, the type of refactoring applied and the associated details.
- **Sonar issues:** contains the list of SonarQube issues such that the anti-patterns and the code smess.
- **Sonar rules:** contains the list of rules monitored by SonarQube.

3.2 Data Preparation

As mentioned, since the real case production environment slightly differs from the aforementioned dataset due to some constraints imposed by the adopted CI/CD tools, that imposes us to have data aggregated at push granularity instead of commit granularity, the Technical Debt Dataset has first been processed and synthetically modified to match the push granularity by aggregating subsequent commits with windows of varying lengths. Aggregation of numerical features has been executed in some cases by averaging the numerical values while in other cases selecting only the min/max values, depending on the meaning of the feature in the context of software development.

More precisely, in order to create the proper dataset to train machine learning models, we consider only some of the available tables, namely GIT_COMMITS, GIT_COMMITS_CHANGES, SONAR_ISSUES, SONAR_MEASURES and SZZ_FAULT_INDUCING_COMMITS. The choice of using only some tables and, consequently, sonly some features among those available has been done to match the features actually collected in the real case infrastructure. Tables are related as in the Entity Relation schema depicted in Fig. 1. According to such schema, data are prepared as follow.

Firstly, we join GIT_COMMITS with SONAR_MEASURES on *projectID* and *commitHash* since they have the same granularity. Then, given that for each commit hash in the GIT_COMMITS table there are more commit changes in the GIT_COMMITS_CHANGES table (one for each file changed), we aggregate commit changes at commit hash level and compute sum and mean for commit changes features *linesAdded, linesRemoved, nloc, complexity* and *tokenCount* and count for *changeType* (Rename, Delete, Modify, Unknown, Add). Thus, we merge GIT_COMMITS_CHANGES with the previously prepared dataset aggregated at commit hash level and, then, merge the resulting dataset with SONAR_ISSUES by adding a label defining if the issues were created or closed within each commit hash. Here, we consider only sonar issues associated with commits that

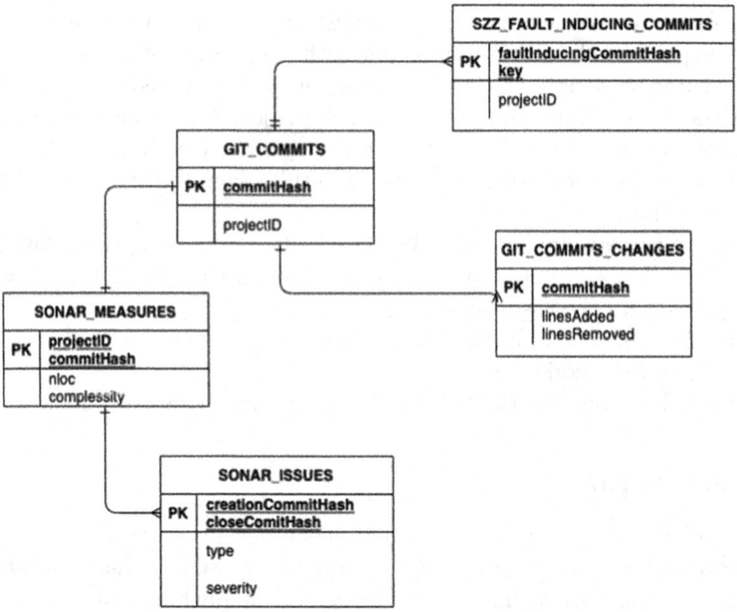

Fig. 1. List of the features with their correlation with dataset label.

induced them and we aggregate only some relevant features, namely *severity, startLine* and *effort.* Finally, we merge the resulting dataset with SONAR_ISSUES at *projectID.*

Over these feature engineered dataset, we then add the label for the final goal of detecting fault inducing commits. To this attempt, we use the SZZ_FAULT_INDUCING_COMMITS table, from which we extract all and only those commits that induced a bug. The label is assigned by the author of the dataset following their own implementation of the SZZ algorithm [18] (The Open-SZZ [20]). The SZZ [21] algorithm tries to identify the fault-inducing commits from a project's version history. The algorithm was developed in 2005 and has since been adopted in more than 200 empirical studies [22,23]. The algorithm is based on Git's blame/annotate feature and assumes that the fault-inducing commit of a fault is known. Usually this is done by combining data from an issue tracker and from Git's log command.

3.3 Feature Engineering and Selection

Once the dataset has been reduced to the required granularity and some preliminary features have been computed as described, data are prepared for machine learning models. First of all, in order to remove missing values, numerical and categorical variable are imputed using respectively the median and the mode values. After imputation, categorical variable are converted into numerical with an ordinal encoder. Variable with zero variance are removed and finally the dataset is balanced with respect to the fault inducing class. Indeed, after data preparation, there were 517 commits associated with the fault inducing class and 78341 commits non associated with the fault inducing class. Thus, data are subsampled to match the dimensionality of the positive class.

In addition, dataset's features have undergone a selection process that involves studying the correlation between each feature with respect to the dataset label, as shown in Fig. 2. The process consisted of a Recursive Feature Elimination (RFE) [19] technique that allows to select the best number of features using as cutoff the F1-score drop. In particular, we train several RF classifiers increasing number of feature by following the order of feature importance as computed in Fig. 2. For each classifier trained, we measure the F1-score and then we plot the values of the F1-score registered with the varying number of features. In Fig. 3 we can see the result of such RFE process. It is possible to see as the best performance are reached with 18 features, with an average F1-score of 0.786. This allows us to reduce the dimensionality of data by only keeping those features valuable to the model.

Table 1. Detail of selected features

Feature name	Description	Aggregation	Source
tokenCount	Token count of functions	Sum, mean	PyDriller
Complexity	Cyclomatic complexity	Sum	PyDriller
nloc	Lines of code of the file	Sum, mean	PyDriller
linesAdded	Number of lines added	Sum, mean	PyDriller
linesRemoved	Number of lines removed	Sum, mean	PyDriller
modificationType	Type of changed applied (modify, delete, add, rename)	Count	PyDriller
filesChanged	Number of modified files	Count	PyDriller
Effort	Time needed to solve the issues	Sum	SonarQube
classComplexity	Complexity of classes in commits	Count	SonarQube
Severity	Severity level of the issues	Max	SonarQube

From hence, the final set of features selected for training is described in Table 1. The RFE process allowed us to select only 18 features. in Table 1 we can see the feature name, the description, the aggregations and the source. Each feature is considered once per each aggregation, thus, as an example, the *tokenCount* feature is considered twice, both as sum of token count of each commit and as mean of token count of each commit. Moreover, the feature *modificationType*, given its categorical nature, is considered as a unique feature for each category it can assume (modify, delete, unknown, add, rename).

It is interesting to notice as, among all the information available coming from SonarQube and Git, the most important features are related to commit size (e.g. number of lines added/removed, lines of code in files, number of token

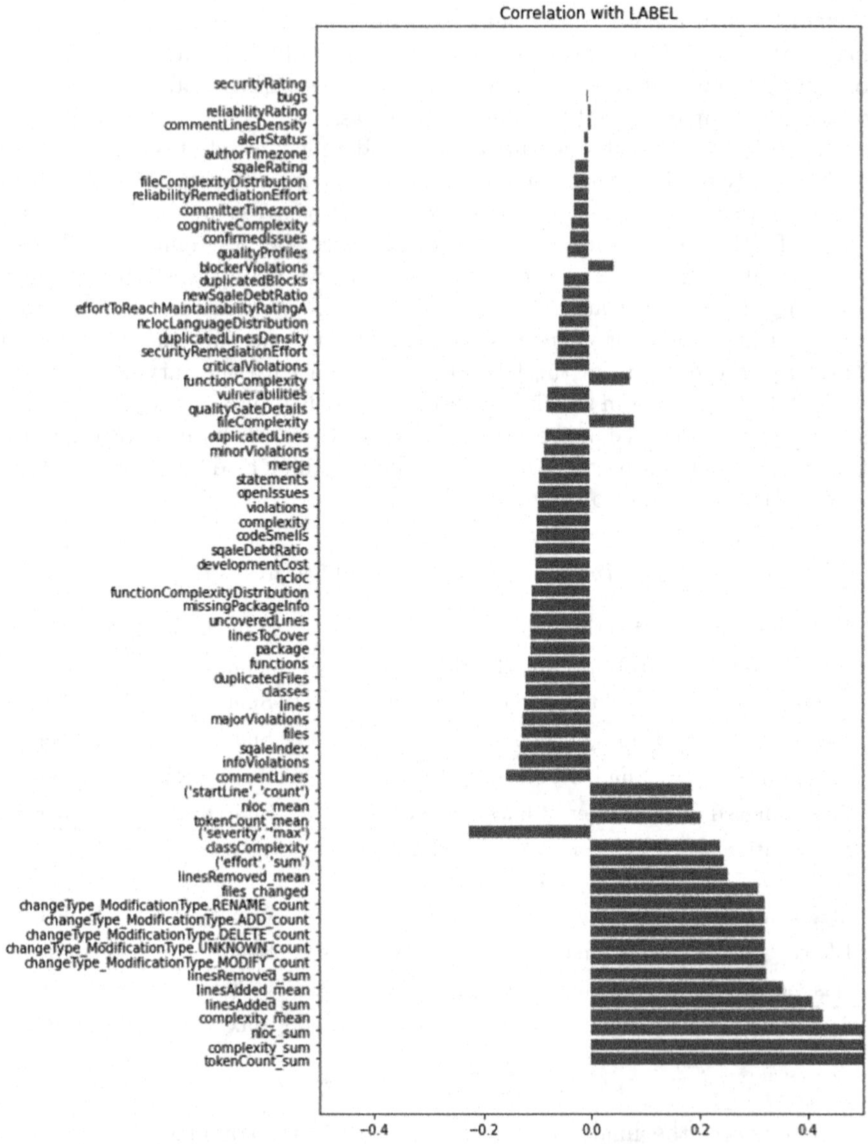

Fig. 2. List of the features with their correlation with dataset label.

in function, type of change applied) and to the type and the effort to restore the sonar issue. This seems to be somehow intuitively explainable if we consider that it is more probable to insert logical bug in code when a lot of changes are performed with respect to when very small changes are applied.

Finally, once features as been prepared and selected, as mentioned, since in the real case scenario data are aggregated at push level, instead of commit level,

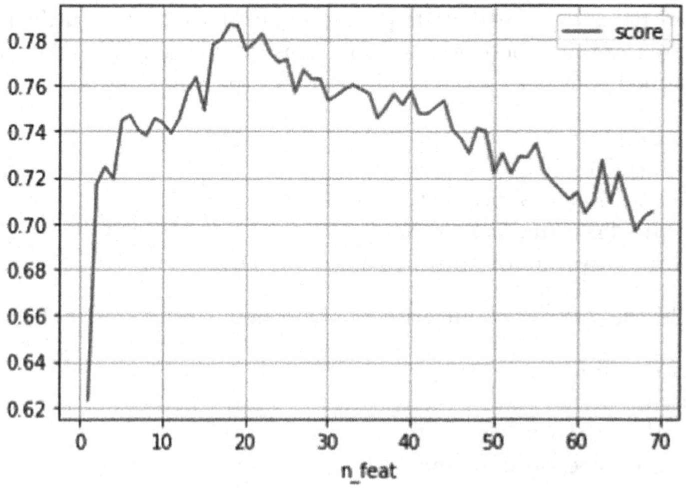

Fig. 3. F1-score values per number of features used during training.

we aggregate subsequent commits to replicate the push granularity. To aggregate the features we create a set of windows with lengths varying from 1 to 4 in a random way. We choose to create the windows sizes randomly since, by analyzing the real case scenario data, we discovered that data does not follow a particular distribution. In Fig. 4 we can see the distribution of the windows sizes used to aggregate commits. After aggregation the number of element in the positive class were 257, against 299 elements in the negative class.

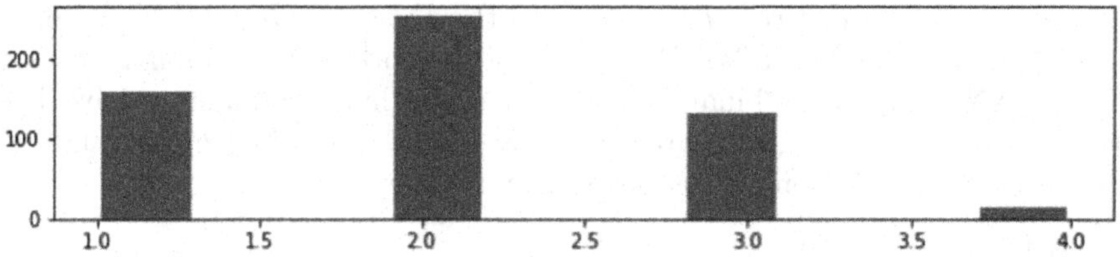

Fig. 4. Windows size distribution

3.4 The Models

The models chosen for continuous defect prediction are the ones mostly used in scientific research, such as in [13,16]. In particular, we tested RF and ANN. To test the performance of the two models we split the dataset into train and test sets, with the 80/20 ratio rule.

As far as RF is concerned, its hyperparameters have been identified by means of grid search optimization over a 5-fold cross validation. The grid search has been performed considering the combination of the following values:

- **Criterion:** entropy, gini
- **Bootstrap:** True, False
- **Number of Estimators:** 100, 250
- **Maximum tree depth:** 10, None
- **Minimum number of samples per splitting:** 2, 3.

After the grid search optimization the following parameters has been selected:

- **Criterion:** gini
- **Bootstrap:** yes
- **Number of Estimators:** 250
- **Maximum tree depth:** None
- **Minimum number of samples for splitting:** 3.

The overall performance on the test set are shown in Table 2.

Table 2. Performance of Random Forest

Class	Precision	Recall	F1-score	support
0	0.92	0.91	0.91	76
1	0.89	0.90	0.90	63

Where the *True Negatives (TN)* are 57 and the *True Positives (TP)* are 69 whereas the *False Positives (FP)* are 7 and the *False Negatives (FN)* are 6.

The other model tested is a Dense Neural Network (DNN), a particular case of the ANN, trained for binary classification. Its hyperparameters have been identified by means of grid search optimization over a 5-fold cross validation that check a combination of the following parameters:

- **Optimizer:** AdaDelta, Adam
- **Learning rate:** 0.01, 0.1
- **Maximum Number of epochs:** 128
- **BatchSize:** 8, 16, 32.

Early stopping criterion has been applied to avoid overfitting and select the number of epochs. The optimization resulted in the following selection:

- **Optimizer:** Adam
- **Learning rate:** 0.01
- **Number of epochs:** 5
- **BatchSize:** 8.

The network architecture is composed of a dense layer with *relu* activation function and an output dimension equal to 64 and 1344 parameters, a dropout layer with a 10% of dropout and a final dense layer with a *softmax* activation function and an output dimension equal to 2 and 130 parameters. The network has been trained with categorical cross entropy as loss function and accuracy as metric. Performance of the DNN model on the test set is shown in Table 3.

Table 3. Performance of dense neural network

Class	Precision	Recall	F1-score	support
0	0.90	0.71	0.79	76
1	0.72	0.91	0.81	63

Where the *True Negatives (TN)* are 53 and the *True Positives (TP)* are 58 whereas the *False Positives (FP)* are 22 and the *False Negatives (FN)* are 6.

As shown above, performance of the RF is better than the one of the DNN, especially when comparing the precision and the recall metrics of the positive class. Indeed, the RF model outperforms the DNN when considering all the metrics.

3.5 The Monitoring Dashboard

According to the results of the trained classifiers, the RF model has been deployed and used in a production environment. In order to visualize the predictions of the model and keep track of all the operations performed in the different software projects, each project has been connected to the model and results have been recorded in a database to be visualized. Thus, a monitoring dashboard has been designed to easily read the results of the analysis. Given the high number of data collected daily, we include in the dashboard distributions and time series charts, in order to give a synoptic point of view of the software projects' status. In Fig. 5 there is an example of the dashboard developed.

In details, the dashboard firstly includes some global metrics that resume the operations performed in the different code repositories over which the extraction and prediction algorithms have been connected. In particular the global metrics included are:

- **Number of commits:** total number of commits analyzed by the system.
- **Lines added:** number of code lines added in the analyzed commits.
- **Lines removed:** number of code lines removed in the analyzed commits.
- **Files changed:** number of files modified in the analyzed commits.
- **Total bugs:** number of bugs identified by the machine learning algorithm in the analyzed commits.

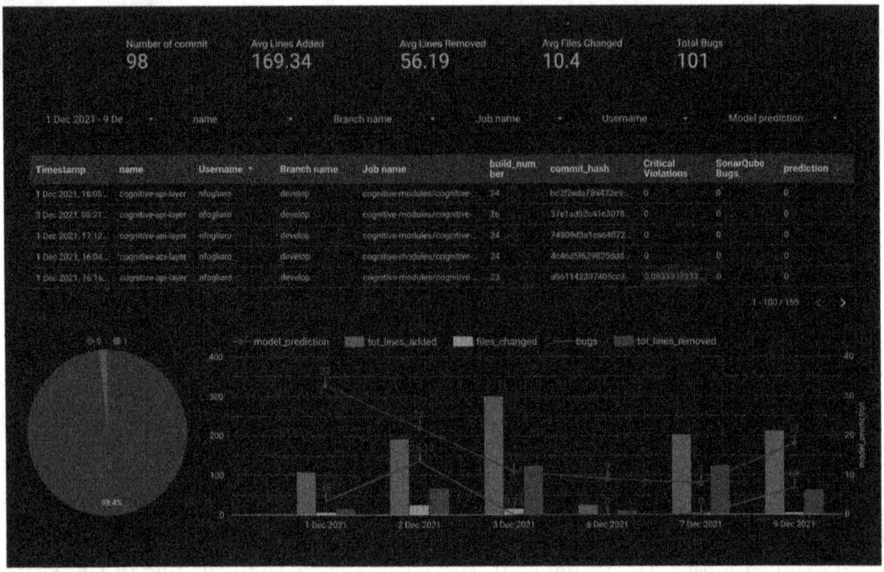

Fig. 5. Example of dashboard's plots and charts

The dashboard also includes a detailed tables that contains some references useful to reconstruct the history of each commit, such as the username, the branch name, the Jenkins job name, the commit hash, the critical violations and the bugs detected by SonarQube. All these informations are correlated with the model prediction, so that it is easy when the model detect a bug to identify the project, the branch and the authors of the interested commit.

Then, with a pie chart it is possible to easily understand the percentage of commits with a possible bug and with a time series chart it is possible to see the trend of detected bug together with some other important features, such as number of lines added, number of files changed and number of lines removed.

Finally, the dashboard gives the user the possibility to filter the content in order to reduce the number of visualized data and change the dimensions of the analysis. The available filters are based on date range, name of the repository, branch name, Jenkins job name, username and model prediction. In this way, all the charts and metrics previously described can be recomputed with specific filters, thus deeply exploring each project according to different dimensions.

The developed dashboard has not given only the possibility to detect bugs in real time, but also the chance to evaluate the quality of the software projects. Indeed, thanks to the different charts and filters, it has been possible to identify projects or branches with more bugs, which generally means that are more complex projects/branches or projects/branches for which the requirements are not well defined. Moreover, it has been possible to monitor also the resources that contribute to software projects. As an example, it has been possible to identify resources that usually do not commit RFEquently, but only in case of large changes or improvements in team's code quality.

4 Infrastructural Considerations

To conclude, we present some considerations related to the infrastructure that we set-up to serve the proposed framework.

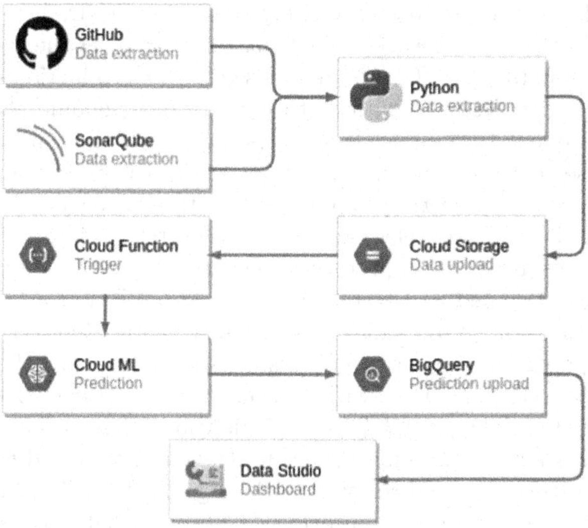

Fig. 6. Architecture of the proposed framework.

We deployed the services using Google Cloud Platform [28] infrastructure. As depicted in Fig. 6, the proposed framework requires to retrieve data both from GitHub and SonarQube. GitHub and SonarQube information are analyzed by means of a Python [29] framework called PyDriller that aims at mining software repositories by easily extracting information from any Git repository, such as commits, developers, modification, diffs and source codes, and quickly export CSV file. On a scheduled basis, we retrieved data from Git repositories by means of such framework and we uploaded them on Google Cloud Storage [30], which is a blob-based storage service. This action triggers a Google Cloud Function [31], which is a scalable and serverless functions as a service that, in turn, invokes Google Vertex AI Prediction [32] service for model predictions. Google Vertex AI is Google's unified platform for building, deploy and scale machine learning models over which we deployed the RF models trained and fine tuned. The results are then saved to Google BigQuery [33], a serverless, highly scalable multicloud data warehouse, and made available for visualization by means of a Data Studio [34] dashboard.

5 Conclusions

The goal of this research was that of defining a framework to detect bugs in software projects' commits in a change-level defect prediction scenario. In order to define such framework, we firstly analyzed the state of the art for machine learning algorithms applied to support CI/CD operations, with a focus on continuous defect prediction. The analysis of the state of the art allowed us to define the main machine learning approach to defect prediction, the main publicly available datasets and some related works. Thus, we selected an approach and a public dataset that fit our needs to create the aforementioned framework. However, differently from the related works that focus on processing the logs of CI tools, given the constraints set by CI/CD tools used in our production environments, we needed to preprocess the dataset to consider an agglomerations of record based on subsequent commits. Thus, we preprocessed the dataset in order to match real case scenario granularity. Once data has been prepared, they have undergone a feature engineering step. From the state of the art, indeed, emerged that properly collecting and selecting features is extremely important within this context. Thus, we used a RFE process to give importance to features and select them. Then, we designed and tested two models: a RF and a DNN both with grid search over 5-fold cross validation for hyperparameters optimization and early stopping for DNN. Experimental results showed that, on the preprocessed dataset, RF outperformed DNN, with an average F1-score over the positive class of 0.91 against 0.81. Thus, we define a Google Cloud based architecture to host our framework for real time monitoring, that allowed to link different software projects to the RF model and register all the logs produced in order to visualize the results. We also design a monitoring dashboard, that allowed us to derive important insights and evaluate software quality.

The developed framework is extremely useful, especially thanks to the synoptic point of view that provides, however some enhancements can be performed. As an example, some future developments could involve the augmentation of the features with user-specific information to make the model learning user-patterns. Other future developments are related to a posterior analysis of the machine learning models. Indeed, we couldn't train a model on a real dataset and a manual analysis of the results showed that this is the reason why the model produces some false positive. Thus, validating the results of the models and retrain the model with a real dataset could enhance the model's performance and allow for a better usage of the framework.

References

1. Ebert, C., Gallardo, G., Hernantes, J., Serrano, N.: DevOps. IEEE Softw. **33**(3), 94–100 (2016)
2. Virmani, M.: Understanding DevOps & bridging the gap from continuous integration to continuous delivery. In: Fifth International Conference on the Innovative Computing Technology (INTECH 2015), pp. 78–82. IEEE, Galcia (2015)
3. Madeyski, L., Kawalerowicz, M.: Continuous defect prediction: the idea and a related dataset. In: 2017 IEEE/ACM 14th International Conference on Mining Software Repositories (MSR), pp. 515–518. IEEE, Buenos Aires (2017)

4. Nogueira, A.F., Ribeiro, J.C., Zenha-Rela, M.A., Craske, A.: Improving la redoute's CI/CD pipeline and devops processes by applying machine learning techniques. In: 2018 11th International Conference on the Quality of Information and Communications Technology (QUATIC), pp. 282–286. IEEE, Coimbra (2018)
5. D'Ambros, M., Lanza, M., Robbe, R.: An extensive comparison of bug prediction approaches. In: Proceedings of 7th IEEE Working Conference on Mining Software Repositories, pp. 31–41. IEEE, Cape Town (2010)
6. Gyimothy, T., Ferenc, R., Siket, I.: Empirical validation of object-oriented metrics on open source software for fault prediction. IEEE Trans. Softw. Eng. **31**(10), 897–910 (2005)
7. Hassan, A.: Predicting faults using the complexity of code changes. In: Proceedings of the 31st International Conference on Software Engineering, pp. 78–88. IEEE, Vancouver (2009)
8. Hassan, A., Holt, R.: The top ten list: dynamic fault prediction. In: Proceedings of the 21st IEEE International Conference on Software Maintenance, pp. 263–272. IEEE, Budapest (2005)
9. Madeyski, L., Jureczko, M.: Which process metrics can significantly improve defect prediction models? An empirical study. Softw. Qual. J. **23**(3), 393–422 (2015)
10. Kamei, Y., et al.: A large-scale empirical study of just-in-time quality assurance. TSE **39**(6), 757–773 (2013)
11. Alnor, N., Khleel, A., Nehéz, K.: Comprehensive study on machine learning techniques for software bug prediction. Int. J. Adv. Comput. Sci. Appl. **12**(8) (2021)
12. Yang, X., Lo, D., Xia, X., Zhang, Y., Sun, J.: Deep learning for just-in-time defect prediction. In: 2015 IEEE International Conference on Software Quality. Reliability and Security, pp. 17–26. IEEE, Vancouver (2015)
13. Li, Y., Wang, S., Nguyen, T. N., Nguyen, S. V.: Improving bug detection via context-based code representation learning and attention based neural networks. In: Proceedings of the ACM on Programming Languages, pp. 1–30. Association for Computing Machinery, New York (2019)
14. Hammouri, A., Hammad, M., Alnabhan, M., Alsarayrah, F.: Software bug prediction using machine learning approach. Int. J. Adv. Comput. Sci. Appl. **9**(2), 78–83 (2018)
15. Pandey, S.K., Mishra, R.B., Triphathi, A.K.: Software bug prediction prototype using Bayesian network classifier: a comprehensive model. Proc. Comput. Sci. **132**, 1412–1421 (2018)
16. Uqaili, I.U.N., Ahsan, S.N.: Machine learning based prediction of complex bugs in source code. Int. Arab J. Inf. Technol. **17**(1), 26–37 (2020)
17. Islam, M.J., Pan, P., Nguyen, G., Rajan, H.: A comprehensive study on deep learning bug characteristics. In: Proceedings of the 2019 27th ACM Joint Meeting on European Software Engineering Conference and Symposium on the Foundations of Software Engineering, pp. 1–11. Association for Computing Machinery, Tallin (2019)
18. Lenarduzzi, V., Saarimaki, N., Taibi, D.: The technical debt dataset. In: Proceedings of the Fifteenth International Conference on Predictive Models and Data Analytics in Software Engineering, pp. 1–2. Association for Computing Machinery, New York (2019)
19. Guyon, I., Weston, J., Barnhill, S., Vapnik, V.: Gene selection for cancer classification using support vector machines. Mach. Learn. **46**, 389–422 (2002)
20. Pellegrini, L., Lenarduzzi, V., Taibi, D.: OpenSZZ: a free, open-source, web-accessible implementation of the SZZ algorithm. In: Proceedings of the 28th Inter-

national Conference on Program Comprehension, pp. 446–450. Association for Computing Machinery, New York (2020)
21. Zeller, A., Sliwerski, J., Zimmermann, T.: When do changes induce fixes?. In: Proceedings of the 2005 International Workshop on Mining Software Repositories, pp. 1–5. Association for Computing Machinery, St. lOUSI, mISSURI (2005)
22. Robles, G., Rodriguez-Perez, G., Gonzalez-Barahona, J.M.: Reproducibility and credibility in empirical software engineering: a case study based on a systematic literature review of the use of the SZZ algorithm. Inf. Softw. Technol. **99**, 164–176 (2018)
23. da Costa, D.A., McIntosh, S., Shang, W., Kulesza, U., Coelho, R., Hassan, A.E.: A framework for evaluating the results of the SZZ approach for identifying bug-introducing changes. IEEE Trans. Softw. Eng. **43**(7), 641–657 (2017)
24. Spadini, D., Aniche, M., Bacchelli, A.: PyDriller: python framework for mining software repositories. In: Joint European Software Engineering Conference and Symposium on the Foundations of Software Engineering (ESEC/FSE), pp. 908–911. Association for Computing Machinery, New York (2018)
25. Tsantalis, N., Mansouri, M., Eshkevari, L. M., Mazinanian, D., Dig, D.: Accurate and efficient refactoring detection in commit history. In: Proceedings of the 40th International Conference on Software Engineering (ICSE 2018), pp. 483–494. Association of Computing Machinery, New York (2018)
26. GitHub Homepage. https://github.com/. Accessed 30 Sep 2021
27. Jira Homepage. https://www.atlassian.com/it/software/jira. Accessed 30 Sep 2021
28. Google Cloud Platform Homepage. https://cloud.google.com. Accessed 30 Sep 2021
29. Python Homepage. https://www.python.com. Accessed 30 Sep 2021
30. Google Cloud Storage Homepage. https://cloud.google.com/storage. Accessed 30 Sep 2021
31. Google Cloud Functions Homepage. https://cloud.google.com/functions. Accessed 30 Sep 2021
32. Google Cloud Vertex AI Homepage. https://cloud.google.com/vertex-ai. Accessed 30 Sep 2021
33. Google Cloud BigQuery Homepage. https://cloud.google.com/bigquery. Accessed 30 Sep 2021
34. Data Studio Homepage. https://datastudio.google.com/. Accessed 30 Sep 2021
35. Jenkins Homepage. https://www.jenkins.io/. Accessed 30 Sep 2021
36. SonarQube Homepage. https://www.sonarqube.org/. Accessed 30 Sep 2021
37. Ptidej GitHub Repository. https://github.com/ptidejteam/v5.2. Accessed 30 Sep 2021

AI Applications

Robust Optimization Models For Local Flexibility Characterization of Virtual Power Plants

Allegra De Filippo(✉), Michele Lombardi, and Michela Milano

DISI, University of Bologna, Bologna, Italy
{allegra.defilippo,michele.lombardi2,michela.milano}@unibo.it

Abstract. A typical Virtual Power Plant (VPP) has a distributed architecture, composed by a central control system and decentralized control units, which coordinates and aggregates local resources. A key aspect of these distributed energy systems is the flexibility offered to the market. This flexibility is considered as the difference between the (partially shiftable) load requested to the system and the energy produced by the local available resources, and it is subject to the uncertainty of the renewable production. This work proposes robust day-ahead optimization models to analyze flexibility of different local resource configurations. For each configuration, we consider a Demand Side Management step to shift the requested load in predefined time windows, based on renewable production forecasts. Moreover, two different objective functions are considered: 1) the cost minimization for the use of available resources; 2) the minimization of the exchange with the external grid (i.e. the market). The models are implemented and tested using real data. We provide a comparative analysis on the expected flexibility and costs that can be exploited by a central system to provide value-added services to the market by synergistically managing different configurations of local resources of a VPP.

Keywords: Robust optimization · Uncertainty · Virtual Power Plant

1 Introduction

Energy systems are increasingly converging towards a full integration of Renewable Energy Sources (RES) in the electricity grid. Due to the stochastic nature of RES, it is necessary for these systems to be able to manage the fluctuations of the electricity input. The consequence is the evolution of energy systems in the direction of a greater flexibility, efficiency and reliability: to this end, the concept of Virtual Power Plant (VPP) is outlined to effectively and efficiently integrate Distributed Energy Resources (DER). VPPs are based on the idea of aggregating the capacity of many local DER (i.e. generation, storage, or demand), to create a single operating profile to increase flexibility through the definition of approaches to manage the uncertainty. Indeed, one of the most important aspects of these distributed energy systems is the flexibility that is offered to the

S. Bandini et al. (Eds.): AIxIA 2021, LNAI 13196, pp. 609–623, 2022.
https://doi.org/10.1007/978-3-031-08421-8_42

market as a service. In further details, it is considered as the difference between the (partially shiftable) load requested to the system and the energy produced by the local available resources. This deviation is subject to RES uncertainty and it can change based on local DER configurations. This aspect must be properly modeled and taken into account, to better coordinate the local resources of a VPP.

This work aims to analyze local flexibilities, based on energy prices and different configurations of local DER. Generally, a VPP system is composed by different levels of aggregation: 1) different local VPPs composed by DERs and 2) a central aggregator that communicates with the market. We propose robust day-ahead optimization models to be employed in the Energy Management System (EMS) of local VPPs to estimate the flexibility towards the aggregator (and the market), based on RES forecasts. The proposed models are composed by two steps: the first step is designed to optimize the load demand shift based on the uncertainty of RES production using a robust (scenario-based) approach; while the second one tries to fully cover the *optimally shifted* energy demand by avoiding the loss of energy produced by RES generators. Both these steps are considered for different configurations of local DER. Moreover, each configuration is analyzed for two different objective functions: 1) the cost minimization for the use of available DERs (respecting the technical constraints); 2) the minimization of the exchange with the external grid (i.e. the market). In other terms, the second case analyzes the local behavior of a VPP when it tries to maximize the use of internal DER to satisfy the requested load.

In this paper we propose the following main contributions: (1) a robust optimization approach for planning different DER power flows in presence of renewable production uncertainty; (2) the development of different real case study configurations to test the approach; (3) a comparative analysis on the expected flexibility offered by different configurations of local VPPs and a comparative assessment of expected local management costs. This work represents a first step to understand and model, through robust approaches, how local flexibility can be exploited by a central system (e.g. an aggregator) that interfaces at run-time with the market to provide value-added services by synergistically managing local resources.

2 Related Work

Energy systems are subject to uncertainty, due to the presence of renewable sources. The progressive shift towards decentralized generation in power distribution networks has made the problem of optimal DERs operation increasingly constrained. This challenge can be met by using new and different concepts like VPP, which is based on the idea of aggregating the capacity of many DERs, (i.e. generation, storage, or demand) to create a single operating profile and to manage the uncertainty (as shown in Fig. 1) [3].

In a virtual power plant EMS, the load shifts can be planned the day-ahead based on RES production forecast. Moreover, based on actual energy prices and

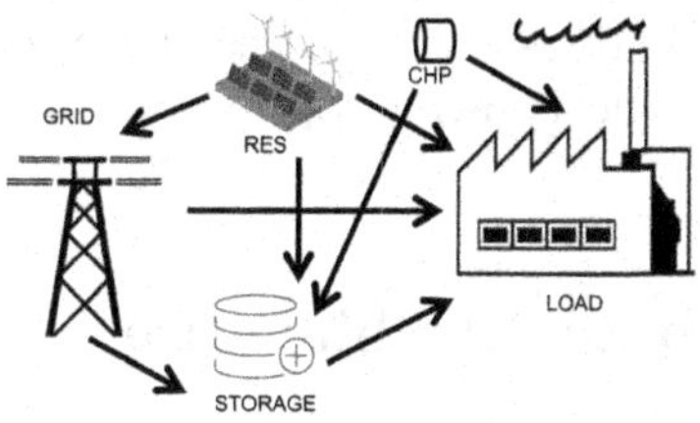

Fig. 1. A typical local Virtual Power Plant and its available DERs

on the availability of DERs, the EMS of a VPP decides: how much energy should be produced; which generators should be used for the required energy; whether the surplus energy should be stored or sold to the energy market; the load shifts planned the day-ahead.

Optimizing the use of energy can lead to significant economic benefits, and improve the efficiency and stability of the electric system. In recent works (see e.g. [16] and [14]) an EMS for controlling a VPP is presented, with the objective to manage the power flows for minimizing the electricity generation costs, and avoiding the loss of energy produced by renewable energy sources.

Optimization techniques such as Demand Side Management (DSM) can bridge the gap between production and real consumption in the energy management of complex systems (e.g. VPP) to reduce operating costs. These techniques can increase energy efficiency by moving part of the energy consumption during non-peak hours [15]. In addition to environmental benefits, DSM mechanisms provide end users with the opportunity to reduce electricity costs by responding to market prices. To this end, optimization models [4,5] have been developed to support political decision makers in defining sustainable business models and energy tariffs.

Even if optimization techniques have a long tradition in supporting planning and operational decisions in the energy sector, the recent literature highlights the need for increasing both the scope and the granularity of the decisions [7], including new factors like distributed generation by renewable sources and uncertainty. Both the most popular methods to deal with uncertainty in mathematical programming (i.e., robust optimization and stochastic programming) have been widely applied in energy systems [12,17,18]. One of the most used assumptions is that the distribution of future uncertainty is available for sampling, e.g. thanks to historical data and/or predictive models. In particular, the assumption that the distribution of future uncertainty is independent of current decisions is present in a variety of applications [8,11]. The assessment of uncertainty in the modeling of distributed energy systems has received considerable attention in recent works (e.g. [3]) for forecasting flexibility of VPPs. The flexibility of a local system therefore consists in the ability to quickly modulate and compensate for the variations in power required. It is a precious feature for the energy system: through rapidity in adapting to the quantity of required energy, it is possible to better follow the price of energy on the market. Furthermore, to improve system performance, it is possible to estimate the flexibility offered by making strategic decisions to improve the real-time optimization of the aggregated energy schedule [6].

3 VPP: A Distributed Architecture

A VPP has generally a distributed architecture: it consists of a central control system and decentralized control units, which coordinate and aggregate local resources (see Fig. 2). It can provide support for the provision of balancing, regulation and modulation services by responding to price signals. The final purpose of a VPP can be twofold: 1) offering aggregated flexibility towards the aggregator (central aggregation), and 2) balancing locally consumption and production for a reduction of costs and an increase in flexibility (local aggregation).

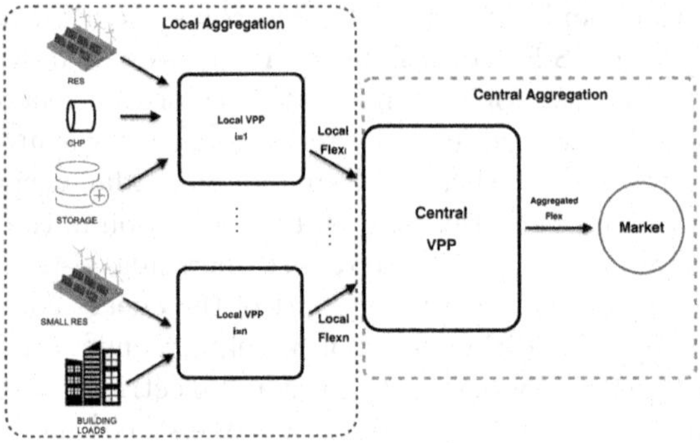

Fig. 2. A VPP distributed architecture

In this paper, we focus on the local aggregation and, based on different DER configurations, we use a two-step robust optimization model to evaluate the degrees of flexibility offered by local VPPs to a central aggregator and the market.

4 Model Description

4.1 Modeling of Uncertainties

In a VPP, the source of uncertainty is due to the presence of load and renewable production forecast.

Formally, we assume that the error for load demand forecast can be considered an independent random variable: this is a reasonable hypothesis, provided that our predictor is good enough. This allows to define our uncertainty range based on confidence intervals. In particular, we assume that the errors follow roughly a Normal distribution $N(0, \sigma^2)$, and that the variance for each timestamp is such that the 95% confidence interval corresponds to 20% of the estimated load. Formally, we have that $1.96\sigma = 0.2P_{Load}(t)$; in practice, this simply means that the δ_{Load} parameters used to obtain our four scenarios is equal to $0.2P_{Load}(t)$, as in [10].

We consider as a RES prediction the average hourly global solar radiation from [13] based on the period of recorded data (summer) in [9]. We then assume that the prediction errors in each timestamp can be modeled again as random variables. Specifically, we assume normally distributed variables with a variance such that the 95% confidence interval corresponds to $\pm 10\%$ of the prediction value. In other words, our δ_{PV} parameter for timestamp t is equal to $0.1P_{PV}(t)$.

The formalization of the local EMS model with its objective functions, the power balance constraints, and the dynamic model of the generation units are presented in the next subsections. All problems are modeled via Mixed Integer Programming (MIP) formulations.

4.2 Model and Components

We propose an optimization model for the VPP EMS that is composed by two steps: the first produces optimized demand shifts ($\tilde{L}$) by assuming as input the predictions for the solar power ($\hat{R}$) generation profile and for the demand load profile ($\hat{L}$) with a fixed percentage of allowed demand shift; the second step tries to fully cover the *optimally shifted* energy demand by avoiding the loss of energy produced by RES generators, for different configurations of local VPPs. Each configuration is analyzed with or without the possibility of the DSM step and for all case studies, two different objective functions are considered: 1) the cost minimization for the use of available resources (respecting the technical constraints); 2) the minimization of the exchange with the external grid (i.e. the market).

A local VPP is modeled as an entity connected to set G of "nodes" (i.e. DERs like generators, storage units, ...). Each x_g^k variable represents the flow at timestamp k from a node g to the VPP (if positive) or in the reverse direction (if negative). We assume the index 0 refers to a node representing the storage units, 1 to RES production and 2 to the external grid. The exchange with the external grid represents the energy that the VPP can buy/sell to the market. All flows must respect the physical bounds $\underline{x}_g^k$ and $\overline{x}_g^k$. The c^k variable represents the cost accumulated at timestamp k (with c_g^k being the unit cost of each flow). The uncertainty is specified via a random variable whose components are the load to be satisfied $\tilde{L}^k$ and the renewable energy flow $\tilde{x}_R^k$. The current state is encoded by the (variable) storage charge γ^k. Let Ω be a set of robust scenarios ω for $\xi = (\xi^0, \dots \xi^{n-1})$ and we consider our decision variables for each given scenario ω.

In the next subsection, the model is presented for each component of the system.

4.3 Modeling of RES Production

We use a robust approach to model uncertainty, which stems from 1) prediction errors in the solar power profile; 2) uncontrollable deviations from the planned demand shifts. For each of these quantities, the range of uncertainty is specified via a lower and an upper bound (for each timestamp), which can be obtained for example by estimating confidence intervals. We use these bounds to define a limited number of scenarios to calculate the optimized demand shifts that minimizes the expectation of the daily operating costs or the exchange with the external grid.

$$x_{1,\omega}^{k+1} = \hat{R}_k + \xi_{R,\omega}^k \qquad \forall \omega \in \Omega, \forall k = 1, \dots n \tag{1}$$

4.4 Modeling of Storage Systems

The development of battery systems has increased over the last few years to cover the use of renewable energy sources when they are not available. Our model for the battery system is based on the level of energy stored at each timestamp k as a function of the amount of energy charged or discharged from the unit.

$x_{0,\omega}^k$ is the energy exchanged between the storage system and the VPP. We consider a battery charge γ^k to define for each timestamp the current state of the battery system. The initial battery charge γ_ω^0 is identical for all scenarios. The battery upper limit is Γ and η is the charging/discharging efficiency: they are employed to specify the limits of the flow from/to the storage.

$$\underline{x}_0 \leq x_{0,\omega}^k \leq \overline{x}_0 \qquad \forall \omega \in \Omega, \forall k = 1, \dots n \tag{2}$$

$$0 \leq \gamma_\omega^k \leq \Gamma \qquad \forall k = 1, \dots n \tag{3}$$

$$\gamma_\omega^{k+1} = \gamma_\omega^k + \eta x_{0,\omega}^k \quad \forall \omega \in \Omega, \forall k = 1, \dots n-1 \tag{4}$$

4.5 External Grid

The variable $x_{2,\omega}^k$ represents the current power exchanged with the grid for each scenario and for each timestamp (i.e. the energy bought/sold from/to the electricity market). We assume bounds given by the net capacity from literature [2] based on real data for the maximum input/output net capacity.

$$\underline{x}_2 \leq x_{2,\omega}^k \leq \overline{x}_2 \qquad \forall \omega \in \Omega, \quad \forall k = 1, \dots n \tag{5}$$

4.6 Modeling of Generator Units

We consider a Combined Heat and Power (CHP) dispatchable generator, with an associated fuel cost. Our approach should decide the amount $x_{g,\omega}^k$ of generated CHP power for each scenario and for each timestamp. We assume bounds based on real generation data [2,9]. In our approach we treat CHP decisions in each timestamp as *independent*, because we assume that each timestamp is long enough to decide independently (from the previous timestamp) whether to switch on or off the generator. Therefore, we can model the generated CHP power with:

$$\underline{x}_g \leq x_{g,\omega}^k \leq \overline{x}_g \qquad \forall \omega \in \Omega, \ \ \forall k = 1, \ldots n, \ \ \forall g = 2, \ldots n_g \tag{6}$$

We consider traditional generator indices starting from 3 to the number of total available generators n_g.

4.7 Demand Side Management

The DSM of our VPP model aims to modify the temporal consumption patterns, leaving the total amount of required daily energy constant. The degree of modification is modeled by shifts that are optimized by the first step of our EMS. We assume that the total energy consumption on the whole optimization horizon is constant. More specifically, we assume that the consumption stays unchanged also *over multiple sub-periods of the horizon*: this a possible way to state that demand shifts can make only local alterations of the demand load. Formally, let T_n be the set of timestamps for the n-th sub-period, the shifted load is given by:

$$\tilde{L}_{\omega}^{k+1} = \hat{L}_k + \delta_k \pm \xi_{L,\omega}^k \quad \forall \omega \in \Omega, \forall k = 1, \ldots n \tag{7}$$

$$\sum_{k=t}^{t+m} \delta_k = 0 \qquad \forall t = 1, \ldots n - m \tag{8}$$

$$\underline{\delta}^k \leq \delta_k \leq \overline{\delta}^k \qquad \forall k = 1, \ldots n \tag{9}$$

where $\tilde{L}_{\omega}^{k+1}$) represents the amount of shifted demand, and $\hat{L}_k$ is the originally planned load for timestamp k (part of the model input). The amount of shifted demand is bounded by two quantities $\underline{\delta}^k$ and $\overline{\delta}^k$. By properly adjusting the two bounds, we can ensure that the consumption can reduce/increase in each timestamp by (e.g.) a maximum of 10% of the original expected load. Deciding the value of the δ_k variables is the main goal of our day-ahead optimization first step.

4.8 Power Balance

In general, ensuring power balance imposes that the total power generation must equal the load demand, $\tilde{L}_{\omega}^{k+1}$), in all timestamps and for all scenarios.

In this work, the load demand that must be satisfied is the *optimally shifted* demand of (day-ahead) step of our model. At any point in time, the overall shifted load is covered by an energy mix considering the generation from the internal sources, the storage system, and energy bought from the market. Energy sold to the grid and stored to the battery system should be subtracted from the power balance. Overall, we have:

$$\tilde{L}^k_\omega = \sum_{g \in G} x^k_{g,\omega} \qquad \forall \omega \in \Omega, \forall k = 1, \ldots n, \quad \forall tg = 0, \ldots n_g \tag{10}$$

4.9 Objective Functions

The first objective function of our EMS is the minimization of the expected operational costs z of the VPP, over a time horizon (T). The objective function is formulated as:

$$\min \& \frac{1}{|\Omega|} \sum_{\omega \in \Omega} \sum_{g \in G} \sum_{k=1}^{n} c^k_g x^k_{g,\omega} \tag{11}$$

where c^k_g is a parameter that represents the hourly cost of each DER (i.e. the electricity market cost for the grid, the storage maintenance cost, and the CHP cost).

The second objective function is the minimization of the expected exchange with the external grid (i.e. the flexibility offered to the market):

$$\min \& \frac{1}{|\Omega|} \sum_{\omega \in \Omega} \sum_{k=1}^{n} x^k_{2,\omega} \tag{12}$$

where the index 2 indicates the external grid. By minimizing the exchange with the external grid, we are forcing the local system to maximize the use of its internal DERs.

5 Case Studies

The model is implemented and tested using real data and our case study is based on a Public Dataset[1]. From this dataset we assume electric load demand and photovoltaic production forecasts, upper and lower limits for generating units and the initial status of storage units.

5.1 Dataset Description and Local VPP Configurations

The dataset presents 100 individual profiles of load demand with a time step of 5 min resolution from 00:00 to 23:00. We consider aggregated profiles with timestamp of 1 h and we use them as forecasted load. The Photovoltaic (PV) production is based on the same dataset with profiles for different sizes of PV

[1] www.enwl.co.uk/lvns.

units but for the same sun irradiance (i.e. the same shape but different amplitude due to the different size of the PV panels used). We use also in this case the PV production as forecasted production. The electricity hourly prices have been obtained based on data from the Italian national energy market management corporation[2] (GME) in €/MWh. The CHP (diesel) price is taken from the Italian Ministry of Economic Development[3] and is assumed as a constant for all the time horizon (one day in our model) as assumed in literature [1] and from [9].

Our models are evaluated over 30 different scenarios, obtained by sampling the random variables for the loads and PV generation in the VPP model. We aggregate data since we consider 96 time timestamps (each 15 min). We solve our MIPs using Gurobi solver. The time limit is 100 s. We assume physical bounds on CHP due to its Electrical Capability, the initial battery states and the efficiency values are based on real generation data and we assume there are physical bounds for storage system always based on real data [2,9]. In Fig. 3, we show the four local configurations analyzed in this work. For each of them, we consider two different objective functions with or without DSM step.

6 Experimental Results and Discussion

The first macro case study minimizes the energy management costs, while the second macro case study minimizes the use of the external grid (in terms of energy exchanged with the market) to meet the load required by the VPP in each time step. For both case studies, all the configurations (represented in Fig. 3) are analyzed with and without the DSM optimization step.

In the first configuration, the EMS satisfied the required load only through photovoltaic production or by buying energy from the external grid (the market). In this configuration, the surplus of energy produced by RES is sold to the market.

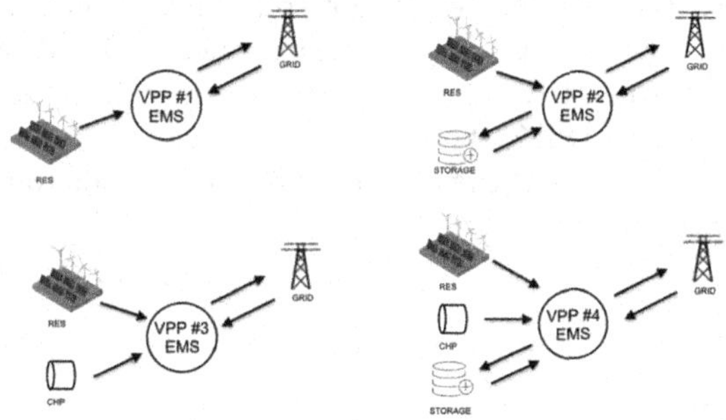

Fig. 3. Local VPP configurations

[2] http://www.mercatoelettrico.org/En/Default.aspx.

[3] http://dgsaie.mise.gov.it/.

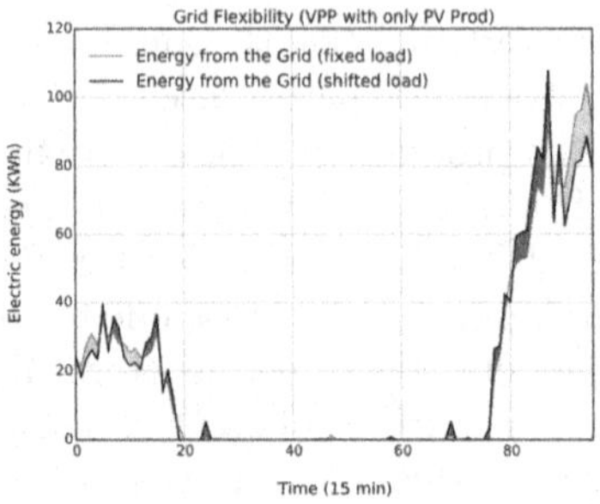

Fig. 4. Configuration 1: Flexibility with cost minimization

In Fig. 4 we can observe that the energy to be bought from the grid decreases (green areas) when the DSM allows to lower the load consumption peaks. In this VPP configuration, the possibility of energy exchange with the grid (i.e. the total flexibility of the system) is therefore given only by the photovoltaic production. Indeed, the case with grid minimization is equivalent to those in Fig. 4.

In the second configuration, the EMS can satisfy the required load through PV production, a storage system and the grid: it is interesting to analyze the use of the storage to satisfy the load in both the cases with different objective functions.

Figure 5 shows the total flexibility with and without DSM: it is possible to see that, w.r.t the previous configuration, in the central part of the time horizon there is almost no demand for energy from the grid, as the use of storage is convenient in terms of cost. This means that the EMS is able to store the surplus of energy from the PV production in order to avoid buying the required energy from the grid. Moreover, for the configurations that include the storage system, we show in detail the energy exchange with the grid and the storage, in order to underline the differences among the configurations considered. Due to the presence of the storage system, we can notice a different behavior based on the objective function considered and on the presence of DSM step: the storage system is more used to satisfy the load if we try to minimize the exchange with the grid. Moreover, with DSM, the use of the storage is greater, and this allows a further decrease in the use of the external grid. This leads to lower operational costs for the EMS.

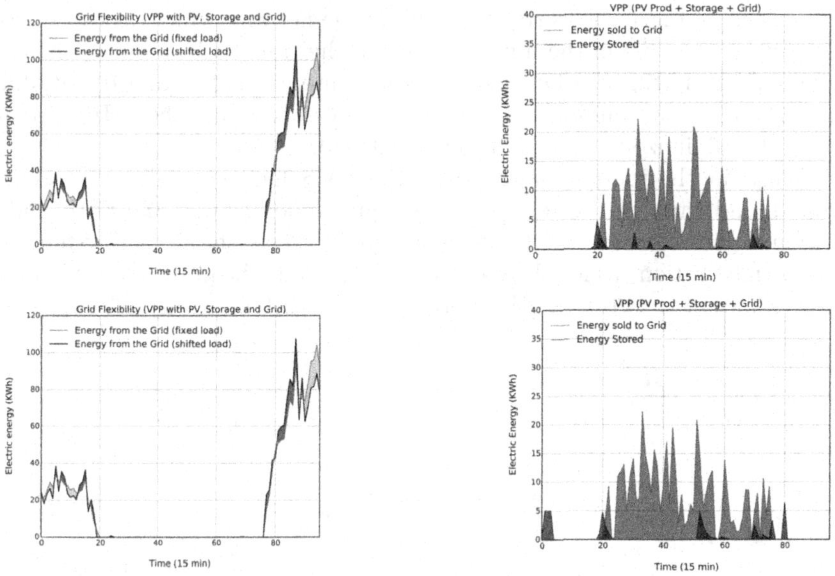

Fig. 5. Configuration 2: (left) Flexibility. (right) Grid and Storage. (up) case with cost minimization. (down) case with grid minimization

In the third configuration, the EMS has the possibility of satisfying the load through photovoltaic production, CHP generators and the external grid. Also in this case, due to the storage absence, the only way to use any surplus produced from renewables is the sale it to the market.

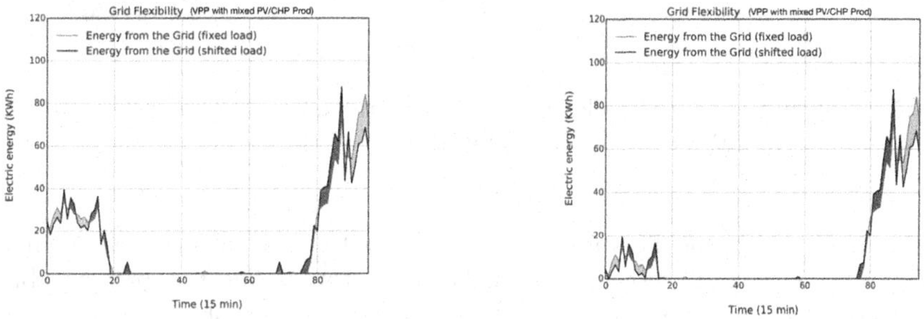

Fig. 6. Configuration 3: (left) Flexibility with cost minimization. (right) Flexibility with grid minimization

Thanks to the mixed production, in this configuration it is possible to see how the range of flexibility of the external network increases in cases with and without shift of the load (see Fig. 6). It is possible to see that, compared to or in Fig. 4, the contribution of the network drops significantly when CHP production occurs. Finally, Fig. 6 shows the flexibility of the network which, as can be seen, has a very low profile in the first few steps of the time horizon unlike the other configurations. In this third configuration it is interesting to analyze that, differently from the cost minimization case, it is necessary to use the CHP generator in order to minimize the use of the external grid.

Finally, in the fourth configuration the EMS has the ability to meet the required load through the mixed production of photovoltaic and CHP and, in addition to the external grid, it has the possibility to use the storage system. Also in this configuration (as for the second configuration) the graphs of the different energy values of the grid and the storage are shown for each timestamp.

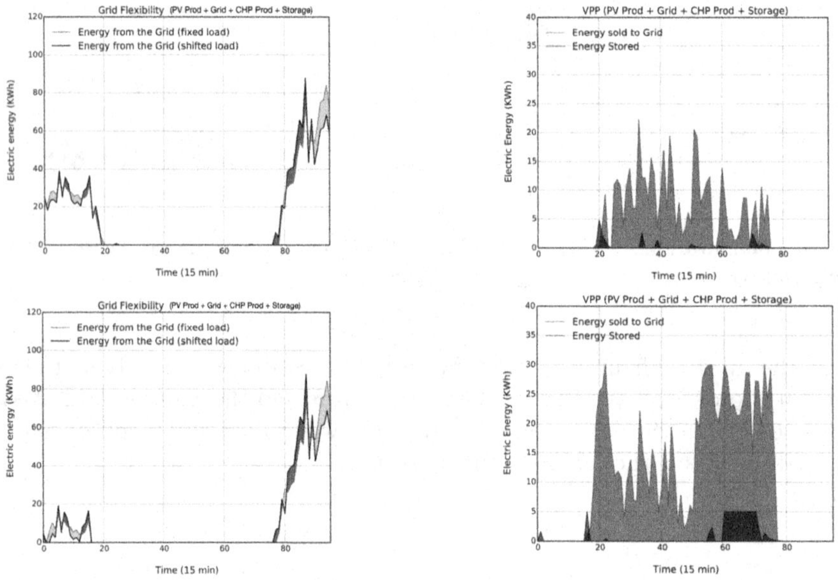

Fig. 7. Configuration 4: (left) Flexibility. (right) Grid and Storage. (up) case with cost minimization. (down) case with grid minimization

Figure 7 shows the flexibility of the grid with and without DSM. In this configuration, it is interesting to show how the storage and the grid are able to differently manage the surplus of energy produced by the photovoltaic system.

6.1 Cost Comparison

The following table summarizes the costs (in K€) over the entire time horizon (one day) for the management of the VPP in the various configurations with and without DSM. In black color we show the costs of the management of all the VPP components, while in red color we show the costs of energy purchase from the grid. In the two macro case studies with different objective functions, it is possible to note the contribution of the CHP generator which allows to satisfy the required load with a mix of productions with lower costs than the case with only storage, photovoltaic and grid.

Local configuration	Cost minimization		Grid exchange minimization	
	Fixed load	Shifted load	Fixed load	Shifted load
1	83.82 (83.82)	83.80 (83.80)	83.82 (83.82)	83.82 (83.82)
2	83.29 (94.43)	83.00 (93.99)	83.35 (93.30)	83.77 (92.49)
3	83.75 (74.94)	83.87 (74.77)	94.13 (55.41)	90.90 (54.01)
4	82.81 (73.67)	82.01 (73.13)	100.92 (54.48)	85.62 (53.18)

Based on all the configurations, the possibility of DSM step allows a further margin of improvement in terms of flexibility: in other terms, it allows to move the load in some time slots respecting the constraints and by lowering load peaks of consumption.

7 Conclusion

The assessment of uncertainty in the modeling of distributed energy systems like VPPs has received considerable attention in recent works for forecasting flexibility. The flexibility of a system consists in the ability to quickly modulate and compensate for the variations in energy required: through rapidity in adapting to the quantity of energy required, it is possible to better follow the price of energy on the market, thus offering the energy produced to the market. Moreover, DSM programs can provide advantages to the energy system: in periods of peak loads even a limited reduction in demand can lead to significant reductions in energy prices on the market.

In this work, we analyze local flexibilities, based on energy prices and different configurations of local VPPs. We propose robust day-ahead optimization models to be employed in the EMS of a local VPP to estimate its flexibility towards the market, based on RES and load forecasts.

We propose the following main contributions: (1) a robust optimization approach for planning different DER power flows and flexibility in presence of renewable production uncertainty; (2) the development of different real case study configurations to test the models; (3) a comparative analysis on the expected flexibility offered by different configurations of local VPPs and a comparative assessment of expected local management costs.

The results underline the importance of the storage systems to modulate the use of the external grid, the possibility to exploit a mixed (conventional and renewable) energy production, and the importance of a DSM step to optimize load shift in order to avoid peaks of consumption. Finally, this work represents a first step to understand and model, through robust approaches, how local flexibility can be exploited by a central system (e.g. an aggregator) that interfaces at run-time with the market to provide value-added services by synergistically managing local resources.

Acknowledgements. This work has been partially supported by the VIRTUS Project (CCSEB00094).

References

1. Aloini, D., Crisostomi, E., Raugi, M., Rizzo, R.: Optimal power scheduling in a virtual power plant. In: 2011 2nd IEEE PES International Conference and Exhibition on Innovative Smart Grid Technologies, pp. 1–7, December 2011
2. Bai, H., Miao, S., Ran, X., Ye, C.: Optimal dispatch strategy of a virtual power plant containing battery switch stations in a unified electricity market. Energies **8**(3), 2268–2289 (2015). http://www.mdpi.com/1996-1073/8/3/2268
3. Bianchi, S., De Filippo, A., Magnani, S., Mosaico, G., Silvestro, F.: Virtus project: a scalable aggregation platform for the intelligent virtual management of distributed energy resources. Energies **14**(12), 3663 (2021)
4. De Filippo, A., Lombardi, M., Milano, M.: Non-linear optimization of business models in the electricity market. In: Quimper, C.-G. (ed.) CPAIOR 2016. LNCS, vol. 9676, pp. 81–97. Springer, Cham (2016). https://doi.org/10.1007/978-3-319-33954-2_7
5. De Filippo, A., Lombardi, M., Milano, M.: User-aware electricity price optimization for the competitive market. Energies **10**(9), 1378 (2017)
6. De Filippo, A., Lombardi, M., Milano, M.: Methods for off-line/on-line optimization under uncertainty. In: IJCAI, pp. 1270–1276 (2018)
7. De Filippo, A., Lombardi, M., Milano, M.: Off-line and on-line optimization under uncertainty: a case study on energy management. In: van Hoeve, W.-J. (ed.) CPAIOR 2018. LNCS, vol. 10848, pp. 100–116. Springer, Cham (2018). https://doi.org/10.1007/978-3-319-93031-2_8
8. De Filippo, A., Lombardi, M., Milano, M.: How to tame your anticipatory algorithm. In: Proceedings of the 28th International Joint Conference on Artificial Intelligence, pp. 1071–1077. AAAI Press (2019)
9. Espinosa, A., Ochoa, L.: Dissemination document "low voltage networks models and low carbon technology profiles". Technical report. University of Manchester, June 2015
10. Gamou, S., Yokoyama, R., Ito, K.: Optimal unit sizing of cogeneration systems in consideration of uncertain energy demands as continuous random variables. Energy Convers. Manag. **43**(9), 1349–1361 (2002)
11. Hentenryck, P.V., Bent, R.: Online Stochastic Combinatorial Optimization. The MIT Press, Cambridge (2009)
12. Jurković, K., Pandšić, H., Kuzle, I.: Review on unit commitment under uncertainty approaches. In: 2015 38th International Convention on Information and Communication Technology, Electronics and Microelectronics (MIPRO), pp. 1093–1097. IEEE (2015)
13. Kaplanis, S., Kaplani, E.: A model to predict expected mean and stochastic hourly global solar radiation I(h;nj) values. Renew. Energy **32**(8), 1414–1425 (2007)
14. Lombardi, P., Powalko, M., Rudion, K.: Optimal operation of a virtual power plant. In: Power & Energy Society General Meeting, PES 2009, pp. 1–6. IEEE (2009)

15. Palensky, P., Dietrich, D.: Demand side management: demand response, intelligent energy systems, and smart loads. IEEE Trans. Ind. Inform. **7**(3), 381–388 (2011)
16. Palma-Behnke, R., Benavides, C., Aranda, E., Llanos, J., Sáez, D.: Energy management system for a renewable based microgrid with a demand side management mechanism. In: 2011 IEEE Symposium on Computational Intelligence Applications in Smart Grid (CIASG), pp. 1–8, April 2011
17. Reddy, S.S., Sandeep, V., Jung, C.M.: Review of stochastic optimization methods for smart grid. Front. Energy 1–13 (2017)
18. Zhou, Z., Zhang, J., Liu, P., Li, Z., Georgiadis, M.C., Pistikopoulos, E.N.: A two-stage stochastic programming model for the optimal design of distributed energy systems. Appl. Energy **103**, 135–144 (2013)

Explainable Artificial Intelligence for Technology Policy Making Using Attribution Networks

Feras A. Batarseh[1,2(✉)], Dominick Perini[1], Qasim Wani[1], and Laura Freeman[2]

[1] Bradley Department of Electrical and Computer Engineering, Virginia Tech, Arlington, VA 22203, USA
{batarseh,perindom,qasim}@vt.edu
[2] Hume Center for National Security and Technology, Virginia Tech, Arlington, VA 22203, USA
laura.freeman@vt.edu

Abstract. In this manuscript, we propose an alternative to conventional policy making procedures. The presented policy pipeline leverages intelligent methods that factor for causal relations and economic factors to produce explainable outcomes. Attribution-based methods for analyzing the effects of technology policies are deployed for all American states. Legal codes are analyzed using natural language processing methods to detect similarity, and K-nearest neighbor (Knn) is applied to group laws by influence on state's technological descriptors, such as broadband and internet use. Additionally, we classify which laws are excitatory and which ones are inhibitory regarding the overall quality of technology services. Our pipeline allows for explaining the 'goodness of a policy' using task-based and end-to-end learning; a notion that has not been explored prior. Data are collected from multiple state statutes, intelligent models are developed, experimental work is performed, and the results are presented and discussed.

Keywords: XAI · Public policy · Attributions · Data-driven law

1 Introduction and Motivation

Conventional policy making approaches to evaluations and forecasting have been grappling with *alternative* methods, but the availability of big data and advances in software and hardware systems pose new challenges. These include dealing with the sheer volume of spatiotemporal data, lengthy lists of factors available to explain economic and contextual relationships (i.e. associated collinearities), and the need to move beyond static and linear models to be relevant in complex and real-world situations. Artificial Intelligence (AI) has been offered as an alternative to address many of these challenges. Several authors have strongly

Supported by the Commonwealth Cyber Initiative (CCI) at Virginia Tech.

S. Bandini et al. (Eds.): AIxIA 2021, LNAI 13196, pp. 624–637, 2022.
https://doi.org/10.1007/978-3-031-08421-8_43

advocated the use of big data and AI to uncover increasingly complex relationships for forecasting purposes [1]. The law research community is catching on [2], but is further challenged by the speed of AI advances (such as deep learning and genetic algorithms), i.e. new techniques emerge every month [3]. Traditional policy making models - such as ad hoc, linear and non-linear econometric specifications and Bayesian approaches - have certain advantages, e.g. good accuracy in the macro context, but their applicability to micro- or state/county/city-levels remains barely explored. Furthermore, traditional approaches employ ex-post data on events, whereas ex-ante modeling of uncertainties and counter-factuals are likely required for accurate and on-time information critical to decision making during policy crafting. An aspect that we target in our pipeline.

Using AI without explainability could exacerbates the problem [4], policy makers are especially critical of approaches that don't show how the outcome was reached (even if the outcome is better), also more importantly, transparency and accountability regarding laws is critical in the eye of the public and to the overall goal of enforcing them in society. The topic of XAI gained traction in 2016, when the US Defense Advanced Research Projects Agency (DARPA) started a program with the same name [5]. Accordingly, in our study, eXplainable AI's (XAI) goal is unveiling key features responsible for deciding (using an deep learning algorithms) whether a law is expected to increase (excitatory) or decrease (inhibitory) Metrics of Interest (MoIs) - i.e. technology descriptors in a state.

1.1 AI-Driven Law and Policy

The adoption of data-driven methods for policy making is challenged by AI assurance hurdles, according to Batarseh et al. [6], AI assurance is defined as: "A process that is applied at all stages of the AI engineering lifecycle ensuring that any intelligent system is producing outcomes that are valid, verified, data-driven, trustworthy and explainable to a layman, ethical in the context of its deployment, unbiased in its learning, and fair to its users" [6]. Explainability, a key pillar in assurance, is especially important in policy making at government. As one of the main producers of data in the country [7], the U.S. government is still lagging behind in injecting more data science and AI into its software systems and its processes. Explainability nonetheless, is critical in improving overall accountability, openness, and effectiveness of policy making in the United States and around the world. The work presented in this paper presents a generic pipeline that enables that, with an application to technology policy at state level, although it could be expanded to other geographical aggregations or other policy domains. Multiple works have presented the use of intelligent methods for public policy [1,8,10] however, most present methods to evaluate and predict policies using random features, predictions, and decision recommendations based on that (such as what is in Fig. 1); however, without considering counterfactuals, models will fall short. Moreover, it is critical to consider the factors that lead to whether a policy [9] is successful or not in accomplishing its goals.

In our pipeline, we identify key features responsible for determining if a policy is inhibitory or excitatory (regarding desired outcomes). We expect that

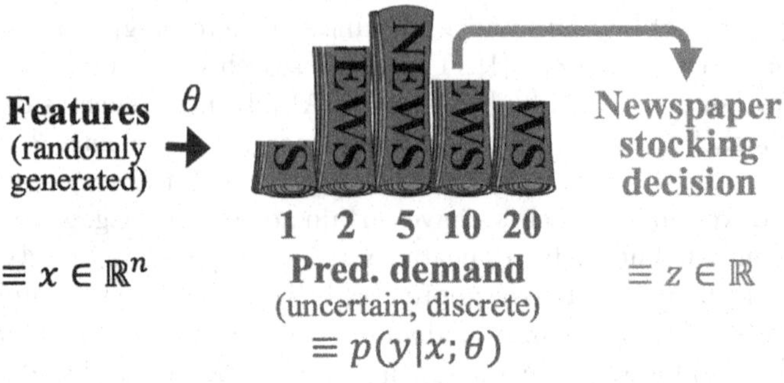

Fig. 1. Conventional data-driven policy making methods

law codes (text) will have a significant effect, therefore, we decided to analyze them using Natural Language Processing (NLP). However, we also expect to see some patterns being picked up in different contexts. Attribution is being used for feature selection. For instance, our model might illustrate that land size doesn't really effect policy $p1$ in determining broadband data for one state, but does for another, while employment rates can be a better indicator whether policy $p2$ would be impactful or not. Besides using neural networks to classify policies, we also present methods in our pipeline that point to causation and attribution - these are presented next.

1.2 Causality Through Attributions

Based on our review of existing work, no previous paper explicitly studied technology-related laws using deep learning techniques. As a result, we collected, merged, and synthesized a dataset that represents 733 policies passed by various states in the past decade (2010–2021). The main challenge in social and legal data is annotation; i.e. how to effectively measure 'goodness' of a policy? how to quantify laws' causality? or how to load 'goodness' values into AI algorithms such as ethics and trustworthiness? Since the policies considered in this study are reflective of technology data, we measured changes (*derivative*) in different MoI and their attributions, such as (a) broadband data, (b) internet usage over time, and (c) state's satellite access, to quantify the *effectiveness* of enacted technology policies at any given state. The dataset consists of 50+ MoIs describing the states, policies, and other contextual information. Every law and variable has an associated self-generated label: *excitatory* or *inhibitory*. More formally, the dataset D consists of m policies where each policy $z_i = (x_i, y_i)$ is a tuple of features and corresponding label based on some user defined MoI. D is passed on as an input to the neural network model which comprises of a Multi-Layer Perception (MLP) setup. D is split into training and test/validation datasets with a ratio of 17:20. The model is trained using Stochastic gradient descent (SGD) [11] of batch size of eight with batch-normalization to reduce correlation between hidden layers. The presented model is cross-validated on five hold-out sets. Once the model is trained, we verify the importance of individual neurons using gradient-based attributions (presented in Sect. 2.3). Attributions are a way of highlighting contribution (i.e. causation) of individual neurons in a network; a notion that can increase model's explainability. Attributions assume a fixed model and therefore can represent changes in prediction by probing the model. An intuitive approach is by occlusion, i.e. increasing the window size of a perturbation to see variance in prediction. This is -as expected- computationally exhaustive for deeper networks. Different approaches have been tested, but the most used ones include perturbations based on network gradients [12]. Generally, policy models deal with interesting causal inferences since there's a non-zero probability that multiple laws are related by either topic or some other legislature or geographical context. If one considers correlation or association amongst the MoIs included, multiple relationships would emerge, none of which are expected to be identifiable as causal though. In the context of deep learning, to understand cause-effect, one has to open the *black box* and identify variables that fire nodes across the network and have a more prominent effect on the outputs - thus, understanding which laws are more effective than others, and also allowing for explainability of outcomes to policy makers. Nonetheless, generating a numerical measure (such as Spearman or Pearson) from a highly textual and contextual dataset has multiple obvious shortcomings; accordingly, we decided to follow the ladder of causality [13] and aim at identifying the cause-effect of laws and MoIs.

2 Methods

This section introduces the methods that constitute the contributed policy pipeline, including NLP, Knn, attributions, and neural networks.

2.1 Deep Learning for Legal Analysis

Policy generations in general deals with sparse input of data. To be able to realize an effective mapping of laws to MoI, we're limited by not just the sparsity of data, but also their amount. The lack of data makes training deep networks a sub-optimal approach due to their over-parameterized nature and tendency to memorize patterns throughout the data. To prevent this, we can encode some latent information not directly available to the model such as how individual laws are connected to each other [2]. After cleaning the data, a *Knn* model is applied to the laws to enable the labeling of laws by similarity of their multiple descriptors (technological and environmental). For instance, for our main technology variable, *broadband levels in a state*, we measure the change in it relevant to the change in environmental/economic descriptors, however, that only shows a linear correlation between the two, therefore, a measure like attribution is critical to calculating the direct effect of a law and an environmental descriptor on the state (pipeline illustrated in Fig. 2). We explore four kinds of gradient based attribution calculations within deep learning [12]:

1. Input*Gradient: this method was at first proposed as a technique to improve the sharpness of attribution maps. Attribution is computed by extracting the (signed) partial derivatives of the output with respect to the input and multiplying them with the input itself.
2. Integrated Gradients: this method measures the mean derivative of each feature between input and output. It computes the partial derivatives of the output with respect to each input feature. However, while Gradient*Input computes a single derivative, evaluated at the provided input x, Integrated Gradients computes the *average* x gradient while the input varies along a linear path from a baseline to x. The baseline is often set to be zero.
3. DeepLIFT: DeepLIFT approximates the outcome from Integrated Gradients and quantifies it in a single step by replacing the gradient at each non-linearity with its average gradient. DeepLIFT is most often a good approximation of Integrated Gradients. This holds for various tasks, especially when employing simple models. However, DeepLIFT diverges from Integrated Gradients and fails to produce meaningful results when applied to Recurrent Neural Networks (RNNs) with multiplicative interactions.
4. Layer-wise Propagation/Conductance [14]: this method is computed with a backward pass on the network. The overall idea is to see what layer conducts the highest pixel-wise decomposition; i.e. to understand the contribution of a single pixel of an image x to the prediction $f(x)$ made by a classifier f. The algorithm starts at the output layer and assigns the relevance of the target neuron = the output of the neuron itself, and the relevance of all other neurons to zero.

All four measures provide a better indicator (*sensitivity*) to attribution than the standard perturbation methods or back propagation indicators within deep learning.

2.2 NLP for Law

Public policies and laws in technology are often deemed to be lagging behind technological advancement [1]. In the wake of a global pandemic, policy making has been scrutinized and public trust in opinion-based policy making has been diminished. It is more important than ever to begin integrating intelligent systems into the policy evaluation and advocacy process. Evidence-based approaches facilitate policy making in a manner that is more relative to the scientific method, beginning with initial hypotheses and evaluating them based on experimentation. On the contrary, opinion-based policy making is typically based on a limited and selective use of evidence or untested views of individuals or groups, based on ideology, prejudice, or speculative conjecture [1,9], and [10]. Within AI, NLP specifically stands out given that all laws and policies are presented in a textual format. In our work, we experimented with two very prominent NLP approaches: Term Frequency-Inverse Document Frequency (TF-IDF) and Global Vectors for Word Representation (GloVe). Additionally, we considered using Bidirectional Encoder Representations from Transformers (BERT)

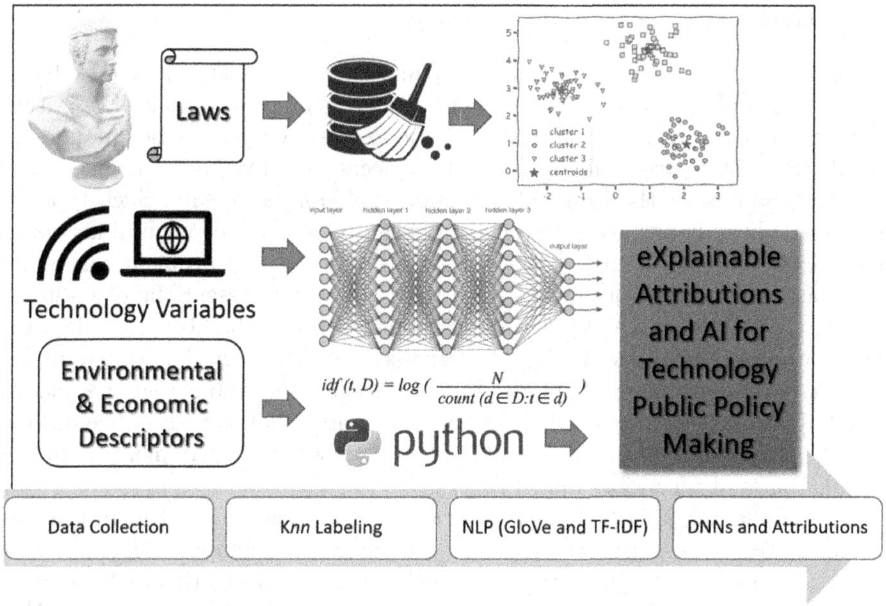

Fig. 2. The proposed technology policy pipeline

[15]; however, given its bi-directional nature, it was deemed not appropriate for the problem at hand. Although BERT might yield better accuracy scores, the nature of law codes' text is different than that of social media or other forms that might carry higher variability and less structure. TF-IDF [16] is an information retrieval technique that weighs a term's frequency (TF) and its inverse document frequency (IDF). Each word or term that occurs in the text has its respective TF and IDF scores. The product of the TF and IDF scores of a term is called the TF-IDF weight of that term. For a term t in document d, the weight $Wt.d$ of term t in document d is given by:

$$Wt.d = TFt.d * log(N/DFt) \tag{1}$$

where: $TFt.d$ is the number of occurrences of t in document d; DFt is the number of documents containing the term t; and N is the total number of documents in the corpus.

The second NLP model, GloVe [17], is an unsupervised learning algorithm for obtaining vector representations of text. Training is performed on aggregated global word-word co-occurrence statistics from a text corpus, and the results illustrate linear substructures and patterns of the word vector space. GloVe is trained on the non-zero entries of a global word-word co-occurrence matrix, which tabulates how frequently words co-occur with one another in a corpus. Generating this matrix requires a single-pass through the entire corpus. The tools provided in the GloVe Python package automate the collection and preparation of co-occurrence statistics for input into the model, which is what we used in this study.

2.3 Attribution Networks for Policy

We have formulated the problem of explainability of policies as a task based end-to-end problem. The overall objective is to be able to 'explain' the critical features in determining changes in MoIs associated with a particular law. To enable that notion, we assume that we have access to a fixed network-like model that well represents the range of possibilities a MoI can create. Such types of expressive, heavily-parameterized networks can be seen in deep neural networks. Thus, explainability is elicited as a local and a global task problem, where the local task is generating a model M_{local} that can well represent the distribution of MoI for a given policy X_i^{law} and the global task is to be able to explain the most important features of M_{local} in representing MoI [12]. The policy maker doesn't particularly care about the local task since their objectives are mostly situated around global tasks. It is important to note that some sacrifice in local model performance M_{local} is acceptable in cases where it maximally improves the outcomes of the global model M_{global}.

Fundamentally, this concept is in practice in regularization. But in the case of our study, we need the result of M_{local} to be able to compute M_{global}, which is computed through a recently developed technique of algorithms focused on understanding contributions of individual neurons and input features of a DNN [12], namely: attributions. Attributions are a way of determining if given some prediction $y \in Y$ and associated input $x \in X$, *what nodes were most responsible for making that prediction?* This can be thought of as a measure of suppression and incitement of individual nodes of a network where a suppressing node should indicate that it had a *negative* effect on a particular prediction while an incited node illustrates "responsibility" for making a particular prediction. Incitement and suppression are a way of measuring what nodes are being activated through one forward and backward pass of M_{local}, as the corresponding output is captured by some model M_{global}. This can be formulated as a task-learning explainability problem:

$$M_{global} = argmax_{m \in \{M_{local}\}} Attribute(m) \quad (2)$$

Accordingly, as we aim to maximise M_{global}. The goal of this study is to identify the most prevalent MoIs across the technology policy spectrum with a maximized M_{global}, and to allocate the most suitable NLP model for policy evaluations and decision support within the defined domain.

2.4 Measuring Similarity Using Nearest Neighbors

All data are wrangled, cleaned, and merged using date and by state, the state code data has the direct wording of each law. Such legal information is rich with keywords and policy motivations, which would be a significant challenge for NLP to make *direct* steady inferences from, so we chose to first apply Knn to identify laws that have similar "language" or legal reasoning. An approach to abstracting the *text data* into a *numeric feature* that could be used as an input to the model is critical to quantifying the laws and deriving AI-driven results and recommendations. Using Knn, inhibitory laws are assigned a 0, excitatory laws are assigned a 1, and laws that don't have a label are assigned a −1 (i.e. not enough information to classify). The Knn method leverages *Euclidean Distance* (*ED*) as the main measure of distance between the laws:

$$ED = Sqrt(\sum_{i=0}^{n}(x1_i - x2_i)^2) \tag{3}$$

Multiple data cluster sizes are deployed, $k = 1$, $k = 4$, $k = 20$, and $k = 100$, given the high number of rules, data variables, laws, environmental descriptors, the model performed best at $k = 20$, therefore, we captured the Knn outputs at $k = 20$ (results are as shown in Fig. 3) and inputted that to the neural network (as shown in Fig. 2). Larger versions of the figures are available on the project's GitHub page: https://github.com/AI-VTRC/AIassurance.

3 Experimental Work

Three forms of data are collected, (1) Legislative data, (2) Technology data, and (3) Environmental and Economic descriptors data. The legislative data are collected from The Pew Trusts site [18]. The data downloaded include the header, the code title, the year the code was enacted, the respective state, the state code, and summaries written by legal scholars. In order to make the system as reproducible as possible, the summaries were excluded from the data. Technology data are collected to identify how citizens use technology across the country. The purpose of using this information is to understand trends in American technology, how technology trends change over time, and how people use technology differently in different parts of the country. We collected data on computer use counts, laptop use counts, number of civilians with a tablet, number of civilians with a smart watch, internet hours at home and at work, internet use by age and gender, as well as internet applications data such as email, blogs, social networks, streaming, and other technology measures - we collected a sum of 50 technology MoIs. Merged with the legislative data, our goal was to develop a big data set that can represent the overall status of the technological and legal context in the country, but we didn't stop there, the challenge of dark data started looming as we explored the data, and we thought that maybe other variables (non-technological) have a stronger attribution or causation to the policies that ought to be crafted, and for that, we collected multiple environmental descriptors. Environmental and economic descriptors present a way to enrich the physical location and technological information encoded in the data. By adding numeric features that describe the environment, -hence the name environmental descriptors- the model can learn more than just obvious legislative or state data. When dealing with technology such as broadband, for example, an important consideration to lawmakers would be the size of a state. The policies that work for a state like Delaware wouldn't have the same impact on states such as Texas or Montana, simply because there are very different considerations for that technology in bigger states with lower population densities and more mountainous terrain for instance. State funds and federal funds of technology research was one environmental descriptor that we chose to also collect because the amount of funding a state has for technology research and development from the government likely differentiates states that have good infrastructure from those that don't. We did an exhaustive search for all relevant descriptors, a list of descriptors (MoIs) included in the study is as follows: state population, amount of funding for state government, federal state funding, total funding (sum of federal and state), per capita funding, monthly unemployment rate, median household income, GDP, percent Of 4-Year-olds enrolled in state funded pre-k, percent of 25 years and over who have completed high school/bachelors/graduate school, number of state traffic fatalities per month, total renewable energy net generation (thousand kilowatt-hours), violent crime rate per 100,000 population, degree granting higher education institutions, alternative fuel vehicles in use, state/federal intergovernmental expenditures, debt, and revenue: total (in thousands of dollars), and top 1 percent income share across every state. The results of the pipeline and its evaluations are presented in the next section.

4 Results and Policy Discussions

This section presents the outcomes of the proposed pipeline. Although TF-IDF is an easy-to-understand method, the complexity of GloVe is evidently needed to capture the high variance in the laws and their associated descriptors. Accordingly, GloVe had a superior performance when compared with TF-IDF in labeling the laws and assigning them as inhibitory or excitatory; much less laws through GloVe were assigned not classified (-1). Knn and both NLP models' outcomes are inputted to the neural network.

The neural network model is executed twice, once with GloVe and another with TF-IDF, the results of the four different attributions are shown in Figs. 4 (TF-IDF) and 5 (GloVe). GloVe classifications with Knn are more suited to providing higher attributions, while TF-IDF provided more variance in the attributions of the laws. Across both models, as the figures show, Layer Conductance provided higher attribution scores for most variables, while Input*Gradient and Integrated Gradients performed in a similar manner to each other in both cases. The outcomes of GloVe are applied to state-level policies, Table 1 shows the

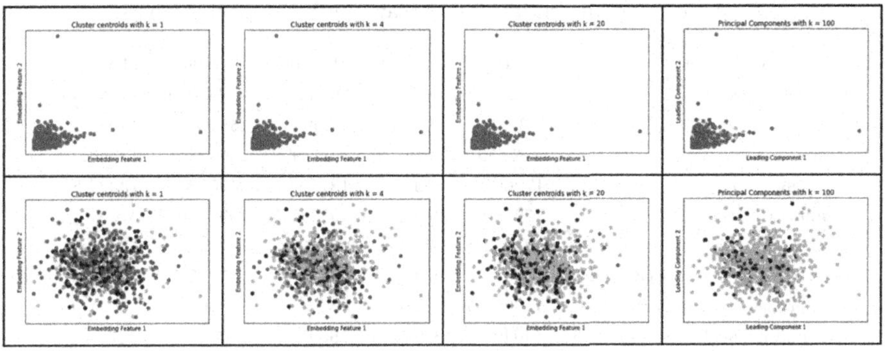

Fig. 3. Knn Clustering of TF-IDF (row 1) vs. GloVe (row 2)

differential effects of five example laws on the environmental descriptors, the comparison is between years before the law was enacted, and years after the law was enacted; the change in values as processed by the pipeline are generated in thousands, positive numbers indicate a positive impact of the law based on what was intended by its passing, vs. a negative impact, while some variables had 0 or a N/A due to missing data or the inability of the model to classify that data point. For instance, one can observe that desktop/tablet/TV use rates are heavily influenced by the policies, whether a policy drives a reduction or an increase however differentiates between states and laws. One can also observe that some MoIs are effected by a law in one state and not in another, the number of satellite users is an example; i.e. heavily effected in VA and not effected in AR. Lastly, some MoIs don't have an attribution value with the enacted law, such as the number of users selling online goods in states like CA and ME.

The overall loss for the model is *0.0036* and the best number of training epochs to reach the outcome = *58*. Five state laws (Table 1) are presented as examples to illustrate the outcomes of the pipeline:

- Maine Rev. (35-A) State §9204-A: Duties of authority [19]
- California Gov. Code §14051: Activities [20]
- Arkansas Code §25-4-125: State broadband manager [21]
- Virginia Code §56-484.31: Attachment of small cell facilities on government-owned structures [22]
- Minnesota State §237.761: Alternative regulation plan; service [23]

For full statutes text, refer to [19–22], and [23].

Table 1. The differential effect of laws on MoIs for five states

Metric of interest	VA code	AR code	MN code	CA code	ME code
desktop_use	−99325.5	23349	79003.5	−1061039	4473.5
laptop_use	−3837	20593.5	−49944	155193	19796.5
tablet_use	−86159	26183.5	−94190.5	286488.5	15446.5
mobile_use	170606	81951	121362.5	2405237.5	73324.5
smartTV_use	169680	96958	198518.5	1603350.5	57054
wearable_use	281462.5	52381.5	97349	1024740	42402.5
internet_Users_above3Years	73048.5	92306	52378.5	637618.5	36374
internetUsers_above15Years	116094.5	92180	83904.5	603508.5	32071
homeInternetUsers	14649	97046.5	78697.5	899716.5	38700.5
workInternetUsers	196614.5	59814	79541.5	416734.5	23265
schoolInternetUsers	−15459	4006.5	12980.5	77529.5	4449.5
cafeInternetUsers	35731.5	46360	6583.5	7767.5	−18469
alternativeHomeInternetUsers	421953.5	36872.5	61572	-78804	3715.5
travelInternetUsers	204247	138220	13431.5	1668491.5	31614
publicInternetUsers	118581.5	41979.5	−81240.5	−217151.5	−31681.5
anyHomeInternetUsers	149695.5	57579.5	53282.5	130091	7712.5
internetAtHome	138017	62173.5	60430	264719	16426
noInternetAtHome	12598	−36236	−42293.5	−302557	−22310.5
homeEverOnline	−15865.5	−2785.5	−150.5	−105185.5	−6756
noNeedInternet	3675.5	−28429	−17956	−99298.5	−6934.5
noExpensiveInternet	−13156	1937.5	−28506.5	−166029	−9296.5
noComputerInternet	−980.5	−4556.5	−4904.5	−18545	−1076.5
noPrivateSectorInternet	2219.5	3082.5	0	16173.5	−1698.5
useInternetElsewhere	8189.5	1283.5	3434.5	−29588	−1400.5
unavailableInternet	17395.5	−3493	-5703	−24972.5	2535.5
mobileDataUsers	249634.5	76423.5	55843.5	297460.5	12093
wiredHighSpeedUsers	65883	50448.5	44682.5	804949.5	22567.5
satelliteUsers	18894	63	−19959.5	62623	2929
dialUpUsers	−7501.5	-3201.5	−4243.5	−13990.5	−2345.5
internetPrivateISP	93895.5	61785.5	34471.5	328519.5	17390.5
internetPublicISP	19353.5	−5222.5	5559	−89602	−1273
internetIncluded	173	−1328.5	12103.5	−60919	−1987.5
internetPublicFree	2017.5	−376.5	−5025.5	−58816	−474.5
emailUsers	198097	100576	87540	485308	21772
textIMUsers	300326	121088.5	137552.5	919272	38262
socialNetUsers	115804	72491.5	111240	912497	37362
publishUsers	7731.5	30335.5	−123353	—	—
onlineConferenceUsers	149012	97078	28777	1158742.5	50934.5
videoUsers	273268.5	111730.5	233313	638598	32866.5
teleworkUsers	206729.5	39985.5	40179	122642	11529
jobSearchUsers	−23028.5	32867.5	44330.5	−658953.5	−30821.5
onlineClassUsers	196571.5	20823	−19199.5	−313777.5	−1937.5
financeUsers	302077.5	84563.5	183449	432568	55407
eCommerceUsers	286875	86705.5	93545	224439.5	39579.5
sellingGoodsUsers	67787	11497	4862.5	—	—
iotUsers	150353	59856	146997.5	620224	18151.5

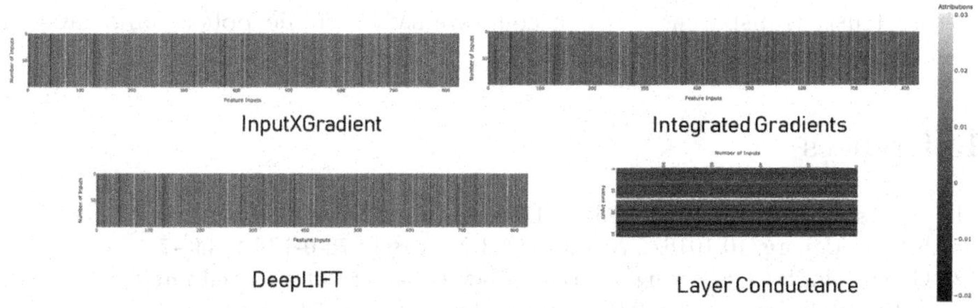

Fig. 4. TF-IDF attributions results

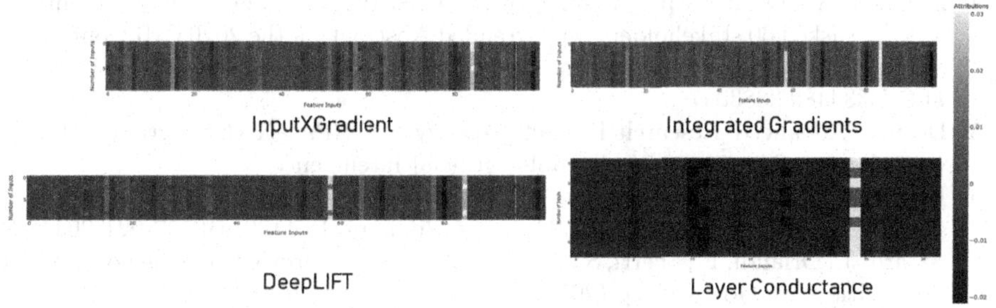

Fig. 5. GloVe attributions results

5 Conclusion

As it is illustrated, the difference between the five laws, variance amongst states' technological spectra, and the multiple contextual MoIs lead to a very high variability in the results of our model; which clearly leads to different effects on crafting these laws by state. A different challenge would be to claim whether a policy is "good" or "bad", accordingly, we decided to avoid such binary conclusions. Classifying good/bad policies requires further analysis such as studying causal effects and collecting more data. Generalization of AI results depends on the level of data abstraction, more abstraction creates more spurious representations. However, in some cases, simpler models (such as the neural network deployed) may do the trick equally well, if not better in some cases. Our pipeline nonetheless, is where the strength of the proposed approach lies, it allows for the consumption of 50+ variables, analyzes text, and enables the optimized results mentioned. This manuscript aims to provide a guideline for other domain-specific datasets, and as this work could be expanded to more MoIs, more laws, and could be tested with more AI models, we believe that the quantified manner that our pipeline can present laws in can majorly help policy makers avoid dark data issues, detect blind spots, understand related attributions and causal relations of policies on their communities, and craft more evidence-based policies; a notion that is critically needed (especially in this age of many black swan events) to restore trust, transparency, and accountability in public policies and laws in America and all around the world.

References

1. Batarseh, F.A., Yang, R.: Federal Data Science. Elsevier's Academic Press (2018). https://doi.org/10.1016/C2016-0-03293-X. ISBN 978-0-12-812443-7
2. Greenstein, S.: Preserving the rule of law in the era of artificial intelligence (AI). Artif. Intell. Law 1–33 (2021). https://doi.org/10.1007/s10506-021-09294-4
3. Schintler, L.A., McNeely, C.L. (eds.): Encyclopedia of Big Data (2021). ISBN 978-3-319-32009-0
4. Brennen, A.: What do people really want when they say they want "explainable AI?" We asked 60 stakeholders. In: Extended Abstracts of the 2020 CHI Conference on Human Factors in Computing Systems, pp. 1–7 (2020). https://doi.org/10.1145/3334480.3383047
5. Defense Advanced Research Projects Agency (DARPA) XAI Program. https://www.darpa.mil/program/explainable-artificial-intelligence
6. Batarseh, F.A., Freeman, L., Huang, C.-H.: A survey on artificial intelligence assurance. J. Big Data **8**(1), 1–30 (2021). https://doi.org/10.1186/s40537-021-00445-7
7. Attard, J., Orlandi, F., Scerri, S., Auer, S.: A systematic review of open government data initiatives. Gov. Inf. Q. (2015)
8. Batarseh, F., Yang, R., Deng, L.: A comprehensive model for management and validation of federal big data analytical systems. J. Big Data Anal. (2017). https://doi.org/10.1186/s41044-016-0017
9. Kim, H., Trimi, S., Chung, J.: Big data applications in the government sector. Commun. ACM **57**(3) (2014). https://doi.org/10.1145/2500873
10. Al-Qaheri, H., Banerjee, S.: Design and implementation of a *policy recommender system* towards social innovation: an experience with *hybrid machine learning*. In: Abraham, A., Jiang, X.H., Snášel, V., Pan, J.-S. (eds.) Intelligent Data Analysis and Applications. AISC, vol. 370, pp. 237–250. Springer, Cham (2015). https://doi.org/10.1007/978-3-319-21206-7_21
11. Zinkevich, M., Weimer, M., Li, L., Smola, A.: Parallelized stochastic gradient descent. In: Advances in Neural Information Processing Systems 23 (NIPS) (2010)
12. Oztireli, A.C., Ancona, M., Ceolini, E., Gross, M.: Towards better understanding of gradient-based attribution methods for deep neural networks. In: Proceedings of ICLR 2018. https://doi.org/10.17863/CAM.47233
13. Pearl, J., Mackenzie, D.: The Book of Why. Penguin Books, Harlow (2019). 9780141982410
14. Bach, S., Binder, A., Montavon, G., Klauschen, F., Müller, K.-R., Samek, W.: On pixel-wise explanations for non-linear classifier decisions by layer-wise relevance propagation. PLoS ONE **10**(7), e0130140 (2015). https://doi.org/10.1371/journal.pone.0130140
15. Devlin, J., Chang, M., Lee, K., Toutanova, K.: BERT: Pre-training of Deep Bidirectional Transformers for Language Understanding. arXiv:1810.04805
16. Sammut, C., Webb, G.I.: TF–IDF. In: Sammut, C., Webb, G.I. (eds.) Encyclopedia of Machine Learning, pp. 986–987. Springer, Boston (2011). https://doi.org/10.1007/978-0-387-30164-8_832
17. Pennington, J., Socher, R., Manning, C: GloVe: Global Vectors for Word Representation (2014). https://nlp.stanford.edu/projects/glove/

18. Pew Research Center. https://www.pewtrusts.org/en/
19. Maine State Code §9204: Chapter 93: Advaned Technology Infrastructure. https://legislature.maine.gov/statutes/35-A/title35-Asec9204-A.html
20. California State Code §14051. https://law.justia.com/codes/california/2020/code-gov/title-2/division-3/part-5/chapter-1/article-3/section-14051/
21. Arkansas State Code §25-4-125: Title 25, State Government Chapter 4, Department of Information Systems. www.arkansas.gov/dis/newsroom/index.php
22. Virginia State Code §56-484.31: Attachment of small cell facilities on government-owned structures. Powers of Commission not restricted; rules and regulations. https://law.lis.virginia.gov/vacode/title56/chapter15.1/section56-484.31/
23. Minnesota State Code §237.773: Minnesota Statutes Telecommunications (Ch. 237, 238). https://www.revisor.mn.gov/statutes/cite/237

A Comparative Study of AI Search Methods for Personalised Cancer Therapy Synthesis in COPASI

Marco Esposito(✉) and Leonardo Picchiami

Computer Science Department, Sapienza University of Rome,
via Salaria 113, 00198 Rome, Italy
{esposito,picchiami}@di.uniroma1.it

Abstract. In recent years, optimisation methods in precision medicine have gained much attention thanks to their ability to tackle relevant problems arising from clinical practice effectively. One of the most compelling challenges in this area is designing computational methods for personalising pharmacological treatments, especially for high-impact diseases, due to the large potential impact on the whole healthcare field. In this work, we address the problem of computing safe and effective personalised therapies for Colorectal Cancer (CRC), one of the deadliest forms of tumour for adult humans. We exploit a recent System Biology Markup Language (SBML) mechanistic model of the tumour growth and of the immune response to two drugs and define a simulation-based, non-linear, constrained optimisation problem for automatically synthesising personalised therapies for any given virtual patient. We present a methodology, proposed in our earlier work, that uses a single tool, namely `COPASI`, to define and solve the optimisation problem. We extend our previous experimental evaluation of the approach by comparing all optimisation algorithms provided by `COPASI` and performing an in-depth analysis of the results, which provides new and practical insights on the ability of the different algorithms to solve the problem.

1 Introduction

The rapid scientific and technological recent advances in Artificial Intelligence (AI) has seen in medicine a dominant field of application. On the one hand, the growing availability of quantitative models of the human patho-physiology, which are gradually obtaining certification from authorities (such as FDA, EMA, see *e.g.*, [15,69]) as they become more and more accurate, inspires an increasing number of applications of computational techniques in the healthcare field. On the other hand, novel computational methods, known under the term Silico Clinical Trials (ISCTs), exploit intelligent simulation-based optimisation techniques to enable precision medicine, making it possible, *e.g.*, to design personalised pharmacological therapies and assess their safety and efficacy. ISCTs make use of Virtual Patients (VPs), which are typically derived by parametrising Virtual

S. Bandini et al. (Eds.): AIxIA 2021, LNAI 13196, pp. 638–654, 2022.
https://doi.org/10.1007/978-3-031-08421-8_44

Physiological Human (VPH) models [63], which in turn capture the Pharmaco-Kinetics/Dynamics (PKPD), *i.e.*, the absorption of drugs and their interaction with the patient's organism, and are designed to consider physiological differences that occur from one person to the other and induce different evolution of the disease and response to drugs.

From a formal point of view, VPH can be seen as *hybrid systems*, where systems of parametric Ordinary Differential Equations (ODEs) describe the dynamics of biological quantities, state and time events capture discrete dynamics, and parameters encode the inter-patient variability. Among the various modelling languages in which VPH models are defined and distributed, System Biology Markup Language (SBML) [21], an XML-based open-standard language, is the most widespread (see, *e.g.*, the BioModels database [28]).

`COPASI` [29] is one of the several existing tools for the design and analysis of SBML models and one of the most complete. It supports several tasks, ranging from the modelling and simulation of biological processes to parameter optimisation and estimation. `COPASI` is open-source software and provides a graphical user interface and Application Program Interfaces (APIs) for several programming languages.

1.1 Motivation

Pharmacological therapies, especially for high-impact and chronic diseases, are generally considerably expensive and toxic. Thanks to the use of ISCTs, we can simulate the effects of a large number of candidate therapies without the risks and costs of *in vivo* experiments on human patients, with the goal of finding the best one for each individual. Given a VPH model and a particular VP, the task of computing a personalised pharmacological therapy that maximises the efficacy of the treatment and its safety is a hard one. It is often the case, in fact, that high dosing regimens have high chances of yielding effective therapies, but provide low safety due to drug toxicity. Furthermore, the number of all possible therapies of interest is generally enormous, growing combinatorially in the number of drugs and the duration of the treatment. Naïve approaches to the modelling of the problem and the search for the best personalised therapy fail to explore such space effectively and within time bounds compatible with clinical practice. Given the complexity of the task, it is unclear what search strategy is the most promising, even if considering a particular VPH model or a single VP. Generally, the search space is highly constrained, and the objectives are conflicting and strongly non-linear.

1.2 Contribution

In this paper, we extend [13,14] by providing a fully formal definition of the optimisation problem and performing an in-depth experimental evaluation on the performance of optimisation methods included in `COPASI`, considering all available algorithms and providing new quantitative analyses and insights. We make use of a large population of VPs generated along the lines of [32], and design, within the Colorectal Cancer (CRC) model, a parametric Therapy Template Model (TTM) that describes therapies of interest as well as safety constraints over them. This methodology enables the integration of the whole modelling and optimisation workflow within a single tool, `COPASI`, and the use of several search algorithms to find the optimal personalised therapy for any given VP.

1.3 Paper Outline

The paper is organised as follows. In Sect. 2 we recall the state of the art on ISCTs, optimisation and parameter estimation for VPH models, Sect. 3 describes the CRC VPH model and in Sect. 4 we describe how we modelled the therapies to enable the parameter optimisation approach. Then, in Sect. 5 we formalise the optimisation problem and in Sect. 6 we present and discuss the results of the experimental comparison of all parameter optimisation algorithms implemented in `COPASI` when applied to our problem. Finally, in Sect. 7 we draw our conclusions.

2 State of the Art

A preliminary study for this work has been performed in [14]. In that work, the feasibility of the approach has been studied using a simpler therapy template model and a smaller number of algorithms. The problem of synthesising personalised therapies using VPH models has been approached with a variety of techniques, *e.g.*, reinforcement learning [22] and genetic and evolutionary algorithms [8,23,53,61]. A simulation-based backtracking algorithm has been proposed in [47,64] for the problem of computing an optimal personalised therapy for assisted reproduction (an area where therapeutic success depends on many factors hard to be manually taken under control [20,30,31]) on a patient *digital twin*, defined as the subset of the VPs of a complete population best matching (up to a used-defined error threshold) the human patient clinical data. One of the most studied problems in systems biology is the estimation of unknown model parameters to fit experimental data. [58,59,71,72] present several specialised optimisation algorithms for this task. Real-world case studies include [1,10,54,57]. Several tools are explicitly designed to solve parameter optimisation problems in systems biology; the most notable are AMICI [18], AMIGO2 [2], MEIGO [12], PESTO [67], Data2Dynamics [55], dMod [24], pyABC [25] and SBML2Julia [27]. Most of these use SBML and allow the definition of the optimisation problem via the PEtab [60] open standard. There exists a large number of SBML simulators. Among the most commonly used, besides `COPASI`, we mention BioUML [26] and LibRoadRunner [66]. SBML2Modelica [33] is a tool that focuses on the interoperability between systems biology and (hybrid) Cyber-Physical Systems (CPSs) domains by automatically translating SBML models to Modelica [17] and the FMI/FMU open standard. This enables the exploitation of well-established techniques for CPS optimisation and verification. For instance, it is possible to use backtracking optimisation algorithms [37] that exploit the efficient storing and retrieval of intermediate simulator states [65], as well as verification algorithms for systems also in presence of uncontrollable events (*e.g.*, [42–46,51]). The solution of large-scale optimisation problems via logic- [3], automata- [11] or constraint-based [56] formalisms (*e.g.*, [6,7,35,36,48] among others) has been largely studied in the literature, on several industry-relevant application domains (*e.g.*, [9,19,39,49,50,52] among others). However, when the problem model is a complex VPH model, such approaches cannot be applied, since the model cannot be accurately defined an it is only available as a simulable black-box. The problem of finding an optimal therapy can be stated as an optimal planning model in hybrid domains. In fact, the VPH models we considered are hybrid systems whose inputs are discrete event sequences [38,40]. Existing approaches to solve this problem [4,5,16,70] are not applicable in our setting, as symbolic methods fail to capture the complexity of large ODE-based VPH real-world models.

3 VPH Model of the Immune Response to Colorectal Cancer

The VPH model proposed in [32] describes the dynamics of the growth of CRC and the immune response of the patient's immune system. The model also includes the PKPD of two drugs, namely Atezolizumab and Cibisatamab, and the patient's response to their administration. The change of the tumour size over time, as well as the total amount of drugs administered, can be observed via simulation thanks to dedicated model variables.

As it is common for models of this kind, the dynamics of the tumour growth and the immune system's response to the drugs vary significantly from patient to patient. The CRC model presents 23 real-valued parameters, which jointly define the space of possible human patients. An assignment to those parameters represents a possible patient, and the evolution of their biological quantities can be computed by simulation.

However, as discussed in [41,68], not all assignments yield patients that are of interest and plausible. In this model, it may be the case that a particular assignment leads to a patient that does not develop a tumour or that shows dynamics that are incompatible with the laws of biology. We used the approach from [63] to compute a population of physiologically admissible VPs. We adopted the admissibility criteria from [32], *i.e.*, admissible patients must develop a tumour of a given size within 8000 days and have plausible dynamics.

We filtered out all VPs that showed no response to the two drugs among the whole virtual population. In this model, in fact, 85% of all admissible patients lack the biological characteristic to take advantage of immunotherapy. We excluded such patients because our ultimate goal is to assess the ability of optimisation algorithms to synthesise effective treatments and not to study the efficacy of the drugs over the whole population (as done in [32]). Including non-responding VPs in the population would significantly alter the results since no optimisation technique could ever find an effective therapy.

In our experiments, we considered 25 VPs sampled at random among responding VPs in the population.

Figure 1 shows the relative growth of the tumour in such VPs, without any drug administration. It can be observed that for all of them the condition gets progressively worse over time. The CRC model makes it possible to simulate any therapy over a given VP. However, safety constraints exist over therapies (defined thanks to clinical trials on human patients), which deal with the toxicity of the drugs. In particular, it is not safe to administer more than 24 mg/kg of Atezolizumab and 160 mg of Cibisatamab in a single dose or cumulatively within a certain period (four weeks for Atezolizumab and three weeks for Cibisatamab).

In general, any VP is simulated for 400 days from the day in which the tumour has reached the given threshold (one of the 23 parameters). Such a period is deemed long enough to verify whether patients respond positively to therapies or not.

Figure 1 shows the relative growth of the tumour diameter in the 25 VPs we used in our experiments when no therapy is administered. For all of them, the condition get worse and worse over time.

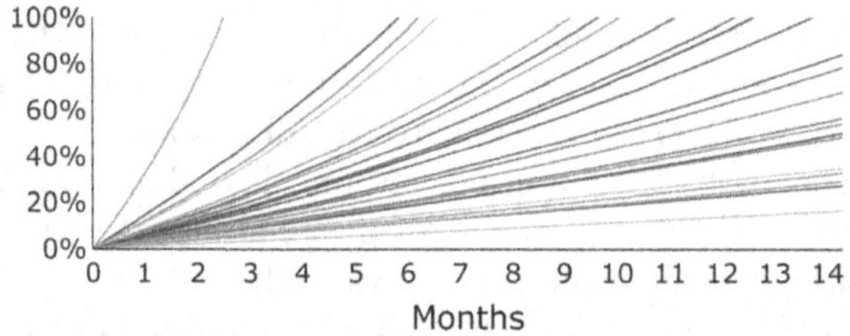

Fig. 1. Relative growth of tumour size in the 25 patients without therapy.

4 Modelling the Therapies

A therapy consists in a function mapping each time instant within a finite interval to the quantity of each drug administered at that time. Instead of considering every instant as a candidate for administration, we restrict the domain of such function to a finite set of instants, defined depending on the possible dosing regimens of the involving drugs. For example, in our case study, drugs are administered on a weekly basis. Indeed, although the admissible doses for a drug are, for obvious reasons, only a finite number, in order to enable the use of the off-the-shelf solver `COPASI`, which does not support discrete decision variables, we defined decision variables for doses as real values (within given bounds). This is not a limitation in practice, as we know, from background knowledge, that small differences in drug doses produce very similar, often indistinguishable, model behaviours. When an optimal therapy (with continuous dose values) is found, we round the quantity of drugs envisioned at each decision point to the closest discrete legal value and simulate the revised therapy once more to double check that performs similarly.

We define a TTM, *i.e.*, a parametric SBML model that represents the skeleton of all the therapies that are deemed of interest for our purposes. A desirable template model should meet a set of requirements.

Number of parameters. The number of parameters of the template must be as low as possible. The optimisation problem generally gets harder and harder as the parameter space gets larger since there may be a combinatorial explosion in the number of possible therapies.

Expressiveness. The template model should be able to represent the largest possible portion of the therapies that are of interest. Since the goal is to find the optimal therapy, the set of expressible therapies should include it.

Constraints and symmetries. The number of constraints that define the space of admissible therapies should be as low as possible. Ideally, any assignment of the parameters should encode a therapy that is safe and of interest. Moreover, it would be desirable not to have symmetries (see, *e.g.*, [34]), *i.e.*, different parameter assignments that correspond to the same actual therapy.

Regularity and Explainability. The therapies that the template model can express must be as regular as possible. Very irregular therapies (*e.g.*, doses changing drastically from week to week) may violate clinical guidelines and fail to obtain the physician's trust, which is crucial as the ultimate responsibility for the treatment lies on them.

Integration. The therapy template model must be described using the SBML language and integrated within the CRC model.

We designed a therapy template model that offers a good trade-off between all the requirements. We define 32 parameters: 30 of them, $(d_a^1, \ldots, d_a^{15}, d_c^1, \ldots, d_c^{15})$, are real-valued and define the doses of each drug that can be administered during each of the 15 4-week periods, while the remaining two, f_a and f_c, are integer numbers that define the minimum distance between administration of, respectively, Atezolizumab and Cibisatamab. For each drug x, the administered dose at week $k \in [1, 57]$, denoted by $\text{adm}_x(\tau, k)$, is equal to $d_x^m \times \text{a}(x, k)$, where $m = \lceil k/4 \rceil$ and $\text{a}(x, k)$ is 1 if $k \bmod f_x = 1$ and 0 otherwise.

Within this therapy template, we model the safety requirements about the maximum dose that can be administered in a single day as simple bound constraints (aka box constraints) over the 30 dose parameters.

The other two safety requirements, which limit the total quantity of drug administered within a certain period, can be conveniently modelled as non-linear constraints. Although COPASI supports the definition of non-linear constraints in the optimisation problem, they are only evaluated after the simulation and not symbolically. Hence, the most straightforward way to model them is as functional (*i.e.*, black-box) constraints as follows. Let τ be a therapy. We introduce two new variables in the model, denoted by $\text{safety}_a(\tau, t)$ and $\text{safety}_c(\tau, t)$, which, at time t, will hold 0 if the safety constraint over, respectively Atezolizumab and Cibisatamab is satisfied and a positive number otherwise.

We introduce an additional linear constraint enforcing the feasible therapies to administer at least one of the two drugs within the first week.

The proposed model has a relatively low number of parameters and expresses very regular, explainable, and credible therapies. In fact, the modelled therapies meet the current clinical guidelines, as the doses varies at most every 4 weeks.

We described this therapy template model using the SBML language and integrated it into the model. Therefore, the resulting VPH model has 55 parameters that can be governed: 23 of them define the VPs and the remaining 32 define the space of therapies.

Finally, we note that our template model is able to represent all therapies for CRC (involving Atezolizumab and Cibisatamab) that have been tested in past clinical trials and that are summarised in [32].

5 Optimisation

Given a VP λ in the set of all possible VPs $\Lambda \subseteq \mathbf{R}^{23}$, let t_0 be the starting time of therapies for λ, $H = t_0 + 400$ be the time horizon of the therapies for λ, and $\mathrm{T} = \mathbf{R}^{30} \times \mathbf{N}^2$ be the space of the TTM parameters. We want to compute a therapy τ which is optimal under two conflicting objectives: maximising the efficacy and minimising the total quantity of administered drugs. We first define the *ineff* Key Performance Indicator (KPI), a measure of the *inefficacy* of a therapy τ, as

$$\text{ineff}\,(\lambda, \tau, H) = \frac{\text{tumoursize}\,(\lambda, \tau, H)^2}{\text{tumoursize}\,(\lambda, \tau, t_0)},$$

where $\text{tumoursize}\,(\lambda, \tau, t)$ is a model variable that holds the diameter of the tumour (in millimetres) at any time t during the simulation. The square at the numerator is a heuristic way to strongly penalise (*i.e.*, to assign much higher inefficacy values to) therapies which fail to bring the tumour to a sufficiently small size within the horizon.

We now define a measure of the quantity of drugs that is administered with therapy τ. Thanks to the safety constraints on each drug, we know the maximum total amounts of each drug that can be administered while still keeping the therapy safe. Let Max_a and Max_c be such values. We define

$$\text{totdrugs}\,(\tau, H) = \left(\frac{1}{2} \times \frac{\text{total}_a\,(\tau, H)}{\text{Max}_a} + \frac{1}{2} \times \frac{\text{total}_c\,(\tau, H)}{\text{Max}_c}\right)$$

where $\text{total}_a\,(\tau, t)$ and $\text{total}_c\,(\tau, t)$ are model variables that hold the total quantity of, respectively, Atezolizumab and Cibisatamab administered up to time t with therapy τ.

Given the maximum single-day doses μ_a and μ_c, we can now define the personalised therapy synthesis problem over therapies $\tau = \left(\{d_a\}_1^{15}, \{d_c\}_1^{15}, f_a, f_c\right) \in \mathrm{T}$ as

$$
\begin{aligned}
\tau^* = \quad & \underset{\tau=\left(\{d_a\}_1^{15},\{d_c\}_1^{15},f_a,f_c\right)\in \mathrm{T}}{\operatorname{argmin}} \quad \alpha \times \operatorname{ineff}(\lambda,\tau,H) + \beta \times \operatorname{totdrugs}(\tau,H) && (1)\\
& \text{subject to} \\
& 0 \le d_a^i \le \mu_a \qquad \forall\, i \in [1,15] && (2)\\
& 0 \le d_c^i \le \mu_c \qquad \forall\, i \in [1,15] && (3)\\
& 1 \le f_a \le 6 && (4)\\
& 1 \le f_c \le 6 && (5)\\
& \operatorname{safety}_a(\tau,H) = 0 && (6)\\
& \operatorname{safety}_c(\tau,H) = 0 && (7)\\
& d_a^1 + d_c^1 > 0 && (8)
\end{aligned}
$$

where α, β are strictly positive real numbers, constraints (2) to (5) model the bounds over the parameter values, (6) and (7) model the safety constraints over drug administrations, and constraint (8) ensures that at least one of the two drugs is administered in the first week. In fact, regardless of the frequency of administration of drug x, if d_x^1 is > 0, the therapy administers a dose equal to d_x^1 at day 1.

5.1 Optimisation Algorithms

We consider all optimisation algorithm implemented in COPASI. We exclude from the experimental comparison those algorithms that, in preliminary experiments failed, on all 25 VPs, to compute a therapy with better objective value than the reference therapy from [32]. Such algorithms are pure gradient-descent methods like Levenberg-Marquardt and Truncated Newton. We can explain their failure in this particular problem by observing that our objective function is highly non-linear and the space is constrained. Not being able to escape from local minima and unfeasible regions is likely to make the problem too hard for such algorithms. The remaining algorithms are:

1. Random Search
2. Praxis
3. Steepest Descent
4. Nelder Mead
5. Evolutionary Strategy SR
6. Evolutionary Programming
7. Scatter Search
8. Genetic Algorithm
9. Differential Evolution
10. Particle Swarm Optimisation
11. Hooke & Jeeves

The details and features of each algorithm can be found at http://copasi.org/Support/User_Manual/Methods/Optimization_Methods/.

6 Results

This section shows the outcome of the execution of all search algorithms over the 25 VPs. In order to mimic a real clinical setting, we assigned to each experiment a time budget of 1 h. All experiments were run on two identical machines equipped with Intel (R) Xeon (R) 8-core CPU E5430 and 32 GB RAM. As for the choice of values for the hyperparameters of each algorithm, we applied three criteria uniformly: (1) the minimum objective value improvement for convergence was set to 0.1 for all algorithms that support it; (2) for all population-based algorithms the population size was set to 64 (double the number of parameters, a typical choice); (3) for genetic and evolutionary algorithm the number of generations was set to 25 (in order to guarantee convergence within 1 h). For each algorithm, we run the optimisation using the reference therapy described in [32] as the starting point. Such therapy administers the maximum allowed doses of both drugs. Since the total amount of drugs is much easier to minimise than the inefficacy of the therapy, we set the α and β coefficient of the objective function (1) (Sect. 5) to, respectively, 0.9 and 10. We found, via preliminary experiments, that such values provide the proper balance between the two KPIs. Figure 2 shows the mean objective value over all VPs for all algorithms. The plot highlights the contribution of each KPI to the objective value. We note that Praxis, Steepest Descent and Nelder Mead perform sensibly worse than Random Search, which we treat as a baseline.

Figure 3a and 3b provide different perspectives on the optimisation results, focusing on one KPI each. In Fig. 3a we compared the average relative variation of the tumour diameter over 400 days with the reference therapy and with each algorithm. On average, the tumour diameter increases by 1.2% with the reference therapy, while generally decreases with the optimised therapies. Most population-based algorithms manage to compute therapies which systematically reduce the tumour size, while Hooke & Jeeves achieves the best results, producing a therapy that reduces the tumour diameter by 25.8% on average. Figure 3b shows the average savings in terms of total drug amounts achieved by the optimised therapies with respect to the reference therapy. The optimised therapies computed by our baseline algorithm, Random Search, already achieves a mean reduction of 72% of the amount of administered drugs, while all the therapies computed with Scatter Search and Hooke & Jeeves use less than 3% of the amount of drugs used by the reference therapy. The poor performance of the Nelder-Mead, Praxis and Steepest Descent algorithms may be explained by the naïve handling of the bound and functional constraints. In fact, these algorithms were not designed to work in constrained space and the `COPASI` implementation does not employ sophisticated strategies to apply whenever constraints are found to be violated.

Figure 4 shows the three algorithm that were able to compute the best therapy for at least one VPs. For each algorithm, the figure shows the number of virtual patients for which it computed the best personalised therapy. Hooke & Jeeves computes the best therapy (according to the objective function) for 22 out of 25 VPs. This implies that such algorithm always dominates all the others (see Fig. 2).

Figure 5 shows the Response Evaluation Criteria in Solid Tumors (RECIST) classification of the VPs with the reference therapy and with the optimal ther-

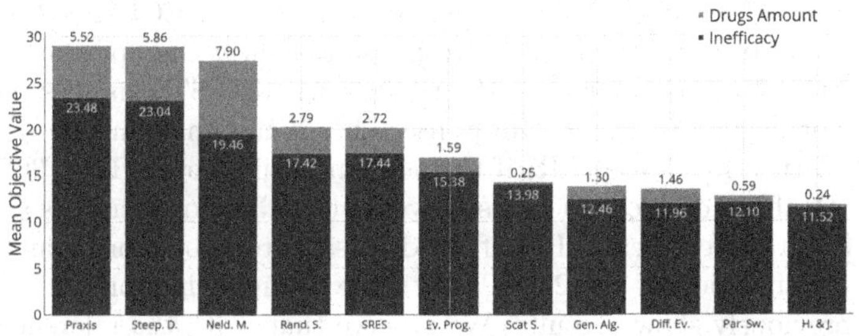

Fig. 2. Objective value and relative KPIs values for all algorithms, averaged over all VPs.

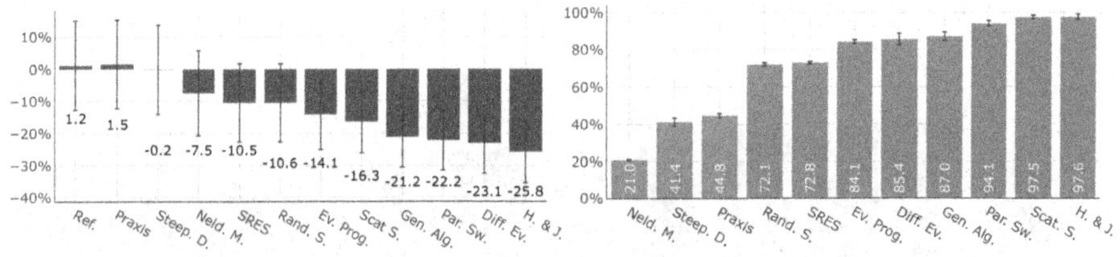

(a) Relative variation of tumour diameter.

(b) Mean amount of drugs saved.

Fig. 3. Tumour size reduction and drugs saving with optimised therapies.

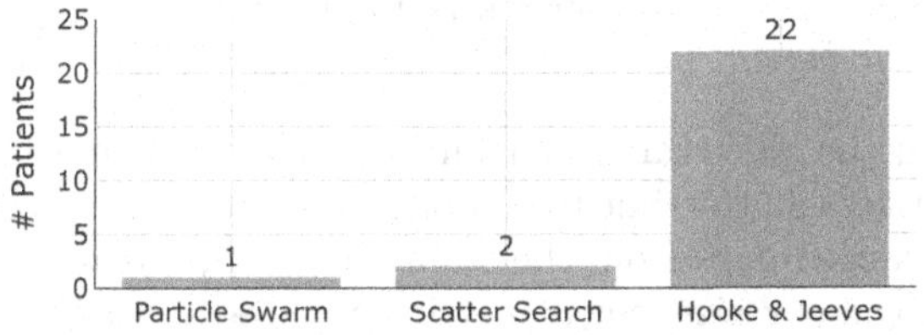

Fig. 4. Algorithms ranking by number of best-treated VPs.

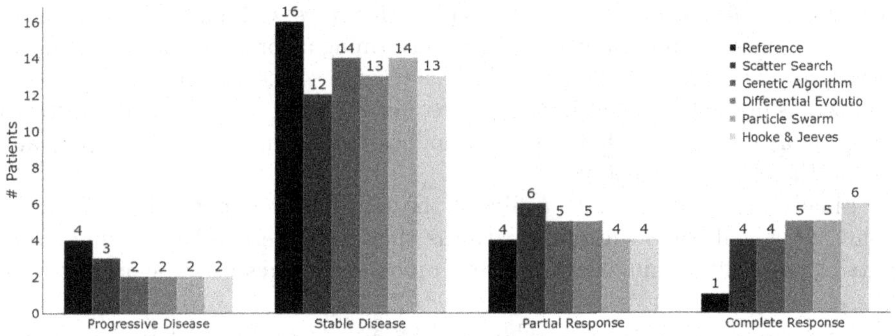

Fig. 5. RECIST results with each algorithm.

apies computed by the five top-performing algorithms. RECIST [62] is a set of classification criteria for the patients response to cancer therapies, based on the final diameter of the tumour after the treatment. RECIST classifies patients in four different classes: Complete Response (CR) if the final tumour diameter is <10 mm, Partial Response (PR) if the tumour shrinks by at least 30%, Stable Disease (SD) if the diameter decreases by less than 30% or increases at most by 20% and Progressive Disease (PD) if the diameter grows by more than 20%. The RECIST classification of the 25 VPs with the optimal therapies are consistent with the previously shown results. We observe that, with the reference therapy only one VP reaches the CR class, while this number grows up to 6 with Hooke & Jeeves. Conversely, we note that the number of VPs in the two worst classes, PD and SD significantly decreases when passing from the reference to the optimised therapies.

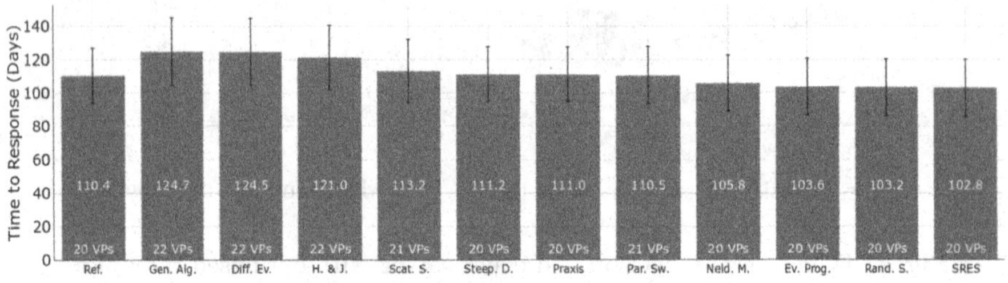

Fig. 6. Mean time to response.

We compared the algorithms over an important metric usually observed in the clinical practice, *i.e.*, the time to response to treatment. Indeed, we computed the number of elapsed days from the beginning of the treatment until the first decrease of the tumour size. Such metric provides a crucial feedback on the effectiveness of a therapy, and is strictly linked with the patient's probability of surviving. Figure 6 shows the mean time to response for the reference therapy and for the optimised ones. Unsurprisingly, the quickest response, on average, is achieved by those algorithms that compute therapies with high drugs doses. In fact, as discussed later, many of the top-performing algorithms (in term of mean objective value) produce therapies that delay most of the administrations to the final weeks of the treatment in order to reduce the total amount of administered drugs. This was a somewhat expected finding, as this metric does not play any role in the objective function.

Finally, we quantitatively analysed the therapies computed by each algorithm. Our goal was identifying patterns that characterise the therapies computed by each algorithm in order to better interpret the result of the optimisation phase.

We computed five metrics, whose values are shown in Table 1: the average number of weeks in which at least one drug is administered to the patient (column "Any" in the table), the average number of weeks in which both drugs

Table 1. Statistics over the best therapies computed with each algorithm.

Algorithm	#Admin		Dose		Max weeks w/out adm
	Any	Both	Ate	Cibi	
Ref	30.0	5.0	24.0 mg/kg	160.0 mg	3.0
Diff. Ev.	6.84 ± 0.85	1.16 ± 0.28	15.34 mg/kg	91.42 mg	23.0 ± 3.05
Ev. Prog.	12.28 ± 0.75	5.08 ± 0.5	7.07 mg/kg	53.95 mg	7.44 ± 0.52
Gen. Alg.	5.52 ± 0.76	0.76 ± 0.19	16.26 mg/kg	116.69 mg	27.08 ± 3.05
H.&J.	13.36 ± 1.16	1.08 ± 0.2	2.19 mg/kg	0.74 mg	10.04 ± 2.48
Neld. M.	15.0 ± 0.0	15.0 ± 0.0	20.59 mg/kg	154.07 mg	4.0 ± 0.0
Part. Sw.	11.84 ± 0.91	4.44 ± 0.72	3.4 mg/kg	15.56 mg	9.6 ± 1.66
Praxis	28.08 ± 0.08	4.04 ± 0.04	5.79 mg/kg	145.43 mg	3.0 ± 0.0
Rand. S.	12.16 ± 0.81	8.8 ± 0.6	10.72 mg/kg	74.71 mg	5.64 ± 0.13
SRES	16.08 ± 1.01	7.68 ± 0.97	9.42 mg/kg	61.65 mg	4.88 ± 0.09
Scat. S.	25.36 ± 2.24	7.28 ± 1.06	0.61 mg/kg	3.98 mg	5.0 ± 0.59
Steep. D.	28.52 ± 0.44	4.32 ± 0.26	5.91 mg/kg	153.96 mg	3.0 ± 0.0

are administered (column "Both"), the average dose of Atezolizumab and of Cibisatamab (respectively columns "Ate" and "Cibi"), and the average length of the longest period without any drug administrations. The best-performing algorithm, Hooke & Jeeves, produces therapies that, on average, administer low doses of drugs regularly throughout the 57 weeks (one administration every 4.3 weeks). The Particle Swarm Optimisation algorithm produces very similar therapies, though with fewer administrations (11.84 vs 13.36) and a much higher average dose of Cibisatamab (15.56 mg vs 0.74 mg). Differential Evolution and Genetic Algorithm compute drastically different therapies. As Table 1 shows, they envision fewer administrations, but at higher doses. We also note that the average maximum number of weeks without any administration for therapies computed by these algorithms is the maximum among all algorithms (23 and 27.08). This implies that the drug administrations take place, on average, at the beginning and, by the most part, at the end of the 400-day period. We observe that this trait is consistent to the high *time to response* values of these two algorithms shown in Fig. 6, as the optimised therapies tend to be lighter within the first months. Scatter Search, according to Fig. 3b, is the algorithm that, on average, achieves the second-to-lowest total amount of administered drugs, although it produces therapies with a strategy that is different from the one shown for Hooke & Jeeves. In fact, while the drug dosages are similar, the number of administrations, and in particular of weeks in which both drugs are used, is sensibly higher. The Evolutionary Programming and SRES algorithms yield reasonably regular therapies but, as Fig. 3b shows, only achieve slightly better performances than Random Search in term of total amount of administered drugs. Finally, the remaining algorithms produce therapies that, proceeding from Random Search to Praxis, tend to be more and more similar to the reference therapy, hence very regular, with a very high administration frequency, and with high doses.

The model and whole source code of our experimental evaluation is publicly available at https://bitbucket.org/mclab/crc-therapy-synthesis-aixia.

7 Conclusions

In this work, we performed a complete comparative study of the optimisation algorithms implemented in COPASI for the computation of personalised pharmacological cancer therapies. We exploited an SBML model of Colorectal Cancer to design an ISCT and implemented the whole approach within COPASI. We established a set of desirable characteristics of therapies and designed a non-trivial TTM, which parametrises the space of all therapies of interest and enables the use of standard parameter optimisation methods. Our experimental results show that COPASI implementations of gradient-based algorithms fail to solve the problem at hand, while algorithms of different families achieve quite diverse results, ranging from poor to excellent, with notable divergences in the characteristics of the computed optimised therapies. We conclude that simulation-based optimisation methods appear to be well-suited to approach the problem of computing personalised therapies and suggest that they may represent a highly effective tool for achieving precision medicine.

Acknowledgements. This work was partially supported by: Italian Ministry of University and Research under grant "Dipartimenti di eccellenza 2018–2022" of the Department of Computer Science of Sapienza University of Rome. INdAM "GNCS Project 2020"; Sapienza University projects RG11816436BD4F21, RG11916B892E54DB, RP11916B8665242F; Lazio POR FESR projects E84G20000150006, F83G17000830007.

References

1. Audigier, C., et al.: Parameter estimation for personalization of liver tumor radiofrequency ablation. In: Yoshida, H., Näppi, J., Saini, S. (eds.) ABD-MICCAI 2014. LNCS, pp. 3–12. Springer, Cham (2014). https://doi.org/10.1007/978-3-319-13692-9_1
2. Balsa-Canto, E., et al.: AMIGO2, a toolbox for dynamic modeling, optimization and control in systems biology. Bioinformatics **32**(21), 3357–3359 (2016)
3. Barrett, C., Tinelli, C.: Satisfiability modulo theories. In: Clarke, E., Henzinger, T., Veith, H., Bloem, R. (eds.) Handbook of Model Checking, pp. 305–343. Springer, Cham (2018). https://doi.org/10.1007/978-3-319-10575-8_11
4. Bogomolov, S., et al.: Planning as model checking in hybrid domains. In: AAAI 2014. AAAI (2014)
5. Bogomolov, S., et al.: PDDL+ planning with hybrid automata: foundations of translating must behavior. In: ICAPS 2015. AAAI (2015)
6. Cadoli, M., Mancini, T.: Combining relational algebra, SQL, constraint modelling, and local search. TPLP **7**(1–2), 37–65 (2007)
7. Cadoli, M., Mancini, T., Patrizi, F.: SAT as an effective solving technology for constraint problems. In: Esposito, F., Raś, Z.W., Malerba, D., Semeraro, G. (eds.) ISMIS 2006. LNCS (LNAI), vol. 4203, pp. 540–549. Springer, Heidelberg (2006). https://doi.org/10.1007/11875604_61

8. Cassidy, T., Craig, M.: Determinants of combination GM-CSF immunotherapy and oncolytic virotherapy success identified through in silico treatment personalization. PLoS Comput. Biol. **15**(11), e1007495 (2019)
9. Chen, Q., et al.: MILP, pseudo-boolean, and OMT solvers for optimal fault-tolerant placements of relay nodes in mission critical wireless networks. Fundam. Inform. **174**(3–4), 229–258 (2020)
10. Chen, T., et al.: Optimal dosing of cancer chemotherapy using model predictive control and moving horizon state/parameter estimation. Comput. Methods Programs Biomed. **108**(3), 973–983 (2012)
11. Clarke, E., et al.: Handbook of Model Checking. Springer, Cham (2016). https://doi.org/10.1007/978-3-319-10575-8
12. Egea, J.A., et al.: MEIGO: an open-source software suite based on metaheuristics for global optimization in systems biology and bioinformatics. BMC Bioinform. **15**(1), 1–9 (2014)
13. Esposito, M., Picchiami, L.: Intelligent search for personalized cancer therapy synthesis: an experimental comparison. In: RCRA 2021, CEUR W.P., vol. 3065. CEUR (2021)
14. Esposito, M., Picchiami, L.: Simulation-based synthesis of personalised therapies for colorectal cancer. In: OVERLAY 2021, CEUR W.P., vol. 2987. CEUR (2021)
15. European Medicines Agency. Reporting of physiologically based pharmacokinetic (PBPK) modelling and simulation (2019). https://www.ema.europa.eu/en/reporting-physiologically-based-pharmacokinetic-pbpk-modelling-simulation. EMA/CHMP/458101/2016
16. Fox, M., Long, D.: Modelling mixed discrete-continuous domains for planning. JAIR **27**, 235–297 (2006)
17. Fritzson, P., Engelson, V.: Modelica—a unified object-oriented language for system modeling and simulation. In: Jul, E. (ed.) ECOOP 1998. LNCS, vol. 1445, pp. 67–90. Springer, Heidelberg (1998). https://doi.org/10.1007/BFb0054087
18. Fröhlich, F., et al.: AMICI: high-performance sensitivity analysis for large ordinary differential equation models. Bioinformatics **37**(20), 3676–3677 (2021)
19. Hayes, B., et al.: Residential demand management using individualised demand aware price policies. IEEE Trans. Smart Grid **8**(3), 1284–1294 (2017)
20. Hengartner, M., et al.: Negative affect is unrelated to fluctuations in hormone levels across the menstrual cycle: evidence from a multisite observational study across two successive cycles. J. Psycho. Res. **99**, 21–27 (2017)
21. Hucka, M., et al.: The systems biology markup language (SBML): language specification for level 3 version 2 core. JIB **15**(1) (2018)
22. Jalalimanesh, A., et al.: Simulation-based optimization of radiotherapy: agent-based modeling and reinforcement learning. Math. Comput. Simul. **133**, 235–248 (2017)
23. Jenner, A.L., et al.: Optimising hydrogel release profiles for viro-immunotherapy using oncolytic adenovirus expressing IL-12 and GM-CSF with immature dendritic cells. Appl. Sci. **10**(8), 2872 (2020)
24. Kaschek, D., et al.: Dynamic modeling, parameter estimation, and uncertainty analysis in R. J. Stat. Softw. **88**(1), 1–32 (2019)
25. Klinger, E., et al.: pyABC: distributed, likelihood-free inference. Bioinformatics **34**(20), 3591–3593 (2018)
26. Kolpakov, F., et al.: BioUML: an integrated environment for systems biology and collaborative analysis of biomedical data. Nucleic Acids Res. **47**(W1), W225–W233 (2019)

27. Lang, P.F., et al.: SBML2Julia: interfacing SBML with efficient nonlinear Julia modelling and solution tools for parameter optimization. arXiv preprint arXiv:2011.02597 (2020)
28. Le Novère, N., et al.: BioModels database: a free, centralized database of curated, published, quantitative kinetic models of biochemical and cellular systems. Nucleic Acids Res. **34**(Suppl. 1) (2006)
29. Lee, C., et al.: COPASI - a complex pathway simulator. Bioinformatics **22**(24), 3067–3074 (2006)
30. Leeners, B., et al.: Lack of associations between female hormone levels and visuospatial working memory, divided attention and cognitive bias across two consecutive menstrual cycles. Front. Behav. Neuro. **11**, 120 (2017)
31. Leeners, B., et al.: Associations between natural physiological and supraphysiological estradiol levels and stress perception. Front. Psycol. **10**, 1296 (2019)
32. Ma, H., et al.: Combination therapy with T cell engager and PD-L1 blockade enhances the antitumor potency of T cells as predicted by a QSP model. J. Immunother. Cancer **8**(2) (2020)
33. Maggioli, F., et al.: SBML2Modelica: integrating biochemical models within open-standard simulation ecosystems. Bioinformatics **36**(7), 2165–2172 (2020)
34. Mancini, T., Cadoli, M.: Detecting and breaking symmetries by reasoning on problem specifications. In: Zucker, J.-D., Saitta, L. (eds.) SARA 2005. LNCS (LNAI), vol. 3607, pp. 165–181. Springer, Heidelberg (2005). https://doi.org/10.1007/11527862_12
35. Mancini, T., et al.: Evaluating ASP and commercial solvers on the CSPLib. Constraints **13**(4), 407–436 (2008)
36. Mancini, T., et al.: Combinatorial problem solving over relational databases: view synthesis through constraint-based local search. In: SAC 2012. ACM (2012)
37. Mancini, T., Mari, F., Massini, A., Melatti, I., Merli, F., Tronci, E.: System level formal verification via model checking driven simulation. In: Sharygina, N., Veith, H. (eds.) CAV 2013. LNCS, vol. 8044, pp. 296–312. Springer, Heidelberg (2013). https://doi.org/10.1007/978-3-642-39799-8_21
38. Mancini, T., et al.: Anytime system level verification via random exhaustive hardware in the loop simulation. In: DSD 2014. IEEE (2014)
39. Mancini, T., et al.: Demand-aware price policy synthesis and verification services for smart grids. In: SmartGridComm 2014. IEEE (2014)
40. Mancini, T., et al.: System level formal verification via distributed multi-core hardware in the loop simulation. In: PDP 2014. IEEE (2014)
41. Mancini, T., Tronci, E., Salvo, I., Mari, F., Massini, A., Melatti, I.: Computing biological model parameters by parallel statistical model checking. In: Ortuño, F., Rojas, I. (eds.) IWBBIO 2015. LNCS, vol. 9044, pp. 542–554. Springer, Cham (2015). https://doi.org/10.1007/978-3-319-16480-9_52
42. Mancini, T., et al.: SyLVaaS: system level formal verification as a service. In: PDP 2015. IEEE (2015)
43. Mancini, T., et al.: User flexibility aware price policy synthesis for smart grids. In: DSD 2015. IEEE (2015)
44. Mancini, T., et al.: Anytime system level verification via parallel random exhaustive hardware in the loop simulation. Microprocess. Microsyst. **41**, 12–28 (2016)
45. Mancini, T., et al.: SyLVaaS: system level formal verification as a service. Fundam. Inform. **149**(1–2), 101–132 (2016)
46. Mancini, T., et al.: On minimising the maximum expected verification time. Inf. Proc. Lett. **122**, 8–16 (2017)

47. Mancini, T., et al.: Computing personalised treatments through in silico clinical trials. A case study on downregulation in assisted reproduction. In: RCRA 2018, CEUR W.P., vol. 2271. CEUR (2018)
48. Mancini, T., Mari, F., Melatti, I., Salvo, I., Tronci, E.: An efficient algorithm for network vulnerability analysis under malicious attacks. In: Ceci, M., Japkowicz, N., Liu, J., Papadopoulos, G.A., Raś, Z.W. (eds.) ISMIS 2018. LNCS (LNAI), vol. 11177, pp. 302–312. Springer, Cham (2018). https://doi.org/10.1007/978-3-030-01851-1_29
49. Mancini, T., et al.: Optimal fault-tolerant placement of relay nodes in a mission critical wireless network. In: RCRA 2018, CEUR W.P., vol. 2271. CEUR (2018)
50. Mancini, T., et al.: Parallel statistical model checking for safety verification in smart grids. In: SmartGridComm 2018. IEEE (2018)
51. Mancini, T., et al.: Any-horizon uniform random sampling and enumeration of constrained scenarios for simulation-based formal verification. IEEE TSE (2021)
52. Melatti, I., et al.: A two-layer near-optimal strategy for substation constraint management via home batteries. IEEE Trans. Ind. Electron. **69**, 8566–8578 (2021)
53. Noman, N., Moscato, P.: Designing optimal combination therapy for personalised glioma treatment. Memetic Comput. **12**(4), 317–329 (2020)
54. Raissi, M., et al.: On parameter estimation approaches for predicting disease transmission through optimization, deep learning and statistical inference methods. Lett. Biomathematics **6**(2), 1–26 (2019)
55. Raue, A., et al.: Data2dynamics: a modeling environment tailored to parameter estimation in dynamical systems. Bioinformatics **31**(21), 3558–3560 (2015)
56. Rossi, F., et al. (eds.): Handbook of Constraint Programming. Elsevier (2006)
57. Sánchez, O.D., et al.: Parameter estimation of a meal glucose-insulin model for TIDM patients from therapy historical data. IET Syst. Biol. **13**(1), 8–15 (2019)
58. Schälte, Y., et al.: Evaluation of derivative-free optimizers for parameter estimation in systems biology. IFAC-PapersOnLine **51**(19), 98–101 (2018)
59. Schmiester, L., et al.: Efficient gradient-based parameter estimation for dynamic models using qualitative data. Bioinformatics (2021). https://doi.org/10.1093/bioinformatics/btab512
60. Schmiester, L., et al.: PEtab-interoperable specification of parameter estimation problems in systems biology. PLoS Comput. Biol. **17**(1), e1008646 (2021)
61. Schmucker, R., et al.: Combination treatment optimization using a pan-cancer pathway model. bioRxiv (2020)
62. Schwartz, L.H., et al.: RECIST 1.1—update and clarification: from the RECIST committee. Eur. J. Cancer **62**, 132–137 (2016)
63. Sinisi, S., et al.: Complete populations of virtual patients for in silico clinical trials. Bioinformatics **36**(22–23), 5465–5472 (2020)
64. Sinisi, S., et al.: Optimal personalised treatment computation through in silico clinical trials on patient digital twins. Fundam. Inform. **174**(3–4), 283–310 (2020)
65. Sinisi, S., et al.: Reconciling interoperability with efficient verification and validation within open source simulation environments. Simul. Model. Pract. Theory **109** (2021)
66. Somogyi, E., et al.: libRoadRunner: a high performance SBML simulation and analysis library. Bioinformatics **31**(20), 3315–3321 (2015)
67. Stapor, P., et al.: PESTO: parameter estimation toolbox. Bioinformatics **34**(4), 705–707 (2018)
68. Tronci, E., et al.: Patient-specific models from inter-patient biological models and clinical records. In: FMCAD 2014. IEEE (2014)

69. U.S.A. Food and Drug Administration. Physiologically based pharmacokinetic analyses - format and content guidance for industry. FDA-2016-D-3969 (2018)
70. Vallati, M., et al.: Efficient macroscopic urban traffic models for reducing congestion: a PDDL+ planning approach. In: AAAI 2016. AAAI (2016)
71. Villaverde, A.F., et al.: Benchmarking optimization methods for parameter estimation in large kinetic models. Bioinformatics **35**(5), 830–838 (2019)
72. Yazdani, A., et al.: Systems biology informed deep learning for inferring parameters and hidden dynamics. PLoS Comput. Biol. **16**(11), e1007575 (2020)

Effective Analysis of Industry-Relevant Cyber-Physical Systems via Statistical Model Checking

Angela Pappagallo(✉)

Computer Science Department, Sapienza University of Rome, Rome, Italy
angela.pappagallo@istat.it

Abstract. Many autonomous Cyber-Physical Systems (*e.g.*, devices for Internet of Things, Unmanned Autonomous Vehicles, medical devices, etc.) are mission-critical (*i.e.*, errors result in loss of money) or safety-critical (*i.e.*, errors result in damage or even death for humans). This motivates research on efficient formal verification methods for such Cyber-Physical Systems.

Unfortunately, this is not an easy task, as verifying a Cyber-Physical System entails evaluating a huge number of scenarios (*scenario explosion*). Furthermore, a unified mathematical model for the (discrete) cyber part and the (continuous) physical part is currently not available. Such obstructions may be mitigated by using Statistical Model Checking, which uses statistical methods to sample the set of scenarios while basing on possibly black-box models of the System Under Verification.

In this paper, we review 5 recent real-world and industry-relevant case studies from the literature that involved usage of Statistical Model Checking. Such case studies range on very different application areas, namely: i) intelligent services for peak shaving in smart grids, ii) In-Silico Clinical Trial for medical services, iii) applications for wireless sensor networks; iv) aircraft data networks; v) plug-in electric vehicles. This shows the maturity, feasibility and flexibility of Statistical Model Checking when applied to real-world case studies.

1 Introduction

A Cyber-Physical System (CPS) is a system where a (continuous) physical system (*plant*) is controlled and/or monitored by a (discrete) software. The deployment of autonomous CPSs [4], such as, *e.g.*, devices for Internet of Things (IoT) [10,87], Unmanned Autonomous Vehicles [35] and medical devices [18], has been speeding up for the last decades, with a projected 1.1 trillion USD global speding on IoT only [81]. For many of such CPSs, it is important to rule out errors [19,20], especially bugs in the software part, since such bugs may lead to:

– loss of money in *mission-critical systems* [9]. This is the case, *e.g.*, in aerospace: as an example, in 1996 the Ariane 5 [5] rocket was destroyed after launch due to a type conversion error in the software, resulting in a 500 M$ loss;

S. Bandini et al. (Eds.): AIxIA 2021, LNAI 13196, pp. 655–670, 2022.
https://doi.org/10.1007/978-3-031-08421-8_45

- death of serious injury for people in *safety-critical systems* [65]. This is the case, *e.g.*, for medical devices.

As standard testing could not provide the required degree of correctness assurance, this motivates research on efficient formal verification methods [13]. There are multiple challenges to overcome when formally verifying a CPS [14], *e.g.*, the huge number of scenarios to be evaluated (*scenario explosion*, *e.g.*, [46,49–51]), which is hard to tackle also using High-Performance Computing (HPC) [48,52,53,57,63]. Furthermore, we miss a unified mathematical model for the discrete cyber part and the continuous physical part [38,42]. Such issues make it hard to apply analytical approaches based on logics (*e.g.*, [11,12,26,44,45]) or automata (*e.g.*, [3,17,43,59]).

Statistical Model Checking (SMC) [41] holds the promise to overcome this obstacle by using statistical methods to sample the set of scenarios up to desired accuracy and precision [15,27,28], while possibly relying on black-box models of the System Under Verification (SUV) (*i.e.*, the full system encompassing both the software and the plant) [2,6].

In this paper, we review 5 recent real-world and industry-relevant case studies from the literature that involved usage of SMC. Such case studies range on very different application areas, namely:

- verification of an intelligent service for peak shaving in smart grids;
- generation of Virtual Patients (VPs) to enable In-Silico Clinical Trial (ISCT) for medical services (Virtual Physiological Human [31,36]);
- verification of maneuvers correctness for an autonomous drone navigating system;
- estimation of the probabilities for successfully communication and energy saving for the Bluetooth protocol;
- estimation of performance parameters for the leader election protocol used in the IEEE 1394 standard.

This shows the feasibility and flexibility of SMC when applied to real-world case studies. Two preliminary versions of this paper has been presented in [67, 68]. With respect to [68], we discuss more case studies, by also providing more details about methodologies and results. With respect to [67], we replaced the last three case studies with other more recent ones from the literature. For a complete survey of SMC methodologies themselves, see, *e.g.*, [1,8,69,73].

2 Industrial Case Studies for Statistical Model Checking

This section discusses some recent real-world and industry-relevant problems that have been solved by using SMC or SMC-based methodologies. Namely, Sect. 2.1 shows an application in the field of intelligent services for smart grids, Sect. 2.2 presents an SMC-based methodology used for enabling ISCT in Virtual Physiological Human (VPH), Sect. 2.3 illustrates how SMC may be used in the field of autonomous drone navigation, Sect. 2.4 discusses results on verifying properties of the Bluetooth protocol and finally Sect. 2.5 computes interesting numerical properties of the leader election protocol used in IEEE 1394 (also known as FireWire).

2.1 Peak Shaving in Smart Grids

An Electric Distribution Network (EDN) [71] is composed of several substations, where each substation serves a set of residential houses. By using the measurements taken from the home electricity mains (Advanced Metering Infrastructure, AMI), we know each house power demand, with periodicity at least one hour. Our objective is to reduce costs for the Distribution System Operator (DSO), by limiting the demand drawn at some or all substations of the EDN at times of peak demand (*peak shaving* [72]). In fact, this reduces costs of buying energy from the market at times of peak electricity price (which involves usage of peak power plants [64]), and reduces overloading of network components during times of peak demand (thus reducing substations aging), or during periods when the system is weakened due to line/transformer maintenance or other outages [83].

Many work in the literature address the problem above, see, *e.g.*, [21,32,34, 76,86]. In this paper, we focus on the methodology in [29,55,56,62], for which a verification based on SMC techniques is available. Namely, in that line of research the problem of achieving peak shaving is counteracted by proposing the two following intelligent services (for an high-level schema, see Fig. 1).

1. The first service (EDN Virtual Tomography, EVT) computes time-varying upper bounds for the aggregated electricity demand resulting from the residential houses U connected to a given EDN substation s. As a result, if the aggregated demand of s is kept below such upper bounds, the DSO will save in the maintenance costs for s, as well as in energy production costs.
2. The second service (Demand-Aware Price Policy, DAPP) computes individualised time-varying upper bounds for each residential house in U. If a residential user keeps its demand below the bounds computed by DAPP, then a low energy tariff is applied, otherwise an high tariff is applied. Note that, in order to do this, residential users must perform *load shifting*, by consuming more electricity when the bound is high and less electricity when the bound is low. As a result, if all residential users succeeds in keeping their demand below the given bounds, the aggregated demand on s will be below the bound computed by EVT.

However, there is no guarantee that residential users will be able to perform load shifting so as to stay below the bounds computed by DAPP. In [54], a domain-specific statistical model checker named Aggregated Power Demand-Analyzer (APD-A) is designed, in order to compute the probability of violations of the bounds on the aggregated demand on s, given probabilistic deviations from the expected power demand (again, computed by DAPP) of each single house. More in detail, APD-A takes in input:

1. the time T on which to perform the evaluation (usually, one month divide in time-slots of one hour);
2. for each user $u \in U$, the *Expected Power Profile (EPP)* $p_u : T \to \mathbf{R}$, i.e., a function taking as input a time-slot in $t \in T$ and returning the power demand $p_u(t)$ (in kW) of user u in t; such demand is a further output of DAPP and

is always below the power bound for u in t (i.e., $p_u(t) \leq P_u(t)$, being $P_u(t)$ the upper bound output by DAPP, for all $u \in U, t \in T$;
3. a probabilistic model dev_u for users deviations from deviations from EPPs, i.e., $\int_a^b dev_u(x)dx =$ is the probability that actual power demand of u in any time-slot $t \in T$ is in $[(1+a)p_u(t), (1+b)p_u(t)]$ (e.g., $\int_{-0.02}^{0.02} dev_u(x)dx =$ probability that actual power demand of u in any time-slot $t \in T$ deviates at most by 2% from EPP of u);
4. the substation safety requirements, i.e., $p_s : T \to \mathbf{R}$ s.t., for each $t \in T$, the DSO wants the aggregated demand on s to be below $p_s(t)$;
5. parameters for the output probability distribution $0 < \delta, \varepsilon < 1$ and $\gamma \in \mathbf{R}$, i.e., the output values must be correct up to tolerance ε with statistical confidence $1 - \delta$, and the output probability distribution is discretized with step γ.

As an output, APD-A returns the probability distribution for the aggregated demand on s resulting from EPPs disturbed with the given probabilistic disturbance model dev_u. To this aim, APD-A relies on a parallel version (for cluster of computers with distributed memory) of the Optimal Approximation Algorithm (OAA) from [28]. Figure 2 shows the resulting output of APD-A for a group of 186 real-world houses in Denmark.

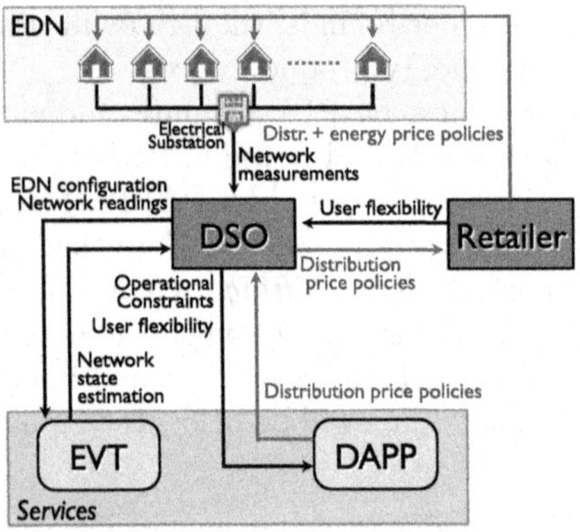

Fig. 1. Intelligent systems for smart grids [29]

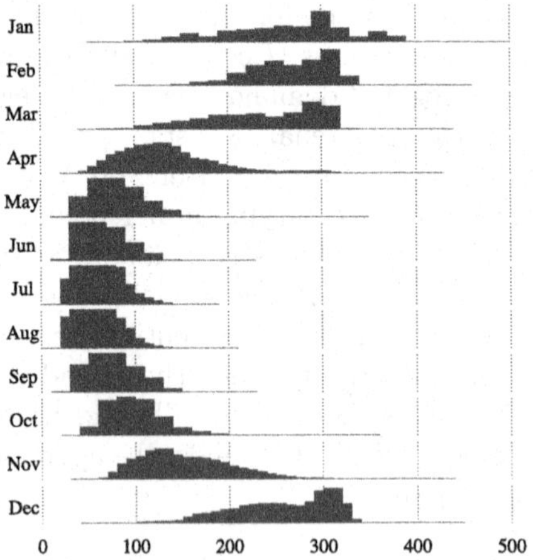

Fig. 2. Results for aggregated power demand-analyzer from [54].

2.2 Virtual Patients for In-Silico Clinical Trials

One of the most complex problems in Medicine is assessing safety and efficacy of pharmacological drugs, medical devices and, more in general, treatment strategies [75]. In the last years, a wide research area called ISCT has been developed [7,70], with the aim to approach such a problem via Computer Science techniques. By prioritizing the successive *in vivo* experimentations, this would decrease time and cost of the overall process, reduce animal and human testing, and enable precision medicine [22,37,84,85].

A key enabler to carry out an ISCT is the availability of a population of VPs, *i.e.*, a set computational models of the physiology of interest and of the Pharmacokinetics/Pharmacodynamics (PK/PD) of the relevant pharmacological compounds on which to perform computer simulations.

However, to guarantee compelling evidence of safety and efficacy of the therapy under assessment, such a population of VP must be *representative* of the entire spectrum of human phenotypes. This includes the possible individual differences in physiology and the different possible reactions to the external stimuli (*e.g.*, drug administrations).

Such computational, *quantitative, personalized* models of the human physiology and drugs PK/PD are typically derived in two steps. First, quantitative *inter-individual* VPH models are derived from *qualitative* knowledge from, *e.g.*, available repositories [23,33], and are often formalized in terms of systems of *parametric* differential equations (for continuous-time models) or different equations (for discrete-time models). Different assignments to such (*real valued*) parameters yield different time courses (aka trajectories) of the modeled biological quantities, and different reactions to the same stimuli. Thus, a quantitative VPH model combined with a parameter assignment is regarded as a *Virtual Patient (VP)*, representing a *human phenotype*. Such VPs can then be *simulated* (typically as black-box systems via numerical simulators, given the complexity of the differential equations) to assess the values of proper metrics of the therapy of interest, *e.g.*, expected safety and efficacy (*In-Silico Clinical Trials*, ISCT).

Unfortunately, computing VPs is all but easy. Indeed, most of the legal assignments to a VPH model do yield model trajectories which clearly *violate* human physiology. This is because such models are often over-parameterised, and *unknown* inter-dependency constraints among the various parameters do exist. Also, parameters are often introduced to model not-well-understood biological mechanisms (see, *e.g.*, [58,82]), or to abstract away details that are not needed to be modeled accurately to perform the planned verification activity. Also in this case, a random assignment to such parameters would yield, with very high probability, an overall model behavior which is clearly non-admissible from a biological standpoint.

The major obstacle is thus to automatically recognize whether a model parameter assignment is a (physiologically admissible) VP, and to *search* for such VPs in the (typically huge real-valued) space of model parameter assignments.

However this is not enough. Indeed, since, in order to carry out an ISCT we need a population of VPs *representative* of the entire spectrum of the phenotypes entailed by the VPH model, we need to search for *all* VPs satisfying the physiological admissibility criterion. Furthermore, since complex VPH models are often non-identifiable, it is often the case that several parameter assignments yield VPs which have *indistinguishable* (with respect to some given tolerance) trajectories under *all* time series of external stimuli (*e.g.*, drug administrations).

The presence, in the computed population, of such indistinguishable VPs would be a major source of redundancy, hence inefficiency of the verification process, and should be avoided.

In [78], SMC-based techniques are used to drive *global search* (intelligently guided by an *heuristic*) in the VPs parameters space. Namely, starting from a (non-identifiable) VPH model and suitable biological and medical knowledge elicited from experts to formally define what a *physiologically admissible* trajectory is, such techniques compute a population of VPs which is representative of the entire spectrum of phenotypes entailed by the model and does not contain indistinguishable VPs, up to the user-requested *statistical guarantees*. Namely, given user-defined constants $\varepsilon, \delta \in (0, 1)$, when the algorithm terminates, the probability that further sampling will yield a VP showing an *unknown* phenotype (*i.e.*, a phenotype not already included in the population computed so far) is $\leq \varepsilon$ with statistical confidence $\geq 1 - \delta$.

The effectiveness of such approach has been proven on GynCycle [74], a non-identifiable model of the female Hypothalamic Pituitary Gonadal (HPG) axis, consisting of 33 highly non-linear stiff ordinary differential equations. Namely, a population of 4,830,264 VPs (each one being an assignment to 75 real-valued parameters) was generated and stratified into 7 levels (at different granularity of behaviours). Figure 4 shows the possible time courses of the Estradiol hormone in the different VP layers The representativeness of such VPs was assessed against 86 retrospective health records from Pfizer, Hannover Medical School and University Hospital of Lausanne. Figure 3 shows that the datasets are respectively covered by such VPs within Average Normalised Mean Absolute Error (ANMAE) of 15%, 20%, and 35%.

The computed population of VPs was then used in [47,80] to compute, again *in silico*, optimal robust personalised treatments for assisted reproduction, an area currently showing many factors that can be hardly kept under full control [30,39,40]. Namely, *digital twins* of human patients were computed by selecting those VPs best matching clinical measurements on them, and a black-box simulator of the VPH model in [74] was driven [77] via intelligent backtracking on such digital twins.

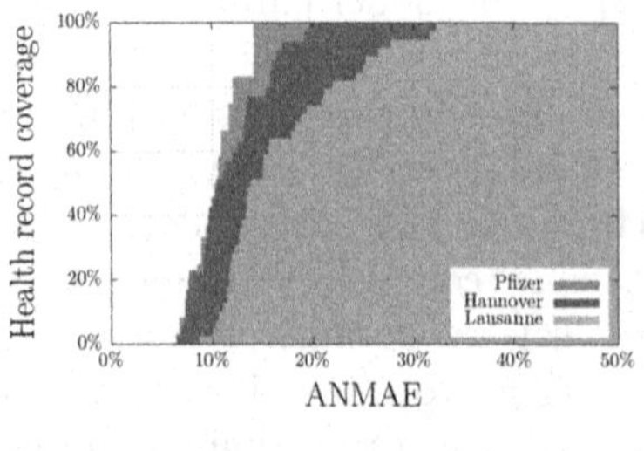

Fig. 3. Results for virtual patients coverage from [78]

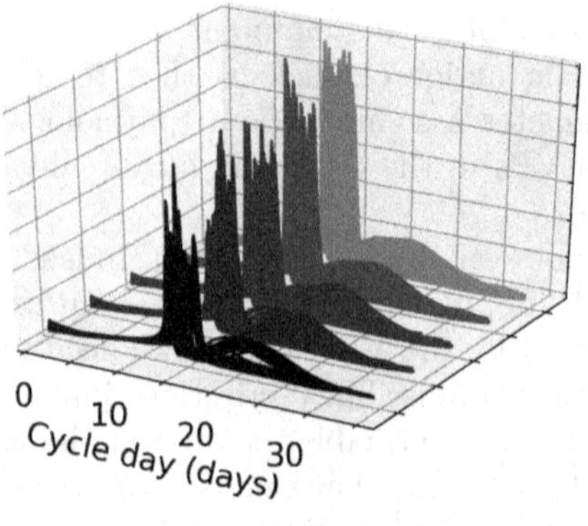

Fig. 4. Estradiol [79]

2.3 Autonomous Drone Navigation

In this section we discuss the verification of a navigation mission of the quadcopter in Fig. 5 [24] presented in [25].

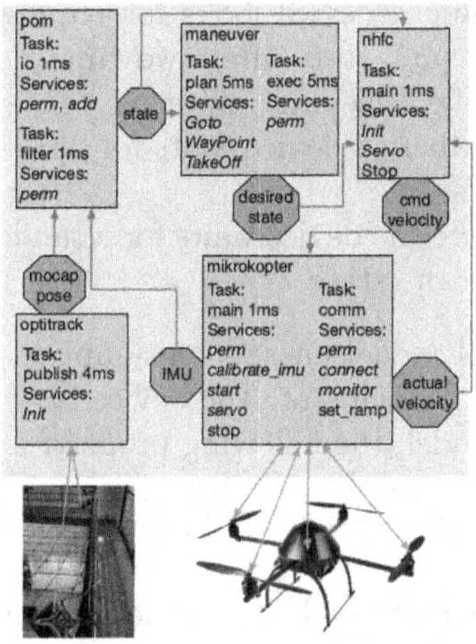

Fig. 5. Quadcopter from [25]

For our purposes, we may focus on the following components of the quadcopter:

- MIKROKOPTER: is the component in charge of the quad-copter low-level hardware. The quadcopter is controlled by applying a velocity to each propeller;
- NHFC (Near Hovering Flight Controller), is the core of the flight controller. Every ms it reads the actual velocity the current position and the desired position (from MANEUVER) and produces the proper command for MIKROKOPTER;
- MANEUVER: is the navigation component. Every 5 ms, given a position or waypoints to navigate to, it computes a trajectory to reach it.

Here we focus on the verification of an important property which must be fulfilled by the quadcopter in order to avoid accidents. Namely, with high probability, there must be a value of t s.t., when requests are sent to maneuver, after t seconds the previously requested activities from MIKROKOPTER and NHFC have already started executing (*readiness*). To this aim, several values for t have been tried from 1ms. As a result, for values less than 7ms, there is a non-negligible probability of violation, for 7ms the requested probability is between 0.98 and 0.99 and for $t \geq 8$ the requested probability is at least 0.99. Finally, in [25] it is also noted that, the greater t, the less number of sampled runs of the systems must be taken by UPPAAL-SMC in order to compute the probability value.

2.4 Bluetooth Protocol

Bluetooth is a wireless telecommunication protocolespecially tailored for short-distance communication. In [16], a simple model of the protocol is proposed. Such model is composed of three modalities for each Bluetooth device.

- The "scan" state, where a device looks for requests. If a request is found, then it goes to the "reply" state after two time slots (a slot is 0.3125 ms). Otherwise, it goes in the "sleeping" state.
- The "sleeping" state, where a device waits for 2012 time slots to save energy, before going back to "scan".
- The "reply" state, where the device waits for a random amount of time before coming back to the "scan" state.

Moreover, authors in [16] model energy consumption with a clock whose rate may change depending on which state the device is.

Starting from such model, the following properties are verified:

- Is there an high probability of replying within 70000 time units after a request?
- Is there an high probability of being in sleeping state for 70000 time units with a limited energy budget (*i.e.*, 4000 energy units)?

In both cases, an extension of UPPAAL-SMC able to handle Constant Slope Time Automata (CSTA) was used to compute the above defined probabilities. Namely, distribution of the probability over the bound given in argument was computed. The results are in Fig. 6, showing the cumulative probability of successfully communicating as a function of time, and Fig. 7, showing the cumulative probability of not running out of energy as a function of energy.

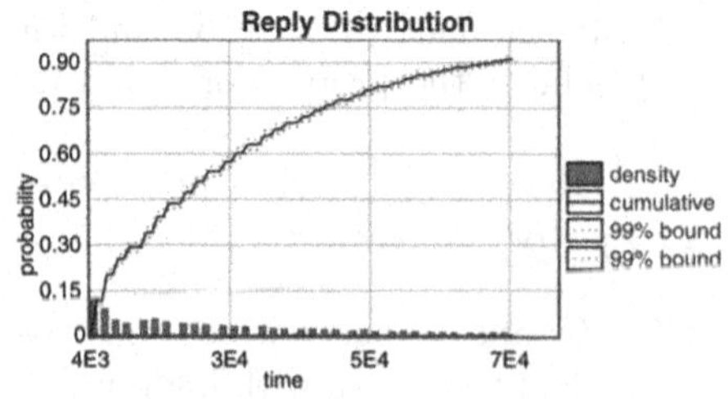

Fig. 6. Cumulative bluetooth replying probability from [16]

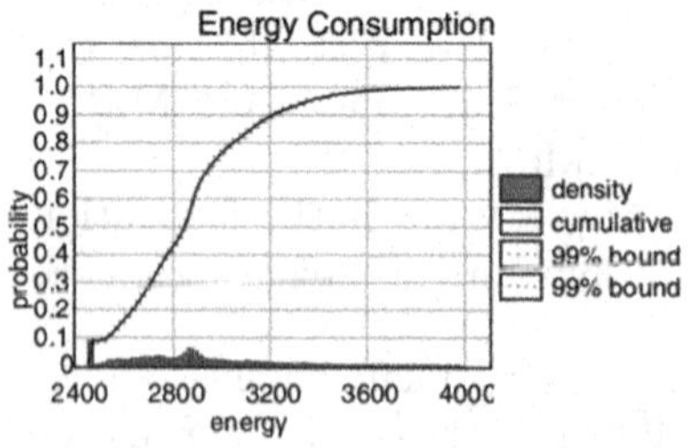

Fig. 7. Cumulative bluetooth energy-saving probability from [16]

2.5 Leader Election Protocol in IEEE 1394

IEEE 1394 (also called FireWire, i.LINK and Lynx) is a standard for connecting hot plug-and-play multimedia devices. Devices are connected in pairs by two unidirectional channels, which may result in arbitrary topologies. The protocol organizes such topologies in a dynamic tree where the root is decided by an election leader protocol (to be repeated for each addition or elimination of a device) and controls the access to the communication bus.

In [60,61], the SBIP model checker [66] is used to verify of some properties of the leader election protocol used in IEEE 1394 via SMC. In fact, the leader election protocol used by IEEE 1394 is in itself probabilistic, since when two devices are asking to be leader at the same time (*contention*), the collision is resolved by having the device repeat the operation after a random amount of time. Furthermore, in the IEEE 1394 model discussed in [60,61] probability is also used to model environment disturbances, *e.g.*, the fact that requests among devices may be either fast or slow with a given probability.

In order to perform the verification, in [60,61] 3 topologies are selected with 2, 3 and 5 devices (and the channels they use to communicate). Both the topologies for 2 and 3 devices are chains (1 is connected with 2, which is also connected with 3), whilst the topology for 5 devices includes a fork (both 4 and 5 communicate with 3). For such topologies, the following properties in Metric Temporal Logic (MTL) have been verified:

- Is it true with high probability that the leader election procedure converges within t_1 time units? That is, will one of the devices eventually become a leader and all the other devices become slaves? This is investigated using multiple values for t, till when a t^* satisfying the property is found.
- With high probability, is it true that the leader election procedure converges within $t \leq t^*$ time units if no contention occurs? This is again performed by using multiple values for t.
- Will a contention eventually occur with high probability during the election phase, *i.e.*, within t^* computed above?
- With high probability, will a given device i eventually become the leader?

Verification results for the first two properties are shown in Fig. 8 (first property is show on top, second on bottom), where t_1, t_2, t_3 highlight the resulting (converging) values for t^* when 2, 3 and 5 devices (respectively) are considered in the verification. As expected, the more devices are involved, the highest the time needed to elect a leader. As for the third property, the results show that it does not inly depends on the numebr of devices, but also on the network topology. In fact, the probability of contention decreases when passing from 2 devices to 3 devices (from 49% to 14%), but then increases in the 5 devices topology, where probability of contention is 29%. Finally, for the fourth property, we have that topology is more important the number of devices. In fact, for 2 devices the probability that any of them becomes the leader is essentially the same (50.7% vs. 49.3%). For 3 devices, the device 2 (the only one which communicates with both the other devices) has 92% probability of becoming the leader, and the remaining 8% is almost evenly spread between the other two devices. For 5 devices, device 2 has 40% probability, while device 3 has 60% probability of becoming leader (probabilities for other devices are 0). This is again due to the fact that, while device 2 communicate with 1 and 3, device 3 communicates with 2, 4 and 5.

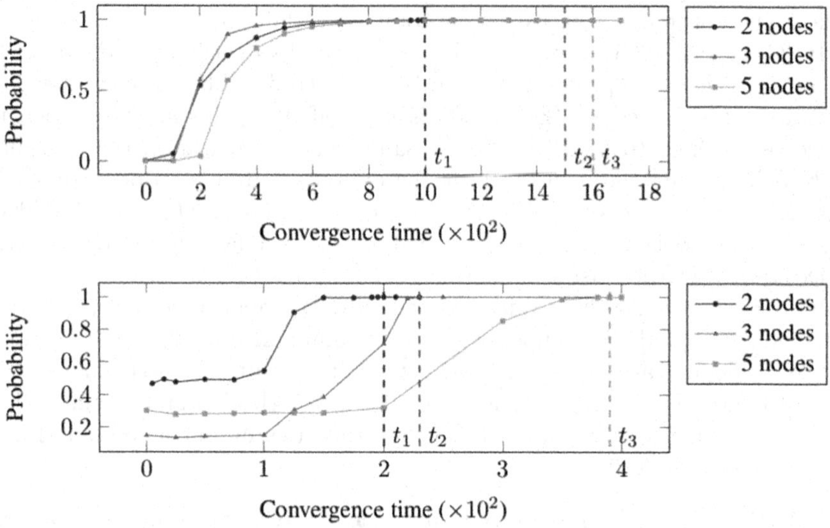

Fig. 8. Results for FireWire verification from [60,61]

3 Conclusions

In this work, we have reviewed some recent real-world problems that were solved using SMC-based techniques. Such problems were taken from very different application areas:

- smart grid intelligent services, in order to compute the probability of EDN substations to be overloaded, when residential users may deviate from their expected power profiles;
- Virtual Physiological Human, to generate a population of VPs for ISCT of drugs, medical devices and treatment strategies, s.t. such population is complete and not over-representative;
- autonomous drone navigation systems, in order to verify that the maneuvers control is successfully scheduled with high probability in case of probabilistic disturbances;
- communication protocols such as the Bluetooth protocol, in order to verify that communication is successfully carried out and that energy is saved when no devices are communicating;

- interface standard such as the IEEE 1394 (also known as FirWire), in order to estimate performance parameters for the leader election protocol used as part of the standard.

In previous versions of this paper it was also shown that the other application areas are possible:

- wireless sensor networks, in order to find the smallest bound for clock synchronization accuracy of an audio streaming application;
- aircraft data network (AFDX, Avionics Full-Duplex Switched Ethernet), in order to estimate network latency under different system parameters such as frame size, Bandwidth Allocation Gap (BAG) and number of Virtual Links (VLs);
- Plug-in Electric Vehicles, in order to estimate the probability of failures during the recharging process.

This results show that SMC is a mature methodology which can be successfully applied to real-world meaningful problems.

References

1. Agha, G., Palmskog, K.: A survey of statistical model checking. ACM Trans. Model. Comput. Simul. **28**(1), 1–39 (2018)
2. Aichernig, B.K., Tappler, M.: Probabilistic black-box reachability checking (extended version). Form. Methods Syst. Des. **54**(3), 416–448 (2019). https://doi.org/10.1007/s10703-019-00333-0
3. Alimguzhin, V., Mari, F., Melatti, I., Salvo, I., Tronci, E.: Linearizing discrete-time hybrid systems. EEE Trans. Automat. Contr. **62**(10), 5357–5364 (2017)
4. Alur, R.: Principles of Cyber-Physical Systems. MIT Press, Cambridge (2015)
5. ARIANE 5 Flight 501 Failure (1996). https://www-users.cse.umn.edu/arnold/disasters/ariane5rep.html
6. Ashok, P., Daca, P., Křetínský, J., Weininger, M.: Statistical model checking: black or white? In: Margaria, T., Steffen, B. (eds.) ISoLA 2020. LNCS, vol. 12476, pp. 331–349. Springer, Cham (2020). https://doi.org/10.1007/978-3-030-61362-4_19
7. Avicenna Project: In silico clinical trials: how computer simulation will transform the biomedical industry (2016). http://avicenna-isct.org/wp-content/uploads/2016/01/AvicennaRoadmapPDF-27-01-16.pdf
8. Bakir, M.E., Gheorghe, M., Konur, S., Stannett, M.: Comparative analysis of statistical model checking tools. In: Leporati, A., Rozenberg, G., Salomaa, A., Zandron, C. (eds.) CMC 2016. LNCS, vol. 10105, pp. 119–135. Springer, Cham (2017). https://doi.org/10.1007/978-3-319-54072-6_8
9. Banerjee, A., Venkatasubramanian, K.K., Mukherjee, T., Gupta, S.K.S.: Ensuring safety, security, and sustainability of mission-critical cyber-physical systems. Proc. IEEE **100**(1), 283–299 (2012)
10. Bordel, B., Alcarria, R., Robles, T., Martín, D.: Cyber-physical systems: extending pervasive sensing from control theory to the internet of things. Pervasive Mob. Comput. **40**, 156–184 (2017)
11. Cadoli, M., Mancini, T.: Combining relational algebra, SQL, constraint modelling, and local search. Theory Pract. Log. Program. **7**(1–2), 37–65 (2007)

12. Cadoli, M., Mancini, T., Patrizi, F.: SAT as an effective solving technology for constraint problems. In: Esposito, F., Raś, Z.W., Malerba, D., Semeraro, G. (eds.) ISMIS 2006. LNCS (LNAI), vol. 4203, pp. 540–549. Springer, Heidelberg (2006). https://doi.org/10.1007/11875604_61
13. Clarke, E.M., Wing, J.M.: Formal methods: state of the art and future directions. ACM Comput. Surv. **28**(4), 626–643 (1996)
14. Clarke, E.M., Zuliani, P.: Statistical model checking for cyber-physical systems. In: Bultan, T., Hsiung, P.-A. (eds.) ATVA 2011. LNCS, vol. 6996, pp. 1–12. Springer, Heidelberg (2011). https://doi.org/10.1007/978-3-642-24372-1_1
15. Dagum, P., Karp, R., Luby, M., Ross, S.: An optimal algorithm for Monte Carlo estimation. SIAM J. Comput. **29**(5), 1484–1496 (2000)
16. David, A., Larsen, K.G., Legay, A., Mikučionis, M., Wang, Z.: Time for statistical model checking of real-time systems. In: Gopalakrishnan, G., Qadeer, S. (eds.) CAV 2011. LNCS, vol. 6806, pp. 349–355. Springer, Heidelberg (2011). https://doi.org/10.1007/978-3-642-22110-1_27
17. Della Penna, G., Intrigila, B., Melatti, I., Tronci, E., Venturini Zilli, M.: Bounded probabilistic model checking with the Murφ verifier. In: FMCAD 2004. IEEE (2004)
18. Dey, N., Ashour, A.S., Shi, F., Fong, S.J., Tavares, J.M.R.S.: Medical cyber-physical systems: a survey. J. Med. Syst. **42**(4), 1–13 (2018). https://doi.org/10.1007/s10916-018-0921-x
19. Ding, K., Ding, S., Morozov, A., Fabarisov, T., Janschek, K.: On-line error detection and mitigation for time-series data of cyber-physical systems using deep learning based methods. In: 2019 15th European Dependable Computing Conference (EDCC), pp. 7–14 (2019)
20. Dowdeswell, B., Sinha, R., MacDonell, S.G.: Finding faults: a scoping study of fault diagnostics for industrial cyber-physical systems. J. Syst. Softw. **168**, 110638 (2020)
21. Erdinc, O., Tascikaraoglu, A., Paterakis, N.G., Catalao, J.P.S.: Novel incentive mechanism for end-users enrolled in DLC-based demand response programs within stochastic planning context. IEEE Trans. Industr. Electron. **66**(2), 1476–1487 (2019)
22. European Medicines Agency: Reporting of physiologically based pharmacokinetic (PBPK) modelling and simulation. EMA/CHMP/458101/2016 (2019)
23. Fabregat, A., et al.: The reactome pathway knowledgebase. Nucleic Acids Res. **46**(D1), D649–D655 (2018)
24. Foughali, M.: Toward a correct-and-scalable verification of concurrent robotic systems: insights on formalisms and tools. In: 2017 17th International Conference on Application of Concurrency to System Design (ACSD), pp. 29–38 (2017)
25. Foughali, M., Ingrand, F., Seceleanu, C.: Statistical model checking of complex robotic systems. In: Biondi, F., Given-Wilson, T., Legay, A. (eds.) SPIN 2019. LNCS, vol. 11636, pp. 114–134. Springer, Cham (2019). https://doi.org/10.1007/978-3-030-30923-7_7
26. Gottlob, G., Greco, G., Mancini, T.: Conditional constraint satisfaction: logical foundations and complexity. In: IJCAI 2007 (2007)
27. Grosu, R., Smolka, S.A.: Quantitative model checking. ISoLA **2004**, 6 (2004)
28. Grosu, R., Smolka, S.A.: Monte Carlo model checking. In: Halbwachs, N., Zuck, L.D. (eds.) TACAS 2005. LNCS, vol. 3440, pp. 271–286. Springer, Heidelberg (2005). https://doi.org/10.1007/978-3-540-31980-1_18

29. Hayes, B., Melatti, I., Mancini, T., Prodanovic, M., Tronci, E.: Residential demand management using individualized demand aware price policies. IEEE Trans. Smart Grid **8**(3), 1284–1294 (2016)
30. Hengartner, M.P., et al.: Negative affect is unrelated to fluctuations in hormone levels across the menstrual cycle: evidence from a multisite observational study across two successive cycles. J. Psychosom. Res. **99**, 21–27 (2017)
31. Hunter, P., et al.: A vision and strategy for the virtual physiological human in 2010 and beyond. Philos. Trans. Math. Phys. Eng. Sci. **368**, 2595–2614 (2010)
32. Jindal, A., Bhambhu, B.S., Singh, M., Kumar, N., Naik, K.: A heuristic-based appliance scheduling scheme for smart homes. IEEE Trans. Industr. Inf. **16**(5), 3242–3255 (2020)
33. Kanehisa, M., Furumichi, M., Tanabe, M., Sato, Y., Morishima, K.: KEGG: new perspectives on genomes, pathways, diseases and drugs. Nucleic Acids Res. **45**(D1), D353–D361 (2017)
34. Kement, C.E., Gultekin, H., Tavli, B.: A holistic analysis of privacy-aware smart grid demand response. IEEE Trans. Industr. Electron. **68**(8), 7631–7641 (2021)
35. Koch, W., Mancuso, R., West, R., Bestavros, A.: Reinforcement learning for UAV attitude control. ACM Trans. Cyber-Phys. Syst. **3**(2), 1–21 (2019)
36. Kohl, P., Noble, D.: Systems biology and the virtual physiological human. Mol. Syst. Biol. **5**(1), 292 (2009)
37. Krieken, J.H.: Precision medicine. J. Hematop. **6**(1), 1 (2013). https://doi.org/10.1007/s12308-013-0176-x
38. Lee, E.A.: Fundamental limits of cyber-physical systems modeling. ACM Trans. Cyber-Phys. Syst. **1**(1), 1–26 (2016)
39. Leeners, B., et al.: Associations between natural physiological and supraphysiological estradiol levels and stress perception. Front. Psycol. **10**, 1296 (2019)
40. Leeners, B., et al.: Lack of associations between female hormone levels and visuospatial working memory, divided attention and cognitive bias across two consecutive menstrual cycles. Front. Behav. Neurosci. **11**, 120 (2017)
41. Legay, A., Delahaye, B., Bensalem, S.: Statistical model checking: an overview. In: Barringer, H., Falcone, Y., Finkbeiner, B., Havelund, K., Lee, I., Pace, G., Roşu, G., Sokolsky, O., Tillmann, N. (eds.) RV 2010. LNCS, vol. 6418, pp. 122–135. Springer, Heidelberg (2010). https://doi.org/10.1007/978-3-642-16612-9_11
42. Maggioli, F., Mancini, T., Tronci, E.: SBML2Modelica: integrating biochemical models within open-standard simulation ecosystems. Bioinformatics **36**(7), 2165–2172 (2020)
43. Mancini, T., Cadoli, M.: Detecting and breaking symmetries by reasoning on problem specifications. In: Zucker, J.-D., Saitta, L. (eds.) SARA 2005. LNCS (LNAI), vol. 3607, pp. 165–181. Springer, Heidelberg (2005). https://doi.org/10.1007/11527862_12
44. Mancini, T., Micaletto, D., Patrizi, F., et al.: Evaluating ASP and Commercial Solvers on the CSPLib. Constraints **13**, 407–436 (2008). https://doi.org/10.1007/s10601-007-9028-6
45. Mancini, T., Flener, P., Pearson, J.K.: Combinatorial problem solving over relational databases: view synthesis through constraint-based local search. In: SAC 2012. ACM (2012)
46. Mancini, T., Mari, F., Massini, A., Melatti, I., Merli, F., Tronci, E.: System level formal verification via model checking driven simulation. In: Sharygina, N., Veith, H. (eds.) CAV 2013. LNCS, vol. 8044, pp. 296–312. Springer, Heidelberg (2013). https://doi.org/10.1007/978-3-642-39799-8_21

47. Mancini, T., et al.: Computing personalised treatments through in silico clinical trials. A case study on downregulation in assisted reproduction. In: RCRA 2018, vol. 2271 of CEUR W.P. CEUR (2018)
48. Mancini, T., Mari, F., Massini, A., Melatti, I., Salvo, I., Tronci, E.: On minimising the maximum expected verification time. Inf. Process. Lett. **122**, 8–16 (2017)
49. Mancini, T., Mari, F., Massini, A., Melatti, I., Tronci, E.: Anytime system level verification via random exhaustive hardware in the loop simulation. In: DSD 2014. IEEE (2014)
50. Mancini, T., Mari, F., Massini, A., Melatti, I., Tronci, E.: System level formal verification via distributed multi-core hardware in the loop simulation. In: PDP 2014. IEEE (2014)
51. Mancini, T., Mari, F., Massini, A., Melatti, I., Tronci, E.: SyLVaaS: system level formal verification as a service. In: PDP 2015. IEEE (2015)
52. Mancini, T., Mari, F., Massini, A., Melatti, I., Tronci, E.: Anytime system level verification via parallel random exhaustive hardware in the loop simulation. Microprocess. Microsyst. **41**, 12–28 (2016)
53. Mancini, T., Mari, F., Massini, A., Melatti, I., Tronci, E.: SyLVaaS: system level formal verification as a service. Fundam. Inform. **149**(1–2), 101–132 (2016)
54. Mancini, T., et al.: Parallel statistical model checking for safety verification in smart grids. In: SmartGridComm 2018. IEEE (2018)
55. Mancini, T., et al.: Demand-aware price policy synthesis and verification services for smart grids. In: SmartGridComm 2014. IEEE (2014)
56. Mancini, T., et al.: User flexibility aware price policy synthesis for smart grids. In: DSD 2015. IEEE (2015)
57. Mancini, T., Melatti, I., Tronci, E.: Any-horizon uniform random sampling and enumeration of constrained scenarios for simulation-based formal verification. IEEE TSE (2021)
58. Mancini, T., Tronci, E., Salvo, I., Mari, F., Massini, A., Melatti, I.: Computing biological model parameters by parallel statistical model checking. In: Ortuño, F., Rojas, I. (eds.) IWBBIO 2015. LNCS, vol. 9044, pp. 542–554. Springer, Cham (2015). https://doi.org/10.1007/978-3-319-16480-9_52
59. Mari, F., Melatti, I., Salvo, I., Tronci, E.: Synthesis of quantized feedback control software for discrete time linear hybrid systems. In: Touili, T., Cook, B., Jackson, P. (eds.) CAV 2010. LNCS, vol. 6174, pp. 180–195. Springer, Heidelberg (2010). https://doi.org/10.1007/978-3-642-14295-6_20
60. Mediouni, B.L., Nouri, A., Bozga, M., Dellabani, M., Legay, A., Bensalem, S.: $\mathcal{S}$BIP 2.0: statistical model checking stochastic real-time systems. In: Lahiri, S.K., Wang, C. (eds.) ATVA 2018. LNCS, vol. 11138, pp. 536–542. Springer, Cham (2018). https://doi.org/10.1007/978-3-030-01090-4_33
61. Mediouni, B.L., Nouri, A., Bozga, M., Dellabani, M., Combaz, J., Legay, A., Bensalem, S.: Sbip 2.0: statistical model checking stochastic real-time systems. Technical Report TR-2018-5, Verimag Research Report (2018)
62. Melatti, I., Mari, F., Mancini, T., Prodanovic, M., Tronci, E.: A two-layer near-optimal strategy for substation constraint management via home batteries. IEEE Trans. Ind. Electron. **69**(8), 8566–8578 (2021)
63. Melatti, I., Palmer, R., Sawaya, G., et al.: Parallel and distributed model checking in Eddy. Int. J. Softw. Tools Technol. Transfer **11**, 13–25 (2009). https://doi.org/10.1007/s10009-008-0094-x

64. Milewski, J., Szczęśniak, A., Lewandowski, J.: Dynamic characteristics of auxiliary equipment of SOFC/SOEC hydrogen peak power plant. IERI Procedia **9**, 82–87 (2014). International Conference on Environment Systems Science and Engineering (ESSE 2014)
65. Mitchell, R., Chen, I.-R.: Behavior rule specification-based intrusion detection for safety critical medical cyber physical systems. IEEE Trans. Dependable Secure Comput. **12**(1), 16–30 (2015)
66. Nouri, A., Legay, A., Bensalem, S., Bozga, M.: SBIP: a statistical model checking extension for the BIP framework. In: Statistical Model Checking Workshop, SMC (2013)
67. Pappagallo, A.: Statistical model checking as an effective technology to formally analyze industry-relevant cyber-physical systems. In: Benedictis, R.D., et al. (eds.) Proceedings of IPS2021 and RCRA2021, vol. 3065 of CEUR Workshop Proceedings. CEUR-WS.org (2021)
68. Pappagallo, A.: Statistical model checking for the analysis of mission- and safety-critical cyber-physical systems. In: 3rd Workshop on Artificial Intelligence and Formal Verification, Logic, Automata, and Synthesis (OVERLAY 2021), volume to appear of CEUR Workshop Proceedings. CEUR-WS.org (2021)
69. Pappagallo, A., Massini, A., Tronci, E.: Monte Carlo based statistical model checking of cyber-physical systems: a review. Information **11**(12), 588 (2020)
70. Pappalardo, F., Russo, G., Tshinanu, F.M., Viceconti, M.: In silico clinical trials: concepts and early adoptions. Brief. Bioinform. **20**(5), 1699–1708 (2019)
71. Patrick, D.R., Fardo, S.W.: Electrical Distribution Systems. Second edn., Pearson Professional Education (2009)
72. Pimm, A.J., Cockerill, T.T., Taylor, P.G.: The potential for peak shaving on low voltage distribution networks using electricity storage. J. Energy Storage **16**, 231–242 (2018)
73. Reijsbergen, D., de Boer, P.-T., Scheinhardt, W., Haverkort, B.: On hypothesis testing for statistical model checking. Int. J. Softw. Tools Technol. Transfer **17**(4), 377–395 (2014). https://doi.org/10.1007/s10009-014-0350-1
74. Röblitz, S., et al.: A mathematical model of the human menstrual cycle for the administration of GnRH analogues. J. Theor. Biol. **321**, 8–27 (2013)
75. Rogers, W., Hutchison, K.: Evidence-based medicine in theory and practice: epistemological and normative issues. In: Schramme, T., Edwards, S. (eds.) Handbook of the Philosophy of Medicine, pp. 851–872. Springer, Dordrecht (2017). https://doi.org/10.1007/978-94-017-8688-1_40
76. Saad, A., Youssef, T., Elsayed, A.T., Amin, A., Abdalla, O.H., Mohammed, O.: Data-centric hierarchical distributed model predictive control for smart grid energy management. IEEE Trans. Industr. Inf. **15**(7), 4086–4098 (2019)
77. Sinisi, S., Alimguzhin, V., Mancini, T., Tronci, E.: Reconciling interoperability with efficient verification and validation within open source simulation environments. Simul. Model. Pract. Theory **109**, 102277 (2021)
78. Sinisi, S., Alimguzhin, V., Mancini, T., Tronci, E., Leeners, B.: Complete populations of virtual patients for in silico clinical trials. Bioinformatics **36**(22–23), 5465–5472 (2020)
79. Sinisi, S., Alimguzhin, V., Mancini, T., Tronci, E., Leeners, B.: Complete populations of virtual patients for in silico clinical trials. Bioinformatics **36**(22–23), 5465–5472 (2021)
80. Sinisi, S., Alimguzhin, V., Mancini, T., Tronci, E., Mari, F., Leeners, B.: Optimal personalised treatment computation through in silico clinical trials on patient digital twins. Fundam. Inform. **174**(3–4), 283–310 (2020)

81. Statistics on IoT Spending (2021). https://www.statista.com/topics/2637/internet-of-things/
82. Tronci, E., et al.: Patient-specific models from inter-patient biological models and clinical records. In: FMCAD 2014. IEEE (2014)
83. Uddin, M., Romlie, M.F., Abdullah, M.F., Abd Halim, S., Kwang, T.C.: A review on peak load shaving strategies. Renew. Sustain. Energy Rev. **82**, 3323–3332 (2018)
84. U.S.A. Food and Drug Administration: Reporting of computational modeling studies in medical device submissions. FDA-2013-D-1530 (2016)
85. U.S.A. Food and Drug Administration: Physiologically based pharmacokinetic analyses - format and content guidance for industry. FDA-2016-D-3969 (2018)
86. Zhang, N., Leibowicz, B.D., Hanasusanto, G.A.: Optimal residential battery storage operations using robust data-driven dynamic programming. IEEE Trans. Smart Grid **11**(2), 1771–1780 (2020)
87. Zimmerling, M., Mottola, L., Kumar, P., Ferrari, F., Thiele, L.: Adaptive real-time communication for wireless cyber-physical systems. ACM Trans. Cyber-Phys. Syst. **1**(2), 1–29 (2017)

An ASP-Based Approach to Scheduling Pre-operative Assessment Clinic

Simone Caruso[1], Giuseppe Galatà[2], Marco Maratea[1(✉)], Marco Mochi[1,2], and Ivan Porro[2]

[1] University of Genoa, Genova, Italy
{simone.caruso,marco.maratea,marco.mochi}@unige.it
[2] SurgiQ srl, Genova, Italy
{giuseppe.galata,marco.mochi,ivan.porro}@surgiq.com

Abstract. The problem of scheduling Pre-Operative Assessment Clinic (PAC) consists of assigning patients to a day for the exams needed before a surgical procedure, taking into account patients with different priority levels, due dates, and operators availability. Realizing a satisfying schedule is of upmost importance for a clinic, since delay in PAC can cause delay in the subsequent phases, causing a decrease in patients' satisfaction. In this paper, we divide the problem in two sub-problems: In the first sub-problem patients are assigned to a day taking into account a default list of exams; then, in the second sub-problem, having the actual list of exams needed by each patient, we use the results of the first sub-problem to assign a starting time to each exam. We first present a mathematical formulation for both problems. Then, we present solutions based on Answer Set Programming (ASP): The first solution is a genuine ASP encoding of the sub-problems, while the second introduces domain-specific optimizations. Experiments show that both solutions provide satisfying results in short time, while the second is able to prove optimality faster.

Keywords: Healthcare · Pre-Operative Assessment Clinic scheduling · Answer set programming

1 Introduction

The Pre-Operative Assessment Clinic (PAC) scheduling problem is the task of assigning patients to a day, in which the patient will be examined and prepared to a surgical operation, taking in account patients with different priority levels, due dates, and operators availability. The PAC consists of several exams needed by patients to ensure they are well prepared for their operation. This allows patients to stay at home until the morning of the surgery, instead of being admitted to the hospital one or two days before the scheduled operation; moreover, reducing waiting time between the exams increase patient satisfaction [34] and avoid the cancellation of the surgery [22].

The problem is divided into two sub-problems [19]: In the first sub-problem, patients are assigned to a day taking into account a default list of exams, and the

S. Bandini et al. (Eds.): AIxIA 2021, LNAI 13196, pp. 671–688, 2022.
https://doi.org/10.1007/978-3-031-08421-8_46

solution has to schedule patients before their due date and prioritize the assignments to patients with higher priority. In the second sub-problem, the scheduler assigns a starting time to each exam needed by the patients, considering the available operators and the duration of the exams. A proper solution to the PAC scheduling problem is vital to improve the degree of patients' satisfaction and to reduce surgical complications. Complex combinatorial problems, possibly involving optimizations, such as the PAC problem, are usually the target applications of AI languages such as Answer Set Programming (ASP). Indeed ASP, thanks to its readability and the availability of efficient solvers [2,10,25,27], has been successfully employed for solving hard combinatorial problems in several research areas, and it has been also employed to solve many scheduling problems [1,4,5,15,16,18,35], also in industrial contexts (see, e.g., [3,20,21,37] for detailed descriptions of ASP applications).

In this paper, we first present a mathematical formulation of both sub-problems: In the solution of the first sub-problem, the scheduler minimizes the number of unassigned patients. Then, we propose a solution to the second sub-problem, using as input of the problem the result of the first one and minimizing the time each patient stays at the hospital. We then apply ASP to solve the PAC scheduling problem, by presenting two ASP encodings for the sub-problems, and run an experimental analysis on PAC benchmarks with realistic sizes and parameters inspired from data seen in literature, varying the number of patients to schedule and the available operators. Overall, results using the state-of-the-art ASP solver CLINGO [24] show that ASP is a suitable solving methodology also for the PAC scheduling problem, even if often it takes a considerable amount of time to prove the optimality of the solution of the second sub-problem. Thus, we finally apply domain-specific optimizations, still expressed as ASP rules, which consider the time slots in which exams can be effectively performed by patients, that help to reduce the overall running time significantly.

The paper is then structured as follows. Sections 2 and 3 present an informal description of the problem and a precise, mathematical formulation, respectively. Then, Sect. 4 shows our ASP encodings for both phases, whose experimental evaluation is presented in Sect. 5. Domain-specific optimizations are introduced and evaluated in Sect. 6. The paper ends by discussing related work and conclusions in Sect. 7 and 8, respectively.

2 Problem Description

Since the schedule of the PAC day must be scheduled as soon as possible, this problem is typically divided in two phases: In the first phase, since we deal with this sub-problem before the actual PAC day, the clinics do not know which exams each patient will require, thus, as typically done in hospitals, we consider that each patient requires a default list of exams according to his specialty, i.e. the lists of exams are equal for patients requiring the same specialty but differ among specialties, and the scheduler assigns the day of PAC without considering the starting time of the exams. Thus, in the first sub-problem the solution assigns patients overestimating the duration and the number of exams needed. In particular, all the optional exams, such as exams required by smokers or patients with diabetes, are assigned to all the patients in the first phase. The overestimation is important in order to have a second sub-problem which is not unsatisfiable. Then, when the operation day is closer, the hospital knows exactly the exams needed by each patient and can assign the starting time of each exam. Going in more details, the first sub-problem consists of scheduling appointments in a range of days for patients requiring surgical operation. Each patient is linked to a due date, a target day, and a priority level: The due date is the maximum day in which (s)he can be assigned, the target day is the optimal day in which schedule the appointment, while the solution prioritizes patients with higher priority level. There are several exam areas, corresponding to the locations in which patients will be examined. Each exam area needs operators to be activated and has a limited time of usage. Each operator can activate three different exam areas, but they can be assigned to just one exam area for each day. The solution must assign the operators to the exam areas, to activate them, and the day of PAC to patients, ensuring that the total time of usage of each exam location is lower than its limit. Since in this first sub-problem the list of exams needed by patients is not the final list, i.e. just the first and the last exam are the same for every patient, and in the second sub-problem some exams could be added, the solution schedules patients leaving some unused time to each exam area. An optimal solution minimizes the number of unassigned patients, giving priority to patients with higher priority levels, and ties are broken by minimizing the difference between the day assigned and the target day of each patient, giving again precedence to patients with higher priority.

In the second sub-problem, patients are linked to their real exams, so the solution has to assign the starting time of each exam, having the first sub-problem already assigned the day. The input consists of registrations, exams needed by patients and the exam areas activated. Exams are ordered, so the solution must assign the starting time of each exam respecting their order and their duration, by considering that each exam area can be used by one patient at a time. Finally, the solution minimizes the difference between the starting time of the first exam and the last exam of each patient.

3 Formalization of the PAC Scheduling Problem

In this section, we provide a mathematical formulation of the two sub-problems.

Definition 1 (first PAC sub-problem). *Let*

- R *be a finite set of registrations;*
- $E = \{e_1, \ldots, e_m\}$ *be a set of* m *exams;*
- $EL = \{el_1, \ldots, el_n\}$ *be a set of* n *exam locations;*
- O *be a finite set of operators;*
- $D = \{t : t \in [1..14]\}$ *be the set of all days;*
- $\delta : R \mapsto \{1, 2, 3, 4\}$ *be a function associating a registration to a priority;*

- $\rho : R \times E \mapsto \mathbb{N}$ *be a function associating a registration and an exam to a duration such that for a registration* r *and an exam* e *if* $\rho(r,e) > 0$ *then the registration* r *requires the exam* e*;*
- $\epsilon : D \mapsto \mathbb{N}$ *be a function associating a day to the number of registration assigned in the day* d*;*
- $\zeta : \mathbb{N} \times oe2 \mapsto \mathbb{N}$ *be a function such that* $\zeta(n) = (ts * \epsilon(n)) - (oe2 * \epsilon * (\epsilon - 1))$*;*
- $\omega : R \mapsto \mathbb{D}$ *be a function associating a registration to a due date;*
- $\lambda : R \mapsto \mathbb{D}$ *be a function associating a registration to a target day;*
- $\sigma : E \mapsto \mathbb{EL}$ *be a function associating an exam to the exam location;*
- $\Delta : EL \times D \mapsto \mathbb{N}$ *be a function associating an exam location to the maximum sum of exams lengths assignable to the exam location;*
- $\tau : EL \times D \mapsto \mathbb{N}$ *be a function associating an exam location and a day to the required number of operators to be activated, such that* $\tau(el, d) = n$ *if the exam location* el *in the day* d *requires* n *operators to be activated;*
- $\theta : O \times EL \times D \mapsto \{0, 1\}$ *be a function such that* $\theta(o, el, d) = 1$ *if the operator* o *is assigned to the exam location* el *in the day* d*, and* 0 *otherwise;*
- oe1 *be a constant used to decrease the maximum sum of exam lengths assignable to the exam locations;*
- $oe2$ *be a constant used to decrease the maximum sum of exams duration assignable to a day;*
- ts *be a constant that is equal to the number of time slots.*

Let $x : R \times D \mapsto \{0, 1\}$ *be a function such that* $x(r, d) = 1$ *if the registration* r *is assigned to the day* d*, and* 0 *otherwise. Moreover, for a given* x*, let* $A_x = \{(r, d) : r \in R, d \in D, x(r, d) = 1\}$.

Then, given sets R*,* E*,* EL*,* O*,*D*, and functions* δ*,* ρ*,* ϵ*,* ω*,* λ*,* σ*,* Δ*,* τ*,* θ*, the first PAC sub-problem is defined as the problem of finding a schedule* x*, such that*

(c_1) $|\{d : x(r, d) = 1\}| \leq 1 \quad \forall r \in R, d \leq \omega(r)$;
(c_2) $|\{d : x(r, d) = 1\}| = 0 \quad \forall r \in R, d > \omega(r)$;
(c_3) $|\{o : \theta(o, el, d) = 1\}| = \tau(el, d) \quad \forall\, (r, d) \in Ax, \rho(r, e) > 0, el = \sigma(e)$;
(c_4) $|\{el : \theta(o, el, d)\}| \leq 1 \quad \forall o \in O, \forall d \in D$;
(c_5) $\sum\limits_{x(r,d)=1, \sigma(e)=el} \rho(r, e) \leq \Delta(el, d)/oe1 \quad \forall\, el \in EL, t \in T$;
(c_6) $\sum\limits_{x(r,d)=1, \forall e \in E} \rho(r, e) \leq \zeta(\epsilon(d), oe2) \quad \forall\, d \in D$;

Condition (c_1) ensures that each registration is assigned at most one time in the days before the due date associated to the registration. Condition (c_2) ensures that each registration is not assigned in a day after the due date associated to the registration. Condition (c_3) ensures that for each exam location used by at least one registration, the required number of operators are assigned Condition (c_4) ensures that each operator is assigned to at most one exam location in each day. Condition (c_5) ensures that the sum of all the durations of the exams associated to an exam location in a day is less or equal to the maximum time assignable to that exam location divided by the value $oe1$. Condition (c_6) ensures that the sum of all exam durations in a day is less than a value obtained with the number of registrations assigned in the day and the value oe2.

Definition 2 (Unassigned registrations). *Given a solution x, let $U_x^{pr} = \{r : r \in R, \delta(r) = pr, r \notin A_x\}$. Intuitively, U_x^{pr} represents the set of registrations of priority pr that were not assigned to any day.*

Definition 3 (Distance target day). *Given a solution x, let $t_x^{pr} = \sum_{x(r,d) \in A_x, \delta(r)=pr} \mid d - \lambda(r) \mid$. Intuitively, t^{pr_x} represents the sum of the distance between the day assigned to the registrations of priority pr and the target day associated.*

Definition 4. *A solution x is said to dominate a solution x' if $|U_x^{pr}| < |U_{x'}^{pr}|$ for the biggest pr for which $|U_x^{pr}| \neq |U_{x'}^{pr}|$ or if $|U_x^{pr}| = |U_{x'}^{pr}|$ for all the pr and $|t_x^{pr}| < |t_{x'}^{pr}|$ for the biggest pr for which $|t_x^{pr}| \neq |t_{x'}^{pr}|$.*

Definition 5 (second PAC sub-problem). *Let*

- *$T = \{t : t \in [1..ts]\}$ be the set of all time slots;*
- *$\beta : R \times E \mapsto \mathbb{N}$ be a function associating a registration and an exam to a value corresponding to the order in which the exam must be assigned.*
- *$\gamma : EL \mapsto \mathbb{N}$ be a function associating an exam location to the starting time of the exam location;*
- *$\xi : EL \mapsto \mathbb{N}$ be a function associating an exam location to the ending time of the exam location;*
- *$\mu : EL \mapsto \mathbb{N}$ be a function associating an exam location and a day to the maximum number of registration that can be assigned concurrently.*

Let $x : R \times E \times EL \times T \mapsto \{0, 1\}$ be a function such that $x(r, e, el, t) = 1$ if the registration r and the exam e are assigned to the exam location el in the time slot t, and 0 otherwise. Moreover, for a given x let $A_x = \{(r, e, el, t) : r \in R, e \in E, el \in EL, d \in D, x(r, e, el, t) = 1\}$.

Then, given sets R, E, EL, T, and functions ρ, β, γ, ξ, μ, the second PAC sub-problem is defined as the problem of finding a schedule x, such that

(c_7) $|\{t : x(r, e, el, t) = 1, t \in T\}| = 1 \quad \forall e \in E, \forall r \in R, \rho(r, e) > 0, \sigma(e) = el;$
(c_8) $\gamma(el) \leq t \leq \xi(el) - \beta(r, e) \quad \forall (r, e, el, t) \in A_x.$
(c_9) $x(r, e, el, t) = 0 \quad \forall (r, e', el, t') \in A_x, \forall e \in E, \rho(r, e') = d, \forall t \in T, t' \leq t < t' + d;$
(c_{10}) $t > t' \quad \forall (r, e, el, t) \in A_x, (r, e', el, t') \in A_x, \beta(r, e) > \beta(r, e');$
(c_{11}) $|\{r : x(r, e, el, t) = 1, r \in R, e \in E\}| = \mu(el) \quad \forall el \in EL, t \in T;$

Condition (c_7) ensures that each exam is assigned exactly once. Condition (c_8) ensures that each exam is assigned after the starting time of the required exam location and before the closing time of the required exam location minus the duration of the exam. Condition (c_9) ensures that for each registration each exam is assigned after that the exam before is ended. Condition (c_{10}) ensures that each exam is assigned after the exams with lower order. Condition (c_{11}) ensures that the number of exams assigned to a location is lower than the maximum availability for each location in any time slot.

```
{x(RID,PR,TOTDUR,DAY) : day(DAY), DAY < DUEDATE} 1 :- reg(RID,PR,TARGET,TOTDUR,DUEDATE).
:- x(RID,_,_,DAY), exam(RID,FORNID,_), not examLoc(FORNID,_,_,DAY,_).
res(RID,FORNID,DAY,DUR) :- x(RID,PR,_,DAY), exam(RID,FORNID,DUR).
:- N1 = #count{FORNID: res(RID,FORNID,_,_)},N2 = #count{FORNID: exam(RID,FORNID,_,_)},
     x(RID,_,_,_), N1 != N2.
:- #sum{DUR, RID: res(RID,FORNID,DAY,DUR)} > NHOURS/oe1, examLoc(FORNID,_,NHOURS,DAY,N).
:- #sum{TOTDUR, RID: x(RID,_,TOTDUR,DAY)} = M, #count{RID: x(RID,_,_,DAY)} = N, day(DAY), M
     > ((ts*N)-(oe2*N*(N+1))), N>1.
{operator(ID, FORNID, DAY) : operators(ID, FORNID, DAY)} == NOP :- examLoc(FORNID, NOP, _,
     DAY,_), res(REGID, FORNID, DAY, _).
:- operator(ID,FORNID1,DAY), operator(ID,FORNID2,DAY), FORNID1 < FORNID2.
unassignedP1(N) :- M = #count {RID: x(RID,1,_,_)}, N = totRegsP1 - M.
unassignedP2(N) :- M = #count {RID: x(RID,2,_,_)}, N = totRegsP2 - M.
unassignedP3(N) :- M = #count {RID: x(RID,3,_,_)}, N = totRegsP3 - M.
unassignedP4(N) :- M = #count {RID: x(RID,4,_,_)}, N = totRegsP4 - M.
:~ unassignedP1(N). [N@8]
:~ unassignedP2(N). [N@7]
:~ unassignedP3(N). [N@6]
:~ unassignedP4(N). [N@5]
:~ x(RID,1,_,DAY), reg(RID,_,TARGET,_,_). [|DAY-TARGET|@4,RID]
:~ x(RID,2,_,DAY), reg(RID,_,TARGET,_,_). [|DAY-TARGET|@3,RID]
:~ x(RID,3,_,DAY), reg(RID,_,TARGET,_,_). [|DAY-TARGET|@2,RID]
:~ x(RID,4,_,DAY), reg(RID,_,TARGET,_,_). [|DAY-TARGET|@1,RID]
```

Fig. 1. ASP encoding of the first sub-problem

Definition 6 (Time in hospital). *Given a solution x, let*

$$m_x = \sum_{r \in R, x(r,0,el,t) \in A_x, x(r,23,el,t') \in A_x} t' + \rho(r,23) - t.$$

Intuitively, m_x represents the sum of the difference between the ending time of the last exam and the starting time of the first exam of each registration.

Definition 7. *A solution x is said to dominate a solution x' if $m_x < m_{x'}$.*

4 ASP Encoding

In this section we present the ASP encoding for the two sub-problems, in two separate sub-sections.

4.1 ASP Encoding for the First PAC Sub-problem

We assume the reader is familiar with syntax and semantics of ASP. Starting from the specifications in the previous section, here we present the ASP encoding for the first sub-problem, based on the input language of CLINGO [23]. For details about syntax and semantics of ASP programs we refer the reader to [9].

Data Model. The input data is specified by means of the following atoms:

- Instances of `reg(RID, PR, TARGET, TOTDUR, DUEDATE)` represent the registrations, characterized by an id (`RID`), the priority level (`PR`), the ideal day in which the patient should be assigned (`TARGET`), the sum of the durations of the exams needed by the patient (`TOTDUR`), and the due date (`DUEDATE`).

- Instances of exam(RID, FORNID, DUR) represent the exams needed by the patients identified by an id (RID), the exam area (FORNID), and the duration (DUR).
- Instances of examLoc(FORNID, NOP, NHOURS, DAY, N) represent the exam areas, characterized by an id (FORNID), which requires NOP operators to be activated, which is active for a certain time (NHOURS) in a day (DAY), and can be concurrently assigned up to N patients.
- Instances of operators(ID, FORNID, DAY) represent the operators, characterized by an id (ID), who can be assigned to the exam ares (FORNID) in a day (DAY).
- Instances of day(DAY) represent the available days.

The output is an assignment represented by an atom of the form x(RID, PR, TOTDUR, DAY), where the intuitive meaning is that the exams of registration with id RID and priority level PR is assigned to the day DAY and has a total duration of exams equal to TOTDUR.

Encoding. The related encoding is shown in Fig. 1, and is described in the following. To simplify the description, we denote as r_i the rule appearing at line i of Fig. 1.

Rule r_1 assigns registrations to a day. The assignment is made assigning a day that is before the due date. Rule r_2 checks that every registration is assigned to a day with all the exams area needed to be activated. Rule r_3 derives an auxiliary atom that is used later in other rules. In particular, the new atom is used to get the duration of the visit for each patient and for each exam area. Then, rule r_4 checks that the number of needed exams and the number of res atoms created are the same. Rule r_5 is used to ensure that each exam area is used for a total amount of time that is lower than its limit divided by the oe1 constant, in order to overestimate the required time for the visits. Rule r_6 is used to be sure to not assign too many patients in the first sub-problem to a particular day. So, it overestimates the time needed by each patient, the degree of the overestimation can be changed by using different oe2 values. Rule r_7 assigns operators to the required exam areas. Rule r_8 checks that each operator is assigned to just one exam area in every day. Rules from r_9 to r_{12} are needed to derive auxiliary atoms that are used later on in optimization. In particular, they are used to count how many patients with different priorities are not assigned to a day. Weak constraints from r_{13} and r_{16} are used to minimize the number of unassigned registrations according to their priority. Finally, weak constraints from r_{17} and r_{20} minimize the difference between the assigned and target day of each patient, giving precedence to higher priorities.

4.2 ASP Encoding for the Second PAC Sub-problem

Data Model. The input data is the same of the first sub-problem for the atoms exam and time, while other atoms are changed:

```
{x(RID,FORNID,ST,ST+DUR,DAY) : examLoc(FORNID,DAY,FORNST,FORNET,_), time(ST), ST >= FORNST,
     ST <= FORNET-DUR} = 1 :- reg(RID,DAY), esame(RID,FORNID,DUR).
:- x(RID,FORNID1,ST1,_,_), x(RID,FORNID2,ST2,_,_), phase(FORNID1,ORD1), phase(FORNID2,ORD2),
     ORD2 < ORD1, ST1 < ST2.
:- #count{FORNID: x(RID,FORNID,ST,ET,DAY), T >= ST, T < ET} > 1, reg(RID,DAY), time(T).
:- #count{FORNID: x(RID,FORNID,ST,ET,DAY), T >= ST, T < ET} > N, examLoc(FORNID,DAY,_,_,N),
     time(T).
:~ reg(RID,_), x(RID,0,ST,_,_), x(RID,23,_,ET,_). [ET-ST@1, RID]
```

Fig. 2. ASP encoding of the second sub-problem

- Instances of `reg(RID, DAY)` represent the registrations, characterized by an id (`RID`) assigned to a day (`DAY`).
- Instances of `examLoc(FORNID, DAY, FORNST, FORNET, N)` represent the exam areas, characterized by an id (`FORNID`), which in a day (`DAY`) has a starting time and closing time respectively equals to `FORNST` and `FORNET`, which is active for a certain value of time (`NHOURS`) in a day (`DAY`), and can provide the exam to `N` patients.
- Instances of `phase(FORNID, ORD)` represent the order (`ORD`) of the exams provided by the exam area characterized by an id (`FORNID`).

The output is represented by an atom of the form `x(RID, FORNID, ST, ET, DAY)`, where the intuitive meaning is that the exam of the registration with id `RID` is in exam area `FORNID`, starts at time `ST` and ends at time `ET`, on the day `DAY`.

Encoding. The encoding consists of the rules reported in Fig. 2. Rule r_1 assigns a starting and an ending time to each exam needed by every patient, checking that the time in which is assigned is inside the opening time of the required exam area. Rule r_2 ensures that the order between the exams is respected. Rules r_3 checks that each patient is assigned to at most one exam for every time slot. Then, rule r_4 checks that each exam area provides the exam to at most `N` patients for every time slot. Finally, rule r_5 minimizes the difference between the ending time of the last exam and the starting time of the first exam of each patient.

5 Experimental Results

In this section, we report the results of an empirical analysis of the PAC scheduling problem via ASP. For the first sub-problem, data have been randomly generated using parameters inspired by literature and real world data, then the results of the first sub-problem have been used as input for the second sub-problem. The experiments were run on a AMD Ryzen 5 2600 CPU @ 3.40 GHz with 16 GB of physical RAM. The ASP system used was CLINGO [23] 5.4.0, using parameters *--restart-on-model* for faster optimization and *--parallel-mode 8* for parallel execution. This setting is the result of a preliminary analysis done also with other parameters, e.g., `--opt-strategy=usc` for optimization. The time limit was set to 300 s for both sub-problems.

PAC Benchmarks. Data are based on the sizes and parameters of a typical middle sized hospital, with 24 different exam areas. For the benchmarks we considered the constants $oe1$ and $oe2$ equal to 2 and 5, respectively. The values of the constants $oe1$ and $oe2$ are used to overestimate the required resources, by adding limits to the assignments to exam locations, for avoiding solutions of the first sub-problem that could lead to unsatisfiable problems in the second sub-problem. Thus, we set the two variables in a safe range, while a hospital could decide to decrease the values of oe1 and oe2 to increase the number of patients assignable in the first sub-problem. The solution schedules patients in a range of 14 days, for each day there are 60 time slots, thus the constant ts is set to 60, corresponding to 5 min per time slot. To test scalability we generated 3 different benchmarks of different dimensions. Each benchmark was tested 5 times with different randomly generated input.

In particular, each patient is linked to a surgical specialty, and needs a number of exams between 5 and 13, according to the specialty, while the duration of each exam varies between 3 and 6 time slots. The priorities of the registrations have been generated from an even distribution of four possible values (with weights of 0.25 for registrations having priority 1, 2, 3, and 4, respectively). For all the benchmarks, there are 24 exam areas and the operators, that are 35, can be assigned to 3 different exam areas. So, by increasing the number of patients while maintaining fixed the number of operators, we tested different scenarios with low, medium and high requests.

For the second sub-problem, we used the results of the first sub-problem as input. Thus, the number of patients and the exam locations activated depend on the assignment of the solution of the first sub-problem. Patients require all the same first and last exam, while the other exams required by each patient are linked to an order that is randomly assigned and that must be respected by the scheduler. In the second sub-problem clinics know the actual list of exams needed by patients: To simulate this scenario, we randomly added and discarded the optional exams assigned to patients in the first sub-problem. For example, optional exams are needed by patients that are over 65 years old or smokers. 5 instances for each benchmark have been generated, each corresponding to the assignments of 14 days.

Results for the First Sub-problem. The first optimization criteria in the PAC scheduling sub-problem is to assign as many patients as possible, starting from patients with higher priority. Our solution is able to assign a day to 201 patients out of 217 patients with highest priority; moreover, the scheduler is able to assign all or all but one patients with the highest priority in 12 out of 15 instances tested. Instances with 80 patients are more difficult, since in this scenario the number of operators is not enough to deal with the high number of patients.

In Table 1 are summarized the results obtained in this first sub-problem, in particular, the table shows the average number of patients from the 5 instances assigned with 40, 60, and 80 patients according to their priority level.

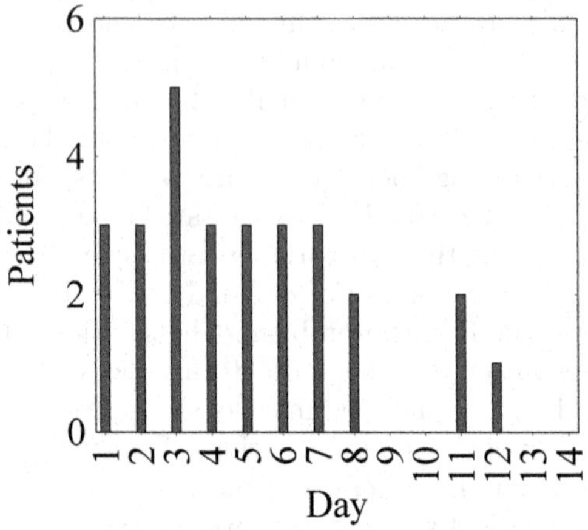

Fig. 3. Number of patients assigned to each day by the scheduler with 40 patients as input

Table 1. Percentage of assigned patients according to their priority level

Total #Patients	%P1 assigned	%P2 assigned	%P3 assigned	%P4 assigned
40	94%	85%	77%	66%
60	90%	69%	20%	13%
80	67%	22%	14%	10%

The second optimization criteria is to have an assigned day that is as much near as possible to the target day. This optimization criteria is able to assign patients with higher priority near to their target day while; instead, for patients with lower priorities, quality decreases. This is due to two reasons: The first one is that there are more optimization criteria with higher priorities, then, the scheduler already tries to assign as many patients as possible, without taking into account the target days of the patients, and the second one is that some patients have a target day in a day without their exam locations available, so, even in an optimal solution the assigned day to some patients would not be in the target day.

Figure 3 reports the result obtained by the scheduler with one of the instances with 40 patients as input. What can be seen from the graph is that some patients are assigned in days 11 and 12, while in days 9 and 10 there are no patients assigned. This can be explained by the fact that the scheduler tries to assign as many patients as possible and do not try to assign as soon as possible the patients. Moreover, in some days patients can not be assigned due to the unavailability of the exam locations required. In particular, in the assignments in Fig. 3, patients that are assigned in day 11 could not be assigned to another day, because that day is the only day with the exam locations they required.

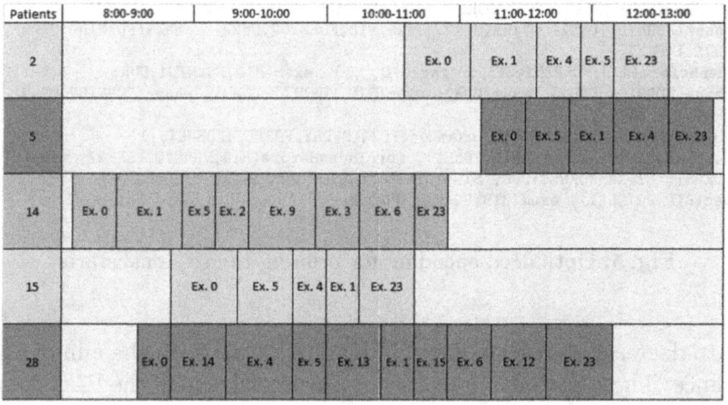

Fig. 4. Representations of the assignments of the starting time of the different exam locations of each patient in a single day

Results for the Second Sub-problem. In the second sub-problem the solution assigns the starting time of each exam of the patients. The input is taken from the results obtained in the first sub-problem. The solution minimizes the difference between the ending time of the last exam and the starting time of the first exam. While minimizing this value the solution tries to minimize the time spent in the hospital by all patients. In this sub-problem the scheduler is able to reach an optimal solution in 13 out of 15 instances tested. While the average total duration of the exams for each patient is 37 time slots, the solution finds a schedule that allows patients to have an average time in hospital that is just 38.5 time slots.

The results are obtained on average in 152, 186, 220 s in the instances with 40, 60 and, 80 patients, respectively. Figure 4 represents the starting times assigned to each patient in a particular day. The patients that must be scheduled are the same that are assigned by the first sub-problem in this day; the scheduler of the second sub-problem minimizes the waiting times of each patient.

As can be seen in Fig. 4 the scheduler is able to assign all patients optimally; indeed, all patients have no waiting time between each exam and thus the time spent in the hospital is reduced to the minimum, while respecting the constraints of the sub-problem, e.g., each exam location is assigned to at most one patient for each time slot.

6 Domain Specific Optimizations

Results show that ASP is a suitable methodology for solving the PAC problem. However, in the second sub-problem, we noted that our encoder is able to find the optimal solution in every instance in a short time but then the solver needs a large amount of time to prove optimality. For this reason, we decided to perform some domain specific optimizations, presented in the following two paragraphs,

```
6 forbiddenAfter(RID,FORNID1,ST+DUR1) :- reg(RID,_,_), exam(RID,FORNID1,DUR1),
      phase(FORNID1,ORD1), #sum{DUR2: exam(RID,FORNID2,DUR2), phase(FORNID2,ORD2), ORD2 >
      ORD1 } = ST.
7 forbiddenBefore(RID,FORNID1,ST) :- reg(RID,_,_), exam(RID,FORNID1,DUR1),
      phase(FORNID1,ORD1), #sum{DUR2: exam(RID,FORNID2,DUR2), phase(FORNID2,ORD2), ORD2 <
      ORD1 } = ST.
8 {x(REGID,FORNID,ST,ST+DUR,DAY): examLoc(FORNID,DAY,FORNST,FORNET,_),
      forbiddenAfter(RID,FORNID,FORB1), forbiddenBefore(RID,FORNID,FORB2), time(ST), ST >=
      FORNST, ST <= FORNET-DUR, ST <= lastTimeSlot-FORB1, ST > FORB2 } = 1 :-
      reg(RID,PRI,DAY), exam(RID,FORNID,DUR).
```

Fig. 5. Optimized encoding for pruning the sessions' starts

in order to decrease the grounding and planning time with the aim of improving performance. These optimizations rely on the knowledge of the PAC domain and the possibility of pruning impossible solutions already in the grounding process, as the results in the third paragraph show.

Pruning of Exams' Starting Time Slots. As shown in Fig. 2, in r_1 the starting time of the exams is guessed between all the available daily time slots, expressed by the atom `time(ST)`. Given that the exams must be assigned following an order, it is known the minimum number of time slots that each patient need to stay before and after each exam. Thus, the guess rule can be improved by reducing the number of possible starting time slots of each exam with the following constraints:

- an exam cannot start in a time slot if the remaining time slots are less than the minimum amount of time slots required to complete all the following exams;
- an exam cannot start in a time slot if the time slots before are less than the minimum amount of time slots required to complete the previous exams.

The encoding for pruning the exams' starting time slots is reported in Fig. 5. In rules r_6 and r_7 two new atoms `forbiddenAfter` and `forbiddenBefore` are defined as the minimum amount of time slots needed by each patient after (before) each exam. The minimum amount of time slots required by the exams after (before) each exam is obtained by computing the sum of the duration of the exams with the greater (lower) phase value. In r_8 the two new atoms are used in the guess rule, so that the starting time is after the value computed by the rule r_6 and after the difference between `lastTimeSlot`, that corresponds to the last time slot, and the value computed by r_7.

Minimization with Lower Bound. As it can be seen in Fig. 2, rule r_5 minimizes the time spent in the hospital by each patient, computed as the difference between the ending time of the last exam and the starting time of the first exam. However, the time spent in the hospital by each patient cannot be lower than the sum of the duration of all the required exams. Therefore, the minimization rule can be improved by computing the minimum time required by each patient and using it as a lower bound, so that solutions below this value are pruned.

```
9  cost(RID, TOT) :- TOT = #sum{DUR,FORNID : exam(RID,FORNID,DUR)}, reg(RID,_,_).
10 :~ x(RID,0,ST,_,_),x(RID,23,_,ET,_), cost(RID,TOT), ET-ST-TOT >= 0. [ ET-ST-TOT@1, RID]
```

Fig. 6. Optimized minimization rule

Table 2. Comparison of the mean time required to reach the optimal solution in the three scenarios with the different versions of the encoding for the second sub-problem

#Patients	ENC (s)	ENC+OPT1 (s)	ENC+OPT2 (s)	ENC+OPT1+OPT2 (s)
40	152	54	5	1
60	186	54	5	1
80	220	77	7	2
Percentage optimal	86,7%	100%	100%	100%

The enconding with the optimized weak constraint is shown in Fig. 6. In rule r_9, the minimum length of time to fully complete all the exams for each patient is computed as the sum of the duration of all the exams and the new auxiliary atom `cost(RID, TOT)` is defined. The weak constraint, in rule r_{10}, minimizes the difference between the planned total time (i.e. the difference between ending time and starting time of the last and first exam) and the lower bound previously computed, activating the weak constraint only when the difference is greater or equal than zero.

Results. In Table 2 the time to reach the optimal solution with the basic encoding, defined as ENC, and with the different optimizations, defined as OPT1 and OPT2, respectively, are reported. In particular, we define ENC+OPT1 as the encoder obtained by adding the rules in Fig. 5 to the encoder defined in Fig. 2 and by dropping the rule r_1 in Fig. 2, ENC+OPT2 as the encoder obtained by adding the rules in Fig. 6 to the encoder defined in Fig. 2 and by dropping the rule r_5 in Fig. 2, and ENC+OPT1+OPT2 as the encoder obtained by adding both optimizations. From Table 2, it can be noted that, while the original encoder is able to reach the optimal solution with 87% of the instances, all the encoders utilizing the different optimizations are able to reach the optimal solution on all instances. Moreover, ENC+OPT1 gives better performance than ENC, in particular, is able to prune a lot of possible solutions thanks to the new rules but, as we previously noted, some time is still spent computing solutions below the known lower bound. With ENC+OPT2, the performance increases noticeably, leading to the optimal solution in a few seconds. While adding either OPT1 and OPT2 led to better results, being able to reach an optimal solution in all the instances in up to 2 s, further increasing the performance.

7 Related Work

This paper is an extended and revised version of a paper appearing in the CEUR proceedings [13], having the following main improvements: (*i*) a mathematical formulation of the two phases of the problem (Sect. 3), which could be a starting point for testing other languages and tools from experts, (*ii*) domain-specific optimizations to the previous encoding, and a related experimental analysis, focused on improving the grounding phase of the ASP solver (Sect. 6), and (*iii*) a more complete related work section, that now includes also recent studies in which ASP has been employed to closely related scheduling problems (reported below).

The section is organized in two paragraphs: the first is focused on alternative methods for solving the PAC problem, while the second mentions works in which ASP has been employed to closely related scheduling problems.

Solving the PAC Problem. The work in [19] used two simulation models to analyse the difficulties of planning in the context of PAC and to determine the resources needed to reduce waiting times and long access times. The models were tested in a large university hospital and the results were validated measuring the level of patient satisfaction. [38] used a Lean quality improvement process changing the process and the standard routine. For example, patients were not asked to move from a room to another for the visits, but patients were placed in a room, and remained there for the duration of their assessment. This and other changes to the processes led to the decrease of the average lead time for patients and to the number of patients required to return the next day to complete the visits. [22,34,39], and, [40] studied the importance of implementing the PAC and the positive results obtained by having less waiting time between the exams and for the visit to the hospital. In particular, while different clinics follow different guidelines, implementing PAC has proved to be an important tool to avoid the cancellation of the surgeries and to significantly reduce the risk associated with the surgery.

Solving Scheduling Problems with ASP. ASP has been successfully used for solving hard combinatorial and application scheduling problems in several research areas. In the Healthcare domain (see, e.g., [3] for a recent survey), the first solved problem was the *Nurse Scheduling Problem* [4,5,18], where the goal is to create a scheduling for nurses working in hospital units. Then, the problem of assigning operating rooms to patients, denoted as *Operating Room Scheduling* [16,17], has been treated, and further extended to include bed management [15]. More recent problems include the *Chemotherepy Treatment Scheduling* problem [14], in which patients are assigned a chair or a bed for their treatments, and the *Rehabilitation Scheduling Problem* [12], which assigns patients to operators in rehabilitation sessions. The current paper is the only one which deals with the pre-operative phase, and presents a two phases approach.

Concerning scheduling problems beyond the Healthcare domain, ASP encoding were proposed for the following problems: *Incremental Scheduling Problem* [8,11,25,26], where the goal is to assign jobs to devices such that their executions do not overlap one another; *Team Building Problem* [35], where the goal is to allocate the available personnel of a seaport for serving the incoming ships; and the *Conference Paper Assignment Problem* [6], which deals with the problem of assigning reviewers in the Program Committee to submitted conference papers. Other relevant papers are Gebser et al. [28], where, in the context of routing driverless transport vehicles, the setup problem of routes such that a collection of transport tasks is accomplished in case of multiple vehicles sharing the same operation area is solved via ASP, in the context of car assembly at Mercedes-Benz Ludwigsfelde GmbH, and the recent survey paper by Falkner et al. [21], where industrial applications dealt with ASP are presented, including those involving scheduling problems.

8 Conclusion

In this paper, we have presented an analysis of the PAC scheduling problem modeled and solved with ASP. We started from a mathematical formulation of the problem, which considers constraints and parameters that can be found in other works, and then presented our ASP solution. The solution is further improved with domain specific optimizations. Results on synthetic data shows that the solution is able to assign a high number of patients with higher priority, and that the domain-specific optimizations help to reduce the time to prove optimality. We are currently working on extending our experiments, and comparing to other languages and tools using the mathematical formulation in Sect. 3. Moreover, we would like also to implement and test other solving procedures, e.g., [31–33,36], considering the relation between ASP and SAT procedures [29,30], whose goal would be to further improve scalability. Finally, we plan to add this solution into a platform of solutions for scheduling problems in Healthcare, similarly to, e.g., [7] in the context of SMT solving.

References

1. Abels, D., Jordi, J., Ostrowski, M., Schaub, T., Toletti, A., Wanko, P.: Train scheduling with hybrid ASP. In: Balduccini, M., Lierler, Y., Woltran, S. (eds.) LPNMR 2019. LNCS, vol. 11481, pp. 3–17. Springer, Cham (2019). https://doi.org/10.1007/978-3-030-20528-7_1
2. Alviano, M., Amendola, G., Dodaro, C., Leone, N., Maratea, M., Ricca, F.: Evaluation of disjunctive programs in WASP. In: Balduccini, M., Lierler, Y., Woltran, S. (eds.) LPNMR 2019. LNCS, vol. 11481, pp. 241–255. Springer, Cham (2019). https://doi.org/10.1007/978-3-030-20528-7_18
3. Alviano, M., et al.: Answer set programming in healthcare: extended overview. In: IPS and RCRA 2020. CEUR Workshop Proceedings, vol. 2745. CEUR-WS.org (2020). http://ceur-ws.org/Vol-2745/paper7.pdf
4. Alviano, M., Dodaro, C., Maratea, M.: An advanced answer set programming encoding for nurse scheduling. In: Esposito, F., Basili, R., Ferilli, S., Lisi, F. (eds.) AI*IA 2017. LNCS, vol. 10640, pp. 468–482. Springer, Cham (2017). https://doi.org/10.1007/978-3-319-70169-1_35
5. Alviano, M., Dodaro, C., Maratea, M.: Nurse (re)scheduling via answer set programming. Intell. Artif. **12**(2), 109–124 (2018)

6. Amendola, G., Dodaro, C., Leone, N., Ricca, F.: On the application of answer set programming to the conference paper assignment problem. In: Adorni, G., Cagnoni, S., Gori, M., Maratea, M. (eds.) AI*IA 2016. LNCS (LNAI), vol. 10037, pp. 164–178. Springer, Cham (2016). https://doi.org/10.1007/978-3-319-49130-1_13
7. Armando, A., Castellini, C., Giunchiglia, E., Idini, M., Maratea, M.: TSAT++: an open platform for satisfiability modulo theories. Electron. Notes Theor. Comput. Sci. **125**(3), 25–36 (2005)
8. Balduccini, M.: Industrial-size scheduling with ASP+CP. In: Delgrande, J.P., Faber, W. (eds.) LPNMR 2011. LNCS (LNAI), vol. 6645, pp. 284–296. Springer, Heidelberg (2011). https://doi.org/10.1007/978-3-642-20895-9_33
9. Calimeri, F., et al.: ASP-Core-2 input language format. Theory Pract. Logic Program. **20**(2), 294–309 (2020)
10. Calimeri, F., Gebser, M., Maratea, M., Ricca, F.: The design of the fifth answer set programming competition. CoRR abs/1405.3710 (2014). http://arxiv.org/abs/1405.3710
11. Calimeri, F., Gebser, M., Maratea, M., Ricca, F.: Design and results of the fifth answer set programming competition. Artif. Intell. **231**, 151–181 (2016)
12. Cardellini, M., et al.: A two-phase ASP encoding for solving rehabilitation scheduling. In: Moschoyiannis, S., Peñaloza, R., Vanthienen, J., Soylu, A., Roman, D. (eds.) RuleML+RR 2021. LNCS, vol. 12851, pp. 111–125. Springer, Cham (2021). https://doi.org/10.1007/978-3-030-91167-6_8
13. Caruso, S., Galatà, G., Maratea, M., Mochi, M., Porro, I.: Scheduling pre-operative assessment clinic via answer set programming. In: Benedictis, R.D., et al. (eds.) Proceedings of the 9th Italian workshop on Planning and Scheduling (IPS 2021) and the 28th International Workshop on "Experimental Evaluation of Algorithms for Solving Problems with Combinatorial Explosion" (RCRA 2021). CEUR Workshop Proceedings, vol. 3065. CEUR-WS.org (2021)
14. Dodaro, C., Galatà, G., Grioni, A., Maratea, M., Mochi, M., Porro, I.: An ASP-based solution to the chemotherapy treatment scheduling problem. Theory Pract. Log. Program. **21**(6), 835–851 (2021)
15. Dodaro, C., Galatà, G., Khan, M.K., Maratea, M., Porro, I.: An ASP-based solution for operating room scheduling with beds management. In: Fodor, P., Montali, M., Calvanese, D., Roman, D. (eds.) RuleML+RR 2019. LNCS, vol. 11784, pp. 67–81. Springer, Cham (2019). https://doi.org/10.1007/978-3-030-31095-0_5
16. Dodaro, C., Galatà, G., Maratea, M., Porro, I.: Operating room scheduling via answer set programming. In: Ghidini, C., Magnini, B., Passerini, A., Traverso, P. (eds.) AI*IA 2018. LNCS (LNAI), vol. 11298, pp. 445–459. Springer, Cham (2018). https://doi.org/10.1007/978-3-030-03840-3_33
17. Dodaro, C., Galatà, G., Maratea, M., Porro, I.: An ASP-based framework for operating room scheduling. Intell. Artif. **13**(1), 63–77 (2019)
18. Dodaro, C., Maratea, M.: Nurse scheduling via answer set programming. In: Balduccini, M., Janhunen, T. (eds.) LPNMR 2017. LNCS (LNAI), vol. 10377, pp. 301–307. Springer, Cham (2017). https://doi.org/10.1007/978-3-319-61660-5_27
19. Edward, G.M., et al.: Simulation to analyse planning difficulties at the preoperative assessment clinic. BJA: Br. J. Anaesthesia **100**(2), 195–202 (2008)
20. Erdem, E., Gelfond, M., Leone, N.: Applications of answer set programming. AI Mag. **37**(3), 53–68 (2016)
21. Falkner, A.A., Friedrich, G., Schekotihin, K., Taupe, R., Teppan, E.C.: Industrial applications of answer set programming. Künstl. Intell. **32**(2–3), 165–176 (2018)

22. Ferschl, M., Tung, A., Sweitzer, B., Huo, D., Glick, D.: Preoperative clinic visits reduce operating room cancellations and delays. Anesthesiology **103**(4), 855–859 (2005)
23. Gebser, M., Kaminski, R., Kaufmann, B., Ostrowski, M., Schaub, T., Wanko, P.: Theory solving made easy with Clingo 5. In: ICLP (Technical Communications). OASICS, vol. 52, pp. 2:1–2:15. Schloss Dagstuhl - Leibniz-Zentrum fuer Informatik (2016)
24. Gebser, M., Kaufmann, B., Schaub, T.: Conflict-driven answer set solving: from theory to practice. Artif. Intell. **187**, 52–89 (2012)
25. Gebser, M., Maratea, M., Ricca, F.: The design of the seventh answer set programming competition. In: Balduccini, M., Janhunen, T. (eds.) LPNMR 2017. LNCS (LNAI), vol. 10377, pp. 3–9. Springer, Cham (2017). https://doi.org/10.1007/978-3-319-61660-5_1
26. Gebser, M., Maratea, M., Ricca, F.: The sixth answer set programming competition. J. Artif. Intell. Res. **60**, 41–95 (2017)
27. Gebser, M., Maratea, M., Ricca, F.: The seventh answer set programming competition: design and results. Theory Pract. Log. Program. **20**(2), 176–204 (2020)
28. Gebser, M., Obermeier, P., Schaub, T., Ratsch-Heitmann, M., Runge, M.: Routing driverless transport vehicles in car assembly with answer set programming. Theory Pract. Log. Program. **18**(3–4), 520–534 (2018). https://doi.org/10.1017/S1471068418000182
29. Giunchiglia, E., Leone, N., Maratea, M.: On the relation among answer set solvers. Ann. Math. Artif. Intell. **53**(1–4), 169–204 (2008)
30. Giunchiglia, E., Maratea, M.: On the relation between answer set and sat procedures (or, between CMODELS and SMODELS). In: Gabbrielli, M., Gupta, G. (eds.) ICLP 2005. LNCS, vol. 3668, pp. 37–51. Springer, Heidelberg (2005). https://doi.org/10.1007/11562931_6
31. Giunchiglia, E., Maratea, M., Tacchella, A.: Dependent and independent variables in propositional satisfiability. In: Flesca, S., Greco, S., Ianni, G., Leone, N. (eds.) JELIA 2002. LNCS (LNAI), vol. 2424, pp. 296–307. Springer, Heidelberg (2002). https://doi.org/10.1007/3-540-45757-7_25
32. Giunchiglia, E., Maratea, M., Tacchella, A.: (In)effectiveness of look-ahead techniques in a modern SAT solver. In: Rossi, F. (ed.) CP 2003. LNCS, vol. 2833, pp. 842–846. Springer, Heidelberg (2003). https://doi.org/10.1007/978-3-540-45193-8_64
33. Giunchiglia, E., Maratea, M., Tacchella, A., Zambonin, D.: Evaluating search heuristics and optimization techniques in propositional satisfiability. In: Goré, R., Leitsch, A., Nipkow, T. (eds.) IJCAR 2001. LNCS, vol. 2083, pp. 347–363. Springer, Heidelberg (2001). https://doi.org/10.1007/3-540-45744-5_26
34. Harnett, M.P., Correll, D., Hurwitz, S., Bader, A., Hepner, D.: Improving efficiency and patient satisfaction in a tertiary teaching hospital preoperative clinic. Anesthesiology **112**(1), 66–72 (2010)
35. Ricca, F., et al.: Team-building with answer set programming in the Gioia-Tauro seaport. Theory Pract. Log. Program. **12**(3), 361–381 (2012)
36. Rosa, E.D., Giunchiglia, E., Maratea, M.: A new approach for solving satisfiability problems with qualitative preferences. In: Ghallab, M., Spyropoulos, C.D., Fakotakis, N., Avouris, N.M. (eds.) ECAI. Frontiers in Artificial Intelligence and Applications, vol. 178, pp. 510–514. IOS Press (2008)
37. Schüller, P.: Answer set programming in linguistics. Künstliche Intell. **32**(2–3), 151–155 (2018). https://doi.org/10.1007/s13218-018-0542-z

38. Stark, C., Gent, A., Kirkland, L.: Improving patient flow in pre-operative assessment. BMJ Open Qual. **4**(1) (2015). https://doi.org/10.1136/bmjquality.u201341.w1226
39. Tariq, H., et al.: Development, functioning, and effectiveness of a preoperative risk assessment clinic. Health Serv. Insights **2016**, 1 (2016). https://doi.org/10.4137/HSI.S40540
40. Woodrum, C.L., Wisniewski, M., Triulzi, D.J., Waters, J.H., Alarcon, L.H., Yazer, M.H.: The effects of a data driven maximum surgical blood ordering schedule on preoperative blood ordering practices. Hematology **22**(9), 571–577 (2017)

Solving the Dial-a-Ride Problem Using an Adapted Genetic Algorithm

Stjepan Zelić[1], Marko Đurasević[2(✉)], Domagoj Jakobović[2], and Lucija Planinić[2]

[1] Hypefy World, Zagreb, Croatia
[2] Faculty of Electrical Engineering and Computing, University of Zagreb, Zagreb, Croatia
{marko.durasevic,domagoj.jakobovic,lucija.planinic}@fer.hr

Abstract. The dial-a-ride problem (DARP) deals with the transportation of people from source to destination locations. One of the most common use cases is in the transportation of elderly or sick people, and as such it represents an important problem to consider. Since DARP is NP-hard, it most often has to be solved using various heuristic methods. Previous studies demonstrated that metaheuristics are suitable for solving this kind of problem. However, in most cases, basic metaheuristics have been considered without any adaptation to the problem, which could potentially limit their performance. Therefore, in this study a GA is proposed and several of its elements adapted for solving DARP. The obtained results show that the proposed algorithm can achieve better results than similar methods from previous studies. Moreover, the experiments demonstrate that the results can be improved by considering some constraints as soft constraints and including them in the cost function to give the algorithm more flexibility in the search.

Keywords: Genetic algorithm · Dial a ride problem · Optimisation

1 Introduction

The dial-a-ride problem (DARP) is a special form of the vehicle routing problem (VRP) that involves the transportation of people rather than goods. In DARP, users make requests to be picked up from a specific location at a specific time and taken to another location by a specific time. The goal of the problem is to schedule a fleet of vehicles to meet the user's needs as much as possible, but also to minimise the duration of the route. DARP has many practical applications in the real world, including door-to-door transportation of elderly or disabled people [5], cab services [13], emergency services [13], and demand-responsive mass transit [11]. Since DARP is a special case of VRP, it also belongs to the category of NP-hard problems. Therefore, there is no known algorithm that provides optimal solutions in a reasonable amount of time. Most of the time, one has to resort to metaheuristics that have proven their strength in many

S. Bandini et al. (Eds.): AIxIA 2021, LNAI 13196, pp. 689–699, 2022.
https://doi.org/10.1007/978-3-031-08421-8_47

areas such as scheduling [16], cryptography [14], rostering [2], transportation [1], and similar.

DARP has already received considerable attention in the literature. One of the first studies dealing with DARP, in which a sequential insertion heuristic is proposed, was done by Jaw et al. [8]. The problem was also addressed in [10] using simulated annealing. Tabu search (TS) was applied in [4] to a problem where travel time must be minimised by considering all user requests. A genetic algorithm (GA) for DARP was proposed in [9] that solves the problem of [4]. The main difference between these works is that several strict constraints are modelled as cost functions that are optimised, which gives some flexibility to GA. Another GA was used in [6], in which the authors test different algorithm configurations. An overview of different DARP models and solution methods can be found in [5]. An extension of DARP that allows users to change vehicles during their trip is solved in [12] using an adaptive large neighbourhood search algorithm. A hyperheuristic approach to solving DARP is proposed in [15]. This method finds the best heuristic strategy for applying simple operators that can be applied to new problems. In [11], an online version of DARP was considered where the optimisation routine runs continuously during system execution. A parallel extension of the TS method for DARP was proposed in [13]. A variant of the problem, where different trip types are studied, is investigated in [7]. In [3], the authors consider a flexible DARP variant in which only a portion of the user requests are predetermined.

The above overview shows that this problem is still intensively researched and many new DARP variants are proposed and investigated. In this paper we consider the original DARP variant described in [4] and [9]. The problem is solved using an adapted GA that incorporates some domain-specific information in its evolutionary process by adapting the solution initialisation procedure and the applied crossover operator. The goal of this research is to gain initial insights that can be used in subsequent studies to further improve the results and that can also be applied to solve the extended DARP variants.

The rest of the paper is organised as follows: Sect. 2 gives an introduction to DARP. The GA adapted for DARP is described in Sect. 3. The experimental setup and the results obtained by the proposed GA are described in Sect. 4. Finally, the conclusion of the paper and future research directions are outlined in Sect. 5.

2 Dial-a-Ride Problem

The DARP under consideration is modelled based on the problem defined in [4,9]. In this problem, there are n customer requests for transportation, given as a list of $2n$ locations. Each request has a pickup location, denoted with item i in the list, and a delivery location (item $n+i$). The locations are modelled as a fully connected graph in which a travel distance d_{ij} is defined between all locations i and j. For each location, there is a time window $[b_i, e_i]$ that defines the service of the request at that location, either for pickup or delivery. Ideally, the service at locations should only occur within these time windows. A service time s_i required at each location is also defined. Each customer request has a specific number of places that the user takes in the vehicle, which are taken at the pickup location and released at the delivery location. Customers also specify a maximum amount of time they would like to spend in the vehicle. To meet user requests, a fleet of m vehicles is available. Each vehicle k starts at the depot location D and returns there after completing all requests. Each vehicle has a constant capacity of C and a maximum route duration. Since it is assumed that all vehicles are identical, both values are the same for all vehicles.

Usually several objectives are considered in DARP, out of which a single cost function is defined as a weighted linear combination of the individual cost functions. The cost functions considered in this study are:

- f_1 - total route duration - the total duration of the routes for all vehicles
- f_2 - total ride time - the total time that the customers spent riding in the vehicles
- f_3 - total wait time - the time that the vehicles spent idle while waiting to service a request
- f_4 - total late time - the total time that the vehicle was late, meaning that it arrived at a location after its defined time window
- f_5 - total amount of ride time violation - the excess amount of time that the customer spend driving in the vehicle above their requested ride time
- f_6 - total maximum route violation - the excess amount of time that the cars spent driving over their given maximum route duration

In [4] only the functions $f_1 - f_3$ were minimised, while the remaining functions were not used because they were modelled as hard constraints (i.e., no lateness was allowed). However, in [9], the authors modelled some constraints as cost functions, which allowed them to obtain better results. The total cost function to be minimised is defined as $f = w_1 \cdot f_1 + w_2 \cdot f_2 + w_3 \cdot f_3 + w_4 \cdot f_4 w_5 \cdot f_5 + w_6 \cdot f_6$. The weights $w_1, \ldots, w_6$ can be freely chosen to determine the significance of each cost function. The magnitudes of the functions f_1 and f_2 are usually similar, while f_3 is usually one order of magnitude smaller. However, the weights have been set as $w_1 = w_2 = w_3 = 1$, since initial experiments have shown that the algorithm nevertheless focuses quite well on optimising the cost function f_3 with such a setting. The cost functions f_4 and f_5 were usually about 5 times smaller than f_1 and f_2, while the cost function f_6 was usually equal to 0. Therefore, their weights were set to $w_4 = w_5 = w_6 = 5$ to focus equally on the cost functions modelling more stricter requirements such as lateness.

3 Genetic Algorithm for DARP

To find solutions to the considered DARP problem, a GA is adapted for it. The solutions are represented by two chromosomes, an integer and a permutation chromosome. The integer chromosome specifies which vehicle each user request is associated with. The permutation chromosome represents the order in which customer requests are processed. Figure 1 represents an example of a problem with 2 vehicles and 5 requests. Since there are 10 requests, this means that values 1–5 in the permutation vector represent pickup requests, while values 6–10 represent delivery requests. In this example, vehicle 0 will first handle the pickup of request 4 and then immediately handle its delivery (request 9). Then the vehicle will handle the second request. Vehicle 1, on the other hand, will first process three pickup requests (requests 2, 3, and 1) and then perform their delivery (requests 8, 7, and 6). The order of the delivery requests does not have to be the same as the order of the pickup requests. This is also clear in the example, because delivery request 7, which corresponds to the pickup request 2, is handled after the delivery request 8, which corresponds to the pickup request 3.

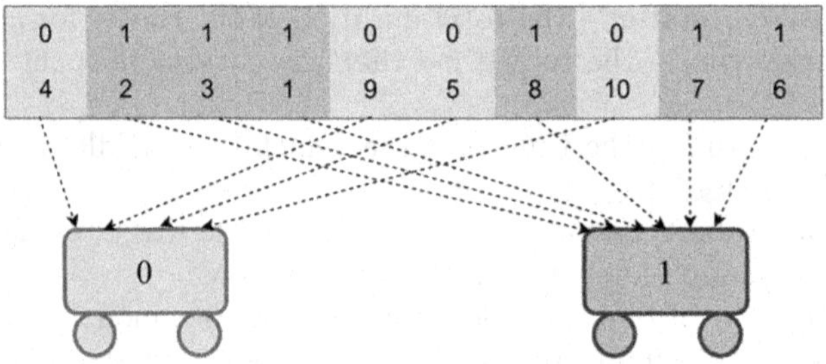

Fig. 1. Solution representation used by the GA

Instead of generating the initial population completely at random, a simple heuristic initialisation was used to construct the initial solutions. The outline of this procedure is shown in Algorithm 1. First, a permutation of requests is randomly generated by ensuring that each pickup request appears before the corresponding delivery request in the solution. Then, the following process is repeated until all requests are served. If the first request in the list is a pickup request, the list of vehicles with free space is first determined. If no such vehicles are available, the request is placed at the end of the list until certain delivery requests are processed and the vehicles free up space for new requests. If there are vehicles with free space, a priority p_i is calculated for each vehicle i and the current request j as

$$p_i = \left| \frac{e_j + b_j}{2} - (t_i + d_{ij}) \right|,$$

where e_j and b_j represent the end and the beginning of the time window, t_i is the current time of the vehicle, and d_ij is the distance between the vehicle and the pickup request location (the time it takes to reach a location is equal to the distance). This priority indicates how close to the middle of the time window the vehicle would arrive. The vehicle with the lowest value is then selected to serve the request. This solution initialisation method has demonstrated to achieve better results in preliminary experiments than if the initial population is generated completely randomly. On the other hand, if the first request in the list is a delivery request, a check is made to see if the corresponding pickup request has already been served. If yes, this delivery request is assigned to the corresponding vehicle. Otherwise, the request is placed back in the list of requests to be considered when its corresponding pickup request is handled.

Algorithm 1. Initial solution construction procedure

requests ← create random permutation of requests
while *requests* not empty **do**
    currentRequest ← first request from *requests*
    if *currentRequest* is a pickup request **then**
        fVehicles ← currently free vehicles
        if *fVehicles* is empty **then**
            Place *currentRequest* at the end of the *requests* list
        else
            for each vehicle v_i in *fVehicles* **do**
                Calculate $p_i = \left|\frac{e_j+b_j}{2} - (t_i + d_{ij})\right|$, where j denotes the location of *currentReqest*
            end for
            selectedVehicle ← select the vehicle with the lowest p_i
            Assign *currentRequest* to *selectedVehicle*
        end if
    else
        if the corresponding pickup request of *currentRequest* is already assigned to a vehicle **then**
            Assign *currentRequest* to the vehicle which contains its corresponding pickup request
        else
            Place *currentRequest* at the end of the *requests* list
        end if
    end if
end while

For the crossover operator an adapted PMX crossover, denoted as partially car mapped crossover (PCMX), is used. Unlike in the PMX crossover, in which two random crossover points are selected, in this variant a number of vehicles are selected and then all the genes associated to those vehicles are copied to the child individual. The remaining genes are then filled in a similar way as it is done in the original PMX crossover by copying over those requests form the second parent which are not yet present in the child individual. Figure 2 shows an example of the crossover performed on a solution for a problem with 10 requests and 2 vehicles. In this case the route for vehicle 1 is copied over from the first parent to the child individual. The requests which belong to the other vehicles are then filled from the second parent. If a request already exists in the child, then it would be mapped in the same way as in PMX to a request which does not exist in the child individual, and that request would be copied to the child.

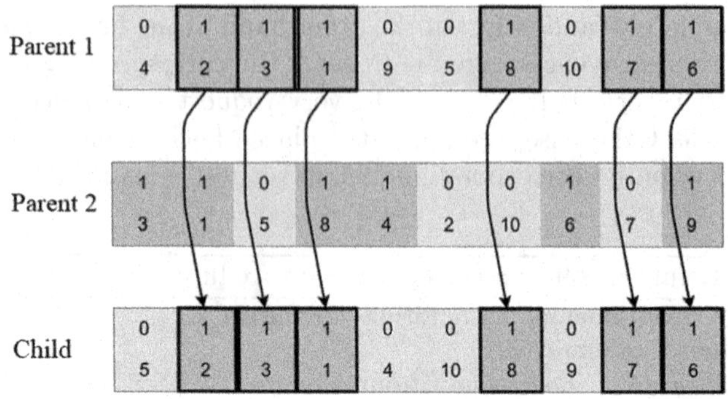

Fig. 2. Example of the PCMX crossover

The mutation is performed by simply swapping the order of the requests for two customers. Two customers are randomly selected (they can be assigned to the same or different vehicles) and then their pickup and delivery requests are swapped. An example of this mutation is shown in Fig. 3. In this example it can be seen that the pickup requests 4 and 2 are swapped, as well as their corresponding delivery requests 9 and 7.

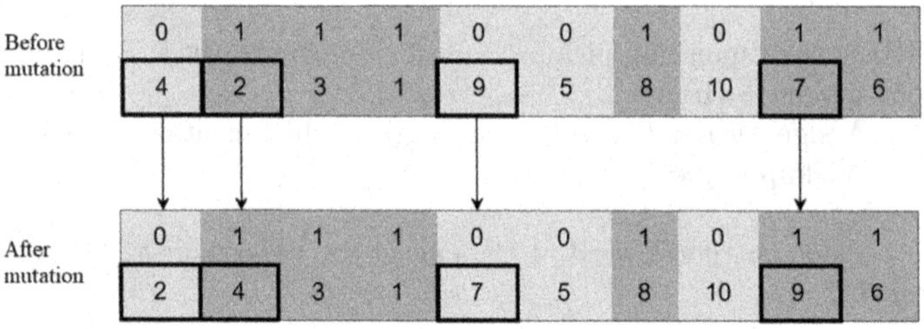

Fig. 3. Example of the swap mutation

It is possible that during evolution a certain number of constraints are not satisfied. Therefore, after each modification of an individual, a procedure is used to check the validity of the solutions and make a correction. First, it is checked whether all delivery requests appear after their respective pickup requests. If this is not the case, the two requests are simply swapped. Second, it checks if the vehicle capacity constraint is satisfied at all points in time. This is determined by finding the point where the capacity constraint is violated in the solution and then moving a delivery request ahead of that point to make room in the vehicle. Using these corrections ensures that the algorithm only works with valid solutions throughout the evolution process.

4 Experimental Study

4.1 Benchmark Setup

The experimental study will be conducted on the dataset which is proposed in [4]. This dataset consists out of 20 problem instances which contain between 24 and 144 customers, and between 3 and 13 vehicles. The instances are divided into two groups, instances from R1a to R10a were generated with narrow time windows, whereas instances from R1b to R10b have been generated with wide time windows. For each instance the GA was executed 10 times. The parameters of the GA were fine tuned in preliminary experiments. A population size of 200 individuals, mutation probability of 0.1, the 5-tournament selection for selecting individuals, and stopping criterion of 1500 generations were used.

The results will be directly compared to the results obtained by previous studies from Cordeau and Laporte [4] and Jorgensen et al. [9]. The results obtained in the previous two studies are summarised in Table 1. It should be outlined that in these studies not all instances were considered, therefore only a subset of instances is denoted in the table.

Table 1. Overview of the results from the literature

Instances	Cordeau and Laporte [4]			Jorgensen et al. [9]		
	Route duration	Waiting time	Ride time	Route duration	Waiting time	Ride time
R1a	1041	252	477	881	211	1095
R2a	1969	470	1367	1985	724	1977
R3a	2779	292	3081	2579	607	3587
R5a	4250	500	5099	3870	833	6154
R9a	3597	94	6251	3155	323	5622
R10a	5006	315	8413	4480	721	7164
R1b	907	143	630	965	321	1042
R2b	1719	198	1214	1565	309	2393
R5b	4296	552	4615	3596	606	6105
R6b	5309	630	6134	4072	449	7347
R7b	1299	102	990	1097	129	1762
R9b	3679	147	5362	3249	487	5581
R10b	4733	113	7969	4041	362	7072
Total	40584	3808	51600	35537	6082	56900

4.2 Results

The results obtained by the proposed GA are shown in Table 2. The table outlines the three main objectives considered in previous studies: route duration, ride time, and waiting time. "Avg." denotes the average of 10 executions obtained for these objectives, while "Best" denotes the value for the objective obtained by the solution with the best fitness. Also, the average values for the late times and ride time violations per customer are given to illustrate how much the obtained solutions violate these constraints. The results in the tables are marked with '†' if they are only better than the results of Cordeau and Laporte, with '*' if they are better than those of Jorgensen et al., with '+' if they are better than the results of both studies, and with '-' if they are worse than the results of both studies. Note that the results for the instances that were not solved in previous studies are not marked. The last row shows the aggregated results for the instances that were also used in the previous studies to make the cumulative results comparable.

Table 2. Overview of the obtained results

Instance	Route duration		Waiting time		Ride time		Late time	Ride time violation
	Avg.	Best	Avg.	Best	Avg.	Best	Avg.	Avg.
R1a	890*	972*	114+	201+	1138–	694†	0.49	0.07
R2a	1601+	1975+	164+	491+	2190–	1969†	0.72	1.60
R3a	2353+	2387+	117+	93+	3487†	2958†	0.34	0.92
R4a	3252	3598	270	548	4635	4495	0.53	1.20
R5a	3813*	3958*	193+	317+	5885†	4790+	0.98	1.32
R6a	4691	4773	279	323	7228	7133	0.92	2.58
R7a	1273	1354	133	162	1571	1295	1.50	0.19
R8a	2271	2254	46	14	3349	2803	0.89	2.86
R9a	3225*	3305*	64†	118†	5835*	5947*	4.72	2.52
R10a	4422*	4518*	97+	102+	8099*	7796*	5.19	4.26
R1b	788*	766*	31+	4+	984†	667†	0.48	0.06
R2b	1499*	1422*	55+	6+	2108†	1733†	0.42	1.32
R3b	2306	2282	69	34	3370	2555	0.34	0.42
R4b	3001	2941	75	38	4353	3636	0.20	0.82
R5b	3749*	3981*	135+	242+	5618†	5130†	0.58	1.34
R6b	4492*	4456*	149+	139+	6653†	6171+	1.13	1.01
R7b	1150*	1120*	19+	10+	1571†	1358†	0.54	1.12
R8b	2329	2355	100	88	3505	2658	0.96	2.17
R9b	3287*	3337*	45+	90+	5962–	5415†	1.88	2.98
R10b	4388*	4442*	66+	70+	7734*	7084*	3.62	2.00
Total	35659*	36637*	1249+	1882+	57264–	51711†	21.08	20.52

The results show that the proposed algorithm can achieve some improvements over the results obtained in the studies of Cordeau and Laporte and Jorgensen et al. For the waiting time cost, the proposed algorithm always obtained better results than both methods. For the route duration cost, the algorithm always obtained better results than the method of Jorgensen et al. Finally, for the ride time cost, better results were obtained for multiple instances than in the study of Cordeau and Laporte, but the overall results obtained for this criterion were worse than in both studies. It should be mentioned that compared to the results of Cordeau and Laporte, the route duration and travel time costs obtained by the proposed method are similar (within a range of 1%). However, we obtained a much smaller value for vehicle waiting time, by a factor of 5. This improvement was possible due to the flexibility provided by treating some constraints as soft constraints (late time). Jorgensen et al. also treated late times as soft constraints. Unfortunately, these values are not reported in the paper and it is not possible to determine the extent to which these constraints were not met. However, the proposed GA was able to achieve better results for the route duration and wait time objectives.

Although the problem was solved by treating late times as soft constraints, it can be noted that the violations of late times and ride times are not very extensive. The average of late times is usually not greater than one minute, and the maximum late time was 5 minutes for instance R10a. On the other hand, the ride time violations were also usually in the range of one or two minutes. Such small violations of constraints should not cause much user dissatisfaction, but should give the algorithm more flexibility in finding better solutions for other criteria. Therefore, it seems to be more beneficial to treat such constraints as soft and optimise them together with the other objectives, as this seems to have a positive effect on the other objectives.

5 Conclusion

The obtained results show that with the initial adjustment of the GA it is possible to improve the results for DARP. For one of the considered criteria the algorithm achieved a significant improvement over the existing results, while the results for the other two criteria were mostly consistent with those of the other studies. This performance was achieved by including more problem-specific elements in the algorithm, but also by allowing some constraints not to be met. Since in this study the problem was addressed only briefly and with only a few adjustments to the algorithm, there is still much room to improve the results through further adjustments and fine-tuning for the problem under consideration.

In future studies, the goal is to test the proposed method on other data sets used in related surveys. It is also intended to adapt the proposed approach to cover other DARP variants not considered in this work. A more thorough study with different metaheuristic algorithms will be conducted to propose alternative and more efficient methods for DARP. Since DARP usually considers multiple objectives simultaneously, another obvious research direction would be to apply multi-objective algorithms.

Acknowledgements. This work has been supported in part by Croatian Science Foundation under the project IP-2019-04-4333.

References

1. Baker, B.M., Ayechew, M.: A genetic algorithm for the vehicle routing problem. Comput. Oper. Res. **30**(5), 787–800 (2003). https://doi.org/10.1016/S0305-0548(02)00051-5. https://www.sciencedirect.com/science/article/pii/S0305054802000515
2. Burke, E.K., Curtois, T., Post, G., Qu, R., Veltman, B.: A hybrid heuristic ordering and variable neighbourhood search for the nurse rostering problem. Eur. J. Oper. Res. **188**(2), 330–341 (2008). https://doi.org/10.1016/j.ejor.2007.04.030. https://www.sciencedirect.com/science/article/pii/S0377221707004390
3. Busing, C., Comis, M., Rauh, F.: The dial-a-ride problem in primary care with flexible scheduling (2021)
4. Cordeau, J.F., Laporte, G.: A tabu search heuristic for the static multi-vehicle dial-a-ride problem. Transp. Res. Part B: Methodol. **37**(6), 579–594 (2003). https://doi.org/10.1016/S0191-2615(02)00045-0. https://www.sciencedirect.com/science/article/pii/S0191261502000450
5. Cordeau, J.F., Laporte, G.: The dial-a-ride problem (DARP): models and algorithms. Ann. OR **153**, 29–46 (2007). https://doi.org/10.1007/s10479-007-0170-8
6. Cubillos, C., Rodriguez, N., Crawford, B.: A study on genetic algorithms for the DARP problem, pp. 498–507 (2007). https://doi.org/10.1007/978-3-540-73053-8_50
7. Dong, X., Rey, D., Waller, S.T.: Dial-a-ride problem with users' accept/reject decisions based on service utilities. Transp. Res. Rec. **2674**(10), 55–67 (2020). https://doi.org/10.1177/0361198120940307. https://doi.org/10.1177/0361198120940307
8. Jaw, J.J., Odoni, A.R., Psaraftis, H.N., Wilson, N.H.: A heuristic algorithm for the multi-vehicle advance request dial-a-ride problem with time windows. Transp. Res. Part B: Methodol. **20**(3), 243–257 (1986). https://doi.org/10.1016/0191-2615(86)90020-2. https://www.sciencedirect.com/science/article/pii/0191261586900202
9. Jorgensen, R., Larsen, J., Bergvinsdottir, K.: Solving the dial-a-ride problem using genetic algorithms. J. Oper. Res. Soc. **58** (2007). https://doi.org/10.1057/palgrave.jors.2602287
10. Baugh Jr, J.W., Kakivaya, G.K.R., Stone, J.R.: Intractability of the dial-a-ride problem and a multiobjective solution using simulated annealing. Eng. Optimiz. **30**(2), 91–123 (1998). https://doi.org/10.1080/03052159808941240. https://doi.org/10.1080/03052159808941240
11. Lois, A., Ziliaskopoulos, A.: Online algorithm for dynamic dial a ride problem and its metrics. Transp. Res. Proc. **24**, 377–384 (2017). https://doi.org/10.1016/j.trpro.2017.05.097. https://www.sciencedirect.com/science/article/pii/S2352146517303782. 3rd Conference on Sustainable Urban Mobility, 3rd CSUM 2016, 26–27 May 2016, Volos, Greece
12. Masson, R., Lehuédé, F., Péton, O.: The dial-a-ride problem with transfers. Comput. Oper. Res. **41**, 12–23 (2014). https://doi.org/10.1016/j.cor.2013.07.020. https://www.sciencedirect.com/science/article/pii/S0305054813001998
13. Pandi, R.R., Ho, S.G., Nagavarapu, S.C., Tripathy, T., Dauwels, J.: GPU-accelerated tabu search algorithm for dial-a-ride problem. In: 2018 21st International Conference on Intelligent Transportation Systems (ITSC), pp. 2519–2524 (2018). https://doi.org/10.1109/ITSC.2018.8569472

14. Picek, S., Jakobovic, D., Miller, J.F., Batina, L., Cupic, M.: Cryptographic Boolean functions: one output, many design criteria. Appl. Soft Comput. **40**, 635–653 (2016). https://doi.org/10.1016/j.asoc.2015.10.066. https://www.sciencedirect.com/science/article/pii/S1568494615007103
15. Urra, E., Cubillos, C., Cabrera-Paniagua, D.: A hyperheuristic for the dial-a-ride problem with time windows **2015**, 1–12 (2015). https://doi.org/10.1155/2015/707056. https://doi.org/10.1155/2015/707056
16. Vlašić, I., Đurasević, M., Jakobović, D.: A comparative study of solution representations for the unrelated machines environment. Comput. Oper. Res. **123**, 105005 (2020). https://doi.org/10.1016/j.cor.2020.105005. https://www.sciencedirect.com/science/article/pii/S0305054820301222

Unstructured Data in Predictive Process Monitoring: Lexicographic and Semantic Mapping to ICD-9-CM Codes for the Home Hospitalization Service

Massimiliano Ronzani[3], Roger Ferrod[1], Chiara Di Francescomarino[3(✉)], Emilio Sulis[1], Roberto Aringhieri[1], Guido Boella[1], Enrico Brunetti[1,2], Luigi Di Caro[1], Mauro Dragoni[3], Chiara Ghidini[3], and Renata Marinello[2]

[1] University of Turin, Turin, Italy
{roger.ferrod,emilio.sulis,roberto.aringhieri,guido.boella, enrico.brunetti,luigi.dicaro}@unito.it
[2] City of Health and Science, Turin, Italy
{ebrunetti,rmarinello}@cittadellasalute.to.it
[3] Fondazione Bruno Kessler, Trento, Italy
{mronzani,dfmchiara,dragoni,ghidini}@fbk.eu

Abstract. The large availability of hospital administrative and clinical data has encouraged the application of Process Mining techniques to the healthcare domain. Predictive Process Monitoring techniques can be used in order to learn from these data related to past historical executions and predict the future of incomplete cases. However, some of these data, possibly the most informative ones, are often available in natural language text, while structured information—extracted from these data—would be more beneficial for training predictive models.

In this paper we focus on the scenario of the Home Hospitalization Service, supporting the team in making decisions on the home hospitalization of a patient, by predicting whether it is likely that a new patient will successfully undergo home hospitalization. We aim at investigating whether, in this scenario, we can take advantage of mapping unstructured textual diagnoses, reported by the doctor in the Emergency Department, into structured information, as the standardized disease ICD-9-CM codes, to provide more accurate predictions. To this aim, we devise two different approaches involving respectively lexicographic and semantic distance for mapping textual diagnoses in ICD-9-CM codes and leverage the structured information for making predictions.

Keywords: Healthcare processes · Predictive process monitoring · Natural language processing · Home hospitalization service

1 Introduction

The improvement of healthcare processes and the support of clinical personnel in making decisions might have an impact on the efficiency of the healthcare

S. Bandini et al. (Eds.): AIxIA 2021, LNAI 13196, pp. 700–715, 2022.
https://doi.org/10.1007/978-3-031-08421-8_48

services, as well as on the quality of the work of the clinical personnel, who sparing time in administrative tasks has more time available for taking care of patients, thus improving the patients' quality of life. Process Mining (PM) [1], which deals with the analysis of business processes based on their behaviour—observed and recorded in event logs—can be a useful instrument in this setting. PM deals with the analysis of business process event logs in different ways [3], including process discovery (i.e., extracting process models from an event log) [1], predictions of the future of ongoing cases [17] and process optimization [1]. PM techniques can be leveraged for the discovery and analysis of both clinical and administrative processes in healthcare. The application of PM techniques is further encouraged by the wide availability of administrative and clinical data in hospitals. These data could be leveraged for discovering (and improving) processes, as well as for supporting hospital teams in making decisions on clinical and administrative issues [4,23]. It often happens that these data are collected in national standard forms and documents, shared among several hospitals on the national area. For instance, in Italy, one of these documents is the Hospital Discharge Form (HDF), which collects information related to the clinical history of a patient during his/her hospitalization. The data collected in the discharge form range from data (with temporal information) related to the hospital admission, discharge and examinations carried out during the hospitalization to data such as the number of days of hospitalization. Unfortunately, however, not all these data are structured. Some of them, possibly the most informative ones, are textual unstructured fields, as in the case of the patients' diagnoses reported by the doctor at the arrival of the patient at the Emergency Department.

In this paper we aim at investigating whether we can take advantage of mapping unstructured data into the structured information provided by the ICD-9-CM[1] taxonomy when making predictions in the scenario of the Home Hospitalization Service. We extend the work in [5], where we investigated a lexicographic distance for mapping textual diagnoses to ICD-9-CM codes, with a semantic distance. We first provide some preliminaries (Sect. 2) and introduce the Home Hospitalization scenario (Sect. 3). In Sect. 4 we report about the proposed approach that aims at (i) mapping unstructured data to ICD-9-CM codes via lexicographic or semantic match; and (ii) leveraging this structured information when making predictions. We report on the evaluations carried out in Sect. 5 and we finally conclude in Sect. 7.

2 Background

In this section we report the background concepts useful for understanding the remainder of the paper.

Predictive Process Monitoring. Predictive Process Monitoring (PPM) [17] is a relatively new branch of PM that aims at predicting at runtime and as early as possible the future development of an ongoing incomplete execution of a process.

[1] https://www.cdc.gov/nchs/icd/icd9cm.htm.

Predictions related to the future of an incomplete process execution (as known as *case*) of state of-the-art approaches can be classified in macro-categories [10]: numeric predictions (e.g., time or cost predictions); categorical predictions (e.g., risk predictions or specific categorical outcome predictions such as the fulfillment or the violation of a certain property); as well as to next activities predictions (e.g, the sequence of future activities, possibly with their payloads).

Together with these techniques, few frameworks have also been recently developed implementing and collecting these techniques, such as for instance Nirdizati [21]. These frameworks take as input a set of past executions and use them to train predictive models to be used for providing users with predictions at runtime. They are usually characterized by two main modules: one for the case encoding, and one for the supervised learning. Each of them can be instantiated with different techniques.

ICD-9-CM. ICD-9-CM is the ninth edition of the *International Classification of Diseases*. It contains a structured standard codification of diseases and procedures that is used internationally both in the management of public health and for statistical and epidemiological purposes.

The ICD-9-CM assigns specific codes (and associated descriptions) to both diseases and procedures. It is organized in the form of a taxonomy, so that each code corresponding to a specific disease variant (subprocedure) is classified as a disease (procedure), which, in turn, is classified as a category of diseases (procedures) and so on. In the case of the diagnoses, each code is composed of five digits: the first three digits represent a high level disease category, the fourth digit indicates the specific disease, while the last digit identifies the specific variant of the disease. In turn, the first three digits are further classified according to number interval ranges corresponding to families of diseases. For instance, the code **410.22** corresponding to the description *Acute myocardial infarction of inferolateral wall, subsequent episode of care* is a leaf of the hierarchy:

- **390–459**: *Diseases of The Circulatory System*
  - **410–414**: *Ischemic Heart Diseases*
    - **410**: *Acute myocardial infarction*
      - **410.2**: *Acute myocardial infarction of inferolateral wall*
        - **410.22**: *Acute myocardial infarction of inferolateral wall, subsequent episode of care*

This simple representation of the taxonomy allows us to select, for a given diagnosis code, the level of abstraction, i.e., the ancestor, among the low levels of the taxonomy, by truncating the last or the last two digits of the ICD-9-CM code.

3 The Home Hospitalization Service Scenario

The Home Hospitalization Service (HHS) of the City of Health and Science (CHS), which has been in operation for over 30 years, has proven to be a valid alternative to hospitalization for a variety of acute and chronic exacerbated diseases [22], such as uncomplicated ischemic stroke, congestive heart failure, exacerbations of chronic obstructive pulmonary disease, onco-hematological diseases with high transfusion requirements, dementia with behavioral disorders [14]. The HHS consists of a multidisciplinary team. The essential criteria for taking care of an acute patient at home are threefold: (i) clinical aspects, e.g., no need for continuous or invasive monitoring of vital parameters, as well as to perform invasive diagnostic-interventions; (ii) geographical aspects (residence in the area of competence of the HHS); (iii) social welfare (constant presence of one or more caregivers, formal or informal). Every year, the service manages about 500 admissions of patients coming in most cases from the same hospital and in small part upon direct request of the General Practitioner (GP). At the end of the treatment period, more than 80% of patients are discharged to the GP, 10.5% die during hospitalization and about 8% is moved to hospital. Over the past 8 years, the percentage of patients unable to continue care management at home has remained constant, despite the increase in clinical complexity and care burden of patients taken into care. In 2018, HHS patients were 492 with a high average age (about 84 years). The overall goal is supporting the HHS team in the timely identification and notification of the patients that can be managed through the HHS, as well as in the efficient management of the HHS processes.

Data Description. The administrative and clinical data available so far for the specific case study are related to Emergency Department Discharge Forms (EDDF) and to the Hospitalization Discharge Forms (HDF) of about 400 CHS patients benefitting from the HHS. The EDDF contains information collected at the Emergency Department (ED) such as: (i) date and time information related to the ED admission, triage, discharge, last and latest update of the anamnesis; (ii) structured information e.g., on the patient triage colour code; and (iii) textual notes e.g., on the diagnosis. The HDF contains instead information about the clinical history of the patient during the hospitalization, such as: (i) date and time information related to e.g., the hospital admission, discharge, main intervention; (ii) structured information related to e.g., patients' data (age, sex, civil status, etc.), number of visits; and (iii) textual information related to e.g., the hospitalization cause and the anamnesis.

4 Approach

In order to support the HHS team in making decisions on the home hospitalization of a patient, the overall idea is applying existing approaches of PPM to the data related to the administrative and clinical management of ED patients. To this aim, patient data need to be transformed into a trace describing the history of the patient and used as features to learn and provide predictions about the home hospitalization of the patient. Most of these data are structured bits of information, while others, equally or more informative, are collected as unstructured text, as for instance the diagnosis informally reported by the doctor when the patient reaches the ED. In order to be able to apply PPM approaches and properly leverage this information when making predictions, we devised the following pipeline:

- we preprocess data so as to generate an event log describing the patient histories (Sect. 4.1);
- we map the informal diagnosis descriptions into the standardized diagnosis codes of the ICD-9-CM taxonomy (Sect. 4.2);
- we leverage the mapped structured ICD-9-CM code or one of its ancestors as a structured feature to be used in making predictions (Sect. 4.3).

4.1 Data Preprocessing and Analysis

The dataset related to the HDFs extracted from the hospital information systems has first been cleaned by removing hospitalizations of few days or "routine" procedures and then joined with the dataset of the ED. The following steps have been then applied to the joined dataset:

- The dataset has been transformed into an event log. The hospital discharge id number has been used as *trace id*. For the HDF data, date and time fields related to the hospital admission, discharge, and to the interventions performed by the patient during the hospitalization have been used as timestamps for the activities `H_admission`, `H_discharge` and for the intervention activities (labelled with the corresponding ICD-9-CM code or with the procedure category they belong to in the ICD-9-CM procedures), respectively. Patient personal data and other structured data, such as the setting of referral, have been added as case attributes. Similarly, for EDDF data, date and time fields related to the ED admission, discharge, triage, anamnesis and diagnostic hypothesis have been used as timestamps for the `ED_admission`, `ED_discharge`, `ED_triage`, `ED_anamnesis`, `ED_diagnostic_hp`, respectively. Diagnosis and other few attributes have been instead used as case attributes. The resulting event log is composed of 413 cases with 270 different paths and 49 different activities.
- In order to be able to make predictions at the time of the discharge from the ED, each trace in the log has been truncated at the time of the activity `ED_discharge`, and the attributes that cannot be known at the time of the ED discharge have been removed, e.g. the attribute `H_number_of_days_in_the_facility`, which is known only at the end of the hospitalization.

Finally, data have been labelled according to whether (i) the patient has been hospitalized at home and the hospitalization had a positive outcome (HH, i.e., Home Hospitalization); or (ii) she/he has been hospitalized in a different ward or the home hospitalization had a negative outcome (NO-HH). Out of the 413 cases, 368 (89%) were labeled with HH and 45 (11%) with NO-HH.

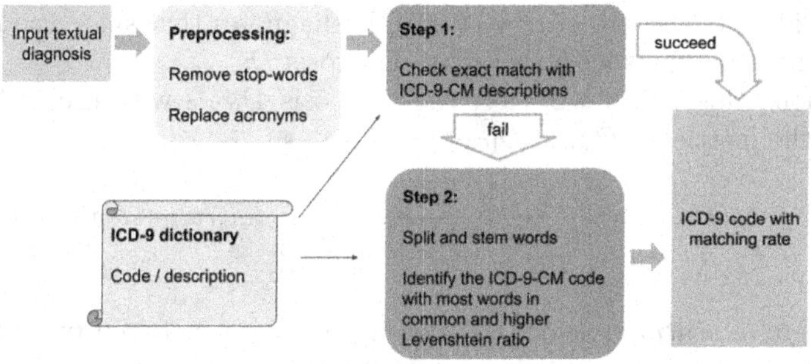

Fig. 1. Overview of the ICD-9-CM mapping pipeline.

4.2 Mapping the Diagnosis Field to the ICD-9-CM Dictionary

In this section we briefly illustrate the Natural Language Processing (NLP) techniques applied to short unstructured textual diagnoses in order to map them to structured ICD-9-CM diagnosis codes. Since all the textual diagnoses we want to decode are in Italian, we refer to the Italian translation of the ICD-9-CM descriptions[2]. This is used to create a description/code dictionary of diseases, after the removal of those codes starting with letter 'E' (supplementary classification of external causes) and 'V' (supplementary classification of factors influencing health status and contact with health services). The technique developed is organized in three steps, which are illustrated in Fig. 1:

- **Preprocessing step:** the input textual diagnosis is preprocessed with the removal of stop-words and proper replacement of acronyms;
- **Step 1:** if the input diagnosis is already exactly matching one of the ICD-9-CM descriptions, then the corresponding code is taken from the dictionary;
- **Step 2:** if in the previous step there is no match, we try to identify among the ICD-9-CM descriptions the closest one to the input diagnosis. To this aim, we can follow a pure *lexicographic* or a *semantic* approach. We detail in the following the two alternative approaches for carrying out **Step 2**.

Lexicographic Approach. In order to identify among the ICD-9-CM descriptions the one closest to the input diagnosis we can go through the following procedure:

- **Step 2 lexicographic:**
  - we stem words[3] in both input and ICD-9-CM diagnoses. Moreover we delete some undefined adjective (e.g. "non specificato" that means unspecified); this is done in order to prefer generic diagnoses to specialized ones.

[2] https://www.salute.gov.it/portale/documentazione/p6_2_2_1.jsp?lingua=italiano&id=2251.

[3] We used snowball stemmer from nlkt package https://www.nltk.org/_modules/nltk/stem/snowball.html.

- we identify the subset of ICD-9-CM diagnoses that share the maximum number of stems with the input diagnosis D_{input}
- among this subset we select the diagnosis D_{ICD9} with the highest value of the metrics $g(D_{\text{input}}, D_{\text{ICD9}})$ defined as

$$g(D_1, D_2) = \frac{1}{len(D_1)len(D_2)} \sum_{\substack{stem_1 \in D_1 \\ stem_2 \in D_2}} lev.ratio(stem_1, stem_2) \tag{1}$$

  where $lev.ratio(s_1, s_2)$ is the Levenshtein ratio between two stems s_1, s_2 and $len(D)$ counts the number of stems composing the sentence D. The denominator normalizes the metrics: since the numerator grows with the number of words in the diagnoses, the metrics is a number between 0 and 1.

Once the input diagnosis is associated to an ICD-9-CM code, we assign a *Lexicographic score* (SC_L) from 0 to 100. This metrics aims at estimating the probability that the mapping is correct. If a match is found in **Step 1**, then $SC_L = 100$; if the mapping comes in **Step 2**, then it is computed as follows:

$$SC_L = \min\left(\omega\, g(D_1, D_2)(1 + r(D_1, D_2)), 100\right) \tag{2}$$

where ω is a weight set to 50, g is the metrics defined in (1) and r is the number of stems in common between diagnoses D_1 and D_2. The quality of this choice for the metrics is investigated in Sect. 5.1.

The value of the *Lexicographic score* will be used to as a filter parameter: when its value is above a certain *Lexicographic score* threshold, we will use the associated ICD-9-CM code, otherwise we will assign a default code "0". The impact of the choice of the *Lexicographic score* threshold on the predictions is inspected in Sect. 5.2.

Semantic Approach. The pipeline proposed above is based uniquely on the Levenshtein lexicographic distance. This means that diagnoses with the same semantics but with a different wording have a high lexicographic distance. For instance, *pyrexia* and *fever*, though having the same semantics, will result in a high lexicographic distance. In the semantic approach, instead, we want to take into account the semantic distance between words and for this we leverage a word embedding model.

For the embedding model we relied on CODER [26], a multilingual model created specifically to deal with medical nomenclature, thanks to the integration of Knowledge Graph, such as UMLS, and mBERT [8]. Behind the functioning of word embeddings lies the principle of distributional semantics, according to which: *"linguistic items with similar distributions have similar meanings"*; therefore, vectors corresponding to similar words will appear close together in the embeddings space. For instance, the vectors of *pyrexia* and *fever* will be rather close in the embedding space. Moreover, we have observed how important it is, in this context, to extend this principle by integrating the information expressed in UMLS in order to correctly compute the similarity between medical terms. This similarity has been calculated on the basis of the cosine distance, which is defined as:

$$vect.distance(w_1, w_2) = 1 - cos(\theta) = 1 - \frac{w_1 \cdot w_2}{\|w_1\|\|w_2\|} \tag{3}$$

where θ is the angle between the vector representation of words w_1 and w_2.

In order to identify among the ICD-9-CM descriptions the one closest to the input diagnosis we can go through the following procedure:

- **Step 2 semantic:**
  - we split input and ICD-9-CM diagnoses in two lists of words and we delete some undefined adjectives (e.g. "non specificato" that means unspecified); this is done in order to prefer generic diagnoses to specialized ones.
  - we identify the subset of ICD-9-CM diagnoses that share with the input diagnosis D_{input} the maximum number of *semantically similar* words. Given two sentences D_1 and D_2, two words $w_1 \in D_1, w_2 \in D_2$ are *semantically similar* when:

$$vect.distance(w_1, w_2) \leq 0.15 \tag{4}$$

  - in this subset we select the diagnosis D_{ICD9} with the highest value of the metrics $h(D_{\text{input}}, D_{\text{ICD9}})$ defined as:

$$h(D_1, D_2) = (1 - Q(\mathbf{v}))(1 - D(\mathbf{v})) \tag{5}$$

    where Q and D are respectively the value of the first quartile and the value of the first decile computed on the population $\mathbf{v}$ of all the semantic distances between the words of the two diagnoses:

$$\mathbf{v} = \{vect.distance(w_1, w_2), \forall\, w_1 \in D_1, w_2 \in D_2\}. \tag{6}$$

    The metrics is a number between 0 and 1.

Similarly to the lexicographic case (2), when the ICD-9-CM code is associated to the input diagnosis we assign a *Semantic score* (SC_S). This score is set to 100 if the diagnosis is matched during **Step 1**, otherwise it is computed with the following formula:

$$SC_S = \min\left(\omega\, h(D_1, D_2)(1 + s(D_1, D_2)), 100\right) \tag{7}$$

where ω is a weight set to 50, h is Eq. (5) and s is the number of semantically similar words in D_1 and D_2, computed as described in Eq. (4). The quality of this choice for the metrics is investigated in Sect. 5.1.

The two pipelines described in this section are used separately to associate the ICD-9-CM code to the input diagnosis; the respective results are then used in the predictive model and their performances are compared in Sect. 5.2.

4.3 Predicting The Home Hospitalization Outcome

The structured data, either extracted from the diagnosis textual fields or already stored in structured fields, can then be provided as input to PPM algorithms that use these features to learn a predictive model. At runtime, when the HHS team has to decide whether a new patient should undergo the home hospitalization, given the features of the new patient, the predictive model will predict whether it is likely that she/he will successfully undergo home hospitalization (HH) or whether it is better to proceed with the hospitalization in another ward (NO-HH). PPM algorithms, e.g., the ones available in Nirdizati [21], a PPM tool that collects a rich set of state-of-the-art approaches based on machine learning algorithms, can be used to train a predictive model able to learn the correlations between variables that describe the patient data and examinations he/she has carried out (features) and the hospitalization at home or in another hospital ward.

5 Evaluation

In this section we evaluate the proposed approach. In detail, we first evaluate the mapping of the textual fields to the ICD-9-CM disease codes (Sect. 5.1) and then the impact of the mapping to ICD-9-CM codes at different levels of abstraction of the ICD-9-CM taxonomy, when making predictions on the home hospitalization outcome (Sect. 5.2).

5.1 ICD-9-CM Mapping Evaluation

In this section we aim at evaluating: (i) the correctness of the ICD-9-CM mappings obtained using the two approaches presented in Sect. 4.2; (ii) whether the *Lexicographic score* and the *Semantic score* are good metrics to evaluate the quality of each ICD-9-CM mapping.

In order to evaluate their correctness, we analyzed the ICD-9-CM mappings given by the two approaches to 490 different textual diagnoses in the dataset. We then asked a domain expert to classify each mapping according to three categories:

- *Good* mapping: the assigned ICD-9-CM code correctly represents the semantics of the textual diagnosis, e.g. "anemia" (anemia) is mapped to code 599.0 corresponding to "altre e non specificate anemie" (other and unspecified anemias)
- *Fair* mapping: the assigned ICD-9-CM code represents only partially the semantics of the textual diagnosis, possibly it represents a superclass, e.g. "leucemia e polmonite" (leukemia and pneumonia) is mapped to code 208.9: "leucemia non specificata" (unspecified leukemia), so we miss the information about pneumonia
- *Bad* mapping: the assigned ICD-9-CM code represents a diagnosis that is uncorrelated to the textual one, e.g. "acufeni" (tinnitus) is mapped to code 706.1: "altre acni" (other acni)

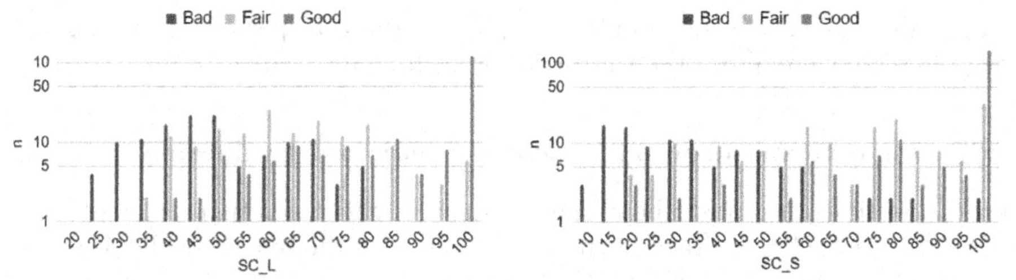

(a) (b)

Fig. 2. Number of diagnoses for *score* values. (a) Lexicographic approach. (b) Semantic approach.

Table 1. Percentage of ICD-9-CM diagnosis mappings with: (a) SC_L value higher than T_L for the lexicographic approach; (b) SC_S value higher than T_S for the semantic approach. The values of the thresholds T_L and T_S are chosen so to filter respectively 100%, 70% and 45% of all the diagnoses.

T_L	tot	*good*	*fair*	*bad*
0	100%	41%	33%	26%
53	70%	38%	23%	9%
70	45%	33%	10%	2%

(a)

T_S	tot	*good*	*fair*	*bad*
0	100%	42%	36%	22%
50	70%	40%	26%	4%
79	45%	33%	11%	1%

(b)

Based on the classification of the domain expert, we found that

- with the lexicographic approach: 41% of the mappings are *good*, 33% are *fair* and 26% are *bad*.
- with the semantic approach: 42% of the mappings are *good*, 36% are *fair* and 22% are *bad* mappings.

This represents a reasonable result. Indeed, by discarding the *bad* mappings we are able to fairly map 74% and 78% of the textual diagnoses for the lexicographic and the semantic approach, respectively. Moreover, we notice that the results returned by the semantic approach are overall better than the ones of the lexicographic approach.

In order to check whether the two *scores* are good metrics to evaluate the quality of the mappings, so as to use these metrics to discriminate the mappings we can trust as features for prediction tasks, we show in Fig. 2) the distributions of the three categories of diagnoses with respect to the relative *score* for each of the two approaches. The plot shows that in both cases most of the *bad* mappings have a low *score* value.

The metrics look reasonably good in separating *bad* mappings and hence, setting a *Lexicographic score* threshold value T_L (respectively *Semantic score* threshold value T_S), they can be used to automatically exclude most of the bad mappings. Table 1 reports for different T_L (T_S) values the percentage of diagnosis mappings that are above the threshold for each quality category.[4]

5.2 Home Hospitalization Outcome Prediction Evaluation

In this section we report about the accuracy of the predictions related to the HHS scenario. The accuracy of the predictions is evaluated using the *Matthews correlation coefficient metric* (MCC) [18] that is defined as follows:

$$\text{MCC} = \frac{TP \times TN - FP \times FN}{\sqrt{(TP+FP)(TP+FN)(TN+FP)(TN+FN)}} \tag{8}$$

where TP, TN, FP, FN are respectively true positive, true negative, false positive and false negative predictions. The MCC metrics ranges from −1 to 1, where a perfect prediction measures 1, a random prediction measures 0 and a completely wrong prediction measures −1. In unbalanced datasets, like ours, where the number of positive and negative traces is very different (368 vs. 45), this metrics is more suitable than others like accuracy and F-measure for measuring the quality of the predictions [7].

In order to evaluate whether structured features, as the ICD-9-CM codes or its ancestors, rather than unstructured ones, as textual diagnoses, can be leveraged to get more accurate predictions, we analyzed and compared the results obtained with different sets of features:

- without the diagnosis (no_diag);
- with the textual diagnosis (text_diag);
- with the ICD-9-CM code assigned to the textual diagnosis or one of its ancestors via the lexicographic match (icd9_diag_lex(all)).
- with the ICD-9-CM code assigned to the textual diagnosis or one of its ancestors via the semantic match (icd9_diag_sem(all)).

These last two cases are further refined in different sub-cases based on two parameters: (i) the threshold values T_L, T_S; for each of them we consider two reference values: one that filters the 70% of the diagnoses ($T_L = 53$, $T_S = 50$) and one that filters the 45% of the diagnoses ($T_L = 70$, $T_S = 79$), see Table 1; and (ii) the level of abstraction of the ICD-9-CM classification, that corresponds to the number of digits that we trim from the right side of the ICD-9-CM codes (see Sect. 2): the higher the number of digits trimmed, the higher the abstraction level in the ICD-9-CM taxonomy. Here we consider two abstraction levels: the full ICD-9-CM code corresponding to the specific diagnosis, and the code with two digits trimmed corresponding to its ancestor diagnosis group.

As predictive model we used a Random Forest classifier on the incomplete traces properly preprocessed as described in Sect. 4.1. Moreover, we tested the predictions assuming we have observed only the first five activities at the ED.

[4] The percentages in Table 1 refer to the number of mappings per diagnosis. Note that these are in principle different from the number of mappings per trace in which the diagnosis appears, since the same diagnosis may appear in more than one trace.

Table 2. Prediction accuracy results obtained with different diagnosis information used in the encoding.

Diagnosis information	Description	avg(MCC)	σ(MCC)	max(MCC)
no_diag	without diagnosis	0.51	0.09	0.65
text_diag	textual diagnosis	0.4	0.1	0.6
icd9_diag_lex_70%-5	ICD-9-CM, lexicographic, $T_L = 53$, 5 digits	0.58	0.05	0.65
icd9_diag_lex_70%-3	ICD-9-CM, lexicographic, $T_L = 53$, 3 digits	0.56	0.07	0.65
icd9_diag_lex_45%-5	ICD-9-CM, lexicographic, $T_L = 70$, 5 digits	0.57	0.05	0.70
icd9_diag_lex_45%-3	ICD-9-CM, lexicographic, $T_L = 70$, 3 digits	0.61	0.04	0.70
icd9_diag_sem_70%-5	ICD-9-CM, semantic, $T_S = 50$, 5 digits	0.56	0.06	0.70
icd9_diag_sem_70%-3	ICD-9-CM, semantic, $T_S = 50$, 3 digits	0.49	0.08	0.65
icd9_diag_sem_45%-5	ICD-9-CM, semantic, $T_S = 79$, 5 digits	0.56	0.07	0.70
icd9_diag_sem_45%-3	ICD-9-CM, semantic match, $T_S = 79$, 3 digits	0.55	0.07	0.65

For the feature encoding we used the frequency-based encoding [16] enriched with trace attribute features. The classifier is trained with 70% of the traces; 10% of the traces is used to perform the hyper-parameter optimization on the MCC metrics (8); and finally the classifier is tested on the remaining 20% of the traces. Due to the non-deterministic trait of the prediction, each experiment is repeated 30 times, and the average value of MCC together with its standard deviation σ are used as reference metrics.

The results are reported in Table 2. The first and the second columns of Table 2 show the diagnosis information used for the prediction and its description. The third and fourth columns contain respectively the mean and the standard deviation σ of the MCC value computed in several (30) tests, while the fifth column contains the maximum values of MCC obtained during the (30) tests.

The worst performance is obtained when the textual diagnosis is used as feature (text_diag), while no_diag performs better than text_diag. This is possibly due to the high variability of the textual information, resulting in noise for the predictive model. On average, the best way of taking into account the diagnosis for the predictions seems to be via the mapped ICD-9-CM codes. Indeed, all the predictions obtained with mapped ICD-9-CM codes, except one (icd9_diag_sem_70%-3), provide better results than the no_diag prediction.

In order to further validate this analysis, we also checked the statistical significance of the identified differences:

$$\begin{array}{rl} \text{no\_diag} > \text{text\_diag} & \text{p-value} < 0.002 \\ \text{all icd9\_diag except icd9\_diag\_sem\_70\%-3} > \text{text\_diag} & \text{p-value} < 10^{-5} \\ \text{all icd9\_diag except icd9\_diag\_sem\_70\%-3} > \text{no\_diag} & \text{p-value} < 0.05 \\ \text{icd9\_diag\_sem\_70\%-3} > \text{text\_diag} & \text{p-value} < 0.006 \end{array}$$

The results confirm that all the mappings based on ICD-9-CM codes—except icd9_diag_sem_70%-3—are significantly higher than no_diag and text_diag, while icd9_diag_sem_70%-3is only significantly better than text_diag.

We further analysed the results obtained with the mappings based on the ICD-9-CM codes by focusing on:

- the approach, i.e., the lexicographic or the semantic approach adopted;
- the threshold values used to filter bad ICD-9-CM mappings, i.e., T_L and T_S: the higher the value of these thresholds, the lower the percentage of bad ICD-9-CM codes mapped;
- the number of digits used of the ICD-9-CM code, corresponding to the level of abstraction of the diagnoses: 5 digits represent detailed diagnosis codes, 3 digits represent groups of diagnoses.

Concerning the approach, the results obtained with the lexicographic approach provide slightly better results than the ones obtained with the semantic approach. However, when comparing the approaches with the same threshold value and number of digits, the difference is overall low and it is not statistically significant—except for icd9_diag_lex_45%-3 (lexicographic, $T_L = 70$, 3 digits) and icd9_diag_lex_70%-3 (lexicographic, $T_L = 50$, 3 digits) that perform better than their semantic-based counterpart (icd9_diag_sem_45%-3 and icd9_diag_sem_70%-3, respectively) with p-value ≤ 0.05. This result is rather surprising considering the evaluation of the matching methods in terms of bad ICD-9-CM codes reported in Sect. 5.1.

Our understanding of this result is that a big part in the prediction performance is given by those ICD-9-CM codes which are classified in the *Fair* category. For example the diagnosis *pneumonia and cough* may be fairly mapped to both *486 pneumonia* and *786.2 cough*, but clearly the first one might be more important in the decision about home hospitalization than the second one. At the moment, however, we have not yet developed a method to select the most relevant sub-diagnosis when a diagnosis is composed of several sub-diagnosis.

Concerning the threshold values used to filter bad mappings, the results do not show any clear trends, although it seems that overall higher thresholds return very close or more accurate results than lower thresholds. This difference is however not statistically significant—except for the case of icd9_diag_lex_45%-3 that presents better results than icd9_diag_lex_70%-3 with a statistical significance.

Finally, concerning the level of abstraction of the ICD-9-CM mappings, we can observe that overall the accuracy obtained with more specific ICD-9-CM codes (5 digits) is higher than the accuracy obtained with more general ICD-9-CM codes (3 digits). This is however not true for icd9_diag_lex_45%-3 (3 digits) that has a significantly higher accuracy than icd9_diag_lex_45%-5 (5 digits).

In general, the statistical analysis shows that there are no significant differences between any of the ICD-9-CM results displayed in Table 2, except for two cases: icd9_diag_lex_45%-3 (lexicographic, $T_L = 70$, 3 digits) performs better than all the other ICD-9-CM mappings with p-value ≤ 0.005 and icd9_diag_sem_70%-3 (semantic, $T_S = 50$, 3 digits) performs worse than all the other mappings with p-value ≤ 0.004.

6 Related Work

The literature related to this work mainly pertains to two research areas: Predictive Process Monitoring (in particular with unstructured data) and the mapping of textual fields to the ICD.

Predictive Process Monitoring approaches can be classified based on the types of prediction they provide: (i) numeric predictions, (ii) outcome–based predictions, and (iii) next activity predictions. In this work we focus on outcome–based predictions, that is related to the fulfilment of a predicate on an ongoing trace, i.e., the outcome of the home hospitalization. Almost all the approaches in this field, rely on implicit models such as machine learning and statistical methods. Maggi et al. [17] report an approach that classifies the fulfilment of a predicate on an ongoing trace by exploiting both control flow and data flow. This work has then been extended in [9,16,24,25]. Di Francescomarino et al. [9] extend the work adding clustering techniques on top of the previous approach. This results in training more classifiers with a smaller subsets of data. Leontjeva et al. [16] treat the execution traces as complex symbolic sequences, while Verenich et al. [25] combine these two approaches. Teinemaa et al. [24] exploit unstructured (textual) information contained in messages exchanged between process instances during execution in order to improve the accuracy of the predictions. Recently in [20] Pegoraro et al. apply natural process language techiniques and LSTM neural networks to integrate information from text documents written in natural language to the prediction model. In this work we borrow the idea of the works in PPM to extract structured information from textual data so as to improve the accuracy of outcome-based predictive models. However, to this aim, we leverage a mapping of textual diagnosis to ICD-9-CM diseases.

The mapping of free text to the ICD classification has been considered in several works. In [2] Akshara et al. provide an automated ICD-9-CM diagnosis prediction integrating structured patients' data together with unstructured clinical text notes. In [13] Gangavarapu et al. present a method for ICD-9-CM code group prediction from unstructured clinical nursing notes, using vector space and topic modeling approaches; in [12] this approach is integrated with a fuzzy similarity cleansing approach to merge anomalous and redundant data. In [19] machine learning and natural language processing approaches are used in the automatic mapping of ICD-10 codes from narrative text fields. In this work the performance of different classical machine learning classifiers are compared in terms of accuracy, precision and recall. In [15] and [11] machine learning techniques are used to map ICD-10 codes from textual death certificates. In [6] recurrent neural networks are used to map ICD-10 codes from Dutch cardiology discharge letters. Differently from all the above state-of-the-art approaches, we focus on Italian textual data and we defined an approach that is able to cope with the available NLP resources.

7 Conclusions

With the purpose of improving prediction accuracy by using structured rather than unstructured information in PPM, we have proposed a pipeline that leverages NLP methods and two different approaches—a lexicographic and a semantic one—for mapping textual fields to an existing dictionary, as in the case of textual fields mapped to ICD-9-CM codes. We have applied the proposed approach to a real-life healthcare scenario related to the HHS, and we have evaluated (i) the quality of the mappings; and (ii) the accuracy of the predictions without using the diagnosis information, using the textual diagnosis information, or using the structured information contained in ICD-9-CM codes. The results are overall reasonable and confirm that having structured rather than unstructured features improves the accuracy of the predictions.

We plan, as future work, to further refine the pipeline devised for mapping textual fields to the ICD-9-CM codes, e.g., by taking into account the fact that some textual descriptions are richer than a single ICD-9-CM code and can hence be mapped to more than one code.

Acknowledgments. This research has been partially carried out within the "Circular Health for Industry" project, funded by "Compagnia San Paolo" under the call "Intelligenza Artificiale, uomo e società".

References

1. van der Aalst, W.M.P.: Process Mining - Data Science in Action. Springer, Heidelberg (2016). https://doi.org/10.1007/978-3-662-49851-4
2. Akshara, P., Shidharth, S., Gokul S., K., Sowmya, K.: Integrating structured and unstructured patient data for ICD9 disease code group prediction. In: 8th ACM IKDD CODS and 26th COMAD, p. 436. Association for Computing Machinery (2021)
3. van der Aalst, W., et al.: Process mining Manifesto. In: Daniel, F., Barkaoui, K., Dustdar, S. (eds.) BPM 2011. LNBIP, vol. 99, pp. 169–194. Springer, Heidelberg (2012). https://doi.org/10.1007/978-3-642-28108-2_19
4. Amantea, I.A., et al.: A process mining application for the analysis of hospital-at-home admissions. Stud. Health Technol. Inform. **270**, 522–526 (2020)
5. Aringhieri, R., et al.: Leveraging structured data in predictive process monitoring: the case of the ICD-9-CM in the scenario of the home hospitalization service. In: Proceedings of the Workshop on Towards Smarter Health Care: Can Artificial Intelligence Help? Co-Located with AIxIA2021. CEUR Workshop Proceedings, vol. 3060, pp. 48–60. CEUR-WS.org (2021)
6. Bagheri, A., Sammani, A., Heijden, P.G., Asselbergs, F., Oberski, D.: Automatic ICD-10 classification of diseases from Dutch discharge letters, pp. 281–289, January 2020
7. Chicco, D., Jurman, G.: The advantages of the Matthews correlation coefficient (MCC) over F1 score and accuracy in binary classification evaluation. BMC Genomics **21**(1), 6 (2020)
8. Devlin, J., Chang, M., Lee, K., Toutanova, K.: BERT: pre-training of deep bidirectional transformers for language understanding. In: Proceedings of, NAACL-HLT 2019, pp. 4171–4186. Association for Computational Linguistics (2019)
9. Di Francescomarino, C., Dumas, M., Maggi, F.M., Teinemaa, I.: Clustering-based predictive process monitoring. IEEE Trans. Serv. Comput. **12**(6), 896–909 (2019)
10. Di Francescomarino, C., Ghidini, C., Maggi, F.M., Milani, F.: Predictive process monitoring methods: which one suits me best? In: Weske, M., Montali, M., Weber, I., vom Brocke, J. (eds.) BPM 2018. LNCS, vol. 11080, pp. 462–479. Springer, Cham (2018). https://doi.org/10.1007/978-3-319-98648-7_27
11. Duarte, F., Martins, B., Pinto, C., Silva, M.: A deep learning method for ICD-10 coding of free-text death certificates, pp. 137–149, August 2017

12. Gangavarapu, T., Jayasimha, A., Krishnan, G.S., Kamath, S.: Predicting ICD-9 code groups with fuzzy similarity based supervised multi-label classification of unstructured clinical nursing notes. Knowl.-Based Syst. **190**, 105321 (2020)
13. Gangavarapu, T., Krishnan, G.S., Kamath, S., Jeganathan, J.: Farsight: long-term disease prediction using unstructured clinical nursing notes. IEEE Trans. Emerg. Top. Comput. **9**(3), 1151–1169 (2021)
14. Isaia, G., Bertone, P., Isaia, G.C., Ricauda, N.: Home care for patients with chronic obstructive pulmonary disease. Arch. Phys. Med. Rehabil. **100**, 664–665 (2010)
15. Koopman, B., Zuccon, G., Nguyen, A., Bergheim, A., Grayson, N.: Automatic ICD-10 classification of cancers from free-text death certificates. Int. J. Med. Inform. **84** (2015)
16. Leontjeva, A., Conforti, R., Di Francescomarino, C., Dumas, M., Maggi, F.M.: Complex symbolic sequence encodings for predictive monitoring of business processes. In: Motahari-Nezhad, H.R., Recker, J., Weidlich, M. (eds.) BPM 2015. LNCS, vol. 9253, pp. 297–313. Springer, Cham (2015). https://doi.org/10.1007/978-3-319-23063-4_21
17. Maggi, F.M., Di Francescomarino, C., Dumas, M., Ghidini, C.: Predictive monitoring of business processes. In: Jarke, M., Mylopoulos, J., Quix, C., Rolland, C., Manolopoulos, Y., Mouratidis, H., Horkoff, J. (eds.) CAiSE 2014. LNCS, vol. 8484, pp. 457–472. Springer, Cham (2014). https://doi.org/10.1007/978-3-319-07881-6_31
18. Matthews, B.: Comparison of the predicted and observed secondary structure of T4 phage lysozyme. Biochimica et Biophysica Acta (BBA) - Protein Struct. **405**(2), 442–451 (1975)
19. Nkolele, R.: Mapping of narrative text fields to ICD-10 codes using natural language processing and machine learning. In: Proceedings of the The Fourth Widening Natural Language Processing Workshop, pp. 131–135. Association for Computational Linguistics, Seattle, July 2020
20. Pegoraro, M., Uysal, M.S., Georgi, D., Aalst, W.: Text-aware predictive monitoring of business processes, April 2021
21. Rizzi, W., Simonetto, L., Di Francescomarino, C., Ghidini, C., Kasekamp, T., Maggi, F.M.: Nirdizati 2.0: new features and redesigned backend. In: Demonstration Track at BPM 2019. CEUR Workshop Proceedings, vol. 2420, pp. 154–158. CEUR-WS.org (2019)
22. Sulis, E., et al.: Monitoring patients with fragilities in the context of de-hospitalization services: an ambient assisted living healthcare framework for e-health applications. In: 23rd ISCT, pp. 216–219. IEEE (2019)
23. Sulis, E., Terna, P., Di Leva, A., Boella, G., Boccuzzi, A.: Agent-oriented decision support system for business processes management with genetic algorithm optimization: an application in healthcare. J. Med. Syst. **44**(9), 1–7 (2020)
24. Teinemaa, I., Dumas, M., Maggi, F.M., Di Francescomarino, C.: Predictive business process monitoring with structured and unstructured data. In: La Rosa, M., Loos, P., Pastor, O. (eds.) BPM 2016. LNCS, vol. 9850, pp. 401–417. Springer, Cham (2016). https://doi.org/10.1007/978-3-319-45348-4_23
25. Verenich, I., Dumas, M., La Rosa, M., Maggi, F.M., Di Francescomarino, C.: Complex symbolic sequence clustering and multiple classifiers for predictive process monitoring. In: Reichert, M., Reijers, H.A. (eds.) BPM 2015. LNBIP, vol. 256, pp. 218–229. Springer, Cham (2016). https://doi.org/10.1007/978-3-319-42887-1_18
26. Yuan, Z., Zhao, Z., Sun, H., Li, J., Wang, F., Yu, S.: Coder: knowledge infused cross-lingual medical term embedding for term normalization (2021)

Author Index

Albarelli, Andrea 297
Amato, Domenico 462
Anderson, Andrew 447
Andrea, Salafia 591
Andresini, Giuseppina 478
Anteghini, Marco 198
Appice, Annalisa 478
Arani, Elahe 515
Aringhieri, Roberto 700
Audrito, Davide 185
Auer, Sören 198
Auletta, Vincenzo 263

Badar, Ahmed 515
Basili, Roberto 228, 564
Batarseh, Feras A. 624
Beraldo, Gloria 32
Bergamasco, Filippo 297
Bianco, Simone 338
Boella, Guido 700
Borhanifard, Zeinab 213
Borroto, Manuel 171
Breazzano, Claudia 228
Brunetti, Enrico 700

Cacciamani, Barbara 564
Calegari, Roberta 91, 104
Capobianco, Roberto 46, 413, 550
Caprari, Riccardo 310
Caputo, Sergio 326
Caruso, Simone 671
Castellano, Giovanna 326
Castro, Giulia 310
Celona, Luigi 338
Cerutti, Federico 377
Cesta, Amedeo 32
Cialdea Mayer, Marta 153
Contissa, Giuseppe 91
Coppola, Antonio 263
Cortellessa, Gabriella 32
Croce, Danilo 228, 564
Cuteri, Bernardo 171

D'Souza, Jennifer 198
De Benedictis, Riccardo 32
De Filippo, Allegra 609
De Magistris, Giorgio 310
Dell'Olio, Domenico 478
Dell'Orletta, Felice 245
Demarchi, Stefano 77
Devaram, Rami Reddy 32
Di Caro, Luigi 185, 700
Di Francescomarino, Chiara 700
dos Santos, Vitor A. P. Martins 198
Dragoni, Mauro 700
Đurasević, Marko 689

Ejbali, Ridha 348
Esposito, Marco 638

Fabio, Sgrò 591
Faili, Heshaam 213
Ferraioli, Diodato 263
Ferrod, Roger 700
Fersini, Elisabetta 279
Fionda, Valeria 123
Freeman, Laura 624
Furukita, Fernanda N. T. 61

Gaglio, Salvatore 490
Galatà, Giuseppe 671
Gallotta, Roberto 46
Gamal, Mahmoud 515
Gasparini, Francesca 279, 359
Ghidini, Chiara 700
Ghogho, Mounir 580
Giammanco, Andrea 490
Giancarlo, Raffaele 462
Giorgio, Lazzarinetti 591
Golestani, Melika 213
Gori, Marco 389, 403
Greco, Francesco 326
Greco, Gianluigi 123
Gregg, David 447

Horta, Vitor A. C. 532
Humphreys, Llio Bryn 185

Iocchi, Luca 310
Iqbal, Haris 515

Jakobović, Domagoj 689

Karami, Hossein 3
Khalifa, Intissar 338, 348

La Rosa, Biagio 550
Lertvittayakumjorn, Piyawat 429
Lo Bosco, Giosué 462
Lo Re, Giuseppe 490
Lombardi, Michele 609

Magdy, Omar 515
Makinwa, Sayo M. 550
Malerba, Donato 478
Malhotra, Sagar 137
Maratea, Marco 671
Marcellino, Fernando J. M. 61
Margiotta, Daniele 564
Marinello, Renata 700
Mastratisi, Marco Antonio 123
Mastrogiovanni, Fulvio 3
Menapace, Marco 77
Mencar, Corrado 326
Miaschi, Alessio 245
Milano, Michela 609
Mileo, Alessandra 532
Mochi, Marco 671
Morana, Marco 490
Moukafih, Youness 580

Napoletano, Paolo 338, 348
Napoli, Christian 310
Nardi, Daniele 310, 413
Nicola, Massarenti 591

Ocana, Jim Martin Catacora 413
Oddi, Angelo 153
Omicini, Andrea 104

Pappagallo, Angela 655
Percassi, Francesco 18
Perini, Dominick 624
Persand, Kaveena 447
Petrovsky, Alexey 338
Petti, Niccolò 326
Pham, Tuan D. 503
Picchiami, Leonardo 638
Picchiotti, Nicola 389, 403
Piccoli, Flavio 338
Pisano, Giuseppe 91, 104
Pistellato, Mara 297
Planinić, Lucija 689
Porro, Ivan 671

Rago, Antonio 429
Rasconi, Riccardo 153
Ravelli, Andrea Amelio 245
Ressi, Dalila 297
Ricca, Francesco 171
Rizzi, Giulia 279
Ronzani, Massimiliano 700
Rotoloni, Marco 564
Russo, Samuele 310

Saibene, Aurora 279, 359
Santucci, Vieri Giuliano 153
Sartor, Gabriele 153
Sartor, Galileo 91
Sartor, Giovanni 91, 104
Sbihi, Nada 580
Scala, Enrico 18
Schettini, Raimondo 338, 348
Serafini, Luciano 137
Shanin, Ivan 338
Sichman, Jaime 61
Smaili, Kamel 580
Solé-Casals, Jordi 359
Staniec, Adrian 515
Sukpanichnant, Purin 429
Sulis, Emilio 185, 700

Tacchella, Armando 77
Tahmasebian, Farnaz 213
Thomas, Antony 3
Toni, Francesca 429

Vallati, Mauro 18
Varma, Arnav 515
Vessio, Gennaro 326

Wani, Qasim 624

Zaied, Mourad 348
Zelić, Stjepan 689
Zollo, Davide 153
Zonooz, Bahram 515

Printed in the United States
by Baker & Taylor Publisher Services